THE REAL ALE PUB GUIDE

2005

Edited by Nicolas Andrews
with
—THE REAL ALE—
RESEARCH TEAM

foulsham
LONDON • NEW YORK • TORONTO • SYDNEY

foulsham
The Publishing House, Bennetts Close,
Cippenham, Berkshire, SL1 5AP, England.

Controlling editor:
Nicolas Andrews

Regional editors and contributors:
Malcolm Rigby
Debra Greenhouse
Martin Kay
John Lyons
MaryRose Johnstone
Nancy Cavill
Malcolm Kinross
Magnus Gardham
Matt Lyons

While every effort has been made to ensure the accuracy of all the information contained within this book, neither the authors nor the publisher can be liable for any errors. The publisher would welcome letters of correction and further information.

ISBN 0-572-03034-7

A CIP record for this book is available from the British Library

Back cover photograph: The White Horse, Hedgerley, Buckinghamshire

Printed in Great Britain by Creative Print & Design (Wales), Ebbw Vale.

CONTENTS

Welcome to *The Real Ale Pub Guide 2005*. We are now in our eighth year and I honestly believe that we are bigger and better than ever before.

In 1997, two of us, a landlord and a newspaper journalist, set out to fill what we perceived to be a gap in the market for an independently produced, critically compiled collection of some of the best pubs in Britain. We focused exclusively on their ability to sell high-quality real ale produced by the nation's regional, local and microbreweries. Starting from scratch, it was quite a task and there were plenty of gaps, but from relatively humble beginnings, I think we are maturing nicely.

We have now built a substantial and constantly expanding network of contributors and regional editors. We have also been helped greatly by the recommendations of a growing number of readers. The brewers and the pubs themselves supply vital updates and extra detail, all of which enables us to put together one of the most comprehensive guides to the best real ale pubs in Britain.

One of the joys of working on this book is that there is always more to discover. We finish each year wishing we had time to add more, disappointed that another new find has missed the deadline. Fortunately, it is soon time to start work on the next edition. So it has proved this time, with many impressive new entries dotted all around the country.

Last year we highlighted the demise of the Brakspear Brewery at Henley-on-Thames and celebrated the survival of McMullen and Sons in Hertfordshire, which has since announced plans for a new brewhouse. This year we can salute the fact that the brewing of Brakspear ales has returned to its home county of Oxfordshire, thanks to the new owner Refresh UK's decision to expand the Wychwood plant at Witney. Other causes for celebration include the return of Theakston to family control and the way that Adnams, Timothy Taylor and a number of other family brewers are all managing to keep up with growing demand. Fuller's is also going from strength to strength, with the Chiswick company now able to boast that it sells more pints of London Pride than Interbrew, the world's biggest brewer, sells of Draught Bass.

As always there are worrying developments. Scottish & Newcastle is closing the famous Fountain Brewery in Edinburgh after 250 years. Its Tyne Brewery is another victim as it attempts to cut costs. And some observers are not yet convinced that the joint venture between S&N and the Caledonian Brewing Company so soon after the latter won the Champion Beer of Britain award for its Deuchars IPA is a wise one in the longer term.

Further south, Greene King's £650 million bid for the Laurel Pub Company, after previously snapping up Morland, Morrell's and others, means that the Suffolk brewer now owns more than 2,000 pubs and is in danger of turning from a respected independent regional producer into a national operator with excessive expansionist plans.

But the whole point of this book has always been to celebrate the work of the smaller brewers who seem to grow in number and increase in ingenuity every year. And the past 12 months have seen some particularly impressive developments.

Northern Brewing has returned the production of real ale to Runcorn for the first time since 1906, Millstone Brewery has become the 15th independent to open in Manchester, Glossop Brewery is up and running and Green Jack is producing again in Suffolk after a two-year break. Wharfedale Brewery in North Yorkshire was officially opened by the Duke of Kent in early 2004; Downtown Brewery has opened in Wiltshire; Southport is the first new brewery on Merseyside for almost 100 years and the Westerham Brewery in Kent is returning real ale production to the town for the first time since 1965.

And so it goes on. For every pub closure or brewery driven out of business, there seem to be more than enough stories of expansion, recovery and boom times to keep the real ale cause a healthy one. New government legislation, including next year's introduction of the Licensing Act to England and Wales and a potential smoking ban surely not too far around the corner, will also help to ensure that the industry cannot stand still.

We believe passionately that real ale is a drink like no other, to be cherished and celebrated, and the fact that you are reading this means we are clearly not alone. The real ale cause will always experience its ups and downs, but the dark keg days of the 1960s and 1970s do certainly seem to be behind us. While it is always hugely disappointing when a pub closes, removes its handpumps or serves up something too warm (or cold), too poorly kept or just too tired, I prefer to think of the glass being half full rather than half empty and to move on in search of something better. For every dud, there is sure to be a gem not far around the corner. And I hope that this book will help you to find it.

HOW IT ALL BEGAN

We have the Romans to thank for bringing beer to Britain in the first century AD, although the drink has its origins in Mesopotamia perhaps as many as 8000 years before that. The first brewer probably stumbled across the secret by accident, perhaps as a result of airborne wild yeast infecting food, but from there it spread to Greece, Egypt and eventually to Rome. While the Roman aristocracy still preferred to drink wine, Caesar's invading army appreciated beer as an important source of nutrition and, with water supplies so often contaminated, native Britons soon found it safer, and no doubt more pleasurable, to drink than water.

Beer and brewing continued to thrive in Britain long after the Romans had gone, and more than 40 breweries were listed in the Domesday Book of 1086. Hops, which impart flavour and aroma, and act as a preservative, were initially introduced from Scandinavia in the middle of the tenth century, but they were not widely used until the fifteenth-century, when they were grown here, primarily in Kent.

Many of the early brewers were monks, and it was in monasteries that brewing techniques were improved and refined, particularly with the introduction of better varieties of barley. During the Reformation, however, and Henry VIII's break with Rome, the monasteries were shut down and their land and assets seized by the Crown. The noble art thus passed into the hands of farmers and owners of estates, who installed private brewhouses to supply beer for farm workers and staff.

Commercial breweries began to appear during the latter part of the sixteenth-century, growing steadily in number until, by the 1870s, some 30,000 were registered in Great Britain. This was a golden age, with beer drinking per head of the population at its all-time peak.

The Beer Act of 1830 had made it easy to obtain a licence to brew and sell beer from home, but increasing taxation on malt and hops made home-brewing less economically viable and so, by the end of the nineteenth-century, the market was dominated by commercial brewers.

One hundred years ago, a brewery was to be found serving almost every local community, but as the market became increasingly competitive and preservation techniques and transport improved, the vast majority went out of business, were bought up or simply faded away. Only about 50 of the independent breweries that were in operation at the turn of the last century still brew today.

Of these, Shepherd Neame Ltd at Faversham in Kent is believed to be the oldest. Beer has been produced on the same site without interruption since the brewery's official foundation in 1698. Britain's oldest surviving brewpub is believed to be the Blue Anchor at Helston in Cornwall. It first became a pub around the middle of the sixteenth-century, although it seems certain that monks were already brewing beer on the premises long before then.

The title of the oldest pub in Britain is disputed, but it probably belongs to the Trip to Jerusalem in Nottingham, part of which is cut into the rock of the castle and dates from 1189. This was once the malthouse for the castle brewery.

Although brewing technology may have progressed over the centuries, the process and basic ingredients have changed very little. Today, real ales still arrive at the pub with live yeast and fermentable sugars present in the brew, allowing the final stages of fermentation to take place in the cellar. This produces a fresh, pert, rounded flavour and natural effervescence. This is real ale at its very best, and part of the proud tradition which spans the centuries.

While market forces, and the price of real estate, see famous names disappearing every year from the brewing map, new, smaller operations are still springing up to replace them. At least 400 breweries are in business today, a considerable improvement on the situation of just 20 years ago.

WHAT WENT WRONG?

Many pubs originally brewed their own beer, often drawing water from a spring or well beneath. But cask-conditioned beers tended to be unreliable and were too often not properly looked after in the cellar.

To overcome this problem, the larger brewers turned to bottles and keg beers which, though bland and characterless by comparison, were consistent and had a much longer shelf life. They were also easy to transport and look after. Huge investments were made in kegs, equipment and advertising and, by the middle of the 1960s, real ale had all but disappeared from the British pub. This was the age of the ubiquitous Watneys Red Barrel, of Worthington E and Double Diamond; the British brewing industry was on the rocks.

Just four brewpubs remained and, as recently as 1985, there were fewer than 150 independent breweries in operation. Lager, too, although a poor imitation of the excellent continental brews, became increasingly popular with British pub-goers, due largely to advertising campaigns which targeted the trend-conscious younger drinker. The national breweries had imposed their corporate will to increase profits at the expense of quality. Real ale sales declined to the verge of extinction.

Though consistent, keg beer is a poor substitute for the natural product. While it starts life as real ale, the beer is filtered, pasteurised and chilled before being poured into containers. This process destroys and removes the yeast, preventing any further fermentation, and ensures that the beer is clear and bright in the keg.

But the beer is now dead. It produces no natural carbon dioxide and lacks the depth of character that cask-conditioned beers offer. In an effort to overcome this problem, it is now frequently served using a mixture of nitrogen and carbon dioxide, which gives the beer a tighter, creamy head in the glass while reducing the overall fizziness associated with carbon dioxide. But it is still a long way from the real thing.

Keg beer is easy to brew, easy to transport, easy to keep and easy to serve. Very little can go wrong so profits are at a premium and craftsmanship plays no part.

THE REAL ALE REVIVAL

Over the past 30 years, due to the dedication of a number of small brewery owners and the campaigning efforts of CAMRA (the Campaign for Real Ale), Britain's excellent real ales have gradually re-emerged and a great heritage of independent breweries is back on the scene. A change in the law known as the Beer Orders helped, too, permitting pubs previously tied to one brewery for all beer supplies to take a guest beer from elsewhere. This increased considerably the potential market for the smaller independent suppliers.

However, problems remain as the big brewers have found a way of fighting back. The Office of Fair Trading conducted a review of the Beer Orders, which was published in December 2000. It found that the larger brewers no longer owned and ran pubs in the traditional way but had sold them, or divided their business into breweries and pub companies.

So none of the big, national brewers now owns enough pubs for the Beer Orders provisions to apply. Traditional giants such as Bass and Whitbread have sold their brewing businesses to Interbrew, a giant international conglomerate, and are concentrating on their leisure interests instead.

This has caused a huge problem for the licensed trade, because the buying power is concentrated in the hands of large pub companies that buy from the big brewers, who can supply large quantities at knockdown prices. The pub companies then sell that beer to their tenants at the full list price and, because the tenant is tied to the pub company for all the beer sold in the pub, he or she has no choice but to buy what the pub company wants to sell at the price it wants to charge.

The same old problem has re-emerged and many tenants are struggling to meet steep targets set by their landlords, the pub companies. These companies, in turn, are increasingly profitable, enabling them to buy up more freehouses or to pounce when struggling smaller breweries with fewer tied houses go under.

While there are some enlightened exceptions among the all-too-dominant pub companies, fewer and fewer pubs are finding themselves able to buy beer from small breweries. In 2003, the Office of Fair Trading refused a request from the Federation of Small Businesses to investigate the rents and drinks prices charged by pub companies. The Chancellor also announced a 1p per pint duty increase, which undid much of the good work of the previous year, when Gordon Brown went to the aid of the smaller independent and micro-brewers by announcing Progressive Beer Duty.

A new licensing Bill will be introduced during 2005 which, while potentially relaxing rigid rules on opening hours, hands more control to local authorities who do not always have the landlord or the pub drinker's best interests at heart. These are still difficult times for the real ale producer and consumer alike.

But it is the imagination and inventiveness of the small independent and micro-brewers that has kept the real ale market alive in Britain and, against whatever odds, no doubt they will continue to do so. Before 1991, very few brewers produced seasonal or occasional ales; these days, very few do not. Today, the 400 independent breweries in Britain provide about 2,000 beers of widely varying styles and character, plus a plethora of one-off special or occasional brews. Wheat, tandoori, garlic, vanilla, honey, melon, coriander, lemon, orange, strawberry and liquorice are just a few of the novel flavours on offer, in addition of course to the whole raft of more traditional beers.

Fortunately, more and more enterprising publicans are now offering these brews and the image of the overweight, ageing and exclusively male real ale drinker is fading as a new generation emerges. Quality, variety and seasonal sensitivity really do count for something and the market should easily be able to support the current crop of independents. Those that produce good brews of consistent quality and possess sufficient marketing and distribution skills can continue to thrive.

But the national brewers have not gone to sleep. Keg beer, dispensed using mixed gases in an effort to mimic the character of real ale, is still gaining ground on the back of multi-million pound marketing campaigns with which no one can compete. The predatory pub companies, too, are highly professional operations that can afford the soaring cost of land and property and can deliver healthy dividends to shareholders at the same time.

Real ale campaigners have fought long and hard to get British beer back to where it is today. Keeping it there is going to be just as much of a challenge.

THE BREWING PROCESS

The brewing process is a delicate one and most brewers inevitably experience occasional problems. The very nature of real ale makes it impossible to produce a consistently uniform product, barrel after barrel, month after month.

Of course, this is part of the attraction for the drinker. There is nothing like the experience of discovering new tastes and drinking sensations, and it places a premium on the skills and experience of both the brewer and the publican. But this inconsistency is something that the makers of bland, uniform keg beers are also keen to emphasise.

The slightest variations in established practice or, more commonly, yeast infections, equipment failures, changes in water or ingredient sources can upset the brewing process and affect the resulting beer. Often, a combination of these elements causes problems. No matter how much care is taken, it is simply not feasible to expect every new brew to taste and behave just the same as it did the last time.

Even renowned, award-winning beers are sometimes unacceptably inconsistent in quality and flavour. Increased demand during the summer months in particular can lead to beer being sent out 'green', before it is really ready.

Barley started the whole process off when it grew wild in Mesopotamia 8,000 years ago, and it is still a vital ingredient for beer-making today. It is soaked in water, then spread over the floor of the malthouse and gently heated to promote germination. This releases sugars, which are vital for fermentation. The barley is constantly raked to ensure even germination throughout. Once the grains start to produce rootlets, they are roasted to prevent further germination. The higher the temperature, the darker the malt will be, and the beer produced from it will consequently be darker, with a more roasted flavour. Pale malt will impart a sweeter, more delicate flavour to the brew.

At the brewery, the malt is passed through rollers in the malt mill, which crush the grains releasing the soluble starch. It is then put in the mash tun, where it is mixed with hot water or 'liquor'. This is known as 'mashing' and converts the soluble starches into fermentable and non-fermentable sugars. Depending on the type of beer required, a mix of malts may be included.

Water used in the brewing process is usually treated in order to remove any unwanted characteristics, and to improve consistency. The 'mash' is thoroughly stirred, then allowed to stand until it becomes clear, when it is known as 'wort'.

The wort is then run into the copper, where it is boiled and hops are added. At this stage, additional ingredients, such as invert sugar to increase fermentability, may be introduced, although purists might consider this an insult to the brewer's art.

There are many different types of hops and different brews use different hops or different combinations of them. They impart the essential bitterness of flavour and aroma and help to prevent infection in the wort. Of the varieties available, those most commonly used in Britain are still the Golding and the Fuggle, although many others are rapidly finding favour.

The wort remains in the copper for a couple of hours before it is passed through the hop back, where the spent hops are removed. On its way to the fermenting vessel, the wort travels through a heat exchanger, where its temperature is reduced to 20°C. This helps to produce optimum conditions for the yeast, as extremes of temperature will either kill it or result in a sluggish fermentation.

The wort is now 'pitched', as yeast is added to the fermenting vessel. It will remain here for around five days, with the yeast feeding on the fermentable sugars while excreting alcohol and producing carbon dioxide.

A thick creamy head of yeast builds up in the fermenting vessel, and this is skimmed and retained for further use. But, as the yeast in the brew becomes tired and much of the sugar is converted to alcohol, the process slows down. Primary fermentation is now over, and it is at this point that beer produced for the keg will go its separate way from real ale.

At this stage, beer is said to be 'green' and the flavour is harsh. The next stage, then, is its transfer to conditioning tanks, where it will remain for several days and much of the remaining sugar will ferment out to produce a more rounded flavour.

At last, the beer is ready to be put into the cask, or 'racked'. By now, any harsh or undesirable flavours will have disappeared and the brew will be crisp and fresh. Finings, which draw the dying yeast cells to the bottom of the cask, are added allowing the beer to clear, or 'drop bright'.

Some fermentable sugars and living yeast cells remain, so the beer continues to ferment gently in the cask. Sometimes, priming sugar will be added to assist this secondary fermentation. Some additional hops may also be added to impart a hoppier aroma to the brew. Once in the pub cellar, the beer will continue to ferment, producing carbon dioxide, which gives real ale its natural vitality. The finings will clear the beer down and the cask will then be tapped, in preparation for use.

This final stage, which is known as cask-conditioning, typically takes two or three days and brings the beer naturally to perfection. The whole process should have taken well over a week, but the beer should now be served as soon as possible.

Assuming that a beer is in the proper condition when it leaves the brewery, plenty of damage can still be done during distribution. Most beers will 'travel', providing that they are properly handled.

The brew within the cask is a living product that must be treated with respect if it is ultimately to be served at its best. Every time a cask is rolled, the finings, which draw all the solid matter to the bottom of the cask, are activated and these will work effectively for approximately five cask rollings. Better-quality finings are available which will allow more cask rollings, but they are significantly more expensive.

Therefore, a cask from a brewer in Scotland arriving at a pub in Cornwall may well have been moved between wholesalers and rolled a number of times. It may also have been in transit too long, having been left in various stores en route, and so be nearing the end of its life even before it arrives. The result will almost certainly be a lifeless, dull brew lacking in any subtlety of flavour.

Extremes of temperature can also prevent a brew from getting into condition properly and dropping clear and bright. Casks may be left in very hot or cold conditions, in warehouses, garages or on the back of vehicles where there is no temperature control equipment. This, too, may result in a brew being damaged before it arrives at the pub and, unfortunately, the publican will not know about this until it is too late.

Co-operation is the key. Regional and larger independent brewers have, for some time, distributed beers from other breweries and an increasing number of the smaller independents are now offering their product wholesale in an effort to improve turnover and distribution. Delivering beers to a brewery in another part of the country, while collecting that brewery's beer for sale with one's own, is obviously of great benefit to both parties.

So, it is very much in a publican's interest to deal directly with the breweries wherever possible and to avoid brews from wholesalers that may arrive via a devious route. It is important, too, to boycott any source of supply if it proves necessary to return more than the occasional cask. Having said that, there are some excellent real ale wholesalers operating in Britain. The key is to find them and then deal with them only, even if this ultimately limits the range of beers on offer.

A small amount of beer is inevitably lost when spilling and tapping each cask and, no matter how carefully it may be stooped, some beer will always be unservable. For this reason, many licensees prefer to buy larger casks in order to minimise wastage, but this often results in casks remaining on-line in the cellar for too long. Once a beer has worked into condition, it will remain at its best for a relatively short period of time. Every pint pulled draws more air into the cask, increasing the rate of oxidisation. If a beer remains on-line for four or five days, although still drinkable, it will be well past its best.

In order to prevent air being taken into the cask, some cellarmen use a cask breather system, which maintains a blanket of carbon dioxide on top of the beer. The gas is at a much lower pressure than that used for the dispensing of keg beer, so there is relatively little absorbence, although it is often detectable as a pint is served.

This method of dispensing beer has become a very contentious issue and there are few hard and fast rules. Many drinkers object to long 'swan necks' or multi-holed sparklers on the end of a hand pump, although some beers are brewed deliberately to be served in this way. Some beer is at its best served through the conventional, slit-type sparkler and short neck, while other brews lose much of their condition and hoppiness if served through any form of sparkler at all. In such cases, the beer should be served straight from the barrel if its subtleties of flavour are to be enjoyed to the full.

Different beers are at their best served in different ways. To insist that all sparklers are an abomination, or that all beer is at its best straight from the wood, is to misunderstand the nature of cask-conditioned beers. Rest assured, there will undoubtedly be something for everyone – and hopefully enough to go round.

HOW TO USE THIS BOOK

The Real Ale Pub Guide is a celebration of the art of brewing in Britain. Our concern, deliberately, is not with the mass-produced market leaders, but with the smaller, independent makers of what we consider to be the real, real ales. For this reason, we do not tell you about the big, multi-national brewers and their products, good or bad. Nor do we tell you about the pubs whose reputation owes more to their location, their cooking or their range of malt whiskies, although we may mention this in passing. This is a book about beer and is aimed squarely at those who love drinking it, who want to know more about it and who want to know where to find it at its best.

The entries within England are arranged alphabetically by county, taking into account the boundary changes that came into force in 1996. Unitary authorities (such as Bristol and Leicester) have been placed in their most logical county. For some border towns and villages the postal address is in one county while the actual pub is over the boundary. We have tried to place all the entries in the counties to which they actually belong, but be prepared for some county-hopping along borders. Scotland and Wales are organised first by region and then alphabetically by town.

Each county contains details first of the breweries (including brewpubs and micro-breweries linked or attached to pubs) within it and then of the pubs themselves, organised alphabetically by town or village. We list as many beers brewed as possible but an increasing number of occasional, seasonal and celebration ales make this an inexact science. You may find a beer not listed here – well, rejoice at the diversity!

We have attempted to give as full an address as possible for pubs and a telephone number in almost every case. Some even have websites, although these may not be too rigorously maintained. Brief directions may also be found within the entry itself but, if you do get lost, a call ahead should keep the inconvenience to a minimum.

For the past few editions, London has been treated slightly differently to the rest of the book. There are more pubs in the capital than anywhere else in the country and a large number of them sell real ale, albeit of varying quality. There are also many chains, such as Wetherspoons, and tied houses owned by the region's brewers, many of which are hard to separate. With this in mind, full entries in London are only given to pubs that we feel truly offer a good selection of interesting beers. Chains and tied houses are listed at the end of each postal area and these are well worth a look, too.

We are expanding our coverage around the country, carrying out many more anonymous inspections and benefiting greatly from the growing number of readers who send us their comments, reports or recommendations. With your help, and that of our developing band of volunteers, we are growing every year.

Our primary aim is to make this guide as useful to people looking for a place to drink good real ale as possible. The criteria for an entry, therefore, is that a selection of real ales is always available, whether the pub is a freehouse, a tied house or belongs to a chain.

Where possible, we have sought to include the licensee's name for we believe that the character and quality of a pub owes much to the person who runs it. Inevitably, these people move on and many enjoy the challenge of taking on a new pub and establishing its place on the map. While every acknowledgement should be made of the nation's finest innkeepers, this is more than just a chance for publicans to see their names in print. We hope that readers will recognise the people who run successful pubs and, as they move, need no other recommendation to visit than that person's name.

Because we believe the beers are the most important thing, we have sought to give an indication of the names and numbers of ales that you are likely to find when you walk through the door. Of course, availability varies and, on some days, the choice will be wider than on others. Nevertheless, a pub that says it has 12 beers on tap should come reasonably close to doing just that. If you discover this is not the case, then we want to know.

There is a short description of the type of pub to be found with each entry. If they specialise in a certain type of food, or have accommodation or other features, we have sought to tell you. However, as this is not the purpose of our guide, we have kept the details to a minimum.

Opening hours are another feature that will vary. An increasing number of pubs are opening for longer and later than was the case just a few years ago. However, we suggest that, if you are proposing to visit in the middle of the afternoon, a telephone call ahead will avoid disappointment.

It would be impossible to include an entry for every real ale pub in the country. Similarly, there are many pubs about which we have heard favourable reports but which we have so far been unable to verify for ourselves. Perhaps, if you get there first, you can let us know what you find by returning one of the questionnaires at the back of the book. If you find a pub that does not live up to your expectations or you know of an absent pub that should be included, we would love to hear from you. Some of the pubs already recommended are highlighted with a 'Reader's Report' logo. Please send us your completed questionnaire, or e-mail realale@foulsham.com with your comments. Many thanks.

Nicolas Andrews

The Real Ale Pub Guide seeks out and promotes Britain's finest beer-drinking establishments. We sincerely hope that every pub featured in this guide will satisfy those who go looking for something a little bit special in their pint glass. We also recognise that taste is a personal thing and so seek to celebrate the marvellous diversity of beers produced by the nation's independent regional and microbrewers. Some pubs, though, are extra special, centres of real ale excellence about which we might all agree.

Last year we introduced a new section highlighting a dozen pubs that we believe are well worth travelling the extra mile to visit. While we would never be so bold as to try to produce a list of the best 12 pubs in Britain, our team of researchers has put its collective head together and has no hesitation in recommending the following as this year's best of the best.

We have tried to spread our selection around Britain and we know that there are many other equally deserving candidates. Next year, we will highlight 12 more. Each of the pubs chosen is marked in the book with a star. We should be delighted to hear your views and your nominations for 2006. But, in the mean time (and in no particular order), we give you *The Real Ale Pub Guide* Twelve of the Best 2005:

The Watermill Inn
Ings, Near Staveley, Kendal, Cumbria
(page 71)
With 14 breweries now flourishing, the Lake District is the real ale capital of Britain. This former mill offers 16 brews to choose from, so is there be anywhere better to toast the industry?

The Oakdale Arms
283 Hermitage Road, Harringay, London N4
(page 230)
A new arrival on the London real ale scene, already winning awards and richly deserving of all the encouragement we can give it.

The Turk's Head
St Agnes, Isles of Scilly
(page 176)
Our favourite pub on these magical islands. Take the booze cruise from St Mary's straight to the pub for a top evening's drinking.

The Boat Inn
The Quay, Ashleworth, Gloucestershire
(page 127)
A friendly, tranquil, long-established Severnside jewel serving beers straight from the barrel.

Pear Tree Inn
Scotland End, Hook Norton, Oxfordshire
(page 307)
Hook Norton beers at their freshest and finest from the tap in the shadow of one of England's best-loved breweries.

The Fat Cat
Sheffield, South Yorkshire
(page 444)
The Kelham Island Brewery tap, so the place to drink Pale Rider, Camra's Champion Beer of Britain 2004, before working through the five guests.

The Three Judges
141 Dumbarton Road, Patrick Cross, Glasgow, Scotland
(page 477)
Our man on the ground reports that this West End favourite is better than ever after a sympathetic refurbishment last year.

Plough and Harrow
Monknash, Near Llantwit Major, Vale of Glamorgan, Wales
(page 503)
A vibrant atmosphere and a splendid selection of real ale, most straight from the barrel. South Wales's finest?

The Priory Arms
83 Lansdowne Way, Stockwell, London SW8
(Page 244)
The capital does not boast many genuine freehouses with such a commitment to the real ale cause, but this one stands out and has won enough awards to prove it.

The Hollybush
Bedmond Lane, Potter's Crouch, Near St Albans, Hertfordshire
(Page 161)
If London Pride is now the most popular real ale in Britain and the licensee here is recognised as among the brewery's finest, can there be a better place to drink Fuller's ales?

The Massingberd Arms
Brinkhill Road, South Ormsby, Louth, Lincolnshire
(Page 216)
A new discovery for us this year which we are anxious to promote from the outset. The range may not be huge, but it is varied and interesting.

And finally...

Lewes, Sussex
(Pages 368–369)
Instead of a twelfth pub, we cheated last year by picking Southwold for the sheer number of top-quality Adnams pubs in the town. The home of Harvey's in Sussex is just as deserving. We list five pubs, but there are others worth checking out, too.

The Twelve of the Best 2004:
The Wenlock Arms, London N1
The Fat Cat, Norwich, Norfolk
Bhurtpore Inn, Aston, Cheshire
The Hobgoblin, Reading, Berkshire
Ship and Mitre, Liverpool, Merseyside
The Royal Oak, London SE1
Red Lion, Snargate, Kent
Red Lion, Ampney St Peter, Gloucestershire
Ram Inn, Cwmann, Mid-Wales
Duke of York, Iddlesleigh, Devon
and Southwold, Suffolk

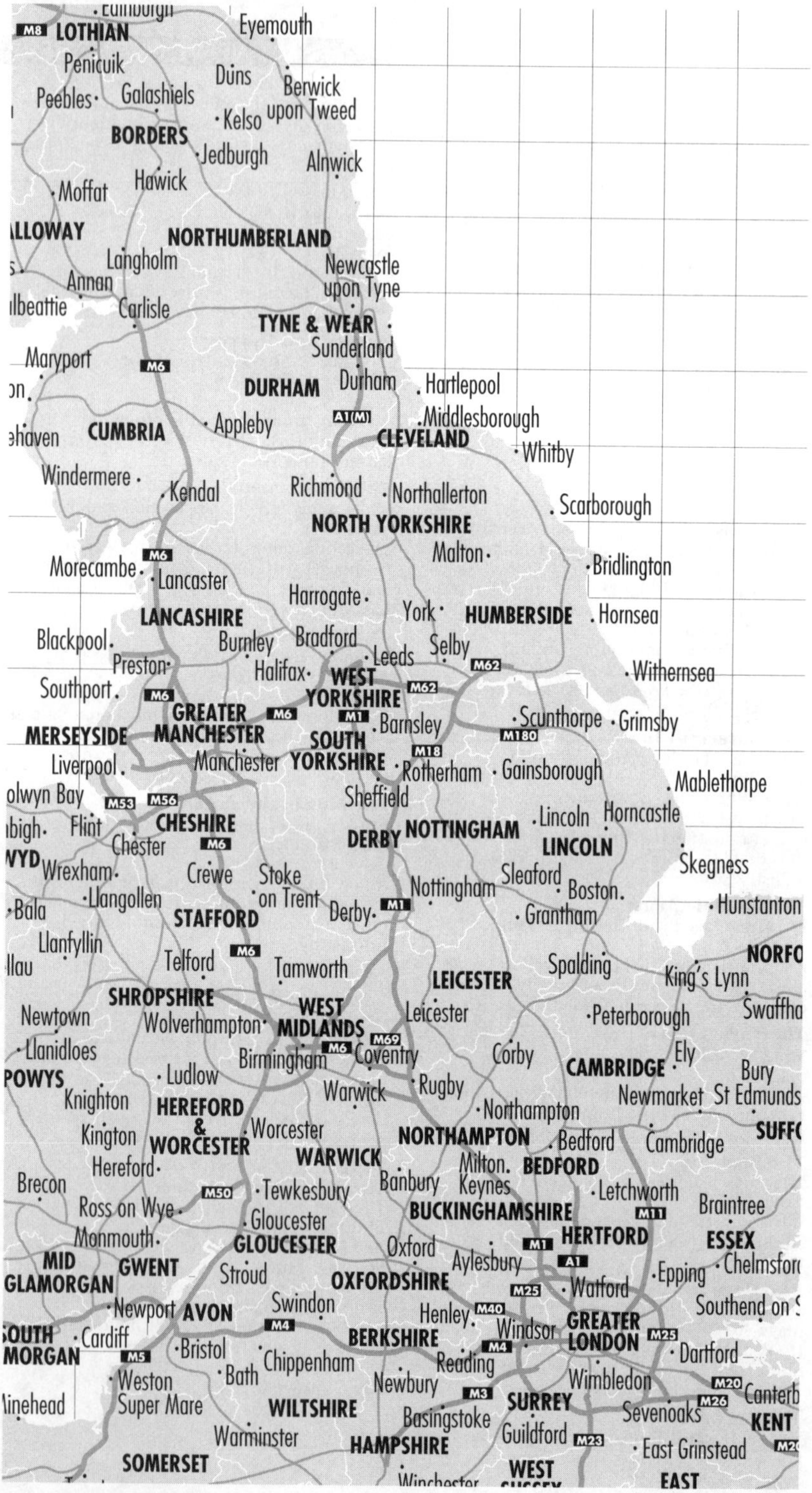

Edinburgh
M8 LOTHIAN
Eyemouth
Penicuik
Duns
Berwick upon Tweed
Peebles
Galashiels
Kelso
BORDERS
Jedburgh
Alnwick
Moffat
Hawick
GALLOWAY
NORTHUMBERLAND
Langholm
Newcastle upon Tyne
Annan
Dalbeattie
Carlisle
TYNE & WEAR
Sunderland
Maryport
M6
DURHAM
Durham
Hartlepool
A1(M)
Middlesborough
Whitehaven
CUMBRIA
Appleby
CLEVELAND
Whitby
Windermere
Kendal
Richmond
Northallerton
Scarborough
NORTH YORKSHIRE
Malton
M6
Bridlington
Morecambe
Lancaster
Harrogate
York
HUMBERSIDE
Hornsea
LANCASHIRE
Blackpool
Burnley
Bradford
Selby
Leeds
M62
Preston
Halifax
WEST YORKSHIRE
M62
Withernsea
Southport
M6
GREATER MANCHESTER
M6
M1
Barnsley
Scunthorpe
Grimsby
MERSEYSIDE
SOUTH YORKSHIRE
M180
M18
Liverpool
Manchester
Rotherham
Gainsborough
Mablethorpe
Colwyn Bay
M53
M56
Sheffield
Denbigh
Flint
CHESHIRE
Lincoln
Horncastle
CLWYD
Chester
M6
DERBY
NOTTINGHAM
LINCOLN
Wrexham
Crewe
Stoke on Trent
Skegness
Llangollen
Nottingham
Sleaford
Boston
Bala
STAFFORD
Derby
M1
Grantham
Hunstanton
Llanfyllin
M6
NORFOLK
Dolgellau
Telford
Tamworth
LEICESTER
Spalding
King's Lynn
SHROPSHIRE
WEST MIDLANDS
Leicester
Swaffham
Newtown
Wolverhampton
MIDLANDS
Peterborough
M69
Llanidloes
M6
Coventry
Corby
Ely
Birmingham
CAMBRIDGE
Bury St Edmunds
POWYS
Ludlow
Rugby
Warwick
Newmarket
Knighton
HEREFORD & WORCESTER
Northampton
SUFFOLK
Kington
Worcester
NORTHAMPTON
Bedford
Cambridge
Hereford
WARWICK
Milton Keynes
BEDFORD
Brecon
M50
Tewkesbury
Banbury
Letchworth
Ross on Wye
BUCKINGHAMSHIRE
Braintree
Gloucester
M11
Monmouth
GLOUCESTER
HERTFORD
ESSEX
MID GLAMORGAN
GWENT
Oxford
M1
Aylesbury
A1
Stroud
Epping
Chelmsford
OXFORDSHIRE
M25
Watford
Newport
AVON
Swindon
Southend on Sea
Henley
M40
SOUTH GLAMORGAN
Cardiff
M4
BERKSHIRE
Windsor
GREATER LONDON
M25
Bristol
M4
Dartford
M5
Chippenham
Reading
Weston Super Mare
Bath
Newbury
Wimbledon
M20
Canterbury
Minehead
M3
SURREY
M26
WILTSHIRE
Basingstoke
Sevenoaks
KENT
Warminster
Guildford
M23
East Grinstead
HAMPSHIRE
M20
SOMERSET
WEST SUSSEX
EAST
Winchester

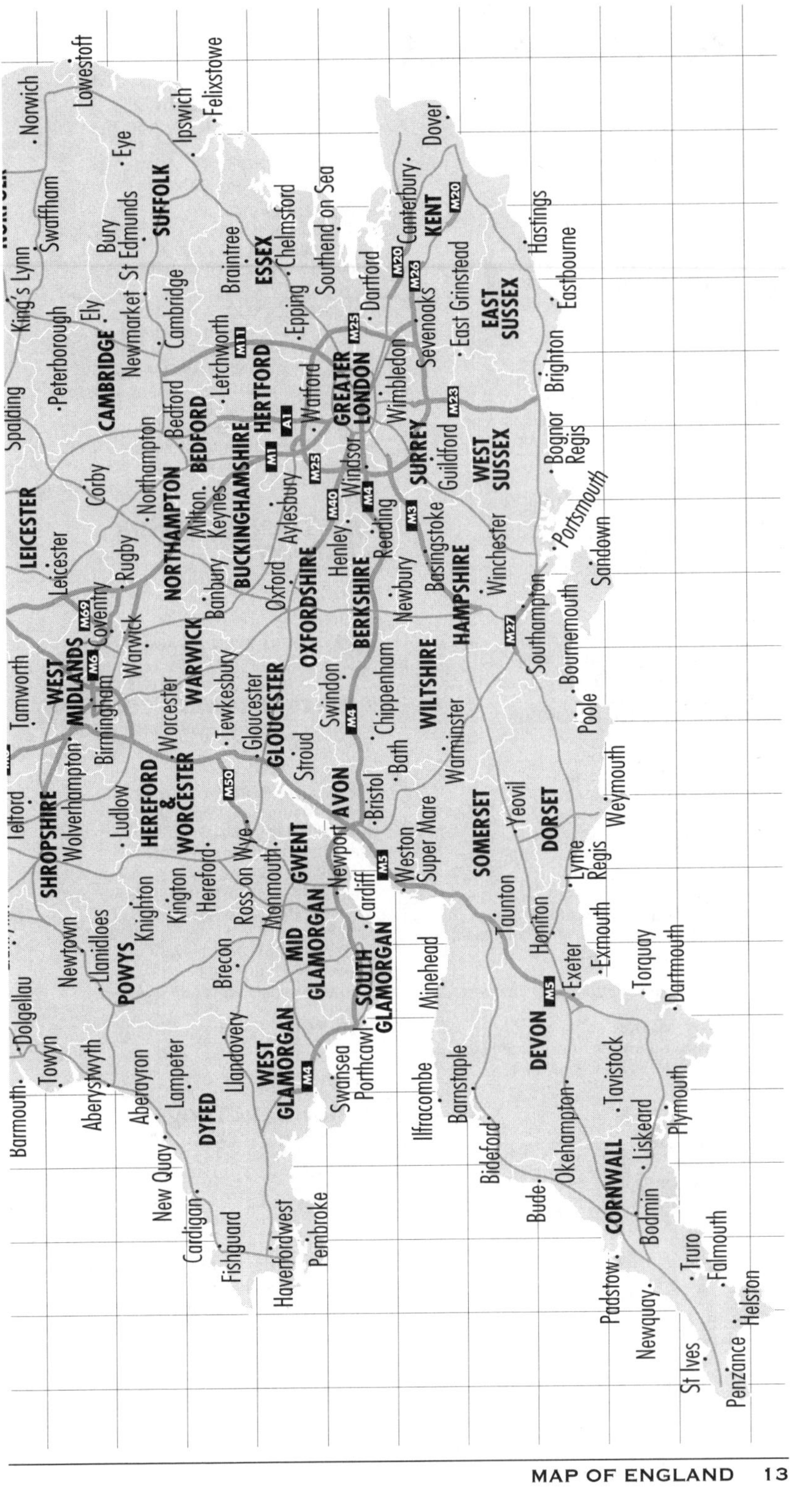

Norwich
Lowestoft
Felixstowe
Ipswich
Eye
Swaffham
King's Lynn
Bury St Edmunds
SUFFOLK
Braintree
Chelmsford
ESSEX
Southend on Sea
Dover
Canterbury
KENT
M20
Hastings
Eastbourne
East Grinstead
EAST SUSSEX
Brighton
Sevenoaks
M26
Dartford
M25
Epping
Cambridge
Newmarket
Ely
Peterborough
CAMBRIDGE
Spalding
Letchworth
M11
HERTFORD
Watford
A1
GREATER LONDON
Wimbledon
M23
Bognor Regis
WEST SUSSEX
SURREY
Guildford
Portsmouth
Sandown
Bedford
BEDFORD
Northampton
M1
M25
Windsor
M4
M3
Basingstoke
Winchester
LEICESTER
Leicester
Corby
Rugby
NORTHAMPTON
Milton Keynes
BUCKINGHAMSHIRE
Aylesbury
M40
Henley
Reading
Banbury
Oxford
OXFORDSHIRE
BERKSHIRE
Newbury
HAMPSHIRE
Southampton
M27
Bournemouth
Poole
Tamworth
WEST MIDLANDS
M6
M69
Coventry
Warwick
WARWICK
Tewkesbury
Gloucester
GLOUCESTER
Swindon
M4
Chippenham
WILTSHIRE
Warminster
Birmingham
Worcester
Wolverhampton
Telford
SHROPSHIRE
Ludlow
HEREFORD & WORCESTER
M50
Stroud
Bath
Bristol
AVON
Weymouth
DORSET
Yeovil
SOMERSET
Lyme Regis
Weston Super Mare
M5
Newport
GWENT
Monmouth
Ross on Wye
Hereford
Kington
Knighton
Llanidloes
Newtown
POWYS
Brecon
MID GLAMORGAN
Cardiff
SOUTH GLAMORGAN
Minehead
Taunton
Honiton
Exmouth
Exeter
M5
Torquay
Dartmouth
DEVON
Dolgellau
Towyn
Barmouth
Aberystwyth
Aberayron
Lampeter
Llandovery
WEST GLAMORGAN
M4
Swansea
Porthcawl
Ilfracombe
Barnstaple
Tavistock
Okehampton
Plymouth
Liskeard
DYFED
New Quay
Cardigan
Fishguard
Haverfordwest
Pembroke
Bideford
Bude
CORNWALL
Bodmin
Padstow
Truro
Falmouth
Newquay
Helston
St Ives
Penzance

THE BREWERIES

B & T BREWERY LTD

The Brewery, Shefford SG17 5DZ
☎ *(01462) 815080*
www.banksandtaylor.com

SHEFFORD BITTER 3.8% ABV
Golden and hoppy with dry hop finish.
SHEFFORD DARK MILD 3.8% ABV
Rich, mellow, dry and hoppy.
DRAGON SLAYER 4.5% ABV
Light-coloured, with subtle malt and hops.
SHEFFORD PALE ALE 4.5% ABV
Hoppy with balancing malt and dry finish.
SHEFFORD OLD DARK 5.0% ABV
Deep red, sweet caramel and malt flavour.
SHEFFORD OLD STRONG 5.0% ABV
Hoppy with bitter malty flavour.
BLACK BAT 6.0% ABV
Ruby black, malt and fruit flavour.
2XS 6.0% ABV
Golden, rich aroma and fruit undertones.
OLD BAT 7.0% ABV
Full-flavoured winter beer with sweetness and a fruity aroma.
Seasonals:
MIDSUMMER ALE 3.5% ABV
Straw-coloured, easy-drinking brew.
BARLEY MOW 3.8% ABV
Quenching hoppy brew.
BEDFORDSHIRE CLANGER 3.8% ABV
Crisp and well-hopped.
SANTA'S SLAYER 4.0% ABV
Sweeter fruit and malt flavour.
TURKEY'S TRAUMA 4.0% ABV
Well-balanced beer.
MADHATTER ALE 4.2% ABV
Malty, copper-coloured with a hoppy nose.
BODYSNATCHER 4.5% ABV
Sweetness with balancing hops.
OXFORD REBELLION 5.0% ABV
Reddish colour, hoppy overtones on a malt finish.
SHEFFORD WHEAT BEER 5.0% ABV
Sharp and refreshing, 50/50 pale and wheat hops.
FROSTBITE 5.5% ABV
Pale gold with hoppy overtones on malt finish.
Plus other regular commemorative and celebratory brews.

CHARLES WELLS LTD

The Eagle Brewery, Havelock Street, Bedford MK40 4LU
☎ *(01234) 272766*
www.charleswells.co.uk

EAGLE 3.6% ABV
Balanced, dry, full-flavoured IPA.
BOMBARDIER 4.3% ABV
Hoppy, well-balanced with dry finish.
Seasonals:
SUMMER SOLSTICE 4.1% ABV
Full-flavoured, refreshingly malty with distinctive bitterness.
LOCK, STOCK AND BARREL 4.3% ABV
Red-brown in colour, intriguing and complex with a bittersweet finish.
BANANA BREAD BEER 4.5% ABV
Dark, golden and intense with banana flavour.
NAKED GOLD 4.5% ABV
Creamy head and pronounced nutty flavour.

OLD STABLES BREWING COMPANY

Sir William Peel, 39 High Street, Sandy SG16 6AA
☎ *(01767) 692151*

STABLE ALE 4.2% ABV
Light, hoppy bitter.

POTTON BREWING COMPANY

10 Shannon Place, Potton, Sandy SG19 2PZ
☎ *(01767) 261042*
www.potton-brewery.co.uk

SHANNON IPA 3.6% ABV
Traditional, hoppy IPA.
PHOENIX 3.8% ABV
Soft, smooth and hoppy.
SHAMBLES 4.3% ABV
Hoppy bitterness with balancing sweetness.
VILLAGE BIKE 4.3% ABV
Hoppy brew.
PRIDE OF POTTON 6.0% ABV
Warming and dry-hopped.
Plus seasonal and occasional brews.

THE PUBS

ASTWICK

Tudor Oaks Lodge

Taylors Road, Astwick, Nr Hitchin SG5 4AZ
☎ *(01462) 834133* Mr E Welek
www.thetudoroakslodge.co.uk

A freehouse serving up to seven real ales from a constantly changing range.

On the Hertfordshire–Bedfordshire border, a fifteenth-century coaching inn with 13 bedrooms and a restaurant. Set around a central courtyard. Food available at lunchtime and evenings. Children allowed, outside seating. Situated off the A1.

OPEN *All day, every day.*

BEDFORD

The Castle

17 Newnham Street, Bedford MK40 3JR
☎ *(01234) 353295* Tom Sahota

A Charles Wells tenancy, with Eagle and Bombardier plus four guest beers available from a range of 12 per year including Greene King Old Speckled Hen, Marston's Pedigree, Young's Special, Brains Bitter and Badger Tanglefoot.

A two-bar pub on the edge of town with a country pub atmosphere. Bar food available at lunchtime and evenings. Garden. Car park, accommodation. Well-behaved children allowed.

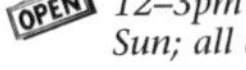 *12–3pm and 5.30–11pm Mon–Thurs and Sun; all day Fri–Sat.*

De Pary's Hotel

45 De Pary's Avenue, Bedford MK40 2UA
☎ *(01234) 352121* Sonia Pollard
www.hotelsinbedford.co.uk

Charles Wells Eagle always available plus a range of guests, often featuring Potton, Nethergate and Crouch Vale Brewery ales or Fuller's London Pride. Beers changed weekly, with an emphasis on smaller breweries.

Owned by Choice Inns, a 25-bedroom hotel with bar and 100-seater restaurant and private function room. Situated near the park. Food available at lunchtimes and evenings Monday to Saturday, and all day Sunday. Large, attractive award-winning garden with children's play area. Beer festivals and fmily fun days.

 *11am–11pm (10.30pm Sun).*

The Embankment Hotel

The Embankment, Bedford MK40 3PD
☎ *(01234) 261332* Lisa Bayley
www.hotelsinbedford.co.uk

Four real ales usually available. CharlesWells Eagle and Bombardier are permanent fixtures, with the other two rotating every couple of weeks.

A nineteenth-century hotel beside the River Ouse. Twenty bedrooms and an 80-seater restaurant. Food served at lunchtime and evenings Mon–Thurs, all day Fri–Sun. Car park at rear, children welcome. Tables and chairs outside for riverside drinking.

 *11am–11pm (10.30pm Sun).*

The Wellington Arms

Wellington Street, Bedford MK40 2JX
☎ *(01234) 308033* Eric Mills
www.wellingtonarms.co.uk

A B&T tied house, with Two Brewers (the house brew) always available, plus up to ten guests including seasonal brews from B&T and other micro-breweries. There is always a mild, a stout and a porter available. Plus four Belgian beers on draught and real cider and perry.

A traditional one-bar street-corner local with wooden floors. Regular local and regional CAMRA Pub of the Year. Large collection of real ale memorabilia, including bottles and pump clips. Filled rolls available at lunchtime. Outside drinking area. Small car park. Live music most Tuesdays. Situated near the prison.

 *12–11pm (10.30pm Sun).*

BIGGLESWADE

The Brown Bear

29 Hitchin Street, Biggleswade SG18 8BE
☎ *(01767) 316161* David Carter

At least four hand pumps, serving a range that might include Shepherd Neame Spitfire, Timothy Taylor Landlord and Fuller's London Pride.

Former freehouse sold by its previous owners to Enterprise Inns and sadly scaling down the real ale emphasis as a result. A two-bar, open-plan town-centre pub with a large non-smoking eating area. Bar snacks available at lunchtime and evenings. On the main street, off the market square.

 *12–3pm and 5–11pm Mon–Fri; 11am–11pm Sat; 7–10.30pm Sun (closed lunchtime).*

The Wheatsheaf

5 Lawrence Road, Biggleswade SG18 0LS
☎ *(01767) 222220*

Greene King IPA and XX Mild regularly available.

Simple, unspoilt, small and friendly one-bar pub known locally for its well-kept beer. Cask Marque award winner. No food. Pub games and Sky TV. Beer garden and children's play area.

 *11am–4pm and 7–11pm Mon–Thurs; 11am–11pm Fri–Sat; 12–10.30pm Sun.*

BROOM

The Cock

23 High Street, Broom
☎ *(01767) 314411* Gerry and Jean Lant

Greene King IPA, Abbot and Ruddles County always available.

A 300-year-old Grade II listed village pub in which the beers are served direct from the barrels in the cellar. Food available 12–2.30pm every day and 7–9pm Monday to Saturday. Children welcome, with family room available. Dogs allowed. Car park. Garden, plus caravan and campsite available. Situated off the A1 at Biggleswade roundabout.

 *12–3pm and 6–11pm Mon–Fri; 12–4pm and 6–11pm Sat; 12–4pm and 7–10.30pm Sun.*

CAMPTON

The White Hart

Mill Lane, Campton, Near Shefford SG17 5NX
☎ *01462 812657* Jerry Cannon

Genuine freehouse with up to six brews available. Hook Norton Best, Marston's Pedigree, Theakston Best and Greene King Ruddles County are usually among them, plus guest ales which could come from any UK independent brewery.

Grade II listed, 300-year-old village freehouse with three bar areas. Run by the same family for more than 30 years. A traditional brick and beam interior including inglenook fireplaces, decorated with rural artefacts and antiquities. No pool table. No juke box. No food except when pre-booked for functions. Children welcome. Large garden with patio, petanque area and children's play area. Large car park. Folk club on Wednesdays. Located off the A507, just outside Shefford.

 *7–11pm Mon–Fri (closed lunchtimes); 12–11pm Sat; 12–3pm and 7–10.30pm Sun.*

CLOPHILL

The Stone Jug

Back Street, Clophill MK45 4BY
☎ *(01525) 860526* Joyce and Vikki Stevens

B&T Shefford always available, plus two guests, changed frequently, from breweries across Britain. Often including local ales from local breweries such as Potton and Tring, but also Nethergate, Archers and many more.

A traditional backstreet country freehouse, built around 1700 as three cottages and converted into a pub in the nineteenth century. One large bar area, front patio and small patio at back. Crib, darts and dominoes. Food available 12–3pm Monday to Saturday. Separate room available for children. Good walking nearby. Between Luton and Bedford, off the A6.

 *12–4pm and 6–11pm Mon–Thurs; 12–11pm Fri; 11am–11pm Sat; 12–10.30pm Sun.*

DUNSTABLE

The Victoria

69 West Street, Dunstable LU6 1ST
☎ *(01582) 662682* Dave and Val Hobbs

Five hand pumps regularly serving a house beer (Victoria Ale) from the Tring Brewery and four guests (approx 200 per year) from independent breweries such as Potton, Fuller's, Young's, Adnams, Everards, Vale, Mauldons, Cottage, Wye Valley, York and Fernandes.

A traditional, friendly single-bar pub next to the police station just outside the town centre. Bar food is served at lunchtimes only (12–3pm), with roasts on Sundays. Well-behaved children allowed. The landlord's policy is to have a session, a premium and a mind-blowing beer always on sale! Regular beer festivals held in the barn at the rear of the pub. Function room. Small patio-style garden with heaters where regular barbecues are held in summer.

 *All day, every day.*

EVERSHOLT

Green Man

Church End, Eversholt MK17 9DU
☎ *(01525) 280293*

Two guest beers are on offer, from a range of independent breweries.

Early Victorian building opposite the church. Food available at lunchtime and evenings (bar snacks all day). Garden with children's play area and aviary. Car park. Two miles from Woburn Abbey.

OPEN *12–11pm (10.30pm Sun).*

EVERTON

The Thornton Arms

1 Potton Road, Everton, Sandy SG19 2LD
☎ *(01767) 681149* Michael Hall
www.the-thornton-arms.co.uk

Charles Wells IPA and Fuller's London Pride usually available, plus guest ales which change all the time, with local micro-breweries supported as much as possible.

A traditional nineteenth-century pub with two bars. Food available 12–2pm, including Sunday roasts. Children allowed until 9pm. Beer garden. Live music. Sunday quiz nights. Located in the centre of the village.

 *12–2.30pm and 6–11pm Mon–Fri; 12–11pm Sat; 12–10.30pm Sun.*

GREAT BARFORD

The Golden Cross

2–4 Bedford Road, Great Barford MK44 3JD
☎ *(01234) 870439 or 871727*
Messrs KP Li, WK Li and LF Li

Greene King IPA, Charles Wells Eagle and Everards Tiger usually available, with other brews appearing occasionally.

A traditional, 150-year-old village pub on the main road with an unconventional twist as the rear lounge bar houses a Chinese restaurant. Only Chinese food is available (not Mon or Tues lunchtimes). Children allowed in restaurant. Outside seating and car park.

12–2.30pm and 5.30–11pm Mon–Fri; 12–11pm Sat; 12–10.30pm Sun.

HARROLD

The Magpie

54 High Street, Harrold, Bedford MK43 7DA
☎ *(01234) 720071*
Norman Wilson and Jean Leeson

A Charles Wells house with Eagle and Bombardier always available plus guests.

A busy, traditional single-bar country pub with beams and open fireplaces. Pool table, garden, car park. Children allowed.

12–3pm and 5–11pm Mon–Fri; 12–11pm Sat; 12–10.30pm Sun.

HENLOW

The Engineers Arms

68 High Street, Henlow SG16 6AA
☎ *(01462) 812284*
Kevin Machin and Claire Sturgeon
www.engineersarms.co.uk

Everards Tiger and something from the Potton Brewery are always available plus an ever-changing range of guests. Up to nine brews may be on offer at any one time (15 per week) and the selection changes daily.

Popular, award-winning two-bar village freehouse with a real fire and pleasant beer terrace. Sky TV in a separate room. Fresh rolls and traditional hot pies available. Children welcome in separate room and garden. Regular beer festivals. The pub is in Henlow village, not Henlow Camp. Off the A507 Hitchin to Bedford road.

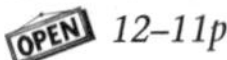
12–11pm (10.30pm Sun).

LEIGHTON BUZZARD

The Crown

72 North Street, Leighton Buzzard LU7 1EN
☎ *(01525) 217770* Dave Maslen

Greene King IPA plus three guest ales usually available and selected from independent or micro-breweries.

A traditional-style pub in a modern building on the outskirts of the town centre. Large island bar. Food served at lunchtime and evenings. Outside seating. Children welcome.

11am–11pm Mon–Sat; 12–10.30pm Sun.

The Stag

1 Heath Road, Leighton Buzzard LU7 8AB
☎ *(01525) 372710*
Peter Fleckney and Cathy Ives
www.thestagph.com

A Fuller's pub with four beers usually available, including three from the brewery range (London Pride, ESB and a seasonal) plus one guest.

A traditional town pub with one wood-panelled bar and a local clientele. Food served Mon–Fri lunchtimes (12–2pm) and evenings (6–9.30pm) plus Saturday (12–9pm) and Sunday (12–6pm). Children not allowed. Outside seating, car park.

12–2.30pm and 6–11pm Mon–Fri; all day Sat–Sun.

LUTON

The Bricklayers Arms

16–18 Hightown Road, Luton LU2 0DD
☎ *(01582) 611017* Alison Taylor

Everards Beacon and Tiger, plus B&T Golden Hatter usually available with two ever-changing guest beers from a wide range of local and regional breweries.

Bare boards and barrels set the tone for this traditional pub, first known to be trading in 1834. Formerly owned by Banks and Taylor. Lunchtime bar snacks served 12–2pm Monday to Friday. Sky TV, car park. Quiz night on Mondays. No children. Close to the railway station.

12–2.30pm and 5–11pm Mon–Thurs; 12–11pm Fri–Sat; 12–10.30pm Sun.

The Globe

26 Union Street, Luton LU1 3AN
☎ *(01582) 728681* Ian Mackay

Greene King IPA usually available, plus two guests from a frequently changing range. More brews are available at the pub's regular beer festivals.

Friendly one-bar street-corner pub, situated just outside the town centre. Strong local support, with bar games and teams a regular feature. All major sporting events shown. Car park plus large patio area. Children allowed at meal times. Food served 11am–3pm Mon–Fri, 10am–3pm Sat.

OPEN *All day, every day.*

Mother Redcap

Latimer Road, Luton LU1 3XD
☎ *(01582) 730913* Bill and Noreen Lauden

A Greene King tied house with IPA and Abbot permanently available, plus one guest such as Greene King Old Speckled Hen or Ruddles Best or County.

A typical drinkers' backstreet local in a traditional building. Outside seating at the front. Car park. Pool, darts, juke box and fruit machines. Bar food lunchtimes (not Sun). Children allowed at lunchtime only.

OPEN *11am–11pm Mon–Sat; 12–10.30pm Sun.*

The Two Brewers

43 Dumfries Street, Luton LU1 5AY
☎ *(01582) 616008* Andy Gill

Two Tring beers always available, plus up to four ever-changing guest ales from Crouch Vale, Iceni, Kitchen, Slater's and Hook Norton, among others.

A welcoming, old-style, backstreet pub two minutes from the town centre. Refurbished by Tring Brewery, although no longer owned by them. Food available 12–3pm Mon–Sat. Children allowed, live music evenings, beer festivals.

OPEN *12–11pm (10.30pm Sun).*

The Wheelwright's Arms

34 Guildford Street, Luton LU1 2NR
☎ *(01582) 759321* Alex Dalgarno

A freehouse with Fuller's ESB and London Pride among the beers always available. Two guests might include something else from Fuller's, perhaps seasonal beers such as Summer Ale, Honey Dew, and Red Fox.

Traditional drinkers' pub in a mid-nineteenth-century building, with one large bar, garden and seating. Food available at lunchtime and evenings. Pool, snooker, darts. Live music very occasionally. Fifteen bedrooms. Children allowed until early evening. Near the bus station.

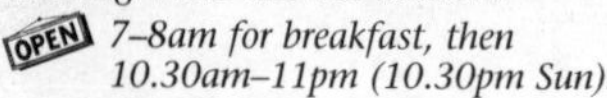
OPEN *7–8am for breakfast, then 10.30am–11pm (10.30pm Sun).*

MILLBROOK VILLAGE

The Chequers at Millbrook

Millbrook Village MK45 2JB
☎ *(01525) 403835* Thomas Polti

Something from Stonehenge (Pigswill, Heel Stone or Body Line) or from Country Life (Old Appledore, Wallop) always available and changed on a weekly basis.

An Italian family-run pub specialising in pasta, chargrilled meat, fish and award-winning coffee. Food served 12–2pm and 7–9pm (Tues to Sat). Children allowed in the restaurant. Car park, beer garden. Located off A507 from Ridgmont.

OPEN *11.30am–2.30pm and 6.30–11pm Tues–Sat (closed Sun and Mon).*

ODELL

The Bell

Horsefair Lane, Odell MK47 7AU
☎ *(01234) 720254* Kyla Benning

A Greene King tied house with IPA and Abbot always available plus Ruddles County and/or Old Speckled Hen and a guest.

Thatched 300-year-old village pub with log fires, five rooms and a large garden (complete with aviary) backing onto the Great Ouse. Good food available 12–2pm daily and 6.30–9.15pm Mon–Sat. Children welcome, car park. Close to Harrold Country Park. North of Bedford, off the A6.

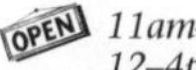
OPEN *11am–3pm and 6–11pm Mon–Sat; 12–4pm and 7–10.30pm Sun.*

POTTON

The Red Lion

1 Station Road, Potton, Sandy SG19 2PZ
☎ *(01767) 262705*

Greene King IPA always available during the summer months, and Greene King Old Speckled Hen during the winter. Plus seasonal guests.

A one-bar drinkers' pub with pool, skittles, big-screen TV and live music. Beer garden. Parking. No food. No children.

OPEN *5–11pm Mon–Fri (7–11pm in winter); all day Sat–Sun and bank holidays.*

RAVENSDEN

The Blacksmith's Arms

Bedford Road, Ravensden
☎ *(01234) 771496* Pat O'Hara

Fuller's London Pride, Greene King IPA and Abbot and Marston's Pedigree permanently available, plus occasional guests in summer.

A family-friendly, food-oriented pub and restaurant in traditional style with beams and fireplaces. Food served throughout opening hours. Garden. Parking. Live music and quiz nights.

 *12–3pm and 6–11pm Mon–Sat; 12–10.30pm Sun.*

RIDGMONT

The Rose & Crown

89 High Street, Ridgmont MK43 0TY
☎ *(01525) 280245* Neil McGregor

Charles Wells Eagle and Bombardier plus Adnams Broadside usually available. Other guests might include Greene King Old Speckled Hen, Everards Tiger or a Young's brew.

A traditional, 300-year-old, two-bar rural pub with food available (12–2pm and 7–9pm). Children allowed. Outside seating to the front and in the enormous rear garden. Car park. Camping and caravan site nearby.

 *10.30am–2.30pm and 6–11pm (10.30pm Sun).*

SANDY

Sir William Peel

39 High Street, Sandy SG16 6AA
☎ *(01767) 680607* Lindsey Hehir

Home of the Old Stables Brewery since 2002. Stable Ale, Black Beauty, Palomino and Bright Bay Best available, plus seasonal brews, Everards Beacon and two guests from other micro-breweries.

Opened in 1838 as the Lord Nelson, this welcoming and traditional pub was renamed after Captain Sir William Peel who, apart from his distinguished military service, built the railway line. Rolls and bar snacks only. Outside seating and car park. Two minutes from the station.

 *12–11pm Mon–Fri; 11am–11pm Sat; 12–10.30pm Sun.*

SHARNBROOK

The Swan with Two Necks

High Street, Sharnbrook MK44 1PM
☎ *(01234) 871585* Mr and Mrs Baxter

Charles Wells Eagle IPA and Bombardier plus Greene King Old Speckled Hen always on offer, as well as one guest beer.

Village pub with food available (snacks and full menu) 12–2.30pm and 6–9pm Mon–Thurs, 12–2.30pm and 6–10pm Fri–Sat, 12–2.30pm Sun (including roasts). Children welcome. Car park.

 *11.30am–3pm and 5–11pm Mon–Fri; all day Sat–Sun.*

SHEFFORD

The Brewery Tap

14 North Bridge Street, Shefford SG17 5DH
☎ *(01462) 628448* Mr D Mortimer

B&T Shefford Bitter, Mild and Dragon Slayer always available plus seasonal B&T brews. Also at least one guest beer, perhaps from Wye Valley or Crouch Vale.

One-bar local beer house. Hot pies and rolls served at lunchtimes. Live music. Children allowed (family room and outside seating). Car park.

 *11.30am–11pm Mon–Sat; 12–10.30pm Sun.*

SHILLINGTON

Musgrave Arms

16 Apsley End Road, Shillington, Hitchin SG5 3LX
☎ *(01462) 872530*

Greene King IPA, Abbot and XX Mild available plus a guest.

Beamed country pub in attractive village. Dining room. Food served at lunchtime and evenings. Garden including petanque pitch plus children's play area.

OPEN *12–3pm and 5–11pm Mon–Fri; 12–11pm Sat; 12–4pm and 7–10.30pm Sun.*

SLAPTON

The Carpenters Arms

Horton Road, Slapton, Nr Leighton Buzzard LU7 4DB
☎ *(01525) 220563* Sam and Barry Smith

A Vale Brewery pub with Notley Ale and Edgar's Golden Ale always available plus others from the brewery and guests from independents around the country.

A refurbished fourteenth-century, thatched ale house bought by Vale in 2001 and smartened up since then. Food available at lunchtime and evenings (not Sun). Buffalo products (steaks and cheese) are a popular feature on the menu – from the farm up the road. Garden. Right on the Bedfordshire–Buckinghamshire border.

 *12–3pm and 7–11pm (10.30pm Sun).*

STUDHAM

The Red Lion

Church Road, Studham LU6 2QA
☎ *(01582) 872530* Debbie and Graham

Five real ales available, perhaps including Greene King Abbot Ale and Old Speckled Hen, Fuller's London Pride and Wadworth 6X, plus a guest such as Black Sheep Bitter or Timothy Taylor Landlord changed on a weekly basis.

Traditional country pub with bar and restaurant food served 12–2.30pm and 6.30–9.30pm but not Sunday evenings or Mondays. Children welcome. Games room with bar billiards plus beer garden. Close to Whipsnade Zoo.

11.30am–3pm and 5–11pm Mon–Fri; 11am–11pm Sat; 12–10.30pm Sun.

TODDINGTON

Oddfellows Arms

Market Square, Toddington, Dunstable LU5 6BP
☎ *(01525) 872021*

Adnams Broadside, Fuller's London Pride and a couple of regularly changing guest beers usually available.

A fifteenth-century pub and restaurant. Food served at lunchtime and evenings (not Sun). Outside seating. Beer festivals.

5–11pm Mon–Tues; 12–3pm and 5–11pm Wed–Sat; 12–3.30pm and 7–10.30pm Sun.

Sow & Pigs

19 Church Square, Toddington, Dunstable LU5 6AA
☎ *(01525) 873089*
www.sowandpigs.co.uk

Greene King IPA and Abbot plus at least one guest.

A nineteenth-century, one-bar pub with real fires. Rolls and bar snacks. No hot food (except soup). Upstairs room available for hire. Accommodation.

All day, every day.

TURVEY

Three Cranes

High Street, Turvey MK43 8EP
☎ *(01234) 881305* Paul Linehan

At least four real ales usually available, including Greene King Abbot and IPA.

Ivy-covered, seventeenth-century coaching inn and restaurant set back from the Bedford to Northampton road. Food available at lunchtime and evenings. Four bedrooms. Garden with children's play area. Car park.

11am–2.30pm and 6–11pm Mon–Sat; 12–3pm and 7–10.30pm Sun.

WINGFIELD

The Plough Inn

Tebworth Road, Wingfield, Leighton Buzzard LU7 9QH
☎ *(01525) 873077* Sue and Jim Carr

A Fuller's house serving Chiswick, London Pride and ESB, together with their seasonal ales, Honey Dew, Summer Ale, Red Fox and Jack Frost. A guest beer is also available.

A thatched olde-English pub with low beams and conservatory. Bar and restaurant food available at lunchtimes and evenings (not Sun evenings). Garden with children's play area. From M1 junction 12, follow the A5120 through Toddington to Houghton Regis. Turn off to Wingfield.

11am–3pm and 5.30–11pm Mon–Sat; 12–3.30pm and 6–10.30pm Sun.

YELDEN

The Chequers

High Street, Yelden MK44 1AW
☎ *(01933) 356383* Alistair Bowie

Thwaites Bitter, Greene King Abbot on gravity, and Fuller's London Pride always available plus two rolling guests such as Wadworth 6X, Tamworthy Real Ale, Pott'n'Gold or any Potton Brewery ale.

A traditional village pub, located close to game shooting venues with real beer, real cider and a real fire! Large beer garden. Food available in separate dining area. Children allowed. Pool, darts, skittles (children welcome to play). Annual beer festival.

5–11pm Mon–Tues (closed lunch); 12–2pm and 5–11pm Wed–Fri; 11am–11pm Sat; 12–10.30pm Sun. 11am–11pm during game shooting season.

THE BREWERIES

BUTTS BREWERY LTD

Unit 6A, Northfield Farm, Wantage Road, Great Shefford, Hungerford RG17 7BY
☎ *(01488) 648133*

JESTER 3.5% ABV
BUTTS BITTER 4.0% ABV
BLACKGUARD 4.5% ABV
BARBUS BARBUS 4.6% ABV
Plus occasional brews.

THE WEST BERKSHIRE BREWERY CO LTD

The Old Bakery, Yattendon, Thatcham RG18 0UE
☎ *(01635) 202968*
www.wbbrew.co.uk

OLD FATHER THAMES 3.4% ABV
MR CHUBB'S LUNCHTIME BITTER 3.7% ABV
MAGG'S MAGNIFICENT MILD 3.8% ABV
GOOD OLD BOY 4.0% ABV
DR HEXTER'S WEDDING ALE 4.1% ABV
FULL CIRCLE 4.5% ABV
DR HEXTER'S HEALER 5.0% ABV
Plus special, seasonal and occasional brews.

THE PUBS

ALDWORTH

The Bell Inn

Aldworth, Nr Reading RG8 9SE
☎ *(01635) 578272* Mr and Mrs IJ Macaulay

Arkells 3B and Kingsdown Ale, West Berkshire Old Tyler and Magnificent Mild always available, plus a monthly ale from West Berkshire.

A small, unaltered inn dating from 1340 in good walking country. Bar food featuring homemade soup, warm filled rolls and ploughman's available at lunchtimes and evenings. Well-behaved children allowed in the tap room. Country garden with adjacent cricket ground. Two miles from Streatley on B4009 to Newbury.

 *11am–3pm, 6–11pm Mon–Sat; 12–3pm and 7–10.30pm Sun (closed all day Mon except bank holidays)*

ASHMANSWORTH

The Plough

Ashmansworth, Nr Newbury RG20 9SL
☎ *(01635) 253047* Oliver Davies

Archers Village, Best and Golden always available plus one guest which might be Butts Barbus Barbus or Morrells Graduate.

A small, traditional pub serving beer direct from the cask. Light bar snacks available 12–1.45pm Wed–Sun. No children. Tiny car park accommodating three cars.

 *12–2pm (not Tues) and 6–11pm Tues–Sat; 12–3pm, 7–10.30pm Sun. Closed all day Mon.*

ASTON

The Flower Pot Hotel

Ferry Lane, Aston, Henley-on-Thames RG9 3DG
☎ *(01491) 574721* AR Read and PM Thatcher

Brakspear Mild, Bitter, Special and Old available, plus seasonal brews.

Built around 1890, the Flower Pot retains its Victorian character. Situated in pleasant countryside close to the river and half a mile from Hambledon Lock. Large garden. Bar food served lunchtimes and evenings. Children welcome. Car park.

OPEN *11am–3pm and 6–11pm (6–10.30 Sun).*

BRACKNELL

The Green Man

Crowthorne Road, Bracknell RG12 7DL
☎ *(01344) 423667* Alan Cannon

Two weekly changing guest beers available. Hundreds of different beers have been served, including Bateman Jolly's Jaunts and Everards Tiger.

A local community pub with two bars. Food available. Pool table, darts. Large garden. No children.

OPEN *11am–11pm (10.30pm Sun)*

BRIMPTON

Three Horseshoes

Brimpton Lane, Brimpton, Reading RG7 4TL
☎ *(0118) 971 2183* Mr and Mrs M Holmes

Arkells 3B and Kingsdown always available, plus specials from Arkells such as Summer Ale and Noel.

Small, country pub with and lounge and public bars, off the A4 between Thatcham and Midgham. Refurbished with disabled access and toilets. Food served 12–2pm every day and 7–9.30pm Mon–Sat. Beer garden. Car park. Well-behaved children welcome.

 *11.30am–2.30pm, 6–11pm Mon–Sat; 12–3pm and 7–10.30pm Sun.*

BROAD LAYING

The Rampant Cat

Broad Laying, Wootton Hill, Newbury RG20 9TP
☎ *(01635) 253474* Mr JP Molyneux

Greene King Abbot Ale and IPA and Fuller's London Pride regularly available, plus a guest beer changed every eight weeks, such as Charles Wells Bombardier.

A well-presented pub with good atmosphere and magnificent gardens, set in beautiful Berkshire countryside. Food served lunchtimes and evenings Tues–Sat, evenings only Mon and lunchtimes only Sun. Car park. Children welcome if eating.

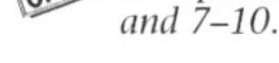
12–3pm and 6–11pm Mon–Sat; 12–3pm and 7–10.30pm Sun.

BURGHCLERE

The Carpenters Arms

Harts Lane, Burghclere, Newbury RG20 9JY
☎ *(01635) 278251* Herbie Clark

An Arkells pub with 3B always on offer, with other Arkells beers such as Kingsdown Ale and seasonals such as Noel, Summer Ale and Moonlight regularly featured.

A tiny country pub with open log fire and beams. Full menu available lunchtimes and evenings (not Sun or Mon evening). Garden, car park. Children allowed. Off the by-pass, over the roundabout, head to Sandringham Memorial Chapel, turn left at the T-Junction, and the pub is on the right.

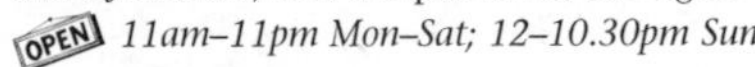
11am–11pm Mon–Sat; 12–10.30pm Sun.

BURGHFIELD COMMON

The Bantam

Omers Rise, Burghfield Common, Reading RG7 3HJ
☎ *(0118) 983 2763* Carron McDermot

An Arkells pub with 3B usually available, plus seasonal Arkells ales.

A drinkers' pub in a modern building, featuring two bars, pool tables, a juke box and fruit machines. No food. Barbecues occasionally held in summer. Garden, car park. Children allowed lunchtimes only, in garden. Call for directions.

11am–11pm Mon–Sat; 12–10.30pm Sun.

CAVERSHAM

The Baron Cadogan

22–4 Prospect Street, Caversham, Reading RG4 8JG
☎ *(0118) 947 0626* Simon Grogan

Three hand pumps serving a constantly changing range of guests, with four or five different beers each week. Regulars include Fuller's London Pride and Shepherd Neame Spitfire. Beers from the Loddon Brewery and Cottage Brewery are also regularly available.

A modern town Wetherspoon's pub with food available all day. Children allowed, if eating, until 6pm

10am–11pm Mon–Sat; 12–10.30pm Sun.

CHIEVELEY

The Olde Red Lion

Green Lane, Chieveley RG20 8XB
☎ *(01635) 248379* Paul Clarke

Arkells 3B and Kingsdown Ale always available plus other, seasonal Arkells brews.

A traditional pub with bar food available 12–2.30pm and 6.30–10pm, plus all day Sunday. Children welcome. Located north off M4 J13, near the services. Dogs and coach parties welcome.

11am–11pm Mon–Sat; 12–10.30pm Sun.

COOKHAM DEAN

Jolly Farmer

Church Road, Cookham Dean, Maidenhead SL6 9PD
☎ *(01628) 482905* David and Laura Kelsey
www.jollyfarmercookhamdean.co.uk

Four hand pumps serve beers such as Young's Bitter and Brakspear Bitter, and guests from breweries such as Rebellion and Hop Back.

Traditional two-bar country pub near the church. Separate restaurant with food available every lunchtime, and from 7–9pm in the evening (not Sun or Mon). Large garden. The pub is owned by the village.

11.30am–11pm Mon–Sat; 12–10.30pm Sun.

DONNINGTON

The Fox & Hounds

Oxford Road, Donnington, Newbury RG14 3AP
☎ *(01635) 40540* Julia Megarry

An Arkells pub where 3B is always on offer, plus Arkells seasonal ales on a regular basis.

Small country pub with open fire, live music and garden patio. Food served in the 50-seater restaurant. Food available 12–2.30pm and 7–9.30pm. Small private dining room/meeting room. Car park. Children allowed in restaurant. Close to J13 of M4.

 *11am–11pm Mon–Sat; 12–10.30pm Sun.*

ETON

Waterman's Arms

Brocas Street, Eton, Windsor SL4 6BW
☎ *(01753) 861001* Mr Lever

Fuller's London Pride, Hogs Back Traditional English Ale and Brakspear Bitter always available. Also Addlestone's Cloudy Cider.

An old English-style pub, dating from 1542, close to the river. Small beer garden. Food is served in a separate restaurant at lunchtimes and evenings Mon–Fri and all day at weekends with a roast on Sunday. Daily fresh fish a speciality. Children welcome.

 *11am–11pm Mon–Sat; 12–10.30pm Sun.*

FRILSHAM

Pot Kiln

Frilsham, Yattendon RG18 0XX
☎ *(01635) 201366* Philip Gent

West Berkshire Brick Kiln Bitter only available here, plus Greene King Morland Original, Arkells 3B and others. Seasonal brews and specials, usually from West Berkshire brewery.

A traditional pub with the West Berkshire micro-brewery in an out-building at the back. Food available 12–2pm and 7–9.30pm. Large garden. Children allowed. From Newbury take B4009 into Hermitage. Turn right at The Fox, follow Yattendon sign. Take second turning on right and continue for a mile. Pub is on the right.

 *12–2.30pm and 6.30–11pm Mon–Sat (closed Tues); 12–3pm and 7–10.30pm Sun.*

HOLYPORT

The Belgian Arms

Holyport Street, Holyport, Maidenhead SL6 2JR
☎ *(01628) 634468* Alfred G Morgan

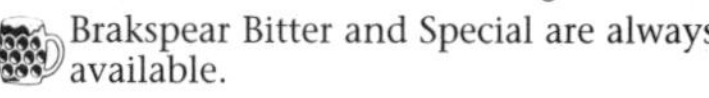

Brakspear Bitter and Special are always available.

A new licensee will be running this pub as from summer 2004, so some details may change. A typical English country pub situated next to the village pond, with a 250-year-old wisteria plant at the pub's entrance. Cosy in wintertime. Conservatory leading on to attractive beer garden where large willows screen a view of the village green. Food served 12–2pm and 7–9.30pm on weekdays and 12–2pm Sun. Children allowed in the conservatory but not in the bar area. Car park. From Junction 8/9 on M4 follow signs for Maidenhead, then take A330 Ascot/ Bracknell road, turn left at Holyport Green and left again at the village pond.

11–3pm and 5.30–11pm Mon–Sat; 12–3pm and 7–10.30pm Sun.

HURLEY

The Dew Drop Inn

Batts Green, Honey Lane, Hurley SL6 6RB
☎ *(01628) 824327* CH and BD Morley

Brakspear Bitter, Special and a seasonal ale regularly available.

An award-winning cottage-style country pub, refurbished and sensitively extended, in an idyllic woodland setting. Fresh, home-cooked food served every lunchtime and evening (not Sun evening). Large car park and garden. Well-behaved children welcome. To find the pub, look for a sharp turning halfway along Honey Lane with a smaller lane leading off. Follow this for 300 yards. Pub will be found on the right-hand side.

12–3pm and 6–11pm Mon–Sat; 12–3pm and 7–10.30pm Sun.

HURST

Green Man

Hinton Road, Hurst, Twyford RG10 0BP
☎ *(0118) 934 2599* Mr Gordon Guile

Brakspear Bitter and Special generally available, as well as seasonal beers.

A classic country pub dating back to the seventeenth century. Two drinking areas and a non-smoking restaurant. You can book a table through their website.

11–3pm and 5.30–11pm Mon–Sat; 12–3pm and 6–10.30pm Sun.

LITTLEWICK GREEN

The Cricketers

Coronation Road, Littlewick Green SL6 3RA
☎ *(01628) 822888* Mr Hickman

Badger Best, King & Barnes Sussex and Tanglefoot usually available.

A traditional village pub situated on the village green close to the old Bath Road (A4). Recently refurbished and now a Hall & Woodhouse tied house. Food available. Cricket regularly played at weekends. Children allowed. Bed and breakfast available.

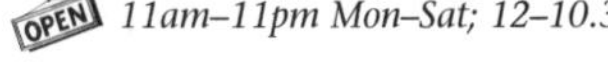
11am–11pm Mon–Sat; 12–10.30pm Sun.

LOWER INKPEN

The Swan Inn

Lower Inkpen, Hungerford RG17 9DX
☎ *(01488) 668326* Mary Harris
www.theswaninn-organics.co.uk

Butts Brewery's Traditional, Blackguard Jester and West Berkshire Magg's Magnificent Mild regularly available.

A traditional seventeenth-century village hotel with 'freehouse' bar. West Berkshire CAMRA Pub of the Year 2000. Ten bedrooms and a restaurant. AA and English Tourist Board recommended. Bar food also available with organic food a speciality. Organic farm shop and butchery on the premises. Children allowed.

11am–2.30pm and 7–11pm Mon–Sat; 12–3pm and 7–10.30pm Sun.

NEWBURY

The Coopers Arms

Bartholomew Street, Newbury RG14 5LL
☎ *(01635) 47469* David Reid

Tied to Arkells, with 2B and 3B always on offer.

Town-centre locals' pub in an old-style building. Pool and darts. Car park. No children. Call for directions.

11am–11pm Mon–Sat; 12–10.30pm Sun.

The Monument

57 Northbrook Street, Newbury RG14 1AN
☎ *(01635) 41964* Simon Owens
www.themonumentonline.co.uk

Butts Traditional, Butts Barbus Barbus, Greene King Old Speckled Hen and Theakston Old Peculiar usually available, with Gale's HSB an occasional guest.

This 350-year-old pub is the oldest in Newbury. Good food available all day and evening, including roasts on Sundays. Children and dogs very welcome. Live music Tues and Wed, plus a quiz night on Thursday. Covered and heated garden open in summer – the roof is removable. Free juke box with range of 400 CDs and a free internet facility (with a two-drink minimum purchase).

11am–11pm Mon–Sat; 12–10.30pm Sun.

The Red House

12 Hampton Road, Newbury RG14 6DB
☎ *(01635) 30584* Mr and Mrs Andrews

West Berkshire Mr Chubb's usually available, plus one guest, changed monthly, often from a local brewer.

A local drinkers' pub, with pool and football teams. No food, no garden, no parking, no children.

6-11pm Mon–Fri (closed lunchtimes); 11am–11pm Sat–Sun.

The Woodpecker

Wash Water, Newbury RG20 0LU
☎ *(01635) 43027* Andrew and Janet Cover

An Arkells pub with 2B and 3B usually available, plus occasional beers such as Moonlight, Summer Ale or Noel Ale.

Old-fashioned beamed pub with no music, pool or games, just good food and drink! Non-smoking dining area. Outside seating at the front of the pub. Two car parks. No children. No credit cards.

11.15am–2.45pm and 6–11pm Mon–Sat; 12–4pm and 7–10.30pm Sun.

PINKNEYS GREEN

The Stag & Hounds

Lee Lane, Pinkneys Green, Maidenhead SL6 6NU
☎ *(01628) 630268* Caroline Saunders

A freehouse with four hand pumps serving Charles Wells Bombardier and a seasonal beer from Rebellion always on offer, plus guest beers from other independent breweries.

A friendly pub in a rural location, with a clientele mainly over the age of 30. Homemade food available 12–2.30pm and 6–9pm. Function room and huge garden. Children allowed.

11am–3pm and 6–11pm Mon–Thurs; 11am–11pm Fri–Sat; 12–10.30pm Sun.

READING

Back of Beyond

104–8 Kings Road, Reading RG4 8DT
☎ *(0118) 959 5906* Jason Lord

Beers from Loddon Brewery and Cottage Brewery frequently available. Guest ales are chosen from a list of about fifty breweries including Archers, Hogs Back, Shepherd Neame and Rebellion.

A traditional JD Wetherspoon's pub with garden, located five minutes from the railway station. Food available all day. Well behaved children allowed.

 *10am–11pm Mon–Sat; 12–10.30pm Sun.*

Corn Stores

10 Forbury Road, Reading RG1 1SE
☎ *0118 951 2340* Fayze Ghaly

Fuller's Chiswick Bitter, London Pride and ESB always available.

Town pub on three floors converted from Walter Parsons seed merchants warehouse. The Il Gusto Italian restaurant is on the first floor. The whole place is decorated with seed merchant memorabilia. Reading Science Fiction Group meet here on Monday evenings.

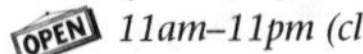 *11am–11pm (closed Sun).*

The Hobgoblin

2 Broad Street, Reading RG1 2BH
☎ *(01734) 508119* Rob Wain

Ales consist of three beers from the West Berkshire Brewery and five ever-changing guests from other micros. Westons cider or perry also available.

Small, intimate town-centre pub serving a wide range of ales. Victorian interior decorated with breweriana. No juke box, but background alernative/indie.

11am–11pm Mon–Sat; 12–10.30pm Sun.

The Hop Leaf

163–5 Southampton Street, Reading RG1 2QZ
☎ *(0118) 931 4700*
Debbie and Malcolm Purvis

Five hand pumps serve a range of Hop Back ales, usually including Summer Lightning, GFB, Best, Crop Circle and Entire Stout. A further three hand pumps serve guest ales, usually from local breweries. A real cider is also served.

Refurbished pub in a late Victorian building on the edge of the town centre. Full bar menu available lunchtimes and evenings Tues–Sun, limited menu served Mon. Pub games played, including skittles, darts and bar billards. Children and well-behaved pets allowed.

11am–11pm Mon–Sat; 12–10.30pm Sun.

Retreat

8 St. Johns Street, Reading RG1 4EN
☎ *(0118) 957 1593*
Bernie Whiten and Jane Marston

Six hand pumps with Ringwood Best and Caledonian Deuchars IPA usually available and four ever-changing guest ales.

Bustling, two-bar pub situated away from the town centre. Good range of real ales sold in the front bar, pool played in the back bar.

11am–3pm and 5–11pm Mon–Thurs; 11am–11pm Fri-Sat; 12–10.30pm Sun.

Sweeney & Todd

10 Castle Street, Reading RG1 7RD
☎ *(0118) 958 6466* Catherine J Hayward

Wadworth 6X, Hall & Woodhouse Tanglefoot and Adnams bitter usually available, plus one guest which might include a beer from Wadworth or West Bershire breweries.

A traditional 'pie and pint' pub. A huge range of pies is served all day in the dedicated restaurant. Food available 12–10.30pm (not Sun). Children allowed in the restaurant.

11am–11pm Mon–Sat (closed Sun).

SHINFIELD

Bell & Bottle

School Green, Shinfield, Reading RG2 9EE
☎ *(0118) 988 3563*
Antony James, Stuart Hodges, Jem Dance

Four ales generally available including Wadworth 6X, Archers Best, Loddon Hoppit and Morrells Grumpy Cow.

A traditional pub with restaurant. Children and dogs welcome.

11.30am–11.30pm Mon–Sat; 12–10.30pm Sun.

SILCHESTER

The Calleva Arms

Silchester Common, Silchester, Reading RG7 2PH
☎ *(0118) 970 0305*
Simon and Sharon Bumpstead

A Gale's pub with HSB, Butser Bitter and Best always on offer, plus one guest ale from another SIBA brewery.

A village pub with beams and open fires. Separate dining area and conservatory. Beer garden. Car park. Children allowed.

11am–3pm and 5.30–11pm Mon–Fri; 11am–11pm Sat; 12–10.30pm Sun.

SINDLESHAM

The Walter Arms

Bearwood Road, Sindlesham, Wokingham RG41 5BP
☎ *(0118) 978 0260* Brian Howard

Adnams Broadside and Fuller's London Pride usually available, plus a guest ale such as Shepherd Neame Spitfire, Young's Special or Greene King Ruddles County.

Upmarket pub with three open fires. Popular with business diners for pre-ordering and rapid service – food is served 12–2.30pm and 6.15–9.30pm (booking essential). Only fresh produce used, with traditional dishes a speciality in the evenings. 'Fish Called Walter' is the adjacent fresh fish and seafood restaurant, open lunchtimes 12–3pm Wed–Fri and 7–10pTues–Sat (booking essential). Garden, parking for 80 cars. No children under 14. Situated on the main road.

12–3pm and 5–11pm Mon–Sat; 12–4.30pm Sun.

SLOUGH

The Rose & Crown

213 High Street, Slough SL1 1NB
☎ *(01753) 521114* Mr Jobling

A freehouse with four pumps serving a range of guest beers, which may include ales from Archers or Springhead breweries.

Traditional town pub with two small bars. Patio at front, garden at rear. No food. No children

11am–11pm Mon–Sat; 12–10.30pm Sun.

SONNING

The Bull

High Street, Sonning, Reading RG4 6UP
☎ *(0118) 969 3901*
Christine and Dennis Mason

A George Gale tied house, always serving Gale's HSB, Best and Butser, plus seasonal specials such as Swing Low.

Sixteenth-century village inn separated from the church next door by a patio and courtyard garden. One large lounge bar and a separate locals bar. There is also a non-smoking restaurant. Log fires. Food available lunchtimes and evenings. Children allowed.

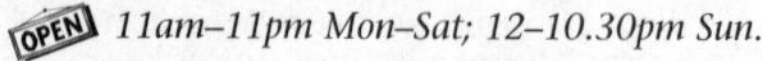
11am–11pm Mon–Sat; 12–10.30pm Sun.

STANFORD DINGLEY

The Boot

Stanford Dingley, Reading RG7 6LT
☎ *(0118) 974 4292* John Haley

Real ales rotated fortnightly usually from Loddon, Archers or West Berkshire breweries.

A traditional, eighteenth-century olde-worlde freehouse. Bar food available (12–2.15pm and 7–9.15pm). Children welcome.

11am–3pm and 6–11pm (7–10.30pm Sun).

The Bull

Stanford Dingley, Reading RG7 6LS
☎ *0998 974 4409* Robert and Kate Archard and Robin and Carol Walker
www.thebullatstanforddingley.co.uk

West Berkshire Skiff, Good Old Boy and Dr Hexter's Healer often available, plus something from Brakspear, and Lodden Hoppit.

Traditional family-owned fifteenth-century freehouse in centre of village, with two bars, a dining room and six bed and breakfast rooms. Menu offers excellent food at pub, not restaurant, prices. Food served 12–2.30pm and 6.30–9.30pm Mon–Sat, 12–2.30pm and 7–9pm Sun (no food Sun evenings in winter). Children welcome, as long as the parents behave! Classic-car owners and motorsport enthusiasts particularly welcome. There is a large garden with lots of tables for summer.

12–3pm and 6–11pm Mon–Sat; 12–3pm and 7–10.30pm Sun.

SUNNINGDALE

The Nags Head

28 High Street, Sunningdale SL5 0NG
☎ *(01344) 622725* Dave and Denise West

Harveys XX Mild, Sussex Pale Ale and Sussex Best Bitter usually available plus a seasonal brew.

Traditional village pub and the only Harveys pub in Berkshire. Games-orientated public bar and spacious lounge bar. Cask Marque award. 'Pub grub' with daily special served 12–2pm Mon–Sat. Car park. Well-behaved children welcome in lounge bar. Play equipment in large garden. Between A30/A329 in Sunningdale village, nearly opposite the church.

11.30am–11pm Mon–Sat; 12–10.30pm Sun.

SUNNINGHILL

The Dukes Head

Upper Village Road, Sunninghill SL5 7AG
☎ *(01344) 626949* Philip Durrant

Greene King IPA and Abbot usually available, plus two handpumps for guest ales or a Greene King seasonal ale when available.

A traditional village pub specialising in Thai food (12–2.30pm and 6–10pm). Owned by Greene King. Well-behaved children allowed. Upper Village Road runs parallel to the High Street. A beer festival is held once a year.

 *11am–11pm Mon–Sat; 12–10.30pm Sun.*

THATCHAM

The White Hart

2 High Street, Thatcham RG19 3JD
☎ *(01635) 863251* Des Williams

Three hand pumps with Greene King Abbot Ale always available, and guest ales such as Greene King Old Speckled Hen.

Town-centre pub, catering for business people at lunchtimes and locals in the evenings. Lounge bar with dining area. Food served lunchtimes Mon–Fri and Sun. No darts, pool or TV. Parking at rear and street parking. No children.

 *11am–11pm Mon–Fri; 11am–3.30pm and 7–11pm Sat; 12–3.30pm and 7–10.30pm Sun.*

THEALE

The Red Lion

5 Church Street, Theale, Reading RG7 5BU
☎ *(0118) 930 2394* Carron Crabtree

Marston's Pedigree and Greene King IPA is usually available, plus guest beers such as Greene King Old Speckled Hen or Abbot Ale.

Village pub with beams, two fires and an old-fashioned cosy atmosphere. Food served 12–2pm Mon–Sat and 12–2.30pm Sun. Small garden, skittle alley (converted for dining during busy periods). Children allowed, and can use skittle alley if not in use. Situated off the High Street.

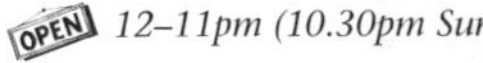 *12–11pm (10.30pm Sun).*

TIDMARSH

The Greyhound

The Street, Tidmarsh RG8 8ER
☎ *(0118) 984 3557* Paul and Ann Woodford

Fuller's London Pride, ESB and Chiswick Bitter usually availble with a changing guest ale every two weeks

A traditional thatched twelfth-century village pub serving food at lunchtimes. Food available 12–2.30pm Mon–Fri; 12–3pm Sat; 12–8pm Sun. Children allowed. On the main A340.

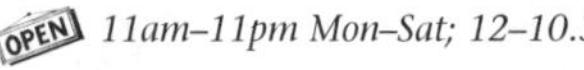 *11am–11pm Mon–Sat; 12–10.30pm Sun.*

TWYFORD

The Duke of Wellington

27 High Street, Twyford RG10 9AG
☎ *(0118) 9340456* Karen and Bill Suter

A Brakspear tenancy selling Bitter and Special, and a seasonal beer when available.

Village local with separate public and lounge bars, a large beer garden with children's play equipment and an outside patio. Traditional pub food available Mon–Sat 12–2pm. Children allowed. Car park at rear. Situated in the village centre, 100 metres from the traffic lights.

 *11.30am–2.30pm and 5–11pm Mon–Fri; 11am–11pm Sat; 12–10.30pm Sun.*

The Golden Cross

38 Waltham Road, Twyford, Reading RG10 9EG
☎ *(0118) 934 0180* Mark Grey

Three hand pumps with Fuller's London Pride and a beer from West Berkshire usually available, plus a guest beer.

A locals' pub with restaurant area and beer garden. Food served every lunchtime and Tues–Sat evenings. Children allowed in the garden and restaurant only.

 *11.30am–11pm Mon–Fri; 11am–11pm Sat; 12–10.30pm Sun.*

WALTHAM ST LAWRENCE

Bell

The Street, Waltham St Lawrence RG10 0JJ
☎ *(0118) 934 1788* Glen Glenister

Two house beers usually available, No. 1 is brewed by West Berkshire, and Ding Dong is brewed by Loddon brewery. Three changing guest ales are also available, all from regional independents.

Fourteenth-century half-timbered inn opposite the village church. Two drinking areas and a restaurant. Lots of oak panelling and beams.

 *11.30am–3pm and 5–11pm Mon–Fri; 11–11pm Sat; 12–10.30pm Sun.*

WARFIELD

The Cricketers

Cricketers Lane, Warfield RG42 6JT
☎ *(01344) 882910* Dawn and Paul Chance

Greene King IPA and Abbot always available, plus one guest from breweries such as Wadworths or Batemans

A small, rural pub situated in a quiet country lane. Three bars – public, saloon and middle – separate restaurant and garden. Food available 12–3pm and 6–9pm Mon–Fri; 12–9pm Sat–Sun plus Sunday carvery from 12–3pm. Children welcome, play area in garden. Car park. Follow the B3022 from Bracknell towards Windsor and Cricketers Lane is found on the right-hand side of a sharp bend.

 *11.30am–11pm Mon–Sat; 12–10.30pm Sun.*

WHITE WALTHAM

The Beehive

Waltham Road, White Waltham SL6 3SH
☎ *(01628) 822877* Guy Martin
www.thebeehive-pub.com

Brakspear Bitter, Fuller's London Pride and Greene King Abbot Ale usually available, plus guest ales including beers from Loddon and Rebellion breweries.

A rural pub with two large gardens, one south-facing overlooking cricket pitch, and a separate restaurant. Cask Marque award winner. Food available lunchtimes and evenings, and all day at weekends until 9.30pm (8.30pm Sun). Children welcome. Monthly quiz nights.

 *11.30am–11pm Mon–Sat 12–10.30pm Sun.*

WINDSOR

Carpenters Arms

4 Market Street, Windsor SL4 1PB
☎ *(01753) 755961* Cilla Palmer

A constantly changing range of five ales is generally available, usually from craft brewers.

Traditional Victorian town pub situated in the cobbled streets between the guildhall and the castle. There are three drinking areas on three levels. A pub since 1518, the cellars reputedly have passages leading into Windsor Castle.

 *11am–11pm Mon–Sat; 12–10.30pm Sun.*

WINDSOR FOREST

The Duke of Edinburgh

Woodside Road, Windsor Forest SL4 2DP
☎ *(01344) 882736* Nicholas Tilt

Tied to Arkells, with 2B, 3B and Kingsdown Ale always available, plus seasonal Arkells beers.

Traditional 100-year-old pub with restaurant. Public, saloon and back bar – lots of different nooks and crannies! Food available. Garden and car park. Call for directions.

 *11am–11pm Mon–Sat; 12–10.30pm Sun.*

WOKINGHAM

Wheelwright's Arms

Davis Way, St Nicholas Hurst, Wokingham RG10 0TR
☎ *(0118) 934 4100* Kevin Morley

Four Wadworth brews always available, plus guest ales which may include Adnams Broadside, Badger Tanglefoot and others. Guests are changed monthly.

A traditional pub dating from the 1850s with low beams and a real fire. Quiz night on Monday. Food available 12–2pm and 6.30–9pm (not Sunday evening or Monday evening). Children allowed in restaurant only.

 *11am–3pm and 5–11pm Mon–Thurs (open all day bank holidays); 11am–11pm Fri–Sat; 12–4pm and 7–10.30pm Sun.*

THE BREWERIES

THE CHILTERN BREWERY

Nash Lee Road, Terrick, Aylesbury HP17 0TQ
☎ *(01296) 613647*
www.chilternbrewery.co.uk

CHILTERN ALE 3.7% ABV

GOLDEN SOVEREIGN 3.7% ABV
Summer.

BEECHWOOD BITTER 4.3% ABV

GLAD TIDINGS 4.6% ABV
Winter.

THREE HUNDREDS OLD ALE 4.9% ABV
Winter.

REBELLION BEER CO

Bencombe Farm, Marlow Bottom SL7 3LT
☎ *(01628) 476594*

IPA 3.7% ABV

SMUGGLER 4.1% ABV

BLONDE 4.3% ABV

OVERDRAFT 4.3% ABV

MUTINY 4.5% ABV

ROASTED NUTS 4.6 ABV

ZEBEDEE 4.7% ABV

RED 4.7% ABV

Plus other seasonal and occasional brews.

VALE BREWERY CO. LTD

Thame Road, Haddenham HP17 8BY
☎ *(01844) 290008*

BLACK SWAN MILD 3.3% ABV

NOTLEY ALE 3.3% ABV

BEST BITTER 3.7% ABV

WYCHERT BITTER 3.9% ABV

BLACK BEAUTY 4.3% ABV

EDGAR'S GOLDEN ALE 4.3% ABV

SPECIAL BITTER 4.5% ABV

GRUMPLING OLD ALE 4.6% ABV

Plus seasonal and occasional brews.

THE PUBS

ASHENDEN

Gatehangers

Lower End, Ashenden HP18 0HE
☎ *(01296) 651296* Mrs Crisp

Two hand pumps serve beers such as Greene King IPA, Brakspear Bitter and Young's Bitter.

A 300-year-old, busy country pub with a traditional atmosphere. Beamed in part with open fires and a large L-shaped bar. Food served at lunchtime (not Mon and Wed) and evenings. Car park and garden. Children allowed. Accommodation. Between the A41 and A418 west of Aylesbury, near the church. Twenty minutes to Oxford.

OPEN *12–2.30pm and 6–11pm (10.30pm Sun).*

ASHERIDGE

The Asheridge Arms

Asheridge, Chesham HP5 2UX
☎ *(01494) 758263* Peter George

A freehouse, with Fuller's London Pride and Charles Wells Bombardier or IPA usually available plus a guest, changed weekly, from an independent or micro-brewery. Recent ales have come from Adnams, Cottage, Exmoor, Orkney, Rebellion and Arundel breweries.

Changed its name in 2003 from the Blue Ball. A traditional, family-run pub with a mixed clientele. Built in 1821, in a hamlet two miles north of Chesham. Non-smoking function room, big garden. Food served at lunchtime and evenings (not Sun). Children allowed in dining area. Annual beer festival held in June with up to 30 real ales available.

OPEN *12–2.30pm and 5.30–11pm Mon–Thurs; 12–11pm Fri–Sat; 12–10.30pm Sun.*

AYLESBURY

The Grapes

36 Market Square, Aylesbury HP20 1TW
☎ *(01296) 483735* Nic Swanson

A Greene King tied house with IPA always available.

A locals' haven in the town centre. Food served 12–3pm daily. Car parking available in adjacent multi-storey.

OPEN *12–11pm; (closed Sun).*

BEACONSFIELD

The Greyhound

33 Windsor End, Beaconsfield HP9 2JN
☎ *(01494) 673823* Maggie Miller

A Rebellion beer is usually available with guest ales from breweries such as Rebellion and Adnams.

A traditional two-bar public house with separate dining area. Food served at lunchtime and evenings (not Sun and Mon). No children. Beer garden

OPEN *11–3pm and 5–11pm (6–10.30pm Sun).*

BELLINGDON

The Bull

Bellingdon HP5 2XU
☎ *(01494) 758163* Carl and Kathy Slaughter

Young's Bitter and Adnams Broadside are among the brews usually available.

Country pub with one bar and beams, formerly a coaching inn. Food available at lunchtime and evenings. Garden, car park, occasional live music. Children allowed.

OPEN *11am–11pm Mon–Sat; 12–10.30pm Sun.*

BLEDLOW

The Lions of Bledlow

Church End, Bledlow, Princes Risborough HP27 9PE
☎ *(01844) 343345* Mark McKeown

A freehouse with Wadworth 6X and Marston's Pedigree usually available, and perhaps Brakspear, Burton Bridge or Slaters. In addition, at least one local ale such as Loddon Hoppit, Vale Wychert or Rebellion Mutiny is also available.

Sixteenth-century, traditional, rambling pub with beams and stone floors. One long bar with two rooms. Food available at lunchtime and evenings – there is a separate dining area. Garden, car park. Children allowed in dining area only. Look for the brown tourist sign at the bottom of B4009.

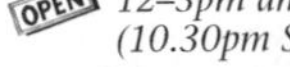 *12–3pm and 6–11pm Mon–Sat (10.30pm Sun).*

CADMORE END

Old Ship

Marlow Road, Cadmore End, High Wycombe HP14 3PF
☎ *(01494) 883496* Philip Butt

A freehouse offering Brakspear Bitter plus three rotating guests served straight from the cask in the cellar. These may well include something from the local Vale Brewery.

Restored seventeenth-century, two-roomed pub just off the M40. Food served at lunchtime and evenings (not Sun). Outside terrace and garden. Children welcome.

 *11am–3pm (not Mon) and 5.30–11pm; 12–3pm and 7–10.30pm Sun.*

CHEARSLEY

The Bell Inn

The Green, Chearsley, Aylesbury HP18 0DJ
☎ *(01844) 208077* Peter and Susan Grimsdell

A Fuller's pub with Chiswick, London Pride, ESB and seasonal brews available.

A pretty, thatched pub set on the village green with open fires and plenty of beams. Food available at most lunchtimes and evenings (not Mon; Sun lunch only). Large garden with children's play area. Barbecues in summer.

 *12–2.30pm (not Mon except bank holidays) and 6–11pm (10.30pm Sun); (may open longer in summer).*

CHENIES

The Red Lion

Chenies Village, Rickmansworth WD3 6ED
☎ *(01923) 282722* Mike Norris

A freehouse with Lion Pride, brewed especially for the pub by Rebellion, plus Wadworth 6X and Vale Best Bitter usually available. Other locally brewed beers often available.

In Buckinghamshire, but with a Hertfordshire postal address. Owner-run, traditional pub that sells food, not a restaurant that sells beer! Front bar, back room and snug. Home-cooked meals served 12–2pm and 6.30–10pm (until 9.30pm Sun). No children. Car park. Outside seating. From J18 on M25, pub is off the A404 between Little Chalfont and Chorleywood.

 *11am–2.30pm and 5.30–11pm (6.30–10.30pm Sun).*

CHESHAM

The Black Horse

The Vale, Chesham HP5 3MS
☎ *(01494) 784656* Mick Goodchild

Three ales available which might include Greene King Old Speckled Hen, Fuller's London Pride or Adnams Best.

A fourteenth-century coaching inn just outside Chesham (with certified ghosts!), mainly operating as a restaurant. Large garden. No children allowed in bar area.

OPEN *12–3pm and 6–11pm (7–10.30pm Sun).*

The Queens Head

120 Church Street, Old Chesham HP5 1JD
☎ *(01494) 778690* Mr John Swift

Fuller's brews such as London Pride and ESB are usually on offer, together with Brakspear Bitter and seasonal Fuller's ales when available.

A traditional two-bar family pub beside the River Chess, offering English and Thai food in the bar (lunchtime and evenings). There is also a Thai restaurant upstairs. Outside drinking area. Children allowed.

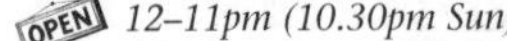 *12–11pm (10.30pm Sun).*

COLESHILL

The Red Lion

Village Road, Coleshill HP7 0LH
☎ *(01494) 727020* John Ullman

Greene King IPA or Banks's Bitter always available plus a guest, changed weekly and usually from a local brewery. Vale Wychert Ale, Rebellion Smuggler and Morrells Varsity are regular favourites.

A village pub with beams and open fires. Home-cooked food available at lunchtime and evenings (not Sun). Garden front and back, with children's area. Car park. Coleshill signposted at Water Tower on A355 Amersham–Beaconsfield road, pub is along the village road, opposite pond and church.

11am–3pm and 5.30–11pm Mon–Fri; 11am–11pm Sat; 12–4.30pm and 7–10.30pm Sun.

CUBLINGTON

The Unicorn

High Street, Cublington LU7 0LQ
☎ *(01296) 681261* Shaun Walls, John Gregory and Steve George

A freehouse with Shepherd Neame Spitfire and Greene King IPA usually available, plus a guest ale such as Timothy Taylor Landlord.

A traditional country pub dating from 1600 with open fires and low beams in the main bar. Non-smoking restaurant. Bar food including specials available lunchtimes and evenings seven days a week 12–4pm and 6–9.30pm. Car park and garden. Children allowed. Dogs welcome.

12–11pm (10.30pm Sun).

DENHAM

The Falcon Inn

Village Road, Denham, Uxbridge UB9 5BE
☎ *(01895) 832125*
David Brench and Marilyn Heath

Real ales available include Marston's Pedigree, Timothy Taylor Landlord and a guest beer such as Charles Wells Bombadier.

Award-winning sixteenth-century inn located in a preservation village. Pub and restaurant areas. Popular with walkers, the Colne Valley Regional Park is nearby. Bed and breakfast available. Food served 12–2.30pm and 6.30–9.30pm Mon–Sat; 12–3pm and 7–9.30pm Sun.

12–3pm, 5.30–11pm Mon–Fri (5–11pm Fri); 11am–11pm Sat; 12–10.30pm Sun.

EASINGTON

The Mole & Chicken

Easington, Nr Long Crendon HP18 9EY
☎ *(01844) 208387* Shane Ellis
www.moleandchicken.co.uk

A freehouse with Greene King Old Speckled Hen and IPA and something from Hook Norton usually available, plus one guest. Fuller's London Pride is often featured, with Wychwood The Dog's Bollocks also a favourite.

A country pub and restaurant, with a slate floor, two fireplaces, and an oak bar, plus oak and antique pine furniture. Good food available. Beer garden with views over Oxford. Summer barbecues. Car park and accommodation. Children allowed. Call for directions.

12–3pm and 6–11pm Mon–Sat; 12–10.30pm Sun.

FARNHAM COMMON

The Foresters

The Broadway, Beaconsfield Road, Farnham Common SL2 3QQ
☎ *(01753) 643340* Tony Jackson

Fuller's London Pride is usually available and one frequently changing guest ale which may include Hop Back Summer Lightning or Adnams Regatta.

A cafe-style bar and restaurant. Popular with walkers as Burnham Beeches is nearby. Menu changes daily, Meals are served 12–2.30pm and 6.30–10pm (12–10pm Sat).

12–2.30pm and 6.30–10pm Mon–Fri; 12–10pm Sat; 11am–11pm and 12–10.30pm Sun.

FORTY GREEN

The Royal Standard of England

Brindle Lane, Forty Green, Beaconsfield HP9 1XT
☎ *(01494) 673382* Cyril Cain

Brakspear Bitter, Fuller's London Pride and Marston's Pedigree usually available, plus two guest ales which may include beers from Wychwood, Rebellion or Vale.

Justifiably claims to be one of the oldest pubs in England. It changed its name when Charles II hid in the rafters after the Battle of Worcester in 1651. Full of beams, log fires and cosy corners. Food available at lunchtime and evenings. Large car park and plenty of outside seating. Children allowed in family room.

11am–3pm and 5.30–11pm Mon–Sat; 12–3pm and 7–10.30pm Sun.

FRIETH

The Prince Albert

Moors End, Frieth, Henley-on-Thames RG9 6PY
☎ *(01494) 881683* Colin, Paul and Fiona Lacy

Brakspear Bitter and Special always available.

A family-run seventeenth-century country pub, refurbished, with original features restored, and with increasing emphasis on the food, which is served 11–2.30pm and 6.30–9.30pm. Large beer garden. Children welcome. From Lane End, turn left before the Frieth signs, towards Fingest.

11am–11pm Mon–Sat; 12–10.30pm Sun.

GAWCOTT

The Cuckoo's Nest

Back Street, Gawcott MK18 4HN
☎ *(01280) 812092* Bruce and Kate Harden

A Vale tied house with Best, Special and Notley Ale usually available plus a guest ale.

Popular pub in the village where Sir Gilbert Scott was born. Garden. Children welcome. Quiz on Sun. Annual beer festival over Easter weekend. South of Buckingham.

11am–3pm (not Mon except bank holidays) and 5–11pm Mon–Thurs; 11am–11pm Fri–Sat; 12–10.30pm Sun.

HADDENHAM

The Rising Sun

9 Thame Road, Haddenham HP17 8EN
☎ *(01844) 291744* Mike and Cilla Addley

A freehouse with Vale Wychert Ale and Vale Best usually on sale. Guest beers are from a range of micro-breweries such as Banks and Taylor, and other beers from Vale Brewery.

A village pub, on the main road from Thame to Aylesbury. Very much a drinker's pub, with bar snacks only. Beer garden. Children allowed until 7.30pm.

11am–3pm and 5–11pm Mon–Thurs; 11am–11pm Fri–Sat; 12–10.30pm Sun.

HAMBLEDEN

Stag & Huntsman

Hambleden, Henley-on-Thames RG9 6RP
☎ *(01491) 571227*
Henry Smith and Andrew Stokes

A freehouse with Rebellion IPA, Wadworth 6X and a regularly changing guest from Rebellion or other micro-brewery.

Popular pub near the church in a typically English National Trust village. Bar and restaurant food available at lunchtime and evenings (not Sun evening). Three bars and dining room. Accommodation. Garden. Children welcome in eating areas.

11am–2.30pm and 6–11pm Mon–Fri; 11–3pm and 6–11pm Sat; 12–3pm and 7–10.30pm Sun.

HEDGERLEY

White Horse

Village Lane, Hedgerley SL2 3UY
☎ *(01753 643225)*
Dot Hobbs, Janet and Kevin Brooker

Genuine freehouse serving approx 1,000 different real ales annually. Seven at any one time, all drawn from the cask. Real cider and Belgian draught beer also available

Award-winning, family-run, fifteenth-century village local. Two bars. Food served at lunchtime. Annual beer festival in late May. No machines, no music. Garden and outside seating. Bird sanctuary nearby.

11am–2.30pm and 5.30–11pm Mon–Fri; 11am–11pm Sat; 12–10.30pm Sun.

IBSTONE

The Fox

The Common, Ibstone, Stokenchurch HP14 3GG
☎ *(01491) 638289* Bob Cook (manager)
www.thefoxofibstonehotel.co.uk

Greene King Ruddles County and IPA usually available plus a guest ale such as Greene King Old Speckled Hen or Abbot Ale.

A 300-year-old traditional country inn. Two bars with low beams and log fires. Bar and restaurant food available at lunchtime and evenings. Garden with patio area. Accommodation. Children allowed. Wedding and conference facilities available for hire. Off M40 J5.

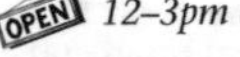

12–3pm and 6–11pm (10.30pm Sun).

LEY HILL

The Swan

Ley Hill, Near Chesham HP5 1UT
☎ *(01494) 783075* David and Natalia Allen
www.swan-ley-hill.com

Adnam's Best, Young's Bitter, Marston's Pedigree, Fuller's London Pride and Timothy Taylor Landlord available, plus a couple of rotating guests such as Woodforde's Wherry, Hook Norton Best, King and Barnes Sussex, Oakham JHB, Jennings Cumberland, Black Sheep Bitter, Harvey's Best, Bateman's XB, Wychwood Hobgoblin, Caledonian Deuchars IPA and many more.

A characterful village inn dating from 1520, close to the Hertfordshire border. Low beams and log fires. Divided into two, with a bar on one side and a restaurant on the other. Outside seating to the front, where the pub looks onto a cricket pitch, golf course and common. Good food served 12–2.15pm and 6.45–9.15pm (not Sun evening). Children welcome during the day.

12–3pm and 5–11pm Mon–Sat; 12–4pm and 7–10.30pm Sun (all day Sat and Sun in summer).

LITTLE MARLOW

The King's Head

Church Road, Little Marlow SL7 3RZ
☎ *(01628) 484407* Tim Pegrum

Up to five real ales available. Fuller's London Pride, Timothy Taylor Landlord and something from Brakspear always available. Others, changed every three to four weeks, might include Wadworth 6X, Caledonian Deuchars IPA, Adnams Broadside and beers from Rebellion, Vale and Eccleshall breweries.

Seventeenth-century village pub situated between Marlow and Bourne End. One large, comfortable bar, a non-smoking dining room, and a function room for 50–80 people. Food is served at lunchtime and evenings Mon–Sat and all day Sun. Garden. Children welcome.

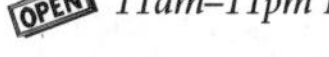

11am–11pm Mon–Sat; 12–10.30pm Sun.

LITTLE MISSENDEN

The Crown

Little Missenden HP7 0QD
☎ *(01494) 862571* Trevor How

A freehouse with four beers on pumps and occasionally one from the wood. Adnams Bitter, Brakspear Special and Fuller's London Pride usually available plus guests, changed twice weekly, which might include something from Greene King, Gale's, Hop Back, Woodforde's, Bateman, Rebellion or Vale breweries.

A country pub off the A413 coming from Amersham towards Aylesbury, with one bar and two real fires. Mixed clientele, no juke box or machines. Large garden, close to the river. Food served at lunchtime only. Children allowed, but not in bar area. Run by the same family for nearly a century.

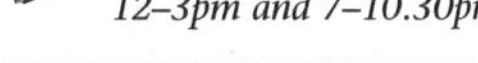

11am–2.30pm and 6–11pm Mon–Sat; 12–3pm and 7–10.30pm Sun.

LITTLEWORTH COMMON

The Jolly Woodman

Littleworth Road, Littleworth Common, Burnham SL1 8PF
☎ *(01753) 644350* Sue Fish

Six beers always available which may include Brakspear Bitter, Gale's HSB, Greene King Abbot Ale and Timothy Taylor Landlord.

A traditional seventeenth-century pub in the middle of Burnham Beeches. Lovely walks all around. Beer garden. Food available at lunchtime and evenings. Children allowed until 8pm.

11am–11pm Mon–Sat; 12–10.30pm Sun.

LOUDWATER

Derehams Inn

5 Derehams Lane, Loudwater, High Wycombe HP10 9RH
☎ *(01494) 530965*
Graham and Margaret Sturgess

At least six beers always available including Fuller's London Pride, Young's Bitter, Brakspear Bitter. Three or four guests may include something from Rebellion, Hook Norton, Fuller's and a mild.

Small and cosy local freehouse. Bar food on weekdays at lunchtime. Car park, garden. Children allowed in the restaurant area. Less than a mile from M40 J3.

11.30am–3pm and 5.30–11pm Mon–Thurs; 11am–11pm Fri–Sat; 12–10.30pm Sun.

MARLOW

The Chequers

51–3 High Street, Marlow SL7 1BA
☎ *(01628) 482053* Paul

Brakspear Bitter and Special plus seasonal brews available.

Village pub with two bars and a function room. Small patio on the High Street. Food available every lunchtime and Mon–Thurs evenings. Cask Marque accredited. Children allowed if eating until 6pm. DJ on Fri and Sat.

11am–11pm Mon–Thurs; 11am–1am Fri–Sat; 12–10.30pm Sun.

The Prince of Wales

1 Mill Road, Marlow SL7 1PX
☎ *(01628) 482970* Robert Robson

Fuller's London Pride, Brakspear Bitter and Adnams Bitter always available plus a rotating guest changed frequently which may come from Rebellion, B & T or another local brewery.

A traditional pub just off the high street, with no juke box, pool, darts or alcopops. Food served at lunchtime and evenings (Thai food only in evenings). Separate dining area. Accommodation. Children not allowed in the bar area. Outside patio. Car park.

11am–11pm Mon–Sat; 12–10.30pm Sun.

The Two Brewers

St Peters Street, Marlow SL7 1NQ
☎ *(01628) 484140* Clive and Barry Mason

Brakspear Bitter and Fuller's London Pride are usually available, plus a beer from Rebellion such as IPA or Blonde.

Traditional pub in a 300-year-old building, with beams and fires. Patio, barn at the back and tables outside, near the river. Food is available, and there is a 50-seater restaurant. Children allowed.

11am–11pm Mon–Sat; 12–10.30pm Sun.

MARLOW BOTTOM

Three Horseshoes

Wycombe Road, Marlow Bottom, Marlow SL7 3RA
☎ *(01628) 483109* Nigel Douglas

Six beers from the local Rebellion Brewery always on sale. IPA and Mild always available.

Country pub with one large main bar incorporating a conservatory and two smaller drinking areas near the main entrance. Exposed brickwork and beams give the pub a rustic feel. Extensive lunchtime and evening menu. Food served 12–3pm and 5.45–9pm Mon–Thurs; 12–4.45pm and 5.45–9.30pm Fri–Sat; 12–4pm Sun.

11am–3pm and 5–11pm Mon–Thurs; 11am–11pm Fri– Sat; 12–4pm and 7–10.30pm Sun; (Open all day bank holidays).

NEW BRADWELL

The New Inn

2 Bradwell Road, New Bradwell, Milton Keynes MK13 0EN
☎ *(01908) 312094* Scott Daubney

Four real ales always available, usually Adnams Broadside, Greene King Old Speckled Hen, Charles Wells Eagle and Bombardier.

Canalside, family-run traditional pub with beer garden, between Newport Pagnell and Wolverton. Food available in a separate 70-seater restaurant, 12–2.45pm and 6–8.45pm Mon–Sat, plus 12–3.45pm Sun. Restaurant available for dinner-dances on Fri–Sat. Children allowed.

12–11pm (10.30pm Sun).

NEWPORT PAGNELL

The Bull Inn

33 Tickford Street, Newport Pagnell MK16 9AE
☎ *(01908) 610325* Miss Jennie Lloyd

A freehouse usually serving about five real ales at any one time, with a minimum of two changed each week. Favourites include Young's Special, Fuller's London Pride, Wadworth 6X and Adnams and Bateman brews. Others might be Shepherd Neame Spitfire, Hampshire Pride of Romsey, Jennings Sneck Lifter, Burton Bridge Top Dog Stout and Ridleys ESX Best, to name but a few.

An old-fashioned coaching inn, just like pubs used to be! No music in lounge. Food at lunchtimes and evenings. Children allowed in restaurant only, if eating. Accommodation. Function room available for hire. Take M1, junction 14; pub next door to the Aston Martin Lagonda factory.

11.30am–2.30pm and 5–11pm Mon–Fri; 11am–11pm Sat; 12–10.30pm Sun.

The Green Man

92 Silver Street, Newport Pagnell MK16 0EG
☎ *(01908) 611914*
Tom Thompson

Greene King IPA and Adnams Bitter are among the three or four beers usually available.

Busy backstreet bar with patio, serving food at lunchtimes only.

12–11pm (10.30pm Sun).

NORTH CRAWLEY

The Cock Inn

16 High Street, North Crawley, Newport Pagnell MK16 9LH
☎ *(01234) 391222* Susan Warterton
www.northcrawley.com/the_cock.htm

A Charles Wells pub with Eagle IPA and Greene King Old Speckled Hen usually available plus a guest ale whick may include beers from Adnams, Marston's or Wadworth.

An oak-beamed pub, built around 1460, next to the church in the village square. A broad cross-section of customers. Two bars and a family room. Bar and restaurant food served at lunchtime and evenings (except Sun). Children allowed in family room. Regular theme nights and live music.

12–3pm and 6–11pm (7–10.30pm Sun).

OLD AMERSHAM

The Kings Arms

30 High Street, Old Amersham HP7 0DJ
☎ *(01494) 726333* John Jennison
www.kingsarmsamersham.co.uk

A freehouse with Rebellion IPA and Burton Ale on hand pump always available, plus two weekly changing guests from breweries such as Brakspear, Young's and Vale, served direct from casks behind the bar.

A 500-year-old coaching inn, where Oliver Cromwell allegedly once stayed. No TV, no music. Featured in *Four Weddings and a Funeral* as 'The Lucky Boatman'. Food is available in the pub at lunchtimes only, but the restaurant is open Tues–Sat for lunch and dinner, and for Sunday lunch (menus available on website). Car park, beer garden. Small non-smoking area for children.

11am–11pm Mon–Sat; 12–10.30pm Sun.

PENN STREET

Hit or Miss

Penn Street, Amersham HP7 0PX
☎ *(01494) 713109* Michael and Mary Macken
www.hitormissinn.co.uk

A Hall & Woodhouse tied house usually serving Best and King & Barnes Sussex, plus seasonal beers such as Fursty Ferret or Tanglefoot.

Idyllic country pub dating from 1730 situated opposite the cricket ground. Several drinking areas and restaurant with low beams and inglenook fireplace. Cricketing memorabilia decorate the walls. Meals are served 12–2.30pm and 6.45–9.30pm Mon–Sat; 12–8pm Sun.

 *11am–11pm Mon–Sat; 12–10.30pm Sun.*

PRESTWOOD

The King's Head

188 Wycombe Road, Prestwood HP16 0HJ
☎ *(01494) 868101* Malcolm and Dee Eden

A Greene King pub with the brewery's ales always available, including Abbot Ale and IPA. Greene King Old Speckled Hen or Triumph may also be available.

An old pub on the edge of the village. Tastefully refurbished. Food served at lunchtime and evenings. Large car park. Large garden with children's play area and barbecue. Take the A4128 from High Wycombe.

 *12–11pm (10.30pm Sun).*

SHERINGTON

The White Hart

1 Gun Lane, Sherington, Newport Pagnell MK16 9PE
☎ *(01908 611953)* Keith Shepherd
www.whitehartsherington.com

Young's Bitter and Fuller's London Pride usually available and three ever-changing guest ales.

Three-hundred-year-old, award-winning, two-bar freehouse, hotel and restaurant. Wide variety of food served lunchtime and evenenings (not Sun). Large garden. Luxury accomodation in converted barn. Annual May bank holiday three-day beer and sausage festival.

 *12–3pm and 5–11pm Mon–Sat; (7–10.30pm Sun).*

STOKE POGES

Rose & Crown

Hollybush Hill, Stoke Poges SL2 4PW
☎ *(01753) 662148* Ronald Holloran

A Greene King tied house with IPA and Morland Original always available. Abbot and Ruddles County are usually rotated on the third pump.

A traditional village pub with food served at lunchtimes. Well-behaved children allowed. Garden with children's play area.

OPEN *11am–3pm and 5.30–11pm (10.30pm Sun).*

STONY STRATFORD

Vaults Bar

The Bull Hotel, 64 High Street, Stony Stratford MK11 1AQ
☎ *(01908) 567104* Paul Wareing

Fuller's London Pride, Young's Special, Eldridge Pope Royal Oak, Wadworth 6X and Adnams Bitter usually available. One guest beer is also available from a very varied list. Timothy Taylor Landlord is the one repeat beer.

Simple, characterful bar in imposing Georgian coaching inn, prominently located in the High Street. Food available 12–10pm. Car park. Children welcome although there are no special facilities. Live music. Accommodation.

OPEN *12–11pm (10.30pm Sun).*

THE LEE

The Cock & Rabbit

The Lee, Great Missenden HP16 9LZ
☎ *(01494) 837540*
Jian Franco and Victoria Parola

The permanent beer is Cock and Rabbit Bitter (brewed by Greene King). Other beers available may include Greene King IPA, Abbot Ale and Triumph.

A classic English pub with an Italian flavour. Facilites include a restaurant called Grazie Mille (a thousand thank yous), dining area and garden lounge. Food served lunchtimes and evenings, seven days a week. Large garden. Children allowed.

 *12–2.30pm and 6–11pm Mon–Sat; 12–3pm and 7–10.30pm Sun.*

The Old Swan

Swan Lane, The Lee, Great Missenden HP16 9NU
☎ *(01494) 837239* Sean Michaelson-Yeats

A freehouse, with Adnams Bitter and Young's Bitter usually available and a guest ale such as Archers Village Bitter.

A traditional sixteenth-century dining pub in the Chiltern Hills. Off the beaten track, it lies between Tring, Chesham, Great Missenden and Wendover. Four inter-connecting rooms. Food served at lunchtime and evenings, with fresh fish a speciality. Restaurant area. Large garden with children's play area.

 *12–3.30pm and 6–11pm Mon–Sat; 12–7pm Sun (12–10.30pm Sun in summer).*

THORNBOROUGH

The Lone Tree

Bletchley Road, Thornborough MK18 2DZ
☎ *(01280) 812334* Nichole McDonald
www.thelonetree.co.uk

Five hand pumps deliver a constantly changing range of ales from independent brewers across the country.

Small roadside pub with a large choice of food available at lunchtime and evenings. Car park and garden. Supervised children allowed.

 *12–3pm and 5.30–11pm Mon–Sat; 12–10.30pm Sun.*

WENDOVER

The Red Lion Hotel

9 The High Street, Wendover HP22 6DU
☎ *(01296) 622266* Tim Cutting

Young's Special, Brakspear Pale Ale and Adnams Bitter usually available, plus one monthly changing guest purchased through the Beer Seller.

A seventeenth-century coaching inn situated in beautiful Chilterns countryside, ideal for walkers. Another pub with Oliver Cromwell connections (see The Kings Arms, Old Amersham). One bar, open fires, outside seating. Very busy restaurant serving fresh food all day every day, plus separate bar food available at lunchtimes and evenings. Children allowed. Accommodation. Function room.

7am for breakfast; 11am–11pm.

WESTON TURVILLE

The Chequers Inn

35 Church Lane, Weston Turville HP22 5SJ
☎ *(01296) 612079* Christian Wioland
www.aylesburyvale.net/aylesbury/chequers

Fuller's London Pride, Adnams Bitter and Wadworth 6X usually available. Guest ales may include beers from breweries such as Black Sheep, Brakspear, Bateman or Hook Norton.

Sixteenth-century country inn with stone floors, real fires and two bars. Bar and (French-influenced) restaurant food available at lunchtime and evenings (not Mon). Two dining rooms. Live music outside sometimes during summer. Car park. Function room. Children allowed. Near the church, but ring for directions, as can be difficult to find.

 *12–3pm (not Mon) and 6–11pm (7–10.30pm Sun).*

WHEELER END

The Chequers

Bullocks Farm Lane, Wheeler End, High Wycombe HP14 3NH
☎ *(01494) 883070*
Stephen Warner and Anna Kaiser
http://chequers.tablesir.com/

A Fuller's inn with London Pride and ESB always available, plus a Fuller's seasonal ale. There is also a monthly guest ale from breweries such as Adnams, Hardys & Hansons, Timothy Taylor or Jennings.

A traditional seventeenth-century pub with attractive beer gardens and inglenook fireplace. Home-cooked food, freshly prepared on the premises, served lunchtime and evenings (not Sun evenings). Candlelit restaurant. Children welcome in the restaurant. Dog-friendly. Beer garden and patio. Car park at rear.

 *11am–3pm and 5.30–11pm Mon–Fri; 11am–11pm Sat; 12–10.30pm Sun.*

WING

The Cock Inn

26 High Street, Wing, Leighton Buzzard LU7 0NR
☎ *(01296) 688214*
Alberto Marcucci and Stuart Mosley

Four weekly changing guest beers available from independent or micro-breweries which may include beers from Woodforde's, Thwaites, Brains or Cottage.

Privately owned, fine English country pub with log fires and good home-cooked food available every lunchtime and evening in a separate restaurant and at the bar. Car park. Children welcome, high chairs available. Garden with play area.

11.30am–3pm and 6–11pm Mon–Sat; 12–3pm and 7–10.30pm Sun.

THE BREWERIES

CITY OF CAMBRIDGE BREWERY LTD

Ely Road, Chittering, Cambridge CB5 9PH
☎ *(01223) 864864*
www.cambridge-brewery.co.uk

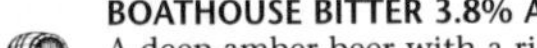

BOATHOUSE BITTER 3.8% ABV
A deep amber beer with a rich, chocolatey nose, supported by a little citrus hoppiness.

RUTHERFORD IPA 3.8% ABV
A copper-coloured IPA. A good clean bitterness with an aroma of floral and citrus notes.

HOBSON'S CHOICE 4.1% ABV
A light golden bitter with a pronounced hop aroma, contributing to the refreshing bitter aftertaste.

SUNSET SQUARE 4.4% ABV
A smooth, crisp-tasting golden-coloured beer with a strong aroma. A blend of Atom Splitter and Hobson's Choice.

ATOM SPLITTER 4.7% ABV
Amber-coloured beer with plenty of character. Bursting with First Gold hoppiness.

DARWINS DOWNFALL 5.0% ABV
A blended ruby-golden-coloured fruity-flavour bitter with a tangy aftertaste.

PARKERS PORTER 5.3% ABV
A dark rich ruby-coloured fruity-flavoured bitter with a tangy aftertaste.

Seasonal:

JET BLACK 3.7% ABV
Uniquely styled black beer, mild but full in flavour and body. Available throughout the year.

EASTER BUNNY 3.8% ABV
Brewed for Easter. A rich amber bitter with a hoppy nose and smooth aftertaste. Available March–May.

TRINITY 4.3% ABV
A full-flavoured blend of Boathouse and Atom Splitter, creating a lovely red beer with a subtle citrus nose and a hint of roast barley flavour. Available April–July.

MICH'AELMAS 4.6% ABV
Christmas ale. A deep reddish blend of Porter and Best Bitter creating a diverse mix of hops and malt not normally placed together. Ideal for the season. Available September–December.

PATRON SAINT 4.7% ABV
Brewed to celebrate St. George's Day on the 23rd April. An amber beer with a rich malty nose backed by a hint of orange. Available in April.

HOLLY HEAVEN 5.2% ABV
A wonderfully full-bodied, full-flavoured Christmas beer. Deep rich copper in colour, with well-balanced malt and hops, both of which are present in abundance. Available October–December.

BRAMLING TRADITIONAL 5.5% ABV
Bramling hops are used to give attractive fruit flavour. Available October–March.

ELGOOD AND SONS LTD

North Brink Brewery, Wisbech PE13 1LW
☎ *(01945) 583160*
www.elgoods-brewery.co.uk

BLACK DOG MILD 3.6% ABV
Malty, dark mild with good balance.

CAMBRIDGE BITTER 3.8% ABV
Malt fruit flavours with dry finish.

PAGEANT ALE 4.3% ABV
Rounded, balanced and bittersweet.

GOLDEN NEWT 4.6% ABV
Dry and hoppy.

GREYHOUND 5.2% ABV

BITTERSWEET FLAVOUR.

Plus a large range of seasonal and occasional brews.

THE FENLAND BREWERY

4, Prospect Way, Chatteris PE16 6TY
☎ *(01354) 696776*
www.fuggle.demon.co.uk/fenland

FBB 4.0% ABV

DOCTOR'S ORDERS 5.0% ABV

RUDOLPH'S ROCKET FUEL 5.5% ABV

MILTON BREWERY CAMBRIDGE LTD

Unit 111, Norman Industrial Estate, Cambridge Road, Milton CB4 6AT
☎ *(01223) 226198*
www.miltonbrewery.co.uk

MINOTAUR 3.3% ABV
Dark mild with rich chocolate malt flavour.

PEGASUS 4.1% ABV
Hoppy with balancing fruit, malt finish.

ELECTRA 4.5% ABV
Malty sweetness and powerful bitter finish.

CYCLOPS 5.3% ABV

Seasonals:

JUPITER 3.5% ABV
A spring/summer session beer.

NEPTUNE 3.8% ABV
Crisp autumn/winter brew.

MAMMON 7.0% ABV
Dark winter warmer for December.

7 Wonders Range:

ARTEMIS 3.7% ABV

ZEUS 4.2% ABV

BABYLON 4.4% ABV
Rounded malt and fruit flavours.

PHAROS 4.7% ABV

MAUSOLEUM 4.9% ABV

PYRAMID 4.9% ABV

COLOSSUS 5.6% ABV

The Imperator Range:
Seven beers named after Roman Emperors.

OAKHAM ALES

80 Westgate, Peterborough PE1 2AA
☎ *(01733) 358300*
www.oakham-ales.co.uk

JEFFREY HUDSON BITTER 3.8% ABV
WHITE DWARF 4.3% ABV
Slightly cloudy wheat beer.
BISHOP'S FAREWELL 4.6% ABV
BLACK HOLE PORTER 5.5% ABV
Seasonals:
FIVE LEAVES LEFT 4.5% ABV
Autumn/winter brew.
HELTER SKELTER 5.0% ABV
MOMPESSON'S GOLD 5.0% ABV
OLD TOSSPOT 5.2% ABV
Brewed Sept–May.
Plus one-off brews for special occasions.

ROCKINGHAM ALES

c/o 25 Wansford Road, Elton PE8 6RZ
☎ *(01832) 280722*
www.rockinghamales.co.uk

FOREST GOLD 3.9% ABV
A1 AMBER ALE 4.0% ABV
SAXON CROSS 4.1% ABV
FRUITS OF THE FOREST 4.2% ABV
DARK FOREST 5.0% ABV
Seasonals:
FINESHADE 3.8% ABV
Autumn.
SANITY CLAUSE 4.3% ABV
Christmas brew.
OLD HERBACEOUS 4.5% ABV
Winter brew.

THE PUBS

ABINGTON PIGOTTS

The Pig & Abbot

High Street, Abington Pigotts, Nr Royston
☎ *(01763) 853515*
Miss Nicola Grundy and Mrs Pat Thomson

Adnams Best and Broadside and Fuller's London Pride always available, plus a constantly changing guest. Examples of ales served recently include Adnams Oyster, Woodforde's Wherry, Elgood's Cambridge Bitter, Nethergate Suffolk County and City of Cambridge Boathouse Bitter.

Cosy, olde-worlde country pub with open fire, beams and a relaxed, friendly atmosphere. Home-cooked food to appeal to all tastes served 12–2pm and 7–9pm Mon–Fri and 12–3pm and 7–9.30pm Sat–Sun. Restaurant, beer gardens. Children welcome, and high chairs are available. Car park. Turn off the A1198 to Bassingbourn and look for signs.

12–3pm and 6–11pm Mon–Fri; 12–11pm Sat; 12–10.30pm Sun.

ASHTON

The Chequered Skipper

The Green, Ashton, Nr Arundel, Peterborough
☎ *(01832) 273494* Colin Campbell

Oakham JHB is a permanent feature, and the four weekly changing guests (250 in the last three years) could include beers such as Black Sheep Bitter, Bateman XXXB, Adnams Broadside or Slaters Premium.

One-bar pub, traditional on the outside but modern inside. Full green, back garden, restaurant. Occasional live music on Bank Holidays. Children allowed.

11.30am–3pm and 6–11pm Mon–Fri; 11am–11pm Sat; 12–10.30pm Sun.

BOXWORTH

The Golden Ball

High Street, Boxworth CB3 8LY
☎ *(01954) 267397* Hilary Paddock

Beers available include Adnams Broadside and Greene King IPA. Guests include Greene King Old Speckled Hen, Ruddles County, Potton Village Bike and many more.

Typical country pub in good walking area. Bar and restaurant food at lunchtime and evenings, with interesting and upmarket fare. Meeting room, car park. Large garden with separate entrance. Children allowed. Ten miles from Cambridge, six miles from St Ives.

11.30am–2.30pm and 6.30–11pm.

BRANDON CREEK

The Ship

Brandon Creek, Downham Market PE38 0PP
☎ *(01353) 676228* Mr N Mott

A regularly changing range of guest beers which often features something from Adnams, Fuller's, Woodforde's and Shepherd Neame.

Situated by the River Ouse with easy river and road access. Quality food is available, non-smoking restaurant (reservations recommended). Children welcome.

12–3pm and 5.30–11pm Mon–Thurs; 12–11pm Fri–Sat; 12–10.30pm Sun.

CAMBRIDGE

The Bird in Hand

73 Newmarket Road, Cambridge CB5 8EG
☎ *(01223) 351919* Trevor Critchlow
www.bird-in-hand.fsnet.co.uk

Greene King IPA, XX Dark Mild, Old Speckled Hen and Ruddles County always on offer, plus one guest, changed every two months, such as Brakspear Bitter, Black Sheep Bitter or Jennings Cocker Hoop.

Traditional one-bar town pub with garden. No games or music. A French chef prepares the food on the French menu. Children not allowed.

 *12–2pm and 5–11pm Mon–Thurs; 12–11pm Fri–Sun (10.30pm Sun).*

Cambridge Blue

85–7 Gwydir Street, Cambridge CB1 2LG
☎ *(01223) 361382* Chris and Debbie Lloyd

At least six beers always available, focusing on Cambridgeshire and East Anglia breweries. Favourites include City of Cambridge Hobson's Choice and other ales in their range, plus beers from the Milton brewery, such as Pegasus or from Adnams and Elgood's. Always open to suggestions.

Terraced side-street pub, totally non-smoking and mobiles-free, with large garden and two bars. Healthy bar food at lunchtimes and evenings, seven days a week. Children allowed in conservatory area until 9pm. Off Mill Road on the city side of railway bridge.

12–2.30pm (3.30pm Sat) and 6–11pm.

The Dobblers Inn

184 Sturton Street, Cambridge CB1 2QF
☎ *(01223) 576092* Miss Emma Mitchell

A Charles Wells tenancy, with Eagle IPA and Bombardier plus Adnams Broadside always available as customer favourites. Guest ales include Badger Tanglefoot, Wadworth 6X, seasonal ales and even Charles Wells Banana Bread Beer.

Welcoming, lively backstreet boozer, ten minutes from the Grafton Centre. The blooming beer garden is regularly used for barbecues in summer. Sky Sports (3 screens), gaming machines, juke box, pool table and bar billiards. Smoking allowed throughout, with extraction and two air filters maintaining a clean and pleasant atmosphere.

 *12–11pm (10.30pm Sun).*

The Elm Tree

42 Orchard Street, Cambridge CB1 1JT
☎ *(01223) 363005* John Simons

A Charles Wells tenancy with Bombardier and Eagle IPA always on offer. Two guest beers, such as Adnams Best, Broadside or Marston's Pedigree, are changed regularly.

A traditional one-bar pub in a back street off the city centre, near Grafton Shopping Centre, with large-screen TV and lots of table games (including chess). Rolls only served. No children allowed. Live music.

12–2.30pm and 4 or 5–11.30pm Mon–Thurs; 11am–11pm Fri–Sat; 12–10.30pm Sun.

The Free Press

Prospect Row, Cambridge CB1 1DU
☎ *(01223) 368337*
Donna and Martin Thornton

A Greene King tied house with Abbot, IPA and XX Dark Mild always available, plus two guests changed regularly.

A famous East Anglian real ale house, the first pub in Cambridge to stock real ales when the revival began. A very traditional atmosphere, with table games available and a courtyard beer garden. Genuine homemade hot and cold bar food available 12–2pm and 6–8.30pm Mon–Fri, 12–3pm and 6–8.30pm Sat, and 12–2.30pm Sun. Has been totally non-smoking for 12 years and is now mobiles-free as well. Children welcome. Located near Grafton Shopping Centre.

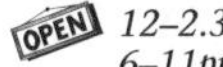 *12–2.30pm Mon–Fri; 12–3pm Sat–Sun; 6–11pm Mon–Sat; 7–10.30pm Sun.*

The Kingston Arms

33 Kingston Street, Cambridge CB1 2NU
☎ *(01223) 319414* Jane Fairhall

Regularly serving up to ten real ales on hand pumps. Hop Back Summer Lightning and Entire Stout, Elgood's Black Dog Mild, Timothy Taylor Landlord, Crouch Vale Brewer's Gold and Oakham JHB usually feature plus guest beers changed on a weekly basis.

A friendly pub, winner of many awards and with a good mix of locals and visitors. No music or machines, just a natural buzz! Free internet access is available with two PCs available in the bar, or bring your own lap-top and take advantage of the wireless access point. Traditional English food served from 12–2pm and 6–9pm, with a good wine list. Tables can be pre-booked. Garden open in summer. Children under 14 allowed in the garden until 9pm. Situated just off Mill Road, 15 minutes' walk from city centre.

 *12–2.30pm and 5–11pm (closed Mon lunch); all day Sat–Sun.*

The Locomotive

44 Mill Road, Cambridge CB1 2AS
☎ *(01223) 322190* Mr Foster

Greene King IPA and Adnams Broadside permanently available, plus a regularly changing guest ale.

Situated near the University, with a student-based clientele. One bar, air-conditioned function room, large-screen TV for sports. Parking at rear. Thai food available in the evenings on a trial basis. Children allowed until 7pm.

OPEN *11am–11pm Mon–Sat; 12–10.30pm Sun.*

Live and Let Live

40 Mawson Road, Cambridge CB1 2EA
☎ *(01223) 460261* Peter Wiffin

Seven hand pumps serve Adnams Bitter, Everards Tiger and Nethergate Umbel Ale as regular beers, along with an ever-changing guest list, including beers from Oakham, Milton, Tring, B&T and Mighty Oak. An eighth pump serves a locally produced real cider, Cassels. Several mini beer festivals held throughout the year.

Situated in central Cambridge, just off Mill Road, popular with students, business people and locals alike. The pub is 120 years old with a single bar, wooden furniture , floors and panelling plus real gas lighting. Beer and railway memorabilia. Live music on Saturday nights by a local busker. Extensive home-cooked menu with several vegetarian options available lunchtimes until 2pm and evenings until 9pm (not Sun evenings). Children allowed in eating area. Street parking.

OPEN *11.30am–2.30pm daily; 5.30–11pm Mon–Fri; 6–11pm Sat; 7–10.30pm Sun.*

The Portland Arms

129 Chesterton Road, Cambridge CB4 3BA
☎ *(01223) 357268* David Thompson

A Greene King tenancy. Greene King IPA, Abbot, XX Mild and Ruddles Best are always on offer, and there are always two non-Greene King beers available as well, such as Black Sheep Bitter, Jennings Bitter, Badger Tanglefoot and Everards Tiger.

A pub with three bars, one a traditional saloon, one a music venue (100 capacity), and one an internet bar/café with five terminals. Food served in all areas, especially the saloon. Garden and parking. Children allowed. Situated on the outer Ring Road (A10).

OPEN *11am–11pm Mon–Sat; 12–10.30pm Sun.*

St Radegund

129 King Street, Cambridge CB1 1LD
☎ *(01223) 311794* Terry Kavanagh

One of the few true freehouses in Cambridge, where Milton St Radegund Habit Ale, Fuller's London Pride and Shepherd Neame Spitfire are always available. Occasional guest beers also served.

The smallest pub in Cambridge. No juke box, no games machines. Background jazz music. Filled rolls only. Children not allowed. Opposite the Wesley church in King Street.

OPEN *5–11pm Mon–Fri; 12–11pm Sat; 12–2pm and 6.30–10.30pm Sun.*

Tap & Spile

14 Mill Lane, Cambridge CB2 1RX
☎ *(01223) 357026* Peter Snellgrover

Approx 300 beers per year (nine at any one time) including brews from Adnams, Bateman, Black Sheep, Thwaites, Ushers, Nethergate and many other independent breweries.

Traditional alehouse with oak floors and exposed brickwork in picturesque setting right next to the river (perhaps the biggest beer garden in England?). Punting station nearby. Bar food at lunchtime.

OPEN *11am–11pm Mon–Sat; 12–3pm and 7–10.30pm Sun.*

Wrestlers

337 Newmarket Road, Cambridge CB5 8JE
☎ *(01223) 566553* Tom Goode

A house tied to Charles Wells, with Eagle IPA and Bombardier always served, plus two guest beers changed fortnightly. Favoured breweries include Lees, Archers, Caledonian and Adnams.

The pub specialises in Thai food. Children allowed.

OPEN *12–3pm and 5–11pm Mon–Sat; closed Sun.*

CASTLE CAMPS

The Cock Inn

High Street, Castle Camps, Cambridge CB1 6SN
☎ *(01799) 584207* Mr Puell

A freehouse always serving Greene King IPA and Abbot plus a guest beer, which may be Fuller's London Pride, something from Nethergate or Shepherd Neame Spitfire. Changed weekly.

An olde-worlde two-bar drinkers' pub. Food available most evenings and Sun lunchtime. Children allowed. Accommodation available.

OPEN *12–2pm and 7–11pm Sun–Fri; 12–11pm Sat.*

DOGSTHORPE

The Blue Bell Inn

St Pauls Road, Dogsthorpe, Peterborough PE1 3RZ
☎ *(01733) 554890* Mr PR and Mrs TL Smith

Elgood's Black Dog Mild, Cambridge Bitter and Greyhound usually available with a weekly changing guest beer such as Bateman XXXB and beers from Hook Norton, Adnams and Burton Bridge.

Good old-fashioned character to this listed, sixteenth-century, Elgood's tied house. Food served 11am–2pm Mon–Fri, but not bank holidays. Car park. Children permitted in small lobby room and garden. Located on the junction of Welland Road/St Pauls Road, near to Dogsthorpe Fire H.Q.

OPEN *11am–2.30pm and 6–11pm Mon–Fri; 11.30am–3pm and 6–11pm Sat; 12–3pm and 7–10.30pm Sun.*

DUXFORD

The Plough Inn

59 St Peters St, Duxford, Cambridge
☎ *(01223) 833170* Julie Nicholls

Everards Tiger, Original and Beacon, and Adnams Bitter always on offer, plus one guest, perhaps another Adnams beer.

Thatched village pub with beer garden. Food available 12–2pm and 5–9pm Mon–Fri, and 12–6pm Sat–Sun. Live music Saturday. Children welcome (bouncy castle in garden!). Car park.

OPEN *11am–3pm and 5–11pm Mon–Thurs; 11am–11pm Fri–Sat; 12–10.30pm Sun.*

ELY

The Fountain

1 Silver Street, Ely CB7 4JF
☎ *(01353) 663122* John Borland

A freehouse with Adnams Bitter and Broadside or Regatta plus Fuller's London Pride as permanent fixtures. A guest beer, changed frequently, could well be Charles Wells Bombardier.

A Victorian pub near the cathedral, renovated and modernised. No food. Children allowed until 9pm.

OPEN *5–11.30pm Mon–Fri; 12–2pm and 6–11.30pm Sat; 12–2pm and 7–11pm Sun.*

GLINTON

The Blue Bell

10 High Street, Glinton, Peterborough PE6 7LS
☎ *(01733) 252285* Mr Mills

Tied to Greene King brewery and permanently serving IPA and Abbot Ale. Guests from various breweries also available.

A village pub with separate dining area. Food served at lunchtime and evenings. Children allowed.

OPEN *12–2.30pm and 5.30–11pm Mon–Thurs; 12–11pm Fri–Sat; 12–10.30pm Sun.*

GRAVELEY

The Three Horseshoes

23 High Street, Graveley, Huntingdon PE18 9PL
☎ *(01480) 830992* Alfred Barrett

A freehouse with three pumps serving a variety of beers, which change weekly, mainly from independent breweries such as Marston's, Adnams and others.

A very old country inn, with no juke box or pool tables. Non-smoking restaurant. Food at lunchtime and evening. Children allowed.

OPEN *11am–3pm and 6–11pm Mon–Sat; 12–2pm and 7–11pm Sun.*

HINXTON

The Red Lion

32 High Street, Hinxton, Cambridge CB10 1QX
☎ *(01799) 530601* Linda Crawford

A freehouse with Adnams Bitter and Woodforde's Wherry Best always on sale. There is also one guest.

A sixteenth-century coaching inn half a mile south of junction 9 off the M11, with one bar and a non-smoking restaurant. Food served at lunchtime. Children allowed.

OPEN *11am–2.30pm and 6–11pm Mon–Sat; 12–2.30pm and 7–10.30pm Sun.*

HOLYWELL

The Ferryboat Inn

Holywell PE27 4TG
☎ *(01480) 463227*
David and Niamh Baynham

Tied to Greene King, with IPA and Abbot always available. Additional beers, mainly available in the summer months, include Greene King Old Speckled Hen and Ruddles County.

A remote pub in a rural setting down a country lane and overlooking the River Great Ouse. Ring for directions, if needed! Food-oriented, with meals available all day. Large bar and eating area with function room. Children welcome.

OPEN *11.30am–11pm Mon–Sat; 12–10.30pm Sun.*

HUNTINGDON

The Old Bridge Hotel

1 High Street, Huntingdon PE29 3TQ
☎ *(01480) 424300* Martin Lee

Adnams Best and City of Cambridge Hobson's Choice are always available, along with a guest beer.

A smart town-centre hotel that features a busy and welcoming bar. Restaurant meals and bar snacks served every day, with full afternoon teas. Well-behaved children allowed. Occasional live entertainment.

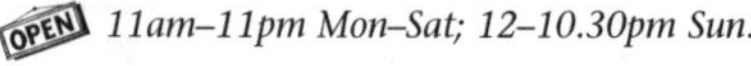
11am–11pm Mon–Sat; 12–10.30pm Sun.

KEYSTON

The Pheasant

Keyston, Huntingdon PE18 0RE
☎ *(01832) 710241* Jonathan Dargue

Adnams Bitter always available, plus two guests from a changing selection, with brews from Potton, City of Cambridge and other local micro-breweries appearing regularly.

A thatched inn in a quiet village, with oak beams and large open fires. Quality food served in the pub, and in the small restaurant. Food available lunchtimes and evenings. Car park. Children welcome.

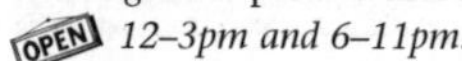
12–3pm and 6–11pm.

LEIGHTON BROMSWOLD

The Green Man

37 The Avenue, Leighton Bromswold, Nr Huntingdon PE18 0SH
☎ *(01480) 890238* Ms Toni Hanagan

Nethergate Bitter always available plus three guest beers (200 per year) perhaps from Adnams, Young's, Robinson's, Shepherd Neame, Brakspear, Fuller's, Wychwood, Shepherd Neame or Timothy Taylor.

Seventeenth-century, detached public house with a collection of water jugs and memorabilia. Bar food available at lunchtime and evenings. Open fire, car park, garden, children's room. Skittles played. One mile off the A14.

12–3pm and 7–11pm; closed Mon.

LITTLE GRANSDEN

The Chequers

71 Main Road, Little Gransden, Sandy SG19 3DW
☎ *(01767) 677348* Mr R Mitchell

Adnams Bitter is permanently available, and there is one constantly changing guest beer, from breweries such as Milton, Church End, Wye Valley and Nethergate.

Friendly pub with tap room, lounge, games room and large garden. No food. Children welcome until 9pm. Car park. Close to the Bedfordshire border.

12–2.30pm and 5–11pm Mon–Fri; 11am– 11pm Sat; 12–2pm and 7–10.30pm Sun.

LONGSTOWE

The Red House

Old North Road, Longstowe PB3 7UT
☎ *(01954) 718480* Gillian Willis

A freehouse with Potton Shambles a permanent feature. Two guests, changed every few weeks, include favourites such as Greene King Ruddles County and beers from Nethergate.

Traditional rural pub with one bar, garden and separate restaurant. No games. Live music occasionally on Sundays. Car parking. Children welcome.

12–2.30pm and 5.30–11pm (10.30pm Sun).

MADINGLEY

The Three Horseshoes

Madingley CB3 8AB
☎ *(01954) 210221* Richard Stokes

Adnams Best is a permanent feature, with two guests also served, City of Cambridge being a regular.

A thatched inn with a bar and large garden. Imaginative food served in the bar, garden and conservatory-restaurant. Meals available 12–2pm and 6.30–9.30pm daily. Car park. Children welcome.

11.30am–2.30pm and 6–11pm Mon–Sat; 12–3pm and 7–10.30pm Sun.

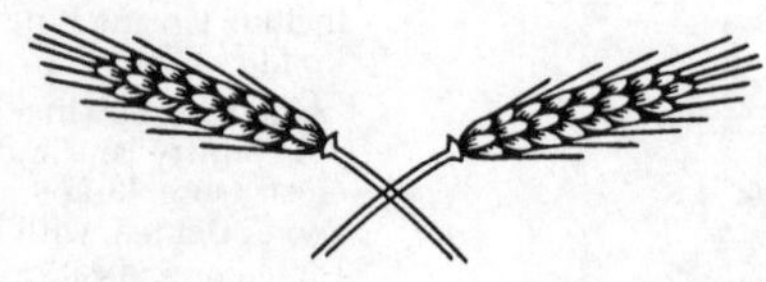

MARCH

The Rose & Crown

41 St Peters Road, March PE15 9NA
☎ *(01354) 652879* Mr D Evans

At least seven traditional beers served from a menu that changes on a daily basis. Archers Village and a mild are usually available and around 300 different ales feature each year, including some imported ones, plus traditional ciders and perry. The pub also stocks over 100 whiskies.

A 150-year-old suburban pub with a non-smoking lounge. Winner of a CAMRA gold award. No juke box, no videos, no television, just a good old-fashioned atmosphere. Outside patio area.

12–2.30pm and 7–11pm Mon–Fri (closed Wed lunchtime); 12–3pm and 7–11pm Sat–Sun (10.30pm Sun).

MILTON

The Waggon & Horses

39 High Street, Milton CB4 6DF
☎ *(01223) 860313*
Nick and Mandy Winnington

Elgood's Cambridge Bitter, Black Dog Mild, Golden Newt and Greyhound Strong Bitter usually available, plus one guest ale from a varied range.

Imposing 1930s mock-Tudor building set back from the main road. Large child-friendly garden to rear. Note hat collection and eclectic pictures on walls. Bar billiards and darts. Children allowed in pub under supervision (9pm curfew), as are animals on a lead. Car park.

12–2.30pm and 5–11pm Mon–Fri; 12–4pm and 6–11pm Sat; 12–3pm and 7–10.30pm Sun.

NEEDINGWORTH

The Queen's Head

30 High Street, Needingworth, Nr Huntingdon PE17 2SA
☎ *(01480) 463946* Mr and Mrs Vann

Six beers always available including Smiles Best, Woodforde's Wherry Best and Hop Back Summer Lightning. Approximately 100 guests per year including Timothy Taylor Landlord, Parish Somerby Premium, Butterknowle Conciliation, Hook Norton Best, Chiltern Beechwood, Sarah Hughes Dark Ruby Mild and brews from Wild's brewery.

Friendly pub. Bar snacks served 12–8pm. Car park and garden. Children allowed in lounge bar. Close to St Ives.

12–11pm.

NEWTON

Queen's Head

Fowlmere Road, Newton, Nr Cambridge CB2 5PG
☎ *(01223) 870436* Mr David Short

Has specialised in Adnams beers for over 30 years. Best Bitter and Broadside always available, plus seasonal winter ale, Regatta (the seasonal summer ale) and Tally Ho! on Bonfire Night and at Christmas.

A typical early eighteenth-century pub beside the village green. Bar food at lunchtime and evenings. Car park, children's room, various bar games. Three miles from M11 junction 10; less than two miles off the A10 at Harston.

11.30am–2.30pm and 6–11pm Mon–Sat; 12–2.30pm and 7–10.30pm Sun.

OLD WESTON

The Swan

Main Road, Old Weston, Huntingdon PE17 5LL
☎ *(01832) 293400* Jim Taylor

Greene King Abbot, Adnams Best and Broadside are always available in this freehouse, along with two guest beers each week. Hook Norton Old Hooky is regularly featured.

A beamed restaurant/pub with a central bar. Fish and chip night each Wednesday. Children allowed.

6.30–11.30pm Mon–Fri; 11am–11pm Sat; 12–10.30pm Sun.

PETERBOROUGH

Bogart's Bar and Grill

17 North Street, Peterborough PE1 2RA
☎ *(01733) 349995*

Six beers always available from a varied selection (300+ per year) usually ranging from a mild at 3.0% to 5.5% ABV. Regional beer festival at the start of each month, featuring brewers from a specific part of the UK. Real cider also available.

Bogart's was built at the turn of the century and now has a wide-ranging clientele. The horseshoe-shaped bar is decorated with film posters and Humphrey Bogart features prominently. Background music but no juke box or pool table. Bar food at lunchtime. Car park opposite and beer garden. No children. Located off the main Lincoln Road.

11am–11pm Mon–Sat; closed Sun.

The Brewery Tap

80 Westgate, Peterborough PE1 2AA
☎ *(01733) 358500*
Stuart Wright and Jamie Howley

A freehouse associated with the Oakham Ales brewery, which brews on site and can be observed through a glass wall. Up to 12 pumps serving Oakham JHB, Bishop's Farewell and White Dwarf as permanent fixtures plus guests from all over the country.

An open-plan 500-seater pub with relaxed sofa seating area and restaurant-style food served at pub prices at lunchtime and in the evenings. Thai cuisine. Extended opening hours on Fri and Sat. Over 18s only.

 *12–11pm Mon–Thurs; 12–1.30am Fri–Sat; 12–10.30pm Sun.*

Charters Bar

Town Bridge, Peterborough PE1 1DG
☎ *(01733) 315700* Stuart Wright
www.bluesontheboat.co.uk

Twelve hand pumps serve four permanent and eight guest ales. Oakham JHB and Bishop's Farewell, Timothy Taylor Landlord and Hop Back Summer Lightning are always available, and the guest beers (approx. 500 per year) are from as many independent breweries as possible.

A floating converted Dutch barge moored on the River Nene by the bridge in the centre of Peterborough. Oriental bar food is served at lunchtimes, and there is an oriental restaurant on the upper deck. Landscaped beer garden next to the river. Late-night live blues club Fri and Sat nights until 2am.

 *12–11pm (1.30am Fri–Sat).*

Coalheavers Arms

5 Park Street, Fletton, Peterborough PE2 9BH
☎ *(01733) 565664*

Milton Brewery ales including Minotaur, Jupiter and Pegasus plus guest beers from smaller breweries. An Autumn beer festival took place in September 2004.

Back-street boozer relaunched in 2002 by a local consortium including the Milton Brewery. No food. Outside seating. In the south of the city.

 *12–2.30pm and 5.30–11pm Mon–Thurs. All day Fri–Sat. 12–3pm and 7–10.30pm Sun.*

The Golden Pheasant

1 Main Road, Etton, Peterborough PE6 7DA
☎ *(01733) 252387* David McLennan

Hop Back Summer Lightning, Oakham Jeffrey Hudson Bitter, Woodforde's Wherry and Adnams Broadside are always available, plus six guests, two of which are changed every fortnight. Regular favourites include Timothy Taylor Landlord, Bateman XXXB, Woodforde's Great Eastern and Nelson's Revenge. Rare malts and brandies plus exclusive wines also served. Annual beer festival on first weekend of September features over 20 beers.

This pub in an old Georgian rectory is set in an acre and a half of gardens, with a 100-seater marquee permanently available for functions. Food is available 12–2.30pm and 6.30–9.30pm Mon–Sat, plus 12–6pm Sun. The gourmet restaurant, where booking is advisable, features in the *Good Food Guide,* and food is also served in the bar and conservatory. Boules, barbecues, large car park. Children are welcome, and there are family facilities outside. Located close to 'Green Wheel' cycle route.

 *12–3pm and 5–11pm Mon–Thurs (closed Mon lunch); all day Fri–Sun. Open all day, every day in summer (closed Mon lunch).*

Hand & Heart

12 Highbury Street, Peterborough PE1 3BE
☎ *(01733) 564653* Eamon Bracken

Two or three guests are on offer, changed weekly, from a range including Wolf Granny Wouldn't Like It, Barnsley IPA, Black Dog Stout and Kelham Island Pride of Sheffield.

A local community pub retaining many original 1930s features, with friendly, warm atmosphere. Open fire, wooden floor and large beer garden with lawn and flowers. Crib, darts and dominoes, but no juke box. Sandwiches and rolls are available on request. Children welcome in lounge bar until 6pm. Located 15 minutes' walk from town centre, off Lincoln Road.

 *11am–11pm Mon–Sat; 12–10.30pm Sun.*

ST IVES

The Royal Oak

13 Crown Street, St Ives PE27 4EB
☎ *(01480) 462586* Angie Davies

Four real ales usually available including Wadworth 6X, plus one rotating guest from a wide selection.

Built in 1502 and now a grade II listed building, this traditional-style pub in the town centre features a single bar. Food is served from 12–4pm daily. Children allowed until 7pm. Car park, beer garden.

11am–11pm Mon–Sat; 12–10.30pm Sun.

SIX MILE BOTTOM

Green Man Inn

London Road, Six Mile Bottom CB8 0UF
☎ *(01638) 570373* James Ramselle

At least three beers always available, including Greene King IPA and Adnams Best Bitter, and a guest beer, such as Nethergate Umbel Ale.

Award-winning, historical, old-fashioned friendly country inn, with open log fire in the bar. Candlelit dining room with famous giant horseracing mural, delightful flower garden, terrace and petanque court. Lunch served 12–2pm Tues–Sun and dinner 6.30–9pm Tues–Sat. Internet services. Car park. Located on the A1304 near Newmarket.

 *11.30am–2.30pm and 5.30–11pm Tues–Sat; 12–4.30pm Sun (closed Sun evening and all day Mon).*

STOW CUM QUY

Prince Albert

Newmarket Road, Stow cum Quy CB5 9AQ
☎ *(01223) 811294* Mr and Mrs Henderson

Five beers always available including Greene King IPA. Guests might include Ash Vine Bitter, Stormforce Ten, Worzel Wallop and Shardlow Reverend Eaton's Ale.

Lively roadside pub built in 1830. Bar and restaurant food served at lunchtime and weekend evenings. Private functions catered for. Car park and garden. Children allowed. Just off A14 on the Newmarket road (A1303).

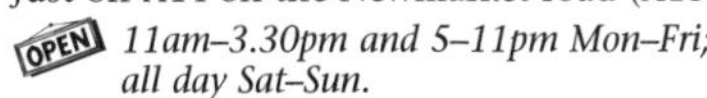
11am–3.30pm and 5–11pm Mon–Fri; all day Sat–Sun.

White Swan

Main Street, Stow cum Quy CB5 9AB
☎ *(01223) 811821* Mr A Cocker

Among those beers always available are Greene King IPA, Adnams Best, Shepherd Neame Spitfire and Woodforde's Wherry Best plus a guest beer changed fortnightly. Regulars include Everards Tiger, Fuller's London Pride and something from Charles Wells.

A freehouse and restaurant with one small public bar. No smoking. Food served at lunchtime and Tues–Sun evenings. Children allowed but no facilities for them.

11am–3pm and 6–11pm Tues–Sat; 12–3pm and 7–10.30pm Sun.

THRIPLOW

The Green Man

2 Lower Street, Thriplow SG8 7RJ
☎ *(01763) 208855* Ian Parr

A freehouse offering an ever-changing selection of up to four real ales. Beers from Milton, Slaters and Oakham have been featured, but brews from almost any brewery could be served.

Open-plan, two-bar pub by the village green with small non-smoking dining area. Formerly Charles Wells. Bar and restaurant food available at lunchtime and evenings (not Sunday). Car park and garden. Children allowed with well-behaved parents! Turn off the A505 near the Imperial War Museum, Duxford.

12–3pm and 6–11pm Tues–Sat; 12–3pm Sun (closed Sun evening and all day Mon).

WHITTLESEY

The Boat Inn

2 Ramsey Road, Whittlesey, Nr Peterborough PE7 1DR
☎ *(01733)* 202488 Philip Quinn

An Elgood's Brewery tied house with two real ales usually available. Cambridge Bitter and Pageant Ale are the likely suspects.

A seventeenth-century traditional pub on a site mentioned in the Domesday Book. Large informal bar, plus separate lounge featuring the bow of a boat as the bar. Bed and breakfast accommodation. No food (except breakfasts for those staying). Large car park and garden featuring children's play area. Ask for directions on reaching Whittlesey.

12–11pm (10.30pm Sun) every day except 4–11pm Tues.

WISBECH

The Rose Tavern

53 North Brink, Wisbech PE13 1JX
☎ *(01945) 588335*
David O'Connell and Sarah Dodd

Up to nine real ales available, from brewers small and large nationwide with the range changing every couple of days.

A 200-year-old listed building forming a comfortable, one-roomed pub on the banks of the River Nene. The closest pub to Elgood's Brewery. Garden, wheelchair access, traditional pub games, accommodation, children welcome. Beer festival held on the last weekend in June. Follow National Trust signs to Peckover House, then another 250 yards towards Elgood's Brewery.

12–3pm and 6–11pm (7–10.30pm Sun).

WOODSTON

Palmerston Arms

82 Oundle Road, Woodston, Peterborough PE2 9PA
☎ *(01733) 565865* Mr D McLennan

A freehouse offering up to ten real ales. Hop Back Summer Lightning and Bateman XB are always available plus rotating guest beers including Shepherd Neame Spitfire, Church End Vicar's Ruin and RCH Pitchfork.

A traditional pub with lounge and public bar. All beers served straight from the barrel in the cellar. No food. No children.

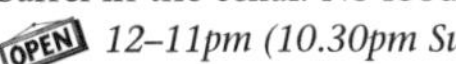
12–11pm (10.30pm Sun).

YARWELL

The Angel

59 Main Street, Yarwell, Peterborough PE8 6PR
☎ *(01780) 782582* Mrs Pamela Turner

A freehouse with Banks's Best always available. One guest, changed weekly, might be something like Harveys Sussex Best Bitter or Fenland Doctor's Orders.

Traditional two-bar village pub with beams and fires. Pool table, skittles, fruit machine. Bar meals available. Garden. Children allowed in family room.

12–2.30pm and 6.30–11pm Mon–Fri (closed Mon evenings); 12–3pm and 6.30–11pm Sat; 12–3pm and 7–10pm Sun.

THE BREWERIES

RW RANDALL LTD

PO Box 154, Vauxlaurens Brewery, St Julian's Avenue, St Peter Port, Guernsey GY1 3JG
☎ *(01481) 720134*

MILD 3.4% ABV
ISLAND GOLD 3.8% ABV
PALE ALE 3.8% ABV
PATOIS 4.8% ABV
STOUT 5.5% ABV
Plus occasional brews.

TIPSY TOAD BREWERY

La Grande Route de St Pierre, St Peter's Village, Jersey JE3 7AA
☎ *(01534) 485556*

TIPSY TOAD ALE 3.8% ABV
JIMMY'S BITTER 4.2% ABV
Plus seasonal and occasional brews. Also:
GUERNSEY BRAYE MILD 3.8% ABV
GUERNSEY PIRATES ALE 4.2% ABV
GUERNSEY SUNBEAM BITTER 4.2% ABV

THE PUBS

JERSEY

GROUVILLE

Seymour Inn

La Rocque, Grouville, Jersey JE3 9BU
☎ *(01534) 854558* Gary Boner

Guernsey Sunbeam and Tipsy Toad Jimmy's Bitter usually available. Occasional and seasonal brews from Tipsy Toad are also served.

Traditional country pub with two lounges, bar and beer garden. Food 12–2pm and 6–8pm Mon–Sat. Car park. Children welcome.

10am–11pm Mon–Sat; 11am–11pm Sun.

ST BRELADE

The Old Smugglers Inn

Ouaisne Bay, St Brelade, Jersey JE3 8AW
☎ *(01534) 741510* Nigel Godfrey

A genuine freehouse serving two guest ales which change daily, perhaps including Greene King Abbot and something from Ringwood or Young's.

Close to the beach and dating from the eighteenth century, this pub has no music or fruit machines. Food is served every day and there is a non-smoking dining area. Children welcome.

All day, every day.

ST HELIER

Lamplighter

9 Mulcaster Street, St Helier, Jersey JE2 3NJ
☎ *(01534) 723119* Sean Murphy

Five or six real ales usually available including Ringwood Best and Fortyniner, Charles Wells Bombardier and Wadworth 6X. Seasonal and occasional guests also feature.

Gas-lit pub with old wooden beams, rafters and soft, pewter bar top. Refurbished in July 2003 but with the character still intact. Live sport on satellite TV. Food 12–2.15pm and 5.30–8pm Mon–Thurs, 12–2.15pm Fri, 12–3pm Sat and 12–4pm Sun. Children welcome. Close to St Helier bus station.

10am–11pm Mon–Sat; 11am–11pm Sun.

The Prince of Wales Tavern

French Lane, St Helier, Jersey JE2 4SL
☎ *(01534) 737378* Graeme Channing

Tied to Randalls, mainly serving beers from the big national breweries but Ringwood Best also features and plans for a fifth ale may have been realised.

A small, one-bar, eighteenth-century tavern in the middle of St Helier with character and ambience and a beautiful beer garden. No TV, no pool, no juke box, just background music. Food 11.30am–2.15pm Mon–Fri. No children. Next to the central market.

10am–11.30pm Mon–Sat; 11.30am–2.30pm Sun.

ST LAWRENCE

The British Union

Main Road, St Lawrence, Jersey JE3 1NL
☎ *(01534) 861070* Mark Finch

Something from the Tipsy Toad Brewery is always available.

An open-plan pub with two bars and games room. Small beer garden. Food at lunchtime and evenings. Children allowed. Opposite St Lawrence Church.

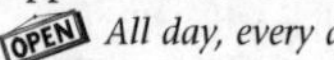

All day, every day.

ST OUEN

Le Moulin de Lecq

Greve de Lecq, St Ouen, Jersey JE3 2DT
☎ *(01534) 482818* Caroline Byrne

A freehouse offering Guernsey Sunbeam and guest ales such as Greene King Old Speckled Hen and Abbot or a Ringwood brew.

Built around a twelfth-century flour mill with working parts still on view inside and outside the bar. One bar and small upstairs lounge, large outside seating area and adventure playground with a bouncy castle. Summer barbecues. Food served at lunchtime and evenings (except Sun). Children welcome.

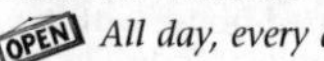

All day, every day.

ST PETER'S VILLAGE

The Star

La Grande Route de St Pierre, St Peter's Village, Jersey JE3 7AA
☎ *(01534) 485556* John Dryhurst

Home of The Tipsy Toad Brewery. Jimmy's Bitter is always available plus the seasonal or occasional brews.

Jersey's first brewpub, opened in 1992 and situated in renovated and restored Victorian premises. The result is a cosy pub with a family atmosphere. The brewing process can be observed through a wall of windows. Bar food is available at lunchtime and evenings. Family room and conservatory, outdoor children's play area. Baby-changing facilities and disabled toilets. Live music every weekend.

11am–11pm.

GUERNSEY

CASTEL

Hotel Fleur du Jardin

Kings Mills, Castel, Guernsey GY5 7JT
☎ *(01481) 257996* Keith Read
www.fleurdujardin.guernsey.net

A local brew such as Guernsey Sunbeam is always available, plus a guest beer.

Fifteenth-century country inn with olde-worlde atmosphere, serving bar and restaurant meals at lunchtimes and evenings. A lovely beer garden with al fresco dining at lunchtimes. Car park. Children welcome.

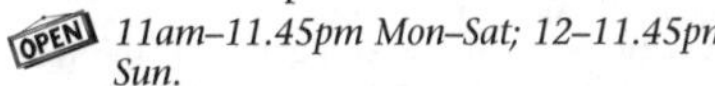

11am–11.45pm Mon–Sat; 12–11.45pm Sun.

FOREST

Venture Inn

New Road, (Rue de la Villiaze), Forest, Guernsey GY8 0HG
☎ *(01481) 263211* Tony and Kay Mollet

Randall's Patois usually available plus seasonal or occasional brews.

Country pub in the heart of the farming community. Log fire in the lounge bar during winter months. Big-screen TV, pool and darts in the public bar. Food served May–Sept, 12–2pm and 6–9pm Mon–Sat; Oct–Apr, 12–2pm Mon–Thurs, 12–2pm and 6–9pm Fri–Sat. Car park. Children's menu.

10.30am–11.45pm Mon–Sat.

ST MARTINS

The Captain's Hotel

La Fosse, St Martins, Guernsey GY4 6EF
☎ *(01481) 238990* Alison Delamare

A Guernsey Brewery tied house with a guest ale changing monthly.

A traditional locals' pub, which is popular with tourists. Outside tables. Petanque pitch. Food served in the bar and in separate bistro – parties catered for. Children and dogs allowed.

10am–11.45pm.

ST PETER PORT

Albion House Tavern

Church Square, St Peter Port, Guernsey GY1 2LD
☎ *(01481) 723518* Amanda Roberts

A Guernsey Brewery house with Sunbeam always available.

Spread over two floors with a large nautical-themed bar downstairs, sports bar and wine bar upstairs with pool tables. Food available every lunchtime and Mon–Thurs evenings. Children allowed. Situated right beside the Church, the pub actually features in *The Guinness Book of Records* as the pub closest to a Church in the UK!

10.30am–11.45pm Mon–Sat; 12–3.30pm Sun (closed Sun evening).

The Banker's Draught

The Pollet, St Peter Port, Guernsey GY1 1WL
☎ *(01481) 723855* Glen Pontin

A Guernsey Brewery tied house with Sunbeam usually available.

A big pub with varied clientele – business people, tourists and families. Video games machines and video juke box, live bands occasionally. Food served at lunchtime only. Children allowed.

10am–11.45pm Mon–Thurs; 10am–12.45am Fri–Sat; 12–7pm Sun.

Cock & Bull

2 Lower Hauteville, St Peter Port, Guernsey
☎ *(01481) 722660* Stephen Taylor

Ringwood Best Bitter, Fortyniner and VB Sipping Bull (brewed exclusively for the pub) usually available, plus guests from breweries such as Stonehenge, Shepherd Neame, Hop Back, Rebellion, Greene King, Orkney, Crouch Vale, and many others.

Large, friendly pub on three levels, with one bar. The varied clientele includes plenty of university students and rugby supporters. Quarterly beer festivals held. Irish music provided by the landlord and his wife often features on Thursday nights (with a little Irish dancing thrown in!). Acoustic music on Tuesday nights. Food served lunchtimes Mon–Sat. Pool room, big-screen TV. Situated at the top of Cornet Street, on the way to Victor Hugo's house, and close to the Mignot Plateau, which offers one of the best views of Castle Cornet and the Harbour.

11.30am–2.30pm and 4–11.45pm Mon–Thurs; 11.30am–12.45am Fri–Sat; closed Sun.

The Cornerstone Café Bar

2 La Tour Beauregard, St Peter Port, Guernsey GY1 1LQ
☎ *(01481) 713832* William Cann

A freehouse with three hand pumps. Beers from the nearby Randall's brewery are among those often featured, plus Tipsy Toad Jimmy's Bitter and guest brews such as Wadworth 6X, Fuller's London Pride, Badger Best and Tanglefoot, Adnams Broadside, Bateman XXXB, Young's Bitter and Greene King Old Speckled Hen.

A former restaurant and sister pub of The Drunken Duck, popular with locals. Comprehensive menu offering local fresh fish and bar food specials, daily roasts, homemade soups and chilli. Sandwiches and baguettes made while you wait. Food is served 8am–2.30pm and 6–8.30pm Mon–Fri, 10am–2.30pm and 6–8.30pm Sat, and 10am–2.30pm Sun. Menu also available in French. Occasional live music, dart board and amusing jokes in the toilets.

 *8am–12.45am Mon–Fri; 10am–12.45am Sat; 10am–3.30pm Sun.*

The Drunken Duck

La Charroterie, St Peter Port, Guernsey GY1 1EL
☎ *(01481) 725045* Cyril Dunne

The range on offer at this freehouse varies, with brews such as Wadworth 6X, Fuller's London Pride, Thwaites Lancaster Bomber, Badger Best and Tanglefoot, Adnams Broadside, Bateman XXXB, Young's Bitter and Greene King Old Speckled Hen and IPA, to name but a few.

A small, friendly pub, still painted yellow! Appeals to young and old alike, and is popular with a wide range of customers. Big-screen TV for major sporting events, separate, quiet back bar. Food available Mon–Fri lunchtimes. Ample parking from 5pm and at weekends. Occasional live music, dart board and more amusing jokes in the toilets.

 *11am–12.45am Mon–Sat; 12–11pm Sun.*

The Ship & Crown

Pier Steps, The Esplanade, St Peter Port, Guernsey
☎ *(01482) 721368* Mark Pontin

Guernsey Sunbeam, Fuller's London Pride and Wadworth 6X usually available plus one from a range of 15–20 guests constantly rotated.

Large, lively, single-bar town pub with excellent views over the harbour. Walls covered in pictures of local shipwrecks and local history, including the German occupation during WW2. Food served 11am–3pm Mon–Sat, plus 12–3pm and 6–10pm Sun, with local fish and crab a speciality. Car park. Children welcome until 3pm.

 *10am–12.45am Mon–Sat; 12pm–12.45am Sun.*

ST PETERS

Longfrie Inn

Route du Longfrie, St Peters, Guernsey GY7 9RX
☎ *(01481) 263107* Peter and Jill Wright

A Guernsey Brewery tied house with a range of traditional real ales always available.

A food-oriented pub with beams and log fires in winter. Beer garden. Live music. Very large car Park. Children welcome.

OPEN *11am–11.45pm (summer); 12–3pm and 5.30–11.45pm (winter).*

ST SAMPSON

Blind O'Reilly's

South Side, St Sampson, Guernsey GY2 4QH
☎ *(01481) 244503* Mark O'Reilly

A Guernsey Brewery tied house with Randall's Mild and Sunbeam usually available.

A pub in two halves, with the front an Irish theme bar and the back a traditional family pub. Live music, festivals and entertainment. Food available at lunchtime. Children allowed.

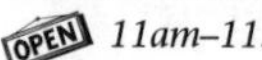 *11am–11.45pm.*

Pony Inn

Les Capelles, St Sampsons, Guernsey GY2 4GX
☎ *(01481) 244374* Isoken Ogbeide

A Guernsey Brewery tied house with either Sunbeam or Pirates Ale always available.

A family-orientated two-bar pub with conservatory, patio, play area, Playstations and TV-screen games. Child-free zone for those who prefer a peaceful pint. Live music every Friday. Car park. Food available.

 *10.30am–11.45pm.*

VALE

Houmet Tavern

Grande Havre, Vale, Guernsey GY6 8JR
☎ *(01481) 242214* Antony Green

A Guernsey Brewery tied house with one guest, changed every couple of weeks. Seasonal and special brews are sometimes featured, but the guest could be from anywhere.

Comfortable lounge bar overlooking the sea. No smoking in the conservatory. Darts, pool, bar billiards. Beer garden. Car park. Food available Mon–Sat lunchtimes and Tues, Wed, Fri, Sat evenings. Children allowed, and there is a special children's menu available.

 *10am–11.45pm.*

THE BREWERIES

BEARTOWN BREWERY

Bromley House, Spindle Street, Congleton CW12 1QN
☎ *(01260) 299964*
www.beartownbrewery.co.uk

GOLDIE HOPS 3.5% ABV
KODIAK GOLD 3.8% ABV
BEAR ASS 4.0% ABV
Aromatic, with smooth, dry malty flavour.
BEARSKINFUL 4.2% ABV
Golden, dry sharp flavour, with a hoppy, rich malt aftertaste.
POLAR ECLIPSE 4.8% ABV
Rich dark oatmeal stout.
BLACK BEAR 5.0% ABV
Smooth, dark ruby mild.
BRUINS RUIN 5.0% ABV
Golden, smooth and full-flavoured.
WHEAT BEER 5.0% ABV
Crisp, refreshing award winner.
Plus a range of speciality brews.

COACH HOUSE BREWING CO. LTD

Wharf Street, Howley, Warrington WA1 2DQ
☎ *(01925) 232800*
www.beer.u-net.com

COACHMAN'S BEST BITTER 3.7% ABV
Smooth, rich malt flavour, with some fruit.
GUNPOWDER STRONG MILD 3.8% ABV
Full flavour, with slight bitter aftertaste.
OSTLERS SUMMER PALE ALE 3.8% ABV
SQUIRES GOLD SPRING ALE 4.2% ABV
INNKEEPER'S SPECIAL RESERVE 4.5% ABV
Crisp and malty with balancing hops.
POSTHORN PREMIUM 5.0% ABV
Rich, smooth and complex.
TAVERNERS AUTUMN ALE 5.0% ABV
BLUNDERBUSS OLD PORTER 5.5% ABV
ANNIVERSARY ALE 6.0% ABV
Strong ale brewed once a year.
Plus seasonal brews.

FREDERIC ROBINSON LTD

Unicorn Brewery, Stockport SK1 1JJ
☎ *(0161) 480 6571*
www.frederic-robinson.com

HATTERS 3.3% ABV
Fresh, with malt throughout.
OLD STOCKPORT BITTER 3.5% ABV
Golden, with a hoppy flavour.
HARTLEYS XB 4.0% ABV
Malt flavour with hoppy bitterness.
BEST BITTER 4.2% ABV
Light in colour with a bitter hop taste and aroma.
FREDERIC'S 5.0% ABV
Smooth and well-balanced.
OLD TOM 8.5% ABV
Superb, mellow winter warmer.

THE KHEAN BREWING CO.

Unit 4, Royle Park, Royle Street, Congleton CW12 1JJ
☎ *(01260) 272144*

ALL-ROUNDER 3.9% ABV
Light golden, creamy tasting, smooth session beer with a very pleasant bitter finish.
VILLAGE GREEN 4.0% ABV
Pale golden bitter refreshingly dry with a very pleasant flowery finish.
CAUGHT BEHIND 4.2% ABV
Smooth, traditional, easy-drinking stout with a dry-roasted barley flavour.
LEG SPINNER 4.4% ABV
Gold-coloured beer with a sharp flavour and a strong bitter finish.
SEAMER 4.5% ABV
Conker-coloured smooth ale with a balanced malt and hops flavour, leaving a bitter aftertaste.

PARADISE BREWING COMPANY

Unit 2, The Old Creamery, Wrenbury Road, Wrenbury, Nantwich CW5 8EX
☎ *(01270) 780916*

MARBURY MILD 3.6% ABV
ASTON LIGHT 3.8% ABV
WRENBURY ALE 4.0% ABV
Slightly dark, crisp aftertaste.
PARADISE GOLD 4.4% ABV
Lovely gold, well-hopped beer.
WYBUNBURY RED 4.5% ABV
Reddish full-bodied beer.
DABBER'S GOLD 5.0% ABV
Golden wheat beer.
RUM OLD ALE 6.0% ABV
Dark, mature, strong and well balanced.
Plus bottled beers, seasonal and celebration ales.

THE STORM BREWING CO.

2 Waterside, Macclesfield SK11 7HJ
☎ *(01625) 431234*

BEAUFORTS 3.8% ABV
BITTER EXPERIENCE 4.0% ABV
DESERT STORM 4.0% ABV
ALE FORCE 4.2% ABV
HURRICANE HUBERT 4.5% ABV
WINDGATHER 4.5% ABV
SILK OF AMNESIA 4.7% ABV
STORM DAMAGE 4.7% ABV

WEETWOOD ALES LTD

The Brewery, Weetwood Grange, Tarporley CW6 0NQ
☎ *(01829) 752377*
www.weetwoodales.co.uk

BEST BITTER 3.8% ABV
EASTGATE ALE 4.2% ABV
Golden, with fruity hoppiness.
OLD DOG PREMIUM BITTER 4.5% ABV
Deep colour, smooth and rich.
AMBUSH 4.8% ABV
OAST-HOUSE GOLD 5.0% ABV
Pale and hoppy with a dry finish.

THE PUBS

ALDFORD

Grosvenor Arms
Chester Road, Aldford, Chester, CH3 6HJ
☎ *(01244) 620228 Fax: (01244) 620247*
www.grosvenorarms-aldford.co.uk

Regular beers are: Caledonian Deuchars IPA, Flower's IPA and Robinson's Best Bitter, plus two rotating guest beers.

The Grosvenor is a charming Victorian pub in the village of Aldford on the Duke of Westminster's estate. It has well-spaced rooms and a great outside terrace leading into a small but very pleasing garden, which in turn leads onto the village green. The locals are very fond of it. Children welcome if supervised until 6pm. Food is served daily 12–10pm (9pm on Sundays).

11.30am–11.00pm Mon–Sat; 12–10.30pm Sun.

APPLETON THORN

Appleton Thorn Village Hall
Stretton Road, Appleton Thorn, Nr Warrington WA4 4RT
☎ *(01925) 268370* Mrs Karen Howard

Five real ales always available, always different (over 1,500 served in last three years).

A charitable village club operated voluntarily by local residents. Membership not required for entry, though new members always welcome (£4 per year). Car park, garden, playing field, bowling green, pool and darts. Children welcome. From M6 Jct 20 or M56 Jct 10, follow signs for Appleton Thorn. Hall is 100m west of village church. 1995 CAMRA national club of the year.

8.30–11pm Thurs–Sat; 8.30–10.30pm Sun. Open lunchtimes (1–4pm) on first Sunday of each month.

ASTON

Bhurtpore Inn
Wrenbury Road, Aston, Nr Nantwich CW5 8DQ
☎ *(01270) 780917* Simon and Nicky George

Hanby Drawwell always available plus ten guest beers (950 to 1000 per year) which may include a brew from Burton Bridge, Weetwood, Adnams, Slaters (Eccleshall), Bateman, Black Sheep and Rudgate. Also real cider and 180 bottled Belgian beers plus three Belgian beers on draught. A real ale drinkers' Mecca !

The family has been connected with this comfortable, traditional, award-winning pub since 1849. Fresh bar and restaurant food at lunchtime and evenings 12–2pm and 6.45–9.30pm Monday to Saturday and Sunday 12–9pm. Car park, beer garden. Well-behaved children allowed in pub at lunchtime and in early evening up to 8pm. Annual beer festivals. Bed and breakfast available (2 rooms). Located 5 miles south of Nantwich, west of the A530, midway between Nantwich and Whitchurch.

12–2.30pm and 6.30–11pm Mon–Sat; 12–10.30pm Sun.

BROXTON

The Egerton Arms
Whitchurch Road, Broxton CH3 9JW
☎ *(01829) 782241* Jim Monaghan

A Burtonwood house, with Top Hat a permanent feature. One guest beer, changed monthly, could be another Burtonwood ale, or a beer such as Ridleys Rumpus or Everards Tiger.

A rural pub on the main road, with one bar and a restaurant. Garden, car park. Children allowed. Seven letting rooms refurbished in 2004. Located 10 miles from Chester on the junction of the A41 and A534.

11am–11pm Mon–Sat; 12–10.30pm Sun.

BUNBURY

Dysarts Arms
Bowes Gate Road, Bunbury, Nr Tarporley CW6 9PH
☎ *01829 260183*

Regular beers are Timothy Taylor Landlord, Thwaites Best Bitter plus three rotating guest beers

A truly classic English village pub with open fires and an abundance of oak furniture. It has a pleasant garden and food is served 12–2.15pm and 6–9.30pm Monday to Friday, 12–9.30pm Saturday and 12–9pm Sunday. Children welcome until 6pm if supervised by parents. Disabled facilities.

11.30am–11.30pm Mon–Sat; 12–10.30pm Sun

CHESTER

The Mill Hotel

Milton Street, Chester CH1 3NF
☎ *(01244) 350035*
www.millhotel.com

CAMRA Millennium Pub of the Year 2000, offering 16 real ales, including three permanently available, Weetwood Best, Coach House Mill Premium and Cains Traditional Bitter. Guests change daily (approx. 1200 served every year) and always include a mild and either a stout or a porter. Requests welcome!

Hotel bar and restaurant on the site of a once-working mill. Bar and restaurant food available at lunchtime and evenings. Canalside patio, restaurant boat lunch and dinner cruises. Accommodation available (130 bedrooms). Non-smoking area. Sky Sports on TV (with sound turned down). Families most welcome. Ample car parking.

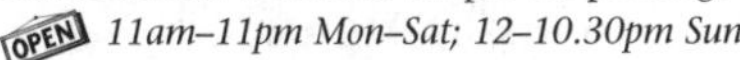 *11am–11pm Mon–Sat; 12–10.30pm Sun.*

Old Harkers

1 Russell Street, Chester CH3 5AL
☎ *(01244) 344525*
www.harkersarms-chester.co.uk

Flower's IPA and Thwaites Best Bitter usually available plus eight guests.

This is an old London-style boozer, only in Chester, with a good reputation for its food. A great meeting place for a pub lunch and at different times you will find half the commercial and professional heart of the city in the bar. Food is served daily from 12–2.30pm and 5–9.30pm (9pm on Sun). No food on Friday evenings. Supervised children allowed until 7pm.

 *11.30am–11pm Mon–Sat; 12–10.30pm Sun.*

The Union Vaults

44 Egerton Street, Chester CH1 3ND
☎ *(01244) 322170* Miss Lee

Former Greenalls pub offering Plassey Bitter from Wrexham plus two guests, which are changed weekly.

A little local alehouse, five minutes from Chester train station, this is a drinkers' pub with one bar. No food. Children allowed.

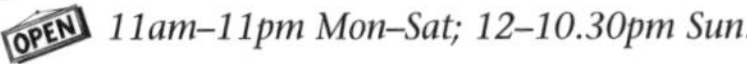 *11am–11pm Mon–Sat; 12–10.30pm Sun.*

CONGLETON

The Beartown Tap

18 Willow Street, Congleton CW12 1RL
☎ *(01260) 270990* Steve King

The Beartown Brewery tap, with the full range of Beartown beers usually available. Six hand-pulled beers available – Wye Valley Brew 69 and Dwan Tipperary are examples of the guests on offer (one, changed weekly). Cider and Belgian beer on draught, plus over 30 bottled Belgian beers.

Traditional drinkers' town pub, quiet (no juke box), with no swearing allowed! Darts, dominoes and crib. Pre-booked meals and buffet are available. Function room. Parking nearby. Children allowed.

 *12–2pm and 4–11pm Mon–Thurs; 12–11pm Fri–Sat; 12–10.30pm Sun.*

The Queen's Head Hotel

Park Lane, Congleton CW12 3DE
☎ *(01260 272546)* Anna and Tony Gunner

Greene King Abbot, IPA and Ruddles County and Marston's Pedigree usually available. Guests may come from Titanic, Coach House, Beowulf, Cottage, Archers, Phoenix and elsewhere. All ales purchased as firkins and changed every 2–3 days.

Owned by London and Edinburgh Inns, a traditional community pub beside the Macclesfield Canal (with moorings). Food served all day. Garden with children's play area. Accommodation.

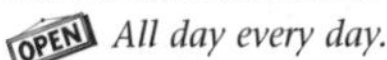 *All day every day.*

CREWE

The Office

1 Pedley Street, Crewe CW2 7AA
☎ *(01270) 251465* Jacqui and Rick Woolhouse

Greene King Abbot and Fuller's London Pride always available plus a changing guest.

A modern but relaxed and comfortable atmosphere with one long bar. Recently refurbished. Close to the railway station and local football ground. Food served 12–3pm Monday to Saturday. Children only allowed on football days, if accompanied by parents. Sky Sports and free music every day. To find, take first left after the railway station, then right at first traffic lights.

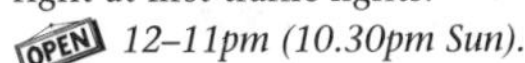 *12–11pm (10.30pm Sun).*

FRODSHAM

Netherton Hall

Chester Road, Frodsham WA6 6UL
☎ *(01928) 732342*

A Jennings brew is a permanent fixture, plus four fine cask ales, perhaps Greene King Abbot and IPA, Timothy Taylor Landlord and something from Adnams.

A typical Cheshire country pub on the main road, with one large bar, half of which is smoking and half non-smoking. Food served at lunchtime and evenings, and all day Sunday. Well-behaved children allowed.

OPEN *11am–11pm Mon–Sat; 12–10.30pm Sun.*

Helter Skelter

31 Church Street, Frodsham WA6 6PN
☎ *(01928) 733361* Mike Toner and Robin Holt

Six real ales always available, including Weetwood Best Bitter (the house bitter) plus five guest beers, changing constantly. There is also one pump serving traditional farmhouse cider.

One-room public bar with restaurant above. Bar and restaurant food at lunchtime and evenings. Restaurant closed Saturday lunchtime and all day Sunday. Parking. Children allowed in restaurant. In the main shopping area, close to British Rail station.

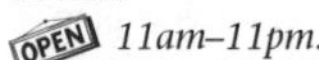
OPEN *11am–11pm.*

GREAT SUTTON

The White Swan Inn

Old Chester Road, Great Sutton, Ellesmere Port CH66 3NZ
☎ *(0151) 339 9284* John and Denise Hardy

Tied to the Burtonwood Brewery, offering five different brews a week, the Burtonwood range plus guests such as Shepherd Neame Bishop's Finger and Jennings Sneck Lifter.

A community local with Sky TV, off the main road (not signposted). Meals served at lunchtimes 11.30am–2pm Mon–Sat (except Tues) and 12–4pm Sun (Sunday roast available: three choices, £4.50). Children allowed only if dining.

OPEN *11.30am–11pm Mon–Sat; 12–10.30pm Sun.*

HALEBANK

The Cock & Trumpet Inn

Halebank Road, Halebank, Widnes WA8 8NB
☎ *(0151) 4253142* Tom Glover (Manager)

Two pumps serve Burtonwood Top Hat plus one guest, changed weekly, which may include Jennings Sneck Lifter or Shepherd Neame Bishop's Finger, though the aim is not to repeat beers.

Fairly modern community pub with two bars (games room and lounge). 'Pub grub' served. Beer garden at back with play area. Barbecues when weather permits. Car park. Children allowed up to 8pm. Located five minutes from Runcorn Bridge, off Ditton Road.

OPEN *11.30am–11pm Mon–Sat; 12–10.30pm Sun.*

HASSALL GREEN

The Romping Donkey

Hassall Green, Sandbach CW11 4YA
☎ *(01270) 765202* Steve Fennel

Greene King Abbot and Robinson's Best Bitter are always featured.

A family-oriented pub with large beer garden. Food available 12–9pm daily, including carvery, bar menu and à la carte meals. Children are welcome. Large car park. Off the main Alsager–Sandbach road, turn left at the New End public house.

OPEN *12–11pm (10.30pm Sun).*

HATCHMERE

Carriers Inn

Delamere Road, Hatchmere, Norley
☎ *(01928) 788258* Karen Ashton

A Burtonwood house with Bitter and Smooth permanently available, plus two monthly changing guests. York Yorkshire Terrier is a regular feature.

A refurbished inn with restaurant and extensive beer garden overlooking the lake. Food available 12–3pm and 6–8pm daily. Pool table. Children allowed, with children's play area provided. Located on the B5152.

OPEN *11am–11pm Mon–Sat; 12–10.30pm Sun.*

HIGHER HURDSFIELD

George & Dragon

61 Rainow Road, Higher Hurdsfield, Macclesfield SK10 2PD
☎ *(01625) 424300* D Molly Harrison

A beer from Storm Brewing Co. is among the brews usually available.

Traditional part-seventeenth-century pub with food served 12–2pm Mon–Fri and Sun. Car park. Children welcome, but no special facilities.

 *12–3pm and 7–11pm Mon–Fri; 7–11pm Sat; 12–3pm and 7.30–10.30pm Sun.*

KINGSLEY

Horseshoe Inn

Hollow Lane, Kingsley WA6 8EF
☎ *(01928) 788466* Ron Varnett

A Burtonwood pub, with Burtonwood Bitter always on offer. One guest, such as Everards Tiger or something from Ridleys, is changed monthly.

Village community pub with an L-shaped bar and open fire. Food is available, and there is a dining area. Patio, car park. Children allowed.

 *12–3pm and 5–11pm (10.30pm Sun).*

LANGLEY

Leather's Smithy

Clarke Lane, Langley, Nr Macclesfield SK11 0NE
☎ *(01260) 252313* Paul McMahon
www.leatherssmithy.co.uk

Charles Wells Bombardier, Theakston Best and Greene King Old Speckled Hen always available, plus one guest changed twice weekly, which could be from any independent brewery. Wherever possible, guest beers are not repeated.

A former smithy (originally run by William Leather), built in the sixteenth century in beautiful surroundings on the edge of Macclesfield Forest overlooking the Ridge Gate Reservoir (fishing possible). Food available at lunchtime and evenings. Also 80 different whiskies. Car park, garden, family/function room.

 *12–3pm and 7–11pm Mon–Sat; 12–10.30pm Sun.*

MACCLESFIELD

The Railway View

Byrons Lane, Macclesfield SK11 7JW
☎ *(01625) 423657* David and Jane Hamilton

A freehouse with beers from Coach House and Cains always available, plus five guests, changed regularly, such as Timothy Taylor Landlord, Charles Wells Bombardier, Sarah Hughes Dark Ruby Mild and Wadworth 6X.

One-bar family pub with beams and log fires. Patio, darts. Children allowed. Ring first for directions.

 *4–11pm Mon–Thurs; 12–11pm Fri; 11am–11pm Sat; 12–10.30pm Sun.*

Waters Green Tavern

96 Waters Green, Macclesfield SK11 6LH
☎ *(01625) 422653* Brian McDermott

Timothy Taylor Landlord and Greene King IPA are always available, plus guests from breweries such as Rooster's, Phoenix, Oakham and Whim, to name but a few.

A traditional pub with a real fire in winter. Home-cooked food served at lunchtime only. Children allowed if dining.

 *11.30am–3pm and 5.30–11pm Mon–Fri; 11am–3pm and 7–11pm Sat; 12–3pm and 7–10.30pm Sun.*

MIDDLEWICH

The Big Lock

Webbs Lane, Middlewich CW10 9DN
☎ *(01606) 833489* Stuart Griffiths

Phoenix Wobbly Bob and Black Sheep Bitter permanently available. The two guests, changed every fortnight and not repeated if possible, could be Marston's Pedigree, Charles Wells Bombardier, or anything from Beartown or Moorhouse.

Traditional pub on the canal bank with outside balcony and benches overlooking the canal. Two public bars, restaurant and function room. Food served at lunchtime and evenings, all day on Sun. Car park. Children allowed. Call for directions.

 *11am–11pm Mon–Sat; 12–10.30pm Sun.*

MOBBERLEY

The Roebuck Inn

Mill Lane, Mobberley WA16 7XH
☎ *(01565) 872757* Dave Robinson

A freehouse with Timothy Taylor Landlord and Greene King Abbot Ale always available, plus guests, changed weekly, that may include Hydes Bitter, Shepherd Neame Spitfire or Elgood's Pageant Ale.

A friendly, refurbished country inn with a contemporary twist. Fresh food served at lunchtime and evenings. Children allowed.

 *12–3pm and 5.30–11pm Mon–Fri; 12–11pm Sat; 12–10.30pm Sun.*

NANTWICH

The Black Lion

29 Welsh Row, Nantwich CW5 5ED
☎ *(01270) 628711* Jill Llewellyn

A three-pump freehouse with Weetwood Old Dog and Best Bitter plus Titanic Premium always available.

A traditional two-bar pub. Food at lunchtime and evenings. No children.

11am–11pm Mon–Sat; 12–10.30 pm Sun.

Oddfellows Arms

97 Welsh Row, Nantwich CW5 5ET
☎ *(01270) 624758* Roger Drinkwater

Tied to Burtonwood, with Burtonwood Bitter and Top Hat always on offer and two guest beers changed every month and three monthly.

Locals' pub, built circa 1640 with beams and open fires. Food served daily at lunch and early evening except Monday. Book for Sunday lunch. Garden. First pub into town from the canal. Children allowed until 9pm if eating. On A53 , the old Chester road from the town centre.

12–3pm and 6–11pm Mon–Thurs (closed Mon lunch); 12–11pm Fri–Sat; 12–4pm and 7–10.30pm Sun.

Wilbraham Arms

58 Welsh Row, Nantwich CW5 5EJ
☎ *(01270) 626419*

Marston's Pedigree and JW Lees Best Bitter always available.

Close to the town centre, near canal, with traditional Georgian frontage, bar and dining area. Bar food available at lunchtime and evenings. Small car park, accommodation. Children allowed in dining room.

12–11pm (10.30pm Sun).

PENKETH

The Ferry Tavern

Station Road, Penketh, Warrington WA5 2UJ
☎ *(01925) 791117* Mr T Maxwell
www.theferrytavern.com

Charles Wells Bombardier always available, plus eight to ten guest beers every week (on three pumps). These could be from breweries such as Cottage, Coach House, Daleside, Caledonian, Rebellion or Brakspear, but beers from all over the country, from Orkney to the Isle of Wight, have been featured. A range of 300 whiskies is also on offer, including 50 Irish varieties (one of the best selections outside Ireland).

Built in the eleventh century, the Ferry Tavern has been an alehouse for 300 years and stands in a unique position on an island between the river Mersey and the St Helens canal. CAMRA Pub of the Year for Cheshire 2002. No food – the emphasis is on real ale. Car park. Children welcome.

12–3pm and 5.30–11pm Mon–Fri; 12–11pm Sat; 12–10.30pm Sun.

RODE HEATH

The Royal Oak

41 Sandbach Road, Rode Heath ST7 3RW
☎ *(01270) 875670* Christopher Forrester

Adnams Bitter or Greene King Abbot always available.

Public house with bar, smoke room, lounge and restaurant. Food served 12–9pm. Children are welcome, and there is a fully equipped play area. Car park. Located on the main Alsager to Sandbach road.

12–11pm (10.30pm Sun).

SANDBACH

Ring O'Bells

17 Wells Street, Sandbach CW11 1GT
☎ *(01270) 765731* Jane Robson

A Burtonwood house with Bitter and Mild permanently available, plus guests during the winter months.

A traditional one-bar locals' pub with darts, pool and a juke box. No food. Children allowed until 6pm.

11am–11pm Mon–Sat; 12–10.30pm Sun.

TUSHINGHAM

The Blue Bell Inn

Bell o'th Hill, Tushingham, Nr Whitchurch SY13 4QS
☎ *(01948) 662172*
Ginette Hanson and Jeremy Mark Ward

Hanby Drawwell Bitter always available plus one or two others (now up to 80 per year), perhaps including beers from Ma Pardoes Old Swan and Cotleigh breweries.

Dating from 1667, this is said to be one of Cheshire's oldest pub . Friendly and welcoming. No games machines or loud music. Food available at lunchtime and evenings.12–2pm and 6–9pm Tuesday to Saturday and 12–2pm and 7–9pm on Sundays. Car park and garden. Children and dogs always very welcome. No smoking room. Four miles north of Whitchurch on the A41 Chester road.

12–3pm and 6–11pm Tues–Sat; 7–11pm Sun. Closed all day Mon except bank holidays.

WARRINGTON

The Old Town House

Buttermarket Street, Warrington WA1 2NL
☎ *(01925) 242787* Roy Baxter

A five-pump freehouse, always serving Marston's Pedigree and Greene King Old Speckled Hen.

A country town pub with one bar, situated in the main street leading into the town centre. Food served at lunchtime only. Children allowed.

11am–11pm Mon–Sat; 12–10.30pm Sun.

WILLEY MOOR

Willey Moor Lock Tavern

Tarporley Road, Nr Whitchurch SY13 4HF
☎ *(01948) 663274* Mrs Elsie Gilkes

Five guest beers served in summer, two in winter. These may include beers from Beartown, Hanby Ales, Cottage, Weetwood, Coach House, Wood, Springhead or Wychwood breweries.

Situated next to a working lock on the Llangollen Canal, this pub was formerly a lock-keeper's cottage. Food served lunchtimes and evenings. Children welcome: there is a large garden with a play area. Car park. Situated two miles north of Whitchurch on A49. Pub found at end of driveway, pub sign on the road.

12–2.30pm (2pm winter) and 6–11pm Mon–Sat; 12–2.30pm (2pm winter) and 7–10.30pm Sun.

WRENBURY

The Old Creamery

Wrenbury Road, Wrenbury, Nantwich CW5 8EX
☎ *(01270) 780916* John Wood

Home of the Paradise Brewing Company with the full range of Paradise ales always available.

An unusual and fascinating haven for real ale lovers, this is the opposite of a brewpub: a bar inside a brewery. The building dates back to 1930 and was part of a powdered milk creamery. Parties of 20 or more catered for by prior arrangement. Two annual beer festivals in July and in between Christmas and New Year when up to 30 different beers are available. Located next to the railway station .

5–7pm Tues–Thurs; 11am–11pm Fri; 12–4pm Sat and Sun.

THE BREWERIES

BLACKAWTON BREWERY
Unit 7, Peninsula Park, Shannon Road, Saltash PL12 6LX
☎ *(01752) 848777*

BITTER 3.8% ABV
Well-hopped. A popular session beer.
WEST COUNTRY GOLD 4.1% ABV
Summer brew. European style. Light and fresh.
44 SPECIAL 4.5% ABV
Full-bodied with rich nutty flavour.
EXHIBITION 4.7% ABV
Pale, soft and fruity.
HEADSTRONG 5.2% ABV
Rich and powerful with fruit flavour. Deceptively smooth.
Plus occasional brews.

BLUE ANCHOR
50 Coinage Street, Helston TR13 8EL
☎ *(01326) 562821*

MIDDLE 5.0% ABV
JUBILEE 4.5% ABV
BRAGGET 6.0% ABV
SPECIAL 6.6% ABV
Plus Easter and Christmas specials.

DOGHOUSE BREWERY
Scorrier, Redruth TR16 5BN
☎ *(01209) 822022*

WET NOSE 3.5% ABV
FIGHTER 4.0% ABV
RETRIEVER 3.9% ABV
STAFFI STOUT 4.7% ABV
DOGFIGHT 4.8% ABV
CORGI 4.5% ABV
BOW WOW 5.0% ABV
DINGO 5.0% ABV

DRIFTWOOD BREWERY
Driftwood Spars Hotel, Quay Road, Trevaunance Cove, St Agnes TR5 0RT
☎ *(01872) 552428*
www.driftwoodspars.com/Brewery.htm

CUCKOO ALE 4.0% ABV

KELTEK BREWERY
Unit 3a, Restormel Industrial Estate, Liddicoat Road, Lostwithiel PL22 0HG
☎ *(01208) 871199*

4K MILD 3.8% ABV
GOLDEN LANCE 3.8% ABV
KELTEK MAGIC 4.2% ABV
KELTEK KING 5.1% ABV
REVENGE 7.0% ABV
BEHEADED 10.0% ABV

THE ORGANIC BREWHOUSE
Unit 1, Higher Bochym Workshops, Cury Cross Lanes, Helston TR12 7AZ
☎ *(01326) 241555*

HALZEPHRON GOLD 3.6% ABV
LIZARD POINT 4.0% ABV
SERPENTINE 4.5% ABV
Malty and hoppy.
BLACK ROCK 4.7% ABV
WOLF ROCK 5.0% ABV
Full-bodied premium bitter.

RING O'BELLS BREWERY
Pennygilliam Industrial Estate, Pennygilliam Way, Launceston PL15 7ED
☎ *(01566) 777787*
www.ringobellsbrewery.co.uk

PORKER'S PRIDE 3.8% ABV
SURF BOAR 4.0% ABV
Seasonals:
BODMIN BOAR 4.3% ABV
ONE AND ALL 4.4% ABV
DRECKLY 4.8% ABV
TIPSY TROTTER 5.1% ABV
A winter ale.
FARMER DRAY 5.5% ABV
SANTA BOAR'S 5.5% ABV
A Christmas ale.
SOZZLED SWINE 5.5% ABV

ST AUSTELL BREWERY CO. LTD
63 Trevarthian Road, St Austell PL25 4BY
☎ *(01726) 74444*
www.staustellbrewery.co.uk

IPA 3.4% ABV
DUCHY BITTER 3.7% ABV
TINNERS 3.7% ABV
BLACK PRINCE 4.0% ABV
TRIBUTE 4.2% ABV
HICKS SPECIAL DRAUGHT 5.0% ABV

SHARP'S BREWERY
Pityme Industrial Estate, Rock, Wadebridge PL27 6NU
☎ *(01208) 862121*

CORNISH COASTER 3.6% ABV
CORNISH JACK 3.8% ABV
DOOM BAR BITTER 4.0% ABV
EDEN ALE 4.2% ABV
OWN 4.4% ABV
WILL'S RESOLVE 4.6% ABV
SPECIAL ALE 5.2% ABV

SKINNER'S BREWING CO.

Riverside View, Newham, Truro TR1 2SU
☎ *(01872) 271885*
www.skinnersbrewery.com

COASTLINER 3.4% ABV
SPRIGGAN ALE 3.8% ABV
BETTY STOGS BITTER 4.0% ABV
HELIGAN HONEY 4.0% ABV
KEEL OVER 4.2% ABV
CORNISH KNOCKER 4.5% ABV
FIGGY'S BREW 4.5% ABV
ICE BLONDE 5.0% ABV
SUMMER BLONDE 5.0% ABV
Plus speciality and occasional brews.

WHEAL ALE BREWERY

Bird in Hand, Trelissick Road, Hayle TR27 4HY
☎ *(01736) 753974*

PARADISE 3.8–4.0% ABV
MILLER'S 4.2–4.4% ABV
SPECKLED PARROT 5.5–6.5% ABV

See also Isles of Scilly (page 175)

THE PUBS

ALTARNUN

The Rising Sun

Altarnun, Nr Launceston PL15 7SN
☎ *(01566) 86636* Mr and Mrs Manson

Six guest beers available, changed weekly, such as brews from Sharp's and Cotleigh, and ales sourced from Cask Force and the Beer Seller.

Sixteenth-century, single-bar freehouse with open fires and slate/hardwood floor. Bar food available at lunchtime and evenings. Ample parking. Children allowed. One mile off the A30, seven miles west of Launceston.

OPEN *11am–3pm and 5.30–11pm Mon–Fri; 11am–11pm Sat; 12–10.30pm Sun. Open all day, every day, during summer season.*

BLISLAND

Blisland Inn

The Green, Blisland, Nr Bodmin PL30 4JF
☎ *(01208) 850739* Gary Marshall

Eight pumps with guests changing every couple of days. Cornish ales are regulars.

Country-style freehouse, with lounge, public bar and family room. CAMRA Cornwall Pub of the Year and CAMRA South West Pub of the Year, both in 2000. Separate dining area for bar food served at lunchtime and evenings. Children allowed in family room.

OPEN *11.30am–11pm Mon–Sat; 12–10.30pm Sun.*

BODMIN

The Masons Arms

Higherbore Street, Bodmin PL31 2JS
☎ *(01208) 72607* Matt Woods

A freehouse with Sharp's Cornish Coaster and Marston's Pedigree always on offer. Three guests are rotated a couple at a time, every four days. Crouch Vale Willie Warmer, Sutton XSB and Robinson's Old Tom are regular favourites.

A traditional Cornish drinkers' pub in a seventeenth-century building, with quiet lounge bar and noisy public bar. No food. Pool, darts, beer garden. Car parking. Children allowed, but not in bar area. Located on the main road, so easy to find.

OPEN *11am–11pm Mon–Sat; 12–10.30pm Sun.*

BOSCASTLE

The Cobweb Inn

Boscastle PL35 0HE
☎ *(01840) 250278* AI and AP Bright

St Austell Tinners, Sharp's Doom Bar and Greene King Abbot permanently available, plus a range of guest ales.

Atmospheric, seventeenth-century freehouse, close to the harbour. Food served lunchtimes and evenings. Car park. Non-smoking family room and restaurant. Outside seating. The pub is across the road from the car park at the bottom of the village, near the harbour.

OPEN *11am–11pm Mon–Fri; 11am–midnight Sat; 12–10.30pm Sun.*

CHARLESTOWN

Rashleigh Arms

Quay Road, Charlestown, St Austell PL25 3NJ
☎ *(01726) 73635*
Neville and Enid Andrews

A St Austell house with Hicks Special Draught, Tribute and Tinners among the beers on offer. Cask Marque award.

A newly refurbished, family-friendly pub where children and well-behaved adults are welcome! Food served 12–9pm every day. Comfortable accommodation available.

OPEN *11am–11pm Mon–Sat; 12–10.30pm Sun.*

CRACKINGTON HAVEN

Coombe Barton Inn

Crackington Haven, Bude EX23 0JG
☎ *(01840) 230345* Nick Cooper
www.coombebartoninn.com

A freehouse offering up to six beers from breweries such as Sharp's, St Austell, Skinner's and Cottage. Cornish ales always available.

A family-run pub next to the beach in a beautiful cove. Food served every day, lunchtimes and evenings, with a children's menu and Sunday carvery. Large family room. Six rooms available for bed and breakfast. Car park.

 *Summer: 11am–11pm Mon–Sat; 12–10.30pm Sun; winter: 11am–3pm and 6–11pm.*

CRANTOCK

Old Albion

Langurroc Road, Crantock, Newquay TR8 5RB
☎ *(01637) 830243*
Mr James Hardy and Miss A Cockcroft

Skinner's and St Austell beers always available. Three guests, changed frequently, might include Fuller's London Pride, Smiles Best and something from Ring O'Bells, plus extra guests in summer.

A country pub, which used to be used for smuggling beer, situated next to the church in Crantock. Homemade food served at lunchtime and evenings in bar area. Children allowed in family room.

 *12–11pm.*

CROWLASS

The Star Inn

Crowlass TR20 8DX
☎ *(01736) 740375* Pete Elvin

Fourteen different brews per week are available at this freehouse. Everards Tiger is regularly served, and Nethergate Umbel and beers from Keltek have also been featured. The landlord always tries to keep a local beer on during the summer.

Locals' village pub in a late Victorian purpose-built hotel. Restaurant/dining area being planned. Pool, darts, occasional live music. Beer garden, car park. Children allowed.

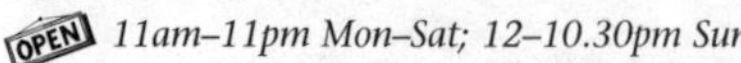 *11am–11pm Mon–Sat; 12–10.30pm Sun.*

CUBERT

The Smuggler's Den Inn

Trebellan, Cubert, Newquay TR8 5PY
☎ *(01637) 830209*
Mr SE Hancock and Mr PB Partridge
www.thesmugglersden.co.uk

Freehouse serving on a permanent basis Smugglers Ale from Skinner's and Trebellan Tipple from Sharp's, both brewed especially for the pub, plus a couple of guests, one of which will be a brew from St Austell.

A sixteenth-century thatched country pub with a reputation locally for good ale, wine and food. Real fires, beer garden with children's play area, function room for private hire. Food available lunchtime from 12pm and evenings from 6pm. Children allowed. Car park. Ale & Pie festival annually in April. Situated on the A3075 Newquay–Redruth road. Turn towards Cubert village and take first left.

 *Summer: 11.30am–11pm (10.30pm Sun). Winter: 11.30am–2.30pm Thurs–Sun (closed lunchtimes Mon–Wed); 6–11pm Mon–Sat; 6–10.30pm Sun.*

EDMONTON

The Quarryman

Edmonton, Wadebridge PL27 7JA
☎ *(01208) 816444* Terrence de-Villiers Kuun

A four-pump freehouse, with guest beers changed every two or three days. Favourites include Skinner's and Sharp's brews plus Timothy Taylor Landlord and Hop Back Summer Lightning.

An old Cornish inn with separate restaurant and bar food. Food served at lunchtime and evenings. Well-behaved children allowed.

OPEN *12–11pm (10.30pm Sun).*

FALMOUTH

The Quayside Inn

41 Arwenack Street, Falmouth TR11 3JQ
☎ *(01326) 312113*
Paul and Katherine Coombes

Up to eight beers always available. Sharp's Special and Doom Bar, Skinner's Cornish Knocker and Heligan Honey permanently served, plus a range of four rotating guests.

Twice-yearly beer festivals at this quayside pub overlooking the harbour. Two bars – comfy upstairs lounge and downstairs real ale bar. Food available all day, every day in summer, and at lunchtimes and evenings in winter (skillet house with food cooked in skillets). Outside seating on quayside. Parking. Children very welcome – children's menu. On Custom House Quay.

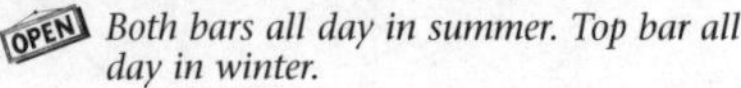 *Both bars all day in summer. Top bar all day in winter.*

GOLANT

The Fisherman's Arms

Fore Street, Golant, Fowey PL23 1LN
☎ *(01726) 832453* Steve and Sue Perry
www.golant.net

Three real ales are always on offer, including Sharp's Doom Bar Bitter.

A village pub on the banks of the River Fowey. Food at lunchtime and evening. Garden. Beer festival every August Bank Holiday weekend. Children and dogs welcome. Near St Austell and the Eden Project.

 *12–3pm and 6–11pm Mon–Fri; 12–11pm Sat; 12–10.30am Sun; all day, every day July–August.*

GORRAN HAVEN

Llawnroc Inn

33 Chute Lane, Gorran Haven, St Austell PL26 6NU
☎ *(01726) 843461*
Alan Freeman and Reg Luff

Four real ales (three in winter) always available, including Llawnroc Ale (exclusively brewed by Sharp's) and Sharp's Doom Bar, plus two guest ales such as Fuller's London Pride, Greene King Abbot or Shepherd Neame Spitfire.

Relaxing, family-run hotel with beautiful sea views and a terraced garden, situated in an old fishing village. Food served 12–1.45pm and 6.30–9.45pm in summer and 12–2pm and 6.30–9pm in winter. Car park. Children welcome. From St Austell continue past Heligan Gardens and after Gorran Haven, turn right.

 *12–11pm (10.30pm Sun).*

GUNNISLAKE

Rising Sun Inn

Calstock Road, Gunnislake PL18 9BX
☎ *(01822) 832201* David and Caroline Heery
www.risingsuninn.co.uk

A freehouse with up to six real ales available including brews from Sharp's and Skinners plus Timothy Taylor Landlord and guests.

A warm and friendly seventeenth-century traditional stone freehouse with two bars and a dining area. Log fires and live music. No TV or games machines. Award-winning beer garden with views over the Tamar valley. Good walking and fishing. Food served 12–2pm daily and 6–9pm (not Sun).

 *12–2pm and 5–11pm Mon–Sat, 12–3pm and 7–10.30pm Sun.*

HAYLE

Bird in Hand

Trelissick Road, Hayle TR27 4HY
☎ *(01736) 753974* Mr Miller

Home of the Wheal Ale Brewery. A range of own brews always available, plus two guest beers, perhaps including Greene King Abbot or Shepherd Neame Spitfire.

An old coach house with one bar. Live music. Food at lunchtime and evenings (summer only). Children allowed.

11am–11pm Mon–Sat; 12–10.30pm Sun.

HELSTON

The Blue Anchor

50 Coinagehall Street, Helston TR13 8EX
☎ *(01326) 562821*

One of only four pubs in Britain which has brewed continuously for centuries and still produces its famous Spingo ales, from a Victorian word for strong beer.

This thatched town pub was originally a monks' rest home in the fifteenth century. Brewing continued on the premises after the Reformation and the Blue Anchor is now believed to be the oldest brewpub in Britain. Garden, children's room, skittle alley, function room. Accommodation available.

 *10.30am–11pm Mon–Sat; 12–10.30pm Sun.*

KILKHAMPTON

The London Inn

Kilkhampton EX23 9QR
☎ *(01288) 321665* Stewart and Lorraine Davey

Sharp's Doom Bar always available, plus one guest.

Sixteenth-century pub with unusual hard-wood bar front. The pub has a reputation for good-quality food, served in the restaurant or the snug, 12–2pm and 6.30–9pm. Beer gardens to front and rear. Children and dogs welcome if kept under control. Ample parking space nearby. Located at the centre of the village on the main A39.

All day, every day.

LAUNCESTON

The Eliot Arms

Tregadillet, Launceston
☎ *(01566) 772051* Sarah Richards

Sharp's Eden and Doom Bar always available, with guests including other Sharp's brews.

Ivy-clad pub with softly lit rooms, open fires, slate floors, high-backed settles and fine Victorian furniture and artefacts. Collection of horse brasses, Masonic regalia and clocks (46, including five grandfather clocks). Food served 12–2pm and 7–9pm, including children's menu. Car park. Children and dogs welcome in front rooms.

 *11am–3pm and 6–11pm Mon–Fri; 11am–11pm Sat; 12–10.30pm Sun.*

LERRYN

The Ship

Lerryn, Nr Lostwithiel PL22 0PT
☎ *(01208) 872374* Mr Packer
www.cornwall-online.co.uk/shipinn-lerryn

Three beers available including Sharp's brews and guests such as Exmoor Gold, Greene King Old Speckled Hen, Fuller's London Pride and Otter Ale.

A pub since the early 1600s, with a wood burner in the bar and slate floors. Bar and restaurant food available at lunchtime and evenings. Set in a quiet riverside village three miles south of Lostwithiel. Car park, garden, accommodation. Children allowed. Dogs welcome in the bar and garden.

 *11.30am–3pm and 6–11pm Mon–Sat; 12–3pm and 7–10.30pm Sun.*

LOSTWITHIEL

The Royal Oak Inn

Duke Street, Lostwithiel PL22 0AG
☎ *(01208) 872552* Mr and Mrs Hine

Marston's Pedigree, Sharp's Own and Fuller's London Pride always available. Orkney Skullsplitter, the Blue Anchor Spingos, Woodforde's Headcracker, Exmoor Gold, Badger Tanglefoot and Best are among the guest beers (50 per year).

A popular thirteenth-century inn catering for all tastes. Bar and restaurant food at lunchtime and evenings. Car park, garden, children's room. Spacious accommodation. Located just off the A390 going into Lostwithiel.

OPEN *11am–11pm.*

NANCENOY

Trengilly Wartha Inn

Nancenoy, Constantine, Nr Falmouth TR11 5RP
☎ *(01326) 340332*
Nigel Logan and Michael MacGuire

Sharp's Cornish Coaster always available, plus a couple of constantly rotating guests which may include brews from Skinner's, Keltek, St Austell or Exmoor.

A country freehouse and restaurant in six acres of valley gardens and meadows. Bar food at lunchtime and evenings, restaurant open in evening. Car park, garden and children's room. Eight bedrooms. Just south of Constantine – follow the signs.

OPEN *11am–2.30pm and 6.30–11pm.*

PENZANCE

Globe & Ale House

Queen Street, Penzance TR18 4BJ
☎ *(01736) 364098* Mr and Mrs Cripps

A freehouse with up to eight real ales always available. Something from local Skinner's and Sharp's usually features, plus a constantly changing range of real ales from any independent or micro-brewery from Cornwall to Orkney!

An alehouse with live music once a week and quiz nights. Food served lunchtimes and evenings, but no separate dining area. No children.

OPEN *11am–11pm Mon–Sat; 12–10.30pm Sun.*

Mounts Bay Inn

Promenade, Wherry Town, Penzance TR18 4NP
☎ *(01736) 360863*
Denis Mayor and Shirley O'Neill

Skinner's Cornish Knocker always available, plus two guests in the summer, changed weekly, which could be from any independent or micro-brewery.

A warm welcome awaits in this characterful olde-worlde pub. Food served lunchtimes and evenings. Local authority car park situated opposite the pub. Quiz nights. No children allowed inside the pub, although welcome on side terrace. Small side terrace with seating.

OPEN *11am–11pm Mon–Sat; 12–10.30pm Sun.*

POLPERRO

The Blue Peter Inn

The Quay, Polperro, Nr Looe PL13 2QZ
☎ *(01503) 272743*
Caroline and Steve Steadman

A selection of Sharp's and St Austell ales permanently available, plus daily guest beers, with the emphasis on smaller independent breweries from all over the country. Local draught scrumpy also served.

Small, atmospheric, traditional pub with beamed ceilings, log fires and a family room. Children and pets welcome. Excellent lunch menu available every day, with local crab and scallops a speciality. Live music Fri and Sat nights plus Sun afternoons. Situated at the end of the fish quay.

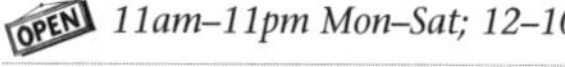
11am–11pm Mon–Sat; 12–10.30pm Sun.

The Old Mill House

Mill Hill, Polperro PL13 2RP
☎ *(01503) 272362* Jon Aspinall and Jan Perry
www.oldmillhouseinn.com

Freehouse offering Sharp's Special and Old Millhouse Ale plus one guest.

White-painted, homely cottage-style pub. Food available at lunchtimes (in season) from 12pm and from 7pm in the evening. Pool table. Log fire in winter. Well-behaved children and dogs welcome. Car parking for residents only. Accommodation. Garden. Cash point. In the centre of the village.

Summer: 10.30am–11pm (10.30pm Sun). Winter: 12–11pm (10.30pm Sun).

PORT GAVERNE

Port Gaverne Inn

Port Gaverne PL29 3SQ
☎ *(01208) 880244* Mrs Hopehill

Sharp's Doom Bar Bitter and Cornish Coaster permanently available, plus one guest, such as Greene King Abbot or Fuller's London Pride.

Sixteenth-century hotel and bar 100 yards from the sea. Restaurant open in evenings, bar food also served during the day. Garden, car park. Accommodation available (17 rooms and 9 cottages/flats). Children allowed in garden and designated areas.

11am–2.30pm and 6–11pm Mon–Thurs; 11am–11pm Fri–Sat; 12–10.30pm Sun. All day Easter and throughout summer.

PORTHALLOW

The Five Pilchards

Porthallow, St Keverne, Helston TR12 6PP
☎ *(01326) 280256* Brandon Flynn

A four-pump freehouse with Greene King Abbot Ale and Sharp's Doom Bar always available. Two guests, changed fortnightly, might include favourites Skinner's or Sharp's.

An old Cornish seafaring pub, with conservatory featuring a waterfall. Interesting dispay of ship's accessories, including figure heads, binnacles and telegraphs, plus ship models. Food served lunchtimes and evenings – separate dining area available. Juicing machine which juices whole oranges. Children allowed.

12–2.30pm and 6–11pm.

PORTHLEVEN

Atlantic Inn

Peverell Terrace, Porthleven, Helston TR13 9DZ
☎ *(01326) 562439* Leigh and Adrian Santi

A freehouse, with Skinner's ales such as Figgy's Brew and Coastliner regularly featured.

A traditional seaside pub in a village location (signposted), with live entertainment every Saturday. Food served lunchtimes and evenings from an extensive menu, reasonably priced. Children allowed.

12–11pm (10.30pm Sun).

PORTREATH

Basset Arms

Tregea Terrace, Portreath TR16 4NS
☎ *(01209) 842077* Paula Richards

Sharp's Doom Bar and Marston's Pedigree regularly available.

Warm and friendly pub situated directly opposite Portreath Bay. Food served 12–2pm and 6.30–9.30pm. Car park. Children's play area.

Summer: 11.30am–11pm Mon–Sat; 12–10.30pm Sun. Winter: 11.30am–2.30pm and 6–11pm Mon–Sat; 12–2.30pm and 7–10.30pm Sun.

QUINTRELL DOWNS

The Two Clomes
East Road, Quintrell Downs, Nr Newquay TR8 4PD
☎ *(01637) 871163* Kath/Frank

Approx 100 guest beers per year, three or four at any one time. Beers from Exmoor, Otter, Sharp's, Fuller's and Cains breweries all favoured.

A converted and extended old farm cottage built from Cornish stone with a beer garden and 48-seater restaurant. Open log fires in winter. Bar food available at lunchtime and evenings. Car park. Take the A392 from Newquay to Quintrell Downs, straight on at the roundabout, then second right.

 *12–3pm and 7–11pm (10.30pm Sun).*

ST AGNES

Driftwood Spars Hotel
Trevaunance, Quay Road, St Agnes TR5 0RT
☎ *(01872) 552428/553323*
Gordon and Jill Treleavan
www.driftwoodspars.com

A freehouse serving five permanents including their own Cuckoo Ale plus a couple of brews from Sharp's and one rotating guest.

Built in 1660 as a tin-mining warehouse and ships chandlery, the pub is close to the beach and has stunning sea views. Food served breakfast, lunch and evening. Garden, car park and accommodation. Children and dogs welcome.

OPEN *11am–11pm.*

ST CLEER

The Stag Inn
Fore Street, St Cleer, Liskeard PL14 5DA
☎ *(01579) 342305* Pam Dawson

A seven-pump freehouse, with Sharp's Own, Greene King Abbot and something from Skinner's always available, plus guest ales changed weekly.

A seventeenth-century pub with TV and non-smoking dining area. Food at lunchtimes and evenings. Well-behaved children welcome. En-suite accommodation. Close to the Eden Project.

OPEN *12–11pm (10.30pm Sun).*

ST COLUMB

The Queen & Railway Inn
St Columb Road, St Columb TR9 6QR
☎ *(01726) 860343* Richard Barnes

One frequently changing guest is on offer at this freehouse, usually from a West Country brewery.

Traditional village pub with open fire, one bar and patio. No food. Pool, darts, juke box. Car park. Children allowed in the early evening only.

OPEN *12–(variable closing time in afternoon) and 7pm–11pm (10.30pm Sun).*

ST JUST

The King's Arms
Market Square, St Just, Penzance TR19 7HF
☎ *(01736) 788545* Jan McCall

A St Austell Brewery tied house with Tinners and Tribute always on offer, plus HSD when available, and seasonal St Austell ales. Cask Marque awarded.

A fourteenth-century cosy pub with family atmosphere. One bar with lots of nooks and crannies, low ceilings, open fires. Outside seating at the front, parking on the square. Occasional live music, weekly in summer, free weekly quiz night. Food available lunchtimes and evenings. Children and dogs welcome. Bed and breakfast.

 *11am–11pm Mon–Sat; 12–10.30pm Sun. Plus early opening for breakfast in summer.*

The Star Inn
1 Fore Street, St Just, Penzance TR19 7LL
☎ *(01736) 788767* Peter and Rosie Angwin

A St Austell house with HSD, Tinners, Tribute and Dartmoor generally available.

Old mining pub with a horseshoe bar and artefacts on the walls. Bar food available at lunchtimes all year round, and in the evenings in summer. Accommodation. Children welcome, children's room provided. Beer garden with outside seating.

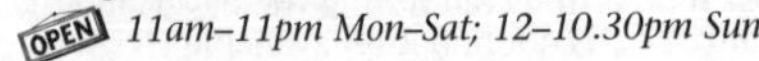 *11am–11pm Mon–Sat; 12–10.30pm Sun.*

STITHIANS

Seven Stars

Church Road, Stithians
☎ *(01209 860003)* Phil Preen

Up to four almost exclusively Cornish real ales such as Sharp's Doom Bar Bitter or Special and Skinner's Betty Stogs Bitter.

Beamed, stone-floored one-room village local which was built as a farmhouse extension in the nineteenth century. Outside drinking area. Food served at lunchtime (not Tues) and Weds–Sat evenings. Saturday night is music night.

12–2.30pm and 7–11pm Mon–Fri; all day Sat; 12–3pm and 7–10.30pm Sun.

STRATTON

King's Arms

Howell's Road, Stratton, Bude EX23 9BX
☎ *(01288) 352396* Steven Peake

A seventeenth-century freehouse serving Sharp's Own and Doom Bar Bitter and Exmoor Ale. Two guests are changed weekly. Traditional cider served during the summer season. Cask marque awarded.

A traditional pub, with quality, value-for-money bar meals served 12–2pm and 6.30–9pm, including a very popular Sunday lunch. Quiz nights on Tuesdays. Well-behaved children and nice dogs are welcome. Ten minutes' drive from beautiful beaches and rugged coastal walks. Accommodation.

12–2pm and 6.30–11pm Mon–Thurs; 11am–11pm Fri–Sat; 12–10.30pm Sun.

TREBARWITH

The Mill House Inn

Trebarwith, Tintagel PL34 0HD
☎ *(01840) 770200*
www.themillhouseinn.co.uk

The three permanent beers include Sharp's Own and Doom Bar Bitter plus a guest ale always available.

A sixteenth-century mill over a trout stream, set in seven acres of woodland half a mile from the sea. Bar and restaurant food available at lunchtime and evenings, featuring excellent cuisine in an informal atmosphere. Car park, garden and terrace. Barbeques on the terrace in summer. Accommodation (all en-suite). Children welcome.

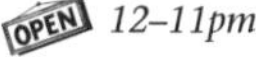
12–11pm.

TREGREHAN

The Britannia Inn

Tregrehan Par, Tregrehan PL24 2SL
☎ *(01726) 812889*
Richard Rogers and Philip Lafferty
www.britanniainn.net

This freehouse has four permanent real ales and two guests.

A very popular, busy pub with two bars, a restaurant and function room. Food served at lunchtime and evenings (all day in season). Children allowed in the dining area. Large beer garden with children's play area. Close to the Eden Project.

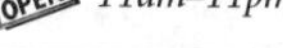
11am–11pm Mon–Sat; 12–10.30pm Sun.

TRESPARRETT

The Horseshoe Inn

Tresparrett, Camelford PL32 9ST
☎ *(01840) 261240* Pat Codack
www.thehorseshoeinn.co.uk

Freehouse serving up to four real ales, perhaps from Sharp's or Skinner's.

A one-bar country pub situated in walking country. Separate dining area, outside seating, food served lunchtime and evening. Darts and pool. Children allowed. Car park. Located off the A39.

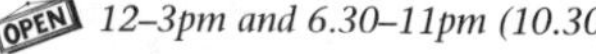
12–3pm and 6.30–11pm (10.30pm Sun).

TRURO

The Old Ale House

7 Quay Street, Truro TR1 2HD
☎ *(01872) 271122* Mark and Bev Jones

A house ale brewed by the local Skinner's brewery, Kiddlywink, is permanently available, plus a range of guest ales served straight from the barrel. Regulars include Wadworth 6X, Sharp's Own, Exmoor Stag and Gold, Cotleigh Tawny and Old Buzzard, Fuller's London Pride and Shepherd Neame Spitfire.

An olde-worlde pub in the town centre with old furniture. *The Good Pub Guide* Beer Pub of the Year 2000. Bar food available at lunchtime and evenings with skillets and hands of bread a speciality. Live music twice a week. Children welcome.

OPEN *11am–11pm Mon–Sat; 12–10.30pm Sun.*

WIDEMOUTH BAY

The Bay View Inn

Marine Drive, Widemouth Bay, Bude EX23 0AW
☎ *(01288) 361273*
Clive Mansell and Alison Carter
www.bayviewinn.co.uk

Freehouse offering up to eight real ales drawn straight from the cask. Skinner's Kitch's Klassic (exclusive to this pub), Skinner's Heligan Honey (brewed using honey from the Lost Garden's apiary), Sharp's Own and Sharp's Doom Bar are always available. The four guests are from breweries such as Cheriton, Ring O'Bells, Butcombe, Otter, Cotleigh, Exmoor and St Austell, and cask-conditioned cider is also served. Regular real ale festivals and promotions are held.

A traditional old-style seaside pub decorated with local views. Two bars, garden, children's play area, large car park. Decking from which to witness the sunsets. Food available at lunchtimes from 12–2.30pm and evenings from 6–9pm. Non-smoking dining and family room. Accommodation with stunning views of the sea. Children allowed in designated rooms.

All day, every day.

ZELAH

Hawkins Arms

High Road, Zelah, Truro TR4 9HU
☎ *(01872) 540339* Ian Spencer-Brown

A freehouse with seven pumps. Mainly beers from the Doghouse brewery but also generally a Skinner's brew and a rotating guest.

A one-bar country-style pub with non-smoking area and beer garden. Food served at lunchtime and evenings. Children allowed. Large car park. Accommodation.

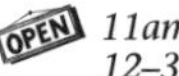
11am–3pm and 6–11pm Mon–Sat; 12–3pm and 7–10.30pm Sun; all day Fri.

ZENNOR

The Tinners Arms

Zennor, St Ives TR27 3BY
☎ *(01736) 796927* David Care

Sharp's Doom Bar and St Austell Tinners are always available, plus two guests straight from the barrel.

Freehouse in a lovely fourteenth-century building, with stone floor, beams and open fires. Function room is used as a family room in bad weather in summer. Food served. Large garden with tables overlooking coastline. Occasional live music. Children allowed, but not in the main bar. Follow the Wayside Museum signs.

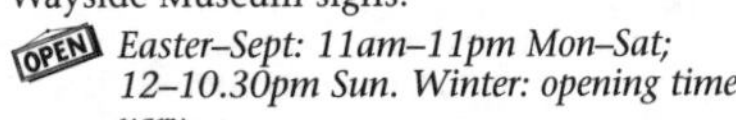
Easter–Sept: 11am–11pm Mon–Sat; 12–10.30pm Sun. Winter: opening times vary.

THE BREWERIES

BARNGATES BREWERY LTD

The Drunken Duck Inn, Barngates, Ambleside LA22 0NG
☎ *(01539) 436575*
www.drunkenduckinn.co.uk

CRACKER ALE 3.9% ABV
TAG LAG 4.4% ABV
CHESTER'S STRONG & UGLY 5.2% ABV

BECKSTONES BREWERY

Upper Beckstones Mill, The Green, Millom, Cumbria LA18 5HL
☎ *(01229) 775294*

LEAT 3.6% ABV
Thirst-quenching, fruity, flowery, modern-style quaffing ale.
IRON TOWN 3.8% ABV
Standard bitter, darker in colour with malty bitter aftertaste.
BORDER STEEANS 4.1% ABV
Scottish-style beer.
BITTACLOUT 4.6% ABV
Pale ale.
HEMACITE 5.5% ABV
Dark strong ale, very malty.

BITTER END BREWPUB

15 Kirkgate, Cockermouth CA13 9PJ
☎ *(01900) 828993*

COCKERSNOOT 3.8% ABV
CUDDY LUGS 4.3% ABV
SKINNER'S OLD STRONG 5.5% ABV

THE CONISTON BREWING CO. LTD

The Forge, Coniston LA21 8HL
☎ *(01539) 441133*
www.conistonbrewery.com

BLUEBIRD BITTER 3.6% ABV
OLD MAN ALE 4.4% ABV
Seasonals:
OPIUM 4.0% ABV
Autumn brew.
BLACKSMITH'S ALE 5.0% ABV
Christmas brew.

DENT BREWERY

Hollins, Cowgill, Dent LA10 5TQ
☎ *(01539) 625326*
www.dentbrewery.co.uk

BITTER 3.7% ABV
Mild hop flavour and slightly sweet.
AVIATOR 4.0% ABV
Full, rounded hop flavour.
RAMSBOTTOM STRONG ALE 4.5% ABV
Medium-dark, caramel flavour.
KAMIKAZE 5.0% ABV
Very pale, good hop flavour and creamy maltiness.
T'OWD TUP 6.0% ABV
Powerful stout. Roast barley, bite and softness.
Plus monthly brews.

DERWENT BREWERY

Units 2a–2b, Station Road Industrial Estate, Silloth, Wigton CA5 4AG
☎ *(01697) 331522*

CARLISLE STATE BITTER 3.7% ABV
PARSON'S PLEDGE 4.0% ABV
TEACHERS PET 4.3% ABV
WHITWELL & MARK PALE ALE 4.4% ABV
BILL MONK 4.5% ABV
Plus occasional brews.

FOXFIELD BREWERY

Prince of Wales, Foxfield, Broughton in Furness LA20 6BX
☎ *(01229) 716238*
www.princeofwalesfoxfield.co.uk

A constantly changing range of ales. The only permanent ale is:
DARK MILD 3.4% ABV

GREAT GABLE BREWING CO.

Wasdale Head Inn, Wasdale Head, Seascale CA20 1EX
☎ *(01946) 726229*
www.greatgablebrewing.com

GABLE 3.7% ABV
WRY'NOSE 4.0% ABV
WASD'ALE 4.4% ABV

HAWKSHEAD BREWERY COMPANY

Town End Farm, Hawkshead LA22 0JU
☎ *(01539) 436111*
www.hawksheadbrewery.co.uk

HAWKSHEAD BITTER 3.7% ABV
Pale, hoppy and bitter.
HAWKSHEAD BEST 4.2% ABV
Red, malty and dry.
HAWKSHEAD PREMIUM 4.8% ABV
Dark with pale chocolate malt.
Plus occasional and seasonal brews.

HESKET NEWMARKET BREWERY

Old Crown Barn, Hesket Newmarket Wigton CA7 8JG
☎ *(01697) 478066*
www.hesketbrewery.co.uk

GREAT COCKUP PORTER 3.0% ABV
Dark, smooth and malty.
BLENCATHRA BITTER 3.2% ABV
Ruby-coloured and hoppy.
SKIDDAW SPECIAL BITTER 3.7% ABV
Gold-coloured and full-flavoured.
HELVELLYN GOLD 4.0% ABV
DORIS'S 90TH BIRTHDAY ALE 4.3% ABV
Full-flavoured, with fruit throughout.
CATBELLS PALE ALE 5.0% ABV
OLD CARROCK STRONG ALE 6.0% ABV
Rich, smooth and strong.

JENNINGS BROS PLC

The Castle Brewery, Cockermouth CA13 9NE
☎ *(01900) 823214*
www.jenningsbrewery.co.uk

JENNINGS DARK MILD 3.1% ABV
JENNINGS BITTER 3.5% ABV
Nutty and mellow, with malt.
OLD SMOOTHY 3.5% ABV
1828 3.8% ABV
CUMBERLAND ALE 4.0% ABV
Gold-coloured, rich and smooth.
CUMBERLAND CREAM 4.0% ABV
CRAG RAT 4.3% ABV
Golden-coloured bitter.
JJ NO 1 4.3% ABV
CROSSBUTTOCK ALE 4.5% ABV
Well-hoppped malt bitter.
RED BREAST 4.5% ABV
COCKER HOOP 4.6% ABV
A well-hopped premium bitter.
SNECK LIFTER 5.1% ABV
Robust and slightly sweet.
Seasonals:
LA'AL COCKLE WARMER 6.5% ABV
Smooth Christmas brew.

LOWESWATER BREWERY

Kirkstile Inn, Loweswater, Cockermouth CA13 0RU
☎ *(01900) 85219*
www.kirkstile.com

MELBREAK BITTER 3.7% ABV
GRASMOOR DARK ALE 4.3% ABV

THE TIRRIL BREWERY

Unit 11, Brougham Hall, Brougham, Penrith CA10 2DE
☎ *(01768) 863219*
www.tirrilbrewery.co.uk

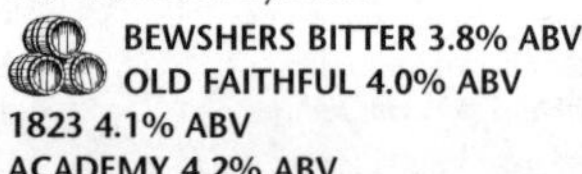

BEWSHERS BITTER 3.8% ABV
OLD FAITHFUL 4.0% ABV
1823 4.1% ABV
ACADEMY 4.2% ABV

YATES BREWERY

Ghyll Farm, Westnewton, Wigton CA7 3NX
☎ *(01697) 321081*
www.yatesbrewery.co.uk

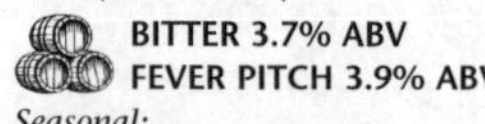

BITTER 3.7% ABV
FEVER PITCH 3.9% ABV
Seasonal:
SUN GODDESS 4.2% ABV
WINTER SUN 4.2% ABV
XB 4.5% ABV
BEST CELLAR 5.6% ABV
SPRING FEVER 4.7% ABV

THE PUBS

ALLONBY

Ship Hotel

Main Street, Allonby CA15 6QF
☎ *(01900) 881017* Steve and Valerie Ward

Yates Bitter and seasonal ales always available.

Overlooking the Solway Firth, a 300-year-old hotel with considerable history. Home-cooked bar meals served at lunchtime 12–3pm and evenings 6–11pm, Sun 6–10.30pm (no food on Mondays during winter). Car park, accommodation. Dogs welcome.

12–3pm and 7–11pm (10.30pm Sun). Closed Monday lunch in winter.

AMBLESIDE

Queens Hotel

Market Place, Ambleside LA22 9BU
☎ *(015394) 32206* John Wrennall
www.queensheadhotelambleside.com

A freehouse with up to six real ales always available with local brews favoured. Jennings Bitter should be one of them while others are likely to come from the same brewery or from Hawkshead, Coniston and Yates.

A Victorian town-centre hotel, with two traditional but recently refurbished bars. Food available 12–9.30pm daily. Smoking and non-smoking areas, and à la carte restaurant. Children welcome. 26 ensuite bedrooms.

11am–11pm Mon–Sat; 12–10.30pm Sun.

APPLEBY

The Royal Oak Inn

Bongate, Appleby CA16 6UB
☎ *(017683) 51463* Tim and Jo Collins

Black Sheep Bitter is among the beers always available, plus 50 guests per year, including such ales as Thwaites Lancaster Bomber and Charles Wells Summer Solstice. Well-chosen range of wines and malt whiskies for non-beer drinkers!

A long white-washed building, roughly 400 years old with lots of character. Bar snacks are available 12–2.30pm, and food from the à la carte menu is served 12–2.30pm and 6–9pm. Large non-smoking dining room and outside terrace. Children welcome. Nine letting rooms. On the B6542 just outside Appleby town centre.

OPEN *11am–11pm Mon–Sat; 12–10.30pm Sun.*

ARMATHWAITE

Fox & Pheasant

Armathwaite, Carlisle CA4 9PY
☎ *(01697) 472400* Neil Pritt

Owned by Robinson's Brewery since 2003 and now exclusively selling their ales. Cumbria Way, Hartleys XB and Double Hop usually available plus a couple of seasonal brews.

A seventeenth-century traditional coaching inn with log fires and beamed ceilings, overlooking the River Eden, in a small village. Outside seating. Food served at lunchtime and evenings in the bar and a separate dining area. Children allowed. En-suite accommodation. On the Carlisle to Settle railway line.

12pm–3pm and 6–11pm Mon–Fri; 12–11pm Sat; 12–10.30pm Sun.

BARNGATES

The Drunken Duck Inn

Barngates, Ambleside LA22 0NG
☎ *(015394) 36347* Stephanie Barton

The home of the Barngates brewery, with Cracker Ale, Tag Lag, Chester's Strong & Ugly plus Jennings Bitter.

Delightful 400-year-old inn, set in beautiful countryside and oozing olde-worlde charm. Tempting restaurant and modern, stylish accommodation. Amusing story behind the pub name – ask the landlady! Food available 12–2.30pm and 6–9pm. Car park. Children are welcome, but there are no special facilities.

11.30am–11pm Mon–Sat; 12–10.30pm Sun.

BRAMPTON

White Lion Hotel

Brampton CA8 1RP

Black Sheep Bitter and a guest ale usually available.

Seventeenth-century former coaching inn in the centre of a busy market town. Log fires, award-winning flower displays. Good food.

11am–11pm (10.30pm Sun)

BROUGHTON IN FURNESS

The Manor Arms

The Square, Broughton in Furness LA20 6HY
☎ *(01229) 716286* David and Scott Varty

Up to eight well-kept real ales available. Brews from Yates, Coniston and Timothy Taylor usually available plus rotating guests changed frequently. New brews, winter warmers – you name it, they have probably served it!

Eighteenth-century traditional family-run freehouse with a welcoming atmosphere. Two real fires. Regular CAMRA pub of the year award-winner. Bar snacks available all day until 10pm. Parking and outside seats overlooking a picturesque market square. En-suite accommodation. Children welcome. Regular beer festivals.

12–11pm (10.30pm Sun).

BROUGHTON MILLS

The Blacksmiths Arms

Broughton Mills, Broughton-in-Furness LA20 6AX
☎ *(01229 716824)* Michael and Sophie Lane
www.theblacksmithsarms.com

Jennings Bitter, Cumberland Ale plus a guest, usually from a local brewery such as Barngates, Coniston or Dent.

Dates from 1577 and still totally unspoilt, in walking country off the A593. Wooden tables and beams, real fires, flagstone floors. Outside seating. Food served at lunchtime and evenings.

All day, every day in summer; 12–2.30pm (not Mon) and 5–11pm (10.30pm Sun) in winter.

CARLISLE

Woodrow Wilsons

48 Botchergate, Carlisle CA1 4RG
☎ *(01228) 819942*
Richard Archibald (Manager)

A Wetherspoon's pub with Greene King Abbot, Derwent Carlisle State Bitter, Thwaites Mild and Shepherd Neame Spitfire always available. Two guests are changed every few days, and may include Hop Back Summer Lightning, Timothy Taylor Landlord or Cotleigh Osprey.

Typical Wetherspoon's town-centre pub in a stone-fronted building. Food available all day. Children not allowed.

11am–11pm Mon–Sat; 12–10.30pm Sun.

CARTMEL

Cavendish Arms

Cavendish Street, Cartmel LA11 6QA
☎ *(01539) 536240* Richard English
www.thecavendisharms.co.uk

Jennings Cumberland and Greene King IPA always available, plus two guests which change every month.

A food-oriented coaching inn, 450 years old, with one large bar. Food available at lunchtime and evenings. Car park, dining room, non-smoking room, seven ensuite bedrooms. Riverside drinking area. Children not allowed in the restaurant during the evenings.

 *11am–11pm Mon–Sat; 12–10pm Sun.*

COCKERMOUTH

The Bitter End

15 Kirkgate, Cockermouth CA13 9PJ
☎ *(01900) 828993* Susan Askey
www.bitterend.co.uk

Home to the Bitter End Brewery with own brews always available. Farmers Ale, Cuddly Lugs and Blue Bell are usually on the menu. Also Jennings Bitter, Cumberland and Sneck Lifter and one or two guests, changed weekly.

A very traditional brewpub with open fires, background music, non-smoking area at lunchtimes. No machines or juke box. Food served at lunchtime and evenings. Children allowed. Tuesday is quiz night.

 *11.30am–2.30pm and 6–11pm Mon–Thurs; 11.30am–3pm and 6–11pm Fri–Sat; 11.30am–3pm and 7–10.30pm Sun.*

The Bush

Main Street, Cockermouth CA13 9JS
☎ *(01900) 822064* Maureen Williamson

A Jennings house with six hand pumps. The full Jennings range is usually on offer, plus one guest which could be any local ale.

A very warm, friendly town-centre pub with open fires. In operation since 1817. Food served at lunchtime only. Children and dogs welcome in the afternoons.

 *11am–11pm Mon–Sat; 12–10.30pm Sun.*

CONISTON

The Black Bull Hotel

1 Yewdale Road, Coniston LA21 8DU
☎ *(01539) 441335/41668* Ronald Bradley (landlord), Les Gott (manager)

A genuine freehouse with the Coniston Brewery behind it. Coniston Bluebird, Bluebird XB, Old Man and Blacksmith's Ale are usually available. Plus seasonals and specials.

A sixteenth-century coaching inn in the centre of Coniston, with one bar, oak beams and log fire. No juke box or fruit machines. Outside seating area. Separate restaurant. Food served all day. Children and dogs welcome. Car park.

 *11am–11pm Mon–Sat; 12–10.30pm Sun.*

The Sun Hotel and 16th Century Inn

Coniston LA21 8HQ
☎ *(01539) 441248* Alan Piper
www.thesunconiston.com

A freehouse with five pumps and a cool cellar! Local brews are regularly featured, with Coniston Bluebird a permanent fixture, plus guests that might include Black Sheep Special, Moorhouse's Black Cat or something from Yates, Barngates and Hawkshead breweries.

This sixteenth-century pub has a nineteenth-century hotel attached, accommodating 25 people in good-value refurbished bedrooms. Situated on rising ground to overlook the village and enjoying excellent mountain views. One bar, a new conservatory and terrace overlooking the beer garden, outside seating at front, side, rear and in garden. Food from à la carte menu and specials board served lunchtimes and evenings in the conservatory restaurant and bar; the wine list has 40 wines. Children and dogs welcome. Situated on the hill leading up to the Old Man of Coniston, 100 yards above Coniston village, turn left at the bridge.

11am–11pm (10.30pm Sun).

CURTHWAITE

The Royal Oak

Curthwaite, Wigton CA7 8BG
☎ *(01228) 710219*

Derwent Carlisle State Bitter is usually on offer, as well as two guest beers.

Seventeenth-century country pub with a non-smoking restaurant. Darts. Children allowed.

 *12–2.30pm and 7–11pm (10.30pm Sun); 11am–11pm Sat.*

DALTON IN FURNESS

Black Dog Inn

Broughton Road, Holmes Green, Dalton in Furness LA15 8JP
☎ *(01229) 462561* Jack Taylor

A genuine freehouse with six constantly changing real ales and four real ciders always served. There is always a Cumbrian brew, a mild and a stout available, plus three more of varying strength and provenace.

An old coaching inn situated at the site of the tollgates on the ancient Furness Abbey to Scotland road. The inn is a local institution, with its homemade food, excellent range of beers and good accommodation. Four beer festivals held each year. Open fires, exposed beams and tiled floors. Patio garden, function room. No games machines or music. Situated just 1km from South Lakes Wildlife Park.

 *Summer: 12–11pm (10.30pm Sun). Winter: 5–11pm Mon–Fri; 12–11pm Sat; 12–10.30pm Sun.*

DENT

The George & Dragon

Main Street, Dent LA10 5QL
☎ *(01539) 625256* Dorothy Goad

Owned by Dent Brewery, with Dent beers always available.

A country pub, with accommodation. Food served lunchtimes and evenings, separate dining area. Children and dogs allowed. Ten miles from junction 37 of the M6.

Summer: 11am–11pm; closed afternoons in winter.

The Sun Inn

Main Street, Dent LA10 5QL
☎ *(01539) 625208* Martin Stafford

Owned by Dent Brewery. So up to five Dent brews always available.

A traditional country pub in the cobbled main street close to the George & Dragon. Friendly atmosphere, large beer garden, pool room, non-smoking dining area. Food served lunchtimes throughout the year and evenings in summertime only. Children allowed till 9pm.

 *Winter: 12–2pm and 7–11pm Mon–Fri; 11am–11pm Sat; 12–10.30pm Sun. Summer: 11am–11pm Mon–Sat; 12–10.30pm Sun.*

ELTERWATER

Britannia Inn

Elterwater, Ambleside LA22 9HP
☎ *(01539) 437210* Clare Woodhead
www.britinn.co.uk

A freehouse with Jennings Bitter, Coniston Bluebird and Timothy Taylor Landlord always on the menu, plus two guests changed every barrel from a variety of local and national breweries.

A quintessential English lakeland inn in the middle of a picturesque village four miles from Ambleside. Around 500 years old. Small oak-beamed rooms with log fires in winter. Food served lunchtimes and evenings, plus snacks all afternoon. Separate dining area. Large outside seating area plus car park. Nine en-suite rooms. Children and dogs welcome. Autumn beer festival, quiz night most Sundays.

 *11am–11pm Mon–Sat; 12–10.30pm Sun. Closed Christmas Day.*

FOXFIELD

The Prince of Wales

Foxfield, Broughton in Furness LA20 6BX
☎ *(01229) 716238* Stuart and Lynda Johnson
www.princeofwalesfoxfield.co.uk

The home of the Foxfield Brewery, which operates from an adjoining converted stables. Up to six hand pumps dispense a constantly changing range of interesting beers. There is usually a mild and something from Tigertops (in Wakefield) or Foxfield breweries, both of which are owned and run by the Johnsons. Draught and bottled Belgian beers, plus a variety of malts and blended whiskeys, are also available.

A 'no-frills' real ale house, for real ale lovers, in the hamlet of Foxfield. Homemade snacks served 12–7pm Fri–Sun. Car park. Bed and breakfast available. Traditional pub games. Located opposite Foxfield station.

 *5–11pm Wed–Thurs; 12–11pm Fri–Sat; 12–10.30pm Sun; closed Mon–Tues.*

GARRIGILL

George & Dragon

Garrigill, Alston CA9 3DS
☎ *(01434 381293)* Julia and Richard Jackson

Black Sheep Bitter and Riggwelter plus a guest ale usually available.

Very rural but popular inn with good atmosphere and good food. Handily placed for the Pennine Way. Food served at lunchtime and evenings. B&B accommodation. Two miles from Alston.

 *All day, every day.*

GRASMERE

The Traveller's Rest

Grasmere, LA22 9RR
☎ *(01539) 435604* R Collins
www.lakedistrictinns.co.uk

Four real ales always available.
A Jennings tied house, so Jennings Bitter, Cumberland and Sneck Lifter are on the menu along with a guest which might be Black Sheep Bitter, Coniston Bluebird or another beer from an independent brewery, according to availability and demand.

A sixteenth-century inn with one bar, beer garden, games room and bed and breakfast (en-suite accommodation). Food served from 12–3pm and 6–9.30pm (winter); 12–9.30pm (summer). Smoking dining area and non-smoking restaurant. Families and dogs always welcome. Half a mile north of Grasmere village, on A591.

 *11am–11pm (10.30pm Sun).*

GREAT CORBY

The Corby Bridge Inn

Great Corby, Carlisle CA4 8LL
☎ *(01228) 560221* Barbara Griffiths

Thwaites Bitter and Mild always available plus a rotating guest, changed at least twice a week, often including Nethergate Old Growler, Charles Wells Bombardier, Fuller's London Pride, Timothy Taylor Landlord, Badger Tanglefoot or a Wychwood brew.

A freehouse built in 1838. Originally a railway hotel. Grade II listed. Approximately four miles from junction 43 of M6. One bar, pool and darts room and non-smoking dining area. Large garden, games area, accommodation. Food served all day Tues–Sun and Bank Holiday Mondays. Well-behaved children welcome.

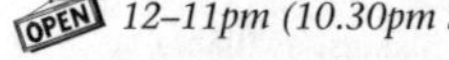 *12–11pm (10.30pm Sun).*

GREAT LANGDALE

Old Dungeon Ghyll Hotel

Great Langdale, Ambleside LA22 9JY
☎ *(01539) 437272* Neil and Jane Walmsley
www.odg.co.uk

Five real ales and scrumpy available in this freehouse. Yates Bitter and Jennings Cumberland Ale always present. Three guests are changed regularly, one barrel at a time. Black Sheep Special is popular, also Theakston Best and Old Peculiar.

An interesting National Trust-owned, listed building with real fire. Food served at lunchtime (12–2pm) and evenings (6–9pm). Children allowed. Accommodation. Outside seating. Seven miles from Ambleside, on the B5343.

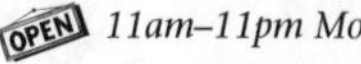 *11am–11pm Mon–Sat; 12–10.30pm Sun.*

GREAT SALKELD

The Highland Drove Inn

Great Salkeld, Nr Penrith CA11 9NA
☎ *(01768) 898349* Donald and Paul Newton
www.highland-drove.co.uk

Theakston Black Bull and John Smiths Bitter always available plus a guest beer.

Friendly, family-run freehouse. Bar, lounge and separate games room plus a restaurant extension serving good food at lunchtime and evenings. Accommodation available.

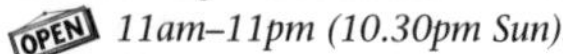 *11am–11pm (10.30pm Sun).*

HAYTON

Stone Inn

Hayton, Brampton, Nr Carlisle CA8 9HR
☎ *(01228) 670498* Johnnie and Susan Tranter

Thwaites Bitter and Mild always available plus occasional seasonal guest ales.

A traditional village pub rebuilt in 1815. Food available for private functions but the focus is on beer. Coach parties can be catered for if booked in advance. The pub has a car park, and is situated seven minutes east of M6 junction 43, just off the A69.

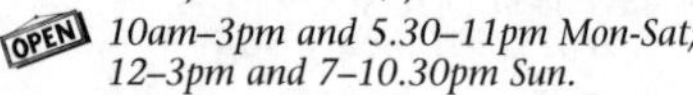 *10am–3pm and 5.30–11pm Mon-Sat; 12–3pm and 7–10.30pm Sun.*

HESKET NEWMARKET

The Old Crown

Hesket Newmarket, Caldbeck, Wigton CA7 8JG
☎ *(01697) 478288* Lou and Linda Hogg
www.theoldcrownpub.co.uk

A freehouse specialising in Hesket Newmarket brews. Up to eight available with Old Carrock Strong Ale, Skiddaw Special, Catbells Pale Ale, Doris's 90th Birthday Ale, Blencathra Bitter and Great Cockup Porter always on the menu.

A small, old-fashioned pub, with two bars, bought by a co-operative of more than 100 locals in 2003. The Hesket Newmarket Brewery is in a barn behind the pub. Food served at lunchtime (Tues–Sun) and evenings (Tues–Sat). Children allowed. On the edge of the Lake District National Park, the only pub in the village. The Prince of Wales dropped in in February 2004!

 *5.30–11pm Mon; 12–3pm and 5.30–11pm Tues–Sat; 12–3pm and 7–10.30pm Sun.*

INGS

12

The Watermill Inn

Ings, Nr Staveley, Kendal LA8 9PY
☎ *(01539) 821309* AF and B Coulthwaite
www.watermillinn.co.uk

Sixteen beers are usually available (500 per year), including Black Sheep Bitter, JW Lees Moonraker, Coniston Bluebird, Jennings Cumberland and Theakston Old Peculiar. Guests may come from the Hop Back, Cotleigh, Ridleys, Shepherd Neame, Exmoor, Summerskills, Coach House, Yates and Wadworth breweries.

Formerly a wood mill, now a traditional, family-run pub full of character with log fires, brasses and beams and a relaxing atmosphere. Two bars. No juke box or games machines. Many times winner of Westmorland Pub of the Year and other prizes. Food served 12–4.30pm and 5–9pm every day. Car park, garden, seats and tables by the river. Disabled toilets. Children allowed in one bar, dogs in the other. Accommodation. From the M6, junction 36, follow the A591 towards Windermere. One mile past the second turning for Staveley. Turn left after the garage, before the church.

 *12–11pm (10.30pm Sun).*

IREBY

The Lion

The Square, Ireby, Carlisle CA5 1EA
☎ *(01697) 371460* Brad and Amanda Leader
www.irebythelion.co.uk

A three-pump freehouse offering Derwent Carlisle State Bitter, Jennings Bitter and a guest, which might come from Yates or Hesket Newmarket.

This traditional village freehouse features oak panels, an open fire and wooden floor. Back bar/games room for pool and darts. Food served at lunchtimes at weekends and every evening except Monday. Children welcome.

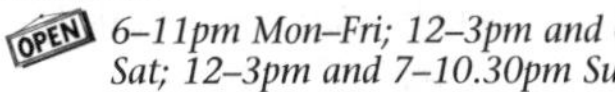 *6–11pm Mon–Fri; 12–3pm and 6–11pm Sat; 12–3pm and 7–10.30pm Sun.*

KENDAL

Burgundy's Wine Bar

19 Lowther Street, Kendal LA9 4DH
☎ *(01539) 733803* Mike Pennington

A freehouse with beers brewed by Derwent Brewery including Kendal Pale Ale and Auld Kendal, plus brews from Yates or another local producer. Guests changed every three days.

Traditional town pub, fromerly the Kendal Labour Exchange, built in the early nineteenth century. Split-level bar with a continental feel and a relaxed atmosphere. Plans for expansion in 2005 will double capacity. No food yet. Live music on Thursdays and Fridays. Beer festival in April. Children allowed. Next to the Town Hall.

 *6.30–11pm Tues–Weds; 11am–3.30pm and 6.30–11pm Thurs–Sat; 7–10.30pm Sun.*

Ring o' Bells

39 Kirkland, Kendal LA9 5AF
☎ *(01539) 720326* Clive Graham
www.ringobellskendal.co.uk

Four real ales usually available, with two regular features and a couple of rotating guests changed every few days.

An unspoilt seventeenth-century pub in the grounds of the parish church. Bar food available at lunchtime and evenings. The non-smoking dining room has room for 14. Parking. Children allowed. Accommodation. Take M6 junction 36, then follow the A590 and A591 to the A6 in Kendal.

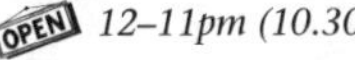 *12–11pm (10.30pm Sun).*

KIRKBY LONSDALE

The Snooty Fox

Main Street, Kirkby Lonsdale LA6 2AH
☎ *(01524) 271308* Stuart Rickard

A freehouse, with Timothy Taylor Landlord and Black Sheep Bitter regularly available, plus a wide range of guest cask ales.

A seventeenth-century inn, with two bars, stonework and beams. Nine en-suite bedrooms. Food at lunchtime and evenings. Children allowed.

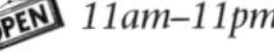 *11am–11pm Mon–Sat; 12–10.30pm Sun.*

KIRKSANTON

King William IV

Kirksanton, Nr Millom LA18 4NN
☎ *(01229) 772009* Pete and Karen Rodger

A freehouse with Jennings Cumberland Ale (@ £1.75) always available, with regular guest ales during the summer season.

A 200-year-old country pub with oak beams and real fires. Four letting rooms available for bed and breakfast. Non-smoking dining area. Food at lunchtime and evenings. Children allowed. On the main road from Millom to Whitehaven.

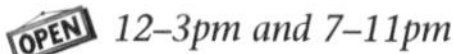
12–3pm and 7–11pm.

LANERCOST

Abbey Bridge Inn

Lanercost, Near Brampton CA8 2HG
☎ *(016977) 2224* Tim and Sue Hatt
www.abbeybridge.co.uk

Traditional inn specialising in Cumbrian beers. Yates Bitter and Coniston Bluebird XB are always available, plus up to two guests. Brews from Hesket Newmarket are frequently served.

Former temperance inn dating from 1832 with two bars featuring stone slab floors and open fires. Food is available at lunchtime and evenings, and there is a non-smoking restaurant. Car park, outside seating, children and dogs allowed. Accommodation. Situated close to Hadrian's Wall, Lanercost Priory and the riverbank.

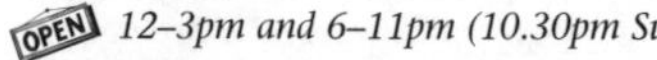
12–3pm and 6–11pm (10.30pm Sun).

MELMERBY

Shepherds' Inn

Melmerby CA10 1HF
☎ *(0870745) 3383*

Jennings Cumberland Ale, Black Sheep Bitter and at least one guest ale usually available. More in summer.

On a popular tourist route between Penrith and Alston, an eighteenth-century village pub with converted barn attached. Highly recommended food served at lunchtime and evenings.

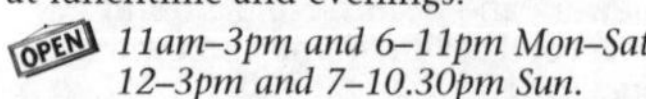
11am–3pm and 6–11pm Mon–Sat; 12–3pm and 7–10.30pm Sun.

NETHER WASDALE

The Screes Inn

Nether Wasdale, Seascale CA20 1ET
☎ *(01946) 726262*
Nick Putnam and Rachel Hughes
www.thescreesinnwasdale.com

A freehouse, with Yates and Black Sheep brews always available. Four guests, changed weekly, come from independents such as Dent.

An eighteenth-century pub with split-level bar, separate dining area, small function room and five en-suite letting rooms. Magnificent views of the fells. Food served all day. Children allowed. Can be tricky to find. Ring for directions, if necessary.

OPEN *All day, every day (except Christmas Day).*

RAVENSTONEDALE

The King's Head Hotel

Ravenstonedale CA17 4NH
☎ *(015396) 23284*

Black Sheep Bitter and at least four guest ales available. An annual beer festival is held in August.

A sixteenth-century inn created out of four cottages. Beams, real fires, no-smoking areas, games and family room. Food served at lunchtime and evenings. Off the A685.

OPEN *11am–11pm Mon–Sat, 12–10.30pm Sun.*

SILLOTH

The Golf Hotel

Criffel Street, Silloth CA7 4AB
☎ *(01697) 331438* Christine Previtali

A freehouse with Derwent Carlisle State Bitter always available plus guests in summer.

A 22-room hotel and restaurant with one bar. Food served. Games machine. Children allowed.

OPEN *11am–11pm Mon–Sat; 12–10.30pm Sun.*

STRAWBERRY BANK

The Mason's Arms

Strawberry Bank, Cartmel Fell LA11 6NW
☎ *(01539) 568486* Helen Parker

Five real ales always available, including Timothy Taylor Landlord and brews from Black Sheep and Hawkshead. Other guests are from all over the country, e.g. Greene King Old Speckled Hen, Caledonian Deuchars IPA and beer from Barngates brewery. Good selection of fruit beers and bottle-conditioned beers. Hoegaarden and Budvar also available.

A rural freehouse set in the middle of nowhere! Slate floor and open fires. Terrace with 12 tables overlooking the valley. Self-catering studio apartments available. Homemade food served at lunchtime and evenings, with a good vegetarian and vegan selection. Children allowed.

 *11.30am–3pm and 6–11pm Mon–Thurs; all day Fri–Sun.*

TALKIN

Blacksmith's Arms

Talkin, Nr Brampton CA8 1LE
☎ *(016977) 3452*
www.blacksmithsarmstalkin.co.uk

Black Sheep Bitter and Coniston Bluebird usually available.

A seventeenth-century blacksmith's and now a freehouse popular with drinkers and diners. Good food served at lunchtime and evenings. Golf course and country park nearby, not far from Hadrian's Wall. Accommodation.

 *12–3pm and 6–11pm (10.30pm Sun)*

TIRRIL

The Queen's Head

Tirril, Penrith CA10 2JF
☎ *(01768) 863219* Chris Tomlinson
www.queensheadinn.co.uk

Offers four beers from the Tirril Brewery, plus one other ale on a guest pump.

A 300-year-old pub, once owned by the Wordsworth family, situated on the B5320, with stone walls and beams. Two bars, Grade II listed. The small village of Tirril once boasted two breweries, one being at this inn. It was closed in 1899, and reopened 100 years later in October 1999 by the present landlord, in an outhouse at the rear of the pub. The brewery moved to nearby Brougham Hall in 2002. The pub itself is a Cask Marque winner. Food served at lunchtime and evenings, with a separate dining area available. Cumbrian Beer and Sausage Festival held annually on second weekend of August. Another festival in February. Children allowed. Seven en-suite rooms.

 *12–3pm and 6–11pm Mon–Fri; 12–11pm Sat; 12–10.30pm Sun.*

TROUTBECK

The Queen's Head Hotel

Troutbeck LA23 1PW
☎ *(01539) 432174* Mark Stewerdson
www.queensheadhotel.com

A freehouse with four guests, which change every few days, and which might include Coniston Bluebird, Old Man Ale, Burton Bridge Amazon or Great Northern.

A food-oriented pub and hotel in a seventeenth-century coaching inn. Nine bedrooms and seating area outside. Food served at lunchtime and evenings. Children allowed.

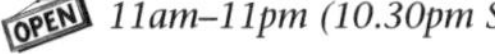 *11am–11pm (10.30pm Sun).*

WALTON

The Centurion Inn

Walton, Nr Brampton CA8 2DH
☎ *(016977) 2438*

Jennings Cumberland and Dark Mild usually available plus a guest.

Known as the Black Bull until 1974, on the actual route of Hadrian's Wall, a family-run community freehouse with non-smoking restaurant and bed and breakfast accommodation. Real fires, beams. Food served at lunchtime and evenings.

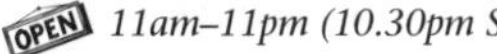 *11am–11pm (10.30pm Sun)*

WASDALE HEAD

Wasdale Head Inn

Wasdale Head, Nr Gosforth CA20 1EX
☎ *(01946) 726229* Howard Christie
www.wasdale.com

Home of the Great Gable Brewery, with the brewery's own beers always available. Beers from other breweries, such as Jennings, Dent, Derwent, Coniston and Foxfield, are also regularly served.

A traditional pub with a beer garden, set in the Lake District National Park. Food served all day until 8.30pm. Children allowed (if on a lead!).

11am–11pm Mon–Sat; 12–10.30pm Sun.

WINTON

The Bay Horse Inn

Winton, Kirkby Stephen CA17 4HS
☎ *(01768) 371451* Derek Parvin

A freehouse offering four real ales, two rotated, and all hand-pulled from the cask. Black Sheep Bitter is always on offer. Varied guests, changed twice weekly, may include Coniston Bluebird or perhaps a Harviestoun brew.

A pub dating from the late 1600s, off the A685, two miles north of Kirkby Stephen. Lounge bar, panelled walls, beams, two open fires, flag floors. Public and lounge bars with central servery. Modern 50-seater dining area. Food served at lunchtime and evenings. Children allowed.

 *12–2pm and 7–11pm (closed Tues lunchtimes). More flexible in summer.*

THE BREWERIES

BRUNSWICK BREWERY

The Brunswick Inn, 1 Railway Terrace, Derby DE1 2RU
☎ *(01332) 290677*

MILD 3.6% ABV
TRIPLE HOP 4.0% ABV
SECOND BREW 4.2% ABV
RAILWAY PORTER 4.3% ABV
TRIPLE GOLD 4.5% ABV
OLD ACCIDENTAL 5.0% ABV

EDALE BREWERY CO. LTD

Ruskin Villa, Hope Road, Edale, Hope Valley S33 7ZE
☎ *01433 670289*

KINDER CHALLENGE 3.8% ABV
KINDER TRESPASS 4.0% ABV
KINDER CROSS 4.3% ABV
KINDER DOWNFALL 5.0% ABV
RINGING ROGER 6.0% ABV

GLOSSOP BREWERIES LTD

Unit 8 Waterside Industrial Estate, Waterside, Hadfield, Glossop SK13 1BR
☎ *(07904) 039224*
www.glossopbreweries.com

DEXTER'S BEST BITTER 3.8% ABV
FLETCHER'S CAMPAIGN BITTER 4.3% ABV

LEADMILL BREWERY

Unit 1, Park Hall Farm, Parkhall Road, Denby, Ripley DE5 8PX
☎ *(01332) 883577*

INGOT 3.6% ABV
WILD WEASEL 3.9% ABV
Pale, refreshing and malty.
ARC-LIGHT 4.2% ABV
Dry-hopped, pale and fruity.
ROLLING THUNDER 4.5% ABV
Full-flavoured with some sweetness.
SAIGON 4.5% ABV
Distinctive pale ale.
LINEBACKER 4.6% ABV
Flavoursome, with fruity hop finish.
RED RIVER 4.8% ABV
AGENT ORANGE 4.9% ABV
Balanced and hoppy with subtle honey tones.
FIREBIRD 5.0% ABV
Creamy red ale with a hint of blackcurrant.
NIAGARA 5.0% ABV
Malt flavour throughout and dry-hopped.
APOCALYPSE NOW 5.2% ABV
Inviting, well-balanced flavour with some fruit.

LEATHERBRITCHES CRAFT BREWERY

The Bentley Brook Inn, Fenny Bentley, Ashbourne DE6 1LF
☎ *(01335) 350278*
www.bentleybrookinn.co.uk

GOLDINGS 3.6% ABV
ASHBOURNE 4.0% ABV
BELTER 4.4% ABV
BELT N BRACES 4.4% ABV
HAIRY HELMET 4.7% ABV
BESPOKE 5.0% ABV

JOHN THOMPSON BREWERY

John Thompson Inn, Ingleby Lane, Ingleby, Melbourne DE73 1HW
☎ *(01332) 863033*

JOHN THOMPSON SPECIAL 4.2% ABV
JOHN THOMPSON PORTER 4.5% ABV
JOHN THOMPSON SUMMER GOLD 4.5% ABV

TOWNES BREWERY

Speedwell Inn, Lowgates, Staveley, Chesterfield S43 3TT
☎ *(01246) 472252*

SPEEDWELL BITTER 3.9% ABV
A light, well-hopped and spicy session beer.
BEST LOCKOFORD BITTER 4.0% ABV
IPA 4.5% ABV
PYNOT PORTER 4.5% ABV
Very dark and wholesome.
STAVELEYAN 4.8% ABV
A robust full-flavoured premium bitter.
Plus monthly brews covering a range of styles.

WHIM ALES

Whim Farm, Hartington, Buxton SK17 0AX
☎ *(01298) 84991*

ARBOR LIGHT 3.6% ABV
MAGIC MUSHROOM MILD 3.8% ABV
Very dark and flavoursome.
HARTINGTON BITTER 4.0% ABV
HARTINGTON IPA 4.5% ABV
Plus occasional brews.

THE PUBS

BRAMPTON

The Royal Oak

413 Chatsworth Road, Brampton, Chesterfield S40 2AH
☎ *(01246) 277854* Mr and Mrs M Mount
www.royaloakbrampton.com

A freehouse with a large selection of real ales always available. Seven regulars include Marston's Pedigree, Greene King Ruddles Best, three Theakston brews and two from Whim Ales. Three guests changed weekly.

A traditional local pub with friendly staff and regulars of all ages. Two bars, timber ceilings and an open fire. Live music, quizzes, pub games pool and big-screen TV. Annual music and beer festivals. Jazz on Sunday afternoons. No food. Car park. Children's play area in beer garden.

11.30am–11pm.

BUXWORTH

Navigation Inn

Bugsworth Canal Basin, Buxworth, Nr Whaley Bridge SK23 7NE
☎ *(01663) 732072* Lynda and Alan Hall
www.navigationinn.co.uk

A freehouse with at least four real ales always available. Timothy Taylor Landlord and Marston's Pedigree are regulars plus a range of constantly changing guest beers.

A 200-year-old stone inn on the site of a restored canal basin in Derbyshire's High Peak. Full of interesting memorabilia and canalwares. Lounge bar with log fire, separate restaurant, play area, pets' corner, games room and stone-floored snug. Food served 12–3pm and 5.30–9.30pm Mon–Fri, 12–9.30pm Sat–Sun. Beer festival held at the end of June. En-suite accommodation.

11am–11pm Mon–Sat; 12–10.30pm Sun.

CHESTERFIELD

The Derby Tup

387 Sheffield Road, Whittington Moor, Chesterfield S41 8LS
☎ *(01246) 454316* Mr Hughes

Black Sheep Bitter, Whim Hartington, Timothy Taylor Landlord, Marston's Pedigree and Greene King Abbot always available, plus four pumps serving a constantly changing range of guest ales (500 per year).

Old and original, beamed with three rooms and open fires. Home-cooked food available 11am–2pm daily and 6–8pm Thurs–Sat; Thai, Indian and vegetarian food are specialities. Parking nearby, children allowed. Sunday quiz, occasional live music.

11.30am–3pm and 5–11pm Mon–Tues; 11.30am–11pm Weds–Sat; 12–4pm and 7–10.30pm Sun.

The Market

95 New Square, Chesterfield S40 1AH
☎ *(01246) 273641* Keith Toone

Marston's Pedigree and Greene King Abbot always available. Three guests may include Black Sheep Special, Hop Back Summer Lightning or Ushers Founders Ale.

A one-bar market pub, with dining area in bar. Food served at lunchtime only. Children allowed in the dining area only and if eating.

11am–11pm Mon–Sat; 7.30–10.30pm Sun

The Rutland Arms

23 Stephensons Place, Chesterfield S40 1XL
☎ *(01246) 205857* Paul Young

Tied to Whitbread, serving four ales straight from the barrel and five on pumps. Castle Eden Ale, Caledonian Deuchars IPA, Marston's Pedigree and Greene King Abbot are always on offer plus guests, changed every ten days, which often include Greene King Old Speckled Hen, Bateman XXXB or Black Sheep Best.

Predominantly wooden interior, close to Chesterfield's famous crooked spire church. Real fires in winter. Non-smoking dining area away from the bar. Food served 11am–9pm Mon–Thurs and 11am–7pm Fri–Sun. No children.

11am–11pm Mon–Sat; 12–10.30pm Sun.

CROMFORD

The Boat Inn

Scarthin, Cromford, Matlock DE4 3QF
☎ *(01629) 823282*
Kevin White and Debbie White

A freehouse with a Springhead ale and Marston's Pedigree usually available plus all sorts of guests, from local micro-breweries whenever possible.

A village pub built about 1772, near the market square. A 24-seater restaurant, Frets, has been added. Two bars, log fires, beer garden. Regular music nights and pub quizzes, plus an annual beer festival. Bar snacks at lunchtime and evenings plus Sunday lunches. Children allowed. Dogs welcome.

11.30am–3pm and 6–11pm Mon–Fri; all day Sat–Sun.

DALE ABBEY

The Carpenters Arms

Dale Abbey, Ilkeston DE7 4PP
☎ *(0115) 932 5277* John Heraty

Tied to Punch Retail, with Marston's Pedigree and Adnams Bitter always available, plus two other beers from local and national breweries such as Charles Wells and Greene King.

A traditional village pub in picturesque walking country, family run for 70 years. Children's play area and beer garden, family room and large car park. Food served at lunchtimes and evenings. Children not allowed in bar. Three miles from junction 25 off the M1.

 *12–3pm and 6–11pm (7–10.30pm Sun).*

DENBY

The Old Stables Bar

Unit 5, Park Hall, Park Hall Road, Denby, Nr Ripley DE5 8PX
☎ *(01332) 883577* Richard Creighton

Owned and run by the nearby Leadmill Brewery, with a selection of beers from the huge Leadmill range plus a couple of guests. Up to ten real ales at any one time.

Opened in January 2003 in a 200-year-old stable building. One small bar, sawdust on the floor. Fresh cobs and snacks available. Brewery tours by arrangement. Outside seating. Children welcome until 9pm. One mile south of Denby Pottery.

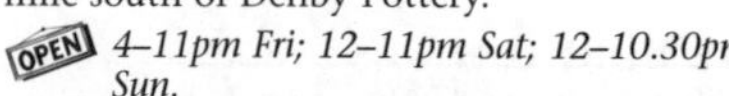

OPEN *4–11pm Fri; 12–11pm Sat; 12–10.30pm Sun.*

DERBY

The Alexandra Hotel

203 Siddals Road, Derby DE1 2QE
☎ *(01332) 293993* Mark Robins

Castle Rock Nottingham Gold, York Yorkshire Terrier and Belvoir Star Bitter are usually available, plus seven ever-changing guests, including a mild.

Built as a coffee and chop house in 1865. Now trading as a comfortable award-winning pub decorated with a railway and brewery theme. Bar food at lunchtimes. Four en-suite bedrooms. Car park and garden. Three minutes' walk from Derby Midland Railway Station.

OPEN *11am–11pm Mon–Sat; 12–3pm and 7–10.30pm Sun.*

The Brunswick Inn

1 Railway Terrace, Derby DE1 2RU
☎ *(01332) 290677* Graham Yates

Fourteen pumps serve beer from all around the country, notably Marston's Pedigree and Timothy Taylor Landlord, plus five or six ales from the on-site brewery.

Built in 1841–2 as the first purpose-built railwaymen's pub in the world. The birthplace of the Railway Institute, an educational establishment for railway workers. It fell into dereliction in the early 1970s and trading ceased in April 1974. The Derbyshire Historic Buildings Trust started restoration work in 1981. The pub reopened in October 1987 and the installation of the brewing plant followed in 1991. The first beer was produced on 11 June that year. Bar food is available at lunchtime. Parking, garden, children's room, non-smoking room, function room.

OPEN *11am–11pm Mon–Sat; 12–10.30pm Sun.*

The Crompton Tavern

46 Crompton Street, Derby DE1 1NX
☎ *(01332) 733629* Mr and Mrs Bailey

Marston's Pedigree and Timothy Taylor Landlord always available plus four guest beers (200 per year) perhaps from Fuller's, Coach House, Kelham Island, Banks & Taylor or Burton Bridge breweries. A porter or stout is normally available.

A small pub just outside the city centre. Popular with locals and students. Cobs and sandwiches available daily. Car park and garden. Children allowed in garden.

OPEN *11am–11pm Mon–Sat; 12–10.30pm Sun.*

The Falstaff

74 Silver Hill Road, Normanton, Derby DE23 6UJ
☎ *(01332) 342902* Adrian Parkes

Four real ales are permanently on offer. Greene King Abbot Ale is almost always on tap, as is Leatherbritches Hairy Helmet. Two other local beers are also available, one around 5% ABV and one 5.2% or above.

A friendly, 125-year-old former hotel and former brewery tucked away in the back streets of Derby. One main bar serves three rooms. Real fire in lounge. Outside seating area. Children welcome. Wheelchair access if required. From the city, take the Normanton Road to the painted island, turn right, take the first available right, then the next right.

OPEN *12–11pm (10.30pm Sun).*

The Flowerpot

25 King Street, Derby DE1 3DZ
☎ *(012332) 204955* S Manners

Marston's Pedigree and Hook Norton Old Hooky always available plus at least seven (and sometimes 14) guest beers (500+ per year) from all over the United Kingdom. The widest choice of real ale in Derby.

A traditional friendly town pub with parts of the building dating from the late seventeenth century. Age range of regulars is 18 to 95. Ground-level cellar bar has a unique 'beer wall', through which customers can see ale being cared for and dispensed. Homemade bar food served at lunchtime through to evening. Garden area. Function suite with capacity for up to 250 people. Wheelchair access to all areas. Children welcome till 7.30pm. Car park 30 yards away. Situated on the A6 just off the inner ring road, 300 yards north of the Cathedral.

OPEN *11am–11pm Mon–Sat; 12–10.30pm Sun.*

The Friargate

114 Friargate, Derby DE1 1EX
☎ *(01332) 297065* Roger Myring

A freehouse serving Marston's Pedigree straight from the barrel plus up to eight others. Regulars come from Rooster's, Whim and Oakham breweries.

A quiet town pub with one main bar. Acoustic music on Wednesdays. Food served at lunchtime (not Sun). No children.

OPEN *11am–11pm Mon–Sat; 12–3pm and 7–10.30pm Sun.*

The Rowditch Inn

246 Uttoxeter New Road, Derby DE22 3LL
☎ *(01332) 343123* Mr Birkin

A freehouse with at least four real ales always available, including Marston's Pedigree and Hardys & Hansons Kimberley Classic and Kimberley Best Bitter, plus a wide range of rotating guests.

A traditional beer house with one bar, non-smoking area, snug and beer garden. No food, no children. Regular beer festivals. On the main road.

OPEN *12–2pm Thurs–Sun; 7–11pm daily (10.30pm Sun).*

The Smithfield

Meadow Road, Derby DE1 2BH
☎ *(01332) 370429* Roger and Penny Myring
www.thesmithfield.co.uk

A freehouse with Whim Hartington IPA and either Whim Arbor Light or Oakham JHB available, plus up to five guests changing two or three times a week. Fuller's London Pride and beers from Rooster's and Oakham regularly featured.

Traditional, friendly atmosphere. Lounge with open fire and pub games plus a family room. Food served 12–2pm only. Children allowed until 8pm. Ring for directions.

OPEN *11am–11pm Mon–Sat; 12–10.30pm Sun.*

FENNY BENTLEY

The Bentley Brook Inn

Fenny Bentley, Ashbourne DE6 1LF
☎ *(01335) 350278* Mrs Jeanne Allingham
www.bentleybrookinn.co.uk

Home to the Leatherbritches Craft Brewery, Fenny's Restaurant and Leatherbritches Fine Food shop. Leatherbritches cask and bottle-conditioned beers, brewed on site, are always available, plus Marston's Pedigree and guest beers. Up to six real ales at any one time with the menu changing daily.

A traditional, family-run, country inn (AA 2 star, 12 en-suite rooms) with large garden, children's play area and kitchen herb garden and nursery open to the public. Permanent marquee. Food served 12–9pm. Annual beer festival (100 beers, ten bands) on bank holiday at end of May. Two miles north of Ashbourne.

OPEN *All day, every day.*

The Coach & Horses

Fenny Bentley DE6 1LB
☎ *(01335) 350246* John and Matthew Dawson

A family-run freehouse offering a continually changing range of award-winning cask ales. Marston's Pedigree always available, plus three guests, which may include Abbeydale Moonshine, Coniston Bluebird or Timothy Taylor Landlord.

A traditional seventeenth-century coaching inn with background music and beer garden. Food served every day 12–9pm. Winner of Derbyshire Food and Drink Award 2003. Children welcome.

OPEN *11am–11pm.*

FOOLOW

The Bull's Head Inn

Foolow, Eyam, Hope Valley
☎ *(01433) 630873* Les Bond

Black Sheep Bitter and Shepherd Neame Spitfire plus one or two other brews usually available.

Claims to be the prettiest pub in the Peak District! Good food available 12–2.30pm and 6.30–9pm. Children, dogs and muddy boots welcome. Three delightful en-suite bedrooms. Car park. Take the A623 through Stoney Middleton towards Chapel-en-le-Frith, turn right for Foolow.

OPEN *12–3pm and 6–11pm (10.30pm Sun).*

GLOSSOP

The Old Glove Works

Riverside Mill, George Street, Glossop SK13 8AY
☎ *(01457) 858432*
www.thegloveworksglossop.com

Six ever-changing real ales always available, from breweries such as Wye Valley, Shaws, Abbeydale, Kelham Island and Whim Ales.

A grown-up environment, appealing to the over 25s. Food available 12–2pm Mon–Fri. Two outside riverside drinking areas. Live entertainment Thurs and Sun, resident DJ playing music from the 60s–80s Friday and Saturday.

OPEN *12–8pm Mon–Wed; 12–11pm Thurs; 12pm–12am Fri–Sat (no admission after 10.45pm); 12–10.30pm Sun.*

HEMINGTON

The Jolly Sailor

Main Street, Hemington, Derby DE74 2RB
☎ *(01332) 810448* Margaret and Peter Frame

Five real ales always available, including Greene King Abbot, Marston's Pedigree and Kelham Island Gold and a mild plus two rotating guests, which could be something like Abbeydale Absolution, Fuller's ESB, Whim Hartington IPA, Timothy Taylor Landlord, Oakham Jeffery Hudson Bitter, Bateman XXXB or something from Burton Bridge.

A seventeenth-century village pub, full of character and with a hospitable atmosphere. Run by the same couple for 14 years. Food is served 12–2pm Mon–Sat. The two patios are heated. No children's facilities. Car park. Next to Castle Donington (Junction 24 on M1).

OPEN *11.30am–2.30pm and 4.30–11pm Mon–Fri; 11.30am–11pm Sat; 12–10.30pm Sun.*

HOPE

The Woodroffe Arms Hotel

1 Castleton Road, Hope, Hope Valley S33 6SB
☎ *(01433) 620351* Barry Thomson

Marston's Pedigree permanently available.

Attractive one-bar pub with traditional log fires, conservatory restaurant, outside seating and patio with swings for children. Food available every lunchtime and evening with £4.95 specials available Mon–Sat lunchtimes. Children allowed.

OPEN *11.30am–11pm Mon–Sat; 12–10.30pm Sun.*

HORSLEY WOODHOUSE

Old Oak Inn

176 Main Street, Horsley Woodhouse, Ilkeston DE7 6AW
☎ *(01332) 780672* Roger and Frances Warren

Now owned by the Leadmill Brewery with a selection from the brewery's range of 40-plus beers, plus a couple of constantly changing guests. Nine real ales at any one time.

A 150-year-old former village freehouse bought by the brewery in October 2003 and saved from potential demolition. Three rooms, covered courtyard with garden and field behind. Skittle alley. Beer festivals held in May and December. Fresh cobs and bar snacks available. Children welcome in the back rooms.

OPEN *5–11pm Mon–Thurs; 4–11pm Fri; 12–11pm Sat; 12–10.30pm Sun.*

ILKESTON

Spring Cottage

1 Fulwood Street, Ilkeston DE7 8AZ
☎ *(0115) 932 3153* Mr Wootton

Tied to Punch Taverns, with two guests changed daily, that may include Wadworth 6X, Marston's Pedigree, Greene King Abbot Ale and Old Speckled Hen or Shepherd Neame Spitfire.

A traditional town pub with two bars and background music. Children's room. The lounge doubles as a dining area. Food at lunchtime and evenings. Children allowed. Near the main shopping area on one-way system.

OPEN *11am–3pm and 6–11pm Mon–Thur; 11am–4pm and 6–11pm Fri; 11am–5pm and 7–11pm Sat; 12–3pm and 7–10.30pm Sun.*

ILKESTON JUNCTION

Dewdrop

24 Station Street, Ilkeston Junction DE7 5TE
☎ *(0115) 9329684* Graham Sargerson (Sarge)
www.eggpie.com

Up to five real ales always available, including Timothy Taylor Best and Middleton Pale Ale (brewed for the pub by Rooster's) plus beers from Glentworth, Rooster's, Kelham Island, Abbeydale, Oakham, Nottingham, Mallard, Ossett, Maypole and Archers. All are sourced directly from the breweries. The Polish beer Zywiec is also served, plus a range of continental bottled beers and occasionally farmhouse cider.

Large, unspoilt award-winning pub dating from 1884 beside the railway station and still with many original features. The tap room has a free 1960s jukebox and pool table, the lounge is the place for good conversation by the fire. Food served at all times, with hot black pudding cobs a speciality. Outside seating in the 1950s beer yard. Unrestricted parking. East of town on the A6096, by the railway bridge. Erewash Valley Pub of the Year 2004.

 *12–2.30pm and 7–11pm Mon–Fri; 12–4.30pm and 7–11pm Sat–Sun.*

INGLEBY

John Thompson Inn

Ingleby, Melbourne DE73 1HW
☎ *(01332) 862469* John Thompson

Home of the John Thompson Brewery, which re-introduced brewing to Derbyshire in 1977. JTS XXX Bitter plus the seasonal ale always available.

Converted fifteenth-century oak-beamed farmhouse, with a collection of paintings and antiques. Food served from the carvery lunchtimes only. Close to the River Trent. Car park. Children's room and large garden.

 *10.30am–2.30pm and 7–11pm Mon–Sat; 12–2.30pm and 7–10.30pm Sun.*

KIRK IRETON

The Barley Mow Inn

Main Street, Kirk Ireton, Ashbourne DE6 3JP
☎ *(01335) 370306* Mary Short

Up to five real ales usually available. These might include Hartington IPA, Hook Norton Old Hooky and brews from Cottage, Storm, Leatherbritches and Burton Bridge. Farmhouse cider also served.

Seventeenth-century village inn with unspoilt interior. Beers served straight from the stillage behind the bar. Real fire. Rolls available at lunchtime. Children are permitted inside the pub at lunchtime, but there are no special facilities. Garden area at front. Car park. En-suite accommodation.

12–2pm and 7–11pm (10.30pm Sun).

KNIVETON

The Red Lion

Main Street, Kniveton, Ashbourne DE6 1JH
☎ *(01335) 345554* Susan Lyon and James Pugh

A freehouse with something from the Black Sheep Brewery always on offer, plus one guest.

A small, traditional village pub with separate dining room. Background music only. Food served at lunchtime and evenings. Children welcome. Close to Carsington Water.

 *12–2pm and 7–11pm Mon–Fri; 11am–11pm Sat; 12–10.30pm Sun.*

MAKENEY

The Holly Bush Inn

Holly Bush Lane, Makeney, Milford DE56 0RX
☎ *(01332) 841729* JJK Bilbie

Marston's Pedigree and Ruddles County (Greene King) always available plus four (200+ per year) guests that may include Brains Dark, Exmoor Gold, Fuller's ESB, Marston's Owd Roger, Greene King Abbot and Old Speckled Hen, Timothy Taylor Landlord and brews from Bateman. Also scrumpy cider.

A Grade II listed former farmhouse with flagstone floors and open fires. Bar food at lunchtime, barbecues in summer. Regular beer festivals. Car park and children's room. Private parties welcome. Just off the main A6 at Milford, opposite the Makeney Hotel.

 *12–3pm and 5–11pm Mon–Thurs; 12–11pm Fri–Sun.*

MARSH LANE

The George Inn

46 Lightwood Road, Marsh Lane, Eckington
☎ *(01246) 433178* Martyn and Christa

A regularly changing guest beer available perhaps from Everards, Robinson's, Young's, Bateman and others, all 4.2% ABV or above and served in over-sized glasses.

Village freehouse with taproom and lounge, each with real fire and free of any machines or music. Outside seating at front and small garden to rear. No food. Car park. Children welcome during the day. Dogs welcome.

1–4pm and 7–11pm Mon–Sat; 12–3pm and 7–10.30pm Sun.

MATLOCK

The Thorntree Inn

48 Jackson Road, Matlock DE4 3JG
☎ *(01629) 582923* Philip John Sismey

Timothy Taylor Landlord is always on offer, plus one guest, which might come from Black Sheep or any one of a number of different breweries. Twice-yearly real ale festival held.

Traditional country-style community pub with a large covered patio, heated on chilly evenings, offering unrivalled views over the valley. Food available 12–1.45pm Wed–Sat, 7–8.30pm Tues–Sat and 12–5.30pm Sun. Children allowed on the patio, but no special facilities. From Crown Square in Matlock, go up the hill on Bank Road, turn into Smedley Street, then second right into Smith Road, and the pub is at the top on the left.

7–11pm Mon–Tues; 12–2.30pm and 7–11pm Wed–Sat; 12–10.30pm Sun.

MELBOURNE

The Bluebell Inn

53 Church Street, Melbourne DE73 1EJ
☎ *(01332) 865764* Kevin Morgan

Owned by Shardlow, with Shardlow Reverend Eaton's Ale, Goldenhop and Best Bitter always on offer. One guest, changed weekly, might be something like Brunswick The Usual, Everards Tiger, Shardlow Five Bells or a beer from Springhead.

Traditional family pub frequented by good drinkers! Bar snacks available, plus meals in the small restaurant. Patio, barbecue. Four en-suite letting rooms. Accompanied children allowed. Situated near Melbourne Hall.

11am–11pm Mon–Sat; 12–10.30pm Sun.

The Paddock Hotel

222 Station Road, Melbourne DE73 1BQ
☎ *(01332) 862566*
Linda and Harvey Goodchild
www.smoothhound.co.uk/hotels/paddockhotel.html

A freehouse with Shardlow's Reverend Eaton, Marston's Pedigree and Timothy Taylor Landlord usually available.

A small pub within a family-run hotel with seven en-suite bedrooms and a non-smoking restaurant. Two warm and friendly bars. Food served 6.30–9pm Mon–Sat and 12–4pm Sun. Children allowed. On the outskirts of the village. Secure parking.

OPEN *5.30–11pm Mon–Fri; all day Sat–Sun.*

OCKBROOK

The Royal Oak

55 Green Lane, Ockbrook DE72 3SE
☎ *(01332) 662378* Olive Wilson

Three guest beers are changed up to five times a week, and may include brews from Shardlow, Whim, Brewsters or Burton Bridge.

Village pub built in 1762. The landlady has run the pub for over 50 years! Lunch is available every day, plus evening meals 6–8pm Mon–Fri, and there is a separate dining area. Function room with bar, two beer gardens (one for adults, one for children), darts, car park. Annual beer festival in October. Children allowed at lunchtimes only.

11.30am–2.30pm and 6.30–11pm (10.30pm Sun).

OLD TUPTON

The Royal Oak Inn

Derby Road, Old Tupton, Chesterfield S42 6LA
☎ *(01246) 862180* John Angus

Greene King Old Speckled Hen always available plus four guests, changed weekly, often including Whim Hartington IPA, Greene King Ruddles County, Charles Wells Bombardier or Tomintoul Witches Cauldron.

A 100-year-old freehouse with three rooms. Food at lunchtime and evenings. No children. Three miles south of Chesterfield.

12–3pm and 5–11pm Mon–Thur; 11am–11pm Fri–Sat; 12–3pm and 7–10.30pm Sun.

OVER HADDON

Lathkil Hotel

School Lane, Over Haddon, Nr Bakewell DE45 1JE
☎ *(01629) 812501* Robert Grigor-Taylor
www.lathkil.co.uk

A freehouse featuring up to five real ales. Whim Hartington Bitter, Charles Wells Bombadier plus guest brews from Cottage, Springhead, Adnams, Fullers and Marston's Pedigree change frequently.

A pub with stunning views over the Dales. Occasional TV for sporting events. Food served in the bar at lunchtime and evenings and the restaurant in the evenings only. Children allowed at lunchtimes only. Four en-suite bedrooms. Two miles from Bakewell.

 *11.30am–3pm and 7–11pm Mon–Fri; 11.30am–11pm Sat; 12–10.30pm Sun. Winter opening hours may vary.*

ROWARTH

Little Mill Inn

Rowarth, High Peak SK22 1EB
☎ *(01663) 743178* Mr Barnes

A freehouse always offering Banks's Bitter, Marston's Pedigree, Camerons Strongarm and Hardys & Hansons Kimberley Best. A guest beer, changed weekly, may well be Hartleys SB (Robinson's).

An old-style pub in the middle of nowhere with a waterwheel at the side. Two bars, live music twice a week, quiz and bingo nights. Upstairs restaurant area. Food served all day. Children allowed. Isolated, but fully signposted.

 *11am–11pm Mon–Sat; 12–10.30pm Sun.*

SHARDLOW

The Old Crown Inn

Cavendish Bridge, Nr Shardlow DE72 2HL
☎ *(01332) 792392* Mrs Monique Johns

Owned by the Burtonwood Brewery so with Burtonwood brews and others from Jennings, plus Marston's Pedigree and a couple of guests changed weekly.

An eighteenth-century olde-worlde traditional inn serving homemade food and a good range of beers. Displays of old advertising on the walls and water jugs hanging from the ceiling. Food available 12–2pm Mon–Sat and 12–3pm Sun. Two en-suite bedrooms. Car park. Children allowed (children's menu available). Located off the A50 Junction 1, signposted Shardlow. Turn left just before the bridge over the River Trent, close to Shardlow Marina.

 *11am–3pm and 5–11pm Mon–Sat; 12–4pm and 7–10.30pm Sun. All day in summer.*

SMALLEY

The Bell Inn

Main Road, Smalley, Ilkeston DE7 6EF
☎ *(01332) 880635* Angela Bonsall

A freehouse with seven or eight real ales available at any one time. Adnams Broadside and ales from Mallard, Rooster's, Bateman, Crouch Vale, Nottingham and Whim Hartington regularly on offer plus Marston's Pedigree.

A two-roomed, Victorian-style pub. Food available 11.30am–2pm and 6–9pm (8.30pm Sun). Accommodation. Children welcome in the garden.

 *11.30am–2.30pm and 5–11pm Mon–Fri; all day Sat–Sun.*

STAVELEY

Speedwell Inn

Lowgates, Staveley, Chesterfield S43 3TT
☎ *(01246) 472252* Alan Wood

A freehouse whose owners run the Townes Brewery on the premises. At least four Townes brews, such as Sunshine and Golden Bud always available, plus occasional guests.

A traditional pub with occasional live music. Non-smoking area. No food. No children. Local CAMRA Pub of the Season for Winter 1999 and Pub of the Year 2000.

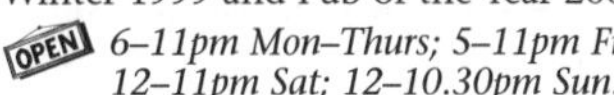 *6–11pm Mon–Thurs; 5–11pm Fri; 12–11pm Sat; 12–10.30pm Sun.*

SWINSCOE

The Dog & Partridge Country Inn

Swinscoe, Ashbourne DE6 2HS
☎ *(01335) 343183* Mr MJ Stelfox
www.dogandpartridge.co.uk

Greene King Old Speckled Hen and Marston's Pedigree usually available, plus one or two guest beers changed on a weekly basis.

Seventeenth-century inn, with olde-worlde beamed bar and log fire in winter. Restaurant and garden. Cosy lounges and sunny conservatory. Bar and restaurant food available all day, including breakfasts. Car park. Indoor and outdoor children's play areas, highchairs and special children's menu. Six miles from Alton Towers on the A52 between Ashbourne and Leek.

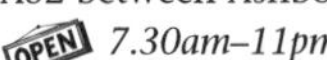 *7.30am–11pm.*

TICKNALL

The Staff of Life

7 High Street, Ticknall DE73 1JH
☎ *(01332) 862479* Christopher Nix
www.thestaffoflife.co.uk

Up to six real ales usually available. Marston's Pedigree, Timothy Taylor Landlord, Hop Back Summer Lightning and Greene King Old Speckled Hen are regulars. The guests rotate regularly.

A sixteenth-century oak-beamed genuine freehouse refurbished in early 2004. Bar and restaurant food at lunchtime and evenings, home-cooked British foods a speciality. Car park, beer garden and children's room. Now also offers accommodation. Families welcome, disabled facilities. At the south end of the village at the intersection between the main street and the Ashby-de-la-Zouch road.

11.30am–2.30pm and 6–11pm Mon–Fri; 11am–3pm and 6–11pm Sat; 12–3pm and 6–10.30pm Sun.

TIDESWELL

The George Hotel

Commercial Road, Tideswell, Buxton SK17 8NU
☎ *(01298) 871382* Mr Norris

A pub tied to Hardys & Hansons Kimberley Brewery, so with Kimberley Best and Classic always available. Also four guest beers, changed every six to eight weeks, including Hardys & Hansons seasonal ales.

A coaching house dating back to 1730, with separate dining area. Food served at lunchtime and evenings. Children allowed.

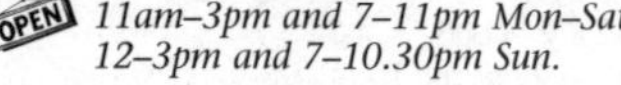
11am–3pm and 7–11pm Mon–Sat; 12–3pm and 7–10.30pm Sun.

WARDLOW MIRES

Three Stags' Heads

Wardlow Mires, Tideswell SK17 8RW
☎ *(01298) 872268* Mr and Mrs Fuller

Broadstone Brewery's Bitter, Abbeydale Black Lurcher (brewed exclusively for The Three Stags' Heads), Absolution and Matins permanently available, plus occasional guests.

A small seventeenth-century Peak District farmhouse pub with stone-flagged bar and its own pottery workshop. Unspoilt, with no frills, no piped muzak, no games machines. Live folk/Irish music at weekends. Bar food at lunchtime and evenings. Car park. Older children allowed (no babes-in-arms or toddlers). On the A623 at the junction with the B6465.

7–11pm Fri; 11am–11pm Sat; 12–10.30pm Sun (closed during the week).

WHALEY BRIDGE

Shepherd's Arms

7 Old Road, Whaley Bridge, High Peak SK23 7HR
☎ *(01663) 732384* Mr and Mrs Smith

A Marston's tenancy, where Banks's Mild, Marston's Bitter and Pedigree are always available, plus one guest beer, changed monthly.

Old-fashioned, traditional, family-orientated pub, with beautiful large beer garden. Bar snacks available. Children allowed. Families and dogs welcome.

4–11pm Mon (12–11pm bank hols); 2–11pm Tues–Fri; 12–11pm Sat; 12–10.30pm Sun.

WHITEHOUGH

The Oddfellows Arms

Whitehead Lane, Whitehough, Chinley, High Peak SK23 6EJ
☎ *(01663) 750306*
Miss JA Newton and Mr A Holland

Tied to Marston's, so always offers Marston's Bitter and Pedigree, plus one guest, changed monthly.

A one-bar country pub. Food served 12–7pm Mon–Sat and 12–5pm Sun. Children allowed.

11am–11pm Mon–Sat; 12–10.30pm Sun.

WOOLLEY MOOR

The White Horse Inn

Badger Lane, Woolley Moor, Alfreton DE55 6FG
☎ *(01246) 590319*
Forest Kimble and Keith Hurst
www.the-whitehorse-inn.co.uk

A freehouse with three or four real ales which often include Jennings Lakeland or Cumberland, Ruddles Best Bitter, Adnams Broadside, Black Sheep Bitter and Fuller's London Pride.

A two-bar pub with non-smoking areas in main lounge and conservatory for dining. Adventure playground, football goalposts, outside seating on three patios with 25 tables, disabled facilities. Food usually served 12–2pm and 6–9pm Mon–Sat and 12–8pm Sun. Hours more limited in January and February.

12–3pm and 6–11pm Mon–Sat; 12–10.30pm Sun.

THE BREWERIES

BARUM BREWERY

c/o Reform Inn, Reform Road, Pilton, Barnstaple EX31 1PD
☎ *(01271) 329994*
www.barumbrewery.co.uk

XTC 3.9% ABV
JESTER 4.2% ABV
ORIGINAL 4.4% ABV
BREAKFAST 5.0% ABV
Hoppy bitterness throughout.
FIRING SQUAD 5.3% ABV
CHALLENGER 5.6% ABV
Seasonals:
GOLD 4.0% ABV
Summer only.
MILD 4.2% ABV
LIQUID LUNCH 4.6% ABV
DARK STAR 4.8% ABV
BARUMBURG 5.1% ABV
TECHNICAL HITCH 5.3% ABV
BARNSTABLASTA 6.6% ABV
Winter only.

THE BEER ENGINE

Sweetham, Newton St Cyres, Nr Exeter EX5 5AX
☎ *(01392) 851282*
www.thebeerengine.co.uk

RAIL ALE 3.8% ABV
Amber-coloured, malty nose and flavour of fruit.
PISTON BITTER 4.3% ABV
Sweetness throughout, with some bitterness in the finish.
SLEEPER HEAVY 5.4% ABV
Red, with fruit, sweetness and some bitterness.
Seasonals:
RETURN TICKET 3.4% ABV
GOLDEN ARROW 4.6% ABV
PORTER 4.7% ABV
WHISTLEMAS 6.7% ABV

BLACKDOWN BREWERY

Units C5/C6 Dunkeswell Business Park, Dunkeswell, Honiton, Devon EX14 0RA
☎ *(01404) 891122*

BLACKDOWN BITTER 3.8% ABV
BLACKDOWN GOLD 4.3% ABV
BLACKDOWN PREMIUM 4.7% ABV
DARK SIDE 5.0% ABV
Plus seasonals.

THE BRANSCOMBE VALE BREWERY

Great Seaside Farm, Branscombe EX12 3DP
☎ *(01297) 680511*

BRANOC 3.8% ABV
Golden and malty with a light hop finish.
DRAYMANS BEST BITTER 4.2% ABV
BRANSCOMBE VALE BEST 4.6% ABV
House beer, may be sold under different names.
Seasonals:
ANNIVERSARY ALE 4.6% ABV
Light-coloured with clean, crisp hoppy flavour, Feb only.
HELLS BELLES 4.8% ABV
Oct–Mar. Smooth, mellow and hoppy.
SUMMA THAT 5.0% ABV
Golden, light and hoppy throughout, Mar–Oct.
YO HO HO 6.0% ABV
From November onwards. Fruity, and flavour packed.
Plus occasional brews.

CLEARWATER BREWERY

2 Devon Units, Hatchmoor Industrial Estate, Torrington EX38 7HP
☎ *(01805) 625242*

CAVALIER 4.0% ABV
TORRIDGE BEST 4.4% ABV
1646 4.8% ABV
OLIVER'S NECTAR 5.2% ABV
Plus occasional brews.

COUNTRY LIFE BREWERY

The Big Sheep, Abbotsham, Bideford EX39 5AP
☎ *(01237) 420808*

OLD APPLEDORE 3.7% ABV
Dark red colour and quenching.
WALLOP 4.4% ABV
Pale, easy-quaffing, summer brew.
GOLDEN PIG 4.7% ABV
Gold-coloured and well rounded.
COUNTRY BUMPKIN 6.0% ABV
Dark with malty sweetness.
Plus occasionals.

EXE VALLEY BREWERY

Silverton, Exeter EX5 4HF
☎ *(01392) 860406; Fax: (01392) 861001*

EXE VALLEY BITTER 3.7% ABV
A full-bodied bitter based on an old West Country recipe.

BARRON'S HOPSIT 4.1% ABV
A well-hopped bitter using Challenger hops.

DOB'S BEST BITTER 4.1% ABV
A finely balanced bitter with that extra touch of hops.

DEVON GLORY 4.7% ABV
A distinctive beer made from the finest Devon malt.

MR SHEPPARD'S CROOK 4.7% ABV
Premium bitter, full flavour of Devon malt and Challenger hops.

EXETER OLD BITTER 4.8% ABV
A smooth, well-hopped, strong beer.

Seasonals:

DEVON SUMMER 3.9% ABV
SPRING BEER 4.3% ABV
AUTUMN GLORY 4.5% ABV
DEVON DAWN 4.5% ABV
WINTER GLOW 6.0% ABV

Occasionals:

BARRON'S DARK 4.1% ABV
HOPE 4.3% ABV
CURATES CHOICE 4.8% ABV

THE JOLLYBOAT BREWERY

The Coach House, Buttgarden Street, Bideford EX39 2AU
☎ *(01237) 424343*

GRENVILLE'S RENOWN 3.8% ABV
FREEBOOTER 4.0% ABV

MAINBRACE 4.2% ABV
Light chestnut colour, late hopped for aroma.

PLUNDER 4.8% ABV
Dark red with Caribbean flavours. Fuggles hop.

PRIVATEER 4.8% ABV
Full-flavoured and hoppy. Mixed hop.

Seasonals:

BUCCANEERS 3.7% ABV
Nut-brown colour and hoppy. Summer.

CONTRABAND 5.8% ABV
Christmastide feasting ale/porter. Cascade hop.

Plus occasional brews.

MCBRIDE'S BREWERY

63 East Street, Newton Abbot TQ12 2JP
☎ *(01626) 353451*

MISCHIEF 4.2% ABV
RASCAL 4.6% ABV

O'HANLON'S BREWING CO.

Great Barton Farm, Clyst St Lawrence EX5 2NY
☎ *(01404) 822 412*
www.ohanlons.co.uk

FIREFLY 3.7% ABV
WHEATBEER 4.0% ABV
BLAKELEY'S BEST NO.1 4.2% ABV
DRY STOUT 4.2% ABV
MYRICA ALE 4.2% ABV
PORT STOUT 4.5% ABV
RED ALE 4.5% ABV
YELLOWHAMMER 4.2% ABV
ORGANIC RYE 5.0% ABV

ROYAL OAK 5.0% ABV
Formerly Eldridge Pope brew.

THOMAS HARDY 11.7% ABV
Bottle only. Formerly Eldridge Pope.

Plus seasonal brews.

OTTER BREWERY

Mathayes Farm, Luppit, Honiton EX14 4SA
☎ *(01404) 891285*
www.otterbrewery.com

BITTER 3.6% ABV
Pale brown. Hoppy, fruity aroma.

BRIGHT 4.3% ABV
Light and delicate with long malty finish.

ALE 4.5% ABV
OTTER CLAUS 5.0% ABV

HEAD 5.8% ABV
Smooth, strong and malty.

POINTS WEST BREWERY

Plymouth College of Further Education, Kings Road, Devonport, Plymouth PL1 5QG
☎ *(01752) 305700*

KITCHEN PORTER 4.4% ABV

DRAKE'S DRUM 4.8% ABV
Heavier bodied but still hoppy.

Seasonals:

ROOSTER 7.5% ABV
Brewed at Christmas, this is a Monastic Ale based on Monasteries in Belgium.

PRINCETOWN BREWERIES LTD

Tavistock Road, Princetown PL20 6QF
☎ *(01822) 890789*

DARTMOOR IPA/BEST 4.0% ABV
Pale, refreshing and hoppy.

JAIL ALE 4.8% ABV
Also available in bottles.

SCATTOR ROCK BREWERY

Unit 5, Gidley's Meadow, Christow, Exeter EX6 7QB
☎ *(01647) 252120*
www.scattorrockbrewery.com

SCATTY BITTER 3.8% ABV
TEIGN VALLEY TIPPLE 4.0% ABV
TOM COBLEY 4.2% ABV
DEVONIAN 4.5% ABV
GOLDEN VALLEY 4.6% ABV
VALLEY STOMPER 5.0% ABV
Plus the Tor Collection: two brews each month, named after local Tors.

SUMMERSKILLS BREWERY

Unit 15, Pomphlett Farm Industrial Estate, Broxton Drive, Billacombe, Plymouth PL9 7BG
☎ *(01752) 481283*
www.summerskills.co.uk

CELLAR VEE/BBB 3.7% ABV
Well-balanced.
BEST BITTER 4.3% ABV
Pale, with malty flavour and honey hints.
TAMAR 4.3% ABV
WHISTLEBELLY VENGEANCE 4.7% ABV
Dark ruby colour. Hop, dark malt and liquorice flavour.
INDIANA'S BONES 5.6% ABV
Rich, dark winter warmer.
Seasonals:
HOPSCOTCH 4.1% ABV
O'SUMMERSKILLS SHAMROCK STOUT 4.4% ABV
DEVON PILLS LOUTENBERG 4.5% ABV
DUNE PALE ALE 4.5% ABV
MENACING DENNIS 4.5% ABV
Robust and clean flavour.
WINTER WARMER 4.6% ABV
NINJA BEER 5.0% ABV
Winter ale. Rich and golden, with soft malt, hops and toffee flavour.

SUTTON BREWING COMPANY

31 Commercial Road, Coxside, Plymouth PL4 0LE
☎ *(01752) 205010*

DARTMOUTH PRIDE 3.8% ABV
PLYMOUTH PRIDE 3.8% ABV
XSB 4.2% ABV
WILD BLONDE 4.4% ABV
SUTTON COMFORT 4.5% ABV
BUMBLEBEE 4.5% ABV
MEDIVA STOUT 5.0% ABV
Seasonals:
HOPNOSIS 4.5% ABV
A summer ale.
EDDYSTONE LIGHT 4.8% ABV
KNICKADROPPA GLORY 5.5% ABV
A winter warmer.

TEIGNWORTHY BREWERY,

The Maltings, Teign Road, Newton Abbot TQ12 4AA
☎ *(01626) 332066*

REEL ALE 4.0% ABV
Hoppy, dry session beer.
SPRING TIDE 4.3% ABV
Sweet, copper-coloured brew, with hops throughout.
OLD MOGGIE 4.4% ABV
Golden, hoppy, citrus ale, ideal for hot summer weather.
BEACHCOMBER 4.5% ABV
Light in colour with citrus taste.
MALTSTERS ALE 5.0% ABV
Winter ale, rich and dark but highly drinkable.
CHRISTMAS CRACKER 6.0% ABV
Smooth rich seasonal brew.
Plus occasional brews.

THE PUBS

ABBOTSKERSWELL

Court Farm Inn

Wilton Way, Abbotskerswell, Newton Abbot TQ12 5NY
☎ *(01626) 361866* Mr Parker

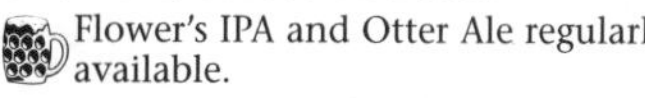

Flower's IPA and Otter Ale regularly available.

Large, busy and foody. Typical Devonshire longhouse with two bars. Food-led. Children welcome. Garden. Car park.

12–2pm and 6–9pm Mon–Sat; 12–8pm Sun.

APPLEDORE

Beaver Inn

Irsha Street, Appledore, Nr Bideford EX39 1RY
☎ *(01237) 474822* Graham Stone

Three real ales are usually on offer – but changing regularly.

Popular town pub with a wonderful location overlooking the estuary. Food lunchtime and evening. Children welcome. Patio with view of the sea. Pool table.

11am–3pm and 6–11pm Mon-Thur; all day Fri–Sun.

Coach and Horses

5 Market Street, Appledore, Nr Bideford EX39 1PW
☎ *(01237) 474470* Mandi Cloke

Freehouse serving Country Life's Old Appledore plus four other real ales perhaps Shepherd Neame Spitfire or Charles Wells Lock, Stock and Barrel.

Cosy backstreet pub – a traditional seventeenth century alehouse with real fire, real food and a warm welcome. Food served all day. Children welcome. Beer garden. Accommodation. Park on the quay.

10am–11pm Mon-Sat; 12–10.30pm Sun.

AXMOUTH

Harbour Inn

Axmouth, Seaton EX12 4AF
☎ *(01297) 20371* David Squire

Freehouse offering Otter Ale, Flower's Original and Flower's IPA.

A twelfth-century traditional-style pub with a large games room attractive to families. Food every session except Sunday night in the winter – home-produced lamb is the speciality. Children welcome. Car park. Garden. Pool table and skittle alley.

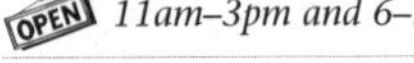

11am–3pm and 6–11pm.

The Ship Inn

Axmouth, Seaton EX14 4AF
☎ *(01297) 21838*
Christopher and Jane Chapman

Young's Special and Otter Bitter are permanents.

Pleasant pub, covered in creeper, with a resident owl and a variety of different rooms – one with a display of dolls. Food. Children welcome. Garden and car park. Skittle alley.

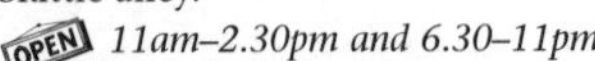

11am–2.30pm and 6.30–11pm.

BARNSTAPLE

The Check Inn

Castle Street, Barnstaple EX31 1DR
☎ *(01271) 375964* Steve and Mary Miller

Six hand pumps offer a constantly changing range of beers, direct from independent breweries around the UK. Also beer served on gravity.

A true freehouse with one bar, a friendly, local atmosphere and the usual pub games. Music (mainly blues/rock) on alternate Fri–Sat evenings. Car park. Children welcome.

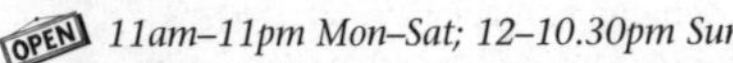

11am–11pm Mon–Sat; 12–10.30pm Sun.

BEER

Barrel O'Beer

Fore Street, Beer EX12 3EQ
☎ *(01297) 20099* Roberta Hunt

A freehouse offering Timothy Taylor Landlord, Fuller's London Pride, and two beers from Exe Valley, plus seasonals.

A family-run pub with a friendly welcome to all, serving real ale and local sea food. A clean and unfussy pub in historic fishing village. Food is locally sourced when possible. Children over 5 are welcome.

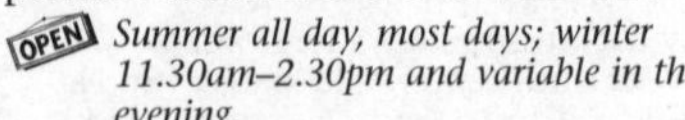

Summer all day, most days; winter 11.30am–2.30pm and variable in the evening.

BELSTONE

Tors

Belstone, Okehampton EX20 1QZ
☎ *(01837) 840689* Ann and Tony Cooper

Freehouse offering Sharp's Doom Bar and something from Palmers brewery.

Unpretentious country local in pleasant Dartmoor village. Popular with walkers. One bar. Reasonably priced food in every session. Accommodation. Children allowed in non-smoking dining area. Darts. Patio.

11am–3pm and 6–11pm Mon–Sat; 12–4pm and 7–10.30pm Sun; all day, every day in the summer.

BIDEFORD

The Kings Arms

The Quay, Bideford EX39 2HW
☎ *(01237) 475196* Paul Phipps

Jollyboat Grenville Renowned, Cotleigh Tawny and Greene King Abbot Ale are generally available.

Pleasant market-town pub in a building dating from 1560, with beams and log fires. One big bar, patio. Food served lunchtimes. Children allowed.

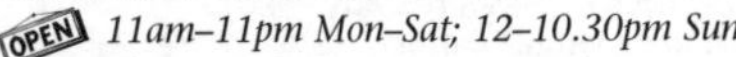

11am–11pm Mon–Sat; 12–10.30pm Sun.

BISH MILL

Bish Mill

Near South Molton EX36 3QF
☎ *(01769) 550944* Robert Sunley

Freehouse serving Oliver's Nectar and Cavalier from the Clearwater Brewery, plus Fuller's London Pride.

A warm, welcoming character pub with a large games room. Food. Small beer garden and small car park.

12–3pm and 6–11pm.

BLACKAWTON

The George Inn

Main Street, Blackawton, Totnes TQ9 7BG
☎ *(01803) 712342* Vic Hall and Ruth Coe

Teignworthy Spring Tide and Princetown Jail Ale always on sale in this freehouse. Guest beers change frequently, and often include Harviestoun Belgian White, Wychwood Hobgoblin, Heather Froach Ale, Palmers 200 or IPA.

An old village pub with eating area in the lounge bar. Four en-suite bed and breakfast rooms. Beer garden. Live bands occasionally. Food served at lunchtime and in the evening, with local produce used whenever possible. Children welcome.

12–2.30pm and 6.30–11pm Mon–Thur; 12–11pm Fri–Sun in the winter; 12–11pm every day in the summer.

BRANSCOMBE

The Fountain Head

Branscombe EX12 3AG
☎ *(01297) 680359* Mrs Luxton

Branscombe Vale Branoc, Hells Belles and Summa That often available. Guests (60 per year) include Hook Norton Old Hooky, Crouch Vale Millennium Gold and Freeminer Speculation Ale.

A fourteenth-century pub at the top of the village with flagstone floors, log fires and wood panelling. The lounge bar was formerly the village blacksmith's. Food at lunchtime and evenings. Car park, outside seating, non-smoking area and children's room. Self-catering accommodation.

 *11.30am–2.30pm and 6.30–11pm Mon–Sat; 12–3pm and 7–10.30pm Sun.*

The Mason Arms

Branscombe Village EX12 3DJ
☎ *(01297) 680300*
Murray Inglis and Mark Thompson

Five real ales always available including brews from Barum, Exmoor, Cottage, Cotleigh, Exe Valley, O'Hanlon's and further afield. An annual beer festival takes place each July.

Originally a one-bar Devon cider house in the middle of a row of cottages, now a thatched freehouse comprising the lot. Beams, slate floors, stone walls and open fires. Front terrace and side garden. Good food served at lunchtime and evenings. A 17-mile drive from Exeter and a 12-minute walk from the sea. Accommodation.

 *11am–11pm (12-10,30pm Sun).*

BRENDON

The Rockford Inn

Brendon, Nr Lynton EX35 6PT
☎ *(01598) 741214* Barrie Jon Marden

Three real ales on offer over a summer weekend, otherwise generally two. Rockford Ale from St Austell is a popular one.

Seventeenth-century riverside inn, in quiet village at the heart of Exmoor. Food served 12–2.30pm and 7–9pm. Small beer garden and accommodation. Car park. Children's room.

 *12–3pm and 6–11pm Mon–Fri; 12–11pm Sat; 12–3pm and 6.30–10.30pm Sun.*

BROADHEMPSTON

Coppa Dolla Inn

Broadhempston, Totnes TQ9 6BD
☎ *(01803) 812455* Philip Saint

A freehouse with two guest ales, changed every two weeks, always available. These will usually include a local or regional bitter.

A country pub with restaurant area and delightful beer garden. Food at lunchtime and evenings. Children allowed. Easy to find, once you're in Broadhempston.

 *11.30am–3pm and 6.30–11pm (10.30pm Sun).*

BUCKFASTLEIGH

The White Hart

2 Plymouth Road, Buckfastleigh TQ11 0DA
☎ *(01364) 642337* Geoff Hutchings

A freehouse with Teignworthy Beachcomber, Gale's HSB and a house ale always on the menu, plus one guest, changed every two days.

An olde-worlde pub, Grade II listed, with flagstone floors and log fires. One bar, background music. Partitioned dining area and family room. Food served at lunchtime and evenings (not Sun evening). Three bed and breakfast rooms (two en-suite). Children allowed.

 *12–11pm Mon-Sat (10.30pm Sun).*

CHAGFORD

Bullers Arms

7 Mill Street, Chagford TQ13 8AW
☎ *(01647) 432348*
Alex and Karen Duxbury-Watkinson

An Enterprise tenancy offering four real ales in the summer and three in the winter, usually something from either Otter or Butcombe.

Pleasant friendly local with an open space feel in Dartmoor market town. Accommodation. Food every session. Children welcome. Court yard. Darts.

 *11am–3pm and 5–11pm Mon–Thur; all day Fri–Sun.*

CHIPSHOP

The Chipshop Inn

Chipshop, Gulworthy, Tavistock Pl19 8NT
☎ *(01822) 832322* S Kirkham

Freehouse offering Sharp's Doom Bar as a permanent and two guests, which may include Fuller's London Pride or Shepherd Neame Spitfire.

A traditional and friendly rural pub in Dartmoor. Food every session, and yes they do serve chips! Garden and car park. Children allowed. Skittle alley and darts.

 *12–2.30pm and 5–11pm Mon–Fri; 12–11pm Sat; 12–10.30 Sun.*

CHITTLEHAMPTON

The Bell

The Square, Chittlehampton EX37 9QL
☎ *(01769) 540368* Mr and Mrs Jones

Eight or nine real ales always available, from breweries such as Cotleigh, Clearwater, Greene King or any independent brewery. Range of 150 different whiskies are also available.

Village community pub in an unusual building on the Square, overlooking the church. Food available. Non-smoking conservatory, dining area, garden, orchard, skittle alley and function room. Children, and dogs on leads, are allowed.

 *11am–3pm and 6–11pm Mon–Fri; 11am–11pm Sat; 12–10.30pm Sun.*

CHUDLEIGH

Bishop Lacy

Fore Street, Chudleigh TQ13 0HY
☎ *(01626) 854585* Robin Bishop

Freehouse offering O'Hanlon's Firefly and Skinner's Cornish Knocker on a regular basis, also Princetown Jail Ale served from the barrel. Plus one or two guests.

An old pub, covered in flowers in the summer, with a strong reputation. Food served lunchtime and evening. Children and dogs welcome. One or two beer festivals each year.

 *11am–11pm Mon–Sat; 12–10.30pm Sun.*

COCKWOOD

Anchor Inn

Cockwood, Nr Starcross EX6 8RA
☎ *(01626) 890203* Terry Morgan

Otter Ale, Fuller's London Pride, Greene King Abbot and Old Speckled Hen and Wadworth 6X are permanents.

A charming low-ceiling pub furnished in dark wood. Delightful vine-covered terrace overlooking the harbour. Food led – previously won best food pub UK – speciality seafood. Best Seafood Pub 2003. Children welcome. Car park.

 *11am–11pm Mon–Sat; 12–10.30pm Sun.*

COLEFORD

New Inn

Coleford, Crediton EX17 5BZ
☎ *(01363) 84242* Mr PS Butt

A freehouse with Bodmin Boar by Ring O' Bells and Badger Best permanently available.

A thirteenth-century thatched pub, with lots of oak beams. Restaurant and bar meals available. Food served lunchtimes and evenings. Six luxury bedrooms. Well-behaved children allowed.

 *12–2.30pm and 6–11pm Mon–Sat; 7–10.30pm Sun.*

COLYTON

Gerrard Arms

Rosemary Lane, Colyton EX24 6LN
☎ *(01297) 552588* Roy Turner

A freehouse offering a couple of real ales including Branscombe Vale Branoc.

Cosy one-bar local in pleasant village. Food available every lunchtime, also every evening in the summer but only Fri and Sat nights in the winter. Children welcome. Garden. Skittle alley.

 *11am–3pm and 6–11pm Mon–Sat; 12–3pm and 7–10.30pm Sun.*

COMBEINTEIGNHEAD

The Wild Goose

Combeinteignhead, Newton Abbot TQ12 4RA
☎ *(01626) 872241* Jerry and Kate

A freehouse offering 40 different real ales a month. Regularly featured are Otter Bright, Princetown Jail Ale, Teignworthy Springtide, Skinner's Betty Stogs and Exe Valley Devon Glory, plus ales from other independent West Country brewers.

A seventeenth-century, traditional, family-run country village pub with real open fires. Extensive menu with an emphasis on homemade fare, with fresh fish and vegetarian dishes always available. Separate dining room and beer garden.

 *11.30am–2.30pm and 6.30–11pm Mon–Sat; 12–3pm and 7–10.30pm Sun.*

COMBE MARTIN

The Castle Inn

High Street, Combe Martin EX34 0HS
☎ *(01271) 883706*
Alan and Sharon Stephenson

Four and sometimes five real ales are available at this freehouse.

A village pub, with one bar and a big-screen TV. Bar food served 12–9pm seven days a week. Restaurant open Thur, Fri and Sat evenings. Large car park and garden. Children and dogs allowed.

 *12–11pm (10.30pm Sun).*

Ye Olde George & Dragon

Castle Street, Combe Martin EX34 0HX
☎ *(01271) 882282* Craig Davey

A freehouse with beers from Barum and St Austell always served.

Village pub, club and restaurant in a 400-year-old building, with three bars. Meals served throughout. Pool, darts, patio. Children allowed. Ring for directions, as it is easy to miss.

 *4–11pm Mon–Wed; 4pm–1am Thurs–Sat; 12–10.30pm Sun.*

CREDITON

The Crediton Inn

28A Mill Street, Crediton EX17 1EZ
☎ *(01363) 772882* Diane Heggadon

A freehouse with Sharp's Doom Bar Bitter always available, plus three guests changed every two days. Examples include Branscombe Vale Branoc and Teignworthy Reel Ale.

A friendly local, with skittle alley and function room. Bar meals and snacks. No children.

 *11am–11pm Mon–Sat; 12–2pm and 7–10.30pm Sun.*

DARTMOUTH

The Cherub Inn

13 Higher Street, Dartmouth TQ6 9RB
☎ *(01803) 832571* Laurie Scott
www.the-cherub.co.uk

A freehouse with Cherub Best Bitter (Summerskills) and three other real ales that change every month. These are typically from Brakspear, Cains, Everards, Exmoor, Jennings, Shepherd Neame or Young's.

A 600-year-old pub, very small with beams and open fire. Air-conditioned cellar. Bar food at lunchtimes and evenings. Over-10s only in the restaurant at certain times, no under-14s in the bar.

 *11am–11pm Mon–Sat; 12–10.30pm Sun.*

DODDISCOMBSLEIGH

The Nobody Inn

Doddiscombsleigh, Nr Exeter EX6 7PS
☎ *(01647) 252394* Nick Borst-Smith

Nobody's House Ale always available plus two guest beers (at least 70 per year) which may include Blackawton Headstrong, Sarah Hughes Dark Ruby Mild, Otter Bitter and RCH East Street Cream.

A sixteenth-century inn with beams and inglenook fireplaces. Food available in the bar at lunchtimes and in the restaurant in the evenings. Speciality cheeses. Car park and garden. Accommodation unsuitable for children under 14. Three miles southwest of Exeter racecourse.

 *12–2.30pm and 6–11pm.*

DUNSFORD

Royal Oak

Dunsford EX6 7DA
☎ *(01647) 252256* Mark Harrison

Greene King Abbot Ale and Princetown Jail Ale are permanent with up to three rotating guest beers.

A light and open Victorian village pub. Accommodation. Food lunchtime and evening. Children welcome. Car park. Garden. Pool.

 *12–2.30pm and 6.30–11pm (7–10.30pm Sun and Mon).*

EXETER

Double Locks Hotel

Canal Bank, Exeter EX2 6LT
☎ *(01392) 256947* Jenny Hale

Young's Bitter, Special, Waggle Dance and Winter Warmer are always available. There will be beers from the Jollyboat, Scattor Rock, O'Hanlon's and Otter breweries, with some guests to make up a choice of about 12 different brews.

The pub is located in a 250-year-old building situated by twin locks on the oldest ship canal in the country. Bar food is available all day. Car park, large garden, volleyball, barbecue in summer and children's room. Located on the south-west edge of the city, through the Marsh Barton Trading Estate.

 *11am–11pm Mon–Sat; 12–10.30pm Sun.*

Great Western Hotel

St David's Station Approach, Exeter EX4 4NU
☎ *(01392) 274039* Mr R Kaushall

Fuller's London Pride, Adnams Broadside and Bitter and a beer from Exe Valley always available, plus a number of guests to make ten different beers during the week and 14 at weekends. These may include favourites such as Orkney Dark Island and Greene King Old Speckled Hen.

A traditional freehouse within a hotel. Exeter and East Devon CAMRA Pub of the Year 2001, South West CAMRA Pub of the Year 2002. Staff pride themselves on looking after their customers. Thirty-five bedrooms with en-suite facilities. Background music. Live music on bank holidays. Food served all day. Children allowed.

 *11am–11pm Mon–Sat; 12–10.30pm Sun.*

EXMOUTH

The Grove

The Esplanade, Exmouth EX15 2AZ
☎ *(01395) 272101* Chris Whitehead

A Young's pub offering Bitter, Special and Triple A, plus Smiles IPA.

A quiet pub with one bar downstairs and another upstairs for eating. Food at lunchtime and evenings. Children allowed.

11am–11pm Mon–Sat; 12–10.30pm Sun.

GEORGEHAM

The Rock Inn

Rock Hill, Georgeham EX33 1JW
☎ *(01271) 890322* Mr and Mrs Scutts

Up to six real ales usually available. Greene King Abbot, Fuller's London Pride and Cotleigh Golden Eagle are permanently served. There are usually two guest beers from local breweries such as Cotleigh and Barum.

A 400-year-old inn one mile from the sea. Bar food available at lunchtime and evenings. North Devon Pub Food Silver Award winner in 2000 and 2001. Car park, garden and conservatory. Children's room and children's area.

 *11am–4pm and 6–11pm Mon–Fri; all day Sat–Sun.*

HALWELL

Old Inn

Halwell, Nr Totnes TQ9 7JA
☎ *(01803) 712329* Mr Crowther

A freehouse with RCH East Street Cream always on offer. There is also one guest, changed sporadically.

A food and beer pub, with dining area and background music. Food at lunchtime and evenings. Accommodation. Children allowed.

 *11am–3pm and 6–11pm Mon–Sat; 12–3pm and 6–10.30pm Sun.*

HATHERLEIGH

Tally Ho Country Inn

14 Market Street, Hatherleigh EX20 3JN
☎ *(01837) 810306* Ady Taylor

Offers Cavalier, Torridge Best and Oliver's Nectar from the Clearwater brewery.

An inn that used to be the town bakery. Bar and restaurant food available at lunchtime and evenings. Garden, accommodation. Children allowed.

 *11am–2.30pm and 6–11pm.*

HOLBETON

Mildmay Colours

Holbeton, Plymouth PL8 1NA
☎ *(01752) 830248* Louise Price

Mildmay Colours Best (Skinner's) always on the menu in this freehouse. One guest, changed weekly, is sourced locally.

A traditional country pub with upstairs dining and bar area. Occasional rock and jazz bands. Food at lunchtime and evenings. Children allowed.

 *11am–3pm and 6–11pm Mon–Sat; 12–3pm and 7–10.30pm Sun.*

HORNDON

The Elephant's Nest

Horndon, Nr Mary Tavy PL19 9NQ
☎ *(01822) 810273* Peter Wolfes

Palmers IPA and Copper, St Austell HSD always available, plus one changing guest, perhaps Exmoor Gold or Otter Bright. Also draught cider.

This sixteenth-century Dartmoor inn with a large garden and log fires has a collection of 'Elephant's Nests' written in different languages on the beams in chalk. Bar food and à la carte menu at lunchtime and evenings. Car park and children's room. Large garden includes cricket pitch and overlooks Dartmoor. Travel along the A386 into Mary Tavy. Take the road signposted Horndon for just under two miles.

 *12–3pm and 6–11pm Tues–Sat; 12–3pm Sun; closed Sun evening and Mon.*

HORSEBRIDGE

The Royal Inn

Horsebridge TL19 8PJ
☎ *(01822) 870214* Catherine Eaton

A freehouse with a Cotleigh and a Sharp's brew always available. Two guests also offered in the summer.

An old pub with open fires, patio and beer garden. Food at lunchtime and evenings. Children allowed at lunchtime only.

12–3pm and 6.30–11pm (10.30pm Sun).

IDDESLEIGH

Duke of York

Iddesleigh EX19 8BG
☎ *(01837) 810253* J Stewart

A freehouse, with all real ales served straight from the barrel; no pumps used. Adnams Broadside and Cotleigh Tawny are always available, plus numerous guest beers which change daily. Wye Valley brews are a favourite.

A pub in a rural setting (ring for directions!). Occasional live music. Separate dining area. Food served all day. Children allowed.

11am–11pm Mon–Sat; 12–10.30pm Sun.

INSTOW

The Quay

Marine Parade, Instow EX39 4HY
☎ *(01271) 860624* Steven Lock

Ales from the pub's own Fremington micro-brewery are regularly among the beers on offer.

Traditional seaside pub overlooking estuary of River Torridge, with an emphasis on real ale and food, especially seafood. Impromptu live music. Outside seating, restaurant. Children allowed.

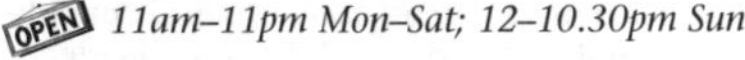
OPEN *11am–11pm Mon–Sat; 12–10.30pm Sun.*

LAPFORD

The Old Malt Scoop Inn

Lapford, Nr Crediton EX17 6PZ
☎ *(01363) 83330* Colin Comasso

Marston's Pedigree, Otter Best, Sharp's Doom Bar and Special Ale, plus a couple of guests. Also traditional cider.

This sixteenth-century freehouse is open for morning coffee, bar snacks, meals and cream teas. There are inglenook fireplaces, beamed ceilings, panelled walls, skittle alley, beer garden, patio areas and car park. Children are allowed in the sun lounge and one of the bars. Lapford is on the A377 between Crediton and Barnstaple. Follow brown tourist signs near village. The inn is at the centre of the village, opposite the church.

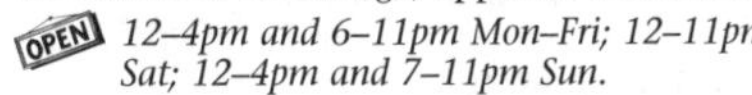
OPEN *12–4pm and 6–11pm Mon–Fri; 12–11pm Sat; 12–4pm and 7–11pm Sun.*

LOWER ASHTON

The Manor Inn

Lower Ashton, Teign Valley, Nr Exeter EX6 7QL
☎ *(01647) 252304* GW and CMS Mann

A freehouse with Teignworthy Reel Ale, RCH Pitchfork and Princetown Jail Ale always on offer, plus one guest, which could be from anywhere!

Informal rural pub in the heart of the scenic Teign Valley. No games machines, no piped music, just good conversation! There is an emphasis on food, served 12–1.30pm and 7–9.30pm Tues–Sun (until 9pm Sun). Children allowed in garden only. Car park. Located on the B3193, about five miles from Chudleigh.

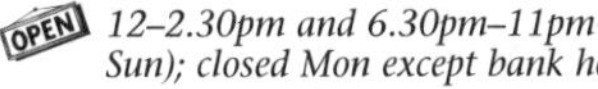
OPEN *12–2.30pm and 6.30pm–11pm (10.30pm Sun); closed Mon except bank holidays.*

LYMPSTONE

Redwing

Church Road, Lympstone EX8 5JT
☎ *(01395) 222156* Dave and Jackie Moir

Greene King Abbot, Palmers IPA and Otter Bitter are permanents, plus one guest.

Atmospheric local in attractive village on the River Exe estuary. Home-cooked food every session except Sunday evening. Children over 5 welcome in the restaurant area. Garden and car park.

OPEN *11am–3pm and 6–11pm Mon–Fri; all day Sat–Sun.*

MARY TAVY

The Mary Tavy Inn

Lane Head, Mary Tavy PL19 9PN
☎ *(01822) 810326* Mr Brown

Freehouse serving Princetown Jail Ale and two guests, quite likely something from Sharp's.

Unpretentious and welcoming roadside community pub. Children welcome. Food every session. Accommodation. Garden and car park. Pool and darts. On the A386.

OPEN *12–2.30pm and 6–11pm; closed Mon lunchtime.*

MONKLEY

The Bell Inn

Monkley EX39 5JS
☎ *(01805) 622338* Sue Smith and Jock Tierney

A freehouse with beers from Barum Brewery permanently available, plus two monthly guests, with ales from Clearwater and West Berkshire regular favourites.

Fifteenth-century thatched village pub with dining area. Food served 12–9pm. Pool and darts, live music, garden. Accommodation available – a single, a double and a twin. Car park. Children allowed.

OPEN *12–11pm (10.30pm Sun).*

MORTEHOE

The Chichester Arms

Chapel Hill, Mortehoe, Woolacombe EX34 7DU
☎ *(01271) 870411* John and Marsha Huxtable

Barum Original and a Cottage brew always available plus one guest from a local micro.

Mortehoe's original village inn, built as a vicarage in 1620. Converted in 1820, it is basically unchanged since and is still partly gas lit, although it does also have its own electricity generator. Food served 12–2pm and 6–9pm every day. Children's room and garden. Car park.

*Winter: 12–2.30pm and 6.30–11pm Mon–Fri; 12–11pm Sat; 12–10.30pm Sun. Summer: 11.30am–11pm Mon–Sat; 12–10.30pm Sun.*

NEWTON ABBOT

Dartmouth Inn

63 East Street, Newton Abbot TQ12 2JP
☎ *(01626) 353451* Francis McBride

Princetown Dartmoor IPA plus four regularly changing guest beers (up to 500 per year) may include RCH East Street Cream, Sarah Hughes Dark Ruby Mild, Teignworthy Springtide and Sutton Knickerdroppa Glory. Plus their own brews Mischief and Rascal.

This 450-year-old pub is reputed to be the oldest inn in Newton Abbot. Beautiful beer garden, a previous Bloom of Britain winner. The pub has also won the regional CAMRA Pub of the Year award on several occasions. Five minutes' walk from the station. Bed and breakfast.

11am–11pm Mon–Sat; 12–10.30pm Sun.

NEWTON POPPLEFORD

Cannon Inn

High Street, Newton Poppleford EX10 0DW
☎ *(01395) 568266* Tony Pitcher

Ringwood Best is on permanently and there is one rotating guest.

Welcoming village pub with a nautical flavour; pictures of ships on the walls and a fishing boat hanging from the ceiling in the bar. Food lunchtime and evening. Accommodation. Children welcome. Garden and car park. Skittle alley and pool table. Live music every other Sun.

*11.30am–2.30pm and 5–11pm Mon–Sat; 12–3pm and 7–10.30pm Sun.*

NEWTON ST CYRES

The Beer Engine

Sweetham, Newton St Cyres, Nr Exeter EX5 5AX
☎ *(01392) 851282 Fax (01392) 851876*
Peter and Jill Hawksley
www.thebeerengine.co.uk

Rail Ale, Piston Bitter and Sleeper Heavy brewed on the premises and always available. Seasonals brewed occasionally.

The brewery was established along with a cellar bar in the basement of a former station hotel in 1983. It has now expanded to produce three brews and supplies a couple of local pubs and wholesalers. Homemade food available at lunchtime and evenings. Car park, garden. Children allowed.

*11am–11pm Mon–Sat; 12–10.30pm Sun.*

NORTH TAWTON

Fountain Inn

Exeter Street, North Tawton EX20 2HB
☎ *(01837) 82551* Lesley Whitehouse

A freehouse with St Austell Daylight Robbery, Charles Wells Bombardier, and Greene King Old Speckled Hen always available.

A large, lively and friendly pub. Separate, non-smoking dining area. Food at lunchtime and evenings. Well-behaved children allowed.

*11.30am–2.30pm and 5.30–11pm Mon–Fri; all day Sat–Sun.*

Railway Inn

Whiddon Down Road, North Tawton EX20 2BE
☎ *(01837) 82789* Claire Bolt

A freehouse with Teignworthy Reel Ale always available. Regular guests include Teignworthy Beachcomber, Adnams Broadside and ales from Skinner's.

An old country inn, on the main road but slightly hidden, with one bar and dining area. Bar snacks and evening meals. Children allowed.

*12–3pm (not Mon) and 6–11pm Mon–Sat; 12–3pm and 7–10.30pm Sun.*

OKEHAMPTON

Plymouth Inn

26 West Street, Okehampton EX20 1HH
☎ *(01837) 53633* Geoff and Jill Hoather

A freehouse, with beers served straight from the barrel. Accent on brews from the West Country, though others are often featured.

A country-style town pub with restaurant, beer garden and function room. Local CAMRA Pub of the Year 2002. Mini beer festivals and occasional folk bands. Food at lunchtime and evenings. Children allowed; function room doubles as children's room.

*12–11pm (10.30pm Sun).*

OSSABOROUGH

The Old Mill

Ossaborough, Woolacombe EX34 7HJ
☎ *(01271) 870237* D Huxtable

A beer from the Barum brewery is usually available.

Once a mill, this seventeenth-century country pub has plenty of olde-worlde charm and retains many decorative features. Food is served 12–2pm and 6–9pm. Children welcome, outdoor play area. Barbecue and carvery every day in the summer. Car park. Take the first right-hand turning out of Woolacombe.

 *Winter: 12–3pm and 6–11pm (10.30pm Sun); Summer: 11am–11pm (10.30pm Sun).*

OTTERY ST MARY

The Kings Arms

Gold Street, Ottery St Mary EX10 1GT
☎ *(01404) 812486* Graham Hudson

Branscombe Vale Summa That and Branoc are generally available, plus Hells Belles in the winter.

Unpretentious town-centre local with large-screen TV. Car Park. Pool and darts. Two beer festivals held each year. Karaoke Sun evening.

 *6–11pm Mon–Fri; 11am–11pm Sat; 12–10.30pm Sun.*

PETER TAVY

Peter Tavy Inn

Peter Tavy, Tavistock PL19 9NN
☎ *(01822) 810348*

Freehouse serving Princetown Jail Ale, Sharp's Doom Bar and Summerskills Tamar on a permanent basis plus two guest beers.

A charming fifteenth century inn serving good food and real ale in an attractive Dartmoor village. Two large rooms. Children welcome. Garden and car park. A couple of miles off the A386.

 *12–3pm and 6–11pm (10.30pm Sun).*

PILTON

The Reform Inn

Reform Street, Pilton, Barnstaple EX31 9PD
☎ *(01271) 323164* Esther Hatch

A wide variety of Barum ales always available.

The Reform Inn offers a pool table, darts and shove ha'penny. The Barum Brewery is situated behind the pub, but is separately owned.

 *11.30am–11.30pm (10.30pm Sun).*

PLYMOUTH

The Clifton

35 Clifton Street, Greenbank, Plymouth PL4 8JB
☎ *(01752) 266563* Mr Clark

Clifton Classic (house beer brewed by Summerskills) always on offer. Two guests, changed weekly, may include beers from anywhere in the UK, with Orkney Dark Island a particular favourite.

A locals' pub, with one bar and Sky TV for football. No food. No children. Not far from the railway station.

3.30–11pm Mon–Thurs; 11am–11pm Fri–Sat; 12–10.30pm Sun.

The Prince Maurice

3 Church Hill, Eggbuckland, Plymouth PL6 5RJ
☎ *(01752) 771515* Rick and Anne Dodds

Eight real ales always available, including Badger Tanglefoot, Summerskills Best and Adnams Broadside, plus many and various guest beers.

Small, seventeenth-century freehouse with two bars and log fires. Local CAMRA Pub of the Year 1994, 1995, 2000 and 2001. Weekday lunchtime bar snacks. Car park, patio.

 *11am–3pm and 7–11pm Mon–Thurs; all day Fri–Sat; 12–4pm and 7–10.30pm Sun.*

Porters

20 Looe Street, Plymouth PL4 0EA
☎ *(01752) 662485* Denise Vessey

Six real ales are available, changed every two or three days. Sharp's Doom Bar, Greene King Old Speckled Hen and Fuller's London Pride regularly featured.

A town-centre pub with exposed brickwork and lots of bric-à-brac. Background music. Raised area at top of pub for eating. Beer garden. Food served at lunchtimes and evenings. Children allowed.

12–11pm Mon–Sat (9pm Sun).

Thistle Park Brewhouse

32 Commercial Road, Plymouth PL4 0LE
☎ *(01752) 204890* Quentin and Debbie Style

A brewpub with ales from the Sutton Brewing Company always served. Brewing began in 1993.

Polished wooden floors, maritime relics and oil paintings by a local artist. Bar food and a range of South African cuisine served at lunchtime and evenings. Parking, patio. Live bands.

12pm–2am (12.30am Sun).

PLYMSTOCK

The Boringdon Arms

13 Boringdon Terrace, Turnchapel, Nr Plymstock PL9 9TQ
☎ *(01752) 402053* Barry Elliott
www.bori.co.uk.

Butcombe Bitter and RCH Pitchfork always available plus four guests beers (250 per year) from Orkney (north), Butts (south), Skinner's (west), Scott's (east) and all points in between.

An ex-quarrymaster's house with a good atmosphere. No juke box. Live music on Saturday nights. CAMRA's first Plymouth Pub of the Year, and Plymouth CAMRA's Pub of the Year for 1999/2000. Bar food available at lunchtime and evenings. Conservatory and beer garden in the old quarry to the rear of the pub. Accommodation. Bi-monthly beer festivals. Located at the centre of the village, four miles south-east of Plymouth, on south coast footpath. Signposted from the A379.

11am–11pm Mon–Sat; 12–10.30pm Sun.

PRINCETOWN

The Prince of Wales

Tavistock Road, Princetown PL20 6QF
☎ *(01822) 890219* Mr and Mrs Baker

Princetown Jail Ale and Dartmoor IPA are always available, as well as one guest, with beers from St Austell a regular feature.

Family-run bar in a 150-year-old building, full of character. Food available all day, and there is a small restaurant. Children allowed. En-suite bed and breakfast. Car park.

11am–11pm Mon–Sat; 12–10.30pm Sun.

RINGMORE

The Journey's End

Ringmore, Nr Kingsbridge TQ7 4HL
☎ *(01548) 810205* Mark Genders

Four West Country ales changing regularly – just three in the winter.

A thirteenth-century inn with flagstone floors and open fires. Bar and restaurant food served at lunchtime and evenings. Conservatory, car park, garden, non-smoking dining room. Accommodation.

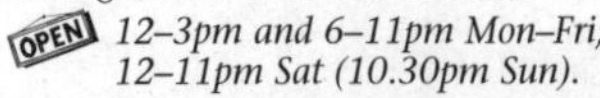
12–3pm and 6–11pm Mon–Fri; 12–11pm Sat (10.30pm Sun).

ST GILES IN THE WOOD

The Cranford Inn

St Giles In The Wood, Torrington EX38 7LA
☎ *(01805) 623309*
Paul Owens and Nicola Newcombe

Exmoor Ale and Gold are permanent, with one changing guest.

Food-oriented country pub in a converted farmhouse, with restaurant, garden and patio. Car parking. Children allowed. On the B3227, the only pub on the road!

12–2.30pm and 6–11pm (10.30pm Sun).

SIDBURY

Red Lion

Fore Street, Sidbury EX10 0SD
☎ *(01395) 597313* Colin Isaacson

Freehouse serving Adnams Bitter and Wadworth 6X on a permanent basis, plus one guest sourced locally.

Friendly traditional local, former coaching inn, with wooden beams and brasses. Food served in both sessions. Children welcome. Garden. Darts and skittles. Accommodation. Occasional beer festival.

12–3pm and 6–11pm Mon–Fri; all day Sat; 12–3pm and 7–10.30pm Sun.

SIDMOUTH

The Swan Inn

37 York Street, Sidmouth EX10 8BY
☎ *(01395) 512849* Adrian Ricketts

A Young's pub offering the full range.

A traditional pub. Local fish is a speciality. Garden. Two real ale festivals in the summer.

11am–2.30pm (3pm Sat) and 5.30–11pm (10.30pm Sun).

SILVERTON

Silverton Inn

Fore Street, Silverton, Nr Exeter EX5 4HP
☎ *(01392) 860196* Shane Radmore

Exe Valley Dob's Best Bitter always available, plus a guest. Greene King Abbot is a favourite.

Traditional, cosy wooden pub between Exeter and Tiverton with easy access to sea coasts and shopping towns. Food available evenings. Well-equipped luxury rooms are available. Nearby parking, beer garden. Killerton House, a National Trust property, is close.

11.30am–3pm and 6–11pm.

SLAPTON

The Tower Inn

Slapton, Nr Kingsbridge TQ7 2PN
☎ *(01548) 580216*
Andrew and Annette Hammett

Adnams Best, Badger Tanglefoot and St Austell Tribute usually available plus a couple of guests.

A fourteenth-century inn offering accommodation and a superb garden. Bar and restaurant food available at lunchtime and evenings. Car park. Hidden in the centre of the village at the foot of the old ruined tower.

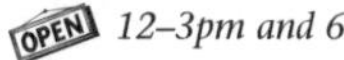 *12–3pm and 6–11pm.*

SOUTH ZEAL

Oxenham Arms

South Zeal, Okehampton EX20 2JT
☎ *(01837) 840244* Paul Lucas

Freehouse always offering a beer from the Sharp's brewery and also one other, straight from the barrel.

One of the oldest inns in Devon, first licensed in 1477, located in interesting Dartmoor village. Accommodation. Food every session. Children welcome. Garden.

 *11am–3pm and 5–11pm Mon–Sat; 12–2.30pm and 7–10.30pm Sun.*

STAVERTON

Sea Trout Inn

Staverton, Nr Totnes TQ9 6PA
☎ *(01803) 762274*
Nick and Nicky Brookland

A Palmers pub offering IPA, Gold and 200.

Many people's idea of the idyllic Devon inn. Nice local feel to public bar and a large lounge bar. Food served every session – on very big plates! Children welcome. Car park and garden. Accommodation.

 *11am–3pm and 6–11pm Mon–Sat; 12–3pm and 7–10.30pm Sun.*

STICKLEPATH

Devonshire Inn

Sticklepath, Okehampton EX20 2NW
☎ *(01837) 840626*
John and Ann Verner-Jeffreys

Freehouse serving St Austell Tinners and Hicks Special Draught straight from the barrel and cooled from passing stream.

Thatched pub with loads of character. Keys hang from low beams, and there is a big fireplace and strange photographs. Food if ordered in advance, also bar snacks. Children allowed but not in bar area. Car park. Garden. Dogs welcome. Accommodation only with dogs. Bar billiards and other games.

 *11am–3pm and 5–11pm Mon–Thur; all day Fri–Sat; 12–3pm and 7–10.30pm Sun.*

STOKENHAM

The Tradesman's Arms

Stokenham, Kingsbridge TQ7 2SZ
☎ *(01548) 580313*
Nick and Rebecca Abbott
www.thetradesmansarms.co.uk

Brakspear bitter always available plus a guest beer from a local brewery if possible.

Welcoming, picturesque country pub, well known locally for its imaginative and interesting food. Good range of malt whiskies. Food served every session except Sun and Mon nights in the winter. Car park. Situated 100 yards off the A379 Kingsbridge to Dartmouth road.

 *11.30am–3pm and 6–11pm Mon–Fri; 11.30am–3pm and 6.30–11pm Sat; 12–3pm and 7–10.30pm Sun. Open all day Sat–Sun in good summer weather.*

TAVISTOCK

The Halfway House

Grenofen, Tavistock PL19 9ER
☎ *(01822) 612960* Peter Jones

A freehouse with Sharp's Doom Bar Ale, Sharp's Special, Fuller's London Pride and Shepherd Neame Spitfire always available, plus one guest.

A country inn on the A386. Public bar. Background music. Separate dining and lounge bar. Food, emphasis on the home made, served every lunchtime and evening. Children allowed. Pets welcome. En-suite accommodation available.

 *11.30am–2.30pm and 5.30–11pm Mon–Sat; 12–3pm and 6.30–10.30pm Sun.*

TEIGNMOUTH

The Blue Anchor

Teign Street, Teignmouth TQ14 8EG
☎ *(01626) 772741* Paul Fellows

A freehouse serving Adnams Broadside, Marston's Pedigree and Teignworthy Reel Ale. Three guests, changed two or three times a week, include favourites such as Greene King Abbot, Fuller's ESB or something from Bateman or Branscombe Vale.

A small, very boozy, locals' pub. Old, with log fire. Rolls only. No children. Beer garden.

 *11am–11pm Mon–Sat; 12–10.30pm Sun.*

The Golden Lion

85 Bitton Park Road, Teignmouth TQ14 9BY
☎ *(01626) 776442* John Hardy

At least two guest beers (approx 50 per year) usually available from regional brewers such as Teignworthy or Exe Valley.

This is a locals' pub on the main road just out of the town with a public and lounge bar. Darts and pool are played. Bar food is available at lunchtime and evenings. Small car park. Children not allowed.

 *12–4pm and 6–11pm (10.30pm Sun).*

TOPSHAM

Bridge Inn

Bridge Hill, Topsham, Nr Exeter EX3 0QQ
☎ *(01392) 873862*
Mrs Caroline Cheffers-Heard
www.cheffers.co.uk.

Nine or ten real ales usually available, which may include Branscombe Vale Branoc, Exe Valley Exeter Old, Otter Ale, Blackawton West Country and a O'Hanlon's brew, plus seasonal brews from local breweries.

This sixteenth-century pub overlooking the River Clyst has been in the same family since 1897 through four generations. Simple bar food at lunchtime. Car park. Two miles from M5 junction 30. Topsham is signposted from the exit. In Topsham, follow the yellow signpost (A376) to Exmouth.

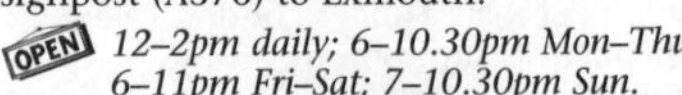 *12–2pm daily; 6–10.30pm Mon–Thurs; 6–11pm Fri–Sat; 7–10.30pm Sun.*

TORQUAY

Chelston Manor

Old Mill Road, Torquay TQ2 6HW
☎ *(01803) 605142* Nina and Mark

Fuller's London Pride always available, and two guests such as Wadworth 6X, Marston's Pedigree or Sharp's Doom Bar.

Unique olde-worlde pub in the heart of Torquay. Home-cooked meals served 12–2.30pm and 6–9.30pm daily. Large walled beer garden. Car park. Children welcome. Follow sign for Chelston and Cockington Village.

 *11am–3pm and 5.30–11pm Mon–Thurs; all day Fri–Sun. Open all day, every day June–Sept.*

Crown & Sceptre

2 Petitor Road, St Marychurch, Torquay TQ1 4QA
☎ *(01803) 328290* Mr R Wheeler

Eight real ales always available, including Fuller's London Pride, Young's Special, Marston's Pedigree and Greene King Old Speckled Hen. Plus two guest ales from around the country.

A traditional pub with two bars, children's room and garden. Live music. Food at lunchtimes only. Children allowed.

 *11am–3pm and 5.30–11pm Mon–Thur; 11am–11pm Fri; 11am–4pm and 6.30–11pm Sat; 12–4pm and 7–10.30pm Sun.*

TUCKENHAY

Maltsters Arms

Bow Creek, Tuckenhay TQ9 7EQ
☎ *(01803) 732350*
Quentin and Denise Thwaites
www.tuckenhay.com

A freehouse with Princetown Dartmoor IPA always available. Two or three guests also served, with regulars including brews from Teignworthy, Scattor Rock, Blackawton, Cottage and Exmoor. Over 100 different guest ales served last year. Young's Special London Ale (bottle conditioned) is also stocked.

A traditional country pub with separate eating area overlooking the river. Bed and breakfast, with themed bedrooms. Barbecues on the river bank. Occasional live music. Food served 12–3pm and 6.30–9.30pm every day (except Christmas Day). Children allowed in certain areas. In the middle of nowhere. If you manage to find Tuckenhay, you'll find the pub.

 *11am–11pm Mon–Sat; 12–10.30pm Sun (12–2pm Christmas Day).*

UMBERLEIGH

The Rising Sun

Umberleigh EX37 9DU
☎ *(01769) 560447* Malcolm Andrew Hogg

Cotleigh Tawny Bitter and Barn Owl are available on a permanent basis.

Inn in a traditional building, with restaurant, patio and nine bedrooms. Local folk musicians have jamming sessions every Monday (not Bank Holidays). Car park. Children allowed. On the A377 between Barnstaple and Exeter.

11.30am–3pm and 6–11pm (10.30pm Sun).

WEST DOWN

The Crown Inn

The Square, West Down
☎ *(01271) 862790* Russ Trueman

Barum Original usually available plus one guest beer (two in the summer). This might be another Barum beer, Wadworth 6X, Greene King Abbot Ale, Marston's Pedigree or local ales of interest.

A small seventeenth-century village pub with open fire, non-smoking area and delightful garden. Food served in separate restaurant 12–2pm and 6–10pm. Children welcome. Accommodation. Car park. Follow tourist signs between Braunton and Ilfracombe and Lynton Cross and Mullacott Cross.

12–3pm and 6–11pm Mon–Sat; 12–4pm and 7–10.30pm Sun.

WESTWARD HO!

Pig on the Hill

West Pusehill, Westward Ho!, Bideford EX39 5AH
☎ *(01237) 425889* Simon Curtis

The original home to the Country Life Brewery, with the four beers rotated on the pumps. Bottle versions of the home brews also available.

Friendly country inn in rural setting with food available each session. Garden, terrace and children's play area. Games room and giant TV. Petanque club.

12–3pm and 6.30–11pm Mon–Sat; 12–3pm and 7–10.30pm Sun.

WHIDDON DOWN

Post Inn

Exeter Road, Whiddon Down, Okehampton EX20 2QT
☎ *(01647) 231242* Miriam Short

Freehouse always offering three or four local brews but always changing, perhaps something from Exe Valley or Scattor Rock.

Popular roadside pub. Serves a nice pint but also food-orientated. One bar for three areas. Children welcome. Car park. Patio.

11am–11pm Mon–Sat (closed all day Tues); 12–10.30pm Sun.

WHIMPLE

New Fountain Inn

Church Road, Whimple, Exeter EX5 2TA
☎ *(01404) 822350* Paul Mallett

A freehouse with Teignworthy, O'Hanlon and Branscombe Vale beers usually on the menu. Guest beers (one from the barrel) come from local independent breweries.

A family-run village inn split into two tiers, the top one used for eating. Food served at lunchtime and evenings. Children and dogs welcome. Heritage centre on the site.

12–2.30pm and 6.30–11pm Mon–Sat; 12–2.30pm and 7–10.30pm Sun.

WINKLEIGH

The Kings Arms

Fore Street, Winkleigh EX19 8HQ
☎ *(01837) 83384* Julia Franklin and Chris Guy

Flower's IPA, Butcombe Best and Skinner's Cornish Knocker are usually available.

Traditional, thatched country pub in pretty village. Food available all day, every day. Children welcome, but no special facilities. Follow signs 'To the village'.

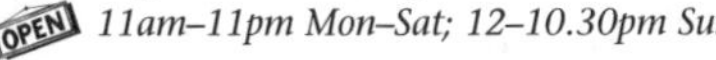
11am–11pm Mon–Sat; 12–10.30pm Sun.

The Royal Oak

The Square, Winkleigh, Dolton EX19 8QF
☎ *(01805) 804288* Myfanwy Jones

Fuller's London Pride and Princetown Dartmoor Best are permanent.

Large village pub in a fourteenth/sixteenth-century building, with restaurant, two main bars and snug. Food served. Pool table, darts, skittles, garden. Car parking available. At the end of the village.

12–11pm every day (closed Wed lunchtime and Tue).

YARDE DOWN

Poltimore Arms

Yarde Down, South Molton EX36 3HA
☎ *(01598) 710381* Richard Austen

A freehouse with real ales served straight from the barrel. Cotleigh Tawny Ale is always available, and during the summer there may well be a guest.

Dates back to 1600. Has its own generator for electricity. Food served; a very large menu. Children allowed. In the middle of nowhere; best to ring for directions.

12–2.30pm and 6.30–11pm Mon–Sat; 12–2.30pm and 7–10.30pm Sun.

THE BREWERIES

DORSET BREWING COMPANY (THE QUAY BREWERY)
Brewers Quay, Hope Square, Weymouth DT4 8TR
☎ *(01305) 777515*

WEYMOUTH HARBOUR MASTER 3.6% ABV
Rounded and easy-drinking.
SUMMER KNIGHT 3.8% ABV
Award-winning wheat beer. Available May–Oct.
WEYMOUTH BEST BITTER 4.0% ABV
Gold and well-balanced.
WEYMOUTH JD 1742 4.2% ABV
Quenching bittersweet flavour.
QUAY STEAM BEER 4.5% ABV
Aromatic and full-flavoured. American hops.
JURASSIC 4.7% ABV
DURDLE DOOR 5.0% ABV
SILENT KNIGHT 5.9% ABV
Dark wheat beer.
Plus occasional beers.

GOLDFINCH BREWERY
47 High East Street, Dorchester DT1 1HU
☎ *(01305) 264020*

TOM BROWN'S BITTER 4.0% ABV
Hoppy throughout.
FLASHMAN'S CLOUT 4.5% ABV
Balanced and flavoursome.
MIDNIGHT SUN 4.5% ABV
Occasional.
MIDNIGHT BLINDER 5.0% ABV
Sweet malt with balancing hoppiness.
Plus occasional brews.

HALL AND WOODHOUSE BREWERY (BADGER)
Blandford St Mary, Blandford Forum DT11 9LS
☎ *(01258) 452141*
www.tanglefoot.co.uk

BEST BITTER 4.0% ABV
Fruity with refreshing finish.
CHAMPION 4.6% ABV
Delicate hop and citrus flavours.
TANGLEFOOT 5.1% ABV
Pale, full fruit, with bittersweet finish.

JC AND RH PALMER
Palmers Brewery, West Bay Road, Bridport DT6 4JA
☎ *(01308) 422396*
www.palmersbrewery.com

BRIDPORT BITTER 3.2% ABV
Refreshing, with hops and bitterness throughout.
COPPER ALE 3.7% ABV
Session ale, with fruit throughout.
DORSET GOLD 4.5% ABV
Golden with delicate fruity hoppiness.
BEST BITTER 4.2% ABV
Well-balanced and good hop character.
200 5.0% ABV
Smooth, full-flavoured and complex.
TALLY HO! 5.5% ABV
Nutty and distinctive.

THE PUBS

BEAMINSTER

The Greyhound Inn
11 The Square, Beaminster DT8 3AW
☎ *(01308) 862496* Peter Smith

A Palmers house offering Tally Ho!, 200, IPA and Copper Ale.

Small, warm and friendly pub set right on the town square. Food every session. Children welcome. Traditional games such as table skittles and darts. Parking on the square.

 *11.30am–3pm and 6.30–11pm Mon–Thur; 11.30am–3pm and 5–11pm Fri; all day Sat and Sun.*

BENVILLE

The Talbot Arms
Benville, Dorchester DT2 0NN
☎ *(01935) 83381* Brian Dash

A freehouse serving Branscombe Vale Drayman's Best Bitter, plus one guest, which may be another beer from Branscombe Vale, or one from a wide range of other breweries.

A country pub/restaurant with beer garden. Food served at lunchtime and evenings. Campsite. Children allowed.

OPEN *11am–11pm.*

BOURNEMOUTH

The Goat & Tricycle

27–9 West Hill Road, Bournemouth BH2 5PF
☎ *(01202) 314220* James and Trish Blake

Wadworth 6X, Henry's Original IPA and JCB always available, plus seven regularly changing guests.

A traditional pub with family area and courtyard. No juke box, background music only. No children in the bar. Food served lunchtimes and evenings.

OPEN *12–3pm and 6–11pm Mon–Sat; 12–3pm and 7–10.30pm Sun.*

Moon in the Square

4–8 Exeter Road, Bournemouth BH2 5AQ
☎ *(01202) 652090* Dave and Terri Lea

Four guest real ales always available, with Shepherd Neame Spitfire a regular feature.

A traditional Wetherspoon's pub with non-smoking bar. Food served all day. Beer garden. Disabled facilities. Children welcome.

OPEN *All day, every day.*

BRADPOLE

The King's Head Inn

Bradpole, Bridport DT6 3DS
☎ *01308 422520* Barry Lurkins

A Palmers house, with Palmers IPA and Copper Ale permanently available. Other beers from Palmers, such as 200, Tally Ho! and Dorset Gold, appear as guests.

Traditional 400-year-old village pub with two bars and a dining area. Food available. Entertainment and quiz nights once a month. Garden and patio. Two letting rooms. Car parking. Well-behaved children and dogs allowed. On the main road from Bridport to Yeovil.

11am–2.30pm and 6–11pm Mon–Sat; 12–2.30pm and 6–10.30pm Sun.

BRANKSOME

Branksome Railway Hotel

429 Poole Road, Branksome, Poole BH12 1DQ
☎ *(01202) 769555*
Bill Whiteley and Debbie Ellery

An Enterprise pub with a weekly guest beer policy. Hampshire Strong's Best always available, plus two changing guests from Cottage, Hop Back, Brains, Fuller's, Jennings and many more.

Victorian pub built in 1894. Two bars, games including pool and darts. Live music/disco at weekends, Sunday afternoon entertainment a must! Sunday lunches. B&B in large, comfortable en-suite accommodation. Located on the A35, opposite Branksome Railway Station.

OPEN *All day, every day.*

BRIDPORT

The Crown Inn

59 West Bay Road, Bridport DT6 4AX
☎ *(01308) 422037*
Ian Hendry and Karen Phillips

Tied to Palmers, with a range of the brewery's beers available (Bridport Bitter, IPA, 200).

Family-run pub in a very old building on the edge of town. One bar, dining area, garden and rear patio. Food available all day. Live music most Saturdays. Children allowed. On the main A35, look out for the entrance 50 yards on right-hand side of the B3157.

OPEN *12–11pm (10.30pm Sun).*

BUCKLAND NEWTON

Gaggle of Geese

Buckland Newton, Nr Dorchester DT2 7BS
☎ *(01300) 345249* Trevor and Janet Marpole

Freehouse serving Badger Best, Butcombe Best, Ringwood Fortyniner and Best.

A community country pub decorated with unusual objects and anything goose-like. Internet access for customers. Holds two geese auctions a year. Food every session. Well-behaved children welcome. Garden and car park. Skittle alley and darts.

OPEN *12–2.30pm and 6.30–11pm.*

BURTON BRADSTOCK

Anchor Inn

High Street, Burton Bradstock, Nr Bridport DT6 4QF
☎ *(01308) 897228* John Plunkett

Three real ales usually available including Wychwood's Hobgoblin.

Pleasant gastropub that specialises in shellfish. Food every session. Children welcome. Patio and car park. Accommodation. Table skittles and darts.

OPEN *All day, every day.*

CATTISTOCK

The Fox & Hounds

Duck Street, Cattistock
☎ *(01300) 320444* David Hubling

Palmers IPA, Copper and 200 or Gold always available plus occasional guests.

A fifteenth-century village inn with large fires, flagstones and a separate restaurant. Relaxing atmosphere. Bar and restaurant food available at lunchtime and evenings. Parking, garden and play area opposite. Campsite nearby. Accommodation. On the A37, look out for the sign for Cattistock, just past the Clay Pigeon Cafe from Yeovil or the sign on the road from Dorchester.

OPEN *12–2.30pm and 6.30–11pm.*

CERNE ABBAS

Royal Oak

23 Long Street, Cerne Abbas DT2 7JG
☎ *(01300) 341797* David Birch

Freehouse with Greene King Speckled Hen and Butcombe Best as permanents, plus three other guest beers.

A low-ceilinged sixteenth century pub decorated with brasses and cups. A friendly comfortable tourist gastropub that hasn't lost its character. Children welcome. Courtyard. Located in the centre of the village.

11.30am–3pm and 6.30–11pm.

CHARMOUTH

The Royal Oak

The Street, Charmouth DT6 6PE
☎ *(01297) 560277* Mr and Mrs Prosser

Tied to Palmers, with Bridport Bitter, Copper and IPA always on offer, plus 200 occasionally.

A village pub built in the 1870s, with beams, open fires in winter and one through bar. Bar snacks available. Children allowed.

12–3.30pm and 7–11pm (10.30pm Sun).

CHETNOLE

The Chetnole Inn

Chetnole, Sherborne DT9 6NU
☎ *(01935) 872337* David and Jane

A freehouse with Branscombe Vale Branoc Ale, Butcombe Bitter and Palmers IPA permanently available, plus a range of guest beers.

A two-bar village pub with background music and occasional small live bands. Beer garden and dining area. Food served at lunchtime and evenings, except Wednesdays. Children welcome. Opposite the church.

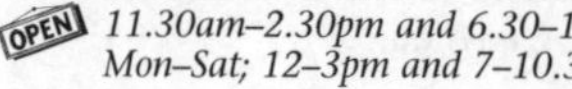
11.30am–2.30pm and 6.30–11pm Mon–Sat; 12–3pm and 7–10.30pm Sun.

CHIDEOCK

The Anchor Inn

Seatown, Chideock, Bridport DT6 6JU
☎ *(01297) 489215* Paul Wiscombe
www.theanchorinn.co.uk

A Palmers house with IPA and Palmers 200 permanently available, plus Tally Ho! and Copper occasionally.

Situated in the centre of a little cove, nestled under the Golden Cap Cliff which is the highest point on the south coast. A World Heritage site, area of outstanding natural beauty, with National Trust land all around. Food available all day in summer, lunchtimes and evenings in winter. Well-behaved children and dogs allowed. Beer garden with terraces overlooking the sea and the south west coastal path. Accommodation. From A35 travel south to Chideock.

Summer (end May–September): all day, every day. Winter: 11am–2.30pm and 6–11pm (10.30pm Sun).

CHILD OKEFORD

Saxon Inn

Gold Hill, Child Okeford DT11 8HD
☎ *(01258) 860310* Peter and Helen

Three real ales always available, including Ringwood Best, something from Butcombe, and a variety of popular brews from around the country.

A friendly, traditional, old village pub with two cosy log fires. Good, tasty, home-cooked food from a varied menu served every day except Sunday evenings. At the rear of the pub is a country garden with ample seating.

12–2.30pm and 7–11pm Mon–Fri; 12–3pm and 7–11pm Sat; 12–10.30pm Sun.

CHRISTCHURCH

The Ship

48 High Street, Christchurch
☎ *(01202) 484308* Nicole Thomas

Ringwood Fortyniner and Best and Greene King Abbot Ale are always on offer, plus occasional guests.

Steeped in history, with a welcoming atmosphere and excellent staff, this claims to be the oldest (and busiest!) pub in Christchurch. Recently refurbished. A wide range of traditional and special food, mostly homemade, is served lunchtimes and every evening in the summer, lunchtimes only in winter. Children welcome. Patio area. Car park. Situated on main street opposite Woolworths.

11am–11pm Mon–Sat; 12–10.30pm Sun.

CHURCH KNOWLE

The New Inn

Church Knowle, Wareham BH20 5NQ
☎ *(01929) 480357* Mr M Estop

Wadworth 6X is a permanent fixture, and the one guest beer might be something like Greene King Old Speckled Hen.

Beamed sixteenth-century food-oriented pub that has been run by the same family since 1985 (they also run The Farmer's Arms, Lower Apperley, Glos), and has featured in several food guidebooks. Part stone, part thatched, with fires in winter, two bars and non-smoking dining area. Garden, car park. Children allowed in one bar.

 *11am–3pm and 6–11pm (10.30pm Sun); opening hours change in winter, so call first to confirm.*

CORFE CASTLE

The Fox Inn

8 West Street, Corfe Castle BH20 5HD
☎ *(01929) 480449* AL Brown

A freehouse generally serving about four real ales straight from the barrel at any one time. Fuller's London Pride, Greene King Old Speckled Hen and Wadworth 6X are regulars.

A traditional, old-fashioned, olde-worlde pub dating back to 1568. A long and narrow building with a garden overlooking the castle. Food every session.

 *11am–3pm (2.30pm in the winter) and 6.30–11pm.*

The Greyhound

The Square, Corfe Castle BH20 5EZ
☎ *(01929) 480205* Jacci Pestana

Seven real ales are always available but changing every couple of weeks. Fuller's London Pride, Black Sheep Bitter and Timothy Taylor Landlord are some of the favourites.

An interesting inn with lots of small rooms including a family room with games. There is a lovely terrace and beer garden just by the entrance to the castle. Children, cyclists, walkers and dogs are all welcome. Accommodation. Food every session, barbecues in the summer, and a weekend carvery. Music at weekends. Beer festivals in May and September with over 40 real ales.

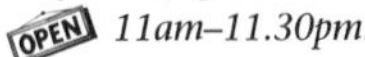 *11am–11.30pm.*

CORFE MULLEN

Coventry Arms

Mill Street, Corfe Mullen BH21 3RH
☎ *(01258) 857284* John Hugo

Freehouse serving local beers straight from the barrel, including Ringwood Best and Fortyniner, plus other guests as available.

An old-style, one-bar country pub with food served at lunchtime and evenings in a separate dining area. Children allowed. Located on the main A31.

 *10am–3pm and 5–11pm Mon–Fri; all day Sat–Sun.*

CORSCOMBE

The Fox Inn

Corscombe, Nr Beaminster DT2 0NS
☎ *(01935) 891330* Clive Webb

Exmoor Ale and Butcombe Bitter are the permanent beers here, with one guest ale in the summer.

Sixteenth-century thatched country pub, with log fire, flagstone floors and beams. No music. A wide variety of food is served in the pub's four dining areas. Garden, car park. Four letting rooms. Well-behaved children allowed. On the Halstock road, on the outskirts of Corscombe.

 *12–3pm and 7–11pm (10.30pm Sun) (afternoon closing times may vary).*

CRANBORNE

The Sheaf of Arrows

The Square, Cranborne BH21 5PR
☎ *(01725) 517456*
Craig Adams and Wendy McLaren

Ringwood Best Bitter regularly available plus four constantly changing guest beers.

Small, friendly village local with lots of passing trade. Open fires in both bars. Garden and skittle alley. Home-cooked food served 12–2pm and 7–9pm daily. Accommodation.

 *12–3pm and 6–11pm Mon–Thur (closed Mon lunchtime); 12–11pm Fri–Sun.*

DORCHESTER

Blue Raddle

Church Street, Dorchester DT1 1JN
☎ *(01305) 267762* Michael Sharpe

Otter Ale is a permanent with three regularly changing guests.

Small, market-town pub. Food served 12–2pm Tues–Sat and in the evening Wed–Sat. No children.

 *11.30am–3pm and 7–11pm Mon–Sat; 12–3pm Sun.*

Tom Brown's

47 High East Street, Dorchester DT1 1HU
☎ *(01305) 264020* Alan Finch

Home to the Goldfinch brewery, generally three of their beers are available.

A locals' pub. Darts.

 *11am–3pm and 5.30–11pm Mon–Thur; all day Fri–Sat; 12–4pm and 7–10.30pm Sun.*

EAST CHALDON

Sailor's Return

East Chaldon, Dorchester DT2 8DN
☎ *(01305) 853847* Michael Pollard

Freehouse with Strongs from Hampshire Brewery and Ringwood Best as permanents and four constantly changing guests, Badger Tanglefoot a favourite.

An eighteenth-century thatched pub in wonderful countryside and close to Lulworth Cove. Food lunchtime and evening. Children allowed in restaurant, dogs in bar. Car park. Garden. Spring bank holiday beer festival.

 *Winter: 11am–2.30pm and 6.30–11pm; summer: 11am–11pm.*

EVERSHOT

Acorn Inn

28 Fore Street, Evershot DT2 0JW
☎ *(01935) 83228* Todd Moffat

A freehouse serving Branscombe Vale Draymans Best and Branoc, plus Ringwood Best.

A sixteenth century inn with basic traditional bar for locals and a posher non-smoking side for residents. Thomas Hardy connection – Tess of the D'Urbervilles stayed here. Food every session. Garden and car park. Skittles, pool, darts and table football.

11am–11pm.

EYPE

The New Inn

Eype DT6 6AP
☎ *(01308) 423254* Steve Tuck

A Palmers tied house, with four pumps serving the range of Palmers brews, changed regularly.

Village pub in a traditional building. Food is available, and there is a separate dining area. Garden, patio. Small car park. Children allowed.

12–3pm and 6–11pm Mon–Sat; 12–3pm and 7–10.30pm Sun.

GILLINGHAM

Phoenix Inn

The Square, Gillingham SP8 4AY
☎ *(01747) 823277* Adrian Clarke

Badger Sussex Bitter and Best always available plus one seasonal.

Friendly town-centre local with one bar and a dining area. Food every session. Well-behaved children welcome. Patio. Shove ha'penny.

10am–2.30pm (3pm Sat) and 7–11pm; 12–3pm and 7–10.30pm Sun.

HINTON ST MARY

The White Horse

Hinton St Mary, Sturminster Newton DT10 1NA
☎ *(01258) 472723* Mr T Spooner-Green

A freehouse serving a wide range of real ales (two per week) on a rotating basis including Ringwood Best and True Glory plus brews from Tisbury and Cottage Breweries. One light beer (under 3.9% ABV) and one heavy (over 4% ABV) always available. On Fridays one real ale is selected for a special offer at £1.50 per pint.

A busy nineteenth-century pub. Public bar, lounge bar and beer garden. Restaurant area in the lounge with à la carte menu and specials plus Sunday roasts. Food served at lunchtime and evenings. Children allowed.

11.45am–3pm and 6.15–11pm Mon–Sat; 12–3pm and 7–10.30pm Sun.

HURN

Avon Causeway Hotel

Hurn, Christchurch BH23 6AS
☎ *(01202) 482714* Keith Perks

Up to seven real ales available, including Wadworth 6X, Ringwood Best and Old Thumper, plus guests. Traditional cider also on offer.

A quaint country hotel, ten minutes from Bournemouth. Formerly Hurn railway station, the pub is decorated with lots of railway bric-à-brac. CAMRA and Cask Marque approved. Food served at lunchtime and evenings in a separate large lounge. Murder mystery nights are a feature, and make use of an old Victorian carriage. Beer garden with large children's play area. Inside, children are allowed in dining area only.

All day, every day.

LANGTON HERRING

The Elm Tree Inn

Langton Herring, Weymouth DT3 4HU
☎ *(01305) 871257* Mr Brickle

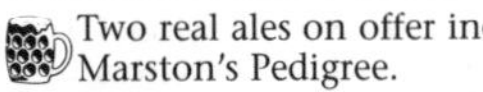
Two real ales on offer including Marston's Pedigree.

Traditional old country inn, close to Chesil beach and set in quiet village. Nice garden. Food every session. Children welcome. On the B3154 between Abbotsbury and Weymouth.

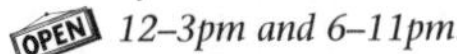
12–3pm and 6–11pm.

LODERS

The Loders Arms

Loders, Nr Bridport DT6 3SA
☎ *(01308) 422431* Jane Legg

Palmers 200, IPA and Bridport Bitter are always available.

Country village pub, a traditional Dorset longhouse, over 200 years old. Food served. Fires, dining area, garden, patio and car park. Two letting rooms, occasional live music in garden. Children allowed.

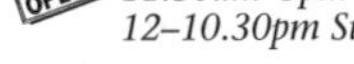
11.30am–3pm and 6–11pm Mon–Sat; 12–10.30pm Sun.

LOWER BURTON

The Sun Inn

Lower Burton, Nr Dorchester DT2 7RX
☎ *(01305) 250445* Robin Maddex

Three to five constantly changing cask ales available.

A traditional coaching inn with the motto 'Good Beer and Good Cheer'. Garden and disabled facilities. Carvery and bar menu served 12–2.30pm and 6.30–10pm Mon–Sat and 12–9.30pm Sun. Car park. Children's menu and high chairs available. Situated half a mile from Dorchester town centre on the Sherbourne road.

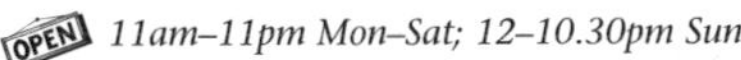
11am–11pm Mon–Sat; 12–10.30pm Sun.

LYME REGIS

The Nag's Head

Silver Street, Lyme Regis DT7 3HS
☎ *(01297) 442312* Mrs Hamon

A freehouse with up to four ales available, perhaps including Ringwood Best.

A traditional one-bar pub with background music and beer garden. Separate dining area. Food served Sunday lunchtime.

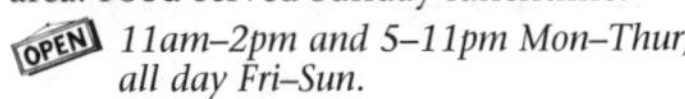
11am–2pm and 5–11pm Mon–Thur; all day Fri–Sun.

The Volunteer Inn

31 Broad Street, Lyme Regis DT7 3QE
☎ *(01297) 442214* JP O'Donnell

Fuller's London Pride and house ale Donegal which is brewed by Branscombe Vale are always available. Two constantly changing guest ales served. Regulars include St Austell IPA, Otter Bitter and Ale, Exmoor Ale and Sharp's Doom Bar.

A small, friendly pub with separate dining area and extensive bar menu; the emphasis is on food, drink and conversation. Food available 12–2pm and 6–9pm Tues–Sat, 12–2pm Sun. Children allowed in the dining area only. Located on the main high street, at the top of the hill.

11am–11pm Mon–Sat; 12–10.30pm Sun.

MARSHWOOD

The Bottle Inn

Marshwood, Bridport DT6 5QJ
☎ *(01297) 678254* Shane Pym

Freehouse serving Otter Bitter on a permanent basis. Greene King Old Speckled Hen is a regular and there are often brews from the Quay and Branscombe Vale breweries – generally four available at any time.

A quirky, unspoilt thatched pub built in 1585. Famous for nettle-eating competition. Sells organic coke and has a good range of vegetarian meals on its menu. Garden with strange horse in playground. Car park. Skittle alley. Children welcome. On the B3165 between Crewkerne and Lyme Regis.

12–3pm and 6.30–11pm; closed Mon in the winter.

NETTLECOMBE

Marquis of Lorne Inn

Nettlecombe, Nr Bridport DT6 3SY
☎ *(01308) 485236* Julie and David Woodrosse

A Palmers pub with Palmers 200, IPA and Copper permanently served.

Country pub with two bars and a restaurant, in a sixteenth-century farmhouse. The only pub in Dorset that is a member of the Campaign for Real Food, so the focus is on homemade food using local produce. Log fires in winter. Occasional live folk music. Large garden. Car park for 50. Seven double en-suite letting rooms. Children allowed. Half a mile from Powerstock.

 *12–2.30pm and 6.30–11pm Mon–Sat; all day Sun.*

NORTH WOOTTON

The Three Elms

North Wootton, Nr Sherborne DT9 5JW
☎ *(01935) 812881* Mr and Mrs Manning

Fuller's London Pride, Otter Bitter and Butcombe brews always available.

This busy rural roadside pub contains a large collection of 1,500 diecast model cars and lorries in display cabinets around the walls. Bar and restaurant food, including a large vegetarian selection, available at lunchtime and evenings. Children allowed. Accommodation. Situated on the A3030 Sherborne to Sturminster Newton road, two miles from Sherborne.

 *11am–2.30pm Mon–Sat, 12–3pm Sun; 6.30–11pm Mon–Thurs, 6–11pm Fri–Sat, 7–10.30pm Sun.*

PLUSH

The Brace of Pheasants

Plush DT2 7RQ
☎ *(01300) 348357* Toby and Suzie Albu

A freehouse with either Fuller's London Pride or Ringwood Best always available, plus two weekly rotated guests, perhaps ales from Butcombe or Adnams.

A sixteenth-century thatched village inn. Private dining/conference room, non-smoking restaurant area, large garden. Bar meals and snacks and à la carte restaurant food served lunchtimes and evenings. Well-mannered children and dogs allowed. Situated off B3142 Dorchester/Sherborne road.

 *12–2.30pm and 7–11pm Tue–Sat; 12–3pm and 7–10.30pm Sun; closed Mon.*

POOLE

Bermuda Triangle Freehouse

Parr Street, Lower Parkstone, Poole BH14 0JY
☎ *(01202) 748087* Gisela Crane

Four real ales constantly changing. Likes to support micros such as Stonehenge and Dark Star.

An interesting theme pub. Three German lagers on draught. Good music, great atmosphere. Bar food at lunchtime. Car park. Near Ashley Cross.

12–3pm and 5.30–11pm Mon–Fri; all day Sat–Sun.

The Blue Boar

29 Market Close, Poole BH15 1NE
☎ *(01202) 682247 Fax (01202) 661875*
Jim and Sheila Kellaway and
Tim and Clare Welford
www.blueboarpub.co.uk

A freehouse with five real ales available. Cottage Southern Bitter is a permanent feature, and the constantly changing guests are from independent breweries.

An unusual three-storey pub in a restored eighteenth-century listed mansion. Cellar bar with live music on Fri and Sun, open-floor music night on Wed, DJ (rock/blues/cajun/jazz/folk/chart) on Sat night. Food served 11.30am–2pm, and 5-8pm Mon-Fri. Pub games (shove ha'penny, darts), children's certificate while meals are served. Comfortable lounge bar on ground floor. Conference facility with bar on first floor.

 *11am–3pm and 5–11pm Mon–Fri; all day Sat and Sun.*

The Brewhouse

68 High Street, Poole BH15 1DA
☎ *(01202) 685288* Paul Slocombe

Tied to Milk Street Brewery, with Milk Street Mermaid and Beer always on offer.

A welcoming pub with a varied clientele. Pool table and darts team. Pub has narrow frontage on High Street, so could easily be missed.

All day, every day.

Hogs Head

35–7 High Street, Poole BH15 1AB
☎ *(01202) 670520* Sheila Killeen

A Hogshead-managed pub with Ringwood Best, Fuller's London Pride and Caledonian Deuchars IPA always available.

Town pub in a very old building. Air-conditioned, with excellent staff, games machines, log fires and non-smoking area. Food served 12–9pm. Recently refurbished. Children not allowed. To find the pub, face the High Street and walk towards the Quay from the Dolphin Centre.

OPEN *11am–11pm Mon–Sat; 12–10.30pm Sun.*

Sandacres Free House

3 Banks Road, Sandbanks, Poole BH13 7PW
☎ *(01202) 707244* Peter Fay (Manager)
www.thesandacres.co.uk

Ringwood Best and Fortyniner and Greene King Old Speckled Hen permanently available, plus two guests, usually from smaller local breweries such as Palmers.

A modern-style waterside pub in Poole Harbour with lovely views. One large bar, children's area, outside seating. Disabled facilities with no steps. Food served at lunchtimes and evenings. Children allowed until 9pm.

11.30am–3pm and 6–11pm Mon–Sat; 12–3pm and 7–10.30pm Sun.

PULHAM

Halsey Arms

Pulham, Dorchester DT2 7DZ
☎ *(01258) 817344* Tony and Sharon Carpenter

A freehouse serving five constantly changing beers, may include Greene King Old Speckled Hen and Fuller's London Pride.

A traditional pub with a friendly atmosphere – everyone welcome! Wide-ranging menu available, including carvery on Sunday lunchtimes, children's and over-60s' menus plus a good range of sandwiches. Happy hour. Large car park.

OPEN *12–3pm and 6–11pm Mon–Fri; 11am–11pm Sat; 12–10.30pm Sun.*

SANDFORD ORCAS

The Mitre Inn

Sandford Orcas DT9 4RU
☎ *(01963) 220271*
Cheryl Holloway and Allen Page

Greene King Abbot Ale and IPA and Charles Wells Bombardier are generally available.

Friendly country local in charming village. Flagstoned floors, armchairs and bookshelf in bar. Fresh food using local produce served every session except Monday evening. Children welcome. Car park. Garden.

11.30am–2.30pm and 7–11pm Mon–Sat; 12–3pm and 7–10.30 Sun.

SHAFTESBURY

Ship Inn

Bleke Street, Shaftesbury SP7 8JZ
☎ *(01747) 853219* Mark Tilbrook

Badger Tanglefoot and Best always available plus one constantly changing guest.

An old-style pub in attractive building and lots of small rooms. Decorated with plenty of pictures of ships. Food every session except Sunday night. Children welcome. Garden. Games including crib, pool, darts and boules.

OPEN *11am–11pm Mon–Sat; 12–10.30pm Sun.*

SHERBORNE

Britannia

Westbury, Sherborne DT9 3EH
☎ *(01935) 813300*
John and Emily Bolwell

Ringwood Best and Shepherd Neame Spitfire regularly available plus one guest perhaps Cornish Rebellion from Redruth.

Friendly town local just round the corner from the abbey. The pub was originally built in 1743 as a school for the poor girls of the town. Public bar and lounge. Accommodation. Food at lunchtime and evening. Children welcome during the day. Car park. Skittle alley.

OPEN *11am–2pm and 6–11pm Mon–Sat; 12–3pm and 7–10.30pm Sun.*

The Digby Tap

Cooks Lane, Sherborne DT9 3NS
☎ *(01935) 813148* Peter LeFevre

Twenty different beers served each week from a range of 100 per year. Brews from the Sharp's, Teignworthy, Ringwood, Exmoor, Otter and Cottage breweries, plus many other regional producers.

A traditional, local, one-bar pub with flagstone floors. Bar snacks available at lunchtime (not on Sundays). Children are allowed at lunchtime only. Just 100 yards from the abbey, towards the railway station.

OPEN *11am–2.30pm and 5.30–11pm Mon–Sat; 12–2.30pm and 7–10.30pm Sun.*

Skippers

1 Terrace View, Sherborne DT9 3HE
☎ *(01935) 812753* Chris Frowde

A Wadworth pub serving Henry's IPA and 6X, Butcombe Bitter as a permanent guest and one other changing ale.

Pleasant town local. Decorated with toy farm animals, school photos, a ten-shilling note and a letter from Margaret Thatcher – like a free museum! Food every session, large menu but retaining significant drinking area. Children welcome. Beer garden and car park. Just off the A30.

OPEN *11am–3pm and 6–11pm Mon–Sat; 12–3pm and 7–10.30pm Sun.*

SHROTON

The Cricketers

Shroton, Nr Blandford Forum DT11 8QD
☎ *(01258) 860421* George and Carol Cowie

Butcombe bitter is a regular, with many guest ales from various breweries, including Wychwood, Shepherd Neame, Brakspear, Palmers, Quay and Hook Norton.

Very friendly freehouse with pretty, sheltered garden and children's play area, situated between village green and Hambledon Hill. Good for walking. Well-known locally for good food from blackboard menu, available lunchtimes and evenings seven days a week. One luxury en-suite bed and breakfast garden room. Children allowed. Large beer garden. Located just off the A350 between Blandford and Shaftbury.

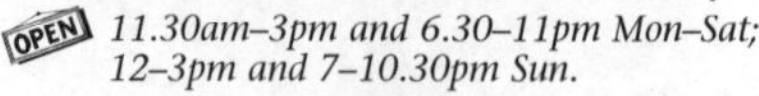

OPEN *11.30am–3pm and 6.30–11pm Mon–Sat; 12–3pm and 7–10.30pm Sun.*

SPYWAY

The Spyway Inn

Spyway, Askerswell, Dorchester DT2 9EP
☎ *(01308) 485250* Mr and Mrs Cox

Otter Ale and Weymouth from the Quay brewery are permanents.

Old smugglers' lookout, situated in glorious Dorset countryside. Atmospheric bars with oak beams. Good walks from the pub. Terrace and garden. Food served every session. Large car park. Separate dining room for families. Camping area.

OPEN *12–3pm and 6–11pm (10.30pm Sun).*

STOKE ABBOTT

New Inn

Stoke Abbott, Near Beaminster DT8 3JW
☎ *(01308) 868333* Mike Webb

A Palmers house selling 200, IPA, Copper and Tally Ho! in the winter.

Quiet traditional country pub in pretty village – a place to go to get away from it all (mobile-phone free). Pleasant garden with hatch to buy your beer. Food every session – tables do get booked up. Children and dogs welcome. Car park.

OPEN *11.30am–3pm and 6.30–11pm Mon–Sat; 12–3pm and 6.30–10.30pm Sun.*

STOURTON CAUNDLE

Trooper

Stourton Caundle, Sturminster Newton DT10 2JW
☎ *(01963) 362405* Roger and Rachel Paull

A freehouse with two real ales always on offer perhaps something from Ringwood, Butcombe, Exmoor, Otter, Young's, Fuller's or Flower's.

A very small pub with two bars. Snacks served at lunchtime. Children welcome. Situated off the main road.

OPEN *12–2.30pm and 7–11pm (closed Monday lunchtimes except on bank holidays).*

STRATTON

Saxon Arms

The Square, Stratton, Near Dorchester DT2 9WG
☎ *(01305) 260020* Ian Barrett

Freehouse offering Saxon Ale (brewed specially by Palmers), Palmers Best, London Pride and a guest.

Based in a large new building, the pub surprisingly has a thatched roof, and should age well. Located just off the A37 in the new part of the village. Food. Garden and car park. Children welcome in dining area. Try a dish of the Chilli Puffs with your pint!

OPEN *11am–2.30pm and 5.30–11pm Mon–Sat; 12–3pm and 6–10.30pm Sun.*

STUDLAND

The Banks Arms

Manor Road, Studland BH19 3AU
☎ *(01929) 450225* Mr and Mrs Lightbown

A freehouse with nine pumps. The one permanent beer is chosen at the annual beer festival, held every August and featuring beers from 30 breweries. The winner remains a permanent fixture for the whole year. The eight guests, changed daily, might be from breweries such as Cottage, Smiles, Wychwood or Badger.

Country village inn overlooking the sea, with two fires, beams and dining area. The only pub in the village! Award-winning food available. Fruit machine, live music, garden. Car park. Eight en-suite letting rooms. Children allowed.

 *11am–11pm Mon–Sat; 12–10.30pm Sun.*

SWANAGE

The Red Lion

63 High Street, Swanage BH19 2LY
☎ *(01929) 423533* Wolf and Amanda Strong

Ringwood Best and Greene King Old Speckled Hen are permanent beers and in the summer there are generally about four other guest ales served straight from the barrel, quite possibly Adnams Best or Timothy Taylor Landlord.

A traditional and cosy family-run local. Food served lunchtime and evening during the summer. Car park and garden. Children welcome. Pool and darts.

 *All day, every day.*

TARRANT MONKTON

The Langton Arms

Tarrant Monkton, Nr Blandford DT11 8RX
☎ *(01258) 830225* Barbara Cassins
www.thelangtonarms.co.uk

A freehouse serving 30 different guest ales every month through four real ale pumps. A fifth pump permanently serves The Langton's Best, brewed by Hop Back.

An attractive seventeenth-century thatched inn with a separate restaurant (evenings only). Bar food available lunchtime and evenings. Car park, garden, children's room and play area. Accommodation. Less than two miles off the A354 Blandford to Salisbury road, five miles north of Blandford.

 *All day, every day.*

TRENT

The Rose & Crown

Trent, Nr Sherborne DT9 4SL
☎ *(01935) 850776* Mr and Mrs Phillips

Butcombe Best and Sharp's Doom Bar always available plus two guest beers possibly including something from the Hop Back or Exmoor breweries.

A fifteenth-century part-thatched freehouse opposite Trent church. Bar and restaurant food available at lunchtime and evenings. Car park, garden, children's room and playground. Less than two miles north of the A30 between Sherborne and Yeovil.

 *12–3pm and 7–11pm; closed Sun evening and Mon.*

VERWOOD

Albion Inn

Station Road, Verwood BH31 7LB
☎ *(01202) 825267* Rex Neville

An Enterprise Inns pub, with Ringwood Best Bitter always available.

A traditional two-bar layout. Was previously a railway-owned hotel. Food served at lunchtime and evenings. Patio and garden plus children's garden.

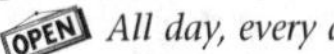 *All day, every day.*

WAYTOWN

Hare and Hounds

Waytown, Bridport DT6 5LQ
☎ *(01308) 488203* Ron Hobson and Cherry Ball

A Palmers tenancy offering IPA and Copper Ale plus 200 as a guest in the summer.

A classic unspoilt and friendly country pub with wonderful views from the beer garden. Recently refurbished. Food available every session except Sun and Mon nights. Children welcome, play equipment outside. Car park. Darts, quiz nights in winter. Difficult to find, off the B30668 between Bridport and Beaminster.

 *11.30am–2.30pm and 6.30 (7 in the winter)–11pm.*

WEST STAFFORD

The Wise Man

West Stafford, Near Dorchester DT2 8AG
☎ *(01305) 263694* Robert Henderson

Ringwood Best is a permanent plus three regularly changing guests.

Pretty thatched pub in pleasant village. Prides itself on its food, fish a speciality, booking advisable. Family room. Beer garden and car park.

 *12–3pm and 6–11pm.*

WESTBOURNE

The Porterhouse

113 Poole Road, Westbourne BH4 9BG
☎ *(01202) 768586* Tony Day

Ringwood Best, Fortyniner, Old Thumper and a seasonal always available, plus regular guests changed every few days such as Fuller's London Pride, Everards Mild, Hop Back Summer Lightning or Hogs Back Hop Garden Gold – in all more than a hundred last year.

Former wine bar, now a traditional one-bar pub on the main road. Food served at lunchtime only. No children under 14.

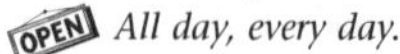
All day, every day.

WEYMOUTH

The Boot

High Street West, Weymouth DT4 8JH
☎ *(01305 770327* Giles Emley

A Ringwood tied house, featuring the full range including Best Bitter, Fortyniner, Old Thumper, Porter and seasonal brews, plus a wide range of guests on an additional pump. Real cider also served.

With foundations dating from 1346, and in business since the seventeenth century, this is the oldest pub in Weymouth. One bar area with comfortable rooms for sitting at either end. Also seating on the pavement outside. Behind the fire station.

All day every day.

King's Arms

15 Trinity Road, Weymouth DT4 8TJ
☎ *(01305) 770055* Mr and Mrs Glynn

Ringwood Best and Fortyniner always available.

An olde-worlde quayside pub with separate dining area. Two bars, pool table. Food served every lunchtime and Wed–Sat evenings. Children and dogs allowed.

All day, every day.

The Weatherbury Freehouse

7 Carlton Road North, Weymouth DT4 7PX
☎ *(01305) 786040* Mr and Mrs Hannah

Fuller's London Pride is a permanent with three changing guests that may include something from Butcombe or Palmers.

A busy town local in a residential position. Bar and restaurant food available at lunchtime and evenings. Car park, patio and dining area (where children are allowed). Accommodation. Dart board and pool table. Coming in to Weymouth, turn right off the Dorchester road.

12–11pm (10.30pm Sun).

WINKTON

The Lamb Inn

Burley Road, Winkton BH23 7AN
☎ *(01425) 672427* Mr and Mrs J Haywood

Four real ale pumps, one serving Fuller's London Pride, the others with a range of ales such as Ringwood Best Bitter or Fortyniner.

Situated on the edge of the New Forest, this pub has a lounge and public bar. Bar and restaurant food available at lunchtime and evenings. Car park and garden. Children are allowed in the restaurant and garden.

11am–3pm and 5–11pm Mon–Fri; 11am–11pm Sat; 12–10.30pm Sun.

WORTH MATRAVERS

The Square & Compass

Worth Matravers, Nr Swanage BH19 3LF
☎ *(01929) 439229* Charles Newman

Freehouse with Ringwood Best on permanently and up to four guests depending on the time of year – perhaps Tanglefoot or something from Hop Back.

An old-fashioned but very popular place, this has been a pub for more than 300 years. Excellent views of the sea. Basic food such as pasties. Garden. Games in the winter. Children welcome.

12–3pm and 6–11pm (closed Sun evenings) in the winter; all day in the summer.

WYKE REGIS

The Wyke Smugglers

76 Portland Road, Wyke Regis, Weymouth DT4 9AB
☎ *(01305) 760010* Mick Neville

Greene King Old Speckled Hen always available plus two real ales served as guests which change weekly.

A local drinkers' pub, sport orientated. No food. No children.

11am–2.30pm and 6–11.30pm.

YETMINSTER

The White Hart

High Street, Yetminster DT9 6LF
☎ *(01935) 872338* Mr Baysfield

Two or three real ales on offer, usually something from Otter, Butcombe or Ringwood.

A sixteenth century thatched village pub with one long bar in three bits and a pool table in the conservatory. Decorated in an interestingly unconventional way. Food lunchtime and evening. Car park. Skittle alley. Cottage lets. Village is just a few miles off the A37.

12–2.30pm and 7–11pm.

THE BREWERIES

CASTLE EDEN & CAMERON'S BREWING CO

Lion Brewery, Hartlepool TS24 7QS
☎ *(01429) 266666*

NIMMOS 3X 3.6% ABV
CASTLE EDEN BITTER 3.9% ABV
CASTLE EDEN CLASSIC 4.0% ABV
CASTLE EDEN ALE 4.2% ABV
NIMMO'S XXXX 4.4% ABV
Seasonals:
SPRING KNIGHTS 4.0% ABV
SUMMER KNIGHTS 4.0% ABV
AUTUMN KNIGHTS 4.2% ABV
WINTER ROYAL KNIGHTS 5.0% ABV

DERWENT ROSE BREWRY

The Grey Horse, 115 Sherburn Terrace, Consett DH8 6HE
☎ *(01207) 502585*
www.thegreyhorse.co.uk

MUTTON CLOG 3.8% ABV
PADDYS DELIGHT 3.8% ABV
STEEL TOWN 3.8% ABV
TARGET ALE 4.0% ABV
POTT CLOCK 4.2% ABV
RED DUST 4.2% ABV
SWORDMAKER 4.5% ABV
ANGELS ALE 5.0% ABV
C2C 5.0% ABV
DERWENT DEEP 5.0% ABV
DEVILS DIP 9.0% ABV

THE DURHAM BREWERY

Unit 5a, Bowburn North Industrial Est., Bowburn DH6 5PF
☎ *(0191) 377 1991*
www.durham-brewery.co.uk

The White Range:
SUNSTROKE 3.6% ABV
Summer ale.
GREEN GODDESS 3.8% ABV
Refreshing and spicy.
MAGUS 3.8% ABV
Pale, well-hopped lager-style beer.
WHITE GOLD 4.0% ABV
Light, refreshing with citrus fruit.
Plus 10 other regular beers.
The Gold Range:
MORNINGSONG 2.5% ABV
FROSTBITE 3.6% ABV
Winter ale.
CATHEDRAL GOLD 4.5% ABV
PRIORS GOLD 4.5% ABV
MAGNIFICAT 6.5% ABV
The Dark Range:
BONNY LASS 3.9% ABV
BLACK VELVET 4.0% ABV
CANNY LAD 4.3% ABV
EVENSONG 5.0% ABV
BLACK ABBOT 5.5% ABV
SANCTUARY 6.0% ABV

THE PUBS

BARNARD CASTLE

The Black Horse Hotel

10 Newgate, Barnard Castle DL12 8NG
☎ *(01833) 637234* Mr Landon

Castle Eden pub with Castle Eden Bitter and Nimmo's XXXX always on offer.

Rural pub in a stone building dating from the seventeenth century, formerly a coaching inn. Food available – the pub is famous for its steaks. Function room, pool room, snug area and private dining area for small parties. Occasional live music. Car park at rear. Five letting rooms. Children allowed.

OPEN *7–11pm Mon–Tues; varies on Wed–Thurs; 11am–11pm Fri–Sat; 12–10.30pm Sun.*

BILLY ROW

Dun Cow Inn (Cow Tail)

Old White Lea, Billy Row, Crook
Steve Parkin

One or two Darwin beers regularly available from a changing selection which may include Richmond Ale.

Established in 1740, this pub is only open four nights a week and has a unique atmosphere. 'A bit of a good crack.' The current licensee has been here since 1960. Car park. Well-behaved children welcome.

OPEN *8–11pm Wed, Fri, Sat; 8–10.30pm Sun.*

BISHOP AUCKLAND

Newton Cap

Newton Cap Bank, Bishop Auckland DA14 7PX
☎ *(01388) 605445* Christine Peart

Tied to Castle Eden. One guest ale, changed monthly, is available, and the policy is not to repeat beers if possible.

This has been a pub since the nineteenth century. Pool room, lounge, patio. No food. Car parking space available. Accompanied children allowed, but not in evenings. Situated on the outskirts of town, two miles from the bus station.

OPEN *12–4pm and 7–11pm (10.30pm Sun); closed Tues lunch.*

BOLAM

The Countryman

Bolam, Nr Darlington DL2 2UP
☎ *(01388) 834577* Paul Stabler

Black Sheep Bitter, Theakston Best and a guest ale (Greene King Old Speckled Hen?) usually available. Guests will increasingly be sourced from local breweries.

A 150-year-old one-bar country pub, with beams and coal fires, that reopened at Easter 2004 after almost two years standing vacant and unoccupied. Food available. Garden, car park for 50 cars. Children allowed. On the A68 between Darlington and West Buckland.

 *Ring ahead to check.*

CONSETT

The Grey Horse

115 Sherburn Terrace, Consett DH8 6NE
☎ *(01207) 502585* Mr and Mrs Conroy
www.thegreyhorse.co.uk

Home of the Derwent Rose Brewery, with home beers brewed and always available on the premises, plus up to four other ales.

A brewpub with traditional interior including two log fires in winter. No juke box or loud music. Snacks available, including famous lunchtime doorstep 'sarnies'. No children.

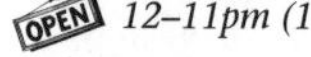 *12–11pm (10.30pm Sun).*

CROXDALE

The Daleside Arms

Front Street, Croxdale, Durham DH6 5HY
☎ *(01388) 814165* Mr Patterson

A freehouse with Black Sheep Special and Mordue Workie Ticket always available. Four guest beers, which change weekly, include other favourites from Mordue, Black Sheep and Border breweries.

A village pub in a country setting, with en-suite accommodation and two bars (a pub/lounge and restaurant). Food served at lunchtimes only. Children allowed.

OPEN *2–11pm Mon–Fri; all day Sat–Sun.*

DARLINGTON

Number Twenty 2

Coniscliffe Road, Darlington DL3 7RG
☎ *(01325) 354590* Mr Wilkinson

Ten ales including Hambleton Nightmare, White Boar and Old Raby always available plus guests (500 per year) such as Dent Ramsbottom, Hadrian Gladiator and Butterknowle Conciliation.

Traditional town-centre freehouse. Food available at lunchtimes, 12–2pm. Parking nearby, children allowed.

OPEN *11am–11pm.*

The Railway Tavern

8 High Northgate, Darlington DL1 1UN
☎ *(01325) 464963* Mr C Greenhow

Tied to Enterprise, this pub offers Wadworth 6X and Bateman XXXB on a fairly regular basis. Guests include beers from Durham, Mordue, Timothy Taylor, Northumberland, Rudgate, Marston Moor and others.

This small local pub was probably the first 'Railway Inn' in the world, as it is situated 150 metres from the first passenger station in the world. The land on which it stands was owned by the Pease family, founders of the Darlington–Stockton Railway. On the main road through Darlington, the pub has two bars, one of which has pool and darts, and features live music on Friday nights. Children allowed if supervised.

OPEN *12–11pm.*

Tap & Spile

99 Bondgate, Darlington DL3 7JY
☎ *(01325) 381679* Marian Holtby

Caledonian Deuchars IPA always available, plus up to four guests which regularly include Marston's Pedigree among many others.

Traditional town-centre pub with two bars, a function room and live music Thurs–Sun. Bar food available Mon–Sat lunchtime. Children allowed if eating. Outside café pavement licence. Disabled facilities.

OPEN *11.30am–11pm Mon–Thurs; 11.30am–midnight Fri–Sat; 12–11pm Sun.*

DURHAM

Ye Old Elm Tree

12 Crossgate, Durham DH1 4PS
☎ *(0191) 386 4621* Mr Dave Cruddace

Regular guests, two rotating every two weeks, may include Fuller's London Pride, Greene King Old Speckled Hen or Bateman XXXB.

An alehouse dating from 1601, situated in the centre of Durham city, off Framwellgate Bridge. Two guest rooms, beer garden and patio. The bar is built round an elm tree. Quiz and folk nights held. Light snacks at lunchtime and evenings. Children allowed.

 *12–3pm and 6–11pm Mon–Fri; 11am–11pm Sat; 12–4pm and 7–10.30pm Sun.*

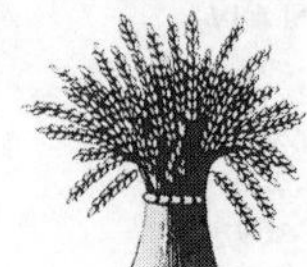

FOREST IN TEESDALE

The High Force Hotel

Forest in Teesdale DL12 0XH
☎ *(01833) 622222* Gary Wilson

Home of the High Force brewery with three own brews always available.

A country hotel, which is easy to find, serving food at lunchtime and evenings. Children allowed.

 *11am–11pm Mon–Sat; 12–10.30pm Sun. Opening hours subject to seasonal variation.*

FRAMWELLGATE MOOR

Tap & Spile

27 Front Street, Framwellgate Moor, Durham DH1 5EE
☎ *(0191) 386 5451* Lesley Fyfe
www.tapandspile.co.uk

Up to eight beers available. Marston's Pedigree and Fuller's London Pride are usually among them but the range changes constantly.

A traditional pub with a main bar, (bookable) family room, non-smoking room and games room for darts and billiards. Pet-friendly. Bar snacks only. Children allowed until 9pm. Beer festivals planned. Two miles north of Durham city centre, on the old A1.

 *12–3pm and 6–11pm Mon–Sat; 12–3pm and 7–10.30pm Sun.*

GREAT LUMLEY

The Old England

Front Street, Great Lumley, Nr Chester le Street DH3 4JB
☎ *(0191) 388 5257* Mr Barkess

Three or four different ales a week are available in this freehouse, with a good mix of nationals and micro-breweries from all over the country. Regular guests include Hop Back Summer Lightning and brews from Caledonian and Wychwood.

A pub/restaurant set off the road, with a 200-seat lounge, 150-seat bar, separate dining area, darts, dominoes, pool. Food served mostly during evenings, lunchtime at weekends. Children allowed in dining area.

11am–11pm Mon–Sat; 12–10.30pm Sun.

HARTLEPOOL

Tavern

56 Church Street, Hartlepool TS24 7DX
☎ *(01429) 222400* Chris Sewell

Camerons Strongarm and three guest beers regularly available such as Orkney Dark Island or something from the Jennings range.

Traditional town-centre one-bar pub with upstairs, open-plan dining area. Home-cooked food served 11am–2pm and 5–8pm Mon–Sat, 12–4pm Sun. Children welcome until 8pm and they eat half price. Situated close to the railway station.

 *11am–3pm and 5–11pm Mon–Fri; 11am–11pm Sat; 12–3pm and 7–10.30pm Sun.*

KIRK MERRINGTON

The Half Moon Inn

Crowther Place, Kirk Merrington, Nr Spennymoor DL16 7JL
☎ *(01388) 811598* Mrs Crooks

Something from Durham Brewery always available in this freehouse. Favourite guest beers might come from the Kitchen Brewery, or include Elgood's Black Dog and Hart Squirrels Hoards. Anything and everything has been tried.

A traditional pub on the village green, with one room, games area and car park. Bar meals at lunchtime and evening. Children allowed up to 8pm.

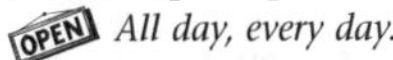 *All day, every day.*

MIDDLESTONE VILLAGE

The Ship Inn

Low Row, Middlestone Village, Bishop Auckland DL14 8AB
☎ *(01388) 810904* Graham Snaith
www.downourlocal.com/ship

A freehouse with up to six real ales available. Timothy Taylor Landlord is a regular fixture and ales from local breweries such as Durham, Daleside and Big Lamp are popular. The range changes constantly.

A well-appointed traditional pub with a small bar and lounge. Built into the hillside in walking country, it offers panoramic views. CAMRA North East Pub of the Year 2001 and 2002. Restaurant on first-floor balcony doubles as a function room. Food served every day except Tues. Children allowed if parents are eating. Spring and winter beer festivals. See website for directions.

 *4–11pm Mon–Thurs; 12–11pm Fri–Sat; 12–10.30pm Sun.*

NEASHAM

The Fox and Hounds

24 Teesway, Neasham, Darlington DL2 1QP
☎ *(01325) 720350*
Bev Hayman and Brenda Whear

Two or three real ales always on offer. Black Sheep Special is a regular, plus rotating guests from Timothy Taylor, Greene King, Ridleys, Charles Wells and Jennings, to name but a few.

Country pub on the banks of the River Tees. Bar, conservatory and restaurant area. Food served 11.30am–2pm and 6–9.30pm Tues–Sun. Free children's meals (when adults eat) from 6–7pm. Children's play area.

All day, every day in summer; 11.30am–2.30pm and 6–11pm Tues–Sat, 12–10.30pm Sun in winter. Closed on Mondays.

NEWTON AYCLIFFE

The Blacksmith's Arms

Preston-le-Skerne, Newton Aycliffe DL5 6JH
☎ *(01325) 314873*
Brenda Whear and Bev Hayman

Black Sheep Special always available. Plus two local beers rotated each week (100 per year). Favourites come from Hambleton, Barnsley and a range of micro-brewers.

A country pub in the middle of farmland, in an isolated position two miles from Newton Aycliffe. Two bars, a one-acre beer garden, rabbits and a plant nursery. Ice creams served. Food available at lunchtime and evenings, outdoors in summer. Children allowed (free children's menu 6–7pm).

All day, every day in summer; 12–3pm and 6.30–11pm in winter.

NO PLACE

Beamish Mary Inn

No Place, Nr Stanley DH9 0QH
☎ *(0191) 370 0237* Graham Ford

Black Sheep Special and Bitter and Jennings Cumberland Ale always available, plus three guests often including No Place, a beer brewed specially by Big Lamp Brewery. Others come from small local breweries.

Over 100 years old, this pub is a throw-back from the Beamish Museum housing many interesting artefacts. Live music four nights a week in the converted stables of the old barn. Food served 12–2pm and 7–9.30pm in a separate restaurant area. B&B. Children allowed.

12–3pm and 6–11pm Mon–Thurs; all day Fri–Sun.

NORTH BITCHBURN

Famous Red Lion

North Bitchburn Terrace, Nr Crook DL15 8AL
☎ *(01388) 763561* Mr Keith Young

A freehouse with three real ales always available. A house brew (Jenny Ale) is a regular fixture plus brews from Cameron, Northumberland, Black Sheep, Timothy Taylor, Rudgate, Hart and Derwent breweries which change every week.

An easy-to-find, typical, olde-worlde inn, stone-built with open fires, one bar, a beamed ceiling, small patio and a separate restaurant. Food served 12–2pm (not Mon) and 7–9.30pm. Families welcome, car park at rear.

12–3pm (not Mon) and 6.30–11pm (10.30pm Sun).

ROOKHOPE

The Rookhope Inn

Rookhope, Near Stanhope DL13 2BG
☎ *(01388) 517215* Chris Jones
www.rookhope.com

A freehouse offering a choice of two Jennings beers plus a constantly changing guest ale.

A seventeenth-century listed pub with log fires, real beams and a resident ghost. Live music at weekends. Three rooms: lounge bar, games bar and dining room. Hot food and sandwiches served all day. Five en-suite bedrooms. Mountain bike and tandem hire (on the coast-to-coast cycle route). Home to two Dalmatian dogs.

All day, every day (late licence Fri–Sat).

SEDGEFIELD

The Dun Cow Inn

43 Front Street, Sedgefield TS21 3AT
☎ *(01740) 620894* Geoff Rayner

Three guest ales always available, from breweries such as Black Sheep, Camerons, Marston's, Hart, Daleside, Hambleton, Northumberland, Castle Eden and Jennings.

A pretty old building with two large bars and a separate restaurant. Six en-suite letting rooms. Food available 12–2pm and 6–9.30pm. Car park. Children welcome. Situated in the centre of the village, identifiable by its impressive flowers and shrubs all year round.

11am–3pm and 6–11pm Mon–Sat; 11.30am–3pm and 7–10.30pm Sun.

SHADFORTH

The Plough Inn

South Side, Shadforth, Durham DH6 1LL
☎ *(0191) 372 0375* Jane Barber

A freehouse with a varied and ever-changing range of beers, which change once or twice a week. Regular guests, which now number in the hundreds, come mainly from independents and micro-breweries. You name it, they've probably served it!

A small, traditional country pub, with one bar and lounge. No food. Children allowed.

 *6.30–11pm Mon–Fri; 11am–11pm Sat; 12–10.30pm Sun.*

TANTOBIE

The Highlander

White-le-Head, Tantobie, Nr Stanley DH9 9SN
☎ *(01207) 232416* Mr CD Wright

Up to 100 beers per year changed weekly including something from Thwaites, Timothy Taylor, Black Sheep and Marston's, plus beers from many other smaller breweries as available.

One bar has games and music (pool, darts, etc). Also a small lounge and dining area. Hot food available on weekday evenings and weekend afternoons. Car park, beer garden and function room. Children welcome. Occasional accommodation. Ring to check. One mile off the A692 between Tantobie and Flint Hill.

 *7.30–11pm Mon–Fri; 12.30–3pm and 7.30–11pm Sat–Sun.*

THE BREWERIES

BLANCHFIELD'S BREWERY

The Nest, Ashington Heights, Durham Road, Rochford SS4 3AE
☎ *(01702) 530053*
www.blanchfields-brewing.com

BLACK BULL MILD 3.6% ABV

BULL BEST BITTER 3.9% ABV

WHITE BULL 4.4% ABV

RAGING BULL BITTER 4.9% ABV

CROUCH VALE BREWERY LTD

12 Redhills Road, South Woodham Ferrers, Chelmsford CM3 5UP
☎ *(01245) 322744*
www.crouch-vale.co.uk

ESSEX BOYS BITTER 3.5% ABV
Plenty of malt and hop flavour.

BLACKWATER MILD 3.7% ABV
Smooth, dark and malty.

BREWERS GOLD 4.0% ABV
Hoppy with tropical fruit aromas.

CROUCH BEST 4.0% ABV
Malt and fruit, some hops.

ANCHOR STREET PORTER 4.9% ABV
Rounded, roast barley flavour.

Plus around two dozen seasonal brews.

FAMOUS RAILWAY BREWERY

The Famous Railway Tavern, 58 Station Road, Brightlingsea CO7 0DT
☎ *(01206) 302581*
www.geocities.com/famousrailway

CRAB & WINKLE MILD 3.7% ABV

SPRAT & OYSTER BITTER 4.3% ABV

BLADDERWRACK STOUT 4.7% ABV

THE FELSTAR BREWERY

Felsted Vineyard, Crix Green, Felsted CM6 3JT
☎ *(01245) 361 504*

HOP-HOP-HURRAY 4.0% ABV

CHICK CHAT 4.1% ABV

HOPPIN' HEN 4.5% ABV

HOPSIN 4.6% ABV

FELSTAR WHEAT 4.8% ABV
Wheat beer.

GOOD KNIGHT 5.0% ABV
Strong mild.

DARK WHEAT 5.4% ABV
Wheat beer.

LORD ESSEX 5.4% ABV
An Old ale.

HOWLIN' HEN 6.5% ABV
Stout.

Plus a range of bottled ales.
Brewery is also retail outlet and customers can drink on site.

GRAY AND SONS

Rignals Lane, Galleywood, Chelmsford CM2 8RE
☎ *(01245) 475181*
www.grayandsons.co.uk

Not strictly 'brewers' now (although they were from 1828 to 1974) Grays deserve a mention here for their 49 tenanted houses all serving at least two cask ales from the likes of Greene King, Adnams and Mighty Oak. On top of this, publicans can choose from eight or so guests each month from a variety of independents and can even 'nominate' their regulars' favourite brews from the ever-widening selection available through wholesalers. See the website for a full list of Gray's houses.

MALDON BREWING CO. LTD

The Stable Brewery, Silver Street, Maldon CM9 4QE
☎ *(01621) 840925*

BLUE BOAR BITTER 4.0% ABV
Malty, uses 1st Gold hops.

HOTEL PORTER 4.2% ABV
A dark beer of 'stout' character.

PUCKS FOLLY 4.2% ABV
A light beer with lots of Goldings hops and a hint of grapefruit.

MIGHTY OAK BREWING CO.

14b West Station Yard, Spital Road, Maldon CM9 6TW
☎ *(01621) 843713*
www.mightyoakbrewery.co.uk

IPA 3.5% ABV
Pale golden. Good hoppy bitterness.

OSCAR WILDE 3.7% ABV
Mellow and nutty dark mild.

MALDON GOLD 3.8% ABV
Light golden ale with biscuity malt flavours.

BURNTWOOD BITTER 4.0% ABV
Deep copper-coloured, clean bitterness and complex malt flavours.

SIMPLY THE BEST 4.4% ABV
A tawny-coloured ale with crisp, light bitterness.

ENGLISH OAK 4.8% ABV
Full malt amber ale with strong hop finish.

HIGH AND MIGHTY 6.5% ABV
Deep tawny ale reminiscent of a barley wine.

Plus 12 (monthly) seasonal brews and 'two new brews a month'.

TD RIDLEY AND SONS LTD

Hartford End Brewery, Mill Lane, Chelmsford CM3 1JZ
☎ *(01371) 820316*
www.ridleys.co.uk

RIDLEY'S IPA 3.5% ABV
Crisp, traditional 'India Pale Ale' with hoppy aroma.

TOLLY COBBOLD MILD 3.5% ABV
A dark mild with smooth, chocolate malt flavour.

TOLLY COBBOLD ORIGINAL 3.8% ABV
A smooth, malty-tasting bitter with a hint of sweetness.

PROSPECT 4.1% ABV
Rich golden ale.

RUMPUS 4.5% ABV
Ruby, with smooth nutty character.

OLD BOB 5.1% ABV
Smooth, rich, full-bodied premium ale with a spicy flavour.

Plus monthly specials and occasional brews.

THE PUBS

BARKING

The Britannia

1 Church Road, Barking, IG11 8PR
☎ *(020) 8594 1305* John and Rita Pells

A Young's pub with Special and Bitter always available, plus a winter warmer from October and various specials in summer.

An old-fashioned community alehouse with public bar, saloon/lounge bar and snug. Patio. Food available at lunchtime and evenings. No children. Can be extremely difficult to find – ring if need be.

 *11am –3pm and 5–11.30pm Mon–Fri; all day Sat–Sun.*

BASILDON

The Moon on the Square

1–15 Market Square, Basildon SS14 1DF
☎ *(01268) 520360*
Samantha Taylor and Jason Harris

A Wetherspoon's pub. At least eight beers, with Shepherd Neame Spitfire and Greene King Abbot always available. Guests changed weekly, from a list that includes, Adnams Clipper, Badger Tanglefoot, Hook Norton, Charles Wells Bombardier, Ringwood Fortyniner, amongst many other independents.

A busy market pub (note early opening) with one large bar. A mixed clientele of business customers and lunchtime shoppers. Food served all day. Children allowed only at tables.

 *8am –11pm Mon–Sat; 10am–10.30pm Sun.*

BILLERICAY

The Coach & Horses

36 Chapel Street, Billericay CM12 9LU
☎ *(01277) 622873* Terry Roberts

Greene King IPA and Abbot and Adnams Bitter always available, plus weekly changing guest beers. Tries to stock independent breweries' beers whenever possible.

A town pub with one bar. Friendly locals and good regular clientele. Food available 12–2.20pm and 6–9pm Mon–Sat, Sunday lunch 12–7pm. Patio garden. No children in pub. Next to Waitrose.

 *All day Mon–Sat; 12–10.30pm Sun.*

BIRDBROOK

The Plough

The Street, Birdbrook CO9 4BJ
☎ *(01440) 785336* Jan Walton

Adnams Best and Greene King IPA always available, plus rotating guest beers.

A sixteenth-century thatched freehouse with a very low beamed ceiling. Three interlinking bars with pool table; safe beer garden. Food served lunchtimes and evenings Tues–Sat. Friday is fish and chips night. Sunday food arrangements vary with season – ring first. Children allowed. Follow signs to Birdbrook from A1017.

 *12–3pm and 6.30–11pm Mon–Sat; 12– 4pm and 7–10.30pm Sun.*

BLACK NOTLEY

The Vine Inn

105 The Street, Black Notley, Nr Braintree CM77 8LL
☎ *(01376) 324269* Tony Keogh

Adnams Bitter and Broadside always available plus a weekly guest from small independents and micros, generally following Adnam's monthly 'Brewery in Focus', but also open to regulars' requests.

A country freehouse dating from 1640 with an old barn end, a minstrel's gallery and lots of beams. Main area is split 50/50, bar and restaurant. Food served at lunchtime and evenings. Children allowed in restaurant (for meals) and on patio. A couple of miles outside Braintree on the Notley Road

 *12–2.30pm and 6.30–11pm Mon–Sat; 12–4pm and 7–10.30pm Sun.*

BRENTWOOD

The Swan

123 High Street, Brentwood CM14 4RX
☎ *(01277) 211848* Duncan Kenny

Young's Special, Fuller's London Pride, Brakspear Bitter and Greene King IPA always available on hand pump, plus up to four weekly changing guests such as Adnams Broadside, Shepherd Neame Spitfire and seasonal ales from all over the UK served on gravity.

A thirteenth-century pub with a friendly atmosphere. Mainly a locals' pub with quiet background music. Food served lunchtimes and generally 6–8pm evenings, but parties catered for outside these hours. Small patio garden. No children.

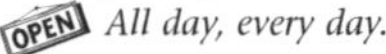 *All day, every day.*

BRIGHTLINGSEA

The Famous Railway Tavern

58 Station Road, Brightlingsea CO7 0DT
☎ *(01206) 302581* David English

Brewpub with home brews plus Crouch Vale Best, a dark mild, a stout and a real cider always available, plus up to five guests from local breweries. Gravity-fed in winter.

A friendly, traditional pub with real fire and floorboards. No fruit machines or juke box in the public bar. Garden, children's room. Table football, shove ha'penny, darts, cribbage, dominoes. Campsite opposite, 11 pubs within walking distance. Buskers' afternoon held once a month between October and April. Annual cider festival held during first week of May.

 *5–11pm Mon–Thurs; 3–11pm Fri; 12–11pm Sat; 12–3pm and 7–10.30pm Sun.*

BURNHAM-ON-CROUCH

The Anchor Hotel

The Quay, Burnham-on-Crouch CM0 8AT
☎ *(01621) 782117* Kevin Veal

Greene King IPA and Adnams and Crouch Vale brews usually available, plus three guests from breweries such as Titanic Youngs or Ridleys. Seasonal ales also stocked.

A locals' pub with a broad clientele in a small seaside town with seating on the sea wall. Two bars, two dining areas (one non-smoking). Food available at lunchtime and evenings. Children allowed.

All day, every day.

The Queen's Head

Providence, Burnham-on-Crouch CM0 8JU
☎ *(01621) 784825* Alison and Stewart Mawer
www.queensheadburnham.co.uk

A Gray's house with Greene King IPA and Abbot always available plus an interesting guest. This house has won awards for its well-kept cellar.

A bijou back-street pub with a family atmosphere, traditional pub games and pool table. Beer garden. The sort of pub where there is always something interesting to catch the eye, and conversations are open to all. Food served lunchtimes (12–2.30pm) and evenings (6.30–8.45pm) except Tuesdays. Well-behaved children welcome until 8.30pm.
Providence is a narrow turning off the High Street, opposite the Clock Tower and there is a public car park over the road from the pub.

 *11am–4pm and 6–11pm Mon–Sat; 11am–4pm and 7–10.30pm Sun.*

The Ship Inn

High Street, Burnham-on-Crouch CM0 8AA
☎ *(01621) 785057* Tony and Brenda Tofari

An Adnams house with Southwold Bitter and Broadside always available, plus the same brewery's Regatta through the summer, and various other guests through the rest of the year.

A recently refurbished country town pub with open-plan bar, but clever separation of eating and drinking areas. Outside seating on the quiet High Street. En-suite accommodation. Food served lunchtimes (12–2.30pm) and evenings (7–9.30pm). Well-behaved children allowed at restaurant tables.

 *11am–4pm and 6–11pm Mon–Sat; 11am–4pm and 7–10.30pm Sun.*

CHELMSFORD

The Cricketers

143 Moulsham Street, Chelmsford CM2 0JT
☎ *(01245) 261157* Mr Harley

A Gray's house with Greene King IPA and Abbot always available plus two guests from Mighty Oak and others.

A city-centre local with pool table and Sky Sports. Bar food served at lunchtimes.

11am–11pm Mon–Sat; 12–10.30pm Sun.

The Endeavour

Duke Street, Chelmsford CM2 6AW
☎ *(01245) 257717* Mike Mitchell
www.pickapub.co.uk/theendeavour.htm

A Gray's house with Greene King IPA and Abbot, and Mighty Oak Maldon Gold always available plus two guests, with Woodforde's Wherry a regular visitor.

A cosy seventeenth century pub with original features and large open fire. Recently refurbished and with two bars. Originally named to commemorate Cook's ship, it also celebrates the Space Shuttle of the same name. The pub also boasts a rare 'Russian Black' terrier bitch. Theme nights every so often. Food served Mon–Sat lunchtimes with specials. Fresh fish from Lowestoft on Fridays and steak night on Saturdays. Sunday lunch. Booking essential for Sat evening and Sun lunch.

11am–11pm Mon–Sat; 12–10.30pm Sun.

The Railway Tavern

Duke Street, Chelmsford CM2 0AS
☎ *(01245) 356995* Chris and Rick Day

A Gray's house with Greene King IPA and Abbot always available plus two guests from around the country, and a draught cider.

A long, narrow pub with interesting features and where maximum use has been made of the available space, situated immediately opposite the main station entrance. Busy at lunchtimes and early evenings, with traditional pub games for quieter hours. Secluded beer garden. Food served Mon–Sat lunchtimes only (12–2.30pm), with specials changed daily. Children in beer garden only.

12–11pm Mon–Sat; 12–4pm and 7–10.30pm Sun.

The Queen's Head

30 Lower Anchor Street, Chelmsford CM2 0AS
☎ *(01245) 265181* Mike Collins

A Crouch Vale-owned house. Crouch Vale Best and multiple award-winning Brewer's Gold always available, plus guests (500 a year), always including a mild, stout or porter. Guests come from a range of independent breweries such as Buffy's, St Peters, RCH, Skinner's and Orkney.

A traditional alehouse a mile from the cricket ground. Built in 1895 but totally refurbished – one bar with real fires, courtyard and beer garden. Pub games, no music. Food available Mon–Sat lunchtimes only, with homemade pies and locally produced beer sausages a speciality. No children.

12–11pm Mon–Sat; 12–10.30pm Sun.

The White Horse

25 Townfield Street, Chelmsford CM1 1QJ
☎ *(01245) 269556* Rob Furber

Up to nine cask-conditioned ales served at this pub managed by Wessex Taverns. Greene King Old Speckled Hen, IPA and Abbot, Adnams Bitter and Broadside and Young's Bitter usually available, plus guests.

Award-winning, comfortable one-bar pub with a plethora of traditional pub games. Bar food available at lunchtime. An ideal drop-in after an arduous journey! Turn right from the rear of the railway station.

All day, every day.

COLCHESTER

The Bricklayers

27 Bergholt Road, Colchester CO4 5AA
☎ *(01206) 852008* Fred Beasey

An award-winning Adnams pub featuring the full range of the brewery's beers plus up to three wide-ranging guest ales.

Two-bar town pub not far from the station. Food served Sun–Fri lunchtimes. Conservatory and outside seating, non-smoking area. Good Sunday lunch 12–2pm.

11am–3pm and 5.30–11pm Mon–Thur; all day Fri–Sat; 12–3pm and 7–10.30pm Sun.

Odd One Out

28 Mersea Road, Colchester CO2 7ET
☎ *(01206) 578140* John Parrick

Ridleys Prospect, Archers Best and a dark ale always available plus up to four guests which will mainly be East Anglian beers. Also up to three traditional ciders, always including one organic cider (Crones).

Friendly pub about 100 yards up the Mersea Road from St Botolph's roundabout. A traditional drinkers' alehouse with garden. Also has a good range of whiskies.

4.30–11pm Mon–Thurs; 11am–11pm Fri–Sat; 12–10.30pm Sun.

The Hospital Arms

123–5 Crouch Street, Colchester CO3 3HA
☎ *(01206) 573572* Mike Blackmore

An Adnams' tied house with Bitter and Broadside, and Fuller's London Pride always available along with a selection of two or more other Adnams brews. On top of this, there are constantly changing guests from independents.

Traditional English alehouse with soft background music. Bar food served lunchtimes. Outside patio. Children allowed in the garden only. Just outside the town centre, opposite the Essex County Hospital, on Lexden Road. Traditionally known as Ward 9 by the hospital staff regulars (the hospital itself has eight wards!).

OPEN *All day, every day.*

COXTIE GREEN

The White Horse

173 Coxtie Green Road, Coxtie Green, Brentwood CM14 5PX
☎ *(01277) 372410* David Hastings

Ridleys Rumpus, Fuller's London Pride and Adnams Bitter always available, plus three rotating guests such Hop Back Summer Lightning, Timothy Taylor Landlord or Crouch Vale or Mighty Oak brews. Over 100 guest beers served every year.

A semi-rural pub, with public bar and lounge. Darts. Large garden. Barbecues in summer, some children's facilities in the garden. Food served lunchtimes Mon–Sat. Situated off the A128 towards Ongar.

OPEN *All day, every day.*

EPPING

The Moletrap

Tawney Common, Epping CM16 7PU
☎ *(01992) 522394* Mr and Mrs Kirtley

A freehouse with Fuller's London Pride always available plus ever-changing guests from all over the country with the emphasis on independent and micro-breweries.

A 250-year-old listed building which has been extended. Outside seating. Food served at lunchtime and evenings. Well-behaved children allowed. Down a rural country lane, but only five minutes' drive from Epping.

OPEN *Winter: 11.30am–2.30pm and 6.30–11pm. Summer: 11.30am–3pm and 6–11pm.*

FEERING

The Sun Inn

3 Feering Hill, Feering, Nr Kelvedon CO5 9NH
☎ *(01376) 570442* Charlie and Kim Scicluna
www.suninnfeering.com

Six ever-changing beers (six on-line at any time and up to 20 different per week). The emphasis is firmly on the more unusual micro-breweries – see website for weekly details of what's on at present and coming up. Some 40–60 beers are in the cellar waiting to reach their peak at any time and a total of nearly 600 different ales are served each year.

A heavily timbered former mansion, richly decorated with carved beams and open fires. Bar and restaurant food is available at lunchtime and evenings. Car park and garden. Small functions (up to 28 persons) catered for. Turn off the Kelvedon bypass when coming from the north or south.

OPEN *12–3pm and 6–11pm Mon–Sat; 12–3pm and 7–10.30pm Sun.*

FINCHINGFIELD

The Red Lion

6 Church Hilll, Finchingfield CM7 4NN
☎ *(01371) 810400* Frank Tyler

A Ridleys pub with IPA and Old Bob always on offer, plus one monthly changing beer, usually another Ridleys brew such as Rumpus or Prospect.

Country village pub, a fifteenth-century coaching inn, with one bar and two gardens. Food is available, and there is a non-smoking restaurant. Live music on bank holidays. Car park. Four letting rooms. Children allowed.

OPEN *11am–11pm Mon–Sat; 12–10.30pm Sun.*

FYFIELD

The Queen's Head

Queen Street, Fyfield, Ongar CM5 0RY
☎ *(01277) 899231*
Daniel Lamprecht and Penelope Miers

Timothy Taylor Landlord plus Adnams Best and Broadside always available plus three constantly changing guests from a range of independent and micro-breweries.

A friendly freehouse dating from the fifteenth century, with riverside garden and open fires. Food served seven days a week (not Sun evening). No children under 14 years allowed in the bar.

OPEN *11am–3.30pm and 6–11pm Mon–Sat; 12–3.30pm and 7–10.30pm Sun.*

GESTINGTHORPE

The Pheasant

Audley End, Gestingthorpe CO9 3AU
☎ *(01787) 461196* Ian and Kay Crane

Greene King IPA plus Adnams Best are always available, and a guest beer is usually on offer.

Multi-roomed, 400-year-old freehouse with exposed beams, open fires and a warm friendly atmosphere. There is one bar and two non-smoking dining areas. Comprehensive menu of home-cooked food available every lunchtime (except Mon), with roast and bar snacks on Sunday. Garden with extensive views over the Essex countryside. Car park. Children are welcome: the pub has a children's play area and a children's menu. Well signposted, just north of Halstead, the only pub in the village. Monthly theme night (mostly Thursdays – ring for details).

OPEN *12–3pm and 6–11pm Mon–Fri; 12–3.30pm and 6–11pm Sat; 12–4pm and 7–10.30pm Sun.*

HATFIELD BROAD OAK

The Cock Inn

High Street, Hatfield Broad Oak CM22 7HF
☎ *(01279) 718306*
Pam Holcroft and Dave Sulway

Adnams Best and Fuller's London Pride always available, plus guests.

A traditional country freehouse with open fires, non-smoking area, private function room, car park, disabled access and outside seating. Food served at lunchtime and evenings. Well-behaved children allowed.

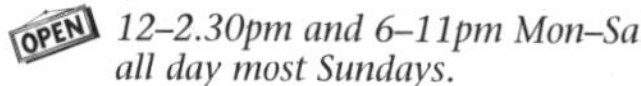
OPEN *12–2.30pm and 6–11pm Mon–Sat; all day most Sundays.*

HERONGATE TYE

The Old Dog Inn

Billericay Road, Herongate Tye, Brentwood CM13 3SD
☎ *(01277) 810337* Sheila Murphy

Ridleys IPA, Fuller's London Pride and Greene King Abbot always available and something from Mauldons, Adnams and Crouch Vale (perm any two from three). Also two or three regularly changing guests, such as Shepherd Neame Spitfire or Hop Back Summer Lightning. A total of at least seven real ales available at any time.

A sixteenth-century family-owned and -run Essex weatherboard pub. One bar, garden, background music only. Food served at lunchtime and evenings in a separate dining area. Well-behaved children allowed. Located off the A128 Brentwood/Tilbury Road.

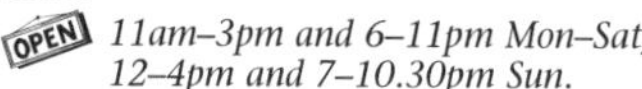
OPEN *11am–3pm and 6–11pm Mon–Sat; 12–4pm and 7–10.30pm Sun.*

HIGH RODING

The Black Lion

3 The Street, High Roding, Great Dunmow CM6 1NT
☎ *(01371) 872847* John Devine

A Ridleys tied house, so Ridleys IPA, Rumpus and Old Bob always on.

Built in 1397, this olde-worlde country village pub features beams and open fires. Food is served and there is a non-smoking dining area. Children welcome – the pub has a children's enclosed garden. Lawned area, car park. On the main B4187.

OPEN *12–3pm and 6–11pm Mon–Fri; 11am–11pm Sat; 12–10.30pm Sun.*

HORNDON ON THE HILL

The Bell Inn

High Road, Horndon On The Hill SS17 8LD
☎ *(01375) 642463 John Vereker*
www.bell-inn.co.uk

Greene King IPA usually available, with regularly changing guest beers such as Hop Back Summer Lightning, Crouch Vale Millennium Gold, Young's Special, Shepherd Neame Spitfire, Slaters Top Totty, Mighty Oak Burntwood and Greene King Ruddles County.

Attractive 600-year-old village inn. Courtyard filled with hanging baskets in summer. Award-winning restaurant and bar food available lunchtimes and evenings (except bank holiday Mondays) – see website for today's menu. Car park. Children welcome in the restaurant and bar eating area.

OPEN *11am–2.30pm and 5.30–11pm Mon–Fri; 11am–3pm and 6–11pm Sat; 12–4pm and 7–10.30pm Sun.*

HUTTON

Chequers

213 Rayleigh Road, Hutton, Brentwood CM13 1PJ
☎ *(01277) 224980* Peter Waters

Greene King IPA always available plus a range of guest ales served on one pump. Tends towards the lighter brews.

A seventeenth-century coaching house. Two cosy bars, beer garden, main road location. Bar snacks available at lunchtime. Children allowed. Situated on the main A129 road.

OPEN *All day, every day.*

ILFORD

The Rose & Crown

16 Ilford Hill, Ilford IG1 2DA
☎ *(020) 8478 7104*

Marston's Pedigree and Adnams Best always available along with a monthly selection which might include Shepherd Neame Spitfire or a special brew. Three guest pumps.

A town pub just off the high street with beams and log fires. One bar with dining area and a small terrace. Food available 12–3pm Mon–Fri. Children allowed if eating.

OPEN *11am–11pm Mon–Sat; 12–10.30pm Sun.*

LEIGH-ON-SEA

The Broker Free House

213–17 Leigh Road, Leigh-on-Sea SS9 1JA
☎ *(01702) 471932*
Alan and Elaine Gloyne and family
www.brokerfreehouse.co.uk

Shepherd Neame Spitfire, Ridleys Tolly Original and Young's Tiger always available, plus two guests which regularly include Fuller's London Pride, Young's Bitter and beers from Mighty Oak, Woodforde's, Harveys, Mansfield, Bateman and Cottage breweries. Often serves 14 different beers over 10 days.

A family-run, family-friendly freehouse, catering for 18–102 year olds! One big bar, beer garden, children's licence and dedicated children's area. Sunday night is live music or quiz night. Food served at lunchtime and evenings (except Sunday evenings). Children allowed.

 *11am–3pm and 6–11pm Mon–Wed; 11am–11pm Thurs–Sat; 12–10.30pm Sun.*

The Elms

1060 London Road, Leigh-on-Sea SS9 3ND
☎ *(01702) 474687* Greg Borgatz

Shepherd Neame Spitfire always available, plus more than 100 guests every year from smaller breweries such as Ridleys. Beer festival.

A Wetherspoon's pub. Modern bar with an old-looking exterior. Outside seating. Non-smoking area. Food served 10am–10pm. Well-behaved children up to 6pm.

OPEN *All day, every day.*

LITTLE CLACTON

The Apple Tree

The Street, Little Clacton CO16 9LF
☎ *(01255) 861026* Paul Lead and Alan Short

Fuller's London Pride, Adnams Southwold Bitter and Might Oak Oscar Wilde are regularly available, plus seasonal guest beers. A total of three real ales available at any time. All beers are served straight from the barrel.

A traditional freehouse with both smoking and non-smoking bars. Food served in a separate non-smoking restaurant at lunchtimes and Friday and Saturday evenings. Car park and garden. Follow the 'old' road into Clacton (i.e. not the bypass).

OPEN *12–11pm (10.30pm Sun). Sun evenings in winter.*

LITTLE OAKLEY

Ye Olde Cherry Tree Inn

Clacton Road, Little Oakley, Harwich CO12 5JH
☎ *(01255) 880333* Steve and Julie Chandler
www.cherrytreepub.com

Adnams Best and Broadside and Fuller's London Pride always available, plus two rotating guest, one session and one heavier brew, changing weekly.

A traditional country pub with traditional pub games. One bar, beer garden and children's play area. Friendly, family atmosphere, overlooking the sea. Bistro-style restaurant with non-smoking area open Tues–Sat lunchtimes and evenings; bar food served 12–2pm and 7–9pm. Colchester and North East Essex CAMRA Pub of the Year 2000 and 2001. Cask Marque winner. Children allowed.

 *11am–2.30pm and 5–11pm Mon–Fri; all day (subject to trade) Sat–Sun.*

LITTLE TOTHAM

The Swan

School Road, Little Totham CM9 8LB
☎ *(01621) 892689* John Pascoe
www.theswanpublichouse.co.uk

A freehouse with a reputation for real ale. Top nine always available Mighty Oak Oscar Wilde Mild, Totham Parva, English Oak and Maldon Gold, Crouch Vale Brewer's Gold, Adnams Southwold Bitter, Fuller's London Pride, Greene King Abbot and IPA. Four guests which often include Nethergate Augustinian, Hop Back Summer Lightning, Triple FFF Pressed Rat and Warthog and Mauldons Peggotty's Porter. All beers dispensed straight from the barrel, can have up to 25 barrels in the cellar at one time.

CAMRA Pub of the Year 2002 and NFU Countryside Rural Pub of the Year 2003, this is a traditional English country pub in a Grade II listed building with heavy beams, low ceilings and a large open fire. Food available every lunchtime. Separate dining area. Non-smoking area. Free camping and caravanning is available to customers. House Rule: no swearing. Dress Code: no vests/ singlets/backwards hats. Children welcome – with well-behaved parents! Muddy boots and dogs welcome. Situated off the B1022 Colchester–Maldon road, near Tiptree.

11am–11pm Mon–Sat; 12–10.30pm Sun.

LITTLEBURY

The Queen's Head

High Street, Littlebury, Nr Saffron Walden CB11 4TD
☎ *(01799) 522251* Martin Housden

A Greene King tied house with IPA and Ruddles Best permanently available, plus guest beers.

A sixteenth-century coaching inn with exposed beams, a snug and two open fires. Good food available lunchtimes and evenings, all home-cooked using freshly prepared ingredients to create interesting restaurant-style meals rather than typical pub grub. Non-smoking area, car park, garden. Accommodation. Children allowed. On the B1383, between Newport and junction 9 of the M11.

12–4pm and 5.30–11pm Mon–Thurs; 12–11pm Fri–Sat; 12–3pm and 7–10.30pm Sun.

MALDON

The White Horse

26 High Street, Maldon CM9 5PJ
☎ *(01621) 851708* Gary and Wendy Cooper

A Shepherd Neame tied house. So, Bishop's Finger, Spitfire and Master Brew always available plus one rotating guest.

A typical high-street pub offering homemade food at lunchtime and evenings, with specials changed daily. Patio. Pool table. Children allowed. B & B accommodation.

OPEN *All day, every day.*

MANNINGTREE

Manningtree Station Buffet

Station Road, Lawford, Manningtree CO11 2LH
☎ *(01206) 391114* Mr Paul Sankey

Adnams Best and IPA permanently available, plus two guest ales.

A station buffet, built in 1846. Food served all day in a 24-seater restaurant. Restaurant menu in evenings, pies and breakfast until 2.30pm. Children allowed.

OPEN *5.30am–11pm Mon–Fri; 7am–11pm Sat; 8am–3pm Sun.*

MILL GREEN

The Viper

Mill Green Road, Mill Green, Nr Ingatestone CM4 0PT
☎ *(01277) 352010* Mr RDM Beard

Five regularly changing real ales always available, including a mild. These may be from Mighty Oak, Nethergate, Wolf, Crouch Vale, Oakham, Ridleys or other breweries around the country. A traditional cider is always available.

A small, traditional, unspoilt country pub with award-winning garden. Bar food available at lunchtime. Car park. Children allowed in garden only. Take the Ivy Barn road off the A12. Turn off at Margaretting. Two miles north-west of Ingatestone.

OPEN *12–3pm and 6–11pm Mon–Sat; 12–3pm and 7–10.30pm Sun.*

MORETON

The Nag's Head

Church Road, Moreton, Nr Ongar CM5 0LF
☎ *(01277) 890239* Richard Keep

A Ridleys tied house serving IPA, Prospect, Old Bob and Rumpus.

A country pub with food served at lunchtimes and evenings in a separate dining area.

OPEN *11.30am–3.30pm and 6–11pm Mon–Fri; all day Sat–Sun (all day Fri–Sun in Summer).*

NAVESTOCK HEATH

The Plough Inn

Sabines Road, Navestock Heath RM4 1HD
☎ *(01277) 372296*

Marston's Pedigree and Fuller's London Pride among the beers always available in a varied selection of eight real ales (100+ per year) chosen from all across the land.

A one-bar public house with a small dining room and family room. Background music, no juke box, machines or pool table. Bar snacks and meals are available at lunchtime and evenings (except Sunday and Monday). Car park, two gardens, children allowed. The pub is difficult to find, so ring for directions.

11am–11pm Mon–Sat; 12–10.30pm Sun.

ONGAR

The Royal Oak

High Street, Ongar CM5 9DX
☎ *(01277) 363893* Terry Butcher

Ridleys IPA and Prospect are always on offer.

Traditional local boozer. No food. Darts, folk club every other Tuesday. Children not allowed. Car park.

11.30am–3pm and 5.30–11pm Mon–Thurs; 11am–11pm Fri–Sat; 12–10.30pm Sun.

ORSETT

The Foxhound

High Road, Orsett RM16 3ER
☎ *(01375) 891295* Jackie Firman

Tied house with one pump offering a regularly changing guest beer, perhaps from Elgood's, Fuller's, O'Hanlon's, Everards, Charles Wells, York, Millennium, Hampshire, Phoenix or Shepherd Neame, among others.

Traditional, two-bar country pub with local pictures and memorabilia covering the walls. Saloon lounge bar with open fire and 'tree'. Bar and restaurant food available every lunchtime and Wed–Sat evenings. Traditional roasts on Sundays. Darts and pub games in public bar. Dogs welcome. Patio. Large car park. Well-behaved children welcome in the restaurant.

11am–3.30pm and 6–11pm Mon–Fri; 11am–11pm Sat; 12–3.30pm and 7–10.30pm Sun.

PEBMARSH

The King's Head

The Street, Pebmarsh, Nr Halstead CO9 2NH
☎ *(01787) 269306* Jackie and Graham Tufnell

Greene King IPA always available plus three constantly changing guest ales.

A richly timbered freehouse dating from around 1450, with restaurant, large bar area and pool room. Homemade meals available at lunchtimes and evenings – fresh fish, Mexican and American dishes complement a range of traditional food, including Sunday roasts. Barbecues in season. Large car park, outside seating for over 100 on the forecourt and patio, and in the beer garden. Bouncy castle and other outdoor games for children. One mile off the A131 Halstead to Sudbury road.

12–3pm and 6–11pm Tues–Sat (closed Mondays); 12–6pm Sun (closed Sun evening).

PLESHEY

The White Horse

The Street, Pleshey, Chelmsford CM3 1HA
☎ *(01245) 237281* Mike and Jan Smail

Young's PA, Triple A and Waggle Dance and a selection of Smiles ales always available.

A village pub in very picturesque historic village. One bar and two eating areas, large garden, car park. Food served at lunchtime and evenings during the week and all day at weekends. Children allowed.

11am–3pm and 7–11pm Mon–Sat; 12–4pm Sun (closed Sun evening).

RADWINTER

The Plough Inn

Radwinter, Nr Saffron Walden CB10 2TL
☎ *(01799) 599222*

A freehouse with Adnams Best and Greene King IPA always available, plus two or three rotating guests such as Oakhill Mendip Gold, Jennings Cumberland Ale, Shepherd Neame Spitfire, Timothy Taylor Landlord, Nethergate Golden Gate and Hop Back Summer Lightning.

A seventeenth-century country freehouse with heavy emphasis on food and accommodation. Non-smoking area in the restaurant. Food available at lunchtime and evenings. Children and dogs welcome. At the junction of B1053 and B1054, four miles east of Saffron Walden.

12–3pm and 6.30–11pm (10.30pm Sun).

RICKLING GREEN

The Cricketer's Arms

Rickling Green, Quendon, Saffron Walden CB11 3YG
☎ *(01799) 543210* Tim Proctor
www.cricketers.demon.co.uk

A freehouse with three guest ales always available from a list including Wadworth 6X, Fuller's ESB, one best bitter and one dark mild. The focus is on stronger brews. Also a selection of Belgian beers.

A heavily timbered building dating from 1590, ten en-suite bedrooms, three dining rooms (one non-smoking). Food served daily at lunchtime and evenings. Children not allowed in the main bar area. Facing the cricket green, just off the B1383 at Quendon.

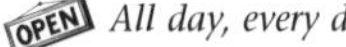 *All day, every day.*

RIDGEWELL

The White Horse

Mill Road, Ridgewell CO9 4SG
☎ *(01440) 785532* Robin Briggs

A freehouse serving a constantly changing range of real ales, which may include Fuller's London Pride or brews from Young's, Shepherd Neame, Hop Back, Cottage or other smaller breweries.

A rural village pub with games room, pool table and darts. Single bar covered in old pennies (4,200 in all). Large restaurant, beer garden and car park. Food served at lunchtime and evenings. Children allowed. Located on the A1017 between Halstead and Haverhill.

 *6–11pm Tues; 11am–3pm and 6–11pm Wed–Sat; 12–10.30pm Sun (closed all day Mon except bank holidays).*

ROCHFORD

The Golden Lion

35 North Street, Rochford SS4 1AB
☎ *(01702) 545487* Sue Williams

Greene King Abbot and Timothy Taylor Landlord always available, plus four guests ales which constantly change. The emphasis is on unusual brews from smaller breweries, and one dark ale is always served. Scrumpy is a permanent feature.

A sixteenth-century traditional-style freehouse with one bar with beams and brasses and a small beer garden. South East Essex CAMRA Pub of the Year 2003. Well-behaved dogs welcome.

OPEN *12–11pm.*

ROMFORD

The Moon & Stars

103 South Street, Romford, RM1 1NX
☎ *(01708) 730117* Sarah Saye

A Wetherspoon's pub with Greene King Abbot and Shepherd Neame Spitfire among the beers always available. Four guest ales change on a weekly basis.

Large bar, non-smoking dining area, outside seating, disabled facilities. Food available all day. Children allowed outside only.

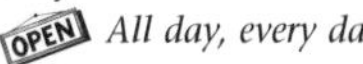 *All day, every day.*

SHALFORD

The George Inn

The Street, Shalford CM7 5HH
☎ *(01371) 850207* Mr and Mrs D Buckman

Greene King IPA and Old Speckled Hen and Adnams Broadside always available, plus one changing guest. Regular guests include Badger Best, Morrells Trinity and Shepherd Neame Spitfire.

A country pub, over 500 years old, with restaurant and bar areas. Food available lunchtimes and evenings, including Sunday roasts. Children welcome if eating. Patio and ample parking. Situated on the main road from Braintree to Wethersfield.

 *12–3pm and 6.30–11pm (closed Sunday evening).*

SOUTHEND-ON-SEA

Cork & Cheese

10 Talza Way, Victoria Plaza, Southend-on-Sea SS2 5BG
☎ *(01702) 616914* John Murray

Nethergate IPA always available plus guests from all micro-breweries (over 2,350 in last ten years).

An alehouse with a cosmopolitan trade. Local CAMRA Pub of the Year 2002. Separate dining area for bar and restaurant meals. Food available at lunchtime. Multi-storey car park nearby. Patio in summer. Children allowed in the restaurant. Located on the basement floor of the Victoria Circus shopping centre in Southend.

OPEN *11am–11pm Mon–Sat; closed Sun.*

Last Post

Weston Road, Southend-on-Sea SS1 1AS
☎ *(01702) 431682* Robin Duberley

Greene King Abbot always available, plus up to six daily-changing guests such as Greene King Old Speckled Hen or Hop Back Summer Lightning. Anything and everything from brewers of real ale considered.

A busy two-bar operation with disabled access and toilets. No music, a real drinkers' pub. Two non-smoking areas. Food served all day, every day. No children. Opposite the railway station.

10am–11pm.

SOUTHMINSTER

The Station Arms

39 Station Road, Southminster CM0 7EW
☎ *(01621) 772225* Martin Park

Crouch Vale Brewer's Gold and Adnams Bitter always available, plus three guest beers from a range of small independent brewers.

A welcoming, one-bar, Essex weatherboard pub with open fire and traditional pub furniture. CAMRA Dengie and Maldon Pub of the Year 2001. Pub games played. Restaurant and courtyard to the rear. Food served in restaurant Thurs–Sat evenings only. Street parking. No children. Three beer festivals held each year, with 30 real ales at each. Just 200 yards from Southminster railway station.

12–2.30pm and 6–11pm Mon–Fri; 12–11pm Sat; 12–4pm and 7–10.30pm Sun.

STANFORD RIVERS

The Woodman

155 London Road, Stanford Rivers, Ongar
☎ *(01277) 362019* Peter Benefield

Shepherd Neame Master Brew, Spitfire and Bishop's Finger regularly available.

Wooden-clad, fourteenth-century inn set in three acres. Food served all day. Car park. Children's play area.

11am–11pm Mon–Sat; 12–10.30pm Sun.

STISTED

The Dolphin

Stisted, Braintree CM7 8EU
☎ *(01376) 321143* George James

Tied to Ridleys, with IPA and ESX Best always on offer, plus other Ridleys beers such as Fisherman's Whopper.

Traditional locals' pub – three cottages knocked into one. Food available. Beer garden, car park. Children not allowed. On the main A120 from Stansted and Colchester.

12–3pm and 6–11pm Mon–Sat; 12–3pm and 7–10.30pm Sun.

STOCK

The Hoop

21 High Street, Stock CM4 9BD
☎ *(01277) 841137* Albert and David Kitchen

Up to ten beers available. Brews from Adnams, Crouch Vale, Wadworth and Charles Wells always served. Guests from Bateman, Archers, Ringwood, Hop Back, Jennings, Exmoor, Fuller's, Marston's, Nethergate, Rooster's and Shepherd Neame.

The pub has been adapted from some late fifteenth-century beamed cottages. There is an extensive beer garden to the rear. Bar food available all day. Barbecues at weekends in summer, weather permitting. Parking. Children not allowed. Take the B1007 from the A12 Chelmsford bypass, then take the Galleywood–Billericay turn-off.

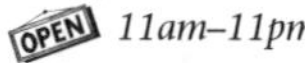
11am–11pm.

STOW MARIES

The Prince of Wales

Woodham Road, Stow Maries CM3 6SA
☎ *(01621) 828971* Robert Walster

Fuller's Chiswick always available plus any four guests (too many to count) including a mild and a stout/porter from small independent and the better regional brewers.

A traditional Essex weatherboard pub with real fires and Victorian bakehouse. Bar food available at lunchtime and evenings. Car park, garden and family room. Under two miles from South Woodham Ferrers on the road to Cold Norton.

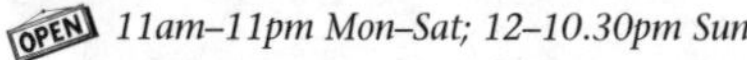
11am–11pm Mon–Sat; 12–10.30pm Sun.

TENDRING

The Cherry Tree

Crow Lane, Tendring CO16 9AP
☎ *(01255) 830340* Mr Whitnell

Greene King IPA, Abbot and Adnams Best always available, plus a regularly changing guest.

An olde-worlde pub and restaurant. One bar, big garden. Food served at lunchtime and evenings. Well-behaved children allowed.

11am–3pm and 6–11pm Mon–Sat; all day Sun.

TOOT HILL

The Green Man and Courtyard Restaurant

Toot Hill, Nr Ongar CM5 9SD
☎ *(01992) 522255* Diane Whitworth

Crouch Vale Best always available plus two guests changing twice weekly including, perhaps, an Adnams brew or Fuller's London Pride. No strong bitters over 4.3% ABV.

A country freehouse with two restaurants, one bar, courtyard and beer garden. Food served at lunchtime and evenings. Children aged 11+ allowed. Five letting rooms available 2005.

 *11am–3pm and 6–11pm (10.30pm Sun).*

WENDENS AMBO

The Bell

Royston Road, Wendens Ambo CB11 4JY
☎ *(01799) 540382* Elizabeth Fetzer

Adnams' Bitter and Broadside always available plus three or four guests from small independents and micro-breweries.

Built in 1576, beamed with open fires in winter. Home-cooked food available 12–2pm and 6–9pm Mon–Fri, 12–3pm and 6–9pm Sat, 12–3pm Sun (no food Sun evenings except through summer). Extensive wine list. Car park, dining terrace overlooking pond, three and a half acres of landscaped gardens with wilderness walk to river. Children's golf. Family-friendly garden with areas of water inaccessible to toddlers.

 *11.30am–2.30pm and 5–11pm Mon–Thurs; all day Fri–Sun.*

WHITE RODING

The Black Horse

Chelmsford Road, White Roding CM6 1RF
☎ *(01279) 876322* Michael Miller

A Ridleys house with IPA and Old Bob always on offer.

A traditional family-oriented country pub with two bars, a non-smoking dining room and beer garden. Bar food and full à la carte menu available with fish a speciality. No food on Sunday evenings. Well-behaved children allowed.

 *5.30–11pm Mon; 11.30am–3pm and 5.30–11pm Tues–Fri; 11.30am–3pm and 6–11pm Sat; 12–3pm and 7–10.30pm Sun.*

WITHAM

The Woolpack

7 Church Street, Witham CM8 2JP
☎ *(01376) 511195* Lynda Thomas

Greene King IPA and Charles Wells Eagle always available, plus one constantly changing guest ale from a wide range.

A small community locals' drinking pub. Team oriented (darts, pool, cribbage etc). Bar snacks available at lunchtime. No children.

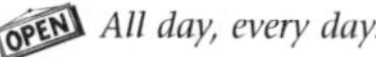 *All day, every day.*

WOODFORD GREEN

The Cricketers

299–301 High Road, Woodford Green IG8 9HQ
☎ *(020) 8504 2734* Mr and Mrs Woolridge

Owned by McMullen, so AK Original, and Country Best Bitter always served, with specials and seasonals when available.

A semi-rural pub with lounge and public bars and beer garden. Food available 12–2pm Mon–Sat, with OAP specials Mon–Thurs. Children allowed till 6.30pm in the lounge bar only. Situated near the statue of Winston Churchill.

 *11am–11pm Mon–Fri; 11.30am–11pm Sat; 12–10.30pm Sun.*

WOODHAM FERRERS

The Bell Inn

Main Road, Woodham Ferrers, Chelmsford CM3 8RF
☎ *(01245) 320443* DL Giles and S Rowe

Ridleys IPA and Adnams Bitter regularly available, plus five guest beers often from Ridleys, Adnams, Mauldons, Crouch Vale or Cottage.

Friendly village pub with cosy bars and open fire in winter. Freshly cooked food served 12–2.30pm and 7–10pm Mon–Fri, 12–10pm Sat–Sun. Car park. No children.

 *11am–3pm and 6–11pm Mon–Fri; 11am–11pm Sat; 12–10.30pm Sun.*

WOODHAM WALTER

The Bell

The Street, Woodham Walter, Maldon CM9 6RF
☎ *(01245) 223437* Tony Lorrimore

A freehouse with Greene King IPA permanently available, plus two guest pumps serving real ales from a wide range with around six different ales per month from the smaller independent and micro-breweries.

A traditional sixteenth-century village inn with beams, one large bar and non-smoking dining room. No machines. Background music from the 1930s and 1940s. Beer garden. Food available lunchtimes and evenings in a separate dining room. Children allowed.

 *12–3pm and 6–11pm Mon–Sat; 12–4pm and 7–10.30pm Sun.*

GLOUCESTERSHIRE

THE BREWERIES

BATH ALES LTD
Siston Lane, Webbs Heath, Bristol BS30 5LX
☎ *(0117) 961 5122*
www.bathales.com

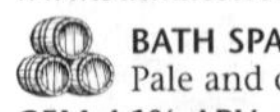

BATH SPA 3.7% ABV
Pale and quenching.
GEM 4.1% ABV
Well-rounded flavours with balancing hops.
BARNSTORMER 4.5% ABV
Roast malt flavour with some fruitiness.
FESTIVITY 5.0% ABV
Award winning – rich, dark and warming.
SPA EXTRA 5.0% ABV
A golden beer with bags of hop character and a bitter finish.
RARE HARE 5.2% ABV
Dry and clean on the palate.
Plus seasonal brews.

DONNINGTON BREWERY
Upper Swell, Stow-on-the-Wold GL54 1EP
☎ *(01451) 830603*

BB 3.6% ABV
Plenty of flavour for gravity.
SBA 4.4% ABV
Smooth and malty.

FREEMINER BREWERY LTD
Whimsey Road, Stem Mills, Cinderford GL14 3JA
☎ *(01594) 827989*
www.freeminer.com

BITTER 4.0% ABV
IRON BREW 4.2% ABV
SPECULATION ALE 4.8% ABV
GOLD STANDARD 5.0% ABV
SHAKEMANTLE GINGER ALE 5.0% ABV
DEEP SHAFT 6.2% ABV
Seasonals:
STRIP AND AT IT 4.0% ABV
Summer brew.
Plus occasionals.

GOFF'S BREWERY LTD
9 Isbourne Way, Winchcombe GL54 5NS
☎ *(01242) 603383*
www.goffs.biz

JOUSTER 4.0% ABV
Fruity, with hop flavours.
TOURNAMENT 4.0% ABV
Amber thirst-quenching bitter with delicate floral aroma.
WHITE KNIGHT 4.7% ABV
Pale, with hoppiness throughout.
Plus eight ales from the round table.

NORTH COTSWOLD BREWERY
Unit 3, Ditchford Farm, Moreton-in-Marsh GL56 9RD
☎ *(01608) 663947*

SOLSTICE 3.7% ABV
Straw coloured and lightly hopped.
GENESIS 4.0% ABV
Full bodied with refreshing taste.
FOUR SHIRES 4.2% ABV
Copper coloured, balanced hop flavour.
XMAS SPECIAL 4.4% ABV
Dark with smooth malty taste.

SMILES BREWING CO. LTD
Colston Yard, Colston Street, Bristol BS1 5BD
☎ *(0117) 929 9308*
www.smiles.co.uk

ORIGINAL 3.8% ABV
BEST BITTER 4.1% ABV
Well-rounded, hop, fruit and malt flavours.
BRISTOL IPA 4.5% ABV
With a delicate aroma.
HERITAGE 5.2% ABV
Dark and rich with roast malt character.
Plus monthly brews.

STANWAY BREWERY
Stanway, Cheltenham GL54 5PQ
☎ *(01386) 584320*
www.stanwaybrewery.co.uk

COTTESWOLD GOLD 3.9% ABV
Light refreshing ale only brewed in summer.
LORDS-A-LEAPING 4.5% ABV
Winter ale.
STANNEY BITTER 4.5% ABV
Quenching, with hoppiness throughout.

ULEY BREWERY LTD
The Old Brewery, The Street, Uley, Dursley GL11 5TB
☎ *(01453) 860120*

HOGSHEAD PALE ALE 3.5% ABV
Light in colour and well-hopped.
ULEY BITTER 4.0% ABV
Balanced and full-flavoured.
LAURIE LEE'S BITTER 4.5% ABV
OLD RIC 4.5% ABV
OLD SPOT 5.0% ABV
Flagship ale. Powerful malt flavour with fruit and hops.
PIG'S EAR 5.0% ABV
Smooth IPA.

WICKWAR BREWERY CO.

The Old Cider Mill, Station Road, Wickwar GL12 8NB
☎ *(01454) 294168*
www.wickwarbrewing.co.uk

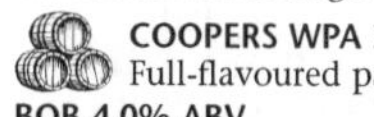

COOPERS WPA 3.5% ABV
Full-flavoured pale ale.

BOB 4.0% ABV
Characterful and well-balanced.

COTSWOLD WAY 4.2% ABV
Rich amber, smooth, well-balanced beer.

OLD ARNOLD 4.6% ABV

OLD MERRYFORD ALE 4.8% ABV
Flavoursome, with hoppy fruit aroma.

MR PERRETT'S TRADITIONAL STOUT 5.9% ABV
A powerful stout with a liquorice and chocolate taste.

STATION PORTER 6.1%ABV
Intricate, well-rounded blend of flavours.

Plus seasonal and occasional brews.

THE PUBS

AMPNEY ST PETER

Red Lion

Ampney St Peter, Cirencester GL7 1SL
☎ *(01285) 851596* John Barnard

Freehouse serving Hook Norton Best plus Timothy Taylor Landlord at the weekend.

A unique little gem of a pub, 400 years old. Only three different landlords since 1887, present one (very friendly) has been here since 1975. Two small rooms, one in which the beer is served. No lager. Car park. Children allowed in the games room.

6–10pm Mon–Thur; 6–11pm Fri–Sat; 7–10.30pm Sun; also lunchtimes at the weekend and bank holidays.

APPERLEY

Coal House Inn

Gabb Lane, Apperley GL19 4DN
☎ *(01452) 780211* Mrs McDonald

Wickwar BOB always available plus two changing guests.

A country freehouse on the east bank of the River Severn. Home-cooked food served lunchtimes and evenings. 'Portuguese Steak on a Stone' a speciality. Large car parks and riverside garden. Children allowed. Moorings for boats (24 hours). Apperley is signposted on B4213 south of Tewkesbury. Follow signs for Coalhouse Wharf from village centre.

April–Sept: 12–2.30pm and 6–11pm; Oct–Mar: 12–2.30pm and 7–11pm; 12–3pm and 7–10.30pm Sun (all year).

ASHLEWORTH

12

The Boat Inn

The Quay, Ashleworth GL19 4HZ
☎ *(01452) 700272* Mrs Nicholls

Always something from the Wye Valley and RCH breweries plus at least another two constantly changing guest beers, perhaps from the Church End, Hook Norton, Arkells or Hobsons breweries.

A small fifteenth-century cottage pub on the banks of the River Severn which has remained in the same family for 400 years. Rolls available at lunchtime. Car park and garden. Children allowed. Ashleworth is signposted off the A417 north of Gloucester. The Quay is signed from the village.

April–Sept: 11.30am–2.30pm and 6.30–11pm Mon–Sat, closed Mon and Wed lunchtime; 12–3pm and 7–10.30pm Sun; Oct–Mar: 11.30am–2.30pm Thurs–Tues, closed Mon, Wed and Thur lunchtime; 7–11pm Mon–Sat; 12–3pm and 7–10.30pm Sun.

AVENING

The Bell

29 High Street, Avening, Tetbury GL8 8NF
☎ *(01453) 836422*
Tony Seward and Simon Taylor

A freehouse with Wickwar BOB usually available plus two guests.

A traditional Cotswold pub with log fire, dining area and garden. Food served at lunchtime and evenings, every day. Children allowed.

12–3pm and 6–11pm (10.30pm Sun).

AWRE

The Red Hart Inn

Awre, Newnham GL14 1EW
☎ *(01594) 510220* Gerry Bedwell

A freehouse with Fuller's London Pride generally available, plus two guests changing weekly. Examples include something from Wickwar, Archer's or Goff's. The landlord's policy is to support smaller breweries as much as possible.

A beamed hostelry dating from 1483 with one bar area. Non-smoking area. Outside seating in front garden. Bar snacks and à la carte menu available at lunchtime and evenings. Children allowed until 8pm, if well supervised. Set in a tranquil hamlet environment. Turn off A48 between Newnham and Blakeney.

6.30–11pm Mon (check in the winter); 12–3pm and 6.30–11pm Tues–Sat; 12–3pm and 7–10.30pm Sun.

BEDMINSTER

Robert Fitzharding

24 Cannon Street, Bedminster, Bristol BS3 1BN
☎ *(0117) 966 2757* Neil Sykes

A Wetherspoon's pub with Butcombe Gold always available. Four guest pumps serve a range of 30 guests every quarter. Examples include Coniston Bluebird, Exmoor Beast, Caledonian Deuchars IPA or something from Burton Bridge.

A city suburb pub with non-smoking area. Two beer festivals held each year. Food served all day. Children welcome until 6pm.

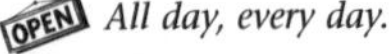
All day, every day.

BIRDLIP

The Golden Heart Inn

Nettleton Bottom, Nr Birdlip GL4 8LA
☎ *(01242) 870261*
Mr D Morgan and Miss C Stevens

Timothy Taylor Landlord and Golden Best and something from Young's and Archers always available, plus guest beers.

A sixteenth-century pub with stone floors, beams and bric-à-brac. Bar food available at lunchtime and evenings. The menu features both traditional dishes and exotic fare such as ostrich, crocodile and kangaroo, and there is also an emphasis on English meats from prize-winning stock. Beer festivals held on May and August bank holidays, featuring over 40 real ales plus cider and perry. Live music, barbecues, camping. Also has en-suite accommodation available. Car park, garden, children's room and function room. Situated on the A417 between Cheltenham, Gloucester and Cirencester, two miles from Birdlip.

11am–3pm and 5.30–11pm Mon–Thurs; 11am–11pm Fri–Sat; 12–10.30pm Sun; summer all day every day.

BISHOPSTON

The Annexe

Seymour Road, Bishopston, Bristol BS7 9EQ
☎ *(0117) 949 3931* Teresa Rogers

Smiles Best, Marston's Pedigree and Greene King IPA are permanent plus one guest changing daily.

A town pub with disabled access, children's room, garden, darts etc. Bar food available at lunchtime and restaurant food in the evenings. Children allowed until 8.30pm in the conservatory only.

11.30am–2.30pm and 6–11pm Mon–Fri; 11.30am–11pm Sat; 12–10.30pm Sun.

BLAISDON

The Red Hart Inn

Blaisdon, Nr Longhope GL17 0AH
☎ *(01452) 830477* Guy Wilkins

Hook Norton Best Bitter regularly available plus three guest beers perhaps from Uley, Wickwar, Berkeley, Freeminer, Goff's, RCH, Timothy Taylor, Wood, Eccleshall, Exmoor, Otter, Hop Back, Adnams, Cotleigh or Greene King.

Traditional English village pub with stone floor, low-beamed ceiling and open fire. Large bar area and separate non-smoking restaurant with food available 12–2pm and 7–9pm Sun–Thurs, 12–2pm and 7–9.30pm Fri–Sat. Barbecue and large garden with children's play area. Car park. Unattended children in the bar are sold as slaves.

12–2.30pm and 6–11pm Mon–Sat; 12–3pm and 7–10.30pm Sun.

BLEDINGTON

The Kings Head Inn

The Green, Bledington OX7 6XQ
☎ *(01608) 658365*
Archie and Nicola Orr-Ewing

A beer from Hook Norton usually available, plus two guest beers which may include Shepherd Neame Spitfire, Timothy Taylor Landlord, Uley Old Spot or Pig's Ear, Wychwood Hobgoblin or Fiddlers Elbow, Smiles Best, Adnams Broadside amongst many others.

Quintessential, fifteenth-century Cotswold stone inn located on the village green with brook and attendant ducks. Retains olde-worlde charm of pews, settles, flagstone floors, beams, antique furnishings and inglenook fireplace. Tasteful accommodation. Food served 12–2pm and 7–9.45pm. Children welcome, under supervision, in the garden room. Large car park. On the B4450.

11am–2.30pm and 6–11pm Mon–Sat; 12–3pm and 7–10.30pm Sun.

BLOCKLEY

Great Western Arms

Station Road, Blockley GL56 9DT
☎ *(01386) 700362* John Ferguson

Hook Norton brews plus one guest changing every month.

Typical unpretentious local in classic Cotswold pretty village. Food every session. Children welcome. Garden and car park. Darts and pool.

11.30am–3pm and 6–11pm; all day Sun in the summer.

BOX

The Halfway Inn

Minchinhampton, Box, Stroud GL6 9AE
☎ *(01453) 832631* Matthew Walker

Greene King IPA, a Smiles seasonal and Butcombe Best always available, plus a guest. Also Black Rat Scrumpy cider.

A prettily situated freehouse with refurbished bar and 70-seat restaurant. Landscaped garden with giant chessboard and Jenga.

 *Closed Monday; summer: 12–11pm Tues–Sun; winter: 12–3pm and 6–11pm Tues–Thurs; 5–11pm Fri; 12–11pm Sat–Sun.*

BREAM

The Rising Sun

High Street, Bream, Forest of Dean GL15 6JF
☎ *(01594) 564555* Peter and Julie Hicks

A freehouse serving Goff's Jouster, one of the Freeminer beers and at least two guest ales.

A friendly traditional pub that won CAMRA Forest of Dean pub of the year in 2002 and 2003. Annual beer festival in October. Food every session. Children and dogs welcome. Car park and garden. Darts.

 *12–2.30pm and 6.30–11pm Mon–Fri; all day Sat–Sun.*

BRISTOL

The Bag O'Nails

141 St Georges Road, Hotwells, Bristol BS1 5UW
☎ *(0117) 940 6776* James Dean
www.bagonails.org.uk

Up to six different beers served on a guest basis (over 300 offered in two years). Always supplied by smaller, independent breweries. The pub's own web page gives details of beers stocked at any one time.

A small, quiet, gas-lit city-centre pub with one bar. Situated just 25 yards from the Dock. Simple lunches only, served 12–2pm. No children.

 *12–2.15pm and 5.30–11pm Mon–Thurs; all day Fri–Sun.*

The Bell Inn

21 Alfred Place, Kingsdown, Bristol BS2 8HD
☎ *(0117) 907 7563* Anna Luke

A freehouse regularly offering Abbey Bellringer and Sharp's Own. Also RCH Pitchfork plus occasional guests.

A proper, traditional English pub with a warm and friendly atmosphere. Customers an eclectic mix of all ages. Candlelight in the evenings. No food. No children. Situated off St Michael's Hill, at the back of the BRI hospital.

 *4.30-11pm Mon–Tues and Thurs–Fri; 12–11pm Wed; 4–11pm Sat; 7–10.30pm Sun.*

The Bridge Inn

16 Passage Street, Bristol BS2 0JF
☎ *(0117) 949 9967* Robert Clarke

Freehouse that has Bath SPA and Gem as permanents, plus occasional guests, perhaps something from RCH or Hop Back.

The smallest pub in Bristol, it has office-based clientele during the day and a mixed bunch in the evening. Basic pub food at lunchtime but the emphasis is on the beer.

11.30am–11pm Mon–Fri; 12–11pm Sat; 7–10.30pm Sun.

Cadbury House

68 Richmond Road, Montpelier, Bristol BS6 5EW
☎ *(0117) 924 7874* Claire Trick

Sharp's Doom Bar and Bath Ales Gem always available plus one rotating guest, perhaps Greene King Old Speckled Hen.

A locals' pub in a residential area. Clientele a mix of regulars and students. Large beer garden. Bar meals lunchtime and evening. Children allowed until 9pm.

All day, every day.

The Cat & Wheel

207 Cheltenham Road, Bristol
☎ *(0117) 942 7862*
Scott Waldron and Jim Hill

A Mole's pub with Mole's Tap Bitter always on offer.

A two-bar pub, famous for its pig-racing nights! One bar has a traditional, relaxed atmosphere, while the other is student-oriented, with pool and juke box. No food. Bands and singers on Fridays 9–11pm – no door charge. Children not allowed.

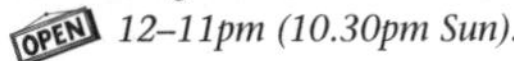 *12–11pm (10.30pm Sun).*

GLOUCESTERSHIRE

Commercial Rooms

43–5 Corn Street, Bristol BS1 1HT
☎ *(0117) 927 9681*

A freehouse serving Butcombe Bitter and Gold plus two guests changing constantly, at least nine different beers in a week.

A town-centre pub with twice-yearly beer festivals in April and October. Food served all day. Children allowed until 6pm.

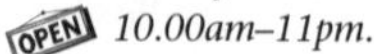
10.00am–11pm.

Cornubia

142 Temple Street, Bristol BS1 6EN
☎ *(0117) 925 4415* Jason Champion

A freehouse offering up to five constantly changing beers from a range of hundreds per year, specialising in micro-breweries from around the country. A dark mild, porter or stout is usually available.

A Georgian listed building situated just behind the old Courage Brewery site, 10 minutes' walk from Temple Meads Station. Traditional town-centre pub atmosphere. Food served lunchtime Mon–Fri. Well-behaved children allowed.

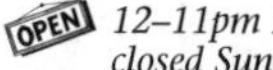
12–11pm Mon–Fri; 5.30–11pm Sat; closed Sun.

Coronation

18 Dean Lane, Southville, Bristol BS3 1DD
☎ *(0117) 9409044*

Six beers from the Hop Back brewery.

A relaxed and busy local. Pizzas served in the evening. Supervised children welcome during the day. Chess and draughts to play.

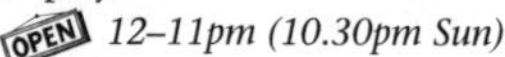
12–11pm (10.30pm Sun).

Hare On The Hill

41 Thomas Street North, Kingsdown
☎ *(0117) 9081982* James Blackwell

Bath Ales SPA, Gem, Barnstormer, SPA Extra (summer) and Festivity (winter) usually available with one or two guest beers, all above 4.8% ABV. Their own Rare Hare is also offered and they specialise in beer swaps.

Popular, Bath Ales award-winning pub. Bar food served lunchtimes and evenings. Sunday roasts 12.30–3.30pm. Well-behaved children welcome, but no special facilities.

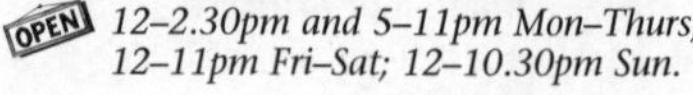
12–2.30pm and 5–11pm Mon–Thurs; 12–11pm Fri–Sat; 12–10.30pm Sun.

The Highbury Vaults

164 St Michael's Hill, Cotham, Bristol BS2 8DE
☎ *(0117) 973 3203* Bradd Francis

A Young's tied house serving Young's Bitter, Special and seasonal ales, plus Smiles Best and Heritage and Brains SA.

Very traditional pub set in the heart of university land with no music, fruit machines, pool tables etc. Lots of atmosphere for young and old, students and locals. Cheap bar food available at lunchtime and evenings (nothing fried). Heated rear garden. Children allowed in garden.

12–11pm (10.30pm Sun).

The Hope and Anchor

38 Jacobs Wells Road, Clifton, Bristol BS8 1DR
☎ *(0117) 9292987*
Nikki Hughes and David Medway

A freehouse offering up to six different real ales, changing all the time but quite likely something from Bath Ales or a micro-brewery such as Blindmans Brewery.

A laid-back, almost intellectual atmosphere with wooden floors, wooden tables and sophisticated haircuts. Food all day, every day. Beer garden at back. Chess and backgammon.

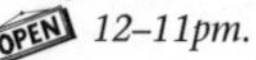
12–11pm.

Horts

49 Broad Street, Bristol BS1 2EP
☎ *(0117) 9252520* Craig Davey

Smiles Best, Young's Bitter, Special and Waggledance are permanents, plus one or two guest ales. Real cider.

A deceptively large city-centre pub that still manages to maintain atmosphere. Food, but not Fri and Sun nights. Pool tables. Small patio area.

All day, every day.

The King's Head

60 Victoria Street, Bristol BS1 6DE
☎ *(0117) 9277860* Jane Wakeham

Four real ales are served including Sharp's Doom Bar and Cornish Coaster.

Small narrow city pub with a comforting atmosphere. Part of the bar has a wooden tramcar design complete with bells and mirrors. Food available Mon–Fri 12–2pm.

11am–11pm Mon–Fri; 7.30–11pm Sat; 12–3pm and 7–10.30pm Sun.

Knowle Hotel

Leighton Road, Knowle, Bristol BS4 2LL
☎ *(0117) 9777019* Mathew and Sarah Williams

Marston's Pedigree is a permanent, and Shepherd Neame Spitfire and Greene King Abbot are alternated.

A large local, in the middle of a residential area, which is striving to be family friendly. Wonderful views over the city. Reasonably priced food. Children very welcome. Garden. Pool. Quiz night on Tuesday and the occasional casino night.

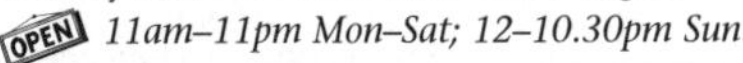
OPEN *11am–11pm Mon–Sat; 12–10.30pm Sun.*

Merchant's Arms

5 Merchant's Road, Hotwells, Bristol BS8 4PZ
☎ *(0117) 9040037* John Sprague

A Bath Ales pub offering SPA, Gem and Barnstormer. Plus one guest and perhaps a seasonal.

Like a pub used to be, a friendly, quaint, no-frills, old-style place for conversation. Limited food. Challenging quiz once a week.

OPEN *12–3pm and 5–11pm Mon–Thur; 12–11pm Fri–Sun.*

The Penny Farthing

115 Whiteladies Road, Clifton, Bristol BS8 2PB
☎ *(0117) 973 3539* Charles Corston

Henry's IPA and 6X from Wadworth, Adnams Broadside, Badger Tanglefoot and Butcombe Bitter are regulars plus three rotating guests. Charles Wells Bombardier is a favourite.

Popular character pub with strange decorations including a penny farthing. One bar. Food at lunchtime but not on Sunday. Small patio.

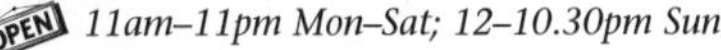
OPEN *11am–11pm Mon–Sat; 12–10.30pm Sun.*

Quinton House

No. 2 Park Place, Clifton, Bristol BS8 1JW
☎ *(0117) 9077858* Gary Russell

Five real ales generally available including Greene King Abbot, Wadworth 6X and Butcombe Bitter.

A cosy little city local with wood-clad walls and a warm atmosphere. Food every lunchtime and up until 8pm in the evening.

OPEN *11.30am–11pm (closed 3–4.30pm Mon–Thur).*

The Royal Oak

50 The Mall, Clifton Village, Bristol BS8 4JG
☎ *(0117) 9738846* Simon Dauncey

Five real ales on offer including Greene King IPA, Sharp's Doom Bar and Cornish Coaster.

A friendly local decorated with sports memorabilia and 1970s Smirnoff posters. Children welcome. Food every session. Darts, dominoes and chess to play.

OPEN *12–11pm Mon–Sat; 12–4pm Sun.*

Shakespeare Tavern

68 Prince Street, Bristol BS1 4QZ
☎ *(0117) 929 7695*

Five real ales on offer including Greene King Abbot, IPA and Old Speckled Hen.

An old pub with a traditional homely feel – open fire, bare floor boards, wood panelling. Food at lunchtime. Small terrace. Board games.

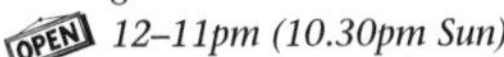
OPEN *12–11pm (10.30pm Sun).*

Smiles Brewery Tap

6–8 Colston Street, Bristol BS1 5BT
☎ *(0117) 921 3668* Rowhan Shadbolt

Smiles Original, Best, Heritage, IPA and seasonal brews available.

A traditional pub atmosphere awaits in this small horseshoe bar with hops adorning the ceiling. Separate non-smoking room and small bar with wood panelling and chequered tiled floor. Hot food served 12–3pm Mon–Sat; sandwiches always available. Children allowed in non-smoking area.

OPEN *11am–11pm Mon–Sat; ring to check time on Sun.*

BROAD CAMPDEN

The Bakers Arms

Broad Campden, Chipping Campden GL55 6UR
☎ *(01386) 840515* Sally and Ray Mayo

Charles Wells Bombardier, Timothy Taylor Landlord and brews from Stanway and Hook Norton always available, plus one rotating guest ale.

A small, friendly Cotswold country pub with open fire. Bar food available every lunchtime and evening; all day in the summer. Car park, garden, patio and children's play area. Non-smoking dining area. In a village between Chipping Campden and Blockley.

OPEN *Summer: 11.30am–11pm Mon–Sat; 12–10.30pm Sun. Winter: 11.30am–2.30pm and 4.45–11pm Mon–Fri; 11.30am–11pm Sat; 12–10.30pm Sun.*

CHARLTON KINGS

Merryfellow

2 School Lane, Charlton Kings, Cheltenham GL53 8AU
☎ *(01242) 525883* Jim Dockree

Five different beers generally available. Greene King IPA, Gale's HSB, Wadworth 6X and beers from Archers and Black Sheep are regulars.

Classic village pub offering value-for-money food and a selection of ales. No food on Monday. Car park, garden, skittle alley, function room and pool table. Children welcome.

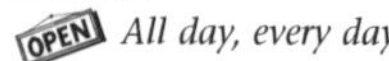 *All day, every day.*

CHELTENHAM

Adam & Eve

10 Townsend Street, Cheltenham GL51 9HD
☎ *(01242) 690030* Mrs Gasson

Arkells 2B, 3B and seasonals always on offer.

Simple side-street pub that could be somebody's front room. Skittle alley and darts. Children allowed in patio area.

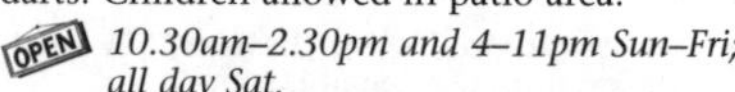 *10.30am–2.30pm and 4–11pm Sun–Fri; all day Sat.*

The Kemble Brewery Inn

27 Fairview Street, Cheltenham GL52 2JF
☎ *(01242) 243446* Dennis Melia

Timothy Taylor Landlord, Wickwar BOB and Cotswold Way, Beowulf Swordsman and Noble are regularly available with one changing guest as well, often Smiles Best.

This small, friendly local with rear courtyard is one of the few remaining real ale pubs in Cheltenham. Situated behind Fowlers motorcycle shop in the Fairview area. Food served 12–2.30pm Sun–Mon, 6–8.30pm Mon–Fri. Children welcome in courtyard.

11.30am–2.30pm and 5.30–11pm Mon–Fri; 11.30am–11pm Sat; 12–4pm and 7–11pm Sun.

Tailors

4 Cambray Place, Cheltenham GL50 1JS
☎ *(01242) 255453* Mrs Cherri Dandridge

A Wadworth-managed house with 6X, IPA and JCB always available.

A comfortable, traditional pub in the town centre, full of character. Cellar bar is a function room. Two lovely beer gardens. Four big-screen TVs. Landlady was a recent finalist in the licensee of the year. Good-value pub meals served Mon–Sat lunchtimes only. Children welcome.

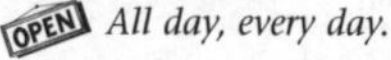 *All day, every day.*

CHIPPING CAMPDEN

The Lygon Arms

High Street, Chipping Camden GL55 6HB
☎ *(01386) 840318* Ivor Potter

Wadworth 6X, Hook Norton Best and Greene King Old Speckled Hen permanently available plus two guests, changing frequently, from any independent brewery.

A sixteenth-century, family-run coaching inn. One bar, non-smoking dining area, courtyard and beer garden, car parking at rear. En-suite accommodation. Homemade, traditional English food from local produce. Children allowed.

 *Winter: 10.30am–2.30/3pm and 6–11pm Mon–Fri; 11am–11pm Sat; 12–10.30pm Sun. Summer: 11am–11pm Mon–Sat; 12–10.30pm Sun.*

The Volunteer

Lower High Street, Chipping Campden GL55 6DY
☎ *(01386) 840688* Mrs H Sinclair

North Cotswold Genesis, Stanway Stanney Bitter and Hook Norton Best always available, plus three guests from all around the country.

A country inn with garden. Food served at lunchtime and evenings. Children allowed. Accommodation.

 *11.30am–3pm and 5–11pm Mon–Fri; 11.30am–3pm and 6–11pm Sat; 12–3pm and 7–10.30pm Sun.*

CHIPPING SODBURY

Beaufort Hunt

Broad Street, Chipping Sodbury, Bristol BS37 6AG
☎ *(01454) 312871* Mr Arnall

Greene King IPA always available plus one guest perhaps Fuller's London Pride.

An olde-style village pub with courtyard. Food available at lunchtime. Children aged 14–18 allowed in lounge bar only if eating. Under 14s not allowed.

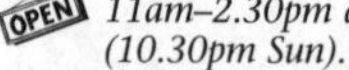 *11am–2.30pm and 5–11pm (10.30pm Sun).*

CIRENCESTER

The Bear Inn

12 Dyer Street, Cirencester GL7 2PF
☎ *(01285) 653472* Lianne

A Mole's Brewery tied house. Mole's Best is always available, plus one guest.

A town-centre pub, refurbished in the style of an old coaching inn. Home-cooked food served at lunchtime and evenings. Children allowed until 6.30pm.

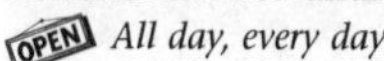 *All day, every day.*

Corinium Hotel

12 Gloucester Street, Cirencester GL7 2DG
☎ *(01285) 659711* Graham Mills

Fuller's London Pride and Shepherd Neame Spitfire generally available, plus one guest beer changing regularly.

A sixteenth-century wool merchant's house, now a hotel, bar and restaurant with Roman theme. Wide selection of food served lunchtimes and evenings. Children welcome in restaurant and garden.

OPEN *11am–11pm (10.30pm Sun).*

The Drillman's Arms

84 Gloucester Road, Cirencester GL7 2JY
☎ *(01285) 653892* Richard Selby

A freehouse serving Archers Best, Wickwar Cotswold Way and Young's bitter plus one guest.

A village pub with log fire and function room. Food served at lunchtime and evenings. Children allowed.

OPEN *11am–3pm and 5.30–11pm Mon–Fri; all day Sat; 11am–4pm and 7–10.30pm Sun.*

Twelve Bells

Lewes Lane, Cirencester GL7 1EA
☎ *(01285) 644549* RJ Ashley

A freehouse serving five different real ales but always changing – more than 350 last year.

A traditional pub offering good beer, good grub in pleasant atmosphere. Don't be fooled by the ordinariness of the outside, this is a real find. One bar with three quieter side rooms. Children welcome. Car park and garden.

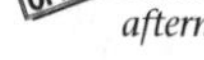

OPEN *11am–11pm (closed for an hour in the afternoon).*

CLEARWELL

The Lamb Inn

The Cross, Clearwell, Coleford GL16 8JU
☎ *(01594) 835441* FJ Yates and SY Lewis

Freeminer Best Bitter always available, with a range of guest beers which may include Goff's Jouster, Bath Ales Gem, or beers from Slater's, Otter, Hampshire, Church End, Wye Valley or Archers.

Nineteenth-century stone-built inn with later additions. No food, machines or music and the beer is served straight from the barrel. Well-behaved children welcome till 8.30pm. Car park. Situated 200 yards from Clearwell Cross on the Newland and Redbrook road.

OPEN *6–11pm Wed–Thurs; 12–3pm and 6–11pm Fri–Sat and bank holidays; 12–3pm and 7–10.30pm Sun.*

COCKLEFORD

Green Dragon Inn

Cockleford, Cowley, Cheltenham GL53 9NW
☎ *(01242) 870271* Mhari Ashwarth

Butcombe Bitter and Hook Norton Best Bitter regularly available, plus one guest, which could be from any one of a range of breweries.

Traditional Cotswold inn with stone-clad floors and roaring log fire in winter. Function room and patio overlooking lake. Accommodation. Food served 12–2.30pm and 6–10pm Mon–Fri, all day over the weekend. Car park. Children's menu and high chairs available.

OPEN *11am–11pm Mon–Sat; 12–10.30pm Sun.*

COLEFORD

The Angel Hotel

Market Place, Coleford GL16 8AE
☎ *(01594) 833113* Barry C Stoakes

Two constantly changing real ales from a range of breweries.

Dating from the sixteenth century and situated in the Forest of Dean, this was once used as a town hall but is now a nine-room hotel with real ale bar. Courtyard and beer garden. Separate nightclub attached. Food served lunchtimes and evenings with sandwiches available during the afternoons. Children welcome if dining, until 7pm.

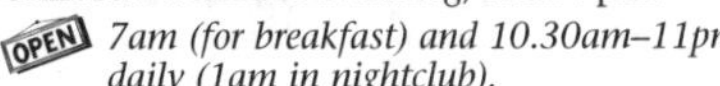

OPEN *7am (for breakfast) and 10.30am–11pm daily (1am in nightclub).*

CRANHAM

The Black Horse Inn

Cranham, Gloucester GL4 8HP
☎ *(01452) 812217* David Job

Four real ales generally available including Wickwar BOB, plus probably something from Archers.

An unspoilt traditional village inn perched on the side of a hill. Cosy lounge, classic country public bar complete with strange stag head, and dining room upstairs. No food on Sunday evening. Car park and garden. Children allowed.

OPEN *12–2.30pm and 6.30–11pm (8–10.30pm Sun). Closed some Mondays in the winter.*

DIDMARTON

The King's Arms

The Street, Didmarton, Nr Badminton GL9 1DT
☎ *(01454) 238245* Zoe Coombe

Uley Bitter and Butcombe Bitter usually available with two guest ales changing regularly.

A coaching inn dating from the seventeenth century, with two bars and a restaurant. The old country pub has been refurbished in an Edwardian style. Accommodation – rooms and self-catering cottages. Food available each session. Children welcome. Well-kept, stone-walled garden with boules piste.

11am–3pm and 6–11pm Mon–Thur; 11am–11pm Fri–Sat; 12–10.30pm Sun.

DUNTISBOURNE ABBOTS

Five Mile House

Gloucester Road, Duntisbourne Abbots, Cirencester GL7 7JR
☎ *(01285) 821432* JW Carrier

A freehouse serving three different distinctive beers of varying strength. Timothy Taylor Landlord is quite often on the list as is Donnington BB and Archers Village.

A traditional country pub with old bar, family room and garden. Food served at lunchtime and evenings in non-smoking restaurant. Well-behaved children allowed.

12–3pm and 6–11pm (7–10.30pm Sun).

DURSLEY

Old Spot Inn

Hill Road, Dursley GL11 4JQ
☎ *(01453) 542870* Stephen Herbert

Six ales always available, with Old Ric from the local Uley brewery a permanent feature. Guests are from Wickwar, Abbey, Bath, Wychwood, Fuller's, Young's, Adnams and many more.

Cosy freehouse with log fires, on the Cotswold Way. Lunches served daily. Secluded garden, boules piste. Clean-air policy. Parking. Four beer festivals every year. Live music Wednesday night. *Morning Advertiser's* Real Ale Pub of the Year 2003.

11am–3pm and 5–11pm Mon–Thurs; all day Fri–Sun.

EBRINGTON

The Ebrington Arms

Ebrington, Nr Chipping Campden GL55 6NH
☎ *(01386) 593223* Barry Leach

Hook Norton Best and Charles Wells Bombardier always available, plus one changing guest perhaps Fuller's London Pride.

An unspoilt traditional Cotswold village pub that has been sympathetically refurnished. Gentle music. Traditional games such as darts and cribbage. Bar and restaurant food at lunchtime and evenings (no food Sun and Mon evenings). Car park and garden. Children allowed in the restaurant only. Accommodation.

11am–2.30pm and 6–11pm Mon–Sat (closed Monday lunchtime); 12–3pm and 7–10.30pm Sun.

FORD

The Plough Inn

Ford, Temple Guiting GL54 5RU
☎ *(01386) 584215* Craig Brown

A Donnington Brewery house always serving BB and SBA.

A thirteenth-century Cotswold stone inn with inglenook fireplace, beams and flagstone floor. Food served at lunchtime and evenings, with a separate dining area. Children allowed. Located on the main road between Stow-on-the-Wold and Tewkesbury, opposite the Jackdaws Castle racing stables.

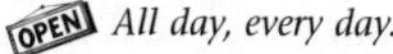
All day, every day.

FORTHAMPTON

Lower Lode Inn

Forthampton, Near Tewkesbury GL19 4RE
☎ *(01684) 293224* Samantha Snape

Freehouse with Hook Norton Old Hooky and Donnington on permanent plus up to four guests depending on the season.

A riverside inn dating from the fifteenth century. Popular with locals but also a destination pub in the summer. Accommodation. Food every session. Car park and garden. Children welcome. Pool, darts.

12–3pm and 6–11pm Mon–Thur; all day Fri–Sun; closed Mon and Tue lunchtime in the winter.

FRAMPTON COTTERELL

The Rising Sun

43 Ryecroft Road, Frampton Cotterell, Nr Bristol BS17 2HN
☎ *(01454) 772330* Kevin Stone

A popular freehouse with Butcombe Bitter, Fuller's London Pride, Wadworth 6X and Henry's IPA always available, with up to 80 guest beers per year.

Small, friendly, single-bar local that likes to support the smaller brewers. Bar food available at lunchtimes, including Sunday lunch. Evening food in the restaurant – a large conservatory.

 *11.30am–3pm and 5.30–11pm Mon–Thurs; 11.30am–11pm Fri–Sat; 12–3pm and 7–10.30pm Sun.*

FRANCE LYNCH

The King's Head

France Lynch, Stroud GL6 8LT
☎ *(01453) 882225* Mike Duff

A freehouse serving Hook Norton and Archers brews, plus a guest beer that changes frequently.

A small, traditional, country pub with large garden. No juke box. Live music every Monday evening. Food served at lunchtime and evenings. Children's play area.

 *12–2.30pm and 6–11pm Mon–Sat; 12–2.30pm and 7–10.30pm Sun.*

GLOUCESTER

Black Swan Inn

68–70 Southgate Street, Gloucester GL1 2DR
☎ *(01452) 523642* Craig Reynolds

Wickwar Cotswold Way is generally available, plus five regularly changing guests, perhaps something from Eccleshall or Boggart Hole Clough.

There's a lively and friendly atmosphere in this refurbished freehouse. One bar. Accommodation. Food every session. Car park and small garden. Children welcome.

11am–11pm Mon–Sat; 6.30–10.30pm Sun.

England's Glory

66–8 London Road, Gloucester GL1 3PB
☎ *(01452) 302948* Alban Joseph

A Wadworth-managed house with IPA, 6X and JCB always available. Also two guests, changing every week, which may include Badger Tanglefoot.

A food-oriented pub on the outskirts of town. Disabled access, non-smoking area, beer garden. Food available at lunchtime and evenings. Children allowed in the non-smoking area only.

 *11.30am–2.30pm and 5–11pm Mon–Fri; all day Sat–Sun.*

The Linden Tree

73–5 Bristol Road, Gloucester GL1 5SN
☎ *(01452) 527869* Gordon Kinnear

Wadworth 6X, Henry's IPA, and JCB always available plus up to four guest beers which may include Badger Tanglefoot.

A true country pub in the heart of Gloucester, south of the city centre. Large refurbished Georgian Grade II listed building. Bar food available at lunchtime and evenings (except Sat and Sun night). Parking, skittle alley, function room. Children allowed if eating. Accommodation. Cask Marque approved. Follow the Bristol road from the M5.

 *11.30am–2.30pm and 6–11pm Mon–Fri; 11am–11pm Sat; 12–10.30pm Sun.*

New Inn Hotel

16 Northgate Street, Gloucester GL1 1SF
☎ *(01452) 522177* Paul and Jeanette Parkin

Generally six different real ales are available, changing all the time but RCH Pitchfork is a popular one.

A friendly, relaxed pub with courtyard. Accommodation. Food every session. Darts.

 *All day, every day; 1am licence Thur–Sat.*

The Regal

32 St Aldate Street, King's Square, Gloucester GL1 1RP
☎ *(01452) 332344* Michael Ayers

A Wetherspoon's pub. Greene King Abbot and Shepherd Neame Spitfire always available plus at least two guests changed on a weekly basis.

A large town pub with non-smoking areas, disabled access and toilets. Beer garden. Food served all day. Children allowed up to 6pm (5pm Saturday). Regular beer festivals.

All day, every day.

GRETTON

The Royal Oak

Gretton Road, Gretton GL54 5EP
☎ *(01242) 604999* Andy Robertson

Owned by Goff's Brewery and serving Jouster, Tournament and White Knight, plus one guest ale changing weekly.

Much bigger than it seems, the pub has a tasteful and light extension. Panoramic views. Huge car park and play area – even has its own tennis court. Food. Children welcome.

 *12–3pm and 6–11pm Mon–Sat; 12–4pm and 7–10.30pm Sun.*

HAM

The Salutation Inn

Ham, Berkeley GL13 9QH
☎ *(01453) 810284* Mrs BS Dailly

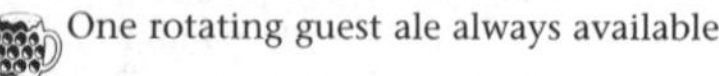
One rotating guest ale always available.

Friendly pub set in pleasant countryside. Situated off the A38 towards Berkeley. Food served 12–2pm and 7–9pm. Children are welcome, but there are no special facilities. Car park.

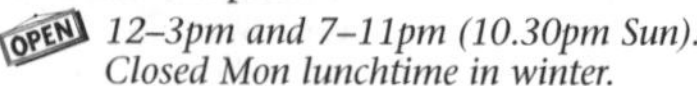
12–3pm and 7–11pm (10.30pm Sun). Closed Mon lunchtime in winter.

HANHAM MILLS

Old Lock & Weir

Hanham Mills, Bristol BS15 3NU
☎ *(0117) 967 3793* Karen State

A freehouse serving a range of up to five quality real ales, including Butcombe Bitter, Wadworth 6X and Greene King Old Speckled Hen plus two guest ales.

A riverside country pub with dining area and garden. Food available at lunchtimes and evenings. Children allowed in dining area and garden only.

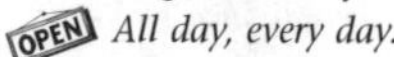
All day, every day.

HAWKESBURY UPTON

The Beaufort Arms

High Street, Hawkesbury Upton GL9 1AU
☎ *(01454) 238217*

Wickwar BOB, plus two or three guest beers which may include Fuller's London Pride, or beers from Bath Ales, Goff's or RCH. More unusual brews are obtained from Ales of the Unexpected.

Traditional Cotswold freehouse with extensive collection of old advertising signs, pub mirrors, bottles and jugs. Dining room and skittle alley. Food served 12–2.30pm and 7–9.30pm every day. Well-behaved children welcome. Disabled facilites. Car park.

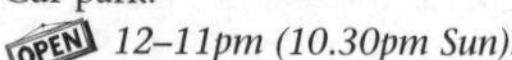
12–11pm (10.30pm Sun).

IRON ACTON

The Rose and Crown

High Street, Iron Acton, Nr Bristol BS37 9UQ
☎ *(01454) 228423* A Didcott

A freehouse with Uley Pig's Ear and Old Spot, Timothy Taylor Landlord and Marston's Pedigree always available.

A traditional and homely local. Accommodation. Children over 14 allowed. Garden. Darts and pool.

5–11pm Mon–Fri; 6–11pm Sat; 12–3pm and 7–10.30pm Sun.

KINGSWOOD

Dinneywicks Inn

The Chippings, Kingswood, Wotton-under-Edge GL12 8RT
☎ *(01453) 843328* Mr and Mrs Thomas

A Wadworth house serving 6X and IPA, with other seasonal guests such as Adnams Broadside.

A refurbished village pub with garden and petanque court. Children allowed.

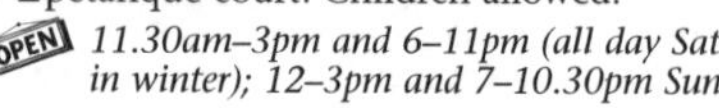
11.30am–3pm and 6–11pm (all day Sat in winter); 12–3pm and 7–10.30pm Sun.

LIME STREET

The Greyhound Inn

Lime Street, Eldersfield GL19 4NX
☎ *(01452) 840381* Matthew and Kate Brown

A freehouse with a Butcombe brew regularly available, plus a weekly changing guest beer from an independent brewery such as Ledbury, Wickwar, Smiles or Oakhill.

A rural country inn with two bars and real fires, skittle alley/function room. Large garden with play area. Food served every lunchtime and evening except Mondays. Children allowed. Look for Lime Street on the map, not Eldersfield!

11.30am–2.30pm Mon–Sat; 12–3pm Sun; 7–11pm Mon; 6–11pm Tues–Sat; 7–10.30pm Sun.

LITTLETON UPON SEVERN

The White Hart Inn

Littleton upon Severn, Nr Bristol BS12 1NR
☎ *(01454) 412275* Howard and Liz Turner

A Young's pub always offering Young's Bitter and Special, plus Waggle Dance in the summer and Winter Warmer for the colder months.

Near the Severn Bridges and Thornbury Castle. Bar food at lunchtime and evenings. Children are welcome in the garden room. Signposted from Elberton village.

12–3pm and 6–11pm Mon–Sat; 12–4pm and 7–10.30pm Sun.

LONGBOROUGH

The Coach & Horses Inn

Longborough Village, Moreton-in-Marsh GL56 0QJ
☎ *(01451) 830325* Connie Emm

A Donnington tied house with XXX and Best Bitter served.

Old, original Cotswold locals' inn in lovely village setting with good views from patio. Children welcome at lunchtime and early evening. Walkers are very welcome, and can eat their own sandwiches on the premises.

 *11am–3pm and 7–11pm (10.30pm Sun).*

LONGHOPE

The Glasshouse Inn

May Hill, Longhope GL17 0NN
☎ *(01452) 830529* Mr S Pugh

A freehouse regularly serving Butcombe brews. Guests served straight from the barrel include ales from Adnams and Hook Norton.

An old-fashioned country pub with garden. Food served at lunchtime and evenings, but not on Sundays. No children under 14 allowed.

 *11.30am–3pm and 6.30–11pm Mon–Sat; 12–3pm and 7–10.30pm Sun.*

LOWER APPERLEY

The Farmer's Arms

Ledbury Road, Lower Apperley GL19 4DR
☎ *(01452) 780307* Maurice Estop

Wadworth 6X and IPA are permanent ales usually with a different guest beer each week; Charles Wells Bombardier is a popular one.

An eighteenth-century inn with one bar, oak beams and open fires. Run by the same family as The New Inn, Church Knowle (Dorset). Bar and restaurant food available at lunchtime and evenings. Car park and garden. B4213 Ledbury Road, four miles south of Tewkesbury.

 *11.30am–2.30pm and 6–11pm Mon–Sat; 12–3pm and 7–10.30pm Sun.*

LYDNEY

The Swan

Pillowell, Lydney Gl15 4QU
☎ *(01594) 562477* The Halford family

Freehouse serving one constantly changing real ale.

A small local set in the centre of the Forest of Dean, welcoming to walkers and cyclists. Food every session. Children welcome. Small car park.

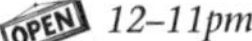 *12–11pm.*

MEYSEY HAMPTON

The Masons Arms

28 High Street, Meysey Hampton, Nr Cirencester GL7 5JT
☎ *(01285) 850164* Andrew and Jane O'Dell

A freehouse offering Hook Norton and two guests, perhaps something from Wickwar or another local brewery.

A village local serving the rural community. No garden but use of the village green alongside. Accommodation. Food every session except Sunday evening. Children welcome until 9pm. Daily papers on batons is a nice touch. Small car park.

 *11.30am–2.45pm and 6–11pm Mon–Sat; 12–4pm and 7–10.30pm Sun (closed Sun evening in the winter).*

MINCHINHAMPTON

The Weighbridge Inn

Longfords, Minchinhampton GL6 9AL
☎ *(01453) 832520* Simon and Jane Hudson

Uley Old Spot and Wadworth 6X usually available with one rotating ale such as Uley Hogshead Bitter.

This part-seventeenth-century building used to serve the local mill and now acts as a community pub. Hundreds of old keys from the mill hang from the ceiling providing a curious decoration. Famous for its 2-in-1 pie – customers choose a second filling to go with cauliflower cheese – a 25-year-old recipe. Food served all day, every day but it is advisable to book. Car park and beer garden. Well-behaved children welcome. Disabled access and toilets. Located half way between Minchinhampton and Nailsworth.

12–11pm (10.30pm Sun).

MORETON-IN-MARSH

Inn on the Marsh

Stow Road, Moreton-in-Marsh GL56 0DW
☎ *(01608) 650709* Wayne Branagh

Banks' Original, Marston's Pedigree and Best are permanents, plus one guest changed every couple of weeks.

Roadside and marshside yellow-stoned building – a locals' pub with some passing trade from the Fosse way. Large conservatory used as a dining area. Food every session. Children welcome. Pub games such as dominoes, also a Dutch game called schoolen. Garden and car park.

 *12–2.30pm and 7–11pm Mon; 11am–2.30pm and 7–11pm Tue; 12–2.30pm and 7–11pm Wed; 12–2.30pm and 6–11pm Thur–Fri; 11.30am–3pm and 6–11pm Sat; 12–3pm and 7–10.30pm Sun.*

NAUNTON

The Black Horse Inn

Naunton, Cheltenham GL54 3AB
☎ *(01451) 850565* Dave and Sheila Gray

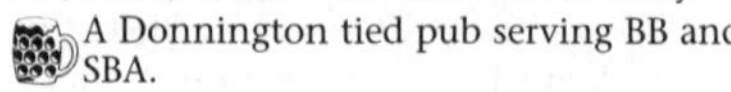

A Donnington tied pub serving BB and SBA.

Small and pleasant country local in pretty Cotswold village – popular with walkers. Food every session except Sun and Mon nights in winter. Patios at front and back. Car park. Children welcome. Darts. Accommodation.

11am–3pm and 6–11pm Mon–Fri; all day Sat–Sun.

NEWLAND

The Ostrich Inn

Newland, Nr Coleford GL16 8NP
☎ *(01594) 833260* Miss Kathryn Horton

Character country pub boasting eight real ales that are changed continuously. Some of the most frequent and popular include Hook Norton Old Hooky, Exmoor Hound Dog, Timothy Taylor Landlord and Uley Pig's Ear.

This thirteenth-century inn opposite the Cathedral of the Forest has beams, log fire, settles and candles. Well-known for its meals using local produce – bar and restaurant food available at lunchtime and evenings. Garden.

12–2.20pm and 6.30–11pm Mon–Fri; 12–3pm and 6–11pm Sat; 12–3pm and 6.30–10.30pm Sun.

OAKRIDGE LYNCH

Butchers Arms

Oakridge Lynch, Nr Stroud GL6 7NZ
☎ *(01285) 760371* PJ Coupe and BE Coupe

Archers Best Bitter, Young's Bitter, Greene King Abbot Ale and Wickwar BOB regularly available plus an occasional guest beer.

Friendly, 200-year-old village pub with log fires, exposed beams and attractive garden. It has been in the same hands for 18 years. Separate restaurant. Food served in the bar each lunchtime and evening (except Sun evening and all day Monday). Restaurant open 7.30–9.30pm Wed–Sat and Sun lunchtimes. Car park. Children welcome in the restaurant and small dedicated room off bar area. Signposted from the Eastcombe to Bisley road.

12–3pm and 6–11pm Mon–Sat; 12–4pm and 7–10.30pm Sun.

OLD SODBURY

Dog Inn

Old Sodbury, Near Bristol BS37 6LZ
☎ *(01454) 312006* John Harris

Wadworth 6X, Wickwar BOB and Fuller's London Pride are permanent features.

Very popular cosy rural pub with plenty of oak beams. Food available lunchtime and evening each day. Juke box. Accommodation. Children welcome in the large garden which includes a play area. Parking.

11am–11pm Mon–Sat; 12–10.30pm Sun.

OLDBURY ON SEVERN

Anchor Inn

Church Road, Oldbury on Severn BS35 1QE
☎ *(01454) 413331* Mark Sorrell

Freehouse offering a Butcombe ale at all times.

A sixteenth-century country pub whose clientele come from far and wide. Two bars and a dining area. Good walks in the area. Boasts one of the largest boules pistes in the country. Children welcome in the dining room. Garden and parking.

11.30am–2.30pm and 6.30–11pm Mon–Fri; open all day Sat–Sun.

PILL

The Star Inn

13 Bank Place, Pill, Nr Bristol BS20 0AQ
☎ *(01275) 374926* Miss Hurst

Archers Best always available plus one guest.

Local village pub with a wide range of customers. Parking. New owners put strong emphasis on food (not Monday). Junction 19 off the M5.

12–3pm and 6–11pm.

POPE'S HILL

The Greyhound Inn

The Slad, Pope's Hill, Gloucester GL14 1JX
☎ *(01452) 760344* Mr Wells

A freehouse serving Timothy Taylor brews. Also two twice-weekly changing guests from any brewery in the UK. Examples are Exmoor Gold, RCH Pitchfork and brews from Cottage, Goff's and Hop Back.

A country pub with restaurant area and garden. Food served at lunchtime and evenings. Children allowed only if they are eating.

11.30am–3.30pm and 5.30–11pm Mon–Sat; 12–3.30pm and 7–10.30pm Sun.

PRESTBURY

The Royal Oak

43 The Burgage, Prestbury, Cheltenham GL52 3DL
☎ *(01242) 522344* Simon Daws

Timothy Taylor Landlord and an ale from the Archers brewery are always on offer plus one changing guest.

Classic old country pub with hops hanging from the beams. It is claimed to be the most haunted pub in Britain and was formerly owned by cricketer Tom Graveney. Bar and dining room – food served every session. Car parking, garden and skittle alley. Children allowed in dining room and garden.

 *11.30am–3pm and 5.30–11pm Mon–Sat; 12–10.30pm Sun.*

PUCKLECHURCH

Rose & Crown

Parkfield Road, Pucklechurch BS16 9PS
☎ *(0117) 9372351* Evan Stewart

A Wadworth house with 6X, IPA and JCB permanently available.

A popular pub that retains its olde-worlde charm in the quaint front bars, with its stone floors and wooden furniture, but is also heavily orientated towards food with the large dining area at the back. Food every lunchtime and evening except Sunday and Monday nights – best to book in advance. Car park, garden and play area. Children allowed in the dining room. Darts and occasional live music.

 *11.30am–3pm and 6–11pm Mon–Sat; 12–4pm and 7–10.30 Sun.*

The Star Inn

37 Castle Road, Pucklechurch BS17 9RF
☎ *(0117) 9372391* Bob Todd

Wadworth 6X always on offer. Also a range of traditional ciders.

A popular and friendly village local that has a real sense of community. Beer festival held third week in June with 25 guest ales. Opposite the playing fields that double as a beer garden. Children welcome. Food every session except Sun evening. Car park. Darts, cribbage, etc.

 *11am–11pm.*

QUEDGELEY

Little Thatch Hotel

Bristol Road, Quedgeley, Gloucester GL2 4PQ
☎ *(01452) 720687* Mrs J McDougall

Three constantly changing beers on offer, perhaps Woodford's Norfolk Nog or something from Goff's or Oakhill.

Black and white timber-frame hotel built in 1350 with recent addition. Food served 12–2pm and 7–9.30pm Mon–Fri and 7–10pm Sat. Car park. Children welcome.

12–2.30pm and 6.30–10.30pm Mon–Fri; 7–10.30pm Sat; 12–3.30pm and 7–10.30pm Sun.

SAPPERTON

The Daneway

Sapperton, Nr Cirencester GL7 6LN
☎ *(01285) 760297*
Elizabeth and Richard Goodfellow

Wadworth house offering 6X, Henry's IPA and JCB all year, plus Wadworth seasonal brews.

Built in 1784, this beamed pub is set in some wonderful Gloucestershire countryside. It features a lounge and public bar, plus small non-smoking family room. No music, machines or pool but traditional pub games. Bar food is available at lunchtime and meals in the evening. Car park, garden, children allowed in family room. Less than two miles off the A419 Stroud–Cirencester road.

 *11am–2.30pm and 6.30–11pm.*

SHEEPSCOMBE

The Butcher's Arms

Sheepscombe, Painswick GL6 7RH
☎ *(01452) 812113*
Johnny and Hilary Johnston

A freehouse with Hook Norton Best always available, plus two constantly changing guests.

A sixteenth-century country pub with panoramic views and sheltered gardens. Bar and restaurant food served lunchtimes and evenings. Car park. Children allowed. Situated off A46 north of Painswick (signposted from main road).

 *11.30am–3pm and 6.30–11pm (10.30pm Sun).*

SLAD

Woolpack Inn

Slad Road, Slad, Stroud GL5 7QA
☎ *(01452) 813429*
Dan Chadwick and Richard Bolton

Uley Bitter, Old Spot, Pig's Ear and Laurie Lee Bitter regularly available. One or two guest beers are usually served, which may include Wickwar Cooper's WPA or Fuller's London Pride. Draught cider offered in the summer months.

The haunt of the late Laurie Lee (*Cider with Rosie*) and situated in the beautiful Slad Valley. Food served 12–2pm and 6–9pm Mon–Sat, 1–4pm (best to book) Sun. Car park. Small garden and terrace. Children welcome.

 *12–3pm and 6–11pm Mon–Fri; 11.30am–11pm Sat; 12–10.30pm Sun.*

SLING

The Miners Arms

Sling, Coleford GL16 8LH
☎ *(01594) 836632* Brian and Yvonne

Two rotating real ales on offer, including beers from local micro-breweries.

Traditional country inn with one bar, in tourist area. Nice walking and views. Large garden, juke box and live music twice a week. Food served all day. A la carte restaurant. Children's play area. Situated on the main road from Chepstow to Coleford and the Forest of Dean.

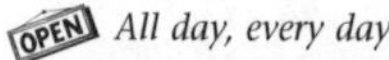 *All day, every day.*

SNOWSHILL

The Snowshill Arms

Snowshill, Broadway WR12 7JU
☎ *(01386) 852653* David J Schad

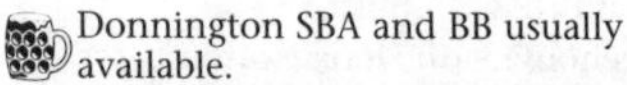

Donnington SBA and BB usually available.

Rural Donnington-owned, family pub in the heart of the Cotswolds. The open-plan bar has a log fire in winter. Food lunchtimes and evenings. Children welcome, with play area in garden for use under parental supervision. Car park.

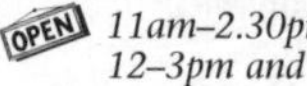 *11am–2.30pm and 6–11pm Mon–Sat; 12–3pm and 7–10.30pm Sun.*

SOUTH WOODCHESTER

The Ram Inn

South Woodchester, Nr Stroud GL5 5EL
☎ *(01453) 873329* Phil McAsey

Wickwar BOB, Uley Old Spot, Archer's Golden and something from the Dwan brewery usually available plus three constantly changing guest beers from around the country. Approximately 400 served each year.

This bustling old Cotswold pub was built around 1601. Beautiful village setting, with wonderful views. Food served 12–2pm and 6–9pm every day. Children welcome. Plenty of outside seating, and real fires in the winter. Car park. Follow brown tourist signs from A46.

All day, every day.

STOW-ON-THE-WOLD

The Golden Ball Inn

Lower Swell, Stow-on-the-Wold GL54 1LF
☎ *(01451) 830247* Steve and Maureen Heath

Tied to the nearby Donnington Brewery, so BB and SBA are always available.

A seventeenth-century, Cotswold stone, village local with log fires in winter. Accommodation available. Typical old pub games played (darts, dominoes, cribbage, Aunt Sally). Bar food served at lunchtime and evenings. Car park and garden. Children and pets welcome. On the B4068, one mile from Stow-on-the-Wold.

 *12–3pm and 6–11pm Mon–Sat; 12–3pm and 7–10.30pm Sun.*

The Queen's Head

The Square, Stow-on-the-Wold GL54 1AS
☎ *(01451) 830563* John Bate

A Donnington house offering both BB and SBA.

Not a restaurant that sells beer but a pub that sells food. One of many inns in this historic market town. Stone floor, hops on the ceiling, and friendly. Food every session in the summer, not Sun and Mon nights in the winter. Attractive patio.

 *11am–11pm in the summer; closed mid-afternoon Mon–Thur in the winter.*

SWINEFORD

The Swan Inn

Bath Road, Swineford, Bitton, Bristol
☎ *(0117) 9323101* Peter Abram

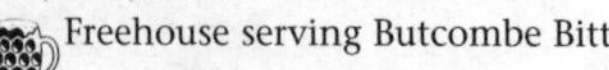

Freehouse serving Butcombe Bitter.

Unpretentious friendly local halfway between Bath and Bristol. One bar, two rooms. Food every session except Sunday evening. Children allowed if eating. Small car park. Small garden.

 *11am–3pm and 5–11pm.*

TEWKESBURY

The Berkeley Arms

8 Church Street, Tewkesbury GL20 5PA
☎ *(01684) 293034* Mr Ian Phillips

Wadworth IPA, 6X and JCB always available, plus a seasonal ale and one guest which may include Badger Tanglefoot, Wadworth Old Timer, Greene King Old Speckled Hen and Charles Wells Bombardier.

A small, homely fifteenth-century pub. Cask Marque accredited. Bar and restaurant food available. Street parking. The restaurant can be hired for functions. Children allowed in the restaurant.

 *11am–3pm and 5–11pm Mon–Thur; all day Fri and Sat; 12–4pm and 7–10.30pm Sun.*

The White Bear

Bredon Road, Tewkesbury GL20 5BU
☎ *(01684) 296614* Gerry and Jane Boazman

A freehouse serving two guest beers from breweries such as Wood, Hook Norton, RCH, Wyre Piddle and Banks's.

A games-orientated boozer. No food. Children allowed until 8.30pm.

OPEN *All day, every day.*

TODENHAM

The Farriers Arms

Todenham, Moreton-in-Marsh GL56 9PF
☎ *(01608) 650901* Tom and Charlotte Young

A freehouse with Hook Norton Best always available, plus usually two monthly changing guests, perhaps Timothy Taylor, Wye Valley Butty Bach, Shepherd Neame Spitfire, or seasonal and celebration ales.

Seventeenth-century brick-built village pub with inglenook fireplace, beams and wood burner. Prides itself on its food – has won awards – and there is a large restaurant. Front patio, car park, and garden. Children allowed in non-bar areas. Signposted from the A429.

 *12–3pm and 6.30–11pm Mon–Sat; 12–3pm and 7–10.30pm Sun.*

ULEY

Old Crown Inn

The Green, Uley, Dursley GL11 8SN
☎ *(01453) 860502* Miss Morgan

A freehouse with Uley Bitter and Pig's Ear regularly available, plus three weekly changing guests from breweries such as Cotleigh, Greene King, Hook Norton, Hampshire or Hop Back.

A village pub with games room, garden and accommodation. Pub food served at lunchtimes and evenings. Children allowed.

OPEN *11.30am–3pm and 7–11pm (10.30pm Sun).*

WATERLEY BOTTOM

The New Inn

Waterley Bottom, North Nibley, Nr Dursley GL11 6EF
☎ *(01453) 543659* Mrs Cartigny

Greene King Abbot, Cotleigh Tawny, Bath Ales SPA and Gem always available, plus a changing guest (about 100 different beers per year).

A remote freehouse with two bars, set in a beautiful valley. Bar food available at lunchtime and evenings, except Monday and Tuesday. Car park and garden. Beer festival held on the last weekend in June with 18 different ales. Children welcome. From North Nibley, follow signs for Waterley Bottom.

OPEN *7–11pm Mon; 12–2.30pm and 6–11pm Tues–Fri; all day Sat–Sun.*

WESTBURY ON TRYM

The Post Office Tavern

17 Westbury Hill, Westbury on Trym, Bristol BS9 3AH
☎ *(0117) 940 1233* Rodney Duckett

Normally seven beers available. Otter Ale, Bath SPA, Smiles Best, Butcombe Bitter and Fuller's London Pride are regulars, plus various other guests.

Early twentieth-century alehouse full of post office memorabilia. Non-smoking lounge. Bar food lunchtime and evenings. Street parking, small patio. No children under 14. On main road in Westbury village.

 *11am–11pm Mon–Sat; 12–3pm and 7–10.30pm Sun.*

The Prince of Wales

84 Stoke Lane, Westbury on Trym, Bristol BS9 3SP
☎ *(0117) 962 3715* Richard Ellis
www.theprinceatwestbury.co.uk

A freehouse generally serving Fuller's London Pride, Butcombe Bitter, Bath SPA and Brakspear Bitter, plus one guest perhaps Timothy Taylor Landlord.

A friendly and busy real ale local, decorated with cricket memorabilia. Food lunchtime only and Mon–Sat. Garden with children's play area.

OPEN *11am–3pm and 5.30–11pm Mon–Fri; all day Sat; 12–4pm and 7–10.30pm Sun.*

The Victoria Inn

20 Chock Lane, Westbury on Trym, Bristol BS9 3EX
☎ *(0117) 950 0441* Alastair Deas
www.thevictoriapub.co.uk

A Wadworth tied house with 6X and Henry's IPA always available, plus two weekly changing guests such as Butcombe Bitter and seasonal brews.

A village pub with garden. Food available at lunchtime and evenings. Menu on the website. Children allowed.

12–2.30pm and 5.30–11pm.

WHITMINSTER

The Old Forge

Bristol Road, Whitminster GL2 7NY
☎ *(01452) 741306* Mr and Mrs Hardy

Butcombe Bitter, Black Sheep and Greene King IPA normally available plus either Greene King Old Speckled Hen or Wychwood Hobgoblin.

An old, traditional pub with dining area and beer garden. Food served at lunchtime and evenings. Children allowed.

3–11pm Mon (closed Mon lunchtimes); all day the rest of the week.

WINTERBOURNE DOWN

The Golden Heart

Down Road, Winterbourne Down, Bristol BS36 1AU
☎ *(01454) 773152* Peter and Lynette Bevan

Smiles Original and Wadworth 6X permanently available.

A pub that from the outside looks just like a traditional country local – and it is – but there is also a large dining area attached at the back. Food served all day. Car park and huge garden with two play areas. Children allowed in restaurant. Quiz night Wed and 60s, 70s and 80s night on Sun.

12–11pm (10.30pm Sun).

WOOLASTON COMMON

The Rising Sun

Woolaston Common, Lydney GL15 6NU
☎ *(01594) 529282* Phil Brockwell

Wye Valley Bitter and Fuller's London Pride are permanents.

A low-ceiling country pub decorated with currencies from around the world, and with the atmosphere of a freehouse. Food. Car park and garden.

12–2.30pm and 6.30–11pm Mon–Sat; 12–3pm and 7–10.30pm Sun.

THE BREWERIES

BALLARD'S BREWERY LTD

Unit C, The Old Sawmill, Nyewood, Rogate, Petersfield GU31 5HA
☎ *(01730) 821301*
www.ballardsbrewery.org.uk

TROTTON BITTER 3.6%
BEST BITTER 4.2% ABV
NYEWOOD GOLD 5.0% ABV
WASSAIL 6.0% ABV
Malty and powerful, but not over-sweet.
Seasonals and occasionals:
MIDHURST MILD 3.5% ABV
Winter brew, dark and smooth.
GOLDEN BIND 4.2% ABV
ON THE HOP 4.5% ABV
WILD 4.7% ABV
WHEATSHEAF 5.0% ABV
Plus a powerful Christmas ale.

THE CHERITON BREWHOUSE

Cheriton, Alresford SO24 0QQ
☎ *(01962) 771166*

POTS ALE 3.8% ABV
Golden, with hoppiness throughout.
BEST BITTER 4.2% ABV
Pronounced fruit and malt flavour.
DIGGERS GOLD 4.6% ABV
Powerful hoppiness and bitter finish.
Plus seasonal and occasional brews.

GEORGE GALE & CO. LTD

The Hampshire Brewery, Horndean PO8 0DA
☎ *(02392) 571212*
www.gales.co.uk

BUTSER BREW 3.4% ABV
A sweet brew, with fruit throughout.
GB 4.0% ABV
Malt flavour with some fruitiness. Bitter.
WINTER BREW 4.2% ABV
FESTIVAL MILD 4.8% ABV
Sweet and dark, with fruitiness.
HSB 4.8% ABV
Sweet and malty.
Plus seasonal ales.

HAMPSHIRE BREWERY LTD

6–8 Romsey Industrial Estate, Greatbridge Road, Romsey SO51 0HR
☎ *(01794) 830529*
www.hampshirebrewery.com

KING ALFRED'S BITTER 3.8% ABV
Amber, light, refreshing and complex.
STRONGS 3.8% ABV
IRONSIDE 4.2% ABV
Amber, with crisp hop flavour and bitter finish.
LIONHEART 4.5% ABV
Refreshing with subtle hop finish.
PRIDE OF ROMSEY 5.0% ABV
Aromatic with good bitter flavour.
Plus a range of special brews.

ITCHEN VALLEY BREWERY

Unit 4, Shelf House, New Farm Road, Alresford SO24 9QE
☎ *(01962) 735111*
www.itchenvalley.com

GODFATHERS 3.8% ABV
FAGIN'S 4.1% ABV
HAMPSHIRE ROSE 4.2% ABV
Smooth maltiness throughout.
JUDGE JEFFREYS 4.5% ABV
Copper-coloured, rounded with hoppy bitterness. Seasonal.
TEA CLIPPER 4.6% ABV
PURE GOLD 4.8% ABV
WATT TYLER 5.5% ABV
Seasonal brew.
Plus occasional brews.

OAKLEAF BREWING COMPANY

Unit 7, Clarence Wharf Industrial Estate, Mumby Road, Gosport PO12 1AJ
☎ *(02392) 513222*
www.oakleafbrewing.co.uk

FARMHOUSE ALE 3.5% ABV
MAYPOLE MILD 3.8% ABV
OAKLEAF BITTER 3.8% ABV
NUPTU'ALE 4.2% ABV
GREEN GOLD 4.3% ABV
SQUIRREL'S DELIGHT 4.4% ABV
PISTON PORTER 4.6% ABV
HOLE HEARTED 4.7% ABV
I CAN'T BELIEVE IT'S NOT BITTER 4.9% ABV
STOKERS STOUT 5.0% ABV
BLAKE'S GOSPORT BITTER 5.2% ABV
IPA 5.5% ABV
BLAKE'S HEAVEN 7.0% ABV

PORTCHESTER BREWERY

6 Audret Close, Portchester, Fareham PO16 9ER
☎ *(01329) 512918*
www.portchesterbrewery.co.uk

CHASTITY 3.5% ABV
TREBOUCHET 3.9% ABV
Ordinary bitter.
SLINGSHOT 4.2% ABV
CATAPULT 4.8% ABV
Light-coloured, refreshing, strong bitter.
BATTERING RAM 5.0% ABV
Well-hopped, premium English ale.
STOCKING CELLAR 6.3% ABV
Christmas brew.
Plus occasionals.

THE RED SHOOT BREWERY

Toms Lane, Linwood, Ringwood BH24 3QT
☎ *(01425) 475792*

FOREST GOLD 3.8% ABV
TOMS TIPPLE 4.8% ABV

RINGWOOD BREWERY LTD

138 Christchurch Road, Ringwood BH24 3AP
☎ *(01425) 471177*
www.ringwoodbrewery.co.uk

BEST BITTER 3.8% ABV
Sweet malt flavour, becoming dry.
BOLD FORESTER 4.2% ABV
HUFFKIN 4.4% ABV
FORTYNINER 4.9% ABV
Hop and malt flavour with malty finish.
OLD THUMPER 5.6% ABV
Golden with various fruit flavours.
Seasonals:
BOONDOGGLE 4.0% ABV
Available May–September.
XXXX PORTER 4.7% ABV
Full-bodied, winter brew.

TRIPLE FFF BREWING CO.

Old Magpie Works, Unit 3, Station Approach, Four Marks, Alton GU34 4HN
☎ *(01420) 561422*

ALTON'S PRIDE 3.8% ABV
PRESSED RAT AND WARTHOG 3.8% ABV
Dark and malty with hoppy bitterness.
MOONDANCE 4.2% ABV
Golden with fruity, hoppy flavour.
DAZED AND CONFUSED 4.6% ABV
Light and hoppy.
STAIRWAY TO HEAVEN 4.6% ABV
COMFORTABLY NUMB 5.0% ABV
Dark and fruity.
Plus occasionals.

THE PUBS

ANDOVER

The George

Vernham Dean, Andover SP11 0JY
☎ *(01264) 737279* Peter and Pat McKay

A Greene King house with IPA and Old Speckled Hen permanently available, plus one monthly changing guest.

A traditional country village pub with exposed beams. Food available lunchtime and evenings either at the bar or in a separate dining area. Beer garden and front patio.

6–11pm Mon; 12–3pm and 6–11pm Tues–Sat; 12–4pm Sun.

AXFORD

The Crown Inn

Axford, Near Preston Candover, Basingstoke RG25 2DZ
☎ *(01256) 389494* Steve Nicholls

A freehouse with three real ales usually available. Generally something from the Triple FFF brewery in Alton (such as Alton's Pride and Moondance) plus Cheriton Pots Ale.

A busy, two-bar country pub with a warm atmosphere. Homemade food available at lunch and evenings (all day at weekends during summer). Large garden with patio to the rear. Car park. Well-behaved children and dogs welcome. Situated on the Candover Valley road (B3046) between Basingstoke and Arlesford. Five miles from the M3.

12–3pm and 6–11pm Mon–Sat; 12–3pm and 6–10.30pm Sun.

BEAUWORTH

The Milbury's

Beauworth, Alresford SO24 0PB
☎ *(01962) 771248* Ken Rice

A freehouse with Milbury's Best (house beer), Theakston Old Peculiar and Caledonian Deuchars IPA always available. Two guests change every couple of months, and may be something like Timothy Taylor Landlord.

A seventeenth-century country pub with dining area and beer garden. Food available 12–2pm and 6.30–9.30pm Mon–Fri, 12–3pm and 7–9.30pm Sat–Sun. Children allowed.

12–11pm.

BENTWORTH

The Sun Inn

Bentworth, Nr Alton GU34 5JT
☎ *(01420) 562338* Mary Holmes

Ringwood Best, Cheriton Pots Ale, Hampshire Sun (house beer) and Bunces Pigswill always available, plus at least four guest ales changed weekly. Regulars include Ringwood Old Thumper, Badger Best, Brakspear Bitter, Archers Best, Fuller's London Pride, Gale's HSB and Young's Special.

Originally two cottages, now a pretty seventeenth-century country freehouse with three connecting rooms. No music or fruit machines. Stone and wooden floors and real fires. Food available 12–2pm and 7–9.30pm. Children allowed.

12–3pm and 6–11pm Mon–Sat; all day Sun.

BISHOPS WALTHAM

The Hampshire Bowman

Dundridge Lane, Bishops Waltham, Southampton SO32 1GD
☎ *(01489) 892940* Heather Seymour

A freehouse serving a constantly changing range of five ales straight from the cask. Breweries regularly featured include Cheriton, Ringwood, Archers, Stonehenge and Hop Back, to name but a few.

An unspoilt, traditional rural pub with large garden and car park. No music, fruit machines or mobile phones. Food available every lunchtime and Mon–Sat evenings. No children.

 *12–3pm and 6–11pm Mon–Thurs; 12–11pm Fri–Sat; 12–10.30pm Sun.*

CHALTON

The Red Lion

Chalton, Waterlooville PO8 0BG
☎ *(023) 9259 2246* Mr McGee

A Gale's brewery managed house, serving HSB, Butser Bitter and GB plus one rotating guest changed monthly. This might be Marston's Pedigree, Shepherd Neame Spitfire, Charles Wells Bombardier or Wadworth 6X.

Reputed to be the oldest in Hampshire (1147), this country pub with garden overlooks the Downs. Thatched roof, non-smoking lounge and non-smoking dining area. Food available at lunchtime and evenings (not Sunday evenings). Under 14s allowed only if eating. North of Horndean.

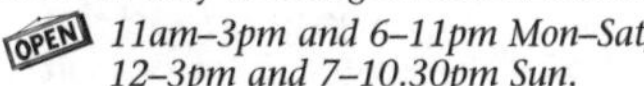 *11am–3pm and 6–11pm Mon–Sat; 12–3pm and 7–10.30pm Sun.*

CHARTER ALLEY

The White Hart

White Hart Lane, Charter Alley, Tadley RG26 5QA
☎ *(01256) 850048* Howard Bradley
www.whitehartcharteralley.com

A freehouse with West Berkshire Magg's Magnificent Mild, Oakleaf Farmhouse Ale, Otter Ale and Timothy Taylor Landlord always available, plus one or two guest beers.

A village pub with dining area, skittle alley, garden and patio. Lots of oak beams. Food available at lunchtime and evenings. Accommodation.

 *12–2.30pm Mon–Sat; 12–3pm Sun; 7–11pm Mon–Sat; 7–10.30pm Sun.*

CHERITON

The Flower Pots Inn

Cheriton, Alresford SO24 0QQ
☎ *(01962) 771318*
Paul Tickner and Jo Bartlett

The Cheriton Brewhouse is situated very close to this pub, hence the full range of Cheriton brews are always available, plus occasional Cheriton specials. The two businesses are run separately though, and this is not the 'brewpub' that it is often mistaken for.

The pub is an unspoilt traditional inn on the edge of the village. Bar food is available every lunchtime and Mon–Sat evenings. Car park, garden, en-suite accommodation. Children not allowed in the pub.

 *12–2.30pm and 6–11pm Mon–Sat; 12–3pm and 7–10.30pm Sun.*

EASTON

The Cricketers Inn

Easton, Near Winchester SO21 1ET
☎ *(01962) 779353* Paul Moffatt
www.cricketers.easton.com

A freehouse serving Ringwood Best and Otter Ale plus a couple of guests changed after every barrel from brewers across the country.

A local village pub with a cricketing theme. Two bars, a drinking terrace and non-smoking dining room. Homemade food served 12–2pm and 7–9pm. Ensuite accommodation, large car park, conference room. Children welcome. Good fishing and walking locally. Between Winchester and Alresford.

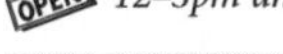 *12–3pm and 6–11pm (7–10.30pm Sun).*

ECCHINSWELL

The Royal Oak

Ecchinswell, Nr Newbury RG20 4UH
☎ *(01635) 298280* Mrs A Noonan and Mr Lay

Two guest ales, changed weekly, are served straight from the cask. Wadworth 6X and Fuller's London Pride are regulars, but other beers are featured if requested by customers!

Small village pub with two bars, a dining area, fireplaces and beams. Food served. Pool, darts, TV, beer garden, car park. Children allowed. Situated just over 7 miles south of Newbury.

12–11pm (10.30pm Sun).

FAREHAM

Osborne View Hotel

67 Hill Head Road, Fareham PO14 3JP
☎ *(01329) 664623* Paul Reynolds

A Hall and Woodhouse (Badger) tied pub with up to eight real ales always available. Badger Best, IPA and Tanglefoot always featured, plus a range of ales from Gribble Brewery.

A seafront pub on three levels. Non-smoking area, sea views, parking. Food available at lunchtimes and evenings, and all day on Sundays. Children and dogs welcome.

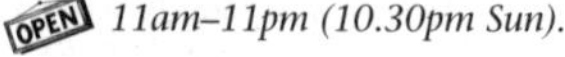 *11am–11pm (10.30pm Sun).*

FARNBOROUGH

The Prince of Wales

184 Rectory Road, Farnborough GU14 8AL
☎ *(01252) 545578* Julie and Peter Moore

Ten-pump freehouse with Hogs Back TEA, Fuller's London Pride, Hall and Woodhouse Tanglefoot, Ringwood Fortyniner and Young's Bitter the permanent beers, plus four guests, continually changing. Session beers below 4.0% ABV appear on a monthly basis. Ales from micro-breweries across the country are featured, plus Brakspear Bitter, Hop Back Summer Lightning and Fuller's Chiswick.

Traditional country drinking pub in an old building on the edge of town. Local CAMRA Pub of the Year 2003. No music, games or darts. Food available Mon–Sat lunchtimes. Marquee outside during summer, car park. Children allowed only in marquee. Round the corner from Farnborough North Station.

 *11.30am–2.30pm and 5.30–11pm Mon–Sat; 12–10.30pm Sun.*

FREEFOLK PRIORS

The Watership Down Inn

Freefolk, Nr Whitchurch RG28 7NJ
☎ *(01256) 892254* Mark and Alison Lodge

Real ale available on five pumps, all serving a constantly changing range of guest ales, usually from smaller breweries. A mild is always available.

Built in 1840, renamed after the Richard Adams novel that was set locally, a one-bar pub with an open fire and pretty garden with many outside tables. Bar and restaurant food available at lunchtime and evenings, plus non-smoking conservatory that seats 30 diners. Car park, new children's play area. Children allowed in the restaurant. On the B3400 between Whitchurch and Overton.

 *11.30am–3pm and 6–11pm (10.30pm Sun).*

FROGHAM

The Forester's Arms

Abbots Well Road, Frogham, Fordingbridge SP6 2JA
☎ *(01425) 652294* Mr M Harding

A Wadworth tied house with 6X, JCB and Henry's IPA always available plus two seasonal or special brews such as Mayhem Odda's Light.

A country inn in the New Forest area. Dartboard, garden with children's play area. Food available at lunchtime and evenings in a separate non-smoking restaurant. Children and dogs welcome.

 *11am–3pm and 6–11pm Mon–Sat; 12–3pm and 7–10.30pm Sun.*

FROXFIELD

The Trooper Inn

Froxfield, Petersfield GU32 1BD
☎ *(01730) 827293* Mr Matini

A freehouse serving Ringwood Fortyniner and Best plus a couple of weekly changing guests from breweries such as Ballard's.

A country pub with dining area, function room and garden. Food available at lunchtime and evenings. There is an eight-bedroom hotel attached to the pub – phone for reservations. Children allowed.

 *11am–3pm and 6–11pm (10.30pm Sun).*

GOSPORT

The Clarence Tavern

1 Clarence Road, Gosport PO12 1AJ
☎ *(023) 9252 9726* Patrick and Teresa Noonan

Beers from the Oakleaf Brewery range are always available. Beer festivals at Easter and August bank holiday.

A Victorian pub with food available all day in separate dining area. Outside terrace seating. Darts. Golf society. Car park. Function room.

11am–11pm (10.30pm Sun).

Queens Hotel

143 Queens Road, Gosport
☎ *(023) 9258 2645* Sue Lampon

Freehouse serving brews from Young's, Rooster's, Ringwood and Hook Norton, plus two rotating guests.

Popular backstreet local, a genuine freehouse, with a good selection of ales. Snacks and rolls served at lunchtimes only. No children.

 *11.30am–2.30pm and 7–11pm Mon–Fri; 11.30am–11pm Sat; 12–3pm and 7–10.30pm Sun.*

HAMBLE

The King & Queen

High Street, Hamble, Southampton SO31 4HA
☎ *(023) 8045 4247* Kelly Smith

An Enterprise Inn with Fuller's London Pride, Wadworth 6X, Adnams Best and Ringwood Fortyniner always available.

A sailing pub with log fires and bar billiards. Serving food at lunchtime and evenings. Children allowed in the lounge.

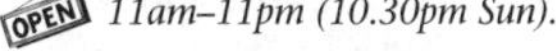
OPEN *11am–11pm (10.30pm Sun).*

HARTLEY WINTNEY

The Wagon & Horses

High Street, Hartley Wintney, Nr Hook RG27 8NX
☎ *(01252) 842119* Neil Scott

A freehouse with Gale's HSB always available, plus two guests, often brews from Ringwood but changing all the time.

A typical village pub with secluded garden. Food available at lunchtime. Children welcome.

OPEN *11am–11pm Mon–Sat; 12–3pm and 7–10.30pm Sun.*

HAWKLEY

The Hawkley Inn

Pococks Lane, Hawkley, Nr Liss GU33 6NE
☎ *(01730) 827205* Al Stringer

Six constantly changing real ales available at any one time, from breweries such as Ballard's, RCH, Itchen Valley, Triple FFF, Ringwood, Beckett's and Weltons, to name but a few. The pub's own cider, Swamp Donkey, is also served.

Small, rural alehouse with fires in winter. Large garden. Discreet blues music and a handsome landlord! Food served from an interesting menu, lunchtime and evening, but not Sun evening. Extremely well-behaved children welcome at lunchtime only. Parking in lane opposite pub. Smokers welcome.

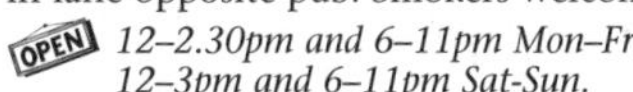
OPEN *12–2.30pm and 6–11pm Mon–Fri; 12–3pm and 6–11pm Sat-Sun.*

HINTON AMPNER

The Hinton Arms

Petersfield Road, Hinton Ampner, Alresford SO24 0NH
☎ *(01962) 771252* Roger and Angela Mattia

Hinton Sportsman brewed specially by the Hampshire Brewery and Fuller's London Pride are permanent plus one or two guests.

Friendly, roadside country freehouse with real open log fire. One very large bar divided into restaurant and public area. Home-cooked food is available lunchtime and evening. Large garden. Children very welcome. Located next door to National Trust property.

OPEN *11am–3pm and 5.30–11pm (10.30pm Sun) in the winter; all day May–Sept.*

HORNDEAN

Ship & Bell Hotel

6 London Road, Horndean, Waterlooville PO8 0BZ
☎ *(023) 9259 2107* Alec and Mary Russell

A Gale's Brewery house serving Butser, HSB and GB plus seasonal specials and a range of other guests perhaps including Everards Tiger.

A village pub with separate dining area and accommodation. Children allowed if eating.

OPEN *All day, every day.*

LASHAM

The Royal Oak

Lasham GU34 5SJ
☎ *(01256) 381213* Lawrence Barwick

A range of guest ales is available, changing on a regular basis. Favourite breweries include Triple FFF, Hop Back and Sharp's.

Village pub in a building dating from 1780, with beams and real fires. Food available. Two bars (lounge and public), attractive beer garden. Children allowed in the lounge. Located next to Lasham Airfield, which is signposted.

OPEN *11am–2.30pm and 6–11pm Mon–Thurs; 11am–11pm Fri–Sat; 12–10.30pm Sun.*

LINWOOD

The Red Shoot Inn & Brewery

Toms Lane, Linwood, Ringwood BH24 3QT
☎ *(01425) 475792* Lee and Lisa Sainsbury

Wadworth 6X and IPA plus Red Shoot's own beers – Forest Gold and Tom's Tipple – usually available. Wadworth seasonal brews also served.

This Wadworth-owned, New Forest pub is home to the Red Shoot Brewery. Food served lunchtimes and evenings. Children and dogs welcome. Family and non-smoking area. Beer festivals in April and October. Live bands Sun. Music quiz Thur. Car park. Signposted from A338 at Ellingham.

 *Winter: 11am–3pm and 6–11pm Mon–Fri; 11am–11pm Sat; 12–10.30pm Sun. Summer: 11am–11pm Mon–Sat; 12–10.30pm Sun.*

LITTLE LONDON

The Plough Inn

Silchester Road, Little London, Tadley RG26 5EP
☎ *(01256) 850628* Mr Brown

A freehouse with Ringwood Best and Ringwood seasonals always available plus a wide selection of guest ales.

Situated on the edge of Pamber Forest, this 330-year-old pub has exposed beams and a secluded garden for summer, log fires in winter. Hot, filled baguettes served at lunchtime and evening. Children allowed.

 *12–2.30pm and 6–11pm Mon–Sat; 12–3pm and 7–10.30pm Sun.*

MEONSTOKE

The Bucks Head

Bucks Head Hill, Meonstoke, Southampton SO32 3NA
☎ *(01489) 877313* Sue Creese

A Greene King house with IPA and Old Speckled Hen always available, plus one guest.

A rural country pub on the banks of the river. Tourist Board recommended with separate restaurant and B&B. Food available at lunchtime and evenings. Well-behaved children and dogs allowed. Situated just off the A32 north of Dropsford

 *11am–3pm and 6–11pm Mon–Fri; all day Sat–Sun and bank holidays.*

MICHELDEVER

Half Moon & Spread Eagle

Winchester Road, Micheldever SO21 3DG
☎ *(01962) 774339*
Richard Tolfree and Christina Nichols

A Greene King tenancy with Greene King ales always available, plus guests.

A popular rural pub with sixteenth-century walls and original beams. Wide selection of bar food and à la carte menu lunchtimes and evenings daily. Large garden and patio overlooking village cricket green. Car park. Less than a mile off the A33, six miles north of Winchester, 12 miles south of Basingstoke.

 *12–3pm and 6–11pm (10.30pm Sun).*

OVINGTON

The Bush Inn

Nr Alresford, Ovington SO24 0RE
☎ *(01962) 732764* Nick and Cath Young

Wadworth 6X, JCB and IPA are permanently available, plus seasonals.

A seventeenth-century up-and-down pub with lots of little rooms and antique memorabilia. Real fires make it cosy in the winter. One main bar in the middle of the pub. Beer garden. Disabled facilites. Reputation for good food, which is available every lunchtime and Mon–Sat evenings. Well-behaved children allowed. Situated off the A31 towards Winchester.

 *11am–3pm and 6–11pm Mon–Sat; 12–3pm and 7–10.30pm Sun.*

PORTCHESTER

The Cormorant

181 Castle Street, Portchester PO16 9QX
☎ *(023) 9237 9374*
Sue Bennett and Dave Dutton,
Mike and Carol Frewing

Fuller's London Pride, Gale's HSB and Ringwood Best are permanent features, and the guest beers may include Hop Back Summer Lightning, Ringwood Fortyniner and Timothy Taylor Landlord.

Originally called The Swan, the pub dates back over 300 years. Large non-smoking restaurant, with food served 12–2.30pm and 6–9.30pm Mon–Sat and 12–5pm Sun. Large car park. Children welcome, but no special facilities. Adjacent to Portchester Castle in a quite, leafy part of Portchester. From A27 from Portsmouth, follow signs for Portchester Castle.

 *11am–11pm Mon–Sat; 12–10.30pm Sun.*

PORTSMOUTH

The Connaught Arms

119 Guildford Road, Fratton, Portsmouth PO1 5EA

☎ *(023) 9264 6455* Debbie Ridley-Hughes

Five beers usually available. Caledonian Deuchars IPA and Hop Back Summer Lightning are permanent, plus guests, perhaps Cheriton Pots Ale, Ringwood Fortyniner or others.

Comfortable pub hidden in the back streets of Fratton, famous for its interesting range of pasties. Bar menu available 11.45am–2.15pm Mon–Sat; pasties available every session. Well-behaved children welcome until 7pm. Situated at the junction of Penhale and Guildford roads.

OPEN *All day, every day.*

The Dolphin

41 High Street, Old Portsmouth PO1 2LV

☎ *(023) 9282 3595*

Pete Croft and Jackie Rumary

Fuller's London Pride, Wadworth 6X, Timothy Taylor Landlord, Gale's HSB, Ringwood Fortyniner, Greene King Abbot and IPA and Adnams Broadside always available.

A sixteenth-century coaching inn with wood and flagstone floors. Historic area with good walks nearby. The pub boasts Nelson's signature on a piece of glass in the bar! A la carte menu and bar food available 12–2.30pm and 6.30–9pm. Small function room and outside patio area. Children allowed. Directly opposite the cathedral in Old Portsmouth.

OPEN *11am–3pm and 6–11pm Mon–Fri; all day Fri–Sun.*

The Tap

17 London Road, North End, Portsmouth PO2 0BQ

☎ *(023) 9261 4861*

Up to 11 beers available including Ruddles Best and Ringwood Old Thumper. Guests (100 per year) could include Ringwood Best, Badger Tanglefoot and Gale's HSB. Micro-breweries particularly favoured.

A one-bar drinking pub in the town centre with no juke box or fruit machines. Formerly the brewery tap for the now defunct Southsea Brewery. Bar meals available at lunchtime. Street parking opposite, small yard, disabled toilet. Children not allowed.

10.30am–11pm Mon–Sat; 12–10.30pm Sun.

The Wellington

62 High Street, Portsmouth PO1 2LY

☎ *(023) 9281 8965* Ms K Blake

Young's Special and Greene King IPA available plus one guest from a brewery such as Fuller's.

A traditional community pub with a friendly atmosphere and a reputation for good food, served at lunchtime and four evenings per week, plus full Sunday lunch. Patio garden. Use the harbour entrance. Children allowed.

OPEN *11am–11pm (10.30pm Sun).*

Wetherspoons: The Isambard Kingdom Brunel

2 Guildhall Walk, Portsmouth PO1 2DD

☎ *(023) 9229 5112* Karen and Mark Saunders

Eight to ten real ales served including Hop Back Summer Lightning, Ringwood Fortyniner and Shepherd Neame Spitfire. Quality ales at Wetherspoon prices.

A friendly town pub in a Grade II listed building. Food served all day with meal deals available. Non-smoking area. Cask Marque approved. Children's licence. Conference rooms for hire. Outside drinking in the summer. Near the Guildhall.

OPEN *10am–11pm Mon–Sat; 12–10.30pm Sun.*

The Winchester Arms

99 Winchester Road, Portsmouth PO2 7PS

☎ *(023) 9266 2443* Paul Fewings

Beers from Oakleaf Brewery always served, with Nuptu'Ale, Blake's Gosport Bitter and Hole Hearted (Beer of Hampshire 2002) permanently available.

Small, backstreet, community village pub, where everybody is treated as a friend. Live music from local musicians every Sunday, with occasional karaoke and discos. Light-hearted pub quiz every Monday evening, darts, football and cricket teams. Wed night, open mike. Non-smoking area, children allowed in snug, tap and patio garden.

OPEN *4–11pm Mon; 11am–11pm Tues–Sat; 12–10.30pm Sun.*

PRIORS DEAN

The White Horse Inn

Priors Dean, Nr Petersfield GU32 1DA
☎ *(01420) 588387* Paula and Georgina Stuart
www.stuartinns.com

Gale's tied house serving HSB, Butser and various Gale's seasonals plus Ringwood Fortyniner. Four or five permanents and two or three rotating guests.

An olde-world pub untouched for years, with log fires and ticking clocks. Two bars and a restaurant. Food available at lunchtime and evening (not Sun evening). Children welcome in restaurant. Car park and garden. June beer festival with up to 40 ales, live music and camping. Tricky to find. Between Petersfield and Alton, five miles from Petersfield, seven miles from Alton.

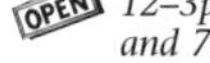
12–3pm and 6–11pm Mon–Sat; 12–3pm and 7–10.30pm Sun.

RINGWOOD

Inn on the Furlong

12 Meeting House Lane, Ringwood BH24 1EY
☎ *(01425) 475139*

A Ringwood Brewery pub, so Best, Fortyniner and Old Thumper available, plus a seasonal beer.

An old building with log fire, conservatory and beer garden. Food available at lunchtime. Children allowed.

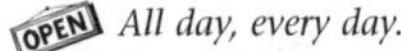
All day, every day.

ROTHERWICK

The Falcon

The Street, Rotherwick, Hook RG27 9BL
☎ *(01256) 762586*

A choice of three real ales is offered, Fuller's London Pride, Adnams Best and a weekly changing guest ale.

A traditional family-run village pub/restaurant with a large garden and car park. Food available 12–2pm and 7–9.30pm Mon–Sat, 12–2pm and 7–9pm Sun. Children allowed, but not in bar area. No high chairs.

11am–2.30pm and 6–11pm Mon–Sat; 12–10.30pm Sun.

SELBORNE

The Selborne Arms

High Street, Selborne GU34 3JR
☎ *(01420) 511247* Nick & Hayley Carter
www.selbornearms.co.uk

A freehouse with Ringwood Fortyniner and Cheriton Pots Ale always on offer, plus guests from a wide range of local breweries.

Traditional village pub in a seventeenth-century building, with original beams, log fires, garden and children's play area. Two separate bars and a small dining room. A wide range of imaginative food is served. Cask Marque approved. Between Alton and Liss on B3006.

11am–3pm and 6–11pm Mon–Sat; 12–10.30pm Sun.

SHEDFIELD

The Wheatsheaf Inn

Botley Road, Shedfield, Southampton SO32 2JG
☎ *(01329) 833024*
Tim Shepherd and Jo Bartlett

A freehouse serving Cheriton Pots Ale plus beers from Oakleaf, Ringwood and many other local micro-breweries.

A country pub with garden. Food available at lunchtime. There is a beer festival held on the late Spring Bank Holiday weekend. Jazz and blues every Saturday night.

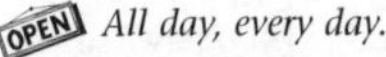
All day, every day.

SOUTHAMPTON

The Alexandra

6 Bellevue Road, Southampton SO15 2AY
☎ *(023) 8033 5071*
Kiren Bennett and Alison Cole

A leased house with Fuller's London Pride, Timothy Taylor Landlord and Ringwood Best always available, plus a weekly changing guest ale, such as Brains SA, Shepherd Neame Spitfire or Greene King Old Speckled Hen.

A traditional city-centre pub with heated beer garden and a dedicated fooball following. Big-screen TV, darts, table football. Food available at lunchtimes. Children permitted in garden at weekends, until 7pm.

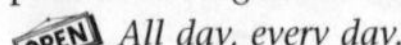
All day, every day.

Bevois Castle

63 Onslow Road, Bevois Valley, Southampton SO14 OJL
☎ *(023) 8033 0350* Dave and Sandy Bulpitt

Three beers from the Hampshire Brewery plus a rotating guest.

Small, traditional pub with real fire. Darts and pool. Strong football following. Full menu available 11am–2pm. Courtyard garden. No children's facilities. Car park.

OPEN *11am–11pm (10.30pm Sun).*

The Crown Inn

9 Highcrown Street, Southampton SO17 1QE
☎ *(023) 8031 5033* Jackie Hahyer

An Enterprise house with Fuller's London Pride and something from Ringwood among the beers always available, plus a rotating guest ale, often Hampshire Strongs Best Bitter.

A city pub and restaurant with food available at lunchtime and evenings. No children under 14 allowed.

OPEN *11am–11pm Mon–Sat; 12–10.30pm Sun.*

The Duke of Wellington

36 Bugle Street, Southampton SO14 2AH
☎ *(023) 8033 9222* Mr R Rose

A Wadworth house offering the full range of Wadworth ales, plus three constantly changing guests.

Built in the twelfth century, this is the oldest pub in Southampton. Cask Marque approved. Food available in a separate dining area at lunchtimes and evenings Mon–Sat and lunchtimes only Sun. Function room. Children welcome in the dining area.

OPEN *All day, every day.*

The Eagle

1 Palmerston Road, Southampton SO14 1LL
☎ *(023) 8033 3825* Bob Warren

An Enterprise tenancy with Wadworth 6X and Fuller's London Pride always available, plus four guests from a range of ales such as Gale's HSB, Greene King Abbot and Old Speckled Hen.

A traditional town-centre pub with darts and pool. Food available at lunchtime. No children.

OPEN *All day, every day.*

The Standing Order

30 High Street, Southampton SO14 3HT
☎ *(023) 8022 2121* Paul Goble

A Wetherspoon's pub with Ringwood Fortyniner and Shepherd Neame Spitfire always available, plus about ten different guests per week.

A traditional high-street pub with non-smoking area. Food available all day. No children.

OPEN *10am–11pm Mon–Sat; 12–10.30pm Sun.*

The Stile

163 University Road, Southampton SO17 1TS
☎ *(023) 8058 1124* Andy Ebdy

Five constantly changing real ales.

A city-based student pub with food served all day. Beer garden. Children welcome for dining.

OPEN *11am–11pm.*

Waterloo Arms

101 Waterloo Road, Southampton SO15 3BS
☎ *(023) 8022 0022* Robert and Linda Roach

A Hop Back pub serving Summer Lightning, GFB, Entire Stout, Crop Circle and Best, plus guests rotated weekly on one pump, perhaps King and Barnes Festive, Woodforde's Wherry or something from the Hampshire Brewery.

A local, traditional, village pub with conservatory and garden. Food available 12–3pm and 7–9pm. Children allowed.

OPEN *All day, every day.*

SOUTHSEA

The Artillery Arms

Hester Road, Southsea, Portsmouth PO4 8HB
☎ *(023) 92733610* Kevin Smith

A freehouse with seven real ales usually available: Gale's GB and HSB, Cheriton Village Elder, Ringwood Old Thumper and Fortyniner plus a guest changed every week.

A traditional, two-bar local community pub with garden. Food available at lunchtimes (not Mon). Beer festival held at the end of May. Small parking area.

OPEN *12–3pm and 6–11pm Mon–Thurs; 12–11pm Fri–Sat; 12–10.30pm Sun.*

The Old Oyster House

291 Lockway Road, Southsea, Portsmouth PO4 8LH
☎ *(023) 9282 7456*
Cath Robertson and Gareth Bridgman

Two or three real ales on offer including perhaps Summer Lightning, Abbot Ale or something from the Ringwood Brewery. Traditional draught cider also on offer.

Friendly, comfortable and busy pub with separate games bar for pool, darts, table football and big-screen Sky Sports. Large garden and patio. Food available lunchtime and evening. Large public car park opposite. Located at the end of a mile-long cul de sac near university sports ground.

 *Winter: 4–11pm Mon–Thur; 12–11pm Fri–Sat; 12–10.30pm Sun. Summer: 12–11pm Mon–Sat; (10.30pm Sun).*

Wine Vaults

43–7 Albert Road, Southsea PO5 2SF
☎ *(023) 9286 4712* Mike Hughes

Twelve hand pumps serve a range of ales including Fuller's London Pride and beers from Archers, Young's, Greene King, Itchen Valley, Ringwood, Hampshire and Suthwyk breweries.

Friendly, traditional pub with varied clientele and good atmosphere. Food is served 12–9pm daily, and there is also a brasserie menu. Well-behaved over 5s welcome, but there are no special facilities. Located directly opposite Kings Theatre.

 *12–11pm (10.30pm Sun).*

TITCHFIELD

The Wheatsheaf Inn

1 East Street, Titchfield, Fareham PO14 4AD
☎ *(01329) 842965* Adrienne De Noia

A freehouse serving Fuller's London Pride and Woodforde's Wherry plus two guests changed weekly. Examples may include Hook Norton Best and Exmoor Gold.

A village pub with dining area, open fire, patio and garden. Food available at lunchtime and evenings. Children allowed in the dining area only.

 *12–3pm and 6–11pm Mon–Thurs; all day Fri; 12–3pm and 6–11pm Sat; 12–3pm and 7–10.30pm Sun.*

WEYHILL

Weyhill Fair

Weyhill Road, Weyhill, Nr Andover SP11 0PP
☎ *(01264) 773631* Mr and Mrs Rayner
www.weyhillfair.co.uk

Fuller's London Pride, Chiswick and seasonal beers always available, plus three guests (approx. 200 per year) including brews from Ringwood, Burton Bridge and Hop Back.

A friendly local freehouse offering bar food at lunchtime and evenings (except Sun evening). Cask Marque award winner. Small function room. Beer festival in July. Car park, garden and non-smoking family room. Close to Hawk Conservancy and Thruxton circuit. On the A342 west of Andover.

 *11am–3pm and 6–11pm Mon–Thurs; 11am–3pm and 5–11pm Fri; 11am–3pm and 6–11pm Sat; 12–3pm and 7–10.30pm Sun.*

WHITSBURY

The Cartwheel

Whitsbury Road, Whitsbury, Nr Fordingbridge SP6 3PZ
☎ *(01725) 518362* David Watt

A Ringwood pub serving a range from the brewery plus one guest changing regularly.

A relaxed bar with exposed beams and open fire, in good walking country. Bar and restaurant food available at lunchtime and evenings. Car park and garden. Children allowed in the restaurant. Beer festival once a year. Turn west out of Salisbury onto the Fordingbridge road at Breamore. Signposted from the A338.

 *11am–2.30pm and 6–11pm; all day Sun in summer.*

WINCHESTER

The Old Gaol House

11 Jewry Street, Winchester SO23 8RZ
☎ *01962 850095* Gareth Hughes

Shepherd Neame Spitfire, Greene King Abbot and Hop Back Summer Lightning are among the beers permanently served, plus four guests from a wide range of independent breweries.

Large pub offering food 10am–10pm Mon–Sat and 12–9.30pm Sun. Accompanied children welcome 12–5pm if eating, with children's menu, high chairs and baby-changing facilities available.

 *10am–11pm Mon–Sat (10.30pm Sun).*

THE BREWERIES

DUNN PLOWMAN BREWERY

Ye Olde Tavern, Victoria Road, Kington HR5 3BX
☎ *01544 231933*

TAVERN BITTER 3.5% ABV
BREWHOUSE BITTER 3.8% ABV
EARLY RISER 4.0% ABV
STING HONEY BEER 4.2% ABV
KINGDOM BITTER 4.5% ABV
OLD JAKE STOUT 4.8% ABV
SHIRE HORSE ALE 5.5% ABV
CROOKED FURROW 6.5% ABV

SHOES BREWERY

Three Horse Shoes Inn, Norton Canon, Hereford HR4 7BH
☎ *(01544) 318275*

NORTON ALE 3.6% ABV
CANON BITTER 4.1% ABV

SPINNING DOG BREWERY

88 St Owen Street, Hereford HR1 2DQ
☎ *(01432) 342125*

CHASE YOUR TAIL 3.6% ABV
An easy quaffer.
MUTLEY'S MONGREL 3.9% ABV
A blend of three hops, giving a pleasant aroma.
HEREFORD CATHEDRAL BITTER 4.0% ABV
MUTLEY'S DARK 4.0% ABV
PIT STOP 4.0% ABV
TOP DOG 4.2% ABV
A premium, full-bodied ale.
MUTLEY'S OATMEAL STOUT 4.4% ABV
CELTIC GOLD 4.5% ABV
HARVEST MOON 4.5% ABV
MUTLEY'S RESERVE 4.9% ABV
MUTTS NUTTS 5.0% ABV
SANTA PAWS 5.2% ABV
A seasonal Christmas ale.

WYE VALLEY BREWERY

Stoke Lacey, Bromyard, Hereford, HR74HG
☎ *(01885) 490505*
www.wyevalleybrewery.co.uk

BITTER 3.7% ABV
HEREFORD PALE ALE 4.0% ABV
BUTTY BACH 4.5% ABV
Dorothy Goodbody's selection:
SPRINGTIME ALE 4.0% ABV
GOLDEN ALE 4.2% ABV
AUTUMN DELIGHT 4.4% ABV
WHOLESOME STOUT 4.6% ABV
WINTER TIPPLE 4.7% ABV
COUNTRY ALE 6.0% ABV

THE PUBS

ASTON CREWS

The Penny Farthing

Aston Crews, Nr Ross-on-Wye HR9 7LW
☎ *(01989) 750366* Mrs R Blanch, Miss E Mellor and Miss D Mellor

Marston's Pedigree and Bitter and Wadworth 6X always available plus a guest beer (ten per year) which may be Shepherd Neame Spitfire, Greene King Old Speckled Hen or from Robinson's or Hook Norton breweries.

A country inn and restaurant. Bar and restaurant food available at lunchtime and evenings. Car park and garden. Children allowed in the restaurant. Turn off the A40 Ross-on-Wye to Gloucester road at Lea, on to the B4222 (signposted to Newent). The Penny Farthing is one mile down this road.

OPEN *12–3pm and 7–11pm.*

AYMESTRY

The Riverside Inn

Aymestry, Leominster HL6 9ST
☎ *(01568) 708440* Richard Gresko
www.theriversideinn.org

Two real ales usually available. Expect Shropshire Lad or a seasonal brew from Wood's, and Dorothy Goodbody's Golden Ale or something else from the Wye Valley range.

A sixteenth-century rural village pub with one main bar, dining area and a riverside garden which is floodlit at night. Bar and restaurant food available at lunchtime and evenings. Children of all ages permitted in the bar dining area. Function room and car park. Accommodation.

OPEN *11am–3pm and 6–11pm (10.30pm Sun).*

BROMYARD

The Rose & Lion Inn

5 New Road, Bromyard HR7 4AJ
☎ *(01885) 482381* Mrs Herdman

A Wye Valley tied house always serving Bitter, Hereford Pale Ale, Dorothy Goodbody's, Butty Bach and Wholesome Stout. Plus one weekly changing guest, sometimes a seasonal Wye Valley ale such as Springtime, or brews such as Coach House Gunpowder Strong Mild.

An award-winning, two-bar drinking house. Old, traditional building carefully renovated, with garden. No food. Children allowed in the garden only.

OPEN *11am–3pm and 6–11pm Mon–Fri; all day most Sat–Sun.*

DORMINGTON

The Yew Tree

Priors Frome, Dormington HR1 4EH
☎ *(01432) 850467* Len Gee
www.lengees.info

Greene King Old Speckled Hen always available, plus a local beer from Wye Valley, Spinning Dog or another nearby brewery.

This 200-year-old country freehouse and restaurant with log fire and wood burner has beams that are 500 years old. Home-cooked food available at lunchtime and evenings (except Tuesdays). Three bars, 50-seater restaurant, large garden. Car park plus room for coaches. Children allowed.

 *12–2pm and 7–11pm Mon and Wed (closed Tues); 12–2pm and 6–11pm Thurs–Fri; 12–4pm and 6–11pm Sat; 12–4pm and 7–10.30pm Sun.*

FROMES HILL

Wheatsheaf Inn

Fromes Hill, Ledbury HR8 1HT
☎ *(01531) 640888* Mr Mirfin

A brewpub serving Fromes Hill Buckswood Dingle and Overture. Also occasional guests.

A country inn with one bar, dining area and garden. Food served at lunchtime and evenings. Children allowed.

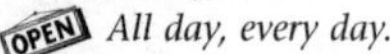 *All day, every day.*

HAMPTON BISHOP

Bunch of Carrots

Hampton Bishop, Hereford HR1 4JR
☎ *(01432) 870237* Paul and Katharine Turner

Hook Norton Best Bitter and three guest beers, often from local breweries, regularly available.

Traditional country inn with open fires and stone-clad floors, beer garden and function room. Situated two miles from Hereford city centre on the B4224, close to the River Wye. Disabled facilities. Carvery and bar food served lunchtimes and evenings. Car park. Children's menu and play area in the garden.

 *11am–3pm and 6–11pm Mon–Sat; 12–4pm and 7–10.30pm Sun.*

HAY-ON-WYE

Bull's Head

Craswall, near Hay on Wye, Herefordshire HR2 0PN
☎ *(01981) 510616*

Wye Valley Butty Bach and guest beers available.

On the Welsh border but just in Herefordshire, nestling at the foot of the Black Hill, in the Black Mountains. Flagstone floors, open fires, excellent atmosphere. High-quality food served at lunchtime and evenings. Popular with walkers. Accommodation (B&B or camping). Isolated, but not to be missed.

 *11am–8.30pm Mon–Fri; 11am–9pm Sat–Sun. Food served from 12pm.*

HEREFORD

The Barrels

69 St Owen Street, Hereford HR1 2JQ
☎ *(01432) 274968* Fran Bowerman

Once the home of the Wye Valley Brewery, this pub still stocks the full range of Wye Valley brews. Also offers one guest ale, such as O'Hanlon's Red.

A town boozer. One of the last multi-roomed public houses in Hereford. Clientele a mix of old regulars and students. Occasional live music. Outside seating and fishpond. Annual beer festival on August bank holiday weekend, during which over 50 beers and ciders are available. No food. No children.

 *All day, every day.*

Lichfield Vaults

11 Church Street, Hereford HR1 2LR
☎ *(01432) 267994* John Cray

Five real ales usually available. Greene King Abbot is a regular, plus two rotating guests.

A traditional, historic town-centre pub with one bar and a mixed clientele. Food served 12–8pm Mon–Sat and 12–6pm Sun. Beer garden, children welcome until 3pm.

OPEN *11am–11pm Mon–Sat; 12–10.30pm Sun.*

The Victory

88 St Owen Street, Hereford HR1 2QD
☎ *(01432) 274998* Jim Kenyon

Home of the Spinning Dog Brewery, with up to eight real ales available, four from Spinning Dog and four from elsewhere. Two annual beer festivals held (May Day and October).

A two-bar boozer with a nautical theme. Live music on Saturday and Sunday evenings. Thursday is curry and quiz night. Beer garden. Food served lunchtimes and evenings Mon–Sat, with vegetarian meals available, and traditional roasts on Sundays 12–5pm. Children allowed. Cask Marque accredited. CAMRA Herefordshire Pub of the Year 2001. The publican runs a visitors' book which is an absolute must for 'tickers'! Brewery tours available. Function room available.

OPEN *All day, every day.*

KINGTON

The Queen's Head

Bridge Street, Kington HR5 3DW
☎ *(01544) 231106* Michael John Hickey

Owned by the nearby Dunn Plowman Brewery and run as the brewery tap, with the full range of brews always available. Brewing no longer takes place on the premises.

A 400-year-old refurbished pub in the old market town. Food available all day Tues–Sun. Beer garden. Petanque court. Accommodation. Children allowed.

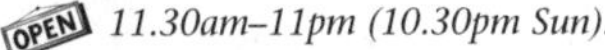
11.30am–11pm (10.30pm Sun).

LEDBURY

The Horseshoe Inn

The Homend, Ledbury HR8 1BP
☎ *(01531) 632770* David Tegg

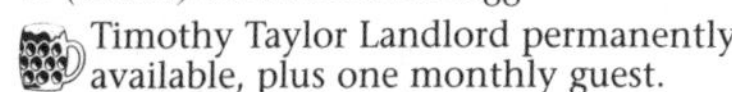
Timothy Taylor Landlord permanently available, plus one monthly guest.

A small family inn in Ledbury town with one bar and garden. Food available at lunchtime only. Children allowed.

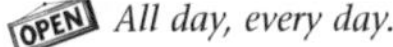
All day, every day.

The Royal Oak Hotel

The Southend, Ledbury HR8 2EY
☎ *(01531) 632110* David Robert Tegg

Marston's Pedigree and Fuller's London Pride usually available, plus a couple of guest beers changed weekly.

Eighteenth-century Georgian coaching hotel situated at the top of the town, refurbished, and featuring exposed beams dating from 1420 and hidden since 1836. Extensive traditional bar menu with many homemade specialities, served in the oak-panelled bar. Off-street parking and quality en-suite accommodation. Well-behaved children and dogs welcome. Function room for hire.

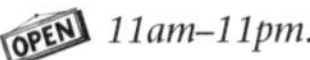
11am–11pm.

LEOMINSTER

The Black Horse Coach House

South Street, Leominster HR6 8JF
☎ *(01568) 611946* Peter Hoare

A freehouse serving Dunn Plowman Black Horse (house ale) and Hobsons Town Crier plus two guests such as Fuller's London Pride, Hobsons Best or other micro-brews. Has served 150 beers over the past 12 months.

A former coaching inn in a traditional building. Two bars, restaurant and garden. Food served every lunchtime and Mon–Sat evenings. Children allowed.

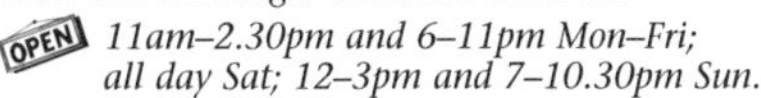
11am–2.30pm and 6–11pm Mon–Fri; all day Sat; 12–3pm and 7–10.30pm Sun.

The Grape Vaults

Broad Street, Leominster HR6 8BS
☎ *(01568) 611404* Julie Saxon

Owned by Avebury Taverns with five real ales usually available. Marston's Pedigree and Banks's Original and Mild are regulars plus two guests, changing constantly, often from micro-breweries.

A small, unspoilt Victorian pub in the town centre with a splendid snug bar. Log fire and no music or games machines. Bar meals available at lunchtime and evenings (not Sun). Children allowed if eating. Close to Leominster Priory.

11am–11pm Mon–Sat; 12–10.30pm Sun.

LETTON

The Swan Inn

Letton, Hereford HR3 6DH
☎ *(01544) 327304* M Boardman

The house bitter is brewed for the pub by Wye Valley Brewery and called Old Swan Bitter (3.7% ABV). A second real ale, which may be Wye Valley's Butty Bach (4.5% ABV) is also usually available.

A traditional roadside freehouse with two bars, a pool table, darts and a beer garden with petanque. No background music. Food available until 9.30pm. Children welcome. Car park. Non-smoking accommodation available. Located on the A438 Hereford–Brecon road, 12 miles out of Hereford.

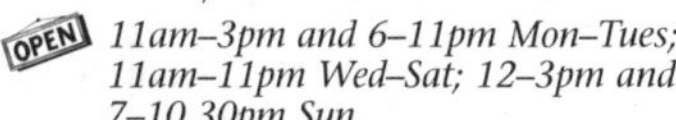
11am–3pm and 6–11pm Mon–Tues; 11am–11pm Wed–Sat; 12–3pm and 7–10.30pm Sun.

MUCH DEWCHURCH

The Black Swan Inn

Much Dewchurch, Hereford HR2 8DJ
☎ *(01981) 540295* A Davies

Brews from Timothy Taylor and Adnams are usually available plus one rotating guest such as Greene King Old Speckled Hen, Fuller's London Pride and Hook Norton Best.

A fourteenth-century freehouse with lounge and public bar. Dining area in lounge. Patio. Food available at lunchtime and evenings. Children allowed.

12–3pm and 6–11pm Mon–Fri; 11.30am–3pm and 6–11pm Sat; 12–3pm and 7–10.30pm Sun.

NORTON CANON

Three Horse Shoes Inn

Norton Canon, Hereford HR4 7BH
☎ *(01544) 318375* Frank Goodwin

Home of the Shoes Brewery, with own brews always available.

Two bars and a games room, with grassed area for summer use. Situated on the A480. No food. Car park. Children welcome.

 *6–11pm Mon–Tues; 12–3pm and 6–11pm Wed–Fri; 11am–11pm Sat; 12–10.30pm Sun.*

ROSS-ON-WYE

The Crown Inn

Gloucester Road, The Lea, Ross-on-Wye HR9 7JZ
☎ *(01989) 750407* Mr F and Mrs S Ellis

Hook Norton Best and RCH Pitchfork permanently available, plus three guests, often from Wye Valley Brewery. Small, independent breweries favoured.

A splendid fifteenth-century country village pub with a warm welcome always assured. One bar, beer garden. Smoking and non-smoking restaurant. Food available Mon–Sun lunchtimes and Tues–Sat evenings. Children allowed. Situated on the A40 from Ross-on-Wye to Gloucester.

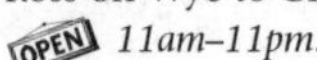 *11am–11pm.*

The Crown & Sceptre

Market Place, Ross-on-Wye HR9 5NX
☎ *(01989) 562765* Les Trute and Sarah Dean

An Enterprise Inn serving Wye Valley Bitter, Fuller's London Pride and Greene King Abbot Ale. A couple of rotating guests such as Greene King Old Speckled Hen, Shepherd Neame Spitfire or Gale's HSB are also available at busy times.

A town pub with a friendly atmosphere and mixed clientele. One bar with smoking and non-smoking areas, patio and garden. Home made food including up to ten specials served all day. Well-behaved children allowed.

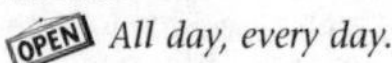 *All day, every day.*

WELLINGTON

The Wellington

Wellington HR4 8AT
☎ *(01432) 830367* Ross Williams

A freehouse with Hobsons Best Bitter among the beers always available, plus two regularly changing guests including Shepherd Neame Spitfire, Robinson's Best, Tomos Watkin OSB, Wood Shropshire Lad and brews from Spinning Dog and Wye Valley.

Traditional single-bar country pub in a Victorian building, with a restaurant in the converted stables. No games, no TV. Beer garden, car park. Children allowed.

OPEN *12–2.30pm and 6–11pm (10.30pm Sun).*

THE BREWERIES

BUNTINGFORD BREWERY CO.

3A Watermill Industrial Estate, Aspenden Road, Buntingford SG9 9JS
☎ *(07956) 246215*
www.buntingford-brewery.co.uk

HIGHWAYMAN BEST BITTER 3.7% ABV
Light brown session beer.

TINKER 4.0% ABV
50/50 blend of Highwayman and Hurricane Force.

HURRICANE FORCE 4.3% ABV
Mid-brown premium bitter.

HERTFORDSHIRE GOLD 4.5% ABV
Golden beer with citrus and hop flavours.

BISHOP 5.0% ABV
Uses lager malt and American hops for clean, crisp lager-style brew.

WATERMILL STOUT 4.8% ABV
Traditional English-style stout. Near black in colour.

Seasonals and occasionals:

THE BUNTINGFORD WITCH PROJECT 4.4% ABV
Dark, but not quite a mild, not quite a stout. Slightly roasted and fruity flavours.

HERTFORDSHIRE HONEY 4.6% ABV
Dark beer brewed with local honey.

GARDEN BARBER BREWERY

PO Box 23, Hertford SG14 3PZ
☎ *(01992) 504167* Steven Johnson

REEDY POPS 4.0% ABV
Bitter mild ale, sold locally and for festivals.

GREEN TYE BREWERY

Green Tye, Much Hadham SG10 6JP
☎ *(01279) 841041*

SHOT IN THE DARK 3.6% ABV
Dark ruby colour with flavour of hops. Available October.

IPA 3.7% ABV
Refreshing, pert hoppiness and dry finish.

MUSTANG MILD 3.7% ABV
Dark mild.

SNOWDROP 3.9% ABV
Quenching, balanced hop flavour, with some sweetness.

FIELD MARSHALL 4.0% ABV

AUTUMN ROSE 4.2% ABV
Red-brown best bitter.

GREEN TIGER 4.2% ABV
Light copper-coloured bitter.

MAD MORRIS 4.2% ABV
Golden and quenching with citrus fruit tanginess.

WHEELBARROW 4.3% ABV
Balanced hop, malt and fruit flavours. Easy drinker.

COAL PORTER 4.5% ABV
Flavour-packed porter. Winter brew.

CONKERER 4.7% ABV
Mid-brown best bitter.

TUMBLEDOWN DICK 5.3% ABV
Strong and hoppy.

MCMULLEN & SONS LTD

The Hertford Brewery, 26 Old Cross, Hertford SG14 1RD
☎ *(01992) 584911*

ORIGINAL AK 3.7% ABV
Light, well-balanced with good hoppiness.

COUNTRY BEST BITTER 4.3% ABV
Hoppy, fruity aroma and flavour.

GLADSTONE 4.3% ABV
Smooth, with finely rounded bitterness.

STRONGHART 7.0% ABV
Powerful, complex, sweet and dark.

Plus seasonal beers.

RED SQUIRREL BREWERY

146 Mimram Road, Herftford SG11 1NN
☎ *(01992) 501100*
www.redsquirrelbrewery.co.uk

BITTER 3.9% ABV
CONSERVATION BITTER 4.1% ABV
IPA 4.1% ABV
NO1 BITTER 4.1% ABV
GOLD 4.2% ABV
SCOTTISH ALE 4.3% ABV
STOUT 4.9% ABV
ENGLISH IPA 5.0% ABV
HONEY PORTER 5.0% ABV
IPA IN THE USA 5.4% ABV

SAWBRIDGEWORTH BREWERY

The Gate, 81 London Road, Sawbridgeworth CM21 9JJ
☎ *(01279) 722313*
www.the-gate-pub.co.uk

IPA 3.6% ABV
SELHURST PARK FLYER 3.7% ABV
TEFLON 3.7% ABV
BROWN BOMBER 3.8% ABV
IS IT YOURSELF 4.2% ABV
STOUT 4.3%
BROOKLANDS EXPRESS 4.6% ABV
LYNNE PEARCE 5% ABV
PILEDRIVER 5.3% ABV

THE TRING BREWERY COMPANY LTD

81–82 Akeman Street, Tring HP23 6AF
☎ *(01442) 890721*
www.tringbrewery.com

SIDE POCKET FOR A TOAD 3.6% ABV
JACK O'LEGS 4.2% ABV
COLLEY'S BLACK DOG 5.2% ABV

Plus occasional and seasonal beers.

VERULAM BREWERY

134 London Road, St Albans AL1 1PQ
☎ *(01727) 766702*

VERULAM SPECIAL 3.8% ABV
A light mild.

VERULAM IPA 4% ABV
A true bitter.

FARMERS JOY 4.5% ABV
A darker ale.

Plus occasional and seasonal beers.

THE PUBS

ALDBURY

The Greyhound

19 Stocks Road, Aldbury, Tring HP23 5RT
☎ *(01442) 851228* Richard Coletta

A Badger (Hall and Woodhouse) Brewery tied pub serving Badger Best, Tanglefoot, IPA and seasonal ales.

A historic inn in a pretty village with an inglenook fireplace, two bars, two dining areas including a non-smoking conservatory, and courtyard garden. Food available every lunchtime and Tuesday to Saturday evenings. Children and dogs welcome. Close to Ashridge forest. Conservatory and accommodation.

OPEN *11am–11pm Mon–Sat; 12–10.30pm Sun.*

Valiant Trooper

Trooper Road, Aldbury, Tring HP23 5RW
☎ *(01442) 851203* Tim O'Gorman

Adnams Bitter, Fuller's London Pride and up to three regularly rotating guest ales.

In the village centre. Exposed beams and open fires. Three rooms. Bar and restaurant food served every lunchtime and Tues–Sat evenings. Outside seating plus garden with children's play area. Dogs welcome.

OPEN *All day, every day.*

AMWELL

Elephant & Castle

Amwell Lane, Amwell, Wheathampstead AL4 8EA
☎ *(01582) 832175*

Greene King brews plus a range of guest ales.

Located in buildings almost 500 years old, with three bars on different levels. There is a 200ft well in the middle of the bar. No music or machines. Bar meals available at lunchtime and evenings (not Sunday or Monday). Car park, two gardens (one for adults only), dining area. Children not allowed in bar. Not easy to find. Ask in Wheathampstead or ring for directions.

OPEN *11am–3pm and 5.30–11pm Mon–Fri; all day Sat–Sun.*

ASHWELL

The Bushel & Strike

Mill Street, Ashwell
☎ *(01462) 742394*
Mrs J Grommann and Mr N Burton

Charles Wells Eagle and Bombardier usually available plus three guest beers which may include Adnams Broadside or Greene King Old Speckled Hen.

Located in a pretty village, a Charles Wells two-bar house with large restaurant, patio, barbecue and small garden. Food served 12–2.30pm Mon–Sun, 7–9pm Mon–Sat. Car park. Special children's menu. Opposite the church.

OPEN *11.30am–3pm and 6–11pm Mon–Sat; 12–10.30pm Sun.*

AYOT ST LAWRENCE

The Brocket Arms

Ayot St Lawrence AL6 9RT
☎ *(01438) 820068* Toby Wingfield-Digby
www.brocketarms.com

Greene King IPA and Abbot Ale, Young's IPA, Adnams Broadside and Fuller's London Pride always available plus a guest beer, changing weekly, from any independent brewery.

A fourteenth-century, oak-beamed, village pub with attractive walled garden and accommodation. Bar and restaurant food served at lunchtime and evenings (except Sunday and Monday nights). Parking. Dogs welcome. Close to Shaw's Corner, home of George Bernard Shaw.

OPEN *11am–11pm.*

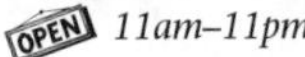

BALDOCK

The Old White Horse

1 Station Road, Baldock SG7 5BS
☎ *(01462) 893168* Margaret Patterson
www.oldwhitehorse.com

An Enterprise Inn with Fuller's London Pride and something from Adnams usually available plus a guest, rotated every couple of months.

A former coaching inn with restaurant specialising in Caribbean and English food. Bar food at lunchtime. Restaurant open from 7pm. Beer garden. Children allowed. Regular beer festivals.

OPEN *11am–3pm Mon–Thurs; all day Fri–Sun.*

BARKWAY

The Tally-Ho

London Road, Barkway, Royston SG8 8EX
☎ *(01763) 848389* Paul Danter

Nine different ales on offer every week, through three barrels at a time. The focus is on a varied spectrum of strengths from breweries nearby and across the country, the local Buntingford Brewery ales among them.

A traditional pub with traditional values – no fruit machines, no pool tables, no music, no TV. Oak-panelled bar with armchairs, a non-smoking restaurant, two gardens and terraces, petanque pitch, car park. Homemade food available 12–2pm and 7–9pm. Children allowed, with well-behaved parents! On the B1368.

 *11.30am–3pm and 5.30–11pm Mon–Fri;12–3pm and 6–11pm Sat; 12–4pm Sun (closed Sun evening).*

BARLEY

The Fox & Hounds

High Street, Barley, Nr Royston SG8 8HU
☎ *(01763) 848459* Caroline Cox

Formerly a brewpub but now owned by Punch Taverns. Two real ales usually available. Greene King IPA and Wadworth 6X are popular choices but the selection rotates regularly.

Parts of the heavily beamed village pub date back to 1450. Formerly known as The Waggon and Horses, the pub has the only gantry still standing in the country, which spans the road and depicts a hunt in progress. Warm and welcoming with an inglenook fireplace and original beams. Darts, games and pool table. Bar and restaurant food is available 12.30–2.30pm daily and 6.30–8.30pm Thurs–Sat. Sunday roasts 12.30–4.30pm. Non-smoking area in dining room. Facilities for parties. Car park, garden, children's room, disabled toilets, baby-changing facilities. Well-behaved children welcome.

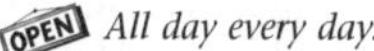 *All day every day.*

BARNET

Moon Under Water

148 High Street, Barnet EN5 5XP
☎ *(020) 8441 9476* Gareth Fleming

A Wetherspoon's pub with Greene King IPA and Abbot plus Shepherd Neame Spitfire always available. Also three guests such as Hop Back Summer Lightning which are changed on a weekly basis.

An olde-worlde town pub with one large bar, a non-smoking dining area and big beer garden. Food available from 11am–10pm. No children.

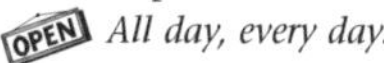 *All day, every day.*

BENINGTON

The Lordship Arms

42 Whempstead Road, Benington
☎ *(01438) 869665* Alan and Daphne

Woodforde's Wherry, Young's Special and Fuller's London Pride always available, plus guest beers (100 per year). Specialises in ales from small independent and micro-breweries. Also draught cider.

A cosy village freehouse with a display of telephone memorabilia. Bar snacks available on weekday lunchtimes. Home-cooked roast lunches served on Sundays (booking advisable). Curry night on Wednesdays. Car park and garden. Children not allowed. Take the A602 exit off the A1(M), turn left. Signposted Aston, Benington.

 *12–3pm and 6–11pm Mon–Sat; 12–3pm and 7–10.30pm Sun.*

BISHOP'S STORTFORD

The Half Moon

31 North Street, Bishop's Stortford CM23 2LD
☎ *(01279) 834500* Fiona Davies

Up to seven real ales available. Caledonian Deuchars IPA, Fuller's London Pride, Wychwood Hobgoblin and Theakston Old Peculiar are regular fixtures with up to three rotating guests changed every month.

A two-bar (one non-smoking) town pub with children's room and beer garden. Food available during the day, with cheese a speciality. Children allowed in children's room. Regular live music and beer festivals. On the corner of North Street and the A1250.

All day, every day.

BUNTINGFORD

The Crown

17 High Street, Buntingford SG9 9AB
☎ *(01763) 271422*

Three real ales usually available. Ridleys IPA and Archers Best plus a guest changed every week or two.

Two-bar pub in the town centre. Covered patio (children welcome) and garden. Food served at lunchtime and evenings. Function room. Theme nights. No pool table or juke box.

12–3pm and 6–11pm (7–10.30pm Sun).

HERTFORDSHIRE

BUSHEY

Swan
25 Park Road, Bushey WD23 3EE
☎ *(0208) 950 2256*
Peter, Gavin and Marian White

Young's Bitter and Special plus Jennings Cumberland and Wadworth 6X always on offer.

A friendly one-bar local in a residential street, built in 1866 and retaining its traditional character. No fruit machine or juke box, just real fires, a dart board and a piano. Bar snacks served.

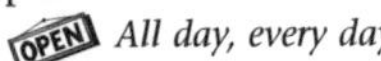
All day, every day.

GREEN TYE

The Prince of Wales
Green Tye, Much Hadham SG10 6JP
☎ *(01279) 842517* Gary Whelan

Home of the Green Tye Brewery, so with beers from the range available plus a guest from an independent brewery.

Former McMullen's tied house turned back into a village freehouse in 1991 and run in conjunction with the Green Tye Brewery since 1999. Food served at lunchtimes. Car park and beer garden. Children allowed. Monthly folk club. Beer festival in May.

12–2.30pm (not Mon) and 5.30–11pm Mon–Fri; all day Sat–Sun.

HARPENDEN

The Carpenter's Arms
14 Cravells Road, Southdown, Harpenden AL5 2JP
☎ *(01582) 460311* John Tibble

Adnams Bitter, Greene King Abbot and another pump featuring a wide range of guests, usually from a local brewery or micro.

Smallest pub in town, but very friendly and full of motoring memorabilia. Run by the same landlord for almost 20 years. Food served at lunchtime. Car park. Outside seating.

11am–3pm and 5.30–11pm Mon–Sat; 12–3pm and 7–10.30pm Sun

Cross Keys
39 High Street, Harpenden AL5 2SD
☎ *(01582) 763989*

Cross Keys Bitter (from Tring Brewery), Timothy Taylor Landlord and Fuller's London Pride available.

Oldest pub in town, situated close to station. Low oak beams and open fires, pewter-topped bar. Snug. Garden. Dogs welcome. Food served at lunchtime (not Sunday).

OPEN *All day every day.*

The Oak Tree
15 Leyton Green, Harpenden AL5 2TG
☎ *(01582) 763850* Mr Needham

Formerly a freehouse, now tied to Charles Wells so with Bombardier and Eagle IPA available. But still serving four guests, perhaps including Adnams Bitter and Jennings Cocker Hoop.

A one-bar town house with seats to the front and patio behind. Home-cooked food available at lunchtime. Children allowed at lunchtimes if eating.

All day, every day.

HERTFORD

The White Horse
33 Castle Street, Hertford SG14 1HH
☎ *(01992) 501950* Nigel Crofts

Fuller's Chiswick, London Pride, ESB and seasonal brews and Adnams Bitter usually available, plus up to six guest beers from micro-brewers the length and breadth of the country. Spring and autumn beer festivals held, each featuring up to 60 micro-brewery beers.

Classic fifteenth-century alehouse, renowned for its selection of cask ales, despite being a Fuller's tied pub. Two bars, and a traditional bar billiards room upstairs. Home-cooked food served 12–2pm Mon–Sat, with roasts on Sunday. Supervised children welcome in the upstairs non-smoking area. Well-behaved dogs always welcome. Near the castle. Outside seating.

12–2.30pm and 5.30–11pm Mon–Thurs; all day Fri–Sun.

HERTINGFORDBURY

The Prince of Wales
244 Hertingfordbury Road, Hertingfordbury, Hertford SG14 2LG
☎ *(01992) 581149* Andrew Thomas

A freehouse with Fuller's London Pride, Greene King IPA, McMullen AK and Wadworth 6X always available.

A one-bar country pub with extension and garden. Food available at lunchtime only. Children allowed. Accommodation.

OPEN *All day, every day.*

HITCHIN

The Sunrunner

24 Bancroft, Hitchin SG4 0NS
☎ *(01462) 440717* Kevin MacNamara

A freehouse with up to nine real ales available. Potton Shannon IPA and Fuller's London Pride are regular fixtures. Up to seven guests, changed daily, from a huge range. Also two real ciders.

Town pub in an old building, with lots of character, beams and one large bar. Original wood floors and fireplaces. Food served 12–2.30pm Mon–Thurs and 12–3pm Fri–Sun. Also 7–9pm Tues and Thurs. Private room available for hire. Children allowed.

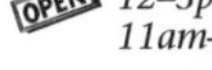
12–3pm and 5.30–11pm Mon–Thurs; 11am–11pm Fri–Sat; 12–10.30pm Sun.

ICKLEFORD

The Cricketers

107 Arlesey Road, Ickleford, Hitchin SG5 3TH
☎ *(01462) 422766* Mathew Walker

A Charles Wells tied house with four beers usually available. These are likely to be Bombardier and Eagle IPA plus Adnams Best and Broadside although other guests do put in an occasional appearance.

A one-bar traditional country pub with wood-burning stove and various nooks and crannies. No food. No children. Accommodation, beer garden, car park quiz nights (Wednesday) and midsummer music festival. At the far end of the village.

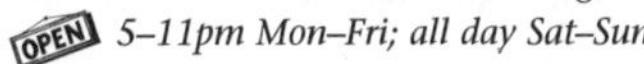
5–11pm Mon–Fri; all day Sat–Sun.

The Plume of Feathers

Upper Green, Ickleford, Hitchin SG5 3YD
☎ *(01462) 432729* Teresa Thompson

Owned by Enterprise Inns, with Fuller's London Pride, Adnams Best, Wadworth 6X and a couple of other brews available from a constantly changing range.

A 300-year-old pub on the village green with dining area and garden. Food available at lunchtime and evenings (not Sun). Well-behaved children allowed. Near the church.

11.30am–3pm and 6–11pm Mon–Thurs; all day Fri–Sun.

KIMPTON

The White Horse

22 High Street, Kimpton SG4 8RJ
☎ *(01438) 832307* Peter and Janet Johnson
www.whitehorsekimpton.co.uk

McMullen AK always available plus at least one guest.

A Grade II listed conversion of three cottages dating from the sixteenth century in the heart of an ancient village. The first was licensed in the 1820s, with an extension to include the rest in 1989. Log fires and a priest hole included. Bar and restaurant food served lunchtime and evenings (except Monday). Theme nights. Outside decked area and garden. Car park.

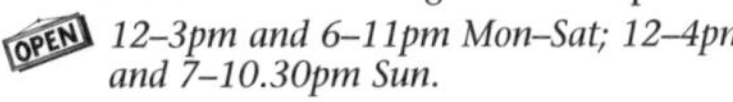
12–3pm and 6–11pm Mon–Sat; 12–4pm and 7–10.30pm Sun.

OLD KNEBWORTH

The Lytton Arms

Park Lane, Old Knebworth SG3 6QB
☎ *(01438) 812312* Anthony Smith

Up to ten real ales usually available with something from Fuller's, Adnams and Mighty Oak among them. The wide-ranging guests change every day. Note also the Belgian beers and malt whiskies.

A traditional freehouse on the edge of Knebworth Park, built in 1837 and completely refurbished in late 2004. Beamed with open fires. Bar food available at lunchtime and evenings (12–5pm on Sundays). Car park, front terrace, rear garden and children's room. Regular beer festivals have resumed four times a year. Located halfway between Knebworth and Codicote.

OPEN *11am–11pm Mon–Sat; 12–10.30pm Sun.*

PERRY GREEN

The Hoops

Perry Green, Much Hadham SG10 6EF
☎ *(01279) 843568* Michael O'Connor
www.thehoopsinn.co.uk

Greene King IPA and Fuller's London Pride always available, plus a guest ale from the Green Tye Brewery.

A seventeenth-century, family-run pub in a small hamlet situated close to the Henry Moore Foundation and Sculpture Park and directly opposite Henry Moore's house. Tastefully extended in keeping with the period. Separate non-smoking dining room. Large garden with outside seating, two patios, barbecue and large car park. Bar and restaurant food available at lunchtime and evenings Mon–Sat, all day Sun. Children allowed.

12–3pm and 6.30–11pm Mon–Sat; 12–10.30pm Sun.

POTTER'S CROUCH

12

The Hollybush

Bedmond Lane, Potter's Crouch, St Albans AL2 3NN
☎ *(01727) 851792* Ray Taylor

Fuller's Chiswick, London Pride and ESB available plus seasonal brews. The licensee is an award-winning Fuller's cellarman and the quality of his beers reflects it.

Spotless pub with a country cottage feel tucked down a back lane between Bedmond and St Albans. One low-beamed bar on two levels with various alcoves and seating areas. Award-winning garden. Simple bar food seved at lunchtimes (not Sunday). Children welcome in the garden only.

 *11.30am–2.30pm and 6–11pm Mon–Fri; 12–2.30pm and 7–11pm Sat; 12–2.30pm and 7–10.30pm Sun.*

PRESTON

The Red Lion

The Green, Preston, Nr Hitchin SG4 7UD
☎ *(01462) 459585* Tim Hunter

Greene King IPA plus an ever-changing range of four guests, from local independents and micros. Recently including brews from Tring, Grand Union, Oakham and Castle Rock.

Award-winning, 200-year-old village green pub with log fires. The first pub in Britain top be owned by the local community. Food served 12–2pm and (usually) 7–9pm. Car park. Large beer garden.

 *12–3pm and 5.30–11pm Mon–Fri; Sat varies; 12–3pm and 7–10.30pm Sun.*

REDBOURN

The Hollybush

Church End, Redbourn, St Albans AL3 7DU
☎ *(01582) 792423*

Adnams Bitter usually available plus three rotating guests from local (Tring and Vale) and regional independents.

Operating since 1696 in a pretty street, this former freehouse is now owned by Brakspear. Open fires and exposed beams. Food available at lunchtime. Hall available for private functions and folk club on Thursdays. Garden. Car park.

 *11am–2.30pm and 5.30–11pm Mon–Fri; 12–3pm and 7–11pm Sat–Sun.*

REED

The Cabinet

High Street, Reed, Nr Royston SG8 8AH
☎ *(01463) 848366*
www.thecabinetatreed.co.uk

Cabinet Bitter plus up to three guests, always changing but often including something from Nethergate.

Sixteenth-century weatherboarded pub with two rooms. Bar and restaurant food served at lunchtime and evenings. Children's room. Large garden. 'A watering hole for 500 years.' On A10 south of Royston.

 *12–3pm and 6–11pm (10pm Sun).*

ROYSTON

The White Bear

49 Kneesworth Street, Royston SG8 5AQ
☎ *(01763) 242458* Shirley Smeeton

Greene King IPA and City of Cambridge Hobson's Choice usually available plus two guests from Tring Brewery and a couple of others from Nethergate, Adnams, Rebellion, Crouch Vale or similar, changed every two or three days.

Town-centre pub close to the railway station. Food served at lunchtime and evening. Front and rear beer gardens. Car park. Accommodation available.

 *11am–11pm Mon–Sat; 12–10.30pm Sun.*

ST ALBANS

The Blacksmith's Arms

56 St Peter's Street, St Albans AL1 3HG
☎ *(01727) 855761* Sue and Noel Keane

Six real ales always available (over 250 a year), with Wadworth 6X and Timothy Taylor Landlord regularly served, plus a wide variety of guests from around the country. The only supplier of City of Cambridge beer in St Albans. Regular Beer of the Month feature, and free tasters on all products. Six Belgian beers also stocked.

A Hogshead pub with one bar. Food served 12–9pm Mon–Thurs, 12–7pm Fri–Sun. Background music. Large garden – children welcome in garden until 5.30pm. Located on the main road.

 *11am–11pm Mon–Sat; 12–10.30pm Sun.*

The Duke of Marlborough

110 Holywell Hill, St Albans AL1 1DH
☎ *(01727) 858982* Andy and Pam Evans

Greene King IPA and Abbot plus Adnams Bitter usually available.

Situated on the main road through St Albans, near the park and Abbey railway station. Two bars. Big-screen TV for sport. Food served all day. Children welcome in beer garden and function room. Car park.

All day, every day.

The Farmer's Boy

134 London Road, St Albans AL1 1PQ
☎ *(01727) 766702* Viv Davies

Home of the Verulam Brewery since 1996, so with Best Bitter, Special, IPA, Farmer's Joy and the seasonal brews available.

A one-bar town brewpub with patio and garden. Food served all day, every day (roasts on Sunday). Children allowed.

All day, every day.

The Garibaldi

61 Albert Street, St Albans AL1 1RT
☎ *(01727) 855046* P Day

A Fuller's pub with four real ales always available plus one rotating guest changed every two weeks.

Backstreet Victorian local with homemade pub food available at lunchtime and Thai food in the evenings. Beer garden. Down Holywell Hill from the town centre, close to the cathedral.

12–11pm (10.30pm Sun).

The Lower Red Lion

34–6 Fishpool Street, St Albans AL3 4RX
☎ *(01727) 855669* Chris, Mary and Alan
www.thelowerredlion.co.uk

Genuine freehouse with up to nine real ales available. Fuller's London Pride and Oakham JHB are consistent fixtures, plus seven guests (at least 750 per year) from all over the country. Two beer festivals held each year.

A two-bar traditional coaching house dating from the seventeenth century in the conservation area of St Albans close to the abbey and Roman Verulamium. A wide-ranging clientele. No music or games machines. Home-cooked food is available 12–2.30pm Mon–Sat and roasts on Sunday. Car park, function room and garden. Accommodation. No children.

12–2.30pm and 5.30–11pm Mon–Fri; 12–11pm Sat; 12–10.30pm Sun.

The Mermaid

98 Hatfield Road, St Albans AL1 3RX
☎ *(01727) 837758*

Former Everards pub, with the brewery's beers still available. Plus Adnams Bitter and other guests from independent and micro-breweries.

Lively pub in a Victorian building with live music at weekends. Limited food served at lunchtime. Outside seating.

All day, every day.

The Plough

Tyttenhanger Green, Nr St Albans AL4 0RW
☎ *(01727) 857777*
Mike and Solveig Barrowman

Fuller's London Pride and ESB always available plus five or six guests, which might include Marston's Pedigree, Greene King IPA, Abbot and Old Speckled Hen, Wadworth 6X, Tring Ridgeway or Timothy Taylor Landlord.

Popular country freehouse in a rural setting on the outskirts of St Albans housed in a building that was once the village bakery. Bar food available at lunchtime only. Real fires. Car park and beer garden.

11.30am–2.30pm (3pm Sat) and 6–11pm Mon–Sat; 12–3pm and 7–10.30pm Sun.

The Rose and Crown

St Michael's Street, St Albans AL3 4SG
☎ *(01727) 851903* Ruth Courtney

Adnams Bitter and Fuller's London Pride available plus a guest, perhaps from Black Sheep or Timothy Taylor.

A sixteenth-century pub in the same part of town as The Lower Red Lion. Beams and open fires. Food (especially speciality sandwiches) served at lunchtime. Live music. Family room. Garden.

11.30am–3pm and 5.30–11pm Mon–Fri (all day in summer); all day Sat–Sun.

The White Lion

91 Sopwell Lane, St Albans AL1 1RN
☎ *(01727) 850540* Gary Jenkins

Fuller's London Pride, Young's Bitter and Greene King IPA usually available plus a couple of weekly rotating guests.

Another fine sixteenth-century St Albans pub, this one located just off Holywell Hill. Two bars. Large garden with children's play area. Summer barbecues. Food served at lunchtime (12–4pm). Live music on Tuesdays and Fridays.

12–3pm and 6–11pm Mon–Thurs; 12–11pm Fri–Sat; 12–10.30pm Sun.

ST PAULS WALDEN

The Strathmore Arms

London Road, St Pauls Walden, Near Hitchen SG4 8BT
☎ *(01438) 871654*

Fullers Chiswick and London Pride plus a rotating range of guest beers from smaller independent breweries. An annual beer festival takes place in September.

On the Bowes-Lyon family estate, CAMRA's Hertfordshire pub of the year for 2004. Refurbished and relaunched with a beer garden and good food served at lunchtime and evenings. Children welcome.

Closed Mon, 12–2.30pm and 5–11pm Tues–Thurs, all day Fri–Sun.

SANDRIDGE

The Green Man

High Street, Sandridge AL4 0NS
☎ *(01727) 854845*

A range including Adnams Bitter and Broadside, Greene King IPA and Abbot and Bateman XXXB. At least three of the beers are served straight from the cask.

Solid red-brick pub built in the 1880s and formerly owned by Benskins. Food served at lunchtime and Friday and Saturday evenings. Family room. Garden. Car park.

11am–3pm and 5.30–11pm Mon–Thurs; 11am–11pm Fri–Sat; 12–10.30pm Sun.

SAWBRIDGEWORTH

The Gate

81 London Road, Sawbridgeworth CM21 9JJ
☎ *(01279) 722313* Gary and Tom Barnett
www.the-gate-pub.co.uk

Home of the Sawbridgeworth Brewery. Nine hand pumps at all times, serving a range of home brews and guests including Greene King Abbot and Timothy Taylor Landlord. More than 2,000 different brews have so far been featured.

A traditional pub with two bars, darts and pool. Food available at lunchtime (Sunday roasts from 12–4pm). Children allowed. Outside seating. Regular beer festivals. Small car park.

11.30am–3pm and 5.30–11pm Mon–Thur; all day Fri–Sat; 12–10.30pm Sun.

STAPLEFORD

Papillon at the Woodhall Arms

17 High Road, Stapleford SG14 3NW
☎ *(01992) 535123* Phil Gonzalez

Charles Wells Eagle IPA and Adnams Bitter are usually served, and the two guests (15–20 beers a month) might be ales from Adnam's, Young's, Everards, Wychwood or Brains.

Food-oriented French/Continental pub/ restaurant. The bar, restaurant and conservatory each seat 50 people, and there is an extra restaurant seating 25, plus a party room for 10. Food available at lunchtime and evenings. Garden and barked play area – children allowed. Car park for 60 cars. Accommodation available in 12 letting rooms. On the A119 between Hertford and Stevenage.

11–3pm and 5–11pm Mon–Sat; 12–4 and 7–10.30pm Sun.

STEVENAGE

Our Mutual Friend

Broadwater Crescent, Stevenage SG2 8EH
☎ *(01438) 312282* Keith Neville

Five or six real ales usually available from independent and micro-brewers, perhaps including a mild. Caledonian Deuchars IPA and Black Sheep Bitter are regulars. Also real cider.

Revitalised, two-room (one for games, one for talking/drinking) pub. Food served at lunchtime. Live music, TV, pool and darts. Beer festivals.

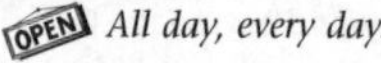
All day, every day.

TONWELL

The Robin Hood & Little John

14 Ware Road, Tonwell SG12 0HN
☎ *(01920) 463352* Mr Harding

A freehouse with up to four beers, perhaps including Hampshire Brewery's Lion Heart, Nethergate Swift or Shepherd Neame Spitfire.

A 300-year-old, traditional village pub two miles from Hertford. One bar on split levels and non-smoking restaurant. B&B. Food available at lunchtime and evenings. Children allowed in the restaurant only.

12–2.30pm and 5.30–11pm Mon–Fri; 12–3pm and 5.30–11pm Sat; 12–3pm and 7–10.30pm Sun.

TRING

The King's Arms

King Street, Tring HP23 6BE
☎ *(01442) 823318*
John Francis, Thomas and Victoria North

A freehouse with five real ales usually available. Wadworth 6X is a permanent fixture plus guests from a wide-ranging list of smaller breweries including local Tring ales.

A traditional town pub built in the 1830s with distinctive Regency architecture and a covered and heated beer garden. Real fires. Home-cooked food available at lunchtime and evenings. Non-smoking area. No machines, music or television. Children allowed at lunchtime only.

12–2.30pm and 7–11pm Mon–Thurs; 12–3pm and 7–11pm Fri; 11.30am–3pm and 7–11pm Sat; 12-4pm and 7–10.30pm Sun.

Robin Hood

1 Brook Street, Tring HP23 5ED
☎ *(01442) 824912*

Fuller's Chiswick, London Pride, ESB and seasonal brews.

Another Hertfordshire pub run by a Fuller's master cellarman (see also The Hollybush, Potter's Crouch). Once a street-corner cottage, with low beams and real fires. Food (especially fish) served at lunchtime and evenings (not Sunday evening). Conservatory, courtyard.

11am–2.30pm and 5.30–11pm Mon–Fri; 11am–3pm and 6.30–11pm Sat; 12–3pm and 7–10.30pm Sun.

WALTHAM CROSS

The Vault

160 High Street, Waltham Cross EN8 7AB
☎ *(01992) 631600* Mr P Laville
www.thevaultinn.co.uk

A freehouse with no permanent beers but a regularly changing selection of up to six real ales that might include brews from Crouch Vale, Clark's or numerous micro-breweries.

Formerly a bank, now a family and food-orientated town-centre pub with separate dining area. Food available at lunchtime and early evenings. Live bands every Thursday plus other live entertainment. Beer terrace. Children allowed during the day.

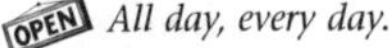 *All day, every day.*

WARESIDE

Chequers Inn

Wareside, Nr Ware SG12 7QY
☎ *(01920) 467010* Douglas Cook

A freehouse with Adnams Best and Broadside usually available plus up to four regularly changing guests such as Archers Dark Mild, Young's Special or Greene King IPA. All beers are served straight from the cask racked behind the bar.

A tiny village pub with parts of the building dating from the thirteenth century and parts from the seventeenth century. Three bars, wooden beams and two open fires. Food available at lunchtime and evenings (not Sunday) in a 40-seater restaurant. Bench seating outside, hog roast on bank holidays. Live band on Sundays. Children allowed. Just outside Ware. Accommodation.

 *12–3pm and 6–11pm Mon–Sat; all day Sun.*

WESTON

The Cricketers

Damask Green Road, Weston SG4 7DA
☎ *(01462) 790273* Tony Szpak
www.rhubarb-inns.co.uk/cricketers00.html

Three real ales usually availble. Fuller's London Pride, Tring Jack O'Legs and Worthington 1744 might comprise a typical trio.

Previously called The Thatched House, now owned by Rhubarb Inns, a two-bar Victorian-style freehouse in a village near Baldock. Garden including petanque pitch and children's play area. Food served at lunchtime and evenings Tues–Sat plus Sunday lunchtime. Car park. Near Junction 9 on the A1(M).

 *12–2.30pm and 5.30–11pm Mon–Fri; all day Sat; 12–4pm and 7–10.30pm Sun.*

WHITWELL

The Maiden's Head

67 High Street, Whitwell, Nr Hitchin SG4 8AH
☎ *(01438) 871392* Mike and Barbara Jones

A McMullen tied house with AK Original and Country Best available plus one guest, changed monthly, perhaps including Shepherd Neame Spitfire, Everards Tiger or Wadworth 6X.

An unspoilt, two-bar village pub in a seventeenth-century timbered building. Large garden. Licensees in place for more than 20 years. Darts and dominoes played. Food available Mon–Sat lunchtimes and Tues–Sat evenings. No children. Between Stevenage and Luton.

OPEN *12–3pm and 5–11pm.*

WIDFORD

The Green Man

High Street, Widford, Ware SG12 8SR
☎ *(01279) 842846* Brian Goodbody

Adnams Bitter and a McMullen ale are the regular beers at this freehouse, plus two guests, changed every two weeks, perhaps from Green Tye, Moor or Mighty Oak.

Traditional pub with one large bar. Darts, pool, beer garden. Food served at lunchtimes (not Monday) only. Children allowed. Car park. Accommodation available. On main road from Bishop's Stortford to Ware.

 *12–3pm and 5.30–11pm Mon–Fri (open 4.30pm Fri); 11am–11pm Sat; 12–10.30pm Sun.*

WILD HILL

The Woodman

45 Wildhill Lane, Wild Hill, Hatfield AL9 6EA
☎ *(01707) 642618* Graham Craig

McMullen ales, Greene King Abbot and IPA available plus three guests from independent and micro-breweries such as Rooster's, Hampshire, Mighty Oak or York.

A popular country village pub with garden. Sandwiches available at lunchtime (no food on Sundays or bank holidays). No children. Car park.

 *11.30am–2.30pm and 5.30–11pm Mon–Sat; 12–2.30pm and 7–10.30pm Sun.*

THE BREWERIES

BUSHY'S BREWERY LTD

Mount Murray, Castletown Road, Braddon IM4 1JE
☎ *(01624) 661244*
www.bushys.com

CASTLETOWN BITTER 3.5% ABV
RUBY MILD 3.5% ABV
BUSHY'S BITTER 3.8% ABV
CELTIBRATION 4.0% ABV
MANANNAN'S CLOAK 4.0% ABV
CLASSIC 4.3% ABV
OLD BUSHY TAIL 4.5% ABV
Seasonals and occasionals:
SUMMER ALE 3.8% ABV
OYSTER STOUT 4.2% ABV
PISTON BREW 4.5% ABV
Brewed for the TT races.
LOVELY JUBBELY 5.2% ABV
Winter brew.

OKELL & SONS LTD

Falcon Brewery, Kewaigue, Douglas IM2 1QG
☎ *(01624) 6661120*
www.okells.co.uk

MILD 3.4% ABV
Rich malt aroma and a hint of Seville oranges.
BITTER 3.7% ABV
Full malt and hop aroma, with a long-lasting dry-ish hoppy complex finish.
MACLIR 4.4% ABV
Heavily hopped.
OLDE SKIPPER 4.5% ABV
Light, golden-coloured beer with a hop and fruit aroma.
Seasonals:
SUMMER STORM 4.2% ABV
Flavours of vanilla and banana.
AUTUMN DAWN 4.4% ABV
Full-bodied light brown beer.
SPRING RAM 4.5% ABV
Rich bittersweet flavour with a complex finish of malt and hops.

THE PUBS

BALLAUGH

The Raven Inn

Main Road, Ballaugh IM7 5EG
☎ *(01624) 897272* Steven Barrett
www.raven-hotel.com

Okells Bitter usually available, plus guest ales changed weekly. Fuller's London Pride is popular.

Small, friendly former coaching inn built in 1780 next to Ballaugh Bridge. Good selection of home-cooked food served Tues–Sat 12–2pm and 5.30–8pm, and Sunday lunchtimes. One main bar with separate dining room and games room. Traditional pub games and TV. Children welcome at lunchtime only. Outside drinking area where occasional barbecues take place. Car park.

12–11pm Sun–Thurs; 12–12.30pm Fri–Sat; closed Mon–Thurs until 3pm in winter.

CASTLETOWN

The Sidings

Station Road, Castletown IM9 1EF
☎ *(01624) 823282* David Quayle

Up to eight real ales available on any one night. Four regular fixtures should include Bushy's Castletown Bitter and Ruby Mild plus Caledonian Deuchars IPA or Greene King IPA. The others might also come from Bushy's or much further afield.

Welcoming, traditional, beer-orientated pub which was once the railway station and is now situated alongside it. Church pews and coal fires. Chip-fat-free atmosphere! Bar snacks served 12–2.30pm. Car park. Beer garden. Children welcome at lunchtime only. A beer festival takes place each July.

11.30am–11pm Sun–Thurs; 11.30am–midnight Fri–Sat.

DOUGLAS

Albert Hotel

3 Chapel Row, Douglas IM1 2BJ
☎ *(01624) 673632* Harry Creevy

Okells Mild, Bitter and Jough Manx Ale (the house bitter) usually served. Occasional brews from Okells may also be available.

Town-centre, popular working man's local next to the bus terminal and close to the quay. No food. No children.

10am–11pm Mon–Thurs; 10am–midnight Fri–Sat; 12–11pm Sun.

Old Market Tavern

Chapel Row, Douglas IM1 2BJ
☎ *(01624) 675202* Breda Watters

Okells Bitter and Bushy's Bitter regularly served.

A friendly atmosphere is to be found in this small, seventeenth-century backstreet tavern, popular with all ages. No food. No children.

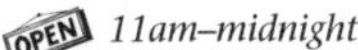 *11am–midnight.*

Saddle Inn

Queen Street, Douglas
☎ *(01624) 673161* Christine Armstrong

Okells Bitter and Mild regularly available, plus guest beers also from Okells.

Friendly quayside pub, popular with locals, visitors and motorcyclists throughout the year. Various memorabilia on display. No food.

 *11.30am–11pm Mon–Thurs; 11.30am–midnight Fri–Sat; 12–11pm Sun.*

LAXEY

Queens Hotel

New Road, Laxey
☎ *(01624) 861195* James Robert Hamer

A freehouse offering Bushy's Ruby Mild, Castletown Bitter and Export, plus two guest beers which might, perhaps, include something from Archers.

Friendly village pub with single, open-plan bar and pool area. Large beer garden and adjacent to the electric railway. Live music on Saturday nights. The Laxey wheel is near by. Toasted sandwiches available. Car park. B&B accommodation available all year.

 *12–11pm Mon–Thurs; 12–12 Fri–Sat; 12–11pm Sun.*

OLD LAXEY

The Shore Hotel

Old Laxey IM4 7DA
☎ *(01624) 861509* Paul and Jill Phillips
www.welcome.to/shorehotel.com

A brewpub, home of the Old Laxey Brewing Company, with Bosun's Bitter always on offer, plus guest appearances for a brew from Okells, Bushy's or Banktop. Brewery tours can be arranged (phone for details).

Friendly eighteenth-century village pub with river frontage close to the harbour and beach, featuring nautical charts, oil paintings of steam drifters and framed pictures of exotic fish from around the world! Food served in the bar or the riverside beer garden 12–2pm. Background music only. Children's play area. Large car park. Midway between Douglas and Ramsey, follow signs to Laxey Harbour,

 *12–11pm Mon–Thurs; 12–12 Fri–Sat; 12–11pm Sun.*

PEEL

The White House

2 Tynwald Road, Peel IM5 1LA
☎ *(01624) 842252* Jamie Keig

A freehouse serving Okells Mild and Bitter, Bushy's Bitter, Flower's Original and Timothy Taylor Landlord plus up to four guests from all over the country.

A traditional family-run pub with one main bar and four small adjoining rooms. CAMRA listed and Cask Marque approved. Live Manx music every Saturday. TV. Light bar snacks served in the bar area. Children allowed until 9pm. Beer garden, function room, car park, TV and pub games.

 *11am–midnight.*

RAMSEY

The Stanley Hotel

West Quay, Ramsey
☎ *(01624) 812258* Colin Clarke

Okells Mild and Bitter are permanent features, plus a guest beer from Okells or anywhere else.

A small pub close to the harbour. No food.

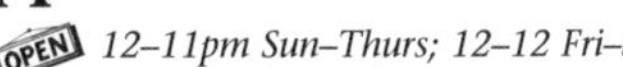 *12–11pm Sun–Thurs; 12–12 Fri–Sat.*

The Trafalgar Hotel

West Quay, Ramsey
☎ *(01624) 814601* James Kneen

Okells Bitter, Cains Mild and Bitter always available, plus a regularly changing guest beer which could be from anywhere in England.

Small, friendly, traditional quayside pub, known for well-kept ales. Cask Marque accredited. No food. Private room available. Children welcome.

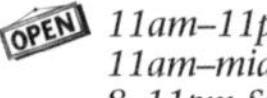 *11am–11pm Mon–Thurs; 11am–midnight Fri–Sat; 12–3pm and 8–11pm Sun.*

THE BREWERIES

GODDARDS BREWERY

Barnsley Farm, Bullen Road, Ryde PO33 1QF
☎ *(01983) 611011*
www.goddards-brewery.co.uk

ALE OF WIGHT 4.0% ABV
Pale, refreshing and fruity.
SPECIAL BITTER 4.0% ABV
Well-balanced with good hoppiness.
FUGGLE DEE DUM 4.8% ABV
Golden, full-bodied and spicily aromatic.
IRON HORSE 4.8% ABV
Dark, with liquorice/chocolate flavour.
DUCK'S FOLLY 5.2% ABV
Light colour, strong and hoppy.
INSPIRATION 5.2% ABV
Floral and exotic.
WINTER WARMER 5.2% ABV
Dark and smooth.

SCARECROW BREWERY

Arreton Barn, c/o Dairymans Daughter, Newport Road, Arreton PO30 3AA
☎ *(01983) 856161*

SCARECROW BEST 4.2% ABV

VENTNOR BREWERY LTD

119 High Street, Ventnor PO38 1LY
☎ *(01983) 856161*
www.ventnorbrewery.co.uk

GOLDEN BITTER 4.0% ABV
Light and fruity. Winner of CAMRA Isle of Wight Beer of the Year 2002.
ADMIRAL'S ALE 4.0% ABV
SUNFIRE 4.3% ABV
OYSTER STOUT 4.5% ABV
WIGHT SPIRIT 5.0% ABV
SANDROCK SMOKED ALE 5.6% ABV
Plus seasonal brews.

YATES BREWERY

The Inn at St Lawrence, Undercliffe Drive, St Lawrence, Ventnor PO38 1XG
☎ *(01983) 854689*
www.yates-brewery.co.uk

UNDERCLIFFE EXPERIENCE 4.1% ABV
GOOD KING SENSELESS 4.5% ABV
HOLY JOE 4.9% ABV
BROADWAY BLITZ 5.5% ABV
Seasonal:
WIGHT WINTER 5.0% ABV

THE PUBS

ARRETON

The Dairyman's Daughter

Arreton Barns, Main Road, Arreton PO30 3AA
☎ *(01983) 539361*
Andrew Gibbs and Jane Simmonds

Up to eight real ales always on tap including the pub's own Scarecrow Ale, brewed on the premises, plus beers from Ventnor, Goddards, Yates of St Lawrence and Badger (Hall & Woodhouse).

A traditional beamed brewpub located in a craft village, with a host of agricultural memorabilia. Large terrace, live traditional music most nights, beer and brewery shop. Top-quality hot and cold food served all day. The village features glass-blowing, woodworking, ceramic crafts, candlemaking, a Saxon church and an ancient carp pond – a good day out for all the family.

10.30am–11pm Mon–Sat; 12–10.30pm Sun.

The White Lion

Main Road, Arreton, Newport PO30 3AA
☎ *(01983) 528479* Chris and Katie Cole
www.white-lion-arreton.com

An Enterprise Inns pub with Fuller's London Pride and Badger Best always available plus an occasional guest.

A 300-year-old coaching inn in a picturesque country village. One bar, two non-smoking restaurants, family room and patio garden. Food served 12–9pm every day. Function room available, car park, children welcome.

OPEN *11am–11pm Mon–Sat; 12–10.30pm Sun.*

BEMBRIDGE

The Crab & Lobster

32 Forelands Field Road, Bembridge PO35 5TR
☎ *(01983) 872244* Richard and Adrian Allan
www.crabandlobsterinn.co.uk

Greene King IPA and Goddards Fuggle Dee Dum always available plus Flower's Original.

Family pub and restaurant overlooking the Bembridge Ledge, with outstanding sea views. Large lounge area, bar and à la carte restaurant featuring locally caught seafood, available all year round (12–2.30pm and 6–11pm). Children and dogs welcome. Car park. Five en-suite rooms available.

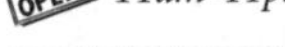 *11am–11pm Mon–Sat; 12–10.30pm Sun.*

BRIGHTSTONE

The Countryman

Limerstone Road, Brightstone
☎ *(01983) 740616* Mr R Frost

Three or four real ales usually available. Badger IPA, Dorset Best and Tanglefoot are all regulars, plus a guest beer in summer, such as Wadworth 6X.

Situated in a countryside setting in the south west of the island, with panoramic views of the coast and sea from the beer garden. Well known locally for food which is available 12–2pm and 6–9.30pm. Car park. Families and dogs welcome. Function room, no-smoking area. Two miles from Brightstone village, about 400 yards along Shorewell Road.

 *11am–3pm and 5.30–11pm.*

CHALE

The Wight Mouse

Church Place, Newport Road, Chale PO38 2H
☎ *(01983) 730431* Roger Burston

Badger Best, Tanglefoot and Champion, Gribble's Fursty Ferret, Harveys Sussex Bitter and Ventnor Golden permanently available. Plus 260 whiskies.

A traditional family pub overlooking the downs to the Needles. Food available all day, every day. Children welcome, there is a covered play area and swings. Front and rear gardens. Plenty of car parking. Accommodation.

11am–11pm Mon–Sat; 12–10.30pm Sun.

COWES

The Anchor Inn

High Street, Cowes PO31 7SA
☎ *(01983) 292823* Andy Taylor

Wadworth 6X and Fuller's London Pride always available plus four guests, usually from local or independent breweries. Goddards Fuggle Dee Dum and Inspiration Ale and Badger Tanglefoot are popular.

A high-street pub built in 1704. Three bars, garden. Stable bar with music Fri–Sat. Food available 12–9.30pm. Children allowed in the garden and middle eating area.

All day, every day.

The Duke of York

Mill Hill Road, Cowes PO31 7BT
☎ *(01983) 295171* Barry Caff

Tied to Whitbread, with Greene King Old Speckled Hen, Goddards Fuggle Dee Dum and Fuller's London Pride permanently featured.

Old-fashioned town pub and restaurant with a maritime theme. Seafood meals are a speciality. Twelve letting rooms. Children allowed. Car park.

11am–11pm (later in summer months) Mon–Sat; 12–10.30pm Sun.

The Globe Inn

The Parade, Cowes PO31 7QJ
☎ *(01983) 293005* André Russell

Wadworth 6X is among the beers always on offer. Two guests are also served, with beers from Goddards, such as Fuggle Dee Dum and Inspiration Ale, regular favourites.

A town pub with a patio. Bar food is served downstairs and there is an à la carte restaurant upstairs. Live music on Sundays. Car park. Children allowed until 7pm.

11am–11pm Mon–Sat; 12–10.30pm Sun.

The Ship & Castle

21 Castle Street, East Cowes PO32 6RB
☎ *(01983) 280967* Mrs Malcolm

Greene King Old Speckled Hen and Marston's Pedigree always available plus guests such as Badger Brewery ales or local brews from Ventnor Brewery. The preference is for independent beers.

A tiny pub with a friendly, traditional atmosphere. No pool or music. No food but the restaurant across the road delivers food to the pub! Well-behaved children allowed.

All day, every day.

GODSHILL

The Griffin Inn

Godshill PO38 3JD
☎ *(01983) 840039* Andrew Still

Greene King Old Speckled Hen and Marston's Pedigree are regular guests, and local beers such as Goddards Special Bitter and Ventnor Golden are also featured.

An open-plan, family pub in a Gothic-style stone building. The superb garden includes a pond, wendy house, play area, basketball hoop, and hedge maze in the shape of a griffin, made up of 2,500 privet trees. Food is served from the Adults' and Children's Menus plus Specials board.

 *10.30am–11pm Mon–Sat; 12–10.30pm Sun.*

HULVASTON

The Sun Inn

Hulvaston, Newport PO30 4EH
☎ *(01983) 741124*
David Gibson and Rachel Tyler

Badger Best always available, plus at least two guests. Regular features include Archers Golden and Wychwood Hobgoblin.

A small 600-year-old thatched pub offering views of the Channel. Log burner and fireplace in winter, plus a very large beer garden for use in summer. Food is available 12–9pm daily, from an extensive menu and daily specials board. Children are welcome until 10pm. Large car park, private room for hire. Curry nights on Tuesday and fortnightly quizes. Dogs welcome in main bar. The pub is located just off the main Military road, five minutes' drive from Chessel Pottery.

 *All day, every day.*

NEWPORT

The Bargeman's Rest

Little London Quay, Newport PO30 5BS
☎ *(01983) 525828*
Dan McCarthy and Debbie Richardson
www.bargemansrest.co.uk

Badger IPA, Best and Tanglefoot available plus a wide range of guests. Local beers are favoured whenever possible.

A huge, traditional seafaring family pub. The two bars are decorated with artefacts of marine interest, and the pub has an outside terrace and a function room. Food is available all day, every day. Children, dogs and muddy boots are all welcome.

OPEN *10.30am–11pm Mon–Sat; 12–10.30pm Sun.*

The Blacksmith's Arms

Calbourne Road, Newport PO30 5SS
☎ *(01983) 529263* Simon Willis

Four real ales are always available, including Badger Best, Tanglefoot and Gribble Fursty Ferret plus a rotating guest ale.

A countryside pub with restaurant and panoramic views of the island and the Solent. Log fires and flagstones. Large garden. Food available (locally-caught seafood) all day, every day. Children welcome.

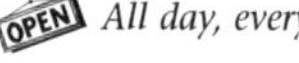 *All day, every day.*

NITON

The Buddle

St Catherine's Road, Niton PO38 2N3
☎ *(01983) 730243* John Bourne

Six real ales always on tap, including Adnams Best (the landlord's favourite, so they never run out!), and a local ale from either the Ventnor Brewery or Yates of St Lawrence. Local wine and cider served when available, together with a wide and interesting selection of soft drinks for the non-drinker.

A sixteenth-century, stone-built former farmhouse with oak beams, flagstone floors and open fires. Good food available at lunchtime and evenings. Car park, dining room and garden with fine views. Children allowed. Near St Catherine's Lighthouse.

 *11am–11pm Mon–Sat; 12–10.30pm Sun.*

NORTHWOOD

The Traveller's Joy

85 Pallance Road, Northwood, Cowes PO31 8LS
☎ *(01983) 298024* Derek Smith
www.tjoy.co.uk

Locally brewed Goddards Special Bitter is the regular ale, plus a range of seven guest ales from all around the country.

Multiple winner of the local branch of CAMRA's Real Ale Pub of the Year. Food is available at lunchtime and evenings and a traditional roast lunch is served on Sundays. There is a large car park and a garden with a patio and children's play area in addition to two children's rooms. On the main Cowes to Yarmouth road.

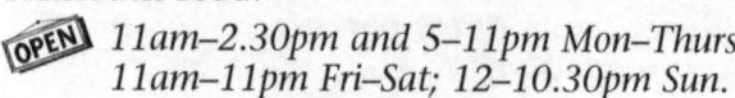 *11am–2.30pm and 5–11pm Mon–Thurs; 11am–11pm Fri–Sat; 12–10.30pm Sun.*

ROOKLEY

The Chequers Inn

Niton Road, Rookley PO38 3NZ
☎ *(01983) 840314* Debbie Lazelle
www.chequersinn-iow.co.uk

Greene King Old Speckled Hen and Gale's HSB are among the permanent features, plus two guests, changed every couple of months.

Traditional pub with beams, log fires and a flagstone floor. Food served all day. Gaming machines, garden with great views, car park. Children allowed – there is a play area and a non-smoking family room.

11am–11pm Mon–Sat; 12–10.30pm Sun.

Rookley Inn

Main Road, Rookley PO38 3LU
☎ *(01983) 721800* Jeff Ledicott

Fuller's London Pride and Greene King Abbot are always on offer. Two guests, changed fortnightly, might include Goddards Fuggle Dee Dum, Ventnor Golden, Ringwood Fortyniner or Badger Tanglefoot.

A family-oriented pub on a holiday park, with stage, restaurant and patio area. Entertainment seven nights a week. Children welcome. From Rookley, take the main road from Newport to Shanklin.

All day, every day (except Christmas Day); late licence till 12.30am.

RYDE

Fowler & Co

41–3 Union Street, Ryde PO33 2LF
☎ *(01983) 812112* Sharon Longley

Tied to Wetherspoon's, with Shepherd Neame Spitfire, Greene King Abbot and Ventnor Golden among the beers always available. Of the twelve pumps, three or four serve guest ales, changing every couple of days, with favourites including Hop Back Summer Lightning, Badger Tanglefoot and Charles Wells Bombardier.

Traditional town pub with non-smoking areas. Food available. Children allowed until 8pm.

10am–11pm Mon–Sat; 12–10.30pm Sun.

The Railway

68 St Johns Road, Ryde PO33 2RT
☎ *(01983) 615405*
Janet Brown and Garret True

Greene King IPA, Oakleaf Farmhouse and Adnams Broadside always available. Plus a rotating guest ale which changes weekly.

An olde-worlde pub with flagstone floor, stone walls, beamed ceiling and open fire. Food available at weekends only (12–4pm and 6–9pm). Well-behaved children allowed. No car park. Situated opposite St John's railway station.

11am–11pm Mon–Sat; 12–10.30pm Sun.

The Simeon Arms

Simeon Street, Ryde PO33 1JG
☎ *(01983) 614954* Jamie Clarke

Wadworth 6X is always on offer, and the weekly changing guest is often a beer from Goddards.

Locals' backstreet drinking pub with one bar, function room, darts, shove ha'penny and the best petanque on the island! Food available at lunchtime and Fri and Sat evenings. Garden with outside seating. Live music Fri/Sat. Children allowed in function room.

11am–3pm and 6–11pm Mon–Fri; 11am–11pm Sat; 12–10.30pm Sun.

The Wishing Well

Pondwell Hill, Ryde PO33 1PX
☎ *(01983) 613222* Mr Adrian Allen

Goddards Fuggle Dee Dum is permanently available. Two guests might be something like Greene King Abbot and IPA, or something from Ventnor.

Family pub with one main bar, fireplace, patio and wishing well. Elevated decking gives superb views down the valley to the sea. Games room with pool table and TV. Food served 12–2.30pm and 6–9.30pm. New disabled facilities. Children and dogs allowed. Car park.

11am–11pm Mon–Sat; 12–10.30pm Sun.

ST LAWRENCE

The Inn at St Lawrence

Undercliffe Drive, St Lawrence, Ventnor PO38 1XG
☎ *(01983) 853938* James Collins

Home of the Yates Brewery, with a range of home brewed beers always available. Also occasional guests from Hall & Woodhouse and Ventnor.

An old coaching inn, converted from stables. One bar, separate restaurant, raised outdoor decking area with sea views. Food available every lunchtime and evening. Children allowed. Disabled facilities. Located on the A3055.

11am–3pm and 6.30–11pm (10.30pm Sun).

SANDOWN

The Castle Inn

12–14 Fitzroy Street, Sandown PO36 8HY
☎ *(01983) 403169* Penny Wooly

A freehouse with Wadworth 6X, Gale's HSB and Ventnor Golden always served, plus two guests such as Charles Wells Bombardier or Marston's Pedigree.

Drinkers' town pub with patio. Bar snacks served. No children.

OPEN *12–11pm (10.30pm Sun).*

SHANKLIN

Billy Bunters Freehouse and Restaurant

64 High Street, Shanklin PO37 6JN
☎ *(01983) 867241* Marc Richards

A freehouse with a choice of four real ales, including locally brewed as well as mainland favourites such as Fuller's London Pride and Greene King Old Speckled Hen, plus hand-pulled mild.

Family-friendly, medium-sized town pub with separate non-smoking restaurant upstairs. Live music every Friday and Billy Special Steak Night every Wednesday. Food is served all day (booking recommended). Located on the edge of Shanklin Old Village, opposite the Tourist Office and Theatre.

OPEN *11am–11pm Mon–Sat; 12–10.30pm Sun.*

The Crab Inn

High Street, Shanklin PO37 6NS
☎ *(01983) 862363* Derry Derbyshire

Something from Goddards is always available here, and one monthly changing guest beer is also served.

Traditional family dining pub with patio, built in the seventeenth century. No music, games or TV. Children allowed.

OPEN *11am–11pm Mon–Sat; 12–10.30pm Sun.*

The Steamer Inn

Shanklin Esplanade, Shanklin PO37 6BS
☎ *(01983) 862641* Duncan Scott (Manager)

Ventnor Golden, Badger Best and Tanglefoot and Goddards Fuggle Dee Dum permanently available, plus two guests which might include Greene King Abbot, Adnams Regatta (in summer) or a Yates of St Lawrence ale.

A nautical theme which includes memorabilia and a seafront terrace. Get 'wrecked' here!! Food, including local seafood, available all day in summer, lunchtimes and evenings in winter. Children welcome, children's menu available.

OPEN *11am–11pm Mon–Sat; 12–10.30pm Sun.*

The Village Inn

Old Village Church Road, Shanklin PO37 6NU
☎ *(01983) 862764* Paul Ottley

Ventnor Golden permanently available, plus a guest ale.

A two-bar pub with beams and fireplaces. Children welcome, separate family bar upstairs. Food available 12–2.30pm and 6–10pm daily. Beer garden.

OPEN *11am–11pm Mon–Sat; 12–10.30pm Sun.*

TOTLAND BAY

The Broadway Inn

The Broadway, Totland Bay PO39 0BL
☎ *(01983) 755333* Kim Miller

All three of the island's breweries are represented here, with Gypsy, an exclusive brew from Ventnor Brewery, Goddards Fuggle Dee Dum and house ale Broadway Blitz (5.5% ABV), brewed exclusively for the pub by Yates of St Lawrence. Guest ales are also served, as well as a selection of premium beers such as Hoegaarden, San Miguel and Warsteiner on tap.

A two-bar public house offering a wide range of quality ales for the discerning customer. Children welcome until 9pm. Food available, beer garden, live music two nights per week. The pub is pet friendly, as there is a large 'Hooch' in residence!

11am–11pm Mon–Sat; 12–10.30pm Sun.

Highdown Inn

Highdown Lane, Totland Bay PO39 0HY
☎ *01983 752450*
Miss S White and Mr NK Ballantyne
www.highdowninn.com

Three real ales are always available. Ushers Best Bitter is a permanent feature, and the guests might be something like Greene King Abbot or IPA.

Ideal ramblers' pub, nestling at the foot of Tennyson Down, only half a mile from Alum Bay and the Needles. Muddy boots and dogs welcome! Known locally as a pub for good food and real ales. Runner-up in the Ushers Food Competition. Food available in the newly decorated non-smoking restaurant, two small bars or garden patio area. Children are catered for with their own menu and play area within a large garden. En-suite accommodation also available throughout the year, offering comfortable rooms with countryside views. Follow Alum Bay Old Road to Freshwater Bay.

Winter: 11am–3pm and 6–11pm; potentially all day in summer.

VENTNOR

The Spyglass

The Esplanade, Ventnor PO38 1JX
☎ *(01983) 855338* Neil and Stephanie Gibbs

Badger Best and Tanglefoot and Ventnor Golden always available, plus three guests. Goddards Fuggle Dee Dum and beers from Yates of St Lawrence, Badger (Hall & Woodhouse), Ventnor Ales and Scarecrow are often available. Two real ale festivals every year, in spring and October.

A seafaring pub situated on the sea wall. Food available 12–9.30pm Mon–Sat and 12–9pm Sun. Large outside terraces. Children, dogs and muddy boots welcome. Live music every evening.

11am–11pm Mon–Sat; 12–10.30pm Sun.

The Volunteer Inn

30 Victoria Street, Ventnor PO38 1ES
☎ *(01983) 852537* Mike and Heather Janvrin

Leased from Victoria Inns with up to eight regularly changing ales. The locally produced Ventnor Golden Bitter is always available, plus other local brews, Greene King Old Speckled Hen and Abbot Ale.

This award-winning freehouse is the smallest pub on the island, and a haven for adult drinkers. Traditional wooden floors, lively conversation and gourmet pickled eggs, but no chips, children, fruit machines or juke box. Annual October beerfest with over 24 real ales. Muddy boots and (cat-proof) dogs welcome.

All day, every day.

WHIPPINGHAM

Folly Inn

Folly Lane, Whippingham PO32 6NB
☎ *(01983) 297171*
Andy and Cheryl (managers)

Four pumps serve a range of real ales, changed seasonally, including brews from Goddards, Greene King Old Speckled Hen and Wadworth 6X.

Open-plan country pub seating 200, with large patio, garden area and breathtaking views. Non-smoking dining area, full menu and specials board (lunches served from 12 noon). Live music Fri and Sat in summer. Based on a river mooring for 230 boats and pontoon with mooring – a water taxi runs from the pontoon to the mooring during summer. Showers available 24 hours. Children allowed. Well signposted.

9am (for breakfasts)–11pm (10.30pm Sun).

WROXALL

The Four Seasons Inn

2 Clarence Road, Wroxhall PO38 3BY
☎ *(01983) 854701* Richard and Sonia Lowe

Ringwood Best and Greene King Abbot usually available. Alternatives by popular demand.

A pub with a warm welcome for children and dogs. Food available in the bar or in a separate non-smoking restaurant. Beer garden with outside seating, car park. Located off the main road but visible from it, on the junction with Manor Road.

11am–3pm and 5.30–11pm Mon–Fri; 11am–11pm Sat; 12–10.30pm Sun.

YARMOUTH

The Bugle Coaching Inn

The Square, Yarmouth PO41 0NS
☎ *(01983) 760272* Ray Benwell
www.buglecoachinginn.co.uk

Greene King Old Speckled Hen is a permanent feature, as is a local favourite, Bugle Bitter, brewed on the island to The Bugle's own recipe. Two guests usually available.

Seventeenth-century coaching inn fronting the town square, with two bars and a beer garden. Food is available, including a specials menu featuring locally caught fresh fish. Nine letting bedrooms. Children always welcome. Non-smoking areas. Car park.

OPEN *All day, every day.*

The Wheatsheaf

Bridge Road, Yarmouth PO41 0PH
☎ *(01983) 760456* Mrs Keen

Goddards Fuggle Dee Dum, Wadworth 6X, Greene King Old Speckled Hen and a Brakspear bitter usually available.

A traditional, food-oriented former coaching house with two bar areas, separate eating area, two family areas, conservatory and garden. An extensive menu is available at lunchtime and evenings. Children allowed. Near the ferry.

OPEN *All day, every day.*

THE BREWERY

ALES OF SCILLY

Higher Trenoweth, St Mary's TR21 0NS
☎ *(01720) 422419*

MAIDEN VOYAGE 3.8% ABV
THREE SHEETS 4.2% ABV
SCUPPERED 4.7% ABV
Specials:
NATURAL BEAUTY 4.2% ABV
Summer.
Plus Christmas and seasonal specials.

THE PUBS

ST MARY'S

Atlantic Inn

Hugh Street, St Mary's TR21 0HY
☎ *(01720) 422323* John McKetterick

There are always at least four pumps dedicated to real ale at this brewery-owned pub in the heart of Hugh Town on St Mary's. St Austell IPA, Tribute, HSD and Tinners Aleare regulars but the selection varies according to the brewery's output.

A tiny outdoor terrace (a real sun-trap) overlooks the harbour – at high tide the water literally laps at the walls. The one large bar with low, beamed ceilings and a smattering of nautical memorabilia attracts a mix of tourists and locals. Connected to the bar is a spacious restaurant serving tourist favourites including fresh crab sandwiches; food is served at lunchtime and evenings, seven days a week. Children are welcome.

OPEN *11am–11pm Mon–Sat; 12–10.30pm Sun.*

Bishop & Wolf

Hugh Street, St Mary's TR21 0LL
☎ *(01720) 422790* Alex and Blanche Alexander

You'll find three pumps serving real ales at this St Austell tied pub in the centre of bustling Hugh Town. Like its sister pub, the nearby Atlantic Inn, it serves a selection of well-kept Cornish-brewed St Austell beers such as Tinners Ale, Tribute and HSD, depending on what the brewery supplies.

There is one main bar with a smaller, non-smoking area and a large, licensed restaurant upstairs. Food is served lunchtime and evenings every day, and children are welcome.

OPEN *11am–11pm (10.30pm Sun).*

Mermaid Inn

The Bank, St Mary's TR21 0HY
☎ *(01720) 422701*
Irene Connolly and Ray Brown

As well as Greene King IPA you'll always find one pump dedicated to local beer from the Ales of Scilly brewery at this Unique Pub Company hostelry.

This quay-side pub is always busy with locals, sailors and tourists – many of whom arrive on the Scilly Isles' main island, St Mary's, on the ferry which docks just around the corner. The decor is strictly nautical with bits of boats on the walls and flags signed by visiting sailors adorning the ceiling. There is one main bar, a restaurant upstairs and a cellar bar, open in the summer only. Children are welcome and food is served every day, lunchtime and evenings.

OPEN *11am–11pm (10.30pm Sun).*

Old Town Inn

Old Town Lane, St Mary's TR21 0NN.
☎ *(01720) 422442* Nicholas Smith

This freehouse always serves three real ales, two of them regulars – Scuppered and Natural Beauty – which come from nearby island brewery, the Ales of Scilly. The other is likely to be a guest ale with a Cornish flavour, perhaps something from small brewer Sharp's, based at Rock near Wadebridge.

The Old Town Inn opened as a pub in 1996 but the building, which was once a wood workshop belonging to the local Ennor Castle estate, dates back to 1744. Inside are original old beams and a wood-burning stove. There are two beer gardens and a games room featuring two bowling alleys – children are welcome. There is also a function suite attached to the pub and the landlord plans to open B&B accommodation in spring 2005. The pub attracts a mixture of locals and tourists, and serves food at lunchtime and evenings, seven days a week.

OPEN *12–3pm and 6–11pm Mon–Sat (10.30pm Sun).*

Scillonian Club

The Parade, St Mary's TR21 0LP
☎ *(01720) 422720* Mark Twynham

Beer from the local Ales of Scilly Brewery is always available on one pump; the other regular beer here is Tribute, from St Austell. An occasional guest ale is available, too.

This former private club is a freehouse now open to annual and short-stay members alike. It costs £1 to join for a month – pay as you order your beer and sign the guest book – to enjoy subsidised beer prices (around 50p a pint cheaper than most pubs in the islands). Housed on the first floor of a terraced house in Hugh Town, St Mary's, the club has an open-plan bar that includes a games area with pool tables and sofas. There is occasional live music; upstairs in the Lyonnesse bar there is a 60-seat restaurant with views of the harbour.

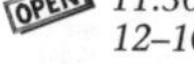
11.30am–11pm Mon–Sat; 12–10.30pm Sun.

ST AGNES

12

Turk's Head

St Agnes TR22 0PL
☎ *(01720) 422434* John Dart

Two guest ales, changing frequently, are always on offer at this popular freehouse. Cornish ales from small brewers are favoured – especially beers from the islands' own brewery, the Ales of Scilly – as well as Truro brewer Skinner's and Turk's Ale, brewed by St Austell.

This welcoming pub on the sparsely populated island of St Agnes is about a half-hour boat ride from the main island of St Mary's and well worth the sometimes choppy journey. Situated bang on the quayside, the Turk's Head used to be home to a lifeboat station. It has been a pub since 1974 but the stone building dates from much earlier times. It has a main bar, a garden bar overlooking the sea and a restaurant room, as well as a raised beer garden and benches outside the pub, which can be overflowing with customers on sunny afternoons. Food is served every day, at lunchtimes and evenings (all day in the height of the summer season) – its pasties are legendary. Children are welcome.

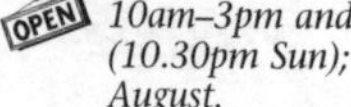
10am–3pm and 6pm–11pm Mon–Sat (10.30pm Sun); open all day in July and August.

TRESCO

New Inn

New Grimsby, Tresco TR24 0QE
☎ *(01720) 422844*
Alan Baptist and Robin Lawson

Up to four pumps dedicated to real ale at this island freehouse. Beers from Skinner's and the local Ales of Scilly brewery on St Mary's. Occasional guest ales are served and beer festivals are held twice a year, in May and September.

Part of a row of workers' cottages in the village of New Grimsby. Leased from the Duchy of Cornwall by the Dorrien Smith Family, who also own the island's hotel. The main bar area includes comfy battered leather sofas, pool table and dartboard; the beer garden has views of nearby island Bryher. In recent years the New Inn hotel has been extended to include a café and an outdoor swimming pool which is open to pub guests. Food is served from 12–3pm and from 7pm–9pm (6pm in high season). Breakfast is also available in high season. Children are welcome in the pub until 9pm.

All day every day.

P & D J GOACHER

Unit 8, Tovil Green Business Park, Tovil, Maidstone ME15 6TA
☎ *(01622) 682112*

REAL MILD ALE 3.4% ABV
Malt taste, slightly bitter.

FINE LIGHT ALE 3.7% ABV
Light with hops and some balancing malt.

SPECIAL 3.8% ABV
House beer as requested.

BEST DARK ALE 4.1% ABV
Darker bitter brew with malt flavours.

CROWN IMPERIAL STOUT 4.5% ABV
Classic and very drinkable Irish-style stout.

GOLD STAR 5.1% ABV
Powerful pale ale.

OLD 1066 ALE 6.7%
Strong, dark winter ale.

HOPDAEMON BREWERY CO

18A–18B Canterbury Hill, Tyler Hill, Canterbury CT2 9LS
☎ *(01227) 784962*

GOLDEN BRAID 3.7% ABV

INCUBUS 4.0% ABV

SKRIMSHANDER IPA 4.5% ABV

GREEN DAEMON 5.0% ABV

LEVIATHAN 6.0% ABV

Special:

GOLDEN DOVE 5% ABV

LARKINS BREWERY LTD

Larkins Farm, Chiddingstone, Edenbridge TN8 7BB
☎ *(01892) 870328*

TRADITIONAL ALE 3.4% ABV
Tawny-coloured drinkers' drink.

CHIDDINGSTONE BITTER 4.0% ABV
Copper red with a malty finish.

BEST BITTER 4.4% ABV
Flavoursome with surprising bitterness.

PORTER 5.2% ABV
Fruit, roast malt and complex finish.

MILLIS BREWING COMPANY LTD

48 Vigilant Way, Riverview Park, Gravesend, DA12 4PP
☎ *(01474) 566903*
www.millis-brewing.com

MILLIS BITTER 3.9% ABV
Copper-coloured ale with a pale crystal malt base, balanced by tart tangy fruit flavours and Kentish-grown crops.

CAPALL DUBH 4.3% ABV
Full-bodied straw-coloured premium beer.

DARTFORD WOBBLER 4.3% ABV
Tawny-coloured full-bodied beer with complex malt and hop flavours.

KENTISH RED ALE 4.3% ABV
Complex malt, hops and fruit notes.

THIEVES 'N' FAKIRS 4.3% ABV
Complex fruit, hops and malt tasting beer. Full-bodied, long, clean bitter finish.

Occasional/seasonal range:

BANDRAOI BITTER 4.8% ABV

BURNING SUN 4.8% ABV

RAMSGATE BREWERY

The Ramsgate Royal Harbour Brewhouse & Bakers, 98 Harbour Parade, Ramsgate CT11 8LP
☎ *(01843) 594758/594659*
www.ramsgatebrewhouse.com

GADDS' NO 7 RAMSGATE BITTER 3.8% ABV

MILD ALE 4.0% ABV

GADDS' NO5 RAMSGATE BEST 4.4% ABV

RAMSGATE BROWN ALE 4.8% ABV

GADDS' NO3 RAMSGATE PALE ALE 5.0% ABV

DOGBOLTER WINTER PORTER 5.6% ABV

SHEPHERD NEAME LTD

17 Court Street, Faversham ME13 7AX
☎ *(01795) 532206*
www.shepherd-neame.co.uk

MASTER BREW BITTER 3.7% ABV
Clean, dry, refreshing session bitter with a touch of sweetness.

BEST BITTER 4.1% ABV
Biscuity sweetness meets fruity bitterness.

EARLY BIRD SPRING HOP ALE 4.3% ABV
Light gold beer that is full bodied and refreshing with malty undertones.

LATE RED AUTUMN HOP ALE 4.5% ABV
A balance of rich, dark malt flavours and strong, robust hoppiness.

SPITFIRE PREMIUM KENTISH STRONG ALE 4.5% ABV
Golden ale with a hint of toffee, citrus and fruity spiciness.

WHITSTABLE BAY ORGANIC ALE 4.5% ABV
Light beer with a bittersweet flavour, floral overtones and a dry finish.

GOLDINGS SUMMER HOP ALE 4.7% ABV
Floral scented with a unique biscuity taste.

BISHOPS FINGER KENTISH STRONG ALE 5% ABV
Fruity flavour, full-bodied and nut-brown.

SWAN ON THE GREEN

The Green, West Peckham, Maidstone ME18 5JW
☎ *(01622) 812271*
www.swan-on-the-green.co.uk

GINGER SWAN 3.6% ABV
Pale ale flavoured with ginger and other spices.

O.F.MILD 3.6% ABV
'Old-fashioned' mild ale.

WHOOPER PALE 3.6% ABV
Straw coloured and lightly hopped with USA Cascade for a subtle fruity aroma.

BLONDE 4% ABV
Clean and refreshing.

TRUMPETER 4% ABV
Typical English ale colour-hopped with UK Target and First Gold.

SWAN ON THE PORTSIDE 4.2% ABV
Darker ale with a smooth flavour. A bottle of port is added to each cask.

WEISSE 4.5% ABV
Slightly spicy Continental style.

BEWICK SWAN 5.3% ABV
Heavyweight premium bitter.

THE PUBS

ASHFORD

Hooden on the Hill

Silver Hill Road, Willesborough Lees, Ashford TN24 0NY
☎ *(01233) 662226*
Howard Lapish and Kelly Loft

Young's Bitter and Greene King IPA always available, plus a usually stronger guest beer.

Oldest and busiest pub in suburban Ashford, beamed and candlelit with hops in the ceiling and worth escaping the town centre to enjoy, or simply to witness regular customers forming an orderly queue to be served! One bar, friendly staff and menu specialising in Mexican food. Full range of Gales country wines generally in stock. Food available 12–2pm and 6–10pm Mon–Sat; 12–10pm Sun. Children and dogs allowed. Large garden. Leave town-centre one-way system heading east on A292 (Hythe Road), and shortly before reaching M20 turn left into Lees Road at Esso service station. Lees Road becomes Silver Hill Road and pub is on left about 300 yards after underpassing M20.

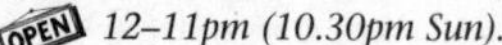
12–11pm (10.30pm Sun).

BADLESMERE

The Red Lion

Ashford Road, Badlesmere, Faversham ME13 0NX
☎ *(01233) 740320* Moira Anderson

Shepherd Neame Master Brew, Fuller's London Pride and Greene King Abbot Ale always available, with Timothy Taylor Landlord and Hop Back Summer Lightning popular among guest beers. A mild is usually on tap Easter to late summer.

Sixteenth-century village local with one bar offering wide selection of traditional games. Food available 12–3pm and 7–9pm (not Sun or Mon); traditional Sunday roast. Children and dogs allowed. Large garden housing sheep. On A251.

12–3pm and 6–11pm Mon–Thurs; 12–11pm Fri–Sat; 12–10.30pm Sun.

BARFRESTONE

The Yew Tree Inn

Barfrestone, Dover CT15 7JH
☎ *(01304) 831619* Peter and Kathryn Garstin
www.barfrestone.co.uk

Genuine freehouse with four beers always available, including a mild. Strong emphasis on local breweries, Ramsgate (Gadds) and Hopdaemon in particular, although a vast range from throughout the country is stocked during year.

Unspoilt traditional village pub with wooden floors and pine-scrubbed tables; built only in 1927 because of a fire to the previous building, but giving the impression of being much older. One bar and two other rooms, both of which are designated non-smoking areas. Food available 12–2.15pm and 7–9.15pm Tues–Sat; 12–2.15pm Sun, with traditional roast. Children allowed but not in bar; dog-friendly; tethering bar for horses outside. Patio garden. Long two miles north-east of A2; look for the yew tree! OS:264501.

5–11pm Mon; 12–3pm and 5–11pm Tues–Thurs; 12–11pm Fri–Sat; 12–10.30pm Sun.

BEXLEYHEATH

Robin Hood & Little John

78 Lion Road, Bexleyheath DA6 8PF
☎ *(020) 8303 1128* Ray Johnson

A freehouse serving eight cask-conditioned beers. Brains Reverend James, Harveys Best, Fuller's London Pride, Adnams Best and Brakspear Bitter are regular features, the other two brews change every month.

A one-bar, village-type pub with wood panel walls and old Singer sewing machine tables. Beer garden. Food available at lunchtime only, Mon–Sat. No children. Off Bexleyheath Broadway.

11am–3.30pm and 5.30–11pm (7–11pm Sat; 7–10.30pm Sun).

Wrong Un

234–6 The Broadway, Bexleyheath,
☎ *(0208) 298 0439* Timothy Shepherd

Hop Back Summer Lightning and Greene King Abbot Ale regularly available plus four or five guest beers such as Shepherd Neame Spitfire, Bateman XXXB, Brains SA, Hook Norton Old Hooky, Hop Back Thunderstorm or something from Marston's.

Light, spacious pub with relaxed atmosphere and large non-smoking area. Extensive menu available 10am–10pm Mon–Sat, 12–10.30pm Sun. Disabled facilities. Car park. No children.

OPEN *10am–11pm Mon–Sat; 12–10.30pm Sun.*

BLUE BELL HILL

The Lower Bell

201 Old Chatham Road, Blue Bell Hill, Aylesford ME20 7EF
☎ *(01634) 861127* Laurence Walker

Greene King tied house offering IPA and Abbot Ale permanently, with up to two other beers from the brewery's portfolio, but note the landlord accepts it would be folly, strengthwise, to pit Greene King Old Speckled Hen against Abbot Ale – so he doesn't!

Built about 100 years ago, the pub gets its name from a bell signalling system used by stagecoaches on the single-track road to the top of the hill. One bar, separate dining area and non-smoking restaurant/function suite on two levels. Food available 12–2.30pm and 6–9.30pm, with traditional roast Sun lunchtime. Homemade pies and fresh fish are specialities. Children allowed but not dogs. Patio garden. At foot of sliproad west of A229 (Blue Bell Hill).

OPEN *11am–11pm Mon–Sat; 12–10.30pm Sun.*

BOUGHTON ALUPH

The Flying Horse

The Lees, Boughton Aluph, Ashford TN25 4HH
☎ *(01233) 620914* Simon Chicken

Fuller's London Pride and Greene King IPA always available, plus two other beers, with Shepherd Neame Spitfire proving a good seller.

Fifteenth-century beamed pub on edge of cricket green with two natural wells rediscovered under small back bar. Two bars and restaurant; accommodation. Food available 12–3pm and 6–9pm (not Mon). Children allowed in restaurant only. Garden. Just off A251 at Boughton Lees (despite Boughton Aluph address).

OPEN *12–11pm (10.30pm Sun).*

BOUGHTON MONCHELSEA

The Cock Inn

Heath Road, Boughton Monchelsea, Maidstone ME17 4JD
☎ *(01622) 743166* Dave and Jo Whitehurst

Young's tied house offering Bitter and Special permanently, with Waggle Dance or Winter Warmer in addition, depending on the time of year.

Built in 1604 by the Canterbury Diocese as a lodging house, it had become a pub by the late eighteenth century. One extended beamed bar and separate dining area, where seafood is the speciality. Food available 12–2.30pm and 6–9pm Mon–Sat; 12–4pm Sun, with traditional roast. Children under 14 allowed in restaurant only; dog-friendly. Small outdoor drinking area. On B2163.

OPEN *11am–11pm Mon–Sat; 12–10.30pm Sun.*

BOXLEY

The King's Arms

The Street, Boxley, Maidstone ME14 3DR
☎ *(01622) 755177* Helen and Jon Sutton
www.pubsinkent.com/kingsarms

Fuller's London Pride, Adnams Bitter, Greene King IPA and Gale's HSB always available.

Village pub mindful of good causes, with some parts of the building dating from the twelfth century. One open bar in two distinct sections, with hops prevalent. Food available 12–2pm and 7–9pm Mon–Fri; 12–9pm Sat–Sun, with traditional Sunday roast 'until it runs out'. Children allowed; dog-friendly. Large garden. Best approached from A229 junction with M20 (J7).

OPEN *11am–11pm Mon–Sat; 12–10.30pm Sun.*

BOYDEN GATE

The Gate Inn Marshside

Marshside, Chislet, Canterbury CT3 4EB
☎ *(01227) 860498* Chris Smith

Shepherd Neame tied house offering Master Brew Bitter and Spitfire permanently, with whatever seasonal beer is appropriate, all served directly from the cask.

Parts of the pub are 200 years old, but not the 'beams' in the single hopped bar. Couple of side rooms, too, all with tiled floors and illustrating that this has long been the centre of village life, from rugby and distance running to mummers' plays each Christmas. Food available 11am–2pm and 6–9pm Mon–Sat; 12–2pm and 7–9pm Sun. No food Mon and Tues evenings in winter. Well-behaved children and dogs allowed. Large garden complete with stream and ducks, though 'canard' was not seen on the menu! Long mile south of A299 (Thanet Way). OS:220656.

11am–2.30pm and 6–11pm Mon–Sat; 12–4pm and 7–10.30pm Sun.

BROMLEY

The Red Lion

10 North Road, Bromley, BR1 3LG
☎ *(020) 8460 2691*
Chris and Siobhan Humphrey

Greene King Abbot and IPA plus something from Harveys always available. The two guest pumps offer a wide selection of ales from various breweries, changed at least twice weekly.

Friendly local offering food Mon–Sat.

11am–11pm (10.30pm Sun).

CANTERBURY

The Canterbury Tales

12 The Friars, Canterbury CT1 2AS
☎ *(01227) 768594* Jacqui and Mark Tunbridge

Shepherd Neame Spitfire, Fuller's London Pride and Greene King IPA always available, plus a changing guest beer.

Lively country-style eighteenth-century pub in town-centre setting, used by locals as well as actors from the Marlowe Theatre, opposite. Bar food available 12–9pm Tue–Sat; 12–4pm Sun, with traditional roast, and Mon. The Aztec, a separate restaurant upstairs, opens 6–9.30pm and specialises in both North and South American dishes. Dogs allowed; children also, but not in main bar. Nearest railway station is Canterbury West.

11am–11pm Mon–Sat; 12–10.30pm Sun.

The Phoenix

67 Old Dover Road, Canterbury CT1 3DB
☎ *(01227) 464220* Linda Barker
www.thephoenix-canterbury.co.uk

Young's Bitter, Charles Wells Bombardier and Greene King Abbot Ale always available, plus a mild served directly from the cask. In addition, there are four regularly changing guest beers.

Pub with a friendly atmosphere built in 1962 after the Bridge House Tavern, formerly on the site, burnt down. One large bar; accommodation. Monday night is (board) games night! Food available 11am–9.30pm Mon–Wed, Fri and Sat; 11am–4pm Thu; 12–9.30pm Sun, with traditional roast. No children or dogs. Terraced outdoor drinking area. South-east of town centre, close to county cricket ground.

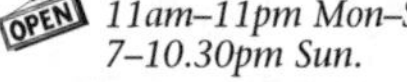
11am–11pm Mon–Sat; 12–4pm and 7–10.30pm Sun.

The Unicorn

61 St Dunstan's Street, Canterbury CT2 8BS
☎ *(01227) 463187* Lorenzo Carnevale-Maffé

Shepherd Neame Master Brew Bitter always available, plus three other beers that change weekly, with Timothy Taylor Landlord and products from local breweries often featured.

Welcoming pub in listed building dating from 1604, with one large bar housing bar billiards table. Food available 12–2pm and 6–8pm Mon–Fri; 12–3pm and 6–8pm Sat; 12–3pm Sun, with traditional roast. Children allowed, at discretion of landlord, until 7.30pm. Large garden. On A290 near Canterbury West railway station, north-west of city centre.

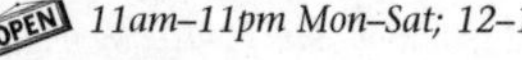
11am–11pm Mon–Sat; 12–10.30pm Sun.

CAPEL

The Dovecote Inn

Alders Road, Capel, Tonbridge TN12 6SU
☎ *(01892) 835966* George and Jenny Schneider

Genuine freehouse with five beers available, served directly from the cask: Harveys Sussex Best Bitter, Larkins Chiddingstone, Adnams Broadside and Badger (King and Barnes) Sussex Bitter permanently, plus an ever-changing guest.

Situated among picturesque terraced cottages, this friendly village pub is about 200 years old. One beamed, seriously hopped bar and non-smoking dining area. Food available 12–2pm and 6–9pm Mon–Sat; 12–3pm Sun, with traditional roast. Children allowed but not dogs. Large garden with play area (and dovecote!) and separate paved patio. Short mile west of, and signed from, A228 between Tonbridge and Paddock Wood.

12–3pm and 5.30–11pm Mon–Fri; 12–4pm and 6–11pm Sat; 12–4pm and 7–10.30pm Sun. All day at weekends in summer.

CHARING

The Bowl Inn

Egg Hill Road, Charing, Ashford TN27 0HG
☎ *(01233) 712256* Alan and Sue Paine
www.bowlinn.co.uk

Fuller's London Pride always available, plus three other beers, regularly featuring Adnams, Harveys and less familiar brews such as Sharp's Doom Bar, Woodforde's Wherry and many more.

Traditional country pub on top of North Downs above Charing, built as a farmhouse in 1512 and converted to a brewhouse in 1606. One extended bar area with revolving hexagonal pool table. Bar snacks served until 9.30pm every day. Kent-cured ham a speciality. Log fires in winter, large rural garden and heated patio in summer. Annual beer festival in mid-July. Signed from A20 and A252. OS:950515.

 *5–11pm Mon–Thurs; 12–11pm Fri–Sat; 12–10.30pm Sun.*

CHATHAM

The Alexandra

43 Railway Street, Chatham ME4 6PL
☎ *(01634) 300084*
Craig Geddes and Lynne Charles

Shepherd Neame tied house offering Master Brew Bitter and Spitfire permanently, with whatever seasonal beer is appropriate.

Victorian pub renovated to include quiet room off the one airy bar, conservatory and upstairs function room. Food available 12–3pm and 5–8pm Mon–Fri; 12–9pm Sat; 12–7pm Sun, with traditional roast. Children allowed in conservatory and garden until 8pm; dogs in garden only. Effectively situated on traffic island just down from Chatham railway station.

 *11am–11pm Mon–Sat; 12–10.30pm Sun.*

The Tap & Tin

24 Railway Street, Chatham ME4 4JT
☎ *(01634) 847926* Dave Gould

Greene King IPA, Abbot Ale and Old Speckled Hen usually available, plus up to three other beers, one of which is often Goacher's Gold Star.

Lively pub just down hill from Chatham railway station and with largely young clientele. Four bars: one on ground floor, one in pool room and two upstairs. Snacks only. Dogs allowed; children in patio area only. On edge of one-way system, under arches; A2 passes overhead.

OPEN *12–11pm Mon–Wed; 12–1am Thurs–Sat; 2–10.30pm Sun.*

CHIDDINGSTONE HOATH

The Rock Inn

Ryewell Hill, Hoath Corner, Chiddingstone, Edenbridge TN8 7BS
☎ *(01892) 870296* Shaw Kew

The only Larkins tied house, less than two miles from the brewery and offering Traditional Ale permanently and Best or Porter, depending on the season.

A 450-year-old rural drinkers' pub that should not be missed. Two bars, one with a distinctive brick floor, large wood-burning stove and octagonal, wooden pump handles. Food available 12–2pm and 7–9pm Tues–Sat. Dogs allowed but not children. Garden. Long two miles south of B2027. OS:497431.

 *11.30am–3pm and 6–11pm Tues–Sat; 12–3pm and 7–10.30pm Sun.*

CLAYGATE

The White Hart

Benover Road, Claygate, Marden TN12 9PL
☎ *(01892) 730313* Russell and Sue Roberts
www.thewhitehart.biz

Genuine freehouse with Adnams Bitter, Fuller's London Pride and Goacher's Fine Light Ale permanent fixtures on hand pump, and a varying guest beer served directly from the cask.

Victorian pub with two bars and separate restaurant area, run by a man fiercely loyal to the contacts (e.g. Phil Goacher) he has made in his years in the trade, and for whom nothing seems too much trouble. Succulent food available 12–2.30pm and 7–9.30pm, with traditional Sunday roast. Children and dogs allowed. Massive garden. On B2162, three miles east of Paddock Wood.

 *11am–11pm Mon–Sat; 12–10.30pm Sun.*

COWDEN

The Fountain

30 High Street, Cowden, Edenbridge TN8 7JG
☎ *(01342) 850528* Maria and John E'Vanson
www.harveys.org.uk/t1fountain.htm

Harveys tied house offering Sussex Pale Ale and Sussex Best Bitter permanently, with any of the brewery's other products flowing from the third hand pump.

Seventeenth-century village pub with two small oak-beamed bars and separate dining area. Restaurant-style food at pub prices available 12–2.30pm and 7–9.30pm Tue–Sat; 12–2.30pm Sun, with traditional roast. Children not encouraged; dogs allowed. Large rear garden; small front patio. Barely a quarter of a mile from East Sussex boundary, short mile north of A264. OS:465404.

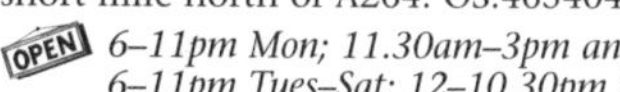 *6–11pm Mon; 11.30am–3pm and 6–11pm Tues–Sat; 12–10.30pm Sun.*

DARTFORD

The Malt Shovel

3 Darenth Road, Dartford DA1 1LP
☎ *(01322) 224381*
Steve Huggett and Josephine Stewart

Young's tied house since 1983 offering Bitter, Triple A and Special permanently, with seasonal brews and beers from Smiles also regularly on tap.

Beer has been sold on the site since 1873, while parts of the tap room date back 200 years before that. Two low-ceilinged bars and conservatory strongly favoured by diners. Food available 12–2pm Mon–Sat; 6.30–8.30pm Tue–Sat; 12.30–2.30pm Sun, traditional roast only. Children and dogs allowed. Patio garden. Only just outside town centre, but safe from the weekend 'strolling masses'. Close to A226, east side of town.

 *11am–2.30pm and 5–11pm Mon–Thurs; 11am–11pm Fri and Sat; 12–3pm and 7–10.30pm Sun.*

The Wat Tyler

80 High Street, Dartford DA1 1DE
☎ *(01322) 272546* Michael Aynge

Brains Bitter always available, plus three other beers.

One long bar and separate dining area; accommodation. Food available 12–9pm Mon–Sat. Children allowed; dogs discouraged. On eastern fringe of pedestrian precinct, but landlord thankfully offers nothing to encourage clientele associated with town-centre drinking in Kent.

 *10am–11pm Mon–Sat; 12–10.30pm Sun.*

DOVER

The Mogul

5–6 Chapel Place, Dover CT17 9AS
☎ *(01304) 205072* Frank and Charlie Franklin

A true freehouse with three or four beers always available, served directly from the cask. Range constantly changing, but brews from Oakham are among the most popular.

Unspoilt pub licensed at least since 1882, with wooden floors and log-burning stove. One bar and non-smoking room at back where traditional games such as quoits and table skittles may be played. Sandwiches available from lunchtime to early evening. No children's licence; dogs allowed. Terraced garden at rear. Not the easiest of places to locate, but in a town such as Dover, it really is worth making the effort to do so. From Snargate/York Street roundabout, take first left off York Street, first left again, then follow road round between car parks. Close to A256/A20 junction. OS:318412.

OPEN *11am–11pm Mon–Sat; 12–10.30pm Sun.*

EAST FARLEIGH

The Farleigh Bull

Lower Road, East Farleigh, Maidstone ME15 0HD
☎ *(01622) 726282* Tim and Sarah Benger
www.farleigh-bull.co.uk.

Adnams Bitter, Fuller's London Pride and Shepherd Neame Master Brew Bitter and Spitfire always available, with at least one low-gravity product from Goacher's certain to feature among two other rotating beers.

Victorian pub that has self-contained function room and large L-shaped bar. Food available 12–3pm and 7–9.30pm Mon–Sat; 12–4pm Sun, with traditional roasts on menu daily; times likely to expand. Live music Sunday evenings. Children and dogs allowed. Large garden, secure children's play area and patio. On B2010, two miles south-west of Maidstone.

 *11am–11pm Mon–Sat; 12–10.30pm Sun.*

EAST MALLING

The Rising Sun

125 Mill Street, East Malling ME19 6BX
☎ *(01732) 843284*
Peter Kemp and Paul Fincham

Freehouse where products from Goacher's and Shepherd Neame are usually available, plus a third beer from virtually anywhere, though generally a stronger one.

Locals' pub in a terrace of mill cottages with one U-shaped bar. Vast selection of standard-priced single-malt whiskies. Food available 12–2.15pm Mon–Fri; then only snacks until late afternoon. Dogs allowed but not children. Large paved garden. League darts played every weekday evening. Short mile south of A20. OS:697572.

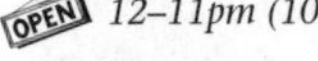 *12–11pm (10.30pm Sun).*

EDENBRIDGE

The King and Queen

81 High Street, Edenbridge TN8 5AU
☎ *(01732) 862139* Jenny Edney

Shepherd Neame tied house offering Best Bitter and Spitfire permanently, with whatever seasonal beer is appropriate.

Dating back to 1650, this welcoming pub has one beamed and hopped bar, separate dining area, several nooks and crannies and real fires. Food 12–2.30pm daily, with traditional Sunday roast, and 7–9pm Sat (phone to ask on other evenings). Familes welcome, though a sign above the bar warns 'Children left unattended will be sold to the circus' – riled, Jenny could be awesome; dogs discouraged. Garden. On B2026, southern end of town.

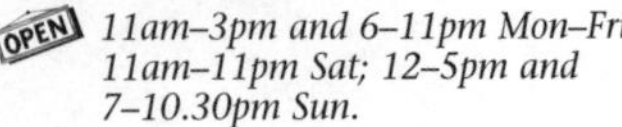 *11am–3pm and 6–11pm Mon–Fri; 11am–11pm Sat; 12–5pm and 7–10.30pm Sun.*

ELHAM

The Rose and Crown

High Street, Elham, Canterbury CT4 6TD
☎ *(01303) 840226*
Denise and Gerard McNicholas
www.roseandcrown.co.uk

Harveys Sussex Best Bitter, Hopdaemon Golden Braid and Greene King Ruddles Best always available, plus a guest beer that could come from anywhere.

Sixteenth-century village inn with extensive beamed bar; accommodation. Full à la carte, bar food and fresh fish menus available 12–2pm and 6.30–9pm (7–9pm Sun) in lounge bar or non-smoking restaurant; traditional roast Sunday lunchtime, and evening 'if there's any left over'. Children and dogs allowed. Patio garden. On B2065.

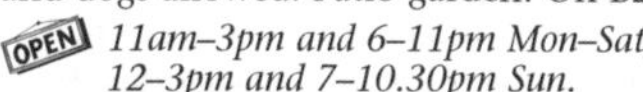
11am–3pm and 6–11pm Mon–Sat; 12–3pm and 7–10.30pm Sun.

FAIRSEAT

The Vigo Inn

Gravesend Road, Fairseat, Sevenoaks TN15 7JL
☎ *(01732) 822547* Peter and Peta Ashwell

Young's and Harveys products permanently occupy four of the five hand pumps, the other being reserved for a variable guest beer.

An old drovers' inn, now completely non-smoking, with two bars: one built in the fifteenth century, the other in the sixteenth. Simple food and bar snacks available. A must for anybody who values the traditions of a no-nonsense English pub. Located on the North Downs Way, on the A227, a country mile north-east of A20.

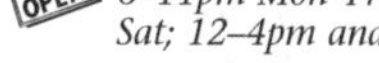
6–11pm Mon–Fri; 12–4pm and 6–11pm Sat; 12–4pm and 7–10.30pm Sun.

FARNBOROUGH

The Woodman

50 High Street, Farnborough BR6 7BA
☎ *(01689) 852663* Sharon Pritchard

Shepherd Neame Master Brew, Spitfire and a seasonal brew always available.

A village pub in a quiet location, with a large garden, grapevine canopy and many hanging baskets, window boxes and tubs. Food served 12–2pm and 7–9pm Mon–Sat and lunchtime roasts every Sunday. Children welcome. Car park. Located just off the A21, three miles from Bromley, signposted 'Farnborough Village'.

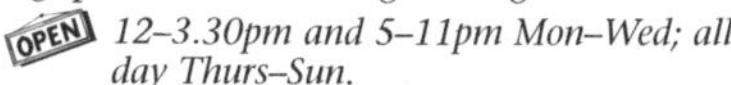
12–3.30pm and 5–11pm Mon–Wed; all day Thurs–Sun.

FARNINGHAM

The Chequers

High Street, Farningham, Dartford DA4 0DT
☎ *(01322) 865222*
Alan Vowls and Karen Jefferies

Fuller's London Pride and ESB and Timothy Taylor Landlord always available, with something from Oakham virtually certain to feature among up to six other beers from smaller breweries.

Three-hundred-year-old beamed village pub with one bar, close to River Darenth in Brands Hatch area. Food available 12–2.30pm Mon–Sat. Children and dogs allowed. Street-corner site about 250 yards from A20.

11am–11pm Mon–Sat; 12–10.30pm Sun.

FAVERSHAM

The Anchor Inn

52 Abbey Street, Faversham ME13 7BP
☎ *(01795) 536471* Nat Victor

Shepherd Neame tied house offering Master Brew Bitter, Best Bitter and Spitfire permanently, with whatever seasonal beer is appropriate.

Seventeenth-century pub, long associated with the brewery. Two bar areas, one of which is a 26-seat non-smoking restaurant with à la carte menu. Food available 12–3pm and 7–9.30pm Tue–Sat; 12–3.30pm Sun, with traditional roast. Game, fish and shellfish dishes are specialities. Children allowed at landlord's discretion; dog-friendly. Large garden. North of town centre, close to Standard Quay.

12–3pm and 6–11pm Mon; 12–11pm Tues–Sat; 12–10.30pm Sun.

The Crown & Anchor

41 The Mall, Faversham ME13 8JN
☎ *(01795) 532812* Marion M Koncsik

Shepherd Neame tied house offering Master Brew Bitter permanently. Best Bitter and Spitfire are added to coincide with brewery's hop festival.

The pub was already serving beer when Shepherd Neame acquired it in 1859. One L-shaped bar and separate games room. Food available 12–2.30pm Mon–Fri. Goulash is a speciality. Just off A2, south of town centre.

10.30am–3pm and 5.30–11pm Mon–Fri; 10.30am–4pm and 6–11pm Sat; 12–2.30pm and 7–10.30pm Sun.

The Elephant Inn

31 The Mall, Faversham ME13 8JN
☎ *(01795) 590157* David Hooper

A genuine freehouse that usually has five hand pumps dispensing a constantly changing range of beers, including those of the Nelson Brewery.

Traditional locals' pub with friendly atmosphere. A single bar plus games room. Pub snacks available from noon until near closing Mon–Sat; traditional Sunday roast 12–4pm. Children welcome in spruced-up garden that acts as a pleasant sun trap and all areas away from the bar; dogs allowed. Between A2 and railway, south of town centre.

 *3–11pm Mon–Thurs; 12–11pm Fri–Sat; 12–10.30pm Sun.*

The Shipwright's Arms

Hollowshore, off Ham Road, Oare, Faversham ME13 7TU
☎ *(01795) 590088* Derek and Ruth Cole

Genuine freehouse serving beers only from Kent breweries directly from the cask. Goacher's Dark Mild, Original and Shipwrecked (the house ale) plus Hopdaemon Incubus and Golden Braid are regular features.

Unspoilt seventeenth-century former smugglers' inn with one service bar, lots of nooks and crannies and non-smoking area. Food available 12–2.30pm every day and 7–9pm (not Sun); traditional Sunday roast. Large garden. Children allowed in designated areas. On Ham Marshes, long mile north of Faversham; follow signs for Oare, then for the pub itself. OS:017636.

 *Summer: 11am–3pm and 6–11pm Mon–Fri; 11am–4pm and 6–11pm Sat; 12–10.30pm Sun. Winter: As summer, but closed Mon and 4–6pm Sun. May close early on winter evenings if no customers (wise to phone first).*

FOLKESTONE

The Lifeboat

42 North Street, Folkestone CT19 6AD
☎ *(01303) 243958* Muriel Wootton

A true freehouse with Fuller's London Pride always available, plus up to five other beers, including the products of Kent micro-breweries 'if we can get them'.

Classic backstreet locals' local in listed building on the fringes of what tourist area Folkestone has left, run by former licensee of nearest pub to Old Trafford (mention Duncan Edwards and watch Muriel's eyes light up). Beer has been sold on site since sixteenth century. One beamed bar with neither juke box nor fruit machines. Food available 12–3pm and 6–9pm; traditional roast Sunday lunchtime. Dogs allowed; children until 8pm. Garden. About 100 yards from seafront; follow signs to Folkestone Harbour, while they still have some meaning.

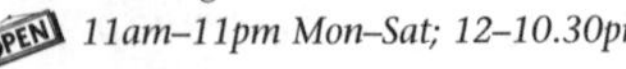 *11am–11pm Mon–Sat; 12–10.30pm Sun.*

GILLINGHAM

The Dog & Bone

21 Jeffrey Street, Gillingham ME7 1DE
☎ *(01634) 576829* David Skinner

Four constantly changing beers always available, with styles and strengths to suit everyone. Priced identically.

Traditional pub with one L-shaped bar, large conservatory/dining area and games room. Bar food available 12–2.30pm Tues–Sat; restaurant meals Tues–Sat from 6pm; traditional Sunday roast 12–2.30pm. Garden. On corner of James Street, few minutes from Gillingham railway station.

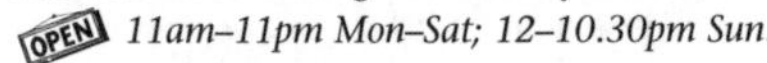 *11am–11pm Mon–Sat; 12–10.30pm Sun.*

The Frog & Toad

Burnt Oak Terrace, Gillingham ME7 1DR
☎ *(01634) 852231* John Brice
www.thefrogandtoad.com

Fuller's London Pride always available, plus three other regularly changing beers. Priced identically. Belgian beers also available.

Lively one-bar street-corner freehouse with no fruit machines or juke boxes. Good-value, freshly made sandwiches. Children and dogs allowed in the large garden only. Two annual beer festivals. Virtually due north of Gillingham railway station.

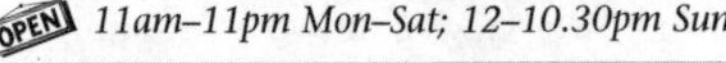 *11am–11pm Mon–Sat; 12–10.30pm Sun.*

The Will Adams

73 Saxton Street, Gillingham ME7 5EG
☎ *(01634) 575902* Peter and Julie Lodge

Hop Back Summer Lightning always available, plus up to four more beers on bank holiday weekends, two at other times.

One-bar local that was originally the Anglo Saxon; renamed by present licencees. Will Adams was a famous local explorer. Burgers, homemade chillis and pies available 12–2pm Sat only. Dogs allowed. Situated on corner of Lock Street at High Street end of Canterbury Street.

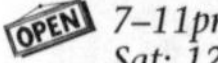 *7–11pm Mon–Fri; 12–3pm and 7–11pm Sat; 12–4pm and 8–10.30pm Sun.*

GOUDHURST

The Green Cross

Station Road, Goudhurst TN17 1HA
☎ *(01580) 211200* Lou and Caroline Lizzi

Genuine freehouse with Larkins Traditional Ale, Harveys Sussex Best Bitter and Shepherd Neame Master Brew Bitter always available.

Built as station hotel on western edge of village and as such provides welcome space away from endless traffic congestion. One basic bar and separate restaurant area, where seafood is the speciality. Food available 12–3pm and 7–9.30pm; traditional Sunday roast. Children allowed but not dogs. Small garden. On A262.

11.30am–3pm and 6.30–11pm Mon–Sat; 12–3pm and 7–10.30pm Sun, but closed Sunday evenings in winter (wise to phone first).

GRAVESEND

The Crown & Thistle

44 The Terrace, Gravesend DA12 2BJ
☎ *(01474) 326049*
Phil Bennett and Jackie Hall
www.crownandthistle.org.uk

Freehouse with Daleside Shrimpers and four other beers usually available, one of which will be above 5% ABV. The fact that in the first 20 months of his tenure, the landlord turned round some 800 different beers speaks for itself about the range.

Pub since 1849 and probably the best-kept secret in town, at least until it was named CAMRA national Pub of the Year for 2004. One beamed bar, separate hopped and non-smoking dining area and run by a Gravesend local with a terrific feel for beer and who is eager to put something back into his locale and already does a vast amount of fund-raising for the RNLI. Bar snacks, Chinese and Thai food available 12–3pm with Indian, Chinese and Thai food – to eat in or to take away – an evening feature from 6–10pm. Children welcome, but are asked to leave by 9pm if not eating; dog-friendly. Large, paved, south-facing garden. Situated in narrow corridor between A226 and River Thames. OS:651743.

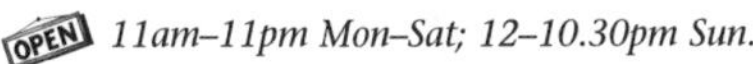
11am–11pm Mon–Sat; 12–10.30pm Sun.

The Jolly Drayman

1 Love Lane, Wellington Street, Gravesend DA12 1JA
☎ *(01474) 352355* Tim and Andrea Fordred
www.jollydrayman.com

Everards Tiger Best Bitter always available, plus up to three other beers, ranging from 3.5% to 5.5% ABV in strength.

Country-style pub in town-centre location and a pub since 1843. Housed in part of Wellington Brewery building. One beamed bar, airy conservatory and separate dining area; accommodation. Food available 12–2.30pm Mon–Sat; 12–4pm Sun, including traditional roast; 7–9.30pm Tues–Sun. Children not allowed in bar but well-behaved dogs are. Garden. Just south of A226.

11.30am–11pm Mon–Sat; 12–10.30pm Sun.

The Somerset Arms

10 Darnley Road, Gravesend DA11 0RU
☎ *(01474) 533837* Edward and Pat Kerr

Six beers always available from a range of hundreds per year, the tied landlord making best of being allowed 'guest' brews.

Former Fremlins street-corner pub, now tied to Enterprise Inns and catering for all tastes. One large U-shaped bar, but with quiet nooks and crannies in which to ease away the pains caused by town-centre shopping. Homemade fresh food available 11am–3pm Mon–Sat. No children in evening nor dogs at any time. Discos Friday and Saturday nights, but an over-21 restriction deters the marauding masses; you can still enjoy the beer. Close to Gravesend railway station on B262, on south-west fringes of one-way system.

11am–midnight.

GREAT CHART

The Hoodeners Horse

The Street, Great Chart, Ashford TN23 3AN
☎ *(01233) 625583* Ralph Johnson

Young's Special always available, plus one rotating guest.

Old English pub with one bar decorated with hops. Varied menu specialising in Mexican food. Full range of Gale's country wines generally in stock. Food available 12–2pm and 6–10pm Mon–Sat; 12–3pm and 5–9pm Sun. Children allowed. Garden. Situated in middle of village on former route of A28.

11am–3pm and 5–11pm Mon–Thurs; 11am–11pm Fri–Sat; 11am–10.30pm Sun.

HALSTEAD

The Rose & Crown

Otford Lane, Halstead, Sevenoaks TN14 7EA
☎ *(01959) 533120* Joy Brushneen

Genuine freehouse with Larkins Traditional Ale and a Harveys beer generally available, plus four other beers. Otter and Cotleigh products are often featured.

Victorian Grade II listed building with two bars; primarily a drinkers' pub. Food available 12–2pm Mon–Fri. Children preferred in the enclosed garden or pool room but, like dogs, are not discouraged from the bar areas if well behaved (or on leads). Short mile west of A224, opposite primary school.

 *12–11pm (10.30pm Sun).*

HARVEL

Amazon & Tiger

Harvel Street, Harvel, Meopham DA13 0DE
☎ *(01474) 814705* Mick Whitehouse

Genuine freehouse with three beers varying on a weekly basis.

Typical village pub that caters for all age groups. Two bars. Food available 12–2.30pm Mon–Sat; 7–9pm Fri and Sat; 12–4pm Sun, with traditional roast. Children and dogs allowed. Garden overlooking cricket ground. Headquarters and spiritual home of Harvel Hash House Harriers, 'the drinking club with a running problem'. Short mile east of A227.

 *12–3pm and 6–11pm Mon–Thurs; 12–11pm Fri–Sat; 12–10.30pm Sun.*

HOOK GREEN

The Elephant's Head

Furnace Lane, Hook Green, Lamberhurst TN3 8LJ
☎ *(01892) 890279* George, Sue and Gina May

Harveys tied house offering Sussex Pale Ale, Sussex Best Bitter and Armada Ale permanently, with any of the brewery's seasonal products, except for Knots of May Light Mild.

Built as farm dwelling in 1489, this splendidly isolated stone building gained its present name and full licence in 1808. Two beamed and hopped bars, one with a cosy off-shoot, separate dining area and airy conservatory. Food available 12–2.30pm daily, with traditional roast on Sunday; 7–9.30pm Tues–Thu; 6.30–9.30pm Fri and Sat. A barbecue may be hired for private functions. Children and dogs on leads allowed. Large garden with paved patio. On B2169, long mile west of Lamberhurst; half a mile from East Sussex boundary.

 *Summer: 11am–3pm and 5–11pm Mon–Fri; 11am–11pm Sat; 12–10.30pm Sun; no afternoon closing, however, during school summer holidays (except perhaps, if it's raining). Winter: As summer, but lunchtime opening 12 all week.*

IGHTHAM COMMON

The Old House

Redwell, Ightham TN15 9EE
☎ *(01732) 882383* Richard Boulter

Genuine freehouse with Daleside Shrimpers, Otter Bitter and Oakham Jeffrey Hudson Bitter always available, plus one or two others, all served lovingly directly from the cask.

Words cannot describe this Grade II listed building that, despite its limited opening hours, deserves to be in every beer/pub guide, whatever the parameters. Two bars: one beamed and dating from the seventeenth century with a vast open fire, the other – more of a 'snug' – a couple of hundred years younger. More than 100 single-malt whiskies. No food. Dogs allowed; children also if kept tethered. No sign outside; look for a row (lit at night) of cottages on the north side of the lane. Less than half a mile from both the A25 and A227. OS:590559.

 *7–9pm Tues; 7pm–closing Wed–Mon; 12–3pm Sat and Sun.*

LADDINGFORD

The Chequers Inn

Lees Road, Laddingford, Nr Yalding ME18 6BP
☎ *(01622) 871266* Charles and Tracey Leaver

Adnams Bitter, Fuller's London Pride and Young's Bitter always available, plus two guest ales.

Built in the fifteenth century, this weatherboarded building has been a farmhouse in its time. One oak-beamed bar leading to patio and at times a large marquee; accommodation. Food available 12–2.30pm and 7–9.30pm, with traditional Sunday roast. Children and dogs allowed. Large garden with livestock and an extensive play area. Award-winning flower displays in summer. Annual real ale festival held every April. A mile east of A228, south-south-west of Yalding.

 *12–3pm and 5–11pm Mon–Fri; 12–11pm Sat; 12–10.30pm Sun.*

LEEDS

The George Inn

4 Lower Street, Leeds, Maidstone ME17 1RN
☎ *(01622) 861314* Alan and Diane Cooper

Shepherd Neame tied house offering Master Brew and Spitfire permanently, with the appropriate seasonal beer.

Built in 1692 and nearest pub to Leeds Castle, but don't let that put you off! Two bars and separate dining area; accommodation. Food available 12–10pm; traditional roast all day Sunday. Children and dogs allowed. Garden. On B2163.

OPEN *11am–11pm Mon–Sat; 12–10.30pm Sun.*

LUDDESDOWN

The Cock Inn

Henley Street, Luddesdown, Gravesend DA13 0XB
☎ *(01474) 814208* Denise and Andrew Turner

Freehouse with Adnams Bitter always available, plus up to six other beers from almost anywhere.

Sixteenth-century traditional beamed and hopped two-bar pub set in idyllic countryside on North Downs escarpment, complete with open fires. No hot food, but doorstep sandwiches available 12–2.30pm Mon–Sat, while a seafood stall is a permanent feature in car park at weekends. No children inside pub, please; dogs more than welcome. Many pubs display personalised tankards; here, the cannines enjoy individualised treat boxes – how marvellous! The pub is biker-friendly, too. Conservatory and small garden. A long half mile east of B2009 and Sole Street station, from which there is a direct footpath. OS:664672.

OPEN *12–11pm (10.30pm Sun).*

MAIDSTONE

The Pilot

24 Upper Stone Street, Maidstone ME15 6EU
☎ *(01622) 691162*
Heather Banks and Laurence Francis

Harveys tied house offering Sussex XX Mild Ale, Sussex Best Bitter and Armada Ale permanently, plus whatever seasonal beer is appropriate on the fourth hand pump.

The county town's little marvel. Grade II listed building that houses all things good about country pubs in an urban location. Two bars, with a third room tucked away for peace and quiet should you need it. Food available 12–2pm Mon–Fri; 12–3pm Sat; 7–9pm Mon–Sat; only live acoustic music most Sunday afternoons! Children and dogs allowed. Garden with some 'interesting' brickwork – see landlord for details. In one-way system on A229 leaving town southwards, but sufficiently far from drinking halls not to attract the weekend blundering chunderers.

OPEN *12–3pm and 6–11pm Mon–Fri; 12–4pm and 7–11pm Sat; 12–5pm and 7–10.30pm Sun.*

The Rifle Volunteers

28 Wyatt Street, Maidstone ME14 1EU
☎ *(01622) 758891* Alan and Wendy Marlow

One of only two Goacher's tied houses, offering realistically priced Real Mild Ale, Fine Light Ale and Crown Imperial Stout permanently.

Street-corner local in Grade II listed building. One basic bar. Food available 12–2pm. No children; dogs tolerated. Patio garden. On junction of Union Street close to town centre, but offers nothing to attract weekend 'strollers'.

OPEN *11am–3pm and 6–11pm Mon–Sat; 12–3pm and 7–10.30pm Sun.*

MARGATE

The Orb

243 Ramsgate Road, Margate CT9 4EU
☎ *(01843) 220663* Dennis McGrellis

Shepherd Neame tied house offering Master Brew Bitter permanently, with Best Bitter, Spitfire or whatever seasonal beer is appropriate.

Built at the end of the fifteenth century, this pub is situated on the town's outskirts close to a large hospital. One bar, separate dining area and games room. Food available 12–2.30pm Mon–Fri; 12–5pm Sun, with traditional roast. Children allowed only if eating; dog-friendly. Outside drinking area. On A254.

OPEN *11am–11pm Mon–Sat; 12–10.30pm Sun.*

The Spread Eagle

25 Victoria Road, Margate CT9 1LW
☎ *(01843) 293396* Renny Dobbs

Greene King IPA and Abbot Ale always available, plus a guest beer.

Traditional Victorian backstreet local with one bar and dining area. Food available 11am–2.30pm Mon–Sat. Children allowed until 8pm. Just off B2055, behind St John's church.

11am–3pm and 5–11pm Mon–Fri; 11am–11pm Sat; 12–10.30pm Sun.

MARSH GREEN

The Wheatsheaf Inn

Marsh Green Road, Marsh Green, Edenbridge TN8 5QL
☎ *(01732) 864091* Neil Foster
www.thewheatsheaf.net

Genuine freehouse with Harveys Sussex Best Bitter always available, with up to six constantly changing other beers. Among the favourites are Fuller's London Pride, Everards Tiger Best Bitter and other brews from Harveys.

Built around the middle of the nineteenth century, this traditional village pub has one large, circular bar with numerous serving areas and several small off-shoots. Food available 12–2pm and 7–9.30pm Mon–Fri; 12–2.30pm and 7–9.30pm Sat; 12–2.30pm, with traditional roast, and 7–9pm Sun. Children and dogs allowed, all kept on leads, please. Conservatory and garden. Only just in Kent, on B2028.

11am–11pm Mon–Sat; 12–10.30pm Sun.

OAD STREET

The Plough & Harrow

Oad Street, Borden, Sittingbourne ME9 8LB
☎ *(01795) 843351* Mark and Neil Lockyer

Greene King IPA and Abbot and Shepherd Neame Master Brew Bitter always available, plus a range of guest beers, often from Young's or Shepherd Neame. Priced identically (and very reasonably), whatever the strength.

Small country pub with two bars littered with breweriana. Food available 12–2pm daily. Garden with children's area. Off A249 near M2 J5.

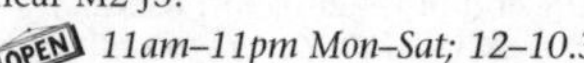
11am–11pm Mon–Sat; 12–10.30pm Sun.

OLD ROMNEY

The Rose & Crown

Swamp Road, Old Romney, Romney Marsh TN29 9SQ
☎ *(01797) 367500*
Kevin Campbell and Laurie and June Harrison
www.roseandcrown-oldromney.co.uk

Greene King XX Mild, IPA and Abbot Ale always available, plus two guests, often featuring Young's Bitter, Fuller's London Pride and Timothy Taylor Landlord.

Built towards the end of the seventeenth century and a pub since 1806. Two bars, conservatory and separate games room; accommodation. Food available 12–2pm and 7–9.15pm (not Sun evenings in winter); traditional Sunday roast. Children and dogs allowed. Large garden. Signed from A259.

11.30am–11pm Mon–Sat; 12–10.30pm Sun.

PECKHAM BUSH

Bush, Blackbird & Thrush

194 Bush Road, Peckham Bush, East Peckham TN12 5LN
☎ *(01622) 871349* Natalie and Jon Surtees

Shepherd Neame tied house offering Master Brew Bitter and Spitfire permanently, with whatever seasonal beer is appropriate, all served directly from the cask.

Fourteenth-century building that stands alone amid spacious farmland. One beamed bar and separate non-smoking restaurant area. Food available 12–2pm and 6.30–9pm Tues–Sat; 12–2.30pm Sun, with traditional roast. Children and dogs allowed, the pub having its own hound, Bremner, who, despite the landlord supporting Leeds United, will 'bite yer leg' only if seriously provoked. Massive garden with plenty of activities for children. Long half-mile west of A228, north of East Peckham village. OS:663499.

12–3pm and 6pm–closing.

PETTS WOOD

Sovereign of the Seas

109 Queensway, Petts Wood, Orpington BR5 1DG
☎ *(01689) 891606* Robert Barfoot

A Wetherspoon's pub with Shepherd Neame Spitfire among the brews always available. Two guests might include Hop Back Summer Lightning or Timothy Taylor Landlord. Guests changed weekly.

A community pub with one big bar, a non-smoking dining area and disabled facilities. Outside patios in summer. Food available all day. No children.

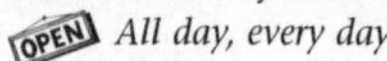
All day, every day.

PLAXTOL

The Papermakers Arms

The Street, Plaxtol, Sevenoaks TN15 0QL
☎ *(01732) 810407*
Michael Crompton and Vicky Colborne

Greene King IPA and Fuller's London Pride always available, with a third beer that changes 'barrel by barrel'.

Smart pub in picturesque medieval village, the Edwardian building providing a spacious bar and resultant relaxed atmosphere. Non-smoking dining area. Food available 12–2pm and 6.30–9pm Mon–Fri; 12–2.30 and 6.30–9.30pm Sat; 12–2.30pm Sun, with traditional roast. Children and dogs allowed. Patio garden with play area. Short mile east of A227. OS:605535.

 *12–3pm and 6–11pm Mon–Sat; 12–4pm and 7–10.30pm Sun.*

RAINHAM

The Mackland Arms

213 Station Road, Rainham ME8 7PS
☎ *(01634) 232178* Dave and Janet Ward

Shepherd Neame tied house offering Master Brew Bitter, Best Bitter and Spitfire permanently, with whatever seasonal beer is appropriate.

Very popular small pub with one L-shaped bar and friendly licencees. No food or children; dogs allowed. Beer garden and patio. On B2004, close to Rainham railway station.

 *10am–11pm Mon–Sat; 12–10.30pm Sun.*

RAMSGATE

The Artillery Arms

36 West Cliff Road, Ramsgate CT11 9JS
☎ *(01843) 853282* Chris and Michele Parry

Genuine freehouse with Charles Wells Bombardier Premium Bitter always available, plus four other beers on a constantly rotating basis.

Small street-corner hostelry with welcoming atmosphere and justifiably CAMRA Thanet Pub of the Year for 2002 and 2003. Grade II listed building constructed at start of the nineteenth century, featuring leaded stained-glass windows depicting Royal Artillery horseback scenes, hand-painted by soldiers after the Napoleonic Wars. No hot food but doorstep sandwiches made fresh to order nearly all day Mon–Sat. No children. Close to marina, perhaps 200 yards from seafront.

12–11pm (10.30pm Sun).

RECULVER

The King Ethelbert Inn

Reculver Lane, Reculver CT6 6SU
☎ *(01227) 374368*
Andrew Edwards and Anne Thornton

Shepherd Neame Master Brew Bitter always available, plus up to two other beers, one of which is usually from a Kent micro-brewery.

Built in 1843, this is a reliable pub for seasiders and walkers alike, being on Saxon Shore Way and overlooking the Thames estuary. One circular beamed bar with large dining area. Food available 12–3pm and 6–9pm Mon–Sat; 12–5pm, with traditional roast, and 6.30–9pm Sun. No food Sun–Wed evenings in winter. Children allowed until 9pm; dogs, on a lead, any time. Patio garden. Long mile north of A299 (Thanet Way).

11am–11pm Mon–Sat; 12–10.30pm Sun.

ROCHESTER

The Britannia Bar Café

376 High Street, Rochester ME1 1DJ
☎ *(01634) 815204* John Baker and Colin Boyes
www.britannia-bar-cafe.co.uk

Young's Bitter and Special always available, plus a guest beer that changes maybe twice a week.

This pub has one bar and a sunny patio. Breakfast available 10–11.45am Mon–Sat, then snacks, sandwiches and meals until 3pm; roast only on Sundays, 12–3pm. Close to seamless join between Chatham and Rochester High Streets, just east of Rochester railway station on corner of Hospital Lane.

10am–11pm Mon–Sat; 12–10.30pm Sun.

The Cooper's Arms

10 St Margarets Street, Rochester ME1 1TL
☎ *(01634) 404298*
Michael and Annette Hamill

Freehouse with three beers always available.

Mentioned in the Domesday Book, this weatherboard pub is thought to be the oldest inn in Kent. Two bars with lots of interesting objects. Original fire place. Food available 12–2pm Mon–Sat. Children allowed in garden and paved terrace area; dogs in pub but not when food is being served. Barbeques on Friday nights in summer. Behind High Street, near castle and cathedral at Rochester Bridge end.

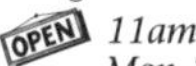 *11am–2.30pm and 5.30–11pm Mon–Thurs; 11am–11pm Fri and Sat; 12–10.30pm Sun.*

The Man of Kent

6–8 John Street, Rochester ME1 1YN
☎ *(01634) 818771* Jay and Mel Sandmann

Five ever-changing beers available at any one time, with Kent micro-breweries strongly favoured. Priced identically, whatever the strength.

Street-corner local with one L-shaped bar and a variety of traditional games on hand. Bar snacks (baguettes, etc) available 'until they run out' and, like the beer, at a standard, very reasonable, price. Children allowed in garden only. Behind police station, close to Star Hill junction at end of Rochester High Street 'proper'.

OPEN *12–11pm (10.30pm Sun).*

SITTINGBOURNE

The Red Lion

58 High Street, Sittingbourne ME10 4BP
☎ *(01795) 472706*
Michael Betts and Alison Miller

Fuller's London Pride, Greene King IPA and Shepherd Neame Spitfire always available, plus up to three other beers.

Fourteenth-century former coaching inn with a wealth of history and a myriad of famous visitors over the years. Now a busy town-centre pub with one long bar and separate dining area, which gel together in the evening, when pizza and pasta help to create a relaxed atmosphere. Good range of Gale's country wines. Food available 12–2.30pm and 6–10pm Mon–Sat; 12–3pm Sun, with traditional roast. No children or dogs inside, but they can be accommodated in garden courtyard. On historical route of A2, which now bypasses town centre.

11.30am–3.30pm and 5.30–11pm Mon–Sat; 12–3.30pm and 7–10.30pm Sun.

SMARDEN

The Chequers Inn

The Street, Smarden, Ashford TN27 8QA
☎ *(01233) 770217* Lisa and Charles Bullock

Harveys Sussex Best Bitter and Adnams Bitter always available, plus two other beers, one usually from a Kent or East Sussex brewery.

Timber-framed pub built in 1385, with beamed bars and three dining areas, two of which are smoke-free zones; accommodation. Food available 11am–2.30pm and 6–9.30pm Mon–Sat; 12–3pm Sun, including traditional roast. Children and dogs allowed. Large garden with delightful pond, offering best of rural tranquility. On B2077.

OPEN *11am–11pm Mon–Sat; 12–10.30pm Sun.*

SNARGATE

The Red Lion

Snargate, Romney Marsh TN29 9UQ
☎ *(01797) 344648* Doris Jemison

Up to five beers available directly from the cask, Kent breweries (Goacher's in particular) virtually guaranteed to be featured.

Unspoilt sixteenth-century pub bursting with character. One bar and a couple of side rooms, all adorned with local items of interest. No food. Gale's country wines an innovative feature. Even if Doris sold only Doubtful Diamond, Dread Barrel or Cavern Peg, this would not be a pub to miss. Children welcome but not in main bar. Large garden. On B2080 about a mile south-east of Appledore station.

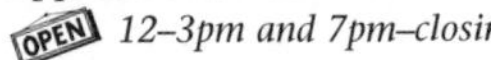
OPEN *12–3pm and 7pm–closing.*

SOUTHFLEET

The Wheatsheaf

8 Highcross Road, Southfleet, Westwood DA13 9PH
☎ *(01474) 833210* Gerry and Nick Cox
www.kent2do.com/wheatsheaf

Owned by Punch Taverns, with five real ales available. Fuller's London Pride, Charles Wells Bombardier, Greene King IPA and Old Speckled Hen are likely to be among them.

Beamed village pub that dates from 1408 and run by the same family for the past 15 years. One extended bar dominated by hops and separate restaurant area that doubles as function room. Food available 12–2.30pm and 7–9.30pm (7–9pm Sun), with traditional roast Sunday lunchtime. Children and dogs allowed, the latter encouraged to stay away from diners, please. Large garden; equally impressive pond. Still at the bottom of the crib league after many years of trying. Long mile south of A2.

OPEN *11am–11pm Mon–Sat; 12–10.30pm Sun.*

SPELDHURST

The George & Dragon

Speldhurst Hill, Speldhurst, Tunbridge Wells TN3 0NN
☎ *(01892) 863125* Patrick Churchward

Freehouse with Harveys Sussex Pale Ale, Harveys Sussex Best Bitter and Larkins Traditional Ale always available, plus up to three other beers, with Harveys and Larkins seasonal brews often featuring during winter months.

Originally a Wealden hall house, built at the beginning of the thirteenth century but understandably modified since. Now a family-friendly pub comprising two bars, separate dining area on ground floor and an impressive restaurant upstairs which, when added in 1582, cost the princely sum of what is now £6.80! Food available 12–3pm Mon; 12–3pm and 7–9pm Tues–Sat; 12–5pm Sun, with traditional roast. Children and dogs allowed. Two outdoor drinking areas: one paved, one grassed. Two miles both west of A26 and north of A264. OS:554414.

OPEN *11am–11pm Mon–Sat; 12–10.30pm Sun.*

SUTTON VALENCE

The Swan

Broad Street, Sutton Valence, Maidstone ME17 3AJ
☎ *(01622) 843212* Richard and Linda Gray

Up to four beers available directly from the cask: Fuller's London Pride, Adnams Bitter and Shepherd Neame Master Brew Bitter permanently, the other varying but with an emphasis on local brews.

Grade II listed building constructed in 1367 with Grade I stable block at rear, which became an inn 100 years later. One bar, separate restaurant area and a landlord who believes vehemently in the historic values of an English pub. Food available 12–2.30pm (not Tues) and 7–10pm (9.30pm Wed and Fri) Mon–Sat and 12.30–3pm (4pm by arrangement), traditional roast only, Sun. Children allowed. Garden. Eastern-most pub in village enjoying panoramic views over Kent Weald.

12–3pm (not Tues) and 6–11pm Mon–Thurs and Sat; 12–11pm Fri; 12–10.30pm Sun.

TENTERDEN

The William Caxton

West Cross, Tenterden TN30 6JR
☎ *(01580) 763142* Giles Davies

Shepherd Neame tied house offering Master Brew Bitter and Spitfire permanently, with whatever seasonal beer is appropriate.

Built in 1580 and probably the only pub in town not dominated by youth. Two beamed bars with hops prevalent and separate non-smoking dining area; accommodation. Food available 12–2.30pm (12–3pm Sat and Sun) and 7–10pm (7–9pm Sun); traditional Sunday roast. Children and dogs allowed. Garden. On junction of A28 and B2082.

OPEN *11am–11pm Mon–Sat; 12–10.30pm Sun.*

TONBRIDGE

The New Drum

54 Lavender Hill, Tonbridge TN9 2AU
☎ *(01732) 365044* Matt and Anthony Spencer

Genuine freehouse with Harveys Sussex Best Bitter and Marston's Pedigree always available, plus two other beers.

Traditional backstreet local that began life as two terraced cottages, with one L-shaped bar and mixed clientele. No food. Children and dogs allowed. For its location, the pub has an unexpectedly large garden, and patio. South of the railway and town centre, therefore relatively safe from weekend 'revelry', but it can be crowded when live football is being televised. North off A2014.

OPEN *11am–11pm Mon–Sat; 12–10.30pm Sun.*

TROTTISCLIFFE

The Plough

Taylors Lane, Trottiscliffe, West Malling ME19 5DR
☎ *(01732) 822233* David and Anne Dyer

Harveys Sussex Best Bitter, Adnams Bitter and Fuller's London Pride always available.

Built originally as two farm cottages in 1483 and licensed since 1817. Two beamed bars. Food available 12–2.30pm Mon–Sat; 6.30–8.30pm Tues–Sat; 12–3pm Sun, with traditional roast. Children and dogs allowed. Small patio. Village (pronounced Trosley) lies a mile north of A20, near junction of M20 and M26.

OPEN *11.30am–3pm and 6 (6.30 Sat)–11pm Mon–Sat; 12–3pm Sun.*

TUNBRIDGE WELLS

The Crystal Palace

69 Camden Road, Tunbridge Wells TN1 2QL
☎ *(01892) 548412*
Christopher and May Goodes

Harveys tied house offering Sussex Pale Ale and Sussex Best Bitter permanently, with any of the brewery's seasonal products.

A lot of time and money has been spent knocking this street-corner pub into shape, resulting in a welcoming, spacious, extended one-bar establishment, with light-coloured wooden flooring that helps to provide a very airy atmosphere. Food available 12–3pm; traditional roast only Sun. Children allowed away from serving area; dogs can go anywhere. Garden that is grassed, paved AND decked! Just north-east of Teenage Terrace, but the new landlord is sufficiently proud of his acquisition to eliminate undesirables virtually on sight, and has no problem with establishing reputation of running a 'clean' pub, safe for everyone. He should be applauded.

OPEN *11am–11pm Mon–Sat; 12–9pm Sun.*

The Rose & Crown

47 Grosvenor Road, Tunbridge Wells TN1 2AY
☎ *(01892) 522427* Peter and Jill Beech

Greene King IPA and Wadworth 6X always available, plus three other beers, one of which is usually a mild while the other two are bitters: one below 4% ABV, one above. These are changed barrel by barrel and the landlord, who certainly knows his stuff, is hopeful of adding a sixth hand pump shortly.

Street-corner Victorian pub in the town centre, with two connecting bars that are partitioned for events such as darts and bar billiards matches. Food, including doorstep sandwiches, available 12–2pm; traditional roast only Sun. Again, the landlord is optimistic that this will extend to evenings – best to phone and inquire. Customers must be over 21, but dogs – of all ages – are allowed. Just north of main shopping precinct which, combined with the age restriction, makes it an enjoyable place to drink on weekend evenings, as well as at any other time. On A26.

 *10.30am–11pm Mon–Sat; 12–10.30pm Sun.*

UNDERRIVER

The White Rock Inn

Carter's Hill, Underriver, Sevenoaks TN15 0SB
☎ *(01732) 833112* Frank and Maria Scott

Genuine freehouse with Harveys Sussex Best Bitter and Fuller's London Pride always available, plus a third beer that could come from anywhere – the landlord drinks the 'real' stuff himself, tends it like he would a baby and is open to suggestions as to where to go to next to add some variety.

Oldest part of the pub dates back to 1820, but there were buildings on the site for hundreds of years before that. Two beamed and hopped bars, one of which is designated non-smoking, similarly smog-free restaurant and separate games area. Food available 12–2pm and 7–9.30pm Mon–Sat; 12–2pm, with traditional roast, and 7–9pm Sun. Fresh fish and Aberdeen Angus steaks are specialities. Children allowed only if eating; no dogs. Extensive garden and patio. Two miles (by road) east of A21, midway between Sevenoaks and Tonbridge. OS:556521.

OPEN *12–3pm and 6–11pm Mon–Sat; 12–3pm and 7–10.30pm Sun.*

UPPER UPNOR

The Tudor Rose

29 High Street, Upper Upnor, Rochester ME2 4XG
☎ *(01634) 715305* Roger Rennie

Freehouse with Young's Bitter and Special usually available, plus four other beers that constantly change.

A 430-year-old pub with one main bar, several off-shoots and 20-seat restaurant. Food available 12–2.30pm Mon–Sat; 7–9.30pm Tues–Sat. Children allowed. Large walled garden with play area. Half a mile river side of A228; follow signs for Upnor Castle.

 *11am–11pm Mon–Sat; 12–4pm and 7–10.30pm Sun.*

WEST MALLING

The Lobster Pot

47 Swan Street, West Malling ME19 6JU
☎ *(01732) 843265* JK Taverns
www.thelobsterpot.co.uk

Up to six beers available, the emphasis being on local – particularly Goacher's and Shepherd Neame – and lesser-known micro-breweries.

Traditional 300-year-old pub run by enthusiastic, knowledgeable (though sadly anonymous), Cumbrian landlord. Two bars, dining area and function room. Food available 12–2pm Mon–Sat; 7–9pm Tues–Thurs; 7–9.30pm Fri and Sat; 12–3pm Sun, with traditional roast. Children allowed in restaurant only; dogs 'not barred'. Just off A228, on corner of Police Station Road!

 *12–2.30pm and 5–11pm Mon–Sat; 12–4pm and 7–10.30pm Sun.*

WEST PECKHAM

The Swan on the Green

The Green, West Peckham, Maidstone ME18 5JW
☎ *(01622) 812271*
Gordon Milligan and Michelle Harris
www.swan-on-the-green.co.uk

Brewpub, with the extensive range of beers produced on the premises always available. Seasonals and specials also brewed, any celebration being excuse enough.

Country pub at heart of small village community with emphasis on good food and beer brewed by a man (Gordon) who seems at total peace with his lot. First licensed in 1685 but, for a pub with beams, hops and a wooden floor, it has a deceptively modern feel in its one extended light bar. Food available 12–2.15pm and 7.15–9.15pm Mon–Sat; 12–2.15pm Sun, with traditional roast. Children and dogs allowed. Seated drinking area outside the pub, as well as across the road on the Green itself. Short mile west of A228. OS:644524.

11am–3pm and 6–11pm Mon–Fri; 11am–4pm and 6–11pm Sat; 12–4pm and 7–10.30pm Sun. Times may differ seasonally and if there are cricket matches or other events on the Green.

WHITSTABLE

The Old Neptune

Marine Terrace, Whitstable CT5 1EJ
☎ *(01227) 272262* Keith Flynn

Fuller's London Pride always available, plus one other beer.

Weatherboarded pub dating from the middle of the nineteenth century, complemented by authentic Thomson and Wootton Brewery windows and floor and bar that slope towards Whitstable Bay. Mixture of 'fast' foods, char-grilled steaks and fish fresh from harbour available 12–6pm throughout summer, but at weekends only in winter. No children. Outside drinking area. Adjacent to beach.

11am–11pm Mon–Fri; 12–10.30pm Sun.

The Ship Centurion Arminius

111 High Street, Whitstable, CT5 1AY
☎ *(01227) 264740*
Janet, Roland and Armin Birks

Freehouse with Adnams Bitter and Elgood's Black Dog Mild always available, plus two frequently changing guest beers, one of which is usually a stronger bitter. The only place in Whitstable where cask mild is available. Genuine continental lagers also served. Cask Marque holders.

One-bar town pub, first licensed in 1750, with sun lounge/24-seat dining area, where children with well-behaved parents are allowed at all times. Home-cooked snacks available 12–3pm and 6–9pm Mon–Fri; light, leftover menu 12–3pm Sat; no food Sun except seafood selection on bar at lunchtime. Live music every Thurs. Four TVs. On B2205, west end of town.

11am–11pm Mon–Sat; 12–7pm Sun.

WITTERSHAM

The Swan Inn

1 Swan Street, Wittersham TN30 7PH
☎ *(01797) 270913* Ray Pratt and Angela Baker
www.swan-wittersham.co.uk

Harveys Sussex Best Bitter, Goacher's Real Mild Ale and Fine Light Ale permanent fixtures on hand pump, with up to four other beers – either brewed locally or 'unusual offerings' from elsewhere – available directly from the cask.

An old drovers' pub on Isle of Oxney and only just in Kent, this focal point for the village has a landlord passionate about draught beer. Two bars. Food available 12–2pm Wed–Mon; 6–9pm Wed–Sat and 7–9pm Sun; traditional Sunday roast. Children and dogs allowed. Beer garden. On B2082, about five miles north of Rye.

11am–11pm Mon–Sat; 12–10.30pm Sun.

WOODLANDS

The Rising Sun

Cotmans Ash Lane, Woodlands, Nr Kemsing, Sevenoaks TN15 6XD
☎ *(01959) 522683* Peter and Michelle Hunter

Genuine freehouse that offers an amazing range of real beers. Five are usually available, which may reduce to four in the worst of the winter; the pump clips offer a treasure trove.

Once in the door of this heavily beamed 400-year-old pub, you won't want to leave; it is a reviving experience. One long bar and separate dining area, with additional nooks and crannies should you want to escape from the open fire that offers warmth for the 30-year-old African grey parrot the licensees inherited. Food available 12–2pm and 7–9.30pm, with traditional – wait for it – 'home-reared' Sunday roast that is served in the evening if there is any left from lunchtime. Dogs, children, muddy boots and probably pet goats allowed, the future of the countryside being of obvious importance to anybody involved in any way with the pub. Large garden with ample facilities for children. Off the beaten track very close to North Downs Way, but, like a handful of other watering holes in the county (see Chiddingstone Hoath, Fairseat, Ightham Common and Snargate), it is seriously worth the effort digging out if you believe that nostalgia is not what it used to be! Best approached by turning off A20 at West Kingsdown opposite Portobello Inn (road signed to Knatts Valley) into School Lane, then three miles of rural roads. OS:563599.

OPEN *11am–3pm and 6–11pm Mon–Sat; 12–3pm and 7–10.30pm Sun.*

WORTH

The St Crispin Inn

The Street, Worth, Deal CT14 0DF
☎ *(01304) 612081* Paul Piddock

Shepherd Neame Master Brew Bitter always available, plus up to two other beers.

Busy oak-beamed pub built in 1420 and licensed since 1690. One large open bar and separate restaurant area; accommodation. Food available 11.30am–2.15pm and 6–9.30pm Mon–Sat; 12–2.15pm, with traditional roast, and 7–9.30pm Sun. Fish and steak specialities. Children and dogs allowed. Large garden. Short half-mile east of A258.

OPEN *11am–3pm and 6–11pm Mon–Sat; 12–3pm and 7–10.30pm Sun; no afternoon closing July–Aug.*

Adlington

Jennings Cumberland ✓

Cracker

John Smiths Smooth ✓

Arizona

Wards Best Bitter

BLACKPOOL BREWERY CO.

Unit 6 The Old Dairy, George Street, Blackpool FY1 3RP
☎ *(01253) 304999*

GOLDEN SMILE 3.7% ABV
Award-winning brew, full-flavoured with hoppy undertones.
BLACKPOOL BITTER 4.0% ABV
A golden blend of strength and flavour that is an original experience.
BPA (BLACKPOOL PALE ALE) 4.2% ABV
Blackpool's very own Pale Ale. Proven to be a great favourite with the North West real ale aficionados.
Seasonal:
BLACK DIAMOND MILD 3.4% ABV
CHRISTMAS LIGHTS 3.9% ABV
SWEET FA 3.9% ABV
LIGHTSOUT 4.4% ABV

THE BOWLAND BEER CO LTD

The Bowland Brewery, Bashall Barn, Twitter Lane, Bashall Town, Clitheroe BB7 3LQ
☎ *(01200) 428825*
www.bowlandbrewery.com

BOWLAND GOLD 3.8% ABV
Citrus flavours.
HUNTERS MOON 3.9% ABV
BOWLAND OAK 4.0% ABV
BOWLAND BLACK 4.3% ABV
Malt loaf and liquorice flavours.
HEADLESS PEG 4.5% ABV
COLD TURKEY 5.0% ABV

BRYSON'S BREWS

1 Summerside, 25 Oxcliffe Road, Heysham LA3 1PU
☎ *(01524) 852150*
www.brysonsbrews.co.uk

MILD 3.5% ABV
SHIFTING SANDS 3.8% ABV
MEMORIAL 4.0% ABV
Summer brew.
CASTLE 4.1% ABV
Spring brew.
BARROWS 4.2% ABV
SHRIMPERS STOUT 4.7% ABV
PRIORY 5.7% ABV
Winter brew.
Plus other one-offs and specials.

GREENFIELD REAL ALE BREWERY

Unit 8 Waterside Mills, Greenfield, Saddleworth OL3 7PF
☎ *(01457) 879789*

CELEBRATION 4.0% ABV
DOVESTONES BITTER 4.0% ABV
GREENFIELD ALE 4.0% ABV
BILLS 'OR' JACKS 4.1% ABV
DELPH DONKEY 4.1% ABV
DOBCROSS BITTER 4.2% ABV
ICE BREAKER 4.2% ABV
JABETHS BITTER 4.2% ABV
PRIDE OF ENGLAND 4.2% ABV
UPPERMILL ALE 4.2% ABV
BRASSED OFF 4.4% ABV
FRIEZLAND ALE 4.4% ABV
LONGWOOD THUMP 4.5% ABV
Plus seasonal beers and for special events to order

HART BREWERY

The Cartford Hotel, Cartford Lane, Little Eccleston, Preston PR3 0YP
☎ *(01995) 671686*

ICE MAIDEN 4.0% ABV
SQUIRREL'S HOARD 4.0% ABV
AMBASSADOR 4.2% ABV
GENESIS 4.2% ABV
NEMESIS 4.5% ABV
VAL(ADDICTION) 4.8% ABV
COBBLESTONE 5.0% ABV
EXCALIBUR 5.0% ABV
CESTRIAN HART 5.2% ABV
STEAMIN' JACK 5.5% ABV
Plus seasonal brews.

THE MILLSTONE BREWERY LIMITED

Unit 4, Vale Mill, Micklehurst Road, Mossley OL5 9JL
☎ *(01457) 835835*

Permanent:
A MILLER'S ALE 3.8% ABV
THREE SHIRES BITTER 4.0% ABV
GRAIN STORM 4.3% ABV
MILLSTONE EDGE 4.4% ABV
Plus seasonal brews

MOONSTONE BREWERY

The Ministry of Ale, 9 Trafalgar Street, Burnley BB11 1TQ
☎ *(01282) 830909*

BLACK STAR 3.4% ABV
SUNSTONE ANNIVERSARY ALE 3.8% ABV
TIGER'S EYE 3.8% ABV
TRUMPINGTON BITTER 4.2% ABV
CRAGGY'S WOBBLE 4.5% ABV
MOONSTONE DARK 4.5% ABV
RED JASPER 6.0% ABV

MOORHOUSE'S BREWERY LTD

4 Moorhouse Street, Burnley BB11 5EN
☎ *(01282) 422864*

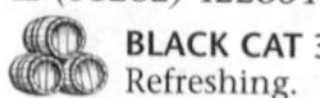

BLACK CAT 3.4% ABV
Refreshing.

PREMIER BITTER 3.7% ABV
Full-flavoured with good hoppiness.

PRIDE OF PENDLE 4.1% ABV
Smooth and well-rounded.

PENDLE WITCHES BREW 5.1% ABV
Complex, sweet malt and fruit flavour.

PICKS BREWERY

Red Lion Hotel, Willows Lane, Greenhowarth, Accrington BB5 3SJ
☎ *(01254) 233194*

MOORGATE MILD 3.5% ABV
PALE ALE 3.7% ABV
BEDLAM BITTER 3.9% ABV
LIONS MANE 4.2% ABV
PORTER 4.5% ABV
LIONS PRIDE 5.4% ABV

PICTISH BREWERY

Unit 9, Canalside Industrial Estate, Woodbine Street East, Rochdale OL16 5LB
☎ *(01706) 522227*
www.pictish-brewing.co.uk

BREWER'S GOLD 3.8% ABV
Spicy hop aroma.

CELTIC WARRIOR 4.2% ABV
Mid-brown premium ale.

Plus seasonals.

PORTER BREWING COMPANY

84 Hud Rake, Haslingden, Rossendale BB4 5AF
☎ *(01706) 214021*

DARK MILD 3.3% ABV
BITTER 3.8% ABV
ROSSENDALE ALE 4.2% ABV
PORTER 5.0% ABV
SUNSHINE 5.3% ABV

Plus occasional and seasonal brews.

RAMSBOTTOM BREWERY

Back Square Street, Bolton Road, Ramsbottom BL0 9FZ
☎ *(0773) 950 7416*

FREEFALL 3.8% ABV
OLD GROUND MILD 3.8% ABV
RAMMY MILE 3.8% ABV
TOWER BITTER 4.0% ABV
PROVIDENT 4.5% ABV

Seasonals:

HAYMAKER 4.1% ABV
Available July/August.

SANTA SPECIAL 5.0% ABV

RED ROSE BREWERY

Royal Hotel, Station Road, Great Harwood BB6 7BA
☎ *(01254) 877373*

BOWLEY BEST BETTER 3.7% ABV
BLACKPOOL BELLE 4.0% ABV
FELIX 4.2% ABV
OLD BEN 4.3% ABV
THE LANCASHIRE & YORKSHIRE ALEWAY 4.5% ABV
OLD DEMDYKE 4.6% ABV
CARE TAKER OF HISTORY 6.0% ABV

THE THREE B'S BREWERY

Laneside Works, Stockclough Lane, Fennicowles, Blackburn BB2 5JR
☎ *(01254) 207686*

STOKERS SLAK 3.6% ABV
BOBBIN'S BITTER 3.8% ABV
TACKLER'S TIPPLE 4.3% ABV
PINCH NOGGIN 4.6% ABV

KNOCKER UP 4.8% ABV
Porter.

SHUTTLE ALE 5.2% ABV

Plus occasional beers.

DANIEL THWAITES BREWERY

PO Box 50, Star Brewery, Syke Street, Blackburn BB1 5BU
☎ *(01254) 686870*
Fax (01254) 686944
www.thwaites.co.uk

THWAITES DARK MILD 3.3% ABV
THWAITES ORIGINAL 3.6% ABV
THOROUGHBRED 4.0% ABV
LANCASTER BOMBER 4.4% ABV

Seasonals:

BLOOMIN ALE 3.9% ABV
CRAFTSMAN 4.2% ABV
LIBERATION ALE 4.5% ABV
GOOD ELF 4.9% ABV

THE PUBS

ACCRINGTON

The George Hotel

185 Blackburn Road, Accrington BB5 0AF
☎ *(01254) 383441*

Four beers always available from an ever-changing list that might include Titanic Stout, Cains FA and Goose Eye Bitter.

A friendly freehouse with an open-plan bar area and separate restaurant in converted stables. Bar and restaurant food available at lunchtime and evenings. Street parking, garden/patio area. Children allowed. Accommodation. Close to the railway and bus stations.

OPEN *12–11pm (10.30pm Sun).*

ARKHOLME

The Bay Horse Hotel

Arkholme, Carnforth
☎ *(015242) 21425)* Peter Dawson Jackson

A guest beer usually available, perhaps Greene King Abbot Ale, Greene King Old Speckled Hen, Everards Tiger or one of several other regular beers.

Typical, unspoilt country pub. Food served Tues–Sun lunchtimes and every evening. Car park. Children welcome. From junction 35 of the M6, follow the Kirkby Lonsdale sign for 5 miles.

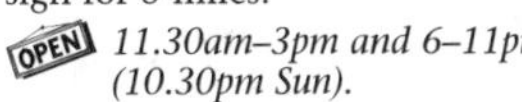

OPEN *11.30am–3pm and 6–11pm (10.30pm Sun).*

BISPHAM GREEN

The Eagle & Child

Malt Kiln Lane , Bispham Green, Nr Ormskirk L40 3SG
☎ *(01257) 462297* Monica Evans

A freehouse with two permanent beers Moorhouse's Black Cat Mild and Thwaites Bitter always available. Also five rotating guests, perhaps from Cottage, Phoenix, Rudgate, Timothy Taylor, Derwent, Fuller's, Hawkshead, Blackpool.

An old-fashioned country pub with flagstone floors, old furniture, bowling green, croquet lawn, beer garden. Food at lunchtime and evenings12–2pm and 6–8.30pm (9pm on Fri–Sat). Large function room available to hire. Children allowed.

OPEN *12–3pm and 5.30–11pm Mon–Sat; all day Sun.*

BLACKBURN

The Cellar Bar

39–41 King Street, Blackburn
☎ *(01254) 698111* Dan Hook

Two regularly changing beers available often from Moorhouse's, Three B's, Castle Eden, Dent, Jennings or RCH.

Buried underground in the first mayor of Blackburn's family home and the oldest Georgian house in the town, this pub has a cosy atmosphere, real fire, live music and the biggest beer garden in Blackburn. No food. Car park. Children welcome.

OPEN *11am–11pm Mon–Tues; 11am–1am Wed–Fri; 7pm–1am Sat; 7–10.30pm Sun.*

The Postal Order

15 Darwen Street, Blackburn BB2 2BY
☎ *(01254) 676400* Neil and Sharon Longley

A Wetherspoon's pub serving several guest ales. Thwaites Mild is a regular, and other guests might include Exmoor Fox, Gale's GB and Cotleigh Barn Owl.

A large, traditional town pub near the Cathedral. One long bar with two separate areas. Non-smoking dining area. Food served all day. Children welcome.

OPEN *All day, every day.*

BLACK LANE ENDS

The Hare & Hounds Inn

Black Lane Ends, Colne BB8 7EP
☎ *(01282) 863070* Betty Holmes

A freehouse serving up to six real ales at any one time including Timothy Taylor Golden Best and Landlord plus Black Sheep Bitter on a regular basis, plus one guest beer.

A country pub with panoramic views on the Carleton to Colne road. One bar, real log fires, stone and wood floors and beams. Non-smoking area. Food available 12–9pm every day. Children welcome. Beer garden. An ideal spot for walkers as there are lots of public footpaths leading from the pub.

OPEN *All day, every day (from 12 noon).*

BLACKPOOL

The Shovels

260 Common Edge Road, Blackpool FY4 5DH
☎ *(01253) 762702* Steve and Helen Norris

Theakston Best Bitter plus five guest beers always available from breweries such as Hart. Micro-breweries favoured whenever possible. Annual beer festival held in the last week of October/first week of November, with up to 80 cask ales.

A steak 'n' ale pub in a suburban location. CAMRA Blackpool Fylde, & Wyre Pub of the Year 2001 and 2003. One bar, non-smoking area, real fire, front patio, disabled access/toilet. Dining area, conservatory. Food served 12–9.30pm. Children allowed, but not in bar. Just off the M55 on main road from Blackpool to Lytham St Annes.

OPEN *11.30am–11pm Mon–Sat and 12–10.30pm Sunday.*

BRETHERTON

The Blue Anchor Inn

21 South Road, Bretherton, Nr Leyland PR26 9AB
☎ *(01772) 600270* Michele Fielden

Timothy Taylor Landlord, Marston's Pedigree and Moorhouse's Black Cat are among the beers always available, and the three guests might be something from Hart, Phoenix, Marston's, Moorhouse's, Boggart Hole Clough, Cottage or Blackpool.

Busy traditional village pub with large beer garden and play area. Food served 11.30am–2pm and 5–9.30pm Mon–Fri and all day at weekends. Children welcome. Car park.

 *11.30am–3pm and 5–11pm Mon–Fri; 11.30am–11pm Sat–Sun.*

BURNLEY

The Ministry of Ale

9 Trafalgar Street, Burnley BB11 1TQ
☎ *(01282) 830909* Michael Jacques

Home of the Moonstone Brewery, with two home ales always available, plus at least two guests which could be a Moonstone special or a beer from any independent brewery, but especially local ones such as Phoenix, Bank Top and Moorhouse's.

A modern café-style brewpub situated on the edge of town. No food. No children.

OPEN *5–11pm Mon–Thurs (closed lunchtimes); 12–11pm Fri–Sat; 12–10.30pm Sun.*

The Sparrow Hawk Hotel

Church Street, Burnley BB11 2DN
☎ *(01282) 421551* Mr Jeffrey Mallinson

A freehouse always offering a choice of eight or more cask ales, including guest bitters, stouts, porters and ciders from breweries throughout the country as well as northern favourites.

A country-style inn in the town centre. Two bars, restaurant and accommodation. Food served at lunchtime and evenings. Entertainment Thurs–Sun.

OPEN *11am–3pm and 6–11pm Mon–Thurs; all day Fri–Sun.*

CHORLEY

Malt 'n' Hops

50–2 Friday Street, Chorley PR6 0AH
☎ *(01257) 260967* Christa and Lawrence

Timothy Taylor Landlord and Barnsley IPA and one dark beer always available plus eight guest beers (at least one changed every day) perhaps including something from Pictish, Slaters, Cains, Moorhouse's, Wheetwood and many other breweries.

A Victorian-style, one-bar pub ideal for trainspotters. Bar food available on order at lunchtime. Parking. Children allowed with responsible parents. Just 200 yards behind the Manchester to Preston railway station.

OPEN *All day, every day.*

CLAYTON-LE-MOORS

The Albion

243 Whalley Road, Clayton-le-Moors, Accrington BB5 5HD
☎ *(01254) 238585* Mr Clive Nightingale

Freehouse with up to four real ales available usually from local micro-breweries such as Three B's and Bank Top.

A traditional real ale pub. Recently refurbished with a new bar area and wood panelling and redecorated throughout. Plans to brew its own ale . Beer garden. Mooring spot for barges on the Liverpool to Leeds canal. Food served but check availability first. Children allowed in the garden only.

OPEN *5–11pm Mon–Tues; all day Wed–Sun.*

CLITHEROE

The New Inn

Parson Lane, Clitheroe BB7 2JN
☎ *(01200) 423312* Mr and Mrs Lees

A Whitbread house with a guest beer policy serving Fuller's London Pride, Marston's Pedigree and a Moorhouse's brew plus a guest, changed weekly, from smaller breweries if possible. Beers featured have included Greene King Abbot, Gale's HSB and Wadworth 6X.

An old English pub with one bar and an open fire. Four adjoining rooms, plus a non-smoking room. No music or games, but folk club on Friday nights. Children allowed in designated area. No food.

OPEN *All day, every day.*

CLIVIGER

Queens

412 Burnley Road, Cliviger, Nr Burnley
☎ *(01282) 436712* Alec Heap

Three guest beers usually available from a wide range of micro-breweries.

Simple alehouse. No pool table, juke box or bandits. No food. Children welcome, but there are no special facilities.

OPEN *1–11pm Mon–Sat; 12–10.30pm Sun.*

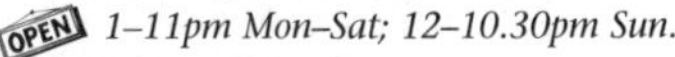

CRAWSHAWBOOTH

The White Bull

612 Burnley Road, Crawshawbooth BB4 8AJ
☎ *(01706) 260394* Chhanu Miah

Formerly tied to Beartown, now a freehouse with three permanent real ales and one guest.

Quiet traditional village pub. Old building, with beams, Indian restaurant upstairs (no food in the pub) and beer garden. Children allowed. Car park.

OPEN *5–11pm Mon–Fri; 12–11pm Sat; 12–10.30pm Sun.*

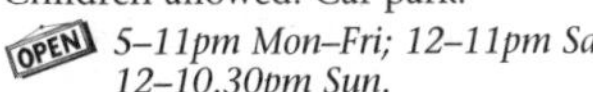

CROSTON

The Black Horse

Westhead Road, Croston, Nr Chorley PR5 7RQ
☎ *(01772) 600338* Mr G Conroy

Six traditional cask bitters and one mild always available, from breweries such as Black Sheep, Caledonian, Jennings, Moorhouse's, Greene King and Timothy Taylor, plus smaller micro-breweries. Two beer festivals held each year around April and October.

This traditional village freehouse serves bar and restaurant food at lunchtimes and evenings, at very competitive prices. Car park, beer garden, children's play area, bowling green and French boules pitch are all available, and specially organised parties and meals can be catered for. In the village of Croston, close to Chorley and midway between Preston and Southport.

OPEN *All day, every day.*

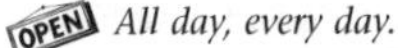

DALTON

The Beacon Inn

Beacon Lane, Dalton WN8 7RR
☎ *(01695) 632607* Kevin Balke

Jennings Mild, Bitter and Cumberland regularly available plus a guest beer which may include Fuller's London Pride or something from Castle Eden.

Acquired by Jennings in 1999, this country pub is much used by ramblers as it is situated by Ashurst Beacon Point. Also handy for Beacon Golf Club. Food served 12–2pm Tues–Sat, 12–5pm Sun. Car park. Large beer garden. Children welcome.

OPEN *12–11pm (10.30pm Sun).*

DARWEN

Black Horse

72 Redearth Road, Darwen BB3 2AF
☎ *(01254) 873040*
www.the blackun.co.uk

Four real ales available including Bank Top Flat Cap and generally obscure guests. Beer festivals held in spring and autumn.

Local community pub off the A666. Food served at lunchtimes. Outside seating.

OPEN *12–11pm Mon–Sat, 12–10.30pm Sun.*

Greenfield Inn

Lower Barn Street, Darwen BB3 2HQ
☎ *(01254) 703945* Carol Wood

Timothy Taylor Landlord, Greene King Abbot and Charles Wells Bombardier always available, plus two guests.

A traditional one-room pub with beer garden. Food served at lunchtime and evenings. Children allowed. Situated on the outskirts of Darwen.

OPEN *12–11pm (10.30pm Sun).*

ENTWHISTLE

The Strawbury Duck

Overshores Road, Entwhistle, Bolton BL7 0LU
☎ *(01204) 852013* Roger and Lisa Boardman

Eight real ales available at all times. Moorhouse's Pendle Witches, Timothy Taylor Landlord and Black Sheep Special are permanent fixtures, and a wide variety of guests are also served. Regulars include Greene King Old Speckled Hen, Marston's Pedigree and ales from Brains or Caledonian including seasonals.

A 300-year-old pub situated next to Entwhistle Railway Station. One bar, several dining areas, pool room, non-smoking room, beer garden, accommodation. Food served 12–9.30pm Mon–Thurs, all day Fri–Sun. Children welcome, with special menu and crayons available.

OPEN *11am–11pm Mon–Sat; 12–10.30pm Sun.*

FLEETWOOD

Wyre Lounge Bar

Marine Hall, The Esplanade, Fleetwood FY7 6HF
☎ *(01253) 771141*

Eight beers always available including Moorhouse's brews. Also 200+ guest beers per year which may come from Young's, Charles Wells, Banks's and Timothy Taylor.

Part of the Marine Hall Sports Complex in Fleetwood. Food available at lunchtime. Car park, garden, function room. No children.

OPEN *11am–4.30pm and 7–11pm Mon–Sat; 12–4pm and 7–10.30pm Sun.*

GREAT HARWOOD

The Dog & Otter

Cliffe Lane, Great Harwood, Blackburn BB6 7PG
☎ *(01254) 885760* Catherine Darnley

A Jennings-managed house with Jennings Bitter and Cumberland Ale always available, plus two rotating guest ales, perhaps Fuller's London Pride or a Marston's brew.

A traditional pub dating back to 1750 with two bar areas.
Restaurant and a patio area with outside tables with outdoor heaters, lights and plants. Traditional pub food including specials served 12–2 pm and 5–9pm. Children allowed.

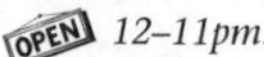
OPEN *12–11pm.*

The Royal Hotel

Station Road, Great Harwood, Blackburn BB6 7BA
☎ *(01254) 883541* Janice and Peter Boothe
www.rock-n-royal.co.uk

A freehouse with seven constantly changing beers (over 350 per year) from a varied selection from around the UK. Regular guests include brews from Phoenix, Hart, Anglo-Dutch, Barngates, Three B's, Picks and Cropton. An eighth hand pump serves draught Sarsparilla (non-alcoholic).

A Victorian pub/hotel with public bar, separate dining area, separate live music area and beer garden. English Tourist Council 3-diamond accommodation. Food available. No football, no discos, no karaoke! Live music Fri, musicians' jam sessions Mon (mainly blues and folk). Children allowed. Great Harwood is between Blackburn, Accrington and Clitheroe.

OPEN *12–11pm (10.30pm Sun).*

HASLINGDEN

The Griffin Inn

84 Hud Rake, Haslingden, Rossendale BB4 5AF
☎ *(01706) 214021* David Porter

Home of the Porter Brewing Company. A brewpub with Dark Mild, Bitter, Porter, Sunshine and Rossendale Ale brewed and served on the premises.

A traditional no-frills alehouse and local community pub on the northern edge of town. No music or TV. No food. No children.

OPEN *All day, every day.*

HESKIN

The Farmer's Arms

85 Wood Lane, Heskin PR7 5NP
☎ *(01257) 451276* Andrew Rothwell
www.farmersarms.co.uk

Castle Eden Ale and Timothy Taylor Landlord are among the beers always available, and the one guest may be something like Marston's Pedigree.

A quaint, white, flowery country village pub in an eighteenth-century building. Food served all day every day – there is a non-smoking dining area. Well-behaved children allowed. Beer garden, car park. Situated off Junction 27 of M56 on B5250

OPEN *12–11pm (10.30pm Sun).*

LANCASTER

The Waterwitch

The Towpath, Aldcliffe Road, Lancaster LA1 1SU
☎ *(01524) 63828*

Up to eight real ales always available, almost exclusively from local independent breweries. Bryson's, Hart, Thwaites and Abbey often feature. Plus bottled beers and wheat and fruit beers on draught.

A genuine canalside inn converted from a stable block in 1978. Real fires, no-smoking areas and garden. Upstairs restaurant. Good food available 12–3pm and 6–9.30pm Mon–Sat, 12–6pm Sun. Live music on Sunday nights.

OPEN *11am–11pm Mon–Sat, 12–10.30pm Sun.*

LEA TOWN

The Saddle Inn

Sidgreaves Lane, Lea Town, Preston PR4 0RS
☎ *(01772) 726616* Carole Buck

A Thwaites tied house, with Thwaites Bitter and Lancaster Bomber permanently featured, plus one seasonal guest beer.

Traditional country pub. Food served all day until 9pm Mon–Sat and until 8pm Sun. Children are welcome, and there is a children's play area. Large car park.

OPEN *All day, every day.*

LITTLE ECCLESTON

The Cartford Hotel

Cartford Lane, Little Eccleston, Preston PR3 0YP
☎ *(01995) 670166* Andrew Mellodew

The Hart Brewery operates from the premises producing a range of 16 beers for sale in the hotel and some local freehouses. Fuller's London Pride and Timothy Taylor Landlord are also regularly available plus a range of over 3,000 other beers so far, served on a guest basis.

An award-winning, 400-year-old family pub. One large bar, large garden with children's play area. Quiet eating area with food available at lunchtime and evenings. Children allowed. Brewery tours by appointment. Car park. Games room. Accommodation.

 *12–3pm and 6.30–11pm Mon–Sat; all day Sun.*

LONGTON

The Dolphin Inn

Marsh Lane, Longton, Preston PR4 5JY
☎ *01772 261 2032* Miss Zena Slinger

Freehouse serving four cask ales including Timothy Taylor Landlord, Greene King IPA and guest ales changing every few days.

A traditional country pub with two bars including one suited to families that leads to a conservatory. Children's play area. Real fire. Food served all day until 8pm includes daily specials and a children's menu. Situated on the Ribble Way and thus an ideal base for walkers.

 *All day, every day.*

LYTHAM

The Taps

12–15 Henry Street, Lytham FY8 5LE
☎ *(01253) 736226* Ian Rigg
www.thetaps.com

Up to eight real ales available on a typical night, two permanent fixtures (including a house brew from Titanic) and six frequently rotating guests from a vast selection of breweries located all over the British Isles. A mild is usually available.

An olde-English town pub with one bar and coal fires. The yard behind is heated. Viewing cellar. Disabled facilities and toilets. Food served at lunchtime only Mon–Sat. Children allowed only if dining.

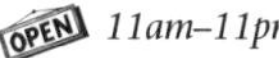 *11am–11pm.*

ORMSKIRK

The Hayfield

County Road, Ormskirk L39 1NN
☎ *(01695) 571157* Godfrey Hedges

Cains Mild is among the beers always on offer, plus eight guests from a variety of breweries, including Jennings, Phoenix, Slaters (Eccleshall), Rooster's, Black Sheep, Weetwood, Moorhouse's and Robinson's.

Busy freehouse with a warm, friendly atmosphere. Food served 12–3pm and 5.30–8.30pm Mon–Sat plus 12–7.30pm Sun. No children's facilities. Car park. On the main A59 road in Ormskirk.

12–11pm (10.30pm Sun).

The Queen's Head

30 Moor Street, Ormskirk L39 2AQ
☎ *(01695) 574380* Gerry Fleming

Up to four guest ales available including Fuller's London Pride, Shepherd Neame Bishop's Finger and Spitfire, Black Sheep Special or Wychwood The Dog's Bollocks.

A traditional one-bar pub with beer garden. Annual themed beer festival. Food 12–2pm Mon–Sat. Well-behaved children allowed.

All day, every day.

POULTON LE FYLDE

Thatched House

12 Ball Street, Poulton le Fylde FY6 7BG
Brian and Valerie Ballentine

Regular beers include Charles Wells Bombardier and Theakston Best Bitter plus two regularly changing guest beers one of which is usually from the Hart Brewery.

Its unusal location in the graveyard of the parish church in the centre of town means that your are always guaranteed of a warm welcome in this award winning and unspoilt traditional pub. No food, children or music.

11am–11pm Mon–Sat; 12–10.30pm Sun.

PRESTON

The Hogshead

Moss Cottage, Fylde Road, Preston PR1 2XQ
☎ *(01772) 252870*
Steven Leyshon (assistant manager)

Caledonian Deuchars IPA, Timothy Taylor Landlord, Black Sheep Bitter and Marston's Pedigree always available, plus two rotating guest ales.

Drinkers' pub in a listed building on the outskirts of town. Food available 12–9pm Sun–Thurs and 12–8pm Fri–Sat. Beer garden and patio. Children not allowed. Parking available. Annual beer festivals held.

11.30am–11pm Mon–Sat; 12–10.30pm Sun.

The Old Black Bull

35 Friargate, Preston PR1 2AT
☎ *(01772) 823397* Stan Eaton

A beer from Cains is among those permanently served. The eight guest beers are changed every couple of days, and might include Timothy Taylor Landlord and Fuller's London Pride.

Old traditional pub in the town centre. Food served until 4pm. Pool and darts, patio. Live music on Saturday nights. Children allowed during the daytime.

 *10.30am–11pm Mon–Sat; 12–10.30pm Sun.*

The Stanley Arms

Lancaster Road, Preston PR1 1DA
☎ *(01772) 254004* Anthony Quinn

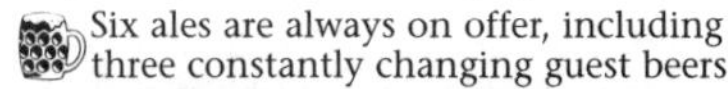
Six ales are always on offer, including three constantly changing guest beers.

A traditional pub in a Grade II listed building. Food available 11am–7pm Mon–Sat and 12.30–6pm Sun. Big-screen TV. The restaurant on the second floor is available for hire.

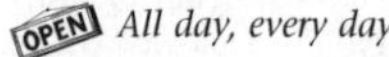 *All day, every day.*

UPHOLLAND

The White Lion

10 Church Street, Upholland WN8 0ND
☎ *(01695) 622727* Paul Tilling

Tied to Thwaites, so Thwaites Best Bitter permanently available, plus a guest changed every couple of weeks.

Village pub built in the sixteenth century, with many of the original features still present. Plans to serve food (ring to check). Traditional pub games such as darts and dominoes, big-screen TV. Non-smoking dining area, beer garden and car park. Children welcome. Functions catered for.

4–11pm Mon–Wed; 12–11pm Thurs–Sat; 12–10.30pm Sun.

WHALLEY

The Swan Hotel

62 King Street, Whalley BB7 9SN
☎ *(01254) 822195* Liz and Sara White

Four cask ales always available, including one changing guest.

A small, friendly, family-run hotel. Food served 12–3pm and 5–8.45pm Mon–Thurs, 12–3pm and 5–7.45pm Fri, 12–7.45pm Sat, and 12–6.45pm Sun. Well-behaved children allowed until 6pm. Car park.

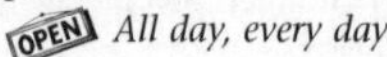 *All day, every day.*

WHARLES

The Eagle & Child Inn

Church Road, Wharles, Nr Kirkham
☎ *(01772) 690312* Brian Tatham

Two guest beers regularly available perhaps from Clark's, Wadworth or Eccleshall.

Relaxed atmosphere and lovely antiques in this Grade II listed thatched country inn (circa 1650) on the Fylde coast. No food. Large car park. Well-behaved children welcome, subject to licensing regulations.

7–11pm Mon–Sat; 12–4pm and 7–10.30pm Sun.

WHEELTON

The Dresser's Arms

9 Briers Brow, Wheelton, Chorley PR6 8HD
☎ *(01254) 830041* Steve and Trudie Turner

A true freehouse with eight hand pumps serving one or two Old Wheelton brews at any one time, plus a selection of ales from Timothy Taylor, Phoenix, Hart, Pictish and any local micro-brewery. The Old Wheelton Brewery is located on the same premises, but operates independently.

A village pub with oak beams, real fires and a cosy atmosphere. Food available with separate Cantonese restaurant upstairs. Beer garden. Car park. Children allowed.

11am–11pm Mon–Sat; 12–10.30pm Sun.

WRIGHTINGTON

Hinds Head

Mossy Lea Road, Wrightington, Nr Wigan WN6 9RN
☎ *(01257) 421168* Mr Ferro

Two guest ales always available such as Greene King Old Speckled Hen.

A big traditional pub with restaurant, beer garden and bowling green. Food available. Children allowed.

11am–2.30pm Tues–Thurs; 5.30–11pm Mon–Thurs; all day Fri–Sun.

THE BREWERIES

BELVOIR BREWERY LTD
6b Woodhill Industries, Nottingham Lane, Old Dalby LE14 3LX
☎ *(01664) 823455*
www.belvoirbrewery.co.uk

WHIPPLING GOLDEN BITTER 3.6% ABV
Light, refreshing and hoppy.
STAR BITTER 3.9% ABV
Citrus fruit and hoppy flavour.
BEAVER 4.3% ABV
Smooth, balanced with malt flavour and bitter finish.
PEACOCK'S GLORY 4.7% ABV
Golden, fruity and hoppy.
Plus occasional brews.

BLENCOWE BREWERY
The Exeter Arms, Main Street, Barrowden, Rutland LE15 8EQ
☎ *(01572) 747247*

BARROWDEN BOYS 3.6% ABV
BEACH BOYS 3.8% ABV
LOVER BOYS 3.8% ABV
YOUNG BOYS 4.1% ABV
DANNY BOY 4.5% ABV
STRONG BOYS 5.0% ABV

BREWSTERS BREWING CO. LTD
Penn Lane, Stathern, Melton Mowbray LE14 4JA
☎ *(01949) 861868*
www.brewsters.co.uk

HOPHEAD 3.6% ABV
MARQUIS 3.8% ABV
MONTY'S MILD 4.0% ABV
BITTER 4.2% ABV
VPA 4.5% ABV
BELLYDANCER 5.2% ABV
Plus seasonals.

DOW BRIDGE BREWERY
2–3 Rugby Road, Catthorpe, Lutterworth LE17 6DA
☎ *(01788) 869121*

BONUM MILD 3.5% ABV
Traditional dark mild. Roast malt flavour with chocolate hints.
BITTER 3.8% ABV
Well-hopped session bitter.
RATAE'D 4.3% ABV
Straw coloured. Strong hop aroma, with bitter hop finish.
FOSSE ALE 4.8% ABV
Occasional festival brew. Rounded fruity bitter.

EVERARDS BREWERY LTD
Castle Acres, Narborough LE19 5BY
☎ *(0116) 2014100*
www.everards.co.uk

BEACON BITTER 3.8% ABV
Award-winning, fresh, clean taste.
TIGER BEST BITTER 4.2% ABV
Good body, dry hopped.
OLD ORIGINAL 5.2% ABV
Copper-brown and sweetish.
Plus seasonal beers.

THE FEATHERSTONE BREWERY
Unit 3 King Street Buildings, King Street, Enderby LE9 5NT
☎ *(0116) 275 0952*

HOWS HOWLER 3.6% ABV
BEST BITTER 4.2% ABV
STAGE ALE 4.8% ABV
VULCAN 5.1% ABV
Special:
KINGSTONE BITTER 7.2% ABV

THE GRAINSTORE BREWERY
Davises Brewing Co. Ltd, Station Approach, Oakham LE15 6RE
☎ *(01572) 770065 (Brewery tours)*

RUTLAND PANTHER 3.4% ABV
COOKING BITTER 3.6% ABV
Golden and well-balanced.
TRIPLE B 4.2% ABV
Malty sweetness with balancing hop flavours.
STEAMIN' BILLY BITTER 4.3% ABV
TEN FIFTY 5.0% ABV
Easy-drinking sweet maltiness, with bitter finish.
Seasonals:
GOLD 4.5% ABV
SPRINGTIME 4.5% ABV
THREE KINGS 4.5% ABV
TUPPING ALE 4.5% ABV
WINTER NIP 7.3% ABV

LANGTON BREWERY
The Bell Inn, Main Street, East Langton, Market Harborough LE16 7TW
☎ *(01858) 545278*
www.thebellinn.co.uk

CAUDLE BITTER 3.9% ABV
BOWLER STRONG ALE 4.8% ABV

PARISH BREWERY
6 Main Street, Burrough-on-the-Hill, Melton Mowbray, Leicester LE14 2JQ
☎ *(01664) 454801*

PARISH MILD 3.9% ABV
FARM GOLD 4.0% ABV
PARISH SPECIAL BITTER 4.1% ABV
BURROUGH BITTER 4.8% ABV
BAZ'S BONCE BLOWER 11.0% ABV

SHARDLOW BREWING CO. LTD

Old Brewery Stables, British Waterways Yard, Cavendish Bridge DE72 2HL
☎ *(01332) 799188*

CHANCELLOR'S REVENGE 3.6% ABV
CAVENDISH DARK 3.7% ABV
SPECIAL BITTER 3.9% ABV
GOLDENHOP 4.1% ABV
KILN HOUSE 4.1% ABV
NARROWBOAT 4.3% ABV
OLD STABLE BREW 4.4% ABV
CAVENDISH GOLD 4.5% ABV
REVEREND EATON'S 4.5% ABV
MAYFLY 4.8% ABV
Pale premium bitter.
FIVE BELLS 5.0% ABV
Ruby-coloured with bittersweet finish.
PLATINUM BLONDE 5.0% ABV
WHISTLE STOP 5.0 ABV
FROSTBITE 6.0% ABV
CHRISTMAS ALE.
Plus occasional brews.

WICKED HATHERN BREWERY

46 Derby Road, Hathern, Loughborough LE12 5LD
☎ *(01509) 842585*

HAWTHORN GOLD 3.5% ABV
WHB (WICKED HATHERN BITTER) 3.8% ABV
SOAR HEAD 4.8% ABV

THE PUBS

ASHBY DE LA ZOUCH

The Ashby Court Hotel

34 Wood Street, Ashby de la Zouch LE65 1EL
☎ *(01530) 415176* Paul

A freehouse with real ales from Shardlow plus various guest beers.

Mock-Tudor town pub with spacious restaurant. Ten en-suite letting rooms. Accompanied children allowed. Car park.

11.30am–2.30pm and 5–11pm Mon–Thurs; 11.30am–11pm Fri–Sat; 12–10.30pm Sun.

AYLESTONE

The Black Horse

65 Narrow Lane, Aylestone
☎ *(0116) 283 2811* Stuart and Pauline Fraser

Everards Beacon, Tiger, Original and seasonal ales always on offer, plus guest beers from Old English Ale Club.

Village community pub in a nineteenth-century building, recently refurbished. Lounge, bar, non-smoking snug, function room, long alley skittles, garden. Food available.

12–2.30pm and 5–11pm Mon–Thurs; 12–11pm Fri–Sat; 12–4pm and 7–10.30pm Sun.

BARROW ON SOAR

The Navigation

Mill Lane, Barrow on Soar LE12 8LQ
☎ *(01509) 412842* Pete Lane

Old Laxey Bosun Bitter, Belvoir Star Bitter, Marston's Pedigree and Banks's Bitter are the beers always on offer, and the two guests, changed every three or four days, might feature Greene King Abbot, Shepherd Neame Bishop's Finger or Spitfire, or Morrells Varsity.

Village pub on the river, with garden for 75 people. Food is available, and there is a non-smoking dining area. The pub has two darts teams. Children allowed. Can be difficult to find, so ask locally or phone for directions.

11am–11pm Mon–Sat; 12–10.30pm Sun.

BARROWDEN

The Exeter Arms

Main Street, Barrowden, Rutland LE15 8EQ
☎ *(01572) 747247 Mr Peter Blencowe*
www.exeterarms.com

Home of the Blencowe Brewing Company. A full range of brews is always available (and only sold here). Also various guests such as Fuller's London Pride, Greene King IPA and seasonal ales from various brewers. The aim is only to repeat the guest beers a maximum of three times a year.

A very traditional country pub, situated off the beaten track. One bar, huge garden. Brewery tours by appointment only. Food available Tues–Sun lunchtimes and Tues–Sat evenings. Accommodation consists of two twin rooms and one double. Children allowed. Ring for directions.

11am–2.30pm and 6–11pm (10.30pm Sun, closed Mon lunchtime).

EAST LANGTON

The Bell Inn

Main Street, East Langton, Market Harborough
☎ *(01858) 545278*
www.thebellinn.co.uk

Home of the Langton Brewery. Home brews always available plus a range of real ales. Greene King Abbot and IPA, Timothy Taylor Landlord, Marston's Pedigree and Jennings ales are regular features but unusual brews are stocked whenever possible. Also a good range of wines.

A traditional county pub in the heart of the Leicestershire countryside. Friendly village pub atmosphere. Freshly prepared food available every lunchtime and evening, from light bites to full meals. Traditional roasts on Sundays. Accommodation. Located 5 miles north of Market Harborough on the B6047.

11am–2.30pm and 7–11pm (10.30pm Sun).

FRISBY ON THE WREAKE

The Bell Inn

2 Main Street, Frisby on the Wreake LE7 2NJ
☎ *(01664) 434237* Mr Wells

A freehouse with Charles Wells Bombardier, Greene King Abbot and IPA among the beers permanently available, plus two guests.

A 250-year-old village pub. One bar serves two rooms. Outside seating and conservatory restaurant. Food served at lunchtime and evenings. Children allowed if eating.

12–2.30pm and 6–11pm (10.30pm Sun).

GLENFIELD

The Dominion

Tournament Road, Glenfield
☎ *(0116) 231 3789* Peter Flaherty

An Everards pub with Beacon and Tiger constantly available, plus one guest, perhaps Everards Original, or a seasonal beer.

Estate community pub offering pool, snooker, darts and games machines. Food served. Garden and patio, car park. Children allowed.

11am–3pm and 5–11pm Mon–Thurs; 11am–11pm Fri–Sat; 12–10.30pm Sun.

GLOOSTON

The Old Barn Inn

Andrews Lane, Glooston, Nr Market Harborough LE16 7ST
☎ *(01858) 545215* Phillip Buswell

Four beers (30 per year) always available from brewers such as Adnams, Hook Norton, Fuller's, Wadworth, Oakhill, Nene Valley, Ridley, Bateman, Thwaites, Leatherbritches, Mauldons, Cotleigh and Greene King.

A sixteenth-century village pub in rural location with a log fire, no juke box or games machines. Bar and restaurant food available in evenings and Sunday lunchtime. Car park. Catering for parties, receptions and meetings. Well-behaved children and dogs welcome. Accommodation. On an old Roman road between Hallaton and Tur Langton.

12–2.30pm Tues–Sun; 7–11pm Mon–Sat; 7–10.30pm Sun.

HOSE

The Rose & Crown

43 Bolton Lane, Hose LE14 4JE
☎ *(01949) 860424* Brian Morley

Greene King Abbot and IPA are permanently available, plus three other real ales, changing constantly.

Not easy to find at the back of the village, this modernised open-plan bar has an olde-worlde lounge with open fire, attractive bar with darts and pool plus background music. Beamed restaurant open Thurs–Sun is available for functions. Large car park and gardens.

12–2.30pm and 7–11pm (5–11pm Fri); closed Mon, Tues, Wed lunchtimes.

KIRBY MUXLOE

The Royal Oak

Main Street, Kirby Muxloe, Leicester LE9 2AN
☎ *(0116) 239 3166* Mr Jackson

An Everards house with Tiger, Beacon and Old Original always available. Also two guest pumps serving beers such as Greene King Abbot Ale, Nethergate Old Growler or an Adnams brew.

A food-oriented village pub. Modern building with traditional decor. Function facilities. Disabled access. Garden. Food available at lunchtime and evenings. Children allowed.

11am–3pm and 5.30–11pm (10.30pm Sun).

LEICESTER

The Ale Wagon

27 Rutland Street, Leicester LE1 1RE
☎ *(0116) 262 3330* Stephen Hoskins

A Hoskins Brewery house with four Hoskins ales always available, plus two or three guests from other micro-breweries.

A 1930s red brick corner pub, originally built as a hotel. Food available lunchtimes and evenings. Located on the corner of Rutland Street and Charles Street.

OPEN *11am–11pm Mon–Sat; 12–10.30pm Sun.*

The Barley Mow

93 Granby Street, Leicester LE1 6SB
☎ *(0116) 254 4663* Lee Boyd (manager)

Everards Tiger and Beacon are always on offer. Lazy Daze, also from Everards, is often featured as one of the two weekly changing guests, and beers such as Jennings Cocker Hoop and Clark's Ram's Revenge have also been served.

Regulars' pub in the city, with one main bar and another upstairs, used when necessary. Food available. Karaoke on Wednesdays. No children allowed. One minute from the station on the way to the city centre.

 *11am–11pm Mon–Fri; 12–11pm Sat; closed Sun.*

The Globe

43 Silver Street, Leicester LE1 5EU
☎ *(0116) 262 9819* Hugh and Janet Kerr

Tied to Everards, so Beacon, Tiger and Original are pemanent fixtures. Occasional and seasonal beers such as Everards Lazy Daze put in appearances, alongside guests from further afield.

Built in 1723, this regular local drinkers' pub has two bar areas and a snug. Gas lighting. Children not allowed. Food served every day 12–7pm. Function room with bar upstairs available for hire. Close to The Shires shopping centre.

OPEN *11am–11pm Mon–Sat; 12–10.30pm Sun.*

The Hat & Beaver

60 Highcross Street, Leicester LE1 4NN
☎ *(0116) 2622157* Anthony Cartwright

Hardys & Hansons tied house serving Mild, Best Bitter and Olde Trip plus seasonal and occasional ales.

Traditional nineteenth-century town-centre pub with two rooms. Pub games. Filled cob rolls available at lunchtimes and on request. Children allowed until 6pm. On the edge of the city.

OPEN *12–3pm and 6–11pm Mon–Thur; 12–11pm Fri–Sat; 12–10.30pm Sun.*

Molly O'Gradys

14 Hotel Street, Leicester LE1 5AW
☎ *(0116) 251 8992*
Siobhan Corrigan and Michael Reeves

Everards Beacon and Tiger are always available at this Everards pub.

Traditional city-centre drinkers' pub in an old building, with fireplaces and wooden interior, known for its live music. Food served at lunchtimes, six days a week. Children not allowed. Situated just off the market place.

 *11am–11pm Mon–Thurs; 11am–1am Fri–Sat; 12–10.30pm Sun.*

The North Bridge Tavern

Frog Island, Leicester LE3 5AG
☎ *(0116) 251 2508* Rod Woodward

A freehouse with Marston's Pedigree always available plus one guest, often from a small local brewery.

A food-oriented town pub. One bar, function room. Non-smoking dining area. Traditional building with disabled access. Food available all day. Children allowed.

OPEN *All day, every day.*

The Swan & Rushes

19 Infirmary Square, Leicester LE1 5WR
☎ *(0116) 233 9167* Grant Cook

Hardys & Hansons Kimberley Best Bitter and Oakham JHB permanently available, plus up to five guests which often include Oakham Bishop's Farewell, Burton Bridge Golden Delicious, Newby Wyke White Squall, Hardys & Hansons Kimberley Mild. There is usually a mild on at least one pump. No nationals. Seasonal beers come from all over the UK. Also a range of imported beers including ales from the Czech Republic and Belgium, and 150 top-quality bottled beers

A triangular pub, built in the 1920s, with a comfortable interior and a small garden with outside seating. Food available every lunchtime and Mon–Sat evenings. Weekly quiz nights, occasional live entertainment. Located at the southern end of Oxford Street.

OPEN *12–11pm (10.30pm Sun).*

LOUGHBOROUGH

The Albion Inn

Canal Bank, Loughborough LE11 1QA
☎ *(01509) 213952* Mr Hartley

Robinson's Best, Brains Dark and something from the Wicked Hathern Brewery always available plus guests such as Shepherd Neame Spitfire and Early Bird, Black Sheep Special or brews from Greene King.

A traditional two-bar pub with garden, situated on the canal bank. Disabled access. Food available at lunchtimes and early evenings. Well-behaved children allowed. Car park.

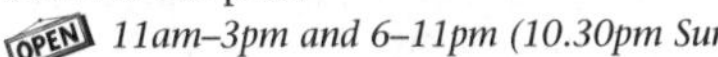
11am–3pm and 6–11pm (10.30pm Sun).

The Swan in the Rushes

21 The Rushes, Loughborough LE11 5BE
☎ *(01509) 217014* Ian Bogie
www.tynemill.co.uk

Castle Rock Rushes Gold and Rock Harvest Pale Ale plus Archers Golden always available. Six guest beers generally include a mild and brews from anywhere and everywhere. About 20 different guest beers are sold each week.

A cosmopolitan town-centre alehouse, smart yet down to earth, with a friendly atmosphere. Home-cooked bar food served lunchtimes and weekday evenings. Two bars and one non-smoking room. Function room, car park and accommodation. Children allowed in designated areas. Two beer festivals held annually, in spring and November. On the A6, behind Sainsbury's.

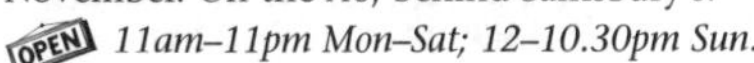
11am–11pm Mon–Sat; 12–10.30pm Sun.

Tap & Mallet

36 Nottingham Road, Loughborough LE11 1EU
☎ *(01509) 210028* Steve Booth

Marston's Pedigree permanently available, plus five guests. Regulars include beers from Abbeydale, Archers, Brewster's, Church End, Cottage, Hook Norton, Mallard, Rooster's, Shardlow, Stonehenge, Oakham and Oldershaw, to name but a few. Traditional scrumpy also served.

The pub features a good selection of well-kept beers, plus a large garden, which includes a children's play area and pets' corner with rabbits and birds.

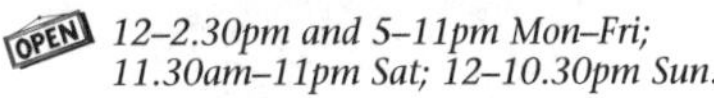
12–2.30pm and 5–11pm Mon–Fri; 11.30am–11pm Sat; 12–10.30pm Sun.

The Three Nuns

30 Churchgate, Loughborough LE11 1UD
☎ *(01509) 611989* Steve Wesson

An Everards pub serving Tiger, Beacon and Original, plus two guests, changed every six weeks, often including Everards Lazy Daze and Perfick.

The second oldest pub in town, with wood-panelled interior. Food available. Live rock bands on Saturdays. Garden seating area, car park. Children allowed until 8pm.

11am–11pm Mon–Sat; 12–10.30pm Sun.

MARKET BOSWORTH

Ye Olde Red Lion

1 Park Street, Market Bosworth CV13 0LL
☎ *(01455) 291713* Eddie Davies

Tied to Banks's, with Bitter and Original plus Marston's Pedigree among the beers always on offer. The two guests are changed every few days, and include something from Frankton Bagby once a month, with beers from Church End, Lloyds and Cottage making regular appearances. Seasonal and celebration ales are also featured.

Small market-town pub, over 400 years old, very close to the countryside. Beams and fires in winter. Food is served every day at lunchtime, plus Tues–Sat evening, and there is a non-smoking dining area. Live jazz once a month, quiz night on first Sunday of month, Irish music four times a year (call for details). Patio, car park, four letting rooms. Children allowed.

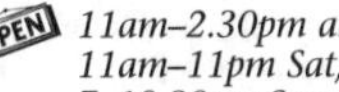
11am–2.30pm and 5.30–11pm Mon–Fri; 11am–11pm Sat; 11am–3pm and 7–10.30pm Sun.

MEDBOURNE

The Nevill Arms

Medbourne, Market Harborough LE16 8EE
☎ *(01858) 565288* Mr and Mrs N Hall

A freehouse with Adnams Bitter, Greene King Abbot and Fuller's London Pride always available plus two guests changing every month. Guests are often seasonal.

A traditional, two-bar country pub. Outside seating on benches near a brook. Bed and breakfast accommodation available in 6-bedroom cottage next door. Bar food served at lunchtime and evenings. Function room available for hire (suitable for weddings and parties for up to 70 people). Well-behaved children allowed.

12–2.30pm and 6–11pm Mon–Sat; 12–3pm and 7–10.30pm Sun.

OADBY

The Cow & Plough

Stoughton Farm Park, Gartree Road, Oadby LE2 2FB
☎ *(0116) 272 0852* Barry and Elisabeth Lount

A freehouse with an ever-changing range of beers, many from micro-breweries. Home of Steamin' Billy beers (brewed by Grainstore), with Grand Prix Mild and Steamin' Billy Bitter always available. Steamin' Billy seasonals include BSB, Country Bitter, Lazy Summer and Skydiver.

A converted barn on a working farm, with ornate Victorian bar and large non-smoking conservatory. Twice CAMRA East Midlands Pub of the Year. A restaurant has been added in a converted dairy with sandwiches and fresh, modern English food available at lunchtime and evenings. Bar snacks in the pub. Large car park.

5–10pm Monday; 12–3pm and 5–11pm Tues–Fri; 12–11pm Sat; 12–5pm and 7–10pm Sun.

OAKHAM

The Grainstore Brewery Tap

Station Approach, Oakham, Rutland LE15 6RE
☎ *(01572) 770065 Tony Davis*

The home of The Grainstore Brewery, so Cooking Bitter, Triple B, Ten Fifty and Rutland Panther are always available plus Steamin' Billy on a guest basis along with other seasonal ales.

A traditional three-storey old grainstore, situated next to the railway station. One bar; outside seating. Live jazz on Sunday afternoons once a month. Brewery tours by appointment. Pub grub at lunchtimes only. The Rutland Beer Festival is held over the August bank holiday. Next to the railway station.

11.30am–11pm Mon–Sat; 12–10.30pm Sun.

OLD DALBY

The Crown Inn

Debdale Hill, Old Dalby, Nr Melton Mowbray LE14 3LF
☎ *(01664) 823134* Alan and Lorraine Hale

Four real ales available, some served straight from the cask behind the bar. These are likely to include Marston's Pedigree, Charles Wells Bombadier and Theakston Old Peculiar. Regular guests are featured, often from the local Belvoir brewery.

Built in 1590, a pub with six small rooms, oak beams, open fires, antique furniture and prints. Large patio and terrace with orchard at bottom of the garden. Beer served from cellar near back door. Bar and restaurant food served at lunchtime (not Mon) and evenings (not Sun or Mon). Car park, petanque pitch. Children welcome. Many special events throughout the year. From Nottingham on the A606, turn right at Nether Broughton for Old Dalby.

6–11pm Mon; 12–3pm and 6–11pm Tues–Sat; 12–3pm and 7–10.30pm Sun.

SADDINGTON

The Queens Head

Main Street, Saddington
☎ *(0116) 2402536*
Christine and Steve Bebbington

Everards Beacon and Tiger always available, plus alternating guests.

A nicely situated, award-winning country inn and restaurant, under new management from 2003. The garden has lovely views over Saddington Reservoir. Previous Leicestershire Tourist Board Pub Meal of the Year winner. Food served 12–2pm and 6.30–9pm, but not on Sunday evenings. Large car park. Situated near to Fleckney.

11am–3pm and 5.30–11pm (10.30pm Sun).

SHAWELL

White Swan Inn

Main Street, Shawell, Nr Lutterworth LE17 6AG
☎ *(01788) 860357* Mike and Susan Walker

Greene King Abbot and IPA always available, plus a regularly changing guest ale.

Built in the main street of a small hamlet in around 1700, it retains many original features. Local skittles in the bar. Non-smoking restaurant and separate dining area for smokers. Seating to the front of the pub. Food served all opening times. Accommodation available, including log cabins. Car park. Children welcome. Located 5 minutes from M1, M6, A14 and A5.

7–11pm Tues–Sat; 12–3pm Sun (closed all day Mon, Tues–Sat lunchtimes and Sun evenings).

SHEARSBY

Chandler's Arms

Village Green, Shearsby, Nr Lutterworth LE17 6PL
☎ *(0116) 247 8384* Mr Ward

Fuller's London Pride and Marston's Pedigree and Bitter always available plus four guests. Beers featured include Greene King Abbot, Wadworth 6X, Exmoor Gold or brews from Timothy Taylor or Jennings.

A seventeenth-century red-brick pub overlooking the village green, with a three-tier prize-winning garden. Two lounges. AA recommended. International cuisine served at lunchtime and evenings. Children allowed.

OPEN *12–2.30pm and 6.30–11pm (10.30pm Sun).*

SMISBY

The Anwell Inn (also known as Mother Hubbard)

Anwell Lane, Smisby, Ashby de la Zouch LE65 2TA
☎ *(01530) 413604* Chris and Kathleen

Three real ales always available. Favourites include Ruddles brews and Marston's Pedigree.

An olde-worlde pub situated in the heart of a farming community, known locally as The Mother Hubbard in honour of the previous landlady. Exposed beams and a bar built from old church fittings. Separate restaurant/function room. Food available 12–2.30pm Wed–Sat; 6–9.30pm Mon–Sat; 12–6pm Sun. Children allowed until 9.30pm, if eating. Beer garden with barbecue area.

OPEN *12–2.30pm Wed–Sat (closed Mon–Tues lunch); 5.30–11pm Mon–Sat; 12–6pm Sun.*

SOMERBY

The Old Brewery Inn

High Street, Somerby, Leicester LE14 2PZ
☎ *(01664) 454777* Wendy and Mick Farmer

Freehouse serving a range of locally brewed ales, including Parish beers such as Baz's Bonce Blower (11% ABV). Guest beers are also available, perhaps Greene King IPA or Bateman XXXB .

Fifteenth-century coaching inn with a large bar and a non-smoking dining room. Good home-cooked food served Tues–Sun. Walled garden with bouncy castle. Accommodation.

OPEN *12–2.30pm and 6–11pm Mon–Sat (closed Mon lunch); 12–10.30pm Sun.*

The Stilton Cheese Inn

High Street, Somerby LE14 2QB
☎ *(01664) 454394* Jeff Evans

Five real ales always on offer. Marston's Pedigree and Grainstore Ten Fifty are among the regulars, plus two constantly changing guest beers, mainly from local micro-breweries. Guest cider on hand pump also available, as well as over 25 malt whiskies and a good wine list.

A sixteenth-century stone freehouse, with beams, two rooms (one non-smoking) and an upstairs restaurant seating 40. Decorated throughout with dried hops and hunting prints. The beams are covered in pump clips from previous guest beers. Food served daily 12–2pm and 6–9pm. Children allowed. Small patio with seating for 20. B&B facilities were planned at the time of going to press.

OPEN *12–3pm and 6–11pm Mon–Sat; 12–3pm and 7–10.30pm Sun.*

SUTTON BASSETT

The Queen's Head

Main Street, Sutton Bassett, Market Harborough LE16 8HP
☎ *(01858) 463530* Melvyn Foot

A freehouse with up to eight real ales including Timothy Taylor Landlord, Adnams Bitter and Greene King IPA plus a selection of guests running into hundreds of different brews each year.

A friendly country pub with traditional decor, real fires, front and back bars. Disabled facilities on ground floor. Patio, beer garden and petanque court. Food served at lunchtime and evenings. Large parties and functions catered for. Children allowed. Prettily situated with views of the Welland valley. Annual beer festival.

OPEN *12–2.30pm and 5–11.30pm Mon–Fri; all day Sat–Sun.*

THORPE SATCHVILLE

The Fox Inn

Main Street, Thorpe Satchville, Melton Mowbray LE14 2DQ
☎ *(01664) 840257* Kevin and Denise

A freehouse offering John O'Gaunt Robin a Tiptoe and Coat O' Red, plus another guest.

Country pub built in 1938. Two bars, games room , skittle alley and petanque courts. Food is available Tues–Sun 12.30–2pm and 7–9pm. Beer garden and patio. Children welcome. Large car park. Between Melton Mowbray and Market Harborough on the B6047.

OPEN *12–3pm and 6–11pm (10.30pm Sun); closed Mon lunch.*

THURNBY

The Swallow

Station Road, Thurnby LE7 9PU
☎ *(0116) 241 9087* Ross Allibone

Everards Tiger, Beacon and Old Original are always served at this Everards tied house. The two guests might include Greene King Old Speckled Hen, something from Adnams, or seasonals like Everards Lazy Daze.

Community pub built in the sixties, with two bars, conservatory, garden and play area. Food is served, and there is a non-smoking restaurant area. Live music Sat and Sun evenings. Disabled facilities, car park. Children allowed until 8pm.

 *11.30am–11pm Mon–Fri; 11am–11pm Sat; 12–10.30pm Sun.*

WALCOTE

The Black Horse

Lutterworth Road, Walcote LE17 4JU
☎ *(01455) 552684* Mrs Tinker

Timothy Taylor Landlord, Greene King Abbot and Oakham Jeffrey Hudson Bitter always available plus two guest beers (75 per year) always from independent breweries.

A one-bar village pub. Bar and restaurant food available at lunchtime and evenings. Authentic Thai cooking. Car park, garden and children's room. One mile east of M1 junction 20.

 *6.30–11pm Mon–Thurs; 12–2pm and 5.30–11pm Fri; 6.30–11pm Sat; 12–3.30pm and 6.30–10.30pm Sun.*

WALTHAM-ON-THE-WOLDS

The Marquis of Granby

High Street, Waltham-on-the-Wolds LE14 4HA
☎ *(01664) 464212* Melanie Dawson

An Everards pub with Tiger and Original plus something from Adnams permanently available, together with one guest, changed every couple of weeks, often a beer from Everards such as Perfick.

A 400-year-old village pub with beams and fires. Food served. Occasional live music. Garden and patio. Children allowed.

 *12–2.30pm and 5.30–11.30pm Mon–Fri; 11am–11pm Sat; 12–10.30pm Sun.*

WIGSTON MAGNA

The Horse & Trumpet

Bull Head Street, Wigston Magna LE18 1PB
☎ *(0116) 288 6290* Andy Moone

Tied to Everards, and always featuring Original, Tiger and Beacon.

Characterful community local in a very old building, with one open-plan bar. Food served at lunchtimes. Live music on Thurs evenings. Patio, skittle alley, function room, car park. No children.

 *11am–2.30pm and 5–11pm Mon–Fri; 11am–2.30pm and 6–11pm Sat; 12–4pm and 7–10.30pm Sun.*

WYMESWOLD

The Hammer & Pincers

5 East Road, Wymeswold, Loughborough LE12 6ST
☎ *(01509) 880735* Mrs T Williomson

A freehouse with Ruddles County and Marston's Pedigree always on offer, plus one weekly changing guest from the Grainstore brewery, such as Ten Fifty or Gold.

Traditional country village pub dating from the sixteenth century, with beams and fires. Food available. Garden, patio and car park. Children allowed.

 *12–2.30pm and 6–11pm Mon–Fri; 12–3pm and 6–11pm Sat; 12–3pm and 7–10.30pm Sun.*

The Three Crowns

45 Far Street, Wymeswold, Loughborough LE12 6TZ
☎ *(01509) 880153* Wayne and Amanda Sharpe

Marston's Pedigree, Adnams Bitter and Highgate Dark Mild are permanent features. The two guests, changed regularly, are often beers from Castle Rock (such as Hemlock), Belvoir (such as Whippling), Springhead or Archers , but other breweries also feature.

Country pub, over 300 years old, with original beams, open fires and a traditional atmosphere. Food available at lunchtimes and Tues–Sat evenings. One bar, lounge, snug and non-smoking eating area, decked beer garden and car park. Families and pets welcome. Function room available. Quiz nights (first Monday in the month) and occasional live music. In the middle of the village, opposite the church.

OPEN *12–3pm and 5.30–11pm Mon–Sat; 12–3pm and 7–10.30pm Sun.*

THE BREWERIES

BLUE BELL BREWERY
Cranesgate South, Whaplode St Catherine, Spalding PE12 6SN
☎ *(01406) 701000*
www.bluebellbrewery.co.uk

SESSION ALE 3.7% ABV
OLDE HONESTY 4.1% ABV
OLDE FASHIONED 4.8% ABV
Plus seasonal ales.

THE BLUE COW BREWERY
29 High Street, South Witham, Nr Grantham NG33 5QB
☎ *(01572) 768432*

THIRLWELL'S BEST 3.8% ABV
WITHAM WOBBLER 4.5% ABV

GEORGE BATEMAN & SON LTD
Salem Bridge Brewery, Mill Lane, Wainfleet, Skegness PE24 4JE
☎ *(01754) 880317*
www.bateman.co.uk

DARK MILD 3.0% ABV
Dark and fruity, some roast malt, hoppy finish.
XB 3.7% ABV
Distinctive, refreshing dry bitterness.
SALEM PORTER 4.7% ABV
Dry, nutty, rich malt and superb hop flavours.
XXXB 4.8% ABV
Multi-faceted malt and fruit character.
Plus a seasonal and special selection.

DARKTRIBE BREWERY
25 Doncaster Road, Gunness, Scunthorpe DN15 8TG
☎ *(01724) 782324*
www.darktribe.co.uk

DIXIE'S MILD 3.6% ABV
Dark, tasty award-winner.
HONEY MILD 3.6% ABV
Dark with a hint of honey.
FULL AHEAD 3.8% ABV
Dry-hopped bitter.
ALBACORE 4.0% ABV
Beautifully pale and hoppy.
RED DUSTER 4.0% ABV
STERN WHEELER 4.2% ABV
BUCKET HITCH 4.4% ABV
DIXIE'S BOLLARDS 4.5% ABV
Ginger beer.
DR GRIFFIN'S MERMAID 4.5% ABV
OLD GAFFER 4.5% ABV
GALLEON 4.7% ABV
Popular award-winner.
TWIN SCREW 5.1% ABV
MIDNIGHT RUNNER 6.5% ABV
DARK DESTROYER 9.7% ABV

FUGELESTOU ALES
Fulstow Brewery, 6 Northway, Fulstow, Louth, North Lincs LN11 0XH
☎ *(01507) 363642*

FULSTOW COMMON 3.8%
WAT PASTURE 4.3%
SWEATING SICKNESS 6.1%
SUMERHEADE 4.7%
Beer names have come from an early medieval enclosure map of Fugelestou (Fulstow) apart from Sweating Sickness which is what the plague was called at the time.

HIGHWOOD BREWERY LTD
Melton Highwood, Barnetby DN38 6AA
☎ *(01472) 255500*
www.tom-wood.com

TOM WOOD BEST BITTER 3.5% ABV
Well-hopped and refreshing.
TOM WOOD SHEPHERD'S DELIGHT 4.0% ABV
Easy-quaffing and full-flavoured.
TOM WOOD HARVEST 4.3% ABV
Soft and full-flavoured.
TOM WOOD OLD TIMBER 4.5% ABV
Smooth and full-flavoured.
TOM WOOD BOMBER COUNTY 4.8% ABV
Red, with good hoppy flavour.
Seasonals:
TOM WOOD BARN DANCE 4.2% ABV
TOM WOOD LINCOLNSHIRE LEGEND 4.2% ABV
Good, hoppy bitterness throughout.
TOM WOOD SUMMER DAYS 4.4% ABV

NEWBY WYKE BREWERY
Willoughby Arms Cottages, Station Road, Little Bytham NG33 4RA
☎ *(01780) 411119*
www.newbywyke.co.uk

SIDEWINDER 3.8% ABV
GRANTHAM GOLD 4.2% ABV
STAMFORD GOLD 4.4% ABV
BEAR ISLAND 4.6% ABV
WHITE SQUALL 4.8% ABV
CHELSEA PALE 5.5% ABV
Plus seasonals and occasionals.

OLDERSHAW BREWERY
12 Harrowby Hall Estate, Grantham NG31 9HB
☎ *(01476) 572135*
www.oldershawbrewery.co.uk

HIGH DYKE 3.9% ABV
Gold-coloured with good hoppiness.
NEWTON'S DROP 4.1% ABV
Golden and hoppy.
CASKADE 4.2% ABV
Light, clean-tasting.
ERMINE ALE 4.2% ABV
Pale and refreshing hoppiness.
AHTANUM GOLD 4.3% ABV
New Zealand hops.
REGAL BLONDE 4.4% ABV
Cask-conditioned lager.
OLD BOY 4.8% ABV
Golden chestnut colour with good balance.
Plus a large range of occasional and special brews.

POACHERS BREWERY

Unit 4 Camp Road, Witham St Hughs, Lincoln LN6 97W
☎ *(01522) 668889*

SUMMA SHY TALK BITTER 3.7% ABV
POACHERS PRIDE 4.0% ABV
POACHERS DEN 4.2% ABV
POACHERS TRAIL 4.2% ABV
POACHERS DICK 4.5% ABV

RIVERSIDE BREWERY

Unit 1 Church Lane, Wainfleet, Skegness PE24 4BY
☎ *(01754) 881288*
www.wainfleet.info/shops/brewery-riverside.htm

MAJOR 3.9% ABV
DESERT RAT 4.8% ABV

WILLY'S BREWERY

17 High Cliff Road, Cleethorpes DN35 8RQ
☎ *(01472) 602145*

WILLY'S ORIGINAL 3.7% ABV
WILLY'S LAST RESORT 4.3% ABV
WILLY'S WEISS BOUY 5.0% ABV
Pronounced 'vice boy'!
WILLY'S OLD GROYNE 6.2% ABV
Plus seasonals and celebration ales.

THE PUBS

ALLINGTON

The Welby Arms

The Green, Allington, Grantham NG32 2EA
☎ *(01400) 281361* Matt Rose and Anna Cragg

Six real ales usually available. Timothy Taylor Landlord, Ringwood Old Thumper, Badger Tanglefoot and Phoenix Wobbly Bob often feature.

A traditional freehouse on the village green with beams, log fires and terrace. Two bars, snug and 70-seater restaurant. Disabled access. Baguettes or soup available at lunchtime in the bar, plus restaurant food 12–2pm and 6.30–9pm. En-suite accommodation. Well-behaved children welcome at lunchtimes. Car park. Close to the Vale of Belvoir and Belvoir Castle.

12–2.30pm (3pm Sat, 4pm Sun) and 6–11pm (10.30pm Sun).

AUBOURN

The Royal Oak

Royal Oak Lane, Aubourn, Lincoln LN5 9DT
☎ *(01522) 788291*
Robert Varley and Rachael Blakebrough
www.royaloakaubourn.co.uk

Bateman XB, Greene King Abbot and Adnams Broadside and Timothy Taylor Landlord always available plus a guest beer changed twice a week.

A traditional village pub with character, open fires and beams. One bar, two rooms and separate restaurant. Bar food available 12–2pm (2.30pm Sun) and 6.30 or 7–9pm. Car park and heated patio plus private orchard and beer garden. Weekly quiz nights. Functions catered for. Children welcome until 8.30pm. South of Lincoln, off the A46.

12–2.30pm and 7–11pm (6.30–11pm Fri–Sat; 7–10.30pm Sun).

BARNACK

The Millstone Inn

Millstone Lane, Barnack, Nr Stamford PE9 3ET
☎ *(01780) 740296* Roger and Gill Wood

Everards Old Original and Tiger plus Adnams Bitter usually available, plus regularly changing guest beers supplied by Everards.

The inn was built in 1672 of Barnack rag stone which was quarried nearby. The interior is olde-worlde with beamed ceilings. Walled courtyard. Food served 11.30am–2pm Mon–Sun and 6.30–9pm Mon–Sat. Children welcome. Car park.

11.30am–2.30pm and 5–11pm Mon–Fri; 11am–11pm Sat; 12–10.30pm Sun.

BELCHFORD

The Bluebell Inn

Main Road, Belchford LN9 6LQ
☎ *(01507) 533602 Darren and Shona Jackson*

Black Sheep Best, Greene King IPA and Flowers Original available, with plans to extend the range in future.

A village pub full of character on the Louth road north of Horncastle. No-smoking restaurant serves imaginative food 12–2pm Tues–Sun and 6.30–9pm Tues–Sat. Garden, accommodation, children welcome.

11.30am–2.30pm and 6.30–11pm Tues–Sat; 12–4pm Sun (closed Sun night and Mon).

BOSTON

The Carpenter's Arms

Witham Street, Boston PE21 6PU
☎ *(01205) 362840* Peter Reid

A Bateman house with XB always available plus two changing guests which are often other Bateman brews but also sometimes Marston's Pedigree, Greene King IPA or Old Speckled Hen, Tanners Jack and others.

A traditional one-bar town pub with games room, a real fire and outside seating during summer months. Food available 7–10pm Mon (spice night), 12–2pm and 4–7pm Wed–Fri, 12–5pm Sat–Sun. Well-behaved children allowed.

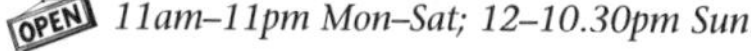
11am–11pm Mon–Sat; 12–10.30pm Sun.

The Eagle

144 West Street, Boston PE21 8RE
☎ *(01205) 361116* Andrew Rudolf

Five real ales usually available perhaps including Banks's Bitter, Castle Rock Harvest Pale, Everards Tiger, Bateman XXXB, Adnams Broadside and Hop Back Summer Lightning. May operate up to eight real ales during beer festivals.

A traditional local on the outskirts of Boston town centre. Two bars (one public, one lounge), real fires, pool room and function room (the venue for monthly meetings of the folk club). Regular beer festivals held throughout the year and brewery trips. Unconfirmed plans to serve food (phone to check).

 *11am–11pm Mon–Sat; 12–10.30pm Sun.*

BRANT BROUGHTON

The Generous Briton

72 High Street, Brant Broughton LN5 0RZ
☎ *(01400) 272119* Ian Philip

Adnams Bitter, Bateman XB and Greene King IPA usually available.

A rural pub of the year, reopened in 2002, with exposed brick and beamed ceilings. Food available at lunchtime and evening. Piped music.

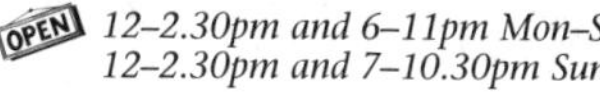
12–2.30pm and 6–11pm Mon–Sat; 12–2.30pm and 7–10.30pm Sun.

CAYTHORPE

The Red Lion Inn

62 High Street, Caythorpe, Grantham NG32 3DN
☎ *(01400) 272632* Ann Roberts

A freehouse serving Adnams Best plus up to three guests from every possible brewery. Glentworth and Slaters (Eccleshall) brews are particular favourites.

A seventeenth-century traditional country inn with two gardens and two bars. No music or games machines. Disabled access. Food available at lunchtime and evenings in a separate restaurant. Children allowed in the restaurant and one of the bars only.

 *11am–2.30pm and 6–11pm (10.30pm Sun).*

DYKE

The Wishing Well Inn

Main Street, Dyke, Bourne PE10 0AF
☎ *(01778) 422970* Mrs Gallacher

Everards Tiger and Greene King Abbot usually available plus three constantly changing beers from micro-breweries around the country.

Attractive country inn with accommodation and a large restaurant. Food served 12–2pm and 6.30–9pm daily. Children welcome. Large car park. One mile north of Bourne, off A15. Look for signs.

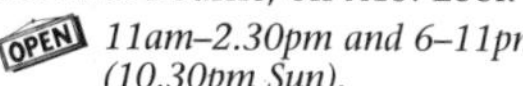
11am–2.30pm and 6–11pm (10.30pm Sun).

FROGNALL

The Goat

155 Spalding Road, Frognall, Market Deeping, Nr Peterborough PE6 8SA
☎ *(01778) 347629* Graham Stokes

Five or six real ales available from a wide variety of micro-breweries and brewpubs nationwide.

A country pub dating from 1647. Full bar menu served every lunchtime and evening, including seasonal specials as available. Functions catered for. Car park, large beer garden with play equipment, family dining area. Situated on the B1525 between Market Deeping and Spalding.

11.30am–2.30pm (3pm Sat) and 6–11pm Mon–Sat; 12–3pm and 6–10.30pm Sun.

GAINSBOROUGH

The Eight Jolly Brewers

Ship Court, Caskgate Street, Gainsborough DN21 2DL
☎ *(01427) 677128* Martin Langdale

Eight real ales usually available. Brews from Broadstone and Glentworth are permanent fixtures plus six guests changed daily from a wide range of micro-breweries.

A 300-year-old town-centre freehouse with two bars in a traditional building. Small outdoor area and patio. Non-smoking room. No food. No children. Private room available. Located near the Guildhall. Easy parking.

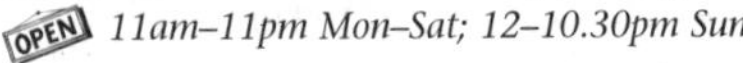
11am–11pm Mon–Sat; 12–10.30pm Sun.

GRAINTHORPE

The Black Horse Inn

Mill Lane, Grainthorpe, Louth LN11 78U
☎ *(01472) 388229* Mrs Donaghue

Beer from the Donoghue Brewery always available, plus Tom Wood Best and Fuller's London Pride. The guests could be something like Badger Tanglefoot or Greene King Abbot.

A cosy country village pub with a real ale theme. Open fires, beer garden with children's area. Food served every evening and at lunchtime at weekends and during the summer. Children allowed, if eating.

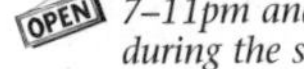
7–11pm and lunchtime at weekends and during the summer.

GRANTHAM

The Blue Bull

64 Westgate, Grantham NG31 6LA
☎ *(01476) 570929* Mr P Mitchell

Three cask ales always available, always including something from Newby Wyke, plus two other guest beers, perhaps from Greene King, Black Sheep or Shepherd Neame.

Pub dating from the 1850s. Bar food available at lunchtimes. Car park. Children allowed. Three minutes from the main line BR railway station.

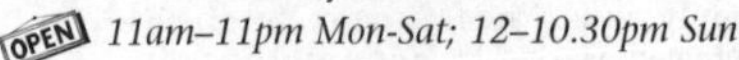
11am–11pm Mon-Sat; 12–10.30pm Sun.

HARMSTON

The Thorold Arms

High Street, Harmston, Lincoln LN5 9SN
☎ *(01522) 720358*
Julie Haycraft and Alison Welch
www.thoroldarms.co.uk

Four guest ales always on offer, one of which will be a Lincolnshire brew, while the other three could be any independent ales.

A rural pub with traditional decor and log fire. Disabled access and toilets. Food available at lunchtime (including Sunday roast) and evenings in a separate dining area. Small functions catered for. No children.

OPEN *12–3pm and 6–11pm (10.30pm Sun).*

KIRKBY ON BAIN

The Ebrington Arms

Main Street, Kirkby on Bain, Woodhall Spa LN10 6YT
☎ *(01526) 354560*

Bateman XB and Greene King Abbot Ale permanently available plus two guest ales from breweries such as Timothy Taylor, Woodforde's, Hook Norton, Fuller's and Bateman.

A typical English country pub with a strong local and seasonal trade and a reputation locally for good beer and good food. Bar food available 12–2pm every day and 7–9pm Tues–Sat. Traditional roasts on Sundays. Children allowed until 9pm. Pets also welcome. Large beer garden. Car park.

OPEN *12–2.30pm and 7–11pm Mon–Thurs; 12–2.30pm and 6.30–11pm Fri–Sat; 12–3pm and 7–11pm Sun.*

LAUGHTERTON

The Friendship Inn

Main Road, Laugherton, Lincoln LN21 2JZ
☎ *(01427) 718681* Diane Humphreys

A freehouse with Marston's Pedigree always available, plus guests, which may well be something from Brewster's, Slaters (Eccleshall) or another micro-brewery.

A traditional, friendly one-bar village pub. Log fires, garden, disabled access. Food available at lunchtime and evenings (except Sun evening) in a designated dining area. Children allowed.

OPEN *11.30am–2.30pm and 6–11pm Mon–Sat; 12–3pm and 7–10.30pm Sun.*

LINCOLN

The Golden Eagle

21 High Street, Lincoln LN5 8BD
☎ *(01522) 521058* James and Liz Middleton

A freehouse with Everards Beacon and Bateman XB always available plus one real cider. Four guest ales, rotating continually.

A locals' pub with two bars, one with no music or games machines, half a mile from the city centre. Snacks menu served 11am–7pm Mon–Fri. Car park and garden. Children not allowed in the pub.

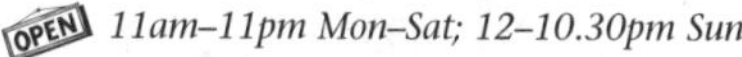
11am–11pm Mon–Sat; 12–10.30pm Sun.

The Portland

50 Portland Street, Lincoln LN5 7JX
☎ *(01522) 560564* Will and Lisa Stevenson

Seven real ales always on offer, including Greene King IPA. The rest, including a mild, change every few days.

Relaxed, games-orientated two-room pub with music and TV. Recently refurbished. Beer garden. Bar food available 12–2pm. Children welcome in beer garden. Car park. Off the high street, close to the train station and football ground.

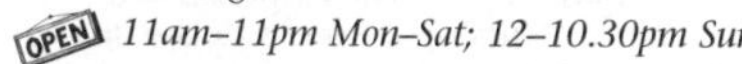
11am–11pm Mon–Sat; 12–10.30pm Sun.

Sippers Freehouse

26 Melville Street, Lincoln LN5 7HW
☎ *(01522) 527612* Joan Keightley

Hop Back GFB and Summer Lightning plus Marston's Pedigree always available plus three regularly changing guest beers (mostly from micro-breweries).

Traditional city-centre pub. Food served lunchtime and evenings Mon–Sat, lunchtime only Sun. Private functions catered for. Families welcome with children until 8.30pm.

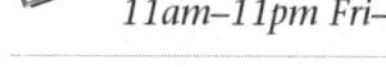
11am–3pm and 5–11pm Mon–Thurs; 11am–11pm Fri–Sat; 7–10.30pm Sun.

The Tap & Spile

21 Hungate, Lincoln LN1 1ES
☎ *(01522) 534015* Mr and Mrs Kay

Eight beers always available but the range changes daily. Approx 150 brews per year including Charles Wells Fargo, Thwaites Craftsman and Greene King IPA.

Formerly the White Horse, a city-centre pub with stone and wood floors, bare brick and plaster walls. Bar food available at lunchtime. Pay and display car park opposite. Children not allowed. At the top of the high street turn left, then 200 yards on the left near the police station.

OPEN *11am–11pm Mon–Sat; 12–3pm and 7–10.30pm Sun.*

The Victoria

6 Union Road, Lincoln LN1 3BJ
☎ *(01522) 536048* Neil Renshaw
www.tynemill.co.uk/lincoln/victoria6.htm

Up to nine beers always available including a mild, Castle Rock Harvest Gold, Timothy Taylor Landlord and Bateman XB. Plus guests (up to 1,000 per year) including Orkney Raven Ale, Brains Bitter, Exmoor Gold, Hop Back Summer Lightning and Adnams brews.

A traditional, two-bar Victorian terraced pub with a small patio, in the city by the west gate of the castle. Bar food available 12–2.30pm Mon–Fri, 11am–2.30pm Sat and 12–2pm Sun. Regular beer festivals and brewery feature nights. Attached cottage for rent. Next to the castle.

OPEN *11am–11pm Mon–Sat; 12–10.30pm Sun.*

LITTLE BYTHAM

The Willoughby Arms

Station Road, Little Bytham, Grantham NG33 4RA
☎ *(01780) 410276* Tony Shilling
www.willoughbyarms.co.uk

A freehouse with three real ales brewed by Newby Wyke Brewery at the rear of the pub, always on offer. Three ever-changing guest beers also available, all from micro-breweries from around the country.

Beamed country pub, around 150 years old, with open fire and garden with superb views over open countryside. Bar meals are available every lunchtime and evening, and there is a non-smoking dining room. Live music several times a month, especially during the twice-yearly beer and music festivals held over bank holiday weekends at the end of May and August. Six mini beer festivals are also held during the year. En-suite accommodation available. Six miles north of Stamford.

OPEN *12–2pm and 5–11pm Mon–Fri; 12–11pm Sat; 12–10.30pm Sun.*

LOUTH

Masons Arms Hotel

Cornmarket, Louth LN11 9PY
☎ *(01507) 609525* Ron Smith
www.themasons.co.uk

Bateman's XB and XXXB, Sam Smith Old Brewery Bitter, Timothy Taylor Landlord and Fuller's London Pride among the brews usually available.

Grade II listed, family-run town centre hotel on the market square. Food served 12–2pm and from 6.30pm every day. Children and dogs welcome, car park.

OPEN *10am–11pm Mon–Sat, 10am–5.30pm Sun.*

The Woodman Inn

134 Eastgate, Louth LN11 9AA
☎ *(01507) 602100* Dave Kilgour

Greene King Abbot always available plus two guests. Among those featured are Wadworth 6X, Charles Wells Bombardier and brews from Cotleigh and Abbeydale. Other specials from micro-breweries stocked when possible.

Situated on the edge of town, this pub has a film theme. Two bars, one a live rock and blues music venue. Food available at lunchtime only. Children allowed.

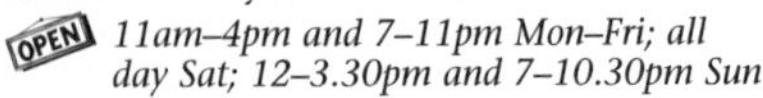

11am–4pm and 7–11pm Mon–Fri; all day Sat; 12–3.30pm and 7–10.30pm Sun.

NORTH KELSEY

The Butchers Arms

Middle Street, North Kelsey, Market Rasen LN7 6EH
☎ *(01652) 678002* Steve Cooper

A freehouse predominantly serving Tom Wood Highwood beers, plus one constantly changing guest.

A small, old-style village pub. One bar. No music or games. Outside seating. Sandwiches, salads and ploughmans available at weekends. Children allowed.

4–11pm Mon–Fri; 12–11pm Sat–Sun.

ROTHWELL

The Blacksmith's Arms

Hillrise, Rothwell LN7 6AZ
☎ *(01472) 371300* Richard and Julie Sandham

A constantly changing range of real ales from local and national micro-breweries is served.

A 400-year-old haunted pub, formerly a blacksmiths, with oak beams, real fires and candles. Bar and restaurant food available at lunchtime and evenings, and all day at weekends. Car park, garden and function room/entertainment room. Restaurant open Fri–Sat evenings from 7pm and Sunday lunchtimes from 12. Two miles off the A46 between Caistor and Swallow.

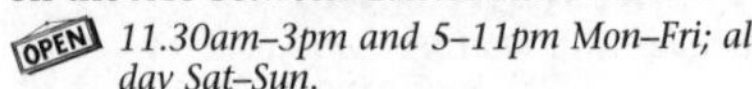

11.30am–3pm and 5–11pm Mon–Fri; all day Sat–Sun.

SCAMBLESBY

The Green Man

Old Main Road, Scamblesby, Louth LN11 9XG
☎ *(01507) 343282* Tim and Anne Eyre

An ever-changing selection of real ales always available. Regular features include Black Sheep Bitter plus Young's and Cottage brews.

A country pub with lounge and public bar. Sky TV. Pub meals served 12–8.30pm Mon–Sat, 12–7.30pm Sun. Children allowed.

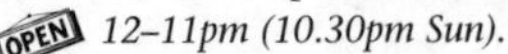

12–11pm (10.30pm Sun).

SKEGNESS

The Vine Hotel

Vine Road, Seacroft, Skegness PE25 3DB
☎ *(01754) 610611* Nigel Dorman

Bateman cask ales are a permanent feature, including XB, XXXB and Mild, plus a monthly guest beer.

Claiming to be the oldest and most famous hotel in Skegness, it dates from the 1770s. RAC/AA 3-star Best Western Hotel set in tranquil gardens, boasting two cosy bars with wooden beams and open fires, a fine dining restaurant alongside and 24 en-suite rooms. Food served 12–2.15pm and 6–9.15pm Mon–Fri, 12–9.15pm Sat–Sun. Extensive parking. Children welcome. At the southern end of Skegness.

11am–11pm Mon–Sat; 12–10.30pm Sun.

SOUTH ORMSBY

Massingberd Arms

12

Brinkhill Road, South Ormsby, Louth LN11 8QS
☎ *(01507) 480492 Kate Bowskill*

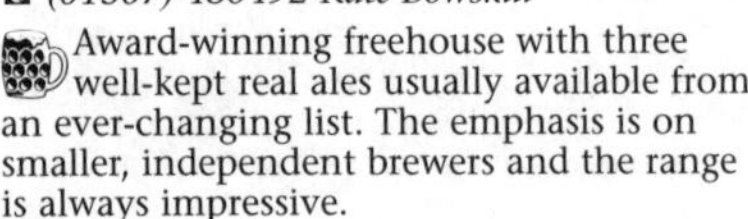

Award-winning freehouse with three well-kept real ales usually available from an ever-changing list. The emphasis is on smaller, independent brewers and the range is always impressive.

A welcoming and atmospheric seventeenth-century pub set in a hamlet of 26 people, surrounded by beautiful Lincolnshire Wolds countryside and parkland. Good food served 12–2pm Tues–Sun and 6.30–8.30pm Mon–Sat. Garden, no-smoking area. Beer festival held in the second week of August. Not far from the A16.

12–3pm Tues–Sat and 6–11pm Mon–Sat; 12–5.30pm and 7–10.30pm Sun.

SOUTH WITHAM

The Blue Cow Inn

29 High Street, South Witham, Near Grantham NG33 5QB
☎ *(01572) 768432* Dick and Julia Thirlwell
www.thebluecowinn.co.uk

Home of The Blue Cow brewery since 1997, with two home-brewed ales available. Thirlwell's Best and Cuddy Bitter are the regulars.

A heavily beamed, thirteenth-century freehouse with stone floors and log fires. Food available every lunchtime and evening in the bar and in a separate restaurant area. Carvery on Sundays. No juke boxes or pool tables. Accommodation commended by the English Tourist Board. Large car park. Chauffeur service for parties of eight or more using the restaurant. Situated eight miles south of Grantham, less than a mile off the A1.

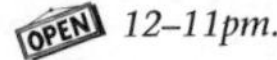

12–11pm.

SPALDING

The Lincolnshire Poacher

11 Double Street, Spalding PE11 2AA
☎ *(01775) 766490* Gary Bettles

Four real ales available at any one time, including three constantly changing guests.

A large, airy pub with two bars. Food available at lunchtimes and early evenings (5.30–7.30pm). Children allowed. Large patio with tables and seating.

11am–11pm Mon–Sat; 12–10.30pm Sun.

STAMFORD

The Green Man

29 Scotgate, Stamford PR9 2YQ
☎ *(01780) 753598* Tony Shilling

Six real ales always available, usually including Stamford Gold, a house ale brewed by Newby Wyke, Rooster's Man of Green and Oakham's Two Tanners plus guests from breweries far and wide. Two beer festivals held every year: one at Easter for four days and one in September for three days.

Olde-worlde pub with oak beams, low ceilings and wooden floors. Food available at lunchtimes. Children allowed until 7pm. Beer garden. Located on the old A1 through Stamford.

11am–11pm Mon–Sat; 12–10.30pm Sun.

The Periwig

7 All Saints Place, Red Lion Square, Stamford PE9 2AG
☎ *01780 762169* William Fry

A freehouse offering Oakham JHB, Hop Back Summer Lightning, Adnams Southwold and Fuller's London Pride, plus two guests (six per week), usually including something from Oakham, though Abbeydale Moonshine and RCH Pitchfork are also regulars.

A town pub in a seventeenth-century building with modernised interior. Food available 12–2.30pm Mon–Sat. Live band once a month. Beer festivals twice a year (call for details). Children allowed.

11am–11pm Mon–Tues; 11am–12pm Wed–Thurs; 11am–12.30am Fri–Sat; 12–10.30pm Sun.

TETFORD

White Hart Inn

East Road, Tetford LN9 6QQ
☎ *(01507) 533255* Mrs V Garnett

Freehouse serving Adnams Bitter, Fuller's London Pride, Greene King Abbot and a guest beer.

Opposite the church in the heart of the village, a beamed pub with several bars. The main bar is at the back with a huge settee in front of an open fire. Food served 12–2pm and 7–9pm Tues–Sun. Fish fresh from Grimsby on Fri and Sat. Accommodation, outside seating, no smoking and children welcome in the lounge bar. Dogs welcome. Walking country.

7–11pm Mon; 12–3pm and 7–11pm Tues–Sun.

WHAPLODE ST CATHERINE

Bluebell Inn

Cranesgate South, Whaplode St Catherine, Spalding PE12 6SN
☎ *(01406) 540300* John Lusher

Two Bluebell Brewery brews produced on the premises plus a guest from further afield.

A pub and non-smoking restaurant with one main bar. Pool and darts. Beer garden with occasional barbecues in summer. Separate restaurant open Tues–Fri evenings, Sat lunchtime and evenings and all day Sun. Children allowed. Brewery visits arranged. Situated in the middle of nowhere, seven miles from Spalding, so do ring for directions.

7–11pm Tues–Fri; 12–4pm and 7–11pm Sat; 12–10.30pm Sun.

WOOLSTHORPE-BY-BELVOIR

The Chequers

Main Street, Woolsthorpe-by-Belvoir, Grantham NG32 1LV
☎ *(01476) 870701* Justin Chad
www.chequers-inn.net

A freehouse with Hardy and Hanson's Kimberley Best and Olde Trip, Adnams Best and Fuller's London Pride always available, plus two guest ales rotated regularly to include bees from Batemans, Brewsters and other local breweries.

A seventeenth-century country pub with olde-worlde decor. Open fires, beams, snug and separate restaurant. Five-acre garden and private cricket field. Four en-suite bedrooms. Restaurant food available 12–2.30pm and 7–9.30pm Mon–Sat and 12–3pm Sun. Children allowed.

12–3pm and 5.30–11pm Mon–Sat; 12–5.30pm Sun.

THE BREWERIES

BATTERSEA BREWERY COMPANY

43 Glycena Road, Battersea SW11 5TP
☎ *(020) 7978 7978*

BATTERSEA BITTER 4.0% ABV
Copper-coloured with hints of malt.
POWER STATION PORTER 4.9% ABV
Dark, dry, traditional London beer.
Plus seasonal ales

FULLER, SMITH & TURNER PLC

Griffin Brewery, Chiswick Lane South, W4 2QB
☎ *(020) 8996 2000*
www.fullers.co.uk

CHISWICK BITTER 3.5% ABV
Quenching, with flowery hop character.
LONDON PRIDE 4.1% ABV
Smooth and rounded, with excellent balance.
ESB 5.5% ABV
Powerful, rounded and well-balanced.
Seasonals:
SUMMER ALE 3.9% ABV
May–Aug. Lager-style beer.
HONEY DEW 4.3% ABV
March–May. Golden smooth and honeyed sweetness.
JACK FROST 4.5% ABV
Winter ale with blueberries among the ingredients.

HAGGARDS BREWERY

c/o The Imperial, 577 King's Road, Chelsea SW6 2EH
☎ *(020) 7731 3780*

HORNY ALE 4.3% ABV
Light, balanced, easy-drinking, with bittersweet finish.
Plus Imperial Ale occasionally.

PITFIELD BREWERY

The Beer Shop, 14 Pitfield Street, Hoxton N1 6EY
☎ *(020) 7739 3701*
www.pitfieldbeershop.co.uk

ORIGINAL BITTER 3.7% ABV
EAST KENT GOLDINGS 4.2% ABV
ECO WARRIOR 4.5% ABV
HOXTON HEAVY 4.8% ABV
BLACK EAGLE 5.0% ABV
SHOREDITCH STOUT 5.0% ABV
Plus seasonal and occasional brews.
Certified organic brewery.

YOUNG & CO.

The Ram Brewery, High Street, Wandsworth SW18 4JD
☎ *(020) 8875 7000*
www.youngs.co.uk

BITTER 3.7% ABV
Pale and bitter throughout.
TRIPLE 'A' 4.0% ABV
Light, easy-quaffer.
SPECIAL LONDON ALE 4.5% ABV
Excellent balance of malt and hops. Revised, slightly lighter recipe.
WAGGLE DANCE 5.0% ABV
Golden, smooth, honeyed flavour.
Seasonals:
DIRTY DICK'S 4.1% ABV
PILSNER 4.0%ABV

THE PUBS

LONDON CENTRAL

EC1

The Artillery Arms

102 Bunhill Row EC1V 8ND
☎ *(020) 7253 4683* Jacqui Eke

A Fuller's pub with Chiswick, London Pride and ESB available plus seasonal brews and a guest ale from a wide range of independent breweries.

An attractive Victorian building tucked away behind Old Street. Named after the Honourable Artillery Company, which is based over the road. Food available 12–3pm Mon–Fri. Upstairs function room.

⊖ Nearest Tube: Old Street.

11am–11pm Mon–Fri; 12–11pm Sat; 12–10.30pm Sun.

The Eagle

139 Farringdon Road EC1
☎ *(020) 7837 1353* Michael Belben

Four hand pumps, with Charles Wells Eagle IPA and Bombardier always available.

A gastro pub with a reputation for good food, which is available 12.30–2.30pm Mon–Fri (3.30pm Sat and Sun) and 6.30–10.30pm Mon–Sat. On a busy main road close to *The Guardian* and *The Observer* newspaper offices. Outside seating.

⊖ Nearest Tube: Farringdon.

12–11pm Mon–Sat; 12–5pm Sun. Closed bank holidays.

Hogshead
171–76 Aldersgate Street EC1
☎ *(020) 7600 5852*

Brakspear Bitter, Fuller's London Pride, Marston's Pedigree and Wadworth 6X always available plus guest beers every month.

A relatively recent addition to the chain on the ground floor of a former office block. Outside drinking on narrow balcony. Food available 12–9pm Mon–Thurs, 12–7pm Fri.

⊖ Nearest Tube: Barbican.

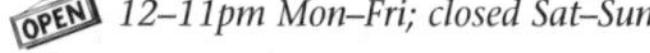 *12–11pm Mon–Fri; closed Sat–Sun.*

Jerusalem Tavern
55 Britton Street, Clerkenwell EC1M 5NA
☎ *(020) 7490 4281* Steven Medniuk

A St Peter's Brewery tied house serving the range of St Peter's brews such as Best Bitter, Strong Bitter, Wheat Beer, Golden Ale, Fruit Beer (elderberry), Summer Ale and Winter Ale. Six available on draught, many more in bottles.

A small, restored eighteenth-century coffee house near Smithfield with plenty of atmosphere, no music or machines. Limited outside seating. Food available at lunchtime from 12–2.30pm and toasted sandwiches in the evenings. Children allowed.

⊖ Nearest Tube: Farringdon.

 *11am–11pm Mon–Fri; 5–11pm Sat, 11am–6pm Sun.*

Melton Mowbray
18 Holborn EC1 2LE
☎ *(020) 7405 7077* Jo Farquhar

A Fuller's house with Chiswick, London Pride, ESB and a seasonal ale available.

Traditional pub on the edge of the City with good food and wine. Home-cooked food served 11am–3pm Mon–Fri. Function room. Monthly quiz nights.

⊖ Nearest Tube: Chancery Lane.

 *11am–11pm Mon–Fri.*

Mulligan's Little House
8 Tysoe Street, Islington EC1
☎ *(020) 7278 7630* Patrick Mulligan

Formerly O'Hanlon's and home of the O'Hanlon's Brewery, which has moved to a site in Devon. Despite the change of ownership, still serving the O'Hanlon's range plus Fuller's Chiswick, London Pride and a guest beer.

Traditional street-corner local close to Sadlers Wells theatre. Some seats outside in summer. Food served 12–3pm and 6–9pm. Children welcome until early evening. Irish folk music on Thursday evenings.

⊖ Nearest Tube: Angel.

 *11am–12am Mon–Fri; 12pm–12am Sat; 12–6pm Sun.*

Sutton Arms
15 Great Sutton Street EC1V 0BX
☎ *(020) 7253 2462*
Michael and Elizabeth Duignan

A freehouse with Fuller's London Pride, Everards Tiger and Greene King IPA likely to be available. A guest beer rotates every three months.

Historic pub in Clerkenwell frequented by a range of City types – builders, artists and designers as well as office workers. Food served 11am–3pm Mon–Fri (booking recommended). Upstairs bar available for private hire from 6.30pm. The whole pub is available for functions at weekends.

⊖ Nearest Tube: Farringdon.

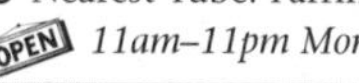 *11am–11pm Mon–Fri.*

Ye Olde Mitre
13 Ely Place, Off Hatton Garden EC1 6JJ
☎ *(020) 7405 4751* Eamon and Kathy Scott

Adnams Bitter, Tetley Bitter and Ind Coope Burton Ale always available on hand pump.

Unspoilt, historic tavern built in 1547 within the grounds of what was the Bishop of Ely's London palace. Two bars. Standing area outside. Upstairs room for hire. Toasted sandwiches and bar snacks served 11am–9.15pm. Down alley off Hatton Garden behind William Hill bookmakers.

⊖ Nearest Tube: Chancery Lane.

 *11am–11pm Mon–Fri; closed Sat–Sun and bank holidays. Opens for the weekend of the Great British Beer Festival in August.*

OTHER REAL ALE PUBS IN EC1

The Betsey Trotwood
(SHEPHERD NEAME)
Farringdon Road EC1R 3BL ☎ *(020) 7253 4285*

The Bishops Finger
(SHEPHERD NEAME)
9–10 West Smithfield EC1 ☎ *(020) 7248 2341*

Butcher's Hook & Cleaver
(FULLER'S)
61–3 West Smithfield EC1A 9DY
☎ *(020) 7600 0615*

City Pride (FULLER'S)
28 Farringdon Lane, Clerkenwell EC1R 3AU
☎ *(020) 7608 0615*

Hogshead
Cowcross Street EC1 ☎ *(020) 7251 3813*

Legion
348 Old Street, EC1 ☎ *(020) 7729 4411*

Sekforde Arms (YOUNG'S)
34 Sekforde Street EC1 0HA ☎ *(020) 7253 3251*

Sir John Oldcastle (WETHERSPOON)
29–35 Farringdon Road EC1M 3JF
☎ *(020) 7242 1013*

The Masque Hunt (WETHERSPOON)
168–72 Old Street EC1V 9PB
☎ *(020) 7251 4195*

Ye Olde Red Cow (SHEPHERD NEAME)
71 Long Lane, Smithfield EC1A 9EJ
☎ *(020) 7726 6137*

One of Two (FULLER'S)
67–9 Cowcross Street, Smithfield EC1M 6BP
☎ *(020) 7250 3414*

EC2

Crowders Well
185 Fore Street, Barbican EC2Y 5EJ
☎ *(020) 7628 8574* Daniel Curtis

A genuine freehouse with a rotating range of up to five real ales always available. The selection varies every week.

A traditional city-centre pub within the Barbican complex, wood-panelled throughout. Bar upstairs, bar and restaurant downstairs. Food available 12–2.30pm. Function room available. Pool table and games machines. Live music up to two nights a week. No children.

⊖ Nearest Tube: Moorgate.

11.30am–11pm Mon–Fri; open some Saturdays, closed Sun.

The Old Doctor Butler's Head
2 Mason's Avenue, Moorgate EC2V 5BY
☎ *(020) 7606 3504* Brendan McBride

Shepherd Neame house with Spitfire, Masterbrew, Bishop's Finger, Best and a seasonal ale available.

Traditional-style pub just off Moorgate with gas lamps in the bar area. Food available at lunchtime or for private diners. First-floor restaurant, second-floor function room for hire.

⊖ Nearest Tube: Moorgate/Bank.

OPEN *11am–11pm Mon–Fri.*

The Phoenix
26 Throgmorton Street, EC2N 2AN
☎ *(020) 7588 7289* Debbie Curran

Four ales usually available, probably including Fuller's London Pride, Adnams Bitter and Caledonian Deuchars IPA.

A former Hogshead now owned by the Laurel Pub Company. Refurbished in December 2003 in traditional style. One bar, non-smoking throughout. Food available 12–9pm Mon–Fri.

⊖ Nearest Tube: Bank.

OPEN *11am–11pm Mon–Fri.*

OTHER REAL ALE PUBS IN EC2

Bill Bentley's (YOUNG'S)
202 Bishopsgate EC2M 4NR
☎ *(020) 7283 1763*

City House
86 Bishopsgate EC2N 4AU ☎ *(020) 7256 8325*

Dirty Dicks
202 Bishopsgate EC2M 4NR
☎ *(020) 7283 5888*

Finch's (YOUNG'S)
12a Finsbury Square EC2A 1AS
☎ *(020) 7588 3311*

Fleetwood (FULLER'S)
36 Wilson Street EC2M 2TE
☎ *(020) 7247 2241*

49 Gresham Street (FULLER'S)
49 Gresham Street EC2 ☎ *(020) 7606 0399*

The Greene Man (WETHERSPOON)
1 Poultry, Bank Station EC2R 8EJ
☎ *(020) 7248 3529*

Hamilton Hall (WETHERSPOON)
Unit 32, Liverpool Street Station EC2M 7PY
☎ *(020) 7247 3579*

One of Two (FULLER'S)
45 Old Broad Street EC2N 12HU
☎ *(020) 7588 4845*

One of Two (FULLER'S)
130 Wood Street EC2V 6DL
☎ *(020) 7600 9642*

Red Herring (FULLER'S)
49 Gresham Street EC2V 7ET
☎ *(020) 7606 0399*

EC3

The Counting House
50 Cornhill EC3V 3PD
☎ *(020) 7283 7123* Peter Biddle

A Fuller's house with five real ales available. Chiswick, London Pride and ESB plus two guests.

Another former bank built in 1893 with a domed ceiling and alabaster walls. One bar, three function rooms. Food available 11am–9pm Mon–Fri.

⊖ Nearest Tube: Bank.

OPEN *11am–11pm Mon–Fri.*

The Crosse Keys

9 Gracechurch Street EC3V 0DR
☎ *(020) 7623 4824* Jason Blower

A Wetherspoon's pub, but one which offers a constantly changing range of up to ten interesting ales from around the UK. These might include Hook Norton First Light, Young's Chocolate Stout or Buchanan's Original (by Robinson's). Fuller's, Ridley's and Hop Back brews are also favoured.

Huge, former Barclays Bank with many original features and an enormous island bar in the middle. Food available all day until 10pm (6pm Sat). Private rooms available, children welcome. Beer festivals held twice a year.

⊖ Nearest Tube: Monument.

OPEN *10am (for breakfast)–11pm Mon–Fri. 10am–7pm Sat.*

The Hoop & Grapes

47 Aldgate High Street EC3
☎ *(020) 7265 5171* Hugh Ede

Fuller's London Pride always available, plus three guests which could well include Timothy Taylor Landlord, Brakspear Special and Best, Badger Best, Adnams Bitter and Extra, Charles Wells Bombardier, Eagle or IPA, Shepherd Neame Spitfire, Hook Norton Old Hooky or Wychwood Hobgoblin or Special. An average of 50 different beers served every year.

A 400-year-old pub just inside the Square Mile. Bar food served every lunchtime 12–3pm, with table service available. No children.

⊖ Nearest Tube: Aldgate.

OPEN *11am–10pm Mon–Wed; 11am–11pm Thurs–Fri; closed Sat–Sun.*

OTHER REAL ALE PUBS IN EC3

Bill Bentley's (YOUNG'S)
5 Minories EC3N 1BJ ☎ *(020) 7481 1779*

Bill Bentley's By The Monument (YOUNG'S)
1 St George's Lane EC3R 8DR
☎ *(020) 7929 2244*

Chamberlain Hotel (FULLER'S)
132 Minories EC3N 1NT ☎ *(020) 7680 1500*

Elephant (YOUNG'S)
119 Fenchurch Street EC3M 5BA
☎ *(020) 7623 8970*

Fine Line (FULLER'S)
124–27 The Minories EC3 1NT
☎ *(020) 7481 8195*

Hog's Head
29 St Mary Axe EC3A 8AA ☎ *(020) 7929 0245*

Hogshead
America Square EC3 ☎ *(020) 7702 2381*

Hung Drawn and Quartered
(FULLER'S)
26–7 Great Tower Street EC3R 5AQ
☎ *(020) 7626 6123*

Lamb Tavern (YOUNG'S)
10–12 Leadenhall Market EC3V 1LR
☎ *(020) 7626 2454*

The Liberty Bounds
(WETHERSPOON)
15 Trinity Square EC3N 4AA
☎ *(020) 7481 0513*

Mint (FULLER'S)
Royal Mint Court, 12 East Smithfield EC3
☎ *(020) 7702 0371*

Swan (FULLER'S)
Ship Tavern Passage, 77–80 Gracechurch Street EC3V 0AS ☎ *(020) 7283 7712*

Three Lords (YOUNG'S)
27 Minories EC3N 1DD ☎ *(020) 7481 4249*

Walrus & Carpenter (YOUNG'S)
45 Monument Street EC3R 8BU
☎ *(020) 7626 3362*

Willy's Wine Bar (YOUNG'S)
107 Fenchurch Street EC3 5JB
☎ *(020) 7480 7289*

Wine Lodge (YOUNG'S)
Sackville House, 145 Fenchurch Street EC3M 6BL
☎ *(020) 7626 0918*

EC4

The Old Bank of England

194 Fleet Street EC4 2LT
☎ *(020) 7430 2255* Victoria Meadows

A Fuller's flagship alehouse with London Pride, Chiswick and ESB always available plus the usual seasonal brews.

An impressive conversion of a Victorian building that was once part of the Bank of England annexed to the law courts. Styled in brass and wood. Two separate rooms for dining (smoking and non-smoking) in which food is available 12–9pm Mon–Thurs and 12–4pm Fri. Full bar menu, including popular pies. No children.

⊖ Nearest Tube: Temple.

OPEN *11am–11pm Mon–Fri; closed Sat–Sun, although available for private party hire.*

Black Friar

174 Queen Victoria Street EC4
☎ *(020) 7236 5650* Karl Becker

Adnams Bitter, Fuller's London Pride, Greene King IPA and Marston's Pedigree available.

Popular and original pub on a triangular site on the edge of The City. Bar food available 12–2.30pm Mon–Fri. Children allowed. Outside standing area.

⊖ Nearest Tube: Blackfriars.

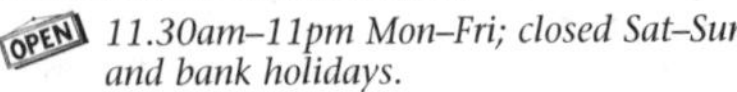
11.30am–11pm Mon–Fri; closed Sat–Sun and bank holidays.

City Retreat

74 Shoe Lane EC4A 3BQ
☎ *(020) 7353 7904* Carol Joyce

Tied to Young's with Bitter, Special and a seasonal brew such as Winter Warmer available.

Very traditional house with one bar and a local feel. The landlady and her son are always behind the bar and many of the customers are regulars. Food available at lunchtime. Functions catered for (at weekends as well).

⊖ Nearest Tube: Chancery Lane.

OPEN *11am–11pm Mon–Fri.*

Mash Tun

80 Farringdon Street EC4A 4BL
☎ *(020) 7353 8808* D Peregrine

A Hall & Woodhouse pub, so serving Sussex Bitter, Best and Tanglefoot.

Formerly known as Samuels, but reverted to its original name of the Hoop and Grapes when saved from demolition and refurbished by the new owners. Now changed again. Outside seating. Restaurant and function room upstairs. Food available all day.

⊖ Nearest Tube: Farringdon.

OPEN *11am–11pm Mon–Fri; available for private hire on Sat.*

Shaws Booksellers

31–4 St Andrew's Hill EC4V 5DE
☎ *(020) 7489 7999* Grant Hawthorne

A Fuller's house with London Pride and a guest ale from either the brewery range or further afield.

A gastro-pub on the ground floor of a building that used to serve the Fleet Street newspaper business. Still with original features but a recent refurbishment has added a more contemporary flavour. Food available until 9pm.

⊖ Nearest Tube: Blackfriars.

OPEN *11am–11pm Mon–Fri.*

The Williamson Tavern

1 Groveland Court EC4
☎ *(020) 7248 5740* Rupert Clarke

Part of the Nicholson's group, with Timothy Taylor Landlord, Adnams Bitter, Greene King IPA and Fuller's London Pride always available plus one guest, changed weekly.

Perhaps London's oldest hostelry and a former home of the Lord Mayor of London, a three-bar pub situated off Bow Lane. Food available 12–9pm. Well-behaved children allowed.

⊖ Nearest Tube: Mansion House.

OPEN *11am–midnight Mon–Fri; closed Sat–Sun.*

OTHER REAL ALE PUBS IN EC4

Banker (FULLER'S)
Cousin Lane EC4R 3TE ☎ *(020) 7283 5206*

Fine Line (FULLER'S)
1 Bow Churchyard EC4M 9PQ
☎ *(020) 7248 3262*

Hogshead
5 Fetter Lane EC4A 1BR ☎ *(020) 7353 1387*

WC1

Calthorpe Arms

252 Gray's Inn Road WC1X 8JR
☎ *(020) 7278 4732* Adrian and Tessa Larner

Popular Young's tenancy serving Bitter, Special and seasonal brews.

One-bar street-corner local. Upstairs dining room. Food served every lunchtime and Monday to Friday evenings. Available for private hire.

⊖ Nearest Tube: Russell Square.

OPEN *11am–11pm Mon–Sat; 12–10.30pm Sun.*

Cittie of Yorke

22 High Holborn WC1V 6BN
☎ *(020) 7242 7670* Stuart Browning

Sam Smith's London flagship, serving Old Brewery Bitter at a competitive price.

Restored pub, impressively huge, with a history dating back to 1430 although it was completely rebuilt in 1923. Enormous back bar with vaulted ceiling, side booths and adjoining wood-panelled room. Cellar bar open in evenings. Bar food available 12–9pm Mon–Sat. Well-behaved children allowed.

⊖ Nearest Tube: Chancery Lane.

OPEN *11.30am–11pm Mon–Sat; closed Sun and bank holidays.*

The College Arms
18 Store Street WC1E 7DH
☎ *(020) 7436 4697* Paul Davies
www.brokenfootinns.com

A freehouse serving Adnams Broadside and Shepherd Neame Spitfire plus one guest rotating monthly, such as Fuller's London Pride.

Formerly The University Tavern, now a one-bar pub with large open-plan basement seating area situated next door to England & Wales College of Law, so very student-oriented. Bare and basic traditional pub, with wooden floors, large-screen TVs and outside seating. Non-smoking area. Recently refurbished. Food available 12–4pm and 5–9pm Mon–Fri, 12–3pm Sat. No children or dogs. Situated off Tottenham Court Road.

⊖ Nearest Tube: Goodge Street.

 *11am–11pm Mon–Sat. Closed Sun except for major sporting events.*

Dolphin Tavern
44 Red Lion Street WC1R 4PF
☎ *(020) 7831 6298* Mr K Charley

An Enterprise Inn with Fuller's London Pride, Young's Bitter and Shephered Neame Spitfire always available plus one guest changed every three months.

A one-bar local close to Conway Hall in Holborn. Food 12–2pm. Off Theobalds Road.

⊖ Nearest Tube: Holborn.

 *11am–11pm Mon–Sat; 12–3pm and 7–10.30pm Sun.*

The King's Arms
11a Northington Street, Bloomsbury WC1N 2JF
☎ *(020) 7405 9107* Clive Gilbert

Greene King IPA, Marston's Pedigree and Wadworth 6X usually available, plus occasional guests but no very strong ales.

A one-bar, office workers' pub in a legal and media professional area. Food available at lunchtime only. No children.

⊖ Nearest Tube: Chancery Lane.

11am–11pm Mon–Fri; closed Sat–Sun.

The Lamb
92–4 Lamb's Conduit Street WC1N 3LZ
☎ *(020) 7405 0713* Michael and Joanne Hehir

Young's brews always available including seasonal ales.

A popular Young's pub in a Grade II listed building with original features and a non-smoking snug. Upstairs dining room. Traditional English pub food available 12–2.30pm and 6–9pm (not Sunday). No children. Outside seating to front and rear.

⊖ Nearest Tube: Russell Square.

11am–11pm Mon–Sat; 12–4pm and 7–10.30pm Sun.

The Museum Tavern
49 Great Russell Street WC1
☎ *(020) 7242 8987* Tony Williamson

Up to six beers usually available, including Fuller's London Pride.

Originally called the Dog and Duck, it changed its name to reflect its location opposite the British Museum. The front and back bars are listed buildings. Food available all day. Outside seating area. No children.

⊖ Nearest Tube: Holborn/Tottenham Court Road.

 *11am–11pm Mon–Sat; 12–10.30pm Sun and bank holidays.*

The Oarsman
2 New Oxford Street WC1A 1EE
☎ *(020) 7404 5009* Leigh Sullivan-Plews

Two real ales always available. Charles Wells Bombardier is a regular but other, more unusual, ales from independent breweries are also served as available.

A small one-bar pub with outside seating. Homemade food available all day. Children allowed.

⊖ Nearest Tube: Tottenham Court Road.

 *12–11pm Mon–Fri; closed Sat–Sun, except for private hire.*

The Old Nick
20–2 Sandland Street WC1R 4PZ
☎ *(020) 7430 9503* Tim Oclee

Now owned by Hall & Woodhouse, so with Badger Best, Tanglefoot and Sussex available plus a guest such as Gribble Fursty Ferret.

Formerly The Three Cups and Young's-owned, changed hands in late 2003 and was recently expanded into the café next door and refurbished. Food served 12–3pm Mon–Fri. Off High Holborn.

⊖ Nearest Tube: Holborn.

 *11am–11pm Mon–Fri (weekend opening planned).*

Overdraught's
6 Dane Street WC1R 4BL
☎ *(020) 7405 6087*

Three real ales usually available, perhaps including Thwaites Best and Forge Smithy, Rebellion Smuggler and something from Greene King.

Tiny, unpretentious street-corner pub beneath residential premises off High Holborn. Separate bar/function room available downstairs. Food served at lunchtime and evenings.

⊖ Nearest Tube: Holborn.

11am–11pm Mon–Fri; closed Sat–Sun.

Pakenham Arms
1 Pakenham Street WC1X 0LA
☎ *(020) 7837 6933* Pat Mulligan

Up to five real ales that might include beers from Fuller's, Young's, Harveys, Slaters, Adnams, Ringwood plus other smaller breweries such as North Yorkshire.

Large, popular local near Mount Pleasant sorting office with extended opening hours as a result. Breakfast, lunch and dinner available. Some brews sold at reduced prices. Outside seating.

⊖ Nearest Tube: King's Cross.

9.30–1.30am Mon–Sun.

Rugby Tavern
19 Great James Street WC1N 3ES
☎ *(020) 7405 1384*

Formerly Fuller's, now Shepherd Neame. Serving Master Brew, Best, Spitfire, Bishop's Finger and seasonal brews such as Early Bird.

Popular locals' pub with central bar. Outside seating. Upstairs dining/function room available for hire. Food available at lunchtime and evenings.

⊖ Nearest Tube: Holborn.

11am–11pm Mon–Fri; 12–3pm and 6–11pm Sat (summer only); closed Sun.

Swan
7 Cosmo Place WC1N 3AP
☎ *(020) 7837 6223*

Up to six real ales available including Greene King IPA and Abbot plus guests.

One-bar pub down pedestrian alley between Southampton Row and Queen's Square. Outside seating. Food available all day.

⊖ Nearest Tube: Russell Square.

11am–11pm Mon–Sat; 12–10.30pm Sun.

OTHER REAL ALE PUBS IN WC1

Dolphin
47 Tonbridge Street WC1H 9DW
☎ *(020) 7692 7116*

Ivy House
8–10 Southampton Row WC1B 4AE
☎ *(020) 7831 6999*

Mabel's Tavern (SHEPHERD NEAME)
Mabledon Place WC1H 9AZ
☎ *(020) 7387 7739*

Penderel's Oak (WETHERSPOON)
283–8 High Holborn, Holborn WC1V 7PF
☎ *(020) 7242 5669*

Skinners Arms
114 Judd Street, WC1H 9NT
☎ *(020) 7837 6521*

WC2

The Crown
43 Monmouth Street WC2H 9DD
☎ *(020) 7836 5861* Mr Brocklebank

An Adnams ale is usually available plus up to four guest ales. Greene King Old Speckled Hen and Marston's Pedigree are regular features.

A traditional, two-bar pub near Seven Dials. Generally quiet, with background music and a mixed clientele. Food available all day. No children.

⊖ Nearest Tube: Leicester Square.

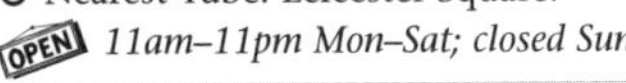
11am–11pm Mon–Sat; closed Sun.

Edgar Wallace
40 Essex Street WC2R 3JE
☎ *(020) 7353 3120* Shane Feeney

Timothy Taylor Landlord is always available, plus three rotating guests such as Adnams Bitter, Fuller's London Pride, Shepherd Neame Spitfire and something from Greene King or Ringwood.

Listed building in legal territory down small side street between the river and the Strand. Popular with barristers and solicitors. Upstairs bar available for hire. Food served 12–8pm.

⊖ Nearest Tube: Temple.

11am–11pm Mon–Fri; closed Sat–Sun.

Knights Templar
95 Chancery Lane WC2A 1DT
☎ *(020) 7831 2660*
Gerard Swards and Steven Morris

Fuller's London Pride, Bateman XXXB, Shepherd Neame Spitfire, Hop Back Summer Lightning and Greene King Abbot available.

Another huge Wetherspoon's conversion right in the legal heart of the city. Food available all day. Non-smoking balcony upstairs.

⊖ Nearest Tube: Chancery Lane.

11am–11pm Mon–Fri; 11am–7pm Sat; closed Sun.

Lamb & Flag
33 Rose Street WC2
☎ *(020) 7497 9504* Terry Archer

Marston's Pedigree, Young's Bitter and Special and one or two guests available.

Popular, Elizabethan pub in the heart of Covent Garden, once known as the Cooper's Arms. Bar food available at lunchtime (12–2pm). Children in eating area only.

⊖ Nearest Tube: Leicester Square.

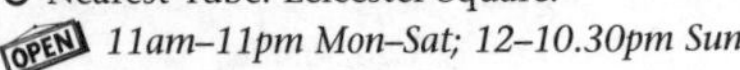
11am–11pm Mon–Sat; 12–10.30pm Sun.

Marquess of Anglesey

39 Bow Street WC2E 7AU
☎ *(020) 7240 3216* Steve Williamson

A Young's house with Bitter, Special and a seasonal ale such as Waggle Dance or Winter Warmer.

In the heart of Covent Garden, opposite the Royal Opera House. Food vailable from 12pm.

⊖ Nearest Tube: Covent Garden.

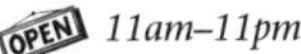
11am–11pm.

Moon Under Water

105–7 Charing Cross Road WC2H 0BP
☎ *(020) 7287 6039* Nic Harper

One of Central London's finer Wetherspoon's establishments serving Fuller's London Pride, Shepherd Neame Spitfire, Greene King Abbot and several other brews. Regular beer festivals.

An impressive conversion of the former Marquee Club. Modern and huge, spread over three floors. Food served all day. No children.

⊖ Nearest Tube: Tottenham Court Road.

OPEN *11am–11pm Mon–Sat; 12–10.30pm Sun.*

The Round House

1 Garrick Street, Covent Garden WC2E 9AR
☎ *(020) 7836 9838* Tim Adams

Greene King IPA, Fuller's London Pride and Young's Bitter often available, plus up to three guests rotated every two weeks from independent and micro-breweries far and wide.

A small, one-bar real ale house in a prominent location with no juke box or machines. Food available all day until 10pm. Children allowed at weekends only.

⊖ Nearest Tube: Leicester Square.

OPEN *11am–11pm Mon–Sat; 12–10.30pm Sun.*

The Round Table

26 St Martin's Court WC2N 4AL
☎ *(020) 7836 6436* Gregory Baird

Charles Wells Bombardier and Fuller's London Pride always on offer plus a guest ale changing every week.

A lively pub with a friendly atmosphere just off Charing Cross Road. Full menu available all day. Children allowed until 7pm. Separate function room available. Comedy on Sunday and Tuesday nights.

⊖ Nearest Tube: Leicester Square.

OPEN *11am–11pm Mon–Sat; 12–10.30pm Sun.*

The Seven Stars

53 Carey Street WC2A 2JB
☎ *(020) 7242 8521* Roxy Beaujolais

Adnams Best and Broadside, Harveys Sussex Best and guest or seasonal ales such as Fuller's Honey Dew or Harveys Tom Paine.

Originally known as The League of Seven Stars in honour of the Dutch sailors who settled in the area, this unspoilt, 402-year-old one-bar freehouse behind the Law Courts was tactfully restored and enhanced a couple of years ago and is now winning awards for its cooking, conviviality and style. Simple but imaginative food available from 12–9pm.

⊖ Nearest Tube: Holborn/Temple.

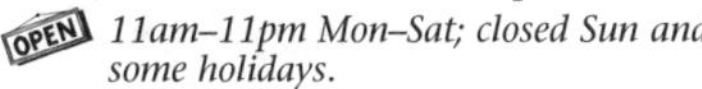
11am–11pm Mon–Sat; closed Sun and some holidays.

Ship & Shovell

1–3 Craven Pasage WC2N 5PH
☎ *(020) 7839 1311* A O'Neill

Owned by Hall & Woodhouse, so Badger IPA, Dorset Best and Tanglefoot always available plus seasonal brews.

Enlarged but still cramped pub on either side of pedestrian passage close to Trafalgar Square. Function room.

⊖ Nearest Tube: Embankment.

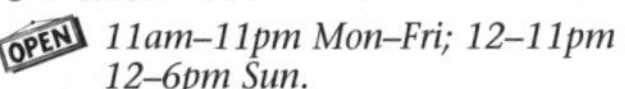
11am–11pm Mon–Fri; 12–11pm Sat; 12–6pm Sun.

OTHER REAL ALE PUBS IN WC2

Columbia Bar (YOUNG'S)
69 Aldwych WC2B 4RW ☎ *(020) 7831 8043*

Fine Line (FULLER'S)
77 Kingsway WC2B 6SR ☎ *(020) 7405 5004*

Hogshead
5 Lisle Street, Leicester Square WC2H 7BF
☎ *(020) 7437 3335*

Hogshead
23 Wellington Street WC2E 7DA
☎ *(020) 7836 6930*

Marquis of Granby
51–2 Chandos Place WC2 ☎ *(020) 7836 7657*

The Moon under Water
(WETHERSPOON)
28 Leicester Square WC2H 7LE
☎ *(020) 7839 2837*

Shakespeare's Head
(WETHERSPOON)
Africa House, 64–8 Kingsway, Holborn WC2B 6BG ☎ *(020) 7404 8846*

LONDON EAST

E1

Brown Bear

139 Leman Street E1 8EY
☎ *(020) 7481 3792* Rob Porter

Fuller's London Pride, Adnams Bitter and a guest beer, changed every week, from an interesting selection of independent breweries.

Well-run traditional one-bar ale house on the edge of the City. Wooden floors and panelling. Food served 11am–9pm. Limited outside seating in summer. Private functions catered for.

⊖ Nearest Tube: Tower Hill/Aldgate East.

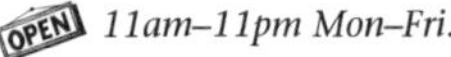
11am–11pm Mon–Fri.

Goodman's Fields

87–91 Mansell Street, E1 8AN
☎ *(020) 7680 2850* Ian Taylorson

A relatively recent addition to the JD Wetherspoon stable, serving five well-kept brews from the usual range. Fuller's London Pride, Shepherd Neame Spitfire and Greene King Abbot are usually available, the other two pumps rotate.

Modern, big and bright ground-floor street-corner location on the edge of the city close to the Tower of London. Named after the owner of the land, which was once a field on which cloth was dried. Food served all day until 9pm (breakfasts from 7.30am, steak club 5–10pm Tuesday; curry club all day Thursday).

⊖ Nearest Tube: Tower Hill.

7.30am–11pm Mon–Fri; 10am–11pm Sat; 10am–10.30pm Sun.

Pride of Spitalfields

3 Heneage Street, Spitalfields E1 5LJ
☎ *(020) 7247 8933* Ann Butler

One or two brews from Fuller's, plus seasonals and weekly changing guests, perhaps including Crouch Vale Best and Hadrian & Border Gladiator.

Friendly, small and comfortable side-street pub just off Brick Lane, attracting a good mixed clientele. Survived serious fire damage in June 2000. Homemade food served at lunchtime. Children welcome. Standing room outside in summer. Turn left out of Aldgate East tube station (Whitechapel Art Gallery end), left again then take the third side street on the left.

⊖ Nearest Tube: Aldgate East.

OPEN *11am–11pm Mon–Sat; 12–10.30pm Sun.*

The Shooting Star

125–9 Middlesex Street E1 7JF
☎ *(020) 7929 6818* Janet Biddle

A Fuller's pub with Chiswick, London Pride, ESB and a seasonal brew usually available.

A seven-year-old pub close to Petticoat Lane. Ground-floor bar plus cellar bar available for hire. Food available 12–8pm Mon–Fri.

⊖ Nearest Tube: Liverpool Street.

11am–11pm Mon–Fri.

OTHER REAL ALE PUBS IN E1

Black Bull
199 Whitechapel Road E1 1DE
☎ *(020) 7247 6707*

The Half Moon (WETHERSPOON)
213–23 Mile End Road, Stepney Green E1 4AA
☎ *(020) 7790 6810*

Mint (FULLER'S)
12 East Smithfield E1 9AP ☎ *(020) 7702 0370*

Thomas More
Thomas More Square, Nesham Street E1W 1YY
☎ *(020) 7702 9222*

The White Swan (SHEPHERD NEAME)
21 Alie Street E1 ☎ *(020) 7702 0448*

E2

The Approach Tavern

47 Approach Road, Bethnal Green E2 9LY
☎ *(020) 8980 2321* Caroline Apperley

A freehouse with Ridleys IPA, Prospect and Old Bob available plus Fuller's London Pride.

A friendly pub with good atmosphere, decorated with photographs. Art gallery, heated beer garden in front. Food available at lunchtime and evenings Tues–Sun. Children and dogs on lead welcome.

⊖ Nearest Tube: Shoreditch.

5–11pm Mon; 12–11pm Tues–Sat; 12–10.30pm Sun.

OTHER REAL ALE PUBS IN E2

The Camden's Head
(WETHERSPOON)
456 Bethnal Green Road, Bethnal Green E2 0EA
☎ *(020) 7613 4263*

E3

The Coborn Arms

8 Coborn Road, Bow E3 2DA
☎ *(020) 8980 3793* Peter and Norma Footman

A Young's pub with Bitter and Special always available.

A large, busy but cosy one-bar locals' pub. Food available 12–2pm and 6–9pm Mon–Fri and 1–9pm Sat–Sun. Outside seating. No children.

⊖ Nearest Tube: Bow Road/Mile End.

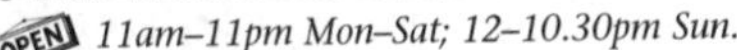
OPEN *11am–11pm Mon–Sat; 12–10.30pm Sun.*

The Crown

223 Grove Road E3
☎ *(020) 8981 9998*
Esther Boulton and Geetie Singh
www.singhboulton.co.uk

One of the few direct outlets for the Pitfield Brewery, who provide a special house ale (Singhboulton), Pitfield Eco Warrior and Shoreditch Stout plus St Peter's Organic Best. Also organic lager and cider.

Organic food and organic drink only at this popular gastro-freehouse opened in 2000 in a Victorian building on a street corner overlooking Victoria Park. Restaurant food and bar snacks available at lunchtime and evenings. Breakfast served at weekends. Outside seating. Upstairs dining rooms available for hire. Children welcome. See also the Duke of Cambridge (N1).

⊖ Nearest Tube: Bow Road/Mile End.

5–11pm Mon; 10.30am–11pm Tues–Fri; 10.30am–11pm Sat; 10.30am–10.30pm Sun.

OTHER REAL ALE PUBS IN E3

The Eleanor Arms

(SHEPHERD NEAME)
460 Old Ford Road, Bow E3 5JP
☎ *(020) 8981 2263*

E4

Kings Ford

250–2 Chingford Mount Road, Chingford E4 8JL
☎ *(020) 8523 9365*

Popular Wetherspoon's pub with the chain staples such as Greene King Abbot, Wadworth 6X, Shepherd Neame Spitfire etc plus three or four guests at any one time.

A busy pub not far from Walthamstow Greyhound Stadium beyond the North Circular Road. Food served all day.

OPEN *11am–11pm Mon–Sat; 12–10.30pm Sun.*

E5

The Anchor & Hope

15 High Hill Ferry, Clapton E5 9HG
☎ *(020) 8806 1730* Leslie Heath

A Fuller's pub, serving ESB and London Pride.

A small, popular, single-bar establishment beside the River Lea near Walthamstow Marshes. No food. Outside seating. Children allowed outside only.

OPEN *11am–3pm and 5.30–11pm Mon–Sat; 12–10.30pm Sun.*

OTHER REAL ALE PUBS IN E5

Princess of Wales (YOUNG'S)

146 Lea Bridge Road, Clapton E5 9QB
☎ *(020) 8533 3463*

E6

Millers Well

419–23 Barking Road, East Ham E6 2JX
☎ *(020) 8471 8404*

A Wetherspoon's pub with six regular brews including Greene King Abbot, Wadworth 6X and Shepherd Neame Spitfire plus a couple of guests.

A former wine bar, converted and extended. Food available all day, every day.

⊖ Nearest Tube: Plaistow.

OPEN *11am–11pm Mon–Sat; 12–10.30pm Sun.*

E7

The Hudson Bay (WETHERSPOON)

1–5 Upton Lane, Forest Gate E7 9PA
☎ *(020) 8471 7702*

E10

The Drum

557–9 Lea Bridge Road, Leyton E10 7EQ
☎ *(020) 8539 9845* Rebecca Brown

A JD Wetherspoon's pub since 1986, serving four regional ales and six interesting guests from around the country at any one time. Greene King Abbot and Shepherd Neame Spitfire are among the staples.

One of the smaller, older members of the chain, refurbished after a fire. A busy local serving food all day (until 10pm). Local CAMRA Pub of the Year 2003. One bar, non-smoking area. Children welcome until 6pm. Beer garden and regular beer festivals.

⊖ Nearest Tube: Walthamstow Central.

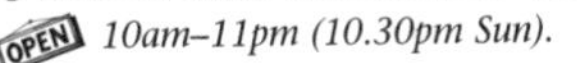
OPEN *10am–11pm (10.30pm Sun).*

King William IV

816 High Road, Leyton E10 6AE
☎ *(020) 8556 2460* Michael Debono

A popular pub with at least five real ales available at any one time. Fuller's London Pride and ESB also always available together with an ever-changing menu of interesting guests sourced from all over the country. Brewing on the premises has recently ceased (hopefully temporarily).

A traditional and genuine East London freehouse with two large bars. Authentic Thai menu available 12–10pm Tues–Sat, 12–9.30pm Sun. Children welcome until 7pm. Quiz on Sunday evenings.

⊖ Nearest Tube: Leyton/Walthamstow Central.

11am–11pm Mon–Sat; 12–10.30pm Sun.

E11

The Birkbeck Tavern

45 Langthorne Road, Leytonstone E11 4HL
☎ *(020) 8539 2584* Roy Leach

A freehouse with a house brew (Rita's Special 4%) named after a previous landlady always available. Plus a minimum of two interesting guests changed daily. At least 250 different brews are served very year.

A friendly, backstreet community pub in a late Victorian building. Two bars, function room and garden. Sandwiches only available 12–6pm. Children allowed in the large garden. Local CAMRA award-winner. Regular beer festivals. Darts and pool.

⊖ Nearest Tube: Leyton.

OPEN *11am–11pm Mon–Sat; 12–10.30pm Sun.*

The Sir Alfred Hitchcock

147 Whipps Cross Road, Leytonstone E11 1NP
☎ *(020) 8532 9662*
Michelle and Jason Flack

A freehouse with three or four real ales usually available, perhaps including Black Sheep Bitter and Fuller's London Pride.

Large, rambling pub opposite Hollow Ponds with several inter-connecting rooms and a rear terrace. Log fires. Refurbished restaurant specialising in steaks, burgers and seafood and serving at lunchtimes (12–3pm Mon–Sat, 1–5pm Sun) and evenings (7–10.30pm Mon–Sat). Quiz nights. Children welcome. Accommodation.

⊖ Nearest Tube: Leytonstone.

OPEN *11am–11pm Mon–Sat; 12–10.30pm Sun.*

OTHER REAL ALE PUBS IN E11

The George (WETHERSPOON)

High Street, Wanstead E11 2RL
☎ *(020) 8989 2921*

The Walnut Tree (WETHERSPOON)

857–61 High Street, Leytonstone E11 1HH
☎ *(020) 8539 2526*

E14

The Grapes

76 Narrow Street, Limehouse E14
☎ *(020) 7987 4396* Barbara Haigh

Adnams Bitter always available, plus Inde Coope Burton Ale and Draught Bass.

Popular, long, narrow riverside pub with a considerable history and splendid views of the Thames. Bar and restaurant food (especially seafood) available at lunchtime and evenings (not Sun evening). Dogs welcome, children and mobile phones not welcome.

⊖ Nearest Tube: Limehouse/Westferry DLR.

OPEN *12–3pm Mon–Sun; 5.30–11pm Mon–Sat; 7–10.30pm Sun.*

The Oporto Tavern

43 West India Dock Road E14 8EZ
☎ *(020) 8987 1530* Steve Baldwin

Three guest beers. Wadworth 6X, Greene King IPA and a Brains brew among those regularly available. Other guests changed monthly.

A traditional male-dominated boozer set in a Victorian building retaining some original features. One bar, TV, darts, pool and racing club. Hot food, including specials, and baguettes available 12–3pm. Children allowed in the paved area at front with bench seating.

⊖ Nearest Tube: Westferry DLR.

OPEN *11am–11pm Mon–Sat; 12–10.30pm Sun.*

OTHER REAL ALE PUBS IN E14

Cat & Canary (FULLER'S)

Building FC2, 1–24 Fisherman's Walk, Canary Wharf E14 4DJ ☎ *(020) 7512 9187*

Fine Line (FULLER'S)

10 Cabot Square, Canary Wharf E14 4QB
☎ *(020) 7513 0255*

Queens Head (YOUNG'S)

8 Flamborough Street E14 7LS
☎ *(020) 7791 2504*

E15

The Golden Grove

146–8 The Grove, Stratford E15 1NS
☎ *(020) 8519 0750* Karen Catchpole

Greene King Old Speckled Hen and Shepherd Neame Spitfire among the five brews always available plus three guests such as Hop Back Summer Lightning but changed almost daily.

A large, popular Wetherspoon's pub with one bar, non-smoking dining area, no music, disabled access and beer garden. Food available all day, 10am–10pm. Children allowed for meals until 6pm. Car park.

⊖ Nearest Tube: Stratford.

OPEN *10am–11pm (10.30pm Sun).*

King Edward VII

47 Broadway, Stratford E15 4BQ
☎ *(020) 8534 2313*
James Eales and John Phillips
www.kingeddy.co.uk

Fuller's London Pride, Charles Wells Bombardier, Greene King Old Speckled Hen and something from Adnams usually available plus two guest brews.

Original, three-bar London tavern dating from 1810 with lots of wood, gas lamps, beams and mirrors. Air-conditioned. Prize quiz nights Sunday and live music nights Thursday. Food served 12–10pm every day (7–10pm in the upstairs restaurant). No children.

⊖ Nearest Tube: Stratford.

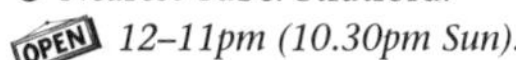

OPEN *12–11pm (10.30pm Sun).*

E17

The Village

31 Orford Road, Walthamstow E17 9NL
☎ *(020) 85214398* Richard Donkin

Five real ales always available, with Fuller's London Pride, Greene King Abbot and Adnams Broadside usually on offer, plus two guests which could come from any independent brewery. Greene King IPA is a favourite.

A residential pub with one bar and a snug area. Large garden. Food available every lunchtime. Children allowed in snug area or the garden until 6pm.

⊖ Nearest Tube: Walthamstow Central.

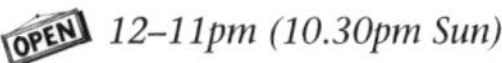

OPEN *12–11pm (10.30pm Sun).*

E18

Hogshead

184 George Lane, South Woodford E18 1AY
☎ *(020) 8989 8542*

LONDON NORTH

N1

Compton Arms

4 Compton Avenue, Islington N1
☎ *(020) 7359 6883* Paul Fairweather

A Greene King pub, so with Abbot and IPA plus seasonal brews always available.

A small, unspoilt local tucked away near Highbury Corner. Food available at lunchtime and evenings (not Tues). Small, part-covered garden. Children by day only.

⊖ Nearest Tube: Highbury and Islington.

OPEN *11am–11pm Mon–Sat; 12–10.30pm Sun.*

Duke of Cambridge

30 St Peter's Street N1 8JT
☎ *(020) 7359 9450*
Esther Boulton and Geetie Singh
www.singhboulton.co.uk

One of the few direct outlets for the Pitfield Brewery, who provide a special house ale (Singhboulton), Pitfield Eco Warrior and Shoreditch Stout plus St Peter's Best. Also organic lager and cider.

Organic food and organic drink only at this popular, street-corner gastro-freehouse which opened in 1998. Restaurant food and bar snacks available at lunchtime and evenings. Outside seating. Children welcome. Sister pub is The Crown, Bow, E3.

⊖ Nearest Tube: Angel.

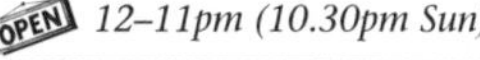

OPEN *12–11pm (10.30pm Sun).*

Marquess Tavern

32 Canonbury Street, Islington N1 2TB
☎ *(020) 7354 2975* Alex Woodoson

Tied to Young's, with Bitter, Special and a seasonal brew always available.

A landmark old music hall tastefully converted and refurbished with many original features. One bar plus separate dining area (available for hire). Food served 12–3pm and 6–10pm Mon–Fri, 12–9pm Sat–Sun.

⊖ Nearest Tube: Highbury and Islington.

OPEN *12–11pm (10.30pm Sun).*

The Prince Arthur

49 Brunswick Place, Charles Square N1 6EB
☎ *(020) 7253 3187* Mr C Dean

A Shepherd Neame house serving Master Brew, Best and Spitfire.

One-bar pub off City Road, built in the seventeenth century and serving the business community. Sandwiches and pies available at lunchtime. Darts.

⊖ Nearest Tube: Old Street.

OPEN *11am–11pm Mon–Fri; 12–6.30pm Sat–Sun.*

The Wenlock Arms

26 Wenlock Road, Hoxton N1 7TA
☎ *(020) 7608 3406* Steven Barnes
www.wenlock-arms.co.uk

A genuine freehouse with up to eight real ales always available. Adnams Best and Pitfield East Kent Goldings always on offer plus a mild. The rest of the menu is an ever-changing selection from brewers up and down the country (see the website for details).

A popular street-corner, one-bar pub with a big real ale reputation. Established in 1835 next door to the Wenlock Brewery, which closed in 1962. Sandwiches and pasties only available. No children after 9pm. Live music on Fri and Sat evening and Sun lunchtime. Quiz on Thurs. Close to the Regents Canal, off City Road.

⊖ Nearest Tube: Old Street/Angel.

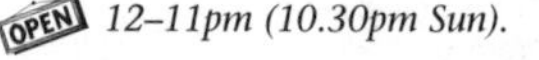
12–11pm (10.30pm Sun).

OTHER REAL ALE PUBS IN N1

The Angel (WETHERSPOON)
3–5 High Street, Islington N1 9LQ
☎ *(020) 7837 2218*

The Barnsbury
209–11 Liverpool Road, Islington N1 1LX
☎ *(020) 7607 5519*

The Crown (FULLER'S)
116 Cloudesley Road, Islington N1 0EB
☎ *(020) 7837 7107*

Drapers Arms
44 Barnsbury Street, Islington N1 1ER
☎ *(020) 7619 0348*

Earl of Radnor (FULLER'S)
106 Mildmay Grove N1
☎ *(020) 7241 0318*

George & Vulture (FULLER'S)
63 Pitfield Street, Hoxton N1 6BU
☎ *(020) 7253 3988*

Hope and Anchor (GREENE KING)
207 Upper Street N1 ☎ *(020) 7354 1312*

The White Swan (WETHERSPOON)
255–6 Upper Street, Islington N1 1RY
☎ *(020) 7288 9050*

N2

Madden's Ale House

130 High Road, East Finchley N2 7ED
☎ *(020) 8444 7444*

Greene King Abbot, Wadworth 6X, Fuller's London Pride and Adnams Broadside always available plus up to eight guests (300 per year) including Ridleys Witchfinder Porter, Ringwood Old Thumper and Fortyniner etc. Also country wines.

A converted shop on the High Road. Bar food available at lunchtime. Children allowed.

⊖ Nearest Tube: East Finchley.

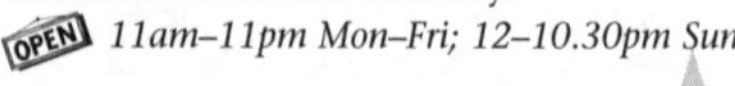
11am–11pm Mon–Fri; 12–10.30pm Sun.

N4

12

The Oakdale Arms

283 Hermitage Road, Harringay N4 1NP
☎ *(020) 8800 2013* Tom Beran
www.individualpubs.co.uk/oakdale

Eight hand pumps serving a wide range of interesting real ales, with Milton Brewery ales always available.

North London's newest freehouse and already winning awards. Regular beer festivals.

⊖ Nearest Tube: Seven Sisters

All day, every day.

The Salisbury

1 Grand Parade, Green Lanes N4 1JX
☎ *(020) 8800 9617* Nick Perry

Fuller's London Pride plus a selection of Ridleys brews including IPA, Rumpus and Old Bob.

Built in 1898, a magnificent and imposing late Victorian inn restored by owners. Spectacular wrought iron entrance leads into three large and impressive bars. Food served at lunchtime (not Mon) and evenings (not Sun or Mon). Function room.

⊖ Nearest Tube: Turnpike Lane/Manor House.

OPEN *12pm–12am Sun–Wed; 12pm–2am Thurs–Sat.*

OTHER REAL ALE PUBS IN N4

The White Lion of Mortimer
(WETHERSPOON)
125–7 Stroud Green Road, Stroud Green N4 3PX
☎ *(020) 7561 8880*

N6

The Flask

77 Highgate West Hill N6 6BU
☎ *(020) 8348 7346* Rupert Reeves

Adnams Broadside, Timothy Taylor Landlord, Hop Back Summer Lightning and Fuller's Chiswick typically available plus guests.

Popular, former coaching inn in the heart of Highgate village. Built in 1663, still with many original features. There is a large paved outside seating area. Food available 12–3pm and 6–10pm (all day on Saturday). Children and dogs welcome.

⊖ Nearest Tube: Highgate.

OPEN *12–11pm (10.30pm Sun).*

OTHER REAL ALE PUBS IN N6

The Gatehouse (WETHERSPOON)
1 North Road, Highgate N6 4BD
☎ *(020) 8340 8054*

N7

The Coronet
338–346 Holloway Road, Holloway N7 6NJ
☎ *(020) 7609 5014* David Leach

A JD Wetherspoon's house with up to ten real ales available. Regulars include Shepherd Neame Spitfire, Greene King Abbot and Theakston Best.

Converted from a cinema in 1996, still with lots of cinema memorabilia and art deco features. Food served all day from 10am. Disabled access, patio area, no music. Children allowed if eating in family area until 9pm.

⊖ Nearest Tube: Holloway Road.

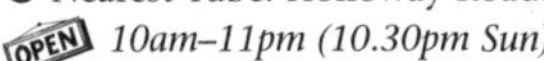
OPEN *10am–11pm (10.30pm Sun).*

N8

The Hogshead
33–5 Crouch End Hill, Crouch End N8 8DH
☎ *(020) 8342 8465* Nichola Cripps

Wadworth 6X, Marston's Pedigree, Fuller's London Pride among the brews always available, plus up to six guests, which might well include Young's Bitter and beers from O'Hanlon's and Shepherd Neame.

A one-bar pub in the heart of Crouch End (so some distance from a Tube). Disabled access, background music, fruit machines, internet games. Food available 12–9pm Mon–Thurs, 12–8pm Fri–Sun. No children.

⊖ Nearest Tube: Finsbury Park.

OPEN *11am–11pm Mon–Sat; 12–10.30pm Sun.*

OTHER REAL ALE PUBS IN N8

The Toll Gate (WETHERSPOON)
26–30 Turnpike Lane N8 0PS
☎ *(020) 8889 9085*

N9

The Lamb Inn
52–4 Church Street, Lower Edmonton N9 9PA
☎ *(020) 8887 0128* Dave and Brenda Andrews

A freehouse with Greene King IPA and Fuller's London Pride among the brews always available, plus up to five guests including, perhaps, Greene King Abbot Ale and Fuller's ESB.

A modern, community pub with one large bar, non-smoking dining area and disabled access. Food available all day. Children allowed.

OPEN *All day, every day.*

N12

Elephant Inn (FULLER'S)
283 Ballards Lane, Finchley N12 8NR
☎ *(020) 8445 0356*

The Tally Ho (WETHERSPOON)
749 High Road, North Finchley N12 0BP
☎ *(020) 8445 4390*

N13

The Whole Hog
430–4 Green Lanes, Palmers Green N13 5XG
☎ *(020) 8882 3597* Paul Shearman

Formerly a Wetherspoon's pub, now under new ownership and serving two guests (six per week) such as Greene King IPA and Abbot or Shepherd Neame Spitfire.

Taken over by the London Inn Group in December 2003, a traditional, friendly pub with two bars, the lower one used only during busy times. Food served from 12–10pm Mon–Sat (9.30pm Sun). Curry night on Thursday. Family area (children allowed until 9pm). Spring and autumn beer festivals.

10am–11pm Mon–Sat; 12–10.30pm Sun.

N14

The New Crown (WETHERSPOON)
80–4 Chase Side, Southgate N14 5PH
☎ *(020) 8882 8758*

N16

The Rochester Castle
145 Stoke Newington High Street, Stoke Newington N16 0YN
☎ *(020) 7249 6016* Jenny Kittermark

Greene King Abbot, Shepherd Neame Spitfire and Fuller's London Pride among the beers always available, plus seven guests selected from the extended Wetherspoon's range. Something changes every day.

A huge Wetherspoon's pub (among the oldest in the chain) with one big bar, patio, disabled access and facilities. No music. Non-smoking dining area in rear conservatory. Food available all day (breakfasts from 10am). Children welcome for meals. Beer garden. Two beer festivals each year.

OPEN *All day, every day.*

The Rose and Crown

199 Stoke Newington Church Street, N16 9ES
☎ *(020) 7254 7497* Mick and Mabel Hill

Independently run but tied to Scottish Courage. The range usually includes Adnams Bitter and Marston's Pedigree plus a guest changed every couple of weeks. Adnams Broadside, Young's Bitter, Charles Wells Bombardier, Greene King Abbot and Old Speckled Hen have all featured.

Former longstanding Truman's street-corner pub built in 1806, rebuilt in 1934 and recently refurbished. Real fires, wooden walls, listed ceiling. Food served at lunchtime (12–2.30pm Mon–Fri, 12–3.30pm Sat–Sun) Children allowed until 7pm. Tuesday is quiz night. Five guest rooms.

 *11.30am–11pm Mon–Sat; 12–10.30pm Sun.*

OTHER REAL ALE PUBS IN N16

The Daniel Defoe (CHARLES WELLS)

102 Stoke Newington Church Street N16
☎ *(020) 7254 2906*

The Shakespeare

Shakespeare's Walk N16 ☎ *(020) 7254 4190*

N17

The New Moon

413 Lordship Lane, Tottenham N17 6AG
☎ *(020) 8801 3496* Tom Connelly

A freehouse with Wyre Piddle Piddle in the Wind always available, plus three guests stocked to customer order. Customers tick a list of suggested ales each month and the ones with the most ticks win! Badger Tanglefoot is popular.

A large town pub with three bars, dining area, patio, disabled access and facilities. Food available at lunchtimes and evenings. Children allowed.

OPEN *All day, every day.*

N18

The Gilpin's Bell (WETHERSPOON)

50–4 Fore Street, Upper Edmonton N18 2SS
☎ *(020) 8884 2744*

N21

The Orange Tree

18 Highfield Road, Winchmore Hill N21 3HD
☎ *(0208) 360 4853 John Maher*

Greene King IPA and Abbot, Ruddles Best and County usually available plus a guest.

Comfortable, traditional one-bar house with pub games and beer garden. Regular CAMRA regional award winner. Food served 12–2.30pm (3.30pm on Sun). Children welcome in beer garden. No car park but plenty of parking nearby. Located off Green Lanes, enter through Carpenter Gardens.

OPEN *12–11pm (10.30pm Sun).*

N22

Wetherspoon's

5 Spouters Corner, High Road, Wood Green N22 6EJ ☎ *(020) 8881 3891*

The Phoenix Bar

Alexandra Palace N22 ☎ *(020) 8365 2121*

LONDON NORTH WEST

NW1

The Albert

11 Princess Road, Primrose Hill NW1
☎ *(020) 7722 1886* Christiane Baehr

Fuller's London Pride, Greene King IPA, Charles Wells Bombardier and a guest ale usually available.

Victorian community pub with a fresh, modern appeal. One bar, garden, conservatory, outside seating at front. Close to the canal. Food served 12–2.30pm and 6–10pm Mon–Fri, all day Sat–Sun. Dogs and children welcome.

⊖ Nearest Tube: Camden Town.

OPEN *11am–11pm Mon–Sat; 12–10.30pm Sun.*

Head of Steam

1 Eversholt Street, Euston NW1 1DN
☎ *(020) 7388 2221* John Craig-Tyler

Nine real ales always available. Shepherd Neame Master Brew, Hop Back Summer Lightning and brews from O'Hanlon's, Cottage, B&T and Brakspear, including one mild, usually featured. Three other brews also served, perhaps from Arundel, Phoenix, Black Sheep, Eccleshall or Barnsley breweries. Monthly beer festivals feature up to 24 beers.

Congenial upstairs freehouse with polished wood floors, featuring regular exhibitions of railway paintings. Food served 12–2.30pm and 5–8pm Mon–Fri, 12–3pm Sat. Children's certificate until 9pm. In front of the bus station outside the mainline railway station.

⊖ Nearest Tube: Euston.

OPEN *11am–11pm Mon–Sat; 12–10.30pm Sun.*

Hogshead

128 Albert Street, Camden NW1 7NE
☎ *(020) 784 1675* Adrian Gill

Caledonian Deuchars IPA and Fuller's London Pride always available.

Relatively recent addition to the chain with a relaxed atmosphere that caters for local workers and residents. Outdoor seating in summer, Sky TV and pool table. Food served daily 12–9pm. Very close to Camden Town tube.

⊖ Nearest Tube: Camden Town.

OPEN *11am–11pm Mon–Sat; 12–10.30pm Sun.*

Spread Eagle

141 Albert Street, Camden NW1 7NB
☎ *(020) 7267 1410* Gill Pipes

A Young's house serving Bitter and Special at all times plus the full seasonal range as appropriate.

Traditional, Victorian pub off Parkway in the heart of Camden, not far from Regents Park and London Zoo. Food served until 7.30pm Mon–Sat and 5pm Sun. Outside seating. No facilities for children.

⊖ Nearest Tube: Camden Town.

OPEN *11am–11pm Mon–Sat; 12–10.30pm Sun.*

Square Tavern

26 Tolmers Square NW1 2PE
☎ *(020) 7388 6010* Rayne McKnight

A Young's house with Bitter, Special and Winter Warmer or Waggle Dance always available.

One main bar, with large outside seating area. Adjoining wine bar serves à la carte food from 12–8.30pm. Tucked away from the traffic just off Hampstead Road.

OPEN *11am–11pm Mon–Fri.*

OTHER REAL ALE PUBS IN NW1

The Engineer

65 Gloucester Avenue, Primrose Hill NW1
☎ *(020) 7722 0950*

The Euston Flyer (FULLER'S)

83–7 Euston Road NW1 2RA
☎ *(020) 7383 0856*

The Lansdowne

90 Gloucester Avenue, Primrose Hill NW1
☎ *(020) 7483 0409*

The Man in the Moon

(WETHERSPOON)
40–2 Chalk Farm Road, Camden NW1 8BG
☎ *(020) 7482 2054*

The Metropolitan Bar

(WETHERSPOON)
7 Station Approach, Marylebone Road NW1 5LA
☎ *(020) 7486 3489*

Queens (YOUNG'S)

49 Regents Park Road, Primrose Hill NW1 8XD
☎ *(020) 7586 9498*

NW2

The Beaten Docket

55–6 Cricklewood Broadway, Cricklewood NW2 3DT
☎ *(020) 8450 2972* John Hand

Shepherd Neame Spitfire and Greene King Abbot always available, plus at least two constantly changing guests from the Wetherspoon's range.

A two-bar Wetherspoon's pub on the A5 (Edgware Road) as it passes through Cricklewood with dining area and patio. Music, but no games. Food available all day. No children.

⊖ Nearest Tube: Kilburn Park.

OPEN *All day, every day.*

NW3

The Duke of Hamilton

23 New End, Hampstead NW3
☎ *(020) 7794 0258* Mary Wooderson

Freehouse serving Fuller's brews plus guests and real cider.

Close to the New End Theatre, a 200-year-old pub that has won several awards thanks to the quality of its beer. Snacks only. Outside seating. Children allowed.

⊖ Nearest Tube: Hampstead

OPEN *12–11pm (10.30pm Sun).*

The Magdala

2A South Hill Park, Hampstead NW3 2SB
☎ *(020) 7435 2503*
Gary Smythe and Sandra Collins

Genuine freehouse with Greene King IPA, Young's Special and Fuller's London Pride always available plus a guest that changes four times a year.

Victorian café, bar and restaurant famed for being the place where Ruth Ellis shot her lover (check out the bullet holes). Two bars, one serving gastro-pub fayre 12–2.30pm and 6–10pm Mon–Fri, all day Sat–Sun. Beer garden. Private restaurant/function room. Right on Hampstead Heath.

⊖ Nearest Tube: Hampstead.

OPEN *11am–11pm Mon–Sat, 12–10.30pm Sun.*

The Spaniards

Spaniards Road, Hampstead NW3
☎ *(020) 8731 6571* Matthew O'Keeffe

Four real ales usually available. Adnams Bitter is a pemanent fixture, the rest rotate. Six-week beer festival held from late February.

Built in 1585, a haunted inn with loads of history and character. The largest beer garden in Hampstead. Car park, children and dogs welcome. No music. Function room. Close to Kenwood House at the north end of Hampstead Heath. Food served 11am–10pm.

OPEN *11am–11pm Mon–Sat; 12–10.30pm Sun.*

OTHER REAL ALE PUBS IN NW3

Flask (YOUNG'S)
14 Flask Walk, Hampstead NW3 1HE
☎ *(020) 7435 4580*

The Hollybush
22 Holly Mount, Hampstead NW3
☎ *(020) 7435 2892*

The Three Horseshoes
(WETHERSPOON)
28 Heath Street, Hampstead NW3 6TE
☎ *(020) 7431 7206*

NW4

Greyhound (YOUNG'S)
Church End NW4 4JT ☎ *(020) 8457 9730*

NW5

The Bull and Last

168 Highgate, Kentish Town NW5 1QS
☎ *(020) 7267 3641* Amanda Rimmer

Greene King IPA and Fuller's London Pride always available.

One-bar former coaching inn built in 1863, now a gastro-pub. Good food served 12–3pm and 6.30–10pm Mon–Fri, 12–10pm Sat–Sun. Upstairs dining room available for functions. Close to Hampstead Heath.

⊖ Nearest Tube: Kentish Town.

OPEN *11am–11pm Mon–Sat; 12–10.30pm Sun.*

The Pineapple

51 Leverton Street, Kentish Town NW5 2NX
☎ *(020) 7284 4631* Francis and Chloe Powell
www.thepineapplelondon.com

Freehouse serving Fuller's London Pride, Marston's Pedigree plus a rotating guest, which might be Adnams Bitter.

Victorian neighbourhood freehouse in a listed building which was saved from closure and sale to a property developer by its regulars, who clubbed together to buy and transform it to great effect. Under new management since May 2002. Food served from 12–2.30pm in the bar downstairs and in the upstairs dining room from 7–10pm (Tues–Sat). Beer garden, conservatory.

⊖ Nearest Tube: Kentish Town.

OPEN *12–11pm Mon–Sat (10.30pm Sun).*

NW6

Queens Arms (YOUNG'S)
1 High Road, Kilburn NW6 4SE
☎ *(020) 7624 5735*

NW8

The Clifton Hotel

96 Clifton Hill, St John's Wood NW8 0JT
☎ *(020) 7372 3427* John Hale

Adnams Best and Fuller's London Pride always available, plus two weekly changing guests such as Timothy Taylor Landlord.

A converted house in St John's Wood with a garden at the front and a patio at the back. A mainly business clientele (average age 25–35ish). Food available 12–3.30pm and 6.30–10pm Mon–Sat and 12–6pm Sun (for traditional roasts). Children allowed if eating, but not at the bar. Situated off Abbey Road, close to Lord's cricket ground.

⊖ Nearest Tube: St John's Wood.

OPEN *11am–11pm (10.30pm Sun).*

NW9

JJ Moons (WETHERSPOON)
553 Kingsbury Road, Kingsbury NW9 9EL
☎ *(020) 8204 9675*

The Moon Under Water
(WETHERSPOON)
10 Varley Parade, Colindale NW9 6RR
☎ *(020) 8200 7611*

NW10

The Coliseum (WETHERSPOON)
25–6 Manor Park Road, Harlesden NW10 4JE
☎ *(020) 8961 6570*

Grand Junction Arms (YOUNG'S)
Canal Bridge, Acton Lane, Willesden NW10 7AD ☎ *(020) 8965 5670*

Green Man (FULLER'S)
109 High Street, Harlesden NW10
☎ *(020) 8965 7307*

The Outside Inn (WETHERSPOON)
312–14 Neasden Lane, Neasden NW10 0AD
☎ *(020) 8452 3140*

William IV
786 Harrow Road, Kensal Green NW10
☎ *(020) 8969 5944*

FURTHER NORTH AND NORTH WEST

HARROW

The Castle

30 West Street, Harrow HA1 3EF
☎ *(020) 8422 3155* Helena Ackroyd

A Fuller's house with London Pride and ESB permanently on offer, plus the seasonal Fuller's ale.

A quiet pub with no music or pool. Central bar and beer garden. Food served 12–9pm Mon–Sat and lunchtime roasts on Sundays. Children and dogs welcome. Follow signs to Harrow School and Harrow on the Hill, West Street is located next to Harrow School Outfitters shop.

 *11am–11pm Mon–Sat; 12–10.30pm Sun.*

The Moon on the Hill

373–5 Station Road, Harrow, HA1 2AW
☎ *(020) 8863 3670* Chris Ollsen

A JD Wetherspoon's pub with up to six guest ales. Shepherd Neame Spitfire, Greene King Abbot Ringwood Fortyniner are among the regulars, but brews from any independent brewery are stocked when possible.

A friendly 12-year-old town-centre pub, with a traditional atmosphere – no music. Food available every day until 10pm. Children allowed if eating until 7pm. Non-smoking area. Beer festivals held twice a year.

 *10am–11pm (10.30pm Sun).*

PINNER

The Village Inn

402–8 Rayners Lane, Pinner HA5 5DY
☎ *(020) 8868 8551* Mark Daniels (Manager)

Shepherd Neame Spitfire permanently available, plus three constantly changing guest ales.

A JD Wetherspoon's house with food available all day, every day. Children allowed, baby-changing facilities provided. Disabled access and facilities. Non-smoking area. Small garden with outside seating. Car park. To find, turn left at the station.

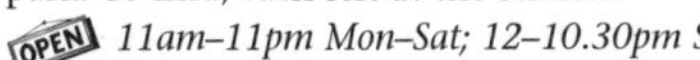 *11am–11pm Mon–Sat; 12–10.30pm Sun.*

STANMORE

The Malthouse

7 Stanmore Hill, Stanmore HA7 3DP
☎ *(020) 8420 7265* Benny Lazar

A freehouse serving a range of up to four constantly changing real ales. Favourites include Timothy Taylor Landlord, Fuller's London Pride and Wadworth 6X.

A modern pub decorated in an old style with character and atmosphere. Late licence. Live music Thurs–Sun. Garden, disabled access. Food available at lunchtimes plus pizzas in the evenings. Children allowed. Theme nights.

 *11am–11pm Mon–Tues; 11am–12am Wed–Thurs; 11am–1am Fri–Sat; 12pm–12am Sun.*

LONDON SOUTH EAST

SE1

Bunch of Grapes

2 St Thomas Street, Borough SE1 9RS
☎ *(020) 7403 2070* Ron and Maggie Wileman

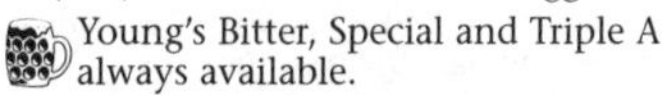 Young's Bitter, Special and Triple A always available.

A busy Young's house close to Guy's Hospital. Beer garden. Bar snacks served at lunchtime (12–2.30pm) and evenings (7–10pm).

⊖ Nearest Tube: London Bridge.

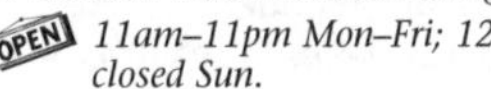 *11am–11pm Mon–Fri; 12–5pm Sat; closed Sun.*

The Fire Station Bar and Restaurant

150 Waterloo Road SE1 8SB
☎ *(020) 7620 2226* Philippe Ha Yeung
www.wizardinns.co.uk

Adnams Best, Fuller's London Pride, Shepherd Neame Spitfire and Young's Special usually available plus a special house brew and occasional and seasonal guests.

Popular conversion of a huge fire station beside Waterloo station. Bar and restaurant food served at lunchtime and evenings (all day at weekends). Children welcome. Function room available for private parties.

⊖ Nearest Tube: Waterloo.

11am–11pm Mon–Sat; 12–10.30pm Sun.

Founders Arms

52 Hopton Street, Blackfriars SE1 9JH
☎ *(020) 7928 1899* Paul and Alex Wakefield

Tied to Young's, with Bitter, Special and either Waggle Dance or Winter Warmer available.

Riverside bar between Blackfriars Bridge and Tate Modern. A concrete construction from the 1970s. One bar, glass front and plenty of outside seating. Superb views of St Paul's etc. Food served all day (breakfast from 9am) every day.

⊖ Nearest Tube: Southwark/Blackfriars

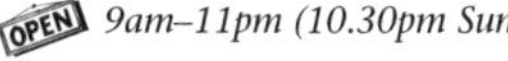 *9am–11pm (10.30pm Sun)*

The George Inn

77 Borough High Street, Borough SE1 1NH
☎ *(020) 7407 2056* George Cunningham
www.georgeinn-southwark.co.uk

Fuller's London Pride, Greene King Abbot and Old Speckled Hen plus a house brew (brewed by Adnams) among the beers always available, plus at least one guest (often seasonal).

A famous galleried seventeenth-century pub, now owned by the National Trust, on a site where a pub has stood for considerably longer. Some say it is older then The Tabard, another famous Southwark pub built in 1307 and demolished in 1875. Four inter-connecting bars open onto a large courtyard. Upstairs restaurant and function rooms available for hire. Food available 12–3pm Mon–Fri (12–4pm Sat–Sun) and 6–9.30pm Mon–Sat in restaurant. Children allowed.

⊖ Nearest Tube: London Bridge.

11am–11pm Mon–Sat; 12–10.30pm Sun.

The Globe Tavern

8 Bedale Street SE1 9AL
☎ *(020) 7407 0043*

An Adnams and Young's brew always available, plus a guest such as Greene King Abbot, Old Speckled Hen or Marston's Pedigree.

A traditional pub close to Borough Market made famous by its appearance in the film *Bridget Jones's Diary*. Background music, bar billiards, game machines. Disabled access. Bar snacks available 12–3pm. No children.

⊖ Nearest Tube: London Bridge.

11am–11pm Mon–Fri; closed Sat–Sun but available for private hire.

Leather Exchange

15 Leathermarket Street SE1 3HN
☎ *(020) 7407 0295* EA Darling

Tied to Fuller's, with London Pride and a seasonal brew available.

Built in 1879 as the London Leather Exchange. The original auctioneers' dining room is now the pub's upstairs dining room, complete with grand piano and real fire in winter. Lively downstairs bar. Good food served 12–3pm and 6–10pm Mon–Fri.

⊖ Nearest Tube: London Bridge

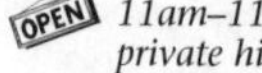
11am–11pm Mon–Fri. Available for private hire at weekends.

Lord Clyde

27 Clennam Street SE1 1ER
☎ *(020) 7407 3397* Michael Fitzpatrick

Young's Bitter, Fuller's London Pride, Adnams Bitter, Shepheard Neame Spitfire and Greene King IPA usually available, although the line-up is altered every couple of months.

There has been an inn on this site for 300 years, though the present building was constructed in 1913. In the Fitzpatrick family for three generations, since 1956. A traditional London 'boozer'. Darts in the backroom bar. Food served all day Mon–Fri (more limited menu at weekends).

⊖ Nearest Tube: Borough

11am–11pm Mon–Fri; 12–5pm and 8–11pm Sat; 12–7pm Sun.

The Market Porter

9 Stoney Street SE1 9AA
☎ *(020) 7407 2495* Tony Hedigan

Harveys Sussex Best always available, plus up to eight often-changing guests (20 per week) from a huge range of independent breweries small and large.

A traditional pub within a rejuvenated Borough Market. The threat of demolition because of the Crossrail project has now receded. Food available at lunchtime. Function room available seven days per week for private functions, meetings, etc. NB early-morning opening.

⊖ Nearest Tube: London Bridge.

6.30–8.30am and 11am–11pm Mon–Sat; 12–10.30pm Sun.

Rose and Crown

47 Columbo Street, Blackfriars SE1 8DP
☎ *(020) 7928 4285* Anna-Maria Quick

Shepherd Neame tied house serving Masterbrew, Best Bitter, Spitfire and a seasonal brew. Winner of the brewery's award for the best-kept beer.

Classic, traditional, 350-year-old pub. Ground-floor bar plus upstairs bar and restaurant area. Large beer garden adjoining church gardens. Food available 12–2.30pm Mon–Fri. Function room available for hire. No children.

⊖ Nearest Tube: Southwark.

11.30am–11pm Mon–Fri.

Royal Oak

44 Tabard Street SE1 4JU
☎ *(020) 7357 7173* Frank Taylor

Well-kept Harveys XX Mild, Pale, Best Bitter and Armada always available, plus seasonal brews.

The capital's only Harveys tied house, tucked away off Borough High Street. An unspoilt oasis and well worth uncovering. Two bars plus upstairs function room. Food available at lunchtime and evenings. No children.

⊖ Nearest Tube: Borough.

11am–11pm Mon–Fri; closed Sat–Sun.

OTHER REAL ALE PUBS IN SE1

Barrow Boy & Banker (FULLER'S)
6–8 Borough High Street SE1 9QQ
☎ *(020) 7403 5415*

The Bridge House (ADNAMS)
218 Tower Bridge Road SE1 2UP
☎ *(020) 7407 5818*

Hog's Head
52 Stamford Street SE1 ☎ *(020) 7261 9642*

Mad Hatter (FULLER'S)
3–7 Stamford Street SE1 9NT
☎ *(020) 7401 9222*

Mulberry Bush (YOUNG'S)
89 Upper Ground SE1 9PP ☎ *(020) 7928 7940*

The Pommeler's Rest
(WETHERSPOON)
196–8 Tower Bridge Road SE1 2UN
☎ *(020) 7378 1399*

Prince William Henry (YOUNG'S)
217 Blackfriars Road SE1 8NL
☎ *(020) 7928 2474*

Ship (FULLER'S)
68 Borough Road SE1 1DX ☎ *(020) 7403 7059*

Simon the Tanner
(SHEPHERD NEAME)
231 Long Lane, Bermondsey SE1 4PR
☎ *(020) 7403 2911*

Wetherspoon's
Metro Central Heights, Newington Causeway, Elephant and Castle SE1 6PB
☎ *(020) 7940 0890*

Wheatsheaf (YOUNG'S)
6 Stoney Street, Borough Market SE1 9AA
☎ *(020) 7407 7242*

SE3

The British Oak
109 Old Dover Road, Blackheath SE3
☎ *(020) 8858 1082*

Princess of Wales
1A Montpelier Row, Blackheath SE3
☎ *(020) 8297 5911*

SE4

The Brockley Barge
(WETHERSPOON)
184 Brockley Road, Brockley SE4 2RR
☎ *(020) 8694 7690*

SE5

Fox on the Hill
149 Denmark Hill, Camberwell SE5 8EH
☎ *(020) 7738 4756* Peter Martin

Shepherd Neame Spitfire and Hop Back Summer Lightning among the brews always available plus a wide range of guests.

A large, modern Wetherspoon's pub with one bar, non-smoking dining area, garden and disabled facilities. Food available all day. Children allowed in the non-smoking area only.

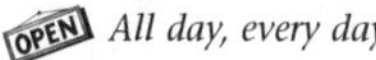

All day, every day.

Hermit's Cave
28 Camberwell Church Street, Camberwell SE5 8QU
☎ *(020) 7703 3188*

Up to 12 beers available including Greene King Old Speckled Hen, Marston's Pedigree, Gale's HSB, Fuller's London Pride and Adnams Best. Micro-brewers provide the guest beers.

Built in 1902, this beamed pub serves bar food at lunchtime and evenings. Street parking. Children not allowed.

OPEN *11am–11pm Mon–Sat; 12–10.30pm Sun.*

SE6

Catford Ram
9 Winslade Way, Catford SE6 4JU
☎ *(020) 8690 6206* Allen and Janice Wadey

A Young's house, so with Bitter, Special and seasonal brews available.

Just off Catford Broadway. The licensees have been at the helm for over 25 years. Raised seating area. Food served at lunchtime and evenings.

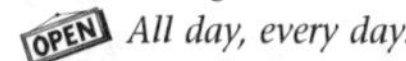

All day, every day.

Rutland Arms
55 Perry Hill, Catford SE6
☎ *(020) 8291 9426* Mrs Christine Baker

Genuine freehouse serving Young's Bitter and Special, Fuller's London Pride and ESB, Adnams Bitter and Broadside.

Spacious pub with live jazz most nights (and Sun lunchtime). Cask Marque approved. Small function room, on-street parking. Bar snacks plus Sunday roasts. Off theSouth Circular Road at Forest Hill.

OPEN *11am–11pm Mon–Sat; 12–10.30pm Sun.*

OTHER REAL ALE PUBS IN SE6

The London & Rye (WETHERSPOON)
109 Rushey Green, Catford SE6 4AF
☎ *(020) 8697 5028*

The Tiger's Head (WETHERSPOON)
350 Bromley Road, Catford SE6 2RZ
☎ *(020) 8698 8645*

SE8

The Dog & Bell
116 Prince Street, Deptford SE8 3JD
☎ *(020) 8692 5664*

Five beers always available. Brews might include Fuller's London Pride and ESB, Shepherd Neame Spitfire, Nethergate Bitter and something from Larkins, Archers or a host of other independents.

Backstreet freehouse built in 1850 and extended more recently. Three connected rooms. Bar food available on weekdays 12–2pm and 6–9pm. Street parking, garden. Children aged 14 and over allowed. Pub quiz (Sun). Tucked away, not far from the railway station.

12–11pm Mon–Sat; 12–3.30pm and 7–10.30pm Sun.

SE9

The Banker's Draft
(WETHERSPOON)
80 High Street, Eltham SE9 1FT
☎ *(020) 8294 1FT*

SE10

Ashburnham Arms
(SHEPHERD NEAME)
25 Ashburnham Grove, Greenwich SE10
☎ *(020) 8692 2007*

Richard I (YOUNG'S)
52–4 Royal Hill, Greenwich SE10 8RT
☎ *(020) 8692 2996*

The Royal George
(SHEPHERD NEAME)
2 Blissett Street, Greenwich SE10 8UP
☎ *(020) 8692 1949*

Spanish Galleon (SHEPHERD NEAME)
48 Greenwich Church Street, Greenwich SE10 9BL ☎ *(020) 8293 0949*

SE11

Prince of Wales
Cleaver Square, Kennington SE11 4EA
☎ *(020) 7735 9916* Louise Stratford

A Shepherd Neame house with Best, Spitfire and a brewery seasonal ale.

Built in 1901, a cosy pub in the corner of an attractive South London square with one bar, open fire in winter, outside seating in summer. Food served 12–2.30pm and 6–9pm.

⊖ Nearest Tube: Kennington.

12–11pm (10.30pm Sun).

OTHER REAL ALE PUBS IN SE11

Court Tavern (SHEPHERD NEAME)
42 Renfrew Road, Lambeth SE11 4NA
☎ *(020) 7840 0878*

SE12

Crown (YOUNG'S)
117 Burnt Ash Hill, Lee SE12 0AJ
☎ *(020) 8857 6607*

The Edmund Halley
(WETHERSPOON)
25–7 Lee Gate Centre, Lee Green SE12 8RG
☎ *(020) 8318 7475*

SE13

The Watch House
198–204 Lewisham High Street, Lewisham SE13 6JP
☎ *(020) 8318 3136* Mark Stevenson

Shepherd Neame Spitfire and Hop Back Summer Lightning among the brews always available plus up to five guests from breweries such as Bateman, JW Lees, Nethergate and Cotleigh.

A town-centre Wetherspoon's pub with a mature clientele. No music. Patio, non-smoking area, disabled facilities. Food available all day. Children allowed until 7pm.

All day, every day.

The Jordan
354 Lewisham High Street, Lewisham SE13 6LE
☎ *(020) 8690 2054* Alan Jordan

Three or four real ales available at any one time, up to 30 each month.

A former Hogshead, more than 100 years old with an old wooden look and feel. One bar, beer garden. Food served Mon–Fri lunchtimes. Five minutes from Ladywell station.

11am–11pm Mon–Sat; 12–10.30pm Sun.

SE15

The Kentish Drovers
(WETHERSPOON)
77–9 Peckham High Street, Peckham SE15 5RS
☎ *(020) 7277 4283*

SE16

Blacksmiths Arms
257 Rotherhithe Street SE16 1EJ
☎ *(020) 7237 1349* Anthony Allan

A Fuller's House with London Pride and ESB plus Adnam's Bitter and a guest ale changed every two weeks.

Next to the Hilton Hotel, a 100-year-old pub with one horseshoe-shaped bar and a games room. Food served each evening from 6pm. Enclosed rear patio garden.

OPEN *12–11pm (10.30pm Sun).*

The Clipper
562 Rotherhithe Street SE16 5EX
☎ *(020) 7237 2022* JR Springate

Greene King Old Speckled Hen and Marston's Pedigree always available, with Adnams Bitter a popular guest.

Opposite the Hilton Hotel, a one-bar pub with restaurant that seats 40. Garden with BBQ facilities. Close to the river. Food served 12–10pm. Available for private hire.

OPEN *11am–11pm Mon–Sat; 12–10.30pm Sun*

OTHER REAL ALE PUBS IN SE16

Moby Dick (FULLER'S)
6 Russell Place, Greenland Dock SE16 1PL
☎ *(020) 7231 5482*

Ship (YOUNG'S)
39–47 St Marychurch Street, Rotherhithe SE16 4JE ☎ *(020) 7237 4103*

The Surrey Docks (WETHERSPOON)
185 Lower Road, Rotherhithe SE16 2LW
☎ *(020) 7394 2832*

SE18

Rose's Free House (aka Prince Albert)
49 Hare Street, Woolwich SE18 6NE
☎ *(020) 8854 1538* Dave Evans

Between three and six brews at any one time, from a huge and varied range. Always changing, with 20–25 different beers a week.

Popular, one-bar, old-style wood-panelled pub. Bar snacks available all day (not Sun), but the clientele is here for the beer! Four twin bedrooms available. One minute from Woolwich Ferry.

OPEN *11am–11pm Mon–Sat; 12–3pm Sun.*

OTHER REAL ALE PUBS IN SE18

The Anglesea Arms
(SHEPHERD NEAME)
91 Woolwich New Road, Woolwich SE18 6EF
☎ *(020) 8317 0834*

The Great Harry (WETHERSPOON)
7–9 Wellington Street, Woolwich SE18 6NY
☎ *(020) 8317 4813*

SE19

The Postal Order (WETHERSPOON)
33 Westow Street, Crystal Palace SE19 3RW
☎ *(020) 8771 3003*

Railway Bell (YOUNG'S)
14 Cawnpore Street SE19 1PF
☎ *(020) 8670 2844*

SE20

Moon & Stars
164–6 High Street, Penge SE20 7QS
☎ *(020) 8776 5680* Rebecca Jordan

Shepherd Neame Spitfire, Greene King IPA and Abbot and Hop Back Summer Lightning among the beers always available, plus up to five guests from a huge list.

A large Wetherspoon's pub in a former cinema. Disabled facilities. Non-smoking dining area, beer garden. Food available all day from 10am. No children. Beer festivals in April and October.

OPEN *10am–11pm (10.30pm Sun)*

SE21

Crown & Greyhound (aka The Dog)
73 Dulwich Village SE21
☎ *(020) 8299 4976* Ann Taylor

Young's Bitter, Fuller's London Pride and an Adnams brew usually available.

Formerly two pubs, this huge refurbished Victorian alehouse sits in the heart of Dulwich. With split-level garden and conservatory. Food available at lunchtime and evenings. Children welcome in parts.

OPEN *11am–11pm Mon–Sat; 12–10.30pm Sun.*

SE22

The Clock House (YOUNG'S)
196a Peckham Rye SE22 9QA
☎ *(020) 8693 2901*

SE23

The Capitol

11–21 London Road, Forest Hill SE23 3TW
☎ *(020) 8291 8920* Jason Kitteringham

Between five and eight real ales always available from the Wetherspoon's range.

Just three years old, another former cinema with many original features retained. One bar, beer garden, non-smoking area. Children welcome until 7pm. Food served 10am–10pm. On the South Circular Road, close to Forest Hill station. Beer festivals held twice a year.

OPEN *10am–11pm (10.30pm Sun).*

OTHER REAL ALE PUBS IN SE23

The Railway Telegraph
(SHEPHERD NEAME)
112 Stanstead Road, Forest Hill SE23 1BS
☎ *(020) 8699 6644*

SE24

Tulse Hill Tavern

150 Norwood Road, Tulse Hill SE24 9AX
☎ *(020) 8674 9754*

SE25

The Alliance

91 High Street, South Norwood SE25 6EA
☎ *(020) 8653 3604* Mr Goodridge

Greene King Abbot, Fuller's London Pride and Shepherd Neame Spitfire alternating on one hand pump plus one guest which might be Timothy Taylor Landlord, Hook Norton Old Hooky, Hop Back Summer Lightning, Cotleigh Barn Owl or another brew from an independent.

A traditional, popular pub built in 1860 with leaded windows and wooden beams. Bar snacks available on weekday lunchtimes. No children's room.

OPEN *11am–11pm Mon–Sat; 12–10.30pm Sun.*

Clifton Arms

21 Clifton Road, South Norwood SE25 6NJ
☎ *(020) 8771 2443* Ian Clarke

Adnams Bitter, Fuller's London Pride, something from Sharp's and a couple of guest beers usually available.

Popular local community pub, close to Selhurst Park, so particularly busy on football days/ evenings. Built in 1863. Food available lunchtime and evenings (Mon–Sat). Beer garden, charity quiz nights, four beer festivals a year.

OPEN *12–11pm (10.30pm Sun).*

Portmanor

Portland Road, South Norwood, SE25 4UF
☎ *(020) 8655 1308* Joan Brendan Kelly

Fuller's London Pride, Greene King Abbot Ale and up to five guest beers regularly available, perhaps from Hogs Back, Flagship or other small independents.

Popular freehouse with a good atmosphere and upstairs restaurant. Food served 11am–3pm and 5–9.30pm Mon–Fri, 12–9pm Sat (7pm Sun). No children. Quiz night (Thurs). Disco at weekends.

OPEN *11am–11pm Mon–Sat; 12–10.30pm Sun.*

OTHER REAL ALE PUBS IN SE25

Goat House (FULLER'S)
2 Penge Road, South Norwood SE25 4EX
☎ *(020) 8778 5752*

The William Stanley
(WETHERSPOON)
7–8 High Street, South Norwood SE25 6EP
☎ *(020) 8653 0678*

SE26

Dulwich Wood House

39 Sydenham Hill SE26 6RS
☎ *(020) 8693 5666* Stephen Harkin

A Young's house with Bitter, Special and the brewery's seasonal ales available.

Built in 1857, designed by Sir Joseph Paxton for a local farmer and leased by Young's since 1889. Traditional, friendly pub with two bars and a large garden plus outside seating at the front. Food served 12–3pm and 6–9pm (12–4pm Sun). Non-smoking restaurant. Car park. Close to Crystal Palace, Sydenham Hill is the nearest station.

OPEN *11am–11pm Mon–Sat; 12–10.30pm Sun.*

The Windmill

125–31 Kirkdale, Sydenham SE26 4QJ
☎ *(020) 8291 8670* Steve Jarvis

A Wetherspoon's pub with Fuller's London Pride and Shepherd Neame Spitfire usually available plus at least three guests.

A former furniture shop occupying spacious premises with non-smoking area and garden. Food available all day.

OPEN *11am–11pm Mon–Sat; 12–10.30pm Sun.*

OTHER REAL ALE PUBS IN SE26

Bricklayers' Arms (YOUNG'S)
189 Dartmouth Road, Sydenham SE26 4QY
☎ *(020) 8699 1260*

SE27

Hope (YOUNG'S)

49 High Street, West Norwood SE27 9JS
☎ *(020) 8670 2035*

LONDON SOUTH WEST

SW1

Buckingham Arms

62 Petty France, Westminster SW1H 9EU
☎ *(020) 7222 3386* Eugene McCaughey

Tied to Young's, with Bitter, Special and either Waggle Dance or Winter Warmer available.

Built in 1780 with one bar and serving a business clientele. No music or pool tables. Food served 12–2.30pm and 6–9pm. Close to Buckingham Palace.

⊖ Nearest Tube: St James's Park

OPEN *11am–11pm Mon–Fri; 11am–5.30pm Sat; 12–5.30pm Sun.*

The Captain's Cabin

4–7 Norris Street SW1Y 4RJ
☎ *(020) 7930 4767* Mervyn and Julie Wood

Greene King IPA and Abbot usually available plus two constantly changing guests.

Two bars with a central staircase and open balcony. Food served all day. Cash-back facilities available! Top bar available for private hire. No children.

⊖ Nearest Tube: Piccadilly Circus.

OPEN *11am–11pm Mon–Sat; 12–10.30pm Sun.*

Cask & Glass

39–41 Palace Street, Victoria SW1
☎ *(020) 7834 7630* Michael McAree

Shepherd Neame house with Spitfire, Best and Masterbrew always available.

The smallest pub in Westminster, mid-Victorian with an olde-worlde ambience. Sandwiches and toasties available at lunchtimes. Outside tables and chairs in summer. Award-winning floral displays. Between Buckingham Palace Road and Victoria Street.

⊖ Nearest Tube: Victoria

OPEN *11am–11pm Mon–Fri; 12–9pm Sat; closed Sun.*

Duke of Wellington

63 Eaton Terrace, Belgravia SW1W 8TR
☎ *(020) 730 1782/3103* John and Helen Bond

Another Shepherd Neame House, with Masterbrew, Spitfire and Bishop's Finger always available.

Set in a former library, late nineteenth century, a friendly and traditional English local. Food served 11am–3pm and 6–9pm Mon–Sat (not Sun). Children welcome. Outside street tables. Three minutes from Sloane Square.

⊖ Nearest Tube: Sloane Square.

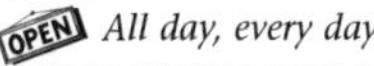
All day, every day.

Jugged Hare

172 Vauxhall Bridge Road, Victoria SW1V 1DX
☎ *(020) 7828 1543* Ben Bagguley

A Fuller's pub serving Chiswick, London Pride, ESB and the seasonal range.

Another bank conversion serving food throughout the day. Gallery available for private hire.

⊖ Nearest Tube: Victoria.

OPEN *11am–11pm Mon–Sat; 12–10.30pm Sun.*

Lord Moon of the Mall

16–18 Whitehall, SW1A 2DY
☎ *(020) 7839 7701* Matt Gold

A Wetherspoon's pub with Fuller's London Pride, Shepherd Neame Spitfire and Greene King Abbot always available, plus up to six guests changed daily.

An impressive former bank with high ceilings, arches and oak fittings. Non-smoking area, disabled facilities. Food available all day from 10am. Children welcome until 5pm. Beer festivals twice a year. Next to the Whitehall Theatre.

⊖ Nearest Tube: Embankment.

OPEN *10am–11pm (10.30pm Sun).*

Morpeth Arms

58 Millbank SW1 4RW
☎ *(020) 7834 6442* Peter Henderson

Tied to Young's with Bitter, Special and Waggle Dance or Winter Warmer.

Traditional pub built in 1845. The cellars were once prison cells. Hot food served 12–4pm, sandwiches until 9pm. Private room for hire. Near Tate Britain.

⊖ Nearest Tube: Pimlico

OPEN *11am–11pm Mon–Sat; 12–10.30pm Sun.*

Nags Head

53 Kinnerton Street SW1
☎ *(020) 7235 1135* Kevin Moran

A freehouse serving Adnams Best and Broadside plus seasonal brews.

Tucked down an attractive mews street off Wilton Place. Two wood-panelled bars on different levels (the bar area is between the two). Some outside seating. Food available all day until 9pm. No mobile phones.

⊖ Nearest Tube: Knightsbridge.

OPEN *All day, every day.*

Rising Sun

46 Ebury Bridge Road, Pimlico SW1W 8PZ
☎ *(020) 7730 4088* Toby Key

Also tied to Young's, with Bitter, Special and one of the two seasonal brews available.

Food served 11am–3pm and 6–9pm Mon–Fri, 12–4pm Sat–Sun. Children welcome. Beer garden at the rear, private room for hire.

⊖ Nearest Tube: Victoria.

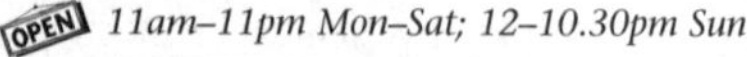
11am–11pm Mon–Sat; 12–10.30pm Sun.

Sanctuary House Hotel

33 Tothill Street SW1 9LA
☎ *(020) 7799 4044* Liz McLelland
www.sanctuaryhousehotel.com

Another Fuller's pub, so with Chiswick, London Pride, ESB and the appropriate seasonal brew available.

Bar attached to small hotel in the heart of Westminster serving food until 9pm every day. Children welcome.

⊖ Nearest Tube: St James's Park.

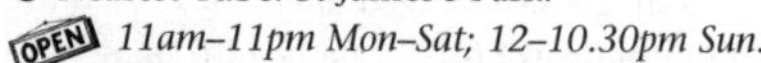
11am–11pm Mon–Sat; 12–10.30pm Sun.

Star Tavern

6 Belgrave Mews West SW1 8HH
☎ *(020) 7235 3019* TJ and Christine Connell

A Fuller's tied pub with Chiswick, London Pride and ESB always available.

Tucked away down a small, cobbled mews street off Belgrave Square. Bars on two floors (upstairs available for functions). Food available at lunchtime (12–2.30pm) and evenings (6–9pm).

⊖ Nearest Tube: Hyde Park Corner/ Knightsbridge.

All day Mon–Fri; 11.30am–3pm and 6.30–11pm Sat; 12–3pm and 7–10.30pm Sun.

Westminster Arms

9 Storey's Gate SW1
☎ *(020) 7222 8520* Gerry and Marie Dolan

A freehouse with a range of real ales always available that might include Adnams Bitter, Greene King Abbot, Wadworth 6X and a special house brew.

A large, busy, politician's pub handy for Westminster, serving restaurant food on weekday lunchtimes (not Wednesdays) and bar snacks at other times. Children in the restaurant only.

⊖ Nearest Tube: St James's Park/ Westminster.

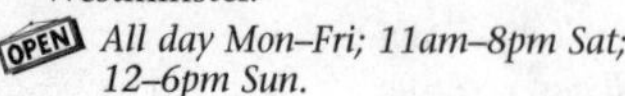
All day Mon–Fri; 11am–8pm Sat; 12–6pm Sun.

Wilton Arms

71 Kinnerton Street, Westminster SW1X 8ER
☎ *(020) 7235 4854* Val Knight

Shepherd Neame Spitfire, Masterbrew and Bishop's Finger.

Opened in 1826, one of two decent pubs on the street (known locally as the Village Pub). Several separate eating and drinking areas, plus a conservatory in the old garden which is available for private hire. Food served 12–10pm Mon–Fri, 12–3pm Sat.

⊖ Nearest Tube: Knightsbridge

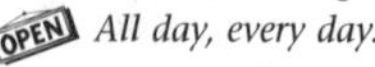
All day, every day.

OTHER REAL ALE PUBS IN SW1

Fox & Hounds (YOUNGS)
29 Passmore Street SW1W 8HR
☎ *(020) 7730 6367*

Grouse & Claret
(HALL & WOODHOUSE)
14–15 Little Chester Street SW1X 7AP
☎ *(020) 7235 3438*

Horse & Groom
(SHEPHERD NEAME)
7 Groom Place, Belgravia SW1X 7BA
☎ *(020) 7235 7949*

Royal Oak (YOUNG'S)
2 Regency Street SW1 4EZ ☎ *(020) 7834 7046*

Wetherspoon's
Unit 5 Victoria Island, Victoria Station SW1V 1JT
☎ *(020) 7931 0445*

The Willow Walk (WETHERSPOON)
25 Wilton Road, Victoria SW1V 1LW
☎ *(020) 78282953*

SW2

The Crown & Sceptre

2a Streatham Hill, Brixton SW2 4AH
☎ *(020) 8671 0843* Sean Pulford

Shepherd Neame Spitfire among the brews always available plus two guests such as Hop Back Summer Lightning and ales from Adnams or Cotleigh.

A Wetherspoon's conversion with a big bar, non-smoking dining area, front and rear patios. Food available all day. Children allowed in the garden only.

⊖ Nearest Tube: Balham.

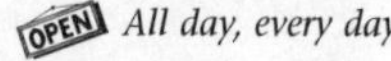
All day, every day.

OTHER REAL ALE PUBS IN SW2

Hope & Anchor (YOUNG'S)
123 Acre Lane, Brixton SW2 5UA
☎ *(020) 7274 1787*

SW3

The Crown
153 Dovehouse Street, Chelsea SW3 6LB
☎ *(020) 7352 9505*
Alan Carroll and Karen Moore

Adnams Best Bitter, Fuller's London Pride plus a guest beer usually available.

Traditional central London pub. Food served 12–3pm Mon–Fri. Well-behaved over 14s welcome. All major sports events shown on plasma screen. Situated 100 yards off Fulham Road, between the Brompton and Royal Marsden hospitals.

⊖ Nearest Tube: South Kensington.

OPEN *11am–11pm Mon–Sat; 12–10.30pm Sun.*

Cooper's Arms
87 Flood Street, Chelsea SW3 5TB
☎ *(020) 7376 3120* Simon and Caroline Lee
www.thecoopers.co.uk

A Young's pub serving Bitter and Special, and Smiles Bristol IPA

Street-corner local just off King's Road. Upstairs function room. Food served 12.30–3pm and 6.30–9.30pm (not Sun evenings).

⊖ Nearest Tube: Sloane Square.

OPEN *11am–11pm Mon–Sat; 12–10.30pm Sun.*

OTHER REAL ALE PUBS IN SW3

Phene Arms
9 Phene Street, Chelsea SW3
☎ *(020)7352 3294*

SW4

Bread & Roses
68 Clapham Manor Street, Clapham SW4 6DZ
☎ *(020) 8498 1779* Peter Dawson
www.breadandrosespub.com

A freehouse owned by the Worker's Beer Company with Workers Ale (a house ale brewed by Smiles), a rotating guest from Adnams and another guest always available.

A bright, modern pub. Bar and function room, front and rear garden, disabled access and toilets. Food available at lunchtime (12–3pm, 4pm on Sat–Sun) and evenings (roasts on Sundays) until 9.30pm. Children allowed until 9pm in the non-smoking conservatory.

⊖ Nearest Tube: Clapham Common/ Clapham North.

OPEN *12–11pm (10.30pm Sun).*

The Windmill on the Common
South Side, Clapham Common SW4 9DE
☎ *(020) 8673 4578* Charles Linney

A Young's house with Bitter, Special and seasonal brews available.

A substantial and popular Victorian pub, built on the site of the home of the founder of Young's brewery. Good accommodation very close to the common. Bar and restaurant food available 12–10pm Mon–Fri (9pm Sat–Sun). Children welcome in the family room, which doubles as a function room available for private hire. Outside seating. En-suite accommodation (29 rooms).

⊖ Nearest Tube: Clapham Common/ Clapham South.

OPEN *11am–11pm Mon–Sat; 12–10.30pm Sun.*

OTHER REAL ALE PUBS IN SW4

Fine Line (FULLER'S)
182–4 Clapham High Street SW4 7UG
☎ *(020) 7622 4436*

SW5

Blackbird (FULLER'S)
209 Earls Court Road SW5 9AR
☎ *(020) 7835 1855*

SW6

The Imperial
577 King's Road SW6 2EH
☎ *(020) 7736 8549* Andrew and Tim Haggard

Haggards Horny Ale and Charles Wells Bombardier always available plus Haggards Imp Ale at select times during the year. The pub lease belongs to the owners of Haggards Brewery and this is the principal outlet for their beers, which are brewed in Battersea.

A bright, airy, modern town pub with covered rear garden. Lively atmosphere. Food served every lunchtime and weekday evenings. Traditional roasts on Sundays. No children. Situated on the junction with Cambria Street.

⊖ Nearest Tube: Fulham Broadway.

OPEN *11am–11pm Mon–Sat; 12–10.30pm Sun.*

The White Horse

1 Parsons Green, Fulham SW6 4UL
☎ *(020) 7736 2115* Mark Dorber
www.whitehorsesw6.com

Harveys Sussex Best, Adnams Broadside and Highgate Mild always available plus a house brew, guests including Rooster's Yankee and all sorts of seasonal brews. Also a wide range of bottled beers from around the world.

A large, comfortable Victorian pub overlooking Parsons Green, known as the 'Sloany Pony' and featuring the non-smoking 'Coach House' restaurant. Brunch is also served on Saturdays, 11am–4pm, and on Sundays. Regular beer festivals, including an Old Ale Festival (last Saturday of November), a Wheat Beer Festival (May) and the 'Beauty of the Hops' competition (June). Function room for private dinner parties, tastings and presentations. Parking, terrace/garden. Children allowed.

⊖ Nearest Tube: Parsons Green.

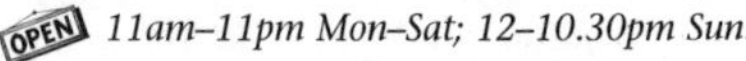
11am–11pm Mon–Sat; 12–10.30pm Sun.

OTHER REAL ALE PUBS IN SW6

Duke of Cumberland (YOUNG'S)
235 New King's Road, Fulham SW6 4XG
☎ *(020) 7736 2777*

SW7

The Anglesea Arms

15 Selwood Terrace, Chelsea SW7 3QG
☎ *(020) 7373 7960* Jenny Podmore
www.angleseaarms.com

Six real ales always available, including Adnams Best and Broadside, Fuller's London Pride and Young's Bitter plus two rotating guests.

A lively, easy-to-find, 200-year-old pub with a traditional atmosphere. No background music or juke box. Food available 12–3pm and 6.30–10pm Mon–Fri, 12–10pm Sat, 12–9.30pm Sun. Wood-panelled dining room open in evenings and at weekends. Heated terraced garden area at front. Cask Marque winner. Children and dogs welcome. Just off the Fulham Road.

⊖ Nearest Tube: South Kensington.

11am–11pm Mon–Sat; 12–10.30pm Sun.

SW8

12

The Priory Arms

83 Lansdowne Way, Stockwell SW8 2PB
☎ *(020) 7622 1884* Gary Morris
www.prioryarms.com

Adnams Bitter, Hop Back Summer Lightning and Harveys Best Bitter always available, plus three guests, mainly from smaller regional breweries and especially micro-breweries.

Popular, genuine freehouse. Regular CAMRA regional pub of the year. Bar food available at lunchtimes, with traditional roasts on Sundays. Quiz night (Sun). Outside seating.

⊖ Nearest Tube: Stockwell.

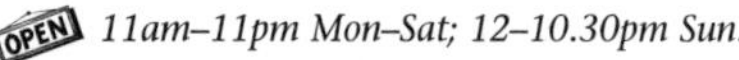
11am–11pm Mon–Sat; 12–10.30pm Sun.

Surprise

16 Southville, South Lambeth SW8 2PP
☎ *(020) 7622 4623* Marie Leo

Owned by Young's, with Bitter, Special and either Waggle Dance or Winter Warmer available.

Traditional one-bar local tucked away down a quiet cul-de-sac off Wandsworth Road. Food served 12–3pm Mon–Sat, 12–4pm Sun. Large patio area, boules pitch. BBQs in summer.

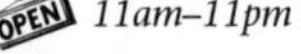
11am–11pm Mon–Sat; 12–10.30pm Sun.

OTHER REAL ALE PUBS IN SW8

The Hope (SHEPHERD NEAME)
7 Heather Close, South Lambeth SW8 3BS
☎ *(020) 7622 2987*

Mawbey Arms (SHEPHERD NEAME)
7 Mawbey Street, Lambeth SW8
☎ *(020) 7622 1936*

Plough Inn (YOUNG'S)
518 Wandsworth Road, Lambeth SW8 3JX
☎ *(020) 7622 2777*

SW9

The Beehive

407–9 Brixton Road, Brixton SW9 7DG
☎ *(020) 7738 3643* Peter Martin

Shepherd Neame Spitfire always available, plus three guests such as Hop Back Summer Lightning, Greene King Abbot or Strawberry Blonde.

A one-bar Wetherspoon's pub with non-smoking dining area, disabled access. Food available all day. No children.

⊖ Nearest Tube: Brixton.

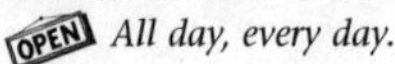
All day, every day.

OTHER REAL ALE PUBS IN SW9

Hogshead
409 Clapham Road SW9 ☎ (020) 7274 2472

Trinity Arms (YOUNG'S)
45 Trinity Gardens, Stockwell SW9 8DR
☎ (020) 7274 4544

SW10

Chelsea Ram
32 Burnaby Street, Chelsea SW10 0PL
☎ (020) 7351 4008 Kristi Ingrilli

A Young's tied house selling Bitter, Special and Waggle Dance or Winter Warmer.

Popular, colourful, cheerful gastro-pub off King's Road. Children welcome. Outside seating. Good food served 12.30–3.30pm and 6.30–10pm (12–9.30pm Sun). Private room, children and dogs welcome. Five minutes from Stamford Bridge.

⊖ Nearest Tube: Fulham Broadway.

OPEN *11am–11pm Mon–Sat; 12–10.30pm Sun.*

Finch's
190 Fulham Road SW10 9PN
☎ (020) 7351 5043 Miss AJ Lowis

Owned by Young's (once owned by Finch's Brewery) with Bitter, Special and seasonal brews available.

A big, traditional football pub with one large bar. Seven minutes from Stamford Bridge. Food served 12–2.30pm and 6–8pm Mon–Sat, 12–3pm Sun.

⊖ Nearest Tube: Fulham Broadway.

OPEN *11am–11pm Mon–Sat; 12–10.30pm Sun.*

OTHER REAL ALE PUBS IN SW10

Fine Line (FULLER'S)
236 Fulham Road SW10 9NB
☎ (020) 7376 5827

The World's End
(HALL & WOODHOUSE)
459 King's Road, Chelsea SW10 0LR
☎ (020) 7376 8946

SW11

The Castle
115 High Street, Battersea SW11 3JR
☎ (020) 7228 8181 Gill Markwell

Tied to Young's with Bitter, Special and either Waggle Dance or Winter Warmer available.

French country farmhouse feel, open fire in the main bar, snug bar with leather sofas. Food served 12–3pm (4.30pm Sun) and 7–10pm daily. Patio beer garden, car park. Snug bar used for private parties.

OPEN *12–11pm.*

OTHER REAL ALE PUBS IN SW11

The Asparagus (WETHERSPOON)
1–13 Falcon Road, Battersea SW11 2PT
☎ (020) 7801 0046

Beehive (FULLER'S)
197 St John's Hill, Wandsworth SW11 1TH
☎ (020) 7207 1267

Duke of Cambridge (YOUNG'S)
228 Battersea Bridge Road SW11 3AA
☎ (020) 7223 5662

Fine Line (FULLER'S)
31–7 Northcote Road, Battersea SW11 1NJ
☎ (020) 7924 7387

The Latchmere
503 Battersea Park Road, Battersea SW11
☎ (020) 7223 3549

Plough (YOUNG'S)
89 St John's Hill, Clapham Junction SW11 1SY
☎ (020) 7228 9136

Woodman (HALL & WOODHOUSE)
60 Battersea High Street SW11 3HX
☎ (020) 7228 2968

SW12

Grove
39 Oldridge Road, Balham SW12 8PN
☎ (020) 8673 6531 Charles Gotto

Young's Bitter, Special and a guest brew always available.

Victorian hotel, now a pub with an oak-floored public bar area, a saloon bar for families and a restaurant. Food served at lunchtime and evenings daily. Popular Sunday roasts, also hog roasts etc on the outside patio area.

⊖ Nearest Tube: Balham/Clapham South.

OPEN *11am–11pm.*

Moon Under Water
194 Balham High Road, Balham SW12 9BP
☎ (020) 8673 0535 James Glover

Hop Back Summer Lightning and Shepherd Neame Spitfire permanently available, plus two guest beers.

A friendly Wetherspoon's local. No music. Large and relatively peaceful non-smoking area. Food served all day, every day. No children.

⊖ Nearest Tube: Balham.

OPEN *11am–11pm Mon–Sat; 12–10.30pm Sun.*

OTHER REAL ALE PUBS IN SW12

Duke of Devonshire (YOUNG'S)
39 Balham High Road SW12 9AN
☎ *(020) 7673 1363*

Jackdaw & Rook (FULLERS)
96–100 Balham High Road SW12 9AA
☎ *(020) 8772 9021*

Nightingale (YOUNG'S)
97 Nightingale Lane, Balham SW12 8NX
☎ *(020) 8673 1637*

SW13

Bulls Head
373 Lonsdale Road, Barnes SW13 9PY
☎ *(020) 8876 5241* Dan and Liz Fleming

A Young's pub serving Bitter, Special, Triple A and seasonal brews such as Winter Warmer as appropriate.

Beside the Thames on the south side of Barnes Bridge with a reputation for live jazz music every evening and on Sundays. Bar and restaurant food available from 12–9pm (12–3pm Sun). Children welcome in eating area. Popular on Boat Race day. Outside seating.

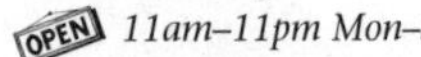
11am–11pm Mon–Sat; 12–10.30pm Sun.

Coach & Horses
27 High Street, Barnes SW13 9LW
☎ *(020) 8876 2695* Nichola Green

A Young's house serving Bitter, Special and seasonal brews.

Popular former coaching inn with large garden. Food available at lunchtime, with barbecues in summer. Function room available for hire. Children welcome in the garden.

11am–11pm Mon–Sat; 12–10.30pm Sun. Hours may be more restricted during the winter.

OTHER REAL ALE PUBS IN SW13

Red Lion (FULLER'S)
2 Castlenau, Barnes SW13 9RU
☎ *(020) 8748 2984*

White Hart (YOUNG'S)
The Terrace, Riverside, Barnes SW13 9NR
☎ *(020) 8876 5177*

SW14

Charlie Butler (YOUNG'S)
40 High Street, Mortlake SW14 8SN
☎ *(020) 8878 2310*

Hare & Hounds (YOUNG'S)
216 Upper Richmond Road, Sheen SW14 8AH
☎ *(020) 8876 4304*

Jolly Gardeners (YOUNG'S)
36 Lower Richmond Road, Mortlake SW14 7EX
☎ *(020) 8876 1721*

Railway Tavern
(HALL & WOODHOUSE)
11 Sheen Lane, Mortlake SW14 8HY
☎ *(020) 8878 7361*

SW15

Green Man
Putney Heath, Putney SW15 3NG
☎ *(020) 8788 8096* Jackie Orr

Tied to Young's with Bitter, Special and one of the two seasonal brews always available.

Recently refurbished, a warm and cosy pub with a large garden. Food served 12–3pm and 6–9.30pm Mon–Fri, 12–9pm Sat and 12–5pm Sun. The heath is on the doorstep.

All day, every day.

The Railway
202 Upper Richmond Road, Putney SW15 6TD
☎ *(020) 8871 4497* Julie Allen

A Wetherspoon's house serving the usual suspects such as Green King Abbot and Shepherd Neame Spitfire plus guests.

Another in the chain, but with a railway theme. Serving standard Wetherspoon's food all day. Non-smoking area, upstairs bar. Children welcome.

⊖ Nearest Tube: East Putney.

11am–11pm Mon–Sat; 12–10.30pm Sun.

OTHER REAL ALE PUBS IN SW15

Angel (YOUNG'S)
11 High Street, Roehampton SW15 4HL
☎ *(020) 8788 1997*

Boathouse (YOUNG'S)
32 Brewhouse Lane, Putney SW15
☎ *(020) 8789 0476*

Duke's Head (YOUNG'S)
8 Lower Richmond Road, Putney SW15 1JN
☎ *(020) 8788 2552*

Half Moon (YOUNG'S)
93 Lower Richmond Road, Putney SW15 1EU
☎ *(020) 8780 9383*

Maltese Cat (YOUNG'S)
Aubyn Square, Roehampton SW15 5NT
☎ *(020) 8876 7534*

P Shannon and Sons (FULLER'S)
46–8 High Street, Putney SW15
☎ *(020) 8780 5437*

Spotted Horse (YOUNG'S)
122 Putney High Street SW15 1RG
☎ *(020) 8788 0246*

Whistle & Flute (FULLER'S)
46–8 High Street, Putney SW15 1SQ
☎ *(020) 8780 5437*

SW16

Bedford Park (YOUNG'S)
233 Streatham High Road, Streatham SW16 6EN
☎ *(020) 8769 2836*

Hogshead
Streatham High Road, Streatham SW16 1DA
☎ *(020) 8696 7582*

The Holland Tringham
(WETHERSPOON)
107–9 Streatham High Road, Streatham SW16 1HJ
☎ *(020) 8769 3062*

The Moon Under Water
(WETHERSPOON)
1327 London Road, Norbury SW16 4AU
☎ *(020) 8765 1235*

Pied Bull (YOUNG'S)
498 Streatham High Road SW16 3BQ
☎ *(020) 8764 4033*

SW17

Castle (YOUNG'S)
38 High Street, Tooting SW17 0RG
☎ *(020) 8672 7018*

Gorringe Park (YOUNG'S)
29 London Road, Tooting SW17 9JR
☎ *(020) 8648 4478*

JJ Moons (WETHERSPOON)
56a High Street, Tooting SW17 0RN
☎ *(020) 8672 4726*

Leather Bottle (YOUNG'S)
538 Garratt Lane, Tooting SW17 0NY
☎ *(020) 8946 2309*

Prince of Wales (YOUNG'S)
646 Garratt Lane, Tooting SW17 0PB
☎ *(020) 8946 2628*

SW18

Alma
499 Old York Road, Wandsworth SW18 1TF
☎ *(020) 8870 2537* Charles Gotto
www.thealma.co.uk

Tenants of Young's, with Bitter, Special and Waggle Dance available plus St George's Ale.

Victorian green-tiled corner building with large open bar and separate restaurnt. Dining room on first floor. Good food served 12–3pm and 6–10pm. Wedding licence held. Private functions catered for.

OPEN *10am–11pm Mon–Sat; 12–10.30pm Sun.*

The Cat's Back
86 Point Pleasant, Wandsworth SW18 1NN
☎ *(020) 8877 0818* Jim Symons

Three real ales always available from Adnams, O'Hanlons, Slaters, Young's and elsewhere.

Small, unique one-bar pub. Food served 12–4pm. Children and dogs welcome.

OPEN *12–11pm (10.30pm Sun)*

Queen Adelaide
35 Putney Bridge Road, Wandsworth SW18 1NP
☎ *(020) 8874 1695* Liam and Karen Sandford

A Young's house with Bitter, Special and a guest ale available.

Old, traditional pub round the corner from the brewery with beer garden including a children's play area and BBQ. Food served 12–2.30pm and weekday evenings, 12–6pm Sat–Sun.

OPEN *All day, every day.*

The Rose & Crown
134 Putney Bridge Road, Wandsworth SW18 1NP
☎ *(020) 8871 4497* Barry O'Hare

Wetherspoon's pub with regulars such as Shepherd Neame Spitfire, Greene King Abbot, Timothy Taylor Landlord and various guests usually available.

Pub with an outside drinking area, non-smoking area, and with food served all day. Children welcome.

⊖ Nearest Tube: East Putney/Putney Bridge.

OPEN *All day, every day.*

Ship
41 Jew's Row, Wandsworth SW18 1TB
☎ *(020) 8870 9667* Charles Gotto

Young's Bitter, Special and seasonal brews available plus St George's Ale.

Popular riverside pub with large conservatory, indoor and outdoor restaurant. The large garden has an outside bar and BBQ facilities. Good food (meat from the Gotto farm) available from noon.

OPEN *10am–11pm Mon–Sat; 12–10.30pm Sun.*

The Spotted Dog
72 Garratt Lane, Wandsworth SW18 4DJ
☎ *(020) 8875 9531* Colin Daniels

Fuller's London Pride and ESB and Greene King IPA and Abbot always available, plus two guests such as Jennings Cocker Hoop, Fuller's Summer Ale and Greene King Centenary. Beers changed weekly.

A traditional one-bar town pub with food available 12–4pm. Disabled facilities. Patio. Children allowed if dining.

OPEN *All day, every day.*

Spread Eagle

71 High Street, Wandsworth SW18 4LB
☎ *(020) 8877 9809* Mr and Mrs Turner

Young's Bitter, Special and Winter Warmer or Waggle Dance always available.

Opposite the brewery in the centre of Wandsworth, a three-bar Victorian ale house. Two function rooms. Food served every day.

OPEN *All day, every day.*

OTHER REAL ALE PUBS IN SW18

Brewer's Inn (YOUNG'S)
147 East Hill, Wandsworth SW18 2QB
☎ *(020) 8874 4128*

Brewery Tap (YOUNG'S)
68 High Street, Wandsworth SW18 2LB
☎ *(020) 8875 7005*

County Arms (YOUNG'S)
345 Trinity Road, Wandsworth SW18 3SH
☎ *(020) 8874 8532*

Crane (YOUNG'S)
14 Armoury Way, Wandsworth SW18 3EZ
☎ *(020) 8874 2450*

Fox & Hounds (YOUNG'S)
29 Passmore Street SW18 8HR
☎ *(020) 7730 6367*

Gardeners Arms (YOUNG'S)
268 Merton Road, Southfields SW18 5JL
☎ *(020) 8874 7624*

Grapes (YOUNG'S)
39 Fairfield Street, Wandsworth SW18 1DX
☎ *(020) 8874 8681*

The Grid Inn (WETHERSPOON)
22 Replingham Road, Southfields SW18 5LS
☎ *(020) 8874 8460*

Halfway House (YOUNG'S)
521 Garratt Lane, Earlsfield SW18 4SR
☎ *(020) 8946 2788*

The Hop Pole (SHEPHERD NEAME)
64 Putney Bridge Road, Wandsworth SW18 1HR
☎ *(020) 8870 8188*

Kings Arms (YOUNG'S)
96 High Street, Wandsworth SW18 4LB
☎ *(020) 8874 1428*

Old Sergeant (YOUNG'S)
104 Garratt Lane, Wandsworth SW18 4DJ
☎ *(020) 8874 4099*

Pig & Whistle (YOUNG'S)
481 Merton Road SW18 5LB
☎ *(020) 8874 1061*

Wheatsheaf (YOUNG'S)
30 Putney Bridge Road, Wandsworth SW18 1HS
☎ *(020) 8874 5753*

SW19

The Brewery Tap

68–9 High Street, Wimbledon Village SW19 5EE
☎ *(020) 8947 9331* John and Heather Grover

Freehouse serving five rotating cask ales from independent breweries, including Fuller's London Pride, Adnams Bitter and three rotating guests, usually one mild and one from the North of England. Cottage, Slaters, Haggards, Battersea, Rebellion and Archers brews have all appeared recently.

Small and cosy one-bar Victorian freehouse in the heart of Wimbledon village. Food available every lunchtime and evenings (Tapas night on Weds). Children allowed.

⊖ Nearest Tube: Wimbledon

OPEN *11am–11pm (10.30pm Sun).*

Crooked Billet

15 Crooked Billet, Wimbledon Common SW19 4RQ
☎ *(020) 8946 4942* Mr and Mrs J Griffin

A Young's house with Bitter, Special and either Winter Warmer or Waggle Dance.

Late seventeenth-century pub with a mock-Tudor interior. One bar plus restaurant. Food served 12.30–3pm and 6.30–10pm. Large outside area and the common is one minute away.

OPEN *11am–11pm Mon–Sat; 12–10.30pm Sun.*

Rose & Crown

55 High Street, Wimbledon SW19 5BA
☎ *(020) 8947 4713* Mr J Messitt

Another Young's house with Bitter, Special and either Winter Warmer or Waggle Dance available.

Dates back to the sixteenth century, in the heart of Wimbledon Village. Recently refurbished, with 13 en-suite bedrooms (more to come). Traditional bar and outside courtyard. Food served 12–3pm and 6.30–10pm. Children welcome.

OPEN *11am–11pm Mon–Sat; 12–10.30pm Sun.*

The Sultan

78 Norman Road, South Wimbledon SW19 1BT
☎ *(020) 8544 9323* Angela Shaw

The only pub in London owned by the Salisbury-based Hop Back Brewery, so serving GFB, Thunderstorm, Summer Lightning, Crop Circle and other seasonal ales.

Two-bar, street-corner local. All beers sold at reduced price (£1.70) on Wednesdays. Garden. Quiz night (Tues). No food. Local CAMRA Pub of the Year 2003.

⊖ Nearest Tube: Colliers Wood/South Wimbledon

OPEN *12–11pm (10.30pm Sun).*

OTHER REAL ALE PUBS IN SW19

Alexandra (YOUNG'S)
33 Wimbledon Hill Road, Wimbledon SW19 7NE
☎ *(020) 8947 7691*

Dog & Fox (YOUNG'S)
24 Wimbledon High Street SW19 5EA
☎ *(020) 8946 6565*

Hand in Hand (YOUNG'S)
6 Crooked Billet, Wimbledon Common SW19 4RQ ☎ *(020) 8946 5720*

Kings Head (YOUNG'S)
18 High Street, Merton SW19 1DN
☎ *(020) 8540 7992*

Princess of Wales (YOUNG'S)
98 Morden Road, Merton SW19 3BP
☎ *(020) 8542 0573*

Wibbas Down Inn (WETHERSPOON)
6–12 Gladstone Road, Wimbledon SW19 1QT
☎ *(020) 8540 6788*

LONDON WEST

W1

Ain't Nothin' But ... Blues Bar

20 Kingly Street W1R 5PZ
☎ *(020) 7287 0514* Rob Bloxham

Adnams Best and Broadside usually available, plus a guest which changes every few days. Recent favourites include Fuller's London Pride and Honey Dew, Young's Waggle Dance, Charles Wells Bombardier, Greene King Old Speckled Hen, Everards Beacon and Tiger, Bateman Salem Porter and brews from Badger and Wychwood.

Central London's only blues bar venue. Good old-fashioned drinkers' bar with mixed clientele. Open late with live music every night. Food served during opening hours. No children. Situated between Regent Street and Carnaby Street behind Hamley's Toy Shop.

⊖ Nearest Tube: Oxford Circus.

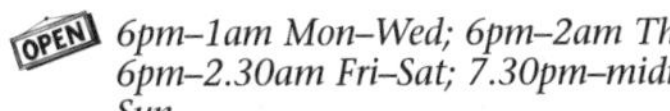
OPEN *6pm–1am Mon–Wed; 6pm–2am Thurs; 6pm–2.30am Fri–Sat; 7.30pm–midnight Sun.*

The Argyll Arms

18 Argyll Street W1 1AA
☎ *(020) 7734 6117* Mike Tayara

Seven beers always available including Wadworth 6X and an ever-changing selection that might feature Everards Daredevil, Hop Back Summer Lightning, Felinfoel Double Dragon, Timothy Taylor Landlord, Charles Wells Bombardier and brews from Jennings, Ringwood or Tomintoul.

A 300-year-old pub just off Oxford Circus owned by the Duke of Argyll. Air-conditioned. Bar and restaurant food available at lunchtime and evenings. Function room, non-smoking area. Children allowed in play area.

⊖ Nearest Tube: Oxford Circus.

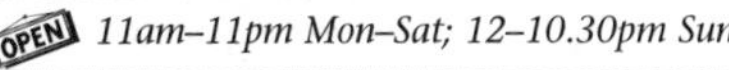
OPEN *11am–11pm Mon–Sat; 12–10.30pm Sun.*

The Carpenters Arms

12 Seymour Place W1H 7NE
☎ *(020) 7723 1050* Sarah Nixon

Fuller's London Pride and Young's Special usually available plus a guest beer such as Hop Back Summer Lightning, Everards Tiger, Wadworth 6X or something from Harveys, Hardys & Hansons or Oakhill.

A charming traditional tavern with a warm welcome. Small and intimate one-bar house which is a great favourite with locals, business people and tourists alike. Food served on weekday lunchtimes. Cask Marque winner.

⊖ Nearest Tube: Edgware Road/Marble Arch.

OPEN *11am–11pm Mon–Sat; 12–10.30pm Sun.*

The Clachan

34 Kingly Street W1R 5LB
☎ *(020) 7734 2659*

A Nicholson's house serving up to four ales that may well include Fuller's London Pride, Greene King IPA, Timothy Taylor Landlord and guests.

Behind Liberty's, just off Carnaby Street, a one-bar central London alehouse with upstairs function room. Food served at lunchtime and evenings.

⊖ Nearest Tube: Oxford Circus.

OPEN *11am–11pm Mon–Sat; closed Sun.*

Golden Eagle

59 Marylebone Lane W1U 2NY
☎ *(020) 7935 3228* Gina Vernon

St Austell Tribute, Greene King IPA and Fuller's London Pride usually available. One guest beer rotated every two months.

A genuine Victorian freehouse five minutes from Oxford Street. Licesned since 1852. One bar. Bar snakcs served 12–2.45pm Mon–Fri. Sing-a-long piano nights (Tue, Thur, Fri).

⊖ Nearest Tube: Bond Street

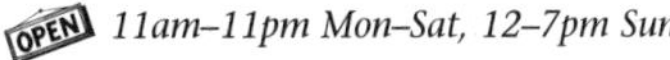
OPEN *11am–11pm Mon–Sat, 12–7pm Sun.*

The Guinea

30 Bruton Place, Mayfair W1J 6NL
☎ *(020) 7409 1728* Carl Smith

A Young's pub serving the brewery's Bitter, Special and seasonal brews (Winter Warmer and Waggle Dance).

Established in 1673 and tucked away in a mews street near Berkeley Square with a fine restaurant next door. Food served 12.30–2.30pm Mon–Fri and 6.30–11pm Mon–Sat.

⊖ Nearest Tube: Bond Street.

OPEN *11am–11pm Mon–Fri; 6.30–11pm Sat; closed Sun and bank holidays.*

Shaston Arms

4–6 Ganton Street W1S 7QN
☎ *(020) 7287 2631* Sally Graham

Owned by Hall & Woodhouse, so serving Badger Best and Tanglefoot, plus King & Barnes Sussex.

Opened in December 2000 in a former wine bar off Carnaby Street. The curious layout sees the bar in one room with much of the seating next door. Food available until 5pm.

⊖ Nearest Tube: Oxford Circus.

OPEN *11am–11pm Mon–Sat; closed Sun.*

The Spice of Life

6 Moor Street, Cambridge Circus, Soho W1D 5NA
☎ *(020) 7437 7013* Andrew Ranum
www.spiceoflifesoho.com

A McMullen's house, with two brewery beers and a guest ale available.

Built in 1898, recently refurbished with two bars. Food available 12–9pm daily. Next to the Palace Theatre (Les Miserables). Live music every night in the basement bar.

⊖ Nearest Tube: Leicester Square.

OPEN *11am–11pm Mon–Sat; 12–10.30pm Sun.*

The Windmill

6–8 Mill Street Mayfair W1R 9TE
☎ *(020) 7491 8050* Pauline Smith
www.windmillmayfair.co.uk

A Young's house with Bitter, Special and one of the two seasonal brews always available.

Cosy, traditional and comfortable ale house with two bars (one non-smoking) and a private room available for hire. Award-winning food served 12–3pm and 6–9.30pm Mon–Fri, 12–4pm Sat. Off Regent Street.

⊖ Nearest Tube: Oxford Circus.

OPEN *11am–11pm Mon–Fri; 12–4pm Sat.*

OTHER REAL ALE PUBS IN W1

Dog & Duck

18 Bateman Street, Soho W1
☎ *(020) 7494 0697*

Fuller's Ale Lodge (FULLER'S)

11 Avery Row, Mayfair W1X 9HA
☎ *(020) 7629 1643*

Hogshead

72 Grafton Way W1 ☎ *(020) 7387 7923*

Jack Horner (FULLER'S)

236 Tottenham Court Road W1P 9AE
☎ *(020) 7636 2868*

The Moon & Sixpence (WETHERSPOON)

183–5 Wardour Street W1V 3FB
☎ *(020) 7734 0037*

The Old Monk

24–6 Maddox Street W1R 9PG
☎ *(020) 7499 3775*

One Tun (YOUNG'S)

58–60 Goodge Street W1T 4ND
☎ *(020) 7209 4105*

Pillars of Hercules

7 Greek Street, Soho W1 ☎ *(020) 7437 1179*

Ship (FULLER'S)

116 Wardour Street W1F 0TT
☎ *(020) 7437 8446*

Sun & 13 Cantons (FULLER'S)

21 Great Pultney Street W1R 3DB
☎ *(020) 7734 0934*

Wargrave Arms (YOUNG'S)

42 Brendon Street W1H 5HS ☎ *(020) 7723 0559*

W2

Archery Tavern

4 Bathurst Street W2 2SD
☎ *(020) 7402 4916* Mac and Louise MacGlade

A Hall & Woodhouse tied pub with Badger Best, Tanglefoot and Sussex Ale always available, plus two occasional guests such as Gribble Black Adder II or Golden Champion Ale.

A three-room, one-bar traditional, friendly pub on the north side of Hyde Park near the riding stables. Quiz night, darts. Food available 12–10pm. Well-behaved children allowed. Outside seating.

⊖ Nearest Tube: Lancaster Gate.

OPEN *11am–11pm Mon–Sat; 12–10.30pm Sun.*

Fountain's Abbey
109 Praed Street W2 1RL
☎ *(020) 7723 2364* David Harrison

Greene King Abbot Ale and Old Speckled Hen plus Charles Wells Bombardier always available, plus one rotating guest ale. Approximately six different guests served every month.

A large, Victorian-style alehouse with outside seating and food available all day. Children allowed until 6pm. Upstairs function room for hire.

⊖ Nearest Tube: Paddington.

OPEN *11am–11pm Mon–Sat; 12–10.30pm Sun.*

The Victoria
10A Strathearn Place, Paddington W2 2NH
☎ *(020) 7724 1191*
Helen Wilson and Chris Cochran

Tied to Fuller's so with Chiswick, London Pride and ESB always available plus a seasonal brew changed quarterly.

Victorian alehouse with many original features and elegant dining and function rooms. Outside patio can cope with 35 people. Quiz night on Tues. Food served 12–3pm and 6–9.30pm Mon–Sat, 12–9pm Sun. Five minutes from Hyde Park.

⊖ Nearest Tube: Paddington

OPEN *11am–11pm (10.30pm Sun)*

OTHER REAL ALE PUBS IN W2

Mad Bishop & Bear (FULLER'S)
1st Floor, The Lawn, Paddington Station W2 1HB ☎ *(020) 7402 2441*

Monkey Puzzle
(HALL & WOODHOUSE)
30 Southwick Street W2 1JQ
☎ *(020) 7723 0143*

Prince Edward
(HALL & WOODHOUSE)
73 Princes Street, Bayswater W2 4NY
☎ *(020) 7727 2221*

The Tyburn (WETHERSPOON)
20 Edgware Road W2 2EN ☎ *(020) 7723 4731*

W3

Kings Head
214 High Street, Acton W3 9NX
☎ *(020) 8992 0282* Dave Connell

Tied to Fuller's so with Chsiwick, London Pride and ESB always available plus a seasonal brew.

Victorian community pub on the high street. One bar, one function room (available for hire). Comedy and live music nights. Sporting events shown. Food served 12–3pm and 6–9pm Mon–Fri, 11am–7pm Sat–Sun.

OPEN *11am–11pm Mon–Sat; 12–10.30pm Sun.*

OTHER REAL ALE PUBS IN W3

Castle (FULLER'S)
Victoria Road, North Acton W3 6UL
☎ *(020) 8992 2027*

Kings Arms (FULLER'S)
Acton Vale, Acton W3 7JT ☎ *(020) 8743 2689*

The Red Lion & Pineapple
(WETHERSPOON)
281 High Street, Acton W3 9PJ
☎ *(020) 8896 2248*

W4

The Bell & Crown
11–13 Thames Road, Strand on the Green, Chiswick W4 3PL
☎ *(020) 8994 4164* Frank McBrearty

A Fuller's tied house with London Pride, Chiswick and ESB permanently on offer. Fuller's seasonal ales served as available.

Backing on to the Thames, with excellent views, this substantial pub has a 40-seater non-smoking dining area/conservatory and outside seating. Food available 12–10pm daily. Children allowed, under supervision.

⊖ Nearest Tube: Gunnersbury.

OPEN *11am–11pm Mon–Sat; 12–10.30pm Sun.*

The George & Devonshire
8 Burlington Lane, Chiswick W4 2QE
☎ *(020) 8994 1859* Tim Lewohl

Another Fuller's tied house with London Pride, Chiswick and ESB permanently on offer. Fuller's seasonal ales served as available.

In a listed sixteenth-century building. Still very traditional. Food served 12–8pm Mon–Fri, 12–4pm Sat–Sun. Car park, beer garden, children welcome. Close to the Fuller's Brewery.

⊖ Nearest Tube: Gunnersbury.

OPEN *11am–11pm Mon–Sat; 12–10.30pm Sun.*

OTHER REAL ALE PUBS IN W4

Crown & Anchor (YOUNG'S)
374 Chiswick High Road, Chiswick W4 5TA
☎ *(020) 8995 2607*

Duke of York (FULLER'S)
107 Devonshire Road, Chiswick W4 2HU
☎ *(020) 8994 4624*

George IV (FULLER'S)
185 Chiswick High Road, Chiswick W4 1DR
☎ *(020) 8994 4624*

Hogshead
34 Chiswick High Road, Chiswick W4
☎ *(020) 8742 0021*

Mawson Arms and Fox & Hounds (FULLER'S)
Mawson Lane, Chiswick W4 2QD
☎ *(020) 8994 2936*

Old Pack Horse (FULLER'S)
434 Chiswick High Road, Chiswick W4 5TF
☎ *(020) 8994 2872*

W5

The Red Lion
13 St Mary's Road, Ealing W5 5RA
☎ *(020) 8567 2541* Jonathan and Victoria Lee

Fuller's Chiswick, London Pride and ESB plus a seasonal brew usually available.

Small, traditional, Grade II listed, one-bar Fuller's pub. No music or machines. Large patio garden. Food served 12–2.30pm and 6–9pm. Children allowed in garden only. Situated opposite Ealing Studios.

⊖ Nearest Tube: Ealing Broadway.

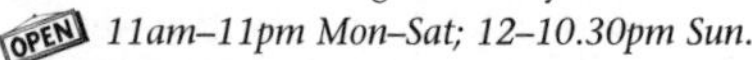
11am–11pm Mon–Sat; 12–10.30pm Sun.

TJ Duffy
282 Northfield Avenue, Ealing W5 4UB
☎ *(020) 8932 1711* Thomas Duffy

Fuller's London Pride always available plus guests from Adnams, Charles Wells, Timothy Taylor etc.

Guest beers are sold at a reduced price on Tuesdays at this west London freehouse. Food served at lunchtimes and evenings. Quiz nights, live music.

⊖ Nearest Tube: Northfields.

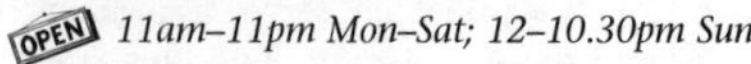
11am–11pm Mon–Sat; 12–10.30pm Sun.

OTHER REAL ALE PUBS IN W5

Castle (FULLER'S)
36 St Mary's Road, Ealing W5 5RG
☎ *(020) 8567 3285*

Fox & Goose Hotel (FULLER'S)
Hanger Lane, Ealing W5 1DP
☎ *(020) 8998 5864*

Hogshead
46–7 The Mall, Ealing W5 3TJ
☎ *(020) 8579 3006*

Plough Inn (FULLER'S)
297 Northfield Avenue, Ealing W5 4XB
☎ *(020) 8567 1416*

Rose & Crown (FULLER'S)
Church Place, St Mary's Road, Ealing W5 4HN
☎ *(020) 8567 2811*

Townhouse (FULLER'S)
The Broadway, Ealing W5 2PH
☎ *(020) 8810 0304*

Wheatsheaf (FULLER'S)
41 Haven Lane, Ealing W5 2HZ
☎ *(020) 8997 5240*

W6

The Andover Arms
57 Aldensley Road, Hammersmith W6 0DL
☎ *(020) 8741 9794* Tom Mahedy

A Fuller's tied house with Chiswick, London Pride and ESB available plus seasonal brews.

Victorian alehouse serving English food on weekday lunchtimes and Thai food Mon–Sat evenings.

⊖ Nearest Tube: Ravenscourt Park.

12–11pm Mon–Sat; 12–4pm and 7–10.30pm Sun.

The Cross Keys
57 Black Lion Lane, Hammersmith W6 9BG
☎ *(020) 8748 3541* Sally Hickson

Fuller's London Pride and a seasonal ale usually available.

A traditional pub with back garden open in summer. Food served 12–3pm and 6–9pm Mon–Fri, 12–4pm Sat–Sun. Live music once a month. Darts and board games. Big screen TV for sports events. Children welcome before 9pm.

⊖ Nearest Tube: Stamford Brook.

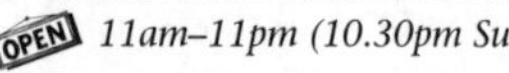
11am–11pm (10.30pm Sun).

Dove
Upper Mall, Hammersmith W6 9TA
☎ *(020) 8748 9474* Alison Juliff

A Fuller's house, with London Pride and ESB always available plus the seasonal brews.

Backing on to the Thames near Hammersmith Bridge. Owned by Fuller's since 1845. Features the smallest bar in Britain, but with plenty of space (inside and out) elsewhere. Bar food available 12–9pm Mon–Sat, 12–4pm Sun. No machines or music.

⊖ Nearest Tube: Hammersmith.

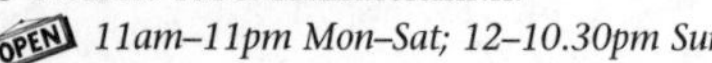
11am–11pm Mon–Sat; 12–10.30pm Sun.

OTHER REAL ALE PUBS IN W6

Blue Anchor
13 Lower Mall, Hammersmith Bridge W6
☎ *(020) 8748 5774*

Brook Green (YOUNG'S)
170 Shepherds Bush Road W6 7PB
☎ *(020) 7603 2516*

Hammersmith Ram (YOUNG'S)
81 King Street, Hammersmith W6 9HW
☎ *(020) 8748 4511*

Latymers (FULLER'S)
157 Hammersmith Road, Hammersmith W6 8BS
☎ *(020) 8748 3446*

Salutation (FULLER'S)
154 King Street, Hammersmith W6 0QU
☎ *(020) 8748 3668*

Thatched House (YOUNG'S)
115 Dalling Road, Hammersmith W6 0ET
☎ *(020) 8748 6174*

The William Morris
(WETHERSPOON)
2–4 King Street, Hammersmith W6 0QA
☎ *(020) 8741 7175*

W7

The Dolphin
13 Lower Boston Road, Hanwell W7 3TX
☎ *(020) 8810 1617* John Connoly

Marston's Pedigree, Brakspear Bitter, Greene King Old Speckled Hen, Fuller's London Pride, Wadworth 6X or Gale's HSB usually available. A guest beer such as Badger Tanglefoot often on offer, too.

Olde-worlde character pub with wooden floors, lovely beer garden and restaurant. Food served 12–2.30pm and 6–9pm Tues–Sun. Kitchen closed Sun evening and Monday. Children welcome, with separate children's menu available. Small car park. Located off one-way system to Uxbridge Road or follow Boston Road to end.

12–11pm (10.30pm Sun).

The Fox
Greene Lane, Olde Hanwell W7
☎ *(020) 8567 3912*

Fuller's London Pride, Timothy Taylor Landlord and Brakspear Bitter plus ever-changing guests.

Freehouse built in 1853 close to the Grand Union Canal serving food at lunchtime and evenings. Garden. Quiz night. Regular live music and beer festivals.

OPEN *11am–11pm Mon–Sat; 12–10.30pm Sun.*

OTHER REAL ALE PUBS IN W7

Viaduct (FULLER'S)
221 Uxbridge Road, Hanwell W7 3TD
☎ *(020) 8567 1362*

White Hart (FULLER'S)
324 Greenford Avenue, Hanwell W7 3DA
☎ *(020) 8578 1708*

W8

Churchill Arms
119 Kensington Church Street W8 7LN
☎ *(020) 7727 4242* Gerry O'Brien

Another Fuller's house, so with Chiswick, London Pride, ESB and seasonal brews available.

A popular, atmospheric, 1930s, award-winning locals' pub with plenty of Churchill family memorabilia (they celebrate his birthday in style). Thai food available. Conservatory.

⊖ Nearest Tube: Notting Hill Gate

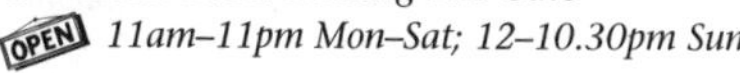
11am–11pm Mon–Sat; 12–10.30pm Sun.

OTHER REAL ALE PUBS IN W8

Britannia (YOUNG'S)
1 Allen Street, Kensington W8 6UX
☎ *(020) 7937 6905*

W9

The Truscott Arms
55 Shirland Road, Maida Vale W9 2JD
☎ *(020) 7286 0310* Barbara Slack

Fuller's London Pride, Greene King IPA and Abbot usually available, plus other Fuller's beers.

Local community pub with one large centre bar. Secluded rear beer garden. Food served 12–3pm and 6–9pm Mon–Sat, plus 12–3pm Sun for traditional roasts and summer barbecues (weather permitting). Children are welcome until 7pm.

⊖ Nearest Tube: Warwick Avenue.

OPEN *11am–11pm Mon–Sat; 12–10.30pm Sun.*

Warrington Hotel
93 Warrington Crescent, Maida Vale W9 1EH
☎ *(020) 7286 2929* J Brandon

Brakspear Special, Young's Special, Fuller's London Pride and ESB usually available, plus one or two guest beers perhaps from Rebellion.

A splendid example of a Victorian public house with art nouveau stained glass, marble bar and fireplace. A family-owned freehouse which has been a popular meeting place for many years. Thai food served in the bar 12–2.30pm and in the upstairs restaurant 6–11pm. No children. Outside seating.

⊖ Nearest Tube: Warwick Avenue.

OPEN *11am–11pm Mon–Sat; 12–10.30pm Sun.*

W11

Duke of Wellington
179 Portobello Road W11 2ED
☎ *(020) 7727 6727* John Joe Murtagh

Tied to Young's with Bitter, Special and either Winter Warmer or Waggle Dance available.

Traditional English pub, 200 years old. One bar. Food served 10am–4pm and 6–9.30pm seven days a week. Close to Portobello Market.

⊖ Nearest Tube: Ladbroke Grove.

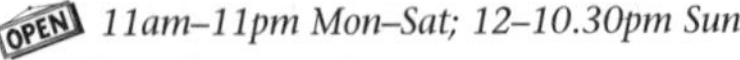
11am–11pm Mon–Sat; 12–10.30pm Sun.

OTHER REAL ALE PUBS IN W11

Elgin
96 Ladbroke Grove W11 1PY
☎ *(020) 7229 5663*

W12

Crown & Sceptre
57 Melina Road, Shepherds Bush W12 9HY
☎ *(020) 8743 6414* Rachel Watson

Owned by Fuller's, with London Pride, a seasonal brew and one guest available.

Cosy gastro-pub in the heart of the local community. Good-sized beer garden, on-street parking. Food served 12–3pm and 6–10pm Mon–Fri, 12–4pm and 6–10pm Sat and 12–4pm and 6–9.30pm Sun.

⊖ Nearest Tube: Goldhawk Road.

OPEN *12–11pm (10.30pm Sun).*

OTHER REAL ALE PUBS IN W12

Vesbar (FULLER'S)
15–19 Goldhawk Road, Shepherds Bush W12 8QQ
☎ *(020) 8762 0215*

W13

Duke of Kent
2 Scotch Common, Ealing W13 8DL
☎ *(020) 8997 5911* Mr and Mrs Elvin

Three real ales usually available, usually from Fuller's, plus one guest.

Grade II listed Georgian pub. Traditional features and modern twists. Beer garden with heated patio. Limited parking, disabled facilities. Food served at lunchtime and evenings daily. Off the A40 at Perivale, just beyond Scotch Common.

OPEN *11.30am–11pm Mon–Sat;, 12–10.30pm Sun.*

OTHER REAL ALE PUBS IN W13

Drayton Court Hotel (FULLER'S)
2 The Avenue, Ealing W13 8PH
☎ *(020) 8997 1019*

W14

Britannia Tap
150 Warwick Road, West Kensington W14 8PS
☎ *(020) 7602 1649* Dale Neil

Tied to Young's with Bitter, Special and either Waggle Dance or Winter Warmer available. Plus a guest such as Smiles' Bristol Bitter.

Tiny pub with award-winning walled garden. Good-priced Thai food available from noon to midnight daily. Five minutes from Olympia.

⊖ Nearest Tube: Kensington

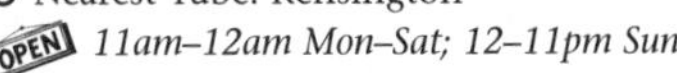
11am–12am Mon–Sat; 12–11pm Sun.

OTHER REAL ALE PUBS IN W14

Seven Stars (FULLER'S)
253 North End Road, Kensington W14 9NS
☎ *(020) 7385 3571*

Warwick Arms (FULLER'S)
160 Warwick Road, Kensington W14 9OS
☎ *(020) 7603 356*

FURTHER WEST

BRENTFORD

The Magpie & Crown
128 High Street, Brentford TW8 8EW
☎ *(020) 8560 5658* Charlie and Steve Bolton

A freehouse with four pumps serving a range of good-priced ales such as Brakspear Bitter, Greene King IPA, something from Cottage and many, many more.

A mock-Tudor pub. One bar. Food served at lunchtime and evenings. No children. Quiz nights on Thursday. Also serves draught European beers, plus ciders and perry.

OPEN *11am–11pm (10.30pm Sun).*

EGHAM

The Crown
38 High Street, Egham TW20 9DP
☎ *(01784) 432608* Lin Bowman

The permanent beers are Adnams Broadside in winter and Adnams Regatta in summer, and the two or three guests, changed weekly, are from a wide range of breweries.

Very busy town pub with one bar, dining area and garden. Plenty of food available! Twice-yearly beer festivals held, with around 10 beers at each. Occasional live music.

OPEN *11.30am–11pm Mon–Sat; 12–10.30pm Sun.*

FELTHAM

Moon on the Square

30 The Centre, Feltham TW13 4AU
☎ *(020) 8893 1293* John Colley

Greene King Abbot is always available, plus four guests changing all the time, from breweries such as Brakspear, Cotleigh, Hook Norton and Exmoor.

One big bar plus non-smoking dining area in which food is available all day. Children allowed until 3pm.

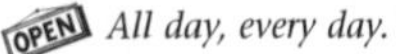

OPEN *All day, every day.*

HEATHROW

The Tap & Spile

Upper Concourse, Terminal One, Heathrow Airport UB5 4PX
☎ *(020) 8897 8418* John Heaphy

Marston's Pedigree always available plus up to nine guest beers (50 per year) including Rooster's Bitter, Charles Wells Eagle, Brains SA, Nethergate IPA and Adnams Best.

Cosy and relaxing refuge with a 1930s feel overlooking the anarchy of the check-in area. Bar food available at lunchtime and evenings. Car park and children's room. On the catering balcony at departure level in terminal one.

OPEN *9–11am for breakfast, then 11am–11pm.*

HOUNSLOW

Moon Under Water

84–6 Staines Road, Hounslow TW3 3LF
☎ *(020) 8572 7506* Peter Johnson

Hop Back Summer Lightning and Greene King Abbot permanently available, plus three to five guests from the extended list which are constantly changing. Brews from Arundel, Cottage and Itchen Valley feature alongside the bigger regionals. Good prices are even cheaper on Monday nights.

A Wetherspoon's pub with non-smoking area, patio, disabled facilities. Food available all day from 10am–10pm (9.30pm Sun). Children allowed until 5pm – separate children's area.

OPEN *10am–11pm (10.30pm Sun).*

ISLEWORTH

The Red Lion

94 Linkfield Road, Isleworth TW7 6QJ
☎ *(020) 8560 1457* Nikki Redding
www.red-lion.info

A freehouse with up to nine real ales available at any one time. Young's Bitter is the house brew. Beer of the Month promotions have featured Harviestoun Bitter and Twisted, Timothy Taylor Landlord, Branscombe Vale Branoc, Otter Ale, Woodforde's Wherry, Marston's Pedigree and Crouch Vale Brewers Gold. Other regular guests include beers from Daleside, Oakham, Hogs Back, Hop Back and Blue Anchor. Tasting notes and knowledgable staff available.

A large, friendly, locals' pub in a back street near the station, situated in an early-Victorian residential area close to Twickenham Rugby Ground and Richmond. Regular live music and a generally relaxed atmosphere. Two bars and a large landscaped garden with regular BBQs in the summer. Corporate hospitality facilities available. Listed in *Time Out* Top 50 Pubs in London 2003. Children allowed in the garden. Quiz night is Thursday. Beer festivals (May and August bank holidays) feature 40 real ales and ciders. B&B planned for Summer 2004.

OPEN *All day, every day.*

LALEHAM

The Feathers

The Broadway, Laleham, Staines TW18 1RZ
☎ *(01784) 453561*
Keith John Graham and Louise Jackson

Fuller's London Pride is a permanent fixture, and the three guest ales might include beers from Hogs Back, Smiles, Adnams, Shepherd Neame, Badger or Hop Back, to name but a few.

Warm, friendly, traditional village pub with a secluded beer garden. An excellent range of freshly cooked meals is served 12–3pm and 6–9pm Mon–Thurs, 12–8.30pm Fri, 12–9.30pm Sat and 12–8pm Sun, and the pub has a separate dining area with two log fires. Children and families welcome. Car park.

OPEN *11am–11pm Mon–Sat; 12–10.30pm Sun.*

STAINES

The Angel Hotel

Angel Mews, High Street, Staines TW18 4EE
☎ *(01784) 452509* John Othick

A freehouse with two beers from Hogs Back and two from Ushers always available, varying according to the season.

A town pub and restaurant with patio and 12 bedrooms. Food available all day.

OPEN *All day, every day.*

The Bells

124 Church Street, Staines TW18 4ZB
☎ *(01784) 454240* Mr and Mrs Winstanley

Tied to Young's, with Young's Special and Triple A always served, plus one guest from Smiles.

Village pub with village atmosphere, with two bars, function room and beer garden. Food available. Children allowed in designated areas.

OPEN *11am–11pm Mon–Sat; 12–10.30pm Sun.*

The George

2–8 High Street, Staines TW18 4EE
☎ *(01784) 462181* Barbara Westwood

Fuller's London Pride and Greene King Abbot among the beers always available plus four guests such as Marston's Pedigree, Shepherd Neame Spitfire and Greene King Old Speckled Hen. Always a good selection of brews from all over the UK. Guests changed frequently.

A large, two-level Wetherspoon's pub. No music, non-smoking dining areas upstairs and down, disabled access and toilets. Food available 10am–10pm Mon–Sat, 10am–9.30pm Sun; alcohol served from 10am except on Sundays. Children allowed, if eating, until 9pm Sun–Thurs and until 6pm Fri–Sat.

OPEN *All day, every day.*

The Hobgoblin

14–16 Church Street, Staines TW18 4EP
☎ *(01784) 452012* Del Woolsgrove

Wychwood Special, Shires XXX and Hobgoblin always available. Three guests could include Marston's Pedigree, Charles Wells Bombardier and beers from Hampshire and Rebellion breweries.

A town-centre, regulars' pub, frequented by the 23–35 age group in evenings, with an older clientele at lunchtimes. An old building with wooden floors and beams, one bar and courtyard. Food available 12–2.30pm. Children allowed in courtyard if open.

OPEN *12–11pm (10.30pm Sun).*

TWICKENHAM

The Eel Pie

9–11 Church Street, Twickenham TW1 3NJ
☎ *(020) 8891 1717* Tom and Kate McAuley

Badger Best, Tanglefoot and IPA and King and Barnes Sussex always available, plus two guests which may include Gribble Brewery's Fursty Ferret or Pig's Ear, or possibly from time to time, Timothy Taylor Landlord, Oakham JHB or Slaters Top Totty.

A cosy, traditional pub with laid-back atmosphere situated just off the main street in Twickenham. A newcomer is welcome either to keep themselves to themselves, or to be the life and soul of the party! Food available 12–4pm daily. Children allowed, children's menu available.

OPEN *11am–11pm Mon–Sat; 12–10.30pm Sun.*

Up 'N' Under

33–5 York Street, Twickenham TW1 3JZ
☎ *(020) 8891 3940* EJF Bourdon (manager)

Up to four real ales stocked, and changed on a monthly basis. Caledonian Deuchars IPA and Fuller's London Pride are favourites.

A stylish, dimly lit bar and gastro-pub serving traditional food, which is available 12–4pm and 6–10pm daily. All sports shown on big-screen TV. Function room, disabled facilities. Children welcome. Two minutes from the station.

OPEN *12–11pm (10.30pm Sun).*

UXBRIDGE

The Load of Hay

Villier Street, Uxbridge UB8 2PU
☎ *(01895) 234676* Gary Carpenter

A freehouse with four real ales always available from breweries such as Archer;s, Woodforde's, Cottage etc – a different one appears each week. Local breweries, micros and small independents favoured, plus Fuller's London Pride.

Approximately 200 years old, situated on the outskirts of town, near the university. University clientele during the daytime, and locals in the evenings. Two bars. Beer garden. Food available every lunchtime and Mon–Sat evenings. Children allowed in the smaller bar area and the garden. In a secluded location – ring for directions if necessary.

OPEN *11am–11pm Mon–Sat; 12–10.30pm Sun.*

The Swan & Bottle

Oxford Road, Uxbridge UB8 1LZ
☎ *(01895) 234047* Claire Chapman

Greene King Old Speckled Hen permanently available plus one guest which changes fortnightly.

A Chef & Brewer pub/restaurant. Family-friendly with children welcome, plus disabled toilet, parking and access. Food available daily. Beer garden.

OPEN *11am–11pm Mon–Sat; 12–10.30pm Sun.*

The Three Tuns

24 High Street, Uxbridge UB8 1JN
☎ *(01895) 233960* Brian Gallagher

Marston's Pedigree, Fuller's London Pride and Adnams Bitter are always on offer.

Traditional town-centre pub with beams, fires, conservatory, beer garden and patio for 80 people. Food available (not Sundays), and there is a separate dining area. Children allowed if eating. Opposite the Tube Station.

OPEN *11am–11pm Mon–Sat; 12–10.30pm Sun.*

THE BREWERIES

3 RIVERS BREWING COMPANY

Unit 12, Vauxhall Industrial Estate, Greg Street, Reddish, Stockport SK5 7BR
☎ *(0161) 477 3333*
www.3riversbrewing.com

G.M.T. 3.8% ABV
Easy-drinking golden session bitter with an underlying malt character supported by a moderate hop bitterness and light floral finish.

SUMMER RAYS 4.0% ABV
A full malt character is supplemented by a very hoppy flavour and notable citrus and floral aroma provided by the American hop cascade.

MANCHESTER IPA 4.2% ABV
Classic Indian pale ale. A light russet amber colour producing a refreshing biscuit-like flavour which is supplemented by a complex citrus finish. Made with genuine Manchester-grown hops.

OXBOW 4.5% ABV
Robust and powerful hoppy bitter with an initial dryness that leads to a spicy character with a prominent aroma and notable citrus aftertaste.

DELTA DARK 4.8% ABV
Strong roast character with hints of treacle toffee and liquorice. The smooth palate gives way to a long and lingering dry bitter finish.

OLD DISREPUTABLE 5.2% ABV
Dark malty brew with distinctive coffee and chocolate traits and a lasting bitter finish.

BANK TOP BREWERY

The Pavillion, Ashworth Lane, Bolton BL1 8RA
☎ *(01204) 595800*
www.banktopbrewery.co.uk

BRYDGE BITTER 3.8% ABV
DARK MILD 4.0% ABV
FLAT CAP 4.0% ABV
GOLD DIGGER 4.0% ABV
GOLDEN BROWN 4.2% ABV
HAKA 4.2% ABV
SAMUEL CROMPTON'S ALE 4.2% ABV
VOLUNTEER BITTER 4.2% ABV
CLIFFHANGER 4.5% ABV
SANTA'S CLAWS 5.0% ABV
SATANIC MILLS 5.0% ABV
SMOKESTACK LIGHTNIN' 5.0% ABV
Plus seasonal brews.

BAZENS' BREWERY

The Rees Bazens' Brewing Co Ltd, Unit 6 Knoll Street Industrial Estate, Knoll Street, Higher Broughton, Salford M7 2BL
☎ *(0161) 708 0247*
www.bazensbrewery.co.uk

BLACK PIG MILD 3.6% ABV
PACIFIC BITTER 3.8% ABV
FLATBAC 4.2% ABV
BAZENS' BEST BITTER 4.3% ABV
SEA GOD 4.3% ABV
GOLDING FLEECE 4.4% ABV
WASS ALE 4.5% ABV
KNOLL ST PORTER 5.2% ABV
Plus seasonal brews.

BOGGART HOLE CLOUGH BREWING COMPANY

13 Brookside Works, Clough Road, Moston, Manchester M9 4FP
☎ *(0161) 277 9666*
www.boggart-brewery.co.uk

BOGGART BITTER 3.8% ABV
BOG STANDARD 4.0% ABV
LOG END 4.0% ABV
ANGEL HILL 4.2% ABV
BOGGART'S BREW 4.3% ABV
THE DARK SIDE 4.4% ABV
SUN DIAL 4.7% ABV
STEAMING BOGGART 9.0% ABV
Plus seasonal brews.

FACER'S BREWERY

6 Knoll Street Industrial Park, Great Clowes Street, The Cliff, Salford M7 2BL
☎ *(0161) 792 7755*
Email dave@facers.co.uk

The brewery was founded in March 2003 by ex-Boddingtons Head Brewer Dave Facer. Premises and brewing plant are shared with Bazens' Brewery in a venture known as the Salford Brewery Syndicate.

NORTHERN COUNTY 3.8% ABV
Standard strength session beer. Light in colour with excellent lacing and a creamy head, the fruity palate has a moreish hop character with orange citrus the predominant impression.

CRABTREE 4.3% ABV
Golden yellow, with a rich and smooth full fruity palate including tangy zest, fruit and elderflower notes, good mouth-feel, and a mellow dry aftertaste. The nose is delightfully hoppy and tempting. It is named to commemorate William Crabtree, the Salford astronomer who, in 1639, was the first to view the transit of Venus across the Sun. This he did but a stone's throw from the site of the Salford Brewery Syndicate, where Facer's beers are brewed.

LANDSLIDE 4.9% ABV
Golden brown in colour with a gentle malt introduction, the bitterness coming through later, enhanced by additional notes including resinous esters, full lemon and orange fruitiness with a hint of cherry and strong mouth-feel.

In addition, there is always a seasonal special available with an ABV of 3.9%. These are available for 2 months at a time and are themed on 'Greats of English Literature'. Specails over the last year included Keats, Scrooge, Prancing Pony, Wordsworth and Chatterley.

J W LEES & CO.

Greengate Brewery, Middleton Junction, Manchester M24 2AX
☎ *(0161) 643 2487*
www.jwlees.co.uk

GB MILD 3.5% ABV
Smooth and sweet, with a malt flavour and a dry finish.

BITTER 4.0% ABV
Refreshing maltiness, with a bitter finish.

MOONRAKER 7.5% ABV
Rounded sweetness, with balancing bitterness.

Plus a changing brew every two months between 4.0% ABV and 5.0% ABV.

JOSEPH HOLT PLC

Derby Brewery, Empire Street, Cheetham, Manchester M3 1JD
☎ *(0161) 834 3285*
www.joseph-holt.com

MILD 3.2% ABV
Malty with good hoppiness.

BITTER 4.0% ABV
Powerful, hoppy and bitter throughout.

HYDES' ANVIL BREWERY LTD

46 Moss Lane West, Manchester M15 5PH
☎ *(0161) 266 1317*
www.hydesbrewery.co.uk

HYDES MILD 3.5% ABV
HYDES LIGHT 3.5% ABV
HYDES BITTER 3.8% ABV
JEKYLL'S GOLD 4.0% ABV

THE LAB BREWERY

Lowes Arms, 301 Hyde Road, Denton M34 3FF
☎ *(0161) 336 3064*

AROMATIC AMBER 3.5% ABV
JET AMBER 3.5% ABV
LOWES IPA 3.8% ABV
OLD ENGLISH ALE 4.5% ABV
BROOMSTAIRS BITTER 4.3% ABV
HAUGHTON WEAVE 4.5% ABV
OLD LANCASTRIAN PORTER 4.5% ABV

LEYDEN BREWING COMPANY

The Lord Raglan, Walmersley Old Road, Nangreaves, Bury BL9 6SP
☎ *(0161) 764 6680*
www.leydenbrewery.com

NANNY FLYER 3.8% ABV
LIGHT BRIGADE 4.2% ABV
CROWNING GLORY 6.8% ABV
Plus seasonals.

MARBLE BREWERY

Marble Arch Inn, 73 Rochdale Road, Manchester M4 4HY
☎ *(0161) 6101073*
www.marblebeers.co.uk

N/4 3.8% ABV
CLOUDY MARBLE 4.0% ABV
MANCHESTER BITTER 4.2% ABV
GINGER MARBLE 4.5% ABV
UNCUT AMBER 4.7% ABV
LAGONDA IPA 5.0% ABV
Plus seasonal brews.

MAYFLOWER BREWERY

Mayflower House, 15 Longendale Road, Standish, Wigan WN6 0UE
☎ *(01257) 400605*
www.mayflowerbrewery.co.uk

BLACK DIAMOND 3.4% ABV
BREWSTERS FIRST 3.8% ABV
MAYFLOWER BEST BITTER 3.8% ABV
AT LAST-CHAMPION ALE 4.0% ABV
WIGAN BIER 4.2% ABV
A WINTERS TALE 4.5% ABV
HIC BIBI 5.0% ABV
Plus seasonal brews.

PHOENIX BREWERY

Oak Brewing Co., Green Lane, Heywood, Greater Manchester OL10 2EP
☎ *(01706) 627009*

BANTAM BITTER 3.5% ABV
OAK BEST BITTER 3.9% ABV
HOPWOOD BITTER 4.3% ABV
OLD OAK ALE 4.5% ABV
THIRSTY MOON 4.6% ABV
BONNEVILLE 4.8% ABV
DOUBLE DAGGER 5.0% ABV
WOBBLY BOB 6.0% ABV
Plus seasonal brews.

SADDLEWORTH BREWERY

Church Inn, Running Hill Gate, Uppermill, Saddleworth OL3 6LW
☎ *(01457) 820902*

SADDLEWORTH MORE 3.8% ABV
AYRTONS ALE 4.1% ABV
Fruity, strawberry blonde, not too bitter.
BERT CORNER 4.1% ABV
BOOMTOWN BITTER 4.1% ABV
HARVEST MOON 4.1% ABV
Some sweetness, but bitter in the finish.
HOPSMACKER 4.1% ABV
PETES DRAGON 4.6% ABV
SADDLEWORTH MORE GOLD 4.6% ABV
SHAFTBENDER 5.4% ABV
Dark porter/stout. Nicknamed The Truth Drug!
CHRISTMAS CAROL 7.4% ABV

SHAWS BREWERY

Park Works, Park Road, Dukinfield SK16 5LX
☎ *(0161) 330 5471*

A five-barrel plant founded in 2002.
BEST BITTER 4.0% ABV
A session beer typical of the north of England with a lingering aftertaste.
PURE GOLD 4.0% ABV
A pale ale with a dry, hoppy finish. Made using American hops.
TAME VALLEY ALE 4.3% ABV
Similar to Best Bitter but with more body and less bite in the aftertaste.
GOLDEN GLOBE 4.5% ABV
Full-bodied and pale. Dry.
IPA 4.8% ABV
Premium pale ale designed to wean the Stella boys!
Plus monthly special ales

THOMAS MCGUINNESS BREWERY

Cask & Feather, 1 Oldham Road, Rochdale OL16 1UA
☎ *(01706) 711476*

FEATHER PLUCKER MILD 3.4% ABV
BEST BITTER 3.8% ABV
SPECIAL RESERVE BITTER 4.0% ABV
JUNCTION BITTER 4.2% ABV
Plus seasonal brews.

THE PUBS

ALTRINCHAM

Old Market Tavern

Old Market Place, Altrincham W14 4DN
☎ *(0161) 927 7062* Ann Marie Holborn

Ten real ales available including Old Market Bitter and one from Phoenix plus a constantly changing selection from brewers such as Hop Back, Archers, Copper Dragon, Robinson's, Oakham, Titanic and Bank Top, to name but a few.

The former town hall in Altrincham, a cosy, old-fashioned but imposing building. No games but live music and a Wednesday quiz night. Food available at lunchtime Mon–Sat. Children welcome. Beer garden. Private parties catered for.

OPEN *12–11pm (10.30pm Sun).*

ASHTON-UNDER-LYNE

The Station

2 Warrington Street, Ashton-under-Lyne OL6 6XB
☎ *(0161) 330 6776* Susan Watson

Marston's Pedigree and Station Bitter (specially brewed) among the beers always available, plus up to six guests perhaps including Timothy Taylor Landlord and Hydes Anvil Bitter.

A traditional Victorian freehouse filled with railway memorabilia. Beer garden, happy hours on weekdays from 3–8pm, 4–8pm Sat and 12–5pm Sun. Entertainment on Friday and Saturday nights. Food served at lunchtime and evenings. Children allowed.

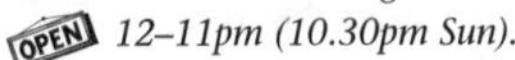

OPEN *12–11pm (10.30pm Sun).*

The Witchwood

152 Old Street, Ashton-under-Lyne OL6 7SF
☎ *(0161) 344 0321*
Pauline Town, Ben and Dan Marshall
www.thewitchwood.co.uk

Freehouse with up to nine real ales available. Joseph Holts Mild and Bitter and Theakston Old Peculiar are among the regulars, plus about five guests changed daily from local and micro-brewers: Phoenix, Coach House, Salamander, Storm, Moorhouse's, Millstone, Burton Bridge … the list goes on.

Award-winning real ale pub and live music venue at least four nights a week. Recently the subject of a management buy-out. Two bars, beer garden. Sandwiches available at lunchtime. No children. Beer festivals at least twice a year. Close to the town centre.

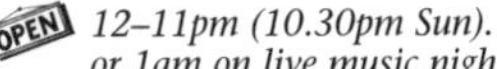

OPEN *12–11pm (10.30pm Sun). Open until 12 or 1am on live music nights.*

ATHERTON

The Pendle Witch

2–4 Warburton Place, Atherton, Manchester M46 0EQ
☎ *(01942) 884537* Joan Houghton

Tied to Moorhouse's with Premier and Pendle Witches Brew always available plus a couple of others, perhaps Moorhouse seasonal ales or specials such as Bursting Bitter, Black Witch, Black Panther, Thunder Struck, Black Cat or Easter Ale.

A 100-year-old cottage pub. Light snacks only available. Beer garden. Children allowed inside in the afternoons or in the garden. Situated off Market Street.

OPEN *All day, every day.*

BOLTON

The Hen & Chickens

Deansgate, Bolton BL1 1EX
☎ *(01204) 389836* Anthony Coyne

Cains Mild and three constantly changing guests ales.

A traditional but smart real ale pub dating back to the early 1800s. Located on the fringe of the town centre close to the bus station. Homemade food served at lunchtime only Mon to Sat (11.30am–2pm). Children allowed at lunchtime only. Entry policy at night.

 *11.30am–11pm Mon–Sat; 7.30pm–10.30pm Sun.*

Howcroft Inn

36 Pool Street, Bolton BL1 2JU
☎ *(01204) 526814* Clive Nightingale

Timothy Taylor Landlord and a Bank Top brew always available plus guests, often from micro-breweries.

A traditional pub five minutes' walk from the town centre on the north side of town. Has appeared on the CAMRA/English Heritage pub interiors list. Beer garden and bowling green. Food served every lunchtime 12–2pm, and on Sundays 12–5pm. Home to perhaps the largest pub beer festival in the country, held in the second week of October, and featuring more than 200 beers. Children allowed.

 *12–11pm (10.30pm Sun).*

BURY

Dusty Miller

87 Crostons Road, Bury BL8 1AL
☎ *(0161) 764 1124* Graeme Jones

A Moorhouse's pub with Premier, Pendle Witches Brew and Black Cat Mild always available plus one weekly changing guest ale.

A traditional local pub. No car park. No children. Located between Walshaw and Bury. Lunch served daily 12–2pm and 5–8pm (Sunday 12–6pm).

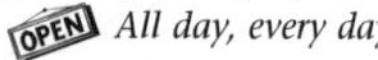 *All day, every day.*

CHEETHAM

The Queen's Arms

4–6 Honey Street, Redbank, Cheetham M8 8RG
☎ *(0161) 834 4239* Dave Price

Eight beers always available, usually including Timothy Taylor Landlord and Phoenix Bantam plus six guests from a constantly changing list. Also a wide range of Belgian beers.

A traditional town pub built in the 1800s and subsequently extended. Bar food available at lunchtime and until 8pm every day. Street parking, children's play area and garden. Five minutes' walk from Manchester Victoria Station.

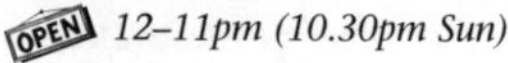 *12–11pm (10.30pm Sun).*

CHORLTON

The Marble Beer House

57 Manchester Road, Chorlton M21 9PW
☎ *(0161) 881 9206* Karen Weldon

A Marble Arch brewery pub, with the totally organic Marble beers always on offer. Two guests, changed every couple of days, include favourites such as Harviestoun Schiehallion and brews from Phoenix. Seasonal Marble beers include Organic Ginger in summer and Organic Chocolate (heavy) in winter.

A café bar with wooden floors and tasteful furniture, reminiscent of an Amsterdam brown café. Conservatory, front seating. No cooked food, but out-of-the-ordinary healthy snacks are available. Children allowed until 5pm. Situated in the heart of Chorlton.

OPEN *12–11pm (10.30pm Sun).*

The Sedge Lynn

21a Manchester Road, Chorlton M21 9PN
☎ *(0161) 860 0141* Bob Crompton

Five beers always available including Marston's Pedigree and something from Titanic Brewery.

A JD Wetherspoon freehouse set in a building with true architectural merit. The pub has a growing reputation for the quality of its real ales and food.

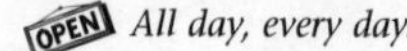 *All day, every day.*

DELPH

Royal Oak Inn

Broad Lane Heights, Delph, Saddleworth OL3 5TX
☎ *(01457) 874460* Michael and Sheila Fancy

A freehouse with Moorhouse's Black Cat Mild and Bitter always available plus four guest ales often including Fuller's London Pride or brews from Black Sheep or Jennings.

Built in 1767 this is an unspoilt pub with low beams, open fires and dining area. Situated in a remote setting off the Delph–Denshaw road, with good views over Saddleworth Moor. Food available Fri–Sun only. Children allowed.

7–11pm Mon–Fri (closed lunchtime); 12–3pm and 7–11pm Sat–Sun.

DENTON

Lowes Arms

301 Hyde Road, Denton M34 3FF
☎ *(0161) 336 3064* Peter and Jillian Wood

A brewpub, home of The LAB Brewery offering four own brews: Haughton Weave, Frog Bog, Broomstairs Bitter and Lowes IPA. Home-brewed seasonals and specials are also served.

A large pub with traditional decor and a friendly atmosphere. Separate lounge, dining area and vault bar. A well-qualified in-house chef provides à la carte meals at lunchtime and evening. Children allowed if eating.

12–3pm and 5–11pm Mon–Thurs; 12–11pm Fri–Sat; 12–10.30pm Sun.

DIDSBURY

Fletcher Moss

1 William Street Didsbury M20 6RQ
☎ *(0161) 438 0073*

A Hydes tied house serving Anvil Light and Bitter.

This pub is one of the best in Hydes' estate. It was extended in 2002 to include a spacious conservatory area. It retains a strong local identity and is popular at weekends as it is one of the few pubs in the area that does not serve food.

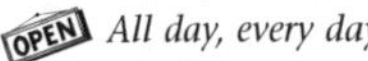
All day, every day.

EDGELEY

Olde Vic

1 Chatham Street, Edgeley, Stockport SK3 9ED
☎ *(0161) 480 2410*
Steve Brannan and Johanne Quinn

Five pumps serve a wide range of constantly changing beers, often switched daily (500 served so far by the current licensees). Chilled Weston's cider is also on offer.

A small, cosy pub with coal fire in the winter and a large, secure beer garden (complete with marquee-style covering for inclement weather!). No food. Two minutes' walk from Stockport railway station.

5–11pm Mon–Fri; 7–11pm Sat; 7–10.30pm Sun (closed every lunchtime).

HANDFORTH

The Railway

Station Road, Handforth, Wilmslow SK9 3AB
☎ *(01625) 523472* Peter and Ann Stacey

Robinson's Best Bitter and Hatters Mild usually available with one other Robinson's beer such as Old Tom (in winter) or another seasonal brew.

Friendly, traditional locals' pub with a tap room and lounge. Non-smoking area. Food served 12–2pm Tues–Fri. Car park. Children welcome at lunchtimes although there are no special facilities. Opposite Handforth railway station. Look out for its hanging baskets in summer.

12–11pm Mon–Sat; 12–3pm and 7–10.30pm Sun.

HAWKSHAW

The Red Lion Hotel

81 Ramsbottom Road, Hawkshaw, Bury BL8 4JS
☎ *(01204) 856600* Carl Owen

A freehouse offering Jennings Bitter and Cumberland Ale and a beer from the Bank Top range, plus a guest from another local brewery, including Phoenix, Three B's and Bazens'.

A traditional pub and restaurant. Bar and restaurant food available. Children allowed.

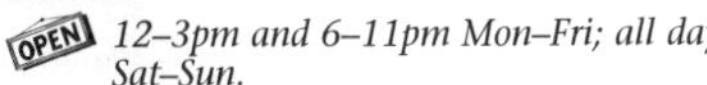
12–3pm and 6–11pm Mon–Fri; all day Sat–Sun.

HEATON CHAPEL

The Hinds Head

Manchester Road, Heaton Chapel, Stockport SK4 2RB
☎ *(0161) 431 9301* Terence Murphy

Greene King Old Speckled Hen, Timothy Taylor Landlord, Marston's Pedigree and Black Sheep Bitter always available, plus one monthly changing guest.

Award-winning pub with extensive lawned beer garden and lovely hanging baskets. CAMRA listed for its beer and food. Meals are served 12–2pm and 7–9pm Mon–Sat and 12–4.30pm Sun. Children welcome at all times in the beer garden and inside the pub if dining. Large car park.

11.30am–11pm Mon–Sat; 12–10.30pm Sun.

HEYWOOD

The Wishing Well

89 York Street, Heywood OL10 4NS
☎ *(01706) 620923* Mr TM Huck

A freehouse with six real ales available. Moorhouse's Millers Brook, Phoenix Navy and White Monk, Black Sheep Bitter and Timothy Taylor Landlord are usually on offer, plus two rotating guests from a vast range of independent and micro-breweries.

A traditional pub with dining area. Food available in a separate restaurant next door open 6.45–9.30pm Tues–Sat. Children allowed.

12–11pm (10.30pm Sun).

HINDLEY

The Edington Arms

186 Ladies Lane, Hindley, Wigan WN2 2QJ
☎ (01942) 259229

A Joseph Holt tied house with Holt Mild and Bitter always available.

An old coaching house with two large, comfortable rooms. No food. Parking and garden. Children allowed. Function room upstairs. Next to Hindley railway station.

All day, every day.

HYDE

The Cheshire Ring

72 Manchester Road, Hyde SK14 2BJ
☎ *(0161) 368 1826*

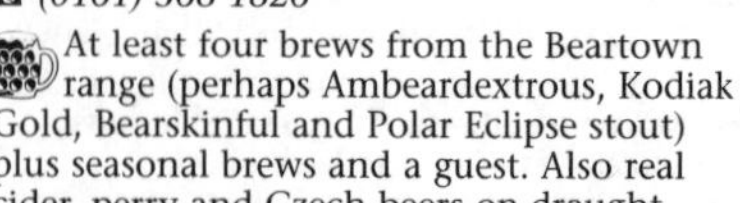

At least four brews from the Beartown range (perhaps Ambeardextrous, Kodiak Gold, Bearskinful and Polar Eclipse stout) plus seasonal brews and a guest. Also real cider, perry and Czech beers on draught.

Bought and reopened by the Beartown Brewery in September 2003 after a year boarded up. Friendly and welcoming with home-cooked food available at lunchtime. Function room, separate non-smoking dining room. Children welcome until 7pm. Accommodation. Close to Hyde Central metro.

All day, every day

The Sportsman

8 Mottram Road, Hyde SK14 2NN
☎ *(0161) 368 5000* Geoff Oliver

A freehouse with Plassey Bitter and Whim Hartington Bitter always available, plus two guests from an ever-changing list including Timothy Taylor Landlord, Whim Magic Mushroom Mild or a Robinson's brew.

A traditional alehouse with open fires. Bar food available at lunchtime. Well-supervised children allowed. Near the railway station at Newton St Hyde Central.

All day, every day.

MANCHESTER

Bar Fringe

8 Swan Street, Manchester M4 5JN
☎ *(0161) 835 3815* Ms Carmen Contreras

A freehouse with four real ales available. Beers from Bank Top and Boggart Hole Clough are permanently featured and the two guests, changed regularly, could be from Spinning Dog, Salamander, Cottage or Derwent breweries. Traditional cider plus draught Belgian and fruit beers are also stocked and there are regular promotional offers. Wide selection of foreign bottled beers, and guest crisps!

A pub on the outskirts of the town centre, in a building over 100 years old, with traditional long, narrow, Belgian brown bar. Food available 12–6pm every day. One bar, pinball table, garden. Three or four beer festivals held every year. Well-behaved children allowed.

12–11pm (10.30pm Sun).

The Lass o'Gowrie

36 Charles Street, Manchester M1 7DB
☎ *(0161) 273 6932* Eleanor Owen

Lass o'Gowrie Ale brewed for the pub by Titanic always available, plus four constantly changing guests such as Black Sheep Bitter and Greene King Old Speckled Hen.

A Victorian tiled pub with gas lighting. Bar food available 12–8pm Mon–Thurs. Refurbished in July 2003. Close to BBC North. Parking nearby. Children allowed.

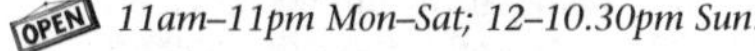

OPEN *11am–11pm Mon–Sat; 12–10.30pm Sun.*

Marble Arch Inn

73 Rochdale Road, Manchester M4 4HY
☎ *(0161) 832 5914* Christine Baldwin
www.marblebeers.co.uk

Claiming to be the only organic brewpub in England, this is the home of the Marble Brewery, with five totally organic ales produced and served on tap. All beers are approved by the Soil Association and the Vegetarian Society. Brewery tours are available. The micro-brewery was installed in December 1998 and turned vegetarian organic in 2000.

A Victorian pub dating from 1888, with mosaic floor and walls of glazed brick with an ornate tile frieze. Bar food available 12–2.30pm Mon–Sat and 4.30–8pm Mon–Fri.

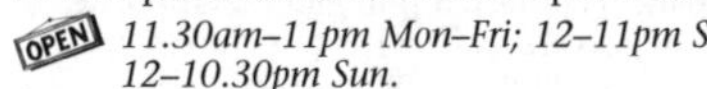

OPEN *11.30am–11pm Mon–Fri; 12–11pm Sat; 12–10.30pm Sun.*

Sand Bar

120 Grosvenor Street, All Saints, Manchester M1 7HL
☎ *(0161) 273 3141* Emma Hodgetts

A freehouse offering a range of brews from Phoenix, Timothy Taylor, Archers, Kelham Island and Burton Bridge. Also selling the biggest range of bottled beers in Manchester (70 in total, mainly German and Belgian).

A city-centre café bar in an old Georgian building. One main bar and benches outside. Sandwiches available 12–5pm Mon–Fri. Children allowed. Located off the A34 by the University.

OPEN *12–11pm Mon–Fri; 6–11pm Sat; closed Sun.*

Sinclairs Oyster Bar

2 Cathedral Gates, Manchester M3 1SW
☎ *(0161) 834 0430*

A Samuel Smith tied house serving Old Brewery Bitter and others.

An old building behind Marks & Spencer that has been moved and rebuilt several times to accommodate modern shopping developments. Heavily timbered throughout, the upstairs bar has two rooms. Downstairs there are many small rooms. A must to visit especially for a break from shopping! Lunches a speciality Mon–Sat.

OPEN *11am–11pm Mon–Sat; 12–10.30pm Sun.*

MIDDLETON

Tandle Hill Tavern

14 Thornham Lane, Slattocks, Middleton, Manchester M24 2SS
☎ *(01706) 345297* Mike

A JW Lees tied house with Mild and Bitter available.

A must on a visit to North Manchester. The pub is set in a rural setting and can be accessed via a rough track/unmetalled road from either Rochdale Road, Royton (A671) or Rochdale Road, Middleton (A664). It is a true surviving example of a country pub situated next to a farm. One of a dying breed. Visitors are made to feel welcome by the landlord and the roaring fires in winter, and the JW Lees beers are the best-kept for miles around. Soup and sandwiches available at lunchtime at weekends only. Good walks locally in Tandle Hill Country Park. Children welcome.

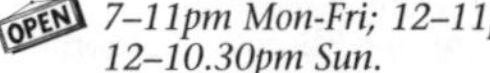

OPEN *7–11pm Mon-Fri; 12–11pm Sat; 12–10.30pm Sun.*

NANGREAVES

The Lord Raglan

Walmersley Old Road, Nangreaves, Bury BL9 6SP
☎ *(0161) 764 6680* Brendan Leyden

The home of the Leyden Brewing Company with the full range of ales brewed on the premises and always available. Will occasionally swap one of the home brews with another local micro-brewery. Two annual beer festivals held late June/early July and in September.

A Victorian two-bar pub and restaurant. Food available 12–2pm and 7–9.30pm Mon–Thurs, 12–2pm and 5–9.30pm Fri and all day Sat–Sun. Beer garden. Car park. Children allowed. Brewery visits by arrangement. Take the M66 to J1 Ramsbottom, turn left onto the A56 and then first left at traffic lights. The pub is just over a mile on the left.

12–2.30pm and 7–11pm Mon–Thurs; 12–2.30pm and 5–11pm Fri; 12–11pm Sat; 12–10.30pm Sun.

OLDHAM

Ashton Arms

28–30 Clegg Street, Oldham OL1 1PL
☎ *(07963) 505393* Jo Potter

A freehouse serving Cains Bitter plus five constantly changing guests from local breweries such as Greenfield, Millstone and Phoenix. Beer festivals are held at Easter and in October.

The centrepiece of this open-plan pub is a large real fire that complements the real ale and real food served by Jo and her staff. Food 12–6pm Mon–Sat. Children welcome.

OPEN *All day, every day.*

ROCHDALE

The Albion Freehouse and Bistro

600 Whitworth Road, Rochdale OL12 0SW
☎ *(01706) 648540* KR Robinson

Timothy Taylor Best and Landlord are the permanent beers here, together with Phoenix Monkey Town Mild, White Monk and JW Lees Bitter. Guest ales from a variety of brewers are also featured and changed regularly.

Traditional three-roomed freehouse with open fires and a welcoming atmosphere. One TV room. No machines. Excellent pub food is available. The 32-seater non-smoking bistro adjoining the pub serves high-quality meals of English and African cuisine. Caters for small weddings, functions, business meeting, etc. On the A671 in the foothills of the Pennines a mile and a half from Rochdale town centre, with nearby moorland making for good walks.

OPEN *12–2.30pm and 5–11pm Mon–Fri; 12–11pm Sat; 12–10.30pm Sun.*

Cask & Feather

1 Oldham Road, Rochdale OL16 1UA
☎ *(01706) 711476* Jackie Grimes

Home of the Thomas McGuinness Brewery, so beers from the range are always available on five hand pumps.

A small brewery founded in 1991 by Thomas McGuinness, who died in early 1993. An old-style castle-fronted pub dating from 1814 and close to the town centre. Bar and restaurant food available at lunchtime and evenings. Parking. Children allowed. Located on the main road near the station.

OPEN *All day, every day.*

Cemetery Inn

470 Bury Road, Rochdale OL11 5EU
☎ *(01706) 645635*
John Ketley and Mark Porter

A freehouse offering a range of beers including Timothy Taylor Best and Landlord plus something from Jennings and Phoenix and up to three guests, changed weekly, from local breweries.

A Victorian pub with log fires, dating from 1865 and recently sympathetically refurbished. Food served daily 12–2.30pm and 5–7.30pm. The menu includes locally sourced sausages and Lancashire cheeses. Children allowed until 7.30pm.

OPEN *All day, every day.*

SALFORD

The Crescent

20 The Crescent, Salford M5 4PF
☎ *(0161) 736 5600* Mrs J Davies

Crescent Bitter (house beer) always available plus up to ten others (150 per year) primarily from local breweries, including Oak, Moorhouse's, Titanic and Marston's. Other guests from all around the country. Occasional beer festivals.

A sprawling pub with a comfortable atmosphere, frequented by students and locals alike. Bar food available at lunchtime. Car park. Traditional pub games. Opposite Salford University. The nearest station is Salford Crescent, on the main A6.

OPEN *12–11pm Mon–Fri; 7.30–11pm Sat; 12–3pm and 7.30–10.30pm Sun.*

Eagle Inn (The Lamp Oil)

18 Collier Street, Greengate, Salford M3 7DW
☎ *(0161) 832 4919* Muriel Craig

A Joseph Holt tied house serving Mild and Bitter.

A classic example of a backstreet boozer with a unique friendly atmosphere. There are three small rooms including a tap room, a games room and a snug. Ask about why it is affectionately known as the Lamp Oil .

OPEN *11am–11pm Mon-Sat; 12–10.30pm Sun.*

STALYBRIDGE

The Buffet Bar

Stalybridge Railway Station, Stalybridge SK15 1RF
☎ *(0161) 303 0007* John Hesketh

Seven or eight real ales available, including a constantly changing range of guest beers from independent breweries. Around 4,850 guest beers served in the past seven years.

A unique and authentic buffet bar built in 1865 with a real fire, real ale and real people! Bar food available at most times. Parking. Children allowed. On platform one at Stalybridge railway station.

11am–11pm Mon–Sat; 12–10.30pm Sun.

Q Inn

3–5 Market Street, Stalybridge SK15 2AL
☎ *(0161) 303 9157* Ray Calland

A Hydes Brewery tied house serving the two Hydes beers plus one weekly changing guest.

The pub with the shortest name in Britain forms part of the Stalybridge Eight – eight pubs in the town offering 37 different beers. Brick walls and a flagstone floor. Quiz night on Wednesdays, rock night on Mondays and Thursdays . No children. Large beer garden. A short walk from the railway station.

 *4–11pm Mon–Wed; 11am–11pm Thurs–Sat; 12–10.30pm Sun.*

The White House

1 Water Street, Stalybridge SK15 2AG
☎ *(0161) 303 2288* Ray and Sheena Calland

A Hydes Brewery tied house serving the full range of Hydes beers, including Dark Mild from the Craft range.

A traditional pub with low ceilings, refurbished and very comfortable. Full menu available. No children.

11am–11pm Mon–Sat; 12–10.30pm Sun.

STRINES

The Sportsman's Arms

105 Strines Road, Strines SK6 7GE
☎ *(0161) 427 2888* Sue and Joe Stockton

Something from Cains always available, plus a guest changed every two weeks from any independent brewery.

A 200-year-old, two-roomed pub with a lounge/dining room and a snug. Wonderful views over the Goyt Valley and an ideal base for walking in the Peak District and Peak Forest canal. Home-cooked food available 12–2pm and 6–9pm Mon–Sat and 12–8pm Sun. Car park, garden. Take the A626 from Stockport and then the B6101.

 *12–3pm and 5–11pm Mon–Fri; all day Sat–Sun.*

STOCKPORT

The Crown Inn

154 Heaton Lane, Heaton Norris, Stockport SK4 1AR
☎ *(0161) 429 0549* Graham Mascord
www.thecrown.org

Ten hand pumps serve a varied and interesting choice of real ales. There are dedicated pumps for Bank Top, Phoenix, Pictish, Whim and Jennings, and many of the independent breweries in the UK are also featured. Micro-breweries also favoured. A range of 15 malt whiskies is also available, plus real cider.

Very cosy, old-fashioned multi-rooomed boozer just off Mersey Square, with the focus on real ale for the real ale lover. Hot and cold snacks available during opening hours. Live music.

 *12–3pm and 6–11pm Mon–Thurs; 12.30–11pm Fri–Sat; 7.30–10.30pm Sun.*

UPPERMILL

The Church Inn and Belfry Function Suite

Church Lane, Off Church Road, Uppermill, Saddleworth
☎ *(01457) 820902 or 872415*
Julian Paul Taylor

Home of the Saddleworth Brewery with all brews usually available, plus occasional guest beers. Brewery visits by arrangement.

A country freehouse set in a beautiful, historic location with panoramic views and a lovely patio area. Peacocks, horses, ducks, geese, cats, dogs and hens too. Caters for all age groups. Log fires in winter. Non-smoking room. Food served lunchtimes and evenings Mon–Fri and all day Sat–Sun. Children welcome. Car park. Situated in Uppermill village, turn into New Street and continue to Church Road. Pub will be found near the church.

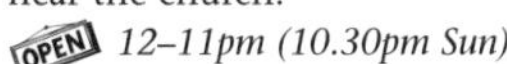 *12–11pm (10.30pm Sun).*

WIGAN

The Beer Engine

69 Poolstock, Wigan WN3 5DF
☎ *(01942) 321820* John Moran

Moorhouse's Pendle Witches Brew and Beer Engine Bitter always available plus up to five guest beers (186 per year) with the emphasis on supporting the smaller brewer.

Food available 12–2pm Mon–Fri and 12–6pm Sat–Sun. Function room with a capacity of 250 for hire. Three full-size snooker tables and a pool table. Crown green bowling. Annual beer, pie and music festival in October. Children allowed. Well known in Wigan, five minutes' walk from the railway station and town centre.

OPEN *11am–11pm Mon–Sat; 12–10.30pm Sun.*

Moon Under Water

Market Place, Wigan WN1 1PE
☎ *(01942) 323437* Paul Hammond

A JD Wetherspoon's pub with Cains Mild among the beers always available, plus two guests often from East-West Ales, perhaps Brakspear Bee Sting. Two annual beer festivals.

A very busy town-centre pub with no music. Food available. No children.

OPEN *All day, every day.*

The Orwell

Wigan Pier, Wallgate, Wigan WN3 4EU
☎ *(01942) 323034* Robin Harston

A freehouse. Three or four guest beers always available from micro-breweries whenever possible. Brews from Pictish, Phoenix, Archers, Ossett and Hanby are regular features.

A tourists' pub on the edge of town on the pier. A converted traditional Victorian cotton warehouse on the Leeds to Liverpool canal. Local CAMRA Pub of the Year 2001 and 2002. Three bars, non-smoking dining area, baby changing facilities, disabled toilets, passenger lift to all floors. Two large function rooms available for hire. Benches outside. Food available lunchtimes 12–2.30pm and Sunday carvery 1–6pm. Children allowed.

OPEN *All day, every day Easter to October; all day Fri–Sun at other times.*

The Tudor House Hotel

New Market Street, Wigan
☎ *(01942) 700296* Mr Miller

A freehouse with Moorhouse's Pendle Witches Brew among the beers always available plus up to four guests including Everards Tiger, Hop Back Summer Lightning, Wychwood Hobgoblin, O'Hanlon's Summer Gold and Phoenix Wobbly Bob.

Predominantly a student pub with open fires, a beer garden and accommodation. Food available at lunchtime and evenings. Children allowed during the day.

OPEN *All day, every day.*

THE BREWERIES

CAMBRINUS CRAFT BREWERY

Home Farm, Knowsley Park, Knowsley L34 4AQ
☎ *(0151) 546 2226*

HERALD 3.7% ABV
A light refreshing summer ale.
YARDSTICK 4.0% ABV
A coloured, malty best mild.
DELIVERANCE 4.2% ABV
A hoppy, dry bitter with a moreish aftertaste.
ENDURANCE 4.3% ABV
An IPA-style beer, smooth, hoppy and oaky.
Plus seasonals and specials.

ROBERT CAIN BREWERY LTD

The Robert Cain Brewery, Stanhope Street, Liverpool L8 5XJ
☎ *(0151) 709 8734*
www.cainsbeers.com

DARK MILD 3.2% ABV
BEST BITTER 4.0% ABV
CAINS FA 5.0% ABV
Plus seasonal brews.

WAPPING BEERS

The Baltic Fleet, 33A Wapping, Liverpool L1 8DQ
☎ *(0151) 709 3116*

WAPPING BITTER 3.6% ABV
SUMMER ALE 4.2% ABV
BALTIC EXTRA 4.5% ABV

THE PUBS

BEBINGTON

Traveller's Rest Hotel

169 Mount Road, Bebington, Wirral L63 8PJ
☎ *(0151) 608 2988* Alan Irving

Greene King Abbot and Cains Traditional always available, plus two guests from breweries such as Timothy Taylor, Enville, Wye Valley, Hart and Cumberland.

A rural village pub bordering fields with a view of Wales. Open fires, non-smoking lounge. Food available. No children.

OPEN *All day, every day.*

BIRKENHEAD

The Crown & Cushion

60 Market Street, Birkenhead L41 5BT
☎ *(0151) 647 8870* Sue Foster

Cains Bitter permanently available, plus a guest ale changed every week, perhaps Highgate Dark Mild or Greene King Old Speckled Hen.

A traditional town-centre community pub. Free sandwiches available. All-day happy hours. Children allowed until 7pm. Close to the town hall and Mersey ferries, two minutes from Hamilton Square station.

OPEN *All day, every day.*

The Crown Hotel

128 Conway Street, Birkenhead L41 6JE
☎ *(0151) 647 0589* Kevin Oates

Ten cask ales usually available, with regulars being Cains Traditional Bitter and Mild.

A typical old alehouse. Bar food available. Parking, darts/meeting room, beer garden. Children allowed. Head for Birkenhead town centre, not far from the Birkenhead tunnel (Europa Park).

OPEN *11.30am–11pm Mon–Sat; 12–3pm and 7–10.30pm Sun.*

The Dispensary

20 Chester Street, Birkenhead CH41 5DQ
☎ *(0151) 649 8259* Katie Banks
www.cainsbeers.com/pubs/thedispensary.html

A Cains tied house, with Traditional and Dark Mild always available, plus a selection of seasonal and special ales.

A modern, refurbished building with raised glass ceiling. Formerly a chemist, hence the name. Used to be known as The Chester Arms. No food. Small beer garden. No children.

OPEN *All day, every day.*

MERSEYSIDE

The Old Colonial

167 Bridge Street, Birkenhead CH41 1AY
☎ *(0151) 650 1110* Jayne Loftus

Cains Traditional Bitter, Mild and Doctor Duncan's IPA, plus seasonal brews usually available.

A friendly, traditional pub. Cask Marque award winner. Food served 12–3pm and 5–7pm Mon–Fri; 12–3pm Sat–Sun. Car park. Children welcome until 7pm, but no special facilities.

 *12–11pm (10.30pm Sun).*

FORMBY

Freshfield Hotel

Massams Lane, Formby L37 7BF
☎ *(01704) 874871*
Greg Byrne and Julie Evans (managers)

Moorhouse's Black Cat Mild, Black Sheep Bitter, Timothy Taylor Landlord and Castle Eden Ale are among the brews usually available, plus six constantly changing guest beers, wherever possible ordered by customer request.

A traditional pub with polished wooden floor and log fire. Beer garden and separate music/conference room at rear. Food served 12–2pm Mon–Fri and 12–4pm Sat–Sun. Car park. No children.

OPEN *12–11pm (10.30pm Sun).*

IRBY

Shippons Inn

Thingwall Road, Irby, Wirral CH61 3UA
☎ *(0151) 648 0449* Stephen Thompson

Thwaites Best, Thoroughbred and Lancaster Bomber always available, plus regularly changing guests.

A rustic pub with beams and stone floor. Food available 12–2.30pm. No children.

OPEN *All day, every day.*

LIVERPOOL

The Baltic Fleet

33A Wapping, Liverpool L1 8DQ
☎ *(0151) 709 3116* Simon Holt
www.wappingbeers.com

A brewpub, home of Wapping Beers, with a range of four home-brewed ales always available plus three guests from micro and regional brewers. A mild is usually on the menu.

Town pub in a 150-year-old painted Victorian building next to the Albert Dock and featuring beams and fireplaces. A network of tunnels, reputedly haunted, leads from the cellar to the docks, and guided tours are available by appointment. Food served in the bar 12–2pm Mon–Sat and in the first-floor restaurant 6–9pm Tues–Thurs, 6–10pm Fri–Sat and 12–4pm Sun. Children allowed in restaurant only until 8pm.

OPEN *12–11pm Mon–Fri; 11.30am–11pm Sat; 12–10.30pm Sun.*

The Brewery Tap

Stanhope Street, Liverpool L8 5XJ
☎ *(0151) 709 2129* Sally Clarke
www.cainsbeers.com/pubs/brewerytap.html

Tied to the Robert Cain brewery, so Cains Bitter, Dark Mild, 2008 and Formidable Ale (FA) always available, plus seasonal and special brews such as Sundowner and Doctor Duncan's IPA.

Built in 1869 and refurbished in January 2004, but with the original character retained. One bar, food available 11.30am–5.30pm. Children allowed if eating. Large car park opposite.

OPEN *All day, every day.*

The Cambridge

Mulberry Street, Liverpool L7 7EE
☎ *(0151) 708 7150* Lorraine Loates

Burtonwood Bitter and Top Hat always available, plus one ever-changing guest.

One of the few traditional pubs in the area, this has a friendly atmosphere and is popular with students and lecturers. Food available 11.30am–2pm Mon–Fri. No children. Outside drinking area.

OPEN *11.30am–11pm (10.30pm Sun).*

The Cambridge Pub

28 Picton Road, Liverpool L15 4LH
☎ *(0151) 280 5126* Joan Adali

A freehouse with Chester's Mild among the brews always available, plus two twice-monthly changing guests.

A modern pub with music. No food. No children.

OPEN *All day, every day.*

Dr Duncan

St John's Building, St John's Lane, Liverpool L1
☎ *(0151) 709 5100* Fiona Watkins

A Cains pub with Traditional, Doctor Duncan's IPA, Formidable Ale and Dark Mild permanently served, plus four guests, changed daily. Cains seasonal ales are usually available, and beers such as Eccleshall Top Totty, Mauldons Midsummer Gold and Oakham White Dwarf are featured. Rooster's Maax is brewed for especially for the pub.

City-centre pub in a traditional listed building from the turn of the last century. Food served throughout the pub, and there is a non-smoking dining area. Function rooms, patio. Beer festivals held every two or three months, usually with a theme (e.g. wheat, Belgian, German). Children allowed up to 7pm in non-smoking area.

OPEN *11.30am–11pm Mon–Sat; 12–10.30 Sun.*

Everyman Bistro

5–9 Hope Street, Liverpool L1 9BH
☎ *(0151) 708 9545* Joe Power (Bar Manager); Alan Crowe (General Manager)
www.everyman.co.uk

A freehouse with a Cains beer always available, plus a constantly changing range of guests, usually including Timothy Taylor Landlord, Marston's Pedigree, Black Sheep Bitter or a beer from Castle Eden.

A lively pub with a bohemian atmosphere, situated between the cathedrals. Popular with an eclectic mix of people. Food always available – menu, with meat and vegetarian options, changes twice daily (choices can be limited outside main lunchtime and evening periods). More of a pub than a bistro after 8pm. Children allowed until 9pm.

OPEN *Bistro: 12–midnight Mon–Wed; 12–1am Thurs; 12–2am Fri–Sat (closed Sun). Foyer Café Bar: 10am–2pm Mon–Fri.*

The Ship & Mitre

133 Dale Street, Liverpool L2 2JH
☎ *(0151) 236 0859*
David Stevenson (manager)

Hydes Anvil Bitter and Dark Mild always available, plus something from Rooster's. Up to eight guests also served (650 different ales per year), plus beers from Belgium, Germany and the Czech Republic on draught.

A town-centre pub, popular with students and council staff. Four-times winner of CAMRA Merseyside Pub of the Year. Good value food served lunchtimes Mon–Fri. The pub has a starred entry in the book *Good Pub Food*. Pay and display car park opposite. Children not allowed. Near the Mersey tunnel entrance, five minutes' walk from Lime Street station and Moorfields station.

 *11.30am–11pm Mon–Fri; 12.30–11pm Sat; 2.30–10.30pm Sun.*

The Swan Inn

86 Wood Street, Liverpool L1 4DQ
☎ *(0151) 709 5281* Clive Briggs

A freehouse with Marston's Pedigree, Phoenix Wobbly Bob and a Cains brew always available, plus three constantly changing guests from breweries such as Hanby Ales, Durham, Cottage, Wye Valley (Dorothy Goodbody's) or Belhaven.

A traditional backstreet pub with wooden floors. Food served in separate dining area. No children. Located off Berry Street at the back of Bold Street

OPEN *All day, every day.*

The Vernon Arms

69 Dale Street, Liverpool L2
☎ *(0151) 236 4525* Joanne Barnes

Coach House Gunpowder is always on offer, and the six guest beers, sometimes changed every day, could be anything from Eccleshall, Cottage or Archers.

Old Victorian one-bar town pub in the business district. Food available. Children allowed until 8pm.

OPEN *11.45am–11pm Mon–Fri; 12–11pm Sat; closed Sun.*

Ye Cracke

13 Rice Street, Liverpool L1 9BB
☎ *(0151) 709 4171* Michael Jones

Oak Best, Phoenix Wobbly Bob, a Cains brew and Timothy Taylor Landlord always available, plus two guests from independent and micro-breweries whenever possible. Examples include Cottage, Weetwood, Wye Valley and Hanby.

A traditional local with beer garden. Food available until 6pm. Children allowed in the pub until 6pm. Located in a back street off Hope Street.

OPEN *All day, every day.*

RAINHILL

The Manor Farm

Mill Lane, Rainhill, Prescot L35 6NE
☎ *(0151) 430 0335* Brian Maguire

A Burtonwood tied house always serving Burtonwood brews. Two other guests from a range including Wyre Piddle Piddle in the Hole.

A traditional seventeenth-century pub with restaurant and beer garden. No juke boxes. Food available. Children allowed.

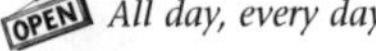 *All day, every day.*

ST HELENS

Beechams Bar

Water Street, St Helens
☎ *(01744) 623420*

A well-established freehouse. Up to seven different cask ales are served, with regulars including Greene King Abbot, Tetley's Cask Bitter and Beechams Crystal Wheat.

Situated under Beecham's clock, this is a traditional real ale house. Merseyside CAMRA Pub of Excellence 2002. Sandwiches available at lunchtimes. Nearby public car park. No children.

 *12–11pm Mon–Sat; closed Sun and bank holidays.*

SOUTHPORT

Barons Bar

The Scarisbrick Hotel, 291 Lord Street, Southport PR8 1NZ
☎ *(01704) 543000* George Sourbutts
www.scarisbrickhotel.co.uk

A freehouse serving a wide variety of up to seven real ales including Flag & Turret, the house brew, at 3.8% ABV. Moorhouse's Pride of Pendle also features, plus guests, changed every couple of days, with the main emphasis on smaller breweries from around the UK.

Refurbished, but retaining a baronial look and feel! The hotel's other facilities can be enjoyed, with 95 bedrooms and plenty of food available. Two annual beer festivals, in May and November. Outside seating in summer. Children allowed in the family room until 6pm. Conference and banqueting facilities. On the main shopping street in the town centre.

 *All day, every day.*

The Berkeley Arms

19 Queens Road, Southport PR9 9HN
☎ *(01704) 500811* Philip Ball

Banks's Bitter, Marston's Pedigree, Adnams Bitter, Camerons Strongarm, Hawkshead Bitter, Moorhouse's Black Cat Mild and Pendle Witches Brew always available, plus one guest beer changed at least once a week.

A family-run freehouse just outside the town centre, anxious to promote the real ale cause, with an extended bar. Music. Pizzas served from 5–11pm. Children allowed. Car park and accommodation. Look behind the fire station.

 *4–11pm Mon–Fri; 12–11pm Sat–Sun.*

Wetherspoons

93 Lord Street, Southport PR8 1RH
☎ *(01704) 530217* Donna Pagett

A Wetherspoon's pub. Regular guest beers served on two pumps include Cotleigh Osprey, Hop Back Summer Lightning and brews from Burton Bridge, Hook Norton, Everards and Banks and Taylor.

An old-fashioned, quiet, drinkers' pub. Food available.

 *All day, every day.*

WAVERTREE

The Willow Bank

329 Smithdown Road, Wavertree, Liverpool L15 3JA
☎ *(0151) 733 5782* Emma Tillotson

Up to seven real ales available at any one time. Regular breweries featured on the guest list include Harviestoun, Caledonian, Wadworth, Arundel, Skinner's, Adnams and Greene King.

A friendly pub, popular with locals, students and real-ale lovers. Two bars. Beer festivals held every three months. Food available 12–3pm and 5–8pm Mon–Fri and 12–6pm Sat–Sun. Beer garden. Quiz nights. Car park. Children allowed in the garden only. Disabled facilities.

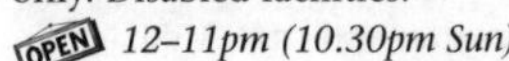 *12–11pm (10.30pm Sun).*

BLUE MOON BREWERY

The Cock Inn, Watton Road, Barford NR6 4AS
☎ (01603) 757646

EASY LIFE 3.8% ABV
DARKSIDE 4.0% ABV
SEA OF TRANQUILITY 4.2% ABV
MOONDANCE 4.7% ABV
HINGHAM HIGH 5.0% ABV
MILK OF AMNESIA 5.2% ABV
Plus seasonals.

THE BRANCASTER BREWERY

Jolly Sailors, Main Road, Brancaster Staithe, Kings Lynn PE31 8BJ
☎ (01485) 210314
www.jollysailors.co.uk

IPA 3.7% ABV
OLD LES 5.0% ABV

BUFFY'S BREWERY

Mardle Hall, Rectory Road, Tivetshall St Mary NR15 2DD
☎ (01379) 676523
www.buffys.co.uk

NORWICH TERRIER 3.6% ABV
Light and quenching with good hop character.
BITTER 3.9% ABV
Easy-drinking, well-hopped brew.
MILD 4.2% ABV
Smooth, dark mild.
POLLY'S FOLLY 4.3% ABV
HOPLEAF 4.5% ABV
IPA 4.6% ABV
NORWEGIAN BLUE 4.9% ABV
ALE 5.5% ABV
Well-rounded and hoppy.
ALE 6.5% ABV
10X 10% ABV

CHALK HILL BREWERY

Rosary Road, Thorpe Hamlet, Norwich NR1 4DA
☎ (01603) 4770778

TAP BITTER 3.6% ABV
CHB 4.2% ABV
DREADNOUGHT 4.9% ABV
FLINTKNAPPERíS MILD 5.0% ABV
OLD TACKLE 5.6% ABV

FOX BREWERY

Fox & Hounds, 22 Station Road, Heacham PE31 7EX
☎ (01485) 570345

PERFICK 3.7% ABV
BRANTHILL BEST 3.8% ABV
HEACHAM GOLD 3.9% ABV
LJB 4.0% ABV
RED KNOCKER 4.2% ABV
BRANTHILL LIGHT 4.3% ABV
GRACE AND FAVOUR 4.4% ABV
CERBERUS STOUT 4.5% ABV
PEDDERS SWAY 5.0% ABV
IPA 5.2% ABV
PUNT GUN 5.9% ABV

HUMPTY DUMPTY BREWING CO

Church Road, Reedham NR13 3TZ
☎ (01493) 701818

NORD ATLANTIC 3.7% ABV
Red-coloured, easy quaffer.
FERRYMAN 3.8% ABV
LITTLE SHARPIE 3.8% ABV
Pale and quenching.
LEMON AND GINGER 4.0% ABV
SWINGBRIDGE ALE 4.0% ABV
TENDER BEHIND 4.0% ABV
Spicy wheat beer.
OPS ON TRAIN 4.1% ABV
Dry-hopped, gold-coloured beer.
UN PETIT DEUX PETITS 4.1% ABV
BRIEF ENCOUNTER 4.3% ABV
CLAUD HAMILTON 4.3% ABV
Oyster stout.
IRON DUKE 4.6% ABV
BUTT JUMPER 4.8% ABV
Sweet malt flavour.
RAILWAY SLEEPER 5.0% ABV
Good hoppy bitterness throughout.

THE ICENI BREWERY

3 Foulden Road, Ickburgh, Mundford IP26 5BJ
☎ (01842) 878922
www.stevedunks.demon.co.uk/iceni

BOADICEA 3.8% ABV
Full-flavoured and hoppy with some fruit.
CELTIC QUEEN 4.0% ABV
FINE SOFT DAY 4.0% ABV
Maple syrup and hops give bittersweet flavour.
FEN TIGER 4.2% ABV
Malty with coriander.
FOUR GRAINS 4.2% ABV
Rounded, fruity flavour.
CÚ CHULAINN 4.3% ABV
Slightly sweet ale.
DEIRDRE OF THE SORROWS 4.4% ABV
Amber and complex.
ROISIN DUBH 4.4% ABV
Dark with sweet flavour.
KIWI 4.5% ABV
Smooth and easy-drinking, with kiwi fruit.
ICENI GOLD 5.0% ABV
WINTER LIGHTNING 5.0% ABV
Light and crisp.
Plus seasonal brews.

REEPHAM BREWERY

Unit 1, Collers Way, Reepham NR10 4SW
☎ *(01603) 871091*

GRANARY BITTER 3.8% ABV
RAPIER PALE ALE 4.2% ABV
NORFOLK WHEATEN 4.5% ABV
VELVET STOUT 4.5% ABV
Plus seasonal brews.

SPECTRUM BREWERY

c/o 23 Briton Way, Wymondham NR18 0TT
☎ *(07949) 254383*
www.spectrumbrewery.co.uk

LIGHT FANTASTIC 3.7% ABV
Golden drinking bitter.
BEZANTS 4.0% ABV
Golden hoppy bitter.
42 4.2% ABV
Hoppyish and pleasant best bitter.
BLACK BUFFLE 4.5% ABV
A vegan stout.
WIZZARD 4.9% ABV
Full-flavoured strong bitter.
OLD STOATWOBBLER 6.0% ABV
Strong, dark and notorious. Also vegan.
TRIP HAZARD 6.5% ABV
Very full-flavoured and fruity. Very strong bitter.
Plus seasonal beers.

TINDALL ALE BREWERY

Toad Lane, Seething NR35 2QE
☎ *(01508) 483844 or 07881658182*

IPA 3.6% ABV
A smooth-tasting pale ale. The goldings hops lead to a delicate, refreshing finish, without lacking on flavour.
SUMMER LOVING 3.6% ABV
A lighter-coloured ale with a Mediterranean taste.
BEST BITTER 3.7% ABV
A good all-round session bitter, a popular ale with a smooth hop taste.
FUGGLED UP 3.7% ABV
A good session bitter with the later addition of the fuggled hop.
MILD 3.7% ABV
A good dark mild – very moreish.
LIBERATOR 3.8% ABV
A lighter ale brewed with cascade hops for a satisfying fruitier finish.
ALLTIME 4% ABV
A slightly stronger session beer.
MUNDHAM MILD 4%
A few extra ingredients makes this slightly stronger dark mild an excellent choice for the connoisseur.
DITCHINGHAM DAM 4.2% ABV
A good dark ale with a subtle hint of ginger.
A SEETHING PINT 4.3% ABV
A lighter ale brewed with cascade hops for a full-flavoured pint.
NORFOLK 'N' GOOD 4.6% ABV
A stronger ale brewed with cascade hops. Light in colour and a fruity finish.
HONEYDO 5% ABV
A lighter ale full of flavour. Laced with Norfolk honey for a distinctive taste sensation.

UNCLE STUART'S BREWERY

Antoma, Pack Lane, Lingwood, Norwich NR13 4PD ☎ *(0773) 201 2112*

PACK LANE 4.0% ABV
CHURCH VIEW 4.7% ABV
BUCKENHAM WOODS 5.6% ABV
STRUMPSHAW FEN 5.7% ABV
CHRISTMAS ALE 7.0% ABV

WINTER'S BREWERY

8 Keelan Close, Norwich NR6 6QZ
☎ *(01603) 787820*
www.wintersbrewery.com

MILD 3.6% ABV
BITTER 3.8% ABV
GOLDEN 4.1% ABV
REVENGE 4.7% ABV
Yellow, with hops throughout; sweet aftertaste.
STORM FORCE 5.3% ABV
Blend of sweetness and malt.
TEMPEST 6.2% ABV

WISSEY VALLEY BREWERY

c/o Grey House, Lynn Road, Stoke Ferry, King's Lynn PE33 9SW ☎ *(01366) 500767*
www.wisseyvalleybrewery.co.uk

WVB 3.6% ABV
RATTY BOB CARTER'S BEST BITTER 3.7% ABV
CAP'N GRUMPY'S BEST BITTER 3.9% ABV
BODGER BROWN 4.0% ABV
OLD WOBBLY 4.2% ABV
WISSEY DAWN 4.3% ABV
BUSTED FLUSH 4.4% ABV
STOKED UP 4.4% ABV
OLD FAITHFUL 4.5% ABV
OLD GRUMPY 4.5% ABV
WISSEY SUNSET 5.0% ABV
GOLDEN RIVET 5.2 ABV

WOLF BREWERY

10 Maurice Gaymer Road, Attleborough NR17 2QZ ☎ *(01953) 457775*
www.wolf-brewery.ltd.uk

GOLDEN JACKAL 3.6% ABV
99 3.7% ABV
WOLF IN SHEEPS CLOTHING 3.8% ABV
Smooth and malty.
WOLF 3.9% ABV
COYOTE BITTER 4.3% ABV
Golden with floral hoppiness.
BIG RED 4.5% ABV
LUPINE 4.5% ABV
STOUT 4.5% ABV
WERWOLF 4.5% ABV
GRANNY WOULDN'T LIKE IT 4.8% ABV
Complex, malty flavour.
WOILD MOILD 4.8% ABV
Dark, smooth and fruity.
PRAIRIE 5.0% ABV
RED & GINGER 5.0% ABV
TIMBER WOLF 5.8% ABV
Plus occasional brews.

WOODFORDE'S NORFOLK ALES

Broadland Brewery, Slad Lane, Woodbastwick, Norwich NR13 6SW
☎ *(01603) 720353*
www.woodfordes.co.uk

MARDLER'S 3.5% ABV
Light, mid-coloured mild.
KETT'S REBELLION 3.6% ABV
WHERRY BITTER 3.8% ABV
Superb, well-hopped session ale.
GREAT EASTERN ALE 4.3% ABV
Golden with malt flavour.
NELSON'S REVENGE 4.5% ABV
NORFOLK NOG 4.6% ABV
Smooth chocolate malt flavour.
ADMIRAL'S RESERVE 5.0 % ABV
Traditional Strong Ale.
HEADCRACKER 7.0% ABV
Fruity and easy to drink for gravity.
NORFOLK NIP 8.5% ABV
Occasional barley wine.
Plus seasonal brews.

THE PUBS

ATTLEBOROUGH

The Griffin Hotel

Attleborough NR17 2AH
☎ *(01953) 452149* Richard Ashbourne

Wolf Best and Coyote plus Greene King Abbot always available. Also two hand pumps serving guest ales from a range of small breweries.

A sixteenth-century freehouse in the centre of town. Beams, log fires, dining area, accommodation. Food available at lunchtime and evenings. Children allowed.

10.30am–3.30pm and 5.30–11pm Mon–Thurs; 11am–11pm Fri–Sat; 10.30am–3.30pm and 5.30–10.30pm Sun.

BARFORD

The Cock Inn

Watton Road, Barford NR9 4AS
☎ *(01603) 757646* Peter Turner

Home of the Blue Moon Brewery, with the home-brewed Hingham, Darkside and Easy Life and either Moondance or Milk of Amnesia always available, plus seasonals and specials, and brews from Spectrum Brewery (which shares the Blue Moon plant).

Two hundred years old with rustic character and lots of nooks and crannies. Two bars, separate dining areas and a beer garden with bowling green and petanque pitch. Food available lunchtimes and evenings. Children allowed at lunchtime only. Situated four miles west of Norwich on the B1108.

12–2.30pm and 6–11pm Mon–Sat; 12–3pm and 7–10.30pm Sun.

BLICKLING

The Buckinghamshire Arms

Blickling, Nr Aylsham NR11 6NF
☎ *(01263) 732133* Robert Dawson-Smith
www.buckinghamshirearms-norfolk.co.uk

Woodforde's Wherry and Blickling (house beer from Woodforde's) plus Adnams brews usually available.

An olde-English, food-oriented freehouse at the gates of Blickling Hall. One large bar, snug, log fires and beer garden. Food available at lunchtimes and evenings in the pub and in a separate restaurant. En-suite accomodation, with four-poster beds. Well-behaved children allowed in the garden, or if eating.

11.30am–3pm and 6.30–11pm.

BRISTON

The John H Stracey

Westend, Briston NR24 2JA
☎ *(01263) 860891* RE Fox

A freehouse with Ruddles County a permanent feature, plus one guest, perhaps Woodforde's Wherry, Greene King Old Speckled Hen or Triumph or something from Reepham.

Country pub, built in 1565, with 46-seat restaurant, fires, beams and oak furniture. Garden and car park. One twin and two double letting rooms available. Children allowed. On the B1354 (Fakenham to Aylsham) in Briston. Special nights.

11am–2.30pm and 6.30–11pm; 12–2.30pm and 7–10.30pm Sun.

BURNHAM THORPE

The Lord Nelson

Walsingham Road, Burnham Thorpe, King's Lynn PE31 8HL
☎ *(01328) 738241 David Thorley*
www.nelsonslocal.co.uk

A Greene King house with Abbot, IPA and beers from Woodforde's always available, all served straight from the barrel.

The pub is well known locally for a unique rum-based drink, Nelson's Blood, and its companion, Lady Hamilton's Nip. Village pub built in 1637 in the birthplace of Nelson, it has stone floors, original oak settles and log fires. Traditional pub games. No bar – customers are served at table. Large beer garden with children's play area. Food available at lunchtime and evenings (not Sunday evening) with the emphasis on local produce (AA Rosette). Children and dogs welcome.

11am–3pm and 6–11pm Mon–Sat; 12–3pm and 7–10.30pm Sun.

BURSTON

The Crown

Crangreen/Millwood Road, Burston IP22 5TW
☎ *(01379) 741257* Mrs Whitehead

Adnams Bitter is always on offer. Guests, often changed two or three times a week, might be something from Hampshire, Old Chimneys or Robinson's.

Rural village pub and restaurant in a late sixteenth-century building, with two bars, fires and beams. Food served. Non-smoking lounge, garden and patio. Children allowed only if eating. There are plans for holiday accommodation with disabled facilities. Car park. On the corner of Crangreen and Millwood Road with large green in front (gypsy cart on green with pub name on!).

Closed Mon–Tues (except for party bookings); 12–2pm and 6.30–10.30pm Wed–Fri; 6.30–11pm Sat (closed Sat lunchtimes except for party bookings); 12–6pm Sun.

CANTLEY

The Cock Tavern

Manor Road, Cantley NR13 3JQ
☎ *(01493) 700895* Mike and Susan Enright

Adnams Best Bitter always available plus four guest beers (100+ per year) including Greene King Abbot and Old Speckled Hen, beers from Iceni Brewery, and many more.

A traditional country pub not far from Norwich with many separate areas, a beamed ceiling and two open fires. Bar food is available at lunchtime and evenings. Car park, garden and children's room. Caravan Club campsite adjacent. Turn right off the A47 (Norwich to Yarmouth road) near Acle, then signposted Cantley. Approx four miles from the turn.

11am–3.30pm and 6–11pm Mon–Fri; 7–11pm Sat; 12–4pm and 7–10.30pm Sun.

COLTISHALL

The Red Lion

77 Church Street, Coltishall NR12 7DW
☎ *(01603) 737402* Mrs Melanie Lamb

Adnams Southwold Bitter and Greene King Abbot Ale usually available plus a guest, often from Woodforde's, who also brew Weaselpis, the house beer.

Olde-worlde, 350-year-old pub full of nooks and crannies, with oak beams and log fires. Food served lunchtimes and evenings Mon–Fri and all day Sat–Sun and bank holidays. Car park. Large beer garden with children's play area, plus indoor soft-play area.

11am–3pm and 5–11pm Mon–Fri; 11am–11pm Sat and bank holidays; 12–10.30pm Sun.

COLTON

The Ugly Bug Inn

High House Farm Lane, Colton, Norwich
☎ *(01603) 880794* Richard Hook

Fuller's London Pride, Greene King Abbot Ale and four guest beers usually available, perhaps from Fuller's, Woodforde's, Elgood's, Archers, Wolf, Iceni or Bateman.

Farm building conversion with informal atmosphere. Restaurant, grounds and lakes in three acres. Food served 12–2pm and 7–9pm daily. Patio dining in summer. Accommodation. Ample parking. Children and dogs welcome.

12–3pm and 5.30–11pm Mon–Thurs; 11am–11pm Fri–Sat; 12–10.30pm Sun.

DOWNHAM MARKET

The Crown Hotel

Bridge Street, Downham Market PE38 9DH
☎ *(01366) 382322*
Messrs Richard Williams and Clive Hughes

A freehouse with Greene King IPA and Abbot, and something from Adnams always available, plus two guests from the likes of Woodforde's, Oldershaw, Elgood's, Iceni, Wolf, Tring and Tom Woods.

An olde-worlde pub dating from the 1600s, with open fires. One bar and two restaurants. Food available at lunchtime and evenings. Accommodation. Function room. Car park. Children welcome. In the centre of Downham Market, just off the High Street.

10am–11pm Mon–Sat; 12–10.30pm Sun.

EAST RUNTON

The White Horse

High Street, East Runton, Nr Cromer NR27 9NX
☎ *(01263) 519530* Tony Morgan

Adnams Bitter and Greene King Abbot always available, plus one or two guests, changed weekly, including beers such as Wolf Mild, Timothy Taylor Landlord, Marston's Pedigree and Reepham brews.

Village family pub, built in 1910. Food served 12–2.30pm and 7–9pm every day in the low season and 12–3pm and 5–9pm through the summer. Two bars, function room, garden/ patio, car park. Live music. Children allowed.

12–3pm and 7–11pm (10.30pm Sun) during low season; 12–11pm (10.30pm Sun) in summer.

ERPINGHAM

The Spread Eagle

Erpingham, Norwich NR11 7QA
☎ *(01263) 761591* Billie Carder

Five real ales are always on offer. Woodforde's Wherry and Nelson's Revenge, plus Adnams Best and Broadside are permanent features, and the guests could include Greene King Abbot or Exmoor Hound Dog. The pub also has an exclusive wine list and offers house wines from around the world.

A traditional pub with open fires, non-smoking dining area, pool room and new garden bar. Live music every Saturday night. Food available at lunchtime and evenings, with roasts on Sundays (booking advisable). Well-behaved children and dogs welcome.

11am–3pm and 6.30–11pm Mon–Sat; 12–3pm and 7–10.30pm Sun (garden bar will remain open on summer afternoons).

FOULDEN

The White Hart Inn

White Hart Street, Foulden, Thetford IP26 5AW
☎ *(01366) 328638* Ann Moss and Sarah Moss

A freehouse serving Greene King IPA and Abbot, plus two guests or customer requests changed twice-weekly.

A family-run, busy village pub with log fires, non-smoking conservatory and beer garden. Biker and dog friendly. Live music on Friday or Saturday. Food available at lunchtime (12.30–2.00pm except Tues) and evenings (7–9.30pm). Children welcome. En-suite accommodation. Monthly live music/theme nights. Two miles from Oxburgh Hall (National Trust). Off the A134 (Thetford to Kings Lynn), 3 miles from Mundford.

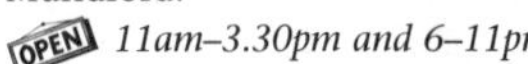
11am–3.30pm and 6–11pm.

GORLESTON

The Cliff Hotel

Gorleston NR31 6DH
☎ *(01493) 662179* Vaughan Cutter

Fuller's London Pride, Greene King IPA, Woodforde's Wherry and Marston's Pedigree usually available.

Hotel with two bars and two restaurants overlooking Gorleston beach and harbour. Food served 12–2.30pm and 7–9.30pm every day. Children welcome in gardens or hotel only, not in the bars. Two car parks.

11am–11pm.

The Short Blue

47 High Street, Gorleston, Great Yarmouth NR31 6RR
☎ *(01493) 602192* Kevin Duffield

Greene King IPA and Adnams Best Bitter always available, plus one regularly changing guest ale. Whenever possible, guest ales are from a local brewery such as Woodforde's.

Dating from 1693, this traditional olde-worlde pub houses carved wood, stained glass and wooden barrels. No juke box or pool table. Food available 12–2pm Mon–Sun and 6–10.30pm Fri. Riverside garden with covered patio, children allowed in the garden only. Roadside parking in Riverside Road.

11am–11pm (10.30pm Sun).

GREAT CRESSINGHAM

The Olde Windmill Inn

Water End, Great Cressingham, Watton IP25 6NN
☎ *(01760) 756232* Caroline and Michael Halls

Greene King IPA and Adnams Best Bitter and Broadside are always available, plus two guests, changed regularly, normally one local beer and one from elsewhere in the UK.

Olde-worlde country pub dating from 1650, with five acres of park land and paddocks, three bars, five family rooms, games room and conservatory. Food is served 12–2pm and 6–10.30pm Mon–Sat, and 12–2pm and 6–10pm Sun. There is an extensive bar menu. Children are welcome in the family rooms, the beer garden and the play area, and the pub has high chairs and a children's menu. Conferences, meetings and private parties are a speciality. Car parks front and back (80 cars). Just off the A1065 Swaffham–Brandon road, or the B1108 Watton–Brandon road.

11.30am–3pm and 6–11pm Mon–Sat; 11.45am–3.30pm and 6pm–10.30pm Sun.

GREAT YARMOUTH

The Mariner's Tavern

69 Howard Street South, Great Yarmouth NR30 1LN
☎ *(01493) 332299* Mr Adams

Fuller's London Pride, Highgate Dark, Greene King Abbot and beers from Adnams always available. One guest changed each weekend. Previous guest beers have included Thwaites Bloomin Ale and Greene King Triumph.

A small traditional pub with log fires. Full bar menu available lunchtimes. Children allowed. Ring for directions.

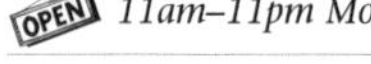
11am–11pm Mon–Sat; 12–10.30pm Sun.

The Red Herring

24–5 Havelock Road, Great Yarmouth NR30 3HQ
☎ *(01493) 853384* Wendy and Dave Woolford

A freehouse serving Greene King IPA and Abbot, plus up to four guest ales from local and national breweries. Old Rosie cask cider also available.

An old-fashioned, country-style pub in a town location. Entertainment on Saturday nights, plus darts and pool. No food. No children. Havelock Road is off St Peter's Road which runs off the sea-front.

12–4pm and 7–11pm Mon–Fri; 11am–4pm and 7–11pm Sat; 12–4pm and 7–10.30pm Sun during quiet season, but mostly open all day through the summer.

GRESSENHALL

The Swan

The Green, Gressenhall, Dereham NR20 4DU
☎ *(01632) 860340* Mr Mansfield

Greene King IPA always available, plus two guests such as Marston's Pedigree or Young's Bitter.

A family-oriented country pub with dining area, log fires and beer garden. Food available at lunchtime and evenings. Children allowed.

12–2.30pm and 6–11pm Mon–Sat; 12–3pm and 7–10.30pm Sun.

HAPPISBURGH

Hill House

Happisburgh NR12 0PW
☎ *(01692) 650004* Clive and Sue Stockton

Buffy's Hill House Elementary Ale, Shepherd Neame Spitfire and two guest beers regularly available, perhaps from Church End, Black Sheep, Wolf, Adnams, Concertina or Ossett.

Coastal coaching inn known for its Sherlock Holmes connection. Restaurant and large garden. Food served 12–2.30pm and 7–9.30pm daily. 'Kids' Bar' open during school holidays. Car park.

Winter: 12–3pm and 7–11pm (10.30pm Sun). Summer: 12–11pm (10.30pm Sun).

HEACHAM

Fox & Hounds

22 Station Road, Heacham PE31 7EX
☎ *(01485) 570345* Mark Bristow

Home of the Fox Brewery with own brews Heacham Gold, Grace & Favour and Red Knob permanently available. Occasional guests and seasonal and special home brews.

A large, traditional 1920s pub with beer garden. Food available 12–2pm and 6–9pm daily. Children allowed. Brewery on site, tours available. Function room.

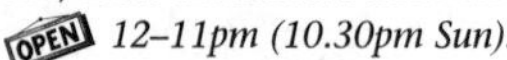
12–11pm (10.30pm Sun).

HILBOROUGH

The Swan

Brandon Road, Hilborough, Thetford IP26 5BW
☎ *(01760) 756380* Jane Roberson

Greene King Abbot and IPA plus a guest brew always available, which changes once a fortnight and may well be a Greene King seasonal or special brew.

An eighteenth-century pub with log fires and many original features. Beer garden, restaurant and en-suite accommodation. Food available 12–2.30pm and 7–9.30pm daily. Children welcome.

11am–3pm and 6.30–11pm Mon–Thurs; 11am–11pm Fri–Sat; 12–3pm and 7–10.30pm Sun.

HINGHAM

The White Hart Hotel

3 Market Place, Hingham, Norwich NR9 4AF
☎ *(01953) 850214* Les and Carol Foster

Greene King IPA and Abbot always available plus two guests.

The only pub in Hingham, this is a family-oriented pub and restaurant with beer garden and accommodation. Food available at lunchtime and evenings. Children allowed.

12–11pm Mon–Sat; 12–5pm and 7–10.30pm Sun.

HOCKWOLD

The Red Lion

Main Street, Hockwold IP26 4NB
☎ *(01842) 828875* Mrs Miles

Greene King IPA always available plus two guests which change fortnightly. A beer festival is held each August bank holiday.

A village pub and restaurant. Children allowed.

 *12–2.30pm and 6–11pm Sun–Fri; 12–11pm Sat.*

INGHAM

The Swan Inn

Mill Road, Ingham NR12 9AB
☎ *(01692) 581099* Sandra and Malcolm Potts

A Woodforde's pub with Wherry, Nelson's Revenge, Great Eastern and Mardler's Mild the permanent beers. One of these is sometimes taken off in order to feature a seasonal or celebration ale.

Fourteenth-century thatched village pub with fireplaces and beams. Food is available, and there is a non-smoking restaurant. Patio, car park, five letting rooms. Children allowed only if eating.

 *Summer: 11am–11pm Mon–Sat; 12–10.30pm Sun. Please call for seasonal opening hours.*

KENNINGHALL

The Red Lion

East Church Street, Kenninghall, Diss NR16 2EP
☎ *(01953) 887849* Mandy and Bruce Berry

A freehouse offering Greene King IPA and Abbot, Woodforde's Wherry and Mardler's, plus one guest, such as a beer from Wolf.

A one-bar village pub with beams, open fires, bare stone floors and floorboards. A listed building with a snug, one of only two snugs in the area. Bar snacks and restaurant food available at lunchtimes and evenings every day. Rear patio garden. Beer garden. Children allowed, but not in the bar area. Bed and breakfast accommodation available.

 *12–3pm and 6.30–11pm Mon–Thurs; 12–11pm Fri–Sat; 12–10.30pm Sun.*

KING'S LYNN

Stuart House Hotel

35 Goodwins Road, King's Lynn PE30 5QX
☎ *(01553) 772169* David Armes
www.stuarthousehotel.co.uk

Adnams Best Bitter and Broadside plus Woodforde's Wherry and Greene King IPA usually available. One guest beer is also served, such as Timothy Taylor Landlord, Fuller's London Pride, Woodforde's Nelson's Revenge, Oakham JHB or Mompesson's Gold. Beer Festival held in grounds at the end of July.

A family-run hotel, quietly situated within its own grounds in the centre of King's Lynn. Cosy bar with a real fire in winter and doors that open on to the garden in summer. Regular entertainment. Bar menu and à la carte restaurant. Food served 7–9.30pm daily. Car park. Well-behaved children welcome until 8.30pm. Pets' corner in garden. Music and events throughout the year – check website for details.

 *6–11pm Mon–Sat; 12–3pm and 6–10.30pm Sun.*

LARLING

The Angel Inn

Larling, Norwich NR16 2QU
☎ *(01953) 717963* Andrew Stammers

Adnams Southwold Bitter and four guest beers usually available, perhaps from Iceni, Woodforde's, Wolf, Mauldons, Orkney or Cottage, changing once or twice a week.

A 400-year-old village pub with quarry-tiled, beamed public bar, real fire and local atmosphere. Two dining rooms. En-suite accommodation. Food served lunchtimes and evenings. Car park. Camping and caravanning. Children welcome in the lounge and picnic area. Small, fenced play area outside. Ideal for quiet outdoor pursuits and handy for Banham Zoo, Snetterton Race Circuit and Sunday Market. Ring for directions.

 *10am–11pm Mon–Sat; 12–10.30pm Sun.*

LITTLE DUNHAM

The Black Swan

The Street, Little Dunham, King's Lynn PE32 2DG
☎ *(01760) 722200* Paul and Christine

A freehouse with three constantly changing real ales always available. Greene King IPA and Abbot are usually featured, plus a constantly changing guest.

A country pub with log fires, restaurant and patio dining. Food available lunchtimes and evenings. Children allowed. Located off the A47.

 *12–2pm Tues–Fri; 6.30–11pm Mon–Fri; 11am–11pm Sat; 12–10.30pm Sun.*

LYNFORD

Lynford Hall

Lynford, Thetford IP26 5HW
☎ *(01842) 878351* Peter Scopes

Woodforde's Wherry, St Peter's Ale and an Iceni brew always available.

Pub located within Lynford Hall, a stately home and tourist attraction open to the public. Separate restaurant and beer garden. Food available. Children allowed.

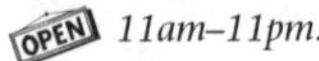 *11am–11pm.*

MUNDFORD

The Crown Hotel

Crown Street, Mundford, Near Thetford IP26 5HQ
☎ *(01362) 637647* Barry Walker

Seven real ales always available including Woodforde's Norfolk Wherry, Marston's Pedigree and Greene King Old Speckled Hen. Guests are changed weekly.

A sixteenth-century beamed freehouse with open fires in winter. Bar and restaurant food available at lunchtime and evenings. Pool and darts, car park, garden, function room, accommodation. Children allowed. On the village green.

OPEN *11am–11pm Mon–Sat; 12–10.30pm Sun.*

NORTHWOLD

The Crown Inn

High Street, Northwold, Thetford IP26 5LA
☎ *(01366) 727317* Gary and Kym Widdicks

A freehouse with four constantly changing real ales always available. Local breweries are favoured, in particular Adnams, Woodforde's and occasionally Iceni.

A traditional village pub with log fires and beer garden. Bar snacks and à la carte food served 12–2.30pm and 6.30–9.30pm Wed–Sun (no food Mon–Tues).

 *12–3pm and 6–11pm Mon–Thurs; 12–11pm Fri–Sat; 12–10.30pm Sun.*

NORWICH

Alexandra Tavern

Stafford Street, Norwich NR2 3BB
☎ *(01603) 627772* JL Little

A freehouse with Chalk Hill Best, Flintknapper's Mild and Tap always available. Guests on two hand pumps tend to be brews such as Exmoor Gold.

A traditional local with log fires in winter. Bar snacks always available, and bar meals are served 12.30–7pm. Children allowed until 7pm.

OPEN *All day, every day.*

Billy Bluelight

27 Hall Road, Norwich NR1 3MQ
☎ *(01603) 623768* Simon Morgan

A Woodforde's house with a good range of Woodforde's ales always available. Mild, Bluelight, Wherry, Great Eastern, Nelson's Revenge, Admiral's Reserve, Norfolk Nog and Headcracker usually on offer, plus seasonals and specials.

Themed 1930s/1940s-style pub. No fruit machine, juke box or pool table. Beer garden with petanque, piste and full-size skittle alley in the function room. Food served lunchtimes and evenings every day. Children welcome until 9pm each day. Located on the junction of Queens and Hall roads.

OPEN *12–11pm (10.30pm Sun).*

Coach & Horses

82 Thorpe Road, Norwich NR1 1BA
☎ *(01603) 477077* Bob Cameron

At least seven constantly changing ales on at any one time. The pub is situated on the same site as Chalk Hill Brewery (tours available by arrangement), so the full range of Chalk Hill ales always on offer.

A 200-year-old traditional pub with an open fire and wooden floors. Wide range of food available 12–9pm Mon-Sat, 11am–8pm Sundays. Well-behaved children welcome. Close to Norwich Station and football ground.

OPEN *11am–11pm (10.30pm Sun).*

The Eaton Cottage

75 Mount Pleasant, Norwich NR2 2DQ
☎ *(01603) 453048*
Mr I Tilbury and Mr M Dormer

Adnams Best, Greene King Abbot, Chalk Hill Best, Fuller's London Pride and Wolf Brewery's Edith Cavell permanently available, plus a guest. Bateman XXXB, Young's Special and Adnams Broadside are among the ales on rotation.

A traditional corner pub, refurbished, with a pool room. Hot snacks (rolls) available all day. Children welcome (under close supervision) until 7pm.

OPEN *12–11pm Mon–Fri; 11.30am–11pm Sat; 12–10.30pm Sun.*

The Fat Cat

49 West End Street, Norwich NR2 4NA
☎ *(01603) 624364*

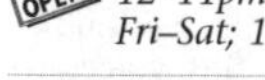
Up to 25 beers available at any one time. Regulars include Timothy Taylor Landlord, Hop Back Summer Lightning and Oakham Bishop's Farewell plus a guest list that now runs into thousands. Belgian beers (four on draught, plus bottles) also stocked.

A traditional Victorian pub decorated with breweriana and pub signs. Filled rolls available at lunchtime. Street parking. Children not allowed.

OPEN *12–11pm Mon–Thurs; 11am–11pm Fri–Sat; 12–10.30pm Sun.*

The Jubilee

26 St Leonards Road, Norwich NR11 4BL
☎ *(01603) 618734*
Tim Wood and Teresa Santos

Fuller's London Pride, Adnams Bitter, Greene King Abbot and IPA are among the beers always available, plus four ever-changing guests.

A traditional freehouse with beer garden and adults' games room. Food available at lunchtime only. Smoke extractors fitted in both bars. Children allowed until 5pm.

OPEN *All day, every day.*

The Kings Arms

22 Hall Road, Norwich NR1 3HQ
☎ *(01603) 766361* John Craft

A freehouse permanently offering Adnams Southwold Best and Broadside, and Wolf Coyote Bitter, plus ten guests. The emphasis is on East Anglian breweries, with beers such as Mauldons Cuckoo and Eatonswill Old, Tindall Best Bitter and Iceni Fine Soft Day being featured. One hand pump is dedicated to fruit beer or spiced ale, changed every three or four days, for example St Peter's Elderberry Beer. Another pump serves a mild, such as Tindall, and is changed every two days. Three beer festivals per year.

One-bar drinkers' pub in the city, a pub since 1834. Non-smoking conservatory. Only rolls are available – customers are encouraged to bring their own food, and cutlery is provided. Courtyard garden. No children. Just off Inner Ring Road, near Sainsbury's.

OPEN *11am–11pm Mon–Sat; 12–10.30pm Sun.*

The Mustard Pot

101 Thorpe Road, Norwich NR1 1TR
☎ *(01603) 432393* Jason Bates

An Adnams house with Best, Broadside and Extra always available, plus Regatta when in season. A range of guest ales such as Charles Wells Summer Solstice or Fuller's London Pride is also served.

A drinkers' pub with beer garden and food available at lunchtime and evenings. No children.

OPEN *All day, every day.*

The Old White Lion

73 Oak Street, Norwich NR3 3AR
☎ *(01603) 620630* Nick Ray (Manager)

Greene King IPA, Woodforde's Wherry, Fuller's London Pride and Adnams Best Bitter always available, plus around eight guest beers every week.

A 450-year-old pub with old beams, slate floors, and lots of wood and brass. Colourfully decorated with flowers on the outside. Candles every evening. Food available 12–10.30pm – phone orders taken. On the inner ring road going anti-clockwise, first left before river on the east side.

OPEN *11am–11pm Mon–Sat; 12–10.30pm Sun.*

The Ribs of Beef

24 Wensum Street, Norwich NR3 1HY
☎ *(01603) 619517* Joolia and Gary Gilvey
www.ribsofbeef.co.uk

A freehouse serving 11 cask ales such as Marston's Pedigree, Woodforde's Wherry and Rib Cracker, Iceni It's a Grand Day and Adnams brews, plus guests changing weekly. These might be something like Brakspear Bee Sting, Hogs Back TEA or Timothy Taylor Landlord.

A popular local situated near the river with private jetty. Food available 12–2.30pm Mon–Fri and 12–5pm Sat–Sun. Children's room.

OPEN *All day, every day.*

Rosary Tavern

95 Rosary Road, Norwich NR1 4BX
☎ *(01603) 666287* Ian and Nina Bushell

At least seven real ales always available. Adnams Best and Black Sheep Best are on permanently plus five constantly changing guests. Also sells real Norfolk cider.

A traditional pub with a friendly atmosphere. Bar food available at lunchtimes only, including roasts on Sun. Car park, beer garden and function room. Easy to find, near the yacht and railway station, and the football ground.

OPEN *11.30am–11pm Mon–Sat; 12–10.30pm Sun.*

St Andrew's Tavern

4 St Andrews Street, Norwich NR2 4AF
☎ *(01603) 614858* Jenny Watt and Alan Allred

An Adnams house serving up to sixteen cask ales, including the full range of Adnams brews. Always an interesting choice of constantly changing guest beers from around the country.

A friendly, traditional pub, close to the city centre. Bar food available at lunchtimes. In the evenings, order your choice of take-away and eat in the pub. Terrace garden with barbecue. Cellar bar available for parties, functions and meetings. Children not allowed. At the junction of Duke Street and St John Maddermarket opposite St Andrews car park.

OPEN *All day Mon–Sat; 12–5pm Sun.*

Seamus O'Rourke's

92 Pottergate, Norwich NR2 1DZ
☎ *(01603) 626627* Phil Adams

A freehouse with Adnams Best and O'Rourke's Revenge (house beer) always available, plus up to eight guests including Charles Wells Bombardier, Wolf Coyote, Iceni Fine Soft Day or a Burton Bridge beer.

Irish sports themed pub with open fires and food available at lunchtime. No children.

OPEN *All day, every day (except Christmas Day 12–3.30pm).*

The Steam Packet

39 Crown Road, Norwich NR1 3DT
☎ *(01603) 441545* Susan Strudwick

An Adnams house with Best Bitter and Broadside always available plus seasonal guest.

A traditional Victorian local built circa 1830 with wooden bar floor and carpeted, non-smoking snug. Hot snacks served all day. Outside seating in summer. Close to castle and city centre, behind Anglia TV.

OPEN *12–11pm Mon–Sat (closed Sunday).*

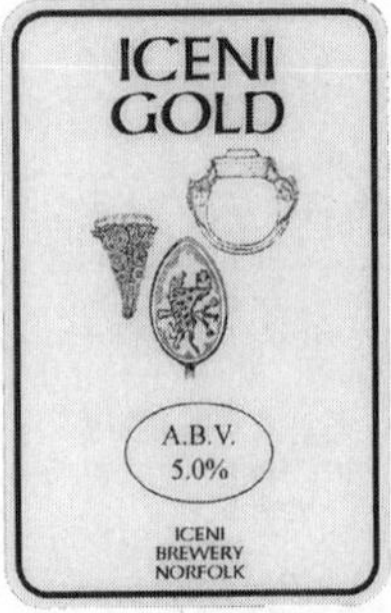

The Trafford Arms

61 Grove Road, Norwich NR1 3RL
☎ *(01603) 628466* Chris and Glynis Higgins
www.traffordarms.co.uk

Adnams Bitter, Woodforde's Mardler's and Barley Boy house bitter brewed by Woodforde's, usually available. A mild is always served and guest beers may include Sarah Hughes Ruby Mild, Burton Bridge Porter, Bateman Dark Mild, Elgood's Black Dog Mild, Timothy Taylor Landlord or brews from Mauldons, Rooster's or Reepham.

A welcoming community pub, just out of the city centre. Cosmopolitan collection of customers from all walks of life. No loud music, just a cacophony of chatting voices. Food served 12–2.30pm and 6–8.30pm Mon–Fri, 12–3pm and 6–8pm Sat, 12–3pm Sun. Limited parking. No children. Situated very close to Sainsbury's on Queens Road.

 *11am–11pm Mon–Sat; 12–10.30pm Sun.*

The York Tavern

1 Leicester Street, Norwich NR22 2AS
☎ *(01603) 620918* Mr Verret

Adnams ales usually available, plus guests such as Wadworth 6X, Marston's Pedigree or Greene King Old Speckled Hen.

An old-fashioned London-style pub with open fires, restaurant and beer garden. Food available at lunchtime and evenings. Children allowed in the restaurant only.

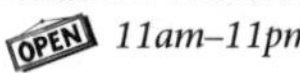 *11am–11pm.*

PULHAM ST MARY

The King's Head

The Street, Pulham St Mary IP21 4RD
☎ *(01379) 676318* Graham Scott

Brews from Buffy's and Adnams always available plus two guests including Marston's Pedigree, Wadworth 6X, Shepherd Neame Spitfire, Woodforde's Wherry and brews from Brains, Robinson's and Fuller's.

Built in the 1600s, this pub has an old oak timber frame with exposed beams. Bar and restaurant food available at lunchtime and evenings. Non-smoking dining area, games room, bowling green, paddock, car park, garden, children's area, accommodation. Off the A140 to Harlesdon, on the B1134.

 *June–Aug: all day, every day. Sept–May: 11.30am–3pm and 5.30–11pm Mon–Fri; all day Sat–Sun.*

REEDHAM

The Railway Tavern

17 The Havaker, Reedham NR13 3HG
☎ *(01493) 700340*
James Lunn and Christina Felix

Adnams ales always available plus many guest beers including those from the local Humpty Dumpty brewery and other small local operations. Beer festivals held in April and September.

A listed Victorian railway hotel freehouse. Two bars. No fruit machines. Bar and restaurant food is available 12–3pm and 6–9pm. Car park, garden and children's room. Accommodation available in separate stable block. Take the A47 south of Acle, then six miles on the B1140. By rail from Norwich, Gt Yarmouth or Lowestoft.

 *12–3pm and 6.30–11pm Mon–Thurs; all day Fri–Sat; normal Sun hours.*

REEPHAM

The Crown

Ollands Road, Reepham, Norwich NR10 4EJ
☎ *(01603) 870964* Mr Good

Greene King Old Speckled Hen and IPA among the beers always available.

A village pub with dining area and beer garden. Food available at lunchtime and evenings. B&B available. Children allowed.

 *12–3pm and 7–11pm Mon; 7–11pm Tues–Fri; 12–5pm and 7–11pm Sat; 12–5pm and 7–10.30pm Sun.*

The Kings Arms

Market Place, Reepham, Norwich NR10 4JJ
☎ *(01603) 870345* Steve Capel

A freehouse with Woodforde's Wherry, Adnams Best and Greene King Abbot permanently available.

A village community pub with restaurant area, courtyard and garden. Jazz on Sundays in summer. Children welcome. Car park.

 *11.30am–3pm and 5.30–11pm (10.30pm Sun); all day Sat–Sun in summer.*

The Old Brewery House Hotel

Market Place, Reepham, Norwich NR10 4JJ
☎ *(01603) 870881* Mike Mansfield

A freehouse with Greene King Abbot, Adnams beers and a house bitter always available, plus one changing guest.

An olde-worlde pub with beams, log fire, restaurant, beer garden and accommodation. Food available at lunchtime and evenings. Children allowed.

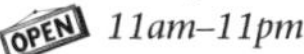 *11am–11pm.*

RINGSTEAD

The Gin Trap Inn

Ringstead, Nr Hunstanton PO36 5JU
☎ *(01485) 525264* Brian and Margaret Harmes

A freehouse with a house beer brewed by Woodforde's called Gin Trap always available, plus Norfolk Nog, Greene King Abbot and an Adnams ale. One other guest served.

A 350-year-old traditional English pub. Dining area, beer garden, self-catering accommodation. Food available at lunchtime and evenings. Children allowed. Ring for directions.

 *11.30am–3pm and 6–11pm Mon–Sat; 12–2.30pm and 6.45–10.30pm Sun (open all day Sun from Whitsun to Sept).*

SHERINGHAM

The Windham Arms

15 Wyndham Street, Sheringham NR26 8BA
☎ *(01263) 822609*
Mike Powell and April Davies

Adnams Best and Broadside and Woodforde's Wherry always available, plus a wide selection of weekly changing guest ales served on three hand pumps (never the same beer twice). An annual beer festival is held on the first weekend in July with 20 different guest beers on offer.

Large pub with restaurant, log fires, beer garden. Food available at lunchtime and evenings. Children allowed.

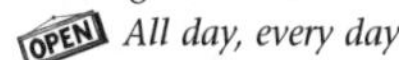 *All day, every day.*

STIFFKEY

The Red Lion

44 Wells Road, Stiffkey, Wells-next-the-Sea NR23 1AJ
☎ *(01328) 830552* Andrew Waddison

A freehouse with Woodforde's Wherry, Greene King IPA and Abbot and Woodforde's Wherry always available, plus a guest – perhaps seasonal Woodforde's ales such as Great Eastern in Summer or Norfolk Nog in Winter, or Elgood's Black Dog Mild, Wolf Best, or something from Nethergate, Green Jack or other local breweries.

An old, rustic pub with tiled floor, log fires and beer garden. Food available at lunchtime and evenings (12– 2.30pm and 6–9.30pm). Children and dogs welcome. Located on the main A149. Half a mile from the sea.

OPEN *11am–3pm and 6–11pm.*

STOWBRIDGE

The Heron

Station Road, Stowbridge, King's Lynn PE34 3PH
☎ *(01366) 384147* The Luckey Family

A freehouse with Greene King IPA and Abbot plus Adnams Best always available. Also three guests including, perhaps, Woodforde's Wherry, Charles Wells Bombardier or Greene King Old Speckled Hen.

A 150-year-old traditional pub with log fires and beer garden. Bar food and separate restaurant food served 12–2pm and 7–9pm. Families welcome. Situated between two rivers, ring for directions if necessary. Riverside moorings available.

 *12–3pm and 5–11pm Mon–Fri; 12–3pm and 6–11pm Sat; 12–3pm and 7–10.30pm Sun.*

SWANTON MORLEY

The Angel

66 Greengate, Swanton Morley, Norwich NR20 4LX
☎ *(01362) 637407*
Avril Evans and Peter Groves

A freehouse with Samuel Smith Old Brewery Bitter and Mighty Oak Oscar Wilde and Maldon Gold always available, plus two guests changed every few days.

A country village pub dating from 1609 with log fires, original beams, beer garden and bowling green. Two bars, pool room. Food available at lunchtimes and evening seven days a week. Children allowed.

 *12–11pm (10.30pm Sun).*

Darby's Freehouse

1 Elsing Road, Swanton Morley, Dereham NR20 4JU
☎ *(01362) 637647*
John Carrick and Louise Battle

A freehouse serving eight real ales. Adnams Best and Broadside, Woodforde's Wherry and Badger Tanglefoot are permanent features, and four guests are changed weekly.

A genuine, family-owned and -run freehouse converted from two derelict farm cottages. Traditional English and Thai cuisine available at lunchtime and evenings. Attached to a nearby farmhouse that offers accommodation and camping. Car park, garden and children's room and playground. Take the B1147 from Dereham to Bawdeswell, turn right on to Elsing Road at Swanton Morley.

 *11.30am–3pm and 6–11pm Mon–Fri; 11am–11pm Sat; 12–10.30pm Sun.*

THORNHAM

The Lifeboat Inn

Ship Lane, Thornham, Hunstanton PE36 6LT
☎ *(01485) 512236* Mr and Mrs Coker

Adnams, Greene King and Woodforde's ales always available plus a couple of guest beers, mainly from small independents.

A sixteenth-century smugglers' alehouse with wood beams, hanging paraffin lamps and open fires overlooking salt marshes. Bar and restaurant food available at lunchtime and evenings. Car park, garden and accommodation. Children allowed. Turn first left when entering the village from Hunstanton.

 *All day, every day.*

TIBENHAM

The Greyhound

The Street, Tibenham NR16 1PZ
☎ *(01379) 677676* David and Colleen Hughes
www.thetibenhamgreyhound.co.uk

Greene King IPA and something from Adnams always on offer, plus two guests, which might be Timothy Taylor Landlord, Shepherd Neame Spitfire, Early Bird or Late Red or Fuller's London Pride, or beers from micro-breweries, changed fortnightly.

A 300-year-old quintessential village pub with oak beams and log fire. The public bar has a dart board and there is a separate pool room. The lounge bar has low beams and a wood fire. Two beer gardens, children's play area and paddock. Large car park. Traditional pub food served all opening hours Wed–Sun. Camping and caravanning facilities.

 *6.30–11pm Mon, Wed, Thurs (closed all day Tues); 12–11pm Fri–Sat; 12–10.30pm Sun.*

TOFT MONKS

Toft Lion

Toft Monks, Nr Beccles NR34 0EP
☎ *(01502) 677702* Jan and Giles Mortimer

Adnams Bitter and a real cask mild are always available, plus an ever-changing selection of guest ales from local and nationwide breweries. Various cask strengths are available, and seasonal ales are featured.

A pub since 1650, this has always been the hub of the community. Good old-fashioned pub with the emphasis on fine ales first and simple, home-cooked food second, served in a convivial atmosphere complete with log fires. En-suite accommodation is available in a double or family room, as you may decide you don't want to go home!

OPEN *12–2.30pm and 6–11pm Mon–Fri (closed Tues lunchtime); 12–2.30pm and 7–11pm Sat; 12–6.30pm Sun. Weekend hours may be extended, especially in summer. Phone for details.*

UPTON

The White Horse

17 Chapel Road, Upton, Norwich
☎ *(01493) 750696* Raymond Norman

Adnams Best, Greene King IPA and St Peter's Best always available, plus two or three guest ales. Emphasis on local breweries; guests come from breweries such as Woodforde's, Wolf, Elgood's, Adnams, Buffy's and Mauldons.

Dating from the nineteenth century, full of character with two inglenook fireplaces, a snug and a main bar with two further rooms. Food available 12–3pm and 6.30–9.30pm daily. Children and dogs welcome. Conservatory. Beer garden with aviary. Regular live music and summer events. Taxi service available for parties.

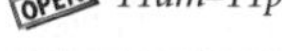

11am–11pm Mon–Sat; 12–10.30pm Sun.

WALSINGHAM

The Bull Inn

Common Place, Shire Hall Plain, Walsingham NR22 6BP
☎ *(01328) 820333* Philip Horan

Ridleys Tolly Original and Marston's Pedigree among the beers always available.

A 600-year-old olde-worlde pub with open fires, restaurant, beer garden and accommodation. Food available at lunchtime and evenings. Children allowed.

11am–3pm and 6–11pm Mon–Sat; 12–3pm and 7–10.30pm Sun.

WARHAM

The Three Horseshoes

Bridge Street, Warham, Wells-next-the-Sea NR23 1NL
☎ *(01328) 710547* Mr Salmon

Woodforde's Wherry and Greene King IPA always available plus a guest (changed each week) such as Greene King Abbot or Old Speckled Hen, Woodforde's Nelson's Revenge and Wadworth 6X.

Traditional cottage pub in the centre of the village with gas lighting and open fires. Bar food available at lunchtime and evenings. Car park, garden, function room, non-smoking room, accommodation. Children allowed.

11.30am–2.30pm and 6–11pm Mon–Sat; 12–3pm and 6–10.30pm Sun.

WEST RUDHAM

The Duke's Head

West Rudham, King's Lynn PE31 8RW
☎ *(01485) 528540* Mr Feltham

A range of Woodforde's ales (usually including Great Eastern, Wherry and Kett's Rebellion) always available. Occasional guests.

A fifteenth-century coaching inn. Food oriented with separate dining area and food available at lunchtime and evenings. Children allowed.

11am–3pm and 7–11pm Mon–Sat (closed Tues); 12–2.30pm and 7–10.30pm Sun.

WEST SOMERTON

The Lion

West Somerton, Great Yarmouth
☎ *(01493) 393289*
Mr GI Milroy and SM Milroy

Greene King IPA and Abbot usually available plus two guest beers, often Hampshire Lionheart and a Mauldons ale.

Traditional country pub with children's room. Food served 11.30am–3pm and 6–9.30pm. Car park.

11.30am–3.30pm and 6–11pm Mon–Sat; 12–3.30pm and 6–10.30pm Sun.

WHINBURGH

The Mustard Pot

Dereham Road, Whinburgh, Dereham NR19 1AA
☎ *(01362) 692179* Ricky and Amanda Fox

A freehouse with Adnams Bitter permanently available, plus guest ales served on four pumps, from local independent breweries.

An old village pub with open fireplace and beer garden. Good pub food available 12–2pm and 6.30–8.45pm Mon–Sat, with Sunday lunches served until 2pm (no food Sun evening). Children welcome.

11am–11pm Mon–Sat; 12–10.30pm Sun.

WINTERTON-ON-SEA

The Fisherman's Return

The Lane, Winterton-on-Sea, Great Yarmouth NR29 4BN
☎ *(01493) 393305* John Findlay
www.fishermans-return.com

A genuine freehouse with Woodforde's Wherry, Norfolk Nog and Great Eastern Best plus Greene King IPA, Adnams Best and Broadside always available and a guest changed seasonally.

A 300-year-old brick and flint pub with open fires and beer garden. Food available 12–2pm and 6.30–9pm daily. Children are welcome, and the pub has a large garden with play equipment, a family room and children's menu (children not allowed in bars). Eight miles north of Great Yarmouth.

 *11am–2.30pm and 6.30–11pm Mon–Fri; all day Sat–Sun.*

WIVETON

The Wiveton Bell

The Green, Wiveton, Blakeney NR25 7TL
☎ *(01263) 740101* John and Lucy Olsen

A freehouse with Adnams Bitter permanently available, plus guests during the summer from local independent breweries such as Wolf.

A traditional, beamed village pub with a non-smoking conservatory restaurant. Beer garden. Adjoining cottage to let. Food available at lunchtimes and evenings. Well-behaved children and dogs welcome.

 *Summer: 12–2.30pm and 6.30–11pm. Winter opening hours vary.*

WOODBASTWICK

The Fur & Feather Inn

Woodbastwick, Norwich NR13 6HQ
☎ *(01603) 720003* Tim and Penny Ridley

The Woodforde's brewery tap, situated next door to the brewery and specialising in the range of Woodforde's ales: Fur and Feather Bitter, Admiral's Reserve, Wherry Best, Mardler's Mild, Great Eastern, Nelson's Revenge, Norfolk Nog and Headcracker.

A thatched country pub/restaurant with beer garden. Food available at lunchtimes and evenings Mon–Sat and all day Sun. Children allowed. Dogs welcome in the garden.

 *11.30am–3pm and 6–11pm Mon–Sat; 12–10.30pm Sun.*

WRENINGHAM

Bird in Hand

Church Road, Wreningham NR16 1BH
☎ *(01508) 489438* Mrs Carol Turner

A freehouse with Woodforde's Wherry, Fuller's London Pride and an Adnams brew always available, plus one guest, perhaps Greene King Abbot.

A traditional pub with wood burners, restaurant and beer garden. Food available at lunchtime and evenings. Children allowed if eating. Ring for directions.

 *11.30am–3pm and 6–11pm Mon–Sat; 12–3pm and 6–10.30pm Sun.*

WYMONDHAM

The Feathers Inn

Town Green, Wymondham, Norfolk NR18 0PN
☎ *(01953) 605675*
Eddie Aldous and Lorna Palmer

A freehouse offering Adnams Best, Greene King Abbot, Marston's Pedigree and Feathers Tickler (brewed for the pub by Elgood's), plus two guests, changed every couple of days, such as Adnams Broadside or something from Nethergate or Burton Bridge.

Regulars' town pub, with one bar and function room. Food available every day 12–2pm and 7.30–9pm. Gaming machines, darts, garden. Children allowed.

 *11am–2.30pm and 7–11pm Mon–Sat (open 6pm Fri); 12–2.30pm and 7–10.30pm Sun.*

THE BREWERIES

FROG ISLAND BREWERY

The Maltings, St James Road, Northampton NN5 5HS
☎ *(01604) 587772*
www.frogislandbrewery.co.uk

BEST BITTER 3.8% ABV
Golden, quenching and well-hopped. Malty finish.

SHOEMAKER 4.2% ABV
Malty with delicate hoppiness and bitter finish.

NATTERJACK 4.8% ABV
Sweet and malty, pale and dangerously drinkable.

FIRE-BELLIED TOAD 5.0% ABV
Pale gold, single hop award winner.

Plus monthly special brews, usually around 5.0% ABV.

THE PUBS

ASHTON

The Chequered Skipper

Ashton, Oundle, Peterborough PE8 5LD
☎ *(01832) 273494* Ian Campbell

Oakham JHB is usually on offer, plus three weekly changing guests from breweries such as Newby Wyke, Gale's and Rockingham.

Thatched freehouse and restaurant in a Rothschild estate village with modern minimalist interior, with stunning village green front drinking area and rear beer garden. Food available at lunchtime and evenings. Events include beer festivals with live music, the World Conker Championships and Morris dancing – phone for details. Children allowed. A mile out of Oundle, just off theA605.

 *11.30am–3pm and 6–11pm Mon–Fri; 11am–11pm Sat; 12–10.30pm Sun.*

BARNWELL

The Montagu Arms

Barnwell, Oundle, Peterborough PE8 5PH
☎ *(01832) 273726* Ian Simmons
www.themontaguarms.co.uk

Adnams Bitter and Broadside served with two or three guest beers such as Ash Vine Hop & Glory, Hop Back Summer Lightning or Shepherd Neame Spitfire.

A traditional country inn built in 1601 and retaining many original features. Heavily beamed bar area and more modern non-smoking restaurant. Food served 12–2.30pm and 7–10pm daily. Free children's facilities include log swings and activity centre. Car park. To be found just past bridge.

 *12–3pm and 6–11.30pm Mon–Fri; 12–11.30pm Sat; 12–10.30pm Sun.*

BRACKLEY

The Greyhound Inn

Milton Malsor, Brackley, Northampton NN7 3AP
☎ *(01604) 858449* Mr and Mrs Rush

At least six beers always available, with Greene King Old Speckled Hen among them.

A fifteenth-century inn, cosy atmosphere with real fires. Large beer garden. Food available. Children allowed. Situated on the main road into the village.

 *All day, every day.*

The Red Lion

Market Square, Brackley, Northampton
☎ *(01280) 701647*

A Charles Wells tied house with Bombardier, Eagle IPA and Lock, Stock and Barrel usually available.

A town-centre pub where they celebrate May Day with a 5.30am champagne breakfast complete with Morris men! Beer festival held each August. Accommodation. Pool table. Food served at lunchtime and evenings. Live music on Fridays.

 *10.30am–11pm Mon–Sat; 12–10.30pm Sun.*

BUGBROOKE

The Wharf Inn

Cornhill Lane, Bugbrooke NN7 3QB
☎ *(01604) 832585* Dave Pownall

A freehouse with Frog Island Best Bitter always on offer, plus two guests, perhaps Greene King Old Speckled Hen or another Frog Island beer.

Canalside pub/restaurant with modern exterior and traditional interior, featuring a giant pile of 10p pieces! There is a balcony for eating, a garden lawned to the canal and a boules area, venue for the Frog Island Boules Competition. Live easy-listening entertainment on Fridays from 9pm. Well-behave children allowed, if eating. 'Busy Bee' canal boat trips run at weekends, or midweek day/evening by private charter (tel 07721 372 569). Situated on the outskirts of the village, heading out towards the A5.

 *12–3pm and 6–11pm Mon–Thur; 11am–11pm Fri–Sat; 12–10.30pm Sun.*

CORBY

Knight's Lodge

Towerhill Road, Corby NN18 0TH
☎ *(01536) 742602* Fred Hope

An Everards house with Tiger, Beacon and Old Original always available. Two other guests including, perhaps, Greene King Old Speckled Hen, Wadworth Farmers Glory or Perfick, Nethergate Old Growler, Everards Equinox, Charles Wells Fargo or Wood Shropshire Lad.

A traditional seventeenth-century inn linked to Rockingham Castle by a network of tunnels. Food available in dining area Fri–Sun. Garden. Children allowed in the dining area if eating, and in the garden.

 *12–3pm and 6–11pm Mon–Thurs; 12–4pm and 6–11pm Fri–Sat; 12–3.30pm and 6–10.30pm Sun.*

DESBOROUGH

The George

79 High Street, Desborough NN14 2NB
☎ *(01536) 760271* Mr Fairy

Tied to Everards, with Beacon and Tiger permanently available. The weekly guest beer might be something from Everards, Greene King Old Speckled Hen, or a winter seasonal ale.

Drinkers' pub in the town centre, with two bars. No food. Pool, darts, skittles and pigeon club. Patio, car park, en-suite letting rooms. Children allowed.

 *12–11pm (10.30pm Sun).*

EASTCOTE

The Eastcote Arms

6 Gayton Road, Eastcote, Towcester NN12 8NG
☎ *(01327) 830731* John and Wendy Hadley

Fuller's London Pride, Adnams Bitter and Greene King IPA always available, plus one guest, constantly changing. An annual beer festival takes place over the Whitsun bank holiday.

A 330-year-old freehouse with dining area and beer garden. Food served at lunchtime and Thurs–Sat evenings. Children allowed in the dining area only. Ring for directions.

 *6–11pm Mon; 12–2.30pm and 6–11pm Tues–Sat; 12–3pm and 7–10.30pm Sun.*

FINEDON

The Bell Inn

Bell Hill, Finedon, Nr Wellingborough NN9 5ND
☎ *(01933) 680332* Denise Willmott

A freehouse with Fuller's London Pride always available, plus three guests perhaps from Woodforde's, Cottage, York or Frog Island.

An ancient pub, apparently dating from 1042. Food served at lunchtime and evenings in dining area. Children allowed.

 *11.30am–3pm and 5.30–11pm Mon–Sat; 12–3pm and 7–10.30pm Sun.*

FOTHERINGHAY

The Falcon Inn

Fotheringhay, Oundle, Peterborough PE8 5HZ
☎ *(01832) 226254* Ray Smikle

Adnams Best Bitter and Old, and Greene King IPA always available, plus one weekly changing guest.

A pub and restaurant in a historic village. Emphasis on good food, served in the pub and restaurant at lunchtimes and evenings. Darts and dominoes, function room, car park. Children allowed.

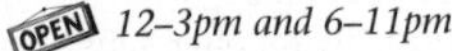 *12–3pm and 6–11pm.*

GAYTON

Eykyn Arms

20 High Street, Gayton, Northampton NN7 3HD
☎ *(01604) 858361* Robert Pattle

Charles Wells Eagle, Greene King IPA and Timothy Taylor Landlord are always available.

Traditional freehouse with accommodation. Non-smoking area. Snacks served by prior arrangement. Car park. Children welcome, but no special facilities.

 *11.30am–2pm and 7–11pm; closed Monday lunchtime.*

GEDDINGTON

The Star Inn

2 Bridge Street, Geddington, Kettering NN14 1AD
☎ *(01536) 742386*
Jim Grimmett and Natalie Britchford

A freehouse with six real ales available, generally including Marston's Pedigree, Wadworth 6X and Fuller's London Pride, plus local brews from Grainstore and Frog Island.

A traditional pub steeped in history set in the heart of Geddington, in front of the Queen Eleanor cross and near the memorial to US fighter pilots. Good range of food, from freshly filled baguettes to pheasant and game dishes, served in separate smoking and non-smoking dining areas. Located off the A43 between Kettering and Corby.

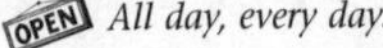 *All day, every day.*

GREAT BRINGTON

The Fox & Hounds

Althorp Coaching Inn, Great Brington, Northampton NN7 4JA
☎ *(01604) 770651* Peter Krempels

A freehouse with 11 real ales always available. Greene King IPA and Abbot are permanent features, and there is usually something from Adnams. Other guests are from all over the country.

A sixteenth-century coaching inn with log fires, exposed beams and stone/wood floors. Dining area and beer garden. Food served at lunchtime and dinner, 'Rosette Standard' cooking. Children and dogs allowed. Walkers and horses welcome. Take the A428 from Northampton past Althorp House, then first left turn before railway bridge.

 *Summer: 11am–11pm Mon–Sat; 12–10.30pm Sun (phone for winter hours).*

GREAT HOUGHTON

The Old Cherry Tree

Cherry Tree Lane, Great Houghton, Northampton NN4 7AT
☎ *(01604) 761399* Richard and Jennie Moore

A Charles Wells house with Bombardier and Eagle always available, plus two rotating guests.

A 500-year-old pub and restaurant, recently rethatched. Two bars, beer garden, car park, function room. Children allowed in the restaurant only. Located off the A428 from Northampton to Bedford. Three miles out of Northampton. Turn right into the village, then first left.

 *12–3pm and 6–11.30pm (10.30pm Sun).*

GRENDON

The Half Moon

42 Main Road, Grendon
☎ *(01933) 663263* Frederick Maffre

Charles Wells Eagle, IPA and one guest beer usually available.

A 300-year-old thatched pub with low ceilings and original beams. Beer garden. Food served lunchtimes and evenings Mon–Sat and Sun lunchtimes only. Car park. Children's menu.

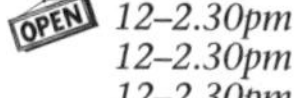 *12–2.30pm and 6–11pm Mon–Fri; 12–2.30pm and 6.30–11pm Sat; 12–2.30pm and 7–10.30pm Sun.*

HIGHAM FERRERS

The Green Dragon

College Street, Higham Ferrers, Rushden NN10 8DZ
☎ *(01933) 312088* Joy Ormond

A freehouse with Fuller's London Pride and Greene King Abbot always available. Guests are numerous and varied and come mostly from small local breweries.

A seventeenth-century coaching inn with open fires, restaurant, beer garden, accommodation. Food served lunchtimes and evenings. Children allowed.

 *12–2.30pm and 5–11pm Mon–Thurs; all day Fri–Sun.*

The Griffin Inn

High Street, Higham Ferrers, Rushden NN10 8BW
☎ *(01933) 312612* Ray Gilbert

Charles Wells Eagle, Greene King Abbot, Fuller's London Pride and Wadworth 6X always available, plus a range of guests constantly changing but often including Marston's Pedigree and Greene King Old Speckled Hen.

A luxurious seventeenth-century freehouse with leather Chesterfield, inglenook fireplace and conservatory. Patio. Food served at lunchtime and evenings in a 50-seater restaurant. Children allowed in the restaurant only.

 *11am–3pm and 5.30–11pm.*

HOLCOT

The White Swan Inn

Main Street, Holcot, Northampton NN6 9SP
☎ *(01604) 781263* David Hodgson

A freehouse with Greene King IPA and a Hook Norton brew always available.

A thatched country pub with two bars, games room and garden. B&B. Food available at lunchtime and evenings. Families welcome.

 *12–2.30pm and 5.30–11pm Mon–Fri; all day Sat–Sun.*

KETTERING

Park House/ The Milestone Restaurant

Kettering Venture Park, Kettering NN15 6XE
☎ *(01536) 523377* Rachael Early

Banks's Bitter and Original always available.

A traditional pub and restaurant. Children allowed.

11.30am–11pm Mon–Sat; 12–10.30pm Sun.

KINGS SUTTON

The Butchers Arms

10 Whittall Street, Kings Sutton, Banbury OX14 3RD
☎ *(01295) 810898* Ian and Lynda Fessey

Tied to Hook Norton, with Best, Old Hooky and occasional and seasonal brews available.

Actually in Northamptonshire, despite the postal address. Set in an ancient village near the River Cherwell and the Oxford Canal. Local brick building with oak beams and real fires. A patio area in front and a beer garden behind. Good food served at lunchtime and evenings.

 *11am–3pm and 6–11pm Mon–Sat. 12–4pm and 7–10.30pm Sun.*

LITCHBOROUGH

The Old Red Lion

Banbury Road, Litchborough, Towcester NN12 8HF
☎ *(01327) 830250* Mr and Mrs O'Shey

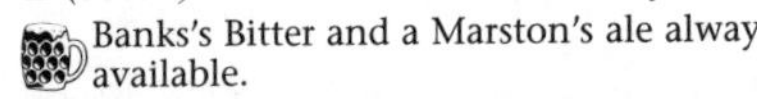

Banks's Bitter and a Marston's ale always available.

A small, 300-year-old pub with log fires and beer garden. Food available Tues–Sat, lunchtime and evenings. Children allowed.

 *11.30am–2.30pm and 6.30–11pm Mon–Sat; 12–3pm and 7–10.30pm Sun.*

LITTLE BRINGTON

Ye Olde Saracen's Head

Little Brington, Northampton NN7 4HS
☎ *(01604) 770640* Richard Williams

Fuller's London Pride, Timothy Taylor Landlord and Greene King IPA always available, plus one changing guest.

The only pub in Little Brington. Open fires and recently refurbished garden. Food available in two dining areas. Children allowed throughout. En-suite accommodation available. Function room available for private hire.

 *12–2.30pm and 6–11pm Mon–Fri; 12–11pm Sat–Sun.*

LITTLE HARROWDEN

The Lamb Inn

Orlingbury Road, Little Harrowden, Wellingborough NN9 5BH
☎ *(01933) 673300* Helen Coates
www.the-lamb-at-harrowden.co.uk

A Charles Wells house with Eagle and Bombardier always available, plus one constantly changing guest.

A traditional seventeenth-century Northampton inn. Skittles table. Live entertainment. Beer garden. Food is available in separate dining area 12–2pm daily, including traditional roasts on Sundays, plus 7–9pm Thurs–Sat. Children allowed until 9pm.

 *12–2.30pm and 6–11pm Mon–Fri; 12–11pm Sat; 12–10.30pm Sun.*

MARSTON ST LAWRENCE

Marston Inn

Marston St Lawrence, Banbury OX17 2DB
☎ *(01295) 711906* Claire Ellis and Paul Parker

Hook Norton tied house with a different guest beer served each month, with Gale's HSB, Shepherd Neame Spitfire, Badger Tanglefoot, Fuller's ESB or Caledonian 80/- among the popular ones.

Fifteenth-century, 'roses-round-the-door' village pub. Converted from three cottages, the pub features oak beams, real fire, two dining rooms (one non-smoking), cosy bar, lounge and gardens. Traditional pub games. Food served 12–2pm Tues–Sun and 7–9.30pm Tues–Sat. Car park. Children welcome in garden or if pre-booked for Sunday lunch.

 *7–11pm Mon; 12–3pm and 7–11pm Tues–Sat; 12–4pm and 7–10.30pm Sun.*

MEARS ASHBY

The Griffin's Head

28 Wilby Road, Mears Ashby, Northampton NN6 0DX
☎ *(01604) 812945* Tom Hewer

Timothy Taylor Landlord, Greene King IPA and Abbot and Adnams Bitter always available, together with a guest ale of the week. A large selection of fine wines also available by the glass.

A traditional old country freehouse with a friendly greeting and wealth of character. Log fire in the winter; non-smoking restaurant serving home-cooked food; beer garden. Food served lunchtimes and evenings. Children welcome if eating.

 *11.30am–3pm and 5.30–11pm Mon–Thurs; 11.30am–11pm Fri; 12–3pm and 6–11pm Sat; 12–10.30pm Sun.*

MILTON KEYNES

The Navigation Inn

Thrupp Wharf, Castlethorpe Road, Cosgrove, Milton Keynes
☎ *(01908) 543156* Mr H Willis

Greene King IPA and Abbot Ale plus two weekly changing guest beers usually available.

Family-run pub set on the Grand Union Canal with unspoilt views over open countryside. Restaurant, sun terrace and family garden. Bar food available lunchtimes and evenings Mon–Sat and all day Sun. Restaurant open evenings only Mon–Sat and all day Sun. Children welcome when dining and in the family garden.

 *12–3pm and 6–11pm Mon–Fri; 12–11pm Sat–Sun.*

NORTHAMPTON

The Malt Shovel Tavern

121 Bridge Street, Northampton NN1 1QF
☎ *(01604) 234212*

Award-winning freehouse with four regular ales, including Frog Island Natterjack, Fuller's London Pride and Banks's Bitter plus up to eight constantly changing guests such as Oakham JHB, Skinner's Cornish Knocker and Timothy Taylor Dark Mild. The emphasis is on beers from micro-breweries.

A traditional pub with beer garden. Food served Mon–Sat lunchtimes 12–2.30pm. Children allowed in the garden only. Located opposite the Carlsberg Brewery.

 *11.30am–3pm and 5–11pm Mon–Sat; 12–3pm and 7–10.30pm Sun.*

Moon On The Square

6 The Parade, Market Place, Northampton NN1 2EE
☎ *(01604) 634062*
Nigel Abbott and Olivia Jenkinson

Marston's Pedigree, Greene King Abbot Ale and Shepherd Neame Spitfire usually available, plus two guest beers from a wide selection supplied by the excellent East-West Ales.

Large city-centre pub with disabled access and no music or games tables. Food served all day, every day. No children.

10.30am–11pm Mon–Sat; 12–10.30pm Sun.

The Old Black Lion

Black Lion Hill, Northampton NN1 1SW
☎ *(01604) 639472* Mr Wilkinson

Frog Island Natterjack is among the beers always served, with other Frog Island beers featured as guests.

Very old building on the outside of the town centre, near the station. Refurbished interior, with one bar, function room and patio. Food available. Children allowed.

11am–11pm Mon–Sat; 12–10.30pm Sun.

ORLINGBURY

The Queen's Arms

11 Isham Road, Orlingbury NN14 1JD
☎ *(01933) 678258*

Up to eight real ales available, with six changing weekly.

A country freehouse and restaurant with beer garden. Food served at lunchtime and evenings. Children allowed.

12–2.30pm and 6–11pm Mon–Fri; all day Sat–Sun.

RAVENSTHORPE

The Chequers

Chequer's Lane, Ravensthorpe NN6 8ER
☎ *(01604) 770379* Gordon Walker

A freehouse with five hand pumps, serving Fuller's London Pride, Greene King Abbot, something from Thwaites and Jennings, plus one guest.

A cosy village pub serving traditional English fare. Restaurant and bar food served lunchtimes and evenings. Beer garden and children's play area – children welcome.

12–3pm and 6–11pm Mon–Fri; all day Sat; 12–3pm and 7–10.30pm Sun.

SOUTHWICK

The Shuckburgh Arms

Main Street, Southwick, Nr Oundle, Peterborough PE8 5BL
☎ *(01832) 274007* Celia Sanders

Fuller's London Pride and Oakham JHB usually available, plus one frequently changing guest from a wide range.

Small, thatched, family-run fifteenth-century freehouse with log fire, beams, and lots of history. Welcoming bar. Darts and dominoes regularly played. Food served 12–2pm and 6–9pm Wed–Sat, 12–5pm Sun. Large car park and patio area. Small family room and children's play equipment in the secure garden. Situated three miles east of Oundle.

6–11pm Mon–Tues; 12–2pm and 6–11pm Wed–Sat; 12–10.30pm Sun. Closed Mon–Tues lunchtimes.

STOKE BRUERNE

The Boat Inn

Stoke Bruerne, Nr Towcester NN12 7SB
☎ *(01604) 862428*
Andrew and Nicholas Woodward
www.boatinn.co.uk

A freehouse with Banks's Bitter, Marston's Bitter, Pedigree and Empire, Frog Island Best Bitter, and Adnams Bitter the permanent beers. One or two beers, often from the Wolverhampton & Dudley Head Brewers' Choice scheme.

Canalside pub, run by the same family since 1877. The original part of building has a thatched roof, stone floors and open fires. Food is available – there is an 80-seater restaurant, plus an extension with lounge bar, bistro and cocktail bar. A 40-seater passenger narrowboat is available for hire for party trips all year. Live music at least once a month and cabarets at Christmas in restaurant. Children allowed. Approximately six minutes from M1 Juntion 15.

 *Summer: 9am–11pm (10.30pm Sun); winter: 9am–3pm and 6–11pm Mon–Thurs; 9am–11pm Fri–Sat; 9am–10.30pm Sun.*

SUDBOROUGH

The Vane Arms

Main Street, Sudborough NN14 3BX
☎ *(01832) 733223* Graeme Walker

Nine different beers changed regularly (150 per year) including Hop Back Summer Lightning, Woodforde's Headcracker, Adnams Broadside, RCH East Street Cream, Oakham Old Tosspot and Bishop's Farewell.

A centuries-old listed thatched village inn. Bar and restaurant food available at lunchtime and evenings. Mexican specials. Car park, games room. Children allowed. Accommodation. Just off the A6116 between Thrapston and Corby.

12–3pm and 5.30–11pm.

SULGRAVE

The Star Inn

Manor Road, Sulgrave OX17 2SA
☎ *(01295) 760389*
Mr and Mrs R Jameson King

Hook Norton Best Bitter and Old Hooky always available plus seasonal Hook Norton ales and a guest beer from a micro- or independent brewery.

Idyllic seventeenth-century country inn on the South Northants/Oxon borders. Flagstone bar and large inglenook fireplace. Separate dining room, vine-covered terrace and benches in the garden. Food served 12–2pm and 6.30–9pm Tues–Sat, 12–3pm Sun (no food Mondays except bank holidays). Car park. Children welcome in non-smoking restaurant and garden. Three en-suite bed and breakfast rooms. Follow brown signs for Sulgrave Manor.

6–11pm Mon; 11am–2.30pm and 6–11pm Tues–Sat; 12–5pm Sun.

TOWCESTER

The Plough Inn

Market Square, Towcester NN12 6BT
☎ *(01327) 350738*
Geraldine, Matthew and Bob Goode

A Charles Wells tied house with Eagle permanently available, plus Adnams Broadside.

Cosy, 400-year-old, award-winning pub which has been in the same hands for over 30 years. Food served 11.30am–10pm and the pub is Egon Ronay recommended. Car park. Children's eating area.

11am–11pm Mon–Sat; 12–10.30pm Sun.

WELLINGBOROUGH

Red Well

16 Silver Street, Wellingborough NN14 1PA
☎ *(01933) 440845*
Steve Frost and Tina Garner

A freehouse with five guest ales always available. Regulars include Hop Back Summer Lightning, Nethergate Old Growler, Greene King Old Speckled Hen, Cotleigh Osprey and Adnams Regatta. Beer festivals held three times a year.

A new-age pub, no music, no games. Separate non-smoking area, disabled access, garden. Food available all day, every day. Children allowed in the garden only.

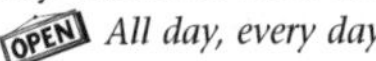
All day, every day.

WOODFORD

The Dukes Arms

High Street, Woodford, Nr Kettering NN14 4HE
☎ *(01832) 732224* Mr and Mrs Keith Wilson

Fuller's London Pride, Greene King Old Speckled Hen, Banks's Best Bitter and Shepherd Neame Spitfire usually available.

Delightful setting for the oldest pub in the village which prides itself on good real ale and down-to-earth food. Garden and restaurant. Food served lunchtimes and evenings. Children welcome, but no special facilities. Car park.

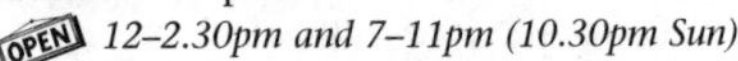
12–2.30pm and 7–11pm (10.30pm Sun).

WOODNEWTON

The White Swan Inn

Main Street, Woodnewton PE8 5EB
☎ *(01780) 470381* David and Susan Hydon

A Bateman house bitter (12 Bore) plus XXXB, Adnams Southwold Bitter and something from Otter usually available, plus one guest.

Friendly pub, situated in the next village to the historic village of Fotheringhay. Boules played in summer. Bar and restaurant food served 12–1.45pm and 7–9pm daily (not Sunday evenings). Car park. Children welcome in garden if supervised (no special facilities).

12–2pm and 7–11pm Tues–Thurs; 12–2pm and 6–11pm Fri; 12–2pm and 6.30–11pm Sat; 12–3pm Sun (closed Sun evening and all day Mon).

HEXAMSHIRE BREWERY

Leafields, Ordley, Hexham NE46 1SX
☎ *(01434) 606577*

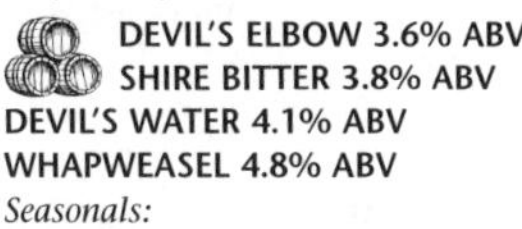

DEVIL'S ELBOW 3.6% ABV
SHIRE BITTER 3.8% ABV
DEVIL'S WATER 4.1% ABV
WHAPWEASEL 4.8% ABV
Seasonals:
OLD HUMBUG 5.5% ABV

THE NORTHUMBERLAND BREWERY

Earth Balance, West Sleekburn Farm, Bomarsund, Bedlington NE22 7AD
☎ *(01670) 822122*
www.northumberlandbrewery.co.uk

CASTLES 3.8% ABV
REIVERS ALE 3.9% ABV
COUNTY 4.0% ABV
KITTY BREWSTER 4.0% ABV
BEDLINGTON TERRIER 4.2% ABV
GNC 4.2% ABV
SECRET KINGDOM ALE 4.3% ABV
THE ORIGINAL NORTHUMBERLAND ALE 4.3% ABV
BEST 4.5% ABV
SHEEPDOG 4.7% ABV

REDBURN BREWERY

Redburn, Bardon Mill, Hexham NE47 7EA
☎ *(01434) 344656*

MITIS 3.5% ABV
Dark brown mild with some sweetness and a hoppy finish.

EBRIUS 3.7% ABV
Pale golden bitter which is full bodied for its strength.

FORTIS 4.3% ABV
A stout that is full bodied and packed with flavour. Initial roast grain flavour leading to coffee overtones and a bitter finish.

SUMMUS 4.4% ABV
Amber best bitter with a malt finish.

OPTIMUS 5.0% ABV
Pale amber premium-strength ale with a fruity character.

VISCUM 5.0% ABV
A dark and full-bodied winter beer.

Other draught beers will be brewed in rotation throughout the year. Bottled-conditioned beers will be available very shortly.

WYLAM BREWERY

South Houghton, Heddon-on-the-Wall NE15 0EZ
☎ *(01661) 853377*
www.wylambrew.co.uk
john@wylambrew.co.uk

HEDONIST 3.8% ABV
Four types of grain are used with Bramling X and Cascade hops. A fine session bitter.

WYLAM BITTER 3.8% ABV
A refreshing lighter version of the 4.4 Rocket using similar ingredients but producing a beer with its own distinctive character.

ALASTAIR GILMOUR'S GOLD TANKARD 4.0% ABV
Made with all gold ingredients; Pale Malt, Golden naked oats, First Gold Hops with a Willamette hop finish. Fresh clean flavour with a hint of grapefruit.

HOPPIN MAD (was Houblon Nouveau) 4.2% ABV
Uses 2002 vacuum-packed hops as the Houblon was so popular.

WYLAM MAGIC 4.2% ABV
A light, crisp refreshing ale made with Amarillo hops and pale malt. Pale gold with a hint of elderflower in the nose. Citrus and spice on the palate with a good bitter finish.

WHISTLE STOP 4.4% ABV
Coppery coloured, slightly maltier with a hop character provided by Challenger and Bramling X hops.

BOHEMIA CZECH RECIPE PILSNER BEER 4.6% ABV
Deep gold in colour with a heady bouquet of layered malt and hops and a deep finish of fruit.

LANDLORD'S CHOICE 4.6% ABV
A complex ale full of interesting flavours and aromas using Styrian Goldings, Fuggles and Hersbrucker hops.

WYLAM HAUGH 4.6% ABV
A dark, satisfying porter which is smooth, full of character and complex. There are hints of chocolate, liquorice and malt. Made with roast, crystal and pale malts, Wye Target and Goldings hops.

SILVER GHOST 5% ABV
Pale and smoothly satisfying, it is made with pale malts, Bramling and Fuggles hops.

THE PUBS

ACOMB

The Miner's Arms
Main Street, Acomb, Hexham NE46 4PW
☎ *(01434) 603909* Joan Crozier

A freehouse serving Yates Bitter and Jennings Bitter, plus a couple of guest ales. Favourites include Durham Brewery ales such as White Velvet, White Gold and Magus or something from Mordue.

An unspoilt old-style stone pub, dating from 1750. Two bar areas, log fire, outside garden and barbecue. Home-cooked food served at lunchtimes (weekends) and evenings (5–9pm). Function facilities. Well-behaved children and dogs allowed until 9pm. At the top of the hill.

5–11pm Mon–Fri (closed lunchtimes); 12–11pm Sat; 12–10.30pm Sun; also open by day Mon–Fri during school holidays and according to demand, and all day on bank holidays.

ALLENDALE

The King's Head Hotel
Market Place, Allendale, Hexham NE47 9BD
☎ *(01434) 683681* Margaret Taylor

A freehouse with Jennings Cumberland Ale and Greene King Abbot always available, plus other Jennings brews and guests such as Timothy Taylor Landlord, Mordue Workie Ticket, Greene King Old Speckled Hen, Marston's Pedigree, Northumberland Cat 'n' Sawdust or one of many Durham Brewery ales.

A cosy former coaching inn with two bars, fires and a function room. No music or games. Food served at lunchtime and evenings. Children allowed. Accommodation.

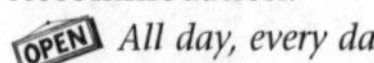
All day, every day.

ALNMOUTH

The Famous Schooner Haunted Hotel & Restaurant
Northumberland Street, Alnmouth NE66 2RS
☎ *(01665) 830216* John Orde (Director)

Schooner Parson's Smyth Ale 3.6% (brewed for the Schooner Hotel) always available plus five guests often featuring Marston's Pedigree, Ruddles County, Charles Wells Bombardier, Border Noggins Nog or Mythic Brews, or other ales from Jennings, Border, Orkney or Northumberland breweries.

A seventeenth-century haunted hotel with Chase Bar and Long Bar, conservatory and terraced beer garden. Two real ale beer festivals held every year at the Whitsun Bank Holiday and the weekend before the August Bank Holiday. Two restaurants with full menus, one specialising in seafood and local game, plus bar food at lunchtimes and all day at weekends and school holidays. Children welcome. Ghostly bouncy castle!

All day, every day.

ALNWICK

The John Bull Inn
12 Howick Street, Alnwick NE66 1UY
☎ *(01665) 602055* David 'Gus' Odlin
www.John-Bull-Inn.co.uk

A freehouse offering three ever-changing guest beers from micro-breweries nationwide, but with an emphasis on locals such as Hadrian and Border, Wylam, Mordue and Jarrow. More than 600 different ales served in four years. Over 80 single-malt whiskies and over 40 Belgian beers also stocked.

Old-fashioned backstreet boozer, purpose-built as a pub in 1831, with walled beer garden. A non-food pub with no music, TV or games machines. Beer festivals in June (phone for further details). Difficult to find – ring for directions, or ask at Tourist Information.

12–3pm and 7–11pm Mon–Fri (closed Wed lunchtime); 11am–3pm and 7–11pm Sat; 12–3pm and 7–10.30pm Sun.

The Market Tavern
Fenkle Street, Alnwick NE66 1HW
☎ *(01665) 602759* Ken Hodgson

Two constantly changing guest ales always available. Jennings Brewery favoured when possible.

A traditional town-centre pub with one bar, restaurant, disabled access and accommodation. Food available at lunchtime and evenings. Children allowed.

All day, every day.

ASHINGTON

The Black Diamond
29 Southview, Ashington NE63 OSF
☎ *(01670) 851500* Paul Gray

Two constantly changing guest ales always available, local breweries featured whenever possible.

Town-centre pub with lounge/diner and public bar. Pool, darts, gaming machines. Separate á la carte restaurant open Tues–Sat evenings and Sun lunch. Four letting rooms. Children allowed. Car park.

11am–11pm Mon–Sat; 12–10.30pm Sun.

Bubbles Wine Bar

58a Station Road, Ashington NE63 9UJ
☎ *(01670) 850800* David Langdown
www.bubblesbar.co.uk

A freehouse with three pumps serving a range of real ales. Too many to list; all breweries stocked as and when available.

A town-centre pub for all ages. One bar, back-yard area, entertainment and discos. Food served at lunchtimes and evenings. There is a nightclub on the premises, open Fri and Sat nights. Children allowed.

10am–11pm Mon–Wed; 10am–midnight Thurs; 10am–2am Fri–Sat; 7am–12.30am Sun.

BEDLINGTON

The Northumberland Arms

112 Front Street East, Bedlington
☎ *(01670) 822754* Mrs Mary Morris

Three regularly changing guest beers served, such as Timothy Taylor Landlord, Fuller's ESB or London Pride, Charles Wells Bombardier, Shepherd Neame Spitfire or Bishop's Finger, Black Sheep Bitter or Special and Bateman XXXB.

Friendly pub with interesting beer range. Food served 11.30am–2.30pm Weds–Sat.

7–11pm Mon–Tues; 11am–11pm Wed–Sat; 12–10.30pm Sun.

BERWICK-UPON-TWEED

Barrels Ale House

Bridge Street, Berwick-upon-Tweed TD15 1ES
☎ *(01289) 308013* Mark Dixon

A freehouse with Fuller's London Pride, Timothy Taylor Landlord and Exmoor Gold the permanent beers, plus five different guests per week, rotated on two hand pumps.

A traditional two-bar pub, one up, one down. Dining area, real fires. Renowned music and comedy venue in basement. Food served at lunchtime and evenings. Children allowed in certain areas. Self-catering accommodation.

All day, every day.

BLYTH

The Joiners Arms

Coomassie Road, Blyth
☎ *(01670) 352852* Mrs Ann Holland

Northumberland Secret Kingdom plus a guest beer usually available.

Small, friendly, one-bar pub with entertainment on Thursday, Saturday and Sunday evenings. Seating area at side of pub. Sandwiches and toasties available. Car park. Children welcome.

12–11pm (10.30pm Sun).

CRAMLINGTON

The Plough

Middle Farm Buildings, Cramlington NE23 9DN
☎ *(01670) 737633* Roy Apps

Four real ales are usually available. Theakston XB is a regular fixture, but the other three rotate from a varied range up to twice a week with an emphasis on local brews.

A two-bar village freehouse with dining area and two beer gardens. Food served every lunchtime, including traditional Sunday roasts. Well-behave children welcome 12–3pm only. Two function rooms. Big-screen TV in bar. Car park.

11am–3pm and 6–11pm Mon–Wed; all day Thurs–Sun.

FEATHERSTONE

The Wallace Arms

Rowfoot, Featherstone, Near Haltwhistle NE49 0JF
☎ *(01434) 321872* Tom Goundry

Jennings Cumberland, Greene King Abbot and IPA are the permanent beers here, plus a guest which changes every couple of weeks.

Traditional country pub rebuilt in 1850 with large beer garden, adjacent to the South Tyne Trail, with one bar, snug and pool room. Two dining areas. Food served 12–2.30pm and 6–9pm every day. Children and dogs welcome. Car park. Two miles from Hadrian's Wall and two miles south of Haltwhistle.

12–3pm and 5.30pm–12am Mon–Fri ; 12pm–12am Sat–Sun.

GREAT WHITTINGTON

The Queens Head Inn

Great Whittington, Newcastle upon Tyne NE19 2HP
☎ *(01434) 672267* Ian J Scott

Queens Head Bitter (brewed by Nick Stafford), Hambleton Best Bitter and Black Sheep Bitter usually available plus one guest. Hambleton Stud, Black Sheep Special, Northumberland Secret Kingdom and Durham Magus feature frequently.

A fifteenth-century coaching inn which incorporates a restaurant. Comfortable bar with open fires. Food served Tues–Sat. Car park. Well-behaved children welcome. Situated four miles north of Corbridge, off the Military Road (B6318) towards Newcastle.

12–2.30pm and 6–11pm Tues–Sat; 12–3pm and 7–10.30pm Sun.

HALTWHISTLE

The Black Bull

Market Square, Haltwhistle NE49 0BL
☎ *(01434) 320463* Dave Hutton

Six real ales available at any one time from an expanded range. Big Lamp Prince Bishop is a permanent feature, with the others likely to come from local breweries such as Yates, Hadrian, Hart, Northumberland, Jennings, Mordue, Wylam and Redburn. The selection changes every few days.

A small, quiet freehouse down a cobbled lane from the marketplace with one main bar and a small (non-smoking) side room. No music or machines. Bar and restaurant food available 12–9pm Tues–Sat in summer (12–2.30pm and 5–9pm in winter) and 12–2.30pm Sun. Children allowed at lunchtime only in the smaller area. Two miles from Hadrian's Wall in good walking country.

 *7–11pm Mon; 12–11pm Tues–Sat; 12–10.30pm Sun in summer. Closed 3–5pm in winter.*

HEDLEY ON THE HILL

The Feathers Inn

Hedley on the Hill, Stocksfield NE43 7SW
☎ *(01661) 843607* Marina Atkinson

Mordue Workie Ticket is among the beers always available, plus a couple of guests perhaps from local breweries such as Big Lamp and Northumberland. The range changes frequently.

A traditional, attractive nineteenth-century pub with log fires, beams and stone walls. No music or games but good atmosphere and friendly locals. Outside tables on the village green. Home-cooked food served Tues–Sun evenings and lunchtime at weekends and bank holidays. Children allowed. An annual beer festival is held over Easter, with approximately 20 ales served from the barrel. Village signposted from New Ridley, OS ref 078592.

 *6–11pm Mon–Fri; 12–3pm and 6–11pm Sat; 12–3pm and 7–10.30pm Sun.*

HEXHAM

The Dipton Mill Inn

Dipton Mill Road, Hexham NE46 1YA
☎ *(01434) 606577* Mr Brooker

A freehouse not far from the Hexhamshire brewery, so Hexhamshire beers such as Devil's Elbow, Shire Bitter, Devil's Water and Whapweasel usually available.

An old-fashioned country pub with real fires. No music or games. One bar, garden, disabled access. Food served at lunchtime and evenings. Children allowed.

 *12–2.30pm and 6–11pm Mon–Sat; 12–4.30pm and 7–10.30pm Sun.*

The Tap & Spile

Battle Hill, Hexham NE46 1BA
☎ *(01434) 602039* Sandra Kelf

Black Sheep Best Bitter is always on offer, plus Theakston Best and four guests, changed daily, such as Timothy Taylor Landlord, Jennings Cumberland Ale, Greene King Old Speckled Hen, Ruddles County, Fuller's London Pride, Hook Norton Best, Marston's Pedigree, Exmoor Gold and beers from Mordue, to name but a few!

A pub since 1862, this is a traditional town-centre bar in a listed building. Pub food and snacks served 12–2pm Mon–Sat. Northumbrian music and other live events. Children allowed in one room. Situated on the main road.

 *11am–11pm Mon–Sat; 12–3pm and 7–10.30pm Sun.*

HIGH HORTON

The Three Horseshoes

Hathery Lane, High Horton, Blythe NE24 4HF
☎ *(01670) 822410* Malcolm Farmer

Greene King Abbot is among the permanent beers at this freehouse. The four guests (usually 10–15 different ones each week) might include Greene King Old Speckled Hen, Adnams Broadside, Bateman XXXB, Charles Wells Bombardier or Northumberland Secret Kingdom.

A pub on the outskirts of town, with beamed ceiling, conservatory, restaurant area and beer garden. Food available. Gaming machines. Children allowed. Car park. The pub is a large white building overlooking the A189.

 *11am–11pm Mon–Sat; 12–10.30pm Sun.*

LONGFRAMLINGTON

The Anglers Arms

Weldon Bridge, Longframlington, Morpeth NE65 8AX
☎ *(01665) 570655* John Young

A freehouse offering one guest, changed daily, with an emphasis on seasonal and celebration ales from local breweries. Charles Wells Bombardier is also a favourite.

Seventeenth-century country inn with beams and fireplaces. Food is available, and there is a non-smoking restaurant. Garden, car park, five letting rooms. Children allowed.

 *11am–3pm and 6–11pm Mon–Sat; 12–3pm and 7–10.30pm Sun.*

LOW NEWTON

The Ship Inn

Newton Square, Low Newton, Nr Alnwick NE66 3EL
☎ *(01665) 576262* Christine Forsythe

One or two ales in winter and four in summer changed as often as twice daily. House ales from Wylam, Northumberland and Black Sheep, plus guest ales from around the country.

An unspoilt eighteenth-century seaside village pub in a unique and breathtaking setting. Imaginative bar food at lunchtime, evening menu including varied vegetarian food, fresh local seafood and lobster and meat from local farms. Booking is advisable for food. Outside tables located on the village green, 20 yards from the beach. Live music occasionally. Flat to let sleeping four. Children and dogs welcome.

 *Summer: 11am–11pm Mon–Sat; 12–10.30pm Sun. Winter: phone for opening times.*

MORPETH

Tap & Spile

23 Manchester Street, Morpeth NE61 1BH
☎ *(01670) 513894* Mrs Boyle

Beers from breweries such as Cumberland, Adnams, Black Sheep, Jennings, Bateman and Fuller's. Also celebration and seasonal ales when available.

An old-fashioned pub with small lounge and bar area. Open fires. No food except on special occasions. Children allowed in the lounge only.

 *12–2.30pm and 4.30–11pm Mon–Thurs; all day Fri–Sun.*

SHOTLEY BRIDGE

The Manor House Inn

Carterway Heads, Shotley Bridge, Nr Consett DH8 9LX
☎ *(01207) 255268* Chris and Moira Brown

Four real ales at any one time. Theakston Best, Charles Wells Bombardier and a weekly changing local brew.

A converted 1760s farmhouse, with open log fires in winter. Stunning views over the Derwent Valley. Bar and restaurant food available all day, every day. Large car park, garden, accommodation. Farm shop sells home-produced and other local produce. Children welcome. On the A68 south of Coxbridge.

 *11am–11pm Mon–Sat; 12–10.30pm Sun.*

TWEEDMOUTH

The Angel Inn

11 Brewery Bank, Tweedmouth
☎ *(01289) 303030* Kirsty Turton

Hadrian and Border Brewery's Cowie – a good session ale at 3.6% ABV – usually available plus three guest ales which could be from any independent or micro-brewery. Black Sheep Bitter, Fuller's London Pride, Timothy Taylor Landlord, Hadrian and Border Rampart and Mordue Workie Ticket are all regular features; beers from Iceni brewery are also often available and very popular.

Known locally as the Berwick Rangers supporters' pub, pride is taken over the range and quality of the real ales on offer, as well as the laid-back, friendly atmosphere. Separate lounge and bar. No food. Children welcome, with beer garden for families. Car park. Situated in the main street.

 *5–11pm Mon–Thurs; 12–11pm Fri–Sun.*

WYLAM

The Boat House

Station Road, Wylam NE41 8HR
☎ *(01661) 853431* GN and M Weatherburn

A constantly changing selection of nine real ales is on offer. Timothy Taylor Landlord, Wylam Rocket and Hadrian and Border Farne Island Pale Ale usually available, plus five or six guest beers, often from Hadrian and Border, High House Farm, Castle Eden, Wylam, Marston's or many other independent breweries.

Warm, friendly pub on the south bank of the Tyne. Northumberland CAMRA Pub of the Year in 2003 and 2004. Unspoilt bar with real fire. Home-prepared food served lunchtimes and evenings Mon–Thurs, 12–6pm Fri–Sat and 12–5pm Sun. Car park. Children welcome in the beer garden and lounge until 9pm. Continue through Wylam village, the pub is situated just over the bridge by the railway station.

OPEN *11am–11pm Mon–Sat; 12–10.30pm Sun.*

THE BREWERIES

ALCAZAR BREWING CO.

The Fox & Crown, 33 Church Street, Old Basford, Nottingham NG6 0GA
☎ *(0115) 978 2282*
www.alcazarbrewingco.com

BLACK FOX 3.9% ABV
Summer ale.
ALCAZAR ALE 4.0% ABV
NOTTINGHAM NOG 4.2% ABV
Winter ale.
ALACAZAM 4.4% ABV
NEW DAWN 4.5% ABV
BRUSH BITTER 4.9% ABV
VIXEN'S VICE 5.2% ABV
MAPLE MAGIC 5.5% ABV
Winter brew.
WINDJAMMER IPA 6.0% ABV
Plus the Sherwood Forest selection and other occasional and seasonal brews.

BROADSTONE BREWING CO. LTD

Waterside Brewery, Retford DN22 7ZJ
☎ *(01777) 719797*

BROADSTONE BEST BITTER 3.8% ABV
STONEBRIDGE MILD 4.0% ABV
CHARTER ALE 4.6% ABV
BROADSTONE GOLD 5.0% ABV
WAR HORSE 5.8 % ABV
Winter brew.

CASTLE ROCK BREWERY

Queensbridge Road, The Meadows, Nottingham NG2 1NB
☎ *(0115) 985 1615*
www.castlerockbrewery.co.uk

BLACK GOLD 3.5% ABV
A dark mild ale with a slight bitterness but without undue sweetness.
NOTTINGHAM GOLD 3.5% ABV
A golden beer with a distinct hop character derived from 100% Goldings hops.
HARVEST PALE 3.8% ABV
A pale ale which is well balanced with a pleasant bitterness derived from American hops.
HEMLOCK BITTER 4.0% ABV
The 'superstar' of quaffing ales. Mid strength, full flavoured with fruity notes and a hop finish.
ELSIE MO 4.7% ABV
A blonde and beautiful malt beer, light in colour and refreshing on the palate.
Specials:
SNOWHITE 4.2% ABV
A refreshing single malt beer with a distinctive hop character. Very pale in colour.
NOTTINGHAM DARK STOUT 4.5% ABV
A dark, heavy, well-hopped traditional stout (November–March)
Plus monthly brews in support of The Wildlife Trust.

CAYTHORPE BREWERY

Walnut Cottage, Boat Lane, Hoveringham, NG14 7JP
☎ *(0115) 966 4376*

DOVER BECK BITTER 4.0% ABV
OLD NOTTINGHAM EXTRA PALE ALE 4.2% ABV
BIRTHDAY BREW 4.5% ABV
Plus seasonal and occasional brews.

FELLOWS, MORTON & CLAYTON BREWHOUSE COMPANY

54 Canal Street, Nottingham NG1 7EH
☎ *(0115) 950 6795*
www.fellowsmortonandclayton.co.uk

FELLOWS BITTER 3.9% ABV
POSTHASTE 4.5% ABV

HARDYS & HANSONS PLC

Kimberley Brewery, Nottingham NG16 2NS
☎ *(0115) 938 3611*
www.hardysand hansons.plc.uk

DARK 3.1% ABV
KIMBERLEY BEST MILD 3.1% ABV
Dark red and nutty with good roast malt flavour.
COOL 3.9% ABV
KIMBERLEY BEST BITTER 3.9% ABV
Golden and well-balanced with pleasing bitter flavour.
OLDE TRIP 4.3% ABV

HOLLAND BREWERY

5 Browns Flat, Brewery Street, Kimberley NG16 2JU
☎ *(0115) 938 2685*

GOLDEN BLONDE 4.0% ABV
LIP SMACKER 4.0% ABV
CLOGHOPPER 4.2% ABV
DOUBLE DUTCH 4.5% ABV
HOLLY HOP 4.7% ABV
DUTCH COURAGE 5.0% ABV

MALLARD BREWERY

15 Hartington Avenue, Carlton NG4 3NR
☎ *(0115) 952 1289*
www.mallard-brewery.co.uk

DUCK 'N' DIVE 3.7% ABV
WADDLERS MILD 3.7% ABV
BEST BITTER 4.0% ABV
FEATHERLIGHT 4.1% ABV
DUCKLING 4.2% ABV
SPITTIN' FEATHERS 4.4% ABV
DRAKE 4.5% ABV
OWD DUCK 4.8% ABV
FRIAR DUCK 5.0% ABV
Seasonals and occasionals:
DUCK DOWN STOUT 4.5% ABV
D.A. 5.8% ABV
Complex winter ale.
QUISMAS QUACKER 6.0% ABV
Dark, smoky, coffee-flavoured Christmas ale.

MAYPOLE BREWERY

North Laithes Farm, Wellow Road, Eakring NG22 0AN
☎ *(01623) 871690*

NORMANTON IPA 3.6% ABV
LION'S PRIDE 3.8% ABV
LOXLEY ALE 4.2% ABV
BREW BRITANNIA 4.5% ABV
WELLOW GOLD 4.6% ABV
MAJOR OAK 4.8% ABV
Occasional brews:
CELEBRATION 4.0% ABV
FLANAGAN'S STOUT 4.4% ABV
GHOST TRAIN 4.7% ABV
MAD MILD 4.9% ABV
MACH 2 5.2% ABV

NOTTINGHAM BREWERY

17 St Peter's Street, Radford NG7 3EN
☎ *(0115) 942 2649*
www.nottinghambrewery.com

ROCK BITTER 3.8% ABV
ROCK MILD 3.8% ABV
LEGEND 4.0% ABV
COCK AND HOOP 4.3% ABV
EXTRA PALE ALE 4.2% ABV
DREADNOUGHT 4.5% ABV
BULLION 4.7% ABV
SOOTY OATMEAL STOUT 4.8% ABV
NOTTINGHAM SUPREME 5.2% ABV
Plus specials.

SPRINGHEAD BREWERY

Unit 3, Sutton Workshops, Old Great North Road, Sutton on Trent, Newark NG23 6QS
☎ *(01636) 821000*
www.springheadfineales.co.uk

PURITAN'S PORTER 4.0% ABV
SPRINGHEAD BITTER 4.0% ABV
ROUNDHEAD'S GOLD 4.2% ABV
GOODRICH CASTLE 4.4% ABV
Pale with rosemary flavour.
THE LEVELLER 4.8% ABV
Rich and rounded.
ROARING MEG 5.5% ABV
Pale and sweet with balancing hoppy, dry aftertaste.
Seasonals:
HERSBRUCKER WEIZENBIER 3.6% ABV
Wheat beer. Available Mar–Sept.
CROMWELL'S HAT 6.0% ABV
Oct–Mar. Herby flavours.

THE PUBS

BARNBY IN THE WILLOWS

The Willow Tree

Front Street, Barnby in the Willows, Newark NG24 2SA
☎ *(01636) 626613* Howard Roberts
www.willowtreeinn.co.uk

Two real ales available from a wide range of breweries.

Eighteenth-century Grade II listed village inn with quaint interior and low beams. Cosy log fires and candlelit tables in winter. There is a beautiful floral courtyard, ideal for early-evening drinks in summer. Good food served every evening from 7pm and at weekend lunchtimes as well. Traditional Sunday lunches available. Seven en-suite letting rooms. Children welcome. Occasional jazz evenings. Four miles from Newark.

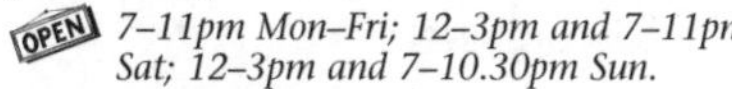
7–11pm Mon–Fri; 12–3pm and 7–11pm Sat; 12–3pm and 7–10.30pm Sun.

BASFORD

The Lion Inn

Mosley Street, Basford, Nottingham NG7 7FG
☎ *(0115) 970 3506* Theresa Singleton

Ten real ales are on offer at this Bateman tenancy, usually including three Bateman ales, plus guests such as Charles Wells Bombardier, Kelham Island Pale Rider, Castle Rock Elsie Mo, Everards Tiger, Bateman XXXB and beers from Nottingham and Mallard. Other seasonal celebration beers on bank holidays, at Christmas and Easter etc.

A traditional pub with wooden floorboards, open fires, beer garden and play area. A broad clientele. Live bands on Fri and Sat nights, plus jazz at Sun lunchtimes. Quiz on Mon, open-mike on Thurs. An extensive menu served at lunchtimes and evenings (lunchtimes only on Sunday). Regular music and beer festivals. Ska music night on first Sunday evening of every month. Children allowed.

OPEN *All day, every day.*

BEESTON

The Victoria Hotel

85 Dovecote Lane, Beeston, Nr Nottingham NG9 1JG
☎ *(0115) 925 4049*
Neil Kelso and Graham Smith

A constantly changing range of 12 cask beers are served, including a mild and a stout or porter. Also 120 whiskies and extensive wine list.

Award-winning Victorian railway pub with high ceilings. Bar and restaurant food is available 12–8.45pm Mon–Sat and 12–7.45pm Sun. The restaurant menu includes a wide vegetarian range. Car park, garden, conference room. Accompanied children allowed in the restaurant and garden until 8pm only. Off Queens Road, behind Beeston railway station.

11am–11pm Mon–Sat; 12–10.30pm Sun.

CARLTON ON TRENT

The Great Northern Inn

Ossington Road, Carlton on Trent, Newark NG23 6NT
☎ *(01636) 821348* Ken and Fran Munro

A freehouse with four pumps serving a range of real ales. No permanent beers but guests might include Timothy Taylor Landlord, Marston's Pedigree or a Bateman ale. Local micro-breweries supported whenever possible, including Springhead, Maypole and Brewsters.

A family-oriented pub with two bars, family room, restaurant, outside playground and large car park. CAMRA Pub of the Season for Spring 2000. Food served at lunchtime and evenings, including a children's menu. Traditional roasts available on Sundays. Located 100 yards from the A1, with easy return access to the A1.

12–2.30pm and 5–11pm Mon–Thurs; all day Fri–Sun and bank holidays.

CAYTHORPE

The Black Horse

29 Main Street, Caythorpe, Nottingham NG14 7ED
☎ *(0115) 966 3520* Miss Sharron Andrews

A freehouse and brewpub with up to four real ales on offer. Home-brewed Dover Beck Bitter is always available, plus guest beers from micro-breweries such as Brewsters and Oldershaw. Timothy Taylor Landlord and Greene King brews are also popular.

A traditional village pub with coal fires, two beamed bar areas, garden and large car park. Freshly prepared food served at lunchtime (Tues–Sat) and evenings (Tues–Fri; booking necessary). No hot food on Sunday lunchtimes, but fresh sandwiches are available. Good location for walkers and cyclists. No children, no music.

12–2.30pm and 5–11pm Tues–Fri; 12–2.30pm and 6–11pm Sat; 12–4pm and 7–10.30pm Sun (8–10.30pm in winter). Closed on Monday except bank holidays.

COLSTON BASSETT

The Martins Arms Inn

School Lane, Colston Bassett NG12 3FD
☎ *(01949) 81361*
Lynne Bryan and Salvatore Inguanta

Seven beers always available (200 per year), with regulars including Marston's Best and Pedigree, Timothy Taylor Landlord and brews from Greene King, Black Sheep and Bateman. Two milds usually featured.

This award-winning village freehouse was built in 1700 as a farmhouse set in 100 acres owned by the local squire. Now set in one acre with original stables surrounded by National Trust parkland. Antique furniture, prints, old beams, Jacobean fireplace and bar. Bar and restaurant food available 12–2pm and 6–10pm (except Sunday). Five of the stables have been converted into an antiques and interiors shop (open 11am–7.30pm). Car park, large garden with croquet, family and function room. Accommodation. On the A46 Newark to Leicester road.

12–3pm (2.30pm in winter) and 6–11pm (10.30pm Sun).

DUNHAM ON TRENT

The Bridge Inn

Main Street, Dunham on Trent, Newark NG22 0TY
☎ *(01777) 228385* David Ollerenshaw

A freehouse with three pumps serving a range of ales, with local breweries featured when possible.

A traditional village pub with two bars, non-smoking restaurant and beer garden. Disabled access. Food available at lunchtime and evenings. No children. On the Lincolnshire border.

 *12–3pm and 5–11pm Mon–Fri; all day Sat–Sun.*

HOVERINGHAM

The Marquis of Granby

Main Street, Hoveringham NG14 7JR
☎ *(0115) 966 3080* Mike Lansdown

A freehouse serving four real ales, changed regularly, with the accent on high ABV. Black Sheep Riggwelter and Greene King Abbot feature regularly.

Old cottage-type country village pub with beams, log fires and beer garden. Hot and cold food served, including traditional Sunday lunch. Pool table. Child-friendly. Car park.

 *5.30–11pm Mon; 11am–3.30pm and 5.30–11pm Tues–Wed; 11am–11pm Thurs–Sat; 12–10.30pm Sun.*

KIMBERLEY

The Nelson & Railway

Station Road, Kimberley NG16 2NR
☎ *(0115) 938 2177* Harry and Mick Burton

Three real ales always available including Hardys & Hansons Kimberley Best and Olde Trip. Also an interesting guest from a range changed once a month.

Opposite the Hardys & Hansons brewery. A Victorian, family-run village pub with dining area, including non-smoking section. Cask Marque accredited. Bar food available 12–2.30pm and 5.30–9pm Mon–Sat, 12–6pm Sun. Car park, garden, skittle alley and games. Accommodation. Children welcome in dining area for meals. One mile north of M1 junction 26.

 *11.30am–11pm Mon–Sat; 12–10.30pm Sun.*

MANSFIELD

Il Rosso

180 Nottingham Road, Mansfield NG18 4AF
☎ *(01623) 623031* Lee Everett

Three real ales are always available and changed every few days. Fuller's London Pride, Black Sheep Bitter, Timothy Taylor Landlord, Greene King Abbot Ale and Old Speckled Hen and Hook Norton Old Hooky regularly feature.

Until recently called The Plough. A welcoming, spacious pub and restaurant situated on the outskirts of Mansfield. Quiz night on Sundays. Big-screen sports. Food served 11am–11pm (12–10.30pm Sun). Car park. Restaurant facilities for babies/children.

9am–11pm (10.30pm Sun).

MAPPERLEY

The Duke of Cambridge

548 Woodborough Road, Mapperley NG3 5FH
☎ *(0115) 962 3083* Mark and Carol Symonds

Three real ales are always available, Marston's Pedigree, Charles Wells Bombardier and one guest changed every few days. Examples of guests served include Springhead Roaring Meg and Cromwell's Hat, Cropton Uncle Sam's, Brewsters Wicked Woman and Caythorpe Dover Beck, plus other exciting ales as available.

Traditional one-room community pub. Food menu available lunchtimes and evenings daily. Function room with pool table, darts and table skittles. Large car park.

 *12–3pm and 6–11pm Mon–Thurs; 12–11pm Fri–Sat; 12–10.30pm Sun.*

NEWARK

The Old Malt Shovel

25 North Gate, Newark NG24 1HD
☎ *(01636) 702036* Tim Purslow

Timothy Taylor Landlord, Adnams Broadside, Everards Tiger and Caledonian Deuchars IPA usually available plus one or two guest beers. These may be from Brewsters, Cains, Black Sheep, York, Rudgate, Glentworth, Hop Back, Cottage, Morrells, Shepherd Neame, Oakham, Exmoor, Badger or many, many other independent breweries from around the UK.

Popular, 400-year-old pub situated 200 yards from the River Trent with lovely walks nearby. Home-cooked food available 12–2.30pm and 5.30–9.30pm Mon–Sat and 12–4pm Sun, both as bar meals and in a continental-style restaurant (non-smoking). Beer garden. Monthly meetings of the RAT (Real Ale Tasting) Society held in pub. Children welcome in the restaurant. Located midway between North Gate and Castle stations.

 *11.30am–3pm and 5.30–11pm Mon–Tues; 11.30am–11pm Wed–Sat; 12–10.30pm Sun.*

NOTTINGHAM

The Bunkers Hill Inn

36–38 Hockley, Nottingham NG1 1FP
☎ *(0115) 910 0114*
Vanessa Frearson and John Rogers

Six real ales usually available. Oakham JHB is generally one of them, plus a mild. Others might include Abbeydale Moonshine, Bateman XB and Kelham Island Pale Rider but the range changes every week.

Drinkers' pub on the outskirts of town, previously a Barclays bank. Two bars, function room and snug (the former bank safe). Food is available at lunchtimes and evenings. Quiz nights, curry nights, open-mike nights and live music. Quiet children allowed. Situated next to the ice arena.

OPEN *12pm–12am (1am Fri–Sat).*

Fellows

54 Canal Street, Nottingham NG1 7EH
☎ *(0115) 950 6795* Keely Williams
www.fellowsmortonandclayton.co.uk

Home of the Fellows, Morton and Clayton Brewhouse Company, with Fellows Bitter and Posthaste always available, plus four guests which might include Timothy Taylor Landlord, Fuller's London Pride or a Castle Eden brew. Other beers from local breweries such as Mallard also feature.

A traditional pub leased from Whitbread with a brewery on the premises. One bar, garden area and restaurant. Food served 11am–9.30pm. Children allowed in the restaurant and garden only. Function room. Near the railway station.

OPEN *All day, every day.*

The Forest Tavern

257 Mansfield Road, Nottingham NG1 3FT
☎ *(0115) 947 5650*
Martin Meyer and Alex Young
www.mazelive.com

Castle Rock Harvest Pale and Greene King Abbot always available plus two guests, usually from Oakham or Castle Rock breweries. The largest range of continental bottled beers in Nottingham plus three Belgian brews on tap.

A continental-style late-licence pub with a live music venue (The Maze) behind it. Folk, country, Americana and blues nights during the week, funk and rock at weekends. Check the website for listings. Food served until half an hour before closing. No children.

OPEN *12pm–12am Mon–Thurs; 12pm–2am Fri–Sat; 12–11.30pm Sun.*

The Golden Fleece

105 Mansfield Road, Nottingham NG1 3FN
☎ *(0115) 947 2843*
Steven and Tracey Greatorex

Up to seven real ales available at any one time, perhaps totalling 20 a week. Marston's Pedigree, Cains Mild, Adnams Bitter, Greene King IPA, Abbot and Old Speckled Hen, Fuller's London Pride and Charles Wells Bombardier are all popular.

A nineteenth-century city centre pub with an L-shaped bar and wooden floor. Snugs and fireplaces. Roof garden available in summer. There is a 40-foot cellar with a glass trap-door visible from the pub. Live music and open-mike nights. Food served 12–7.30pm daily (4pm Sun). Children allowed if eating. Beer festivals held in January and July.

OPEN *All day, every day.*

Playhouse Café Bar

Nottingham Playhouse, Wellington Circus, Nottingham NG1 5AF
☎ *(0115) 941 8467* Andrew Milton-Ayres

Bateman XB, Marston's Pedigree, Fuller's London Pride and Adnams Bitter among those beers always available, plus an ever-changing range of guest beers.

Freshly cooked bar and restaurant food is available from 12–8pm Mon–Sat and 12–2.30pm Sunday. Bookings available on request. Large outdoor seating area. Function room for hire. Children welcome in the restaurant and outside. Adjacent to Nottingham Playhouse and Nottingham Albert Hall.

OPEN *11am–11pm Mon–Sat; 12–10.30pm Sun.*

Lincolnshire Poacher

161–3 Mansfield Road, Nottingham NG1 3FR
☎ *(0115) 941 1584* Paul Montgomery

Bateman XB, XXXB and Victory plus Marston's Pedigree at all times. Also up to five guest beers, mostly from small independent brewers such as Kelham Island, Springhead, Shardlow, Highwood etc.

A traditional alehouse. No juke box, no games machines, lots of conversation. Bar food available at lunchtimes and evenings. Parking and garden. Children allowed at the management's discretion. Just north of the city centre on the left-hand side. On the A612 Newark to Southwell road.

OPEN *11am–3pm and 5–11pm Mon–Thurs; 11am–11pm Fri–Sat; 12–10.30pm Sun.*

The Vat & Fiddle

Queensbridge Road, Nottingham NG2 1NB
☎ *(0115) 985 0611* Neil Trafford

The full range of Castle Rock ales brewed and served on the premises. Plus guest ales such as Archers Golden, Newby Wyke Bear Island or Everards Tiger also available. Micro-breweries favoured.

An old-fashioned alehouse, situated on the edge of Nottingham, near the railway station. Food served 12–3pm daily, plus Mon–Sat 6–8pm. Children allowed if eating.

OPEN *All day, every day.*

Ye Olde Trip to Jerusalem

Brewhouse Yard, Castle Road, Nottingham NG1 6AD
☎ *(0115) 947 3171* Karen Ratcliffe
www.triptojerusalem.com

A Hardys & Hansons tied house with Kimberley Mild, Bitter and Olde Trip always available, plus Marston's Pedigree. Other seasonal Kimberley ales available as guests.

A three-bar pub built inside raw sandstone caves in the Castle Rock, a contender for Britain's oldest inn (1189). Two bars, two courtyards, five rooms. No music or juke box. Food served 11am–6pm Mon–Sat and 12–6pm Sun. Children welcome during food service times, in top bar, snug room or outside only.

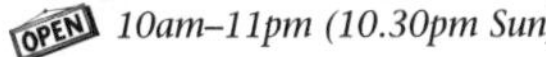
OPEN *10am–11pm (10.30pm Sun).*

OLLERTON

The Olde Red Lion

Eakring Road, Nr Ollerton, Wellow NG22 0EG
☎ *(01623) 861000* Vaughan Mitchell

A freehouse with Maypole Lion's Pride and Shepherd Neame Spitfire always available plus three guests, regularly including Charles Wells Bombardier.

A 400-year-old country village pub. No music or games. Food available at lunchtime and evenings in a separate dining area. Beer garden. Children allowed.

OPEN *11am–3.30pm and 6–11pm Mon–Fri; 11.30am–4pm and 6–11pm Sat; all day Sun. (Hours may vary during the winter.)*

RADCLIFFE ON TRENT

The Royal Oak

Main Road, Radcliffe on Trent NG12 2FD
☎ *(0115) 933 3798* Mark Upton

Six or seven brews usually available including Marston's Pedigree, Timothy Taylor Landlord, Greene King Old Speckled Hen and Castle Eden Ale. Also various guest beers throughout the year, including Exmoor Gold and Black Sheep Bitter. Plus up to four ciders.

A traditional-style eighteenth century pub in the village centre. Cosy lounge and extended public bar, which includes pool table and large-screen TV. No food available at present. Large, private car park. Children welcome until 8pm.

OPEN *11am–11pm Mon–Sat; 12–10.30pm Sun.*

RADFORD

The Plough Inn

17 St Peter's Street, Radford NG7 3EN
☎ *(0115) 942 2649*
Peter Darby and Dave Williams
www.nottinghambrewery.com

Home of the Nottingham Brewery, with Rock Bitter, Mild, Legend, Bullion and EPA brewed on the premises and always available. Up to five rotating guests, either own brews or guests from micro-breweries.

Dating from 1792 but rebuilt, this is a traditional pub with two bars, a dining area and real fires. The brewery was relaunched in autumn 2001. Good food available lunchtimes and evenings including Sunday roasts, curries on Tuesdays. Well-behaved children allowed. Beer garden. Car park. Live music on Thursday nights. Located off Ilkeston Road going out of Nottingham.

OPEN *12–3pm and 5–11pm Mon–Wed; 12–11pm Thurs–Sat; 12–10.30pm Sun.*

RETFORD

Market Hotel

West Carr Road, Ordsall, Nr Retford DN22 7SN
☎ *(01777) 703278* Graham Brunt

Up to eight real ales always available. Shepherd Neame Spitfire, Jennings Sneck Lifter and Thwaites Bitter are regular features plus four ever-changing guest ales generally from local brewers.

Family-run traditionally decorated pub. Bar food available 12–2pm and 6–9.30pm (not Sun). Large car park, non-smoking conservatory restaurant, large banqueting suite. Children welcome. Beer festival in September. Located two minutes through the subway from the railway station.

 *11am–3pm and 6–11pm Mon–Fri; all day Sat; 12–4pm and 7–10.30pm Sun.*

UPPER BROUGHTON

The Golden Fleece

Main Road, Upper Broughton LE14 3BG
☎ *(01664) 822262* Andrew Carnachan

Belvoir Beaver and Marston's Pedigree usually available.

A traditional family pub with beer garden and children's play area, situated on the edge of the Vale of Belvoir. Food served all day, every day. Car park.

 *11am–11pm Mon–Sat; 12–10.30pm Sun.*

UPTON

Cross Keys

Main Street, Upton, Near Newark NG23 5SY
☎ *(01636) 813269* Neil Sharp

Three real ales usually available. Black Sheep Bitter, Adnams Bitter and Fuller's London Pride are regular features.

A seventeenth-century listed freehouse and restaurant. Open fires, beams, brasses etc. The former dovecote has been converted into a restaurant, the tap room has carved pews from Newark parish church. Home-cooked bar food, with an emphasis on Mediterranean-style dishes, fresh fish and tapas, is available 12–2.30pm and 6–9.15pm Tues–Sat, 12–3pm Sun. Car park, garden, children's area, private room for hire.

 *7–11pm Mon; 11am–2.30pm and 6–11pm Tues–Sat; 12–4pm Sun.*

WORKSOP

Mallard

Worksop Railway Station, Station Approach, Worksop S81 7AG
☎ *(01909) 530757* Sarah Cadman

No permanent beers here, just two regularly changing guests from micro- and small breweries.

A Grade II listed building, part of Worksop Station. Occasional beer festivals are held in the cellar bar. Car park. Sandwiches and snacks available. No children.

 *5–11pm Mon–Thurs; 2–11pm Fri; 12–11pm Sat; 12–4pm Sun (closed Sun evening).*

THE BREWERIES

BODICOTE BREWERY

The Plough Inn, 9 High St., Bodicote, Banbury OX15 4BZ
☎ *(01295) 262327*
www.banbury-cross.co.uk/bodicotebrewery

BODICOTE BITTER 3.3% ABV
BODICOTE NO. 9 4.4% ABV
PORTER 5.0% ABV
LIFE SENTENCE 5.1% ABV
XXX 6.2% ABV

THE BRAKSPEAR BREWING COMPANY

Eagle Maltings, The Crofts, Witney OX28 4DP
☎ *(01993) 890800*

BRAKSPEAR BITTER 3.4% ABV
BRAKSPEAR SPECIAL 4.3% ABV

Plus a range of seasonal beers.

BUTLERS BREWERY CO LTD

Wittols Farm, Mapledurham
☎ *(01491) 681974*

BOB (BUTLER'S OXFORDSHIRE BITTER) 3.6% ABV
GRANERY BITTER 4.2% ABV

THE HOOK NORTON BREWERY CO LTD

The Brewery, Hook Norton, Banbury OX15 5NY
☎ *(01608) 737210*

HOOKY DARK 3.2% ABV
BEST BITTER 3.4% ABV
GENERATION 4.0% ABV
OLD HOOKY 4.6% ABV

Plus seasonal ales.

THE LODDON BREWERY

Dunsden Green Farm, Church Lane, Dunsden RG4 9QJ
☎ *(01189) 481111*
www.loddonbrewery.com

KITE MILD 3.2% ABV
HOPPIT CLASSIC BITTER 3.5% ABV
HULLABALOO 4.2% ABV
FERRYMAN'S GOLD 4.4% ABV
BAMBOOZLE 4.8% ABV

Plus seasonal and occasional brews.

OLD LUXTERS WINERY AND BREWERY

Vineyard, Winery and Brewhouse, Hambledon, Henley-on-Thames RG9 6JW
☎ *(01491) 638330*
www.chilternvalley.co.uk/brewery.html

BARN ALE BITTER 4.0% ABV
BARN ALE SPECIAL 4.5% ABV
DARK ROAST 5.0% ABV

Plus a range of bottled beers. Beers are only available from the brewery.

THE WYCHWOOD BREWERY CO LTD

Eagle Maltings, The Crofts, Witney OX28 4DP
☎ *(01993) 702574*
www.wychwood.co.uk

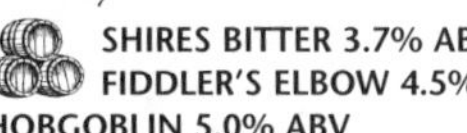
SHIRES BITTER 3.7% ABV
FIDDLER'S ELBOW 4.5% ABV
HOBGOBLIN 5.0% ABV

Plus seasonal and occasional brews.

THE PUBS

ABINGDON

The Old Anchor Inn

1 Saint Helen's Wharf, Abingdon OX14 5EN
☎ *(01235) 521726* Linda and Mike Gillen

A Greene King tied house with Morland Original, Abbot Ale and IPA usually available. In addition, seasonal Greene King beers or a guest beer from breweries such as Caledonian may also be available.

A recently refurbished eighteenth-century building housing one bar and a snug with a stone floor known as The Cabin. Separate wood-panelled dining room. Street parking. Situated on the Thames, 400 yards from the centre of town beside almshouses built in 1447.

12–3pm and 6–11pm Mon–Sat; 12–10.30pm Sun.

BAMPTON

The Romany Inn

Bridge Street, Bampton OX18 2HA
☎ *(01993) 850237* Trevor Johnson

Archers Village usually available, plus guest beers from breweries such as Cottage, Hook Norton, Moles, Charles Wells or Hardys & Hansons.

A seventeenth-century Grade II listed pub with Saxon arches in the cellar. Bar and restaurant food is available at lunchtime and evenings. Car park, garden, picnic tables and children's play area. Accommodation. Bampton is situated on the A4095 Witney to Faringdon road. The pub is in the centre of the village.

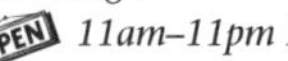
11am–11pm Mon–Sat; 12–10.30pm Sun.

BLOXHAM

The Red Lion Inn

High Street, Bloxham, Banbury OX15 4LX
☎ *(01295) 720352* Mr Doyle

A Fuller's tied house with London Pride always available, plus one other Fuller's seasonal beer or guest beer.

A two-bar village pub with large garden and car park. Food served at lunchtime and evenings (all day Fri, Sat and Sun). Children welcome if eating: children's menu and play area. Facilities available for DIY barbeque, buy food in the pub and cook it yourself.

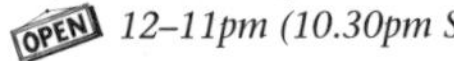 *12–11pm (10.30pm Sun).*

BODICOTE

The Plough Inn

Goose Lane, Bodicote, Banbury OX15 4BZ
☎ *(01295) 262327* James C Blencowe
www.banbury-cross.co.uk/bodicotebrewery

Home of the Bodicote Brewery, which was established in 1982, with Bodicote Bitter and No. 9 always available, plus seasonal specials.

A small village pub with separate lounge/diner and saloon. Early Tudor building, 'cruck' cottage design. Food is available seven days a week from 12–2pm and from 7–9.30pm. Children allowed if eating.

 *11–3pm and 6–11pm Mon–Sat; 12–3pm and 7–10.30pm Sun.*

BRIGHTWELL-CUM-SOTWELL

The Red Lion

Brightwell-cum-Sotwell OX10 0RT
☎ *(01491) 837373* William Prince

West Berkshire Mr Chubb's and Butler's Granery Bitter often available, plus guest ales from other local breweries.

Fifteenth-century thatched freehouse with tables at the front and in the courtyard. Garden and restaurant area. Food served lunchtimes and evenings Tues–Sat, lunchtimes only Sun. Children welcome in the beer garden or restaurant area at lunchtimes only. Car park.

 *11am–3pm and 6–11pm Mon–Sat; 7–10.30pm Sun.*

BURFORD

The Lamb Inn

Sheep Street, Burford OX18 4LR
☎ *(01993) 823155*
Bruno and Rachel Cappuccini

Wadworth 6X, Hook Norton Best Bitter and Adnams regularly available.

A traditional Cotswold inn with log fires and gleaming copper and brass. Tranquil walled garden with a profusion of cottage-garden flowers. Food available daily in bar as well as in dining room and garden. Morning coffee served from 9am, lunches 12–2.30pm (12–3pm Sat and Sun), afternoon teas 3–5.30pm and evening meals 7–9.30pm. Smaller portions available for children. Descending Burford High Street, take the first turning on the left – the pub is the last building on the right.

 *12–3pm and 5.30–11pm Mon–Sat (11.30pm Sat); 12–3pm and 7–10.30pm Sun.*

CHADLINGTON

The Tite Inn

Mill End, Chadlington, Chipping Norton OX7 3NY
☎ *(01608) 676475* Michael Willis
www.titeinn.com

Five real ales always available. Tite Inn Bitter brewed by Wyre Piddle brewery, Young's Bitter and Entire stout by the Hop Back brewery, plus two constantly changing guest ales. A draught cider, usually supplied by Thatchers, is also available.

A sixteenth-century Cotswold stone pub with superb views. Bar and restaurant food available at lunchtimes and evenings. Car park, garden and garden room. Children welcome. Chadlington is just over 2 miles south of Chipping Norton off the A361.

 *12–3pm and 6.30–11pm (10.30pm Sun); closed Mon (except bank holidays).*

CHARLBURY

The Rose & Crown

Market Street, Charlbury, Chipping Norton OX7 3PL
☎ *(01608) 810103* Mr T Page

Young's bitter always available plus five guest beers (100 per year) from breweries such as Lichfield, Coach House, Smiles, Butcombe, Marston's, Timothy Taylor, Robinson's, Badger and Hook Norton. Range of Belgian bottled beers also available.

A popular one-room Victorian pub with a courtyard. No food. Parking, garden and children's room. Located in the town centre.

 *12–11pm Mon–Fri; 11am–11pm Sat; 12–10.30pm Sun.*

CHILDREY

Hatchet

Childrey, Nr Wantage OX12 9UF
☎ *(01235) 751213* Ian James Shaw

Greene King Morland Original Bitter usually available, plus three guest beers from breweries such as Marston's, Greene King or Brains.

Welcoming one-bar village pub. Food served 12–2pm daily. Car park. Garden play area for children.

 *12–2.30pm and 7–11pm Mon–Fri; 12–3pm and 7–11pm Sat; 12–3pm and 7–10.30pm Sun.*

CHIPPING NORTON

The Bell Inn

West Street, Chipping Norton OX7 5ER
☎ *(01608) 642521* Brian Galbraith

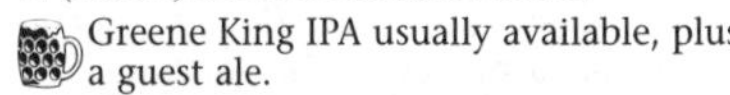

Greene King IPA usually available, plus a guest ale.

Community local in an old stone building, with beams and a wooden floor. Two bars (sports bar and lounge), pool, darts. Food available from a limited menu. Children allowed in the garden only. Car park. On the road from Churchill to Bledington. Accommodation available

 *12–2.30pm and 4.30–11pm Mon–Thurs; 11am–11pm Fri–Sat; 12–10.30pm Sun.*

Stones

Market Place, Chipping Norton OX7 5NH
☎ *(01608) 644466* Brian and Jan Galbraith

A freehouse with Greene King IPA constantly available, plus guest beers from breweries such as Arkells, Archers and Wizard.

Town pub in a listed stone building, with modern interior and traditional values! Annual beer festival (phone for details). Food is available and there is a non-smoking dining area. A good selection of coffees is available. The pub's terrace overlooks the marketplace. Car parking available. Children allowed.

 *10.30am–11pm Mon–Sat; 12–10.30pm Sun.*

CLIFTON

The Duke of Cumberland's Head

Clifton, OX15 0PE
☎ *(01869) 338534* Mick Huntingdon

Hook Norton Bitter usually available plus four or five guest ales from breweries such as Adnams, Caledonian, Black Sheep or Jennings.

Built in the late 1600s, this thatched Oxfordshire village pub serves bar and restaurant food. Car park, attractive gardens, accommodation. Children allowed.

 *12–2.30pm (not Mon), 6.30–10.30pm (11pm Fri–Sat).*

COWLEY

The Original Swan

Oxford Road, Cowley OX4 2LF
☎ *(01865) 778888*
Alex and Janey Peters (Manager)

Tied to Arkells, with Arkells 3B always on offer, plus one guest, often seasonals from Arkells, or celebration ales.

Community pub in a building dating from 1902, with two bars, function room and patio. Food available Mon–Sat lunchtimes only. Occasional live music. Children allowed in lounge bar or outside when accompanied by a responsible adult, until 8pm. Car park.

 *12–2.30pm and 5–11pm Mon–Thurs; 11am–11pm Fri–Sat; 12–10.30pm Sun.*

CROWELL

The Shepherd's Crook

The Green, Crowell, Chinnor OX9 4RR
☎ *(01844) 351431* Mr Scowen

Hook Norton Best, Batham Best, Timothy Taylor Landlord and a seasonal ale from Loddon usually available, plus one other guest ale.

A quiet, one-bar country pub, no music or games. Beer garden. Food served 12–2.30pm and 7–9.30pm. Fish is a speciality. Bookings taken. Children allowed.

 *11.30am–3pm and 5–11pm Mon–Fri; 11am–11pm Sat; 12–10pm Sun.*

EAST HENDRED

Eyston Arms

High Street, East Hendred, Wantage OX12 8JY
☎ *(01235) 833320* George Daily

A free house with Wadworth 6X and Adnams Bitter usually available.

Traditional, beamed village pub with log fire in winter and non-smoking tea room. Darts, dominoes, pool and Aunt Sally. Car park. Bar snacks such as toasties, jacket potatoes and pies available all day. Children welcome until 7pm.

 *11am–3pm and 6–11pm Mon–Fri; 11am–11pm Sat; 12–10.30pm Sun.*

EYNSHAM

The Talbot Inn

Oxford Road, Eynsham OX21 4BT
☎ *(01865) 881348* Charles and Arthur Biggers
www.thetalbotinn.tablesir.com

An Arkells pub with 3B and Kingsdown permanently, plus one seasonal Arkells ale.

Family-run country pub in an eighteenth-century Cotswold stone building, with one bar and a partitioned restaurant. Bar food and an à la carte menu available lunchtimes and evenings, with the emphasis on fresh local produce and fish. Lawn area with seating. Three letting rooms. Children allowed.

OPEN *12–3pm and 5.30–11pm (10.30pm Sun. May close winter Sun evenings).*

FARINGDON

The Bell

Market Place, Faringdon SN7 7HP
☎ *(01367) 240534* Colin Lugg

Wadworth 6X and Henrys IPA always available, plus a seasonal Wadworth ale such as Old Timer, Summersault and Malt and Hops, with JCB served in between.

A sixteenth-century coaching inn, located in the centre of town, with cobbled courtyard recently fully refurbished. AIR-Charter compliant, with smoking in designated areas and ventilation. Well-known for its floral displays in summer. A la carte restaurant and bar food available lunchtimes and evenings. Nine en-suite bedrooms, car park, children welcome. Food served 12–2.15pm and 6–9pm.

 *11am–11pm Mon–Sat; 12–10.30pm Sun.*

FEWCOTT

The White Lion

Fewcott, Bicester OX6 9NZ
☎ *(01869) 346639* Paul and Carol King

Four regularly changing real ales from all over the country.

Cotswold stone, country village community pub. Large beer garden. No food (only bar snacks). Car park. Children welcome. Sky television, pool room.

OPEN *7–11pm Mon–Fri; 12–11pm Sat; 12–4pm and 7–10.30pm Sun.*

FIFIELD

Merrymouth Inn

Stow Road, Fifield OX7 6HR
☎ *(01993) 831652* Mr Andrew Flaherty
www.merrymouthinn.co.uk

A freehouse with Hook Norton Best and one regularly changing guest ale.

An old-style, one-bar pub and restaurant with garden. Large non-smoking areas. Accommodation. Food available 12–2pm and 6.30–9pm. Children allowed.

OPEN *11am–2.30pm and 6–10.30pm Mon–Sat; 12–2.30pm and 7–10.30pm Sun.*

FYFIELD

The White Hart

Main Road, Fyfield, Abingdon OX13 5LW
☎ *(01865 390585)* Susan King

Genuine freehouse with up to five real ales available at any one time. Beers are from independents such as Hook Norton, Bateman, Timothy Taylor, Hampshire, West Berkshire, Loddon and others.

Remarkable fifteenth-century inn in village off the A420. Main room with stone floor and 30-foot beamed ceiling overlooked by a minstrels' gallery. Smaller and snugger, low-ceilinged side bar. Food served at lunchtime and evenings (Curry night on Sun). Large garden with children's play area. Car park.

OPEN *11am–3pm and 6–11pm Mon–Fri; 11am–11pm Sat; 12–10.30pm Sun.*

GREAT TEW

The Falkland Arms

Great Tew OX7 4DB
☎ *(01608) 683653*
Paul Barlow-Heal and Sarah-Jane Courage

Seven beers available from hand pumps at any one time from a range of about 350 per year. Wadworth Henry's IPA, 6X and JCB all favoured. Smaller brewers and some regionals preferred. Also a selection of country wines and draught cider.

A sixteenth-century Oxfordshire village inn with a vast inglenook fireplace, smooth flagstone floor, high-backed settles, oak beams and panelling and sparkling brasses. Bar food 12–2pm daily. Evening food served in a small dining room 7–8pm Mon–Sat, booking essential. Beer garden to the rear of the pub with picturesque view over the Great Tew Estate. Live folk music every Sunday evening. En-suite accommodation. Clay pipes and snuff for sale, in keeping with the picture of a traditional English country inn. Off the B4022, seven miles east of Chipping Norton.

 *11.30am–2.30pm and 6–11pm Mon–Sat; 12–3pm and 7–10.30pm Sun. Open 11.30am–11pm Sat and 12–10.30pm Sun in summer.*

HENLEY-ON-THAMES

Bird in Hand

61 Greys Road, Henley-on-Thames RG9 1SB
☎ *(01491) 575775* Graham Steward

A freehouse with Hook Norton Mild, Brakspear Bitter and Fuller's London Pride usually available, plus guests on two hand pumps, for example beers from Butts, Vale and Cottage breweries.

An old-fashioned one-bar pub. No music, fruit machines or pool table, not even a till! Large garden. Food served at lunchtime only.

 *11.30am–2.30pm and 5–11pm Mon–Fri; 11am–11pm Sat; 12–10.30pm Sun.*

The Horse & Groom

New Street, Henley-on-Thames RG9 2BT
☎ *(01491) 575719* Mr W Honor

A Greene King house with IPA always available, also other Greene King beers such as Morland Original or Old Speckled Hen, and perhaps a seasonal ale such as Triumph. Guest ales from other independent breweries are also sold.

A 150-year-old, traditional, family-run pub in the town centre, close to the river. Three bars and large, award-winning garden. Homemade food served every lunchtime. Children allowed in the garden.

 *11am–11pm Mon–Sat; 12–10.30pm Sun.*

HIGHMOOR

The Dog & Duck

Highmoor, Nettlebed, Henley-on-Thames RG9 5DL
☎ *(01491) 641261* Simon Rudd

A Brakspear tenancy with Brakspear Bitter and Special permanently available.

One-bar country pub with all-over dining area and garden. Food available. Children allowed.

 *11am–3pm and 6–11pm Mon–Sat; (7–10.30pm Sun).*

HOOK NORTON

Pear Tree Inn

12

Scotland End, Hook Norton OX15 5NU
☎ *(01608) 737482*
www.peartree.freeserve.co.uk

The brewery tap for the Hook Norton Brewery, so with Mild, Best, Generation, Old Hooky and seasonal beers available.

An eighteenth-century inn at the end of the brewery lane. One large room with open fires. Attracts mainly local trade, although real ale enthusiasts also come to pay homage. Food served at lunchtime and evenings (not Sun). Service is very friendly and children are made to feel welcome. There is a play area outside for summer visits. Accommodation.

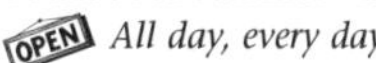 *All day, every day.*

MINSTER LOVELL

Mill and Old Swan

Minster Lovell, Witney OX29 0RN
☎ *(01993) 774441*
Amy Gorden and Marrianne Long

Three Hook Norton beers generally available, including Best, Old Hooky, and a seasonal beer which changes monthly.

Traditional stone built pub situated in the picturesque Windrush valley. Several drinking areas and a restaurant divide up this 600-year-old pub with flagstone floors, exposed beams and log fires in winter.

11am–11pm Mon–Sat; 12–10.30pm Sun.

MURCOTT

The Nut Tree Inn

Murcott, Kidlington OX5 2RE
☎ *(01865) 331253* Dave and Carron Roberts

Hook Norton Best and Adnams Best usually available, plus a guest ale such as Vale Wychert.

Quaint, white, thatched pub with duck pond, set in a peaceful hamlet. Noted for its fine cuisine. Food served 12–2pm Tues–Fri; 12–2.30pm Sat; 12–3pm Sun; 6.30–9.30pm Tues–Sat. Car park. Children welcome in the conservatory or garden.

 *12–2.30pm and 6–11pm Tues–Sat; 12–5pm Sun (closed Sun eve and all day Mon except bank holidays).*

NORTH LEIGH

The Woodman Inn

New Yatt Road, North Leigh, Witney OX8 6TT
☎ *(01993) 881790* Duncan Keith

Wadworth 6X and Hook Norton Best usually available plus two guest beers from breweries such as Adnams, Fuller's, Timothy Taylor, Cotleigh and Charles Wells. The Oxfordshire beer festival takes place here twice a year.

A local village pub on the edge of town, overlooking the Windrush valley. Bar food served at lunchtime and evenings. Car park and garden. Children allowed. Accommodation. Located off the A4095 Witney to Woodstock road.

 *12–3pm and 5.30–11pm Mon–Thurs; 11am–11pm Fri–Sat; 12–10.30pm Sun.*

OXFORD

The Eagle Tavern

28 Magdalen Road, Oxford OX4 1RB
☎ *(01865) 204842* Mr and Mrs Tom Quinn

Arkells 2B and 3B are the permanent beers at this Arkells house.

A refurbished pub in an old building on the outskirts of town, with one bar and garden. Bar snacks available. Occasional live music. Children allowed if kept under control.

11.30am–3pm and 7–11pm (10.30pm Sun).

Folly Bridge Inn

38 Abingdon Road, Oxford OX1 4PD
☎ *(01865) 790106* Roger and Margaret Carter
www.thefollybridge.co.uk

A Wadworth house with 6X, IPA, JCB and seasonal guest beers always available, plus Badger Tanglefoot.

A traditional English pub on the edge of Oxford. Disabled access, patio. Food served at lunchtime and evenings in an environment as smoke-free as possible (there are big smoke extractors). Children allowed.

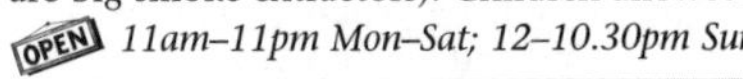
11am–11pm Mon–Sat; 12–10.30pm Sun.

Turf Tavern

4 Bath Place, Oxford OX1 3SU
☎ *(01865) 243235* Darren Kent
www.theturftavern.co.uk

Eleven pumps serve a range of real ales, with favourites including Greene King Abbot and Old Speckled Hen, Gale's HSB and Wadworth 6X, but also more unusual beers from independent breweries around the country (hundreds of different brews every year). Meet the brewer (celebration of ale) at the end of each month. The Turf Tavern Ale house beer is brewed by Titanic. Westons Old Rosie cider is always available.

One of the oldest pubs in Oxford, this is a country-style pub in the city centre. Two bars plus outside alehouse. Three patios kept warm in winter by coal-fired braziers. Food available 12–7.30pm. Children allowed.

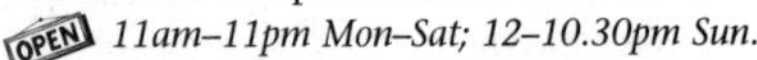
11am–11pm Mon–Sat; 12–10.30pm Sun.

Wharf House

14 Butterwyke Place, St Ebbes, Oxford OX1 1TT
☎ *(01865) 246752* Tony Flatman

Hook Norton Best Bitter and RCH Pitchfork usually available plus two regularly changing guest beers, usually from local breweries such as Oxford, Vale and Rebellion. Farmhouse ciders and a large range of foreign beers also stocked.

Small, basic but friendly pub on the edge of the city centre, close to the Thames. Small car park. Children welcome in the outside seating area, may be allowed inside during bad weather at lunchtime and early evening. Situated at the junction of Thames and Speedwell streets.

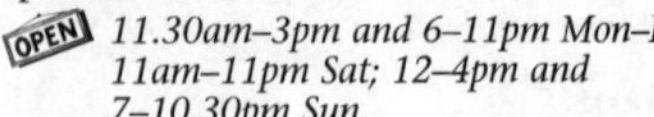
11.30am–3pm and 6–11pm Mon–Fri; 11am–11pm Sat; 12–4pm and 7–10.30pm Sun.

RAMSDEN

The Royal Oak

High Street, Ramsden OX7 3AU
☎ *(01993) 868213* Jon Oldham

West Berkshire Good Old Boy usually available, plus two guest ales from independent breweries such as Hook Norton,Adnams or Butts.

A seventeenth-century former coaching inn situated in a small, charming Cotswold village. Freehouse and restaurant with adjacent accommodation in old stable block. Car park and secluded patio. Ramsden is halfway between Witney and Charlbury off the B4022.

11.30am–3pm and 6.30–11pm Mon–Sat; 12–3pm and 7–10.30pm Sun.

RATLEY

The Rose & Crown

Featherbow Lane, Ratley, Banbury OX15 6DS
☎ *(01295) 678148* Mary and Laura Houguez

A freehouse usually offering Charles Wells Eagle IPA and Bombardier and three other beers such as Greene King Old Speckled Hen and Abbot Ale, plus a beer from another independent brewery.

Small, traditional pub, reputedly dating from 1098. Food served 12–2pm and 7–9.30pm (not Sun or Mon evening). Children are welcome, but no special facilities. The pub is on the MacMillan Way, so walkers are also welcome. Bed and breakfast available (two rooms). Car park. Ratley is a small, picturesque village off the A422 Stratford Road, and the pub is at the far end of the village.

12–2.30pm (not Mon) and 7–11pm (6.30–11pm Fri–Sat); 12–3pm and 7–10.30pm Sun.

SHUTFORD

The George & Dragon

Church Lane, Shutford, Banbury OX15 6PG
☎ *(01295) 780320* Allison Davis
www.georgeandragon.co.uk

Hook Norton Best always available, plus two guest ales such as Adnams Best, Timothy Taylor Landlord, Greene King IPA or Black Sheep Bitter.

A traditional country pub with log-burning stove in winter, beer garden in summer. Food available in an informal restaurant 6–9pm Tues–Sat and 12–2.30pm Sun. Children allowed before 9pm although there are no special facilities. To find Shutford, take the Shipston on Stour road from Banbury.

12–2.30pm and 6–11pm Mon–Sat; 12–10.30pm Sun (closed Mondays except bank holidays).

SOUTH MORETON

The Crown Inn

High Street, South Moreton, Didcot OX11 9AG
☎ *(01235) 812262* Mr and Mrs Cook

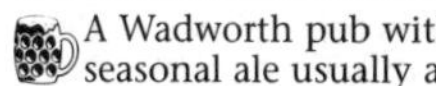
A Wadworth pub with IPA, 6X and a seasonal ale usually available.

An attractive village pub. Bar and restaurant food available. Car park and garden. Children allowed. The village is signposted from both Didcot and Wallingford.

 *11–3pm and 5–11pm Mon–Sat; 12–3pm and 7–11pm Sun.*

SPARSHOLT

The Star Inn

Watery Lane, Sparsholt, Wantage OX12 9PL
☎ *(01235) 751539*
Lee Morgen and Carena Lewis

A Punch Taverns pub selling up to four ales from breweries such Adnams, Timothy Taylor, Young's, Black Sheep or Charles Wells.

A 400-year-old country inn with beams and fireplaces. Food is available, and there is a 30-seater dining room. Eight en-suite letting rooms, converted barn, live music occasionally. Children and dogs allowed.

 *12–3pm and 6–11pm Mon–Fri; 12–11pm Sat; 12–10.30pm Sun.*

STOKE LYNE

The Peyton Arms

Stoke Lyne, Bicester OX27 8SD
☎ *(01869) 345285* Ginette and Angus Stinton

A Hook Norton pub with Mild, Best Bitter and Old Hooky usually available.

Friendly, unspoilt pub situated in a small village. All beers are gravity dispensed. Large garden. Rolls and pies available Fri, Sat and Sun lunchtimes only. Traditional games such as shove ha'penny, Aunt Sally, puzzles and pool. Car park. Children and dogs welcome.

 *12–3pm and 6–11pm (5–11pm Fri); 12–11pm Sat; 12–10.30pm Sun.*

THAME

The Abingdon Arms

21 Cornmarket, Thame OX9 2BL
☎ *(01844) 260332* W Bonner
www.abingdonarms.com

Wadworth 6X, Hook Norton Bitter and Fuller's London Pride usually available, plus two guest beers which may include Vale Wychert Ale or Notley Ale, Hampshire Lionheart or Fuller's ESB.

A sixteenth-century coaching inn which was extensively rebuilt after a fire in 1991. Separate Sky TV, non-smoking section and log fires. Food served lunchtimes and evenings Mon–Fri and all day Sat–Sun. Children welcome, with nappy-changing facilities and high chairs provided, plus play equipment and sand pit. Car park.

 *11am–11pm (10.30pm Sun).*

The Swan Hotel

9 Upper High Street, Thame OX9 3ER
☎ *(01844) 261211* Sue Turnbull
www.swanhotelthame.com

Timothy Taylor Landlord and one Hook Norton brew usually available, plus guest beers perhaps from Rebellion, Shepherd Neame, Wychwood and many more.

A sixteenth-century coaching inn situated in the heart of Thame and retaining many original features. Medieval restaurant, oak-beamed bar, log fire, comfortable Chesterfields and seven en-suite bedrooms. Large, free public car park close by. Children permitted before 8pm away from main bar area, but there are no special facilities.

 *11am–11pm Mon–Sat; 12–10.30pm Sun.*

WANTAGE

The Royal Oak Inn

Newbury Street, Wantage OX12 8DF
☎ *(01235) 763129* Paul Hexter

A beer from West Berkshire Brewery, such as Dr Hexter's Healer, and Wadworth 6X usually available, plus up to six guest ales from independent breweries.

Fair deals and no frills at this freehouse. Navy paraphernalia decorates the bar. All beers served straight from the cask.

 *12–2.30pm and 5.30–11pm (7–11pm Sat); 12–2pm and 7–10.30pm Sun.*

WEST HANNEY

The Lamb Inn

West Hanney OX12 0LA
☎ *(01235) 868917* Ryan Mullins

A freehouse with Wadworth 6X usually available, plus two guests from independent breweries.

A traditional freehouse. One bar, split into two, children's play area, garden. No juke box, but live music once a week. Annual beer festival on August bank holiday. Food served at lunchtime and evenings. Children allowed in the back room and garden.

11am–11pm (3–11pm Mon); 12–10.30pm Sun.

WITNEY

House of Windsor

31 West End, Witney OX8 6NQ
☎ *(01993) 704277*
Prue, Stuart and David Thomas
www.house-of-windsor.co.uk

Timothy Taylor Landlord, Caledonian Deuchars IPA and King & Barnes Sussex Bitter usually available, plus a guest ale from an independent brewery such as Burton Bridge or West Berkshire.

No machines, no pool or darts in this friendly pub. Coal fire in winter. Bar and restaurant food is available Wed–Sat evenings and Sat–Sun lunchtimes. Large beer garden. Children allowed. Off the A40 and straight across two mini-roundabouts.

6–11pm Mon–Fri; 12–3pm and 6–11pm Fri–Sat; 12–10.30pm Sun (closed Mon to Thurs lunchtime)

WOODCOTE

The Highwayman

Exlade Street, Woodcote RG8 0UE
☎ *(01491) 682020* Mrs Murphy

A freehouse with Fuller's London Pride always available. In addition they have up to two guest beers, usually from Loddon or Butlers – the local Woodcote brewery.

Rambling seventeenth-century country inn with two-roomed bar, beams and open fire. Bar and restaurant food available at lunchtime and evenings. Car park, garden, accommodation. Children allowed in restaurant. Signposted from the A4074 Reading to Wallingford Road.

11am–3pm and 6–11pm Mon–Sat; 12–3pm and 7–10.30pm Sun.

THE BREWERIES

ALL NATIONS

Madeley, Telford Shropshire
All Nations is actually a pub, which is already mentioned in the book. They now have a brewer on site and the brewery is called The Worthfield Brewery, same address.

DABLEY ALE 3.8% ABV
Session ale and the house beer at All Nations
OBJ 4.2% ABV
SHROPSHIRE PRIDE 4.5%
Plus seasonals and specials

CORVEDALE BREWERY

The Sun Inn, Corfton, Craven Arms SY7 9DF
☎ *(01584) 861503*
www.thesuninn.netfirms.com/corvedale.htm

NORMAN'S PRIDE 4.3% ABV
SECRET HOP 4.5% ABV
DARK AND DELICIOUS 4.6% ABV

DOLPHIN BREWERY

48 St Michael's Street, Shrewsbury SY1 2EZ
☎ *(01743) 350419*

DOLPHIN BEST 4.0% ABV
DOLPHIN BREW 5.0% ABV

HANBY ALES LTD

New Brewery, Unit C9 Wem Industrial Estate, Soulton Road, Wem SY4 5SD
☎ *(01939) 232432*
www.hanbyales.co.uk

BLACK MAGIC MILD 3.3% ABV
DRAWWELL BITTER 3.9% ABV
Light, golden medium-strength beer.
ALL SEASONS BITTER 4.2% ABV
RAINBOW CHASER 4.3% ABV
Rounded, lagerish style.
SHROPSHIRE STOUT 4.4% ABV
Four malts produce powerful flavours.
WEM SPECIAL 4.4% ABV
Straw-coloured and well-rounded.
CASCADE BITTER 4.5% ABV
Very pale, with clean, refreshing hoppiness.
GOLDEN HONEY 4.5% ABV
SCORPIO PORTER 4.5% ABV
Complex coffee and chocolate flavours.
PREMIUM 4.6% ABV
Amber-coloured, rounded and malty.
OLD WEMIAN 4.9% ABV
TAVERNERS ALE 5.3% ABV
Smooth, fruity full-bodied old ale.
CHERRY BOMB 6.0% ABV
Rich, maraschino cherry taste.
JOYBRINGER 6.0% ABV
Powerful ginger beer. Too easy to drink.
NUTCRACKER BITTER 6.0% ABV
Full-bodied, balanced and distinctive.
Plus seasonal ales and occasional brews.

JOHN ROBERTS BREWING CO

Salop Street, Bishops Castle SY9 5BW
☎ *(01588) 638797*
www.thethreetunsinn.co.uk

SEXTON 3.7% ABV
XXX 4.3% ABV
OFFA'S ALE 4.9% ABV
SCROOGE 6.5% ABV

THE SALOPIAN BREWING CO LTD

The Brewery, 67 Mytton Oak Road, Shrewsbury SY3 8UQ
☎ *(01743) 248414 Fax (01743) 358866*

SHROPSHIRE GOLD 3.8% ABV
Pale, with refreshing fruit and hop flavours.
IRON 4.2% ABV
HEAVEN SENT 4.5% ABV
LEMON DREAM 4.5% ABV
PROUD SALOPIAN 4.5% ABV
PUZZLE 4.8% ABV
Cloudy, white wheat beer.
GOLDEN THREAD 5.0% ABV
Plus seasonal and occasional brews.

SIX BELLS BREWERY

The Six Bells, Church Street, Bishops Castle SY9 5AA
☎ *(01588) 638930*

BIG NEV'S 3.8% ABV
A local favourite.
MARATHON 4.0% ABV
CLOUD NINE 4.2% ABV
Seasonals:
SPRING FORWARD 4.6% ABV
BREW 101 4.8% ABV
CASTLE RUIN 4.8% ABV
FESTIVAL PALE 5.2% ABV
OLD RECUMBENT 5.2% ABV
7 BELLS 5.5% ABV

THE WOOD BREWERY LTD

Wistantow, Craven Arms SY7 8DG
☎ *(01588) 672523*
www.woodbrewery.co.uk

WOOD'S WALLOP 3.4% ABV
Dark, easy-drinking session bitter.
WOOD'S PARISH 4.0% ABV
Light-coloured, refreshing and hoppy.
WOOD'S SPECIAL 4.2% ABV
Well-rounded and fruity with good hoppiness.
SHROPSHIRE LAD 4.5% ABV
Complex and full of flavours.
WOOD'S WONDERFUL 4.8% ABV
Powerful flavours. Excellent winter warmer.
Sam Powell Beers:
SAM POWELL ORIGINAL BITTER 3.7% ABV
Rounded with hop and grain flavours.
OLD SAM 4.6% ABV
Plus seasonal and special brews.

THE WORFIELD BREWING COMPANY LTD

1A The Bullring, Station Lane, Hollybush Road, Bridgenorth WV16 4AR
☎ *(01746) 769606*

HOPSTONE BITTER 4.0% ABV
NAILER'S OBJ 4.2% ABV
SHROPSHIRE PRIDE 4.5% ABV
BURCOTE PREMIUM PALE 4.9% ABV
REYNOLD'S REDNECK 5.5% ABV
An occasional brew.

THE PUBS

ASTON ON CLUN

The Kangaroo Inn

Clun Road, Aston on Clun SY7 8EW
☎ *(01588) 660263* Michelle Harding

A freehouse with Charles Wells Bombardier and Roo Brew (a house beer produced by the Six Bells Brewery) always available, plus Holden's Black Country Mild and up to three guests from local or micro-breweries whenever possible. Examples of previous guests include brews from Cotleigh, Milk Street and RCH.

A prettily situated olde-worlde pub with scenic views. Friendly atmosphere, cosy fire, beer garden and barbecue. Daily newspapers and 'quiet room' available. Food available in separate dining area at lunchtime and evenings. Monthly quizzes, gourmet nights, live music. Children allowed. Email thekangarooinn@yahoo.com for monthly newsletter. Situated on the B4368 towards Clun.

7–11pm Mon–Tues; 12–3pm and 7–11pm Wed–Thurs; all day Fri–Sun.

ATCHAM

Mytton & Mermaid Hotel

Atcham, Shrewsbury
☎ *(01743) 761220* Danny and Ann Ditella

Up to two guest ales, usually offering local real ales such as Wood Shropshire Lad, Six Bells Bishops Castle, or Salopian or Hanby ales.

A casual country house hotel bar with oak floorboards and a large open fireplace. Comfy sofas add to the relaxed feel. Lunches 12–2.30pm, afternoon teas and evening meals from 6.30–10pm. Children welcome. Car park.

11am–11pm (10.30pm Sun).

BISHOPS CASTLE

The Six Bells

Church Street, Bishops Castle SY9 5AA
☎ *(01588) 638930*
Neville Richards and Colin Richards

A freehouse and brewpub, home of The Six Bells Brewery. Four home brews are permanent fixtures plus seasonal ales such as Spring Forward and Old Recumbent when available. An annual beer festival takes place on the second weekend in July.

A Grade II listed building dating mainly from the eighteenth century, tastefully renovated and restored with original fireplaces, stone and timberwork. Food available Thurs–Sun lunchtimes and Thurs–Sat evenings. No music or games. Children allowed. Patio. Brewery tours available.

5–11pm Mon (closed lunchtime); 12–2.30pm and 5–11pm Tues–Fri; all day Sat–Sun.

The Three Tuns Inn

Salop Street, Bishops Castle SY9 5BW
☎ *(01588) 638797*
www.thethreetunsinn.co.uk

A freehouse and former brewpub still serving the Three Tuns range plus seasonals and celebration ales three or four times a year. Annual beer festival in July.

An old-fashioned, town-centre pub dating from 1642. The pub and brewery went their separate ways in 2003, although there are hopes that the new brewery owner will have bought the pub back by the time you read this. Three bars, dining area, garden/yard. Brewery tours and brewery museum. Food available at lunchtime and evenings. Children allowed.

12–3pm and 5–11pm Mon–Thurs; all day Fri–Sun.

BOULDON

The Tally Ho Inn

Bouldon, Nr Craven Arms SY7 9DP
☎ *(01584) 841362* JG Woodward

A selection of real ales always available on one or two hand pumps, featuring a wide variety of independent breweries.

A traditional one-bar village pub with garden. Bar snacks available on weekday evenings and at weekends 12–3pm and from 7pm. Children allowed.

6–11pm Mon; closed Tues–Wed; 6–11pm Thurs–Fri; 12–3pm and 7–11pm Sat; 12–3pm and 7–10.30pm Sun.

BRIDGNORTH

The Bear Inn

Northgate, Bridgnorth WV16 4ET
☎ *(01746) 763250* R Brewer and A Jennings

Timothy Taylor Landlord, Greene King Old Speckled Hen and Abbot and Fuller's London Pride permanently available, plus three daily changing guests from any independent brewery, with Hop Back and Shepherd Neame regular favourites.

A two-bar town pub with large beer garden. Food available at lunchtime only. Accommodation.

1–3pm and 5pm–12am Mon–Sat; 12–3pm and 7–10.30pm Sun.

The Railwayman's Arms

Severn Valley Railway, The Railway Station, Bridgnorth WV16 5DT
☎ *(01746) 764361* Mary Boot

Batham Bitter and Hobsons Best Bitter are always on offer, together with Batham or Hobsons Mild. Three guests, constantly changing, are also served, from breweries such as Hobsons, Holden's, Olde Swan, Burton Bridge, Wye Valley, Cannon Royall, RCH, Stonehenge, Berrow, Cottage, Eccleshall and many, many more from all over the country.

The bar is on Platform One of the Severn Valley Railway's northern terminus and is housed in part of the original station building which dates back to the days of the Great Western Railway. The older part of the bar is the original licensed refreshment room. Filled rolls served at weekends and every day from May to September. Accompanied children welcome until 9pm. Car park.

11.30am–4pm and 6–11pm Mon–Fri; 11am–11pm Sat; 12–10.30pm Sun.

The Swan Inn Hotel and Restaurant

Knowle Sands, Bridgenorth WV16 5JL
☎ *(01746) 763424* Kevin Cooper

A freehouse offering three guest beers (two changed per fortnight), with Wood Shropshire Lad a regular favourite. Others might come from Hanby Ales or Salopian Brewery.

A sixteenth-century inn on the outskirts of Bridgenorth, with one bar and log-burning stoves. Completely refurbished and with views of the Severn valley. Food available 12–2pm and 6–9.30pm. Conservatory, library room, seven letting rooms, beer garden with wishing well. Children welcome. Occasional live music, barbecues in summer. Car park. Two minutes out of town on the B4555.

12–3pm and 6–11pm Mon–Fri; 11am–11pm Sat; 12–10.30pm Sun.

CARDINGTON

The Royal Oak

Cardington, Church Stretton SY6 7JZ
☎ *(01694) 771266* Mike and Dawn Carter

Wood Shropshire Lad, Hobsons Best, Timothy Taylor Landlord and Six Bells Duck and Dive always available.

The oldest pub in Shropshire, this is an unspoilt country freehouse, situated in a picturesque hiking/cycling area. One bar, dining room and patio. Food available Tues–Sun lunchtime and Tues–Sat evenings. Children allowed.

Closed Mon, except bank holidays; 12–3pm and 7–11pm Tues–Sun.

CHURCH ASTON

The Last Inn

Wellington Road, Church Aston, Newport TF10 9EJ
☎ *(01952) 820469* Sheila J Austin

Everards Tiger and Original, Hobsons Best Bitter, Bank's Bitter and Original, and one Salopian ale always available plus two guests which could be Hobsons Town Crier, Marston's Pedigree, Everards Lazy Daze or an ale from Timothy Taylor, Slaters, Cottage, Worfield or Wood.

A busy nineteeth-century country pub with a large conservatory and patio/terrace overlooking the Wrekin and Shropshire countryside. Food available 12–2.30pm and 6–9.30pm Mon–Thurs; 12–2.30pm and 6–10pm Fri–Sat; 12–9.30pm Sun. Large car park. Under 10s welcome in the conservatory and garden up to 8pm.

OPEN *12–11pm (10.30pm Sun).*

CLEOBURY MORTIMER

The King's Arms Hotel

6 Church Street, Cleobury Mortimer DY14 8BS
☎ *(01299) 270252 Brian and Jill Davies*

Hobsons Town Crier and Best are permanently available, with a guest beer from a brewery such as Bathams.

A village pub in a seventeenth-century coaching inn, with beams and fires. Home-cooking with bar snacks, Sunday roasts and restaurant menu available. Six letting rooms including a four-poster bedroom.

11.30am–11pm Mon–Sat; 12–10.30pm Sun.

CLUN

The White Horse Inn

The Square, Clun SY7 8JA
☎ *(01588) 640305* Jack Limond
www.whi-clun.co.uk

Up to six real ales available. Salopian Shropshire Gold, Wye Valley Butty Bach and John Roberts XXX usually available, plus two constantly changing guest beers and a real cider (Weston's First Quality). Cask Marque award winner.

Set in the beautiful Clun Valley, close to the castle, serving homemade meals in the cosy bar or garden. Food served 12–2pm and 6–8.30pm daily. Two letting rooms. Children welcome, but no special facilities. Annual beer festival held on the first weekend in October.

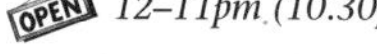 *12–11pm (10.30pm Sun).*

COALBROOKDALE

The Coalbrookdale Inn

12 Wellington Road, Coalbrookdale, Telford TF8 7DX
☎ *(01952) 433953* Dawn Wilcox

Up to seven real ales. Fuller's London Pride and Adnams Broadside usually available plus five guest ales from micro-breweries, both local and across the country.

A traditional, award-winning village pub and restaurant with no fruit machines, pool table or juke box. One bar, plus a non-smoking area, air filtration systems and a small patio area. Food served 12–2pm and 6–8pm Mon–Sat. Small beer garden and car park. Children welcome. On the main road out of Ironbridge.

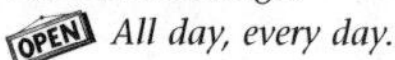 *All day, every day.*

CRAVEN ARMS

The Stokesay Castle Inn

School Road, Craven Arms SY7 9PE
☎ *(01588) 672304* Steve Pitchford

An Enterprise Inns pub, with three or four guest ales on offer, including beers such as Greene King Old Speckled Hen, Timothy Taylor Landlord and Wadworth 6X.

Hotel inn dating from 1894 on the outskirts of Craven Arms village, with oak-panelled restaurant and oak-beamed bar with fireplace. Food served 12–2.30pm and 7–9pm daily, including traditional Sunday roasts. Twelve en-suite rooms. Pool, darts, dominoes. Garden, car park for 36 cars. Children allowed, plus pets by arrangement. From Ludlow, take the first turning right as you enter Craven Arms village. From Shrewsbury, take the last turning on the left in the village. Next to the Secret Hills Discovery Centre (signposted).

OPEN *11am–11pm (10.30pm Sun).*

The Sun Inn

Corfton, Craven Arms SY7 9DF
☎ *(01584) 861503*
Norman, Teresa and Katie Pearce

Home brews Norman's Pride and Secret Hop are permanently available, plus special own brews. These are all available in bottles as well as on draught. Two guests are also served, from micro-breweries such as Cottage and Hanby.

A friendly country freehouse with two bars, a quiet lounge and a non-smoking dining area. Food available 12–2pm and 6–9pm Mon–Sat, 12–3pm and 7–9pm Sun. Exceptionally good disabled facilities, which have been commended by the Heart of England Tourist Board 'Tourism for All' and British Gas's 'Open to All' award, and have made the pub a National Winner of The Ease of Access Award. Children's certificate. Situated on the B4368.

 *12–2.30pm and 6–11pm Mon–Sat; 12–3pm and 7–10.30pm Sun.*

DORRINGTON

The Fox Inn

Great Ryton, Nr Dorrington, Shrewsbury SY5 7LS
☎ *(01743) 718499* Sue and John Owen
www.shropshirepublichouses.co.uk

A freehouse with a rotating selection of real ales available on four hand pumps. Brews from Hobsons, Wood, Marston and Brains regularly featured.

A traditional village freehouse with pub, separate non-smoking restaurant and large car park in a tiny hamlet just outside Condover. Food available 12–2.30pm (except Mon) and 7–9pm. Large beer terrace with one of the best views in Shropshire. No juke box or fruit machines. Children welcome. Beer festival every summer, quiz nights every other Wednesday.

 *12–2.30pm and 7–11pm Mon–Fri; 12–3.30pm and 7–11pm Sat; 12–3.30pm and 7–10.30pm Sun.*

ELLERDINE HEATH

The Royal Oak (The Tiddly)

Ellerdine Heath, Telford TF6 6RL
☎ *(01939) 250300* Barry Colin Malone

Hobsons Bitter, Salopian Shropshire Gold and Wye Valley Hereford Pale Ale usually available, plus two guests from any small independent brewery. Young's Special, Exmoor Gold and Fuller's London Pride make regular appearances.

Lovely country pub in a quiet backwater, yet only a short distance from Telford. Food served during the week 12–2pm and 6–9pm (except Tues), 12–3pm and 5–9pm Sat, 12–2pm and 7–9pm Sun. Children's certificate and play area. Car park. Located halfway between the A53 and A442.

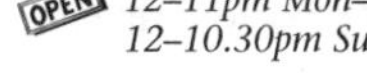
12–11pm Mon–Fri; 11am–11pm Sat; 12–10.30pm Sun.

IRONBRIDGE

The Golden Ball Inn

1 Newbridge Road, Ironbridge, Telford TF8 7BA
☎ *(01952) 432179* Mat Rowland

Timothy Taylor Landlord and Everards Tiger permanently available, plus three guests from local independent breweries, changed twice a week.

Now owned by Punch Taverns but dating from 1728, this pub in a village setting has two bars, a restaurant, a courtyard and garden. Well-behaved children allowed (no play area). Four letting rooms. Car parking. Tucked away, off Madley Road.

12–3pm and 5–11pm Mon–Fri; 11am–11pm Sat; 12–10.30pm Sun.

Ironbridge Brasserie & Wine Bar

29 High Street, Ironbridge, Telford TF8 7AD
☎ *(01952) 432716* Mr Hull

A freehouse with ales from the local Hobsons brewery always available plus two constantly changing guests. Brains SA is a regular feature, among many others.

A village pub/wine bar/restaurant. One bar, dining area and patio. Food available Fri–Sun lunchtime and Tues–Sun evenings. Children allowed.

6.30–11pm Mon–Thurs (closed lunchtimes); 12–2pm and 6.30–11pm Fri–Sun.

LITTLE STRETTON

The Ragleth Inn

Ludlow Road, Little Stretton, Church Stretton SY6 6RB
☎ *(01694) 722711* D Chillcott
www.theraglethinn.co.uk

A freehouse with Hobsons Best always available plus two or more guests that might include Hobsons Mild and/or Old Henry, Wye Valley Butty Bach, Slaters Shining Knight (Eccleshall), Worfield Shropshire Pride or Brains Reverend James. Over 100 malt whiskies also available.

A traditional two-bar country pub with dining area and beer garden with trampolines for children. Limited disabled access. Food available at lunchtime and evenings during the week, all day at weekends. Children and dogs allowed in bar.

12–2.30pm and 6–11pm Mon–Fri; all day Sat–Sun.

LOWTOWN

Black Horse

4 Bridge Street, Lowtown, Bridgnorth
☎ *(01746) 762415*

Two pumps always serve Banks's beers, and seven guest ales, changed daily, might include something from Hobsons, Wood, Holden's, Wychwood or Brakspear.

A 250-year-old village pub in a listed building on the banks of the River Severn. Food is available and there is a non-smoking area. Two bars plus lounge and courtyard, and seating by the river. Live music once a month. Beer festival once a year in summer (call for details). Seven letting rooms. Children allowed. Car park,

6–11pm Mon–Fri; 12–11pm Sat; 12–10.30pm Sun.

MADELEY

All Nations Inn

20 Coalport Road, Madeley, Telford TF7 5DP
☎ *(01952) 585747* James Birtwhistle

Dabley Ale, 3.8% ABV, which is brewed on the premises, is always available. Plus two guests perhaps including Hobson's Mild, Everards Tiger, Hook Norton Old Hooky or an ale from any of the local independent breweries.

A traditional pub with a history of home-brewed ale situated in a unique area close to Ironbridge. One bar with open fires. Large patio area overlooking Blist Hill open-air museum. Rolls and pork pies available. Popular quiz night on Mondays. Car park available, although it is small and steep. Children welcome. Follow signs to Blist Hill (Ironbridge Gorge Museum), the pub is located opposite the museum entrance on the old road which runs above Legges Way.

12–2.30pm and 5–11pm Mon–Thurs; 12–11pm Fri–Sat; 12–10.30pm Sun.

MUCH WENLOCK

The George & Dragon

2 High Street, Much Wenlock TF13 6AA
☎ *(01952) 727312* Milton Monk

A real ale pub with a fine selection of cask ales rotating frequently. Greene King Old Speckled Hen, Abbot and IPA, Hobsons Town Crier, Banks's Original Mild, Adnams Broadside, Charles Wells Bombardier and JW Lees Summer Scorcher are regulars.

Small country town pub, first mentioned in records in 1496, but possibly used by monks since the eleventh century. Food is available 12–2pm and 6–9pm daily, and there is a restaurant area (no restaurant service on Wed and Sun evenings). The pub participates in Shropshire Beer Week Festival. Children allowed. Public car park.

Jun–Sept: 12–11pm (10.30pm Sun). Oct–May: 12–3pm and 6–11pm Mon–Thurs; 12–11pm Fri–Sun (10.30pm Sun).

MUNSLOW

The Crown

Munslow, Craven Arms SY7 9ET
☎ *(01584) 841205* Richard and Jane Arnold
www.crowncountryinn.co.uk

A selection of Holden's and Hobsons ales of different strengths always available, plus seasonal guests from those breweries.

Winner of the best restaurant in Shropshire 2001–02 and 2003–04, with food prepared by a Masterchef of Great Britain served 12–2pm and 7–9pm. Car park. Children welcome. Situated on the B4368 between Aston Munslow and Beambridge.

12–2.30pm and 7–11pm (10.30pm Sun). Closed Monday.

OAKENGATES

Crown Inn

Market Street, Oakengates, Telford TF2 6EA
☎ *(01952) 610888* John Ellis
www.crown.oakengates.com

A freehouse with Hobsons Best Bitter always available plus up to ten ever-changing brews and hand-pulled cider. So far, some 3,000 ales have been served in nine years. Hundreds of breweries featured. Wood, Hanby Ales, Hook Norton, Everards, Wye Valley, Slaters and Beowulf are just a few of the regulars. Only Shropshire beers are sold during the Shropshire Beer Week at the end of July. What are claimed to be the world's biggest pub-based, hand-pulled beer festivals are held twice a year on the first weekends (Thurs–Mon) in May and October, now featuring 34 hand pumps specialising in up to 60 new beers.

A homely, traditional town-centre pub with three drinking areas and a small yard with picnic tables. Landlords dating back to 1835 are listed. Home-cooked food available 12.30–2.15pm Mon–Fri (except August). Telford Acoustic Club meets on Wednesdays, plus quality live music on Thursdy evenings (except August). Classical music on Saturday afternoons. Children allowed in designated areas. Located near the bus and railway stations.

12.30–3pm and 7–11pm Mon–Wed; 12–11pm Thurs–Sat; 12.30–10.30pm Sun.

OLDWOODS

The Romping Cat

Oldwoods, Shrewsbury SY4 3AS
☎ *(01939) 290273* Mr Simcox

A freehouse with Fuller's London Pride among the brews always available, plus four guests from breweries such as Adnams, Bateman or Greene King and local breweries such as Salopian.

A traditional rural pub with one bar, no machines or music. Beer garden. No food. No children.

12–2.30pm Tues and Thurs (closed Mon, Wed and Fri lunchtimes); 6–11pm Mon–Fri; 12–3.30pm and 7–11pm Sat; 12–2.30pm and 7–10.30pm Sun.

PONTESBURY

The Horseshoes Inn

Minsterley Road, Pontesbury, Shrewsbury SY5 0QJ
☎ *(01743) 790278* Mrs Scott

A freehouse with up to four guest ales. Regulars include Fuller's London Pride, but all breweries are featured.

A rural pub with one bar. Food available at lunchtime and evenings. Children allowed if eating. Accommodation.

12–3pm and 7–11pm (10.30pm Sun).

PORT HILL

The Boathouse Inn

New Street, Port Hill, Shrewsbury SY3 8JQ
☎ *(01743) 362965*

Six guest ales are usually served, regularly rotated (15 different ones a week in summer). Examples include regular favourite Marston's Pedigree, Salopian Golden Thread, Greene King Abbot and Old Speckled Hen.

A pub on the outskirts of Shrewsbury town dating from before the seventeenth century, with beams and fireplaces. Food available. Two bars, garden, car park. Children allowed in certain areas.

11am–11pm Mon–Sat; 12–10.30pm Sun.

RATLINGHOPE

The Horseshoe Inn (also known as The Bridge)

Bridges, Nr Ratlinghope SY5 0ST
☎ *(01588) 650260 Colin and Hilary Waring*

Shepherd Neame Spitfire, Adnams Bitter and Timothy Taylor Landlord permanently available.

A 400-year-old countryside pub in an isolated beauty spot. Food available 12–3pm and 6–9pm Mon–Fri; all day Sat–Sun. Children allowed. Beer garden with tables and seating. Phone for directions.

11am–11pm Mon–Sat; 12–10.30pm Sun.

SHIFNAL

The White Hart

High Street, Shifnal TF11 8BH
☎ *(01952) 461161* Andy Koczy

A freehouse serving seven real ales at any one time. The four permanently available are Enville Ale, Wye Valley Butty Bach, Holden's Black Country Bitter and Holden's Mild. The other three pumps serve guest ales, one of which is always a session ale from around the country.

A coaching inn in a traditional timbered building, two bars, beer garden. Local CAMRA Pub of the Year 2002 and 2004, and runner up eight times! Food available 12–2pm Mon–Sat. Children welcome until 7pm.

12–3pm and 6–11pm Mon–Thurs; all day Fri–Sun.

SHREWSBURY

The Dolphin Inn

48 St Michael's Street, Shrewsbury SY1 2EZ
☎ *(01743) 350419* Nigel Morton

Home of the Dolphin Brewery, with Dolphin Best Bitter and Dolphin Brew always available, as well as one or two guest beers from other breweries. Cask cider also served.

A brewpub dedicated to real ales. No lager or beers from national breweries. Traditional decor, wide-ranging, friendly clientele. Coffee available. No food. No children.

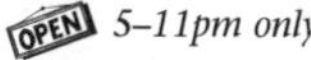
5–11pm only.

The Peacock Inn

42 Wenlock Road, Shrewsbury SY2 6JS
☎ *(01743) 355215* C Roberts

Marston's ales are a speciality here, with Pedigree and Owd Roger always available, plus seasonal brews and other guests such as Banks's Mild on one hand pump.

A pub/restaurant with one bar, beer garden, disabled access. Food available at lunchtime and evenings in separate dining area. Children allowed.

11.30am–3pm and 6–11pm (10.30pm Sun).

The Three Fishes

Fish Street, Shrewsbury SY1 1UR
☎ *(01743) 344793*
David Moss and Victoria Shutt

Five or six real ales usually available. Timothy Taylor Landlord, Fuller's London Pride, and Caledonian Deuchars IPA usually available, plus at least one local guest brew such as Salopian Golden Thread or Minsterly Ale, Six Bells Big Nev's or Cloud Nine, Spinning Dog Mutleys Revenge or beers from Holden's, Hobsons, Hanby, Greene King or Enville.

Seventeenth-century town-centre, completely non-smoking pub, serving a variety of real ales and traditional, homemade meals. One room providing a cosy atmosphere. Food available 12–2.15pm and 6–8.30pm (not Sun). No under 14s.

 *11.30am–3pm and 5–11pm Mon–Thurs; 11.30am–11pm Fri–Sat; 12–4pm and 7–10.30pm Sun.*

UPPER FARMCOTE

The Lion O'Morfe

Upper Farmcote WV15 5PS
☎ *(01746) 710678* Dave Chantler

A freehouse offering six guest beers, usually changed every three days, with Wood Shropshire Lad and beers from Wye Valley, Sheherd Neame, Worfield, Greene King and Banks's regularly featured.

A country pub built in the nineteenth century. Freshly cooked food is available, including a good vegetarian selection, and there is a private, intimate dining room. Two bars, beer garden and car park. Live music weekly. Pool. Children allowed.

 *12–2.30pm (closed Mon lunch) and 7–11pm Mon–Fri; hours vary on Sat/Sun.*

WELLINGTON

The Cock Hotel

148 Holyhead Road, Wellington, Telford TF1 2DL
☎ *(01952) 244954* Peter Arden

A freehouse with eight guests, which might include Hobsons Town Crier, Enville White and occasionally Heaven's Gate, a house brew produced for the hotel by the Salopian Brewery.

A traditional pub with two bars, one non-smoking. No food. No children.

 *4–11pm Mon–Wed; 12–11pm Thurs–Sat; 12–4pm and 7–10.30pm Sun.*

WELSH FRANKTON

The Narrowboat Inn

Welsh Frankton, Oswestry
☎ *(01691) 661051* Colin Hill

Tied to Carlsberg Tetley, but with Charles Wells Bombardier permanently available, plus a weekly changing guest, perhaps featuring beers from Wood and Cottage. The pub's regulars dictate which guests are served.

Country pub and restaurant in the shape of a narrowboat, with low ceiling. Bar at one end, plus non-smoking restaurant. The gardens overlook the canal. Children allowed. Car park. On the main road to Ellesmere.

 *11am–3pm and 6–11pm Mon–Sat; 12–3pm and 6–10.30pm Sun.*

WISTANSTOW

The Plough Inn

Wistanstow, Craven Arms SY7 8DG
☎ *(01588) 673251* Denis and Debbie Harding

The brewery tap to Shropshire's Wood Brewery, serving up to five of their beers, including Plough Inn Bitter which is brewed especially for the pub.

A traditional two-bar country pub with restaurant and patio. Food is prepared on the premises using only local produce to ensure freshness and quality, and is available at lunchtimes and evenings except Sunday evenings. Disabled facilities and toilets. Situated one mile off A49.

 *Closed Mon. 11.30am–2.30pm and 6.30–11pm Tues–Sat; 12–2.30pm and 7–10.30pm Sun.*

WORFIELD

The Dog Inn and Davenports Arms

Main Street, Worfield WV15 5LF
☎ *(01746) 716020* Vic Pocock

Charles Wells Bombardier, Marston's Pedigree and Highgate Mild are among the permanent beers. An occasional guest is also served, with the emphasis on local breweries such as Hobsons, Wood and Hanby.

Seventeenth-century village pub with beams and log burner. Award-winning food served lunchtimes and evenings, often featuring fish and local produce, and there is a non-smoking restaurant. Patio, car park. Occasional live music. Children allowed. Follow signs to Worfield from Bridgenorth Road – the pub is in the village.

 *12–2.30pm and 7–11pm Mon–Sat; 12–3pm and 7–10.30pm Sun.*

ABBEY ALES LTD

The Abbey Brewery, 2 Lansdown Road, Bath BA1 5EE
☎ *(01225) 444437*
www.abbeyales.co.uk

BELLRINGER 4.2% ABV
Golden, hoppy award winner.

BATH STAR 4.5% ABV
Amber, strong hoppy taste.

TWELFTH NIGHT 5.0% ABV
Christmas brew.

WHITE FRIAR 5.0% ABV
Occasional.

BLACK FRIAR 5.0% ABV
Stout.

BERROW BREWERY

Coast Road, Berrow, Burnham-on-Sea TA8 2QU
☎ *(01278) 751345*

BBBB/4BS 3.9% ABV

BERROW PORTER 4.6% ABV
Mellow and fruity.

TOPSY TURVY 5.9% ABV
Golden, fruity and refreshing.

Seasonals:

CARNIVALE 4.6% ABV
Available late Oct–mid Nov.

CHRISTMAS ALE 5.0% ABV
Available Dec–Jan.

BUTCOMBE BREWERY LTD

Butcombe, Bristol BS40 7XQ
☎ *(01275) 472240*

BITTER 4.0% ABV
A dry, clean-tasting bitter with strong hop flavour.

BLOND 4.3% ABV

GOLD 4.7% ABV
Golden and moreish.

COTLEIGH BREWERY

Ford Road, Wiveliscombe, Taunton TA4 2RE
☎ *(01984) 624086*
www.cotleighbrewery.co.uk

TAWNY 3.8% ABV
Flavoursome and well-hopped.

GOLDEN EAGLE 4.2% ABV
A clean golden best bitter.

BARN OWL 4.5% ABV
Smooth, refreshing and hoppy.

OLD BUZZARD 4.8% ABV
Dark, complex winter brew.

Plus occasional and seasonal brews.

COTTAGE BREWING CO.

The Old Cheese Dairy, Lovington, Castle Cary BA7 7PS
☎ *(01963) 240551*

SOUTHERN BITTER 3.7% ABV

BROAD GAUGE BITTER 3.9% ABV

WHEELTAPPERS ALE 4.0% ABV

CHAMPFLOWER 4.2% ABV

SOMERSET AND DORSET ALE 4.4% ABV

GOLDEN ARROW 4.5% ABV

OUR KEN 4.5% ABV

WESTERN GLORY 4.7% ABV

GOLDRUSH 5.0% ABV

HOP AND DROP 5.0% ABV

NORMAN'S CONQUEST MM 5.0% ABV

NORMAN'S CONQUEST 7.0% ABV

Plus monthly special brews.

EXMOOR ALES LTD

The Brewery, Golden Hill, Wiveliscombe, Taunton TA4 2NY
☎ *(01984) 623798*
www.exmoorales.co.uk

ALE 3.8% ABV
Smooth and full-flavoured, with malt throughout.

FOX 4.2% ABV
Easy-drinking and flavour-packed.

GOLD 4.5% ABV
Initially sweet, with a hoppy finish.

HART 4.8% ABV
Malty, with balancing hoppiness.

STAG 5.2% ABV
Well-balanced with lingering finish.

BEAST 6.6% ABV
Dark, with powerful roast malt flavour.

Seasonals:

HOUND DOG 4.0% ABV
Mar–May.

WILD CAT 4.4% ABV
Sept–Nov.

EXMAS 5.0% ABV
Christmas brew.

GLASTONBURY ALES

Grovers Brew House, Unit 10, Wessex Park, Somerton Business Park, Somerton TA11 6SB
☎ *(01458) 272244*

MYSTERY TOR 3.8% ABV

BRUE 4.0% ABV

EXCALIBUR 4.0% ABV

HOLY THORN 4.2% ABV

LADY OF THE LAKE 4.2% ABV

LEY LINE 4.2% ABV

SPRING LOADED 4.4% ABV

HEDGEMONKEY 4.6% ABV

GOLDEN CHALICE 4.8% ABV

FMB 5.0% ABV
A Christmas special.

Only four to five will be brewed at any one time.

JUWARD'S BREWERY

Unit 14G Tonedale Business Park, Wellington TA21 0AW
☎ *(01823) 667909*

SPECIAL MILD 3.8%
BISHOP'S SOMERSET ALE 4.0%
JUWARD'S AMBER 4.1% ABV
JUWARD'S STOUT 4.4% ABV

MILK STREET BREWERY

25 Milk Street, Frome BA11 3DB
☎ *(01373) 467766*

GULP 3.5% ABV
FUNKY MONKEY 4.0% ABV
MERMAID 4.1% ABV
NICKS 4.4% ABV
BEER 5.0% ABV
ELDERFIZZ 5.0% ABV

MOOR BEER COMPANY

Whitley Farm, Whitley Lane, Ashcott, Bridgwater TA7 9QW
☎ *(01458) 210050*
www.moorbeer.co.uk

WITHY CUTTER 3.8% ABV
AVALON SPRINGTIME 4.0% ABV
MERLINS MAGIC 4.3% ABV
PEAT PORTER 4.5% ABV
SOMERLAND GOLD 5.0% ABV
OLD FREDDY WALKER 7.3% ABV
Plus occasional brews.

NEWMANS BREWERY

Meadow Court, Wolvershill Road, Banwell BS29 6DJ
☎ *(01934) 822602*

WOLVERS ALE 4.1% ABV
BITE 4.5% ABV
WOOLLY MAMMOTH 4.5% ABV

ODCOMBE ALES

41 Lower Odcombe, Yeovil BA22 8TX
☎ *(01935) 862591*

LOWER ODCOMBE BITTER 4.0% ABV
DONNE LANE 4.2% ABV
HIGHER ODCOMBE BITTER 4.5% ABV
Seasonals:
BUZZ 4.0% ABV
A honey beer for the summer.
DONKEY PATH 5.4% ABV
Christmas beer.

RCH BREWERY

West Hewish, Nr Weston-super-Mare BS24 6RR
☎ *(01934) 834447*
www.rchbrewery.com

HEWISH IPA 3.6% ABV
Delicate flavours throughout.
PG STEAM 3.9% ABV
Bursting with flavours. Full-bodied for gravity.
PITCHFORK 4.3% ABV
Golden, refreshing and dangerously drinkable.
OLD SLUG PORTER 4.5% ABV
Very dark, traditional porter.
EAST STREET CREAM 5.0% ABV
Refreshing, clean flavour, fruity and deceptive.
DOUBLEHEADER 5.3% ABV
Golden hoppy beer.
FIREBOX 6.0% ABV
Powerful bitter with a multitude of flavours.
SANTA FE' 7.3% ABV
Dark, bittersweet Christmas special.
Plus a monthly beer on a steam theme.

SOMERSET (ELECTRIC) BREWERY

The New Inn, Halse, Near Taunton TA4 3AF
☎ *(01823) 432352*
www.newinnhalse.co.uk

MARK ONE 3.8% ABV
SUNRISE 4.3% ABV
E.S.T. 4.9% ABV

THE PUBS

ASHCOTT

Ring o'Bells

High Street, Ashcott, Bridgwater TA7 9PZ
☎ *(01458) 210232* John Foreman

A freehouse with three hand pumps serving a range of constantly changing real ales. The local Moor Beer Company in Ashcott is regularly supported, plus smaller independents and micros, too many to mention.

A medium-sized village pub with three bars, non-smoking dining area and beer garden. Food available at lunchtime and evenings. Children allowed.

OPEN *12–2.30pm and 7–11pm (10.30pm Sun).*

AXBRIDGE

The Lamb Hotel

The Square, Axbridge BS26 2AP
☎ *(01934) 732253* Sandy Currie

Butcombe Bitter, Blond and Gold, plus a regular guest beer.

Family pub, approximately 400 years old, set in quiet town centre. Opposite beautiful mediaeval building, formerly a hunting lodge, now the museum. One curiosity is the bar that has bottles of wine set in concrete underneath it. Accommodation. Food available except on Sunday night. Children welcome. Parking in market square. Small garden. Skittle alley.

11am–3pm and 6–11pm Mon–Wed; all day Thurs–Sun.

BABCARY

Red Lion

Main Street, Babcary TA11 7ED
☎ *(01458) 223230* Charles Garrard

Hop Back Summer Lightning and Crop Circle regularly available plus one guest, perhaps a beer from the Otter brewery.

A relaxed old-fashioned country pub with large flagstones and thatched roof in remote rural Somerset. Pub skittles and shove ha'penny. Food every session. Car park and garden. Children welcome. Halfway between Shepton Mallet and Yeovil.

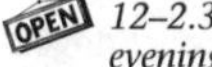
12–2.30pm and 6–11pm. Closed Sunday evening.

BARRINGTON

The Royal Oak

Barrington, Nr Ilminster TA19 0JB
☎ *(01460) 53455* Charlie and Bryony Clarke

Three to four real ales available, changing all the time, but Fuller's London Pride and Butcombe brews are popular.

A sixteenth-century Grade II listed building. Food served lunchtimes and evenings. Car park, garden, skittle alley and function room for larger parties. Follow the National Trust signs for Barrington Court.

12–2.30pm Tues–Fri and 6–11pm Mon–Fri; open all day Sat–Sun.

BATH

The Bell

103 Walcot Street, Bath BA1 5BW
☎ *(01225) 460426* Ian Wood

Abbey Bellringer, Bath Ales Gem and something from Smiles are always available plus seven or eight guests.

Eclectic and lively city-centre pub with music a central focus. One bar and a table football room. Live music three times a week. Beer garden. Vegetarian rolls. Children welcome.

11.30am–11pm Mon–Sat; 12–10.30pm Sun.

Dolphin Inn

103 Locksbrook Road, Lower Weston, Bath BA1 3EN
☎ *(01225) 445048* Gareth Leakey

Marston's Pedigree, Flower's Original, Wadworth 6X and Greene King IPA are permanents.

A friendly and busy community pub, located by the riverside and on the Bath–Bristol cycleway. Food served all day. Children welcome. A range of different rooms including a non-smoking restaurant. Car park and garden. Darts.

11am–11pm Mon–Sat; 12–10.30pm Sun.

The Hobgoblin

47 St James' Parade, Bath BA8 1UZ
☎ *(01225) 460785* Bex Kidger

A freehouse specialising in Wychwood ales, so Hobgoblin and Fiddler's Elbow always available plus three guests.

A lively town pub with a student clientele. Two bars. No food. No children.

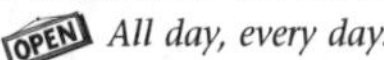
All day, every day.

Hop Pole

7 Albion Buildings, Upper Bristol Road, Bath BA1 3AR
☎ *(01225) 446327* Elaine Dennehy

A Bath Ales pub offering SPA, Gem and Barnstormer plus one weekly changing guest such as Butcombe Gold.

A friendly atmosphere, traditional decor and good food (served lunchtime and evening). Children allowed. Boules in the garden.

All day, every day; winter 12–2.30pm and 5–11pm Mon–Thurs.

The Old Farmhouse

1 Lansdown Road, Bath BA1 5EE
☎ *(01225) 316162* John Bradshaw

Wadworth 6X and IPA, and beers from Butcombe and Abbey Ales always available, plus one occasional guest.

A town pub with two bars, live jazz six nights a week and blues on the seventh. Patio. Food available. Well-behaved children allowed.

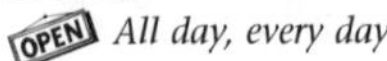
All day, every day.

The Old Green Tree

12 Green Street, Bath BA1 2JZ
☎ *(01225) 448259*
Nick Luke and Tim Bethune

Only stocks draught beer from micro-breweries within a 100-mile radius. Six beers always available including RCH Pitchfork and Wickwar Brand Oak Bitter. Others rotated regularly including brews from Uley, Church End, Otter and Stonehenge.

Small oak-lined city-centre pub. A traditional pub, no recorded music or machines. Bar food at lunchtime. On a small street in city centre between Milsom Street and the post office.

11am–11pm Mon–Sat; 12–10.30pm Sun.

The Pig & Fiddle

2 Saracen Street, Bath BA1 5BR
☎ *(01225) 460868*
Sean Bentley and Jo Humphrey

A freehouse with Abbey Bellringer and something from Bath Ales always available plus three guests, often from Butcombe, Smiles or Badger. Real cider also offered.

Very busy town-centre pub but with relaxed atmosphere. Large beer garden. Bar food available 12–7pm Sun–Thurs and 12–6pm Fri–Sat. Children allowed in garden. Opposite the Hilton Hotel.

11am–11pm Mon–Sat; 12–10.30pm Sun.

The Pulteney Arms

37 Daniel Street, Bathwick, Bath BA2 6ND
☎ *(01225) 463923* Terry and Barbara Coombes

Smiles Best, Young's Bitter, Wadworth 6X, and Fuller's London Pride are generally available, plus one guest that may well be Bath Ales Gem.

An old-fashioned local with sporting links. Various different rooms. Food every lunchtime and Tues–Fri evenings. Darts.

11.30am–3pm and 5.30–11pm Mon–Fri; all day Sat–Sun.

The Salamander

John Street, Bath BA1 2JL
☎ *(01225) 428889* Malcolm Follain

A Bath Ales house, with Bath Gem, SPA and Barnstormer usually available, plus three guest beers, perhaps something like Butcombe Gold or an ale from one of the smaller breweries.

Grade II listed Georgian pub, refurbished but with some original features retained. Food is available and there is a non-smoking area of the bar. Children allowed in restaurant.

11am–11pm.

Star Inn

23 Vineyards, Bath BA1 5NE
☎ *(01225) 425072*
Alan Morgan and Paul Waters

Abbey Bellringer always available plus three rotating guests.

A timeless local with a friendly atmosphere within the wonderful old interior. One bar with four small rooms including 'death row' where the old folk sit. Traditional games such as shove ha'penny.

12–2.30pm and 5.30–11pm Mon–Fri; all day Sat–Sun.

Volunteer Rifleman Arms

3 New Bond Street Place, Bath BA1 1BH
☎ *(01225) 425210* Paul Alvis

Freehouse serving Abbey Ales Bellringer, Mole's Molecatcher, Exmoor Gold and Wickwar BOB as permanents, plus a couple of guests, perhaps Timothy Taylor Landlord.

Cosy little pub tucked away down a back street shopping alley, could be described as a little bit of Amsterdam in the centre of Bath. One bar. Food every session.

11am–11pm.

BAWDRIP

Knowle Inn

115 Bath Road, Bawdrip, Near Bridgwater TA7 8PN
☎ *(01278) 683330* Christina Mathews

Bitters from Otter and Butcombe, Cotleigh Barn Owl, and Camerons Castle Eden are permanents with a couple of guests, quite possibly Wadworth 6X.

A sixteenth century coaching inn with an excellent cellar for keeping beers. Surprisingly big with a number of rooms. Food every session. Accommodation. Children welcome. Large beer garden and car park. Darts. Roadside pub just north of Bridgwater on the A39.

All day, every day.

BLAGDON

New Inn

Church Street, Blagdon BS40 7SB
☎ *(01761) 462475* Anne and Pat McCann

Wadworth IPA, 6X and seasonals plus Butcombe Bitter always available.

Welcoming country pub with fantastic views of Blagdon Lake from the car park. Log fire in the winter. Two out of three bar areas are non-smoking. Children welcome. Garden and large parking area.

 *11am–2.30pm and 7–11pm Tues–Sat; 12–3pm and 7–10.30pm Sun; closed all day Monday.*

Queen Adelaide

High Street, Blagdon BS40 7RA
☎ *(01761) 462573* Terry Beardshaw

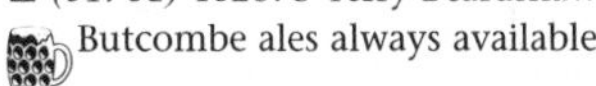

Butcombe ales always available.

Small quaint village pub in a Grade II listed building. Food is served during each session in the one bar. Small beer garden and car park. No children.

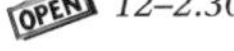 *12–2.30pm and 7–11pm (10.30pm Sun).*

BLEADON

The Queen's Arms

Celtic Way, Bleadon, Nr Weston-super-Mare BS24 ONF
☎ *(01934) 812080* Daniel Pardoe
www.queensarms.co.uk.

A Butcombe pub serving Bitter, Blond and Gold, plus a couple of guests which may include Palmers IPA and Ringwood Old Thumper.

A sixteenth-century freehouse with flagstone floors and settles, specialising in good food and real ales served straight from the barrel. A good stop for refreshment on the Mendip Walk. Food served daily lunchtime and evening, except Sunday evening in the winter when the pub holds a very popular quiz night. Skittle alley also available.

 *11.30am–2.30pm and 5.30–11pm Mon–Fri; 11.30am–11pm Sat; 12–10.30pm Sun.*

BRIDGWATER

Annie's Bar

North Street, Bridgwater TA6 3PW
☎ *(01278) 433053* Mr Truman

A freehouse with Butcombe Bitter and St Austell Tribute constantly available, plus one weekly changing guest, such as a beer from Teignworthy, Stonehenge or Cottage.

Country pub on the outskirts of town in an old, traditional building with beams and fireplaces. Back bar and front bar. Food available (back bar for dining). Garden. Children allowed until 7.30pm.

 *5–11.30pm Mon–Sat; 12–3pm and 6–10.30pm Sun.*

The Fountain Inn

1 West Quay, Bridgwater TA6 3HL
☎ *(01278) 424115*
Roger Gregory and Denise Burgess

Four real ales always available, including Wadworth 6X and Butcombe Bitter.

A traditional one-bar town-centre pub. Background music. Full bar menu available lunchtime only. No children.

 *11am–4pm and 6.30–11pm Mon–Sat; 12–4pm and 7–10.30pm Sun.*

The Horse & Jockey

1 Durleigh Road, Bridgwater TA6 7HU
☎ *(01278) 424283* Ron Chedgey

Beers from Exmoor and Teignworthy are always on offer. Four guests, often changed daily, might include Timothy Taylor Landlord or something from Shepherd Neame.

Out-of-town, traditional pub in a coaching house dating from 1770. Recently extended to make the dining area bigger. Two function rooms. No children.

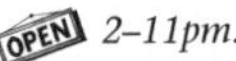 *2–11pm.*

BROADWAY

The Bell Inn

Broadway, Nr Ilminster TA19 9RG
☎ *(01460) 52343* Greg and Jan Knight

A freehouse serving Butcombe Bitter, Exmoor Ale and one guest beer.

Traditional village local with a mixed clientele. Two bars. Accommodation. Food every session. Children allowed. Car park and patio. Pool, skittle and darts.

11am–2.30pm and 5–11pm Mon–Fri; all day Sat–Sun.

BURNHAM ON SEA

The Crown

74 Oxford Street, Burnham on Sea TA8 1EW
☎ *(01278) 782792* Kevin Tippetts

A freehouse with Fuller's London Pride permanently available plus one guest, with Berrow 4Bs a regular. RCH East Street Cream, Hop Back Summer Lightning and Bateman XXXB might also be on offer, plus beers from a wide range of micro-breweries.

Locals' pub just off the town centre, frequented by local sports teams, and hosting six skittles teams and two darts teams. Skittle alley, dartboards, separate pool room. No food. Lounge and public bar, patio area with seating. Children allowed. Car park.

 *4–11pm Mon–Fri; 12–11pm Sat; 12–10.30pm Sun.*

The Royal Clarence Hotel

31 The Esplanade, Burnham on Sea TA8 1BQ
☎ *(01278) 783138* Andrew Neilson

RCH Pitchfork and Butcombe Bitter always available plus one other guest, changed throughout the year.

An old coaching hotel. Hosts occasional beer festivals and cabaret attractions. Bar food available all day. Conference facilities. Parking. Accommodation. Children allowed. Take M5 junction 22, then make for the sea front. The hotel is by the pier.

 *11am–11pm Mon–Sat; 12–10.30pm Sun.*

CANNINGTON

Malt Shovel Inn

Blackmoor Lane, Bradley Green, Cannington TA5 2NE
☎ *(01278) 653432* Jones/Tomlins

Freehouse serving Butcombe Bitter, Exmoor Fox and two changing guest ales.

Old country pub with character and atmosphere – low ceiling, log fire and wide menu. Garden and car park. Children allowed in certain areas. Accommodation. Located a mile outside Cannington.

 *11.30am–3pm and 7–11pm.*

CHARD

The Bell & Crown Inn

Combe Street, Chard TA20 1JP
☎ *(01460) 62470* Michael Hood

Otter Bitter is a permanent fixture, plus four guests, usually from West Country breweries, or seasonal and celebration ales.

A quiet, old-fashioned pub with gas lights. No music. Beer garden. Food available Tues–Sun lunchtime. Children allowed.

 *12–2.30pm (closed Mon lunchtime) and 7–11pm Mon–Fri; 12–3pm and 7–11pm Sat–Sun (10.30pm Sun).*

CHELYNCH

Poacher's Pocket

Chelynch, Shepton Mallet BA4 4PY
☎ *(01749) 880220* Stephanie and Ken Turner

Freehouse serving Cotleigh Tawny, Butcombe Bitter and Wadworth 6X and generally a guest beer.

A traditional village pub with various different rooms off the one bar; has been licensed since the seventeenth century. Food every session. Children and dogs allowed if well-behaved. Skittle alley and shove ha'penny. Folk club once a month. Beer festival end of September. Car park and garden.

 *12–3pm and 6–11pm.*

CHEW MAGNA

The Bear & Swan

13 South Parade, Chew Magna BS40 8SL
☎ *(01275) 331100* Mr Nigel Pushman

Butcombe Bitter is always available plus one guest.

Pub and restaurant at the centre of the village. Food served 12–2pm and 7–9.45pm (not Sun evenings). No children's facilities. Car park.

11am–11pm Mon–Sat; 12–6pm Sun.

CHILCOMPTON

The Somerset Wagon

Broadway, Chilcompton, Radstock, Bath BA3 4JW
☎ *(01761) 232732* Adrian Brixey

A Wadworth pub offering 6X, IPA and seasonals plus Butcombe brews.

The quintessential Somerset pub, and correspondingly popular, with loads of character. One bar. Food every session. Children welcome. Car park and garden.

12–3pm and 5–11pm.

CHISELBOROUGH

The Cat Head Inn

Chiselborough, Stoke sub Hamdon TA14 6TT
☎ *(01935) 881231* Duncan Gordon

An Enterprise pub usually offering bitters from Otter and Butcombe, plus Marston's Pedigree.

A quiet, clean village local with flagstone floors and open fire. Food orientated. Award-winning beer garden. Children welcome.

12–3pm and 6.30–11pm.

CHURCHILL

The Crown Inn

The Batch, Skinners Lane, Churchill, Nr Bristol
☎ *(01934) 852995* Tim Rogers

RCH PG Steam, Hop Back GFB, Bath SPA and Palmers IPA always available straight from the barrel, plus up to three guest beers (100+ per year) to include Exe Valley Devon Glory, Tomintoul Wild Cat, Otter Bright and Hop Back Summer Lightning.

An old pub with small rooms and flagstone floors. Large fires in winter. Food made and prepared to order with fresh local produce when practical, 12–2.30pm. No evening food. Parking, garden, children's room. Children not allowed in bar area. South of Bristol, just off the A38, not far from M5.

 *All day, every day.*

COMBE HAY

The Wheatsheaf

Combe Hay, Near Bath BA2 7EG
☎ *(01225) 833504* Richard Alsworth

A freehouse with Greene King Old Speckled Hen as a regular and two other guest beers changing weekly.

Attractive gastropub in pretty village just south of Bath. Log fires in the winter and barbecues during summer weekends. Large and pleasant garden. Children and dogs welcome. Car park. Accommodation.

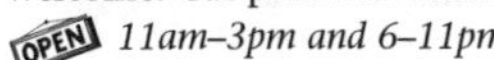 *11am–3pm and 6–11pm.*

COMPTON MARTIN

Ring O' Bells

Compton Martin BS40 6JE
☎ *(01761) 221284* Roger Owen

Freehouse serving a range of real ales including Butcombe Bitter, Blond and Gold, plus a rotating guest such as Fuller's London Pride

A quiet yet busy typical English pub with low ceilings and wooden beams, popular for food. Two bars and a restaurant room with food served at every session. Large car park and garden. Children welcome in family room. Darts and shove ha'penny.

11.30am–2.30pm and 6.30–11pm Mon–Fri; 11.30am–3pm and 6.30–11pm Sat; 12–3pm and 6.30–10.30pm Sun.

CONGRESBURY

The Plough Inn

High Street, Congresbury BS49 5JA
☎ *(01934) 832475* Jackie Armstrong

Two Butcombe brews always available from the Best, Gold and Blond range, plus four rotating guests, often including RCH Double Header. All small breweries are supported.

A 200-year-old alehouse, an old-fashioned ale lover's pub. No food. Children and dogs allowed.

11am–2.30pm and 4.30–11pm Mon–Fri; all day Sat–Sun.

CULMHEAD

Holman Clavel Inn

Culmhead, Taunton TA3 7EA
☎ *(01823) 421432* Cara Lawrence

A freehouse with Butcombe Bitter and Gold always available plus two weekly changing guests.

A fourteenth-century rural pub with garden. Food available at lunchtime and evenings. Children allowed. Dogs welcome.

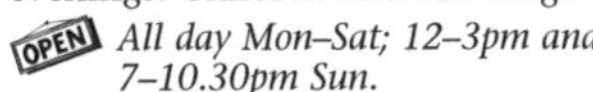 *All day Mon–Sat; 12–3pm and 7–10.30pm Sun.*

DINNINGTON

Dinnington Docks

Lower Street, Dinnington, Nr Hinton St George TA17 8SX
☎ *(01460) 52397* Hilary Hardisty

Freehouse offering Wadworth 6X and Butcombe Bitter plus two or three guests normally from small local breweries.

A friendly village local formerly known as the Rose & Crown. A seventeenth century building containing a selection of pictures, signs and memorabilia relating to its rail and maritime past. Reasonably priced food every session. Children welcome. Play equipment in the garden. Car park and skittle alley. Haircuts in the pub on last Tues night of the month.

11.30am–3.30pm and 6–11pm.

EAST HARPTREE

Castle of Comfort Inn

Castle of Comfort, East Harptree BS40 6DD
☎ *(01761) 221321* Steve and Wendy Crook

A freehouse with Butcombe Best always available plus two or three other real ales, changing weekly.

Pleasant country pub located in the middle of nowhere on the top of the Mendips. On the B3134. Food. Children welcome. Garden and car park. Traditional pub games.

12–3pm and 6–11pm.

EAST LYNG

Rose & Crown

East Lyng, Taunton TA3 5AU
☎ *(01823) 698235* Derek Mason
www.derek.mason.btinternet.co.uk

Freehouse serving Butcombe Bitter and Gold, plus Palmers 200.

A respectable grown-ups' pub with classic lounge furniture – probably a good place to take your mum. Food every session. Accommodation, garden, car park and skittle alley. On the A361 between Glastonbury and Taunton.

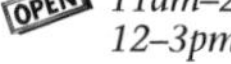 *11am–2.30pm and 6.30–11pm Mon–Sat; 12–3pm and 7–10.30pm Sun.*

EVERCREECH

Bell Inn

Bruton Road, Evercreech BA4 6HY
☎ *(01749) 830287* Stephen and Katie McGrail

Freehouse serving Shepherd Neame Spitfire and Butcombe Bitter as permanents plus one changing guest favouring the micros.

Light and tastefully decorated pub – an unusual mixture of old and new. Opposite the village church that has apparently the most perfect spire in the country. Main bar, restaurant and family area. Accommodation. Food every session except Sunday evening. Children welcome. Car park. Garden. Skittle alley, darts and pool.

 *11.30am–11pm Mon–Sat; 12–10.30pm Sun.*

EXFORD

Exmoor White Horse Inn

Exford, Exmoor TA24 7PY
☎ *01643 831229* Peter Hendrie

Exmoor Ale, Exmoor Gold and Greene King Old Speckled Hen are always available and during the summer there are a couple of guests changing every week.

A sixteenth-century family-run inn with plenty of character, attracting both locals and tourists. Accommodation. Food, lunchtime and evening, has an emphasis on local produce. Car park and terrace overlooking the river. Children welcome up to 9pm. Large selection of malt whiskies.

All day, every day.

FARLEIGH HUNGERFORD

Hungerford Arms

Farleigh Hungerford, Nr Bath BA3 6RX
☎ *(01225) 752411* Stuart Lockley

Freehouse offering Wadworth 6X, Otter Bitter, plus two rotating guests.

An old roadside pub overlooking Farleigh Hungerford Castle. One partitioned bar and a restaurant. Food every session. Children welcome. Car park and patio.

11.30am–3pm and 5.30–11pm Mon–Fri; all day Sat–Sun.

FAULKLAND

Tucker's Grave

Faulkland, Nr Radstock BA3 5FX
☎ *(01373) 834230* Ivan and Glenda Swift

Butcombe Bitter served straight from the cask.

A really traditional rural pub – basic but with plenty of friendly rustic charm. Ploughman's lunch available. Skittle alley and shove ha'penny. Car park and garden.

11am–3pm and 6–11pm (10.30pm Sun).

FROME

The Griffin

25 Milk Street, Frome BA11 3DB
☎ *(01373) 467766*
Nick Branwell and Rick Lyall

Home of the Milk Street Brewery with the full range of the brews always available.

Busy community pub for real ale lovers. No food. No children.

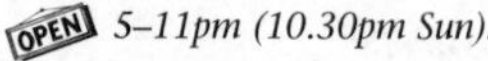 *5–11pm (10.30pm Sun).*

The Horse & Groom

East Woodlands, Frome BA11 5LY
☎ *(01373) 462802* Kathy Barrett

Archers Golden, Branscombe Vale Branoc and a Butcombe brew always available, plus one guest, changing weekly, which might be Bateman XB or a Brakspear brew.

A two-bar country freehouse with log fires, flag floors, restaurant, conservatory and beer garden. Restaurant and bar food available at lunchtime and evenings. Children allowed in the restaurant, lounge and garden only.

11.30am–2.30pm and 6.30–11pm (10.30pm Sun).

GLASTONBURY

Who'd A Thought It

17 Northload Street, Glastonbury BA6 9JJ
☎ *(01458) 834460* Andrew and Eileen Davis

Tied to the Palmers brewery, regularly serving IPA and 200, and occasionally others such as Tally Ho!

A real curiosity of a pub, full of bric-à-brac, old features and loads of character – there's an old red telephone kiosk in the corner, a bike attached to the ceiling and award-winning loos. Strong emphasis on homemade food (every day). Car park and patio. Children allowed in dining area. Accommodation.

 *11am–11pm.*

HALSE

The New Inn

Halse, Near Taunton TA4 3AF
☎ *(01823) 432352* Mark Leadeham
www.newinnhalse.co.uk

Home of the new Somerset (Electric) Brewery, so all their brews served.

An independent and traditional seventeenth century country freehouse. Home-cooked food every session. Many pub games including bar billiards and darts. Well-behaved children and dogs welcome. Garden and car park. Accommodation.

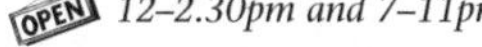 *12–2.30pm and 7–11pm (10.30pm Sun).*

HARDINGTON MOOR

The Royal Oak Inn

Moor Lane, Hardington Moor, Yeovil BA22 9NW
☎ *(01935) 862354* Dave Mitchell

Ales from Butcombe and Branscombe Vale always available plus two guests such as Slaters (Eccleshall) brews. Annual themed beer festival held in May each year.

A rural farmhouse freehouse. Two bars, dining area, beer garden, motorcycle-friendly. Food available Tues–Sun lunchtime and evenings. Children allowed.

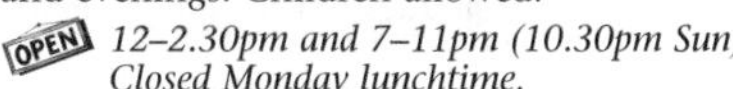 *12–2.30pm and 7–11pm (10.30pm Sun). Closed Monday lunchtime.*

HINTON BLEWITT

Ring O'Bells

Hinton Blewitt, Nr Bristol BS39 5AN
☎ *(01761) 452239* Jon Jenssen

Butcombe Bitter usually available with three guest beers, perhaps Wickwar BOB, Abbey Bellringer, Wadworth 6X or Badger Best.

Traditional country pub with lovely views. Food served 12–2pm and 7–10pm. Car park. Children welcome. Garden.

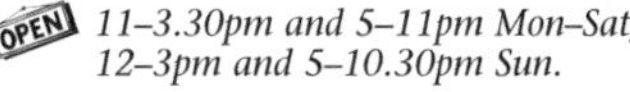 *11–3.30pm and 5–11pm Mon–Sat; 12–3pm and 5–10.30pm Sun.*

HORSINGTON

Half Moon Inn

Horsington, Templecombe BA8 0EF
☎ *(01963) 370140*
Andrew and Philippa Tarling

Freehouse with Wadworth 6X permanently available, plus four or five guests rotating all the time but favouring the stronger ones such as Hop Back Summer Lightning, Badger Tanglefoot and Adnams Broadside.

A typical community country pub that tries to present a traditional front – a pretty exterior, pleasant interior and a friendly atmosphere. Accommodation. Darts, table football and skittle alley. Food every session. Car park and garden.

 *12–2.30pm and 6–11pm Mon Fri; 12–3pm and 6–11pm Sat; 12–3pm and 7–10.30pm Sun.*

HUISH EPISCOPI

The Rose & Crown (Eli's)

Huish Episcopi, Langport TA10 9QT
☎ *(01458) 250494* Eileen Pittard

A freehouse with a Teignworthy ale always available plus three guests of varying strengths usually from local breweries.

A traditional country pub with central servery and lots of smaller adjoining rooms, which has been in the same family for over 130 years. Non-smoking room at lunchtime. Beer garden. Food available at lunchtime and evenings until 8pm. Children allowed.

 *11.30am–2.30pm and 5.30–11pm Mon–Thurs; all day Fri–Sun.*

KELSTON

The Old Crown

Bath Road, Kelston, Nr Bath
☎ *(01225) 423032* C Cole

Butcombe Bitter, Blond and Gold, Bath Ales Gem and Wadworth 6X always available plus Wadworth Old Timer in winter only.

Traditional old-English pub and restaurant with open fire, original flagstones, candle-light and good atmosphere. Food every lunchtime and every evening except Sun and Mon. Car park and garden. No children under 14 inside. On A43 Bitton to Bath road, three miles outside Bath.

 *11.30am–2.30pm and 5–11pm Mon–Fri; all day Sat–Sun.*

KINGSBURY EPISCOPI

The Wyndham Arms

Folly Road, Kingsbury Episcopi, Nr Martock TA12 6AT
☎ *(01935) 823239* Jeremy Dawkins

Fuller's London Pride, something from Teignworthy and a beer from either Butcombe or Otter on offer. Also real cider.

A lovely old-fashioned country pub – comfortable, friendly and laid back. A 400-year-old building with two large open fires and flagstone floors. Food every session. Big garden. Car park. Well-behaved children and dogs welcome. Skittle alley.

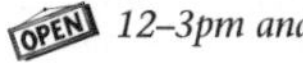
12–3pm and 6.30–11pm.

LANGFORD BUDVILLE

Martlet Inn

Langford Budville, Wellington TA21 0QZ
☎ *(01823) 400262* Vic Bigg

A freehouse with Cotleigh Tawny and Exmoor Ale always available, plus two guests.

A traditional country pub with dining area and beer garden. Food available at lunchtime and evenings. No juke box or games machines. Children allowed in designated areas.

12–2.30pm and 7–11pm Mon–Sat; 12–3pm and 7–10.30pm Sun.

LANGLEY MARSH

The Three Horseshoes

Langley Marsh, Wiveliscombe, Nr Taunton TA4 2UL
☎ *(01984) 623763* John Hopkins

Palmers IPA, Otter Best and Young's Bitter always available plus guest beers which may inclue Harveys Sussex Best and Timothy Taylor Landlord.

An old, unspoilt, no-nonsense traditional pub. No juke box or games machines. Bar and restaurant food is available at lunchtime and evenings. Holiday cottages in grounds. Car park and garden. No children under the age of eight. Follow the B3227 to Wiveliscombe, then follow signs to Langley Marsh.

12–2.30pm and 7–11pm (10.30pm Sun); closed Mondays out of season.

LANGPORT

The Black Swan

North Street, Langport
☎ *(01458) 250355* David and Anita Smith

Butcombe Gold is always available, and Fuller's London Pride alternates with other brews such as Otter.

Characterful inn with restaurant, skittle alley and beer garden. Food served 12–2pm and 7–9.30pm every day except Tuesday. Car park. Children welcome.

11am–2.30pm and 6–11pm Mon–Thur; all day Fri–Sun.

LEIGH COMMON

Hunters Lodge Inn

Leigh Common, Wincanton BA9 8LD
☎ *(01747) 840439* Mr Bent

A freehouse offering Butcombe Gold, Greene King Abbot and Fuller's London Pride.

A country pub with bars, dining area and beer garden. Food available at lunchtime and evenings. Children allowed.

11am–3pm and 6–11pm (10.30pm Sun).

LOWER ODCOMBE

Mason's Arms

41 Lower Odcombe, Yeovil BA22 8TX
☎ *(01935) 862591* Amon Doherty

Home of Odcombe Ales with the two Odcombe Higher and Lower brews produced on the premises and exclusively available in the bar. Also a mild called Donne Lane. Occasional honey beer called Buzz. Other independent ales also available, from breweries such as Otter and Butcombe.

A traditional pub with skittle alley. Food offered Wednesday to Saturday, lunchtime and evening, plus Sunday lunches and special curry nights on Thursdays. Beer garden. Children allowed in the garden. Camping. Accommodation.

7–11pm Mon–Tues (closed lunchtime); 12.30–3pm and 7–11pm Wed–Fri; 12–11pm Sat; 12–3pm and 7–10.30pm Sun.

LUXBOROUGH

Royal Oak of Luxborough

Exmoor National Park, Luxborough, Nr Dunster TA23 0SH
☎ *(01984) 640319* James Waller

A freehouse with Cotleigh Tawny, Exmoor Gold and Palmers 200 and IPA always available plus occasional guest.

An unspoilt rural pub with loads of beams, flagstones etc. Farmhouse tables. Bar food offered at lunchtime, restaurant menu available at both sessions. Car park and beer garden. Children allowed in the restaurant, they must be over 10 for the evening. En-suite accommodation. Off the A396, four miles south of Dunster.

 *12–2.30pm and 6–11pm Mon–Sat; 12–2.30pm and 7–10.30pm Sun.*

MARTOCK

The Nag's Head

East Street, Martock TA12 6NF
☎ *(01935) 823432* Steve Wetherall

A freehouse with Otter Bitter among the brews always available, plus two weekly changing guests such as Timothy Taylor Landlord, RCH East Street Cream, Badger Tanglefoot or other seasonal and celebration ales.

A local village pub with two bars (lounge and public), non-smoking dining area, beer garden, children's play area, accommodation, disabled access at rear. Well-known locally for its good homemade food, available lunchtimes and evenings. Families welcome. Happy hour for food and drink between 6 and 7pm Mon–Fri. Can be difficult to find, but worth it! Phone for directions.

12–2.30pm Tues–Sun (closed Mon lunchtime); 6–11pm daily.

MIDDLEZOY

George Inn

42 Main Road, Middlezoy, Near Taunton TA7 0NN
☎ *(01823) 698215* James and Sonya Enright

A freehouse serving Butcombe Bitter as a permanent and three guests, perhaps a beer from Hop Back, Cottage or Otter.

Lovely country pub in the middle of the Somerset Levels. Stone floors, wooden beams and open fire. Characterful and atmospheric. Food every session except Sun and Mon evenings. Children welcome early in the day. Terrace. Car park. Skittle alley and darts. Easter beer festival. Accommodation – popular with fishermen.

 *12–2.30pm Tues–Fri; 12–3pm Sat–Sun; 7–11pm (10.30pm Sun).*

MIDSOMER NORTON

The White Hart

The Island, Midsomer Norton BA3 2HQ
☎ *(01761) 412957* Malcolm Curtis

Butcombe brews are available on a permanent basis.

Interesting Victorian pub in the centre of town. Lots of different rooms including a skittle alley with full length mural. Food served at lunchtime only – renowned for its ham, egg and chips. Tiny patio. Well-behaved children welcome.

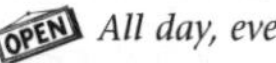 *All day, every day.*

MOORLINCH

The Ring of Bells

Pit Lane, Moorlinch, Nr Bridgwater TA7 9BT
☎ *(01458) 210358* Clive Davies

Freehouse serving Palmers Copper, Otter Ale and Hop Back Summer Lightning or Crop Circle plus a couple of rotating guests, maybe something from Cotleigh, Stonehenge or Exmoor.

Pleasant, friendly and surprisingly spacious village local. Two bars. Food every session. Children welcome. Car park and garden. Skittles, pool and darts. Halfway between Glastonbury and Bridgwater

 *4.30–11pm Mon (closed Mon lunch); 12–11pm Tues–Sat; 12–10.30pm Sun.*

NAILSEA

The Blue Flame Inn

West End, Nailsea BS48 4DE
☎ *(01275) 856910* Mick Davidson

Fuller's London Pride always available plus two or three guest beers at any time, perhaps brews from Archers, Cottage Brewing or RCH.

Charming, 200-year-old real country pub between Nailsea and Clevedon, popular with locals, joggers, riders and walkers. Three rooms and a bar, all with real character. Furnished with mismatched tables and chairs, as far as you can get from high-street theme pubs. Large garden with swings, covered drinking area and a barbecue. Children allowed everywhere except the public bar. Car park. No food.

12–3pm and 6–11pm.

NETTLEBRIDGE

Nettlebridge Inn

Nettlebridge, Nr Oakhill
☎ *(01749) 841360* Mr Piner

Butcombe Bitter regularly available.

Two-bar pub with non-smoking area and lots of hanging baskets in summer. Food served lunchtime and evening, and all day Sunday. Car park. Children welcome.

 *12–3pm and 6–11pm Mon–Sat; all day Sun and bank holidays.*

NORTH CURRY

The Bird in Hand

1 Queen Square, North Curry, Taunton TA3 6LT
☎ *(01823) 490248* James Mogg

A freehouse with Otter Bitter always available, plus one or two constantly changing guests.

A traditional one-bar country pub with log fires and patio, located in attractive village. Food is available during all opening hours in both the bar and the pretty à la carte restaurant. Children allowed.

 *12–3pm and 7–11pm Mon–Fri; 12–4pm and 7–11pm Sat; 12–3pm and 7–10.30pm Sun.*

NORTON ST PHILIP

Fleur de Lys

High Street, Norton St Philip, Nr Bath BA2 7LQ
☎ *(01373) 834333* Simon Shannon

A Wadworth house with 6X and IPA, plus Butcombe Bitter.

An old building and an old-style pub that prides itself on its food. Two bars and a restaurant above. Darts and skittles. Children welcome in one bar. Food served lunchtime and evening seven days a week. Parking.

11am–3pm and 5–11pm Mon–Fri; all day Sat; 12–4pm and 7–10.30pm Sun.

NORTON SUB HAMDON

Lord Nelson

Rectory Lane, Norton Sub Hamdon TA14 6SP
☎ *(01935) 881473* Sue and Dave Gordon

Teignworthy Reel Ale, Greene King IPA and Abbot Ale are served, plus a constantly changing guest beer.

A traditional local village pub with a real fire as well as real beer. Children, dogs and muddy boots welcome. Food available lunchtime and evening every day. Live music once a month. Car park.

 *12–3pm and 6.30–11pm Mon–Fri; 12–11pm Sat; 12–10.30pm Sun.*

OAKHILL

Oakhill Inn

Fosse Road, Oakhill BA3 5HU
☎ *(01749) 840442* Mike Scott

Three real ales changing regularly.

A village local that welcomes families. Situated in the centre of the village, which is a couple of miles north of Shepton Mallet. Food every session. Car park and garden. Darts, pool and shove ha'penny.

 *12–2.30pm and 6–11pm Mon–Fri; 12–4.30pm and 6–11pm Sat–Sun.*

PITMINSTER

The Queen's Arms

Pitminster, Nr Taunton TA3 7AZ
☎ *(01823) 421529*
Bob Cartman and Sharon Isidoro

Cotleigh Tawny, Otter Bitter, Butcombe Bitter and Gold always available plus occasional guest beers.

A traditional stone-built pub with an attached fourteenth-century building. No games machines. Home-cooked food served at lunchtime and evenings. Car park and garden. Children allowed in the lounge, which has books and toys. Follow the signs for Corfe from Taunton and turn right in Corfe.

 *11am–11pm Mon–Sat; 12–10.30pm Sun.*

PITNEY

Halfway House

Pitney, Nr Langport TA10 9AB
☎ *(01458) 252513* J Litchfield

Up to ten beers available, including brews from Teignworthy, Butcombe, Branscombe and Hop Back breweries, plus others.

A very popular real ale pub with flagstone floors and log fires. No music or games machines. Bar food is available at lunchtime and evenings. Car park and garden. Well-behaved children and dogs allowed. CAMRA Somerset Pub of the Year 1997, 2001 and 2003. On the main road between Somerton and Langport (B3153).

 *11.30am–3pm and 5.30–11pm.*

PRIDDY

Queen Victoria Inn

Priddy, Near Wells BA5 3BA
☎ *(01749) 676385* John and Heather Taylor

Freehouse offering Butcombe Bitter, Gold, Blond and Wadworth 6X, plus the occasional guest.

An old-fashioned rural pub with a pleasant atmosphere, real fires and low wooden ceiling. Children and dogs welcome. Car park and garden. Food (focus on the homemade) every session. Darts, bar billiards and shove ha'penny.

12–3pm and 7–11pm Mon–Fri; all day Sat–Sun.

RIMPTON

White Post Inn

Rimpton, Yeovil BI22 8AR
☎ *(01935) 850717* Chris Abrahamsson

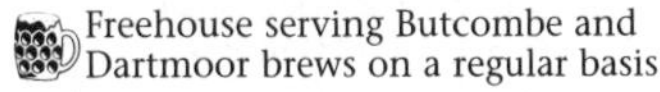
Freehouse serving Butcombe and Dartmoor brews on a regular basis.

Two-bar pub that straddles the Somerset–Dorset border. Lovely views. Swedish landlord and the menu is partly Swedish. Food served every session. Children allowed in certain areas. Car park. Garden.

12–3pm and 6.30–11pm (10.30pm Sun).

RODE

The Bell Inn

13 Frome Road, Rode BA3 6PW
☎ *(01373) 830356* Richard Vestey

A freehouse with Butcombe Bitter regularly available plus two guests.

A food-oriented country pub specialising in seafood. Two bars, dining area and beer garden. Food available at lunchtime and evenings. Children allowed.

12–3pm and 7–11pm (10.30pm Sun).

ROWBERROW

Swan Inn

Rowberrow, Winscombe BS25 1QL
☎ *(01934) 852371* Bob Flaxman

Butcombe Bitter, Blond and Gold always on offer.

Gimmick-free country pub that lets the customers create the atmosphere. Two spacious bars. Parking and garden areas. Food available lunchtime and evening seven days a week. No children under 14. Just off the A38.

12–3pm and 6–11pm Mon–Sat; 12–3pm and 7–10.30pm Sun.

SANDYWAY

Sportsman's Inn

Sandyway, Exmoor EX36 3LU
☎ *(01643) 831109*

Freehouse serving Exmoor Ale and Gold, plus seasonals.

Isolated but cosy pub on the edge of Exmoor between North Molton and Withypool. Curiosities include a well in the middle of the bar. Popular with walkers and riders because of its location. Food every session except Mon and Thurs lunchtimes. Car park. Pool. Accommodation. Children allowed in restaurant.

12–2.30pm and 6.30–11pm (10.30pm Sun).

SHOSCOMBE

The Apple Tree

Shoscombe, Nr Bath BA2 8LF
☎ *(01761) 432263* Mark Bryan

Greene King IPA and Old Speckled Hen are regulars, plus a couple of other real ales.

A quiet and friendly rural pub set in the heart of the village. Food every session from Wed lunchtime to Sun lunchtime. Children welcome. Small car park and garden.

7–11pm Mon–Tues; 12–3pm and 7–11pm Wed–Fri; all day Sat–Sun.

SHURTON

The Shurton Inn

Shurton, Bridgwater TA5 1QE
☎ *(01278) 732695* Mr D Stewart

A freehouse with Exmoor Ale, Otter Bright and Butcombe Bitter always available, plus a guest ale changing weekly. Beer festival held in June.

An unspoilt traditional pub with a large bar, with three seating areas on two levels, a restaurant area and a large beer garden. Home-cooked food available lunchtimes and evenings. Accommodation. Live music once a fortnight. Car park in front and to rear of pub. Children's licence.

12–2.30pm and 6–11pm Mon–Sat; 12–3pm and 7–10.30pm Sun.

SOUTH PETHERTON

Brewers Arms

18 St James Street, South Petherton TA13 5BW
☎ *(01460) 52397* Duncan Webb

Freehouse with Otter Bitter as a permanent and three constantly changing guest beers.

Busy popular community pub in a pleasant town. Beer festivals held last bank holiday in May and August bank holiday. Food every session. Garden. Children welcome. Darts and skittle alley. Close to the A303.

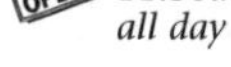
11.30am–2.30pm and 6–11pm Mon–Sat; all day Sun.

SPARKFORD

Sparkford Inn

High Street, Sparkford BA22 7JH
☎ *(01963) 440218* Paul Clayton

Four real ales available at any one time but changing frequently. Brews from Butcombe and Otter are regulars.

A fifteenth-century coaching inn that is quite large yet retains a cosy olde-worlde atmosphere with window seats and interesting furnishing. Food every session. Children welcome. Accommodation. Car park and small garden.

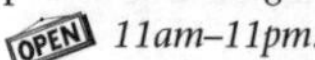
11am–11pm.

STANTON WICK

Carpenters Arms

Stanton Wick, Nr Pensford BS39 4BX
☎ *(01761) 490202* Simon and Sharon Pledge

Freehouse offering Butcombe Bitter and Wadworth 6X.

Quaint traditional pub with restaurant, situated just off the A368. Cosy window seat by large fire. Accommodation and disabled facilities. Food available in bar and restaurant lunchtimes and evening every day. Car park. Children's menu.

11am–11pm Mon–Sat; 12–10.30pm Sun.

TAUNTON

The Eagle Tavern

South Street, Taunton TA1 3AF
☎ *(01823) 275713* Phil Steele and Jo Porter

Otter Bitter is regularly available plus one guest, maybe Timothy Taylor Landlord, London Pride or something from Exmoor.

A country-style pub in the town, with wooden floors and open fire. Beer garden. Food available whenever open. Children not allowed.

5–11pm Mon–Thur; all day Fri–Sun.

The Hankridge Arms

Hankridge Way, Taunton TA1 2LR
☎ *(01823) 444405* Andrew Read

Badger Best and Tanglefoot are permanents, plus one guest beer.

A Grade II listed sixteenth century building bizarrely located in a modern retail park. Handy after a visit to Sainsburys or B&Q. Large fireplace, stone floors and wooden beams. Food all day. Small garden. Car park. No smoking area.

All day, every day.

Mason Arms

Magdalene Street, Taunton TA1 1SG
☎ *(01823) 288916* Jeremy Leyton

Freehouse with Otter Bitter as a permanent and three changing guest ales, usually local.

Cosy old-fashioned town pub with a curious collection of ornaments from antlers to hammers. Food every session except Sunday – soup a speciality. Accommodation in flats.

10.30am–3pm and 5–11pm.

Perkin Warbeck

22 East Street, Taunton TA1 3LP
☎ *(01823) 335830* Ian and Leanne Borsing

A Wetherspoon's pub with Shepherd Neame Spitfire and Greene King Abbot Ale always available, plus up to three regularly changing regional guest ales, often including something from Butcombe.

A two-bar town-centre pub. Non-smoking areas, patio. Food available all day, every day. Children allowed for dining until 5pm.

All day, every day.

TRUDOXHILL

The White Hart

Trudoxhill, Nr Frome BA11 2DT
☎ *(01373) 836324* Gary Dunn

Butcombe Bitter is permanent and there are three guest beers – Wadworth 6X and Palmers Copper are popular.

A sixteenth-century country pub. One bar, restaurant, garden and children's play area. Food available 11.30am–9pm daily. Children allowed.

All day, every day.

WANSTROW

Pub at Wanstrow

Station Road, Wanstrow, Shepton Mallet BA4 4SZ
☎ *(01749) 850455* Paul and Daria Stevens

Blindmans' Mine Beer is constant, Greene King IPA is pretty frequent, and there are four other ales being served, such as Smiles Original or Hop Back Summer Lightning, supporting local breweries as much as possible.

A very friendly little village local with a strong emphasis on the beer. Food every session except Monday and Sunday night. Children allowed. Car park and small garden. Bar billiards, darts and skittle alley.

12–2.30pm and 6–11pm Mon–Sat (closed Mon lunchtimes); 12–2.30pm and 7–10.30pm Sun.

WEDMORE

The New Inn

Combe Batch, Wedmore BS28 4DU
☎ *(01934) 712099* Angela Sayer

A freehouse always serving a Butcombe beer plus a guest ale such as Fuller's London Pride.

A popular little local with interesting corners in the two rooms. Beer garden and small car park. Pool, darts and skittle alley. Children welcome.

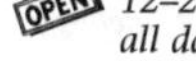
12–2.30pm and 6–11pm Tues–Fri; all day Sat-Sun.

WELLINGTON

The Cottage Inn

Champford Lane, Wellington TA21 8BH
☎ *(01823) 664650* A and L Sullivan

Otter Bitter, Cotleigh Tawny and Fuller's London Pride permanently available, plus one other changing real ale.

Traditional town-centre pub. Pagoda-style garden with seating for 30. Food served 12–2pm daily except Sunday. Children welcome, but no special facilities. Car park. Directions: in Wellington town centre, go past cinema on the left and take the second turning on the left.

11am–3pm and 6–11pm Mon–Sat; 12–4pm and 7–10.30pm Sun.

WELLOW

The Fox & Badger

Railway Lane, Wellow, Bath BA2 8QG
☎ *(01225) 832293* Eric and Susanne Hobbs
www.foxandbadger.co.uk

Butcombe Bitter, Badger Sussex and Best usually available. Traditional ciders also served.

Sixteenth-century pub set in picturesque countryside, with conservatory, courtyard and skittle alley. Food served each lunchtime and evening – specialising in traditional ploughman's lunches with a variety of Cheddars. Ample village parking. Children and dogs welcome.

11.30am–3pm and 6–11pm Mon–Thurs; 11.30am–11pm Fri–Sat; 12–10.30pm Sun.

WELLS

Fountain Inn

1 St Thomas's Street, Wells BA5 2UU
☎ *(01749) 672317* Adrian and Sarah Lawrence

Butcombe Bitter is served.

Popular inn with a good reputation for its food, which is served every session. Non-smoking area. Car park. Children welcome.

12–3pm and 6–11pm (7–10.30pm Sun and 10am–7pm in the winter).

WEST CRANMORE

Strode Arms

West Cranmore, Shepton Mallet BA4 4QJ
☎ *(01749) 880450*
Mr R McBain and Mrs H MacCullum

Wadworth 6X, JCB and Henry's IPA on offer plus one rotating guest.

A traditional and unpretentious country pub overlooking the village duck pond. One main bar and a restaurant. Food every session. Children allowed in restaurant and over 14 in the bar. Car park and garden.

11am–2.30pm and 6–11pm Mon–Sat; 12–3pm and 7–10.30 Sun.

WESTON-SUPER-MARE

Off The Rails

Pub on the Station, Railway Station, Weston-super-Mare BS23 1XY
☎ *(01934) 415109* Mr Hicks

RCH Bitter is constantly available, with two guests, changed weekly – Sharp's Doom Bar is popular.

Traditional pub in a building dating from 1880, with one bar and buffet in the railway station. Food available in the buffet area. Children allowed in the buffet area.

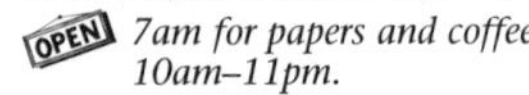
7am for papers and coffee, then 10am–11pm.

The Regency

22–4 Lower Church Road, Weston-super-Mare BS23 2AG
☎ *(01934) 633406* Mark Short

Butcombe Bitter and Charles Wells Bombardier always available, plus occasional guests.

A traditional, comfortable pub with pool room and beer yard. Food available at lunchtimes. Children allowed in the pool room. Situated opposite Weston College.

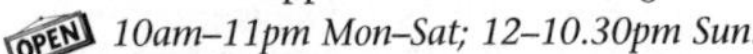
10am–11pm Mon–Sat; 12–10.30pm Sun.

The Woolpack Inn

Shepherds Way, St Georges, Weston-super-Mare BS22 7XE
☎ *(01934) 521670* PW Sampson

Four beers always available, 30 per year, to include Newman's Wolvers and beers from Palmers.

Village freehouse in 200-year-old building. Bar food at lunchtime and à la carte restaurant in the evenings. Car park, conservatory and function room. No children. Off M5, junction 21.

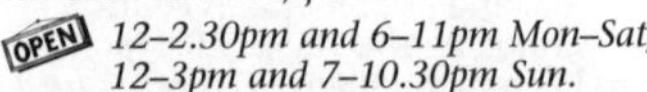
12–2.30pm and 6–11pm Mon–Sat; 12–3pm and 7–10.30pm Sun.

WILLITON

The Forester's Arms Hotel

Long Street, Williton, Taunton TA20 3PX
☎ *(01984) 632508* K Watts

A freehouse with Cotleigh Tawny always available, plus three or four others.

A two-bar village pub with dining area, beer garden, accommodation. Pool room and two dart boards. Food served at lunchtime and evenings. Children allowed during the daytime.

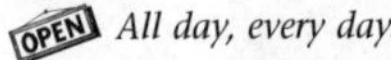
All day, every day.

WINCANTON

The Bear Inn

12 Market Place, Wincanton BA9 9LP
☎ *(01963) 32581* Ian Wainwright

A freehouse with Greene King Abbot always available plus three guests. Regulars include Ringwood Best and Fortyniner, Butcombe and many more.

An old coaching inn with food available at lunchtime and evenings in a separate dining area. Accommodation. Children allowed.

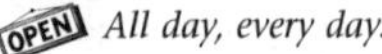
All day, every day.

WINDMILL HILL

The Square & Compass

Windmill Hill, Nr Ilminster TA19 9NX
☎ *(01823) 480467* Chris Slow

Exmoor Ale permanently available plus two or three guests.

Traditional country pub with comfortable and friendly atmosphere. The landlord has added a 250-seat venue for parties and festivals. Food. Children and dogs welcome. Car park and gardens.

12–3pm and 6.30–11pm (closed Tues, Wed, Thurs lunchtimes).

WINSFORD

Royal Oak Inn

Winsford, Exmoor National Park, Nr Minehead TA24 7JE
☎ *(01643) 851455* Charles Steven

Freehouse offering brews from Brakspear and Butcombe.

A cosy twelfth-century thatched inn situated in a beautiful village. Two bars and a quiet atmosphere. Accommodation. Food served lunchtime and evening. Car park and small garden. Children allowed in the back bar.

11am–3pm and 7–11pm Mon–Thurs; all day Fri–Sun in the summer.

WIVELISCOMBE

The Bear Inn

10 North Street, Wiveliscombe TA4 2JY
☎ *(01984) 623537* Mr A and Mrs H Harvey

Cotleigh Tawny and Golden Eagle, plus Otter Bitter regularly available, plus one guest beer.

Welcoming locals' pub with large, well-laid-out garden and patio. Food served 12–2.30pm and 6–9pm daily. Take-away pizza menu 5–9pm. Car park. Family room and large, safe beer garden with children's play equipment. Pool table. Disabled toilets.

OPEN *11am–11pm Mon–Sat; 12–10.30pm Sun.*

WOOKEY

Burcott Inn

Wookey Road, Wookey, Nr Wells BA5 1NJ
☎ *(01749 673874)* Ian Stead

Three cask-conditioned ales offered in the summer, two in the winter. Sharp's Doom Bar often available, also something from Cotleigh, Branscombe or Teignworthy but more than 60 different beers tried in a year.

Old stone traditional pub with real beer, real fires and real homemade food. Two bars in one large room. Food available except Sun and Mon evening. Children welcome in games room, garden and restaurant. Parking and large garden. Traditional games such as darts, cribbage and shove ha'penny.

11.30am–2.30pm and 6–11pm Mon–Fri; 12–3pm and 6–11pm Sat; 12–3pm and 7–10.30pm Sun.

WOOKEY HOLE

Wookey Hole Inn

Wookey Hole, Nr Wells BA5 1BP
☎ *(01749) 676677*
Peter Miller and Jessica White

Four constantly rotating ales are on offer here, perhaps something from the Milk Street Brewery.

From the outside this looks like an ordinary pub, from the inside it has a very different and modern feel. Open-plan, it is a pub that is almost a restaurant. High-quality, competitively priced, food. Accommodation with rooms in a Japanese style. Well-behaved children welcome. Board games. Live music Fri and Sun nights. Large garden with sculptures and a fountain. Car park. It won the Bristol & District CAMRA Pub of the Year for 2003.

12–3pm and 6–11pm Mon–Sat (the restaurant stays open a further hour); 12–4pm Sun.

WRANTAGE

The Canal Inn

Wrantage, Near Taunton TA3 6DF
☎ *(01823) 480210* Claire Paul

Freehouse serving Canal Inn Bitter (specially brewed by Blackdown Brewery), Glastonbury Ale and at least two more West Country beers. Also 16 different Belgian beers. Draught cider.

Friendly and pleasant country pub with resident house parrot. Food, sourced locally, every session except Sun night and Mon lunchtime. Children welcome. Large beer garden with chickens. Skittle alley. Car park. On the A372.

12–2.30pm except Mon; 5–11.30pm Mon–Fri; 7–11pm Sat–Sun.

YEOVIL

The Armoury

1 The Park, Yeovil BA20 1DY
☎ *(01935) 471047* Mark Deegan

Wadworth 6X, IPA and a Butcombe brew always available plus one guest ale such as Adnams Broadside.

A traditional real ale house with one environmentally controlled bar. Patio and skittle alley. Food available at lunchtime and evenings. Children allowed in one bar.

11.30am–2.30pm and 6–11pm Mon–Thurs; all day Fri–Sun.

THE BREWERIES

BEOWULF BREWING COMPANY

Forest of Mercia, Chasewater Country Park, Pool Road, Brownhills WS8 7NL
☎ *(01543) 454067*

BEORMA 3.9% ABV
Excellent session ale. Wonderfully balanced with a malty hint of fruit giving way to a delightful lingering bitterness.
NOBLE BITTER 4.0% ABV
Very bitter, very dry and very drinkable.
WIGLAF 4.3% ABV
Traditional, golden bitter. It has a malty flavour that is married to a particularly pleasing bitterness bursting forth from the three hop varieties used.
CHASEWATER 4.4% ABV
Pale bitter with a traditional hoppy flavour and a lingering bitterness.
SWORDSMAN 4.5% ABV
Bitter beer of fruit and citrus. The beer is pale, dry and crisp and explodes with taste and aroma.
HEROES BITTER 4.7% ABV
Nutty, golden and hoppy with a slight hint of sweetness
MERCIAN SHINE 5.0% ABV
Pale bitter with a fresh, hoppy and fruity aroma and a dry finish. Its bitterness dances on the palate.

BLYTHE BREWERY

Blythe House Farm, Hamstall Ridware, WS15 3QQ

BLYTHE BITTER 4.0% ABV
CHASE BITTER 4.4% ABV
JOHNSON'S ALE 4.4% ABV
PALMER'S POISON 4.5% ABV
OLD HORNY 4.6% ABV

BURTON BRIDGE BREWERY

24 Bridge Street, Burton upon Trent DE14 1SY
☎ *(01283) 510573*

GOLDEN DELICIOUS 3.8% ABV
XL BITTER 4.0% ABV
BRIDGE BITTER 4.2% ABV
PORTER 4.5% ABV
STAIRWAY TO HEAVEN 5.0% ABV
TOP DOG STOUT 5.0% ABV
FESTIVAL ALE 5.5% ABV
Seasonals:
SPRING ALE 4.7% ABV
STAFFORDSHIRE KNOT BROWN ALE 4.8% ABV
BATTLE BREW 5.0% ABV
HEARTY ALE 5.0% ABV
Monthly Gold Medal Ales: all 4.5% ABV.

THE ECCLESHALL BREWING CO LTD

The George Inn, Castle Street, Eccleshall ST21 6DF
☎ *(01785) 850300 Fax (01785) 851452*
www.thegeorgeinn.freeserve.co.uk

MONKEY MAGIC 3.4%
A dark mild.
BITTER 3.6% ABV
Golden amber colour, hoppy with a hint of bitterness.
ORIGINAL 4.0% ABV
A distinctive amber beer, smooth and creamy.
TOP TOTTY 4.0% ABV
A light straw-coloured, fruit-flavoured beer.
PREMIUM 4.4% ABV
Strong, light and creamy. Slightly darker in appearance with a dry texture.
SHINING KNIGHT 4.5% ABV
Oak-coloured, smooth and creamy with a hoppy finish.
SUPREME 4.7% ABV
Light golden colour, fresh and fruity with a hoppy aroma.

LEEK BREWING CO LTD

c/o 12 Bridge End, Leek ST13 8LG
☎ *(01538) 388273*

STAFFORDSHIRE GOLD 3.8% ABV
STAFFORDSHIRE BITTER 4.0% ABV
LEEK PALE ALE 4.3% ABV
BLACK GROUSE 4.4% ABV
ST EDWARDS 4.7% ABV
RUDYARD RUBY ALE 4.8% ABV
DOUBLE SUNSET 5.2% ABV

MARSTON, THOMPSON & EVERSHED PLC

The Brewery, PO Box 26, Shobnall Road, Burton upon Trent DE14 2BW
☎ *(01283) 531131*

BITTER 3.8% ABV
Well-balanced, easy-drinking brew.
PEDIGREE 4.5% ABV
Smooth and rounded.
OWD RODGER 7.6% ABV
Dark and powerful, with some sweetness.
Plus seasonal brews.

MUSEUM BREWERY

Hornington Street, Burton upon Trent DE14 1YQ
☎ *(0845) 600 0598*
www.bass-museum.com

JOULES OF STONE 4.1% ABV
WORTHINGTON E 4.8% ABV
WORTHINGTON'S WHITE SHIELD 5.6% ABV
BILL TIDY COLLECTION 3.5–4.8% ABV
A selection of unique monthly brews carrying humourous names and pictures from the famous cartoonist.

TOWER BREWERY

The Old Water Tower, Walsitch Maltings, Wharf Road, Burton upon Trent DE14 1LX
☎ *(01283) 530695*

THOMAS SALT'S BITTER 3.8% ABV
TOWER BITTER 4.2% ABV
MALTY TOWERS 4.4% ABV
TOWER PALE ALE 4.8% ABV
TOWER OF STRENGTH 7.6% ABV

TOWN HOUSE BREWERY

2 Town House Studios, Town House Farm, Alsager Road, Audley ST7 8JQ
☎ *(0797) 620 9437*

AUDLEY BITTER 3.8% ABV
IPA 3.8% ABV
BARNEY'S STOUT 4.3% ABV
DARK HORSE 4.3% ABV
AUDLEY GOLD 4.5% ABV
MONUMENT ALE 4.6% ABV
TSB: TOWNHOUSE SPECIAL BITTER 5.0% ABV

THE TITANIC BREWERY

Unit 5, Callender Place, Lingard Street, Burslem, Stoke-on-Trent ST6 1JL
☎ *(01782) 823447*
www.titanicbrewery.co.uk

BEST BITTER 3.5% ABV
MILD 3.5% ABV
LIFEBOAT 3.9% ABV
ICEBERG 4.1% ABV
PREMIUM BITTER 4.1% ABV
STOUT 4.5% ABV
WHITE STAR 4.8% ABV
CAPTAIN SMITH'S STRONG ALE 5.2% ABV
Plus monthly concept beers.

THE PUBS

ABBOTS BROMLEY

The Crown Inn

Market Place, Abbots Bromley, Nr Rugeley WS15 3BS
☎ *(01283) 840227* Frank Robertson

Marston's Pedigree usually available, plus guests changed regularly. Greene King Old Speckled Hen and Abbot Ale, Fuller's London Pride, Adnams Broadside and Regatta, Wadworth 6X, brews from Wychwood and seasonal ales may feature.

Traditional village pub, part of which was a nineteenth-century coaching inn, refurbished internally. Food available, including children's menu. Lounge and bar, separate dining area, function room, six letting rooms, garden. Car park. Situated in the centre of the village, so once you've found the village, you've found the pub!

12–3pm and 6–11pm Mon–Fri; 11am–11pm Sat; 12–3pm and 7–10.30pm Sun.

ALSAGERS BANK

The Gresley Arms

High Street, Alsagers Bank ST7 8BQ
☎ *(01782) 720297* Linda Smith

A freehouse offering six regular guests, changed daily, mainly from micro-breweries. Traditional cider/scrumpy also available.

A 220-year-old country village pub that claims to have the best views in Staffordshire – it is high up, and nine counties can be seen, plus the Welsh mountains. One central bar, lounge and games room, dining room, garden and play area. Children allowed. Car park for 30 cars. Three miles from Newcastle under Lyme (look for signs for Alsagers Bank, not Alsagers).

12–3pm and 6–11pm Mon–Sat; 12–10.30pm Sun.

BIGNALL END

The Plough

Ravens Lane, Bignall End, Stoke-on-Trent
☎ *(01782) 720469* Paul Holt

Banks's Bitter permanently available, plus an ever-changing range of guest ales served on four hand pumps, usually from small, local breweries.

A traditional roadside pub. Food available lunchtimes and evenings. Children allowed if eating. Car park. Beer garden.

12–3.30pm and 7–11pm Mon–Thurs; 12–11pm Fri–Sat; 12–10.30pm Sun.

BURTON UPON TRENT

The Alfred

Derby Street, Burton upon Trent DE14 2LD
☎ *(01283) 562178*
Martin Page AMBII and Lesley Greenslade

A Burton Bridge Brewery tenancy with Bridge Bitter, Golden Delicious, Festival Ale, Burton Porter, Mild and XL Bitter permanently available. Plus one constantly changing guest which often includes a Titanic or RCH brew. Leatherbritches and Iceni also supported. Two beer festivals every year: one at Easter and one in November.

A two-bar town pub with dining area and beer garden. Food served every lunchtime and Mon–Sat evenings. Full-sized boules pitch. Children allowed.

12–11pm (10.30pm Sun).

Burton Bridge Inn

Bridge Street, Burton upon Trent DE14 1SY
☎ *(01283) 536596* Kevin McDonald

Home of the Burton Bridge Brewery with Bridge Bitter, Porter and Festival Ale always available. Seasonal ales, such as Summer Ale or Gold Medal Ale and other guests rotated on two pumps including beers from Timothy Taylor and York.

A town brewpub with two rooms (one non-smoking) and a central bar. One room features oak panelling, a quarry-tiled floor and a feature fireplace. Dining area, patio. Food served lunchtimes. Children allowed.

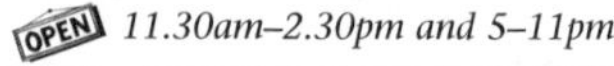 *11.30am–2.30pm and 5–11pm.*

The Devonshire Arms

86 Station Street, Burton upon Trent DE14 1BT
☎ *(01283) 562392* Joseph Stout

A Burton Bridge house with Stairway to Heaven, Bridge Bitter, Golden Delicious and Porter always available plus a frequently changing guest.

A friendly Grade II listed pub dating from the nineteenth century, on the outskirts of Burton. Public and lounge bars decorated with photographs from 1860. Food available 11.30–2.15pm and 5.30–8pm Mon–Thurs and 11.30am–8pm Fri–Sat. Also Sunday lunchtimes for traditional roasts. Children welcome. Non-smoking area, patio. Beer festivals held twice a year. Two minutes from the station.

 *11.30am–2.30pm and 5.30–11pm Mon–Thurs; 11am–11pm Fri–Sat; 12–3pm and 7–10.30pm Sun.*

The Roebuck

Station Street, Burton upon Trent DE14 1BT
☎ *(01283) 568660* Tim and Lisa Salt

Marston's Pedigree, Greene King Abbot and Old Speckled Hen, Adnams Broadside and Ruddles County always available, plus occasional guests.

Fringe-of-town pub with one open-plan room, small patio, accommodation. Bar food, including Staffordshire oatcakes, served 12–2pm Tues–Fri. Weekly quiz. No children.

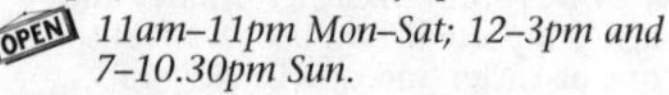 *11am–11pm Mon–Sat; 12–3pm and 7–10.30pm Sun.*

Thomas Sykes Inn

Anglesey Road, Burton upon Trent DE14 3PF
☎ *(01283) 510246* Norman Goddard

A freehouse with Marston's Pedigree usually available, plus seven or eight different guests beers per week.

A town pub born in a stable(!), with a cobblestone floor and brewery memorabilia. Bar and snug. No food. Children allowed.

 *11.30am–2.30pm and 5–11pm Mon–Thurs; all day Fri; 11.30am–2.30pm and 7–11pm Sat; 12–2.30pm and 7–10.30pm Sun.*

CHESLYN HAY

The Woodman Inn

Woodman Lane, Cheslyn Hay WS6 7ES
☎ *(01922) 413686* Mr Arton

Three guest beers, changed weekly, often include Charles Wells Bombardier, but Gale's HSB, Everards Original and Tiger, Bateman XXXB and Marston's Pedigree might also feature.

Traditional village pub dating from the 1870s, with beamed ceiling in the lounge. Having been extended, it has a conservatory, two bars, a non-smoking dining area and garden. Occasional live music. Car park. Children allowed. Can be difficult to find, as it is in a cul-de-sac location, so call for directions.

 *12–3pm and 7–11pm (midnight for diners) Mon–Thurs; 11am–11pm Fri–Sat; 12.30–3pm and 7–11pm Sun.*

CODSALL

Codsall Station

Chapel Lane, Codsall WV8 2EH
☎ *(01902) 847061*

Holden's brews such as Black Country Bitter, Golden Glow and Special plus ever-changing guests.

Located in converted railway buildings and hosting an annual beer festival in September. An award-winning pub with bar, lounge and conservatory. Food available (not Sun evenings).

 *11.30am–2.30pm and 5–11pm Mon–Fri; all day Sat–Sun.*

DOSTHILL

The Fox

105 High Street, Dosthill B77 1LQ
☎ *01827 280847* Mr Gwyn

Greene King Abbot is one of the beers permanently on offer, with the two guests often including something from Church End, or perhaps Fuller's London Pride, Everards Lazy Daze or a Burton Bridge brew.

Village pub on the outskirts of Tamworth in a traditional Victorian building, more than 140 years old. Food available. Lounge and bar, non-smoking dining area, conservatory/restaurant, garden. Children allowed in lounge if eating, but not in the bar. Car park. On the main road out of Tamworth.

 *12–3pm and 6–11pm Mon–Sat; 12–3pm and 7–10.30pm Sun.*

ECCLESHALL

The George Hotel

Castle Street, Eccleshall ST21 6DF
☎ *(01785) 850300* Gerard and Moyra Slater

The Eccleshall Brewery is located on the premises, so the Slaters Ales range of up to six beers are brewed and available here.

Opened in March 1995 by Gerard and Moyra Slater. The beer is brewed by their son, Andrew. The brewery is a 20-barrel plant. The George is a sixteenth-century coaching inn with olde-worlde beams, log fires, real ales, malt whisky. Bar and restaurant food available. Car park. Accommodation. Children and dogs welcome.

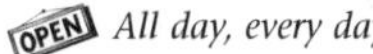
All day, every day.

ETRURIA

The Plough Inn

147 Etruria Road, Stoke-on-Trent ST1 5NS
☎ *(01782) 269445* Rob Ward

A Robinson's tied house serving Hatters Dark Mild, Best Bitter, Double Hop and seasonal ales. Hartleys XB and Old Stockport Bitter might also put in an appearance.

Country-style 150-year-old pub with a collection of valve radios, old TVs, gramophones, telephones, bottled beers and local pictures, plus a preserved classic bus. Originally two cottages, then a greengrocers. Well-known locally for good food, which is available 12–2pm Mon–Sat and 6.30–9pm every day. Small beer garden, car park. Children welcome if dining.

12–2.30pm and 7–11pm Mon–Sat; 7–10.30pm Sun.

FAZELEY

The Plough & Harrow

Atherstone Street, Fazeley B78 3RF
☎ *(01827) 289596* Paul and Lorna Kilby

Two brews always available, including something from Adnams plus a guest, changed weekly.

A 300-year-old one-bar village pub, first licensed in 1801. Beer garden. En-suite accommodation. Restaurant with food served at lunchtime and evenings. Beer garden. Children allowed. Close to Drayton Manor Park, Belfry, Tamworth Castle and the Snowdome.

11.30am–3pm and 5.30–11pm Mon–Thurs; all day Fri–Sun.

GREAT CHATWELL

The Red Lion Inn

Great Chatwell, Nr Newport TF10 9BJ
☎ *(01952) 691366* Mrs Paula Smith

Everards Beacon Bitter and Tiger regularly available, plus three guest beers, perhaps from Charles Wells, Robinson's, Wood, Hook Norton, Mansfield, Shepherd Neame, Eccleshall, Lichfield and many others.

Traditional, ivy-clad pub, attracting a mixed clientele. Food served evenings only Mon–Fri, all day at weekends and bank holidays. Car park. Children's play area with animals and birds.

5.30–11pm Mon–Fri; 12–11pm Sat and bank holidays; 12–10.30pm Sun.

HARRISEAHEAD

The Royal Oak

42 High Street, Harriseahead, Stoke-on-Trent ST7 4JT
☎ *(01782) 513362* Michael Clowes

A true freehouse with three ever-changing guest ales from breweries such as Oakham, Whim and Tower, to name but three. Belgian Leffe and German Erdinger are available on draught, and a wide selection of Belgian bottled beers are also on offer.

A traditional village pub with bar and lounge. Basic bar snacks available. Car park. No children.

7–11pm Mon–Fri; 12–3pm and 7–11pm Sat–Sun.

IPSTONES

The Linden Tree

47 Froghall Road, Ipstones, Stoke-on-Trent ST10 2NA
☎ *(01538) 266370* Graham Roberts
www.thelindentree.co.uk

A freehouse with Timothy Taylor Landlord permanently available, plus two guest ales.

A country pub with separate 50-seater non-smoking restaurant. Beer garden. Food served at lunchtime and evenings. Children allowed.

12–3pm and 6–11pm (10.30pm Sun).

KIDSGROVE

The Blue Bell

25 Hardingswood, Kidsgrove, Stoke-on-Trent ST7 1EG
☎ *(01782) 774052* David Washbrook

A genuine freehouse serving six frequently changing guests (1700 in six years) from small and micro-breweries, including beers from Archers, Whim, Titanic, Oakham, Burton Bridge, Eccleshall, Town House, and many more. Real cider and quality Belgian and German bottled beers also on offer.

Smallish, four-room, out-of-town pub just north of the Potteries, on an island at the junction of the Trent & Mersey and Macclesfield Canals. CAMRA Potteries Pub of the Year 1999, 2000, 2001 and 2003, and CAMRA Staffordshire Pub of the Year 2000, 2001 and 2002. No juke box, no pool, no fruit machines. Outside drinking area to the front and garden to the rear. Basic snacks at weekends. Dog-friendly, no children. Car Park. Five minutes' walk from Kidsgrove Station along canal towpath.

 *7.30–11pm Tues–Fri; 1–4.30pm and 7–11pm Sat; 12–4.30pm and 7–10.30pm Sun; closed Mon except bank holidays.*

KINVER

The Plough & Harrow

High Street, Kinver DY7 6HD
☎ *(01384) 872659* Mrs Shirley

Four pumps serve bitter and three serve mild, with Batham Bitter and Mild always on offer.

Traditional village pub, over 100 years old, with L-shaped lounge and small patio area. Food is available from a limited menu. Live music Thursday evenings. Car park. Well-behaved children allowed. Four miles from Stourbridge.

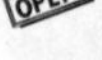 *6–11pm Mon–Thurs; 5–11pm Fri; 11am–11pm Sat; 12–10.30pm Sun.*

LEEK

The Bull's Head

35 St Edward Street, Leek ST13 5DS
☎ *(01538) 370269* Vicki

A freehouse featuring beers from the Leek Brewing Company, two or three at a time, plus occasional guests.

Long, thin pub, with a lively atmosphere at weekends and quieter in the week. Pool table and darts at one end, pin-ball machine at the other. Ample street parking. Children and dogs welcome.

 *5–11pm Mon, Tues, Thurs; 12–11pm Wed and Fri; all day Sat–Sun.*

Den Engel

23 St Edward Street, Leek ST13 5DR
☎ *(01538) 373751* Geoff and Hilary Turner

Four constantly changing guest beers are on offer, and small independents and micros are favoured.

Imposing street-corner building, housing impressive continental-style bar. Excellent beer selection, including over 120 Belgian bottled beers and six Belgian beers on tap. Bar food available Wed–Thurs and Sun evenings, lunchtime and evening Fri and lunchtimes only Sat. A separate restaurant is open Thurs–Sat evenings. Ample street parking.

 *5–11pm Mon–Thurs; 12–11pm Fri–Sat; 12–3pm and 7–10.30pm Sun.*

The Swan Hotel

2 St Edward Street, Leek ST13 5DS
☎ *(01538) 382081* David and Julie Ellerton

Three or four rotating guests on offer. Wadworth 6X, Wychwood Hobgoblin and Robinson's Frederics are regular features, plus seasonal specials.

A four-bar town-style pub in moorlands, with an additional bar called JD's attached, which is a young person's modern themed sports bar. Food served at lunchtime and evenings. Children allowed. Function room. Bridal suite.

 *11am–3pm and 7–11.30pm.*

The Wilkes Head

16 St Edward Street, Leek ST13 5DA
☎ *(01538) 383616*

The Whim Ales flagship pub, with Hartington Bitter and IPA, Magic Mushroom Mild, and Whim Arbor Light always available, plus an ever-changing range of guest ales from around the country. Seasonal ales such as Whim Black Christmas and Old Isaak stocked when available.

An award-winning town pub, famous for its ales. Small and cosy with large beer garden. Children and dogs welcome.

All day, every day.

LICHFIELD

The Hogshead

12–14 Tamworth Street, Lichfield WS13 6JJ
☎ *(01543) 258925* Mia Higgins

Hook Norton Old Hooky, Timothy Taylor Landlord and Marston's Pedigree are among the permanent beers here. Two guests, changed monthly, sometimes include a brew from Lichfield Brewery.

A one-bar drinkers' pub, with food available. Beer festivals held two or three times a year (call for details). Children not allowed. Situated in the town centre.

 *11am–11pm Mon–Sat; 12–10.30pm Sun.*

The Queen's Head
Queen Street, Lichfield WS13 6QD
☎ *(01543) 410932* Roy Harvey

Adnams Best, Timothy Taylor Landlord and Marston's Pedigree always available, plus two guests, rotating weekly, including beers from all over the British Isles.

A traditional, small, backstreet pub. No music, small TV, one games machine. Bar food available at lunchtime (12–2.30pm), but the pub is really famous for its selection of cheeses, of which up to 20 different ones are available all day.

 *All day Mon–Sat; 12–3pm and 7–10.30pm Sun.*

PENKRIDGE

The Star Inn
Market Place, Penkridge, Stafford ST19 5DJ
☎ *(01785) 712513* Rachel and Marcus Riley

Banks's Original and Bitter usually available plus one guest ale from Mansfield or Marston's.

An olde-worlde traditional pub set in a scenic village. Food 12–2.30pm and 5–7pm Tues–Fri, 12–6pm Sat–Sun. Car park.

11am–11pm Mon–Sat; 12–10.30pm Sun.

STAFFORD

The Stafford Arms
43 Railway Street, Stafford
☎ *(01785) 253313* Marie Mullaney

Titanic Best and White Star always available, plus seven guests, a traditional cider and various imported bottled beer.

A traditional pub with bar food available at lunchtimes. West Midlands Charity Pub of the Year 2001, with regular charity events held. Car park, bar billiards. Just by the railway station.

12–11pm Mon–Sat; 12–4pm and 7–10.30pm Sun.

Tap & Spile
Peel Terrace, Stafford ST16 3HE
☎ *(01785) 223563* Mr S Tideswell

A selection of eight constantly changing cask ales always available (around 1000 per year).

A village pub. CAMRA Stafford and Stone Pub of the Year 2002. Non-smoking dining area, beer garden. No food. No children.

All day, every day.

STOKE-ON-TRENT

Hogshead
2–6 Percy Street, Hanley, Stoke-on-Trent ST1 1NF
☎ *(01782) 209585* Brett Ritzkowski

A Whitbread house with an extensive range of cask ales always available. Greene King Old Speckled Hen and Wadworth 6X on permanently, plus a range of six guests such as Titanic Best or Premium. Each month one beer is featured as Beer of the Month on special offer (buy three get one free).

A town pub in a city-centre location. One bar, disabled access and lift. Non-smoking area. Food available all day. Children allowed before 6pm.

All day, every day.

The Tontine Alehouse
20 Tontine Street, Hanley, Stoke-on-Trent ST1 1AQ
☎ *(01782) 263890* Becky Smith

Marston's Pedigree always available, plus four weekly changing guest ales from independent breweries all over the country.

A one-bar, city-centre pub with beer garden. Food served at lunchtime only. Children allowed, if eating.

All day Mon–Sat; closed Sun.

STONE

The Pheasant Inn
Old Road, Stone ST15 8HS
☎ *(01785) 814603* Lynne Keever

A range of traditional cask ales from independent breweries always available.

A Victorian two-bar pub on the outskirts of town, with a dining room and a child-safe beer garden with lockable access though the pub. Darts and traditional pub games. No food at present, though there are plans (phone to check). Children allowed, if accompanied and if eating.

All day, every day.

The Star Inn
Stafford Road, Stone ST15 8QW
☎ *(01785) 813096* Michael Wheeler

Banks's Bitter and Original and Marston's Pedigree always available plus two guests such as Camerons Strongarm.

An edge-of-town pub situated by the canal with access to the towpath. Two bars, garden and patio. Food available all day. Children allowed.

All day, every day.

WHISTON

The Swan Inn

Whiston, Nr Penkridge ST19 5QH
(01785) 716200 Jim Davies

Holden's Bitter and Banks's Original permanently available plus two or three guests mostly from smaller breweries such as Titanic, Church End, Wood, Hanby, Jennings and Slaters. Some 400 different beers served over three years.

Set in six acres in a rural location, this extended pub has a traditional bar, open fireplaces, a non-smoking dining room and a beer garden with children's play area. Food available in the evenings, plus all day Sat–Sun. Children allowed. Car park. Situated two miles off the main road, find Whiston and you find the pub!

OPEN *6–11pm Mon–Fri; all day Sat–Sun.*

THE BREWERIES

ADNAMS & CO. PLC

Sole Bay Brewery, East Green, Southwold IP18 6JW
☎ (01502) 727200
www.adnams.co.uk

BITTER 3.7% ABV
Clean and well-hopped, with fruity flavours.

BROADSIDE 4.7% ABV
Powerful malty brew with balancing hoppiness.

Seasonals:

REGATTA 4.3% ABV
Apr–Aug.

FISHERMAN 4.5% ABV
Sep–end Feb.

TALLY HO % ABV VARIABLE
Dec. Gravity decided on brew day.

Plus other seasonal brews.

EARL SOHAM BREWERY

The Victoria, Earl Soham, Woodbridge IP13 7RT
☎ (01728) 684097
www.earlsohambrewery.co.uk

GANNET MILD 3.0% ABV

VICTORIA BITTER 3.6% ABV

ALBERT ALE 4.6% ABV

Seasonals:

EDWARD ALE 4.0% ABV
Summer only.

SIR ROGER'S PORTER 4.0% ABV
Winter only.

JOLABRUG 5.0% ABV
Christmas ale.

GREEN DRAGON BREWERY

29 Broad Street, Bungay NR35 1EF
☎ (01986) 892681

MILD 3.4% ABV

CHAUCER ALE 3.7% ABV

BRIDGE STREET BITTER 4.5%ABV

DRAGON 5.5% ABV

GREENE KING PLC

Westgate Brewery, Abbot House, Bury St Edmunds IP33 1QT
☎ (01284) 763222
www.greeneking.co.uk

GREEN KING XX MILD 3.0% ABV

IPA 3.6% ABV

RUDDLES COUNTY 4.9% ABV

ABBOT ALE 5.0% ABV

OLD SPECKLED HEN 5.2% ABV

STRONG SUFFOLK VINTAGE ALE 6.0% ABV

HEN'S TOOTH 6.5% ABV

KINGS HEAD BREWERY

132 High Street, Bildeston IP7 7ED
☎ (01449) 741434
www.bildestonkingshead.co.uk

NSB 2.8% ABV
Low-alcohol beer.

BEST BITTER 3.8% ABV

LYNX 3.9% ABV

BLONDIE 4.0% ABV

FIRST GOLD 4.3% ABV

HERSBRUCKER BIER 4.3% ABV

APACHE 4.5% ABV

BILLY 4.8% ABV

CROWDIE 5.0% ABV

JJ'S LEMON BITTER 5.0% ABV

DARK VADER 5.4% ABV
Complex, roast character.

MAULDONS BREWERY

The Blackadder Brewery, 7 Addison Road, Chilton Industrial Estate, Sudbury CO10 2YW
☎ (01787) 311055
www.mauldons.co.uk

MAULDONS BITTER 3.6% ABV

MOLE TRAP 3.8% ABV

DICKENS 4.0% ABV
Pale with hoppy fruit flavour and dry in the aftertaste.

PEGGOTTY'S PORTER 4.1% ABV

PICKWICK BITTER 4.2% ABV
Formerly known as Squires.

SUFFOLK PRIDE 4.8% ABV
Powerful hoppiness throughout.

BLACK ADDER 5.3% ABV
Stout.

WHITE ADDER 5.3% ABV

Plus seasonals.

NETHERGATE BREWERY CO. LTD

11–13 High Street, Clare CO10 8NY
☎ *(01787) 277244*
www.nethergate.co.uk

IPA 3.5% ABV
Clean hop flavour.
PRIORY MILD 3.5% ABV
UMBEL ALE 3.8% ABV
Distinctive hoppy and coriander flavours.
SUFFOLK COUNTY BEST BITTER 4.0% ABV
Malty and bitter.
AUGUSTINIAN ALE 4.5% ABV
OLD GROWLER 5.0% ABV
Soft, chocolate malt flavours.
UMBEL MAGNA 5.0% ABV
Porter with coriander.
Plus monthly seasonal brews.

OLD CANNON BREWERY

86 Cannon Street, Bury St Edmunds IP33 IJP
☎ *(01284) 768769*
www.oldcannon.co.uk

OLD CANNON BEST BITTER 3.8%ABV
POWDER MONKEY 4.6% ABV
GUNNER'S DAUGHTER 5.5% ABV

OLD CHIMNEYS BREWERY

Hopton End Farm, Church Road, Market Weston, Diss IP22 2NX
☎ *(01359) 221013*

MILITARY MILD 3.4% ABV
SWALLOWTAIL IPA 3.6% ABV
Plus seasonal and occasional brews.

OULTON ALES LTD

Oulton Broad Brewery, Unit 2, Harbour Road Industrial Estate, Oulton Road, Lowestoft NR32 3LZ
☎ *(01502) 587905*

OULTON BITTER 3.5% ABV
A hoppy light bitter with a slight malty sweetness and a flowery aroma.
MUTFORD MILD 3.7% ABV
A full-flavoured dark mild. The rich mellow flavour of chocolate and caramel combined with a good hop aroma.
NAUTILUS 4.2% ABV
A traditional IPA, lovely copper colour with well-balanced malt and hops throughout and a developing fruitiness.
WINDSWEPT 4.5% ABV
A dark copper-coloured best bitter with a subtle sweetness with a gentle aroma, perfect for autumn evenings.
EXCELSIOR LT47 4.6% ABV
A light golden ale, fresh on the palate with carefully balanced hops to give a grapefruit and lemony taste and aroma.
GONE FISHING 5% ABV
A dark ruby-coloured premium strong bitter, full-flavoured fruity and malty.
KEELHAUL 6.5% ABV
ROARING BOY 8.5% ABV
Matured for over a year, this strong continental-style light-coloured bitter is deceptively strong.

Seasonal ales:
BEEDAZZLED 4% ABV
A fresh golden ale with malt hops and honey.
SUNRISE 4% ABV
Top-class summer ale brewed with hand-picked elderflowers to give an excellent all-round beer.
WET & WINDY 4.3% ABV
A rich, dark copper-coloured brew with lots of hops, full of flavour with a well-rounded finish.

ST PETER'S BREWERY CO. LTD

St Peter's Hall, St Peter, South Elmham, Bungay NR35 1NQ
☎ *(01986) 782322*
www.stpetersbrewery.co.uk

BEST BITTER 3.7% ABV
EXTRA 4.4% ABV
Hoppy, porter-style beer.
FRUIT BEER (ELDERBERRY) 4.7% ABV
Wheat beer with added elderberry.
FRUIT BEER (GRAPEFRUIT) 4.7% ABV
Refreshing citrus fruit flavour.
GOLDEN ALE 4.7% ABV
MILD 4.7% ABV
Smooth and delicate traditional mild.
SPICED ALE 4.7% ABV
Lemon and ginger flavour.
WHEAT BEER 4.7% ABV
Refreshing and clear with an individual taste.
HONEY PORTER 5.1% ABV
Original-style porter with honey.
OLD STYLE PORTER 5.1% ABV
Original porter. Blend of old ale and younger bitter.
STRONG ALE 5.1% ABV
Smooth, soft and well-rounded.
SUMMER ALE 6.5% ABV

THE PUBS

ALDEBURGH

The Mill Inn

Market Cross Place, Aldeburgh IP15 5BJ
☎ *(01728) 452563* Ted and Sheila Flemming

Tied to Adnams, with Adnams Bitter and Broadside always on offer, plus seasonal Adnams guests, usually Regatta in summer and Fisherman in winter.

Seaside pub in a seventeenth-century building next to the the beach. Food available. Three small bars, restaurant, letting rooms (three doubles, one single). Children allowed.

OPEN *Summer: 11am–11pm Mon–Sat; 12–10.30pm Sun. Winter: 11am–3pm and 6–11pm Mon–Thurs; 11am–11pm Fri–Sat; 12–10.30pm Sun.*

BARHAM

The Sorrel Horse

Old Norwich Road, Barham IP6 0PG
☎ *(01473) 830327* Matthew Smith
www.sorrelhorse.co.uk

Adnams Bitter and Shepherd Neame Spitfire always available. One guest, changed every six months, might be something from Adnams.

Country pub in a building dating from the fifteenth century, with one large bar, beams and open fireplaces. Food is available, and there is a dining area. Garden, eight letting rooms. Very occasional live music. Children's play area. Large car park. Situated opposite the Health Farm.Food served 12–2pm and 6.30–10pm daily.

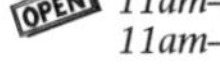 *11am–3pm and 5–11.30pm Mon–Fri; 11am–11.30pm Sat; 12–10.30pm Sun.*

BILDESTON

The Kings Head Hotel

132 High Street, Bildeston, Ipswich IP7 7ED
☎ *(01449) 741434/741719*
James Kevin Harrison

The Kings Head Brewery is located on the same premises, although run as a separate concern. However, Kings Head Best Bitter, First Gold, Billy and Old Chimneys Mild regularly available, plus a guest beer often from Old Chimneys, Iceni, Buffy's, Wolf, Mighty Oak, Mauldons or Nethergate.

Fifteenth-century timber-framed building with original wattle and daub, situated in a small village. Food served 12–3pm and 7–9.30pm daily. Car park. Children welcome. Accommodation and holiday flat available.

 *11am–3pm and 5–11pm Mon–Fri; 11am–11pm Sat; 12–10.30pm Sun.*

BOXFORD

White Hart Inn

Broad Street, Boxford CO10 5DX
☎ *(01787) 211071* Marilyn and Barry Hayton
www.white-hart.co.uk

Greene King IPA and Adnams Broadside regularly available, plus two guest beers perhaps from Adnams, Fuller's, Mauldons, Lidstones, Cottage, Wye Valley, Bartrams, Bateman, Charles Wells or Hobgoblin.

Sixteenth-century village pub with garden and separate non-smoking dining room, home to the local cricket and classic motorcycle clubs. Free quiz night every Sunday. Food served 12–2.30pm and 6–9.30pm Mon–Sat, 12–2.30pm and 7–8.30pm Sun. Children welcome and smaller food portions provided.

 *12–3pm and 6–11pm Mon–Sat; 12–3pm and 7–10.30pm Sun.*

BRANDON

The White Horse

White Horse Street, Brandon IP27 0LB
☎ *(01842) 815767* David Marsh

Ridleys Tolly Original, Greene King IPA and Iceni Fine Soft Day usually available plus a variable number of guests, perhaps from Iceni, Mauldons, Wolf, Nethergate, Old Chimneys or Greene King.

Friendly, family-run freehouse with sporting bias, supporting several darts teams and a successful football team. No food. Car park. Well-behaved children welcome until 8pm. From London Road (by industrial estate), turn into Crown Street. Take the second of two close left turns into White Horse Street.

 *11am–11pm Mon–Sat; 12–10.30pm Sun.*

BROME

The Cornwallis Country Hotel and Restaurant

Brome, Eye IP23 8AJ
☎ *(01379) 870326* Peter Bartlett
www.thecornwallis.com

St Peter's Best Best and Adnams Bitter usually available plus a guest such as Greene King IPA changed every couple of months.

A former Dower House built in 1561, heavily timbered with a well in the bar. Set in 20 acres of gardens with fine yew topiary, water gardens and ducks. Bar and restaurant food served 12–2.30pm and 6–9.30pm (9pm Sun). Children welcome. Sixteen bedrooms and function rooms for private hire. Car parking.

 *7am–11pm (10.30pm Sun).*

BUNGAY

The Chequers Inn

23 Bridge Street, Bungay NR35 1HD
☎ *(01986) 893579* Michael Plunkett

A freehouse with Adnams Best, Fuller's London Pride, Timothy Taylor Landlord and Shepherd Neame Master Brew and Spitfire and Ethel Plunkett Stout always available plus two other real ales, changing frequently.

A seventeenth-century, two-bar traditional town alehouse with log fire, large beer garden and patio. Food available Mon–Sat 12–2.30pm (ish!). Large play area for children. Outside bar facilities available and bandstand for charity events and beer festivals

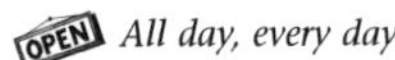 *All day, every day.*

The Green Dragon

29 Broad Street, Bungay NR35 1EE
☎ *(01986) 892681* William and Rob Pickard

Adnams Best is always available and the four beers from the Green Dragon range are brewed and served on the premises.

The pub was bought in 1991 from Brent Walker by William and Rob Pickard. The three-barrel brewery was built and the pub refurbished. Due to increased demand, a second brewery was then built and the capacity expanded to eight barrels. The Green Dragon is a popular pub with a friendly atmosphere. Bar food is available at lunchtime and evenings. Car park, garden, children's room.

OPEN *11am–3pm and 5–11pm Mon–Thurs; 11am–11pm Fri–Sat; 12–3pm and 7–10.30pm Sun.*

BURY ST EDMUNDS

The Old Cannon Brewery

86 Cannon Street, Bury St Edmonds IP33 1JP
☎ *(01284) 768769* Carole Locker

The full range of Old Cannon Brewery beers are brewed on the premises and are permanently available in the pub. Also featuring Adnams Best Bitter, two guest beers usually from local Suffolk or Norfolk independents.

Previously a Victorian brewhouse (brewing stopped in 1917). Now half restaurant, half bar, with unique stainless steel brewery sited in the bar. Brewing again since 2000 with brewings done on Mondays, so pub is closed at lunchtime that day. Food available every other lunchtime and every evening. No children under 14. B&B accommodation. Situated parallel to Northgate Street, off the A14 and five minutes from station.

OPEN *12–3pm Tues–Sun; 5–11pm Mon–Sat; 7–10.30pm Sun.*

The Queen's Head

39 Churchgate Street, Bury St Edmunds IP33 1RG
☎ *(01284) 761554* Don and Jan Rutherford
www.queensheadbury.co.uk

A true freehouse with Adnams Broadside and Best Bitter and Nethergate IPA always available, plus occasional guests. Regular long happy hours, with 50p off selected ales.

Totally refurbished in 2002, this popular town-centre pub has a mixed clientele during the day and a younger crowd in the evenings. One big bar with non-smoking dining area plus conservatory, games room and patio. An extensive menu plus daily specials is available all day, every day. Children welcome everywhere apart from the central bar area.

OPEN *All day, every day.*

The Rose & Crown

48 Whiting Street, Bury St Edmunds IP33 1NP
☎ *(01284) 755934* AP and AE Fayers

Greene King XX Dark Mild, IPA and Abbot are permanently served, plus occasional guests.

An original street-corner local in the same street as the Greene King Brewery. The pub has been with the same family for around 30 years. Food served 12–2pm Mon–Sat.

OPEN *11.30am–11pm Mon–Fri; 11.30am–3pm and 7–11pm Sat; 12–2.30pm and 7–10.30pm Sun.*

CARLTON COLVILLE

The Bell Inn

82 The Street, Carlton Colville, Lowestoft NR33 8JR
☎ *(01502) 582873*

Oulton Bitter and Nautilus always available, plus seasonal specials from Oulton Ales and guest breweries, all served straight from the barrel.

A village pub and restaurant with original flagstone floor and open fires. One long bar, disabled access, beer garden. Food available at lunchtime and evenings. Children allowed.

OPEN *11am–3pm and 4–11pm Mon–Thurs; all day Fri–Sun.*

EARL SOHAM

The Victoria

Earl Soham, Woodbridge IP13 7RL
☎ *(01728) 685758* Paul Hooper

Home to the Earl Soham Brewery, the full range is usually available.

A very traditional pub with tiled floors, wooden decor and several interesting pictures of Queen Victoria. No frills, just good beer, food and conversation. Food served lunchtimes and evenings. Car park. Children welcome. Beer garden.

OPEN *11.30am–3pm and 5.30–11pm Mon–Sat; 12–3pm and 7–10.30pm Sun.*

EAST BERGHOLT

The Red Lion

The Street, East Bergholt CO7 6TB
☎ *(01206) 298332* Rick and Dawn Brogan

Tied to Ridleys, with IPA and Old Bob the permanent beers.

Village country pub, 300–400 years old, with three fireplaces. Two bars – one has restaurant/family room attached. Live music in garden occasionally on bank holidays. Car park, family en-suite letting room. Children allowed in family eating area. Centrally located in the village, close to Flatford Mill and Constable country.

11am–3pm and 6–11pm Mon–Fri; 11am–11pm Sat; 12–10.30pm Sun.

EDWARDSTONE

The White Horse Inn

Mill Green, Edwardstone, Sudbury CO10 5PX
☎ *(01787) 211211* Mrs Baker

A freehouse with Greene King IPA plus a frequently changing mild always available (perhaps Elgood's Black Dog). Also two guests from local breweries or those further afield such as Cottage.

A two-bar village pub with log fires in winter. Beer garden. Caravan and camping club on site for five caravans. There are two self-catering cottages, each sleeping up to six people, in the pub grounds, available for holiday lets. Food available at lunchtime and evenings. Children allowed.

12–2pm Tues–Sun (closed Mon lunchtime); 6.30–11pm Mon–Sat (10.30pm Sun).

FELIXSTOWE

The Half Moon

303 High Street, Walton, Felixstowe
☎ *(01394) 216009* Patrick Wroe

An Adnams tied house, so Adnams beers always available, plus two guests, such as Fuller's London Pride or Everards Tiger.

Old-fashioned, friendly alehouse. No food, no fruit machine, no music. Darts, cribbage, backgammon. Garden, children's play area, car park.

12–2.30pm and 5–11pm Mon–Fri; 12–11pm Sat; 12–3pm and 7–10.30pm Sun.

FRAMSDEN

The Dobermann

The Street, Framsden IP14 6HG
☎ *(01473) 890461* Mrs Sue Frankland

Adnams Best and Broadside always available and guests such as Mauldons Moletrap.

A 400-year-old, traditional thatched and beamed Suffolk village pub. Extensive menu of bar food available. Non-smoking area. Car park, garden, accommodation. No children. Easy to find off B1077.

12–3pm and 7–11pm; closed Mon except bank holidays, and Sunday evenings.

FRECKENHAM

The Golden Boar

The Street, Freckenham, Bury St Edmunds IP28 8HZ
☎ *(01638) 723000* Kate Strachan

A freehouse with four pumps serving a range of real ales. Adnams Best, Woodforde's Wherry and Nethergate brews are regulars, plus specials and seasonals such as Charles Wells Summer Solstice.

The only pub in Freckenham, this is a restored old-style country village pub with old brickwork and fireplaces, separate dining area and garden. Food available at lunchtime and evenings. Children allowed. En-suite accommodation available.

All day Mon–Sat; 12–4pm Sun.

GISLINGHAM

Six Bells

High Street, Gislingham, Eye IP23 8JD
☎ *(01379) 783349* Mr Buttle

A freehouse with Adnams Best Bitter always available plus two guests changing monthly and not repeating, if possible. Shepherd Neame Spitfire and Brakspear ales are examples of previous guests.

A traditional one-bar village pub with non-smoking dining area and disabled facilities. No fruit machines, no pool table. Food available Tues–Sun lunchtimes and evenings. Children allowed. Function room. Situated near Thornham Walks.

12–3pm and 6.30–11pm (10.30pm Sun).

GREAT WENHAM

The Queen's Head

Great Wenham
☎ *(01473) 310590* M Harris

A freehouse with Adnams Best and Greene King IPA and Abbot always on offer, plus one guest, perhaps from Mauldons, Crouch Vale, Woodforde's, Bateman or Fuller's.

Early-Victorian red-brick cottage-style pub in a pleasant rural location, run by the same licensee for fifteen years and catering for a mixed clientele (mainly aged over 25). English and Indian food is served 12–2pm and 7–9pm (not Sun evenings or Mondays), and booking is advisable. An extension has created a non-smoking dining area. Children allowed at lunchtimes only, and not in the bar (advisable to phone in advance). Car park.

 *12–2.30pm and 6.30–11pm Mon–Sat; 12–2.30pm and 7–10.30pm Sun.*

HASKETON

The Turk's Head Inn

Low Road, Hasketon, Woodbridge IP13 6JG
☎ *(01394) 382584* Kirsty Lambert

Ales from Greene King and Adnams always on offer, plus guest beers.

A country village pub with huge log fires and low beams, decorated with brewery memorabilia and antiques. Food available at lunchtimes and evenings, ranging from light snacks to a full menu. Children's menu. No food on Mondays. Beer garden and patio. Camping and caravaning in three acres of meadow. Children welcome.

 *6–11pm Mon (closed Mon lunchtime); 12–3pm and 6–11pm Tues–Sat; 12–4pm and 7–10.30pm Sun.*

IPSWICH

The Cricketers

51 Crown Street, Ipswich IP1 3JA
☎ *(01473) 225910* Nicola Harney

A Wetherspoon's pub. Shepherd Neame Spitfire is among the brews always available plus three guests such as Hop Back Summer Lightning and a range of bottled beers.

A town-centre pub. Large non-smoking area and two beer gardens. Food available all day. Children allowed up to 6pm if eating.

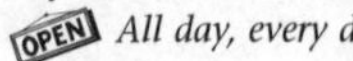 *All day, every day.*

The Dove Street Inn

76 St Helens Street, Ipswich IP4 2LA
☎ *(01473) 211270)*
www.dovestreetinn.co.uk

A huge rotating range of real ales, many from East Anglian brewers such as Adnams, Woodfordes, Mauldons, Crouch Vale etc. But other interesting brews also come from further afield.

A former Tap & Spile relaunched in February 2004 by Real East Anglian Cask Houses Ltd. A beer festival was held in August 2004.

 *12–2.30pm and 5–11pm Mon–Thurs. 12–11pm Fri–Sat. Closed Sun*

The Fat Cat

288 Spring Road, Ipswich IP4 5NL
☎ *(01473) 726524* John Keatley
www.fatcatipswich.co.uk

A freehouse with 16–20 real ales served straight from the barrel and rotating all the time. Woodforde's Wherry and Adnams brews are regular features.

A spit and sawdust pub with wooden floor, no music or machines, but 96-year-old tin pub sign. One bar, beer garden. CAMRA Suffolk Pub of the Year 1998 and 2002. Rolls available at lunchtime. Well-behaved children and dogs allowed. On the outskirts of town.

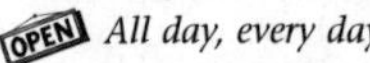 *All day, every day.*

The Steamboat

78 New Cut West, Ipswich IP2 8HW
☎ *(01473) 601902* Alfred Codona

A Ridleys tenancy serving Prospect, Original and IPA, plus one guest from Ridleys, such as Old Bob.

A traditional riverside pub (formerly the Steamboat ticket office) with live music at night. Large beer garden and riverside views. The pub is available for private hire.

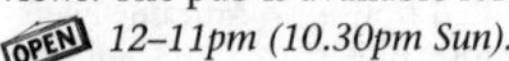 *12–11pm (10.30pm Sun).*

KERSEY

The Bell

Kersey
☎ *(01473) 823229* Paul Denton

Three or four beers always available plus brews from a guest list including Shepherd Neame Spitfire, Fuller's London Pride, Adnams Bitter and Greene King Abbot.

Built in 1380, a timber-framed Tudor-style property with log fires and cobbles. Bar and restaurant food available at lunchtime and evenings. Car park, garden, private dining room. Children allowed. Signposted from Hadleigh.

 *11am–3pm and 6.30–11pm Mon–Sat; 12–3pm and 7–10.30pm Sun.*

LAVENHAM

The Angel Hotel

Market Place, Lavenham CO10 9QZ
☎ *(01787) 247388*
Roy Whitworth and John Barry
www.lavenham.co.uk/angel

Adnams Bitter, Nethergate Suffolk and Old Growler plus Greene King IPA usually available, with one guest beer from a Suffolk brewery changed every month.

Family-run inn in the centre of Lavenham, first licensed in 1420 and specialising in beers from East Anglia. Award-winning food served 12–2.15pm and 6.45–9.15pm Mon–Sun. Bookings advisable for weekends. Children welcome, high chairs supplied. Car park. Eight en-suite bedrooms. No smoking throughout.

OPEN *11am–11pm Mon–Sat; 12–10.30pm Sun.*

LAXFIELD

The King's Head Inn

Gorams Mill Lane, Laxfield, Woodbridge IP13 8DW
☎ *(01986) 798395*
George and Maureen Coleman

An Adnams house with all beers served straight from the barrel in the tap room. Adnams Best, Broadside and Regatta always available plus one of Adnams' seasonal ales.

Known locally as The Low House, this is a well-preserved 600-year-old country village pub. East Anglian and Suffolk CAMRA Pub of the Year 2000. Food served 12–2pm and 7–9pm daily. Beer garden. Music on Tuesdays. Separate dining room and card room. Children allowed in specified areas.

11am–3pm and 6–11pm Mon–Sat; 12–3pm and 7–10.30pm Sun (ring for confirmation).

LOWESTOFT

The Crown Hotel

High Street, Lowestoft NR32 1HR
☎ *(01502) 534808* Chris and Sabrina

Greene King Abbot and IPA are permanent features.

A town pub with wooden floors and winter fires. Food available 12–3pm every day. Patio. Children allowed if eating.

OPEN *All day, every day.*

The Oak Tavern

73 Crown Street West, Lowestoft NR32 1SQ
☎ *(01502) 537246* Jim and Debbie Baldwin

Woodforde's Oak Tavern Ale and Greene King Abbot Ale usually available plus two guest beers, perhaps from Woodforde's, Buffy's, Wolf, Elgood's, Adnams or Bateman breweries.

Friendly community pub, specialising in real ale and Belgian beers, with a separate pool and darts area, plus Sky Sports wide-screen TV. Five minutes from Lowestoft college. Car park. No food. No children.

OPEN *10.30am–11pm.*

Sun Rise Inn

6 Corton Road, Lowestoft NR32 4PL
☎ *(01502) 564616* Danny and Linda Smith

Greene King IPA, Abbot and Old Speckled Hen always available.

Friendly, small hotel with cosy beamed bar, carvery, steakhouse restaurant and 12 en-suite rooms. Food served 12–3.0pm and 6–9pm Mon–Sat, plus 12–3pm Sun, carvery. Car park. Children welcome, but no special facilities. Located off the A12 between Lowestoft and Great Yarmouth. On corner at the turn-off to Corton.

OPEN *11am–11pm Mon–Sat; 12–10.30pm Sun.*

The Triangle Tavern

29 St Peter's Street, Lowestoft NR32 1QA
☎ *(01502) 582711* Bob Vipers

Up to a dozen real ales always available. Home of the Green Jack Brewery (trading as Oulton Ales), so approximately four of the brewery's ales always available plus 6–8 constantly changing guests. Real cider also served.

Owned by the Green Jack Brewing Company and based in the High Street next to the Triangle Market Place, a two-bar pub with real fire. No food (customers are welcome to bring their own). Live music Thurs–Fri nights. Beer festivals held Easter, summer and Christmas. Parking. Brewery tours by arrangement.

OPEN *11am–11pm Mon–Sat; 12–10.30pm Sun.*

Welcome Free House

182 London Road North, Lowestoft NR32 1HB
☎ *(01502) 585500* Gavin Crawford

Adnams Best Bitter and Greene King Abbot Ale usually available, plus guest beers such as Marston's Pedigree, Everards Tiger, Charles Wells Eagle, Greene King Old Speckled Hen, Brakspear Bitter or Elgood's Greyhound.

A traditional real ale town pub. No food. No children.

OPEN *10.30am–4pm and 7.30–11pm (10.30pm Sun).*

MARKET WESTON

The Mill Inn

Bury Road, Market Weston, Near Diss IP22 2PD
☎ *(01359) 221018* Lesley Leacy

Adnams Bitter, Greene King IPA and something from Old Chimneys (usually a bitter and mild, but changes occasionally) are the permanent beers at this freehouse, plus a guest.

Village pub in a nineteenth-century former mill house. Food available 12–2pm (except Mon) and 7–9.30pm. One large bar, garden, patio and restaurant with wood burner. Car park. Children allowed. On the B1111.

 *12–3pm (not Mon) and 5–11pm; 12–3pm and 7–11pm Sun.*

OULTON

The Blue Boad

28 Oulton Street, Oulton, Lowestoft
☎ *(01502) 572160* SJ Battrick

A house beer, Sinbad's Treasure, is a permanent fixture, and the four ever-changing guests (rarely the same twice) have included beers from Buffy's, Humpty Dumpty, Woodforde's, Green Jack and Elgood's.

A pub with two bars (public and lounge), games room, function room, large beer garden, patio and barbecue area. Food served 12–2.30pm and 7–9pm. Children welcome in games room and garden area. Car park.

 *12–3pm and 7–11pm Mon–Thurs; 12–11pm Fri–Sat; 12–3pm and 7–10.30pm Sun.*

PIN MILL

The Butt & Oyster

Pin Mill, Chelmondiston, Ipswich IP9 1JW
☎ *(01473) 780764* Dick Mainwaring

Greene King IPA straight from the barrel, plus Adnams Broadside and Bitter. One guest, changed occasionally.

A sixteenth-century inn with one bar, smoking room and riverside seating area. Food available at lunchtime and evenings. Children allowed.

 *All day, every day in summer; 11am–3pm and 7–11pm Mon–Fri and all day Sat–Sun in winter.*

SNAPE

The Crown Inn

Bridge Road, Snape, Saxmundham IP17 1SL
☎ *(01728 688324)* Diane Maylott

An Adnams pub with Bitter, Broadside and seasonal ales.

Fifteenth-century roadside inn not far from Snape Maltings. Attractive, open, brick-floored bar area with wooden settles plus separate dining room. Beer garden. Three bedrooms. Food at lunchtime and every evening (*Good Pub Guide* Dining Pub of the Year for Suffolk 2004).

12–3pm and 6–11pm (7–10.30pm Sun)

The Golden Key

Priory Road, Snape, Saxmundham IP17 1SG
☎ *(01728 688510)* Max Kissick-Jones

Adnams Bitter, Broadside and seasonal ales such as Regatta and Fisherman.

Another fifteenth-century inn in the heart of the village with beamed open bar with tiled floor plus side room. Terrace with seating in front plus side garden. Accommodation. Food served at lunchtime and evenings (12–2.15pm and 6–9.30pm Mon–Sat, 12–2.15pm and 7–9.30pm Sun). The tenant has been with Adnams for more than 25 years. Children welcome in dining rooms and garden, dogs in bar if on lead.

 *11am–3pm and 6–11pm Mon–Sat; 12–3pm and 7–10.30pm Sun.*

SOUTHWOLD

The Lord Nelson

East Street, Southwold IP18 6ES
☎ *(01502 722079)* John Illston

Adnams Bitter, Broadside and seasonal ales such as Regatta in summer, Fisherman in winter.

Former coaching inn in the heart of the town close to the brewery and the sea. Known locally as The Nellie, decorated with a nautical theme and Nelson memorabilia. Beer patio, disabled access. Food available at lunchtime and evenings. Children and dogs welcome in side room.

 *10.30am–11pm Mon–Sat; 12–10.30pm Sun.*

Harbour Inn

Blackshore, Southwold IP18 6TA
☎ *(01502 722381* Colin Fraser

Adnams Bitter, Broadside and a seasonal ale.

Close to the water, as its name suggests, surrounded by fishermen's huts and other nautical goings-on Food served at lunchtime and evenings. Garden with children's play area. Live music.

All day every day.

STOWMARKET

The Stag Tavern

44–6 Bury Street, Stowmarket IP14 1HF
☎ *(01449) 613980* Phil Rudland

Three real ales on at any time, including Greene King IPA and a weekly changing guest. Guests come from independents such as Nethergate.

A traditional drinker's pub with two bars and traditional pub games and pool table. Food available at lunchtime and early evenings with roast for Sunday lunchtimes. Meeting room, car park, non-smoking area. Well-behaved children allowed.

 *11am–11pm Mon–Sat; 12–10.30pm Sun.*

SWILLAND

The Moon & Mushroom

High Road, Swilland, Ipswich IP6 9LR
☎ *(01473) 785320* Clive John Goodall

Seven real ales from Buffy's, Nethergate, Woodforde's, Wolf and Crouch Vale, all served straight from the barrel.

A fourteenth century timbered 'throw-back in time' pub using traditional methods for ale and food. Vine-covered patio to front. Food served 12–2pm and 6.30–8.15pm Tues–Sat. Children welcome in the garden only.

 *6–11pm Mon; 11am–2.30pm and 6–11pm Tues–Sat; 12–2.30pm and 7–10.30pm Sun.*

WINGFIELD

The De La Pole Arms

Church Road, Wingfield, Diss IP21 5RA
☎ *(01379) 384545*

Tied to St Peter's, with no less than 16 St Peter's beers (on draught or by bottle) always available, including Best Bitter.

A well-restored two-bar dining pub with beams and log fires. Garden, car park. Children allowed. Phone for directions (though once you are in Wingfield, you can't miss the pub!).

12–3pm and 6–11pm Tues–Sat (closed Mon); 12–3pm Sun.

THE BREWERIES

HOGS BACK BREWERY
Units 1–3 Manor Farm Business Centre, The Street, Tongham GU10 1DE
☎ *(01252) 783000*
www.hogsback.co.uk

HAIR OF THE HOG 3.5% ABV

TRADITIONAL ENGLISH ALE 4.2% ABV
Smooth, well-balanced flavours.

HOP GARDEN GOLD 4.6% ABV
Refreshing with good fruity hoppiness.

Plus commemorative and seasonal brews.

LEITH HILL BREWERY
The Plough Inn, Coldharbour Lane, Nr Dorking RH5 6HD
☎ *(01306) 711793*
www.ploughinn.com

CROOKED FURROW 3.6% ABV
Hoppy, light bitter.

TALLYWHACKER 5.6% ABV
Beer with strong roast barley flavour.

PILGRIM ALES
The Old Brewery, West Street, Reigate RH2 9BL
☎ *(01737) 222651*
www.pilgrim.co.uk

SURREY BITTER 3.7% ABV
Hoppy, with a good mixture of flavours.

PORTER 4.0% ABV
Dark with roast malt flavour.

PROGRESS 4.0% ABV
Red and malty.

CRUSADER 4.9% ABV
Gold, with hops and malt flavour.

SPRING BOCK 5.2% ABV
Wheat beer.

Plus seasonal brews.

THE PUBS

ASH

The Dover Arms
31 Guildford Road, Ash GU12 6BQ
☎ *(01252) 326025* Errol George Faulkner

Shepherd Neame Spitfire usually available, plus guest beers from a range of micro-breweries.

Rural village pub with football game, pool and darts. Food served 12–2pm and 7–9pm daily. Car park. Garden. Children welcome.

11.30am–2.30pm and 6–11pm (10.30pm Sun).

BLETCHINGLEY

William IV
Little Common Lane, Bletchingley, Redhill RH1 4QF
☎ *(01883) 743278* Sue Saunders

Fuller's London Pride, Adnams Best, something from Harveys and Greene King Ruddles Best usually available.

An unspoilt Victorian country pub on the edge of the village. Two small bars, dining room and beer garden. Food available at lunchtime and evenings. Children allowed in dining room and garden only.

12–3pm and 6–11pm Mon–Sat; 12–10.30pm Sun.

CARSHALTON

The Racehorse
17 West Street, Carshalton SM5 2PT
☎ *(020) 8647 6818* Julian Norton

A freehouse with Gale's Butser and HSB and Greene King IPA always on offer, plus two guests ales, usually from Fuller's, Marston's or Brakspear.

Locals' pub with two bars, dining area, disabled access and patio. Food available at lunchtime and evenings (not Sunday pm).

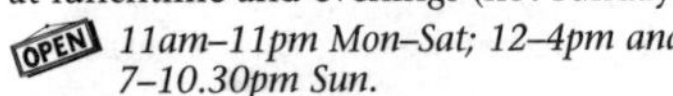
11am–11pm Mon–Sat; 12–4pm and 7–10.30pm Sun.

CHURT

The Crossways Inn
Churt, Nr Farnham GU10 2JE
☎ *(01428) 714323* Paul Ewens

A freehouse with Cheriton Best and Ringwood Fortyniner always available, plus at least four guests, such as Hampshire Lionheart. At least ten different beers are served every week, with more from micro-breweries than not. Also four real ciders from the barrel.

A country village local. Two bars, beer garden. Food available at lunchtime only. Well-behaved children allowed. On the main road.

11am–3.30pm and 5–11pm Mon–Thurs; all day Fri–Sat; 12–4pm and 7–10.30pm Sun.

CLAYGATE

The Griffin

58 Common Road, Claygate, Esher KT10 0HW
☎ *(01372) 463799* Tom Harrington

A freehouse with Fuller's London Pride and Oakham Jeffrey Hudson Bitter always available plus two constantly changing guests. Micro-breweries and smaller independents favoured.

A traditional two-bar village pub with log fires, beer garden and disabled access. Food available every lunchtime plus Friday and Saturday evenings. Children allowed.

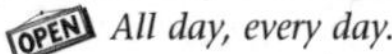 *All day, every day.*

The Swan

Hare Lane, Claygate KT10 9BS
☎ *(01372) 462582* Timothy Kitch

A freehouse with Fuller's London Pride a permanent feature, plus three guest beers, perhaps Greene King IPA or something from Brakspear or Adnams.

A country pub in a building dating from 1804, with beams, Victorian ceiling, 20-foot bar, large garden and a field for use during festivals. Food is available, and there is a Thai restaurant. Annual beer festival in August, usually at the bank holiday (80 beers over four days). Superior en-suite accommodation. Children allowed.

 *11am–11pm Mon–Sat; 12–10.30pm Sun.*

COLDHARBOUR

The Plough Inn

Coldharbour Lane, Coldharbour, Nr Dorking RH5 6HD
☎ *(01306) 711793* Anna and Richard Abrehart
www.ploughinn.com

Six real ales and a real cider always available. Three beers are brewed on the premises under the name of The Leith Hill Brewery. Beers from Ringwood and Shepherd Neame are permanent features, and one guest is changed regularly. Seasonal, special and topical beers, plus farm cider on hand pump, are also on offer.

A traditional family-run seventeenth-century pub in a beautiful rural setting. Allegedly the highest freehouse in south-east England. Bar and restaurant food served every lunchtime and evening. Car parking. Children allowed. High-quality en-suite accommodation. Just over three miles south-west of Dorking.

 *11.30am–11pm Mon–Sat; 12–10.30pm Sun.*

CROYDON

Claret Free House

5 Bingham Corner, Lower Addiscombe Road, Croydon CR0 7AA
☎ *(020) 8656 7452* Mike Callaghan

Palmers IPA, Shepherd Neame Spitfire plus a Cottage brew usually available. Three regularly changing guests are also served (200 per year).

Small, friendly and comfortable community pub. No food. No children. Adjacent to the new Tramlink station.

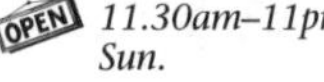 *11.30am–11pm Mon–Sat; 12–10.30pm Sun.*

The George

17 George Street, Croydon CR0 1LA
☎ *(020) 8649 9077*
Caroline Williams and Simon Pitcher

Ridley's Old Bob, Fuller's London Pride, Timothy Taylor Landlord, Shepherd Neame Spitfire and Greene King Abbot are among the beers usually available, plus three or four regularly changed guests.

A Wetherspoon's pub in the town centre, next to the George Street Tramlink stop, converted from a furniture store. Two bars and a non-smoking area. Food served until 10pm.

 *10am–11pm*

The Spread Eagle

39–41 Katherine Street, Croydon
☎ *(020) 8781 1134*
Ashley Hall and Rafal Dulny

Fuller's London Pride, ESB, Chiswick and seasonal ales usually available, plus one guest.

A town-centre Fuller's pub in a converted NatWest bank with a separate function room and large-screen TV. Food served all day.

 *11am–11pm Mon–Sat; 12–10pm Sun.*

DORKING

The King's Arms

45 West Street, Dorking RH4 1BU
☎ *(01306) 883361* Stuart Yeatman

Fuller's London Pride and Greene King IPA always available. Two guests changing every week from micro-breweries and independents – the smaller and more unusual, the better!

A country-style pub in a town location, this is the oldest building in Dorking. More than 500 years old with oak beams, inglenook fireplace, restaurant and courtyard garden. Food available lunchtimes and evenings. Children allowed.

OPEN *11am–11pm (10.30pm Sun).*

EGHAM

The Crown

38 High Street, Egham, TW20 9DP
☎ *(01784) 432608* Linda Bowman

Fuller's London Pride, Greene King Abbot, Adnams Bitter and Broadside plus a weekly guest ale.

A country-style pub, part of the Barracuda chain, with beer gardens front and back, car park and pool table. Beer festivals twice a year. Food available until 9pm Monday to Saturday and 5pm on Sundays.

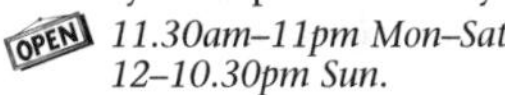
11.30am–11pm Mon–Sat; 12–10.30pm Sun.

ENGLEFIELD GREEN

The Beehive

34 Middle Hill, Englefield Green, Nr Egham TW20 0JQ
☎ *(01784) 431621* Roy McGranaghan

Fuller's London Pride, Hop Back Summer Lightning and Gale's HSB and Best always available plus four guest beers, changing weekly, from breweries such as Adnams, Bateman, Everards, Hoskins & Oldfield, Kemptown, Nethergate, Oldbury, Orkney, Thwaites and Young's. Beer festivals at May and August bank holidays.

A country pub now surrounded by expensive houses. Real homemade food available at lunchtime and evenings. Open log fire in winter. Car park and garden. Just off the A30 between Ferrari's and Royal Holloway College. Children welcome

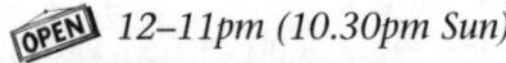
12–11pm (10.30pm Sun).

EPSOM

The Rising Sun

14 Heathcote Road, Epsom KT18 5DX
☎ *(01372) 740809* Ruth Roberts
www.pilgrim.co.uk

Two or three Pilgrim beers usually on draught, plus a guest beer from a small brewery. Black Pearl Stout (from Ireland) and several imported beers are also offered on draught, as well as French cider and at least 35 imported bottled beers.

Originally two cottages, the pub was extended back into the main building at the end of the nineteenth century, and was tastefully redecorated in 1999. Food is available every evening except Sunday, with 'prix fixe' meals on Friday and Saturday evenings using fresh and seasonal produce. Quarterly beer festivals (see website for details). Beer garden. Dogs welcome, plus other animals, including children, if well-behaved. Parking nearby.

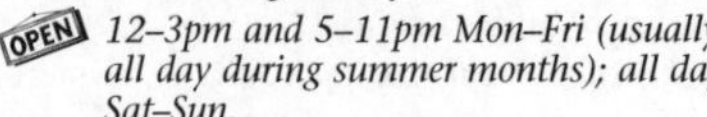
12–3pm and 5–11pm Mon–Fri (usually all day during summer months); all day Sat–Sun.

FARNHAM

The Ball & Wicket

104 Upper Hale Road, Farnham GU9 0PB
☎ *(01252) 735278* Sean Neale

Fuller's London Pride, Young's Ordinary and Hogs Back TEA are the permanent beers here, and an occasional guest is offered.

A friendly, 200-year-old village pub with an open fire and a warm atmosphere. Live entertainment, quiz nights, darts. No food. Children allowed until evening. Car park.

OPEN *4–11pm Mon–Fri; 12–11pm Sat; 12–3pm and 7–10.30pm Sun.*

Exchange

Station Hill, Farnham GU9 8AD
☎ *(01252) 726673*
Terry Devaney and Ms A Fanning

Greene King IPA and Triumph usually available, with one guest such as Ruddles Best, Wadworth 6X or Bateman XXXB.

Traditional bar with garden and patio. Extensive menu, specialising in steaks, available 12–2.30pm and 6.30–9pm daily. Car park. Children welcome, but no special facilities. Located next to Farnham Station.

OPEN *10.30am–3pm and 5.30–11pm Mon–Thurs; all day Fri–Sun.*

The Shepherd & Flock

Moor Park Lane, Farnham GU9 9JB
☎ *(01252) 716675* Stephen Hill

A freehouse with Hogs Back TEA and Ringwood Old Thumper always available plus five guests, such as Hop Back Summer Lightning, Arundel, Triple FFF, Itchen Valley or Welton's brews.

Situated on the outskirts of town, on Europe's biggest inhabited roundabout! A well-known local meeting place, close to the North Downs. Old building with one bar and 50-seater dining room. Food available lunchtimes and evenings. Beer garden. Children allowed in the dining room only.

OPEN *All permitted hours.*

GODALMING

The Anchor Inn

110 Ockford Road, Godalming GU7 1RG
☎ *(01483) 417085* Jos Edmundson

Fuller's London Pride and Shepherd Neame Spitfire are among the beers always available, but this is under review.

A real-ale pub, refurbished, with restored wooden floor and a good mixed clientele. Parking and large rear garden. On the edge of town on the main road.

OPEN *11am–11pm Mon–Sat; 12–10.30pm Sun.*

GUILDFORD

The George Abbot

7–11 High Street, Guildford GU2 4AB
☎ *(01483) 456890* Shaun Harris

The permanent beers here include Fuller's London Pride, Greene King IPA, Hog's Back TEA, Gale's HSB and Marston's Pedigree.

Drinkers' town pub in a traditional building, with beams, fireplaces and a friendly atmosphere. Food available. Fruit and quiz machines. No children.

OPEN *12–11pm (10.30pm Sun).*

KINGSTON-UPON-THAMES

The Canbury Arms,

49 Canbury Park Road, Kingston-upon-Thames KT2 6LQ
☎ *(020) 8288 1882* Paul Adams

Six real ales usually available which may include Wadworth 6X, Greene King Abbot or Old Speckled Hen or Marston's Pedigree. Over 650 beers from more than 100 independent/micro-breweries served so far. Regularly changing real cider and annual Easter cider festival.

Backstreet pub with mock-Tudor interior. Large-screen TV for sport. Extensive reference library. Live music on Friday and Saturday evenings, quiz nights on Sunday. Beer garden with patio. Dog the size of a Shetland pony! No food. Car park with secure motorcycle parking. No children.

OPEN *All permitted hours.*

The Fighting Cocks

56 London Road, Kingston-upon-Thames KT2 6QA
☎ *(020) 8546 5174* Natalie Salt

Wadworth 6X among the brews always available plus two guests such as Marston's Pedigree.

A town pub with wooden floors and panelled walls. Two bars and courtyard. No food. Children allowed.

OPEN *11am–11pm.*

The Kelly Arms

Alfred Road, off Villiers Road, Kingston-upon-Thames KT1 2UB
☎ *(020) 8296 9815* Vanessa McConnon

Four real ales usually available, featuring beers from Wolf, Hogs Back and Cottage breweries, to name but a few. Stowford Press cider from H. Weston also served.

A backstreet locals' pub with a friendly atmosphere. One big bar. Pool table, Tornado football table, darts, pinball, Sky TV. Garden with BBQ. Food available all day, every day. Children allowed if eating or in garden. Functions catered for.

OPEN *11am–11pm Mon–Sat; 12–10.30pm Sun.*

The Willoughby Arms

Willoughby Road, Kingston-upon-Thames KT2 6LN
☎ *(020) 8546 4236* Rick Robinson

Timothy Taylor Landlord, Fuller's London Pride, Caledonian Deuchars IPA and Marston's Pedigree served, plus one guest ale which is sold at £1.60 per pint. HQ of the Kingston branch of the Society of Preservation of Beers from the Wood (meet on Wed night, when all cask ales are £1.50 per pint). Beer festivals held on St George's Day and Hallowe'en.

A refurbished Victorian corner local. Rolls available at lunchtime, barbecues on Sundays (weather permitting). Children allowed in the large garden which has a pond and waterfall. Large-screen TV, bric-à-brac. Quiz night Sundays. Can be difficult to find, so ring if you get lost.

OPEN *10.30am–11pm Mon–Sat; 12–10.30pm Sun.*

KNAPHILL

The Knap

134 High Street, Knaphill GU21 2QH
☎ *(01483) 473374*
Paul Crisp and Elizabeth Williamson

Young's Bitter and Charles Wells Bombardier are served, plus ever-changing guest beers.

A bistro-style country pub, previously known as The Garibaldi. One small bar, beer garden and BBQ. Food available lunchtimes and evenings in a separate dining area. Mexican food is a speciality, but traditional English, Italian and Indian dishes are also served. Live music on alternate Sundays, interspersed with quizzes and other themed nights. Children allowed. On the crossroads of Knaphill High Street.

OPEN *12–11pm.*

NEWDIGATE

Surrey Oaks

Parkgate Road, Newdigate, Dorking RH5 5DZ
☎ *(01306) 631200* Ken Proctor

Ringwood Best, Harveys Sussex and Timothy Taylor's Landlord usually available, plus two guest pumps. Five or six guest beers served each week, from micro-breweries whenever possible, and favourites include beers from O'Hanlons, Dark Star, Bank Top and Cotleigh.

Timber-beamed country pub, original parts of which date back to 1570. Two small bars, one with a magnificent inglenook fireplace and stone-flagged floors. Games room and restaurant. Food served lunchtimes and evenings Tues–Sat; lunchtimes only Sun–Mon. Large car park. Children's play area in garden. Situated one mile from Newdigate village on the Charlwood road.

11.30am–2.30pm and 5.30–11pm Mon–Fri; 11.30am–3pm and 6–11pm Sat; 12–3pm and 7–10.30pm Sun.

NORTH CHEAM

Wetherspoons

552–6 London Road, North Cheam SM3 9AA
☎ *(020) 8644 1808* Dean Kelly

A Wetherspoon's pub with Fuller's London Pride always available plus two guests such as Shepherd Neame Spitfire. Guests changed every three days.

One large bar and non-smoking dining area. Food available all day. Disabled facilities. No children.

All day, every day.

PURLEY

Foxley Hatch

8–9 Russell Hill Road, Purley CR8 2LE
☎ *(020) 8763 9307* Andy Rimmer

A Wetherspoon's pub with Shepherd Neame Spitfire and Greene King Abbot permanently available, plus two guest beers from around the country. Three or four festivals are also held each year offering up to 20 beers at a time.

Friendly, locals' pub free of music and television. Non-smoking area and easy access for the disabled. Food served all day, every day. No children.

11am–11pm Mon–Sat; 12–10.30pm Sun.

PUTTENHAM

The Good Intent

62 The Street, Puttenham, Guildford GU3 1AR
☎ *(01483) 810387* Bill Carpenter

A pub serving only cask-conditioned real ales. Five guests at any one time, including four guests. Favourites are Ringwood Fortyniner, or something from Hog's Back or Hop Back.

A traditional country pub dating from the sixteenth century and situated on the North Downs Way. A wide variety of food is available lunchtimes and evenings (except Sun and Mon evenings), including fish and chips to eat in or take away every Wednesday night, and superb roast Sunday lunch. Enclosed beer garden. Families welcome.

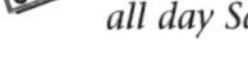
11am–2.30pm and 6–11pm Mon–Fri; all day Sat–Sun.

REDHILL

The Hatch

44 Hatchlands Road, Redhill RH1 6AT
☎ *(01737) 764593* Naomi Newman

A Shepherd Neame house with Bishop's Finger, Spitfire and Master Brew always available, plus up to three seasonal or celebration ales such as Goldings or 1698.

A town pub with horseshoe-shaped bar, log-effect fires and oak beams. Beer garden, front patio, pool room. Food available 12–2pm daily. Families very welcome. Situated on the A25.

12–3pm Mon–Sun; 5.30–11pm Mon–Sat; 7–10.30pm Sun.

RICHMOND

The Triple Crown

15 Kew Foot Road, Richmond TW9 2SS
☎ *(020) 8940 3805*

Fuller's London Pride and Timothy Taylor Landlord regularly available. Four guest beers are also served, from a list running into several hundreds.

Traditional, one-bar house. Food served 12–2.30pm. Children welcome.

11am–11pm Mon–Sat; 12–10.30pm Sun.

SHAMLEY GREEN

The Bricklayer's Arms

The Green, Shamley Green, Guildford GU5 0UA
☎ *(01483) 898377* Debbie Ersser

Shepherd Neame Spitfire constantly available plus one guest from a micro-brewery. There is also a comprehensive wine list.

Situated on the green, this pub underwent a sympathetic refurbishment in summer 2003. Wide and varied menu. Large patio areas surround an ornamental Koi carp pond. Barbecues every weekend, weather permitting. Families welcome.

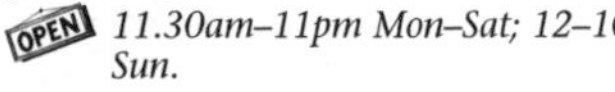
11.30am–11pm Mon–Sat; 12–10.30pm Sun.

SURBITON

Coronation Hall

St Mark's Hill, Surbiton KT6 4TB
☎ *(020) 8390 6164* Emma Wales

A Wetherspoon's pub with Shepherd Neame Spitfire and Fuller's London Pride always available. Three guest pumps changed twice a week, which might include Hop Back Summer Lightning.

Large bar area, non-smoking dining area and disabled facilities. Food available all day. No children.

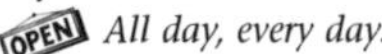
All day, every day.

The Lamb Inn

73 Brighton Road, Surbiton KT6 5NF
☎ *(020) 8390 9229* Ian Stewart

Greene King IPA and Young's Special permanently available plus one guest changed every two or three days. A good choice of regional ales is offered, from the Isle of Wight to the Isle of Man.

A true old-fashioned community locals' pub. Darts, bar games and a friendly welcoming atmosphere. Large beer garden with grassed area for children. Bar food available every lunchtime. Children allowed in the garden only. From J10 of M25, take left turn towards Kingston; eventually you come to Brighton Road.

11am–11pm Mon–Sat; 12–10.30pm Sun.

WEST BYFLEET

The Plough Inn

104 High Road, West Byfleet KT14 7QT
☎ *(01932) 353257* Carol Wells

A freehouse with nine pumps serving ever-changing brews, all from independents.

A traditional two-bar village pub with beams and two log fires. Beer garden, non-smoking conservatory, car park. Food available Mon–Fri 12–2pm. Monthly trivia quiz in winter. Children allowed in conservatory until 7pm.

11am–3pm and 5–11pm (10.30pm Sun).

WEST CLANDON

The Onslow Arms

The Street, West Clandon, Guildford GU4 7TE
☎ *(01483) 222447*

A freehouse with Hogs Back TEA, Charles Wells Bombardier and Shepherd Neame Spitfire always available.

A well-known sixteenth-century coaching inn with four bars and excellent food available at lunchtime and evenings in a restaurant and a rotisserie. Large car park, disabled access. Garden and patio with arbours. Cocktail lounge. Function rooms. Helipad. Children allowed.

All day, every day.

WEYBRIDGE

The Prince of Wales

11 Cross Road, Oatlands, Weybridge KT13 9NX
☎ *(01932) 852082* Brian and Pat Ford

Six pumps, serving Fuller's Chiswick, London Pride and ESB, something from Adnams and a couple of guests. Hogs Back TEA is a particular favourite.

A family-owned local dating from the mid-nineteenth century. Log fires in the winter, quiz nights once a fortnight and excellent home-cooked food served lunchtimes and evenings (lunch only on Sundays).

10.30am–11pm Mon–Sat; 12–10.30pm Sun

WOKING

Wetherspoons

51 Chertsey Road, Woking GU21 5AJ
☎ *(01483) 722818* Gary Hollis

Hogs Back TEA, Shepherd Neame Spitfire and Theakston Best permanently available, plus at least three guest ales.

A one-bar town pub with no music or TV. Front drinking terrace, disabled access and toilets. Food available all day (11am–10pm) with a non-smoking seating area available. No children.

All day, every day.

WOODSTREET VILLAGE

The Royal Oak

89 Oak Hill, Woodstreet Village, Guildford
GU3 3DA
☎ *(01483) 235137* Tony Oliver

A freehouse with Hogs Back TEA always available plus four constantly changing guests, always including a mild. Hop Back Summer Lightning and Cottage Wheeltappers are just two examples from a huge range (nearly 2,000 in nine years). Real cider always available.

A good old-fashioned country pub. One bar, beer garden. Food available Mon–Sat lunchtime. Over 14s only allowed.

 *11am–3pm and 5–11pm Mon–Fri; 11am–3.30pm and 5–11pm Sat; 12–3.30pm and 7–10.30pm Sun.*

WRECCLESHAM

The Bat & Ball

Bat & Ball Lane, Wrecclesham, Farnham
GU10 4RA
☎ *(01252) 792108* Kevin and Sally Macready

Young's Bitter, Hogs Back TEA and a special from Hampshire Brewery permanently available plus three guests from local and national micro-breweries, including Ringwood Fortyniner, Triple FFF and Ballard's.

A pub with restaurant-quality food. Renovated in 2003 with a family area and garden with covered patio. Food available at lunchtime and evenings. Children allowed. Bat & Ball Lane is off Upper Bourne Lane via Sandrock Hill Road.

 *12–11pm (10.30pm Sun).*

The Sandrock

Sandrock Hill Road, Wrecclesham, Farnham
GU10 4NS
☎ *(01252) 715865*
Mr R Mifsud and Miss C Haime

Eight real ale hand pumps to choose from, including beers from Black Country regulars such as Batham, Enville, Holden's and Sarah Hughes, plus a constantly changing selection of guest beers from an ever-increasing range of independent breweries.

Friendly, welcoming freehouse in a pleasant rural setting, though in easy reach of Farnham town centre and road and rail links. Extensive lunch and evening menus offer dishes from around the world, with something to suit all tastes. Food served 12–2.30pm and 6.30–9.30pm Mon–Sat, with traditional Sunday lunch available 12–4pm. Real log fire in the colder months, enclosed patio garden, annual beer festival. Dogs on a lead welcome. Along Farnham bypass towards Alton, left at roundabout onto the A325, left into School Hill, straight across at staggered crossroads into Sandrock Hill Road.

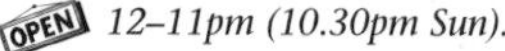
12–11pm (10.30pm Sun).

THE BREWERIES

1648 BREWING CO. LTD
Mill Lane, East Hoathly, East Sussex BN8 6QB
☎ *(01825) 840830*
www.1648brewing.co.uk

1648 ORIGINAL 3.9% ABV
SIGNATURE 4.4% ABV
WARRANT 4.8% ABV
WINTER WARRANT 4.8% ABV

ARUNDEL BREWERY
Unit C7 Ford Airfield Estate, Arundel, West Sussex BN18 0HY
☎ *(01903) 733111*

1999 3.5% ABV
CASTLE 3.8% ABV
Well-balanced and malty with some fruitiness.
ARUNDEL GOLD 4.2% ABV
CLASSIC 4.5% ABV
Malty with some sweetness.
STRONGHOLD 5.0% ABV
Rounded and full-flavoured.
Seasonals:
HAIRY MARY 3.8% ABV
Summer brew.
FOOT SLOGGER 4.4% ABV
Golden seasonal brew.
SUMMER DAZE 4.7% ABV
BLACK BEASTY 4.9% ABV
BULLS EYE 5.0% ABV
Golden seasonal brew.
OLD KNUCKLER 5.5% ABV
All the flavours are here. Winter brew.
Plus other seasonal brews.

BALLARDS BREWERY LTD
Unit C The Old Sawmill, Nyewood, Petersfield GU31 5HA
☎ *(01730) 821301*
www.ballardsbrewery.org.uk

MIDHURST MILD 3.4% ABV
TROTTON 3.6% ABV
BEST BITTER 4.2% ABV
WILD 4.7% ABV
NYEWOOD GOLD 5.0% ABV
WASSAIL 6.0% ABV
Plus seasonal brews.

DARK STAR BREWING CO LTD
Moonhill Farm, Ansty, Haywards Heath RH17 5AH
☎ *(01444) 412311*
www.darkstarbrewing.co.uk

HOPHEAD 3.8% ABV
OVER THE MOON 3.8% ABV
BEST BITTER 4.0% ABV
LANDLORDS WIT 4.1% ABV
ESPRESSO STOUT 4.2% ABV
DARK STAR 5.0% ABV
FESTIVAL 5.0% ABV
PORTER 5.5% ABV
Plus seasonals.

FILO BREWERY
14–15 High Street, Hastings TN34 3EY
☎ *(01424) 425079*
www.thefilo.co.uk

CROFTER'S BEST BITTER 4.0% ABV
FILO GOLD 4.3% ABV
CARDINAL SUSSEX PORTER 4.6% ABV

GRIBBLE BREWERY
The Gribble Inn, Gribble Lane, Oving, Nr Chichester PO22 6BP
☎ *(01243) 786893*
www.gribblebrewery.co.uk

KING AND BARNES MILD 3.5% ABV
FURSTY FERRET 4.0% ABV
Golden with nutty flavour.
GRIBBLE ALE 4.1% ABV
REG'S TIPPLE 5.0% ABV
PLUCKING PHEASANT 5.2% ABV
PORTERHOUSE 5.2% ABV
Malt flavour with a hint of liquorice.
PIGS EAR 5.8% ABV
WOBBLER 7.2% ABV

HARVEY & SONS (LEWES) LTD
The Bridge Wharf Brewery, 6 Cliffe High Street, Lewes, East Sussex BN7 2AH
☎ *(01273) 480209*
www.harveys.org.uk

XX MILD 3.0% ABV
Dark in colour, soft and sweet.
SUSSEX PALE ALE 3.5% ABV
SUSSEX BEST BITTER 4.0% ABV
ARMADA ALE 4.5% ABV
Golden and hoppy, with dryness in the aftertaste.
Plus seasonal brews.

KEMPTOWN BREWERY
Hand in Hand, 33 Upper St Jamesís Street, Brighton BN2 1JN
☎ *(01273) 693070*

BRIGHTON BITTER 3.6% ABV
KEMPTOWN BITER 4.0% ABV
YE OLDE TROUT 4.5% ABV
STAGGERING IN THE DARK 5.2% ABV
OLD GRUMPY 6.2% ABV
December brew.
Plus seasonal and occasional brews.

WJ KING & CO.
3–5 Jubilee Estate, Foundry Lane, Horsham RH13 5EU
☎ *(01403) 272102*
www.kingfamilybrewers.co.uk

HORSHAM BEST BITTER 3.8% ABV
RED RIVER ALE 4.8% ABV
Plus 3 specials each month.

RECTORY ALES LTD

Streat Hill Farm Outbuildings, Streat Hill, Streat Hassocks BN6 8RP
☎ *(01273) 890570*

RECTOR'S PLEASURE 3.8% ABV
RECTOR'S LIGHT RELIEF 4.0% ABV
RECTOR'S REVENGE 5.4% ABV
Plus seasonal brews.

ROTHER VALLEY BREWING CO.

Gate Court Farm, Station Road, Northiam, TN31 6QT
☎ *(01797) 253535*

WEALDEN BITTER 3.7% ABV
SMILD 3.8% ABV
Dark mild.
LEVEL BEST 4.0% ABV
HOPPERS ALE 4.4% ABV
BLUES 5.0% ABV
Winter only.
Plus seasonal and occasional brews.

WELTONS NORTH DOWN BREWERY

1 Rangers Lodge, Oakhill Road, Horsham RH13 5LF
☎ *(01403) 242901*
www.weltons.co.uk

DORKING'S PRIDE 2.8% ABV
NORTH DOWNS 3.8% ABV
OLD COCKY 4.3% ABV
TOWER POWER 5.0% ABV

WHITE BREWING CO.

The 1066 Country Brewery, Pebsham Farm Ind. Est., Pebsham Lane, Bexhill
☎ *(01424) 731066*

1066 COUNTRY ALE 4.0% ABV
M2 4.5% ABV
Available upon request.
WHITE CHRISTMAS 4.5% ABV

THE PUBS

AMBERLEY

The Sportsman's Inn

Crossgates, Amberley, Arundel, West Sussex BN18 9NR
☎ *(01798) 831787* Paul and Amanda Mahon
www.amberleysportsman.co.uk

A freehouse with four real ales always available. Young's Bitter, Fuller's London Pride, Harveys Best, Shepherd Neame Spitfire and Greene King IPA are likely candidates, although the selection changes every two weeks.

An edge-of-village pub with panoramic views over Pulborough Wildbrooks Reserve. Three bars, patio area, dining area in conservatory. Good food served 12–2pm and 6.30–9pm. En-suite bed and breakfast available. Well-behaved children and dogs welcome. Car park. Good walking country.

OPEN *11am–3pm and 6–11pm Mon–Sat; 12–3pm and 7–10.30pm Sun.*

ARLINGTON

The Old Oak Inn

Cane Heath, Arlington, Nr Hailsham, East Sussex BN26 6SJ
☎ *(01323) 482072* Brendan Slattery

Harveys Best Bitter and Badger Best usually available plus one or two guest beers, perhaps from Fuller's, Young's, Adnams or Charles Wells breweries, changed weekly.

Situated between the South Downs and Michelham Priory, a seventeenth-century country freehouse with log fires, oak-beamed bar and restaurant, beer garden and barbecue. Food served 12–2.30pm and 6.30–9.30pm Mon–Fri; 12–9pm Sat–Sun. Large car park. Children welcome, but no special facilities. Barbecues and beer festivals are held during the summer.

OPEN *11am–11pm Mon–Wed; 11am–12am Thurs–Sat; 12–11.30pm Sun.*

ARUNDEL

Arundel Swan Hotel

27–9 High Street, Arundel, West Sussex
☎ *(01903) 882314* Graham Dove

Part of the family-owned George Gale & Co Ltd estate, featuring the award-winning Gale's HSB, plus Gale's GB and Butser. A guest beer is always available, perhaps Hop Back Summer Lightning or Shepherd Neame Spitfire.

Restored to its original Victorian splendour, a very popular meeting place for non-residents, locals and tourists alike. Situated in the heart of Arundel, close to the castle and river. Food served 12–10pm (9.30pm Sun). Car park behind the hotel. Fifteen en-suite rooms.

 *11am–11pm Mon–Sat; 12–10.30pm Sun.*

The King's Arms

36 Tarrant Street, Arundel, West Sussex BN18 9DN
☎ *(01903) 882312* Charlie Malcolmson

A freehouse always serving Fuller's London Pride and Young's Special plus two guests such as Hop Back Summer Lightning, Rye and Coriander or Crop Circle, or brews from Harveys or Cottage. Small producers always well-represented.

A small, country-style pub dating from 1625, situated out of the town centre. Two bars, patio, table seating at the front. Sandwiches available Mon–Thurs lunchtimes, bar menu Fri–Sun lunchtimes. Children allowed.

 *11am–3pm and 5.30–11pm Mon–Fri; 11am–11pm Sat; 12–10.30pm Sun.*

ASHURST

The Fountain Inn

Ashurst, Nr Steyning, West Sussex BN44 3AP
☎ *(01403) 710219*
Mark and Christopher White

Harveys Sussex Best, King Horsham Best Bitter and Marston's Pedigree always on offer, plus a weekly changing guest, perhaps Harveys Sussex Old or Gale's HSB.

An unspoilt sixteenth-century inn with low beams, a flagstone floor and large inglenook fireplace. Picturesque cottage garden and large duck pond. No machines or music. Bar and restaurant food served at lunchtime and evenings (light snacks only Sunday pm and Monday pm). Large car park and garden. Children under 10 not allowed inside the pub. Located on the B2135 north of Steyning.

 *11.30am–2.30pm and 6–11pm Mon–Sat; 12–3pm and 7–10.30pm Sun.*

BALCOMBE

The Cowdray Arms

London Road, Balcombe, Haywards Heath, West Sussex RH17 6QD
☎ *(01444) 811280* Gerry McElhatton

A Greene King tenancy serving Old Speckled Hen, Morland Original, Greene King Abbot and IPA and two guest ales.

A one-bar Victorian pub with a bar, dining room and conservatory restaurant. Large fenced garden. Parking for 60 cars. Food is served lunchtimes and evenings. Situated on the B2036, two minutes from Junction 10a of the M23.

 *11am–3pm and 5.30–11pm Mon–Sat; 12–3pm and 7–10.30pm Sun.*

BATTLE

The Squirrel Inn

North Trade Road, Battle, East Sussex TN33 9LJ
☎ *(01424) 772717* Mr and Mrs Coundley

Harveys ales always available plus several guests (200 per year) including Rother Valley Level Best and brews from Gale's and Mansfield etc. New and seasonal beers ordered as and when available.

An eighteenth-century old drover's pub in beautiful countryside surrounded by fields. Family-run freehouse. Unspoilt public bar with log fires. Restaurant (suitable for functions and weddings). Two large beer gardens, ample parking, purpose-built children's room. Families welcome. Located just outside Battle on the A271.

 *11.30am–3pm and 6–11pm Mon–Thurs; 11.30am–11pm Fri–Sat; 12–10.30pm Sun.*

BECKLEY

The Rose & Crown

Northiam Road, Beckley, Nr Rye, East Sussex TN31 6SE
☎ *(01797) 252161* Alice Holland

Harveys Best, Hook Norton Best, Badger IPA, Timothy Taylor Landlord and Fuller's ESB always available plus two constantly changing guests from independent breweries.

An old coaching inn on a site which has been occupied by a pub since the twelfth century. Dining area, large garden, petanque. Food available at lunchtime and evenings. Well-behaved children allowed.

11.30am–3pm and 5–11pm Mon–Thurs; all day Fri–Sun.

BERWICK VILLAGE

The Cricketers Arms

Berwick Village, Nr Polegate, East Sussex BN26 6SP
☎ *(01323) 870469* Peter Brown

A Harveys tied house with Best Bitter and a seasonal brew usually available.

Three-roomed, cottage-style country pub with stone floors, two open fires and picturesque gardens. Situated near the South Downs Way and very popular with walkers and cyclists. Food served each lunchtime and evening. Car park. Children welcome in designated room. Located west of Drusillas roundabout; signposted to Berwick church.

 *11am–3pm and 6–11pm Mon–Fri; 11am–11pm Sat; 12–10.30pm Sun.*

BEXHILL-ON-SEA

The Rose & Crown

Turkey Road, Bexhill-on-Sea, East Sussex TN39 5HH
☎ *(01424) 214625*
Stephen and Sarah Newman

Greene King Abbot and IPA always available, with Harveys Sussex Best a regularly featured guest. Another guest, changed monthly, could be something like Greene King Ruddles County or Old Speckled Hen.

One bar, dining area, big-screen sports, darts, bar billiards and Bexhill in Bloom-winning beer garden. 'Hungry Horse' menu includes big plate specials and bar snacks. Food is served 12–10pm Mon–Sat and 12–9.30pm Sun. Disabled toilets. Under 14s allowed until 9pm in designated area only.

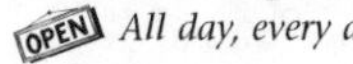 *All day, every day.*

BOGNOR REGIS

Old Barn

42 Felpham Road, Bognor Regis, West Sussex PO22 7DF
☎ *(01243) 821564* Brian Griffith

Ringwood Best Bitter, Shepherd Neame Master Brew and Hop Back Summer Lightning regularly available, plus one or two guest beers perhaps from Hop Back, Gale's, Ringwood, Greene King and others.

Thatched, converted barn on the edge of the village behind Butlin's. Pool, darts and Sky TV. Popular with all ages, locals and Butlin's staff, etc. Food available 11am–7pm. Small car park. Well-behaved children welcome.

11am–11pm Mon–Sat; 12–10.30pm Sun.

BRIGHTON

The Cobbler's Thumb

10 New England Road, Brighton, East Sussex BN1 4GG
☎ *(01273) 605636*
Geoff Eagle and Nicci Wessing

A freehouse serving Harveys Best Bitter, plus at least one other regular and one seasonal ale.

A traditional locals' pub with an Australian theme and speciality drinks. Heated 'outback' beer garden, pool table (free 12–6pm every day), Sky TV, pub games. Occasional music and DJ, pool league and competition. Food available 12–4pm Mon–Fri. Cool dogs welcome.

11am–11pm Mon–Sat; 12–10.30pm Sun.

The Evening Star

55–6 Surrey Street, Brighton, East Sussex BN1 3PB
☎ *(01273) 328931*
Matt and Karen Wickham, Michelle Whitham

The home of the Dark Star Brewing Company, though the brewery is no longer on the same site as the pub. Seven real ales always available, including beers from Dark Star and a rotating guest list. Two real ciders and Belgian beers on draught also served.

A specialist real-ale house with wooden floors. Bar food is available 12–3pm daily. Children not allowed. Just 150 yards from railway station.

12–11pm Mon–Fri; 11.30am–11pm Sat; 12–10.30pm Sun.

Hand In Hand

33 Upper St James's Street, Brighton, East Sussex BN2 1JN
☎ *(01273) 699595* Brenda and Bev Robbins

Home of the Kemptown Brewery with all Kemptown brews usually available, plus Badger Best and Tanglefoot.

Cosy, street-corner pub, probably the smallest tower brewery in England. Food served 12–3pm. No children.

12–11pm (10.30pm Sun).

The Lion & Lobster

24 Sillwood Street, Brighton, East Sussex BN1 2PS
☎ *(01273) 327299* Gary Whelan

A genuine freehouse with five real ales (200 per year). These might include Greene King Abbot, Leadmill Red River, Harveys Best, Gale's HSB or something from Cottage or Dark Star.

A traditional, Irish family-run pub with a great atmosphere. All ages welcome. Bar and restaurant food available 12–3pm and 5–9pm Mon–Thurs, 12–9pm Fri–Sat and 12–6pm Sun. Live music weekly, including jazz and Irish music on Thurs and Sun. Bed and breakfast accommodation. Located 200 yards from the seafront, in between the Bedford Hotel and Norfolk Hotel, just off Western Road.

 *11am–11pm Mon–Wed; 11am–12am Thurs–Sat; 12–11.30pm Sun.*

Prince Albert

48 Trafalgar Street, Brighton, East Sussex BN1 4ED
☎ *(01273) 730499* Chris Steward

Young's Special and a Harveys brew usually available with two guest beers such as Fuller's London Pride, Greene King Old Speckled Hen, Timothy Taylor Landlord or a Bateman or Forge beer.

Large, Grade II listed former Victorian hotel, which was completely refurbished as a pub in 1999. Food served 12–3pm and 5–9pm daily. Children welcome until 5pm. Situated next to Brighton Station, under the Trafalgar Street Bridge.

 *11am–11pm Mon–Sat; 12–10.30pm Sun.*

The Sussex Yeoman

7 Guildford Road, Brighton, East Sussex BN1 3LU
☎ *(01273) 327985* Rosie Dunton

Greene King IPA and Abbot plus a Harveys ale always available. Also occasional seasonal guests.

A trendy pub decorated in orange and blue with a young clientele (25–40) and a relaxed atmosphere. Games nights feature board games, or a pop quiz on Wednesday evenings. Bar snacks and fuller menu available until 9.30pm. No children.

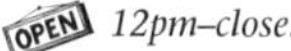 *12pm–close.*

Tap & Spile

67 Upper Gloucester Road, Brighton, East Sussex BN1 3LQ
☎ *(01273) 329540*

Up to four brews. Shepherd Neame Spitfire, Badger Tanglefoot or beers from Bateman and other smaller breweries are among the regular guests. Seasonals and specials as available.

A quaint 1930s-style alehouse, with church pews, wooden floor and a pool room with quarry tiles. A locals' pub, nice and friendly. No food. No children.

 *12–3pm and 5–11pm Mon–Thurs; all day Fri–Sun.*

BURPHAM

The George & Dragon

Burpham, Near Arundel, West Sussex BN18 9RR
☎ *(01903) 883131* James Rose and Kate Holle

Three real ales always available. Harveys Best, King Horsham Best and something from Dark Star are usually on the menu.

Located in a small village two miles from Arundel off the main track, with some of the best views of the Arun valley. Excellent walking all around. Bar and restaurant food available 12–2pm and 7–9.30pm (restaurant evenings and Sunday lunch only). Car park. Children over 12 allowed.

 *11am–2.30pm and 6–11pm Mon–Sat; 12–3pm and 7–10.30pm Sun.*

COMPTON

The Coach & Horses

Compton, Nr Chichester, West Sussex PO18 9HA
☎ *(01705) 631228* David Butler

Fuller's ESB always available plus five guest beers (100s per year) from breweries including Cheriton, Cottage, Hop Back, Dark Star, Oakleaf and Stonehenge.

Situated on the Sussex Downs, a coaching inn built in 1500 with exposed beams and a Victorian extension. Bar and restaurant food is available at lunchtime and evenings. Car parking, garden and skittle alley. Children allowed. Good walking. Take the signed road to Uppark House (B2146).

 *11am–2.30pm and 6–11pm Mon–Sat; 12–3pm and 7–10.30pm Sun.*

CRAWLEY

The Swan Inn

Horsham Road, West Green, Crawley, West Sussex RH11 7AY
☎ *(01293) 527447* Louise and David Baker

Fuller's London Pride always on offer, plus five other guest ales, including one on the back bar. Ales from breweries such as Adnams, Orkney, St Austell, Greene King and Gale's, as well as local breweries King & Co and Dark Star to name but a few. Traditional cider, again on the back bar, served during the summer months. Cask Marque accredited.

A very traditional local with two bars, friendly staff and locals of all ages. Live music every weekend, resident DJ and rock nights throughout the month. Pool table, juke box, darts, cribbage, Sky TV and beer garden. Well-behaved children and dogs welcome. Barbecues throughout the summer and a fortnightly curry night.

OPEN *11am–11pm Mon–Sat; 12–10.30pm Sun.*

DANEHILL

The Coach and Horses

School Lane, Danehill, Nr Haywards Heath, East Sussex RH17 7JF
☎ *(01825) 740369* Ian and Catherine Philpots

Harveys Best, Adnams Bitter and a couple of guests available.

Two-bar cottage-style freehouse with a reputation for good food, served at lunchtime and evenings. Outside garden and terrace with fine views, car park.

OPEN *11.30am–3pm (4pm Sat) and 6–11pm Mon–Sat; 12–4pm and 7–10.30pm Sun.*

EASTBOURNE

The Lamb Inn

36 High Street, Old Town, Eastbourne, East Sussex BN21 1HH
☎ *(01323) 720545* Mrs Hume

Tied to Harveys Brewery, so Harveys Bitter always available.

An old-style, three-bar pub with seating at the side. Food available at lunchtime and evenings. Children allowed.

OPEN *10.30am–3pm and 5.30–close Mon–Thurs; all day Fri–Sat; 12–4pm and 7–10.30pm Sun.*

The Windsor Tavern

165 Langney Road, Eastbourne, East Sussex BN22 8AH
☎ *(01323) 726206* Steve and Debbie Leach

Harvey's Best, Fuller's London Pride, Marston's Pedigree and Shephered Neame Spitfire usually available, plus a guest beer changed regularly.

A quiet, traditional-style pub with a friendly atmosphere close to the town centre and believed to be the oldest alehouse in Eastbourne. The large grassed beer garden hosts barbecues in summer. Good home-cooked food available 12–3pm. Well-behaved children and dogs welcome. Pool table, cribbage.

OPEN *10.30am–11pm Mon–Sat; 12–10.30pm Sun.*

EAST GRINSTEAD

The Ship Inn

Ship Street, East Grinstead, West Sussex RH19 4RG
☎ *(01342) 312089* Chris Phelps

A Young's-owned pub, always serving Young's Bitter, Special and either Winter Warmer or Waggledance (seasonal) plus a couple of guests changed monthly.

A refurbished, traditional English pub with two bars and a huge beer garden. Darts, football and golf teams. Three en-suite bedrooms. Homemade food available Mon–Sat 12–9pm and Sun 12–7pm. Situated at the top of the high street.

OPEN *11am–11pm Mon–Sat; 12–10.30pm Sun.*

EAST HOATHLY

The King's Head

1 High Street, East Hoathly, Lewes, East Sussex BN8 6DR
☎ *(01825) 840238* Robert and Tracie Wallace

Home of the 1648 Brewing Company with 1648 Original and Harveys Best always available plus 1648 Signature and Warrant rotated (new beers are being developed) and a range of guest brews.

A seventeenth-century former coaching inn, now a freehouse and micro-brewery set in a conservation village. Character bar, restaurant, function room, enclosed garden. Home-cooked food served lunchtime and evenings. Period cottage available for letting as holiday accommodation. Children and dogs welcome.

OPEN *11am–4pm and 6–11pm Mon–Sat; 11am–4pm and 7–10.30pm Sun.*

FERNHURST

The King's Arms

Midhurst Road, Fernhurst, West Sussex GU27 3HA
☎ *(01428) 652005* Annabel and Michael Hurst

King's Arms Ale (brewed especially by Ventnor Brewery), Ringwood Best and Hogs Back TEA always available plus two guests, perhaps including Hop Back Summer Lightning, Timothy Taylor Landlord, Ringwood Fortyniner and RCH Pitchfork.

A seventeenth-century freehouse with oak beams and fireplaces. An L-shaped bar with servery to dining area, plus hay barn for live bands, weddings etc. Surrounded by farmland, customers may come by horse or helicopter. Food available at lunchtime and evenings. Children allowed until 7pm, over 14s thereafter.

11.30am–3pm and 5.30–11pm Mon–Sat; 12–3pm only Sun.

FIRLE

The Ram Inn

Firle, Nr Lewes, East Sussex BN8 6NS
☎ *(01273) 858222*
Keith Wooller and Nikki Wooller

Harveys Best Bitter permanently available, plus two regularly changing guest beers perhaps from Otter or Ringwood breweries.

Simple and unspoilt seventeenth-century coaching inn, situated in attractive village. Log fires during the winter months and large enclosed garden. Regular live folk music. Food served 12–5.30pm Mon–Thurs and 12–9pm Fri–Sun. Car park. Families very welcome – special facilities include three children's menus, family room with toys (for use in winter), microwave for heating baby food, nappy changing facilities, high chairs and outdoor play equipment.

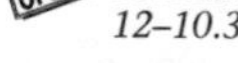
11.30am–11pm Mon–Sat; 12–10.30pm Sun.

FISHBOURNE

The Bull's Head

99 Fishbourne Road, Fishbourne, Nr Chichester, West Sussex PO19 3JP
☎ *(01243) 839895* Roger and Julie Pocock

Gale's HSB, GB and Butser, plus Fuller's London Pride always available, plus a range of changing guest ales.

A converted seventeenth-century farmhouse with a country atmosphere, just one mile from the city centre. Bar and restaurant food available at lunchtime and evenings except Sunday. Car park, garden and children's room. On the A259.

11am–3pm and 5.30–11pm Mon–Fri; 11am–11pm Sat; 12–10.30pm Sun.

FLETCHING

The Griffin Inn

Fletching, Near Uckfield, East Sussex TN22 3SS
☎ *(01825) 722890*
Bridget, Nigel and James Pullen
www.thegriffininn.co.uk

Harveys Best, King Horsham Best and Badger (Hall & Woodhouse) Tanglefoot always available, plus an occasional guest beer.

Sixteenth-century, Grade II listed two-bar coaching inn situated in an unspoilt village. Run by the Pullen family for more than 20 years. Real fires and wood panelling. Two acres of gardens with lovely views towards Sheffield Park. Restaurant and bar food served every lunchtime and evening. Car park. Children welcome. Eight en-suite rooms.

12–3pm and 6–11pm (10.30pm Sun).

FRANT

Abergavenny Arms Hotel

Frant Road, Frant, East Sussex TN3 9DB
☎ *(01892) 750233*
Paul Vallis and Paula Schofield

Four real ales usually available including Fuller's London Pride, Harveys Sussex Best and Greene King Abbot, plus a guest changed every week.

Built in the 1430s, a large, two-bar country inn with non-smoking restaurant. The lounge bar was used as a courtroom in the eighteenth century, with cells in the cellar. Bar and restaurant food available at lunchtime and evenings every day. Three letting rooms (one family suite of two rooms, and one double en-suite). Car park, garden. Children allowed. Easy to find, on the A267 south of Tunbridge Wells.

11am–11pm Mon–Sat; 12–10.30pm Sun.

GRAFFHAM

The Foresters Arms

Graffham, Petworth, West Sussex GU28 0QA
☎ *(01798) 867202* Lloyd Pocock

Cheriton Pots Ale plus four guest beers available which often include Hop Back Summer Lightning, beers from Harveys and an ever-changing selection from local breweries and micros.

Heavily beamed country freehouse dating from circa 1609. Situated at the foot of the South Downs with big log fires in winter and large garden for the summer. Food served every lunchtime and evening. Car park. Children are permitted in certain areas of the bar and restaurant, but there are no special facilities. En-suite accommodation.

11am–2.30pm and 6–11pm Mon–Sat; 12–3pm Sun.

HAILSHAM

The Bricklayers Arms

1 Ersham Road, Hailsham, East Sussex BN27 3LA
☎ *(01323) 841587* C Walker

Brews from Young's and Harveys always available plus a guest ale changed every month.

More than 100 years old, a traditional two-bar pub with fishing, football and chess clubs, darts, pool and bar billiards. Real food available in the bar until 8pm. Interesting beer garden. Children allowed in the garden only. Live music and beer festivals. Five miles from Eastbourne, off the A22.

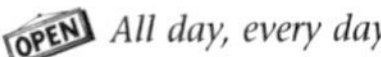
All day, every day.

HALFWAY BRIDGE

Halfway Bridge Inn

Halfway Bridge, Nr Petworth, West Sussex GU28 9BP
☎ *(01798) 861281* Simon and James Hawkins
www.thesussexpub.co.uk

Harvey's Best always available plus two guests (100 per year) changed each week. These could be Cheriton Pots Ale and Gale's HSB or something else from Hampshire or Arundel breweries. Also local cider.

Built in 1710 on the A272 halfway between Midhurst and Petworth, an authentic staging post on the Dover to Winchester road. Four rooms around a central serving area, inglenook fireplace. Bar and restaurant food at lunchtime and evenings. Car park, garden, non-smoking area, traditional games. Children over 10 allowed. Accommodation is available in the converted stable behind the pub.

11–3pm and 6–11pm Mon–Sat; 12–3pm and 7–11pm Sun.

HASTINGS

The Carlisle

Pelham Street, Hastings, East Sussex TN34 1PE
☎ *(01424) 420193* Mike Ford

A freehouse serving brews from various local breweries, including Arundel and White, plus seasonal guests.

A bikers' pub but with a mixed clientele. Rock music, bar games. Large function room. Outside seating on concrete mushrooms. Children allowed until 7pm.

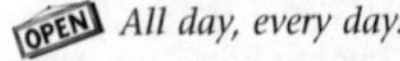
All day, every day.

First In Last Out

14–15 High Street, Hastings, East Sussex TN34 3EY
☎ *(01424) 425079* Mr Bigg
www.thefilo.co.uk

Three beers brewed on the premises, with two always available. Two guest ales such as Hop Back Rye and Coriander, but always changing. Smaller breweries favoured and normally their stronger brews. Occasional beer festivals.

Definitely a real ale house, known locally as FILO, refurbished, with lots of character and charisma. No pool or machines. Food available 12–3pm Mon–Sat. Quizzes or live music on Sunday evenings. Covered outside area with protection from inclement weather! Children allowed during the daytime only.

OPEN *All day, every day.*

HAYWARDS HEATH

The Star

1 The Broadway, Haywards Heath, West Sussex RH16 3AQ
☎ *(01444) 413267* Jason Flexen

Up to 12 beers. Brakspear Bitter, Wadworth 6X, Harveys Sussex and Marston's Pedigree are regularly available, plus guests including Timothy Taylor Landlord and Hop Back Summer Lightning. Monthly '4 for 3' offers on selected ales. Micro beer festival in April (25 ales) and two-week festival in October (50 ales and ciders).

A large, refurbished real ale house in the town centre. Food served all day, every day. Car park and outside seating. Part of the Hogshead pub group.

OPEN *11am–11pm Mon–Sat; normal hours Sun.*

HEATHFIELD

The Prince of Wales

Hailsham Road, Heathfield, East Sussex TN21 8DR
☎ *(01435) 862919* Vivienne and Ted Archer

Regularly changing beers may include Harveys Best, Greene King Abbot Ale and brews from Rother Valley, Wadworth or Charles Wells, as per customer request.

A freehouse partly dating back to the early nineteenth century, when it was used as a drovers' stop-over alehouse. Now enlarged to include two bars, restaurant and conservatory. Food served every day, lunchtime and evenings. Well-behaved children welcome. Car park.

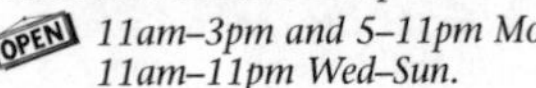
11am–3pm and 5–11pm Mon–Tues; 11am–11pm Wed–Sun.

HERSTMONCEUX

The Brewer's Arms

Gardner Street, Herstmonceux, East Sussex BN27 4LB
☎ *(01323) 832226* Barb and Barry Dimmack

A Greene King pub with IPA and Morland Original always available, plus guest ales and Greene King seasonals.

An Elizabethan pub dating from 1580. Food available 12–2pm and 7–9pm every day except Tuesday. Traditional pub games such as toad-in the-hole and bagatelle. Children under 14 not allowed in the bar, though the pub has a very good decking area and a garden.

 *11am–2.30pm and 6–11pm Mon–Sat; 12–3pm and 7–10.30pm Sun.*

HORSHAM

The Foresters Arms

43 St Leonards Road, Horsham, West Sussex RH13 6EH
☎ *(01403) 254458* Jo Mainstone

Three real ales including brews from Shepherd Neame always available.

A small pub with a large garden for outdoor games which is also child- and dog-friendly. Barbecues, quiz nights, happy hours etc. Food only on special occasions (such as BBQs). Children allowed in garden only.

 *12–3.30pm and 6–11pm Mon–Fri; all day at weekends.*

The Malt Shovel

Springfield Road, Horsham, West Sussex RH12 2PG
☎ *(01403) 254543* Steve Williams

Adnams Bitter, Brakspear Bitter and Black Sheep Bitter always available, plus up to six guests, often including Timothy Taylor Landlord. A beer festival is held in February or March.

A traditional pub with floorboards, real fires, one bar, patio and car park. Food served until 7pm (9.30pm on Mondays). Children over 14 allowed.

All day, every day.

HORSTED KEYNES

The Green Man

The Green, Horsted Keynes, West Sussex RH17 7AS
☎ *(01825) 790656*
Ramsay and Margaret Atkinson

The permanent beers are Greene King IPA, Ruddles County, Old Speckled Hen and Morland Original, and seasonal ales such as Suffolk Summer Ale are also served.

Rural pub with a traditional feel, where a quiet drink and good food can be enjoyed either inside, or out on the green. No gaming machines or pool tables. The background music is usually classical at lunchtimes. Food served 12–2.30pm Mon–Sat and 6.30–9.30pm Tues–Sat, and 12–2.30pm and 7–9pm Sun. There is a small, family dining area (no children under 5 allowed); children under 14 are not allowed in the bar area. Car park.

 *11.30am–3.30pm and 5.30–11pm Mon–Fri; 11.30am–3.30pm and 6–11pm Sat; 12–3.30pm and 6–10.30pm Sun.*

HOVE

Farm Tavern

13 Farm Road, Hove, East Sussex
☎ *(01273) 325902*
Diana Sayers and Colin Peterson

Greene King IPA, Abbot Ale and Old Speckled Hen usually available, plus seasonal Greene King ales.

Hidden little gem of a pub situated near the town centre. Homemade food and bar snacks served 12–3pm and 5–9pm Mon–Fri, 12–6pm at weekends. A recently refurbished upstairs room is available for families with children until 6pm.

 *11am–11pm Mon–Sat; 12–10.30pm Sun.*

Freemasons

Western Road, Hove, East Sussex BN3 1AF
☎ *(01273) 732043* Tanya and Darcy Gander

Greene King IPA always available, plus guests rotating on two pumps. Adnams Broadside and beers from Waggledance and Harveys are regulars.

A bar/restaurant with cocktail bar upstairs. Cask Marque approved. Outside seating. Disabled access and toilets. Food available from 12–9pm Tues–Sat; 12–6pm Sun–Mon; pizzas and tapas available Sun–Mon evenings. Traditional roasts on Sun lunchtimes. Children allowed until 5pm.

12–11pm (10.30pm Sun).

ICKLESHAM

The Queen's Head

Parsonage Lane, Icklesham, Winchelsea, East Sussex TN36 4BL
☎ *(01424) 814552* Ian Mitchell
www.queenshead.com

A freehouse with Greene King IPA and two fortnightly changing guests such as Greene King Abbot, Ringwood Old Thumper and Hop Back Summer Lightning.

A Jacobean pub dating from 1632. Farm implements on ceiling, boules pitch, function room, beer garden overlooking Rye. Food available at lunchtime and evenings. Under 12s allowed until 8.30pm. Situated off the A259.

OPEN *11am–11pm Mon–Sat; 12–10.30pm Sun.*

ISFIELD

The Laughing Fish

Station Road, Isfield, Nr Uckfield, East Sussex TN22 5XB
☎ *(01825) 750349* Linda and Andy Brooks
www.laughingfishonline.co.uk

Greene King IPA, Morland Original and Old Speckled Hen always available, plus at least one changing guest beer.

Rural village pub with real fires, offering genuine home-made food 12–2.30pm and 6.30–9.30pm every day. Sandwiches and light snacks also available. Families welcome. Separate non-smoking dining area, garden, patio and children's play area. Large car park. Situated just off the A26 between Uckfield and Lewes, next door to the Lavender Line Railway HQ at Isfield Station.

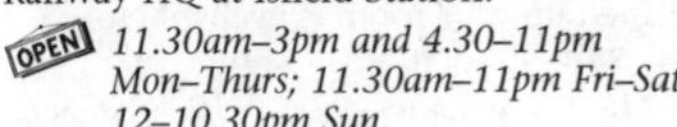

OPEN *11.30am–3pm and 4.30–11pm Mon–Thurs; 11.30am–11pm Fri–Sat; 12–10.30pm Sun.*

LEWES

The Black Horse Inn

55 Western Road, Lewes, East Sussex BN7 1RS
☎ *(01273) 473653* J Mason and J Bowell

Greene King IPA and Abbot usually available plus Morland Original and Old Speckled Hen. A guest ale might be Archers Golden or something from Bateman.

Built in 1800 as a hotel, this is a quiet, two-bar pub situated on the main road through Lewes. Bar billiards, darts, cribbage, walled beer garden. Bar snacks available 12–2pm. No children. Four letting roomss.

OPEN *11am–2.30pm and 5.30–11pm Mon–Fri; 11am–3pm and 6–11pm Sat; 12–3pm and 7–10.30pm Sun.*

The Brewer's Arms

91 High Street, Lewes, East Sussex BN7 1XN
☎ *(01273) 475524* Kevin and Joan Griffin

A freehouse with Harveys Best always available plus up to four real ales constantly rotating. Guests may include beers from Harveys, King, Arundel, Cottage or Rother Valley, to name but a few. Biddenden real cider is also served.

There has been a pub on this site since 1540. Family run, in a central location near the castle. Well-equipped, with two bars. Front bar has non-smoking area while food is being served, and has no piped music. Back bar has pool, darts, toad-in-the-hole, juke box and big-screen TV. Food, including homemade specials, available every day until 6.45pm. Dogs welcome if on a lead.

OPEN *10am–11pm Mon–Sat; 12–10.30pm Sun.*

The Elephant & Castle

White Hill, Lewes, East Sussex BN2 2DJ
☎ *(01273) 473797* Dave Whiting

A freehouse with Harveys Best, Greene King Old Speckled Hen and Charles Wells Bombardier always available.

An old Sussex pub with one bar and a function room. Meeting place for the Bonfire Society. A themed menu is available at lunchtimes only. Children allowed.

OPEN *All day, every day.*

The Gardener's Arms

46 Cliffe High Street, Lewes, East Sussex BN7 2AN
☎ *(01273) 474808* Andy Fitzgerald

A constantly changing range of six real ales from independent breweries across the UK. Harveys Best and others from the local brewery plus Archers Golden are regular features, but more than 800 different brews have been served in the past three years.

A small traditional two-bar street-corner pub opposite Harveys Brewery, sympathetically restored after the 2000 floods. Bar snacks and sandwiches available at lunchtime. Dogs welcome. Handy for shoppers, but country walks nearby.

OPEN *11am–11pm Mon–Sat; 12–10.30pm Sun.*

Snowdrop Inn

199 South Street, Lewes, East Sussex BN7 2BU
☎ *(01273) 471018*

Harveys Best, Hop Back Summer Lightning, Fuller's London Pride and Adnams Broadside could well be among the real ales available.

At the bottom of town, a thriving, friendly local with wooden floors, function/dining room and bars on two levels. Outside yard. Live music. Good food (including vegetarian options) available until 9pm. Children welcome at lunchtimes, plus dogs on a lead.

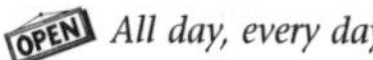
All day, every day.

LINDFIELD

The Linden Tree

47 High Street, Lindfield, Haywards Heath, West Sussex RH16 2HN
☎ *(01444) 482995* Simon Pearce

Ringwood Old Thumper, Harveys Best Bitter, Marston's Pedigree, Arundel Castle and Gale's HSB usually on offer, plus two guests changed every couple of days from breweries such as Dark Star, Weltons (Hepworth and Co) or King.

A traditional inn situated in a village high street. Food available 12–2pm Wed–Sun (Sunday roasts), and 6.30–9.30pm Wed–Sat evenings. No smoking in the restaurant. Public car park within 100 yards. No children. The restaurant is available for hire.

11am–3pm and 6–11pm Mon–Sat;
12–2.30pm and 7.30–10.30pm Sun.

LITLINGTON

The Plough & Harrow

Litlington, Nr Alfriston, East Sussex BN26 5RE
☎ *(01323) 870632* Barry and Ros Richards

Badger Best and Tanglefoot always available plus four guests from a large list including Wadworth 6X, Charles Wells Bombardier and Eagle IPA, Fuller's London Pride and brews from Harveys and Federation.

A fifteenth-century freehouse with oak beams, two bars and a busy restaurant. Bar and restaurant food available. Car park and garden. Children allowed in the restaurant. Three miles south of the A27, two miles from the nearest village (Alfriston).

11am–2.30pm and 6.30–11pm.

MAPLEHURST

The White Horse Inn

Park Lane, Maplehurst, Nr Horsham, West Sussex RH13 6LL
☎ *(01403) 891208* Simon Johnson

A genuine freehouse with Weltons Pride and Joy and Harveys Best always available, plus up to four guests, changed in rotation, such as Hogs Back TEA and brews from King and Dark Star, to name but a few. Small breweries are favoured.

A traditional, 200-year-old three-bar pub in the middle of a Sussex hamlet. No juke box, machines or piped music. Non-smoking area, conservatory, large garden with good views and a children's play area. Food served 12–2pm and 6–9pm daily. Situated less than two miles north of the A272 and south of the A281, five miles from Horsham.

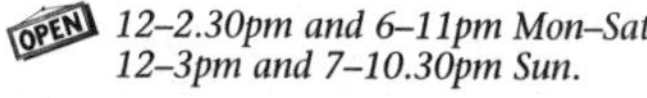
12–2.30pm and 6–11pm Mon–Sat;
12–3pm and 7–10.30pm Sun.

MIDHURST

The Crown Inn

Edinburgh Square, Midhurst, West Sussex GU29 9NL
☎ *(01730) 813462* L Williams and R Cox

Fuller's London Pride and Badger Tanglefoot always available with up to five constantly changing real ales from independent brewers from across the UK. Gravity and hand-pump served.

A sixteenth-century freehouse with wooden floors and open fires. Three bar areas including pool and games room and 50-inch plasma TV in main bar. Courtyard. Behind and below the church in the old part of town.

11am–11pm Mon–Sat; 12–10.30pm Sun.

NUTBOURNE

The Rising Sun

The Street, Nutbourne, Pulborough, West Sussex RH20 2HE
☎ *(01798) 812191* Regan Howard

A freehouse serving Fuller's London Pride, Greene King Abbot and King and Barnes Sussex Ale plus a minimum of two guests such as Harveys Sussex and Hogs Back TEA, or something from an independent such as Cottage.

A 400-year-old pub with Victorian frontage in walking country. Two bars, wooden floors, dining area, mixed clientele with very friendly landlord! Food served at lunchtime and evenings. Children allowed.

11am–3pm and 6–11pm (10.30pm Sun).

NUTHURST

The Black Horse Inn

Nuthurst Street, Nuthurst, West Sussex RH13 6LH
☎ *(01403) 891272*
Clive Henwood and Dave Thomas

Harveys Sussex, Fuller's London Pride, King Horsham and Young's Best usually available, plus guests on up to three pumps, which always include a regional ale and are changed at least twice a week.

A seventeenth-century freehouse with front terrace and stream-side rear beer garden. Lots of original features including a spitroast inglenook fireplace, exposed wattle and daub walls, two bars, one with a Horsham stone floor, a snug and a restaurant. Private room for hire. Food, including daily specials, available 12–2.30pm and 6.30–9.30pm through the week and all day until 9.30pm on Sat and 8.30pm on Sun. Children welcome with menu provided. Dogs also welcome. Beer festivals on bank holidays. Located four miles south of Horsham.

 *12–3pm and 6–11pm Mon–Fri; 12–11pm Sat and bank holidays; 12–10.30pm Sun.*

OLD HEATHFIELD

The Star

Church Street, Old Heathfield, East Sussex TN21 9AH
☎ *(01435) 863570* Mr and Mrs Chappell

Harveys brews and Fuller's London Pride always available plus a guest (50 per year) such as Harviestoun Ptarmigan, Hop Back Summer Lightning, Black Sheep Best; also Daleside Old Legover, Gravesend Shrimpers, NYBC Flying Herbert, Daleside Monkey Wrench and Burton Bridge Hearty Ale etc.

A freehouse built in 1348, licensed in 1388. Original beams and open fires. Famous gardens and views. Bar and restaurant food served at lunchtime and evenings. Car park and garden. Children allowed. At a dead end of a road to the rear of Old Heathfield church.

11.30am–3pm and 5.30–11pm.

OVING

The Gribble Inn

Oving, Nr Chichester, West Sussex PO20 6BP
☎ *(01243) 786893* Brian and Cyn Elderfield

Gribble Ales all available. Wobbler only from September to March.

Picturesque sixteenth-century inn, home to the Gribble Brewery. Traditional country pub, serving good, wholesome home-cooked food at both lunchtime and evenings, seven days a week. Car park, large garden, non-smoking area, children's room, skittle alley.

11am–3pm and 5.30–11pm Mon–Sat; 12–3pm and 7–10.30pm Sun.

PETT

The Two Sawyers

Pett Road, Pett, Nr Hastings, East Sussex TN35 4HB
☎ *(01424) 812255*
Clive Soper and Fred Bramble

Sussex Pett Progress and Brother's Best always available, plus seasonals as available. Weekly changing guests selected from numerous nationwide micro-breweries.

An olde-worlde pub with two bars, comfortable restaurant, large beer garden, children's play area. Live music on Friday nights, quiz night on Wednesday. Food available at lunchtime and evenings. Children allowed in the restaurant, garden or snug.

 *11am–11pm.*

PORTSLADE

The Stanley Arms

47 Wolseley Road, Portslade, East Sussex BN41 1SS
☎ *(01273) 430234* Stephen and Russell Bennett
www.thestanley.com

Three regularly changing beers always available from brewers across the country. As one beer finishes, a different one starts.

Traditional, street-corner pub with attractive garden. Regular CAMRA award winner. Barbecues in summer and live blues/rock music most weekends. Sandwiches available. Children welcome in the lounge and garden until 8pm. Winter, spring and summer beer festivals. Football, cricket and cribbage teams. Situated 400 yards north of Fishersgate station.

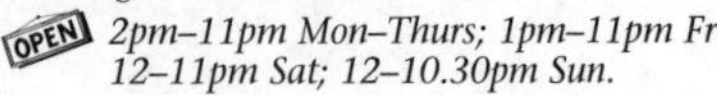
2pm–11pm Mon–Thurs; 1pm–11pm Fri; 12–11pm Sat; 12–10.30pm Sun.

ROBERTSBRIDGE

The Seven Stars Inn

High Street, Robertsbridge, East Sussex TN32 5AJ
☎ *(01580) 880333* Mark Fox and Lisa Conn

Harveys Best Bitter and Old Ale always available, plus Harveys seasonal brews.

Claims to be Britain's oldest haunted pub, dating from the fourteenth century. Homemade food available, including freshly prepared pizzas, 12–2.30pm and 6–9pm Tues–Sat. Sunday carvery 12.30–3.30pm. One bar, dining area, car park and beer garden. In the centre of Robertsbridge.

 *12–11pm*

RUDGWICK

Thurlow Arms

Baynards, Rudgwick, Nr Horsham, West Sussex RH12 3AD
☎ *(01403) 822459* Mr Gibbs

Fuller's London Pride, Hogs Back TEA, Ringwood Best Bitter, Badger Tanglefoot and Dorset Best regularly available.

Large Victorian pub situated on the South Downs Way, with railway memorabilia relating to the closure of Baynards station in 1965. Games room with darts and pool, restaurant, dining rooms and large garden. Food served 12–2pm and 6.15–9.30pm Mon–Fri, 12–2.15pm and 6.15–9.30pm Sat, and 12–2.30pm and 7–9pm Sun. Large car park. Children's play castle and menu.

 *11am–3pm and 6–11pm Mon–Sat; 12–10.30pm Sun.*

RUSTINGTON

The Fletcher Arms

Station Road, Rustington, West Sussex BN16 3AF
☎ *(01903) 784858* Mr and Mrs Baden

Harveys Best, Shepherd Neame Spitfire, Greene King Old Speckled Hen and Ringwood Best always available, plus a daily changing guest beer perhaps from King, Wolf, Ballard's, Wild, Timothy Taylor, Hogs Back, Fuller's, Ringwood, Gale's, or many others from around the country.

Large, friendly, 1920s pub, winner of many awards including Cask Marque. Live entertainment, public and saloon bar and olde-worlde barn. Food available 11.30am–2.30pm and 6–9pm Mon–Sat, 12–2.30pm Sun. Large car park. Large garden with swings and bouncy castle.

OPEN *All day, every day.*

RYE

The Inkerman Arms

Harbour Road, Rye Harbour, Rye, East Sussex TN31 7TQ
☎ *(01797) 222464* Peter and Dawn

A freehouse serving a selection of real ales from one of two local brewers. Guest ales always available.

A traditional pub with one bar, lounge and dining area. Boules pitch, garden. Food served 12–2.20pm and 7–9.20pm daily. Well-behaved children and dogs welcome. Car park.

 *12–3pm Mon (closed Mon evenings); 12–3pm and 7–11pm Tues–Sat; 12–4pm Sun; open all day during summer and bank holidays weekends.*

The Ypres Castle Inn

Gungarden, Rye, East Sussex TN31 7HH
☎ *(01797) 223248*
Tom Cosgrove and Michael Gage
www.yprescastleinn.co.uk

A freehouse with Harveys Bitter always available plus up to four regular guests such as Charles Wells Bombardier, Adnams Broadside, Fuller's London Pride and Timothy Taylor Landlord.

A traditional weatherboarded pub dating from the seventeenth century. No juke box or gaming machines. Non-smoking area, safe garden with lovely river views. Live music Fridays. Food using local produce available at lunchtimes and evenings (except Sunday evening) – reservations recommended. At least ten wines available by the glass. Children allowed in separate area and garden at lunchtime, and until 9pm in an evening, but only if eating.

 *11.30am–3pm and 6–11pm; closed all day Tues and Sun evening, except in July and August; open all day at peak times in summer.*

ST LEONARDS ON SEA

The Dripping Spring

34 Tower Road, St Leonards on Sea, East Sussex RN37 6JE
☎ *(01424) 434055* Mr and Mrs Gillitt

Goacher's Light, Timothy Taylor Best Bitter and Young's Bitter served, plus ales from local breweries. Other guests from as far afield as possible – more than 2,000 guest ales to date.

A small two-bar public house with attractive courtyard to the rear. Sussex CAMRA Pub of the Year 1999, 2000, 2001 and 2003, National CAMRA Pub of the Year runner-up 2001. Bar food available at lunchtime. Car parking. Situated in a side street off the A21.

 *12–11pm Mon–Fri; 11am–11pm Sat; 12–3pm and 7–10.30pm Sun.*

SEAFORD

The Wellington

Steyne Road, Seaford, East Sussex BN25 1HT
☎ *(01323) 890032* Mr Shaw

Fuller's London Pride, Greene King IPA, Abbot and Harveys Best Bitter always available. Also one guest from an independent or micro-brewery, changing daily.

A community pub with two bars and a function room. Parking nearby. Food available at lunchtime only. Children allowed.

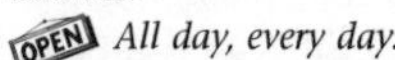 *All day, every day.*

The White Lion

74 Claremont Road, Seaford, East Sussex
☎ *(01323) 892473* Gary Weston

Harveys Sussex Best Bitter, Old, Porter and Fuller's London Pride regularly available, plus one or two guest beers perhaps from Greene King, Shepherd Neame or Harveys.

Friendly, small, family-run hotel by the seafront. Food served every lunchtime and evening. Car park. Large conservatory and separate non-smoking area. Children welcome. En-suite accommodation.

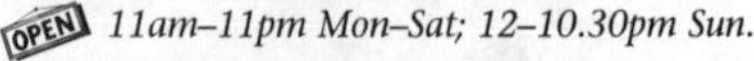 *11am–11pm Mon–Sat; 12–10.30pm Sun.*

SEDLESCOMBE

The Queen's Head

The Green, Sedlescombe, Battle, East Sussex TN33 0QA
☎ *(01424) 870228* Samantha Fisher

Charles Wells Bombardier always available plus Rother Valley Level Best and Flower's Original.

A country pub with beams and brasses, on the village green. Beer garden, car park. Food served 12–2.30pm, including fish and chips, jacket potatoes, baguettes and sandwiches. Traditional Sunday lunch in separate restaurant. Children welcome. Pool table

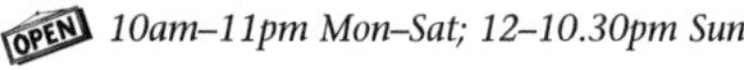 *10am–11pm Mon–Sat; 12–10.30pm Sun.*

SHOREHAM

The Lazy Toad

88 High Street, Shoreham-by-Sea, West Sussex BN43 5DB
☎ *(01273) 441622* Mr Cederberg

Greene King Abbot, Badger Tanglefoot, Shepherd Neame Spitfire and Gale's Festival Mild among the beers always available plus up to three guests.

A small, friendly freehouse with one big bar. Food served only at lunchtime. Children over 14 allowed.

OPEN *All day, every day.*

The Red Lion

Old Shoreham Road, Shoreham-by-Sea, West Sussex BN43 5TE
☎ *(01243) 453171* James and Natalie Parker

Harveys Best Bitter and four or five guest beers regularly available, perhaps from King, Hop Back, Hogs Back, Ringwood, Dark Star, Arundel, Fuller's, Cottage or many more. Annual Easter beer festival features 50–60 beers, live music and barbecue.

Widely considered to be Shoreham's premier country pub, with low beams, inglenook and secluded beer garden. Good atmosphere, full of tales and history. Separate non-smoking eating area. Food served lunchtimes and evenings Mon–Sat, 12–9pm Sun. Children welcome. The car park is situated some distance from the pub: pass the pub on your left, turn left at mini roundabout then first left again. Follow the road to church and the car park is opposite.

OPEN *11.30am–3pm and 5.30–11pm Mon–Fri; 11.30am–11pm Sat; 12–10.30pm Sun.*

STOUGHTON

The Hare & Hounds

Stoughton, West Sussex
☎ *(01705) 631433*

Adnams Broadside, Ringwood Best and Gale's HSB always available plus four guest beers (from an endless list) such as Hop Back Summer Lightning, Timothy Taylor Landlord, Fuller's ESB, Brakspear Bitter, etc.

More than 300 years old, a flint-built pub nestling on the Sussex Downs. Bar food available at lunchtime and evenings. Car park and garden. Children allowed. Signposted at Walberton off the B2146.

 *11am–3pm and 6–11pm Mon–Sat; 12–4pm and 7–10.30pm Sun.*

TARRING

The Vine Inn

High Street, Tarring, Worthing, West Sussex BN14 7NN
☎ *(01903) 202891*
Stephen and Deborah Benson

Badger Dorset Best, Champion Ale and Tanglefoot, King and Barnes Sussex, Ringwood True Glory, Hop Back Summer Lightning and Gribble Inn Fursty Ferret always available, plus guests.

An old-fashioned pub in a listed building dating from 1645. Cask Marque accredited. One bar. Live entertainment on Mondays plus a quiz every Thursday. Enormous garden and courtyard, car park. Food available 12–2.30pm and 5.30–8pm Mon–Fri and 12–2.30pm Sat–Sun. Children and dogs welcome.

 *12–3pm and 6–11pm Mon–Thurs; 11am–11pm Fri–Sat; 12–10.30pm Sun.*

THAKEHAM

The White Lion Inn

The Street, Thakeham Village, West Sussex RH20 3EP
☎ *(01798) 813141* Judi Gehlcken

A freehouse with Greene King Abbot and IPA plus Fuller's London Pride always available, together with one regularly changing guest.

Traditional pub in a Grade II listed building in the centre of a picturesque village. Food is available, and is freshly prepared in an open-plan kitchen.

11am–3pm and 5.30–11pm Mon–Sat; 12–10.30pm Sun.

TICEHURST

The Bull Inn

Dunster Mill Lane, Three Legged Cross, Nr Ticehurst, East Sussex TN5 7HH
☎ *(01580) 200586* Bill Orr and Lisa Tindall

Up to five real ales always available including Harveys Best, Shepherd Neame Spitfire, Greene King Old Speckled Hen and White 1066, plus hundreds of other guests per year including brews from Adnams, Iceni etc.

Whealden Hall House was built between 1385 and 1425 in good walking country and has been a pub for 100 years. There are two bars with an adjoining 50-seater restaurant. Food available at lunchtime and evenings. Large car park, garden, children's play area. Bed and breakfast now available. Coming into Ticehurst from the north on the B2099, turn left beside corner house called Tollgate just before village.

11am–11pm Mon–Sat; 12–10.30pm Sun.

UCKFIELD

Alma

Framfield Road, Uckfield, East Sussex
☎ *(01825) 762232* Mrs Joy Hughes

A Harveys house with Mild, IPA, Best Bitter and seasonal brews usually available.

Traditional, family-run (third generation) pub, with Cask Marque award. Food served 12–2pm Mon–Sat and 6–9pm Mon–Fri. Car park. Separate family and non-smoking rooms.

11am–2.30pm and 6–11pm Mon–Sat; 12–2pm and 7–10.30pm Sun.

The Peacock Inn

Shortbridge, Piltdown, Uckfield, East Sussex TN22 3XA
☎ *(01825) 762463* Matthew Arnold

Harveys Best Bitter, Fuller's London Pride, Greene King Old Speckled Hen and King Horsham Best Bitter are permanent features, and the guest beer might also be from the King Brewery.

A sixteenth-century inn, heavily beamed, with bar, restaurant, inglenook, front and rear garden and patio. Snacks and meals are served 12–2.30pm and 6–10pm, with snacks and afternoon teas available 3–5.30pm. Children are welcome, and the pub has a climbing frame in the rear garden, high chairs and children's menu. Car park. On the A272 Haywards Heath to Lewes road, turn right at Piltdown Garage.

11am–11pm.

WARTLING

The Lamb Inn

Wartling, Nr Herstmonceux, East Sussex BN27 1RY
☎ *(01323) 832116* Robert Farncombe

King Horsham Best and Rother Valley Hoppers Ale always available.

A sixteenth-century pub specialising in fine ales and homemade food. Food available lunchtimes and evenings in the bar and in a separate restaurant; four fresh fish dishes are a daily speciality. Children allowed. Situated one mile from Hertmonceux Castle.

11am–3pm 6–11pm Mon–Fri; all day Sat–Sun.

WEST ASHLING

The Richmond Arms

Mill Road, West Ashling, West Sussex PO18 8EA
☎ *(01243) 575730* Sally Bryan

Greene King Abbot and IPA always available, plus guest ales.

A comfortable and cosy Victorian pub with open fires and a separate restaurant. Patio at the front. Traditional home-cooked bar and à la carte meals available at lunchtime and evenings. Well-behaved children allowed. Functions catered for. Situated one mile from Funtington and three miles from Chichester.

11am–2.30pm and 6–11pm Mon–Sat; 12–4pm and 7–10.30pm Sun.

WEST CHILTINGTON

The Five Bells

Smock Alley, West Chiltington, West Sussex RH20 2QX
☎ *(01798) 812143* Mr Edwards

Five beers always available from an ever-changing range sometimes served straight from the wood. Favoured brewers include Ballard's, Adnams, Bateman, Black Sheep, Brakspear, Bunces, Cheriton, Exmoor, Fuller's, Gale's, Greene King, Guernsey, Harveys, Hogs Back, Hook Norton, Jennings, Rebellion, Palmers, St Austell, Shepherd Neame, Smiles, Samuel Smith, Timothy Taylor and Young's.

An attractive Edwardian-style version of a Sussex farmhouse. Bar and restaurant food available at lunchtime and evenings. Car park, conservatory and beer garden. Well-behaved children allowed. Accommodation available in five en-suite rooms. Ask for directions.

12–3pm and 6–11pm.

WORTHING

The Richard Cobden

2 Cobden Road, Worthing, West Sussex BN11 4BD
☎ *(01903) 236856* John Davies

Greene King IPA and Abbot plus two other real ales always available.

A traditional Victorian alehouse built in 1868. The focus is on the old values of the trade – no fruit machines, no juke box, just old-fashioned sociability and enjoyment of life! Genuine home-cooked food served at lunchtimes (not Sunday).

11am–3pm and 5.30–11pm Mon–Thurs; all day Fri–Sat; 12–3pm and 7–10.30pm Sun.

YAPTON

The Lamb Inn

Bilsham Road, Yapton, Arundel, West Sussex BN18 0JN
☎ *(01243) 551232* Craig Gillett

Harveys Sussex Bitter and Greene King Abbot always available, plus one guest changing regularly.

An edge-of-village pub on the road side. Brick floors, large open fire, non-smoking dining area, car park, garden with children's play area, and petanque/boules. Food served every lunchtime and evening. Children allowed. Located on a minor road between the A259 and Yapton village.

11am–3pm and 5.30–11pm Mon–Thurs; 11am–3pm and 5–11pm Fri; 12–3.30pm and 6–11pm Sat; 12–4.30pm and 6.30–10.30pm Sun. Open all day at weekends during the summer.

The Maypole Inn

Maypole Lane, Yapton, Arundel, West Sussex BN18 0DP
☎ *(01243) 551417* Alan Wingate

A freehouse with a mild, Ringwood Best and Skinner's Betty Stogs always available. Up to five guests from local and West Country micro-breweries.

A country pub with public and lounge bars, log fires, skittle alley, small garden. Bar snacks available at lunchtime and Sunday roasts. Children allowed in the public bar only until 8.30pm.

11.30am–3pm and 5–11pm Mon–Thurs; all day Fri–Sun.

THE BREWERIES

BIG LAMP BREWERS

Big Lamp Brewery, Grange Road, Newburn, Newcastle upon Tyne NE15 8ND
☎ *(0191) 267 1689*

SUNNY DAZE 3.6% ABV
BITTER 3.9% ABV
DOUBLE M 4.3% ABV
SUMMERHILL STOUT 4.4% ABV
PRINCE BISHOP ALE 4.8% ABV
PREMIUM 5.2% ABV
EMBERS 5.5% ABV
KEELMAN BROWN 5.7% ABV
Plus occasional brews.

DARWIN BREWERY

63 Back Tatham St, Sunderland SR1 2QE
☎ *(0191) 514 4746*
www.darwinbrewery.com

SUNDERLAND BEST 3.9% ABV
DURHAM LIGHT ALE 4.0% ABV
EVOLUTION ALE 4.0% ABV
GHOST ALE 4.1% ABV
RICHMOND ALE 4.8% ABV
KILLER BEE 6.0% ABV
Plus a range of specialist beers.

HADRIAN & BORDER BREWERY

Unit 10, Hawick Crescent Industrial Estate, Newcastle upon Tyne NE6 1AS
☎ *(0191) 276 5302*

VALLUM BITTER 3.6% ABV
Rich, golden bitter.
GLADIATOR 3.8% ABV
A rich, dark ruby-coloured session bitter.
FARNE ISLAND 4.0% ABV
Amber-coloured, blended malt and hops.
FLOTSAM 4.0% ABV
Dark golden-coloured.
LEGION ALE 4.2% ABV
SECRET KINGDOM 4.3% ABV
Smooth and full-flavoured, refreshing bitter.
REIVER'S IPA 4.4% ABV
Award-winning bitter with citrus throughout.
CENTURION BITTER 4.5% ABV
Award-winning, pale-coloured, hoppy bitter, fruity and quenching.
NORTHUMBRIAN GOLD 4.5% ABV
JETSAM 4.8% ABV
RAMPART 4.8% ABV
Gold-coloured, flavoursome bitter.

HIGH HOUSE FARM BREWERY

High House Farm, Matfen, Newcastle upon Tyne NE20 0RG
☎ *(01661) 886192*
www.highhousefarmbrewery.co.uk

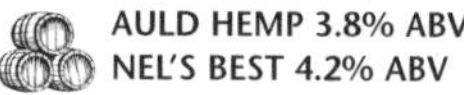

AULD HEMP 3.8% ABV
NEL'S BEST 4.2% ABV

JARROW BREWERY

Robin Hood Inn, Primrose Hill, Jarrow NE32 5UB
☎ *(0191) 428 5454*

JARROW BITTER 3.8% ABV
JOBLING'S SWINGING GIBBET 4.1% ABV
RILEY'S ARMY BITTER 4.3% ABV
VENERABLE BEAD 4.5% ABV
OLD CORNELIUS 4.8% ABV

MORDUE BREWERY

Unit 21a, West Chirton North Industrial Estate, Shiremoor NE29 8SF
☎ *(0191) 296 1879*
www.morduebrewery.com

FIVE BRIDGE BITTER 3.8% ABV
GEORDIE PRIDE 4.2% ABV
WORKIE TICKET 4.5% ABV
RADGIE GADGIE 4.8% ABV
Plus seasonals.

THE PUBS

BYKER

The Cumberland Arms

Off Byker Bank, The Ouseburn, Newcastle upon Tyne NE6 1LD
☎ *(0191) 265 6151* Jo Hodson

A freehouse with an ever-changing selection of ales from local breweries such as Wylam, Jarrow, Mordue, Northumberland and Hexhamshire.

Established in 1832, this is the only country pub in the city of Newcastle. The pub is south facing, has outside seating on a cobbled cul de sac and overlooks the city farm and the Ouseburn Valley. Two bars downstairs. No juke box, pool table, alcopops or piped music. Open fire. Food served 5–11pm Mon–Thurs, 4.30–11pm Fri, 12.30–11pm Sat–Sun. A range of entertainments and bands in upstairs bar, which is available for hire. East over Byker Bridge, right down Byker Bank, second right (cul de sac). Parking.

OPEN *5–11pm Mon–Thurs; 4.30–11pm Fri; 12.30–11pm Sat; 12.30–10.30pm Sun.*

The Free Trade Inn

St Lawrence Road, Byker, Newcastle upon Tyne NE6 1AP
☎ *(0191) 265 5764* Richard Turner

Mordue Workie Ticket and a Mordue seasonal ale always available, plus four guest beers, from local breweries such as Hadrian & Border, Wylam or Cropton.

A traditional town pub with a lovely view of the River Tyne. Two beer gardens, one bar. Sandwiches available. Children allowed during the daytime and early evening only.

OPEN *11am–11pm (10.30pm Sun).*

The Ouseburn Tavern

33 Shields Road, Byker, Newcastle upon Tyne NE6 1DJ
☎ *(0191) 276 5120* Peter Bland

Twelve beers always available from a constantly changing range (450 per year) with Bateman Valiant, Charles Wells Eagle and Black Sheep Bitter among them.

Beamed theme pub with open fires and friendly atmosphere. Bar food available at lunchtime and evenings. Car park. Children allowed. Easy to find.

OPEN *12–11pm (10.30pm Sun).*

FELLING

The Old Fox

13 Carlisle Street, Felling, Gateshead NE10 0HQ
☎ *(0191) 420 0357* Valerie White

A freehouse with Camerons Strong Arm, Fuller's London Pride and something from Durham always available plus a couple of guests from a wide range of brewers changed twice a week. Timothy Taylor Landlord is popular.

A traditional real ale pub in town location, with one main bar, two coal fires, darts, pool and a garden. Bar snacks available all day. Children allowed if eating, up to 7pm. Live entertainment. Bed and breakfast accommodation. Close to the Metro station. Easy access to the coast and central Newcastle.

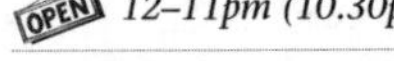
OPEN *12–11pm (10.30pm Sun).*

The Wheatsheaf

26 Carlisle Street, Felling, Gateshead NE10 0HQ
☎ *(0191) 420 0659* Jim Storey

A range of Big Lamp beers such as Bitter, Prince Bishop, Premium Ale, Sandgates or Keelman Bitter always available.

An old-fashioned community pub with one bar. Sandwiches and pies available. Children allowed until 7pm.

OPEN *12–11pm (10.30pm Sun).*

GOSFORTH

Gosforth Hotel

High Street, Gosforth
☎ *(0191) 285 6617* Yvonne Goulden

Charles Wells Bombardier, Fuller's London Pride and Marston's Pedigree always available, plus two guests, such as Black Sheep Bitter, Timothy Taylor Landlord and Shepherd Neame Spitfire.

A busy two-bar pub with a friendly atmosphere. Bar food available 12–2.30pm Mon–Sat. Function room available for hire. Car parking opposite pub. No children.

OPEN *12–11pm (10.30pm Sun).*

HEBBURN

Dougie's Tavern

Blackett Street, Hebburn NE31 1ST
☎ *(0191) 428 4800* James Atherton

Freehouse offering four cask ales, including two ever-changing guests from breweries and micro-breweries all over the UK.

A family-run pub, traditional by day and lively at night. Lunches served. Quiz on Tues, karaoke on Wed, live bands on Thurs, DJ on Fri, Sat and Sun. Children's play equipment in landscaped gardens. Large, floodlit car park.

OPEN *11am–12.30am Mon–Sat; 12–12.30am Sun.*

JARROW

The Robin Hood Inn

Primrose Hill, Jarrow NE32 5UB
☎ *(0191) 428 5454* Alison and Jess McConnell

Home of the Jarrow Brewery, with six Jarrow ales always available plus one guest.

Dating back to 1824, an ex-coaching inn with one public bar, one brewery tap bar, separate Italian restaurant, patio and beer garden overlooking the river. Food available every lunchtime and evening. Children allowed but not in the public bar. Beer festivals in the first week in March and October. Situated a six-minute walk from Fellgate railway station.

OPEN *11am–11pm Mon–Sat; 12–10.30pm Sun.*

JESMOND

The Archer

Archibold Terrace, Jesmond, Newcastle upon Tyne NE2 1DB
☎ *(0191) 281 3010* Richard Norris

Black Sheep Bitter and Caledonian Deuchars IPA always available.

Formerly known as Legendary Yorkshire Heroes and with fewer real ales than before. But a lively refurbished pub within an office complex. Bar food available on weekday lunchtimes. Four pool tables, big-screen sports, live bands Thurs and Sat. Children allowed at lunchtimes only. Five minutes out of Newcastle centre, five minutes from Jesmond Metro.

OPEN *11am–11pm Mon–Sat; 12–10.30pm Sun.*

LOW FELL

The Ale Taster

706 Durham Road, Low Fell, Gateshead NE9 6JA
☎ *(0191) 487 0770* Lawrence Gill

Mordue Workie Ticket and Radgie Gadgie always available plus up to six guests such as Timothy Taylor Landlord or Badger Tanglefoot. Beer festivals held in May and September, serving 30 extra beers.

An old coaching inn with beams and wooden floors, in the town centre. One bar, snug area, large courtyard with play area. Food available until 6pm. Children allowed.

OPEN *11am–11pm Mon–Sat; 12–10.30pm Sun.*

NEWBURN

Keelman

Grange Road, Newburn, Newcastle upon Tyne NE15 8ND
☎ *(0191) 267 1689* Lee Goulding

Big Lamp Bitter, Prince Bishop Ale, Premium, Summerhill Stout plus other Big Lamp brews regularly available.

Superb conversion of ninteenth-century water board building into a traditional family pub. Situated next to the leisure centre in Newburn Country Park, on the River Tyne. Food served daily 12–9pm. Car park, beer garden with children's play area. Accommodation.

 *11am–11pm Mon–Sat; 12–10.30pm Sun.*

NEWCASTLE UPON TYNE

The Bodega

125 Westgate Road, Newcastle upon Tyne NE1 4AG
☎ *(0191) 221 1552* Ben Rea

Mordue Workie Ticket, Geordie Pride and Durham Magus among the brews permanently available, plus two guests from breweries such as Hadrian & Border, Shepherd Neame, Black Sheep and Ridleys. Beers changed every three days.

A traditional real ale pub on the outskirts of the town centre. One bar, food available 11am–2.30pm Mon–Sat and 12–2.30pm Sun. No children.

OPEN *11am–11pm Mon–Sat; 12–10.30pm Sun.*

The Bridge Hotel

Castlegart, Newcastle upon Tyne NE1 1RQ
☎ *(0191) 232 6400* Christine Cromarty

A freehouse with Black Sheep Bitter and Mordue Workie Ticket always featured, plus three constantly changing guest beers, perhaps Hadrian & Border Gladiator, Castle Eden Nimmo's 4X, Hexhamshire Whapweasel, or something from Caledonian, Everards, Ridleys or Adnams.

A 100-year-old town-centre real ale pub with a function room, terrace and garden overlooking the Tyne Bridge and the quayside. Food available at lunchtimes (12–2pm and 12–3pm Sun). Live music in function room, folk club Monday night, jazz on Tuesdays. No children. Situated opposite the castle and above the quayside.

 *11.30am–11pm Mon–Sat; 12–10.30pm Sun.*

The Head of Steam

2 Neville Street, Newcastle upon Tyne NE1 5EN
☎ *(0191) 232 4379* David Campell

A freehouse with Black Sheep Bitter always available plus up to three guests from a wide range of breweries including, among others, Hambleton.

A two-bar, city-centre pub with food available all opening hours. No children.

OPEN *3–11pm Mon–Thurs; 12–11pm Fri–Sat; 12–10.30pm Sun.*

The Hotspur

Haymarket, Newcastle upon Tyne
☎ *(0191) 232 4352* Jim Freeman (manager)

Four guests available, changing once or twice a week. Mordue Workie Ticket and Greene King Ruddles County are among the most popular ales. A wide range is purchased through the Beer Seller.

A very busy pub, part of the T&J Bernard chain, attracting mainly students and young professionals. Food available all day. Wide selection of wines and whiskies. Beer alley with big-screen TV for sport. No children. Located opposite Haymarket Bus Station.

OPEN *11am–11pm Mon–Sat; 12–10.30pm Sun.*

The Tap & Spile
1 Nun Street, Newcastle upon Tyne
☎ *(0191) 232 0026*

Twelve beers always available from a constantly changing range (200 per year) with names such as Durham Canny Lad and Magus, Mordue Workie Ticket and Bateman Yella Belly.

More than 100 years old, with a ground-floor and basement bar. Bar food available at lunchtime. Children allowed for meals. Live bands in the cellar. Two minutes from the railway station and Greys Monument.

 *11am–11pm Mon–Sat; 12–10.30pm Sun.*

The Tut & Shive
52 Clayton Street West, Newcastle upon Tyne NE1 4EX
☎ *(0191) 261 6998*

A Castle Eden ale and Black Sheep Bitter always available.

A friendly, relaxed city-centre pub with a mixed clientele, from students to oaps! Weekly promotional discounts on draught and bottles. No food. Live music up to five nights a week, plus pool knockouts every Sunday. No children. Two minutes from the Central Station.

 *11am–11pm (12–11pm in summer) Mon–Sat; 12–10.30pm Sun.*

NORTH HYLTON

The Three Horseshoes
Washington Road, North Hylton, Sunderland SR5 3HZ
☎ *(0191) 536 4183* Frank Nicol

Four real ales available. Greene King Old Speckled Hen and Caledonian Deuchars IPA always available plus two rotating guests. Annual beer festival held at the end of July.

A traditional 200-year-old country pub with two bars (public and lounge), separate dining area, open fire, pool, darts etc. Food available 12–2.30pm daily and 6–9.30pm (not Sun). Children allowed. Follow signs for Air Museum, by Nissan entrance. B&B accommodation.

 *11am–11pm Mon–Sat; 12–10.30pm Sun.*

NORTH SHIELDS

Chain Locker
New Quay, North Shields NE29 6LQ
☎ *(0191) 258 0147* Peter McAlister

A freehouse with Mordue Workie Ticket and Radgie Gadgie always available plus four daily changing guests including, perhaps, Mordue Five Bridges and Timothy Taylor Landlord.

A riverside pub by a ferry landing on a fresh fish quay. One bar, styled in a nautical theme, plus separate dining area and beer garden. Food available at lunchtime only. Children allowed.

 *11am–11pm (10.30pm Sun).*

The Garricks Head
Saville Street, North Shields NE30 1NT
☎ *(0191) 296 2064* Ken Liddell/Janice Duffin

A genuine freehouse with four pumps all serving a range of weekly changing real ales. Greene King Old Speckled Hen, Charles Wells Bombardier, Marston's Pedigree, Young's Special and Hartleys XB are examples.

A traditional Victorian town pub with one bar, upstairs function room and restaurant. Food available throughout the day. Children welcome in the restaurant only. Live music, karaoke and quiz nights.

 *11am–11pm Mon–Thurs; 11am–midnight Fri–Sat; 12–10.30pm Sun.*

Magnesia Bank
1 Camden Street, North Shields NE30 1NH
☎ *(0191) 257 4831*
Richard, Dee and Kate Slade
www.magnesiabank.com

Durham Magus, Mordue Workie Ticket and Black Sheep Bitter always available plus up to four guests which might include Shepherd Neame Spitfire, Fuller's London Pride or Chiswick, Young's Waggle Dance, Bateman XB or Harviestoun Bitter and Twisted. The selection changes daily.

A true freehouse, family-owned and run and with a long tradition of supporting local micro-breweries. Winner of the *Morning Advertiser*'s Freehouse of Britain 2001. Good range of food, specialising in fresh fish and local lamb and beef, available lunchtimes and evenings Mon–Wed and all day Thurs–Sun. Live music three nights a week. Children allowed until 9pm. Function room available. The pub also has its own flock of lambs. Situated close to North Shields fish quay, opposite the Beacon Centre shoppers' car park.

 *11am–11pm Mon–Wed; 11am–midnight Thurs–Sat; 12–10.30pm Sun.*

The Porthole

11 New Quay, North Shields NE29 6LQ
☎ *(0191) 257 6645* Arthur Reeve

Five beers always available from a large list (156+ per year) that might include Durham Magus, Jarrow Bitter, Mordue Geordie Pride, Hadrian and Border Gladiator and Archer's Best.

An old-fashioned friendly pub with a maritime theme, on the banks of the Tyne. Established in 1854. Bar food served at lunchtime (12–2.30pm). Live music on Weds, Fri and Sun. Car park. Children allowed. Near the North Shields ferry landing, popular with sailors and handy for the metrolink into Newcastle.

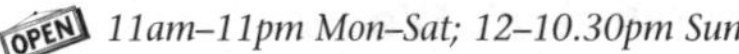
11am–11pm Mon–Sat; 12–10.30pm Sun.

Shiremoor House Farm

Middle Engine Lane, North Shields NE29 8DZ
☎ *(0191) 257 6302* Bill Kerridge

A freehouse with Mordue Workie Ticket always available plus up to five guests such as Moorhouse's Pendle Witches Brew, Jennings Cumberland, Timothy Taylor Landlord or Durham Brewery's Celtic. Beers changed two or three times a week.

A converted farmhouse with two bars, stone floors and separate restaurant. Food available 12–10pm daily. Children allowed.

OPEN *11am–11pm (10.30pm Sun).*

The Tap & Spile

184 Tynemouth Road, North Shields NE30 1EG
☎ *(0191) 257 2523* Mr RM Shacklock

A selection of up to eight real ales always available from a large and varied list. Beers from Harviestoun and Durham breweries usually feature.

A real ale bar with a friendly atmosphere. Bar food served at lunchtime Tues–Sat. Parking. Opposite the magistrates court in North Shields. Beer festivals held four times a year.

OPEN *12–11pm Mon–Fri; 11.30am–11pm Sat; 12–10.30pm Sun.*

RYTON

Ye Olde Cross

Barmoor Lane, Old Ryton Village, Gateshead NE40 3QP
☎ *(0191) 413 4689*
Diane and Dennis Armstrong

The beers on offer usually include Timothy Taylor Landlord, Charles Wells Bombardier, Black Sheep Bitter, Camerons Strongarm and Marston's Pedigree. There is also one guest.

An olde-worlde pub built in 1908 overlooking the village green, with one open-plan room downstairs, restaurant upstairs, and secret garden. No pool, darts or juke box. Bar meals and snacks served downstairs in the pub at all times; the Italian-style restaurant upstairs is open evenings and Sunday lunchtimes. Children welcome. Communal car park.

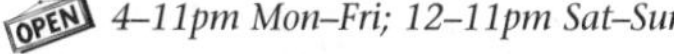
4–11pm Mon–Fri; 12–11pm Sat–Sun.

SOUTH SHIELDS

The Dolly Peel

137 Commercial Road, South Shields NE33 1SQ
☎ *(0191) 427 1441*

Timothy Taylor Landlord and Black Sheep Bitter are always available, plus guest ales from breweries throughout the UK.

A traditional suburban pub with outside seating. Named after an eighteenth-century smuggler – details on request! No juke box, pool table, darts or bandits, just good conversation and excellent beer in pleasant surroundings. Sandwiches available.

OPEN *11am–11pm Mon–Sat; 12–10.30pm Sun.*

Holborn Rose & Crown

Hill Street, South Shields NE33 1RN
☎ *(0191) 455 2379* Bob Overton

Two guest beers usually served, often from Marston's, Bateman, Fuller's, Black Sheep or Mordue breweries.

One-roomed traditional freehouse with beer garden, opposite the old middle docks. Toasted sandwiches available. Children welcome during daytime only.

OPEN *11am–11pm Mon–Sat; 12–10.30pm Sun.*

The Riverside

3 Mill Dam, South Shields NE33 1EQ
☎ *(0191) 422 0411* Paul Hedley

Six real ales always available, including Timothy Taylor Landlord and Black Sheep Special plus two guest beers from micro-breweries around the UK and one cask cider.

Smallish, well-decorated pub offering a friendly welcome. Background music, very busy at weekends, with a clientele mostly over 30. Hot and cold sandwiches available. Close to ferry landing, market place and customs house. Mr Hedley also owns The Trimmers Arms on Commercial Road which was due to open during summer 2004.

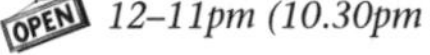
12–11pm (10.30pm Sun).

SUNDERLAND

Fitzgeralds

10–12 Green Terrace, Sunderland SR1 3PZ
☎ *(0191) 567 0852* Matt Alldis

This freehouse held a beer festival a few years ago. It was so successful that it is now run constantly! No permanent ales, just a range of up to ten constantly changing guests, often including brews from Black Sheep, Darwin, Jennings, Hexhamshire and Mordue.

Traditional city-centre bar in an old building with fireplaces. Food is available, and there is a dining area. Quiz machine, beer garden. Children allowed at lunchtimes only.

11am–11pm Mon–Sat; 12–10.30pm Sun.

The Tap & Barrel

Nelson Street, Sunderland SR2 8EF
☎ *(0191) 514 2810* Michael Riley

Everards Tiger and Timothy Taylor Landlord among the brews always available, plus four or five guests from a large selection including Banbury Old Vic and Thwaites Bloomin' Ale. Beers changed weekly.

An old-fashioned pub with two bars and a separate dining area. Food available 4–8pm Mon–Fri and 12–4pm Sat–Sun. Children allowed, if eating.

4–11pm Mon–Fri; all day Sat–Sun.

The Tap & Spile

Salem Street, Hendon, Sunderland
☎ *(0191) 232 0026* Janice Faulder

Nine beers always available from a list of 400+ including North Yorkshire Best, Bateman XB, Charles Wells Bombardier and Marston's Pedigree.

Traditional three-bar alehouse with bare boards and exposed brickwork. Bar food available at lunchtime. Function room. Children allowed in eating area.

11am–11pm Mon–Sat; 12–3pm and 7–10.30pm Sun.

SUNNISIDE

The Potter's Wheel

Sun Street, Sunniside, Newcastle upon Tyne NE16 5EE
☎ *(0191) 488 6255* Liz Donnelly (manager)

Five hand pumps serve permanent beers Timothy Taylor Landlord, Fuller's London Pride and Caledonian Deuchars IPA, plus guests.

Friendly, traditional community pub with bar, lounge, dining area and beer terrace. A 'Britain in Bloom' winner for seven consecutive years. Food served 12–2pm and 5.30–9pm Mon–Sat and 12–7pm Sun. Children's certificate. Car park.

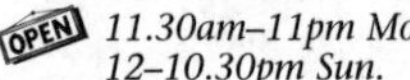
11.30am–11pm Mon–Sat; 12–10.30pm Sun.

WARDLEY

The Green

White Mare Pool, Wardley, Gateshead NE10 8YB
☎ *(0191) 495 0171* Deborah Mackay

A freehouse with six guest ales always available. Timothy Taylor Landlord, Jennings Cumberland, Big Lamp Bitter, Black Sheep Special and Oakham American Blonde are some of the regular features.

A traditional village pub with one bar and one lounge. Patio and restaurant. Disabled facilities. Food available all day, every day. Children allowed in the lounge if eating.

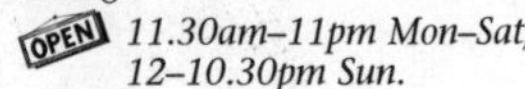
11.30am–11pm Mon–Sat; 12–10.30pm Sun.

WASHINGTON

The Sandpiper

Easby Road, Washington NE38 7NN
☎ *(0191) 416 0038* Lynda Margaret Bewick

Up to six guests such as Marston's Pedigree, Black Sheep Bitter, Fuller's London Pride, something from Daleside or Phoenix Wobbly Bob.

A locals' village community pub with two bars, games area and patio. Charity events held. Food available at lunchtime only. Children allowed until 7pm, if supervised.

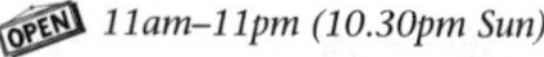
OPEN *11am–11pm (10.30pm Sun).*

WESTMOOR

George Stephenson Inn

Great Lime Road, Westmoor, Newcastle upon Tyne NE12 0NJ
☎ *(0191) 268 1073* Richard Costello

Four real ales are always available, including two constantly changing guests, one of them usually from a local micro-brewery.

A community beer-drinker's pub with lounge, bar and garden. Adult clientele, no games, live music every Wednesday, Thursday and Saturday. No food. No children.

OPEN *12–11pm (10.30pm Sun).*

WHITLEY BAY

The Briar Dene

71 The Links, Whitley Bay NE26 1UE
☎ *(0191) 252 0926* Susan Gibson

Eight different real ales available at any one time always changing and often something new – every day is a beer festival!

Award-winning seafront pub with one bar, family room and lounge. Good food available 12–2.30pm and 6–8.45pm. Large car park.

OPEN *11am–11pm Mon–Sat; 12–10.30pm Sun.*

The Fat Ox

278 Whitley Road, Whitley Bay NE26 2TG
☎ *(0191) 251 3852* Ms JP Cowings

Eight monthly changing real ales on offer, including favourites such as Marston's Pedigree, Black Sheep Bitter and Greene King Old Speckled Hen, plus beers from a wide range of breweries around the UK.

A traditional one-bar town-centre pub with a small beer garden. Live bands on Friday and Saturday nights, big-screen TV. No food. No children. Disabled facilities. In the centre of Whitley Bay.

OPEN *12–11pm Mon–Fri; 11am–11pm Sat; 12–10.30pm Sun.*

THE BREWERIES

CHURCH END BREWERY

109 Ridge Lane, Nuneaton CV10 0RD
☎ *(01827) 713080*

All beers available on a seasonal or occasional basis. No fully permanent ales.

POACHER'S POCKET 3.5% ABV
ALTAR ALE 3.6% ABV
PHEASANT PLUCKER 3.7% ABV
AVON ALE 3.8% ABV
CUTHBERTS 3.8% ABV
GOATS' MILK 3.8% ABV
GRAVEDIGGERS'ALE 3.8% ABV
ANCHOR BITTER 4.0% ABV
SHAKES BEER 4.0% ABV
THINGEE 4.0% ABV
HOP GUN 4.1% ABV
'V' REG 4.1% ABV
ANCHOR GOLD 4.5% ABV
DROP GOAL 4.5% ABV
OLD HERBACIOUS 4.5% ABV
PEWS PORTER 4.5% ABV
RED OCTOBER 4.5% ABV
SHREDDIES 4.5% ABV
WHATEVER HAPPENED TO U-REG? 4.5% ABV
BALOO-THE-BEER 4.6% ABV
STOUT COFFIN 4.6% ABV
SUNSHINE 4.6% ABV
CUTTING ALE 4.8% ABV
SUPER P 4.8% ABV
FALLEN ANGEL 5.0% ABV
INDIA PALE ALE 5.0% ABV
OLD GRAVEL TREADER 5.0% ABV
CHARTER ALE 5.5% ABV
OLD PAL 5.5% ABV
ARTHUR'S WIT 6.0% ABV
OLD FATHER BROWN 6.0% ABV
REST IN PEACE 7.0% ABV

FRANKTON BAGBY BREWERY

The Old Stables, Green Lane, Church Lawford, Rugby CV23 9EF
☎ *(02476) 540770*

DIZZY BLONDE 4.0% ABV
OLD CHESTNUT 4.0% ABV
FAT BOB 4.2% ABV
Summer ale.
JACK O' THE WOOD 4.3% ABV
VILLAGE PRIDE 4.6% ABV
Plus seasonal ales.

WALSH'S BAKEHOUSE BREWERY

Scar Bank, Warwick CV34 5DB
☎ *(01926) 495168*
www.bakehouseales.co.uk

BAKEHOUSE BITTER 3.8% ABV
FLYING TOP 4.4% ABV
OLD GRIDLAP 5.0% ABV

WARWICKSHIRE BEER CO. LTD

Cubbington Brewery, Queen Street, Cubbington, Leamington Spa CV32 7NA
☎ *(01926) 450747*
www.warwickshirebeerco.co.uk

BEST BITTER 3.9% ABV
LADY GODIVA 4.2% ABV
FALSTAFF 4.4% ABV
ST PATRICK'S ALE 4.4% ABV
CASTLE 4.6% ABV
GOLDEN BEAR 4.9% ABV
KING MAKER 5.5% ABV
Plus seasonal and occasional brews.

WIZARD BREWERY

The Norman Knight, Whichford, Shipston on Stour CV36 5PE
☎ *(01608) 684355*
www.thenormanknight.co.uk

APPRENTICE 3.6% ABV
BLACK MAGIC 4.0% ABV
ONE FOR THE TOAD 4.0% ABV
MOTHER IN LAW 4.2% ABV
SORCERER 4.3% ABV
WHITE WITCH 4.8% ABV
DRUID'S FLUID 5.0% ABV
BAH HUMBUG 5.8% ABV

THE PUBS

ALCESTER

Lord Nelson

69 Priory Road, Alcester B49 5EA
☎ *(01789) 762632* Dennis and Brenda Stubbs

Fuller's London Pride usually available, plus two other real ales, varying weekly.

Parts of this pub date back 600 years. There is a mature beer garden, a bar with darts and bar billiards and a restaurant area. Food is available 7–9am, 12–2pm and 7–9pm Mon–Sat, with just lunchtime roasts on Sundays. Car park. Children welcome. Accommodation.

OPEN *12–3pm and 6–11pm Mon–Sat; 12–3pm and 7–10.30pm Sun.*

The Three Tuns

34 High Street, Alcester B49 5AB
☎ *(01789) 762626* P Burdett

Hobsons Best and Goff's Jouster permanently available, plus six guest ales from independent breweries, with Greene King and Salopian brews making regular appearances.

A sixteenth-century public house with open-plan bar, converted back from a wine bar. Beer festivals are held every three months.

OPEN *12–11pm (10.30pm Sun).*

ARMSCOTE

The Fox & Goose

Armscote, Near Stratford-upon-Avon CV37 8DD
☎ *(01608) 682293* Sue Gray
www.foxandgoose.co.uk

A genuine freehouse always serving a house beer, Fox & Goose Bitter, brewed by Brakspear. Plus one or two guests changed every week or two.

Village pub, restaurant and hotel in a 150-year-old stone building adjoining a thatched cottage. Food available 12–2.30pm and 7–9pm. Cosy locals' bar plus smarter dining room. Garden and decking. Four double en-suite letting rooms. Children allowed in restaurant. Private dining facilities. Seven miles south of Stratford.

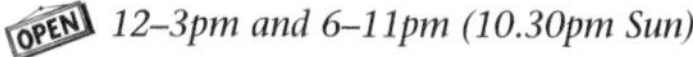
12–3pm and 6–11pm (10.30pm Sun).

ASHBY ST LEDGERS

The Olde Coach House Inn

Ashby St Ledgers, Nr Rugby CV23 8UN
☎ *(01788) 890349* Pete and Christine Ballinger

Everards Old Original always available, plus six guest ales (200 per year) including Hop Back Summer Lightning, Hook Norton Haymaker, Frog Island Natterjack, Adnams Broadside and beers from Frankton Bagby and Timothy Taylor.

An olde-English converted farmhouse in the middle of a historic village. Lots of family tables and small intimate nooks and crannies. Large secure garden for children and plenty of parking space. Bar and restaurant food available 12–3pm and 6–9.30pm. Car park. Accommodation. Three miles from M1 junction 18, close to M6 and M40 and adjacent to A5. Daventry three miles to the south, Rugby four miles to the north.

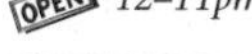
12–11pm (10.30pm Sun).

BEDWORTH

The White Swan

All Saints Square, Bedworth
☎ *(024) 7631 2164* Paul Holden

Charles Wells Eagle, IPA and Bombardier usually served, plus one guest beer such as Greene King Old Speckled Hen, Badger Tanglefoot or Adnams Broadside.

Central pub, catering for mixed clientele of all ages. Food served 12–2pm daily. Car parks close by. Children welcome at lunchtime.

11am–11pm (10.30pm Sun).

BISHOPS TACHBROOK

The Leopard

Oakley Wood Road, Bishops Tachbrook, Nr Leamington Spa CV33 9RN
☎ *(01926) 426466* Ian Richardson

Hook Norton Best, Timothy Taylor Landlord and Greene King Abbot are usually available, plus one changing guest.

Country pub and restaurant in an old A-frame building dating back to 1066. Garden. Food available. Children allowed. Car park.

12–3pm and 6–11pm Mon–Fri; 12–11pm Sat; 12–10.30pm Sun.

CHAPEL END

The Salutation Inn

Chancery Lane, Chapel End, Nuneaton CV10 0PB
☎ *(024) 7632 9360* Carol Martin

Tied to Banks's, with Banks's Bitter always available.

Very old out-of-town pub, formerly a coaching inn. No food. Live entertainment. No children. Car park.

12–11pm (10.30pm Sun).

CHURCH LAWFORD

Old Smithy

Green Lane, Church Lawford, Nr Rugby CU23 9EF
☎ *(024) 7654 2333* John O'Neill

Frankton Bagby Anvil Ale, plus Greene King IPA and Abbot Ale usually available. A guest beer frequently comes from the Frankton Bagby Brewery which adjoins the pub.

Traditional freehouse situated on the village green. Food served lunchtimes and evenings. Car park. Beer garden and children's play area.

11am–3pm and 5.30–11pm Mon–Fri; 11am–11pm Sat; 12–10.30pm Sun.

EDGEHILL

The Castle Inn

Edgehill, Nr Banbury OX15 6DJ
☎ *(01295) 670255* NJ and GA Blann

Hook Norton Best, Generation, Old Hooky and the seasonal brew usually available, plus a guest beer which may be from Shepherd Neame, King & Barnes, Wadworth or Wye Valley.

The inn is situated on the summit of Edgehill near the civil war battle site. Built as a folly in the eighteenth century to commemorate the centenary of the battle, it is a copy of Guy's Tower at Warwick Castle. Food served every session. Car park. Original en-suite bedrooms.

11.15am–2.30pm and 6.15–11pm; open all day Sat–Sun in summer.

GREAT WOLFORD

The Fox & Hounds Inn

Great Wolford CV36 5NQ
☎ *(01608) 674220*
Paul and Veronica Tomlinson
www.thefoxandhoundsinn.com

Hook Norton Best always available plus at least two guest beers each week selected from a wide range.

An unspoilt sixteenth-century village inn with stone-flagged floors, log fires, hops, faded hunting pictures – and an infamous pub sign! Seasonal, local produce used for blackboard specials and bar food menu 12–2pm Tues–Sun and 7–9pm Tues–Sat. Car park, terrace, and charming en-suite bed and breakfast accommodation.

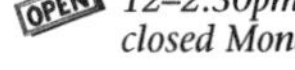
12–2.30pm and 6–11pm (10.30pm Sun); closed Mondays.

HAMPTON LUCY

The Boars Head

Church Street, Hampton Lucy CV35 8BE
☎ *(01789) 840533* M B and Mrs L Waters

Three real ales usually available, including local and national brews from Hook Norton, Shepherd Neame, Warwickshire, Weatheroak, Fuller's, Marston's, Young's, St Austell, Adnams and elsewhere. They change every couple of days.

Traditional English pub with log fire and great atmosphere. Home-cooked food served 12–2pm and 6–9.15pm. Beer garden, car park. Well-behaved children welcome, but no special facilities. Four miles from Stratford, six miles from Warwick.

12–3pm and 6–11pm Mon–Sat; 12–10.30pm Sun.

HARTSHILL

The Anchor Inn

Mancetter Road, Hartshill, Nuneaton CV1 0RT
☎ *(024) 7639 8839* Mark Wade

An Everards pub serving Tiger and Original, plus four guest beers changing weekly.

Pleasant rural pub dating from around the construction of the Coventry canal in 1790, and offering moorings and shower facilities. Close to bridge 29. Large garden, bar and restaurant, summer garden bar, function room. Varied menu available throughout the week (except Sun evening and Mon lunch), plus traditional carvery served Fri–Sat evenings and Sun lunch. Children not allowed in bar after 9pm.

12–2.30pm and 6–11pm Mon–Thurs; all day Fri–Sun; opening times may vary in winter.

HENLEY-IN-ARDEN

The White Swan Hotel

100 High Street, Henley-in-Arden B95 5BY
☎ *(01564) 792623* Nigel May

One guest, changed weekly, might be something like Everards Beacon, Bateman XB, Greene King Old Speckled Hen, Wadworth 6X or a seasonal or celebration ale.

Situated in the centre of the smallest market town in England, this black and white coaching inn dates from 1352. Food available. One bar, restaurant, garden, ten letting rooms. Jazz on Wednesdays. Children allowed. Car park.

11am–11pm Mon–Sat; 12–10.30pm Sun.

ILMINGTON

The Howard Arms

Lower Green, Ilmington CV36 4LT
☎ *(01608) 682226* Gill and Rob Greenstock (landlords), Martin Devereux (manager)
www.howardarms.com

Everards Tiger and North Cotswold Genesis are the permanent ales at this freehouse, which also offers one guest, changed weeky from a local or regional brewer. Marston's Pedigree is a popular choice.

Village pub in a sixteenth-century building with inglenook fireplace. Freshly prepared food using seasonal produce is available from menus that are changed weekly. Served 12–2pm and 7–9pm Mon–Thurs, 12–2pm and 7–9.30pm Fri–Sat, 12–2.30pm and 6.30–8.30pm Sun. Non-smoking areas, garden and terrace, car parking. Three delightful en-suite bedrooms. Children allowed until the early evening only. South of Stratford-on-Avon.

11am–2.30pm and 6–11pm Mon–Sat; 12–10.30pm Sun.

KENILWORTH

The Wyandotte Inn

Park Road, Kenilworth CV8 2GF
No phone Mrs Jaeger

Banks's Bitter plus Marston's Bitter and Pedigree regularly available.

Street-corner local with split-level single room and coal fire in winter. Beer garden. Pool table. Musical events every week. Food served 5–9pm Tues–Fri, all day Sat–Sun. Car park. Children welcome.

5–11pm Mon–Fri; 10am–11pm Sat–Sun and major holidays.

LEAMINGTON SPA

Benjamin Satchwell

112–14 The Parade, Leamington Spa CV32 4AQ
☎ *(01926) 883733* Andy Tompkins

Hop Back Summer Lightning, Greene King Abbot and Shepherd Neame Spitfire are among the permanent beers at this 12-pump pub. The six guests, changed every two days, might include Wyre Piddle Piddle in the Wind, Castle Eden Nimmo's 4X or something from Mordue.

Traditional open-plan Wetherspoon's town pub, holding beer festivals throughout the year (call for details). Food available. No children.

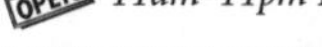 *11am–11pm Mon–Sat; 12–10.30pm Sun.*

LONG LAWFORD

The Sheaf & Sickle

Coventry Road, Long Lawford, Rugby CV23 9DT
☎ *(01788) 544622*
Roger Singh and Ruth Clarkson

Two real ales available from a range of breweries.

An old village coaching inn with saloon, lounge and new à la carte restaurant. Beer garden, private room for hire. Food available during all opening hours. Children welcome. Beer festivals held and parties catered for.

OPEN *12–2.30pm and 6–11pm Mon–Fri; all day Sat–Sun.*

NUNEATON

The Brewery Tap

Ridge Lane, Nuneaton CV10 0RD
☎ *(01827) 713080* Stewart Elliot

Located on the site of the Church End Brewery, serving Gravediggers' Ale plus a range of the Church End ales at the point of production.

A brewery tap room run as a pub. Brewing can be viewed through a window in the bar. Non-smoking. No children. Large, meadow-style garden. Brewery tours (phone for details).

OPEN *11am–11pm Fri–Sat; 12–10.30pm Sun (closed Mon–Thurs).*

RUGBY

The Alexandra Arms

72 James Street, Rugby CV21 2SL
☎ *(01788) 578660* Julian Hardy
www.alexandraarms.co.uk

Greene King IPA and Abbot and Fuller's London Pride always available, plus two guest beers from a wide variety of sources changed every couple of days. Beowolf, Burton Bridge, Church End and Wye Valley brews feature regularly.

Award-winning genuine freehouse built in 1863 with bar billiards, table skittles and pool. Traditional lounge bar. No music or machines. Garden. Food available 12–2.30pm and 5–8pm. No children. Situated near the main post office. An annual beer festival is held on the second weekend of July.

OPEN *11.30am–3pm and 5–11pm Mon–Thurs; 11.30am–11pm Fri–Sat; 12–10.30pm Sun.*

The Three Horseshoes Hotel

Sheep Street, Rugby CV21 3BX
☎ *(01788) 544585* Stephen Jones

Greene King Abbot is among the beers always available, plus one or two guest beers, changed weekly, from an extensive list.

Central refurbished seventeenth-century inn with open fires and beamed restaurant. Food available 12–2pm and 6–9.30pm Mon–Sat and 12–4pm Sun. Car park. Children welcome. Accommodation.

OPEN *11am–11pm Mon–Sat; 12–3pm and 7–10.30pm Sun.*

The Victoria Inn

1 Lower Hillmorton Road, Rugby CV21 3ST
☎ *(01788) 544374* Mrs White

A freehouse with Cottage Champflower always available plus two guests such as Hartley XB (Robinson's), Greene King IPA, Hook Norton and Shepherd Neame brews.

A locals' pub just outside the town centre. Two bars, original mirrors in both rooms. Disabled access. Food available at lunchtime only (notSun). No children.

OPEN *12–2.30pm and 6–11pm Mon–Fri; 12–11pm Sat; 12–2.30pm and 7–10.30pm Sun.*

SHIPSTON-ON-STOUR

The Coach & Horses

16 New Street, Shipston-on-Stour CV36 4EM
☎ *(01608) 661335* Bob Payne

Hook Norton Best always available plus three guests from a long list including Hook Norton Haymaker, Wye Valley Brew 69, Dorothy Goodbody's Summertime Ale and Bateman XXXB and XB.

A 250-year-old village pub in the Cotswolds serving bar and restaurant food at lunchtime and evenings. Car park, garden, accommodation. On the A3400 Birmingham to Oxford road, on the Oxford side of town.

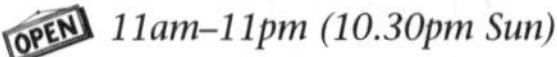 *11am–11pm (10.30pm Sun).*

The Horseshoe Inn

6 Church Street, Shipston-on-Stour CV36 4AP
☎ *(01608) 661225* Terry Falconer

Greene King Ruddles Best always on offer plus a weekly changing guest.

Small town pub with restaurant, in a sixteenth-century Grade II listed building with beams and fires. Fruit machines, live music Wednesdays, beer garden, bed and breakfast. Parking. Children allowed. On the main A34.

 *11am–3pm and 6–11pm Mon–Thurs; 11am–11pm Fri–Sat; 12–10.30pm Sun.*

SHUSTOKE

The Griffin Inn

Church Road, Shustoke B46 2LP
☎ *(01675) 481567* Michael Pugh

Marston's Pedigree, Banks's Mild, Hook Norton Old Hooky and RCH Pitchfork always available.

A large country freehouse with oak beams and open fires set in large grounds. The Church End brewery formerly located next to the pub has moved to Nuneaton. Bar food is available at lunchtime (except Sunday). Car park, garden. Children allowed in the conservatory and grounds. Take the B4114 from Coleshill.

 *12–2.30pm and 7–11pm Mon–Sat; 12–3pm and 7–10.30pm Sun.*

STRATFORD-UPON-AVON

The Queen's Head

53 Ely Street, Stratford-upon-Avon CV37 6LN
☎ *(01789) 204914* Martin Jones

A freehouse with Adnams Bitter among the beers always on offer. Guests are either Highgate Saddlers Celebrated Best Bitter or Greene King IPA in summer, and one extra during winter, for example Wychwood Hobgoblin or Jennings Sneck Lifter.

A good old-fashioned pub in a traditional sixteenth-century building in the centre of Stratford. Food available at lunchtimes only. One bar, beer garden, live music once a month, five B&B rooms. Children allowed until 7pm only.

 *11.30am–11pm Mon–Fri; 11am–11pm Sat; 12–10.30pm Sun.*

STUDLEY

The Little Lark

108 Alcester Road, Studley B80 7NP
☎ *(01527) 853105* Mark Roskell

Ushers Best Bitter and Wadworth 6X always available, plus one guest changed twice weekly. Traditional cider also served.

An interesting selection of printing paraphernalia is a feature in this real ale house. Food available lunchtimes and evenings every day. On the main A435 at the southern end of Studley.

 *12–3pm and 6–11pm Mon–Fri and Sun; 12–11pm Sat.*

WARWICK

The Old Fourpenny Shop Hotel

27–9 Crompton Street, Warwick CV34 6HJ
☎ *(01926) 491360* Jan Richard Siddle

Six guest beers usually served from an extensive selection including RCH Pitchfork, Greene King Abbot and and beers from Church End, Abbey, Frankton Bagby, Warwickshire, Eccleshall, Litchfield, Burton Bridge, Bateman and many others.

Popular real ale house with restaurant. Food served 12–2pm and 7–10pm daily. Car park. Children over 10 years old welcome. Accommodation available, with 11 refurbished bedrooms.

 *12–2.30pm and 5.30–11pm Mon–Thurs; 12–11pm Fri–Sun (10.30pm Sun).*

WHICHFORD

The Norman Knight

Whichford, Shipston-on-Stour CV36 5PE
☎ *(01608) 684621* Mike Garner
www.thenormanknight.co.uk

Four-pump freehouse serving beers from the pub's own Wizard Ales brewery, such as One for the Toad, Mother in Law, Apprentice and Black Magic.

Village pub in a nineteenth-century building, part stone, part brick. Food available. Garden, darts, occasional live music. Self-catering holiday accommodation, caravans and camping. Children allowed. Car park.

 *12–2pm and 7–11pm Mon–Fri; 12–2.30pm and 7–11pm Sat–Sun (closed 10.30pm Sun).*

THE BREWERIES

DANIEL BATHAM & SON LTD

The Delph Brewery, Delph Road, Brierley Hill DY5 2TN
☎ *(01384) 77229*
www.bathams.co.uk

MILD ALE 3.5% ABV
BEST BITTER 4.5% ABV
XXX 6.5% ABV
Christmas ale.

THE BEOWULF BREWING CO.

Waterloo Buildings, 14 Waterloo Road, Yardley, Birmingham B25 8JR
☎ *(0121) 706 4116*

NOBLE BITTER 4.0% ABV
WIGLAF 4.3% ABV
Gold-coloured, with hops and malt.
SWORDSMAN 4.5% ABV
Pale, refreshing and fruity.
HEROES BITTER 4.7% ABV
Golden and hoppy with some sweetness.
MERCIAN SHINE 5.0% ABV
Light in colour, with hoppiness, and dry in the aftertaste.
Plus seasonal brews.

ENVILLE ALES

Enville Brewery, Cox Green, Enville, Stourbridge DX7 5LG
☎ *(01384) 873728*
www.envilleales.com

CHAINMAKER MILD 3.6% ABV
NAILMAKER 4.0% ABV
CZECHMATE SAAZ 4.2% ABV
ENVILLE WHITE 4.2% ABV
ENVILLE ALE 4.5% ABV
GARGOYLE 4.5% ABV
GINGER BEER 4.6% ABV
OLD PORTER 4.8% ABV
PHOENIX IPA 4.8% ABV
Plus special brews.

GOLDTHORN BREWERY & CO.

Imex Unit 60, Sunbeam Street, Wolverhampton WV2 4XA
☎ *(01902) 756920*
www.goldthornbrewery.co.uk

GI'IT SUM OMMER 3.8% ABV
SILVER BULLET 4.0% ABV
WULFRUN GOLD 4.3% ABV
JUNIPER BLONDE 4.5% ABV
TWO TUN BITTER 4.5% ABV
HUMPSHIRE ALE 5.0% ABV
PREMIUM 5.0% ABV
DEADLY NIGHTSHADE 6.0% ABV

HIGHGATE & WALSALL BREWING CO LTD

Sandymount Road, Walsall WS1 3AP
☎ *(01922) 644453*
www.highgatebrewery.com

HIGHGATE DARK MILD 3.4% ABV
World No.1 dark beer champion.
FOX'S NOB 4.0% ABV
HIGHGATE SPECIAL BITTER 3.8% ABV
SADDLERS PREMIUM BEST BITTER 4.3% ABV
Plus huge range of seasonal brews.

HOLDEN'S BREWERY

Hopden Brewery, George Street, Woodsetton, Dudley DY1 4LW
☎ *(01902) 880051*
www.holdensbrewery.co.uk

STOUT 3.5% ABV
Dark with bitter, malty flavour.
MILD 3.7% ABV
Malty and well-balanced.
BITTER 3.9% ABV
Gold-coloured, quenching session beer.
XB 4.1% ABV
Refreshing and hoppy with some sweetness.
SPECIAL 5.1% ABV
Golden, balanced and far too easy to drink.
OLD XL ALE 6.9% ABV
Christmas only.

OLDE SWAN BREWERY

89 Halesowen Road, Netherton, Dudley DY2 9PY
☎ *(01384) 253075*

OLD SWAN ORIGINAL 3.5% ABV
DARK SWAN (MILD) 4.2% ABV
OLD SWAN ENTIRE 4.4% ABV
BUMBLE HOLE 5.2% ABV

RAINBOW BREWERY

73 Birmingham Road, Allesley Village, Coventry, CV5 9GT
☎ *(0124) 7640 2888*

PIDDLEBROOK 3.8% ABV

SARAH HUGHES BREWERY

129 Bilston Street, Sedgley, Dudley DY3 1JE
☎ *(01902) 883380*

PALE AMBER 4.0% ABV
SURPRISE 5.0% ABV
DARK RUBY MILD 6.0% ABV
SNOWFLAKE 8.0% ABV

THE WOLVERHAMPTON & DUDLEY BREWERIES PLC

Park Brewery, Bath Road, Wolverhampton WV1 4NY
☎ *(01902) 711811*
www.fullpint.co.uk

BANKS'S ORIGINAL 3.5% ABV
MANSFIELD CASK DARK MILD 3.5% ABV
MANSFIELD DARK SMOOTH ALE 3.5% ABV
OLD EMPIRE 3.7% ABV
BANKS'S BITTER 3.8% ABV
Hoppy, with a good combination of flavours.
MANSFIELD CASK ALE 3.9% ABV
PEDIGREE 4.5% ABV
Plus monthly specials.

THE PUBS

ALLESLEY

Rainbow Inn

73 Birmingham Road, Allesley Village, Coventry CV5 9GT
☎ *(024) 7640 2888* Jonathan Grote

Piddlebrook brewed and served on the premises plus Greene King IPA and a guest beer changed every week.

Brewing started in October 1994 providing ale only for the pub and a few beer festivals. Production at the two-barrel plant takes place fortnightly. An unpretentious local pub in a village location. Grade II listed building dating from around 1680. Bar and restaurant food served 12–2.30pm and 6–9pm Mon–Fri, 12–4pm Sat and 12–3pm Sun. Parking, garden. Children welcome. Just off the main A45 at Allesley.

OPEN *11am–11pm.*

AMBLECOTE

The Maverick

Brettell Lane, Amblecote, Stourbridge DY8 4BA
☎ *(01384) 824099* Mark Boxley

A freehouse with Banks's Bitter and Mild always available plus one guest from around the country changed three times a week.

A 150-year-old town pub with an American/Mexican/Old West theme. One bar, pool room, beer garden. Bar snacks available all day. Live music on Wednesdays and Fridays. Children allowed. Room for hire. A half-mile out of Stourbridge and close to the canal.

 *3–11pm Mon–Thurs; 12–11pm Fri–Sat; 12–10.30pm Sun.*

The Robin Hood Inn

196 Collis Street, Amblecote, Stourbridge DY8 4EQ
☎ *(01384) 821120*

Batham Bitter, Enville Ale, Everards Beacon, Tiger and Old Original always available plus three guests (120 per year) such as Timothy Taylor Landlord, Badger Tanglefoot, Shepherd Neame Bishop's Finger, Fuller's ESB, Exmoor Gold and Hook Norton Old Hooky.

A family-run, cosy Black Country freehouse. Good beer garden. Non-smoking dining room. Bar and restaurant food available. Parking. Children allowed in the pub when eating. Accommodation.

 *12–3pm and 6–11pm Mon–Sat; 12–10.30pm Sun.*

The Swan

10 Brettell Lane, Amblecote, Stourbridge
☎ *(01384) 76932* Mr G Cook

Three weekly changing guest beers served, from breweries such as Salopian, Oakham, Wylam, Ossett, Olde Swan, Hop Back, Milk Street, Cotleigh, Okells, Outlaw and Blackwater, to name but a few.

A traditional town pub with comfortable lounge, bar, darts and juke box. Beer garden. No food. No children.

 *12–2.30pm and 7–11pm Mon–Fri; 12–11pm Sat; 12–3pm and 7–10.30pm Sun.*

BARSTON

The Bull's Head

Barston Lane, Barston, Solihull B92 0JV
☎ *(01675) 442830* Mr M Bradley

Something from Adnams plus a guest beer regularly available from a large countrywide selection.

Traditional village pub with garden, dating back to the 1490s. Solihull CAMRA Pub of the Year 2000 and 2002. No machines or music. Food served 12–2pm and 7–8.30pm Mon–Sat. The non-smoking restaurant can seat 20 people. Car park. Children welcome.

 *11am–2.30pm and 5.30–11pm Mon–Fri; 11am–11pm Sat; 12–10.30pm Sun.*

BENTLEY

Highgate Hall

Churchill Road, Bentley WS2 0HR
☎ *(01922) 621950* Marie McFadden

A Highgate Brewery house with Mild and Bitter always available.

A locals' pub in the middle of a housing estate. Fairly modern in style with a large car park. No food. No children.

12–11pm (10.30pm Sun).

BERKSWELL

The Bear Inn

Spencer's Lane, Berkswell, Coventry CV7 7BB
☎ *(01676) 533202* Stephen Gamble

Two fixed ales and two guests, changed fortnightly, which might include Marston's Pedigree or Warwickshire Lady Godiva.

A two-bar Chef & Brewer pub in a village location, in a fifteenth-century building. Food is available all day every day and there is a separate dining area. Garden, car park. Children allowed.

 *11am–11pm Mon–Sat; 12–10.30pm Sun.*

BILSTON

The Olde White Rose

20 Lichfield Street, Bilston WV14 0AG
☎ *(01902) 498339* John Denston

Twelve real ale pumps serve the crème de la crème from Shepherd Neame, Hop Back and all the other popular independent and micro-breweries; the list is endless!

Situated in the heart of the Black Country, this is a lounge-style pub, extended to include upstairs restaurant and downstairs bier keller. Food available every day until 9pm. Children allowed, with designated play outside. Beer garden. Easy accessible on the Snowhill–Wolverhampton Metro (tram) although be careful not to confuse it with The White Rose in the same town.

 *12–11pm Mon–Sat; 12–4pm and 7–10.30pm Sun.*

Trumpet

58 High Street, Bilston WV14 0EP
☎ *(01902) 493723* Ann Smith
www.trumpetjazz.org

Holden's Special, Black Country Bitter, Mild and Golden Glow always on offer, plus one guest every week from any one of a range of breweries. Jennings, Hanby Ales, Mauldons, Salopian, Burton Bridge, Cotleigh and many others have been featured.

A live jazz pub that has been entertaining nightly for at least 40 years. Music also played at lunchtime on Sundays. No food at present. Beer garden. Children allowed in the garden only. Car park. Plans for a conservatory. At the top end of the high street.

 *11am–3pm and 7.30–11pm Mon–Sat; 12–3pm and 7–10.30pm Sun.*

BIRMINGHAM

The Anchor

308 Bradford Street, Birmingham B5 6ET
☎ *(0121) 622 4516* Gerry Keane
www.the-anchor-inn@fs.net.co.uk

A freehouse with a constantly changing menu of real ales. At least seven available during the week and up to 12 at weekends. Favourite breweries include Church End, Rooster's, Beowulf and Hobsons. Three major beer festivals held each year (March, May and October), plus themed weekends, e.g. Burns' Night, St Patrick's Day, Easter Beers.

Situated close to the city centre, a well-preserved three-bar pub in a Grade II listed building. Birmingham CAMRA Pub of the Year 2003. Food available at lunchtime and evenings. Children allowed in the beer garden May–October (weather permitting!). Within walking distance of the new Bullring shopping centre.

 *11am–11pm (10.30pm Sun).*

Bartons Arms

144 High Street, Aston, Birmingham B6 4UP
☎ *(0121) 333 5988* Colin Smith

Restored by Oakham Ales and serving Oakham JHB, White Dwarf and Bishop's Farewell plus two rotating guests that usually include a mild.

This Grade II listed pub was built in 1901, and has many impressive features, including decorative tiles and snob screens. Thai food served 12–2.30pm and 5.30–10pm Mon–Sat and 12–7.30pm Sun. On the main A34 at the B4144 junction.

12–11pm Mon–Fri; 11am–11pm Sat; 12–10.30pm Sun.

The City Tavern

38 Bishopsgate Street, Birmingham B15 1EJ
☎ *(0121) 643 8467* Christopher Nicholls

Formerly owned by the Highgate Brewery and still serving Dark Mild, Special Bitter, Saddlers Best, plus at least one guest changed regularly.

Formerly known as the Bulls Head, this Victorian pub has been completely refurbished and its original features restored. Food is available 12–3pm Mon–Fri and there is a function room upstairs on the first floor. Located just off Broad Street in the city centre.

OPEN *12–11pm (10.30pm Sun).*

Figure of Eight

236–9 Broad Street, Birmingham B1 2HG
☎ *(0121) 633 0917* Tom Taylor

Enville Ale and Wadworth 6X usually available in a range of up to 12 real ales. Others are served on a guest basis, and may include beers from breweries such as Enville, Springhead, Wyre Piddle, Timothy Taylor, Hop Back, Hook Norton, Shepherd Neame and Greene King.

Busy JD Wetherspoon's freehouse, popular with all ages, serving the largest number of real ales in the area. Food available 10am–10pm Mon–Sat and 12–9.30pm Sun. No children.

10am–11pm Mon–Sat; 12–10.30pm Sun.

The Old Fox

54 Hurst Street, Birmingham B5 4TD
☎ *(0121) 622 5080 Pat Murray*

Marston's Pedigree and Greene King Old Speckled Hen always available plus two guests, changed twice-weekly, such as Wychwood The Dog's Bollocks, Trash and Tackle or Burton Bridge brews.

An eighteenth-century town freehouse with stained-glass windows, situated in a modern area near the Hippodrome. Food available 12–7.30pm. Outside seating. No children.

11.30am–11pm Mon–Thurs; 11am–2am Fri–Sat; 11.30am–11pm Sun.

The Old Joint Stock

4 Temple Row West, Birmingham B2 5NY
☎ *(0121) 200 1892* Alison Turner

Fuller's London Pride, Chiswick and ESB are permanently available, plus the brewery's seasonal ales and one-off specials. There might also be a guest from Beowulf.

A Fuller's Ale and Pie House. Large pub in traditional style, balcony area, club room and function room for hire. Food served 12–9pm Mon–Sat. Patio area. No children. Function room for hire. Beer festivals held four times a year. Close to the Bullring shopping centre.

OPEN *11am–11pm Mon–Sat; closed Sun and bank holidays.*

The Pavilion

229 Alcester Road South, Kings Heath, Birmingham B14 6DT
☎ *(0121) 441 3286* Peter Galley

Banks's Original and Bitter plus Marston's Pedigree regularly available.

Friendly community local. Food served every lunchtime and evening. Car park. No children.

OPEN *12–11pm (10.30pm Sun).*

BLOXWICH

The Royal Exchange

24 Stafford Road, Bloxwich, Walsall WS3 3NL
☎ *(01922) 494256 Mr Beattie*

Highgate Mild and Bitter are the permanent beers here, and four weekly changing guests might be something from Batham, Bateman or Lichfield.

Community local in Grade II listed building, formerly a coaching inn. Four bars, garden area. Live music Wednesdays and Saturdays. Beer festivals August Bank Holiday and Easter (call to confirm). No food. Well-behaved children allowed. Car park.

OPEN *12–11pm (10.30pm Sun).*

BORDESLEY GREEN

The Tipsy Gent

157 Cherrywood Road, Bordesley Green, Birmingham B9 4XE
☎ *(0121) 772 1858* Paul and Jackie Rackam

A freehouse with Fuller's London Pride among its permanent features, plus one guest, such as Exmoor Gold, changed weekly. Smaller and independent brewers favoured.

A traditional one-bar town pub with stone floors and open fires. Food available Mon–Fri lunchtimes only. Beer garden. No children.

OPEN *11am–11pm (10.30pm Sun).*

BRIERLEY HILL

The Bull & Bladder

10 Delph Road, Brierley Hill DY5 2TN
☎ *(01384) 78293* Mr Wood

Bathams Mild, Best and XXX always available.

Also known as The Vine, this is the brewery tap for Bathams, which is situated behind. A multi-roomed pub with open fires. Bar food available at lunchtime. Car park, garden, children's room.

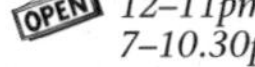 *12–11pm Mon–Sat; 12–4pm and 7–10.30pm Sun.*

CHAPELFIELDS

The Nursery Tavern

38–9 Lord Street, Chapelfields, Coventry CV5 8DA
☎ *(024) 7667 4530* Harry Minton

Four guest ales usually featured from breweries such as Church End, Brewsters, RCH, Springhead and Beowulf.

A small, 150-year-old, village-style pub in a town location. Beams, wooden floors. Bar snacks available Mon–Fri; breakfasts Sat–Sun and Sunday lunches. Children allowed in the back room and garden. The local rugby team drinks here.

 *11am–11pm Mon–Sat; 12–10.30pm Sun.*

COSELEY

Spread Eagle

Birmingham New Road, Coseley, Wolverhampton WV14 9PR
☎ *(01902) 663564* David Mark Ralph

Banks's Original always available, plus a changing range of guest ales.

Separate public bar and lounge, the lounge is comfortably furnished, with live entertainment Mon, Wed, Fri evenings. The public bar has pub games and Sky TV. Bar snacks and restaurant food available 12–3pm and 6–9pm Mon–Sat, 12–3pm Sun. Children welcome and children's menu available. Beer garden with children's play area. Large car park. Functions catered for. Located on the main A4123 Wolverhampton to Birmingham road, approximately 3 miles from Wolverhampton city centre.

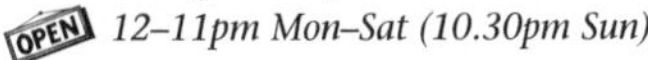 *12–11pm Mon–Sat (10.30pm Sun).*

COVENTRY

The Old Windmill Inn

22–23 Spon Street, Coventry CV1 3BA
☎ *(024) 7625 2183* Robin Addey

Up to six real ales available. Greene King Old Speckled Hen and IPA, Wychwood Hobgoblin and Theakston Old Peculiar are permanent fixtures with a guest changed regularly.

A Grade II listed Tudor building situtated in the city centre. The oldest pub in Coventry with beams, flagstone floor, an old range in one bar, snug rooms and inglenook fireplaces. Food available at lunchtime from 12–2.30pm in non-smoking restaurant. Children allowed in the restaurant only. Private room for hire. Beer festivals.

 *11am–11pm Mon–Sat; 12–3pm and 7–10.30pm Sun.*

CRADLEY HEATH

The Waterfall

132 Waterfall Lane, Cradley Heath B64 6RG
☎ *(0121) 561 3499*
Barbara Woodin and Ray Bowater

Ten beers always available including brews from Bathams. Also Enville Ale, Holden's Special, Hook Norton Old Hooky, Marston's Pedigree and Cains Formidable Ale. Plus guests such as Oak Double Dagger, Titanic White Star and RCH Fiery Liz plus something from Burton Bridge and Wood.

A traditional Black Country pub. Cask Marque accredited. Bar food available at lunchtime and evenings. Car park, garden with waterfall, children's room. Also function room for party and quiz nights, etc. Up the hill from the old Hill Station.

 *12–3pm and 5–11pm Mon–Thurs; all day Fri–Sun.*

WEST MIDLANDS

DUDLEY

Little Barrel

68 High Street, Dudley DY1 1PY
☎ *(01384) 235535*
Brendan Vernon and Chris Sandy

Wadworth 6X always available plus three guests such as Greene King Old Speckled Hen, Holden's XB, Shepherd Neame Bishop's Finger, Wychwood Hobgoblin or King & Barnes brews. Seasonal and celebration beers as available.

A small, traditional town pub with wooden floors. One bar, dining area. Food available at lunchtime only. No children.

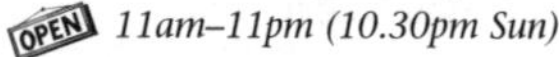
11am–11pm (10.30pm Sun).

The Park Inn

George Street, Woodsetton, Dudley DY1 4LW
☎ *(01902) 661279* A Walford

Four Holden's beers always on offer, plus one monthly changing guest from Holden's.

Traditional pub with open fire and wooden floors. Large bar area and two other rooms. Beer garden, large conservatory. Food served 12–3pm and 6–9pm Mon–Sat; 1–4pm for Sun lunch. Two car parks. Children welcome.

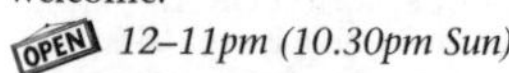
12–11pm (10.30pm Sun).

ENVILLE

The Cat Inn

Bridgenorth Road, Enville DY7 5HA
☎ *(01384) 872209* Lisa Johnson

A freehouse with Enville Ale always on offer. Four weekly changing guests might include Hop Back Summer Lightning or something from Greene King, Sarah Hughes or Ringwood, and where possible the beers are not repeated. A wide range of fruit wines is also available.

Four-bar sixteenth-century village pub with beams and fireplaces. Food is available and there is a non-smoking dining area. Pool room, darts, garden, car park. Children allowed.

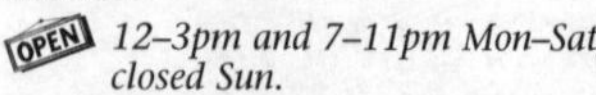
12–3pm and 7–11pm Mon–Sat; closed Sun.

HALESOWEN

Edward VII

88 Stourbridge Road, Halesowen B63 3UP
☎ *(0121) 550 4493* Patrick Villa

Banks's Bitter permanently available plus one guest changing every three weeks. Beers might include Everards Tiger, Enville White or Marston's Bitter.

Beautiful, well-thought-out, comfortable pub/restaurant with two bars and outside seating. Food served every lunchtime and Tues–Sat evenings. Children allowed. Located on the A458, next to Halesowen Town Football Club.

12–3pm and 5–11pm Mon–Thurs; 11am–11pm Fri–Sat; 12–10.30pm Sun.

The Waggon & Horses

21 Stourbridge Road, Halesowen B63 3TU
☎ *(0121) 550 4989* Bob Dummons

Batham Bitter, Nottingham EPA and something from Oakham always available plus up to 11 rotating guests (800 per year) changed after each cask. Two Belgian beers also on draught.

A classic West Midlands Victorian boozer. Bar food available at lunchtime. On the A458.

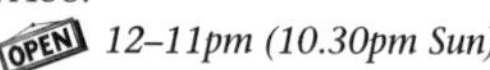
12–11pm (10.30pm Sun).

HIGHGATE

The Lamp Tavern

157 Barford Street, Highgate, Birmingham B5 6AH
☎ *(0121) 622 2599* Eddie Fitzpatrick

A freehouse with Stanway Stanney Bitter, Everards Tiger, Marston's Pedigree and Church End Grave Digger always available, plus one guest pump serving beers such as Shepherd Neame Bishop's Finger or Church End What the Fox's Hat.

A small, friendly village pub situated near the town. Bar snacks available at lunchtime. No children.

All day Mon–Sat; 12–3pm and 8–10.30pm Sun.

HOCKLEY

Black Eagle

16 Factory Road, Hockley, Birmingham B18 5JU
☎ *(0121) 523 4008* Tony Lewis

Marston's Pedigree, Timothy Taylor Landlord and something from Beowulf regularly available plus two guest beers, perhaps from Wye Valley, Church End or Burton Bridge.

Popular award-winning pub with two small front lounges, a large back lounge, snug and restaurant. Original Victorian back bar. Beer garden. Well known locally for good food. Bar meals 12.15–2.30pm and 5.30–9.30pm, restaurant 7–10.30pm. No food on Sunday evenings. Children welcome to eat. Annual beer festival each July. Five minutes by Metro to Soho Benson from Snow Hill.

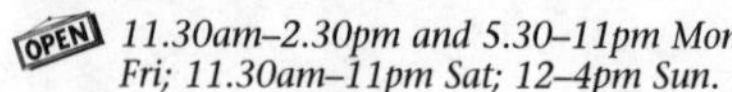
11.30am–2.30pm and 5.30–11pm Mon–Fri; 11.30am–11pm Sat; 12–4pm Sun.

The Church Inn

22 Great Hampton Street, Hockley, Birmingham B18 6AQ
☎ *(0121) 515 1851* Mr Wilkes

Greene King Old Speckled Hen and a Batham ale always available, plus one guest.

A Victorian town pub with one servery and two adjoining rooms. Food available at lunchtime and evenings. Children allowed.

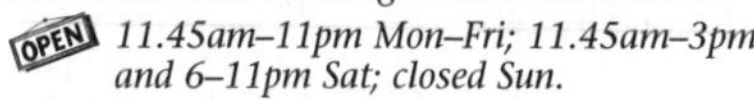

11.45am–11pm Mon–Fri; 11.45am–3pm and 6–11pm Sat; closed Sun.

KNOWLE

The Vaults

St John's Close, Knowle, Solihull B93 0JU
☎ *(01564) 773656*

Six ales always available, including Greene King IPA plus two guests changed frequently from small breweries all around the country. Real cider.

Traditional pub relocated to new premises just off the high street. Food served at lunchtimes. Outside seating.

12–2.30pm and 5–11pm Mon–Fri; all day Sat–Sun.

LOWER GORNAL

The Fountain Inn

8 Temple Street, Lower Gornal DY3 2PE
☎ *(01384) 24277* Alan Davis

Nine real ales always available. Enville Ale, RCH Pitchfork, Hook Norton Old Hooky, Everards Tiger and Greene King Abbot are regular fixtures plus four rotating guests. Two real ciders also served.

A comfortable Victorian freehouse with a warm and pleasant atmosphere. One room with a central bar. Restaurant at the rear with 60 covers; food served 12–9pm Mon–Sat and 12–5pm Sun. Parking, garden. Children allowed in the restaurant area which was once the brewhouse. CAMRA West Midlands Pub of the Year 2003. Two miles from Dudley.

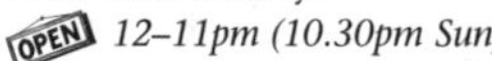

12–11pm (10.30pm Sun).

NETHERTON

The Olde Swan

89 Halesowen Road, Netherton, Dudley DY2 9PY
☎ *(01384) 253075* Mr TJ Newey

A revitalised brewpub, home of the Olde Swan Brewery (formerly known as Ma Pardoe's) with only home brews available, four or five at any one time: Olde Swan Original, Dark Swan, Entire and Bumblebee plus a monthly changing occasional or celebration ale.

One of the original four brewpubs dating from the 1970s, this is a Victorian tower brewery with a pub which is unchanged since 1863, including original mirrored back bar and enamel plate ceiling. Separate bar, lounges and smoking room plus function room. A quiet, real ale drinkers' pub with no juke boxes, games machines or music. Food available 12–2pm and 6–9pm Mon–Sat, and 12–3pm Sun. Courtyard seating. Strictly over 14s only. Brewery tours by arrangement.

11am–11pm Mon–Sat; 12–4pm and 7–10.30pm Sun.

OLDBURY

The Waggon & Horses

17A Church Street, Oldbury B69 3AD
☎ *(0121) 552 5467* Andrew Gale

Brains Reverend James, Enville White and Olde Swan Entire always available plus three guests, often including a traditional mild.

A Victorian, Grade II listed building with tiled walls, copper ceiling and original brewery windows. Two rooms, one non-smoking area. Bar food available 12–3pm. Car parking. Children welcome when eating. Function room with capacity for 40 people. At the corner of Market Street and Church Street in Oldbury town centre, next to the library, opposite the council offices.

12–11pm (10.30pm Sun).

PELSALL

The Sloan Inn

Wolverhampton Road, Pelsall, Walsall WS3 4AD
☎ *(01922) 694696* Miss Catherine Yeats

Highgate Dark Mild and Saddlers Celebrated Best Bitter are always on offer.

The oldest pub in Pelsall, with a homely atmosphere. Food is available 12–2.30pm and 6–9pm Tues–Sat and 12–2.30pm Sun. Children allowed. Car park.

11am–11pm Mon–Sat; 12–10.30pm Sun.

SEDGLEY

The Beacon Hotel

129 Bilston Street, Sedgley, Dudley DY3 1JE
☎ *(01902) 883380* John Hughes

Traditional Victorian brewery tap offering four home-brewed ales from Sarah Hughes: Dark Ruby Mild, Surprise Bitter, Pale Amber and Snowflake (Nov to Feb). Guest beers from an ever-changing selection are also available.

The three-storey Victorian brewery at the rear of the pub houses the Sarah Hughes Brewery, which was restored and reopened in 1987 after a 30-year closure. John Hughes, grandson of Sarah Hughes, discovered his grandmother's recipe for Dark Ruby Mild, and the brewery now supplies around 500 outlets and beer festivals. Brewery tours are available, but booking is essential. Children's room, plus beer garden with play area.

 *12–2.30pm and 5.30–10.45pm Mon–Thur; 12–3pm and 5.30–11pm Fri; 12–3pm and 6–11pm Sat; 12–3pm and 7–10.30pm Sun.*

SHELFIELD

The Four Crosses Inn

1 Green Lane, Shelfield, Walsall WS4 1RN
☎ *(01922) 682518* Mr Holt

A freehouse with Marston's Pedigree and Banks's Bitter and Mild always available, plus two weekly changing guests from smaller and micro-breweries such as Burton Bridge.

A traditional two-bar pub on the outskirts of town. Games in the bar, beer garden. No food. No children.

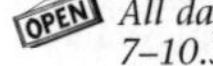 *All day Mon–Sat; 12–3pm and 7–10.30pm Sun.*

SOLIHULL

The Harvester

Tanhouse Farm Road, Solihull B92 9EY
☎ *(0121) 742 0770*
Dawn Bickerton and Philip Jones

Greene King Abbot always available, plus one guest which changes weekly.

A modern community pub with two bars, pool room, dining area in lounge, garden. Food available 12–8pm. Children allowed.

12–11pm (10.30pm Sun).

STOURBRIDGE

Hogshead

21–6 Foster Street, Stourbridge DY8 1EL
☎ *(01384) 371040* David Collins

Fourteen beers including ten guest ales regularly available. Examples include Enville White, Fuller's London Pride, Timothy Taylor Landlord, Marston's Pedigree, Wadworth 6X or something from Black Sheep, Brakspear or many others.

Hogshead original design, town-centre pub with ten beers on long front bar and four gravity-dispensed beers on back bar. Background music during the day, livelier in the evenings. Air-conditioned. Food available all day. Children welcome in designated areas until 8pm. Situated in pedestrian precinct.

 *12–11pm (10.30pm Sun).*

TIPTON

The Port 'n' Ale

178 Horseley Heath, Great Bridge, Tipton DY4 7DS
☎ *(0121) 557 7249* Kevin Taylor

A freehouse with Greene King Abbot, RCH Pitchfork, Moorhouse's Pendle Witches and Badger Tanglefoot always available, plus two guest pumps regularly serving RCH beers or something like Burton Bridge Summer Ale or Cotleigh Barn Ale.

A Victorian pub situated out of town. Bar, lounge and beer garden. Basic food served, including fish and chips and sandwiches. Children allowed in the garden only. Just down the road from Dudley Port railway station.

 *12–3pm and 5–11pm Mon–Fri; 12–11pm Sat; 12–4.30pm and 7–10.30pm Sun.*

The Rising Sun

116 Horseley Road, Tipton DY4 7NH
☎ *(0121) 530 9780* Jacqueline Skidmore

Five real ales usually available, with Oakham JHB a regular fixture and an ever-changing selection perhaps from Church End, Hobsons, Stonehenge, RCH, Kelham Island or elsewhere.

Friendly, award-winning two-bar locals' pub dating from 1865 with large beer garden. No TV or juke box. Food served 12–2pm Mon–Fri with rolls only on Sat. Children welcome in the garden. Close to Owen Street rail and Metro station.

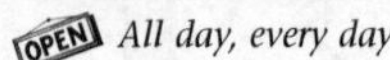 *All day, every day.*

UPPER GORNAL

Britannia Inn

109 Kent Street, Upper Gornal DY3 1UX
☎ *(01902) 883253*

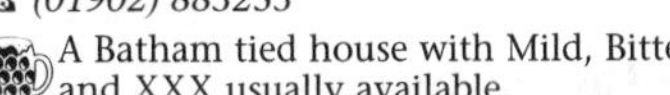

A Batham tied house with Mild, Bitter and XXX usually available.

Main lounge bar, TV room and (non-smoking) tap room. Real fires and outside seating. Loads of character. On the A459 Dudley to Sedgley road.

12–3pm and 7–11pm Mon–Fri; 12–11pm Sat; 12–4pm and 7–10.30pm Sun.

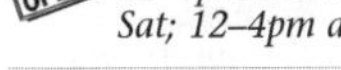

Jolly Crispin

Clarence Street, Upper Gornal DY3 1UZ
☎ *(01902) 672220*
www.jollycrispin.co.uk

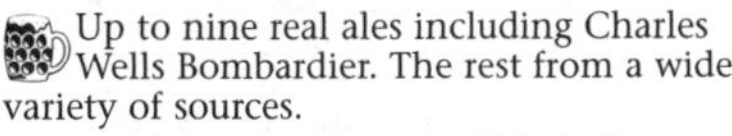

Up to nine real ales including Charles Wells Bombardier. The rest from a wide variety of sources.

An eighteenth-century cobbler's shop, now a genuine freehouse on the 558 bus route. Food available at lunchtimes.

All day, every day.

WALSALL

The Rising Sun

90 Ablewell Street, Walsall WS1 2EU
☎ *(01922) 626575* Reg Turner

A Highgate pub with Mild and Saddlers Celebrated Best Bitter the permanent beers. One guest beer, changed as consumption demands, could be Highgate Fox's Nob or Old Ale, or any one of the Wyre Piddle brews.

Traditional pub in an old building with cobbles outside, on the edge of the town centre. Excellent atmosphere. Food available. Rock-music-oriented at weekends – popular with bikers. Two bars, dining area, massive garden, frequent live music, disco Tues, Fri and Sat – call for details.

12–11pm Mon–Wed; 12–1am Thurs–Sat; 12–10.30pm Sun.

Tap & Spile

5 John Street, Walsall WS2 8AF
☎ *(01922) 627660* John Davies

Charles Wells Eagle IPA usually available plus seven guest beers which change regularly, totalling around 40 per month. These may include beers from Bateman, Wychwood, Arundel, Hoskins, Fuller's, Harviestoun, Hydes, Hop Back, Highwood, Hook Norton, Orkney or any other independent brewery.

Small, traditional backstreet pub with great atmosphere. Friendly staff and chatty customers. Food available 12–2pm Mon, 12–2pm and 6.30–9pm Tues–Sat. Children welcome.

12–3pm and 5.30–11pm Mon–Thurs; 12–11pm Fri–Sat; 12–3pm and 7–10.30pm Sun.

The Wharf

10 Wolverhampton Street, Walsall WS2 8LS
☎ *(01922) 613100* Richard Carr (manager)

Highgate Saddlers Best Bitter and Old Ale usually available plus a guest changed every month.

Town pub in a new building with modern interior and a patio, located on the canal basin in the heart of Walsall. Food available until 4pm. Modern music venue on weekend evenings. Children allowed until 6.30pm. Car park.

11am–11pm Mon–Thurs; 11am–1am Fri; 11am–2am Sat; 12–10.30pm Sun.

WEDNESBURY

The Old Blue Ball

19 Hall End, Wednesbury
☎ *(0121) 556 0197* Jonathan Bradley

Everards Old Original always available, plus three rotating guests from a range including Young's Special, Timothy Taylor Landlord, Fuller's London Pride, Elgood's Cambridge, Greene King Abbot and Wadworth 6X.

Small, friendly, family pub with a small bar, one small lounge and one large lounge. Large garden. Food available Fri–Sat lunchtimes, including barbecues in summer weekends. Sandwiches only Mon–Thurs. Children welcome in the large lounge and beer garden, where there is a climbing frame. From Wednesbury town, look for two churches on a hill. Follow this road and turn right.

12–3pm and 5–11pm Mon–Thurs; 12–11pm Fri; 12–4.30pm and 7–11pm Sat; 12–3.30pm and 7–10.30pm Sun.

The Forge

Franchise Street, Wednesbury WS10 9RG
☎ *(0121) 526 2777* Paul Pugh

Owned by Highgate, with Highgate Mild Ale a permanent fixture. One seasonal guest is also served.

Two-bar community pub, purpose-built in 1935 by Highgate Brewery. No food. Live music Fri, Sat and Sun. Children allowed. Car park. Situated behind IKEA.

 *12–2pm and 5–11pm Mon–Thurs; 11am–11pm Fri–Sun.*

WEST BROMWICH

The Old Crown

56 Sandwell Road, West Bromwich B70 8TG
☎ *(0121) 525 4600* Mr Patel

A freehouse with three hand pumps serving an ever-changing selection of ales such as Timothy Taylor Landlord, Oakham, Enville, Wye Valley, Bathams, St Austell and Burton Bridge ales. RCH Pitchfork and Olde Swan Entire are other favourites.

An open-plan town pub. Food available 12–2pm Mon–Sat and 6–9pm Tues-Sat in a non-smoking area – home-cooked curries, balti and tikka masala are specialities. Children allowed in the non-smoking area only until 9pm.

 *12–4pm and 5–11pm Mon–Thurs; 12–11pm Fri–Sat; 12–4pm and 7–10.30pm Sun.*

The Vine

152 Roebuck Street, West Bromwich B70 6RD
☎ *(0121) 553 2866* Mr Suki Patel
www.sukis.co.uk

A freehouse with one or two real ales always available. Breweries featured include Wood, Lichfield and Wye Valley, among others. The selection changes daily.

A traditional two-bar pub with beams and gardens. Children's play area. Food available at 12–2pm and 5.30–10.30pm Mon–Fri, 12.30–10.30pm Sat–Sun. Barbecues and curries are specialities. Children allowed. Situated out of town.

 *11.30am–2.30pm and 5–11pm Mon–Thurs; all day Fri–Sun.*

WILLENHALL

The Brewer's Droop

44 Wolverhampton Street, Willenhall WV13 2PS
☎ *(01902) 607827*

An Avebury Taverns tenancy with Enville Ale and Charles Wells Eagle IPA always available, plus a range of guests changing twice-weekly, such as Holden's Special and Badger Tanglefoot.

A traditional town-centre pub decorated with bric-à-brac, particularly relating to motorbikes. Two bars, pool table. Food available at lunchtime and evenings. Children allowed until 9pm.

 *12–3.30pm and 6–11pm Mon–Thurs; all day Fri–Sat; 12–4pm and 7–10.30pm Sun.*

The Falcon Inn

Gomer Street West, Willenhall WV13 2NR
☎ *(01902) 633378* Mick Taylor

A freehouse with RCH PG Steam, Pardoe's Dark Swan (from Olde Swan) and Greene King Abbot and Pitchfork always available, plus five guest beers, usually including a stout or a porter. All beers are hand-pulled and served in oversized glasses. Range of malt whiskies also on offer.

A 1930s traditional backstreet pub near the town centre. Walsall CAMRA commended in 2000. Two rooms – bar and lounge – with no price difference! Both rooms are air-filtered. Non-smoking area in lounge. Bar snacks (pies and pasties) available. Beer garden. Plenty of on-street parking.

 *12–11pm (10.30pm Sun).*

WOLLASTON

The Princess

115 Bridgnorth Road, Wollaston, Stourbridge DY8 3NX
☎ *(01384) 443687* Ralph and Kay Vines

Wadworth 6X, Charles Wells Bombardier, Greene King Abbot Ale and Banks's Original are permanent fixtures, plus a monthly changing guest beer.

Single bar with wooden floor, quarry tiles and an interesting selection of mirrors and artefacts. Food served lunchtimes only. Car park. Children welcome, but no special facilities.

 *11am–11pm Mon–Sat; 12–10.30pm Sun.*

The Unicorn

145 Bridgnorth Road, Wollaston, Stourbridge
☎ *(01384) 394823* C John Freeman

Batham Bitter and Mild always available.

A small pub with three rooms and a traditional, cosy, olde-worlde atmosphere. No music. Lovely beer garden. Rolls available at lunchtime. Public car park to the rear. Children welcome until 9pm in the garden and in a specified area of the pub.

 *12–11pm Mon–Sat; 12–4pm and 7–10.30pm Sun.*

WOLVERHAMPTON

Chindit

113 Merridale Road, Wolverhampton
☎ *(01902) 425582* John Ralph Smith

Four guest beers available, changing daily, and totalling around 350 different beers each year. Favourite breweries include Hop Back, Harviestoun, Daleside and Wychwood. The Chindit holds an annual beer festival with over 30 different beers over the May Bank Holiday.

Cosy, two-roomed pub named after a Second World War regiment – the only pub in the world so named. Cask Marque accredited. Live music on Friday evenings and barbecues in summer, weather permitting. Children welcome until 7pm. Play area. Located one mile from city centre, on the west side of Wolverhampton.

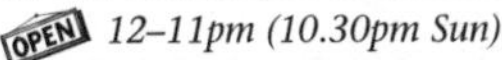

OPEN *12–11pm (10.30pm Sun).*

Great Western

Sun Street, Wolverhampton
☎ *(01902) 351090* Kevin Michael Gould

Batham Bitter, Holden's Mild, Black Country Bitter and Special Bitter regularly available, plus guests.

Friendly pub with non-smoking dining room. Food served 11.45am–2.15pm Mon–Sat. Car park. Situated two minutes' walk from railway station. Children welcome in conservatory if dining.

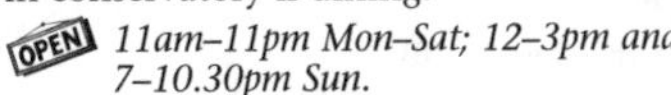

OPEN *11am–11pm Mon–Sat; 12–3pm and 7–10.30pm Sun.*

Moon Under Water

53–5 Lichfield Street, Wolverhampton WV1 1EQ
☎ *(01902) 422447* Edel Crehan

Shepherd Neame Spitfire, Hop Back Summer Lightning and Greene King Abbot Ale permanently available, plus at least two guests. Regular guests include Springhead Roaring Meg and Bitter, Brains SA and Bateman XXXB.

A JD Wetherspoon's pub in the city centre, frequented by locals and shoppers, with a young crowd in the evenings at weekends. Food available all day. Children allowed until 6pm if eating.

OPEN *10am–11pm Mon–Sat; 12–10.30pm Sun.*

Newhampton

Riches Street, Wolverhampton WV6 0DW
☎ *(01902) 745773* Betty Carnegie

Marston's Pedigree, Charles Wells Bombardier and a daily changing guest beer regularly available, such as Timothy Taylor Landlord or something from Enville.

Traditional community pub, an 'oasis' with with bowling green, garden and children's play area. Homemade food served 12–2pm and 6–9pm daily. Children very welcome.

OPEN *11am–11pm Mon–Sat; 12–10.30pm Sun.*

Tap & Spile

35 Princess Street, Wolverhampton WV1 1HD
☎ *(01902) 713319* Michael Stokes

Banks's Bitter and Mild are the permanent beers, plus up to six guest ales which could be from any brewery around the UK.

A locals' town pub with wooden floors, open fire, one main bar and snug rooms. Food available 12–4pm. Beer garden. Children allowed until 7pm.

OPEN *10am–11pm Mon–Sat; 12–10.30pm Sun.*

THE BREWERIES

ARCHERS ALES LTD

Penzance Drive, Churchyard, Swindon SN5 7JL
☎ *(01793) 879929*

VILLAGE BITTER 3.6% ABV
Malty, with hop and fruit notes.
BEST BITTER 4.0% ABV
Bitter with some sweetness.
BLACK JACK PORTER 4.6% ABV
Dark, roasted malt, winter brew.
GOLDEN BITTER 4.7% ABV
Superb balance, a classic beer.
Plus seasonal brews and beers to celebrate the locomotive collection.

ARKELLS BREWERY LTD

Kingsdown Brewery, Swindon SN2 6RU
☎ *(01793) 823026*
www.arkells.com

2B 3.2% ABV
Light and quenching with good bitter hoppiness.
3B 4.0% ABV
Amber, balanced and hoppy.
PETER'S PORTER 4.3% ABV
KINGSDOWN ALE 5.0% ABV
Smooth, rounded and flavour-packed.
Plus seasonal brews.

THE HIDDEN BREWERY

Dinton Road, Wylye, Salisbury SP3 5EU
☎ *(01722) 716440*

OLD SARUM 4.1% ABV
QUEST 4.2% ABV
Plus seasonal brews.

HOBDEN'S WESSEX BREWERY

Farm Cottage, Norton Ferris, Warminster BA12 7HT
☎ *(01985) 844532*

NAUGHTY FERRET 3.5% ABV
CROCKERTON CLASSIC 4.1% ABV
GOLDEN DELIRIOUS 4.5% ABV
WARMINSTER WARRIOR 4.5% ABV
RUSSIAN STOAT 9.0% ABV
Seasonals:
OLD DEVERILL 6.0% ABV
Blackmore Ale's big brother. Rich red colour and a rounded bitter/fruit/malt and hops flavour. Fruitcake in a glass. Once a year.
Plus many occasionals usually with ferret or stoat in the title.

THE HOP BACK BREWERY PLC

Unit 21–4, Batten Road Industrial Estate, Downton, Salisbury SP5 3HU
☎ *(01725) 510986*
www.hopback.co.uk

GFB 3.5% ABV
Smooth and full-flavoured for gravity.
BEST BITTER 4.0% ABV
Well-balanced, easy-drinking.
CROP CIRCLE 4.2% ABV
Pale with wonderful thirst-quenching properties.
ENTIRE STOUT 4.5% ABV
Powerful roast maltiness.
SUMMER LIGHTNING 5.0% ABV
Superb, pale and quenching with good hoppiness.
Plus seasonal and occasional brews.

MOLE'S BREWERY

5 Merlin Way, Bowerhill, Melksham SN12 6TJ
☎ *(01225) 708842*
www.molesbrewery.com

TAP 3.5% ABV
Malty with clean, balancing bitterness.
BEST BITTER 4.0% ABV
Golden with quenching, hoppy finish.
LANDLORD'S CHOICE 4.5% ABV
Darker, with hops, fruit and malt.
RUCKING MOLE 4.5% ABV
Occasional.
MOLENNIUM 4.5% ABV
Fruit, caramel and malty overtones.
MOLECATCHER 5.0% ABV
Seasonals:
BARLEYMOLE 4.2% ABV
Pale, hoppy brew with malty finish.
MOLEGRIP 4.3% ABV
Rounded, balanced autumn ale.
HOLY MOLEY 4.7% ABV
Good malt flavour with hop balance.
MOEL MOEL 6.0% ABV
Winter warmer.

STONEHENGE ALES (BUNCES BREWERY)

The Old Mill, Mill Road, Netheravon, Salisbury SP4 9QB
☎ *(01980) 670631*
www.stonehengeales.sagenet.co.uk

BENCHMARK 3.5% ABV
Malt flavours with good balancing hoppy bitterness.
PIGSWILL 4.0% ABV
Mellow and hoppy.
BODYLINE 4.3% ABV
Darkish beer.
HEEL STONE 4.3% ABV
Quenching fruity flavour.
GREAT BUSTARD 4.8% ABV
DANISH DYNAMITE 5.0% ABV
Golden and far too easy to drink!
Plus seasonal brews.

WADWORTH & CO. LTD

Northgate Brewery, Devizes SN10 1JW
☎ *(01380) 723361*
www.wadworth.co.uk

HENRY'S ORIGINAL IPA 3.6% ABV
Well-balanced and smooth, with malt throughout.

6X 4.3% ABV
Rich, with malt flavours.

JCB 4.7% ABV
Unique palate with chewy bite.

Seasonals:

SUMMERSAULT 4.0% ABV
Quenching, lager-style beer. Summer only.

MALT AND HOPS 4.5% ABV
Sweet and nutty. September.

OLD FATHER TIMER 5.8% ABV
Ripe fruit and hop aromas. December.

THE PUBS

ABBEY MEADS

The Jovial Monk

Highdown Way, St Andrews Ridge, Abbey Meads, Swindon SN25 4YD
☎ *(01793) 728636* Sheila and Oliver Cleary

An Arkells tied house with 2B and 3B permanently available plus seasonals.

A community character-built pub with beams and hard and soft furnishing. Big-screen Sky TV. Food available in separate restaurant area. Children allowed. Patio. Car park. Accommodation. Disabled access. Situated directly behind the Motorola building.

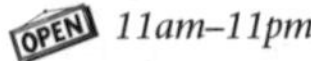

11am–11pm.

AVEBURY

The Red Lion

High Street, Avebury SN8 1RF
☎ *(01672) 539266* Richard Bounds

Greene King Old Speckled Hen, Marston's Pedigree and Flower's IPA generally available.

A large pub handy for the stones. There's an air of efficiency in the variety of different rooms. Accommodation, and it is supposed to be one of Wiltshire's most haunted pubs. Food all day. Car park and patio area.

11am–11pm Mon–Sat; 12–10.30pm Sun.

AXFORD

The Red Lion

Axford, Nr Marlborough SN8 2HA
☎ *(01672) 520271* Seamus Lecky

Hook Norton Best and Fuller's London Pride permanently available plus guest ales from perhaps Butcombe or the Cottage Brewing Company.

A sixteenth-century restaurant and pub with two bars, two beer gardens and a patio. Children allowed.

12–3pm and 6.30–11pm Mon–Sat; 12–3pm and 7–10.30pm Sun.

BERWICK ST JOHN

The Talbot Inn

The Cross, Berwick St John, Nr Shaftsbury SP7 0HA
☎ *(01747) 828222* Peter Hawkins

Wadworth 6X and Ringwood Best Bitter regularly available, plus a guest, alternating perhaps Fuller's London Pride, Greene King Old Speckled Hen, or Hop Back GFB in the summer, and others.

Typical country inn in Chalke Valley below Cranbourne Chase. Food served lunchtimes and evenings Tues–Sat. Car park. Children welcome at lunchtime.

12–2.30pm and 6.30–11pm Mon–Sat; 12–4pm Sun (closed Sun evening).

BOWDEN HILL

The Bell Inn

The Wharf, Bowden Hill, Lacock, Chippenham SN15 2PJ
☎ *(01249) 730308*
Alan and Heather Shepherd

A freehouse with five hand pumps serving Wadworth 6X plus a selection of real ales of varying strengths from local breweries, including smaller and micro-breweries. Farmhouse cider also available.

A traditional rural pub built in converted canal cottages on the edge of a National Trust village. One bar, dining area, beer garden, children's play area. Two boules pistes. Food available every session and all day on Saturday and Sunday. Children allowed.

11.30am–2.30pm and 6–11pm Tues–Fri; all day Sat–Sun; closed all day Monday except Bank Holidays.

The Rising Sun

32 Bowden Hill, Lacock, Nr Chippenham SN15 2PP
☎ *(01249) 730363* Paul and Denise Rogers

Five beers always available including Mole's Tap, Best, Molecatcher, Rucking Mole and Black Rat, plus occasional seasonals.

A Cotswold stone pub with flagstone floors and open fires. Bar food available at lunchtime and evenings (not Sun evening or Mon lunchtime), roasts served on Sun. Car park, garden. Live music Wed evenings plus alternate Sun from 3pm. Children and dogs allowed. Turn into village, then go up Bowden Hill.

12–3pm and 6–11pm Mon–Sat; all day Sun.

BOX HILL

The Quarrymans Arms

Box Hill, Corsham SN13 8HN
☎ *(01225) 743569* John Arundel
www.quarrymans-arms.co.uk.

Wadworth 6X, Mole's Best Bitter and Butcombe Bitter regularly available. Two or three guest beers are also served, often from Bath Ales or Abbey Ales.

A 300-year-old miners' pub, tucked away in the Wiltshire countryside, high above the Colerne Valley. Popular with pot-holers, cavers, walkers and cyclists. Food served 12–3pm and 7–10pm daily. Car park. Children welcome. Very difficult to find, so ring for directions. Accommodation.

11am–3pm and 6–11pm Mon–Thurs; 11am–11pm Fri–Sat; 12–10.30pm Sun.

BRADFORD-ON-AVON

The Beehive

Trowbridge Road, Bradford-on-Avon BA15 1UA
☎ *(01225) 863620* Mrs C Crocker

A freehouse with Butcombe ales always available plus five guests, constantly changing.

A pub situated on the side of the canal. One bar, no music, open fires. Beer garden features a boules pitch and an antique pump dating from 1880. Also open for coffee. Food available every lunchtime except Mon and Tues–Sat evening. Children allowed.

12–2.30pm and 7–11pm (10.30pm Sun).

Bunch of Grapes

14 Silver Street, Bradford-on-Avon BA15 1JY
☎ *(01225) 863877* John Williams

Smiles Best, Young's Bitter and Special, plus a rotating ale from either Young's or Smiles.

Town-centre pub that is supposedly haunted. Food available lunchtime and evening, every day. Children allowed.

12–11pm (10.30pm Sun).

BRATTON

The Duke at Bratton

Bratton, Nr Westbury BA13 4RW
☎ *(01380) 830242* Ian Overend

Mole's Best permanently available plus a rotating guest.

Community village pub close to the Westbury White Horse, which has won awards for its roast lunch and its loos. Food available. Well-behaved children welcome. Garden and car park.

11.30am–3pm and 7–11pm.

BROAD CHALKE

The Queens Head Inn

1 North Street, Broad Chalke, Nr Salisbury SP5 5EN
☎ *(01722) 780344* Mike Craggs

Freehouse serving Greene King IPA, Old Speckled Hen and Ruddles County, plus Wadworth 6X and a guest, which may be Greene King Morland Original.

A popular fifteenth century country local offering food and accommodation as well as the good range of beers. Patio. Large car park. Well-behaved children welcome. Darts.

11am–3pm and 6–11.30pm.

BROKERSWOOD

Kicking Donkey

Brokerswood, Westbury BA13 4EG
☎ *(01373) 823250* Roy King

Freehouse always serving Wadworth 6X, Badger Tanglefoot and Butcombe Bitter, plus a couple of guests, often a beer from Hop Back.

A rustic country pub with stone floors and a terracotta paint effect that highlights the unevenness of the walls. One long bar for two separate areas. Food every session with an à la carte menu in the evening. Children welcome. Garden with bouncy castle and swings. Car park.

11.30am–3pm and 6–11pm Mon–Thur; all day Fri–Sun.

BROUGHTON GIFFORD

Bell on the Common

Broughton Gifford, Nr Melksham SN12 8LX
☎ *(01225) 782309*
Anthony and Dorothy Stanley

A Wadworth pub offering 6X, Henry's IPA and one other from the Wadworth range.

A popular country pub in attractive surroundings and with a prize-winning beer garden. Two bars and a restaurant – food served twice daily, seven days a week. Darts, cribbage, pool and a boules piste. Parking on the edge of the common. Well-behaved children welcome. Winner of the 2002 and 2003 Real Coal Fire Pub of the Year.

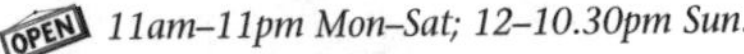
11am–11pm Mon–Sat; 12–10.30pm Sun.

BUSHTON

The Trotting Horse

Bushton, Nr Wootton Bassett SN4 7PX
☎ *(01793) 731338* Richard and Jenny Nickolls

Freehouse with Archers Village and Wadworth 6X as permanents, plus one changing guest.

A friendly and traditional village pub. Food, not Sunday night or Monday, special deals midweek lunchtime. Garden and car park. Games including bar billiards and darts.

12–2pm and 6.30–11pm Mon–Fri;
12–2.30pm and 6.30–11pm Sat;
12–2.30pm and 6.30–10.30pm Sun.

CHARLTON

The Horse & Groom

The Street, Charlton, Malmesbury SN16 9DL
☎ *(01666) 823904* Nicola King

Archers Village and Wadworth 6X always available, plus a guest such as Uley Old Spot, Smiles Best, Abbey Bellringer or Ridleys Spectacular.

A traditional country village pub with beams, fires and wooden floors. Two bars, beer garden, accommodation. Food served at lunchtime and evenings in a separate dining area. Well-behaved children allowed.

12–3pm and 7–11pm Mon–Fri; all day Sat–Sun in the summer.

CHIPPENHAM

Four Seasons

6 Market Place, Chippenham SN15 3HD
☎ *(01249) 444668* Chris Mills

Fuller's ESB and London Pride plus a guest beer.

Pleasant, homely no-frills pub in the centre of town. Food available lunchtime and evening seven days a week. Children allowed if eating with adults. Karaoke Thurs and Sun, music Fri and Sat, music quiz Wed.

11am–11pm Mon–Wed; 11am–1am Thurs–Sat; 12–12 Sun.

Pheasant Inn

Bath Road, Chippenham SN14 OAE
☎ *(01249) 444083*
Kate Partridge and Richard Bennett

Wadworth 6X, IPA and JCB with occasional Wadworth seasonals.

Large edge-of-town pub popular for food and activities. Function room. Skittle alley. Pool. Large-screen TV. Car park. Children welcome.

11am–2.30pm and 6–11pm Mon–Fri;
11am–11pm Sat; 12–10.30pm Sun.

CHRISTIAN MALFORD

Mermaid Inn

Main Road, Christian Malford, Nr Chippenham SN15 4BE
☎ *(01249) 720313* John Gregory

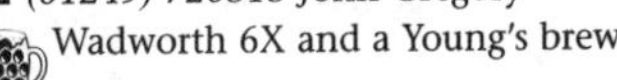
Wadworth 6X and a Young's brew.

Friendly food-led destination pub with good beer and wine. One bar. Food every session. Children welcome. Car park. Garden. Darts and pool.

11.30am–11pm Mon–Sat;
12–10.30pm Sun.

The Rising Sun

Station Road, Christian Malford, Nr Chippenham SN15 4BL
☎ *(01249) 721571* Simon and Sue Woodhead

Freehouse offering Archers Village as a permanent, plus a couple of guests that may include Badger Best or Mole's Rucking Mole.

Pleasant, friendly country pub. Food every session except Monday lunchtime. Children welcome. Garden and car park.

12–2pm and 6.30–11pm Mon–Sat;
12–2pm and 7–10.30pm Sun.

CLYFFE PYPARD

The Goddard Arms

Wood Street, Clyffe Pypard, Swindon SN4 7PY
☎ *(01793) 731386* Raymond Orchard

Freehouse serving Wadworth 6X plus two or three guest beers, favouring the local breweries.

Homely village local with main bar just like an old-fashioned front room. Food. Accommodation. Garden. Car Park. Skittle alley.

12–2.30pm and 7–11pm Mon–Fri; all day Sat–Sun.

COATE

The Sun Inn

Marlborough Road, Coate, Swindon SN3 6AA
☎ *(01793) 523292*
Martin and Lorraine Hobson

An Arkells tied house with 2B and 3B permanently available plus occasionals and seasonals.

A refurbished country pub with family areas (including children's play area), non-smoking areas and large beer garden. Food available. Live music Sun. Quiz night Mon.

 *11am–2.30pm and 6–11pm.*

COMPTON BASSETT

The White Horse

Compton Bassett, Calne SN11 8RG
☎ *(01249) 813118* Catherine Ritchie

Greene King IPA, Wadworth 6X and Adnams Broadside regularly available.

Popular and friendly country pub with a good reputation for food. Meals every session. Children allowed in the restaurant. Large car park. Skittle alley.

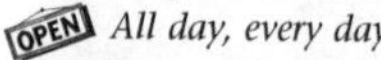 *All day, every day.*

CORSHAM

The Two Pigs

38 Pickwick, Corsham SN13 0HY
☎ *(01249) 712515* Dickie and Ann Doyle

Stonehenge Pigswill always available plus three guests (200 per year) including Church End brews, Hop Back Summer Lightning and Greene King Abbot. Guest ales rotating constantly, two in ABV range 4.1–4.6% and one at 5%+ ABV.

A traditional wood-panelled pub with stone floors. No food. Parking nearby. Covered courtyard. No children. Live blues music on Monday. On the A4 between Chippenham and Bath.

 *7–11pm Mon–Sat; 12–2.30pm and 7–10.30pm Sun.*

CORSLEY

The Cross Keys

Lyes Green, Corsley, Nr Warminster BA12 7PB
☎ *(01373) 832406*
Fraser Carruth and Wayne Carnegie

Wadworth house offering IPA, 6X and seasonal ale plus a rotating guest.

Homely and comfortable village pub. Food available. No children under 14 allowed. Non-smoking and smoking restaurants. Car park and beer garden. Skittle alley and bar games.

 *12–3pm and 6.30–11pm (10.30pm Sun).*

The White Hart

Lane End, Corsley, Nr Warminster BA12 7PH
☎ *(01373) 832805* AE Rimmer

Butcombe Bitter regularly available plus one constantly changing guest.

Welcoming, traditional pub with good mix of clientele and comprehensive menu. Food served lunchtimes and evenings. Car park. Children's room, menu and high chairs.

 *11.30am–depends on custom; 6–11pm Mon–Sat; 12–3pm and 7–10.30pm Sun.*

CORSTON

The Radnor Arms

Corston, Nr Malmesbury SN16 0HD
☎ *(01666) 823389* John Makins

Freehouse offering Hook Norton, Young's Bitter and two rotating guests. Also traditional cider.

A village inn dating from the eighteenth century, serving good food and proper beer. No food on Sun evening. Children welcome. Car park, garden. Darts.

All day, every day.

CORTON

The Dove Inn

Corton, Nr Warminster BA12 0SZ
☎ *(01985) 850109* M and B Wilson
www.thedove.co.uk.

Hop Back GFB and Butcombe Bitter always available plus one guest.

Tastefully refurbished, traditional pub tucked away in a beautiful and tranquil village close to the River Wylye. Restaurant and garden. Food served 12–2.30pm and 7–9.30pm every day. Car park. Children welcome. En-suite accommodation.

 *12–3pm and 6.30–11pm Mon–Sat; 12–4pm and 7–10.30pm Sun.*

CRICKLADE

The White Hart Hotel

High Street, Cricklade SN6 6AA
☎ *(01793) 750206*
William Finch and Norma Brooks

An Arkells tied house with 2B and 3B permanently available, plus Arkells seasonal guests.

An old coaching inn built in 1628, now a small town pub/restaurant. Food available. Live music on Saturday nights. Beer garden. Children allowed but no dogs. Car park. Accommodation.

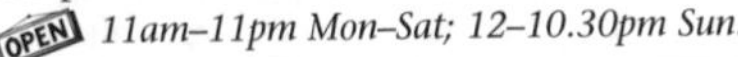
OPEN *11am–11pm Mon–Sat; 12–10.30pm Sun.*

The Red Lion

74 High Street, Cricklade SN6 6DD
☎ *(01793)750776* Mark Whittam

A freehouse offering Butts Bitter, a Mole's brew and eight rotating guests.

There's a homely, characterful, open-spaced feel to this pub on a high street that is littered with inns. Children welcome. Car park. Large garden.

OPEN *12–11pm (10.30pm Sun). 5–11pm Mon–Tues in the winter.*

DAUNTSEY LOCK

The Peterborough Arms

Dauntsey Lock, Nr Lyneham SN15 4HD
☎ *(01249) 890409* Philip Glover

Freehouse serving Wadworth 6X, JCB andHenry's IPA, plus a couple of guests.

A two-bar, traditional country roadside pub with oak beams, fires and antique decorations. Large beer garden. Bar and restaurant menus. Children welcome in restaurant area. Ample parking. Accommodation. Jazz and other themed nights.

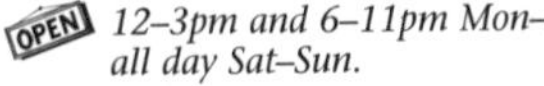
OPEN *12–3pm and 6–11pm Mon–Fri; all day Sat–Sun.*

DERRY HILL

Lansdowne Arms

Church Road, Derry Hill, Nr Calne SN11 9NS
☎ *(01249) 812422*
Michael Lynn and Clare Highton

Wadworth 6X, JCB and Henry's IPA plus seasonals and guests.

An imposing nineteenth-century coaching inn with scenic views across the Avon valley and close to Bowood House. Food available. Car park and garden. Children allowed.

OPEN *All day, every day.*

DEVIZES

The British Lion

9 Estcourt Street, Devizes SN10 1LQ
☎ *(01380) 720665* Michael Dearing

Three or four real ales available but constantly changing. The pub likes to support the West Country micro-breweries as much as it can. Beer range regularly includes stout, porter and mild. A real cider is also permanently served.

A popular single-bar character freehouse. Car park and large, sunny garden at the rear. On the main Swindon (A361) road, opposite The Green.

OPEN *11am–11pm Mon–Sat; all day Sun.*

The Cavalier

Eastleigh Road, Devizes SN10 3EG
☎ *(01380) 723285* Sadie Honeywell

A Wadworth pub offering Henry's IPA and 6X plus seasonals.

A warm welcoming local on an estate. Food. Roast on Sun but no food Sun evening. Children welcome until 8.30pm. Car park and garden. Games include shove ha'penny, darts and pool.

OPEN *11am–11pm.*

The Hare & Hounds

Hare and Hounds Street, Devizes SN10 1LZ
☎ *(01380) 723231* Janet Davies

Wadworth 6X, IPA and seasonals.

A village pub atmosphere in the middle of the town. A public bar and a small lounge. Food at lunchtime only. Children allowed. Small car park. Garden.

OPEN *11am–2.30pm and 7–11pm Mon–Fri; 11am–3pm and 7–11pm Sat; 12–3pm and 7–10.30 Sun.*

The Queen's Head

Dunkirk Hill, Devizes SN10 2BG
☎ *(01380) 723726* Ian and David

A Mole's pub serving Tap and Best.

A friendly edge-of-town local proud of its food, which is served every session. Children welcome. Beer garden. Car park. Skittle alley.

OPEN *12–3pm and 6–11pm.*

Southgate Inn

Potterne Road, Devizes SN10 5BY
☎ *(01380) 722872* Eddie Bonniffini

Hop Back Best, Summer Lightning and GFB are generally available plus three or four guest beers. Also serves the Southgate Special with an ABV of 14.5% and brewed in the States.

Old-fashioned English pub with a warm welcome and lots of nooks and crannies. Food at lunchtime. Garden and small car park. On the A360 Salisbury road out of town.

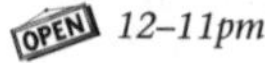 *12–11pm.*

EAST KNOYLE

The Fox & Hounds

The Green, East Knoyle, Salisbury SP3 6BN
☎ *(01747) 830573* Gordon Beck

A Young's tied house with the full range of Young's beers always available, plus one guest which may be from Smiles Brewery or other independents.

A country village pub with beams, slate floors, conservatory and garden. Food available at lunchtime and evenings. Children allowed in the conservatory and garden.

 *11am–2.30pm and 6–11pm (10.30pm Sun).*

EASTERTON

The Royal Oak

11 High Street, Easterton SN10 4PE
☎ *(01380) 812343* Wayne and Jane Nicholas

A Wadworth pub selling 6X, Henry's IPA and one guest beer.

There's a relaxed atmosphere to this seventeenth century thatched inn. Various different rooms. Food. Small garden out the front. Car park. Children welcome. Accommodation.

 *12–2.30pm and 5.30–11pm Mon–Sat; 12–10.30pm Sun.*

EASTON ROYAL

Bruce Arms

Easton Royal, Nr Pewsey SN9 5LR
☎ *(01672) 810216* WJ and JA Butler
www.brucearms.co.uk

Wadworth 6X and Henry's IPA usually available, plus a guest beer.

Popular, traditional pub with many original features, situated on the B3087. Only cheese and onion rolls/sandwiches served lunchtimes and evenings. Car park. Children welcome in lounge, skittle alley or pool room.

 *12–2.30pm and 6–11pm Mon–Sat; 12–2.30pm and 7–10.30pm Sun.*

EBBESBOURN WAKE

The Horseshoe Inn

Ebbesbourne Wake SP5 5JF
☎ *(01722) 780474* Tony Bath

Wadworth 6X, Ringwood Best and Adnams Broadside always available straight from the barrel, plus a guest (12 per year) perhaps from Archers, Stonehenge, or Palmers.

A remote, old-fashioned unspoilt pub hung with old tools of a bygone age. Bar and restaurant food available lunchtime and evenings (except Monday and Sunday night). Car park, garden, accommodation. Children are allowed if eating. From Salisbury (A354), turn right to Bishopston, Broadchalke then on to Ebbesbourne Wake.

 *12–3pm and 6.30–11pm. Closed Monday lunchtime.*

ENFORD

The Swan

Longstreet, Enford, Nr Pewsey SN9 6DD
☎ *(01980) 670338* Paul and Claire Jackson

A good choice of real ales available, changing regularly but usually including brews from Stonehenge and other Wiltshire and West Country breweries.

Old thatched and beamed pub with open fires. Bar food available at lunchtime and evenings. Home-cooked food with local produce. Car park, garden, restaurant. Easy to find.

 *12–3pm and 7–11pm Mon–Sat; 12–4pm and 7–10.30pm Sun.*

FORD

The White Hart

Ford, Nr Chippenham SN14 8RP
☎ *(01249) 782213* Jane Leigh

Wadworth 6X, Flower's IPA and Adnams Bitter are permanent with one guest beer.

Old coaching inn off the A420 on the edge of a river. One main bar, restaurant and lounge. Bar food available at lunchtime. Restaurant open at lunchtime and evenings. Car parks, river terrace, accommodation. Well-behaved children allowed.

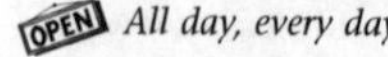 *All day, every day.*

FOVANT

Pembroke Arms

Shaftesbury Road, Fovant, Nr Salisbury SP3 5JH
☎ *(01722) 714201* Janine Trevett

A freehouse serving three real ales including Wadworth 6X and Ringwood Best.

An old country coaching inn decorated with military memorabilia. The village is also famous for its military badges, carved out of the chalk hillside. A restaurant/lounge and a public area. Food every session except Mon evening – Thur is steak night. Children's certificate. Darts and crib. Garden and car park. Accommodation.

 *11am–3pm and 6–11pm.*

FOXHAM

Foxham Inn

Foxham, Nr Chippenham SN15 4NQ
☎ *(01249) 740665*
Ian and Louise Murray-Clarke

A freehouse offering Bath Ales Gem and Wadworth 6X on a permanent basis and one rotating guest.

A traditional village inn – very clean and tidy. One main bar and a dining area. Food every session. Car park, small patio at the front. Well-behaved children welcome.

12–2.30pm and 7–11pm Tues–Thurs; 12–2.30pm and 6.30–11pm Fri–Sat; 12–3pm and 7–10.30pm Sun; closed Mon.

GREAT WISHFORD

Royal Oak Inn

Langford Road, Great Wishford, Nr Salisbury SP2 0PD
☎ *(01722) 790079* Keith and Linda Bidwell

A freehouse serving up to four different real ales, constantly changing, but local breweries such as Hop Back, Ringwood and Stonehenge are favoured.

A friendly, welcoming pub orientated towards food. Car park and garden.

11.30am–2.30pm and 6–11pm Mon–Sat; 12–3pm and 7–10.30pm Sun.

HAMPTWORTH

The Cuckoo Inn

Hamptworth Road, Hamptworth, Nr Salisbury SP5 2DU
☎ *(01794) 390302* Tim Bacon

Wadworth 6X, Ringwood Best, Cheriton Pots Ale, Hop Back Summer Lightning and GFB always available plus up to six guest beers in the summer from a long list including brews from Bunces, Adnams, Ringwood, Hampshire, Shepherd Neame and Cottage breweries.

A 300-year-old thatched pub in the New Forest. Bar food available at lunchtime. Car park, garden, play area, petanque area. Just off the A36 near Hamptworth golf course.

 *11.30am–2.30pm and 6–11pm Mon–Fri; all day Sat, Sun and Bank Holidays.*

HEDDINGTON

The Ivy Inn

Stockley Road, Heddington, Calne SN11 0PL
☎ *(01380) 850276* Andrew Burner

A Wadworth pub selling IPA and 6X, plus sometimes a seasonal.

Picturesque thatched country pub, wooden beams, open fire, perhaps Bob Dylan as background music, with gravity-fed ales. One bar. Food every session. Children welcome. Car park, garden and darts.

 *12–3pm and 6.30–11pm Mon–Sat; 12–5pm and 7–10.30pm Sun.*

HIGHWORTH

The Plough Inn

Lechlade Road, Highworth, Swindon SN6 7HF
☎ *(01793) 762224* Tina Muskett

An Arkells tied house with 2B and Moonlight permanently available.

A locals' country pub. Separate lounge, bar and pool room. Live music some Saturdays. Children allowed. Beer garden. Accommodation. Parking available.

 *5–11pm Mon–Fri (closed lunchtimes); 11am–11pm Sat; 12–10.30pm Sun.*

HILMARTON

The Duke Hotel

Hilmarton, Nr Calne SN11 8SD
☎ *(01249) 760634* Angela Ramirez

An Arkells house with 2B and 3B permanently available, plus an Arkells seasonal ale.

An old-style pub with bar food available, 6–9pm Tues–Sat and 12–2pm Sun. Children allowed. Large beer garden with children's play area. Quiz nights twice a month. Located on the main road between RAF Lyneham and Calne.

OPEN *12–3pm and 6–11pm Mon–Sat; 12–8pm Sun.*

HOLT

Tollgate Inn

Ham Green, Holt, Nr Bradford on Avon BA14 6PX
☎ *(01225) 782326*
Mr A Venables and Miss A Ward-Baptiste

A freehouse that changes its selection twice weekly, using breweries such as West Berkshire, Exmoor, Abbey Ales, Bath Ales and the Quay Brewery.

A country pub that prides itself on its food – local produce freshly cooked, and no chips. Armchairs in the bar give a different but comfortable feel. Accommodation. Car park and garden. No children.

OPEN *11.30am–2.30pm and 5–11pm (10.30pm Sun).*

KILMINGTON

Red Lion Inn

Kilmington, Warminster BA12 6RP
☎ *(01985) 844263* Christopher Gibbs

Freehouse serving Butcombe Bitter and Butts Jester as permanent beers with one rotating guest ale, perhaps Butcombe Gold or Hop Back Summer Lightning.

An unspoilt character country pub that has one bar with a fireplace at either end. Accommodation. Food at lunchtime only. Children welcome until 8pm. Car park. Garden. Darts and shove ha'penny. On the B3092.

OPEN *11.30am–2.30pm and 6.30–11pm Mon–Sat; 12–3pm and 7–10.30pm Sun.*

KINGTON ST MICHAEL

The Jolly Huntsman

Kington St Michael, Chippenham
☎ *(01249) 750305* MI and CVS Lawrence

Wadworth 6X, Sharp's Doom Bar, Wychwood Hobgoblin, Greene King Abbot Ale and IPA regularly served, plus one or two guest beers from a wide selection of independent breweries around the country.

Welcoming village pub with en-suite accommodation. Food served lunchtimes and evenings. Car park. Children welcome.

OPEN *11.30am–2.30pm and 6.30–11pm Mon–Sat; 12–3pm and 7–10.30pm Sun.*

LACOCK

George Inn

4 West Street, Lacock, Nr Chippenham SN15 2LH
☎ *(01249) 730263* John Glass

Wadworth 6X, JCB and Henry's IPA.

A very old inn that has been licensed continuously since 1361, with lots of character including a turn spit in the fireplace. Food every session. Car park and garden. Children allowed.

OPEN *10am–2.30pm and 5–11pm Mon–Fri; all day Sat and Sun.*

LANGLEY BURRELL

Langley Tap

41 The Common, Langley Burrell, Chippenham SN15 4LQ
☎ *(01249) 652707* Mr and Mrs Pakeman

A Wadworth pub serving 6X, Henry's IPA and seasonals, plus an occasional guest.

Known previously as the Brewery Arms it has now returned to its original title. This is a traditional village pub providing real ales and good food at reasonable prices. Meals every session. Children allowed in eating area. Function room. Car park and garden.

OPEN *11am–3pm and 6–11pm Mon–Sat; 12–3pm and 7–10pm Sun.*

LIMPLEY STOKE

Hop Pole

Woods Hill, Limpley Stoke, Nr Bath BA2 7FS
☎ *(01225) 723134* Mich and Bob Williams

A freehouse always serving Butcombe Bitter with one rotating guest ale.

A typical old English village pub characterised by the dried hops hanging from the beams and the wood panelling. Food served lunchtime and evening. Car parking. Children welcome. Large garden overlooking the valley.

OPEN *11am–2.30pm and 6–11pm Mon–Sat; 12–3pm and 7–10.30pm Sun.*

LITTLE CHEVERELL

The Owl

Low Road, Little Cheverell, Devizes SN10 4JS
☎ *(01380) 812263*
Paul Green and Jamie Carter

A freehouse with Wadworth 6X always available plus three constantly changing guests from independent breweries such as Hop Back, Ringwood or Uley.

A country pub with beams and a woodburning stove. One bar, separate dining area. Large streamside beer garden. Food available at lunchtime and evenings. Children allowed. Accommodation.

 *11am–3pm and 6.30–11pm Mon–Sat; 12–4pm and 7–10.30pm Sun. Open all day in the summer.*

LOWER CHICKSGROVE

The Compasses Inn

Lower Chicksgrove, Tisbury, Salisbury SP3 6NB
☎ *(01722) 714318* Alan and Susie Stoneham

A freehouse with Wadworth 6X and Chicksgrove Churl (specially brewed by Wadworth) always available, plus one changing guest.

A beamed pub with open fires and flagstone floors situated in a country hamlet. Small dining area, beer garden, accommodation. Food available Tues–Sun lunchtime and Tues–Sat evenings. Well-behaved children allowed.

 *12–3pm and 6–11pm (10.30pm Sun); closed Mon except bank holidays, but then closed Tues.*

MALMESBURY

The Smoking Dog

62 High Street, Malmesbury SN16 9AT
☎ *(01666) 825823* Ian and Sara Shackleton

Wadworth 6X, Brains SA, Bitter and Reverend James Original, and Archers Best always available, plus at least two guests. These might be Fuller's London Pride or a Young's ale, or seasonal and more obscure ales from smaller breweries.

A traditional small-town pub with log fires, beams and wooden floor. Occasional live music. Food available in an à la carte restaurant, plus bar snacks lunchtime and evening. Beer garden. Children allowed.

OPEN *12–11pm (10.30pm Sun).*

The Three Cups Inn

90 The Triangle, Malmesbury SN16 0AH
☎ *(01666) 823278* Alistair Wilcox

Fuller's London Pride is a permanent plus one revolving guest, perhaps Adnams Best, Smiles or Greene King IPA.

A traditional town pub with lively bar and quieter lounge. Food. Pool, darts and skittle alley.

 *11am–3pm and 5–11pm Mon–Thurs; open all day Fri–Sun.*

MARKET LAVINGTON

The Green Dragon

26–8 High Street, Market Lavington SN10 4AG
☎ *(01380) 813235* Steve Wragg

Wadworth 6X and Henry's IPA available.

A seventeenth century coaching inn and now a friendly village local with a grand exterior and a casual interior. Food lunchtime and evening. Children welcome. Accommodation. Games include boules, skittles, pool and darts. Garden and car park.

 *12–2.30pm and 6.30–11pm Mon–Wed; 12–2.30pm and 5.30–11pm Thurs–Sat; 12–3pm and 7.30–10.30pm Sun.*

MARLBOROUGH

The Bear Hotel

1 High Street, Marlborough SN8 1AA
☎ *(01672) 515047* Andrew and Victoria Hall

Arkells 3B permanently available plus Arkells seasonal guests.

A 200-year-old brick-built town-centre pub designed in the style of a galleon. Food available every day – famous locally for fish and chips. Beer garden. Occasional live music. Children allowed. Function room for medieval banquets. Situated opposite the Town Hall.

 *11am–11pm Mon–Sat; 12–10.30pm Sun.*

MARSTON MEYSEY

The Old Spotted Cow

Marston Meysey SN6 6LQ
☎ *(01285) 810264* James and Denise Kelso

Fuller's London Pride, Wickwar Brand Oak Bitter and Timothy Taylor Landlord usually available, plus a regularly changing mystery guest beer. Sometimes it's guess what it is and you win four pints!

Friendly, attractive, nineteenth-century country inn with large, yet intimate, open stone bar and two feature fireplaces. Situated on the edge of award-winning village. Food served lunchtimes and evenings, every day. Separate restaurant. Car park. Large, safe children's play area with activities. Accommodation. Touring caravan parking facilities.

11.30am–11pm Mon–Sat; 12–10.30pm Sun.

MELKSHAM

The Red Lion

1–3 The City, Melksham SN12 8DA
☎ *(01225) 702960* Margaret Bright

Smiles Best, Sharp's Doom Bar and Shepherd Neame Spitfire regularly available plus one guest.

Grade II listed building dating from 1220, claims to be the only real ale pub in town. Food served 12–2pm Mon–Fri. Car park. No children. Located opposite the Avon Rubber Tyre Factory.

12–2.30pm and 5–11pm Mon–Thurs; 12–11pm Fri–Sat; 12–3pm and 7–10.30pm Sun.

NORTH WROUGHTON

The Check Inn

Woodland View, North Wroughton, Nr Swindon SN4 9AA
☎ *(01793) 845584* Doug Watkins

Eight hand pumps serve a constantly changing range of beers from around the UK and Eire.

Single bar pub with separate lounge (eating) area and extension. Family- and dog-friendly. Traditional pub games and barbecue. Food served lunchtimes and evenings. Accommodation. Car park. Children welcome. Directions: from the A361 Swindon–Devizes, take immediate first right after the dual carriageway over the M4.

11.30am–3.30pm and 6.30–11pm Mon–Thurs; 11.30am–11pm Fri–Sat; 12–10.30pm Sun.

OLD DOWN

The Fox Inn

Inner Down, Old Down, Nr Tockington BS32 4PR
☎ *(01454) 412507*
Philip Biddle and Lynn Fleming

A freehouse serving two constantly changing real ales.

A very traditional pub orientated towards older folk. One bar and children's room. Food every session except Sunday evening. Car park. Small garden and children's play area.

12–3pm and 6–11pm Mon–Sat; all day Sun.

PEWSEY

The Cooper's Arms

37–9 Ball Road, Pewsey SN9 5BL
☎ *(01672) 562495* John Holmes

A freehouse with Wadworth 6X always available, plus three guests, changed weekly, from local breweries.

A thatched country pub in a picturesque area. Food at Sunday lunchtime only. Beer garden. Live music every Friday. Children allowed.

6–11pm Mon–Thurs; 5–11pm Fri; 12–11pm Sat; 12–10.30pm Sun.

PURTON

The Angel

High Street, Purton SN5 9AB
☎ *(01793) 770248*
Dean Dixon and Tommy McKee

An Arkells tied house with 2B and 3B permanently available plus Arkells seasonal guests such as Summer Ale and Noel.

A village pub dating from 1704 with beams and open fireplaces. Food available. Children allowed. Beer garden. Car park.

11am–3pm and 6–11pm Mon–Thurs; 11am–11pm Fri–Sat; 12–10.30pm Sun.

QUEMERFORD

The Talbot Inn

Quemerford, Calne SN11 0AR
☎ *(01249) 812198* Sharon Godwin

Wadworth 6X is regularly available, plus one rotating guest.

A small town pub with a reputation for good food and real ales. One bar, wooden floors, beams, large beer garden and car park. Conservatory doubles as dining area. Food available at lunchtime and evenings. Children allowed in the conservatory and garden only.

12–11pm (10.30pm Sun).

ROWDE

The George & Dragon

High Street, Rowde, Devizes SN10 2PN
☎ *(01380) 723053* Tim Withers

A freehouse with three hand pumps serving just one beer at a time. Real ales from local West Country breweries are featured whenever possible, or other smaller and micro-breweries. Breweries regularly used include Butcombe, Stonehenge and Archers.

A seventeenth-century village pub with beams, wooden floor and open fires. One bar, dining area and beer garden. Food available Tues–Sat lunchtime and evenings. Children allowed.

 *12–3pm and 7–11pm (10.30pm Sun).*

SALISBURY

The Deacon Arms

118 Fisherton Street, Salisbury SP2 7QT
☎ *(01722) 504723* Frank Keay

A freehouse with Hop Back GFB and Summer Lightning and Mole's Best always available, plus occasionals.

A community pub with two bars, wooden floors, open fires in winter and air conditioning in summer. Accomodation. No food. Children allowed.

 *5–11pm Mon–Fri; 12–11pm Sat; 12–10.30pm Sun.*

Devizes Inn

53–5 Devizes Road, Salisbury SP2 7LQ
☎ *(01722) 327842* Brian Corrigan

Ringwood Best and Hop Back GFB permanently available, plus one other real ale, often Hop Back Summer Lightning, but constantly varying.

Locals' town pub near the railway station. En-suite accommodation. No food. Car park. Children welcome.

 *4–11pm Mon–Thurs; 2–11pm Fri; 12–11pm Sat; 12–10.30pm Sun.*

Tom Brown's

225 Wilton Road, Salisbury SP2 7JY
☎ *(01722) 335918* Geoff Price

A Goldfinch Brewery tied house with a range of Goldfinch beers rotated on three pumps and always available: Tom Brown's Best, Flashman's Clout, Midnight Blinder and Midnight Sun.

A basic one-bar town pub for real ale drinkers. No food. No children.

 *6–11pm Mon–Fri; 12–3pm and 6–11pm Sat; 12–3pm and 6–10.30pm Sun.*

The Village Freehouse

33 Wilton Road, Salisbury SP2 7EF
☎ *(01722) 329707* Joe Morris

Timothy Taylor Landlord and Abbey Bellringer are always available. Also three guests, constantly changing, including a mild and a stout or porter.

A small street-corner pub with a friendly atmosphere. Salisbury and South Wiltshire CAMRA Pub of the Year 2001 and 2004. Children allowed. Two minutes from Salisbury railway station.

 *3–11pm Mon; 12–11pm Tues–Sat; 12–10.30pm Sun.*

The Wig & Quill

1 New Street, Salisbury SP1 2PH
☎ *(01722) 335665* Ken Staniforth

A Wadworth tenancy with 6X, JCB and IPA from the wood, a seasonal ale plus a guest ale.

A city-centre pub with an atmosphere that resembles a village local. A mix of the traditional and modern with one bar and three adjoining areas, open fires and beer garden. Food served at lunchtime 12–2.30pm. Children welcome.

 *11am–11pm Mon–Sat; 12–3pm and 7–10.30pm Sun.*

SANDY LANE

The George Inn

Sandy Lane, Nr Chippenham SN15 2PX
☎ *(01380) 850403* Mr Russell

Wadworth pub selling 6X and IPA, plus seasonals.

A traditional village pub with a quiet atmosphere and an emphasis on food (served lunchtime and evening). Children welcome. Car park and garden.

 *12–3.30pm and 7–11pm Mon–Fri; 12–3pm and 6.30–11pm Sat–Sun.*

SHAW

The Golden Fleece

Folly Lane, Shaw, Nr Melksham SN12 8HB
☎ *(01225) 702050* Luke Bate

Fuller's London Pride and Mole's Best are permanents, with one constantly changing guest.

Classic country pub with beams and low ceiling. Quiet but popular. Boasts its own cricket field and team. Food available every session. Garden. Darts. Car park.

12–2.30pm and 6–11pm Mon–Sat; 12–2.30pm and 7–10.30pm Sun.

SHREWTON

The George Inn

London Road, Shrewton, Salisbury SP3 4DH
☎ *(01980) 620341* Tony Clift

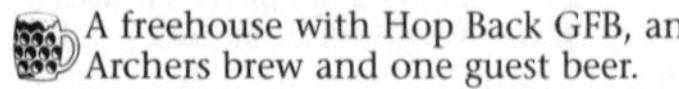
A freehouse with Hop Back GFB, an Archers brew and one guest beer.

A remote country pub with traditional beams, open fires, one main bar, large covered patio area, beer garden, skittle alley and a 26-seater restuarant. Food available at lunchtime and evenings. Children allowed. Beer festival held every August Bank Holiday.

11.30am–3pm and 6–11pm Mon–Fri (closed Tues lunchtime); all day Sat–Sun in summer, regular hours in winter.

SOUTH MARSTON

The Carriers Arms

Highworth Road, South Marston, Nr Swindon
☎ *(01793) 822051* Liz and Jim Sansum

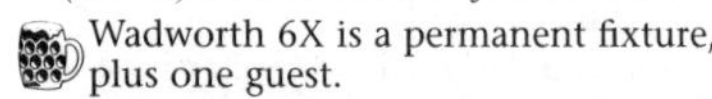
Wadworth 6X is a permanent fixture, plus one guest.

Traditional, village-centre, two-bar pub with separate dining area and patio. Car park. Children welcome when eating, but no special facilities.

12–2.30pm and 6.30–11pm Mon–Sat; 12–3pm and 7–10.30pm Sun.

STAPLEFORD

The Pelican Inn

Warminster Road, Stapleford, Near Salisbury SP3
☎ *(01722) 790241* Robert Worthington

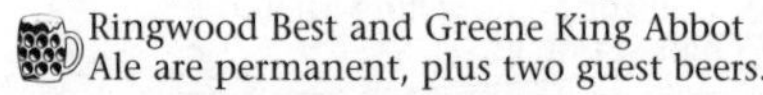
Ringwood Best and Greene King Abbot Ale are permanent, plus two guest beers.

A roadside pub with one long bar. Recent extensions have been made for accommodation. Food. Garden and car park. Children welcome. On the A36.

11.30am–11pm Mon–Sat; 12–10.30pm Sun.

STRATTON ST MARGARET

The Rat Trap

Highworth Road, Stratton SN3 4QS
☎ *(01793) 823282*
Mark and Claire Richardson

An Arkells tied house with 2B and 3B permanently available plus occasional Arkells seasonal guests.

A traditional village two-bar pub with garden. Food available. Pool and darts. Occasional live music. Children allowed. Car park.

12am–3pm and 5–11pm Mon–Fri; all day Sat–Sun.

The Wheatsheaf

Ermin Street, Stratton St Margaret, Swindon SN3 4NH
☎ *(01793) 823149* Alun Rossiter

Arkells 2B and 3B are always on offer, and the one guest is often an Arkells beer.

Small, cosy, clean pub with patio and garden. Rolls served 12–2pm Mon–Fri. Children allowed until 7pm (no special facilities). Car park.

11.30am–2.30pm and 5–11pm Mon–Thur; 11am–11pm Fri–Sat; 12–10.30pm Sun.

SWINDON

The Famous Ale House

146 Redclife Street, Swindon SN2 2BY
☎ *(01793) 522503* Sarah Gibbs

Wadworth 6X and Charles Wells Bombardier always available plus one guest ale.

An olde-worlde locals' community pub. Decorated with football memorabilia. Pool room. One bar, restaurant and garden. Food served lunchtime and evening, except Sunday evening. Live bands Fri and Sat nights. Children allowed in the restaurant and garden.

12–11pm (10.30pm Sun).

The Glue Pot Inn

5 Emlyn Square, Swindon SN1 5BP
☎ *(01793) 523935* Michael Pomery

Tied to the Hop Back brewery serving Crop Circle, Summer Lightning and GFB, plus Mole's Best regularly available, with two to four rotating guests.

A town pub in the centre of Swindon, located by the old railway museum. One small bar, patio. Bar snacks available at lunchtime only. No children.

All day, every day.

The Savoy

38 Regent Street, Swindon SN1 1JL
☎ *(01793) 533970*
Dana and Daniel O'Connell

A Wetherspoon's pub. Greene King Abbot, Archers Best and Shepherd Neame Spitfire always available, plus at least two guest beers (usually three or four), with Archers Golden and Village sometimes featured. Beer festivals held every March and October, with 50 real ales at each.

A one-bar town-centre pub. No music. Games machines. Food available all day. Non-smoking dining area. Children allowed until 6pm.

10am–11pm Mon–Sat; 12–10.30pm Sun.

The Wheatsheaf
32 Newport Street, Old Town, Swindon SN1 3DP
☎ *(01793) 523188*
Michelle and Peter Durnford

A Wadworth house with IPA, 6X, JCB and seasonal brews served.

Traditional town pub with wooden floors and outside seating. Back bar very popular with students. Food available 12–2pm and 6–8.30pm, Sunday lunchtime only. Children welcome. Accommodation.

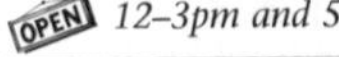 *12–3pm and 5.30–11pm (10.30pm Sun).*

The White Hart
Oxford Road, Swindon SN3 4JD
☎ *(01793) 822272* Derek Rowlands

An Arkells house with 2B and 3B permanently available plus Summer Ale, Noel or other Arkells seasonals on a guest basis.

Situated on the outskirts of Swindon Town, off the A419, this is a three-bar pub with separate non-smoking restaurant plus function room and skittle alley. Big-screen TV. Children allowed in the restaurant only, plus play area outside.

 *11am–3pm and 5–11pm Mon–Fri; all day Sat–Sun.*

TISBURY

Beckford Arms
Fonthill Gifford, Tisbury SP3 6PX
☎ *(01747) 870385* Karen and Eddy Costello

A freehouse serving Timothy Taylor Landlord and Greene King Abbot.

Difficult to find but worth the effort – friendly, light and full of character. Halfway between Hindon and Tisbury, south of A303. Food lunchtime and evening. Accommodation. Pink pool table and darts. Well-behaved children welcome.

 *12–11pm.*

The Boot Inn
High Street, Tisbury, Nr Salisbury SP3 6PS
☎ *(01747) 870363* Mr and Mrs R Turner

Two or three real ales served, always changing. Wadworth 6X is a regular favourite.

The landlord and landlady have been at this typical seventeenth-century village pub for the last 28 years. Bar food every day except Tuesday. Garden and small car park. Darts.

 *11am–2.30pm and 7–11pm; closed Sun evening.*

UPTON LOVELL

Prince Leopold
Upton Lovell, Nr Warminster BA12 0JP
☎ *(01985) 850460*
Graham and Pamela Waldron-Bradley
www.princeleopoldinn.co.uk

Ringwood Best Bitter and a twice-monthly changing guest beer usually available.

Single-bar freehouse, with garden, pleasantly situated by the River Wylye. En-suite accommodation. Food served 12–3pm and 7–9.30pm daily, with a good reputation locally. New restaurant building. Car park. Children welcome.

 *12–3pm and 7–11pm.*

WANBOROUGH

The Black Horse Inn
Wanborough, Swindon SN4 0DQ
☎ *(01793) 790305* Roy Samsum

An Arkells house with 2B and 3B and seasonal guests.

Small and beautiful, with views across the Vale of the White Horse. Large garden and car park. Food available every lunchtime and evening. Children allowed. Marquee available for functions. Located on the Bishopston Road out of Wanborough.

 *12–3pm and 6–11pm (10.30pm Sun).*

The Brewers Arms
High Street, Wanborough SN4 0AE
☎ *(01793) 790707* Darryl Dinwiddy

An Arkells house with 2B and 3B plus an Arkells seasonal ale always available.

A family pub with conservatory, dining area, and large garden featuring a children's play area. Food available lunchtimes and evenings including Sunday roasts. Children welcome.

 *11.30am–2.30pm and 5–11pm Mon–Fri; all day Sat–Sun.*

WARMINSTER

The George Inn

Longbridge Deverill, Warminster BA12 7DG
☎ *(01985) 840396* Nichola Broady

Wadworth 6X permanently available plus two guests changed regularly. Ruddles County, Charles Wells Bombardier, Greene King Old Speckled Hen and brews from breweries such as Brakspear or Butcombe are featured, plus customer recommendations.

A prettily situated pub with the River Wylye running through the large beer garden. Two bars, terrace, function room and accommodation. Children's play area. Bar food is served lunchtimes and evenings, all day at the weekend. Children allowed. Located on the main A350.

 *11am–11pm (10.30pm Sun).*

WILTON

The Bear Inn

12 West Street, Wilton SP2 0DF
☎ *(01722) 742398*
Helen Parsons and Julian Cheeseright

Badgers Best is always served.

A small, homely local with just the one bar. Food available. Pool and darts.

OPEN *11am–2.30pm and 4.30–11pm Mon–Sat; 12–3pm and 6–10.30pm Sun.*

WINTERBOURNE MONKTON

The New Inn

Winterbourne Monkton, Swindon SN4 9NW
☎ *(01672) 539240* Stuart Astbury

Greene King IPA and Wadworth 6X permanently on offer, plus two regularly changing guest beers in the summer and one in the winter.

A traditional country inn, which overlooks Marlborough Downs and is close to Avebury stone circle. Charming restaurant, en-suite accommodation. Food served 12–2.30pm and 7–9pm daily. Car park. Children's play equipment in garden.

OPEN *11.30am–3pm and 6–11pm; closed Mon lunchtime in winter.*

WOOTTON BASSETT

Sally Pusseys Inn

Swindon Road, Wootton Bassett, Swindon SN4 8ET
☎ *(01793) 852430*
Michael Rundall and Nora Thomas

An Arkells tied house with five real ale pumps, and with 2B and 3B permanently available.

A pub/restaurant dating from the nineteenth century, with modern additions. Situated in out-of-town location, not walking distance from anywhere. Close to M4. Food available. Well-behaved children allowed.

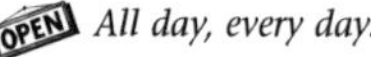 *All day, every day.*

WROUGHTON

The Carter's Rest

High Street, Wroughton SN4 9JU
☎ *(01793) 812288* Alan Dowey

Eight constantly changing real ales always available.

A country village pub with two bars and a patio area. No food. Children allowed.

OPEN *12–2.30pm and 5–11pm Mon–Fri; all day Sat–Sun.*

THE BREWERIES

BRANDY CASK BREWING CO.

25 Bridge Street, Pershore WR10 1AJ
☎ *(01386) 552602*

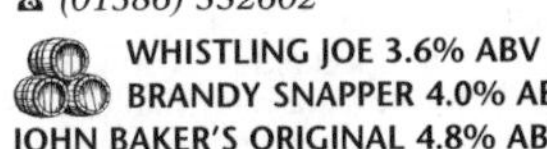

WHISTLING JOE 3.6% ABV
BRANDY SNAPPER 4.0% ABV
JOHN BAKER'S ORIGINAL 4.8% ABV

CANNON ROYALL BREWERY LTD

The Fruiterer's Arms, Uphampton, Ombersley WR9 0JW
☎ *(01905) 621161*
www.cannonroyall.co.uk

FRUITERER'S MILD 3.7% ABV
KINGS SHILLING 3.8% ABV
ARROWHEAD 3.9% ABV
MUZZLELOADER 4.2% ABV

EVESHAM BREWERY

The Green Dragon, 17 Oat Street, Evesham WR11 4PJ
☎ *(01386) 443462*

ASUM ALE 3.8% ABV
ASUM GOLD 5.2% ABV

HOBSONS BREWERY & CO.

Newhouse Farm, Tenbury Road, Cleobury Mortimer, Kidderminster DY14 8RD
☎ *(01299) 270837*
www.hobsons-brewery.co.uk

MILD 3.2% ABV
BEST BITTER 3.8% ABV
Excellent, hoppy session bitter.
TOWN CRIER 4.5% ABV
Smooth, mellow sweetness with balancing hops.
OLD HENRY 5.2% ABV
Darker, smooth and flavoursome.
Plus occasional brews.

MALVERN HILLS BREWERY

15 West Malvern Road, Great Malvern WR14 4ND
☎ *(01684) 560165*
www.malvernhillsbrewery.co.uk

RED EARL 3.7% ABV
BLACK PEAR 4.4% ABV
DOCTOR GULLY'S WINTER ALE 5.2% ABV

ST GEORGE'S BREWING CO. LTD

The Old Bakehouse, Bush Lane, Callow End, Worcester WR2 4TF
☎ *(01905) 831316*
www.stgeorgesbrewery.com

ST.GEORGE'S BITTER 3.7% ABV
Light and refreshing. Brewed using traditional English Barley and local Worcester hops.
GOLD 3.9% ABV
A mellow bitter with a rich colour.
WAR DRUM 4.1% ABV
A pale ale with a multilayered, ripe maltiness and long finish.
PREMIUM 4.3% ABV
Award- winning beer made with English hops.
NIMROD 4.5% ABV
A smoky taste and sharp hopping make for a pronounced character for this traditional ale.
FIRE 4.9% ABV
Increased amounts of roasted and dark malts for full body.
Plus occasional beers.

TEME VALLEY BREWERY

The Talbot Inn, Bromyard Road, Knightwick, Worcester WR6 5PH
☎ *(01886) 821235*
www.temevalley.co.uk

T'OTHER 3.5% ABV
THIS 3.7% ABV
THAT 4.1% ABV

WEATHEROAK BREWERY LTD

Coach and Horses Inn, Weatheroak Hill, Alvechurch, Birmingham B48 7EA
☎ *(0121) 445 4411*
www.weatheroakales.co.uk

LIGHT OAK 3.6% ABV
WEATHEROAK 4.1% ABV
REDWOOD 4.7% ABV
TRIPLE TEE 5.1% ABV

WYRE PIDDLE BREWERY

Highgrove Farm, Pinvin, Nr Pershore WR10 2LF
☎ *(01905) 841853*

PIDDLE IN THE HOLE 3.9% ABV
PIDDLE IN THE WIND 4.2% ABV
Plus occasional and seasonal brews.

THE PUBS

ALVECHURCH

The Coach & Horses Inn

Weatheroak Hill, Alvechurch B48 7EA
☎ *(01564) 823386* Philip Meads

Home of the Weatheroak Brewery with all home brews always available plus Black Sheep Special, Greene King Old Speckled Hen and Wood Special. Regular guests from Frankton Bagby and Slaters.

A country pub set in four acres with separate 100-seater restaurant. Food available 12–2pm and 6–9.30pm Mon–Sat and 12–2.30pm Sun. Local CAMRA Real Ale Pub of the Year winner 2000, 2001 and 2002. Well-behaved children allowed. Large beer garden with outside seating and children's play area. From J3 of the M42, follow signs for Weatheroak.

11.30am–2.30pm and 5.30–11pm Mon–Thurs; 11am–11pm Fri–Sat; 12–10.30pm Sun.

BIRTSMORTON

The Farmer's Arms

Birts Street, Birtsmorton, Malvern WR13 6AP
☎ *(01684) 833308* Miss J and Mrs J Moore

Hook Norton Best and Old Hooky always available plus one guest from breweries such as Wye Valley, Cottage or Cannon Royall.

A traditional two-bar country village freehouse with beer garden. Beams and open fire. Food available at lunchtime and evenings in a separate dining area at one end of the bar. Children allowed. Garden with play area.

 *11am–4pm and 6–11pm Mon–Sat; 12–4pm and 7–10.30pm Sun.*

BISHOP'S FROME

The Chase Inn

4 Bridge Street, Bishop's Frome, Bromyard WR6 5BP
☎ *(01885) 490234* Tony James

Brews from Wye Valley and Black Sheep are among the beers always available at this freehouse.

A family-run country inn built in 1860 with a lounge bar, public bar and dining room that seats 26. Darts and pool. Home-cooked food served 12–9pm Tues–Sat and 12–4pm Sun. Five en-suite bedrooms. Children welcome. Car park. Close to the Frome Valley vineyard. The Malvern Hills are 20 minutes away.

 *12–11pm (10.30pm Sun).*

BRETFORTON

The Fleece Inn

The Cross, Bretforton WR11 5JE
☎ *(01386) 831173* Nigel Smith
www.thefleeceinn.co.uk

Hook Norton and Uley brews always available, plus guests.

Included despite the fact it was extensively damaged by fire in spring 2004 and is unlikely to reopen for 12 months. A remarkable pub, 650 years old and owned by the National Trust who are spending £500,000 restoring it. Fortunately most of the damage was confined to the upper floors and much of the historic contents were rescued. In the meantime, the licensee has opened a temporary bar in the pub's barn. Large garden with children's play area. East of Evesham, in the middle of the village.

 *11am–3pm and 6–11pm Sun–Fri; all day Sat.*

BROADWAY

The Crown & Trumpet Inn

Church Street, Broadway, WR12 7AE
☎ *(01386) 853202* Andrew Scott
www.cotswoldholidays.co.uk

Greene King Old Speckled Hen and Hook Norton Old Hooky always available, plus one rotating guest and a house bitter produced exclusively by the Stanway Brewery. In summer the brew is Cotteswold Gold and in winter Lords-a-Leaping.

A seventeenth-century village inn built from Cotswold stone. Seasonal and homemade dishes cooked on the premises are available at lunchtimes and evenings. Beer garden. Accommodation. Walking parties hosted. Well-behaved children allowed. Live music.

 *11am–2.30pm and 5–11pm Mon–Fri; all day Sat and Sun. Summer hours may vary.*

CASTLEMORTON

The Plume of Feathers

Gloucester Road, Castlemorton WR13 6JB
☎ *(01684) 833554* Emma Harvey

Hobson's Best Bitter and Greene King Old Speckled Hen or Abbot always available plus two guests, which may well come from breweries such as Spinning Dog, Cottage, Wood and Slater's.

A traditional, unspoilt sixteenth-century pub with oak beams in the bar and an open fire in winter. Set in idyllic surroundings looking across Castlemorton common to the Malvern hills. Food available all day, every day. Car park. Children allowed with play area in the garden. On the main Malvern–Gloucester road, on the edge of Castlemorton common.

 *12–11pm (10.30pm Sun).*

DODFORD

The Dodford Inn

Whinfield Road, Dodford, Bromsgrove B61 9BG
☎ *(01527) 832470* Larry Bowen

Three guests available, from breweries such as Titanic, Evesham and Young's. Some 2000 beers served over five years.

A traditional country pub situated in a historic village. Beamed ceilings, very large garden and campsite plus two patios. Food served at lunchtime and evenings. Children allowed.

OPEN *12–3pm and 6–11pm Mon–Fri; all day Sat; 12–3pm and 6–10.30pm Sun.*

DROITWICH

Hadley Bowling Green Inn

Hadley Heath, Hadley, Droitwich WR9 0AR
☎ *(01905) 620294* Richard Everton

Four real ales usually available. Banks Bitter and Original, Marston's Pedigree and Adnams Broadside are regulars plus a guest changed every few weeks.

A recently refurbished country inn set in the heart of Worcestershire. Food served 12–3pm and 6–9pm Mon–Sat and all day Sun (until 9pm). Fourteen en-suite rooms, gardens and one of the oldest bowling greens in the country. Children welcome. Off the M5, junction 6.

11am–3pm and 5–11pm Mon–Fri; all day Sat–Sun.

EVESHAM

The Green Dragon

17 Oat Street, Evesham WR11 4PJ
☎ *(01386) 443462*

Home of the Evesham Brewery. Two Asum brews produced and sold, 'Asum' being the local pronunciation of 'Evesham'. Other guest ales also offered.

The brewery is housed in the old bottle store. A Grade II listed pub with a cosy lounge. Bar and restaurant food is served at lunchtime and evenings. Car park, garden, large function room. Children allowed.

11am–11pm Mon–Thur; 11pm–1am Fri–Sat.

The Queens Head

Iron Cross, Evesham WR11 5SH
☎ *(01386) 871012* Miss Emma Wendon

Greene King IPA, Timothy Taylor Landlord, Wychwood Hobgoblin, Fuller's London Pride and Hook Norton Best Bitter always available, plus one guest.

Rural pub on B4088 Evesham to Alcester road opposite Salford Priors. Food served all day. Children welcome. Car park.

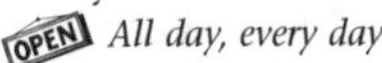
All day, every day.

FERNHILL HEATH

Halfway House

Droitwich Road, Fernhill Heath WR3 8RA
☎ *(01905) 41589* Harry and Norma West

Banks's Original, Marston's Bitter and Pedigree always available plus one monthly changing guest.

A genuine old-fashioned pub with public bar and lounge. Under the same landlord for 12 years with a mostly local clientele. Large beer garden with a new patio. Food available 12–2pm and 6–8.30pm Mon–Sat. Car park. Children allowed. Located on the A38 between Droitwich and Worcester.

11am–3.30pm and 6–midnight.

HANLEY-BROADHEATH

The Fox Inn

Hanley-Broadheath, Tenbury Wells
☎ *(01886) 853189*
James, Ann, Tim and Peter Lawson

Batham Best Bitter and Mild plus Hobsons Best Bitter and Town Crier (or guest ale) are always available.

Set in lovely countryside, part of this black and white beamed family-run pub dates from the sixteenth century. The cosy Phannipa restaurant specialises in authentic Thai cuisine, and serves food 6.30–9.30pm Thurs–Sat and 1–4pm Sun (booking advisable). Games room, large car park and children's play area in beer garden. Children welcome. "Foxstock", a beer and music festival, takes place on the first weekend of August to celebrate the landlord's birthday. Situated on the B4204 Tenbury Wells to Worcester road.

5–11pm Mon–Thurs; all day Fri–Sun and bank holidays.

HANLEY CASTLE

The Three Kings

Church End, Hanley Castle WR8 0BL
☎ *(01684) 592686* Mrs Sheila Roberts

Hobsons and Butcombe brews available plus three guest beers (more than 200 per year) perhaps from Archers, Beowulf, Burton Bridge, Cannon Royall, Goff's, Malvern Hills, St George's, Scattor Rock, Titanic or Weatheroak, to name but a few.

Award-winning, traditional fifteenth-century freehouse that has been in the same family for over 90 years. Bar food available at lunchtime and evenings. Parking, garden, children's room. Accommodation, live music. A beer festival is held in November. Just off the B4211, Upton-upon-Severn to Malvern road. Take the third turn on the left from Upton.

11am–3pm and 7–11pm Mon–Sat; 12–3pm and 7–10.30pm Sun.

WORCESTERSHIRE

KEMPSEY

Walter de Cantelupe Inn

Main Road, Kempsey WR5 3NA
☎ *(01905) 820572* Martin Lloyd-Morris
www.walterdecantelupeinn.com

A freehouse with four real ales usually available. Timothy Taylor Landlord, Cannon Royall Kings Shillings and Everard Beacon are regulars, plus one guest from a wide range which changes every week.

A village pub dating from the early 1700s with wooden beams and stone floors. One bar, non-smoking dining area and walled garden. Food available Tues–Sun lunchtime and evenings, also bank holiday Mondays. Children allowed during the day. Quality en-suite accommodation, car park. Four miles south of Worcester city centre.

12–2.30pm and 6–11pm Tues–Sat; 12–3pm and 7–10.30pm Sun. Also open bank holiday Mondays.

KIDDERMINSTER

The Boar's Head

39 Worcester Street, Kidderminster DY10 1EA
☎ *(01562) 862450* Andy Hipkiss

Banks's Bitter and Original, Camerons Strongarm and Marston's Pedigree always available plus three guests such as Fuller's London Pride, Cains Formidable and Brewery Bitter or a selection from Bateman.

A two-bar town-centre pub with stone floors, beamed ceilings and wood-burning stoves. Small beer garden and all-weather bricked courtyard covered with a glass pyramid. Live bands on Thurs and Sun nights. Food available Mon–Sat 12–3pm. Children allowed in the courtyard only.

12–11pm Mon–Sat; 12–3pm and 7–10.30pm Sun.

The King & Castle

Severn Valley Railway Station, Comberton Hill, Kidderminster
☎ *(01562) 747505* Peter Williamson

Batham Best is among the brews always available plus guest beers (250 per year) from Enville, Hobsons, Hanby, Three Tuns, Timothy Taylor, Holt, Holden's, Berrow, Wood, Burton Bridge and Wye Valley. Wyre Piddle provide a house brew.

The pub is a copy of the Victorian railway refreshment rooms, decorated in the 1930s, GWR-style. Bar food available. Car park and garden. Children allowed until 9pm. Located next to Kidderminster railway station.

11am–4pm and 5–11pm.

The Red Man

92 Blackwell Street, Kidderminster DY10 2DZ
☎ *(01562) 67555* Richard Burgess

Greene King Old Speckled Hen, IPA and Abbot, Adnams Broadside and Timothy Taylor Landlord are always on offer. Guests, changed at least twice a week, might include Timothy Taylor Landlord, brews from Berrow, or seasonal ales such as Smiles Old Tosser (for a week around Pancake Day, with pancakes on the menu!).

A country pub in the town, in a 1930s building, with a focus on traditional ale, traditional fayre and traditional values. Claims to be the only pub of this name in the country. Food available 12–7pm every day. A base for local clog dancers on Mondays in winter. Conservatory, 'tardis' garden, darts, two pool tables, pinball. Children allowed in the conservatory and garden only. Car park.

10am–11pm Mon–Sat; 12–10.30pm Sun.

KNIGHTWICK

The Talbot

Knightwick, Worcester, WR6 5PH
☎ *(01886) 821235*
www.the-talbot.co.uk

Home of the Teme Valley Brewery, so with This, That and T'Other usually available, plus Hobsons Bitter and seasonal brews.

Attractive, 500-year-old country inn standing by the River Teme. Well known locally for its home-produced food. Food available at lunchtimes and some evenings. Car park. Children welcome. Located just off A44 Bromyard to Worcester on B4197 at Knightford Bridge.

11am–11pm Mon–Sat; 12–10.30pm Sun.

MALVERN

Bolly & Bass Bar

Foley Arms Hotel, Worcester Road, Malvern
☎ *(01684) 573397* Nigel Thomas

An ever-changing selection of four guest beers usually available, which may include Shepherd Neame Spitfire, Greene King Old Speckled Hen, Fuller's London Pride or brews from Malvern Hills, Charles Wells, Hook Norton and many others.

Friendly, cosy, locals' pub, situated in the historic Foley Arms Hotel offering live music on Monday nights. Full bar menu available. Car park. Children very welcome. Situated in middle of Malvern on the A449.

12–2.30pm and 5–11pm Mon–Sat; 12–3pm and 7–10.30pm Sun.

Malvern Hills Hotel

Wynds Point, Malvern WR13 6DW
☎ *(01684) 540690* Oswald John Dockery

Hobsons Best Bitter, Black Sheep Best Bitter and Greene King Old Speckled Hen usually available. Two guest beers, which may include Fuller's London Pride, Charles Wells Bombardier, Timothy Taylor Landlord or Wye Valley Butty Bach are also regularly served.

High on the western slopes of the Malverns at British Camp with 'one of the goodliest vistas in England', offering walks with breathtaking views. Warm, traditional oak-panelled lounge bar with sun terrace. Bar food and separate restaurant food available every lunchtime and evening. Car park. Children welcome but no special facilities. Situated on the A449 at British Camp hill fort (also known as the Herefordshire Beacon) midway between Malvern and Ledbury.

 *10am–11pm Mon–Sat; 12–10.30pm Sun.*

OFFENHAM

The Bridge Inn

Offenham, Evesham WR11 8QZ
☎ *(01386) 446565* Paul and Julia Wadsworth

Something from Donnington and Caledonian regularly available plus up to six guest beers from breweries around the country.

Independent, historic one-bar freehouse on the banks of the River Avon. Large riverside patio. Bar and lounge/dining area. Food served 12–2.30pm and 6.30–9pm daily. Car park. Follow signs to Offenham, then brown tourist signs for the riverside pub.

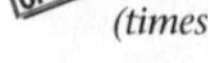 *11am–11pm Mon–Sat; 12–10.30pm Sun (times may vary).*

OMBERSLEY

The Crown & Sandys Arms

Main Road, Ombersley, Worcester WR9 0EW
☎ *(01905) 620252* Richard Everton

Five real ales usually available. Marston's Pedigree and Old Empire, Wood Shropshire Lad and Banks' Bitter are regulars plus guests changed every couple of months.

Seventeenth-century refurbished freehouse with large bar and three busy restaurants. Food served 12–3pm and 6–10pm Mon–Sat and all day (until 9pm) Sun. Luxury en-suite accommodation. Outside patio and gardens. Car park. Children welcome. Off the A499 to Kidderminster.

11am–3pm and 5–11pm Mon–Fri; 11.30am–11pm Sat; 12–10.30pm Sun.

PENSAX

The Bell

Pensax, Abberley WR6 6AE
☎ *(01299) 896677* John and Trudy Greaves

A genuine freehouse with at least five real ales available at any one time. Regulars include Timothy Taylor Best, something from Hobsons plus brews from Cannon Royall, Teme Valley, Wye Valley and Wood. Also draught ciders and perry.

Award-winning, friendly, rural freehouse built in 1883 with various traditional drinking areas and dining room. Large garden, superb views, three real fires in winter. Beer festival held at the end of June. Seasonal home-cooked bar and restaurant food served 12–2pm (not Mon) and 6–9pm on weekdays and 12–4pm Sun. Families welcome. Annual beer festival on the last weekend in June. Camping available across the road. Located on the B4202 Great Witley to Cleobury Mortimer road, between Abberley and Clows Top.

 *5–11pm Mon (closed Mon lunchtimes except bank holidays); 12–2.30pm and 5–11pm Tues–Sat; 12–10.30pm Sun.*

PERSHORE

The Brandy Cask

25 Bridge Street, Pershore, WR10 1AJ
☎ *(01386) 552602* Spencer Cooper

Small craft brewery supplying its own pub with three beers all year round, with occasional out-sales to beer festivals, etc. Greene King Ruddles Best and Marston's Pedigree are served, plus two guest beers, always changing, from small independent breweries.

Town-centre freehouse with lounge bar and restaurant. Food is served at lunchtimes and evenings. Large riverside garden. Annual beer festival around the August bank holiday.

 *11.30am–2.30pm and 7–11pm Mon–Fri; 11.30am–3pm and 7–11pm Sat; 12–3pm and 7–10.30pm Sun.*

SHATTERFORD

The Red Lion Inn

Bridgnorth Road, Shatterford, Nr Kidderminster DY12 1SU
☎ *(01299) 861221* Richard Tweedie

Banks's Mild and Bitter plus Batham Bitter usually available. Two guest beers are also served, often from Wood, Wye Valley, Marston's and Cannon Royall breweries.

Truly rural pub, well known locally for its food. Non-smoking areas and restaurant. Food every lunchtime and evening, including traditional Sunday roasts. Two car parks: one in Worcestershire, the other in Shropshire! Children welcome, with special children's menu available.

 *11.30am–2.30pm and 6.30–11pm Mon–Sat; 12–3pm and 7–10.30pm Sun.*

STOURPORT-ON-SEVERN

The Rising Sun

50 Lombard Street, Stourport-on-Severn DY13 8DU
☎ *(01299) 822530* Robert Hallard

Banks's Original, Bitter and Hanson's Mild plus Marston's Pedigree always available, plus one guest such as Goddards Inspiration. Seasonal and celebration ales served whenever available.

A 200-year-old canalside pub. One bar, small dining area and patio. Food available at lunchtime and evenings (12–4pm Sun). Children allowed in the dining room and patio only.

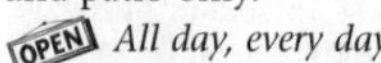 *All day, every day.*

The Wheatsheaf

39 High Street, Stourport-on-Severn DY13 8BS
☎ *(01299) 822613* Mr M Webb

Banks's Mild, Bitter and Hanson's Bitter usually available.

A games-orientated house in the town centre, with relaxing lounge and cosy bar. Food served 10.30am–3pm Mon–Sat and 12–2pm Sun. Children welcome until 9.30pm. Car park.

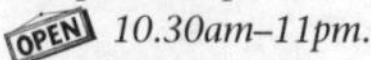 *10.30am–11pm.*

TENBURY WELLS

The Ship Inn

Teme Street, Tenbury Wells WR15 8AE
☎ *(01584) 810269* Michael Hoar

A freehouse with Hobsons Best always available plus a guest beer that changes every week and could come from any brewery in the country.

A seventeenth-century, market-town pub that has been under the same ownership since 1984. The pub has daily deliveries of fresh fish and is renowned for its food, which is served at lunchtimes and evenings every day; there are two separate non-smoking restaurants. Recommended in two good-food guides. Pretty beer garden, accommodation, private room for hire. Children allowed. On the main street, opposite Barclays bank.

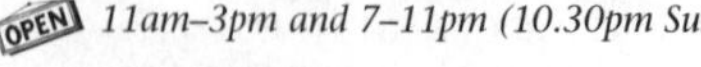 *11am–3pm and 7–11pm (10.30pm Sun).*

UPHAMPTON

The Fruiterer's Arms

Uphampton, Ombersley WR9 0JW
☎ *(01905) 621161*

Cannon Royall brews produced and served on the premises plus a guest beer.

Brewing began in this converted cider house in July 1993 and the maximum output is now 16 barrels per week. The pub has two bars and a log fire in winter. Bar food is served at lunchtime. Car park. Children allowed.

 *12.30–2.30pm and 7–11pm Mon–Fri; 12–3pm and 7–11pm Sat–Sun (10.30pm Sun).*

WORCESTER

The Dragon Inn

The Tything, Worcester WR1 1JT
☎ *(01905) 25845* RM Appleton and SM Malley

A true ale-lovers' paradise. Up to seven ales, a stout and a real cider available year-round. They source their own ales and ciders, and regulars include brews from Beowulf, O'Hanlon's, Church End, Otter, Stonehenge, Oakham, Teme Valley and Cannon Royall, to mention just a few.

Late Georgian, Grade II listed alehouse with L-shaped bar and outside patio area for warm summer days. Food served 12–2pm Mon–Sat. Well-behaved children allowed. Situated a three-minute walk from Foregate Street Station, away from the city centre.

 *12–3pm and 4.30–11pm Mon–Fri; 11am–11pm Sat; 12–3pm and 7–10.30pm Sun.*

The Postal Order

18 Foregate Street, Worcester WR1 1DN
☎ *(01905) 22373* Andrew Hunt

Banks's Mild, Greene King Abbot Ale, Shepherd Neame Spitfire and something from Wyre Piddle always available. Plus up to five guest real ales changed every week. Weston's Old Rosie cider is also served.

An open-plan JD Wetherspoon's house converted from an old telephone exchange (originally a sorting office). Separate non-smoking area, no music. Food available all day. Steak night on Tues, curry night on Thurs. Children welcome until 5pm. Two annual beer festivals. Situated by the train station, opposite the cinema.

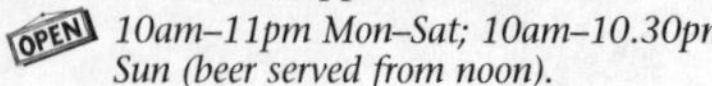 *10am–11pm Mon–Sat; 10am–10.30pm Sun (beer served from noon).*

ABBEY BELLS BREWERY

5 Main Road, Hirst Courtney, Selby, North Yorkshire YO8 8QP
☎ *(0794) 072 6658*
www.abbeybells.co.uk

MONDAY'S CHILD 3.7% ABV
HOPPY DAZE 4.1% ABV
CORDELIA'S GIFT 4.3% ABV
SANTA'S STOCKING FILLER 4.5% ABV
GREASE 4.6% ABV
1911 CELEBRATION ALE 4.8% ABV
ORIGINAL BITTER 5.1% ABV
BLACK SATIN 6.2% ABV

ABBEYDALE BREWERY

Unit 8, Aizlewood Road, Sheffield, South Yorkshire S8 0YX
☎ *(0114) 281 2712*
www.abbeydalebrewery.co.uk

BEST BITTER 4.0% ABV
Smooth and malty with good hoppiness.
MOONSHINE 4.3% ABV
Fruity easy quaffer.
BLACK BISHOP 4.5% ABV
WHITE KNIGHT 4.5% ABV
MATINS 4.7% ABV
Pale and flavoursome for gravity.
ABSOLUTION 5.3% ABV
Golden, smooth and refreshing.
BLACK MASS 6.66% ABV
Stout, with good hoppiness.
LAST RITES 11.0% ABV
Smooth toffee sweetness.
Beerworks beers:
UXB 4.7% ABV
Plus special brews and the Dr Moreton Cure-all range.

ACORN BREWERY

Unit 11, Mitchells Enterprise Centre, Bradberry Back Lane, Wombwell, Barnsley, South Yorkshire S73 8HR
☎ *(01226) 270734*

ACORN BARNSLEY BITTER 3.8% ABV
Brewed using original Barnsley yeast strains. Chestnut in colour, having a well-rounded rich flavour with a lasting bitter finish.
BARNSLEY GOLD 4.3% ABV
Award-winning golden beer – good bitterness level, with a fresh citrus and hop aroma.
OLD MOOR PORTER 4.4% ABV
SIBA Champion Porter of Great Britain 2004. Full-bodied Victorian Porter with hints of liquorice. Initial bitterness gives way to a smooth mellow finish.
Plus seasonal and special brews.

ANGLO-DUTCH BREWERY

Unit 12 Savile Bridge Mills, Mill Street East, Dewsbury, West Yorkshire WF13 6QQ
☎ *(01924) 457772*
www.anglo-dutch-brewery.co.uk

BEST BITTER 3.8% ABV
IMPERIAL PINT 4.0% ABV
KLETSWATER 4.0% ABV
SPIKE'S ON T'WAY 4.2% ABV
GHOST ON THE RIM 4.5% ABV
AT T'GHOUL AND GHOST 5.2% ABV
TABATHA THE KNACKERED 6.0% ABV
Plus seasonal and occasional brews.

THE BLACK SHEEP BREWERY

Wellgarth, Crosshills, Masham, Ripon, North Yorkshire HG4 4EN
☎ *(01765) 689227*
www.blacksheep.co.uk

BEST BITTER 3.8% ABV
Golden, well-hopped and refreshing.
BLACK SHEEP ALE 4.4% ABV
SPECIAL 4.4% ABV
Good body, hoppy and bitter.
YORKSHIRE SQUARE ALE 5.0% ABV
Richly flavoured golden ale.
RIGGWELTER 5.9% ABV
Mouthfilling flavours.

BOAT BREWERY

The Boat Inn, Boat Lane, Allerton Bywater, Castleford, West Yorkshire WF10 2BX
☎ *(01977) 667788*

MAN IN THE BOAT 3.5% ABV
CELESTE 3.8% ABV
NARROWBOAT 4.0% ABV
HELLFIRE JACK 4.2% ABV
OPTIC ILLUSION 4.3% ABV
PEARL DIVER 4.5% ABV
PHESTA 4.5% ABV
GBH 5.0% ABV
NEVISON'S LEAP 5.0% ABV

BRISCOE'S BREWERY

16 Ash Grove, Otley, West Yorkshire LS21 3EL
☎ *(01943) 466515*

ROMBALD'S REVIVER 3.8% ABV
PUDDLED AND BARMY ALE 5.8% ABV

BROWN COW BREWERY

Brown Cow Road, Barlow, Selby, North Yorkshire YO8 8EH
☎ *(01757) 618947*

BROWN COW BITTER 3.8% ABV
Well-hopped traditional session bitter.
MAWDY WARP 3.9% ABV
Ruby well-balanced bitter.
MAIDEN CENTURY 4.0% ABV
A golden and refreshing beer.
WHICH WITCH IS WHICH 4.2% ABV
MANTRA GOLD 4.3% ABV
OLD E'FER 4.4% ABV
Very pale and refreshing with citrus character.
SIMPSONS NUMBER 4 4.4% ABV
Dark and bitter-sweet, full of roast barley character.
HOW NOW 4.5% ABV
Pale, fruity and single hopped.
WOLFHOUND 4.5% ABV
Straw-coloured, full and rounded palate of malt and traditional English hops.
A monthly special is also brewed.

CAPTAIN COOK BREWERY LTD

1 West End, Stokesley, Middlesborough, North Yorkshire TS9 5BL
☎ *(01642) 710263*
www.thecaptaincookbreweryltd.co.uk

SUNSET 4.0% ABV
MIDSHIPS 4.1% ABV
BLACK PORTER 4.4% ABV
SLIPWAY 4.2% ABV

CONCERTINA BREWERY

9a Dolcliffe Road, Mexborough, South Yorkshire S64 9AZ
☎ *(01709) 580841*

BEST BITTER 3.9% ABV
CLUB BITTER 3.9% ABV
OLD DARK ATTIC 3.9% ABV
ONE-EYED JACK 4.0% ABV
BENGAL TIGER 4.6% ABV
DICTATORS 4.7% ABV
ARIEL SQUARE FOUR 5.2% ABV

COPPER DRAGON SKIPTON BREWERY

Snaygill Industrial Estate, Keighley Road, Skipton, North Yorkshire BD23 2QR
☎ *(01756) 702130*
www.copperdragon.uk.com

DARK ALE 3.5% ABV
BEST BITTER 3.8% ABV
GOLDEN PIPPIN 3.9% ABV
SCOTTS 1816 4.1% ABV
CHALLENGER IPA 4.4% ABV

CROPTON BREWERY

Woolcroft, Cropton, Nr Pickering, North Yorkshire YO18 8HH
☎ *(01751) 417330*
www.croptonbrewery.co.uk

KING BILLY 3.6% ABV
ENDEAVOUR ALE 3.8% ABV
TWO PINTS BEST BITTER 4.0% ABV
HONEY GOLD 4.2% ABV
SCORESBY STOUT 4.2% ABV
UNCLE SAM'S BITTER 4.4% ABV
RUDOLPH'S REVENGE 4.6% ABV
YORKSHIRE MOORS BITTER 4.6% ABV
MONKMAN'S SLAUGHTER BITTER 6.0% ABV

CROWN AND WELLINGTON BREWERIES

Hillsborough Hotel, 54–8 Langsett Road, Sheffield, South Yorkshire S6 2UB
☎ *(0114) 232100*
www.crownbrewery.com
(Part of the Edale Brewery Company based in Derbyshire)

WELLINGTON'S CONVICTION 3.8% ABV
HPA 3.9% ABV
WELLINGTON'S MITIGATION 4.2% ABV
LOXLEY GOLD 4.5% ABV
WELLINGTON'S APPEAL 4.8% ABV
STANNINGTON STOUT 5.0% ABV
SAMUEL BERRY'S IPA 5.1% ABV
WELLINGTON'S VOLENTI 5.2% ABV
WELLINGTON'S BEYOND THE CALL 6.0% ABV

DALESIDE BREWERY

Camwal Road, Starbeck, Harrogate, North Yorkshire HG1 4PT
☎ *(01423) 880022*
www.dalesidebrewery.co.uk

BITTER 3.7% ABV
BLONDE 3.9% ABV
OLD LEGOVER 4.1% ABV
OLD LUBRICATION 4.1% ABV
GREEN GRASS OLD ROGUE ALE 4.5% ABV
MONKEY WRENCH 5.3% ABV
MOROCCO ALE 5.5% ABV
RIPON JEWEL ALE 5.8% ABV

EASTWOOD & SANDERS BREWERY (FINE ALES) LTD

The Brewery, Unit 3–5 Heathfield Ind. Est., Heathfield Street, Elland, West Yorkshire HX5 9AE
☎ *(01422) 377677*

FIRST LIGHT 3.5% ABV
A light Yorkshire ale with delicate hop flavours balanced by underlying malt sweetness.

BARGEE 3.8% ABV
A full-flavoured bitter made with four different malts and hops from England and America.

BEST BITTER 4.0% ABV
A dry and aromatic beer made with Maris Otter pale malt and using hops from England and America.

BEYOND THE PALE 4.2% ABV
A pale, golden bitter with a touch of Amber Malt. Pronounced floral hop aroma from the inclusion of North American Cascade hops and a long, dry hoppy finish.

NETTLETHRASHER 4.4% ABV
A deep copper-coloured traditional strong ale, brewed using six different malts with English and American hops.

ELLAND BLACK 4.6% ABV
A very pale premium bitter with grapefruit and citrus top notes in the nose with a bitter yet fruity palate from American hops.

Plus seasonal brews.

THE EGYPTIAN SAND & GRAVEL BREWERY

The Leggers Inn, Stable Buildings, Mill Street East, Dewsbury, West Yorkshire WF12 9BD
☎ *(01924) 502846*

KINAL NO.5 3.8% ABV
MARRIOTS MILD 4.0% ABV
PROSPECT ROAD BITTER 4.0% ABV
GOLDENEYE 700 4.2% ABV
KINAL NO.7 4.2% ABV
PHAROAH'S CURSE 4.6% ABV
KINAL NO.9 5.0% ABV

FERNANDES BREWERY

The Old Malthouse, 5 Avison Yard, Kirkgate, Wakefield, West Yorkshire WF1 1UA
☎ *(01924) 291709*
www.fernandes-brewery.gowyld.com

BOYS BITTER 3.2% ABV
SHAKESPEARES BITTER 3.5% ABV
BEST BITTER 3.8% ABV
MALT SHOVEL MILD 3.8% ABV
TO BE JOYFUL 4.3% ABV
GREEN BULLET 4.5% ABV
WAKEFIELD PRIDE 4.5% ABV
CASCADE 5.0% ABV
DOUBLE SIX 6.0% ABV
EMPRESS OF INDIA 6.0% ABV
MOODIES MILD 6.0% ABV

FRANKLIN'S BREWERY

Bilton Lane, Bilton, Harrogate, North Yorkshire HG1 4DH
☎ *(01423) 322345*

FRANKLIN'S BITTER 3.8% ABV
FRANKLIN'S BLOTTO 4.7% ABV
FRANKLIN'S DT'S 4.7% ABV
MY BETTER HALF 4.8% ABV

FROG AND PARROT BREWHOUSE

64 Division Street, Sheffield, South Yorkshire S1 4GF
☎ *(0114) 272 1280*

ROGER AND OUT 12.6% ABV

GARTON BREWERY

Station House, Station Road, Garton-on-the-Wold, Driffield, East Yorkshire YO25 3EX
☎ *(01377) 252340*

OLD BUFFER 4.5% ABV
Dark mild.

WOLDSMAN BITTER 4.5% ABV
Very light, straw-coloured bitter.

STUNNED MULLET 5.0% ABV
Very deep red bitter.

GOODNIGHT VIENNA 8.0% ABV
Traditional IPA.

LIQUID LOBOTOMY 8.0% ABV
Heavy-duty stout.

Plus seasonals and specials.

GLENTWORTH BREWERY

Glentworth House, Crossfield Lane, Skellow, Doncaster, South Yorkshire DN6 8PL
☎ *(01302) 725555*

LIGHTYEAR 3.9% ABV
NORTHERN STAR 3.9% ABV
BRASSED OFF 4.1% ABV
DONNY ROVER 4.1% ABV
AMBER GAMBLER 4.3% ABV
HAPPY HOOKER 4.3% ABV
DIZZY BLONDE 4.5% ABV
OLD FLAME 4.5% ABV
POT'O GOLD 4.5% ABV
FULL MONTY 5.0% ABV
HENPECKED 5.0% ABV

GOLCAR BREWERY

Swallow Lane, Golcar, Huddersfield, West Yorkshire HD7 4NB
☎ *(01484) 644241*

GOLCAR MILD 3.2% ABV
GOLCAR BITTER 3.8% ABV
WINKLE WARMER 4.2% ABV
Winter ale.

Plus specials

GOODMANHAM BREWERY
Goodmanham Arms, Main Street, Goodmanham, York, North Yorkshire YO43 3JA
☎ *(01430) 873849*

WOLD'S DELIGHT 3.8% ABV
BRANDY MONK 4.2% ABV
MONK'S REVENGE 5.0% ABV

GOOSE EYE BREWERY
Ingrow Bridge, South Street, Keighley, West Yorkshire BD21 5AX
☎ *(01535) 605807*
www.goose-eye-brewery.co.uk

BARMPOT 3.8% ABV
BRONTE BITTER 4.0% ABV
Malty and well-balanced.
NO EYE DEER 4.0% ABV
WHARFEDALE BITTER 4.5% ABV
POMMIE'S REVENGE 5.2% ABV
Straw-coloured, soft and smooth.
Plus occasional brews.

H B CLARK & CO. (SUCCESSORS) LTD
Westgate Brewery, Wakefield, West Yorkshire WF2 9SW
☎ *(01924) 373328*
www.hbclark.co.uk

CLASSIC BLONDE 3.9% ABV
Light ale with hops and fruit throughout.
FESTIVAL ALE 4.2% ABV
Straw-coloured premium ale.
RAM'S REVENGE 4.6% ABV
Rich ruby ale with roast barley and malt.
GOLDEN HORNET 5.0% ABV
Golden fruity ale, with hops throughout.
MULBERRY TREE 5.0% ABV
Strong brew with fruit and hops.
Plus seasonal brews.

HALIFAX STEAM BREWERY
The Conclave, Southgede Works, Hipperholme, Halifax, West Yorkshire HX3 8EF
☎ *(01484) 715074*

MORNING GLORY 3.8% ABV
LILLY FOGG 4.0% ABV
PICKLEHUT IMPOSTER 4.0% ABV
BANTAM 4.1% ABV
COCK O' THE NORTH 4.9% ABV

KELHAM ISLAND BREWERY
23 Alma Street, Sheffield, South Yorkshire S3 8SA
☎ *(0114) 249 4804*
www.kelhambrewery.co.uk

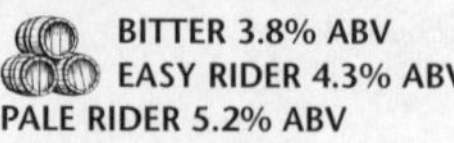
BITTER 3.8% ABV
EASY RIDER 4.3% ABV
PALE RIDER 5.2% ABV
Plus monthly specials.

LINFIT BREWERY
Sair Inn, Lane Top, Linthwaite, Huddersfield, West Yorkshire HD7 5SG
☎ *(01484) 842370*

DARK MILD 3.0% ABV
BITTER 3.7% ABV
CASCADE 4.2% ABV
GOLD MEDAL 4.2% ABV
SPECIAL 4.3% ABV
AUTUMN GOLD 4.7% ABV
ENGLISH GUINEAS STOUT 5.3% ABV
OLD ELI 5.3% ABV
LEADBOILER 6.6% ABV
ENOCH'S HAMMER 8.0% ABV

LITTON ALE BREWERY
Queen's Arms, Litton, Skipton, North Yorkshire BD23 5QJ
☎ *(01756) 770208*

LITTON ALE 3.8%ABV
Standard session beer.
POTTS BECK 4.3%ABV
Hoppier, stronger beer, darker.

MALTON BREWERY
Suddaby's Crown Hotel, Wheelgate, Malton, North Yorkshire YO17 7HP
☎ *(01653) 697580*
www.maltonbrewery.com

DOUBLE CHANCE 3.8% ABV
GOLDEN CHANCE 4.2% ABV
CROWN INN GLORY 4.3% ABV
RYEDALE 4.5% ABV
AULD BOB 6.0% ABV
Plus occasional brews.

NICK STAFFORD HAMBLETON ALES
The Brewery, Holme on Swale, Thirsk, North Yorkshire YO7 4JE
☎ *(01845) 567460*
www.hambletonales.co.uk

BITTER 3.6% ABV
GOLDFIELD 4.2% ABV
STALLION 4.2% ABV
STUD 4.3% ABV
NIGHTMARE 5.0% ABV

NORTH YORKSHIRE BREWING CO.
Pinchinthorpe Hall, Pinchinthorpe, Guisborough, North Yorkshire TS14 8HG
☎ *(01287) 630200*
www.pinchinthorpehall.co.uk

BEST BITTER 3.6% ABV
Pale, refreshing and hoppy.
MILLENNIUM MILD 3.6% ABV
Dark, with caramel hints and hoppy aftertaste.
BORO BEST 4.0% ABV
FOOL'S GOLD 4.6% ABV
Pale, with hops throughout.
FLYING HERBERT 4.7% ABV
Speciality brews:
PRIOR'S ALE 3.6% ABV
Quenching and very hoppy.
ARCHBISHOP LEE'S RUBY ALE 4.0% ABV
Rounded, northern ale.
GOLDEN ALE 4.6% ABV
Powerful hoppiness.
LORD LEE 4.7% ABV
Smooth, full-flavoured malt.
Cosmic beers:
COSMIC GLOW 4.8% ABV
NORTHERN STAR 4.8% ABV
Golden and well-balanced.
SOUTHERN CROSS 4.8% ABV

OAKWELL BREWERY
Pontefract Road, Barnsley, South Yorkshire S71 1EZ
☎ *(01226) 296161*

BARNSLEY BITTER 3.8% ABV
OLD TOM 3.8% ABV

OLD BEAR BREWERY
6 Keighley Road, Crosshilss, Keighley, West Yorkshire BD20 7RN
☎ *(01535) 637451*
www.oldbearbrewery.com

ORIGINAL 3.7–3.9% ABV
HONEY POT 4.4–4.8% ABV
HIBERNATOR 4.8–5.1% ABV

OLD MILL BREWERY
Mill Street, Snaith, Goole, East Yorkshire DN14 9HU
☎ *(01405) 861813*
www.oldmillbrewery.co.uk

TRADITIONAL MILD 3.4% ABV
TRADITIONAL BITTER 3.9% ABV
OLD CURIOSITY 4.5% ABV
BULLION STRONG BITTER 4.7% ABV
Plus seasonal and occasional brews.

OSSETT BREWING COMPANY
Low Mill Road, Ossett, West Yorkshire WF5 8ND
☎ *(01924) 261333*
www.ossett-brewery.co.uk

PALE GOLD 3.8% ABV
SILVER SHADOW 3.9% ABV
SILVER FOX 4.1% ABV
SILVER KING 4.3% ABV
BOBBY DAZZLER 4.5% ABV
SILVER LINK 4.6% ABV
FINE FETTLE 4.8% ABV
EXCELSIOR 5.2% ABV
Plus seasonals and specials.

RAT AND RATCHET BREWERY
40 Chapel Hill, Huddersfield, West Yorkshire HD1 3EB
☎ *(01484) 516734*
www.ratandratchet.co.uk

THE GREAT GNAWTHERN 4.0% ABV
THE GREAT ESCAPE 4.2% ABV
CRATCHET'S CHRISTMAS CRACKER 4.3% ABV

RED LION BREWERY
73 Dewsbury Road, Ossett, West Yorkshire WF5 9NQ
☎ *(01924) 273487*

WHITE LION 4.3% ABV
GOLDEN LION 4.5% ABV
YAKIMA PALE ALE 4.5% ABV
CHARDONNAYLE 5.1% ABV

RIVERHEAD BREWERY
2 Peel Street, Marsden, Huddersfield, West Yorkshire HD7 6BR
☎ *(01484) 841270*
www.riverheadbrewery.co.uk

SPARTH MILD 3.6% ABV
BUTTERLY BITTER 3.8% ABV
DEERHILL PORTER 4.0% ABV
CUPWITH LIGHT BITTER 4.2% ABV
BLACKMOSS STOUT 4.3% ABV
MARCH HAIGH BITTER 4.6% ABV
REDBROOK PREMIUM 5.5% ABV
Plus special brews.

ROOSTER'S BREWERY

Unit 3, Grimbald Park, Wetherby Road, Knaresborough, North Yorkshire HG5 8QA
☎ *(01423) 865959*
www.roosters.co.uk

SPECIAL 3.9% ABV
Pale, with citrus-fruit freshness.
HOOLIGAN 4.3% ABV
Pale, with some hoppy bitterness.
SCORCHER 4.3% ABV
Pale, with citrus flavours and good hoppiness.
YANKEE 4.3% ABV
Pale, soft and fruity.
CREAM 4.7% ABV
Smooth and soft, with fruit flavours.
ROOSTER'S 4.7% ABV
Golden brown, sweet and fruity.
NECTOR 5.0% ABV
Pale, soft, bitter beer. Christmas.
Plus occasional and seasonal brews. Additional brews produced under the Outlaw Brewing Co. label.

RUDGATE BREWERY LTD

2 Centre Park, Marston Business Park, Rudgate, Tockwith, York, North Yorkshire YO26 7QF
☎ *(01423) 358382*
www.rudgate-beers.co.uk

VIKING 3.8% ABV
An easy-drinking session bitter.
BATTLEAXE 4.2% ABV
A robust premium bitter.
RUBY MILD 4.4% ABV
A dark premium mild.
SPECIAL 4.5% ABV
A hoppy pale ale.
WELL BLATHERED 5.0% ABV
A premium golden ale.
Plus monthly brews.

SALAMANDER BREWING CO.

22 Harry Street, Dudley Hill, Bradford, West Yorkshire BD4 9PH
☎ *(01274) 652323*
www.salamanderbrewing.4t.com

BEE'S SPRING BITTER 3.7% ABV
A pale amber-coloured dry-hopped session ale.
OWD AMOS 3.8% ABV
Chestnut-coloured, easy-drinking malty session ale.
SUMMER ALE 3.8%
MUDPUPPY 4.2% ABV
Dark amber, malty and refreshing.
STOUT 4.5% ABV
Brewed with roast and flaked barley.
GENT 4.7% ABV
Russet-coloured premium bitter.
GOLD LAZARUS 4.8% ABV
Pale-coloured with a distinctive aroma of Bramling Cross hops.
HELLBENDER 4.8% ABV
Strong amber ale, with fruit aroma and hoppiness.
HAMMER & TONG 5.0% ABV
Very pale and bitter.

SAMUEL SMITH OLD BREWERY

High Street, Tadcaster, North Yorkshire LS24 9SB
☎ *(01937) 832225*

OLD BREWERY BITTER 4.0% ABV
Rounded and flavoursome.

TIMOTHY TAYLOR & CO. LTD

Knowle Spring Brewery, Keighley, West Yorkshire BD21 1AW
☎ *(01535) 603139*
www.timothy-taylor.co.uk

DARK MILD 3.5% ABV
Mellow and malty with balancing hoppiness.
GOLDEN BEST 3.5% ABV
Balanced, crisp and hoppy.
PORTER 3.8% ABV
Sweeter winter brew.
BEST BITTER 4.0% ABV
Refreshing, hoppy and bitter.
LANDLORD 4.3% ABV
Distinctive combination of malt, hops and fruit.
RAM TAM 4.3% ABV
Landlord with added caramel.

TIGERTOPS BREWERY

22 Oakes Street, Flanshaw, Wakefield, West Yorkshire WF2 9LN
☎ *(01942) 897728*

Constantly changing range of beers with an emphasis on Belgian beer styles.

BLANCH DE NEWLAND 4.6% ABV
Belgian style wheat beer.
WHITE MAX 4.6% ABV
German style wheat beer.

UPPER AGBRIGG BREWERY

Unit 12, Honley Business Centre, New Mill Road, Honley, Holmfirth, West Yorkshire HD9 6QB
☎ *(01484) 660008*

HOLME VALLEY BITTER 3.8% ABV
BLACK BEAUTY PORTER 4.5% ABV
OATMEAL STOUT 5.0% ABV
Plus seasonals, festival specials and a range of German-style bottled beers.

WENSLEYDALE BREWERY

The Forester's Arms, Carlton in Coverdale, Leyburn, North Yorkshire DL8 4BB
☎ *(01969) 640272*

ROWLEY MILD 3.2% ABV
Award-winning beer with chocolate and toffee aromas that lead into a rich and flavoursome ale. The finish is bittersweet.

FORESTERS SESSION BITTER 3.7% ABV
An aromatic, straw-coloured hoppy session beer.

COVERDALE GAMEKEEPER 4.3% ABV
A light copper, very moreish and highly drinkable best bitter with a lingering aftertaste.

BLACK DUB STOUT 4.4% ABV
A black beer brimming with a roasted chocolate aroma.

COVERDALE POACHER 5.0% ABV
A pale, smooth and refreshing beer with quite a dry aftertaste. Citrus flavours dominate both taste and aroma.

WENTWORTH BREWERY LIMITED

The Powerhouse, Gun Park, Wentworth, Rotherham, South Yorkshire S62 7TF
☎ *(01226) 747070*

NEEDLES EYE 3.5% ABV
Beer of the Festival – Leeds CAMRA Beer, Cider and Perry Festival 2001. Beer of the Festival – Sheffield Beer Festival 2001. A traditional Yorkshire light ale.

WPA 4% ABV
Champion Beer of South Yorkshire! – 2000. Best Beer of Festival – Sheffield Beer Festival 1999. Pale-coloured, an extremely well-hopped IPA-style beer with citrus overtones.

BEST BITTER 4.1% ABV
Silver Medal Winner – Oakwood Beer Festival 2000. Mid-brown beer with both hoppy and malty character, a proper traditional beer with hints of citrus fruits in the aftertaste.

WENTWORTH PREMIUM 4.4% ABV
An excellent bitter with a slight treacle aftertaste, medium brown in colour.

ROCK SPALT 4.5% ABV
Straw-coloured, very aromatic, very dry and drinkable. Spalt is the German variety of hop used.

OATMEAL STOUT 4.8% ABV
Bronze Medal Winner overall – National Winter Beer Festival 2003. Silver Medal – Stouts Category National Winter Beer Festival 2003. Gold Medal Winner – Macclesfield and Cheshire Beer Festival 2002. Gold Medal Winner – Cambridge Beer Festival 2002. Bronze Medal Winner – Oakwood Beer Festival 2001. Black, smooth, bucketfuls of roast and chocolate malt with coffee overtones, an outstanding stout!

THE WHALEBONE BREWERY

165 Wincolmlee, Hull, East Yorkshire HU2 0PA
☎ *(01482) 327980*

DIANA MILD 3.5% ABV
Very dark mild with creamy head.

NECKOIL 3.9% ABV
Traditional English bitter, Maris Otter Malt, Target and Fuggles Hops.

MOBY DICK 8.0% ABV
Barley wine.

Plus seasonal ales

WHITELY BRIDGE BREWING CO.

11 Silver Street, Newton Hill, Wakefield, West Yorkshire WF1 2HZ
☎ *(01924) 825836*

SHARP SHOOTER 4.0% ABV
Amber strong ale, strong bitter aftertaste.

EMBERZALE 4.2% ABV
Dark mild – won Best Mild at Doncaster Beerex. Classic mild, burnt aftertaste but sweet flavour.

GUNSLINGERS 4.2% ABV
A ruby dark ale with a rich flavour.

NELLIE'S BITTER 4.2% ABV
Light sweet fruity beer.

BURNING BRIDGES 5.0% ABV
Strong dark bitter beer. Brewer's Choice.

Plus seasonals and specials

WOLD TOP BREWERY

Hunmanby Grange, Wold Newton, Driffield, North Yorkshire YO25 3HS
☎ *(01723) 891636*
www.woldtopbrewery.co.uk

WOLD TOP BITTER 3.7% ABV

FALLINGSTONE 4.2% ABV

MARS MAGIC 4.6% ABV

YORK BREWERY

12 Toft Green, Micklegate, York, North Yorkshire YO1 1JT
☎ *(01904) 621162*
www.yorkbrew.co.uk

STONEWALL 3.7% ABV
Malty with hoppy finish.

BITTER 4.0% ABV
Well-balanced with full bitter flavour.

YORKSHIRE TERRIER 4.2% ABV
Gold-coloured with good bitter finish.

YORK IPA 5.0% ABV
Balanced tawny ale with pleasant finish.

CENTURION'S GHOST ALE 5.4% ABV
Millennium brew.

Plus seasonals.

THE PUBS

ALLERTON BYWATER

The Boat Inn

Boat Lane, Allerton Bywater, Castleford, West Yorkshire WF10 2BX
☎ *(01977) 552216* Kieron Lockwood
www.boatpub.co.uk

All Boat Brewery ales brewed on the premises and permanently available. One other monthly special guest.

A small pub with moorings directly outside. Food available every day in a large restaurant with non-smoking areas. Children allowed.

12–3pm and 6–11pm Mon–Fri; all day Sat–Sun.

BARKISLAND

The Fleece Inn

Ripponden Bank, Barkisland, Halifax, West Yorkshire
☎ *(01422) 822598* Stewart Taylor

Black Sheep Best and Charles Wells Bombardier permanently available plus up to six guest ales. Timothy Taylor Landlord, Black Sheep Special and Riggwelter and Fuller's London Pride are regular features, but different ales are stocked whenever possible.

A country pub with a warm welcome. Beamed ceilings and open fires. Beer garden with impressive views across the Calder valley and Ryburn valley. Food available 12–2.30pm and 6–9pm Mon–Sat, 12–7pm Sun. Live music twice weekly. Children allowed, with play areas outside and inside. Car park.

12–11pm (10.30pm Sun).

BARNSLEY

The Cherry Tree

High Hoyland, Barnsley, South Yorkshire S75 4BE
☎ *(01226) 382541*
Ken Burnett and John Avison

Eastwood & Sanders Bargee and Best Bitter plus Black Sheep Special are among the beers permanently available. Other guests are usually from Eastwood & Sanders.

Country pub with beautiful views. Food available at lunchtime and evenings (all day Sunday). Children allowed. Outside seating. Car park.

12–3pm and 5.30–11pm Mon–Fri; 12–11pm Saturday; 12–10.30pm Sunday.

Miller's Inn

Dearne Hall Road, Low Barugh, Barnsley, South Yorkshire S75 1LX
☎ *(01226) 382888* Colin Myers

A Burtonwood pub serving two Burtonwood brews, one of which changes each month and the other four times a year.

Refurbished in February 2004, a family-friendly waterside village pub with separate non-smoking area, beer garden (overlooking the River Dearne) and children's play area. Food available 12–2pm and 5–8.30pm Mon–Fri and 12–3pm Sun. Various theme nights. The quiz is on Mondays.

12–2.30pm and 5–11pm Mon–Fri; 12–11pm Sat; 12–4 and 7–10.30pm Sun.

BATTYEFORD

Airedale Heifer

53 Stocksbank Road, Battyeford, Mirfield, West Yorkshire WF14 9QB
☎ *(01924) 493547* Melvin Charles

Eastwood & Sanders Bargee permanently available plus occasional seasonal guests.

An old village pub, with food available 12–3pm Tues–Sun. Beer garden. Children allowed. Car park. Live music once a month and odd events throughout the year – call for details or see the website.

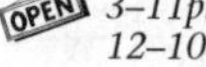
3–11pm Mon; 12–11pm Tues–Sat; 12–10.30pm Sun.

BECK HOLE

Birch Hall Inn

Beck Hole, Goathland, Whitby, North Yorkshire YO22 5LE
☎ *(01947) 896245* Colin and Glenys Jackson
www.beckhole.com

Genuine freehouse with Black Sheep Best Bitter and Theakston Black Bull Bitter always available plus a frequently changing guest, with local brewers strongly favoured.

Licensed since the early nineteenth century, this pub has been run by the same landlords for more than 20 years and offers a memorable step back in time. Much favoured by locals, it has two small bars crammed with memorabilia and separated by a shop which offers produce you thought had died out long ago. Pies and sandwiches available whenever the pub is open. Children allowed in the smaller bar; dogs anywhere. Split-level garden with splendid views over the village. Limited parking, but popular walking country, so travel on foot. Two miles west of A169.

Winter: 11am–3pm Mon –Sat and 7.30–11pm Tues–Sat; 12–3pm and 7.30–10.30pm Sun. Summer (May Day Bank Holiday to end of August): 11am–11pm Mon–Sat; 12–10.30pm Sun.

BRADFORD

The Beehive Inn

583 Halifax Road, Bradford, West Yorkshire BD6 2DU
☎ *(01274) 678550* Kevin Guthrie

At least two guest ales always available, one from a local brewery such as Salamander, Ossett, Eastwood & Sanders, and Daleside. The other guest will be from the Cask Marque seasonal range.

A one-bar locals' pub, with bar snacks available all day. Bradford CAMRA Pub of the Season Spring 2003. Children allowed.

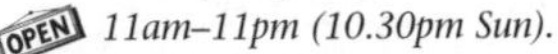
11am–11pm (10.30pm Sun).

The Castle Hotel

20 Grattan Road, Bradford, West Yorkshire BD1 2LU
☎ *(01274) 393166* James Duncan

Mansfield Riding and Riding Mild always available plus seven guest beers (200 per year) from brewers such as Goose Eye, Ridleys, Brains, Moorhouse's, Marston's, Jennings, Wadworth, Shepherd Neame and many more.

A pub built like a castle in 1898. Bar food is served at lunchtime from Monday to Thursday and until 7.30pm on Friday and Saturday. Parking at weekends and evenings. Children not allowed. Located in the city centre.

11.30am–11pm Mon–Sat; closed Sun.

The Corn Dolly

110 Bolton Road, Bradford, West Yorkshire BD1 4DE
☎ *(01274) 720219* Neil Dunkin

Eight beers always available. Moorhouse's Bitter, Black Sheep Bitter, Everards Tiger and something from Timothy Taylor always available, plus four ever-changing guest beers from all over the country, including breweries such as Durham, Ossett, Coach House and Exmoor.

A freehouse with a friendly atmosphere. Bradford CAMRA Pub of the Year 1993,1994, 2000 and 2001. Food is available at lunchtimes Mon–Fri; buffets catered for. Beer garden and car park. Situated just off the city centre (Forster Square).

11.30am–11pm.

The Fighting Cock

21–3 Preston Street, Bradford, West Yorkshire BD7 1JE
☎ *(01274) 726907* Kevin Quill

At least ten beers on sale. Brews from Timothy Taylor and Black Sheep always available plus many guests (200 per year) from Greene King, Fuller's, Archers, Jennings and Ringwood etc.

A friendly back-to-basics original alehouse. Bar food available at lunchtime. Go left on Thornton Road from the former cinema in the city centre, then left again at the lights.

11am–11pm Mon–Sat; 11am–3pm and 7–10.30pm Sun.

Haigy's Bar

31 Lumb Lane, Bradford, West Yorkshire BD8 7QU
☎ *(01274) 731644* David and Yvonne Haig

A genuine freehouse serving Greene King Abbot and up to four other weekly changing real ales, perhaps from Ossett, Oakham and Phoenix breweries.

An edge-of-city centre pub with homely decor. The outside is painted in Bradford City colours. Games, pool, disco at weekends. Disabled access, beer garden. Bar snacks available at lunchtimes. Children allowed in the afternoons only.

5pm–1am Mon–Thurs; 12pm–1am Fri–Sat; 12–7pm Sun (10.30pm Sun if Bradford Bulls or Bradford City are playing at home!).

The Junction Inn

Bolton Road, Bradford, West Yorkshire BD2 4HT
☎ *(01274) 639491* Jim Wright

Samuel Smith OBB, Black Sheep Special and Timothy Taylor Landlord always available plus several guests (130 per year) including Tomintoul Stag, Hop Back Summer Lightning, Fuller's London Pride, Daleside Old Legover, Joseph Holts etc.

A York stone pub with two separate bars, part wood, part flagstone floors, wooden bench seating. A proper no-frills alehouse. Bar food is available. Parking and garden. Follow the 'Idle' signs along Bolton Road for approximately two miles from the city centre.

11.30am–11pm Mon–Sat; 12–3pm and 7–10.30pm Sun.

The New Beehive Inn

171 Westgate, Bradford, West Yorkshire BD1 3AA
☎ *(01274) 721784* William Wagstaff

Kelham Island Bitter, Timothy Taylor Landlord and beers from Barnsley and Ossett are always available, plus up to four guests from independent breweries across the UK. Listed on CAMRA's National Inventory.

A classic Edwardian inn, barely altered over the years, with unique gas lighting. Six separate drinking rooms. Bar food available all day. Children allowed. Accommodation. Situated on the outskirts of the city centre.

12–11pm (10.30pm Sun).

The Shearbridge

111 Great Horton Road, Bradford, West Yorkshire BD7 1PS
☎ *(01274) 732136* David Cheshire

Up to four guests on offer, such as Harviestoun Schiehallion or a Black Sheep ale.

A students' pub with beams, wooden floors and beer garden. There are plans to serve food in the near future. Children welcome.

OPEN *12–11pm (10.30pm Sun).*

Sir Titus Salt

Windsor Baths, Morley Street, Bradford, West Yorkshire BD7 1AQ
☎ *(01274) 732853* Adam Johnson (Manager)

A JD Wetherspoon's pub with Greene King Abbot and Shepherd Neame Spitfire permanently available, plus a selection of regularly changing guests from breweries such as Hook Norton, Highgate, Rooster's, Banks & Taylor and Springhead. Beer festivals held.

A large open pub which used to be a swimming pool! Food available all day every day. Children allowed. Small outside area with seating.

OPEN *10am–11pm.*

BREARTON

The Malt Shovel

Brearton, Harrogate, North Yorkshire HG3 3BX
☎ *(01423) 862929* Leslie Mitchell

Five beers always available – up to 100 guests per year. Favourites include Daleside Bitter, Black Sheep Bitter something from Theakston and other local brews.

A sixteenth-century beamed village freehouse, with beams and open fires in winter. Bar food available 12–2pm and 7–9pm (not Sunday evenings). Car park, garden. Children welcome. Off the B6165, six miles from Harrogate.

OPEN *Closed on Mondays. 12–2.30pm and 6.45–11pm Tues–Sat; 12–2.30pm and 7–10.30pm Sun.*

BRIDLINGTON

The Old Ship Inn

90 St John's Street, Bridlington, East Yorkshire YO16 7JS
☎ *(01262) 670466*

Up to seven beers always available.

A two-bar country pub with dining area and beer garden. Food available. Children allowed.

OPEN *11am–11pm (10.30pm Sun).*

BROMPTON

The Crown Inn

Station Road, Brompton, Northallerton, North Yorkshire DL6 2RE
☎ *(0160) 977 2547 Mrs Addington*

Two guest ales such as Marston's Pedigree in addition to the two regular brews.

A traditional country inn with one bar, coal fires and a small garden. No food. Children allowed.

OPEN *12–3pm and 7–11pm Mon–Thurs; all day Fri–Sun.*

BURLEY

The Fox & Newt

9 Burley Street, Burley, Leeds, West Yorkshire LS3 1LD
☎ *(01132) 432612* Roy Cadman

A wide range of guest ales always available. Regulars include Young's Special, Greene King Abbot, Timothy Taylor Landlord, Wadworth 6X, Marston's Pedigree, Fuller's London Pride and Caledonian 80/-. The beers are changed weekly.

An old-style pub with a wooden floor. Food available at lunchtime only in a separate dining area. Children allowed for lunches only.

OPEN *All day, every day.*

CAWOOD

The Ferry Inn

2 King Street, Cawood, Selby, North Yorkshire YO8 3TL
☎ *(01757) 268515* Steve Kennedy

York Stonewall and Timothy Taylor Landlord are among the beers always available, plus one constantly changing guest ale.

A sixteenth-century village inn with stone floor, beams, log fires and large beer garden overlooking the River Ouse and Cawood's eighteenth-century swing bridge. Bar food available at weekends, 12–2.30pm and 5–9pm. Separate dining area. Children welcome. En-suite accommodation available. Four miles from Selby.

OPEN *12–11pm (10.30pm Sun).*

CHAPEL HADDLESEY

The Jug Inn

Chapel Haddlesey, Selby, North Yorkshire
☎ *(01757) 270307* Paul King

A Brown Cow brew is usually available, plus three guest beers, often from Glentworth, Rudgate, Barnsley, Cropton, Eccleshall, Goose Eye, Kelham Island or Tigertops.

Welcoming village pub with beamed ceilings and open coal fires. Food served 6–9pm daily. South-facing beer garden next to river. Car park.

5.30–11pm Tues–Fri; 12–11pm Sat; 12–10.30pm Sun. Closed all day Mon.

CHAPEL-LE-DALE

The Hill Inn

Chapel-le-Dale, Ingleton, North Yorkshire LA6 3AR
☎ *(015242) 41246* Mrs Sabena Martin

A pub permanently serving Black Sheep Best, Special and Riggwelter plus Dent Bitter and Aviator.

Ancient inn with lots of character, nestling between Ingleborough and Whernside, and close to the White Scar Caves and the Ribblehead Viaduct. Home-cooked food available (phone to check and book), with puddings a speciality! Well-behaved children allowed. Car park.

Opening times vary, depending on the season and level of custom. It is advisable to ring ahead and check.

CHAPELTOWN

The Commercial Inn

107 Station Road, Chapeltown, Sheffield, South Yorkshire S35 2XF
☎ *(0114) 246 9066* Paul Manzies

Wentworth Brewery Best, Needles Eye, WPA and Oatmeal Stout always available plus four guest ales changed continually from a range of independent breweries including Durham, Barnsley, Slaters of Eccleshall and Daleside. Beer festivals twice a year (last weekend in May and November).

A traditional town pub dating from 1889 with one bar serving a lounge, games room and non-smoking snug. Food available 12–2.30pm and 6–9pm Mon–Thurs, 12–9pm Fri–Sat and 12–3pm Sun. No children. Beer garden, car park. Not far from the railway station, just off M1 junction 35. Car park.

12–3pm and 5.30–11pm Mon–Thurs; 12–11pm Fri–Sat; 12–10.30pm Sun.

CRAY

The White Lion

Cray, Skipton, North Yorkshire BD23 5JB
☎ *(01756) 760262* Kevin and Debbie Roe

Four hand pumps all serving a constantly changing range of real ales. Moorhouse's Pendle Witch and Premier, Goose Eye No Eye Deer, Timothy Taylor Landlord, Cottage Champflower, Ossett Silver King, Copper Dragon Best Bitter, Golden Pippin and Pale Ale and Daleside Blonde are among the beers on regular rotation, although many others are also featured. Emphasis on local ales where possible.

Formerly a Drovers' Hostelry dating from the seventeenth century, this is a peaceful pub in the Yorkshire Dales. Situated in a popular walking area of outstanding natural beauty. Food available 12–2pm and 5.45–8.45pm daily, tea and coffee available all day. Outside seating in a beer garden, and also beside the cascading Cray Gill. Superior accommodation with seasonal special offers. Children welcome, baby listening service available to residents. Directions available from Grassington National Park centre.

10am–11pm (10.30pm Sun).

CROPTON

The New Inn

Cropton, Nr Pickering, North Yorkshire YO18 8HH
☎ *(01751) 417330* Philip Lee
www.croptonbrewery.co.uk

Home of the Cropton Brewery, so a selection of at least five Cropton beers always available plus a guest from Thwaites.

Cropton Brewery was established in 1984 in the basement of the New Inn in this tiny moorland village. It owes its existence to the deep-seated local fear that, one day, the harsh moors winter weather would prevent the beer wagon from getting through. The brewery's reputation has since spread and, as demand exceeded capacity, a new purpose-built brewery was constructed in an adjacent quarry. Home-cooked bar and restaurant food is served daily 12–2pm and 6–9pm. Car park, garden, children's room, accommodation. Brewery tours available. Large beer festival held every November.

11am–11pm Mon–Sat; 12–10.30pm Sun.

DENBY DALE

The White Hart

380 Wakefield Road, Denby Dale, Huddersfield, West Yorkshire HD8 8RT
☎ *(01484) 862357* Mrs Donna M Brayshaw

Timothy Taylor Landlord always available, plus two constantly changing guest ales.

Friendly, village-centre pub with an open fire in winter. Beer garden and Tuesday night quiz with free buffet. Homemade food served 12–2.30pm daily. Car park. Children welcome when eating.

OPEN *12–11pm (10.30pm Sun).*

DEWSBURY

The Leggers Inn

Stable Buildings, Mill Street East, Dewsbury, West Yorkshire WF12 9BD
☎ *(01924) 502846*
Mark Wallace and John Smithson

Home of The Egyptian Sand & Gravel brewery with their two most popular home brews, Goldeneye and Marriott Mild, always available, plus Everards Tiger and a Rooster's beer. Four rotating guests plus Hoegaarden and traditional cider on draught.

Situated in an old hay loft in a canal boatyard: pub upstairs, brewery downstairs. Basic food: pies and peas plus sandwiches served all day every day. Live music most Thursdays. Outside seating. Children allowed. Situated past Carlton Cards in Mill Street East, to the right. Can be hard to find so phone for directions.

OPEN *11am–11pm Mon–Sat; 12–10.30pm Sun.*

West Riding Licensed Refreshment Rooms

Dewsbury Railway Station, Wellington Road, Dewsbury, West Yorkshire WF13 1HF
☎ *(01924) 459193*
Challcia Banks and Mike Field

A freehouse with Black Sheep Bitter and Timothy Taylor Landlord always available, plus up to six guests from breweries such as Ossett, Durham, Salamander and the pub's own micro-brewery, Anglo-Dutch. Close links with local breweries.

Situated in the railway station and doubling as a waiting room, this is a real ale pub with one central bar, wooden floors and beer garden. Live music on Thursdays. Music festival venue. Food available every lunchtime, plus Tuesday nights (Pie Nights) and Wednesday nights (Curry Nights). Children allowed in designated areas. On Trans-Pennine route – four trains an hour in each direction.

OPEN *11am–11pm (10.30pm Sun).*

DISHFORTH

The Crown Inn

Main Street, Dishforth, North Yorkshire YO7 3JU
☎ *(01845) 577398* Alison Craddock

Charles Wells Bombardier plus Timothy Taylor Landlord and Golden Best are always on offer, plus four or five guest beers, perhaps Badger Tanglefoot, Greene King Old Speckled Hen, or brews from Durham, Salamander and Goose Eye.

Small country pub with pool room, easily accessible from A1 and A19. Food available 12–3pm and 6–9.30pm Tues–Sun. Children very welcome. Car park. Coach parties welcome (advance notice required for food).

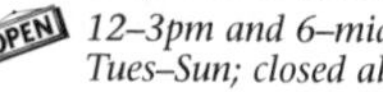

OPEN *12–3pm and 6–midnight (supper licence) Tues–Sun; closed all day Monday.*

DONCASTER

The Salutation

14 South Parade, Doncaster, South Yorkshire DN1 2DR
☎ *(01302) 340705* Aoife Gleeson

A renowned real ale pub with at least two popular guests from breweries such as Young's, Greene King, Adnams and Charles Wells.

A 300-year-old coaching inn with strong connections with Doncaster Racecourse. A one-roomed bar with lots of cosy corners and a real fire in winter. Food available every day – Sunday lunch a speciality. Sunny beer garden and large function room. Coach parties welcome (by appointment).

OPEN *All day, every day.*

DRIFFIELD

The Bell In Driffield

46 Market Place, Driffield, East Yorkshire YO25 6AN
☎ *(01377) 256661* George Riggs

Two or three real ales available during the week with an extra one at weekends from a range of local brews, often including something from Wold Top, Hambleton or Daleside. Plus about 300 malt whiskies.

Characterful and friendly early eighteenth-century coaching inn retaining many original features and run by the same owners for the past 20 years. Food served 12–1.30pm and 7–9.30pm daily. Accommodation. Car park. Disabled access. In the town centre.

OPEN *All day, every day.*

ELLAND

Barge & Barrel

10–20 Park Road, Elland, West Yorkshire HA5 9HB

☎ (01422) 373623 Mark Dalton

Eastwood & Sanders Bargee, John Eastwood Best and Gold Award, Black Sheep Bitter, Shepherd Neame Spitfire, Phoenix Wobbly Bob and Roosters Yankee always available. Plus four constantly changing guests which could be ales from Ossett, Abbeydale or Anglo-Dutch.

A canalside pub, just outside the small town. Food available in non-smoking dining area. Children allowed if eating. Waterside garden. Live music occasionally. Car park.

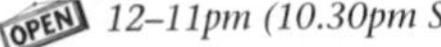

12–11pm (10.30pm Sun).

ELSLACK

The Tempest Arms

Elslack, Nr Skipton, North Yorkshire

☎ *(01282) 842450*

Veronica Clarkson (manager)

Owned by Individual Inns, with Timothy Taylor Landlord and Best Bitter plus Black Sheep Bitter always on offer. Also two local beers from Wharfdale and Copper Dragon. Good range of wines served by the glass and bottle.

A pub situated in glorious countryside. Food served lunchtimes and evenings Mon–Sat and all day on Sunday. Function room for up to 100 guests, plus ten en-suite bedrooms. Just outside Elslack, an ancient hamlet close to the Yorkshire Dales.

11am–11pm Mon–Sat; 12–10.30pm Sun.

EMBSAY

The Elm Tree Inn

5 Elm Tree Square, Embsay, Skipton, North Yorkshire BD23 6RB

☎ *(01756) 790717* Janet Ridd

Goose Eye No Eye Deer permanently available, plus up to six guests such as Fuller's London Pride, Charles Wells Bombardier, Hook Norton Old Hooky, Timothy Taylor Landlord, Caledonian Deuchars IPA or something from Gale's or Adnams.

A traditional country inn in the village square, serving meals every lunchtime 12–2pm and 6–8.30pm Mon; 6–9pm Tues–Wed; 5.30–9pm Thurs–Sat. Non-smoking dining area. Outside seating. Two en-suite accommodation rooms. Car park. Children welcome if eating.

11am–3pm and 5.30–11pm Mon–Sat; 12–3pm and 7.30–10.30pm Sun.

FLAXTON

The Blacksmiths Arms

Flaxton, York, North Yorkshire YO60 7RJ

☎ *(01904) 468210* Mrs Alison Jordan

Black Sheep Bitter and Timothy Taylor Landlord regularly available.

A 250-year-old country freehouse with separate non-smoking dining area serving home-cooked food Tues–Sat evening, lunchtime and evening Sun. Car park. Children welcome.

7–11pm Tues–Sat (closed Mon); 12–3pm and 7–10.30pm Sun.

GOODMANHAM

The Goodmanham Arms

Main Street, Goodmanham, York, North Yorkshire YO43 3JA

☎ *(01430) 873849* Peter Southcott

Home of the Goodmanham Brewery with all three home brews and Black Sheep Bitter permanently available. Regular varied guests.

A freehold country pub on the Wold's Way long distance footpath. Real fires, friendly local clientele and walkers welcome. Bar food available Sat–Sun lunchtimes, plus sandwiches all day every day. Beer garden. Children and dogs welcome.

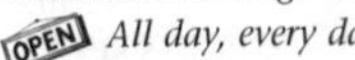

All day, every day

GREETLAND

The Druids Arms

2–4 Spring Lane, Greetland, Halifax, West Yorkshire HX4 8JL

☎ *(01422) 372465* Keith Mallinson

Timothy Taylor Golden Best, Best Bitter and Landlord permanently available plus three constantly changing guest ales. Regular features include: Rooster's Cream, Durham White Sapphire or ales from Halifax Steam or Eastwood & Sanders. Micro-breweries supported.

A homely country pub with comfy sofas, real fires in winter, seating area outside in summer and a friendly atmosphere. No food. Children allowed until 8.30pm. Live music once a month. Car park. May be difficult to find; ring for directions.

5–11pm Mon–Fri; 12–11pm Sat; 12–10.30pm Sun.

GUISBOROUGH

The Tap & Spile

11 Westgate, Guisborough, North Yorkshire TS14 6BG
☎ *(01287) 632983* Angela Booth

Big Lamp Bitter always available plus six guests (200 per year) which may include Hambleton ales and those from Cotleigh, Big Lamp and Durham.

Plenty of olde-worlde charm, a beamed ceiling, non-smoking room, snug and beer garden. Bar food available at lunchtime. Parking. Children allowed. Situated on the main street in Guisborough.

 *11.30am–11pm Mon–Sat; 12–3pm and 7–10.30pm Sun.*

GUNNERSIDE

The Kings Head

Gunnerside, North Yorkshire DL11 6LD
☎ *(01748) 886261*
Steve Stewart and Sam Mealing

Black Sheep Bitter and up to three ever-changing guest ales from all over the country.

Traditional Dales walkers' pub. Hot and cold snacks served at lunchtimes, with home-cooked meals available 7–9pm (booking not necessary). Families welcome.

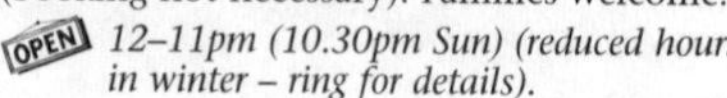 *12–11pm (10.30pm Sun) (reduced hours in winter – ring for details).*

HALIFAX

The Royal Oak

1 Clare Road, Halifax, West Yorkshire HX1 2HX
☎ *(01422) 353661* Chris Dalton

Timothy Taylor Landlord always available, plus five guests, changed every fortnight.

A traditional town pub in a listed building, with one bar and a dining area. Food available at lunchtime only. No children.

OPEN *All day, every day.*

The Three Pigeons

1 Sunfold, South Parade, Halifax, West Yorkshire HX1 2LX
☎ *(01422) 347001* Geoff Amos
www.threepigeons.demon.co.uk

Award-winning, family-run freehouse with seven cask ales on offer. Regulars are Timothy Taylor Landlord and Best Bitter, plus Black Sheep Bitter. Guest ales are drawn from breweries throughout the UK, with mild beers featured on a weekly basis.

A unique, unspoilt 1930s Art Deco pub just a few minutes' walk from the railway station. Real fires, one bar and three parlour rooms. Patio at front. Food available on weekday lunchtimes only, with a curry night on Monday evenings. Children allowed in designated area.

 *12–11pm (10.30pm Sun).*

HAROME

The Star

Harome, Nr Helmsley, North Yorkshire YO62 5JE
☎ *(01439) 770397* Andrew and Jacqui Pern
www.thestaratharome.co.uk

Black Sheep Special always available, plus a guest, often from the local Cropton Brewery but changed every two weeks.

A traditional, fourteenth-century thatched freehouse and Michelin-starred restaurant. One bar and a separate restaurant plus a large beer garden. Food available Tues–Sat 11.30–2pm and 6.30–9.30pm, plus 12–6pm on Sundays. Private dining room and coffee loft. Children welcome. Recently opened hotel opposite. Two miles south of the A170.

 *7.30–11pm Mon; 11.30am–3pm and 6.30–11pm Tues–Sat; 12–10.30pm Sun.*

HARROGATE

The Old Bell Tavern

6 Royal Parade, Harrogate, North Yorkshire HG1 2SZ
☎ *(01423) 507930* Becky Griffiths
www.markettowntaverns.co.uk

Timothy Taylor Landlord, Black Sheep Bitter and Caledonian Deuchars IPA always available, plus five regularly changing guests, from local breweries whenever possible. Also Erdinger WeissBier (a Belgian ale) and two guest Belgian beers, plus a range of Belgian bottled beers.

A traditional period town-centre bar with large non-smoking room. Air conditioned. Food available every day in the bar and in an upstairs dining room/brasserie every day except Sunday. Children allowed in the brasserie only. Situated close to the Pump Room Museum and Valley Gardens.

OPEN *12–11pm (10.30pm Sun).*

The Tap & Spile

Tower Street, Harrogate, North Yorkshire HG1 1HS
☎ *(01423) 526785* Roger Palmer

No permanent beers, but a constantly changing range of guest ales. Rooster's and Rudgate are regular breweries featured, but two new beers are served every week.

A two-bar pub situated just off the town centre. Stone walls, half-carpet in public bar and lounge, one non-smoking, fireplace. Patio at front. Food available at lunchtime only. Children allowed in non-smoking room only.

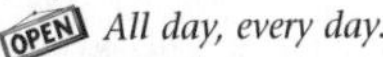
All day, every day.

HAWORTH

The Fleece

Main Street, Haworth, Near Keighley, West Yorkshire BD22 8DA
☎ *(01535) 642172* Melanie Wadwell

The complete range of Timothy Taylor beers (six in all) are always on offer. A Taylor's tied house, but special in that they always stock the complete range and most pubs only stock one or two.

Completely refurbished in 2002, the pub now has a seven en-suite rooms, non-smoking dining area and all new bar area. Food available 12–2pm and 6.30–9pm Mon–Fri; 12–4pm and 6.30–9pm Sat–Sun. Well-behaved children allowed. On Haworth's main cobbled street.

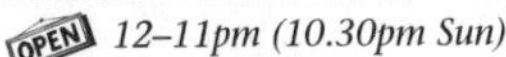
12–11pm (10.30pm Sun).

HEBDEN BRIDGE

The Fox & Goose

9 Heptonstall Road, Hebden Bridge, West Yorkshire HX7 6AZ
☎ *(01422) 842649* Simon and Julia Trapp

Pictish Brewer's Gold is a permanent feature, and the beers on the other three hand pumps, from small independent brewers, change several times a week. Two genuine German pilsner lagers, a range of bottled beers and some 40 whiskies are also served.

A small, friendly three-roomed local. The eclectic mix of customers and the absence of both a juke box and games machines encourage lively conversation! Pool is played in one of the rooms. No food. Well-behaved children are welcome at lunchtimes and in the early evenings, and the owners' dog, Spike, is always on hand to welcome other furry friends.

11.30am–3pm and 7–11pm Mon–Sat (open 6pm Fri); 12–5pm and 7–10.30pm Sun.

The Stubbing Wharf

King Street, Hebden Bridge, West Yorkshire HX7 6LU
☎ *(01422) 844107*
Dean Batty and Shelley Cockayne

Up to four permanent real ales (Timothy Taylor Landlord, Greene King IPA, Black Sheep Bitter and Shepherd Neame Spitfire) plus four guests (12 each week) such as Phoenix Wobbly Bob, Abbeydale Absolution, Archers Golden and Jennings Sneck Lifter or a number of others from Anglo-Dutch, Cottage, Coach House, Cropton, Moorhouse's, Slaters, Springhead, Young's, Wye Valley and elsewhere. Ciders and perry in summer.

Situated on the edge of Hebden Bridge toward Todmorden, this is an eighteenth-century canal- and riverside pub, offering homemade food everyday in summer and at weekends in winter and a function room to seat 50 people. Open-plan bar and dining area. Games night on Monday, Bridge Rats Motorcycle Club meet every Tuesday, Wednesday is acoustic night and quiz night on Thursday. Storytelling and many other regular events. Six miles from Halifax.

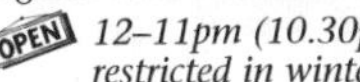
12–11pm (10.30pm Sun) (hours more restricted in winter).

HELPERBY

The Golden Lion Inn

Main Street, Helperby, York, North Yorkshire YO61 2NT
☎ *(01423) 360870* Pippa and Richard Heather

A freehouse with four guest beers always available, including premium and strong beers for adventurous drinkers!

A traditional village country inn with stone floor and two log fires. Bar food always available. Home-cooked meals and 'nibbles' menu available weekends and weekday evenings (except Mon–Tues). A warm welcome for all, including families.

12–11pm (10.30pm Sun).

HOLMFIRTH

The Farmer's Arms

2–4 Liphill Bank Road, Holmfirth, West Yorkshire, HD7 7DE
☎ *(01484) 683713* Damela Greensides

Black Sheep Bitter, Fuller's London Pride, Adnams Bitter and Timothy Taylor Landlord always available, plus a constantly changing guest.

A traditional country village pub where the beer takes priority. No food. Children allowed until 8.30pm. Car park. From Compo's Café take the second turning on the right.

5–11pm Mon–Fri; 12–11pm Sat; 12–10.30pm Sun.

Rose and Crown

7 Victoria Square, Holmfirth, Huddersfield HD9 1DA

Timothy Taylor Best and Landlord, Black Sheep Best, Jennings Cumberland, Moorhouses Black Cat and guest beers available. Held its first beer festival over the bank holiday weekend in August 2004.

An unpretentious drinkers' pub in the middle of the village. Two bars plus a garden. No food.

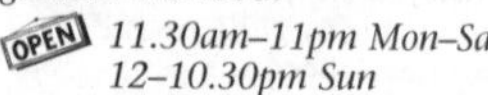

11.30am–11pm Mon–Sat, 12–10.30pm Sun

HORBURY

Boon's

6 Queen Street, Horbury, Wakefield, West Yorkshire WF4 6LP

☎ *(01924) 280442* John Bladen

Timothy Taylor Landlord and Clark's Bitter regularly available, with up to four guest beers often from Adnams, Orkney, Shepherd Neame, Wychwood, Elgood's, Everards, Weltons, Ushers, Thwaites, Rebellion, Nethergate, Jennings, Hoskins, Greene King, Fuller's, Daleside, Bateman or Burton Bridge.

Traditional, single-bar olde-worlde pub with patio and beer garden. Established as a pub c.1710, it retains an open fire, beams and flagged floor. Walls hung with sporting pictures. Children welcome in beer garden and patio only.

OPEN *11am–3pm and 5–11pm Mon–Thur; 11am–11pm Fri–Sat; 12–10.30pm Sun.*

The King's Arms

27 New Street, Horbury, Wakefield, West Yorkshire WF4 6NB

☎ *(01924) 264329* Mike Davidson

A Marston's house with Pedigree, Bitter and others available, plus one guest pump regularly featuring a Banks's ale.

A one-bar village pub with wooden floors in bar area. Pool and games area. Conservatory, dining area, garden. Food currently available 5–7 pm. Children allowed.

OPEN *3–11pm Mon–Thurs; 12–11pm Fri–Sat; 12–4pm and 7–10.30pm Sun.*

HORSFORTH

Town Street Tavern

16–18 Town Street, Horsforth, Leeds, West Yorkshire LS18 4RJ

☎ *(0113) 281 9996*

Lucy Gaunt and Carth Kirsten-Landman

A freehouse with Timothy Taylor Landlord, Black Sheep Bitter and Caledonian Deuchars IPA always available, plus up to six ever-changing guest ales from northern breweries. Also two guest Belgian ales, Erdinger Weiss Bier and over 30 bottled German beers.

A light, airy bar, traditional but with a Continental feel, including a large non-smoking area. Air conditioned. Upstairs brasserie dining room available for private hire. Food available every day. Children are allowed only in the upstairs dining room.

OPEN *12–11pm (10.30pm Sun).*

HUDDERSFIELD

The Old Court Brewhouse

Queen Street, Huddersfield, West Yorkshire HD1 2SL

☎ *(01484) 454035*

Timothy Taylor Landlord and Black Sheep Bitter are among the beers always on offer.

This listed building was formerly the county court. Bar and restaurant food available at lunchtime and evenings (Mon–Sat). Metered parking, garden.

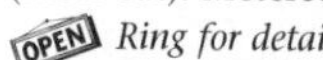

Ring for details.

Rat & Ratchet

40 Chapel Hill, Huddersfield, West Yorkshire HD1 3EB

☎ *(01484) 516734*

Andrew and Maxine Moorehouse

Fourteen ales at all times. Three home brews plus Adnams Best, Bateman Mild, Mansfield Old Baily, Marston's Pedigree, Timothy Taylor Landlord and several more.

The brewery opened here in December 1994. A popular pub with beer festivals and special events held regularly.

OPEN *12–11pm.*

The Star Inn

7 Albert Street, Follyhall, Lockwood HD1 3PJ

☎ *(01484) 545443*

www.thestarinn.info

An impressive selection of real ales including Eastwood &Saunders Best, Timothy Taylor Best and Landlord and a wide range of guests. Beer festivals are regularly held.

A back-street ale house where drinking takes priority. Real fires and beer garden. Off the A616.

OPEN *Closed all day Mon and 12–2pm Tues-Thurs. 12–2pm and 5–11pm Fri, 12–3pm and 6–11pm Sat, 12–3pm and 7–10.30pm Sun.*

HULL

Minerva Hotel

Nelson Street, Hull, East Yorkshire HU1 1XE
☎ *(01482) 326909* Eamon (Scotty) Scott

Up to two guest beers always available – changed weekly. Breweries featured have included Rooster's, Orkney, Caledonian, Young's, Sulwath and Abbeydale. Plus a permanent mild. CAMRA Hull Pub of the Year 2000–2002.

Traditional, nineteenth-century pub built on the banks of the River Humber in 1830 and packed with maritime memorabilia. Four main rooms, plus nooks and possibly the smallest snug in Britain which seats three. Large portions of home-cooked food served lunchtimes and evenings Mon–Thurs, lunchtimes only Fri–Sun. Children welcome if taking a meal. Situated on Nelson Street, facing the river and Victoria pier. Ideal if visiting 'The Deep'.

OPEN *11am–11pm Mon–Sat; 12–10.30pm Sun.*

Springbank Tavern

29 Spring Bank, Hull, East Yorkshire HU3 1AS
☎ *(01482) 581879* Belinda Beaumont

Banks's Original always available plus two guest beers which could be something like Bateman XXXB or Brakspear Special.

A one-room alehouse with traditional games (darts, dominoes and pool). Students and locals provide mixed clientele. Background music, but no juke box. Bar food available 12–2pm daily (12–6pm Sunday). Beer garden. Street parking, disabled facilities. Children allowed in the bar for meals. Just off the city centre.

OPEN *11am–11pm Mon–Sat; 12–10.30pm Sun.*

Ye Olde Black Boy

150 High Street, Hull, East Yorkshire HU1 1PS
☎ *(01482) 326516* Richard and Janette Gant
www.yeoldeblackboy.com

Up to six guest beers available, from breweries such as Caledonian, Hop Back, Titanic, JW Lees, Hydes, Robinson's, Arundel, Gale's and Harviestoun. Hoegaarden and real cider also served.

A historic real-ale pub in the centre of Hull. Cask Marque accredited. Local CAMRA Pub of the Season summer 2002. Light snacks usually available. Function room available for meetings and small private parties (up to 30 people). Situated on the old High Street, next to the river, only 10 minutes' walk from 'The Deep'.

OPEN *12–11pm (10.30pm Sun).*

IDLE

Symposium

7 Albion Road, Idle, Bradford, West Yorkshire BD10 9PY
☎ *(01274) 616587* Karen Harker

Timothy Taylor Landlord always available plus five guests from northern breweries. Also a guest Belgian ale, often Erdinger WeissBier, and a range of over 30 bottled Belgian and German beers.

A traditional ale and wine bar with a non-smoking snug. Separate restaurant with food available every day. Sun terrace available for al fresco drinking and dining. Children allowed at the landlord's discretion. Situated in the centre of Idle village, close to the Green.

12–2.30pm and 5.30–11pm Mon–Thurs; 12–11pm Fri–Sat; 12–10.30pm Sun.

ILKLEY

Bar T'At

7 Cunliffe Road, Ilkley, West Yorkshire LS29 9DZ
☎ *(01943) 608888* Frazer Barnes
www.markettowntaverns.co.uk

Timothy Taylor Landlord always available plus Black Sheep Bitter, Caledonian Deuchars IPA and four guests from northern breweries. Erdinger WeissBier (a Belgian beer) also always on offer and a range of over 30 bottled Belgian and German beers.

A traditional ale and wine bar on two floors. Non-smoking area in the 'cellar'. Food available every day. Children allowed in the 'cellar' only. Adjacent to the central main car park.

OPEN *12–11pm (10.30pm Sun).*

INGLETON

The Wheatsheaf Inn

22 High Street, Ingleton, North Yorkshire LA6 3AD
☎ *(01524) 241275 Mr Thompson*

A freehouse with Black Sheep Bitter, Special and Riggwelter plus Timothy Taylor Golden Best among the beers always available.

An olde-worlde one-bar country pub with dining area and beer garden. Disabled access. Accommodation. Food available at lunchtime and evenings. Children allowed. Good walking country.

OPEN *12–11pm (10.30pm Sun).*

KEIGHLEY

The Old White Bear

6 Keighley Road, Crosshills, Keighley, West Yorkshire BD20 7RN
☎ *(01535) 632115* The Naylor family

One brew produced and served on the premises, plus guests beers such as Timothy Taylor Landlord.

The pub was built in 1735 and retains its original beams. Brewing began in the old stables here in 1993. The current owners took over in 2001. Bar and restaurant food available at lunchtime and evenings. Car park, small garden. Children allowed if kept under control.

 *11.30am–3pm and 5–11pm Mon–Thurs (not Mon lunch); 11.30am–11pm Fri–Sat; 12–4pm and 7–10.30pm Sun.*

The Worth Valley Inn

1 Wesley Place, Halifax Road, Keighley, West Yorkshire BD21 5BB
☎ *(01535) 603539* Trish Binns

Tetley Bitter and a range of changing guest real ales.

Situtated very near to the Keighley and Worth Valley railway, this is a small local with a new landlady which gathers passing trade from the railway. Food available (check for details). Children allowed.

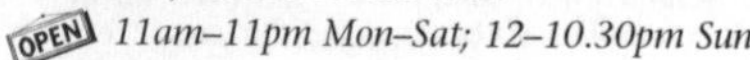 *11am–11pm Mon–Sat; 12–10.30pm Sun.*

KIRKBYMOORSIDE

The George & Dragon Hotel

17 Market Place, Kirkbymoorside, North Yorkshire YO62 6AA
☎ *(01751) 433334* Mrs E Walker

A Black Sheep ale and a selection of guest beers usually available.

Cosy, beamed bar with blazing log fire in winter, plus a collection of cricket, rugby and golf memorabilia for the sports enthusiast. Food served 12–2.15pm and 6.30–9.15pm Mon–Sat and 7–9.15pm Sun. Car park. Children welcome – there is an enclosed garden, but no other special facilities.

 *10am–11pm Mon–Sat; 12–10.30pm Sun.*

KNARESBOROUGH

Blind Jacks

19 Market Place, Knaresborough, North Yorkshire HG5 8AL
☎ *(01423) 869148*
Paul and Debbie Holden-Ridgway

Up to nine real ales always available. Timothy Taylor Landlord, Village Brewer's White Boar (the house beer), Daleside Green Grass Old Rogue Ale and Black Sheep Bitter are always on offer, and the four guests, which always include a mild, regularly feature beers from Rooster's, Daleside, Durham and Boat breweries.

A seventeenth-century listed building, beamed with wooden floors, panelled walls and lots of mirrors. Non-smoking room available. Two cosy upstairs snugs. No food. No children. Parking nearby. Dogs allowed.

 *5.30–11pm Mon; 4–11pm Tues–Thur; 12–11pm Fri–Sat; 12–10.30pm Sun.*

KNOTTINGLEY

The Steam Packet Inn

Racca Green, Knottingley, West Yorkshire WF11 8AT
☎ *(01977) 677266* Donna and Warren Bate

A John Smith's house also stocking a weekly changing guest ale from a wide range.

A small-town pub beside the canal with lounge bar, public bar, function room and beer garden. Food may now be available (ring to confirm). Children allowed but not at the bar.

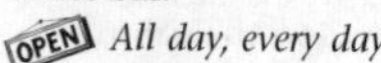 *All day, every day.*

LANGDALE END

Moorcock Inn

Langdale End, Scarborough, North Yorkshire
☎ *(01723) 882268* Susan Mathewson

A Daleside beer and Malton Golden Chance are regularly available, plus a guest beer.

Unspoilt, two-bar country pub with hatch servery. No music or machines. Food served every lunchtime and evening during the summer; Thur–Sun evenings and Sat–Sun lunch in the winter. Well-behaved children welcome until 9pm. Situated at the Scarborough end of Forrest Drive.

 *Summer: 11.30am–2.30pm and 6.30–11pm Mon–Sat; 12–3pm and 7–10.30pm; Winter: 6.30–11pm Wed–Sat; 7–10.30pm Sun (Ring first to be sure).*

LEEDS

The Duck & Drake

43 Kirkgate, Leeds, West Yorkshire LS2 7DR
☎ *(0113) 246 5806* Mr and Mrs Morley

Timothy Taylor Landlord always available plus six guests (300 per year) from breweries including Jennings, Clark's, Exmoor, Rooster's and Pioneer. Also real cider.

A traditional alehouse with wooden floors, coal fires, bare boards and live bands. Bar food served at lunchtime. Get to Leeds market and ask for directions.

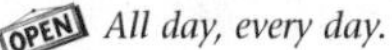 *All day, every day.*

The Eagle Tavern

North Street, Sheepscar, Leeds, West Yorkshire LS2 1AF
☎ *(0113) 245 7146* Mr Vaughan

A Samuel Smith tied house. Old Brewery Bitter always available, plus other seasonal ales.

An 1826 Georgian building close to the city centre. Bar food available at lunchtime and evenings. Occasional live music. Parking. Ten minutes' walk out of the city centre. B&B accommodation.

 *11.30am–2.30pm and 5.30–11pm Mon–Fri; 11.30am–2.30pm and 6–11pm Sat; 12–3pm and 7–10.30pm Sun.*

The Old Vic

17 Whitecote Hill, Leeds, West Yorkshire LS13 3LB
☎ *(0113) 256 1207* Craig Seddon

A freehouse with Timothy Taylor Landlord and Black Sheep Bitter among the brews always available, plus four guests from breweries such as Coach House and Hambleton.

Three rooms plus a function room decorated with old Bramley photographs. Patio. Disabled access and toilets. Situated on the outskirts of town. No food. Well-behaved children allowed.

 *4–11pm Mon–Thurs; 2–11pm Fri; 11am–11pm Sat; 12–3pm and 7–10.30pm Sun.*

LINTHWAITE

Sair Inn

Lane Top, Linthwaite, Huddersfield, West Yorkshire HD7 5SG
☎ *(01484) 842370* Ron Crabtree

Linfit beers are brewed and served on the premises.

Home of the award-winning Linfit Brewery, which began production in 1982 for the Sair Inn and free trade. The pub is a traditional eighteenth-century inn with four rooms, stone floors and open fires. Parking in road. Children allowed in any of the three rooms away from the bar.

 *7–11pm Mon–Thurs; 5–11pm Fri; 12–11pm Sat and public holidays; 12–10.30pm Sun.*

LIVERSEDGE

The Black Bull

37 Halifax Road, Liversedge, West Yorkshire WF15 6JR
☎ *(01924) 403779* Jamie Lawson

The first house owned by the Ossett Brewery, with Pale Gold, Black Bull Bitter, Excelsior and Timothy Taylor Landlord always available. Four rotating guests will include one mild.

A true, traditional ale house with two bars, beamed ceilings, real fires and a non-smoking room. Disabled access at the rear. No food. Children allowed in the afternoons only. Beer garden and car park. Accoustic live music every Tuesday. Situated out of town.

 *12–3pm and 5–11pm Mon–Tues; 12–11pm Wed–Sat; 12–10.30pm Sun.*

The Cross Keys

283 Halifax Road, Liversedge, West Yorkshire WF15 6NE
☎ *(01274) 873294* Paul George Stephenson

Marston's Bitter and Pedigree usually available.

Open-plan, community-style 100-year-old pub, with two bars. Sky TV and regular quiz nights. Food served at weekends. Beer garden, car park, children and walkers welcome.

5–11pm Mon–Fri; 12–11pm Sat–Sun.

LONGWOOD

Dusty Miller

2 Giled Road, Longwood, Huddersfield, West Yorkshire HD4
☎ *(01484) 651763* John Drummond

Black Sheep Special, Eastwood & Sanders Best and Timothy Taylor Landlord and Best always available plus a guest from Phoenix, Golden Hill or Brakspear.

A seventeenth-century village pub for real ale lovers – a drinkers' pub. No food. Children allowed. Patio.

5–11pm Mon–Fri; 11am–11pm Sat; 12–10.30pm Sun.

LUND

The Wellington Inn

19 The Green, Lund, Driffield, East Yorkshire YO25 9TE
☎ *(01377) 217294* Russell Jeffrey

A freehouse with Timothy Taylor Landlord, Black Sheep Best and Wold Top Falling Stone always available, plus one other constantly changing guest ale, usually from local Yorkshire micro-breweries.

A smart, two-bar country village pub with separate restaurant. Cask Marque accredited. York stone floors, three open log fires and small patio. Bar food available at lunchtimes and evenings. Restaurant open in the evenings.

7–11pm Mon; 12–3pm and 7–11pm Tues–Sat (10.30pm Sun).

MALTON

The Kings Head

5 Market Place, Malton, North Yorkshire YO17 7LP
☎ *(01653) 692289* Deborah Watts

One real ale always available, plus two constantly changing guests.

A refurbished modern pub with lounge bar, tap room and upstairs restaurant. A la carte menu and sandwiches available 12–3pm and 6–9pm daily. Live entertainment Fri, disco Sat. The pub is wheelchair-friendly, and children are welcome. There are plans for en-suite accommodation. Car park opposite pub.

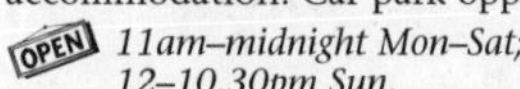
11am–midnight Mon–Sat; 12–10.30pm Sun.

Suddaby's Crown Hotel

Wheelgate, Malton, North Yorkshire YO17 7HP
☎ *(01653) 697580* RN Suddaby
www.suddabys.co.uk

Malton Double Chance, Pickwick's Porter and three other Malton Beers served on a rotational basis, plus at least one guest ale.

The Malton Brewery Company was formed in 1984 in the converted stables behind Suddaby's Crown Hotel. The first pint was pulled in February 1985. The pub is a traditional inn, full of character and located in the town centre. It is popular with locals and visitors alike. No background music or juke box, but pub games and TV showing the latest starting prices for the day's horse racing meetings. Bar food served lunchtime Sat, sandwiches available Mon–Fri lunchtimes. Parking, children's room. Accommodation.

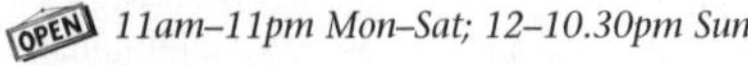
11am–11pm Mon–Sat; 12–10.30pm Sun.

MARSDEN

Riverhead Brewery Tap

2 Peel Street, Marsden, Huddersfield, West Yorkshire HD7 6BR
☎ *(01484) 841270* Philip Holdsworth

Home of the Riverhead Brewery with seven pumps selling only Riverhead ales brewed on the premises.

A real pub for drinking and chatting with no juke box or bandit machines. View into the brewery from the pub to watch the brewing. No food. Beer garden. Three hundred yards from Marsden railway station.

5–11pm Mon–Thurs (closed lunchtimes); 12–11pm Fri; 11am–11pm Sat; 12–10.30pm Sun. Open from noon during the week in July and August.

MELMERBY

The George & Dragon Inn

Main Street, Melmerby, Near Ripon, North Yorkshire HG4 5HA
☎ *(01765) 640970* Mike Halladay

A freehouse with three or four real ales always available. Hambleton Bitter and Greene King IPA are fixtures, plus a weekly changing guest.

Specialising in good ale, wine and food, this pub dates from the 1750s and has two comfortable bars and a small dining room. Real fires, no TV, games machines or juke box. Food available 6.30–9pm Tues–Thurs; 12–2pm and 6.30–9pm Fri–Sun (no food Mon). Children welcome. Car park.

5–11pm Mon–Thurs; 12–2pm and 5–11pm Fri; 12–11pm Sat–Sun.

MEXBOROUGH

The Falcon

12 Main Street, Mexborough, South Yorkshire S64 9DW
☎ *(01709) 513084* Mr Seedring

Old Mill Bitter always available plus several seasonal, celebration or guest ales.

A traditional brewery tap room situated out of the town centre. No food. No children.

All day Mon–Sat; 12–3pm and 7–10.30pm Sun.

MIDDLESBROUGH

Doctor Brown's

135 Corporation Road, Middlesbrough, North Yorkshire TS1 2RR
☎ *(01642) 213213* Tony Linklater

At least four real ales always available, including brews from Black Sheep, Cropton, Jarrow, Hadrian & Border, Wylam, York, Rudgate, Dent and other locals. Plus, from further afield, guests such as Caledonian Deuchars IPA, Greene King Abbot, Marston's Pedigree and more.

A town-centre pub, built in 1867, but a world away from the urban style bars. Live music every Fri and Sat. Food available 12–2pm Sun–Fri. Outdoor café-style seating area (weather permitting!). Disabled facilities, accompanied children for meals. The pub is within easy reach of Middlesbrough centre and Riverside Stadium.

All day, every day.

The Isaac Wilson

61 Wilson Street, Middlesbrough, North Yorkshire TS1 1SB
☎ *(01642) 247708* Norma Hardisty

Up to six guests, with Timothy Taylor Landlord a regular feature.

A town pub with food available 11am–10pm daily. No music or TV. Non-smoking area, disabled access. Children allowed 11am–5pm, if eating.

All day, every day.

NEWPORT

The Crown & Anchor

75 Main Road, Newport, Brough, East Yorkshire HU15 2PR
☎ *(01430) 449757* Phil Ellis

A freehouse, home of the Newport Brewery with a range of home ales always on offer.

A traditional village local with bar food available every evening and Fri–Sun lunchtimes. Outside seating. Children allowed until 8.30pm. Situated one mile from J38 of the M62.

 *3.30–11pm Mon–Thurs; 12–close Fri–Sun*

NORTH DUFFIELD

The King's Arms

Main Street, North Duffield, Selby, North Yorkshire YO8 5RG
☎ *(01757) 288492* Gail and Glen

A freehouse with Black Sheep Bitter always available plus up to three guests such as Timothy Taylor Landlord or ales from Greene King, Adnams or local independent brewers.

A village pub with one bar, beamed ceilings and inglenook fireplace. Bar food available, plus restaurant menu in non-smoking restaurant during evenings only. Children allowed. Beer garden.

12–11pm (10.30pm Sun).

NORTH HOWDEN

Barnes Wallis Inn

Station Road, North Howden, Nr Goole, East Yorkshire DN14 7LF
☎ *(01430) 430639* Philip Teare

Hambleton Best Bitter and Black Sheep Best Bitter regularly served, with a constantly changing range of three guest beers which are rarely repeated unless requested. Previous beers have been from Cottage, Springhead, Salamander, Goose Eye, Rudgates, Brown Cow, Rooster's and many more.

Traditional, small, real ale house with a permanent exhibition of Barnes Wallis (and other) prints. Large main garden and small sheltered one. Barbecue. Food available Sat evening and Sun lunch (bookings only). Large car park. Children welcome, but no special facilities. Situated adjacent to railway station.

5.15–11pm Tues–Fri; 12–11pm Sat; 12–10.30pm Sun.

NORTHALLERTON

Tithe Bar & Brasserie

2 Friarage Street, Northallerton, North Yorkshire DL6 1DP

☎ *(01609) 778482* Graham and Louise Caunt
www.markettowntaverns.co.uk

Timothy Taylor Landlord always available plus Caledonian Deuchars IPA most of the time. Four regularly changing guests might come from Black Sheep, Hambleton, Moorhouse's, Salamander, Rudgate, Ossett, Wentworth, Phoenix, Durham, Rooster's, Daleside, Abbeydale, Eastwood & Sanders or a range of other breweries. Plus Belgian beers.

Built in the old tithe barn of Northallerton, this is a traditional real ale house with large non-smoking area and non-smoking restaurant. Food available 12–2.30pm and 6–7.30pm Mon–Sat and 12–8pm Sun in the bar. The restaurant is open 7–9.30pm Mon–Sat. Children welcome, but not in the bar. Bar games, occasional live music. At the bottom end of town, just off the High Street.

OPEN *12–11pm (10.30pm Sun).*

OLD MIXENDEN

The Hebble Brook

2 Mill Lane, Old Mixenden, Halifax, West Yorkshire HX2 8UH

☎ *(01422) 242059* Teresa Ratcliffe

Black Sheep Special always available plus Old Mill Nellie Dean most of the time. Also up to five guests such as Thwaites Bloomin' Ale or Daniel's Hammer.

A country community pub with lounge and games room. Stone floors in the games room, open fires, wooden ceilings in lounge, garden. Food currently available at lunchtime. No children.

12–3pm and 5.30–11pm Mon–Thurs; all day Fri–Sun.

OSSETT

The Brewer's Pride

Low Mill Road, Healey Road, Ossett, West Yorkshire WF5 8ND

☎ *(01924) 273865*
Matthew Cox, Joanna Cox and Sally Hastewell

Attached to the Ossett Brewery so Excelsior and other brews always available as well as Timothy Taylor Landlord and up to four guests from breweries such as Durham, Phoenix, Rooster's and many more.

A traditional real ale house in a characterful old stone building in the old Healy Mills area. Wood and stone floors. Three rooms. Open fires, pool table in the tap room, beer garden. Brewery tours available. Food available 12–2pm Mon–Sat and Wednesday evenings 7–9.30pm. Children allowed up to 8pm. Annual August bank holiday beer festival.

OPEN *12–3pm and 5.30–11pm Mon–Thurs; all day Fri–Sun and bank holidays.*

The Red Lion

73 Dewsbury Road, Ossett, West Yorkshire WF5 9NQ

☎ *(01924) 273487* Peter Trafford

A brewpub, home of Red Lion Ales, with White Lion and at least one other home ale always available. Plus one guest which may be from breweries such as Phoenix, RCH and Rooster's.

A traditional old English pub with low ceiling, beams, brasses, dining area, and outside seating between the brewery and the pub. Food available every lunchtime and Tues–Sat evening. Sunday roasts available 12–8pm. Children allowed. Located off J40 of the M1, towards Dewsbury.

OPEN *12–11pm (10.30pm Sun).*

OUTWOOD

The Kirklands Hotel

605 Leeds Road, Outwood, Wakefield, West Yorkshire WF1 2LU

☎ *(01924) 826666* CD Cook and CE Cook

Old Mill Bitter and another Old Mill brew, changed monthly.

An olde-worlde hotel built in 1850 with open bar featuring brick fireplaces and a library plus a restaurant. Food served 12–2pm Mon, 12–2pm and 6–9pm Tues–Sat, 12–5pm Sun. Children welcome, but no special facilities. Car park. Situated on main Wakefield to Leeds road, next door to the church in Outwood. Five rooms available.

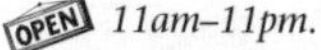

11am–11pm.

PONTEFRACT

The Counting House

Swales Yard, Pontefract, West Yorkshire WF8 1DG

☎ *(01977) 600388* Helen Clayworth

No permanent beers, just a changing range of up to eight ales from breweries such as Black Sheep, Jennings and Old Mill.

A town pub on two levels in a medieval building. Food available at lunchtime only. Children allowed.

OPEN *11am–3pm and 7–11pm (10.30pm Sun).*

POOL-IN-WHARFEDALE

The Hunter's Inn

Harrogate Road, Pool-in-Wharfedale, Nr Otley, North Yorkshire LS21 2PS
☎ *(0113) 284 1090* Geoff Nunn

Seven guest beers always available (300+ per year), including brews from Abbeydale, Black Sheep, Cropton, Daleside, Durham, Enville, Everards, Fuller's, Goose Eye, Hook Norton, Sarah Hughes, Jennings, Kelham Island, Moorhouse's, Oakham, Greene King, Rooster's, Outlaw, Ossett, Rudgate, Slaters (Eccleshall), Hambleton, Black Dog, Marston Moor and many others from all over the country.

Pub with real ale, real fire and real characters, from bikers to business people. Warm, friendly welcome. Bar food available 12–2.30pm every day except Tuesdays. Car park, garden patio with tables and chairs, pool table, juke box, stone fireplace. Children are allowed but not encouraged too much (no play area). One mile from Pool-in-Wharfedale, on the Harrogate road. Seven miles from Harrogate.

OPEN *All day, every day.*

PUDSEY

The Commercial Hotel

48 Chapetown, Pudsey, West Yorkshire LS28 8BS
☎ *(0113) 2577153* Michelle Farr

A freehouse serving a range of real ales.

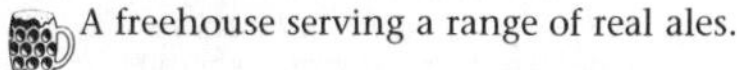

A lively town pub with Friday evening disco, Saturday evening 60s and 70s music and live entertainment once a month. Free dripping and black pudding on the bar on Sundays. Patio. No children.

OPEN *All day, every day.*

QUARMBY

Field Head

Quarmby Road, Quarmby, West Yorkshire HD3 4FB
☎ *(01484) 654581* Russ Beverly

Up to three guest ales from breweries such as Adnams, Bateman, Fuller's and Greene King.

A community village pub built 1920. Live country music on Tuesdays. No food. Children allowed. Beer garden. Car park.

OPEN *4–11pm Mon–Thurs; 3–11pm Fri; 12–11pm Sat; 12–10.30pm Sun.*

RIPON

One Eyed Rat

51 Allhallowgate, Ripon, North Yorkshire HG4 1LQ
☎ *(01765) 607704* Les Moon
www.oneeyedrat.co.uk

Timothy Taylor Landlord and Black Sheep Bitter always available, plus four guests, constantly changing, which may be from Rooster's, Durham, Hambledon, Fuller's or any other independent brewery. No beers from national breweries served. A real freehouse.

Unspoilt, terraced pub, very popular. Superb beer garden. No food, no music, no TV, but fine ales and good conversation. Children allowed in beer garden only.

OPEN *6–11pm Mon–Wed; 12–3.30pm and 6–11pm Thur; 12–3.30pm and 5.30–11pm Fri; 12–11pm Sat; 12–3.30pm and 7–10.30pm Sun.*

RIPPONDEN

The Old Bridge Inn

Priest Lane, Ripponden, Sowerby Bridge, West Yorkshire HX6 4DF
☎ *(01422) 822595* Tim and Lindsay Walker

Moorhouse's Premier, Black Sheep Best Bitter, Timothy Taylor Golden Best, Best Bitter and Landlord regularly available, plus a guest beer which might be from Old Mill, Burton Bridge, Joseph Holt, Fuller's, St Austell or Gale's.

Historic pub in lovely riverside setting. Open fires in winter and flowers in summer. Award-winning window boxes and hanging baskets all year round. Homemade food prepared on the premises: full bar menu on weekday evenings and Sat–Sun lunchtimes; help-yourself carved buffet served during the week. Car park. Children welcome until 8.30pm.

OPEN *12–3pm and 5.30–11pm Mon–Fri; 12–11pm Sat; 12–10.30pm Sun.*

ROBIN HOOD'S BAY

Victoria Hotel

Station Road, Robin Hood's Bay, North Yorkshire YO22 4RL
☎ *(01947) 880205*
Paul Goodenough and Lydia Gibson

Two brews from Camerons are always on offer, plus three frequently changing guests from a wide range of breweries.

Victorian pub with scenic views of the bay. Non-smoking and family room. Food is available. Accommodation, beer garden.

OPEN *Lunchtime and evenings Mon–Thurs; all day Fri–Sun.*

ROTHERHAM

Limes

38 Broom Lane, Rotherham, South Yorkshire
☎ *(01709) 363431* E Daykin

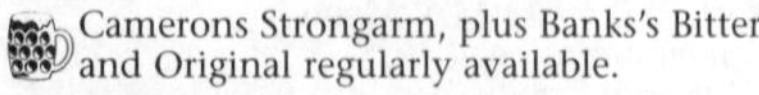
Camerons Strongarm, plus Banks's Bitter and Original regularly available.

This is a popular hotel situated on the outskirts of the town centre with a small hotel atmosphere. Food served all day, every day. Car park. Children welcome, but no special facilities.

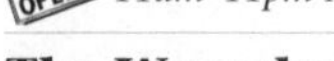
11am–11pm Mon–Sat; 12–10.30pm Sun.

The Waverley

Brinsworth Road, Catcliffe, Rotherham, South Yorkshire S60 5RW
☎ *(01709) 360906* Ron Woodthorpe

A freehouse with four hand pumps serving a range of guest brews. Regular breweries supported include Glentworth, Slaters (Eccleshall), Banks's and Timothy Taylor.

A large suburban pub with separate lounge and children's room, garden and play area. Disabled access and toilets. Food available at lunchtime and evenings. Children allowed in children's room only.

12–4pm and 6–11.30pm Mon–Fri; all day Sat; 12–4pm and 7–10.30pm Sun.

SCARBOROUGH

Cellar's

35–7 Valley Road, Scarborough, North Yorkshire YO11 2LX
☎ *(01723) 367158* Brian Witty

Black Sheep Bitter permanently available, plus two constantly changing guests. Ales from Archers, Slaters, Durham and Rooster's are regularly featured.

A basement real ale bar with holiday flats and a restaurant above. Beer garden and patio, past winner of Scarborough in Bloom Award. Bar food available 5–9pm Mon–Sat and 12–5pm Sun. Children allowed. Live music on Saturdays.

Summer: 11am–11pm Mon–Sat; 12–10.30pm Sun. Winter: 4–11pm (10.30pm Sun).

The Cricketers

119 North Marine Road, Scarborough, North Yorkshire YO1 7HU
☎ *(01723) 365864* Stuart Neilson

Caledonian Deuchars IPA and Timothy Taylor Landlord regularly available, plus three constantly changing guest ales. Also Weston's Old Rosie Cloudy Scrumpy and Hoegaarden available on hand pump.

A friendly real ale pub for anyone. Two bars, sea views, beer garden. Food, specialising in steaks, chilli and Stuart's Steak and Ale Pie, available until 9pm daily. Children allowed. Disabled access and facilities. Situated opposite the Cricket Ground.

12–11pm Mon–Fri; 11am-11pm Sat; 12–10.30pm Sun.

The Highlander Hotel

15–16 The Esplanade, Scarborough, North Yorkshire YO11 2AF
☎ *(01723) 373426* Jim Hobbs
www.thehighlanderhotel.co.uk

Six ales always available, including Greene King IPA plus guests such as Everards Tiger, Shepherd Neame Spitfire, Young's Special, Marston's Pedigree, Charles Wells Bombardier and Bateman's XXB. Plus a large range of whiskies.

On the South Cliff Esplanade, a traditional pub with real fires and real atmosphere. Food available at lunchtime only in a separate dining area. Children allowed until 6pm. Patio. Accommodation.

11am–11pm (10.30pm Sun).

The Hole in the Wall

26–30 Vernon Road, Scarborough, North Yorkshire YO11 2PS
☎ *(01723) 373746* Cheryll Roberts

Four to six guest beers on offer each month, from breweries such as Caledonian, Jennings, Ridleys, Brains, Gale's, Everards, Hydes, Charles Wells, St Austell, Brakspear, Old Mill, Smiles, Aviemore, Bateman and Timothy Taylor, to name but a few!

A traditional wooden-floored real ale pub in a town location. No music, no games. Home-cooked pub grub available all day Mon–Sat, and Sun 12–3pm. Children welcome until 8pm if eating. Dogs welcome.

11am–11pm Mon–Sat; 12–10.30pm Sun.

Indigo Alley

4 North Marine Road, Scarborough, North Yorkshire YO12 7PD
☎ *(01723) 381900* Graham Forrest

A freehouse with six regularly changing guest beers perhaps from Rooster's, Timothy Taylor, Kelham Island or Hambleton, but could be from anywhere in the UK (over 1,000 different ones in three years). Belgian beers such as Leffe (Brun and Blond) and Hoegaarden also stocked.

Wooden-floored, town-centre bar specialising in ever-changing guest beers and live music on Tues, Wed, Thurs and Sun evenings. No food. No children.

3–11pm Mon–Fri; 1–11pm Sat; 1–10.30pm Sun. Extra hours Fri–Sun Jun–Sept.

Old Scalby Mills Hotel

Scalby Mills Road, Scarborough, North Yorkshire YO12 6RP
☎ *(01723) 500449* Keith Dufton

Five real ales usually available. Brains Reverend James and Wychwood Hobgoblin are pemanent fixtures while the three guests come from a wide range of breweries.

A seaside freehouse built in a 400-year-old watermill with the Cleveland Way behind it. Two bars, original stonework and beams. Outside seating areas. Food available 12–6pm. Children allowed until 6pm. Dogs allowed in the smaller of the two bars. Situated near the Sea Life Centre.

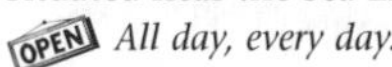 *All day, every day.*

Scholars Bar

Somerset Terrace, Scarborough, North Yorkshire
☎ *(01723) 360084* John Bingham

Four real ales always available, including York Yorkshire Terrier, Charles Wells Bombardier and something from Durham.

Hotel bar featuring a large drinking area with library bar and separate drinking area for those in the know! Home-cooked food served lunchtimes and evenings. Regular jazz club. On the town side of the Bedford Hotel.

 *12–3pm and 5.30–11pm Mon–Thurs; 12–11pm Fri–Sat; 12–10.30pm Sun.*

The Tap & Spile

94 Falsgrave Road, Scarborough, North Yorkshire YO12 5AZ
☎ *(01723) 363837* IM Kilpatrick and V Office

Big Lamp Bitter, Everards Tiger, Timothy Taylor Landlord and Caledonian Deuchars IPA, plus up to five guest beers and a real cider.

A lovely old coaching inn with low beams, old Yorkshire stone floor and non-smoking room. Bar food available 11.30am–3pm Mon–Fri, 11.30am–4.30pm Sat, 12.30–3pm Sun. Car park, garden, children's room. Turn left out of the railway station, going towards the roundabout.

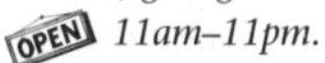 *11am–11pm.*

The Valley Bar

51 Valley Road, Scarborough, North Yorkshire YO11 2LX
☎ *(01723) 372593* Linda and John Soden

Harviestoun Bitter and Twisted and a Theakston brew always available, plus two guests often from local micro-breweries.

A basement bar in a Victorian villa. Live music, quiz nights, occasional theatrical performances and large-screen TV. Pool and function room. Home-cooked food (fresh fish) served at lunchtime and evenings. Ten guest rooms.

OPEN *12–11pm (10.30pm Sun).*

SELBY

The Albion Vaults

1 The Crescent, New Street, Selby, North Yorkshire YO8 4PT
☎ *(01757) 213817* Patrick Mellors

An Old Mill Brewery tied house serving only Old Mill ales. Old Traditional and Bullion always available, plus either Old Curiosity, Springs Eternal or Nellie Dean.

An old dark-wood pub with brick fireplaces, taproom and lounge. Beer garden, disabled access. Food available at lunchtime and evenings. Organises brewery tours of The Old Mill Brewery, which is four miles away, during October–April. Children allowed up to 7pm.

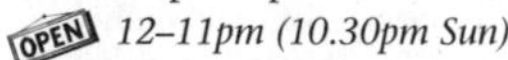 *12–11pm (10.30pm Sun).*

The Royal Oak

70 Ousegate, Selby, North Yorkshire YO8 4NJ
☎ *(01757) 291163* Simon Compton

Three guest pumps with ales such as Timothy Taylor Landlord or Eccleshall Top Totty.

A real ale pub comprising a balance of the traditional and the modern: live music in a Grade II listed building with wooden floors and original beams. Beer garden. No food. Children allowed on Sunday afternoons only.

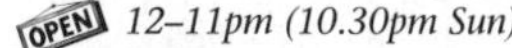 *12–11pm (10.30pm Sun).*

SHEFFIELD

The Broadfield

Abbeydale Road, Sheffield, South Yorkshire S7 1FR
☎ *(0114) 255 0200*
Hannah Creasy and Martin Bedford

Guests such as Greene King Old Speckled Hen, Wadworth 6X and brews from Kelham Island and Black Sheep are served. Only popular beers, such as Kelham Island Pale Rider, are repeated, and requests are encouraged!

A two-bar pub with snooker and pool room and beer garden. Just out of the town centre. Food available 12–7pm daily, plus Sunday breakfast at 11am. Children allowed if eating.

OPEN *11am–11pm Mon–Sat; 11am (for breakfast)–10.30pm Sun.*

Cask & Cutler

1 Henry Street, Infirmary Road, Sheffield, South Yorkshire S3 7EQ
☎ *(0114) 249 2295* Neil Clarke

Up to nine regularly changing guest beers (5,000 beers served to date), including a pale, hoppy bitter, a mild and a stout or porter. Beers are mainly from Durham, Glentworth, Archers, Pictish, Eastwood & Sanders, Wye Valley, Ossett and Oldershaw, plus seasonal specials from all over the country. No nationals. Also serve Weston's Old Rosie cider and a range of over 30 Belgian bottled beers. There is a micro-brewery at the rear of the pub which brews on a small scale, mainly for festivals.

A largely unspoilt street-corner local with two rooms, one non-smoking. Sheffield CAMRA Pub of the Year 2001 (also 1995 and 1999). No music or fruit machines. On-street parking. Real fire in cold weather. Beer garden. Situated 100 yards from Shalesmoor supertram stop. Adjacent to junction of A61 and B6079, one mile north of the city centre.

 *5.30–11pm Mon; 12–2pm and 5.30–11pm Tues–Thur; 12–11pm Fri–Sat; 12–3pm and 7–10.30pm Sun.*

East House

19 Spital Hill, Sheffield, South Yorkshire S4 7LG
☎ *(0114) 272 6916* Rita Fielding

A freehouse with Timothy Taylor Landlord and Abbeydale Moonshine among the beers always available, plus one guest such as Greene King Old Speckled Hen or Timothy Taylor Dark Mild or Golden Best.

A student pub, situated conveniently close to the local curry houses! No food. Children allowed until 8pm.

 *Closed during day; 6–11pm Mon–Sat; 7–10.30pm Sun.*

The Fat Cat

12

23 Alma Street, Sheffield, South Yorkshire S3 8SA
☎ *(0114) 249 4801*
www.thefatcat.co.uk

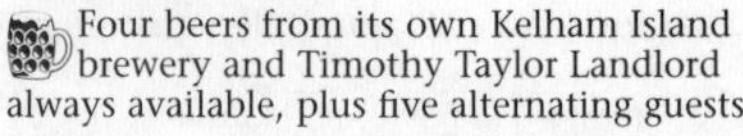

Four beers from its own Kelham Island brewery and Timothy Taylor Landlord always available, plus five alternating guests.

This olde-worlde pub is a Kelham Island Brewery tap, situated a short walk from the city centre, with separate smoking and non-smoking rooms. Voted one of the top five urban pubs in Britain in *The Times,* 1999 and UK Cask Ale Pub of the Year 2004 in *The Morning Advertiser.* No music, no fruit machines. Award-winning home-cooked food is served at lunchtimes, and always includes vegetarian and vegan dishes. Beer garden, open fires. Children- and animal-friendly. Privately owned and fiercely independent!

 *12–3pm and 5.30–11pm Mon–Thurs; 12–11pm Fri–Sat; 12–3pm and 7–10.30pm Sun.*

The Frog & Parrot

Division Street, Sheffield, South Yorkshire S1 4GF
☎ *(0114) 272 1280* Nick Simmonite

A brewpub with Roger and Out (formerly the *Guinness Book of Records* World's Strongest Beer!) always available in third-of-a pint measures, plus Timothy Taylor Landlord, Black Sheep Bitter and Greene King IPA. The two ever-changing guest ales will be from regional and micro-breweries around the country. Hoegaarden and the occasional cask-conditional lager also served.

Traditional, but light and airy, town pub in the heart of the cosmopolitan Devonshire Quarter. Good food served 12–8pm every day, and 'free trade' coffee is always available. Located 100 yards from West Street Supertram stop.

OPEN *11am–11pm (10.30pm Sun).*

The Gardener's Rest

105 Neepsend Lane, Sheffield, South Yorkshire S3 8AT
☎ *(0114) 272 4978* Pat Wilson

Timothy Taylor Landlord, Golden Best, Dark Mild and Best Bitter, Wentworth Needle's Eye and WPA (Wentworth Pale Ale) permanently available, plus four guests from breweries all over the UK plus some from France and Belgium. There is always a wheat and a fruit beer on.

A traditional backstreet pub with modern conservatory and beer garden on the river bank. No juke box but traditional pub games like bar billiards. Disabled access and facilities, non-smoking room. No food. Close to city centre and on bus and tram routes, but ring for directions if necessary.

OPEN *12–11pm (10.30pm Sun).*

The Hillsborough Hotel

54–8 Langsett Road, Sheffield, South Yorkshire S6 2UB
☎ *(0114) 232 2100* Carol Jamieson
www.hillsboroughhotel.com

Owned by the Edale Brewing Company and home of the Wellington (formerly Crown) Brewery with up to eight beers always available. Loxley Gold, Stannington Stout and Hillsborough Pale Ale are brewed on the premises. Edale's Kinder range also available plus guests. Annual beer festival.

A six-room hotel with a dedicated real ale bar run by enthusiasts. Renamed five years ago having been called the Hero and his Horse and then the Wellington. Quiet, traditional atmosphere with no juke box. Baguettes and bar snacks available all opening hours, with a more extensive menu for residents. Well-behaved children allowed. Sun terrace and conservatory. On the super-tram route. Available for private functions.

OPEN *4.30–11pm Thurs–Sun only, plus seven-day residency.*

Kelham Island Tavern

62 Russell Street, Sheffield, South Yorkshire S3 8RW
☎ *(0114) 272 2482*

Up to eight real ales including Barnsley Bitter, Pictish Brewer's Gold and at least one mild.

Rejuvenated pub close to the river. No music or games machines. Food served at lunchtimes. Outside seating.

 *3–11pm Mon; 12–11pm Tues–Sat; 12–3pm and 7–10.30pm Sun.*

The New Barrack Tavern

601 Penistone Road, Sheffield, South Yorkshire S6 2GA
☎ *(0114) 234 9148*

Abbeydale Moonshine, Wentworth WPA, Barnsley Bitter and five guest beers usually available. Breweries featured include Abbeydale, Wentworth, Rooster's, Wye Valley, Kelham Island, Concertina, Swale, Ossett, Rudgate, Okells, Timothy Taylor, Brakspear, Holt, Hydes Anvil, Woodforde's, Beartown, Cains, Oakham, Skinner's, Hop Back, Daleside and many others.

Large, award-winning pub offering a wide selection of draught and bottled beers and excellent food. Regular live music. Non-smoking room and attractive beer garden. Food served 12–2.30pm and 6–8pm Mon–Fri, 12–2.30pm Sat–Sun. Children welcome in the back room and beer garden only.

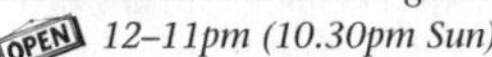 *12–11pm (10.30pm Sun).*

The Old Grindstone

3 Crookes, Sheffield, South Yorkshire S10 1UA
☎ *(0114) 266 0322* Dave Ogden

Up to six guest ales on offer, from a varied range from around the country. Timothy Taylor Landlord, Black Sheep Bitter and Fuller's London Pride are among the likely candidates.

A one-bar local community pub with three log fires. Food available 12–7.45pm Mon–Fri and 12–6.45pm Sat–Sun. Children welcome if dining only.

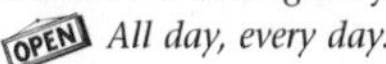 *All day, every day.*

Sheaf View Hotel

25 Gleadless Road, Sheffield, South Yorkshire S2 3AA
☎ *(0114) 249 6455* Alex Tuttle

Barnsley Bitter, Abbeydale Moonshine and Wentworth WPA always available plus up to five guest ales which may be Pictish Celtic Warrior or a brew from Springhead, Phoenix, Glentworth, Berrow, Rudgate or Townes.

A community pub. No food. Non-smoking conservatory. Children allowed in the garden only. Car park. Can be difficult to find so call for directions.

12–11pm (10.30pm Sun).

SHIPLEY

Fanny's Ale & Cider House

63 Saltaire Road, Shipley, Nr Bradford, West Yorkshire
☎ *(01274) 591419* S Marcus Lund

Timothy Taylor Golden Best and Landlord regularly available, plus eight guest beers such as Fuller's London Pride, Timothy Taylor Ram Tam, Black Sheep Bitter, Glentworth Whispers, Daleside Monkey Wrench, Rooster's Yankee or Cream and many others.

Olde-worlde alehouse with wooden floorboards and open fire, full of brewery memorabilia. Gas lighting still used in the lounge bar. Extra seating area upstairs. Free car park nearby. Children welcome at lunchtimes only.

 *5–11pm Mon; 11.30am–11pm Tues–Sat; 12–10.30pm Sun.*

SKIPTON

The Narrow Boat

38 Victoria Street, Skipton, North Yorkshire BD23 1JE
☎ *(01756) 797922* Ian Reid
www.markettowntaverns.co.uk

Timothy Taylor Landlord, Black Sheep Bitter, Caledonian Deuchars IPA and something from the local Copper Dragon brewery always available, plus five regularly changing guests, from local breweries whenever possible. Also Erdinger WeissBier (a Belgian ale), a guest Belgian beer and a range of Belgian bottled beers.

A traditional ale and wine bar with a non-smoking bar area – smoking is permitted in the gallery upstairs. Food available every day 12–3pm and 5–8pm Sun–Thurs. Children allowed. Situated on a quiet cobbled street off the high street, close to the canal basin and train station.

12–11pm (10.30pm Sun).

SOWERBY BRIDGE

The Moorcock Inn

Norland, Sowerby Bridge, West Yorkshire HX6 3RP
☎ *(01422) 832103* Mr Kitson

A freehouse with Samuel Smith Old Brewery Bitter always available plus two guest ales including, perhaps, Coach House Innkeeper's Special Reserve or Phoenix Old Oak Bitter.

A one-bar country pub with wooden beams, restaurant and outside area. Food available at lunchtime and evenings. Children allowed. Disabled access.

12–3pm and 5.30–11pm (10.30pm Sun).

The Moorings

Canal Basin, Sowerby Bridge, West Yorkshire HX6 2AG
☎ *(01422) 833940* Emma O'Connell

Black Sheep Special and Greene King Ruddles County always available plus two constantly changing guests.

A medium-sized pub with good quality beers, food and service. Cask Marque approved. Beams, stone walls, wooden floors. Seating on canal side. Food available at lunchtime and evenings. Children allowed if dining.

 *12–11pm (10.30pm Sun).*

The Navigation Inn

Chapel Lane, Sowerby Bridge, West Yorkshire HX6 3LF
☎ *(01422) 831636* Trish Rushforth

Eastwood & Sanders Best Bitter and Black Sheep Bitter are among the beers usually available, plus guests, often other Eastwood & Sanders brews such as Nettlethrasher and Bargee.

A charming canalside pub with historic fireplace dating from before 1722. Beer garden. Homemade food available 12–2.30pm and 5.30–8.30pm Mon–Sat and 1–6pm Sun.

 *12–3pm and 5.30–11pm Mon–Thurs; 11am–11pm Fri–Sat; 12–10.30pm Sun.*

STAITHES

Captain Cook Inn

60 Staithes Lane, Staithes, Saltburn-by-the-Sea TS13 5AD
☎ *(01947) 840200*
www.captaincookinn.co.uk

Daleside Bitter and a range of guest brews from microbreweries in the Midlands. An annual beer festival in aid of the local lifeboat station is held, usually on the last weekend of July.

Formerly the Station Hotel, set in the fishing village that was home to Captain Cook. Food served in the evenings at weekends only. Children welcome. Garden and accommodation.

 *11am–11pm Mon–Sat, 12–10.30pm Sun.*

STAVELEY

The Royal Oak

Main Street, Staveley, Nr Knaresborough, North Yorkshire HG5 9LD
☎ *(01423) 340267*

Four beers always available plus two guests (25 per year) from small independent breweries.

A typical country pub, cosy, friendly, with open fires and two bars. Bar and restaurant food available at lunchtime and evenings Tues–Sat, and 12–8pm Sun (no food on Monday). Car park, garden, children's play area.

 *12–3pm and 5–11pm Mon–Sat; 12–10.30pm Sun.*

STOKESLEY

The White Swan

1 West End, Stokesley, Middlesbrough, North Yorkshire TS9 5BL
☎ *(01642) 710263* Brian and Julie Skipp

A brewpub with the full range of Captain Cook Brewery beers brewed on site and always available in the pub. Also guests such as Castle Eden Ale.

A market town pub with one bar, open fire, background music and traditional pub games. Brewery on premises, tours available. Ploughman's, homemade pâtés and bar snacks available 12–2.30pm (not Sun).

 *11.30am–3pm and 5.30–11pm Mon–Fri; 11–3pm and 7–11pm Sat; 11–3pm and 7–10.30pm Sun.*

SUTTON UPON DERWENT

St Vincent Arms

Main Street, Sutton upon Derwent, East Yorkshire
☎ *(01904) 608349* Philip Hopwood

Fuller's Chiswick, London Pride and ESB and Timothy Taylor Landlord always available plus guests including Adnams Extra, Old Mill Bitter, Charles Wells Bombardier and seasonal and special ales.

About 200 years old, with white-washed walls. Two bars, four rooms, open fires. Bar and restaurant food available at lunchtime and evenings. Car park, beer garden, non-smoking room. Children allowed. On main road through village.

 *11.30am–3pm and 6–11pm Mon–Sat; 12–3pm and 7–10.30pm Sun.*

THORNE

Canal Tavern

South Parade, Thorne, Doncaster, South Yorkshire DN8 5DZ
☎ *(01405) 813688* D and D Merrington

A freehouse with three guest ales changing weekly and not repeated if at all possible. Examples have included Thwaites Bloomin' Ale, Greene King Triumph and Marston's Pedigree.

A two-bar canalside country pub with dining area. Coal fires in winter, waterside beer garden. Food available at lunchtime and evenings. Children allowed, if eating.

OPEN *All day, every day.*

THORNTON-IN-LONSDALE

The Marton Arms Hotel

Thornton-in-Lonsdale, Nr Ingleton, North Yorkshire LA6 3PB
☎ *(01524) 241281*
Graham Wright and Karen Plant
www.martonarms.co.uk

A freehouse with 15 real ales always on offer. The selection changes every week but Timothy Talor Golden Best, Caledonian Deuchars IPA and Cains Mild are fixtures. Also a selection of over 300 malt whiskies available.

Seventeenth-century coaching inn, now a Grade II listed country house hotel with 12 rooms. Bar billiards, non-smoking area, patio and garden. Children allowed. Car parking. Handy for the Three Peaks in classic Yorkshire Dales country.

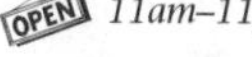
11am–11pm Mon–Sat; 12–10.30pm Sun.

THRESHFIELD

Old Hall Inn

Threshfield, Grassington, Skipton, North Yorkshire
☎ *(01756) 752441* Ronald C Matthews

Timothy Taylor Best Bitter and Landlord regularly available.

Traditional country pub with dining room, patio and beer garden. Food served 12–2pm and 6–9.30pm daily. Car park. Children welcome.

12–3pm and 6–11.30pm Mon–Sat; 12–3pm and 7–10.30pm Sun.

TOCKWITH

The Spotted Ox

Westfield Road, Tockwith, York, North Yorkshire YO26 7PY
☎ *(01423) 358387* Terry and Sue Fellows

A freehouse with a selection of three real ales always available. Timothy Taylor Landlord is among the regulars, plus a weekly changing guest.

A country pub with a snug and tap room. Food available at lunchtime and evenings every day. Beer garden, car park. Forge for hire to the rear. Children allowed. Handy for Wetherby racecourse.

Lunchtime and evenings Mon–Weds; all day Thurs–Sat.

TODMORDEN

Masons

1 Bacup Road, Todmorden, West Yorkshire OL14 7AN
☎ *(01706) 812180* Steve Cranie

Copper Dragon Best Bitter permanently available plus two guests from breweries such as Phoenix, Archers or Moorhouse's.

A traditional drinkers' pub dating from 1830. Beamed ceiling, fireplace. No food. Children allowed. Small beer garden. Pool, darts, Sky TV. Close to Rochdale Canal.

3–11pm Mon–Fri; 12–11pm Sat; 12–10.30pm Sun.

UPPERTHONG

The Royal Oak

19 Towngate, Upperthong, Holmfirth, West Yorkshire HD9 3UX
☎ *(01484) 680568* David Sutton

Timothy Taylor Landlord and Adnams Bitter are usually available, although the landlord might replace the Adnams with a guest if he is in the mood!

A 200-year-old village pub with beamed ceiling and fireplaces. Food available in the non-smoking conservatory, which seats 36, on Tues–Sat evenings (5–9pm) and 12–4pm Sun. Children allowed. garden. Car park. Call for directions.

5–11pm Mon–Sat; 12–10.30pm Sun.

WAKEFIELD

Fernandes Brewery Tap

5 Avison Yard, Kirkgate, Wakefield WF1 1UA
☎ *(01924 369547)* David and Maureen James

Two or three Fernandes brews (including mild) available at any one time plus several guests (approx 500 a year).

Former storeroom for Beverley's Brewery, the micro-brewery was opened in 1997 and the one-bar Brewery Tap on the upper floor two years later. Louis Fernandes built a malt kiln on the site in 1822. Belgian beers, fruit wines and cider. No music, no fruit machines.

5–11pm Mon–Thurs; 11am–11pm Fri–Sat; 12–10.30pm Sun.

The White Hart

77 Westgate End, Wakefield, West Yorkshire WF2 9RL
☎ *(01924) 375887* Ian Bain

Four real ales always available perhaps including Greene King Abbot and IPA, Timothy Taylor Landlord and Rooster's Yankee.

A traditional alehouse with flagstone floors and real log fires in winter. Changed hands in November 2003. All-year-round beer garden, which is covered and heated in winter. Large-screen TV. Children welcome. Five minutes from the station.

12pm–12am (10.30pm Sun).

WALSDEN

The Cross Keys Inn

649 Rochdale Road, Walsden, Todmorden, West Yorkshire
☎ *(01706) 815185* Ken Muir

Timothy Taylor Landlord, Black Sheep Bitter, Charles Wells Bombardier and three weekly changing guest beers usually available.

Lively pub, set on the side of the Rochdale Canal. Food served 12–2pm and 5–8pm Mon–Sat, 12–8pm Sun. Children welcome.

OPEN *12–11pm (10.30pm Sun).*

WEAVERTHORPE

Star Country Inn

Weaverthorpe, Malton, North Yorkshire YO17 8EY
☎ *(01944) 738273* Kate and Mike Baker

Freehouse with four real ales usually available. Wold Top Bitter is a fixture, plus a weekly changing guest.

Traditional country inn, well known locally for good food. Food served 12–2pm every day except Tues and 7–9pm every day except Tues and Sun. Car park. Children welcome, but no special facilities. Accommodation. Four miles from the A64.

7–11pm Mon–Fri; 12–4pm and 7–11pm Sat; 12–4pm and 7–10.30pm Sun.

WENTWORTH

The George & Dragon

85 Main Street, Wentworth, Rotherham, South Yorkshire S62 7TN
☎ *(01226) 742440* Suzanne Jemison

A freehouse always serving Timothy Taylor Landlord, Wentworth IPA and Stout plus a good selection of up to five guests, not repeated if possible, from breweries such as Ossett, Slaters, Springhead, Mighty Oak, Archers, Abbeydale and Kelham Island.

An ward-winning country village pub with two bars, two real fires and stone floors. Food served 11am–2.30pm Mon–Fri, 10am–9pm Sat and 10am–7pm Sun in a separate dining area. Barbecues in summer. Large beer garden with children's play area. Function room available for private hire. Children allowed if eating. Beer festival held every February.

OPEN *10am–11pm (10.30pm Sun).*

WHITBY

Tap & Spile

New Quay Road, Whitby, North Yorkshire YO21 1DH
☎ *(01947) 603937* Peter Fleming

Black Sheep Bitter and Greene King Old Speckled Hen among the beers always available, plus up to three guests. Celebration and seasonal ales served where possible. Lindisfarne fruit wine and Old Rosie traditional cider also on offer.

A two-bar, three-roomed town pub with wooden floors and beams and one non-smoking room. No juke box or pool tables etc. Food available every day from 12–7pm (4pm on Sun). Children allowed in the family room until 9pm. Entertainment most nights (music on Mon, Tues, Wed and Fri at 9pm; quiz on Thurs at 9.30pm; open folk session on Sun at 8.30pm). Located opposite the railway station.

OPEN *All day, every day. Closed 4.30–7pm Sun in winter.*

WOMBWELL

Royal Oak Hotel

13 Burch Street, Wombwell, South Yorkshire
☎ *(01254) 883541* Helen Jones

Five real ales available from a long list including, perhaps, Bateman brews.

A 1920s-style town-centre pub. Bar food available at lunchtime and evenings. Car park, accommodation. Children allowed at restricted times.

OPEN *11am–11pm Mon–Sat; 12–10.30pm Sun.*

WORTLEY

Wortley Arms Hotel

Halifax Road, Wortley, South Yorkshire S35 7DB
☎ *(0114) 288 2245* Brian Morrisey

Timothy Taylor Landlord, Wortley Bitter, Oakwell Barnsley Bitter, Black Sheep Bitter and Riggwelter plus Castle Rock Dark Gold always available, with a guest from Castle Rock. There is a Wildlife Beer of the Month, with a contribution going to the local Wildlife Trust for every pint drunk. Also offers the widest selection of malt whiskies in the area and Weston's real cider on hand pump.

A classic sixteenth-century coaching inn with inglenook fireplace. No background music, no gaming machines. Food served 12–8.30pm Mon–Sat and 12–6.30pm Sun. Car park, children's room, non-smoking room. En-suite accommodation. Popular with walkers and cyclists on Trans-Pennine and Timberland trails.

OPEN *12–11pm (10.30pm Sun).*

YORK

The Ackhorne

9 St Martins Lane, York YO1 6LN
(01904) 671421 Jack Merry

Rooster's Yankee and Caledonian Deuchars IPA plus three guest ales. Regular appearances by Jennings, Hambleton, Wychwood and many others. There is usually a mild available. Plus Weston's Old Rosie cider and a range of foreign bottled beers.

Tucked away down a cobbled alley at the bottom of Micklegate this is a town-centre local. No music or TV, instead there are pub games and conversation! Outside patio to the rear. Food available 12–2.30pm Mon–Sat. Well-behaved children allowed in the lounge or garden areas. Dogs allowed if well-behaved. Located at the bottom of Micklegate, close to the junction with Rougier Street is St Martin's Church. The pub is on the cobbled lane next to the church.

OPEN *12–11pm (10.30pm Sun).*

The Blue Bell

53 Fossgate, York, North Yorkshire YO1 9TF
(01904) 654904 Jim Hardie

Camerons Strongarm Ruby Red, Timothy Taylor Landlord, Greene King Abbot, Caledonian Deuchars IPA and Adnams Bitter always available, plus rotating guests.

The smallest pub in York with an original, untouched, Edwardian interior which dates from 1903, but has been cleaned since! No juke box. Substantial sandwiches available 11am–6pm. No children.

OPEN *11am–11pm Mon–Sat; 12–10.30pm Sun.*

Last Drop Inn

27 Colliergate, York, North Yorkshire
(01904) 621951 Mr and Mrs DE Morgan

York Brewery's first pub, serving Stonewall, Yorkshire Terrier, Centurian's Ghost, Bitter and a seasonal ale, plus one guest beer changed twice a week.

Opened in 2000, this pub has a friendly atmosphere, with wooden floors and panelling. Bar area and lower lounge area. Food available 12–4pm. Situated in the historic heart of York near the top of The Shambles. No juke box, no TV, no children, no pool or darts.

OPEN *All day, every day.*

The Maltings

Tanners Moat, York, North Yorkshire YO1 16HU
(01904) 655387 Maxine Collinge
www.maltings.co.uk

Black Sheep Bitter always available plus six guests changing daily (700 per year). Too many to mention but with an emphasis on small, independent brewers. Beer festivals twice a year. Also Belgian bottled and draught beers, fruit wines and four traditional ciders.

Small city-centre freehouse. Pub grub served at lunchtime. Situated on Lendal Bridge.

OPEN *11am–11pm Mon–Sat; 12–10.30pm Sun.*

Rook and Gaskill

12 Lawrence Street, York, North Yorkshire YO10 3WP
(01904) 674067 Heidi Watkinson

York Brewery pub serving up to four York beers including Terrier, Centurion's Ghost and Stonewall, plus seasonal brews and up to five guests including Caledonian Deuchars IPA and something from Castle Rock.

Locals' pub just outside the city walls, with wooden floor and panelling.No music, children, darts or pool. Food available 12–3pm and 6–8.30pm Tues–Thurs, 12–3pm Fri–Sun. Rook and Gaskill were the last two people to be hanged in York, for stealing sheep. Located outside the city walls, near the Barbican Centre.

OPEN *All day, every day.*

Spread Eagle

98 Walmgate, York, North Yorkshire
(01904) 635868 Ian Taylor

Six beers always available, including Marston's Pedigree, Mansfield Riding Bitter, Banks's Bitter and Original Mild, something from Camerons, plus guests.

Refurbished Victorian-style pub. Full menu available daytimes. Live bands Sunday lunchtimes and weekend evenings. Garden. Children allowed at restricted times.

OPEN *11.30am–11pm Mon–Sat;
12–10.30pm Sun.*

The Tap & Spile

29 Monkgate, York, North Yorkshire
☎ *(01904) 656158* Melanie Merry

Six cask ales always available, with Rooster's Yankee a permanent feature, and Caledonian Deuchars IPA and something from Rudgate usually available. There are regular appearances from Big Lamp, Jennings and Robinson's, to name but a few. Weston's Old Rosie and fruit wines also served.

A traditional pub, with food served Tues–Sun lunchtimes, plus traditional roasts on Sundays. Tea and coffee available all day. Car park, beer garden. Cask Marque accredited. CAMRA award-winning.

OPEN *11.30am–11pm Mon–Sat; 12–10.30pm Sun.*

Three-Legged Mare

18 High Petergate, York, North Yorkshire YO1 7EN
☎ *(01904) 638246* James Butler

York Brewery pub offering Stonewall, Yorkshire Terrier and Centurion's Ghost plus seasonal brews and guests from Castle Rock and elsewhere.

Opened in 2001, a pub combining the traditional values of a local with a cosmopolitan atmosphere. No games machines, TV, juke box or children. For discerning drinkers only. Conservatory and outside drinking area. Award-winning sandwiches served 12–3pm daily. Round the corner from the Minster.

OPEN *All day, every day.*

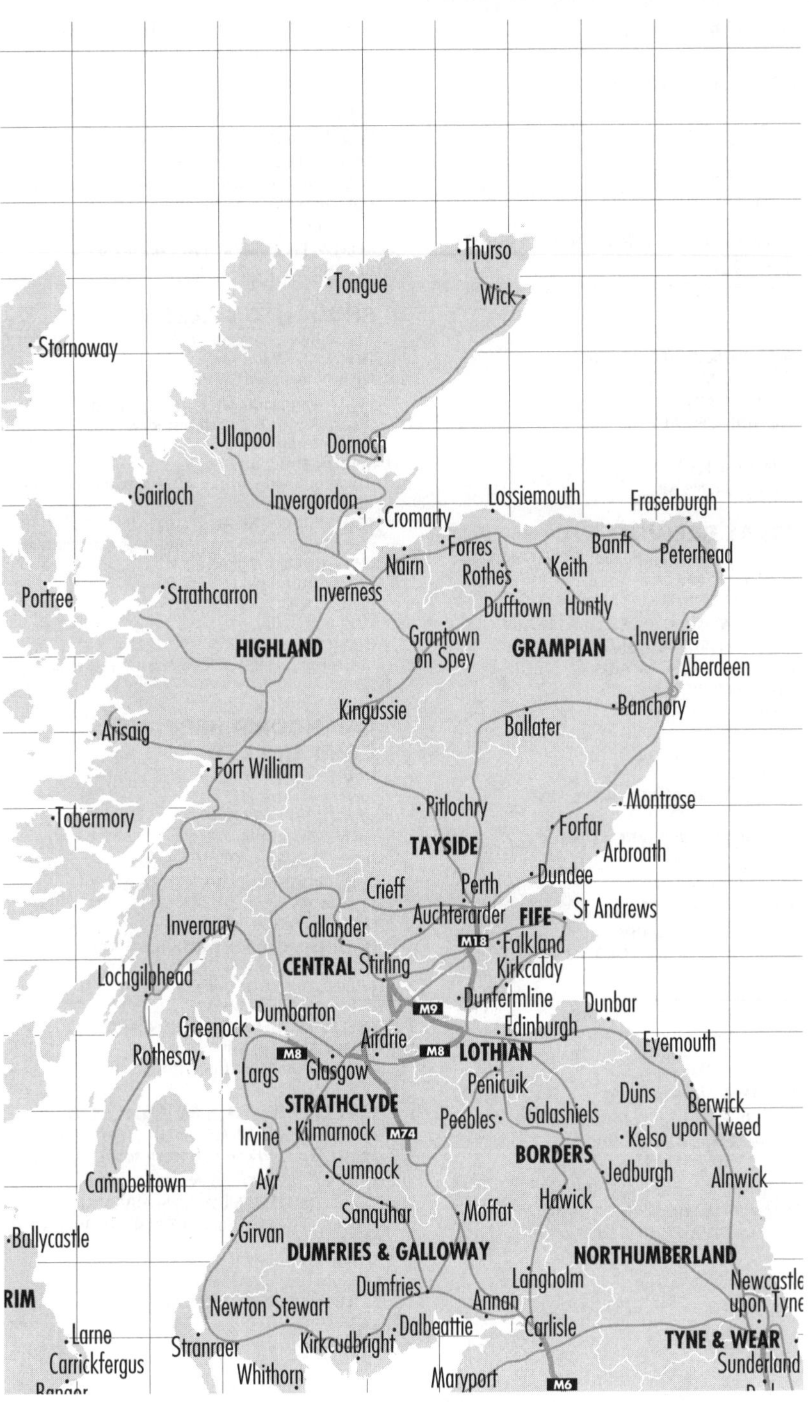
Thurso
Tongue
Wick
Stornoway
Ullapool
Dornoch
Gairloch
Invergordon
Cromarty
Lossiemouth
Fraserburgh
Forres
Banff
Nairn
Rothes
Keith
Peterhead
Portree
Strathcarron
Inverness
Dufftown
Huntly
Grantown on Spey
HIGHLAND
GRAMPIAN
Inverurie
Aberdeen
Kingussie
Banchory
Ballater
Arisaig
Fort William
Pitlochry
Montrose
Tobermory
Forfar
TAYSIDE
Arbroath
Dundee
Crieff
Perth
St Andrews
Auchterarder
FIFE
Inveraray
Callander
M18
Falkland
CENTRAL
Stirling
Kirkcaldy
Lochgilphead
Dunfermline
Dunbar
M9
Dumbarton
Greenock
Edinburgh
Eyemouth
Airdrie
M8
M8
LOTHIAN
Rothesay
Largs
Glasgow
Penicuik
STRATHCLYDE
Duns
Berwick upon Tweed
Galashiels
Peebles
Irvine
Kilmarnock
M74
Kelso
BORDERS
Cumnock
Jedburgh
Alnwick
Ayr
Campbeltown
Hawick
Sanquhar
Moffat
Ballycastle
Girvan
DUMFRIES & GALLOWAY
NORTHUMBERLAND
Langholm
Newcastle upon Tyne
Dumfries
RIM
Annan
Newton Stewart
Dalbeattie
Carlisle
Larne
TYNE & WEAR
Carrickfergus
Stranraer
Kirkcudbright
Sunderland
Whithorn
Maryport
M6

THE BREWERIES

AN TEALLACH ALE

Camusnagaul, Dundonnell, Garve, Ross-shire, Highlands & Islands IV23 2QT
☎ *(01854) 633306*

BEINN DERAG 3.8% ABV
ANTEALLACH ALE 4.2% ABV

THE ISLE OF ARRAN BREWERY CO LTD

Cladach, Brodick, Isle of Arran KA27 8DE
☎ *(01770) 302353*
www.arranbrewery.co.uk

ARRAN ALE 3.8% ABV
DARK 4.3% ABV
'AB' 5.0% ABV
BLONDE 5.0% ABV
Seasonals:
SUNSET 4.4% ABV
FIRESIDE 4.7% ABV

ATLAS BREWERY LTD

Lab Rd, Kinlochleven, Argyll PH50 4SG
☎ *(01855) 831111*
www.atlasbrewery.com

LATITUDE PALE ALE 3.5% ABV
MERIDIAN 4.0% ABV
THREE SISTERS 4.2% ABV
WAYFARER IPA 4.4% ABV
NIMBUS 5.0% ABV
Seasonals:
BLIZZARD 4.7% ABV
Winter only.
TEMPEST WHEAT BEER 4.9% ABV

BELHAVEN BREWERY CO.

Spott Road, Dunbar EH42 1RS
☎ *(01368) 864488*
www.belhaven.co.uk

BEST 3.2% ABV
BEST EXTRA COLD 3.2% ABV
80/- 4.2% ABV
Malty and nutty.
ST ANDREW'S ALE 6.0% ABV
Well-balanced and distinctive with dry after-palate.

BORVE BREWERY

Borve Brew House, Ruthven, Huntley, Aberdeenshire AB54 4SR
☎ *(01466) 760343*

BORVE ALE 4.0% ABV
TALL SHIPS IPA 5.0% ABV
BORVE EXTRA STRONG 10% ABV

BRIDGE OF ALLAN BREWERY

Queen's Lane, Bridge of Allan, Central FK9 4NY
☎ *(01786) 834555*
www.bridgeofallan.co.uk

STIRLING BITTER 3.7% ABV
STIRLING BRIG 4.1% ABV
BANNOCKBURN 4.2% ABV
GLENCOE WILD OAT STOUT 4.5% ABV
LOMOND GOLD 5.0% ABV
Seasonals:
ALEOWEEN PUMPKIN ALE 4.2% ABV
BRAMBLE ALE 4.2% ABV

BROUGHTON ALES LTD

The Brewery, Broughton, Biggar ML12 6HQ
☎ *(01899) 830345*
www.broughtonales.co.uk

GREENMANTLE ALE 3.9% ABV
Maltiness, with bittersweet flavour, and hoppy finish.
MERLIN'S ALE 4.2% ABV
Gold-coloured, with dry hop flavour combined with malt.
SCOTTISH OATMEAL STOUT 4.2% ABV
Powerful, malty flavour and hoppy bitterness.
THE GHILLIE 4.5% ABV
Hoppy fruit flavours throughout.
BLACK DOUGLAS 5.2% ABV
Dark and malty.
OLD JOCK 6.7% ABV
Dark copper-coloured, with fruit and roast flavours.

CAIRNGORM BREWING COMPANY LTD

Unit 12 Dalfaber Estate, Aviemore, Inverness-shire PH22 1PY
☎ *(01479) 812222*
www.cairngormbrewery.com

Aviemore Highland Ales:
HIGHLAND IPA 3.6% ABV
STAG 4.1% ABV
Good hop character.
NESSIE'S MONSTER MASH 4.4% ABV
Malty full-flavoured beer.
CAIRNGORM GOLD 4.5% ABV
Delicious golden beer.
SHEEPSHAGGERS GOLD 4.5% ABV
WILD CAT 5.1% ABV
Complex malt, fruit and hop flavour.

CALEDONIAN BREWING CO.

42 Slateford Road, Edinburgh EH11 1PH
☎ *(0131) 3371286* (Brewery tours)
www.caledonian-brewery.co.uk

DEUCHARS IPA 3.8% ABV
Pale, well-hopped and quenching. Ever-popular.
80/- ALE 4.1% ABV
Golden, full-flavoured award winner.
GOLDEN PROMISE 5.0% ABV
Light-coloured, hoppy organic beer.
Plus monthly special brews.

THE CLOCKWORK BEER CO.

1153–5, Cathcart Road, Glasgow G42
☎ *(0141) 649 0184*

AMBER IPA 3.8% ABV
A contemporary, light IPA which is American hop based.

SPECIAL OF THE MONTH USUALLY 4.1/2% ABV BUT THE STOUT IS 4.2% ABV
Only European (usually British) hops are used in this special. They are brewed throughout the year to suit the season. A few of the specials are repeated regularly due to popularity (e.g. Clockwork Stout and Original Kelpie) while some are repeated on an annual basis (e.g. Harvest Ale). At Christmas they put on a Belgian "White", Christmas Pudding or, as created in 2003, a chocolate-based ale.

RED ALT BEER 4.4% ABV
Based on a Germal Alt beer which is American hop based.

ORIGINAL LAGER 4.8% ABV
Based on a Bavarian-style lager.

HAZY DAZE RANGE OF FRUIT BEERS 5% ABV
Using the 'lagered' beers as a base, this range is secondary-fermented with fresh fruits and spices. The range contains a 'Seriously Ginger' beer and citrus fruits in the summer months to heavier berry fruits in other seasons.

KEY WEISSE BEER 5% ABV
Produced from a half wheat malt, a blend of lager malt and organic wheat flour, while being flavoured with German hops.

RASPBERRY WEISSE 5% ABV
Very dry.

OREGON IPA 5.5% ABV
The strong version of the Amber.

THUNDER & LIGHTNING 6% ABV
The strong version of the Red Alt.

DEVON ALES

Mansfield Arms, 7 Main Street, Sauchie, Nr Alloa, Clackmannanshire FK10 3JR
☎ *(01259) 722020*

DEVON ORIGINAL 3.8% ABV
DEVON THICK BLACK 4.1% ABV
DEVON PRIDE 4.6% ABV

EGLESBRECH BREWING CO.

Eglesbrech @ Behind The Wall, 14 Melville Street, Falkirk FK1 1HZ
☎ *(01324) 633338*
www.behindthewall.co.uk

FALKIRK 400 3.8% ABV
ANTONINE ALE 3.9% ABV
TALL BLONDE 4.0% ABV
EAGLES BREATH SPECIAL ALE 4.1% ABV

FAR NORTH BREWERY

Melvich, Thurso, Caithness & Sutherland KW14 7YJ
☎ *(01641) 531206*
www.smoothound.co.uk/hotels/melvich

REAL MACKAY 3.8% ABV
SPLIT STONE PALE ALE 4.2% ABV
FAST REACTOR 4.8% ABV
EDGE OF DARKNESS 7.0% ABV

FYFE BREWING COMPANY

469 High Street, Kirkcaldy KY1 2SN
☎ *(01592) 264270*

ROPE OF SAND 3.7% ABV
AULD ALLIANCE 4.0% ABV
LION SLAYER 4.2% ABV
FIRST LYTE 4.3% ABV
FYFE FYRE 4.8% ABV
CAULD TURKEY 6.0% ABV

FYNE ALES

Achadunan, Cairndow, Argyll PA26 8BJ
☎ *(01499) 600238*

PIPER'S GOLD 3.8% ABV

MAVERICK 4.2% ABV
Dark and powerful.

HIGHLANDER 4.8% ABV
Full-flavoured and malty.

HARVIESTOUN BREWERY LTD

Hillfoots Business Village, Alva Industrial Estate, Alva, Clackmannanshire FK12 5DQ
☎ *(01259) 769100*

BITTER & TWISTED 3.8% ABV
Blond with clean citrus fruit flavours.

INDIAN SUMMER IPA 4.1% ABV

PTARMIGAN 4.5% ABV
Pale, with Bavarian hops.

SCHIEHALLION 4.8% ABV
Superb, real cask lager.

Plus seasonal and occasional brews.

HEBRIDEAN BREWING CO

18a Bells Road, Stornoway, Isle of Lewis HS1 2RA
☎ *(01851) 700123*
www.hebridean-brewery.co.uk

CLANSMAN 3.9% ABV
ISLANDER 4.8% ABV

HOUSTON BREWERY
South Street, Houston, Renfrewshire PA6 7EN
☎ *(01505) 614528*
www.houston-brewing.co.uk

KILLELLAN 3.7% ABV
BAROCHAN 4.1% ABV
ST PETERS WELL 4.2% ABV
TEXAS 4.5% ABV

THE INVERALMOND BREWERY
1 Inveralmond Way, Inveralmond, Perth PH1 3UQ
☎ *(01738) 449448*
www.inveralmond-brewery.co.uk

INDEPENDENCE 3.8% ABV
Full-flavoured malt and hops with some spiciness.
OSSIAN 4.1% ABV
Golden and hoppy.
THRAPPLEDOUSER 4.3% ABV
Deep golden, refreshing with good hoppiness.
LIA FAIL 4.7% ABV
Smooth, dark and full-flavoured.

ISLAY ALES CO. LTD.
The Brewery, Islay House Square, Bridgend, Isle of Islay PA44 7NZ
☎ *(01496) 810014*

FINLAGGAN ALE 3.7% ABV
Hoppy session bitter.
BLACK ROCK ALE 4.2% ABV
Darker, softer, full-bodied beer.

THE ISLE OF SKYE BREWING CO. (LEANN AN EILEIN) LTD
The Pier, Uig, Portreee, Isle of Skye IV51 9XY
☎ *(01470) 542477* (Brewery tours)
www.skyebrewery.co.uk

YOUNG PRETENDER 4.0% ABV
Gold-coloured and lightly hopped with dry aftertaste.
RED CUILLIN 4.2% ABV
Slightly malty, with some fruit and hoppy finish.
HEBRIDEAN GOLD 4.3% ABV
Smooth with good hoppy bitterness.
BLACK CUILLIN 4.5% ABV
Stout-like, with hints of chocolate and honey.
BLAVEN 5.0% ABV
Golden, fruity and well-balanced.
Plus seasonal brews.

KELBURN BREWING CO. LTD
10 Muriel Lane, Barrhead, Glasgow G7 1QB
☎ *(01505) 329720*
www.kelburnbrewery.com

GOLDI HOPS 3.8% ABV
RED SMIDDY 4.1% ABV
Smooth dry ale.
DARK MOOR 4.5% ABV
CART BLANCHE 5.0% ABV

MOULIN BREWERY
11–13 Kirkmichael Road, Moulin-by-Pitlochry, Perthshire PH16 5EW
☎ *(01796) 472196*
www.moulin.u-net.com

LIGHT ALE 3.7% ABV
BRAVEHEART 4.0% ABV
ALE OF ATHOL 4.5% ABV
OLD REMEDIAL 5.2% ABV
Scottish Tourist Board 2 visitor attraction, tours and shop.*

NEWTONMORE & KINGUSSIE BREWERY LTD
The Royal Hotel, High Street, Kingussie, Inverness-shire PH21 1HX
☎ *(01540) 661898*

NKB3 HIGHLAND MIST 3.6% ABV
NKB1 4.0% ABV
NKB2 PIPER'S BREW 4.2% ABV

THE ORKNEY BREWERY
Quoyloo, Stromness, Orkney KW16 3LT
☎ *(01856) 841802* (Brewery tours)
www.orkneybrewery.co.uk

RAVEN ALE 3.8% ABV
Superb malt, hop, citrus fruit flavours and nuttiness.
DRAGONHEAD STOUT 4.0% ABV
Black, powerful roast maltiness, with nutty flavours.
NORTHERN LIGHT 4.0% ABV
Golden, refreshing and mellow.
RED MACGREGOR 4.0% ABV
Mellow and malty with nut and hoppy finish.
DARK ISLAND 4.6% ABV
Smooth, flavour-packed and easy to drink.
SKULLSPLITTER 8.5% ABV
Beautifully smooth and hoppy with dry finish.
Plus several special brews.

STEWART BREWING LIMITED

33 Montague Street, Newington, Edinburgh EH8 9QS
☎ *(0131) 667-0242*

EDINBURGH NO. 3 4.3% ABV
Premium Scotch Ale.

PENTLAND IPA 4.1% ABV
Premium Pale Ale.

SULWATH BREWERS LTD

The Brewery, 209 King Street, Castle Douglas DG7 1DT
☎ *(01556) 504525*
www.sulwathbrewers.co.uk

CUIL HILL 3.6% ABV
Pale amber, and bursting with fresh malt and hops.

JOHN PAUL JONES 4.0% ABV
Malty occasional brew.

BLACK GALLOWAY 4.4% ABV
Nourishing porter.

CRIFFEL 4.6% ABV
Rounded malt and hop flavours with delicate bitterness.

KNOCKENDOCH 5.0% ABV
Deep roast malt flavour and hoppy aftertaste.

GALLOWAY GOLD 5.0% ABV
Thirst-quenching lager with citrus aftertaste.

Plus occasional brews.

TROSSACHS CRAFT BREWERY

The Lade Inn, Kilmahog, Callander FK11 8HD
☎ *(01877) 330152*
www.theladeinn.com

WAYLADE 3.9% ABV

LADEBACK 4.5% ABV

LADEOUT 5.1% ABV

TRYST BREWERY

Lorne Road, Larbert FK5 4AT
☎ *(01324) 554000*

BROCKVILLE DARK 3.8% ABV
Session ale, light and easy to drink.

BROCKVILLE PALE 3.8% ABV
Session ale, light and easy to drink.

BUCKLED WHEEL 4.1% ABV
Amber bitter.

Plus specials and seasonals

VALHALLA BREWERY

Shetland Refreshments Ltd, Baltasound, Unst, Shetland ZE2 9DX
☎ *(01957) 711658*
www.valhallabrewery.co.uk

WHITE WIFE 3.8% ABV

SIMMER DIM 4.0% ABV

AULD ROCK 4.5% ABV
Smooth, malty and full-bodied robust hoppiness.

THE PUBS

ALLANTON

The Allanton Inn

Allanton, Duns, Berwickshire TD11 3JZ
☎ *(01890) 818260* PR Hunter
www.allantoninn.co.uk

A freehouse with three pumps offering a range that changes weekly, featuring guest ales from small and large Scottish and English breweries. Caledonian Deuchars IPA, Arran Blonde and Fraoch Heather Ale are regulars.

A listed eighteenth-century country coaching inn with pool, darts and a cosy restaurant. Beer garden. Five en-suite bedrooms. Good food served at lunchtimes and evenings. Children welcome. One mile from Chirnside.

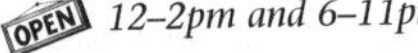 *12–2pm and 6–11pm.*

AUCHENCROW

The Craw Inn

Auchencrow, Berwickshire
☎ *(018907) 61253* Trevor Wilson

Caledonian Deuchars IPA is a regular, plus wide selection of constantly changing guest beers – over 350 in the last four years (count the clips, which all go on display in the bar).

Family-run, eighteenth-century, listed country inn in small, attractive Borders village. Real ale award winner. Bar and restaurant food served noon–2pm (2.30pm Sun) and 6pm (7pm Sun)–9.30pm daily. Car park. Children welcome. En-suite accommodation.

 *12–2.30pm and 6–11pm Mon–Thurs; 12–12 Fri–Sat; 12.30–11pm Sun.*

BONCHESTER BRIDGE

Horse & Hound Hotel

Bonchester Bridge, Hawick TD9 8JN
☎ *(01450) 860645* Rebecca and Marie Hope

Weekly guest beers such as Maclay, Charles Wells, Longstone, Bateman, Jennings, Caledonian, Belhaven or Holt breweries.

A former coaching inn dating from 1704 with comfortable accommodation and non-smoking areas. Bar and restaurant food is available at lunchtime and evenings. Car park. Children's certificate. Hawick is seven miles from Carter Bar on the England–Scotland border.

 *11.30am–3pm and 6–11pm Mon–Fri; 11.30am–midnight Sat–Sun.*

DENHOLM

Auld Cross Keys Inn

Main Street, Denholm, Roxburghshire TD9 8NU
☎ *(01450) 870305* David Mackay Bennett

A freehouse with two or three real ales always available. Black Sheep Bitter, Timothy Taylor Landlord and Caledonian Deuchars IPA are often featured.

A 150-year-old inn with public bar, lounge bar, dining and function room. Meals served lunchtimes and evenings during the week, plus Sunday carvery. Children allowed. Two en-suite rooms available.

 *12pm–12am.*

EYEMOUTH

The Ship Hotel

Harbour Road, Eyemouth, Berwickshire TD14 5HT
☎ *(01890) 750224* Moany and Sue Hubert

Operated by Hubert Hotels, this pub has Caledonian 80/- as a regular, plus one weekly changing guest, usually Caledonian Deuchars IPA or a beer from Hadrian & Border.

A local fishermen's pub and family-run hotel near the harbour, with lounge bar featuring a coal fire, pool table, darts and live music at weekends. The Ship is a landmark in the village, and is mentioned repeatedly in the book *Children of the Sea* by Peter Aitchinson. Separate dining area serves food at lunchtimes and evenings. Children allowed.

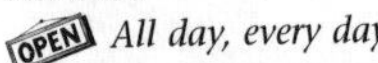 *All day, every day.*

GALASHIELS

Ladhope Inn

33 High Buckholmside, Galashiels, Borders TD1 2HR
☎ *(01896) 752446* Mrs Johnston and Mr Amos

A freehouse with a varied range of constantly changing ales.

On the main road; first pub on the A7. Toasted sandwiches only. Children allowed.

OPEN *All day, every day.*

GREENLAW

Cross Keys Inn

3 The Square, Greenlaw, Duns TD10 6UD
☎ *(01361) 10247* Mary O'Brian

Two real ales always available, regulars including Timothy Taylor Landlord and Caledonian Deuchars IPA.

A very old-fashioned freehouse with one bar and a restaurant area. Food at lunchtime and evenings. Children allowed.

OPEN *Closed daily between 2.30 and 5pm.*

INNERLEITHEN

Traquair Arms Hotel

Traquair Road, Innerleithen, Borders EH44 6PD
☎ *(01896) 830229* Gig and Dianne Johnston

A freehouse with real ales on three pumps offering the local Traquair House Bear Ale on draught. Broughton Greenmantle Ale and 80/- also often available plus occasional others.

A country-style pub with one bar and separate dining area. Food served all day. Children allowed.

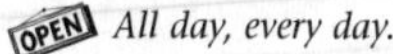 *All day, every day.*

NEWCASTLETON

The Grapes Hotel

16 Douglas Square, Newcastleton, Roxburghshire TD9 0QD
☎ *(01387) 375245* Jim McDonald

Up to eight pumps operating, with Caledonian Deuchars IPA among the beers always available. Guests are changed monthly.

A small hotel with restaurant. Food at lunchtimes and evenings. Children allowed until 8.30pm (residents later).

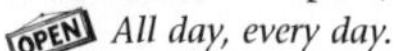 *All day, every day.*

PAXTON

Cross Inn

Paxton, Berwickshire
☎ *(01289) 386267* Mike and Julie Ivison

Freehouse with beers from Northumberland's Wylam Brewery always available, plus a weekly guest ale.

A seventeenth-century village pub with a warm and friendly bar and separate dining room, where children are welcome. Food available all opening hours. Car park. On the Borders Coast and Castles cycle route.

 *12–2.30pm and 6.30–9pm Tues–Sun (closed Mon).*

PEEBLES

Green Tree Hotel

41 Eastgate, Peebles EH45 8AD
☎ *(01721) 720582* Mervyn Edge

Caledonian 80/- is permanently available, plus one or two guest beers such as Timothy Taylor Landlord or something from Broughton Ales.

Lively, traditional hotel bar. Food served 12–2.30pm and 5–8.30pm. Car park. Children welcome.

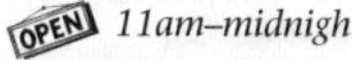 *11am–midnight.*

ST MARY'S LOCH

Tibbie Shiels Inn

St Mary's Loch, Selkirk, Borders TD7 5LH
☎ *(01750) 42231 Mrs Jill Brown*
www.tibbieshielsinn.com

A freehouse offering Broughton Greenmantle Ale and Belhaven 80/-.

A remote nineteenth-century coaching inn beside the loch, with a non-smoking dining area. Food served 12.30–8.15pm. Children allowed.

OPEN *All day, every day (closed Mon–Wed from November–Easter and over Christmas).*

THE PUBS

ALVA

Cross Keys Inn

120 Stirling Street, Alva, Clackmannanshire FK12 5EH
☎ *(01259) 760409* Moira Michie

Owned by Maclay Inns and serving three real ales with the emphasis on Scottish breweries. Maclay Kane's Amber (by Belhaven), Caledonian Deuchars IPA and something from Harviestoun are likely candidates.

A traditional pub with two bars. Popular with locals and visitors alike. Food at lunchtime and evenings. Children allowed. On-street parking. B&B accommodation.

OPEN *All day, every day.*

BRIDGE OF ALLAN

The Queen's Hotel

24 Henderson Street, Bridge of Allan, Stirling, Stirlingshire FK9 4HD
☎ *(01786) 833268* Mr Ross

A freehouse with beers Stirling Brig, Bitter, IPA and Dark Mild from the local Bridge of Allan Brewery permanently available, plus seasonal specials.

A two-bar pub with restaurant and occasional live entertainment. Food at lunchtime and evenings. Children allowed.

OPEN *All day, every day.*

DOLLAR

Castle Campbell Hotel

11 Bridge Street, Dollar, Clackmannanshire FK14 7DE
☎ *(01259) 742519* Richard Nealon
www.castle-campbell.co.uk

A freehouse with real ale on two pumps, Harviestoun Bitter & Twisted plus one changed every couple of weeks.

A traditional, busy hotel (eight rooms, built 1822) with a separate restaurant and lounge bar, with food available in both areas at lunchtimes and evenings. Children welcome.

OPEN *All day, every day.*

The King's Seat

19 Bridge Street, Dollar, Clackmannanshire FK14 7DE
☎ *(01259) 742515* Mr and Mrs Nelson

Harviestoun Bitter & Twisted always available, plus one other guest beer.

A village inn serving families (with a children's certificate). Bar and restaurant food available at lunchtime and evenings. Parking. Dollar is on the main A91 road between Stirling and St Andrews.

OPEN *11am–midnight summer; 11am–11pm winter.*

The Lorne Tavern

17 Argyll Street, Dollar, Clackmannanshire FK14 7AR
☎ *(01259) 743423* Jim Nelson

A freehouse with Harviestoun and Abbeydale brews always available. Two pumps, changed every four days, offer guests which include regulars from the Inveralmond brewery. Others featured include the Maclay range.

A traditional local with separate restaurant. Children allowed in the dining room.

OPEN *All day, every day.*

DUNBLANE

The Tappit Hen

Kirk Street, Dunblane, Perthshire FK15 0AL
☎ *(01786) 825226* Danny Mitchel

Two ales from Belhaven always available, plus five guests, changed weekly.

A community bar with a warm, welcoming atmosphere, situated opposite the cathedral. No food. No children.

OPEN *All day, every day.*

FALKIRK

Behind The Wall Bar and Restaurant

14 Melville Street, Falkirk FK1 1HZ
☎ *(01324) 633338* C Morris
www.behindthewall.co.uk

Home of the Eglesbrech Brewing company with the full range of Eglesbrech beers normally available, including Antonine Ale, Falkirk 400 Commemorative Ale and Tall Blonde. Plus a Caledonian brew and a range of guest beers often from Harviestoun, Caledonian, Broughton, Maclay, Belhaven and Orkney.

Town-centre complex with restaurant, café bar and conservatory. Tex-Mex food served all day. Car park opposite. Children welcome with children's menu available. Heated outdoor terrace. Live music Fri–Sat. Big-screen sports. Bells Football Supporter's Pub of the Year 2003 and Budweiser Quality on Tap Winners 2003.

OPEN *11am–midnight Sun–Thurs; 11am–1am Fri–Sat.*

KILMAHOG

The Lade Inn

Kilmahog, by Callander, FK17 8HD
☎ *(01877) 331878*

Since late 2003 home of the Trossachs Craft Brewery micro-brewery whose exclusive brews include Waylade, LadeBack and LadeOut. Stirling Brig from the not-too-distant Bridge of Allan Brewery and Broughton Ales' Greenmantle session beer are also popular regulars in the log fire-warmed bothy bar, plus wide range of guest ales.

Beer garden, informal ceilidhs most Saturday nights, bar meals, disabled access. Favourite haunt for walkers coming off nearby Ben Ledi and other Trossachs hills.

OPEN *12–3pm and 5–11.45pm Mon–Fri; 12–11.45pm Sat; 12.30–11pm Sun.*

POOL OF MUCKHART

The Muckhart Inn

Pool of Muckhart, Muckhart, Clackmannanshire FK14 7JN
☎ *(01259) 781324* Derek Graham

A freehouse serving Devon Original, Pride and Thick Black plus others.

A one-bar pub with beamed ceilings and log fires. Food at lunchtime and evenings. Children allowed.

OPEN *All day, every day.*

SAUCHIE

Mansfield Arms

7 Main Street, Sauchie, Nr Alloa, Clackmannanshire FK10 3JR
☎ *(01259) 722020* John Gibson

The home of Devon Ales micro-brewery, with three beers brewed and served on the premises.

CAMRA Scottish Pub of the Year in 1993, started brewing in May 1994. The four-barrel brewhouse was built from spare parts and discarded equipment and now produces cask ales in the English tradition. Food is available in the bar until 9pm. Car park, garden. Children allowed. Just north of Alloa.

OPEN *11am–midnight.*

STIRLING

The Birds & Bees

Easter Cornton Road, Causewayhead, Stirling FK9 5PB
☎ *(01786) 463384* Lesley Anderson

A freehouse with three real ales on the menu. Orkney Dark Island always available, plus two guests per week.

A traditional farmhouse-style pub with log fires, beer garden and French boules. Voted one of the best places to eat in local Tourism Awards 2000 – food available lunchtimes and evenings. Children welcome.

OPEN *11am–3pm and 5pm–midnight Mon–Thurs; all day Fri–Sun.*

TILLICOULTRY

The Woolpack

1 Glassford Square, Tillicoultry, Clackmannanshire FK13 6AH
☎ *(01259) 750332* Mr D McGhee

A freehouse with Harviestoun Ptarmigan 85/- and Orkney Dark Island always available. A guest beer, changed every two days, is also offered.

Built around 1700, a one-bar pub with restaurant and children's room. Food served all day. No children in the bar. Off the beaten track, no signposts. Head towards the Glen.

OPEN *All day, every day.*

THE PUBS

BLADNOCH

The Bladnoch Inn
Bladnoch, Wigtown, Wigtownshire DG8 9AB
☎ *(01988 402200)* Peter McLaughlin

Greene King Abbot Ale, Flower's Original plus weekly guest ales.

Two-hundred-year-old country inn and restaurant overlooking the river next to the Bladnoch distillery (guided tours). Food at lunchtime and evenings. Children allowed.

11am–2.30pm and 5–11pm (midnight weekends); all day Sun.

CASTLE DOUGLAS

The Royal Hotel
17 King Street, Castle Douglas, Kirkcudbrightshire DG7 1AA
☎ *(01556) 502040* Mrs Bennett

A freehouse with Orkney Dark Island and Caledonian Deuchars IPA always available.

A small, family-run hotel with two bars and a separate restaurant. Children allowed.

All day, every day.

DALBEATTIE

The Pheasant Hotel
1 Maxwell Street, Dalbeattie DG5 4AH
☎ *(01556) 610345* Elaine McKenzie

Caledonian Deuchars IPA.

A high-street community pub with TV and second-floor dining area. Food at lunchtime and evenings (all day in summer). Children allowed. Friendly mix of local sport fans and out-of-town mountain bikers looking for a rare pint of real ale in Dalbeattie.

All day, every day.

DUMFRIES

Douglas Arms
Friars Vennel, Dumfries DG1 2RQ
☎ *(01387) 256002* Mrs A Whitefield

Broughton Greenmantle Ale, Merlin's Ale, The Ghillie, Black Douglas and Old Jock always available plus one guest beer (150 per year) to include Whim Magic Mushroom Mild and Hartington Bitter.

An old-style pub with a real coal fire. No food available. Situated in the town centre.

11am–11pm Sun–Thurs; 11am–midnight Fri–Sat.

The New Bazaar
38 Whitesands, Dumfries DG1 2RS
☎ *(01387) 268776* George Schneider

A freehouse with four guest beers daily from a list of breweries including Belhaven, Sulwath, Bateman, Adnams, Titanic, Moorhouse's, Tomintoul and Greene King.

A traditional Victorian public house consisting of public bar, lounge, family room and beer garden. The public bar has an old-fashioned gantry stocked with more than 200 malt and other whiskies. Lounge has real coal fire. Food available. Car park. Wheelchair access. The pub overlooks the River Nith.

11am–11pm; (midnight Fri–Sat).

The Ship Inn
St Michael Street, Dumfries DG1 2P7
☎ *(01387) 255189* Mr T Dudgeon

Timothy Taylor Landlord, Greene King Old Speckled Hen, Charles Wells Bombardier, Marston's Pedigree and two regularly changing guest beers usually available, perhaps from Orkney, Everards, Brakspear, Harviestoun, Broughton, Fuller's, Badger, Greene King, Holt, Hook Norton, Hop Back, Jennings or Adnams.

Seven ales on hand pump and four directly from the barrel in this friendly alehouse. No TV or music, just good conversation. No food. No children.

11am–2.30pm and 5–11pm Mon–Sat; 12.30–2.30pm and 6.30–11pm Sun.

Tam O'Shanter
117 Queensberry Street, Dumfries DG1 1BH
☎ *(01387) 254055* Doreen Johnston

Caledonian Deuchars IPA always available plus four guests, changed frequently, from a broad selection.

A traditional pub with upstairs restaurant. Food all day. Children allowed.

All day, every day.

GATEHOUSE OF FLEET

Masonic Arms
Ann Street, Gatehouse of Fleet, Nr Castle Douglas, Kirkcudbrightshire DG7 2HU
☎ *(01557) 814335* Chris and Sue Walker
www.themasonic-arms.co.uk

The Masonic Boom (house ale brewed locally by Sulwath) always available plus two guest ales, often from Timothy Taylor or Theakston.

A traditional, English-style country inn, with one bar and restaurant in conservatory. Food at lunchtime and evenings. Children allowed.

11.30am–2.30pm and 5.30–11.30pm.

GLENLUCE

Kelvin House Hotel

53 Main Street, Glenluce, Newton Stewart, Wigtownshire DG8 0PP
☎ *(01581) 300303* Christine Holmes

A freehouse offering three real ales, one changed once or twice a week. Orkney Red MacGregor and Burtonwood Top Hat always on the menu, with one guest from a good selection that may include Timothy Taylor Landlord and Orkney Dark Island.

A hotel off the A75, with residents' lounge, dining lounge, public bar and restaurant. Food at lunchtime and evenings. Children allowed.

 *11am–3pm and 6–11.30pm.*

HAUGH OF URR

Laurie Arms Hotel

Haugh of Urr, Castle Douglas, Kirkcudbrightshire DG7 3YA
☎ *(01556) 660246* Wullie Rundle

A freehouse offering three real ales including Houston Brewery Killellan on permanently. Regular guests include Caledonian Deuchars IPA and Fuller's London Pride.

An old country pub with log fires and separate dining area. Homemade food at lunchtime and evenings. Children allowed. Outdoor seating.

 *11.45am–2.30pm and 5.30pm–midnight.*

ISLE OF WHITHORN

Steampacket Inn

Harbour Row, Isle of Whithorn DG8 8LL
☎ *(01988) 500334* John Scoular (proprietor)

Theakston XB, Kelburn Goldi Hops plus one other guest beer.

Harbour-side inn and resturant. Down-to-earth bar has wood-burning stove. The name commemorates the steam ships which used to sail between the Isle of Whithorn and Liverpool.

 *11am–11pm (midnight Fri–Sat); 12–11pm Sun. Bar closed 2.30–6pm from October to March.*

KIRKCUDBRIGHT

Selkirk Arms Hotel

High Street, Kirkcudbright, Kirkcudbrightshire DG6 4JG
☎ *(01557) 330209*
www.selkirkarmshotel.co.uk

A freehouse with Sulwath Criffel always available. Two guests, changed weekly, often include beer from Broughton Ales.

A Georgian hotel with public and lounge bars and a bistro. Food at lunchtime and evenings. Children allowed.

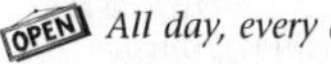 *All day, every day.*

LANGHOLM

The Crown Hotel

High Street, Langholm DG13 0JH
☎ *(01387) 380247*
Mr A Barrie and Ms B Bailey

Orkney brews always available in this freehouse, plus a guest beer changed weekly.

An eighteenth-century coaching house with five bars and a dining area. Food served. Children allowed.

All day, every day.

LOCKERBIE

Somerton House Hotel

35 Carlisle Road, Lockerbie DG11 2DR
☎ *(01576) 202583* Alex Arthur

A freehouse always offering Caledonian Deuchars IPA and Broughton Greenmantle. A guest is changed each week. Favourites include beers from Fuller's, Jennings and Caledonian breweries.

A hotel built in the 1880s with a separate dining area. Food served at lunchtime and evenings. Children allowed.

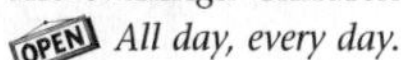 *All day, every day.*

NEWTON STEWART

The Creebridge House Hotel

Newton Stewart, Wigtownshire DG8 6NP
☎ *(01671) 402121* Nikki Cramsie-Smith
www.creebridge.co.uk

A genuine freehouse with Caledonian 80/- and Deuchars IPA usually available. Other favourites might include Timothy Taylor Landlord.

A country-style hotel built in 1760, with one large bar, brasserie and restaurant. Award-winning food available for lunch and dinner. Children's certificate. Beer garden, car park, function room for hire.

 *12–2.30pm Mon–Sun; 6–11pm Mon–Thurs; 6pm–midnight Fri–Sat; 6.30–11pm Sun.*

PORTPATRICK

Harbour House Hotel

53 Main Street, Portpatrick, Stranraer, Wigtownshire DG9 8JW
☎ *(01776) 810456 Ian Cerexhe*
www.harbourhouse.co.uk

A freehouse with Houston Killellan on offer all year round, plus Houston Peter's Well in summer.

Seafront hotel originally used by the Admirality in 1790 as a harbour HQ. Lounge bar; outside seating; separate dining area (non-smoking). Food at lunchtime and evenings. Children allowed. Live music (folk/pop) in bar most weekends Easter–October.

OPEN *11am–11pm Sun–Wed; 11am–midnight Thurs–Sat.*

THORNHILL

Buccleuch & Queensberry Hotel

112 Drumlanrig Street, Thornhill, Dumfriesshire DG3 5LU
☎ *(01848) 330215* David and Naomi Spencer

A freehouse with Caledonian 80/- permanently available, plus one guest, changing weekly, perhaps from Marston's, Timothy Taylor, Orkney, Harviestoun or Jennings, to name but a few.

This 150-year-old hotel stands prominently at the centre of a picturesque conservation village. Traditional old-style lounge bar, log fires and friendly staff. A haven for fishermen, walkers and golfers. Freshly prepared food served every lunchtime and evening. Car park. Children welcome.

OPEN *11am–midnight Mon–Wed; 11am–1am Thurs–Sat; 12.30pm–midnight Sun.*

THE PUBS

ABERDOUR

Cedar Inn
20 Shore Road, Aberdour KY3 0TR
☎ *(01383) 860310* R F Anthistle

Four real ales daily – Harviestoun Bitter & Twisted plus three guests.

A friendly locals' pub, built in the mid-eighteenth century, with two bars and lounge. Food at lunchtime and evenings. Children allowed. Beer gardens. Ten rooms. Live music Fridays.

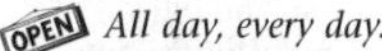
All day, every day.

ANSTRUTHER

Dreel Tavern
16 High Street, Anstruther KY10 3DL
☎ *(01333) 310727* Barry Scarsbrook

A freehouse with two guest beers, changed at least once a week, from Scots breweries.

A sixteenth-century coaching inn offering smoking and non-smoking dining areas, plus a garden bar for summer days. Food available 12–2pm and 5.30–9pm (children's menu until 7pm).

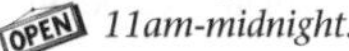
11am-midnight.

CERES

Ceres Inn
The Cross, Ceres, Cupar KY15 5NE
☎ *(01334) 828305* Sharon Hopkinson

Caledonian Deuchars IPA plus guest, often from Belhaven, Harviestoun or Houston Brewery.

Traditional olde-worlde pub, built 1721, with good atmosphere, situated in the centre of Ceres (near St Andrews). Public bar. Restaurant bar. Food served 12–9pm daily. Beer garden. Car park. Children allowed

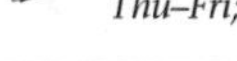
12–11pm Mon–Tues; 12pm–1am Thu–Fri; 12pm–midnight Wed, Sat–Sun.

EARLSFERRY

Golf Tavern (19th Hole)
Links Road, Earlsferry KY9 1AW
☎ *(01333) 330 610* Douglas Duncanson

Caledonian Deuchars IPA, Broughton Greenmantle and an occasional guest beer served.

Small village pub with wood panelling and gas lamps in the bar. Homemade soup and snacks available. Children welcome in the lounge bar until 8pm.

11am–1am in season; 11am–2.30pm and 5pm–1am out of season.

FREUCHIE

Albert Tavern
2 High Street, Freuchie, Fife KY15 7BG
☎ *(01337) 857192* Jim and Pat Kenyon
www.alberttavern.co.uk

Freehouse regularly serving Belhaven 80/- plus up to three frequently changing guests from breweries across Scotland and further afield.

Two-bar, eighteenth-century village coaching inn with small upstairs restaurant bought and transformed in April 2000 by the current landlords, who were former regulars. Outside drinking area, children welcome. Some live entertainment. Food served at lunchtime and evenings. CAMRA 2002 Scottish Pub of the Year.

12–2pm and 5.30–11pm Mon–Thurs; 12pm–1am Fri–Sat; 12.30pm–midnight Sun.

KETTLEBRIDGE

Kettlebridge Inn
9 Cupar Road, Kettlebridge
☎ *(01337) 830232* Paul and Sue Pinkney

Three beers always available from a list that runs into hundreds.

A traditional village coaching inn in Fife golfing country on the A914 road to St Andrews. Open fires, lounge bar and restaurant. Mexican food available at lunchtime and evenings. Street parking. Beer garden. Children welcome.

Closed Mon; 12–2.30pm and 5–11pm Tues–Fri (12am Fri); all day Sat–Sun.

KIRKCALDY

Betty Nicol's
297 High Street, Kirkcaldy KY1 1JL
☎ *(01592) 642083* Sandy Haxton
www.bettynicols.co.uk

A freehouse with Caledonian Deuchars IPA among the beers always available, plus a guest. Greene King Old Speckled Hen, Timothy Taylor Landlord and Fuller's London Pride are regularly featured but many others also stocked as available.

Historic pub with separate lounge for private functions. Bar snacks available.

OPEN *All day, every day.*

Harbour Bar

469 High Street, Kirkcaldy KY1 2SN
☎ *(01592) 264270*

Home of the Fyfe Brewing Company offering the full range of Fyfe beers. Also guests from Belhaven Brewery and elsewhere.

The brewery is located in an old sailworks behind and above the pub. Auld Alliance, the first brew, was launched in May 1995. The plant size is for two and a half barrels, with a ten-barrel per week restriction. The Harbour Bar is a traditional alehouse. Scottish CAMRA Pub of the Year 2000 and runner-up in national awards. Fife CAMRA Pub of the Year for six consecutive years up to 2001. Snacks are available at lunchtime and evenings. Parking. Children not allowed.

 *11am–2.30pm and 5pm–midnight Mon–Thurs; 11am–midnight Fri–Sat; 12.30pm–midnight Sun.*

LESLIE

Burns Tavern

184 High Street, Leslie, Glenrothes KY6 3DB
☎ *(01592) 741345* Archie McCormack

Timothy Taylor Landlord and Caledonian Deuchars IPA regularly served. Wide selection of ales from surrounding local breweries. Customers' requests are welcome.

A very friendly local Scottish pub. Functions catered for and folk club every Wednesday. Snacks available.

All day, every day.

LEVEN

Hawkshill Hotel

Hawkslaw Street, Leven KY8 4LS
☎ *(01333) 427033* Mrs Rossiter

A freehouse with Timothy Taylor Landlord always available, plus a guest beer changed weekly. Favourites include Orkney Dark Island, Exmoor Gold and Kelham Island Pale Rider.

A family inn with function room, separate dining area and beer garden. Food available lunchtimes and evenings. Children allowed.

 *11am–2.30pm and 6pm–midnight Mon–Thurs; 11am–midnight Fri–Sat; 12–12 Sun.*

ST ANDREWS

Drouthy Neebors

209 South Street, St Andrews KY16 9EF
☎ *(01334) 479952* Mr Shug

A Belhaven tied house with St Andrew's and 80/- permanently available plus four guest ales. Regular features include Orkney Dark Island and Raven Ale, plus Ridleys Rumpus.

A real mixed-bag clientele here: students, locals, tourists. Food available. Children allowed. Car parking.

 *11am–midnight Mon–Thurs; 11am–1am Fri–Sat; 12.30pm–midnight Sun.*

THE PUBS

ABERDEEN

Archibald Simpson

5 Castle Street, Aberdeen AB9 8AX
☎ *(01224) 621365* Jason Dullea

Caledonian 80/- and Deuchars IPA regularly served plus one or two guest beers. Tomintoul Wild Cat often available.

It's not difficult to imagine this Grade I listed building as it used to be: a Clydesdale Bank. Now a JD Wetherspoon freehouse situated on the corner of Union and King Streets. Food served all day, every day. Children welcome until 6pm if eating a meal.

11am–midnight Mon–Thurs; 11am–1am Fri–Sat.

The Blue Lamp

121–3 Gallowgate, Aberdeen AB25 1BU
☎ *(01224) 647472* Mr Brown

A freehouse with Caledonian 80/- and Deuchars IPA always available, plus up to five guest beers. Regulars include Isle of Skye Young Pretender and many others from small Scottish breweries.

A pub combining the traditional and the contemporary, with live entertainment at weekends. Two bars, one with an early 1960s feel, the other spacious. Small function room available to hire. Sandwiches only. No children.

 *All day Mon–Sat; 12.30–3.30pm and 6.30–11pm Sun.*

Carriages Bar & Restaurant

The Brentwood Hotel, 101 Crown Street, Aberdeen AB11 6HH
☎ *(01224) 595440/571593* Jim Byers
www.brentwood-hotel.co.uk

Ten real ales always on tap. Caledonian Deuchars IPA and Black Sheep Ale are among the five beers permanently available, plus five guests, changing weekly, such as Marston's Pedigree, Wadworth 6X, Fuller's London Pride, Shepherd Neame Spitfire, Greene King Abbot Ale, Orkney Dark Island or something from Aviemore, Isle of Skye, Tomintoul, Houston or any other independent brewery. Different and unusual ales from independent breweries across the UK are constantly sourced. CAMRA Aberdeen City Pub of the Year 2003.

Carriages is a freehouse, part of the Brentwood Hotel, run by the director/licensee, who is a fount of local knowledge, it has a relaxed, informal atmosphere. A hot buffet lunch is served 12–2pm Mon–Fri; dinner in the restaurant 6–9.45pm Mon–Sun. Car park. Children welcome in lounge area and restaurant, when eating. Special children's menu available.

12–2.30pm and 5pm–midnight Mon–Sat; 6–11pm Sun.

Old Blackfriars

Castle Street, Aberdeen, Grampian AB11 5BB
☎ *(01224) 581922* Fiona Smith

A Belhaven Brewery house with nine real ale pumps. Belhaven 80/- and St Andrew's plus Caledonian 80/-, Deuchars IPA and Inveralmond Ossian permanently available. Up to two guests which may be from breweries such as Orkney, Smiles or Hop Back. Thousands of guest ales have been featured over the years and repeats are avoided.

An 80-year-old city-centre pub in a sixteenth-century building. Original ceiling, old cellar, very traditional atmosphere. Food available in non-smoking dining area at lunchtime. Children allowed for meals only.

 *11am–midnight Mon–Sat; 12.30–11pm Sun.*

The Prince of Wales

7 St Nicholas Lane, Aberdeen AB10 1HF
☎ *(01224) 640597* Steven Christie

A freehouse with house ale from Inveralmond – Prince of Wales Ale – and Caledonian 80/- always on the menu. Four guest beers, changed weekly, may include Isle of Skye Red Cuillin and Young Pretender, Timothy Taylor Landlord or Orkney Dark Island, but ales from other independents also available as and when.

A classic city-centre Victorian bar. No music. Food available at lunchtime. Children allowed.

 *All day, every day.*

J & R Tennent

Aberdeen Airport, Dyce, Aberdeen
☎ *(01224) 722331* J and R Tennent

Two guest beers regularly served, such as Caledonian IPA, 80/- or Marston's Pedigree.

Airport bar. Food served 8am–5pm. Children welcome.

 *8am–9.45pm.*

ELGIN

Sunninghill Hotel

Hay Street, Elgin, Morayshire IV30 1NH
☎ *(01343) 547799* Winnie Rose
www.sunninghillhotel.com

A freehouse offering four real ales. Guests changed weekly but often include Timothy Taylor Landlord, Caledonian Deuchars IPA and beers from Cairngorm Brewing Co.

A hotel lounge bar. Food at lunchtime and evenings. Children allowed.

 *11am–2.30pm and 5–11pm Mon–Thurs (midnight Fri); 11am–midnight Sat; 12.30pm–11pm Sun.*

FINDHORN

Crown & Anchor Inn

Findhorn, Nr Forres, Morayshire IV36 3YF
☎ *(01309) 690243* Mrs Heather Burrell

A freehouse serving at least four real ales and up to seven in summer. Regulars include Timothy Taylor Landlord, Fuller's ESB and Bateman brews.

Built in 1739, a pub offering bed and breakfast accommodation, live entertainment and a lounge area. Food at lunchtime and evenings. Children allowed.

OPEN *All day, every day.*

Kimberley Inn

94 Findhorn, Nr Forres, Morayshire IV36 3YG
☎ *(01309) 690492* Mr John Hessel

A freehouse with real ales changing regularly, including Caledonian Deuchars IPA, Black Sheep Bitter, Orkney The Red MacGregor and guest ales from Orkney, Black Isle or Aviemore.

A village seafood pub with two separate non-smoking areas. Views across the bay, with outside seating and heating. Fresh seafood daily, including 'catch of the day', salmon, langoustines, mussels, and much more! Food served all day, every day in summer, and at lunchtime and evenings during winter. Children welcome until 8pm.

OPEN *All day, every day.*

METHLICK

The Gight House Hotel

Sunnybrae, Methlick, Ellon, Aberdeenshire AB41 7BP
☎ *(01651) 806389* Les Ross
www.gighthousehotel.co.uk

Two real ale pumps serve a regularly changing range of beers, with Hook Norton Old Hooky, Timothy Taylor Landlord, Black Sheep Bitter and Marston's Pedigree all having featured often, plus Scottish brews such as Isle of Skye Red Cuillin.

Not only is the demon drink served in this former Free Kirk manse, there is a putting green on the lawn. Beamed lounge with open fires, restaurant, two conservatories, children's play area. Food served at lunchtime and evenings Mon–Sat and all day Sun.

OPEN *12–2.30pm and 5pm–midnight Mon–Fri; all day Sat–Sun.*

PORTSOY

The Shore Inn

The Old Harbour, Church Street, Portsoy, Banffshire AB45 2QR
☎ *(01261) 842831* Mr Hill

A freehouse with Isle of Skye Red Cuillin among the brews always available. A guest, changed weekly, is also offered.

A traditional, 300-year-old pub, overlooking a seventeenth-century harbour. Separate restaurant. Food all day. Children allowed.

OPEN *All day, every day.*

STONEHAVEN

The Marine Hotel

9–10 Shorehead, Stonehaven AB3 2JY
☎ *(01569) 762155* Mr Phil Duncan

Timothy Taylor ales always available plus five guests (200 per year) perhaps from Orkney, Harviestoun and Tomintoul breweries, plus a wide range of English ales.

The pub overlooks the harbour and has a large bar with a juke box. Bar and restaurant food served at lunchtime and evenings. Local seafood and game. Parking. Follow the signs to the harbour.

OPEN *9am–1am Mon–Sat; 9am–midnight Sun.*

TOMINTOUL

The Glen Avon Hotel

1 The Square, Tomintoul, Ballindalloch, Banffshire AB37 9ET
☎ *(01807) 580218* Robert Claase

A freehouse always offering Tomintoul Wild Cat, Stag and Nessie's Monster Mash. Guest beers changed weekly on two pumps in summer.

A country pub with log fires and separate dining area. Food at lunchtime and evenings. Children allowed.

OPEN *All day, every day.*

THE PUBS

AVIEMORE

Old Bridge Inn

Dalfaber Road, Aviemore, Inverness-shire PH22 1PX
☎ *(01479) 811137* Nigel Reid
www.oldbridgeinn.co.uk

Three rotating real ales usually available at any one time in this freehouse. The menu changes weekly.

Set in a rural location just off the "Ski Road" and next to the River Spey. Separate dining area. Food is available 12–2pm and 6–9pm. Beer garden, adjacent bunk house, car park. Children allowed.

OPEN *All day, every day.*

AVOCH

The Station Hotel

Bridge Street, Avoch, Moray, Ross-shire IV9 8GG
☎ *(01381) 620246* David Graham

A freehouse with two guests, changed twice weekly, from a good range of beers.

A country village pub with two bars and a conservatory. Food at lunchtime and evenings. Children allowed.

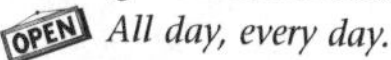
All day, every day.

CARRBRIDGE

Cairn Hotel

Carrbridge, Inverness-shire PH23 3AS
☎ *(01479) 841212* AE Kirk

Black Isle Red Kite, Caledonian 80/- and Deuchars IPA, Isle of Skye Red Cuillin, Aviemore Ruthven and Cairngorm regularly available, plus something perhaps from Houston or Tomintoul.

Family-owned, traditional freehouse in ideal touring area. Situated in the centre of the village, well visited by locals and tourists alike. Food served 12–2.15pm and 6–8.30pm. Car park. Children's certificate. En-suite accommodation.

OPEN *11am–midnight Mon–Fri; 11am–1am Sat; 12.30–11pm Sun.*

FORT WILLIAM

Grog & Gruel

66 High Street, Fort William PH33 6AE
☎ *(01397) 705078* Guy and Ed Daynes
www.grogandgruel.co.uk

Up to eight ales on offer in regular rotation, including beers from the Atlas Brewery in Kinlochleven, Heather and Houston. Seasonal and celebration ales, and occasional festivals.

A traditional town pub in an old building. Bar and restaurant food available. Beer garden. Children allowed daytimes only.

OPEN *12–12 Mon–Wed; 12–1am Thurs–Sat; 12–11pm Sun.*

GLENCOE

Clachaig Inn

Glencoe, Argyll PH49 4HX
☎ *(01855) 811252* Guy Daynes
www.clachaig.com

Beers from Atlas such as Latitude and Three Sisters are regularly featured, together with ales from many other Scottish breweries. Up to eight real ales at any one time, more during regular festivals (e-mailing list to keep you posted).

A pub and hotel, popular with hillwalkers who flock to Glencoe. Food available 12–9pm daily. Children allowed in the lounge bar. Beer garden. Accommodation.

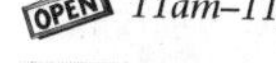
11am–11pm.

INVERNESS

No 27

27 Castle Street, Inverness, Highlands IV2 3DU
☎ *(01463) 241999* Grant Skinner

A freehouse serving two constantly changing real ales which in winter could be Scottish or English ales but in summer are always traditional Scottish ales. Regular breweries featured include Black Isle, An Teallach and Atlas.

A traditional town pub in an old building with wood panelling, stone floor and fireplace. Good bar and restaurant food available. Occasional live music for special events. Children allowed.

OPEN *11am–11pm Mon–Wed; 11am–1am Thurs–Fri; 11am–12.30am Sat; 12.30–11.00pm Sun.*

Blackfriars

93–5 Academy Street, Inverness
☎ *(01463) 233881* Alexander MacDiarmid

Three or four guest beers regularly available, often from Greene King and Black Isle.

Old Scottish alehouse, situated close to Inverness bus and railway stations. Food available. Children's certificate.

 *11am–midnight Mon–Wed; 11am–1am Thur–Fri; 11am–11.45pm Sat; 12.30–11pm Sun.*

Clachnaharry Inn

17–19 High Street, Clachnaharry Road, Inverness IV3 8RB
☎ *(01463) 239806* George Maclean

A freehouse offering six real ales, ranging from Isle of Skye and Black Isle beers to Adnams Broadside and Greene King Abbot.

A traditional old coaching inn next to the railway and canal. Lounge and public bar. CAMRA Inverness Pub of Year 2000–03. The beer garden used to be a train platform. Food served all day. Children allowed in lounge only.

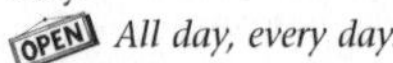

The Heathmount Hotel

Kingsmills Road, Inverness IV2 3JU
☎ *(01463) 235877* Fiona Newton
www.heathmountinn.co.uk

Freehouse where Atlas Three Sisters and Latitude, Black Isles Red Kite and Isle of Skye Red Cuillin are rotated (three real ales on every night).

Victorian building given contemporary revamp. Two bars, seven guest rooms. Smoking and non-smoking areas in the restaurant. Food available all day. Children allowed. Five minutes' walk from city centre.

All day, every day.

ISLE OF ARRAN

Catacol Bay Hotel

Catacol, Lochranza, Brodick, Isle of Arran KA27 8HN
☎ *(01770) 830231* Dave Ashcroft
www.catacol.co.uk

A freehouse with Arran Brewery ales always available plus up to three guest beers.

Easy-going, family-orientated hotel, with lounge bar, dining room and pool and games room. Food all day till 10pm, plus buffet every Sunday 12–4pm. Acoustic music sessions every Friday. The pub has a children's certificate and outdoor play area.

All day, every day.

ISLE OF BUTE

The Russian Tavern at the Port Royal Hotel

37 Marine Road, Port Bannatyne, Isle of Bute PA20 0LW
☎ *(01700) 505073* Dag and Olga Crawford

Usually five ales on any night from four Scots brewers: Arran, Craigmill, Fyne Ales and Kelburn.

The Russian Tavern is unique, a recreation in a waterfront Scottish inn of a pre-Revolutionary Russian bar. Features Russian beer (bottled), kvas (fermented black bread), vodka, 'wines of the Tsars' from Moldova, yoghurt ice cream (or smetana, as used in proper pavlova) and herbal soft drinks (Coca Cola and Irn Bru are banned). Five rooms. Simplest route to Bute is the CalMac ferry from Wemyss Bay. It was good enough for Stella McCartney when she married on the island but if you really must avoid the crowds you'll be relieved to learn the Russian Tavern has five yacht moorings.

All day, every day.

KINGUSSIE

The Royal Hotel

High Street, Kingussie, Inverness-shire PH21 1HX
☎ *(01540) 661898* Fiona McIsaac (manager)

Part of the NKB group (Newtonmore and Kingussie Brewery Limited), and the major outlet for the group's micro-brewery. Three regular home brews from NKB always available, including Piper's Brew and Highland Mist, plus a minimum of three guest ales.

This 52-room hotel has a main bar that holds about 200 people and offers live entertainment at weekends and mid-week in season. Food available until 9.30pm. Beer festival with over 50 real ales on offer held throughout November (special rates available). Well-behaved children and dogs welcome.

All day, every day.

KINLOCHLEVEN

The Tailrace Inn

Riverside Road, Kinlochleven, Argyll PH50 4QH
☎ *(01855) 831777*
Elizabeth Ferguson (manager)

A short walk from the renowned Atlas Brewery, at least two of whose ales are offer at any time in the bar. Other guest ales also served

Live music on Fridays in summer (forget darts, there are musical instruments behind the bar for players who come unprepared). B&B accommodation makes this a popular stopover for West Highland Way walkers.

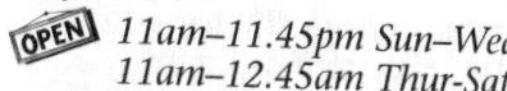
11am–11.45pm Sun–Wed; 11am–12.45am Thur-Sat.

KIRKWALL, ORKNEY

The Bothy Bar, Albert Hotel

Mounthoolie Lane, Kirkwall, Orkney KW15 1JZ
☎ *(01856) 876000*

Orkney Dark Island and Red MacGregor permanently available plus a wide selection of guest beers.

Popular traditional bar with open fire. Famous for hosting 'tunes', impromptu Orcadian folk music sessions. This is where the BBC did the real research for its *Blood of the Vikings* series.

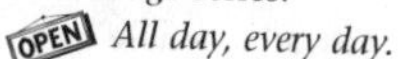
All day, every day.

MELVICH

Melvich Hotel

Melvich, Thurso, Caithness & Sutherland KW14 7YJ
☎ *(01641) 531 206* Peter Martin

Beers from the Far North range are always on offer.

A country hotel with two bars and a restaurant, overlooking the Pentland Firth to Orkney. Food served 6–8.15pm daily. Car park. Children welcome.

OPEN *All day, every day.*

NAIRN

The Invernairne Guest House

Thurlow Road, Nairn, Moray IV12 4EZ
☎ *(01667) 452039* Douglas Mitchell

Isle of Skye Red Cuillin always available plus one or two guests.

A nineteenth-century Italianate-style freehouse with wood-pannelled bar and sea view (garden path leads to the beach). Live jazz Weds nights. Ten rooms. No food.

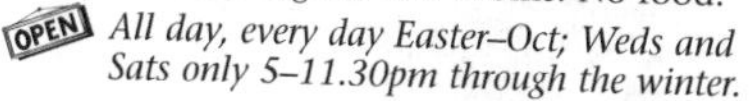
All day, every day Easter–Oct; Weds and Sats only 5–11.30pm through the winter.

ROSEMARKIE

The Plough Inn

High Street, Rosemarkie, Highlands
☎ *(01381) 620164* Rob Brutherstone

A Black Isle Brewery house with Red Kite, Hibernator, Porter and Golden Eye permanently available, plus seasonal guests.

A country village pub dating from 1691. Beer garden. Bar and restaurant food available. Car park. Children allowed.

OPEN *11am–midnight Mon–Thurs; 11am–1am Fri; 11am–11.45pm Sat–Sun.*

SLIGACHAN, ISLE OF SKYE

The Sligachan Hotel

Sligachan, Isle of Skye IV47 8SW
☎ *(01478) 650204* Iain Campbell

A freehouse with five real ale pumps in the public bar. Beers from the Isle of Skye Brewery feature along with a range from Houston and Heather Ales. Also a wide array of malt whiskies.

A 100-year-old building with a large public bar/restaurant. Pool tables, children's play areas and fresh local food.

OPEN *Easter–October and New Year only; 8am–close Mon–Sat; 11am–close Sun.*

STROMNESS, ORKNEY

The Stromness Hotel

The Pier Head, Stromness, Isle of Orkney KW16 3AA
☎ *(01856) 850298* Leona Macleod
www.stromnesshotel.com

A freehouse with Orkney The Red MacGregor and Dark Island always available.

The largest three-star hotel in Orkney, with 42 bedrooms. A separate restaurant serves food at lunchtime and evenings. Children allowed.

OPEN *All day, every day.*

ULLAPOOL

The Ferryboat Inn

Shore Street, Ullapool, Ross-shire IV26 2UJ
☎ *(01854) 612366* Richard Smith

A freehouse offering six real ales. Regulars come from the Orkney brewery, others from further afield such as Wadworth 6X.

An old-fashioned one-bar pub with coal fire and separate restaurant area. Food served at lunchtime and evenings. Children allowed.

OPEN *All day, every day.*

THE PUBS

BELHAVEN

The Mason's Arms

8 High Street, Belhaven, Dunbar, East Lothian EH42 1NP
☎ *(01368) 863700* Peter Sullivan

Belhaven 80/- or St Andrew's Ale usually available, or occasionally Sandy Hunter's Traditional Ale.

Traditional country inn, situated between West Barns and Dunbar. Bar, separate lounge and restaurant. Bar snacks served 12–2pm Mon–Tues, full bar menu 12–2pm and 6.30–9pm Wed–Sun. Children welcome until 9pm, with grass play area set within the beer garden.

12–3pm and 5–11pm Mon–Thurs; 12–1am Fri–Sat; 12–11pm Sun.

EAST LINTON

The Drover's Inn

5 Bridge Street, East Linton, East Lothian EH40 3AG
☎ *(01620) 860298* Alison and John Burns

A freehouse with Adnams Broadside and Caledonian Deuchars IPA always on the menu. Two guests, changed most weeks, include regular choices such as Greene King Abbot, Fuller's London Pride or Orkney Red MacGregor.

An old-fashioned pub-restaurant with one bar. Smoking and non-smoking dining areas and bistro. Live entertainment and folk bands monthly. Food at lunchtime and evenings. Courtesy coach for parties of six or more operates within 25-mile radius. Children allowed.

Summer: 11.30am–11pm Mon–Wed; 11.30am–1am Thurs–Sat; 12.30pm–midnight Sun. Winter: times as above, except closed 2.30pm–5pm Mon–Sat.

EDINBURGH

The Bow Bar

80 West Bow, Edinburgh EH1 2HH
☎ *(0131) 226 7667* Helen McLoughlin

Belhaven 80/-, Caledonian Deuchars IPA and Timothy Taylor Landlord always available, plus five constantly changing guests, including a couple from Scotland and the rest from other independent breweries – from Orkney to Cornwall.

Quite simply one of Edinburgh's – and Scotland's – finest bars. A well-loved and staunchly supported freehouse offering an unparalleled selection of real ales and malt whiskies. Beer festivals usually twice yearly, depending on pressure from the bar's regulars. Pies with gravy stiff as tar at lunchtime. Children not allowed.

OPEN *12–11.30pm Mon–Sat; 12.30–11pm Sun.*

Cambridge Bar

Young Street, Edinburgh, EH2 4JB
☎ *(0131) 225 4266*

Harviestoun Schiehallion and Atlas Nimbus always available. Caledonian 80/- and Deuchars IPA usually on offer, plus one of Edinburgh's most reliable guest beer lists. Expect Timothy Taylor Landlord, Fuller's London Pride, Black Sheep Bitter, Marston's Pedigree, Charles Wells Bombadier and others.

The Cambridge's friendly atmosphere has made it the base for a host of clubs and societies, from cavers to conservationists.

OPEN *12–11.45pm Mon–Sat, 12–11pm Sun.*

Carter's Bar

185 Morrison Street, Edinburgh EH3 8DZ
☎ *(0131) 623 7023* Shane Mallon

Calendonian 80/- and Deuchars IPA permanently available, plus a wide selection of guest ales from all over the UK.

Local bar in the heart of the capital city, with friendly atmosphere downstairs and pleasant, relaxing surroundings in the gallery upstairs. Live music. Food available, including free buffet on Friday evenings. Happy hours 11am–6.30pm Mon–Sat. No children under 14.

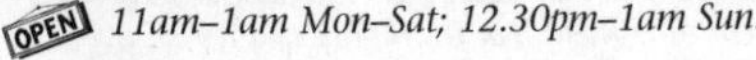
11am–1am Mon–Sat; 12.30pm–1am Sun.

The Cask & Barrel

115 Broughton Street, Edinburgh EH1 3RZ
☎ *(0131) 556 3132* Patrick Mitchell

Harviestoun Bitter & Twisted, Caledonian 80/- and Deuchars IPA are fixtures among a daily line-up of 10 real ales.

A popular horseshoe-style bar pulling in an eclectic bunch of customers. Food available at lunchtime. From the east end of Queen Street, turn left off York Place.

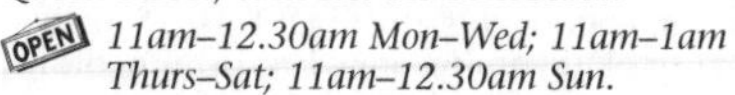
OPEN *11am–12.30am Mon–Wed; 11am–1am Thurs–Sat; 11am–12.30am Sun.*

Cloisters Bar

26 Brougham Street, Edinburgh EH3 9JH
☎ *(0131) 221 9997* Barry Robertson

A freehouse with Greene King IPA, Caledonian 80/-, Deuchars IPA and Timothy Taylor Landlord always available. Five guest ales regularly feature beers from Atlas, Orkney, Harviestoun, Hop Back, Titanic and Oakham breweries. Also a fine range of malt whiskies.

A central, old-fashioned, friendly pub, with no music. Meals are served 12–3pm every day. No children.

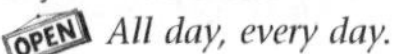
OPEN *All day, every day.*

The Cumberland Bar

1–3 Cumberland Street, Edinburgh EH3 6RT
☎ *(0131) 558 3134*
RD Simpson (owner), A Douglas (manager)

Caledonian Deuchars IPA and 80/-, Timothy Taylor Landlord and Orkney Dark Island always on the menu. The four guests, changed weekly, may include Hop Back Summer Lightning, Fuller's ESB, Greene King Abbot Ale or offerings from Atlas Brewery.

A traditional one-bar alehouse. Food served every lunchtime, with toasties, panninis and soup available in the evenings. Children allowed in part of the bar if under control.

OPEN *All day, every day.*

The Guildford Arms

1 West Register Street, Edinburgh EH2 2AA
☎ *(0131) 556 4312* Paul Cronin

Caledonian 80/-, Deuchars IPA, Orkney Dark Island, Harviestoun Waverley 70/- and Schiehallion permanently available plus seven guest beers (260+ per year) including Traquair Bear Ale and Festival Ale, plus a massive selection from all over England.

A beautiful Jacobean pub. Restaurant food available at lunchtime. At the east end of Princes Street, behind Burger King.

OPEN *11am–11pm Mon–Wed; 11am–midnight Thurs–Sat; 12.30–11pm Sun.*

Halfway House

24 Fleshmarket Close, High Street, Edinburgh EH1 1BX
☎ *(0131) 225 7101* John Ward

Specialising in Scottish breweries with three ales available at any one time. Atlas, Fyne, Harviestoun, Houston, Inveralmond, Kelburn and many others on offer at admirably low prices for cask beer in the Old Town. Look out for brewery 'showcase' weeks during the seven weeks of the Edinburgh Festival. Also a fine range of malt whiskies.

One of the smallest and friendliest pubs in the Old Town, hidden away between Waverley station and the Royal Mile and very close to both. Good value homemade Scots fare including Stovies, Cullen Skink, Haggis. Food available all day, if it hasn't sold out!

OPEN *All day, every day.*

Homes Bar

102 Constitution Street, Leith, Edinburgh EH6 6AW
☎ *(0131) 553 7710* Patrick Fitzgerald

A freehouse with five real ales served on custom-made hand pumps. Guest beers a speciality.

A traditional one-room friendly bar, with interesting decor featuring antiques and memorabilia. Snacks served 12–3pm daily.

OPEN *All day, every day.*

Leslie's Bar

45 Ratcliffe Terrace, Edinburgh EH9 1SU
☎ *(0131) 667 5957* Gavin Blake

A freehouse with real ale on six pumps. Caledonian 80/- and Deuchars IPA, plus Timothy Taylor Landlord and Harviestoun Bitter & Twisted always available. Two guest beers also offered, which often include a Maclay, Atlas or Orkney brew.

Upmarket Victorian local unchanged in over 100 years, with ornate ceiling, old-fashioned gantry and open fire. Original stained glass and numbered serving hatches. One bar. Pies and toasties only. No children. Beer and whisky festivals held twice-yearly. Two miles south of the city centre.

OPEN *11am–11pm Mon–Wed; 11am–11.30pm Thurs; 11am–12.30am Fri–Sat; 12.30–11.30pm Sun.*

Old Chain Pier

32 Trinity Crescent, Edinburgh EH5 3ED
☎ *(0131) 552 1233* Mr Nicol

Caledonian Deuchars IPA, Black Sheep Best Bitter and Timothy Taylor Landlord are more or less permanent fixtures here, plus one guest, changed every two days. Regulars include brews from Harviestoun and Moorhouse's.

A local with very mixed clientele, young and old. Non-smoking area. Food served 12–9.30pm. Children allowed.

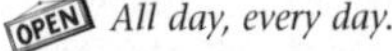
OPEN *All day, every day.*

Ossian's

185 Morrison Street, Edinburgh EH3 8DZ
☎ *(0131) 228 9149* Craig McGhee

A Belhaven house with Caledonian Deuchars IPA and 80/-, Harviestoun Bitter & Twisted, Atlas Latitude and Orkney Dark Island always available plus a guest such as Timothy Taylor Landlord or Ossian's Ale.

A refurbished bar now with two plamsa screens. One main bar and an upstairs gallery. Food served 10am–7pm daily. Private functions catered for. Close to the conference centre on the main road from Haymarket station.

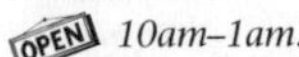
OPEN *10am–1am.*

Royal Ettrick Hotel

13 Ettrick Road, Edinburgh EH10 5BJ
☎ *(0131) 228 6413* Steven Balsillie

Caledonian 80/- and Deuchars IPA plus three guests from a wide range likely to include Timothy Taylor Landlord, Marston's Pedigree or Bateman's XB.

Part of a mansion and conservatory built in 1875 in the leafy suburbs. Bar and restaurant food available at lunchtime and evenings. Morning and afternoon teas also served. Car park, large beer garden, banqueting and conference facilities. Children allowed. Accommodation.

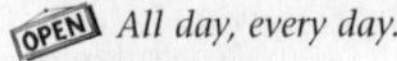
OPEN *All day, every day.*

Southsider

3–7 West Richmond Street, Edinburgh EH8 9EF
☎ *(0131) 667 2003* Mark Leech

Five real ales always available, Caledonian Deuchas IPA among them. The emphasis is on smaller breweries, and a large selection of lager-style beers is also served.

A lounge and public bar, popular with locals and students. Extensive menu available all day until 8pm. Fully refurbished. No children or animals (except guide dogs). Car park in the city centre.

OPEN *11am–midnight Mon–Wed; 11am–1am Thurs–Sat; 12.30pm–midnight Sun.*

The Starbank Inn

64 Laverockbank Road, Edinburgh EH5 3BZ
☎ *(0131) 552 4141* Scott Brown

A freehouse with Belhaven 80/-, Sandy Hunter's Traditional Ale and Timothy Taylor Landlord always available. Five guests, changed weekly, may include Tomintoul brews or those from Aviemore and other small and micro-brewers.

Traditional, old-fashioned pub with one bar, overlooking the River Forth. Separate non-smoking dining area. Food at lunchtime and evenings. Children allowed.

OPEN *All day, every day.*

The Steading

118–20 Biggar Road, Edinburgh EH10 7DU
☎ *(0131) 445 1128* William Store

A freehouse with Caledonian Deuchars IPA, Timothy Taylor Landlord and Orkney and Belhaven brews always available. Plus a guest, changed weekly. Brains Reverend James Original Ale is a favourite.

A country inn with two bars, one smoking, one non-smoking, plus a separate dining area. Food served all day. Children allowed.

OPEN *All day, every day.*

HADDINGTON

Waterside Bistro and Restaurant

1–5 Waterside, Nungate, Haddington, East Lothian EH41 4BE
☎ *(01620) 825674* James Findlay

Regular guests in this freehouse include Belhaven brews, Caledonian Deuchars IPA, Greene King Abbot and Timothy Taylor Landlord.

An old, restored cottage overlooking the River Tyne and the abbey. Separate dining area. Food at lunchtime and evenings. Children allowed.

OPEN *11am–2.30pm and 5–11pm.*

LINLITHGOW

The Four Marys

65 High Street, Linlithgow EH49 7ED
☎ *(01506) 842171* Eve and Ian Forrest

Belhaven 80/- and St Andrew's, Caledonian Deuchars and an Orkney ale always available plus nine guest beers (400 per year) that may include Greene King Old Speckled Hen, and something from Harviestoun or Timothy Taylor.

A traditional pub with antique furniture and stone walls. Local CAMRA Pub of the Year 2000, and *Sunday Mail* Pub of the Year 2002. The bar has masses of mementoes of Mary Queen of Scots, who was born at Linlithgow Palace. Food available lunchtimes and evenings Mon–Fri and all day Sat–Sun. Parking. Children allowed. Two real ale festivals held every year, with 20 real ales at each. Opposite the entrance to Linlithgow Palace.

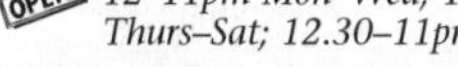

12–11pm Mon–Wed; 12pm–12.45am Thurs–Sat; 12.30–11pm Sun.

West Port Hotel

18–20 West Port, Linlithgow EH49 7AZ
☎ *(01506) 847456* Ian Leask
www.maclay.com/westporthotel.html

Owned by Maclay Inns, with Caledonian Deuchars IPA always available and two other rotating real ales changed on a daily basis.

A 14-bedroom inn with lounge, bar and function room. Food served from 8am–10pm with breakfasts and afternoon tea available as well as lunch and dinner. Car park, families welcome. Close to central Linlithglow and the palace.

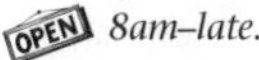

8am–late.

MID-CALDER

Torpichen Arms

36 Bank Street, Mid-Calder, Livingston, West Lothian EH53 0AR
☎ *(01506) 880020* Helen Hill

Caledonian 80/- and Deuchars IPA always available, plus guests, changed weekly. Harviestoun, Nethergate, Robinson's, Tomintoul and Cains breweries are regularly featured.

Old village pub with weekend entertainment. Bed and breakfast. Lunches only. Children allowed until 8.30pm.

All day, every day.

NORTH BERWICK

Nether Abbey Hotel

20 Dirleton Avenue, North Berwick, East Lothian EH39 4BQ
☎ *(01620) 892802* Stirling Stewart
www.netherabbey.co.uk

A freehouse with Caledonian Deuchars IPA always on the menu. Three guests may include Marston's Pedigree, Orkney Dark Island, Kelham Island Pale Rider and Timothy Taylor Landlord.

A hotel with a warm, friendly atmosphere, situated in a leafy Victorian avenue, and run by the Stewart family for the past 40 years. One main bar, brasserie and beer garden, plus first-class accommodation. Food served 12–2.30pm and 6–9.30pm daily (children's menu available). Annual beer festival every February features over 50 ales, plus live music and all-day food. Free parking. Families welcome – the hotel has a children's outdoor play area.

All day, every day.

SOUTH QUEENSFERRY

The Ferry Tap

36 High Street, South Queensferry, Nr Edinburgh EH30 9HN
☎ *(0131) 331 2000* Brian Inglis

A freehouse always offering Caledonian 80/- and Deuchars IPA plus Orkney Dark Island. Guests are changed weekly, one in winter, two in summer.

Old-fashioned real ale house with one bar and lounge. Food served at lunchtimes; snacks only in evenings. No children.

All day, every day.

THE PUBS

AIRDRIE

The Cellar Bar
79 Stirling Street, Airdrie ML6 0AS
☎ *(01236) 764495* George Cairs

Two guest ales always available from the local Belhaven brewery.

A very traditional pub offering a wide range of real ales and 369 malt whiskies. Food available 12–8pm daily. Car park. No children.

OPEN *11am–1am Mon–Sat; 12.30–midnight Sun.*

ARROCHAR

The Village Inn
Shore Road, Arrochar, Argyll and Bute G83 7AX
☎ *(01301) 702279* Jose Andrade
www.maclay.com/villageinn.html

A pub owned by Maclay Inns, with Orkney Dark Island always on the menu. The ever-changing guests may include ales from Fyne.

A 14-bedroom inn on the shores of Loch Long, built in 1827. Food served in bar and restaurant. Children allowed until 8pm. Large beer garden and car park.

OPEN *All day, every day.*

AYR

Burrowfields Café Bar
13 Beresford Terrace, Ayr KA7 2EU
☎ *(01292) 269152* Daniel Kelly

Real ale on three pumps in this freehouse. Regular guests, changed weekly, include brews from Caledonian, Clearwater, Greene King and Cains.

Live music once a week, TV and lounge bar. Food at lunchtime and evenings. Children allowed at lunchtime.

OPEN *All day, every day.*

Geordie's Byre
103 Main Street, Ayr KA8 88U
☎ *(01292) 264325*

Caledonian 80/- and Deuchars IPA always available plus three guest beers (450 per year) from Orkney (Skullsplitter) to Cornwall and Devon (Summerskill Whistle Belly Vengeance).

A friendly freehouse managed by the owners. Decorated with memorabilia and Victoriana. No food. Children not allowed. Located 50 yards from the police headquarters on King Street.

OPEN *11am–11pm (midnight Thurs–Sat); 12.30–11pm Sun.*

BALLOCK

Tullie Inn
Balloch Road, Balloch G83 8SW
☎ *(01389) 752052* Tony James
www.maclay.com/tullieinn.html

Owned by Maclay Inns, with Caledonian Deuchars IPA always available and at least one other real ale changed on a daily basis.

A large inn with 12 bedrooms, public bar and large lounge on the banks of Loch Lomond. Food served all day from 10am. Car park, beer garden, families welcome. Next to the railway station.

OPEN *All day, every day.*

BARRHEAD

Cross Stobs Inn
2–6 Grahamston Road, Barrhead G78 1NS
☎ *(0141) 881 1581*

Kelburn Brewery's Red Smiddy, Goldi Hops and Carte Blanche almost always available, plus guest beers.

Historic local pub.

OPEN *All day, every day.*

BIGGAR

The Crown Inn
109–11 High Street, Biggar, Lanarkshire ML12 6DL
☎ *(01899) 220116* Mr and Mrs A Barrie

A freehouse offering real ale on four pumps, two in each bar. Regular guests include Adnams Broadside, Greene King Old Speckled Hen, Shepherd Neame Spitfire and Wadworth 6X.

A seventeenth-century pub with two bars. Food served all day. Beer garden. Children allowed.

OPEN *All day, every day in summer; lunchtimes and evenings in winter.*

CASTLECARY

Castlecary House Hotel
Main Street, Castlecary, Cumbernauld, Lanarkshire G68 0HB
☎ *(01324) 840233* Mr McMillan
www.castlecaryhotel.com

Freehouse with a good rotation of ales, such as Harviestoun Brooker's Bitter & Twisted, Orkney Dark Island and Houston Peter's Well.

Friendly, family-run hotel with 55 cottage-style bedrooms surrounding the main building, three lounges and a restaurant. Traditional pub food served lunchtimes and evenings, with Camerons Restaurant serving lunch plus à la carte meals in the evening. Children allowed. Just off the A80 between Glasgow and Stirling.

OPEN *All day, every day.*

COVE

Knockderry House Hotel

Shore Road, Cove, Nr Helensburgh, Argyll G84 0NX
☎ *(01436) 842283* Murdo MacLeod

A freehouse with real ale on three pumps plus real cider. Regular guests, changed weekly, include brews from Fyne Ales, Atlas, Kelburn, Belhaven, Harviestoun, Caledonian.

A 10-bedroom hotel on the shores of Loch Long, built in 1851. Open fires and wood panelling abound. Food served in bar and restaurant. Five moorings available. Children allowed and 'dogs in moderation'.

 *All day, every day.*

DARVEL

Loudoun Hill Inn

Darvel, Ayrshire KA17 0LY
☎ *(01560) 320275* Graham and Janet Wellby
www.loudoun-hill-inn.co.uk

Something from Belhaven Brewery is always on offer. The guest beer is changed weekly, and Heather Fraoch Ale and Grozet are usually available in bottles.

An old, one-bar coaching inn with real fire, restaurant and function room. Food served 12–2pm and 5–8pm during opening hours. Well-behaved children welcome. Accommodation available (three en-suite bedrooms). The pub is on the main A71, one mile east of Darvel, and offers access to the Irvine Valley Paths network.

 *12–2.30pm and 5–11pm Mon–Thurs (but closed Tues night, except for residents, and Wed lunch); 12–2.30pm and 5pm–midnight Fri; 12–12 Sat; 12.30–2.30pm and 4.30–11pm Sun.*

DUMBARTON

Cutty Sark

105 High Street, Dumbarton G82 1LF
☎ *(01389) 762509* Mr Fennell

Tied to Punch Taverns, with Belhaven St Andrew's Ale always available. A weekly guest beer might well be Orkney Dark Island.

A town-centre pub with lounge bar and a mixed clientele. Food at lunchtime only. Children allowed.

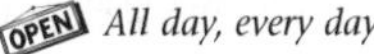 *All day, every day.*

DUNDONALD

Castle View

29 Main Street, Dundonald, Kilmarnock, Ayrshire KA2 9HH
☎ *(01563) 851112* Iain Fisher

Part of the Wilson Boyle development. Caledonian 80/- or Deuchars IPA are regularly featured. Alternatives from Orkney and Harviestoun.

Restaurant-dominated, with two bars. Food at lunchtime and evenings. Children allowed. Just off the B739.

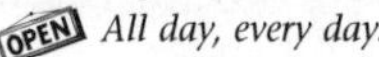 *All day, every day.*

DUNOON

The Coylet Inn

Lock Eck, Dunoon, Argyll PA23 8SG
☎ *(01369) 840426* Richard Addis (proprietor)

As good a place as any to sample Fyne Ales Highlander (4.8% ABV) – the Argyll-brewed beer is this seventeenth Century inn's top seller. Also Deuchars IPA, Caledonian 80/- plus a guest beer, often from Orkney Brewery.

Atmospheric bar has log fire; hotel four rooms. Restaurant and bar meals available. Popular with anglers (Loch Eck fishing permits available from the hotel) and orienteers. Celebrity Warning: this is where Emma Thomson and Greg Wise held their wedding reception in 2003.

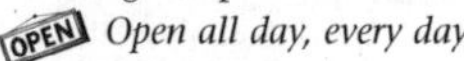 *Open all day, every day.*

FURNACE

Furnace Inn

Furnace, Inverary, Argyll PA32 8XN
☎ *(01499) 500200* Gordon Pirie

A freehouse with four or five beers always available. Guests, changed weekly, often include brews from Orkney and Clearwater.

A country-style pub, with one bar, oak beams and fires. Food served all day. Children allowed.

All day, every day.

GLASGOW

The Bon Accord

153 North Street, Glasgow
☎ *(0141) 248 4427*
Paul McDonagh (proprietor)

At least 10 real ales always available including offerings from Kelburn Brewery, Atlas Brewery, Orkney Brewery. But look out for regular festivals when over 20 brews are on.

The pub that led the reintroduction of real ale to Glasgow in the early 1970s. Remains one of the city's best – and best known – cask ale haunts. Cellar tours can be arranged for groups of 10–15, Mon–Thurs. Good value pub grub; quiz 8pm Weds night; live music 8.30pm Sat night. Home of Clan Pompey, the Scottish Portsmouth FC supporters club.

OPEN *12–11.45pm.*

The Counting House

2 St Vincent Place, Glasgow, Lanarkshire G1 2DH
☎ *(0141) 225 1060* Stuart Coxshall

This JD Wetherspoon house hosts a real ale festival in the spring, when there may be 50 brews on sale. The rest of the time, Caledonian 80/- and Deuchars IPA and Tomintoul Wildcat are among the eight beers always available. Guests change weekly.

A converted Bank of Scotland building with original fixtures and fittings, including the safe. Ninety tables. Food available all day. Children allowed until 7pm, if eating. In the city centre.

OPEN *7.30am–12am Mon–Fri; 10am–12am Sat; 10–12am Sun.*

Maclachlan's Bar

57 West Regent Street, Glasgow G2AE
☎ *(0141) 332 0595*

A range of own brews and Heather Ale always available plus two guests, usually from Scottish breweries.

A very Scottish bar with slate floor and stone bar. Around 100 malt whiskies also available. Food (specialising in venison, pheasant and salmon) available every day. No children.

OPEN *11am–11.45pm Mon–Sat; 12.30–11.45pm Sun.*

Station Bar

55 Port Dundas Road, Glasgow, Lanarkshire
☎ *(0141) 332 3117*
Michael McHugh and George Davie

A freehouse with Caledonian Deuchars IPA always available plus a guest, which might be Caledonian Edinburgh Strong Ale or Fuller's ESB.

A traditional city-centre local with one bar. Snacks, rolls and other tasty food available.

OPEN *All day, every day.*

Tap

1055 Sauchiehall Street, Glasgow G3 7UD
☎ *(0141) 339 0643* Gary Hamilton

Caledonian Deuchars IPA and 80/- usually served, with guest beers such as Heather Ale and Marston's Pedigree.

Traditional bar in a residential area catering mainly for student clientele. Specialising in jazz, with live music at weekends. A light-hearted and welcoming pub favoured by musicians and arty types. Food served 12–9pm. No children. Situated directly opposite Kelvingrove Art Gallery in West End.

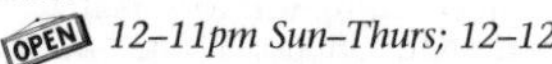

OPEN *12–11pm Sun–Thurs; 12–12 Fri–Sat.*

Taverna (formerly Athena Greek Taverna)

780 Pollokshaws Road, Strathbungo, Glasgow, Lanarkshire G42 2AE
☎ *(0141) 424 0858* Nicholas Geordiades

Six beers always available from a list of 200 guests that may include Otter Bright and beers from Rooster's, Yates, Belhaven, Caledonian and Shardlow breweries.

A café-style bar and adjacent Greek Cypriot restaurant serving Greek and European food. Children allowed. Situated beside Queen's Park railway station, not far from Shawlands Cross.

OPEN *11am–2.30pm and 5–11pm Mon–Sat; closed Sun.*

Tennents Bar

191 Byres Road, Hillhead, Glasgow G12
☎ *(0141) 341 1024* Alison O'Conner

Up to 12 beers available from a guest list (100 per year) that may include Fuller's London Pride, Greene King Old Speckled Hen and Marston's Pedigree.

A large public bar with a friendly atmosphere and no music. Bar food is available at lunchtime and evenings. Adjacent to Glasgow University and Hillhead subway.

OPEN *11am–11pm Mon–Thurs; 11am–midnight Fri–Sat; 12.30–11.30pm Sun.*

The Three Judges

12

141 Dumbarton Road, Partick Cross, Glasgow G11 6PR
☎ *(0141) 337 3055* Helen McCarroll

Caledonian Deuchars IPA always available plus eight guest beers from independent and micro-breweries, old and new.

A lively West End pub. Bar food is served at lunchtime and evenings. Parking available. Near Kelvin Hall underground.

OPEN *11am–11pm Sun–Thurs; 11am–midnight Fri–Sat.*

GOUROCK

Spinnaker Hotel

121 Albert Road, Gourock, Renfrewshire
☎ *(01475) 633107* Stewart McCartney
www.spinnakerhotel.co.uk

Belhaven 80/- regularly available, plus three guest beers – often Caledonian Deuchars IPA, Orkney Dark Island, Harviestoun Bitter & Twisted, but many others.

Small hotel, situated a quarter of a mile west of the town centre, with panoramic views over the River Clyde and Cowal Peninsula. Food available all day every day. Children welcome. Beer garden. Eight guest rooms.

11am–midnight Mon–Thurs; 11am–1.30am Fri–Sat; 12.30pm–12.30am Sun.

HAMILTON

The George Bar

18 Campbell Street, Hamilton, Lanarkshire ML3 6AS
☎ *(01698) 424225* Lynn Adams

A Belhaven pub with Caledonian Deuchars IPA usually available, plus two guests, of which Heather Fraoch Ale is a regular feature.

A friendly, traditional-style, town-centre pub with a non-smoking small back room. Cask Marque award winner. Beer festivals in April and October. Food at lunchtime (12–3pm). Children allowed. Can be tricky to find because of the one-way system! Ten minutes from the station.

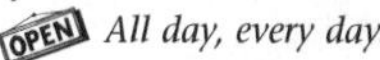
All day, every day.

HOUSTON

The Fox & Hounds

South Street, Houston, Johnstone, Renfrewshire PA6 7EN
☎ *(01505) 612991* Jonathan Wengel

A freehouse and brewpub. Home of the Houston Brewing Company, so home brews are always on the menu, plus guests, changed weekly, such as Isle of Skye Red Cuillin or Coniston Bluebird.

A traditional coaching inn with three bars and a separate restaurant area. Food at lunchtime and evenings. Children allowed.

OPEN *All day, every day.*

INVERARY

The George Hotel

Main Street East, Inverary, Argyll PA32 8TT
☎ *(01499) 302111* Donald Clark

Real ale on up to three pumps in this freehouse. Guests are changed weekly, regulars include Caledonian Deuchars IPA, Orkney Dark Island and others from local producers Fyne Ales and Houston Brewing.

An old-fashioned country house with two bars and a function room. Beer garden. Food served all day. Children allowed.

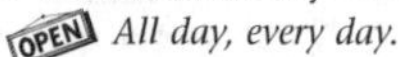
All day, every day.

INVERKIP

Inverkip Hotel

Main Street, Inverkip, Greenock, Renfrewshire PA16 0AS
☎ *(01475) 521478* AW Hardy

Caledonian Deuchars IPA plus guest.

A family-run old coaching inn with dining area and separate restaurant. TV in the public bar. Food at lunchtime and evenings. Children allowed. Popular with boaties from Scotland's biggest marina over the road. Accommodation. Car park.

OPEN *All day, every day.*

JOHNSTONE

Coanes

26 High Street, Johnstone, Renfrewshire PA5 8AH
☎ *(01505) 322925* Michael Coane

A freehouse always offering Caledonian 80/- and Deuchars IPA and Orkney Dark Island. Guests, changed weekly, may include favourites such as Orkney The Red MacGregor, Greene King Abbot Ale, Adnams Broadside or Marston's Pedigree or other occasional features.

An olde-worlde pub with a bar and lounge. Food available at lunchtime and evenings from Wed to Sat. Children allowed up to 8pm if eating.

OPEN *All day, every day.*

KILMARNOCK

The Hunting Lodge

14–16 Glencairn Square, Kilmarnock, Ayrshire KA1 4AH
☎ *(01563) 322920* Mr Little

A freehouse with real ale on up to seven pumps. Caledonian Deuchars IPA and Shepherd Neame Spitfire always available. Guests, changed weekly might include Timothy Taylor Landlord, Greene King Old Speckled Hen and Abbot Ale, and Fuller's London Pride.

Olde-worlde Georgian pub with three bars and a separate eating area. Food at lunchtime and evenings. Children allowed.

11am–3pm and 5pm–midnight Mon–Wed; all day Thurs–Sun.

LARGS

The Clachan Bar

14 Bath Street, Largs, Ayrshire KA30 8BL
☎ *(01475) 672224* Linda Maxwell

Tied to the Belhaven brewery. One real ale always available, such as Belhaven St Andrew's Ale.

A traditional pub with pool room. Bar snacks served 11am–3pm daily, with toasties available all day. Children welcome if eating.

All day, every day.

LOCHWINNOCH

The Brown Bull

33 Main Street, Lochwinnoch, Renfrewshire PA12 4AH
☎ *(01505) 843250* Laura Hunt

Four real ales always on offer from a constantly changing range. More than 400 different brews ae served each year.

Olde-worlde, welcoming one-bar pub built in 1809. Coal fire in winter. Food served 12.30–3pm and 5.30–8pm during the week, 12.30–8.30pm Sun. Children welcome until 8pm.

All day, every day.

PAISLEY

Bull Inn

7 New Street, Paisley, Renfrewshire PA1 1XU
☎ *(0141) 8490472* Alan Murdoch

Owned by Maclay Inns, with Caledonian Deuchars IPA and something from Kelburn and Houston breweries usually available plus at least one other rotating guest changed on a daily basis.

This traditional bar in the centre of town has been a pub since 1901. Small snug rooms. Live sport on TV. Food served 12–3pm and 5–7pm daily.

11am–11pm Mon–Thurs; 11am–midnight Fri–Sat; 12–11pm Sun.

Gabriels

33 Gauze Street, Paisley, Renfrewshire PA1 1EX
☎ *(0141) 887 8204* Michael O'Hare

A freehouse with Caledonian Deuchars IPA and ales from the Houston Brewing Company always available. Guests change weekly and may include Fuller's London Pride, Cotleigh and Harviestoun ales.

An oval bar with traditional decor on the walls. Separate dining area and restaurant. Food all day. Children allowed.

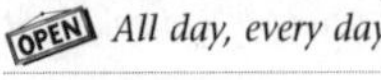
All day, every day.

The Wee Howff

53 High Street, Paisley PA1 2AE
☎ *(0141) 889 2095*

Caledonian Deuchars IPA, Kelburn Goldi Hops plus a changing selection of guest beers.

Down-to-earth drinking bar in the centre of town, but something of a Paisley institution. A tune in honour of the Wee Howff, by piper John 'Stormy' Winter, has been recorded by Strathclyde Police Pipe Band.

All day, every day.

TROON

Dan McKay's Bar

69 Portland Street, Troon KA10 6QU
☎ *(01292) 311079* Dan McKay

A freehouse with Belhaven 80/-, Caledonian 80/- and Deuchars IPA always on offer. Plus a guest beer, changed once or twice a week, which might be Timothy Taylor Landlord, Wadworth 6X, Young's Special or Fuller's London Pride.

Traditional establishment, leaning towards a café bar, with TV, live music and jazz. Food at lunchtime and evenings. Children allowed during the day.

All day, every day.

THE PUBS

ABERNETHY

Cree's Inn

Main Street, Abernethy, Perthshire PH2 9LA
☎ *(01738) 850714* Brian Johnston

A freehouse offering beers on four pumps. The range changes every week, but favourites include Belhaven 80/-, Marston's Pedigree, Greene King Abbot Ale and Caledonian Deuchars IPA and 80/-.

A one-bar country pub with separate restaurant attached, open all day. Children allowed. Accommodation.

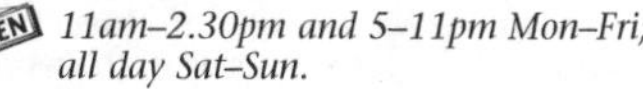
OPEN *11am–2.30pm and 5–11pm Mon–Fri; all day Sat–Sun.*

BLAIR ATHOLL

The Bothy Bar

Atholl Arms Hotel, Old North Road, Blair Atholl, Perthshire
☎ *(01796) 481205*

The sister hotel to the Moulin Hotel, with the full range of Moulin Brewery ales usually available.

This 'bothy' (the word means a place of refuge and comfort) was rebuilt using beams and wood from the old hotel stables. Food served all day. Gardens and children's play area. Disabled access and facilities.

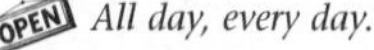
OPEN *All day, every day.*

BLAIRGOWRIE

Ericht Ale House

13 Wellmeadow, Blairgowrie PH10 6ND
☎ *(01250) 872469* Kenneth Fraser (proprietor)

Five real ales available including offerings from Inveralmond Brewery, the Cairngorm Brewing Co, Atlas Brewery and Kelburn.

Former Tayside pub of the year.

OPEN *All day, every day.*

Rosemount Golf Hotel

Golf Course Road, Blairgowrie, Perthshire PH10 6LJ
☎ *(01250) 872604* Alistair C Gibb
www.rosemountgolf.co.uk

A freehouse with two real ales always on offer. Caingorm Stag, Inveralmond Ossian's Ale, Houston Horny Wee Devil and Caledonian Deuchars IPA are recent examples although the selection rotates weekly.

A family-run hotel, with one bar and a dining area with overspill for non-smokers. Function room for hire, car park, children welcome. Good golf, fishing and walking. Food at lunchtime and evenings. Children allowed.

OPEN *All day, every day.*

The Stormont Arms

101 Perth Street, Blairgowrie, Perthshire PH10 6DT
☎ *(01250) 87312* Lewis Forbes Paterson

Three beers usually available often from Caledonian, Inveralmond, Houston, Belhaven, Tomintoul or Orkney.

Traditional pub with lots of mirrors, favoured by sporting types. No food. Car park. No facilities for children.

OPEN *11am–2.30pm and 5–11pm Mon–Thurs; 11am–11pm Fri–Sun.*

BROUGHTY FERRY

Fisherman's Tavern

10–16 Fort Street, Broughty Ferry, Dundee DD5 2AD
☎ *(01382) 775941* Jonathan Stewart

Belhaven 60/-, 70/-, 80/- and St Andrew's Ale always available. Also four guest beers (700 per year) which include Timothy Taylor Landlord, Fuller's London Pride, Arran Ale, Caledonian Deuchars IPA, Harviestoun Brooker's Bitter & Twisted, and Greene King Old Speckled Hen, plus beers from every corner of the UK.

A 300-year-old listed building, formerly a fisherman's cottage. Winner of *Scottish Licence Trade News's* Best Poured Pint in Scotland award in 2001 and *SLTN* Wine by the Glass award 2002. High-quality bar food available: full menu at lunchtimes, snacks in the evening. Live music Thursdays from 10pm. Also 11 en-suite rooms in hotel with walled garden. Children welcome. Situated by the lifeboat station at Broughty Ferry.

OPEN *11am–midnight Mon–Wed; 11am–1am Thurs–Sat; 12.30pm–midnight Sun.*

CARNOUSTIE

The Stag's Head Inn

61 Dundee Street, Carnoustie, Angus DD7 7PN
☎ *(01241) 852265* Mr Duffy

A freehouse with real ale on four pumps. Guest ales, which change constantly, may include Timothy Taylor Landlord, Caledonian 80/- or Orkney Dark Island.

A locals' pub with two bars. Food served at lunchtime and evenings in the summertime. Children only allowed in the pool table area.

OPEN *All day, every day.*

CLOVA

Glen Clova Hotel

Glen Clova, By Kirriemuir, Angus DD8 4QS
☎ *(01575) 550350* June Coventry
www.clova.com

A freehouse with Caledonian Deuchars IPA and 80/- plus Houston Brewery's Texas and St Peter's Well ales always on tap.

A country hotel with food served 12–8.30pm. Accommodation available in 10 en-suite bedrooms and a 32-bed bunk house.

OPEN *All day, every day.*

DUNDEE

Drouthy Neebors

142 Perth Road, Dundee, Angus DD1 4JW
☎ *(01382) 202187* Leon Hunter

Caledonian 80/- always on offer, with Deuchars IPA and other guests regularly featured.

Traditional pub, refurbished, with a friendly, contemporary atmosphere. Good selection of food served 12–8pm Mon–Fri and 12–6pm Sat–Sun. Children welcome during food-service hours.

OPEN *All day, every day.*

Mickey Coyle's

21–3 Old Hawkhill, Dundee
☎ *(01382) 225871* Simon Stansfield

A Maclay Inns house with Caledonian Deuchars IPA and 80/- always available, plus guests, often Bitter & Twisted or Schiehallion from Harviestoun, Isle of Skye's Hebridean Gold, or Cairngorm's Wildcat.

Traditional community pub more popular with staff from nearby university than the students. Food available lunchtimes and evenings Mon–Sat. Car park. Children allowed while food served.

OPEN *11am–3pm and 5pm–midnight Mon–Thurs; 11am–midnight Fri–Sat; 2pm–midnight Sun.*

The Phoenix Bar

103 Nethergate, Dundee, Angus DD1 4DH
☎ *(01382) 200014* Alan Bannerman

A freehouse always offering Orkney Dark Island, Caledonian Deuchars IPA and Timothy Taylor Landlord.

A traditional, one-bar pub with TV and music. Food served lunchtimes and evenings. No children.

OPEN *All day, every day.*

Speedwell Bar

165–7 Perth Road, Dundee, Tayside DD2 1AS
☎ *(01382) 667783* Jonathan Stewart
www.mennies.co.uk

A freehouse with real ale on three pumps. Erdinger Wheat Beer, the world's biggest selling wheat beer (live and cask-conditioned) is permanently available, plus two other ales often including Timothy Taylor Landlord, Fuller's London Pride, Belhaven brews and Caledonian Deuchars IPA.

A truly stunning Edwardian pub, largely unchanged since it was built in 1903, and now rightly recognised as part of the city's architectural heritage. Known locally as Mennies. One bar, two rooms (one non-smoking). Toasties only from behind the bar but drinkers are welcome to bring in pies and pastries from the bakery next door. No children.

OPEN *All day, every day.*

INVERKEILOR

The Chance Inn

Main Street, Inverkeilor, Arbroath, Angus DD11 5RN
☎ *(01241) 830308* Mrs Lee

A freehouse offering three real ales, changed weekly.

Two bars, two recommended restaurants plus accommodation. Food served lunchtimes and evenings. Children allowed. Scottish Tourist Board 3 Star rated, and Tayside CAMRA award winner.

OPEN *12–3pm and 5pm–midnight Tues–Fri; all day Sat–Sun.*

KINROSS

The Muirs Inn

49 Muirs, Kinross
☎ *(01577) 862270* Paul Chinnock
www.themuirsinnkinross.com

A selection of Scottish real ales always available, including Belhaven 80/- plus up to six guest beers (100 per year) perhaps from the Harviestoun or Border breweries. Also Scottish whiskies.

A traditional Scottish country inn. Bar and restaurant food available at lunchtime and evenings. Scottish Licensed Trade Association Food Pub of the Year Finalist 2003. Car park and courtyard. Children allowed. Accommodation. M90 junction 6, then follow signs for the A922. At the T-junction, the inn is diagonally opposite to the right.

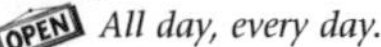
All day, every day.

MEIKLEOUR

Meikleour Hotel

Meikleour, Nr Blairgowrie
☎ *(01250) 883206*

Independence and other Inveralmond Brewery ales regularly available plus selection of guest beers often from south of the border.

Meikleour, off the A93 between Perth and Blairgowrie, is famous for a 100ft high beech hedge, said to be the largest in the world. Beer garden to help you calm down after a visit. Smart hotel and restaurant, bar meals also available. Beer garden.

All day every day

MOULIN

Original Moulin Inn

Moulin Hotel, 11–13 Kirkmichael Road, Moulin, By Pitlochry, Perthshire
☎ *(01796) 472196* Heather Reeves
www.moulinhotel.co.uk

A Moulin Brewery tied house – the brewery is located on the same premises. The full range of Moulin ales (Braveheart; Ale of Athol; Old Remedial; Moulin Light Ale) normally available.

Seventeenth-century coaching inn situated in the village square, with open fires, beams and stone walls. Originally, it was the traditional meeting house for the Parish. Extended in 1880 and again in 1970. Food served all day, every day. Car park. Children welcome away from the bar area.

OPEN *12–11pm Sun–Thurs; 12–11.45pm Fri–Sat.*

MUTHILL

Muthill Village Hotel

Muthill, Nr Crieff PH5 2DA
☎ *(01764) 681451*
Eoin and Elizabeth Haddow (proprietors)

Four guest ales available plus the bar's house ale, Tapsman's Yill (4.2% ABV), brewed by Inveralmond Brewery.

A tapsman is a head drover and the ale's name refers to the history of the eighteenth-century hotel as a stopover for Highand cattle drovers taking their beasts to market in Falkirk. Bar has farming theme and open fire. Plans to establish a Muthill Village Beer Festival. Small hotel and quality restaurant. Real ale fans, though, are drawn by the Bothy Bar.

OPEN *Open all day, every day*

PERTH

Greyfriars

15 South Street, Perth, Perthshire PH2 8PG
☎ *(01738) 633036* Pauline Marshall

A freehouse with Friar's Tipple, the exclusive house ale brewed locally by Inveralmond Brewery, always available. Guests include regular favourites Caledonian Deuchars IPA, Timothy Taylor Landlord and Greene King Old Speckled Hen.

An old-fashioned pub with stone walls and non-smoking dining room upstairs. The clientele tends to be 25 and upwards. Homemade food at lunchtime only. Accompanied children welcome lunchtimes.

OPEN *All day, every day.*

Lovat Hotel

90–2 Glasgow Road, Perth, Tayside PH2 0LT
☎ *(01738) 636555* Mr Graeme Gillon

A freehouse with real ale on three pumps, one rotated each week. The nearby Inveralmond brewery suppplies Lia Fail, Ossian and others.

A large bistro/bar, offering food at lunchtime and evenings. Children welcome. Accommodation. On the outskirts of Perth, a mile from Broxton roundabout.

OPEN *11am–2.30pm and 5pm–11pm.*

Scone Arms

Perth Road, Scone, Perth PH2 6LR
☎ *(01738) 551341*

Free house with ales from Perth's own Inveralmond Brewery, including Independence session beer and Ossian's Ale, plus regular monthly guest brews.

Historic pub, built in 1807, with live music in one bar Sunday afternoons, ceilidhs alternate Sunday evenings.

OPEN *All day, every day.*

STRATHTUMMEL

Loch Tummel Inn

Strathtummel, Nr Pitlochry, Perthshire PH16 5RP
☎ *(01882) 634272* Michael Marsden

A freehouse with Moulin Braveheart always available.

An old coaching in with six bedrooms, loch views and log fires (one in bathroom!). Home-cooked food is served, with smoked salmon a speciality.

OPEN *All day, every day, March–Oct only.*

Whitehaven
CUMBRIA
Windermere
Kendal
Ramsey
Peel
Douglas
M6
Morecambe
Lancaster
LANCASHIRE
Blackpool
Preston
Southport
M6
GREATER MANCHESTER
MERSEYSIDE
Liverpool
Holyhead
Llandudno
Colwyn Bay
M53
M56
Denbigh
Flint
CHESHIRE
Chester
M6
Caernarvon
CLWYD
Wrexham
Crewe
Llangollen
Portmadoc
GWYNEDD
Bala
STAFFORD
Llanfyllin
M6
Barmouth
Dolgellau
Telford
Towyn
SHROPSHIRE
Newtown
Wolverhampton
Aberystwyth
Llanidloes
Ludlow
POWYS
Aberayron
Knighton
HEREFORD & WORCESTER
New Quay
Lampeter
Kington
Cardigan
DYFED
Hereford
Fishguard
Llandovery
Brecon
M50
Ross on Wye
WEST GLAMORGAN
Haverfordwest
Monmouth
MID GLAMORGAN
GWENT
Stroud
Pembroke
M4
Swansea
Newport
AVON
Porthcawl
SOUTH GLAMORGAN
Cardiff
Bristol
M5
Bath
Weston Super Mare
Ilfracombe
Minehead

THE BREWERIES

BRAGDY YNYS MON (ISLE OF ANGLESEY) BREWERY

Cae Cwta Mawr, Lon Cae Cwta, Llangefni, Anglesey LL77 7SD
☎ *(01248) 723801*
www.angleseyale.co.uk

MEDRA 4.0% ABV
WENNOL 4.1% ABV
SOSBAN FACH 4.3% ABV
TARW DU 4.5% ABV
AMNESIA 4.9% ABV

Brewery tours can be arranged.

BRAGDY CEREDIGION BREWERY

2 Brynderwen, Llangrannog SA44 6AD
☎ *(01223) 9654099*

GWRACH DU (BLACK WITCH) 4.0% ABV
Porter.
Y DRAIG AUR (THE GOLD DRAGON) 4.2% ABV
Gold in colour and full-flavoured.
BARCUD COCH (RED KITE) 4.3% ABV
Red in colour, with fruit flavours.
BLODEUWEDD (FLOWER FACE) 4.5% ABV
Organic ale.
YR HEN DARW DU (OLD BLACK BULL) 6.2% ABV
Powerful stout.

BRAIN AND CO. LTD

The Cardiff Brewery, Crawshay Street, Cardiff CF10 5TR
☎ *(029) 2040 2060 (Brewery tours)*
www.sabrain.com

BRAINS DARK 3.5% ABV
Chocolate and nut flavours, dry finish.
BRAINS BITTER 3.7% ABV
Brewed with a combination of malts, Brains' own yeast strain and Fuggles and Goldings hops. The beer has an initial sweet malt flavour with a dry, well-hopped finish.
BUCKLEY'S BEST BITTER 3.7% ABV
A light fragrant nose with a pleasingly hoppy character. Well balanced with nutty overtones.
BRAINS S.A. 4.2% ABV
A distinctly hoppy strong ale brewed to a recipe combining the characteristics of pale and crystal malts with the choicest traditional ale hop varieties.
REVEREND JAMES 4.5% ABV
Full-flavoured and warming, the Reverend James is rich in palate, spicy and aromatic with a deeply satisfying finish.

BRECONSHIRE BREWERY

CH Marlow Ltd, Ffrwdgrech Industrial Estate, Brecon, Powys LD3 8LA
☎ *(01874) 623731*
www.breconshirebrewery.com

BRECON COUNTY ALE 3.7% ABV
Award-winning traditional bitter, hoppy and full flavoured.
GOLDEN VALLEY 4.2% ABV
Award-winning golden ale, refreshing with a 'soft' bitterness.
RED DRAGON 4.7% ABV
Classic red ale, smooth and easy-drinking.
RAMBLERS RUIN 5.0% ABV
Award-winning dark amber traditional strong best bitter.
Seasonal:
WINTER BEACON 5.3% ABV
Strong, golden-coloured winter warmer.

BRYNCELYN BREWERY

Wern Fawr Inn, 47 Wern Road, Ystalyfera, Swansea Valley, SA9 2LX
☎ *(01639) 843625*

BUDDY MARVELLOUS 4.0% ABV
BUDDY'S DELIGHT 4.2% ABV
PEGGY'S BREW 4.2% ABV
CWRW CELYN 4.4% ABV
OH BOY 4.5% ABV
MAYBE BABY 4.5% ABV
CHH 4.5% ABV

BULLMASTIFF BREWERY

14 Bessemer Close, Leckwith, Cardiff CF11 8DL
☎ *(02920) 665292*

WELSH GOLD 3.8% ABV
BEST BITTER 4.0% ABV
JACK THE LAD 4.1% ABV
THOROUGHBRED 4.5% ABV
HARE OF THE DOG 4.6% ABV
WELSH BLACK 4.8%
WELSH RED 4.8%
BRINDLE 5.0% ABV
SON OF A BITCH 6.0% ABV
LEGLESS 11% ABV
Seasonal:
SUMMER MOULT 4.3% ABV
SPRING FEVER 4.5% ABV

CONWY BREWERY LTD
Unit 17 Conwy Morfa Business Park, Ffordd Sampari, Conwy LL32 8HH
☎ *(01492) 585287*
www.conwybrewery.co.uk

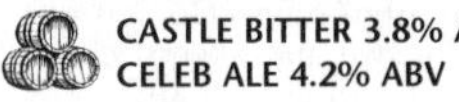

CASTLE BITTER 3.8% ABV
CELEB ALE 4.2% ABV

CWMBRAN BREWERY
Gorse Cottage, Graig Road, Upper Cwmbran, Trofaen NP44 5AS
☎ *(01237) 482543*

CROW VALLEY BITTER 4.2% ABV
Bitter and hoppy.
FOUR SEASONS 4.8% ABV
Light, summer ale.
FULL MALTY 4.8% ABV
Malty cross between a bitter and mild.

FELINFOEL BREWERY CO. LTD
Farmers Row, Felinfoel, Llanelli SA14 8LB
☎ *(01554) 773357*
www.felinfoel-brewery.com

DRAGON BITTER 3.4% ABV
BEST 3.8% ABV
DOUBLE DRAGON 4.2% ABV

NAGS HEAD BREWERY
Nag's Head Inn, Abercych, Boncath, Pembrokeshire
☎ *(01239) 841200*

OLD EMRYS 4.0% ABV

PLASSEY BREWERY
The Plassey, Eyton, Wrexham LL13 0SP
☎ *(01978) 780922 (Brewery tours)*
www.plasseybrewery.co.uk

PLASSEY BITTER 4.0% ABV
FUSILIER 4.5% ABV
CWRW TUDNO 5.0% ABV
DRAGON'S BREATH 6.0% ABV

SHIP & CASTLE BREWERY
High Street, Aberystwyth, Dyfed SY23 1JG
☎ *(01970) 612334*

SHIP ORIGINAL 3.6% ABV
OATMEAL STOUT 4.4% ABV
HARVEST MOON 4.5% ABV
RHEIDOL RESERVE 4.8% ABV
MUTLEY'S REVENGE 4.9% ABV

THE SNOWDONIA BREWERY
Beddgelert Road, Waunfawr, Gwynedd LL55 4AQ
☎ *(01286) 650409*

HAF 5.0% ABV
WELSH HIGHLAND BITTER 5.0% ABV
POTENT 7% ABV
February only.

SWANSEA BREWING COMPANY
Joiner's Arms, 50 Bishopston Road, Bishopston, Swansea SA3 3EJ
☎ *(01792) 232658*

BISHOPSWOOD 4.3% ABV
THREE CLIFFS GOLD 4.7% ABV
ORIGINAL WOOD 5.2% ABV

TOMOS WATKIN
Now brewed c/o Hurns Beer Company
Unit 3 Century Park, Valley Way, Swansea Enterprise Park, Swansea SA6 8RP
☎ *(01792) 560020/797300*

WHOOSH 3.7% ABV
Dark amber beer with light bitterness.
WATKINS BB 4.0% ABV
Malty, with moderate bitter flavour and floral hoppiness.
MERLINS STOUT 4.2% ABV
Dark, with powerful liquorice flavour.
WATKINS OSB 4.5% ABV
Award-winning, malty with delicate hoppiness.
Plus seasonal ales e.g. Cwrw Haf, Cwrw Santa. They have recently launched Watkins OSB and Cwrw Haf in bottles.

WARCOP COUNTRY ALES
Newhouse Farm, St Brides, Wentlooge, Gwent NP10 8SE
☎ *(01633) 680058*

PITSIDE 3.7% ABV
Delicate and malty.
ARC 3.8% ABV
Light, hoppy session beer.
PIT PROP 3.8% ABV
Dark mild.
BLACK AND AMBER 4.0% ABV
Pale ruby bitter.
CASNEWYDD 4.0% ABV
Light, quaffer.
DRILLERS 4.0% ABV
Yellow, with some hoppiness.
HILSTON PREMIER 4.0% ABV
Dry and refreshing.
STEELER'S 4.2% ABV
Malt flavours.
RAIDERS 4.3% ABV
Powerful hoppiness.
ROLLERS 4.3% ABV
Pale ruby bitter.
CUTTERS 4.4% ABV
ZEN 4.4% ABV
FURNACE 4.5% ABV
Malt, dry in the aftertaste.
REFUGE 4.5% ABV
RIGGERS 4.5% ABV
Golden version of Furnace.
PRINTERS 4.6% ABV
ROCKERS 4.8% ABV
DEEP PIT 5.0% ABV
Flavoursome ruby beer.
DOCKER'S 5.0% ABV
Full-bodied, with fruit throughout.
PAINTERS 5.0% ABV

THE PUBS

ABEREDW

The Seven Stars Inn

Aberedw, Builth Wells, Powys LD2 3UW
☎ *(01982) 560494* Ian and Patricia Evans

A freehouse with Wadworth 6X, Brains Reverend James and occasional guests.

A traditional, two-bar olde-worlde inn with log fires, oak beams, no fruit machines or juke box. Beer garden, private room for hire, car park. Former CAMRA regional pub of the year. Bar and restaurant food available all day, including breakfasts. Children welcome. Accommodation.

OPEN *All day every day*

ABERYSTWYTH

The Coopers Arms

Northgate Street, Aberystwyth, Ceredigion SY23 2JT
☎ *(01970) 624050* Mrs Somers

A Felinfoel Brewery tied house with two pumps serving Felinfoel ales and occasional guests.

Live music, no juke box or fruit machines. Well-mixed clientele of locals and students. No food. Children allowed.

OPEN *11am–11pm Mon–Sat; 12–10.30pm Sun.*

The Ship & Castle

High Street, Aberystwyth, Dyfed SY23 1JG
☎ *(01970) 612334* Pete and Dee Fraser

A freehouse and micro-brewery serving own beers plus two guests such as Fuller's London Pride. The guests change weekly.

An old one-bar pub with food available at lunchtime and evenings. Children allowed.

OPEN *11am–11pm Mon–Sat; 12–10.30pm Sun.*

CRICKHOWELL

The Bear Hotel

High Street, Crickhowell, Powys NP8 1BW
☎ *(01873) 810408 www.bearhotel.co.uk*
Stephen Hindmarsh

A freehouse with Brains Reverend James permanently featured, plus two guests.

Fifteenth-century coaching inn, now a hotel with extensive bar and lounge areas. Beer garden, 34 letting rooms. Bar food available every day, 12–2pm and 6-10pm. Restaurant open Tues–Sat evenings only. Dogs and children welcome.

OPEN *11am–3pm and 6–11pm.*

CWMANN

The Ram Inn

Cwmann, Lampeter, Carmarthenshire SA48 8ES
☎ *(01570) 422556* Gary and Sian Pugh

A freehouse offering Archers Golden Bitter plus one or two guest beers changed frequently, from national and smaller breweries.

An old drover's pub one mile outside Lampeter on the Llandovery Road, dating from around 1560, with a dining room, bar and garden. CAMRA Best Pub in Wales 1997 and 4th Best Pub in Britain 1997. Food available at lunchtime and evenings. Children allowed.

OPEN *All day, every day.*

GOGINAN

The Druid Inn

Goginan, Aberystwyth, Ceredigion SY23 3NT
☎ *01970 880650* John and Margaret Howell

A freehouse with three real ales always available. Banks's Bitter and Brains brews are regulars, while other guests changed monthly might include Cottage Champflower Ale.

The building dates back to 1730, when it was used by the local mining community. Bar, pool room, function room. No juke box or games machines. Food available all day in a separate dining room. Children allowed. B&B available. On the A44 heading into Aberystwyth.

OPEN *11am–11pm Mon–Sat; 12–10.30pm Sun.*

HAY ON WYE

The Three Tuns

Hay on Wye, Powys

This is a one-room pub barely able to accomodate two rickety tables but fabulous beer, cider and perry straight from the barrel.

The landlady has been there forever and is quite a character. People often spill out onto the pavement from this pub - as 10 is a crowd inside – especially during the Hay on Wye literary festival, held in the town each year.

OPEN *All day, every day.*

HOWEY

The Drovers Arms

Howey, Llandrindod Wells, Powys LD1 5PT
☎ *(01597) 822508* Henry and Joyce Torz
www.drovers-arms.co.uk

A freehouse serving guest ales such as the ever-popular Wood Shropshire Lad.

A cosy, traditional village inn set in beautiful scenic mid-Wales. The bar lounge has a real log fire and is decorated to a high standard with an emphasis on comfort. Award-winning homemade food served in bar and restaurant. Well-behaved children welcome. Three en-suite rooms, with dinner, bed and breakfast available.

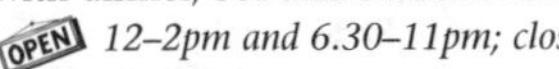 *12–2pm and 6.30–11pm; closed Tues.*

LLANBADARN FYNYDD

The New Inn

Llanbadarn Fynydd, Llandrindod Wells, Powys LD1 6YA
☎ *(01597) 840378* Robert Barton

A freehouse with two real ale pumps changed at least monthly. Wood Shropshire Lad and brews from Eccleshall (Slaters) and Wye Valley are among those usually stocked.

A traditional ale and food house with log fires. Food available lunchtimes and evenings in a separate restaurant. Children allowed. Located on main A483 between Newton and Llandrindod Wells.

 *10.30am–3pm and 5.30–11pm in summer; 12–2.30pm and 7–11pm in winter.*

LLANBEDR

The Red Lion Inn

Llanbedr, Crickhowell, Powys NP8 1SR
☎ *(01873) 810754* Mr Hart

Brains Rev James Original permanently available plus one guest from a range which includes Greene King Abbot Ale, Shepherd Neame Spitfire, Timothy Taylor Landlord, Elgood's Double Swan and Hook Norton and Cottage Brewing Company brews.

A quiet, 300-year-old pub with beams and real fires. Non-smoking room and garden. Nearby campsite situated in a very beautiful spot in the Black Mountains. Home-cooked food available at lunchtimes and evenings in summer and evenings only in winter. Children and dogs welcome. Bootwash provided outside for walkers and up-to-date toilets are always open.

 *7–11pm Mon–Tues; 12–2.30pm and 7–11pm Wed–Fri; 11am–11pm Sat; 12–4pm and 7–10.30pm Sun.*

LLANGORSE

The Castle Inn

Llangorse, Brecon, Powys LD3 7UB
☎ *(01874) 658225* Mr Williams

A freehouse with three pumps serving ales including Breconshire Golden Valley and guests such as Bateman XB, Greene King Old Speckled Hen and many more.

An olde-worlde village inn with a 27-seater restaurant. Food available at lunchtime and evenings. Children allowed under supervision. Outside drinking area with good views.

 *12–3pm and 6–11pm Mon–Fri; 11am–11pm Sat; 12–10.30pm Sun.*

LLANIDLOES

The Red Lion

8 Longbridge Street, Llanidloes, Powys SY18 6EE
☎ *(01686) 412270* Mandy James

A freehouse serving Banks's brews, plus one guest beer.

A modernised, ten-bedroom hotel with a friendly atmosphere. Open fires, patio garden. Restaurant food and bar meals available lunchtimes and evenings. Children allowed in the restaurant only.

11.30am–3pm and 7–11pm (10.30pm Sun).

LLANWRTYD WELLS

Stonecroft Inn

Dolecoed Road, Llanwrtyd Wells, Powys LD5 4RA
☎ *(01591) 610332/610327*
Pete and Jane Brown
www.stonecroft.co.uk

Four regularly changing beers, perhaps from Brains, Dunn Plowman, Wye Valley or Breconshire. Home of the mid-Wales beer festival, held in November.

Welcoming Victorian country pub situated in the smallest town in Britain and popular with cyclists and visitors. One large bar with a real fire, plus large riverside beer garden. Pool, darts, Sky TV. Bar food served Fri–Sun lunchtime (12–3pm) and every evening (6–9pm). Hot basket snacks at other times. Car park. Children welcome. Live music on Saturdays. Accommodation available next door.

 *5–11pm Mon–Thurs; 12–11pm Fri–Sat; 12–10.30pm Sun.*

MACHYNLLETH

The Wynnstay Hotel

Maengwyn Street, Machynlleth, Powys SY20 8AE
☎ *(01654) 702941* Charles Dark

A freehouse with an ever-changing variety of real ales, some big brands such as Greene King Old Speckled Hen and IPA, and Timothy Taylor Landlord, alongside some Welsh brands such as Brains and a representative selection from micro-breweries. Organic ales and seasonal brews included. Also traditional cider on draught.

A comfortable bar in an old coaching inn with very large real open fire. Restaurant (evenings) and quality bar meals (lunchtimes and evenings). Children welcome. Accommodation. Parking.

Main pub: lunchtimes and evenings; Stable bar: 11am–11pm.

MONTGOMERY

The Dragon Hotel

1 Market Square, Montgomery, Powys SY15 6PA
☎ *(01686) 668359* Mark and Sue Michaels
www.dragonhotel.com

A genuine freehouse serving three real ales. Wood's Special and Draught Bass re regulars, plus a guest.

A seventeenth-century family-run coaching inn with 20 rooms a function room and an indoor swimming pool. Food available at lunchtime (12–2pm) and evenings (7–9pm). Traditional jazz on Wednesday evenings. Children allowed.

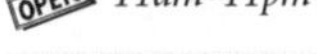 *11am–11pm Mon–Sat; 12–10.30pm Sun.*

PENGENFFORDD

The Castle Inn

Pengenffordd, Talgarth, Powys LD3 0EP
☎ *(01874) 711353* Paul Mountjoy

A freehouse with three pumps serving alternating guest ales. Brains Rev James Original, Shepherd Neame Spitfire and Bateman XXXB are often, plus others from breweries such as Cottage and others.

A rural country inn with separate dining area. B&B, plus barn-style dormitory accommodation in the middle of the hills: a good walking area at 1,000 feet. Food available at lunchtimes and evenings. Children allowed.

 *11am–3pm and 7–11pm (10.30pm Sun).*

PISGAH

The Halfway Inn

Devil's Bridge Road, Pisgah, Aberystwyth, Dyfed SY23 4NE
☎ *(01970) 880631* David Roberts

Badger Dorset Best and Felifoel Double Dragon always available, plus one constantly changing guest during the summer months.

A traditional olde-worlde hostelry 700 feet up with magnificent views of the Cambrian mountains and Rheidol Valley. Bar and restaurant food available at lunchtime and evenings. Pool table. Car park and garden. Children allowed. Accommodation. Free overnight camping for customers. Located halfway along the A4120 Aberystwyth to Devil's Bridge road. Note, this is not the Pisgah near Cardigan.

12–2pm and 6.30–11pm (10.30pm Sun). Times may vary in winter.

RHAYADER

The Cornhill Inn

West Street, Rhayader, Powys LD6 5AB
☎ *(01597) 811015* Rob Wey and Della Bufton

Breconshire's Ramblers Ruin and Red Dragon plus a rotating guest.

Built in 1540, a freehouse with olde-worlde character. Low beams, tiled floors and open fires. Courtyard garden. Bar food available at lunchtimes (12–2.30pm) and evenings (6–8.30pm). Parking. Children and dogs welcome. Accommodation (cottage to let). On the road to Elan Valley.

11am–11pm (10.30pm Sun).

RHYDOWEN

The Alltyrodyn Arms

Rhydowen, Llandysul, Ceredigion SA44 4QB
☎ *(01545) 590319*
Russell Patterson and Chris Sheath

A genuine freehouse serving three or four real ales from a constantly changing list.

A 16th-century pub with open fires, a pool room and beer garden. Bar snacks available during the weeks, restaurant food at weekends. Regular folk music evenings. Children and dogs welcome. Functions catered for. Beer tastings organised. On the A475 between Lampeter and Newcastle Emlyn.

12–11pm Tues–Sat; 12–4pm Sun (closed Mon).

TALYBONT-ON-USK

The Star Inn

Talybont-on-Usk, Brecon, Powys LD3 7YX
☎ *(01874) 676635* Joan Coakham

A constantly changing range of real ales on six pumps, including brews from Felinfoel, Shephered Neame Hancocks and Theakston. A former regional pub of the year.

A 250-year-old riverside and canalside site, with lovely garden. Food is available at lunchtimes (12–2pm) and evenings (7–9pm). Pool room, parking, garden, live music on Wednesdays (a blues festival on the second weekend in August), quiz nights on Mondays. Children welcome. Ensuite accommodation. Less than a mile off the A40 between Brecon and Abergavenny (Brecon six miles, Abergavenny 14 miles).

11am–3pm and 6.30–11pm (all day Saturday).

TREGARON

The Talbot Hotel

Main Square, Tregaron, Ceredigion SY25 6JL
☎ *(01974) 298208* Graham Williams

A freehouse with three hand pumps serving a wide range of real ales.

An old, traditional pub offering a friendly welcome. Beer garden. Open fires, separate restaurant, accommodation, beer garden. Restaurant and bar food available at lunchtime and evenings. Ample parking. Children allowed.

11am–11pm Mon–Sat; 12–10.30pm Sun.

THE PUBS

ABERGELE

The Bull Hotel

Chapel Street, Abergele, Conwy LL22 7AW
☎ *(01745) 832115* Lindsay While

Lees GB Mild and JW Bitter regularly available.

Family-run pub situated just outside Conwy town on the LLanrwst road. Restaurant and music-free main bar. Food served Wed–Mon 11am–2pm and 6–8pm. Car park. Children welcome. Accommodation.

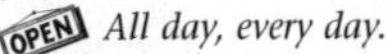
All day, every day.

BANGOR

Belle Vue

Holyhead Road, Bangor, Gwynedd LL57 2EU
☎ *(01248) 364439* Mr Jonathan Lewis

Marston's Pedigree always available, plus a rotating guest.

Lunchtime menu of home-cooked food, including Sunday roasts. Children welcome at lunchtimes.

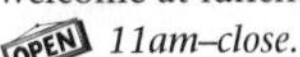
11am–close.

Globe Inn

Albert Street, Bangor, Gwynedd LL57 2EY
☎ *(01248) 362095* Gerallt Williams

Two ales permanently on the pumps, one standard and one premium. Marston's Pedigree and Conwy Brewery's Castle Ale, plus a local guest beer.

Children welcome. Food available.

11am–close.

The Castle

Glanrafon, off High Street, Bangor, Gwynedd LL57 ILP
☎ *(01248) 355866* Christopher Hughes

Part of the Laurel pub company with five hand pumps. Regular guests include Timothy Taylor Landord, Caledonian 80/-, Marston's Pedigree, Wadworth 6X, Brains and Brains SA, plus Hook Norton Old Hooky.

A roomy pub with a large open single floor, dark wood floors, background music. Wheelchair access, well ventilated throughout. Food available 12–3pm. Children allowed until 4pm. Opposite the cathedral, close to the railway station.

12–11pm Mon–Thurs;12–12 Fri–Sat; 12–10.30pm Sun.

The Tap & Spile

Garth Road, Bangor, Gwynedd LL57 2SW
☎ *(01248) 370835* Dean Ibbetson

Greene King IPA, Abbot and Old Speckled Hen, Adnams Best Bitter and Broadside and rotating guests regularly available.

A suburban pub with B&B. Food served lunchtimes and evenings. Located by the pier.

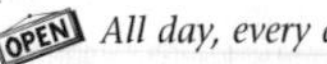
All day, every day.

BETWS-Y-COED

Pont-y-Pair Hotel

Holyhead Road, Betws-y-Coed LL24 OBN
☎ *(01690) 710407* Mr J Carr

Marston's Pedigree and Greene King Abbot Ale usually available.

Small hotel situated in the heart of Snowdonia with lots of rural pursuits close by. Home-cooked food available 12–3pm and 6–9pm daily. Children welcome.

11am–11pm Mon–Sat; 12–10.30pm Sun.

BETWS-YN-RHOS

The Wheatsheaf

Betws-yn-Rhos, Abergele, Conwy LL22 8AW
☎ *(01492) 680218* Raymond Perry

Greene King IPA and Wadworth 6X regularly available.

Located in the Best Kept Village in Wales 2003, this is an inn with an olde-worlde atmosphere and lots of brass, first licensed in 1640. Food every lunchtime and evening. Car park. Beer garden with Wendy house and high chairs available.

12–3pm and 6–11pm Mon–Fri; 12–11pm Sat; 12–10.30pm Sun.

BLAENAU FFESTINIOG

Rhiw Goch Inn

Bron Aber, Transfynydd, Blaenau Ffestiniog LL41 4UY
☎ *(01766) 540374* Mr Bryan Voce

Ales changed either weekly or bi-weekly include Marston's Pedigree, Greene King IPA and a range of others.

Set on a Norwegian log cabin tourist site, which enables the proprietor to keep his selection of real ales going.

12–11pm all year round apart from the quiet month of November when opening hours may be reduced.

BODFARI

Dinorben Arms Inn

Bodfari, Denbigh LL16 4DA
☎ *(01745) 710309* Mr David Rowlands

Marston's Pedigree, Banks's ales and a guest changed every week.

Pretty hillside setting for pub with views of surrounding countryside. Restaurant and carvery meals available with meals also served outdoors on timber framed balconies adorned with hanging baskets. Historic glass-topped well inside the pub. Ample car parking space. The pub is up a winding hilly lane.

 *12–3pm and 6–11pm.*

BROUGHTON

The Spinning Wheel Tavern

The Old Warren, Broughton CH4 OEG
☎ *(01244) 531068* Mr Mike Vernon

Guest beers regularly rotated including Greene King IPA , Fuller's London Pride and Marston's Pedigree.

Family-run pub in a secluded spot well off the main road, with a popular restaurant.

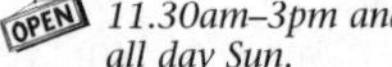 *11.30am–3pm and 6–11pm Mon–Sat; all day Sun.*

BRYNFORD

The Llyn y Mawn Inn

Brynford Hill, Brynford, Flintshire CH8 8AD
☎ *(01352) 714367* Dewi and Annette Lewis

A freehouse serving up to six brews every week. Welsh ales are favoured, plus others from small breweries.

Typical Welsh long house with restaurant and gardens. Real fires, background music. Food available 12–3pm and 6.15–8.15pm weekdays; 12–9.30pm weekends. Booking is advisable for food. Well-behaved children allowed, but not in the bar. Adjacent to the A55 expressway and can be seen from there.

 *12–3pm and 5.30–11pm Mon–Thurs; all day Fri–Sun. All day, every day in summer.*

CADOLE

Colomendy Arms

Gwernaffield Road, Cadole, Mold CH7 5LL
☎ *(01352) 810217* Elsie Butler

Five different guests on pumps. Shepherd Neame Master Brew offered most of the time, with other guest examples including Ridleys Prospect, Orkney The Red McGregor, Shepherd Neame Early Bird, Weetwood ales and a range of others.

Small, cosy, but extremely friendly pub with bar, small lounge and beer garden. Located in tiny village just off the main Mold to Ruthin road.

 *7–11pm Mon–Wed; 6–11pm Thurs; 4–11pm Fri (closed weekday lunchtimes); 12–11pm Sat; 12–10.30pm Sun.*

CAERNARFON

The Alexandra Hotel

North Road, Caernarfon, Gwynedd LL55 1BA
☎ *(01286) 672871* Ken Moulton

A Whitbread tied house serving a range or guests. Regulars include Wadworth 6X, Greene King Old Speckled Hen and Marston's Pedigree.

Tables outside. No food. Children allowed in afternoons only.

OPEN *11am–11pm Mon–Sat; 12–10.30pm Sun.*

The Prince of Wales Hotel

Bangor Street, Caernarfon, Gwynedd LL55 1AR
☎ *(01286) 673367* Mr Gareth Humphreys

Marston's Bitter is always on offer as are Welsh Highland Bitter and Haf, both from the Snowdonia Brewery. The one guest beer could be from any independent brewery.

A traditional pub within a hotel in a townscape setting, half a mile from Caernarfon Castle and half a mile from the yacht marina. An ideal base for Snowdonia and the Irish ferries. Breakfast is served 7–9.30am; lunch 11.30am–2pm and dinner 6–8.30pm and the emphasis is on home cooking. Children and dogs are welcome and the pub has designated family rooms. Car park.

 *11am–11pm Mon–Sat; 12–10.30pm Sun.*

CAERWYS

The Travellers Inn

Pen y Cefn, Caerwys, Mold CH7 5BL
☎ *(01352) 720251* Kevin Jones

A freehouse with Charles Wells Bombardier regularly available plus various other guests rotated on the two remaining pumps. One home brew: Roy Morgan's Original 3.8–3.9% ABV usually on offer.

A family pub and restaurant with food available all day. Children allowed. Located on the A55.

OPEN *11am–11pm Mon–Sat; 12–10.30pm Sun.*

CILCAIN

The White Horse

The Square, Cilcain, Mold, Flintshire CH7 5NN
☎ *(01352) 740142* Mr Peter Jeory

A freehouse with four hand pumps serving a wide range of beers on rotation. Exmoor Gold, Greene King Abbot, Marston's Pedigree and Fuller's London Pride plus numerous others. Others might include beers from Archers or Cottage breweries. The range changes every other day.

A small, cosy, village pub, several hundred years old, spread over four rooms with real fires and beams. No juke box or pool table. Food available at lunchtime and evenings. No children.

12–3pm and 6.30–11pm Mon–Fri; 12–11pm Sat; 12–10.30pm Sun.

CLAWDD-NEWYDD

Glan Lyn Inn

Clawdd-Newydd, Ruthin LL15 2NA
☎ *(01824) 750754* Nigel Cooper

Real ales rotated regularly to include the likes of Wychwood Hobgoblin, Greene King Abbot Ale, Jennings Cumberland and others.

Old-style typical village pub. Food available 6–9pm Thurs/Fri; 4–9pm Sat; 12–4pm Sun.

OPEN *4.30–11pm Mon–Fri; 12–11pm Sat; 12–10.30pm Sun.*

COLWYN BAY

Rhos Fynach

Rhos Promenade, Colwyn Bay LL28 4NG
☎ *(01492) 548185* Mr Robert Skellie

Marston's Pedigree and Banks's Bitter always on offer. Guest ales rotate approximately every two weeks.

Historic pub central to Colwyn Bay, family friendly with spacious beer garden and restaurant. Also caters for weddings and parties. Food served 12–9pm.

OPEN *11am–11pm (10.30pm Sun).*

The White Lion Inn

Llanelian-yn-Rhos, Colwyn Bay, Conwy LL29 8YA
☎ *(01492) 515807* Simon Cole
www.whitelioninn.co.uk

A freehouse with three real ales usually available from a wide range that changes fortnightly.

A traditional stone-built Welsh country inn with slate floor, log fires and beams. Non-smoking dining area and food available at lunchtime and evenings. Children allowed.

OPEN *11.30am–3pm and 6–11pm Mon–Sat; 12–3pm and 6–10.30pm Sun.*

CYMAU

Ye Olde Talbot Inn

Cymau Lane, Cymau, nr Wrexham
☎ *(01978) 761410* WJ Mee

Hydes Anvil Bitter permanently available, plus a changing seasonal beer every two months.

A traditional drinkers' pub. No food. Car park. Children welcome.

OPEN *7–11pm Mon–Fri; 12–4pm and 7–11pm Sat; 12–4pm and 7–10.30pm Sun.*

DENBIGH

The Eagle Inn

Back Row, Denbigh, Denbighshire LL16 3TE
☎ *(01745) 813203* Mrs Karen Williams

A freehouse serving three real ales including Wadworth 6X, Marston's Pedigree and a guest.

A large pub with a snooker room, pool, darts etc. The pub runs quiz nights. Food available at lunchtime. Children allowed if eating.

12–3pm and 6.30–11pm Mon–Fri; 11am–11pm Sat; 12–10.30pm Sun.

DULAS

Pilot Boat Inn

Dulas, Amlwch, Anglesey
☎ *(01248) 410205* Mark Williams

A Robinson's tied house serving Best Bitter.

Traditional country pub in an area of outstanding natural beauty. Popular with locals and tourists alike. Food served 12–9.30pm daily. Car park. Children's menu and play area. Situated on the A5025.

OPEN *11.30am–11pm Mon–Sat; 12–10.30pm Sun.*

FELINHELI

Gardd Fon

Beach Road, Felinheli, Gwynedd LR56 4RD
☎ *(01248) 670359* William Hughes

One permanent bitter, plus a rotating guest, such as Charles Wells Bombardier or Hook Norton Best regularly available.

Friendly, family-run waterside village pub, popular with locals, the sailing fraternity and walkers. Very popular non-smoking bistro; bar food also available. Children welcome. Beer garden overlooking the Menai Strait. Follow signposts to Caernarfon, then signs to Felinheli; the pub is situated down on the waterside.

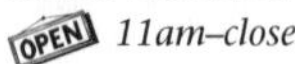
11am–close.

FFRITH

The Poacher's Cottage

High Street, Ffrith, Wrexham LL11 5LH
☎ *(01978) 756465* Mr David Griffiths

Greene King Old Speckled Hen permanently available, plus rotating others such as Marston's Pedigree and Fuller's London Pride.

Old-style pub in countryside setting with open fires. Spacious car park. Restaurant open at same time as pub.

7–11pm Mon–Fri; all day Sat–Sun.

GLYN MYFYR

Crown Inn

Llanfihangel, Glyn Myfry LL21 9UL
☎ *(01490) 420209* Michael Morley

Two pumps in regular use with frequently rotating guests including Phoenix, Wye Valley, Weetwood ales and several smaller micro-breweries.

Winner of local CAMRA branch award for Best Pub of Year 2002 and North Wales, Merseyside and Cheshire regional winner for 2002. Food available – bar meals. Children welcome.

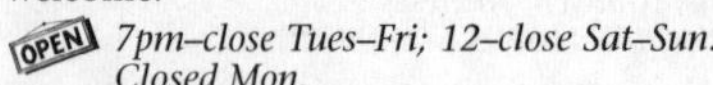
7pm–close Tues–Fri; 12–close Sat–Sun. Closed Mon.

GORSEDD

The Druid Inn

Gorsedd, Holywell, Flintshire CH8 8QZ
☎ *(01352) 710944* Elizabeth Craig

A freehouse usually serving Greene King IPA plus a selection of guests.

A listed twelfth-century long house with oak beams and log fires. The separate non-smoking restaurant serves food every evening and Sunday lunchtime. Children allowed. Located off the A5026, two miles west of Holywell. Private functions catered for.

All day, every day.

GRESFORD

Pant yr Ochain

Old Wrexham Road, Gresford, Wrexham LL12 8TY
☎ *(01978) 853525*
Lindsey du Prole and John Unsworth

Locally brewed Plassey beers permanently available here, plus Timothy Taylor Landlord with others on rotation.

Large pub set in its own grounds with big garden. Several dining areas and food served all day. Attracts clientele from all around the locality and further afield.

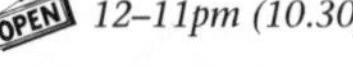
12–11pm (10.30pm Sun)

GWERNAFFIELD

Miner's Arms

Church Lane, Gwernaffield CH7 5DT
☎ *(01352) 740803* Mr P Hammersley

Camerons Bitter and rotating guests including Banks's ales and Marston's Pedigree.

Quiet rural pub in former mining village, catering mainly for local clientele. There is a lounge and bar with darts and pool table. Bar snacks available.

All day, every day.

GWERNYMYNYDD

Owain Glyndwr

Glyndwr Road, Gwernymynydd, Nr Mold, Flintshire CH7 5LP
☎ *(01352) 752967* Richie and Maureen Smith

Ales include Greene King Speckled Hen and Marston's Pedigree.

Rural pub with bed and breakfast accommodation and restaurant offering home-cooked food with good choice of vegetarian meals and Sunday roasts. Log fires and homely atmosphere. There is a pool table.

5–11.30pm Mon–Sat; 12–4pm and 7–10.30pm Sun.

HALKYN

Brittania Inn

Pentre Road, Halkyn, Flintshire CH8 8BS
☎ *(01352) 780272* K Pollitt

A JW Lees house with Traditional Bitter and GB Mild always available, plus a seasonal Lees ale.

A traditional country pub overlooking the Dee and Mersey estuaries – you can see as far as Blackpool Tower! Two bars, a family area, games room and separate conservatory restaurant/function room. Homemade food specialising in local produce available 12–2.30pm and 6.30–9pm Mon–Sun. Children welcome, highchairs available. Small beer garden. Disabled access and facilities. Car park.

11.30am–11pm Mon–Sat; 12–10.30pm Sun.

HOLYWELL

Glan-yr-Afon Inn

Milwr, Holywell, Flintshire CH8 8HE
☎ *(01352) 710052* Mr Pastor

Five real ales at any one time, most from local breweries, including Anglesey and the Plassey, Wrexham.

Children's playground, games room, real fireplace. Bar snacks and restaurant food. B&B, function room, car park.

12–3pm and 5.30–late (supper licence) Mon–Fri; all day Sat–Sun.

LLANDUDNO

The Queen Victoria

Church Walks, Llandudno LL30 2HD
☎ *(01492) 860952* Mr and Mrs Robert Watts

One of the Union Pub Company tenancies serving Banks's brews and up to five others, such as Wychwood Hobgoblin and Everards Tiger. Guests changed every month.

Refurbished inside and out, this is a Victorian pub, comfortable and family-orientated. Food is a speciality with a separate restaurant and bar menu available at lunchtime and evenings. Children allowed. Situated near the pier.

11am–11pm Mon–Sat; 12–10.30pm Sun.

LLANGOLLEN

Corn Mill

Dee Lane, Llangollen LL20 8PN
☎ *(01978) 869555* Mr Andrew Barker
www.cornmill-llangollen.co.uk

Local Plassey beers constantly on the pumps, plus three regularly rotating guests including Timothy Taylor Landlord.

Rural riverside bar full of beams with watermill still turning behind the bar. Opened as a pub in June 2000. Bar and restaurant food available. Children welcome.

12–11pm (10.30pm Sun)

The Sun Inn

49 Regent Street, Llangollen, Denbighshire LL20 8HN
☎ *(01978) 860233*
Alan Adams and Paul Lamb

A freehouse offering six real ales that could well include Weetwood Old Dog and Wye Valley brews. Four Belgian beers and two real ciders also available.

A friendly, lively, beer-drinkers' pub which gets very busy, with a good atmosphere and old-style decor. Take the A5 towards Llangollen. Live music four nights a week – open mic, Mon; jazz, Tues; rock, Thurs; blues/folk Fri.

Summer 11am–11pm Mon–Sat; winter 3–11pm Mon–Fri, 11am–11pm Sat; 12–10.30pm Sun all year round.

LLOC

The Rock Inn

Lloc, Nr Holywell, Flintshire CH8 8RD
☎ *(01352) 710049* T Swift

Burtonwood Bitter and at least one guest bitter always available.

Small friendly, family-run two-bar pub with dining room. Large car park with picnic benches. Food available lunchtimes and evenings except Tues. Children welcome.

12–11pm (10.30pm Sun).

MELIDEN

Melyd Arms

23 Ffordd Talargoch, Meliden LL19 8LA
☎ *(01745) 852005* Frank Del-Pinto

Marston's Bitter permanently available here and rotating guests including Marston's Pedigree and Banks's ales.

Popular village-centre pub with split-level eating area, log fires, pleasant atmosphere.

12–11pm (10.30pm Sun).

MENAI BRIDGE

Victoria Hotel

Telford Road, Menai Bridge LL59 5DR
☎ *(01248) 712309* Mrs Ann Smeaton

Anglesey brew Medra permanently on pumps, plus Mansfield ales also available.

Function room with special licence. Restaurant, garden area, children welcome.

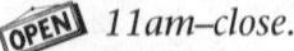
11am–close.

MORFA NEFYN

Cliffs Inn

Beach Road, Morfa Nefyn, Gwynedd LL53 6BY
☎ *(01758) 720356*
Lona Fitzpatrick and Peter Binch

A freehouse with two pumps usually serving one English and one Welsh ale, the Welsh brew usually from Brains.

A food-orientated pub with good beer. Outside patio, food available at lunchtime and evenings in a separate dining area. Children allowed.

12–3pm and 6–11pm (10.30pm Sun)

NORTHOP

Stables Bar at Soughton Hall

Soughton Hall Country House Hotel and Restaurant, Northop, Flintshire CH7 6AB
☎ *(01352) 840577* Mr John Rodenhurst

A freehouse serving real ales from Plassey and monthly rotating guests such as Shepherd Neame and Coach House brews.

An unusual location, set in the old stable block of the hotel complex. The hayloft has been converted into a restaurant. Beer garden and wine shop. Food available at lunchtime and evenings. Children allowed. Located off the A55 Flint/Northop junction.

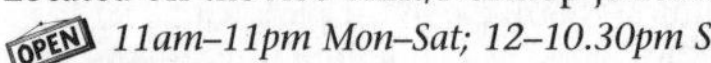
11am–11pm Mon–Sat; 12–10.30pm Sun.

OLD COLWYN

The Red Lion

385 Abergele Road, Old Colwyn, Colwyn Bay, Conwy LL29 9PL
☎ *(01492) 515042* Geoff Hughes

A freehouse serving seven cask ales, five of which are constantly rotated and include Brains SA, Charles Wells Bombardier, Greene King Abbot Ale and Old Speckled Hen, plus many more.

A village pub on the main road with a double lounge bar, open fires and no music in lounge. The public bar has a pool table, TV and juke box. No food. Children not allowed.

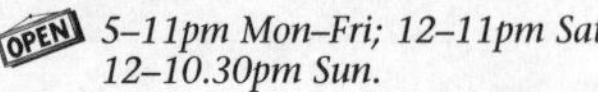
5–11pm Mon–Fri; 12–11pm Sat; 12–10.30pm Sun.

PENTREFOELAS

Giler Arms Hotel

Rhydlydan, Pentrefoelas, Nr Betws-y-Coed LL24 OLL
☎ *(01690) 770612* John and Sue Cowlishaw

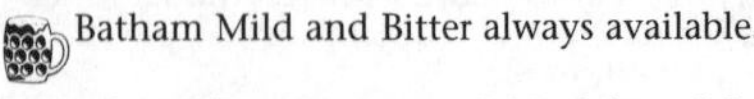
Batham Mild and Bitter always available.

The hotel has a campsite, B&B, fishing lake and restaurant. Children welcome.

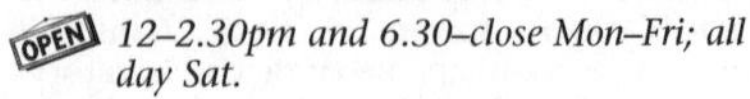
12–2.30pm and 6.30–close Mon–Fri; all day Sat.

PENYSARN

Y Bedol

Penysarn, Anglesey LL69 9YR
☎ *(01407) 832590* Steven and Sheila Hughes

A selection of three Robinson's ales always available.

Warm, friendly pub with beer garden, pool room, karaoke and quiz nights and occasional local Welsh entertainment. Bar food available evenings. Children allowed. Credit cards accepted.

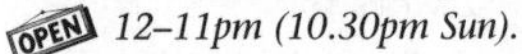
12–11pm (10.30pm Sun).

PONTBLYDDYN

New Inn

Corwen Road, Pontblyddyn, Nr Mold CH7 4HR
☎ *(01352) 771459* Mr D Hunt

Three guests, changed weekly, including a full range such as Highgate, Brains and Weetwood ales.

Child-friendly pub with play area. Food available.

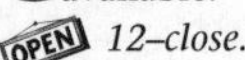
12–close.

PORTHMADOG

Ship Inn

Lombard Street, Porthmadog, Gwynedd LL49 9AP
☎ *(01766) 512990)* Georgina and John Adams

Timothy Taylor Landlord, Greene King IPA and Old Speckled Hen constantly available.

Popular two-roomed inn with separate dining area situated close to the harbour. Food served lunchtimes and evenings. Children welcome. Annual beer festival.

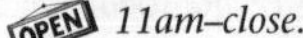
11am–close.

RHEWL

The Drovers Arms

Rhewl, Ruthin, Denbighshire LL15 2UD
☎ *(01824) 703163*
Mr A Givern and Miss A Nancarrow

A freehouse serving two real ales such as Weetwood Eastgate and other guests.

A 300-year-old pub and an old meeting place for drovers. An English Civil War skirmish took place on the bridge outside the pub. Large garden with tables, barbecues in nice weather. Food available at lunchtime and evenings. Well-behaved children allowed. Conservatory and children's safe play area.

12–3pm and 5–11pm Mon–Fri; 12–11pm Sat; 12–10.30pm Sun.

RHYL

Sussex

Sussex Street, Rhyl LL18 15G
☎ *(01745) 362910* Derek Smith

Very wide range of real ales on the pumps, constantly rotating to include guests such as Shepherd Neame Bishop's Finger, Hop Back Summer Lightning, Bateman XXXB and many others.

Designated family dining areas and non-smoking area. Food served 10am–10pm. Children welcome.

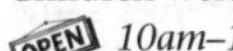
10am–11pm (10.30pm Sun).

RHYD DDU

The Cwellyn Arms

Rhyd Ddu, Gwynedd LL54 6TL
☎ *(01766) 890321)* Graham Bamber

A freehouse serving nine real ales, perhaps Dorothy Goodbody's Warming Wintertime Ale (Wye Valley), Cottage Great Western Ale, Young's Special, Fuller's London Pride, Thwaites Bitter, Wadworth 6X and Old Timer, Coach House Gunpowder Strong Mild or McGuinness Feather Plucker Mild.

A country inn with B&B accommodation and cottages to let. Restaurant, beer garden, children's adventure playground, bunkhouses and camping on nearby 25-acre area leading to Cwellyn Lake. Food available all day every day. At the foot of Mount Snowdon, on the Caernarfon/Beddgelert road.

11am–11pm Mon–Sat; 12–10.30pm Sun.

ROSSETT

The Golden Grove

Llyndir Lane, Burton Green, Rossett
☎ *(01244) 570445* Mr Dennis Ames

Offers five real cask ales, a favourite being Marston's Pedigree. Recently ran a guest beer festival with the likes of Caledonian Deuchars IPA, Highgate Davenport's Bitter, Badger Best and Wadworth 6X, Hook Norton Old Hooky. Also has other regular beers, such as a Banks's Bitter and Marston's.

Family-friendly, warm and cosy, but spacious thirteenth century coaching inn and restaurant, with beamed ceilings, open fires and olde-worlde charm. Large garden area. Unusual location on border between Chester and North Wales. Also offers selection of fine wines.

11.30–11pm Tues–Sun. Open Mon in summer but not winter.

RUTHIN

Red Lion

Cyffylliog, Ruthin, Denbighshire LL15 2DN
☎ *(01824) 710664* Mrs C F Kimberley Jones

JW Lees Bitter regularly available and also seasonal beers from the same brewery.

Friendly, family-run country pub with lots of character. Caters for eveyone, including family meals and bed and breakfast. Food served 7–10pm Mon–Fri and 12–10pm Sat–Sun. Car park. Children welcome.

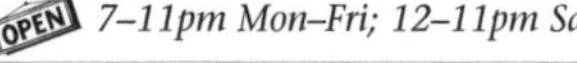
7–11pm Mon–Fri; 12–11pm Sat–Sun.

Three Pigeons

Graigfechan, Ruthin LL15 2EU
☎ *(01824) 703178*
Heather and Morton Roberts

Wide selection of ales changed regularly and including Enville ales and Plassey beers from the local Wrexham brewery, such as Fusilier.

Seventeenth-century inn, well supported by locals. Restaurant open every day except Sunday and Monday evenings. Live music by local bands, plus a drop-in session on a Sunday night. Charity music festivals held in a field with a stage at the back of the pub have raised up to £30,000 for good causes. Camping sites available. Pub offers jugs of beer from the cellar. Families and children welcome.

12–3pm and 5.30–11pm.

ST ASAPH

The Kentigern Arms

High Street, St Asaph LL17 ORG
☎ *(01745) 584157* Mrs Redgrave

A freehouse offering Caledonian 80/- plus maybe another guest.

A seventeenth-century coaching inn with beams and open fires. A separate small room can be used for children or as a dining room. Four bedrooms. Food available. Children allowed.

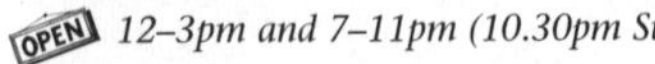
12–3pm and 7–11pm (10.30pm Sun).

SYCHDYN

Glas Fryn

Raikes Lane, Sychdyn, Nr Mold, CH7 6L2
☎ *(01352) 750500* James Meakin
www.glasfryn-mold.co.uk

Timothy Taylor Landlord and local Plassey beers permanently on the pumps, with rotating guests including Shepherd Neame Spitfire, Greene King Old Speckled Hen, Weetwood ales, Ruddles, Phoenix Arizona and a range of others including ales from the new Conwy Brewery. Real ales have been given more prominence here over recent years and the staff encourage customer feedback and try to cater for specific requests.

Glas Fryn is opposite Clwyd Theatr Cymru, Mold. There is a popular and often busy restaurant. Children welcome.

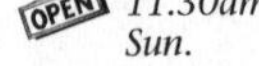
11.30am–close Mon–Sat; 12–10.30pm Sun.

TREUDDYN

Liver Inn

Rhydtalog, Treuddyn, Nr Mold CH7 4NU
☎ *(01824) 780244* Charles and Stuart Dodd

Guest beers change regularly and include Shepherd Neame Spitfire, Greene King Old Speckled Hen and IPA, Jennings Cumberland Bitter and brews from Cottage.

Food available, adult and children's menu. Families welcome.

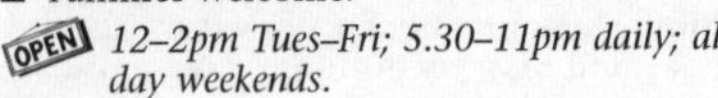
12–2pm Tues–Fri; 5.30–11pm daily; all day weekends.

WAUNFAWR

The Snowdonia Parc Brewpub and Campsite

Beddgelert Road, Waunfawr, Gwynedd LL55 4AQ
☎ *(01286) 650409* Karen Humphreys

A brewpub in which the landlady's son, Gareth, provides the beer, usually to around 5.0% ABV. Marston's Bitter and Pedigree are among a range of guest real ales always available. Up to four beers in total in summer.

A village pub in beautiful surroundings. Campsite, family room. Food available. Play area with play equipment and safety surface. On the A4086 Roman road from Caernarfon to Beddgelert. Nearby terminus for the Welsh Highland Railway from Caernarfon.

11am–11pm Mon–Sat; 11am–10.30pm Sun.

YSCEIFIOG

Fox Inn

Ysceifiog, near Holywell, Flintshire CH8 8NJ
☎ *(01352) 720241* Wendy Langford

Five draught pumps constantly in operation. Greene King Abbot Ale and rotating guests, some from local micro-brewery.

A small village pub which also serves as the village post office on a Friday morning. Bar and lounge, children welcome in the games room. Food served Wed/Thur/Fri evenings and all day Sat and Sun until 9pm.

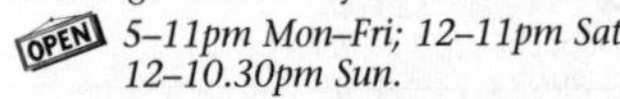
5–11pm Mon–Fri; 12–11pm Sat; 12–10.30pm Sun.

THE PUBS

ABERCRAVE

The Copper Beech Inn

133 Heol Tawe, Abercrave, Swansea Valley SA9 1XS
☎ *(01639) 730269* David Macadam

A family-run freehouse with five guest ales changing weekly. Beers from the nearby Breconshire Brewery, in Brecon, are popular and often featured; others favourites include Tomos Watkin and Brains beers.

A locals' pub, with function room and beer garden. Families welcome. Bar and restaurant food lunchtime and evenings (no food Sunday evening). Accommodation.

11.30am–11.00pm (10.30pm Sun).

ABERTHIN

The Farmer's Arms

Cowbridge Road, Aberthin, Cowbridge, Vale of Glamorgan CF71 7HB
☎ *(01446) 773429*
Simon Fullbrook and Michael Pugh

Wadworth 6X is always on offer plus one guest beer which changes every week. Popular favourites include beers from local Cardiff brewer Bullmastiff and Cottage Brewing Company.

A Victorian detached pub in the heart of the village with one bar, a restaurant and beer garden. Popular with locals and passing trade. Children welcome. Food served lunchtime and evenings.

12–3pm and 6pm–11pm Mon–Sat; 12–3pm and 7pm–10.30pm Sun.

BASSALEG

The Tredegar Arms

4 Caerphilly Road, Bassaleg, Newport NP10 8LB
☎ *(01633) 893247* David Blackborow

A Laurel Pub Company tied house with five hand pumps and up to six beers from the barrel. Brews change weekly but regulars include Shepherd Neame Spitfire and Timothy Taylor Landlord. Popular guests include Hook Norton Old Hooky and Adnams Broadside.

A busy wayside inn, near junction 28 of the M4. Large beer garden, ample car parking. Food available lunchtime and evenings. Children allowed.

11am–11pm Mon–Sat; 12–10.30pm Sun.

BETTWS NEWYDD

The Black Bear Inn and Restaurant

Bettws Newydd, Usk, Monmouthshire NP15 1JN
☎ *(01873) 880701*
Gillian and Stephen Molyneux

A freehouse with between two and four real ales available at any one time, all guests, for example Timothy Taylor Landlord. The range changes every couple of weeks.

An old one-bar country pub with fine restaurant and beer garden. Families welcome. Food available at lunchtime and evenings and all day Sat–Sun. Accommodation. Children allowed. Three miles outside Usk.

12–2pm and 6–11pm Tues–Fri (closed Mon); 12–11pm Sat; 12–10.30pm Sun.

BISHOPSTON

The Joiners' Arms

50 Bishopston Road, Bishopston, Swansea SA3 3EJ
☎ *(01792) 232658*
Ian, Kathleen and Phil Davies

Home of the Swansea Brewing Company. Eight pumps serving seven beers including all the home brews (Bishopswood Bitter, Three Cliffs Gold and Original Wood), plus Marston's Pedigree and a range of guests.

A traditional village pub with mixed clientele, no juke box. Food available at lunchtime and in the evenings. Children allowed. Regular beer festivals held.

11.30am–11pm Mon–Sat; 12–10.30pm Sun.

BLACKMILL

The Ogmore Junction Hotel

Blackmill, Bridgend CF35 6DR
☎ *(01656) 840371* Andrew Taylor

Two pumps including Greene King Old Speckled Hen or a guest beer from smaller brewers on one of the other pumps.

A country pub with beer garden and car park that backs on to the River Ogmore. Food is available lunchtime and evenings. Situated not far from the M4 on the main road to Ogmore Vale. A fortnightly sheep sale is held behind the pub from the end of July to the end of December.

11am–11pm Mon–Sat; 12–10.30pm Sun.

BLAENAVON

Cambrian Inn

Llanover Road, Blaenavon, Torfaen NP4 9HR
☎ *(01495) 790327* Lesley and Ralph Harris

Four pumps dedicated to real ale, two of which regularly serve Brains Bitter and Brains SA. Other beers favoured include Greene King Old Speckled Hen, and Brains Merlin's Oak and Reverend James.

A typical Welsh mining village pub. Darts, pool, cards, etc. No food. Street parking opposite the pub. Children allowed until 7pm in the games room.

6–11pm Mon–Thurs; 12–11pm Sat; 12–10.30pm Sun.

BRIDGEND

The Pen y Bont Inn

Derwen Road, Bridgend CF31 1LH
☎ *(01656) 652266* Ruth and Jim Simpson

Two pumps serving a beer from Brains, which is always available, plus a guest which could be something like Theakston Old Peculiar.

A small, friendly, comfortable pub. Food available 12–6pm Mon–Sat, with fresh rolls served all day Sunday. No children allowed. Located near the railway station – formerly the Railway Hotel.

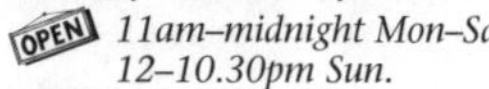

11am–midnight Mon–Sat; 12–10.30pm Sun.

CARDIFF

Cayo Arms

36 Cathedral Road, Cardiff CF11 9LL
☎ *(029) 2039 1910*
Nigel Sandford-Hill (manager)

Run by Celtic Inns, this busy pub has nine real ale pumps on the one bar serving Tomos Watkin ales including BB, OSB, Whoosh and Cwrw Haf. Brains beers such as Reverend James and SA make a regular appearance, and the guest is often from Bullmastiff, another local brewery.

Lively pub with a patio seating area at the front of this converted Victorian townhouse. Expect rugby fixtures to be shown on the screens inside (it's very busy on match days) and to hear Welsh spoken at the bar. Now has bed and breakfast accommodation available; food is served lunchtime and evenings during the week and all day Saturday and Sunday.

12–11pm (10.30pm Sun).

Chapter Bar

Chapter Arts Centre, Market Road, Canton, Cardiff CF5 1QE
☎ *(029) 2031 1050* Dave Morgan (manager)

Four pumps serving three ever-changing guest ales and one with Brains Rev James, plus three regular German weissbeers and pilsners. In addition, the bar is stocked with 250 bottled European beers, including Belgian Leffe and Duval and German ales and pilsners, and an impressive array of single malt whiskies.

Situated in a popular arts centre and cinema, this bar is buzzing with Cardiff's arty crowd on most evenings. Children are welcome. Nearby café in the centre. Popular beer festivals in June and October.

6–11pm Mon–Wed; 5–11pm Thurs; 5pm–12.30am Fri; 6–11pm Sat; 7–11pm Sun.

The Conway Inn

58 Conway Road, Pontcanna, Cardiff CF11 9NW
☎ *(029) 2023 2797*
Eddie and Gaynor Pritchard

There are five real ales always on offer at this corner pub including Greene King IPA and Abbott, Timothy Taylor Landlord, Charles Wells Bombardier and Fuller's London Pride. Guest ales are often available too – favourites include Shepherd Neame Spitfire.

This traditional, Victorian pub can be found on a quiet street corner in the leafy Cardiff suburb of Pontcanna. It has a lounge, bar and outdoor tables and a strong, local following – thanks to its reputation for well-kept real ale. The new landlords are considering introducing occasional beer festivals. No food – basic snacks only at present although this could change under the new management.

12–11pm (10.30pm Sun).

The Gatekeeper

9–10 Westgate Street, Cardiff CF10 1DD
☎ *(029) 2064 6020* James Ace (manager)

A Wetherspoon's pub serving two or three regular cask ales plus up to six guest beers. Regular ales include Brains SA, Arms Park and Dark, and guest beers come from a changing range of small breweries from all over the country.

Just across the road from the Millennium stadium, this is a huge pub on two floors that is nearly always busy, especially on match days. Food served all day, every day until an hour before closing. Children allowed; baby-changing facilities and children's menu provided.

10am–11pm Mon–Sat; 12–10.30pm Sun.

Owain Glyndwr

St John's Street, Cardiff CF10 1XR
☎ *(029) 2022 1980* Glyn White

Five pumps serving regularly changing cask ales including Hook Norton Haymaker, Fuller's London Pride and many others. There is usually Weston's Old Rosie cask cider available too.

This pub has, yet again, been refurbished – this time for the better. The cosy single bar, serving well-kept real ale, is now, once again, to be separated from its noisier cousin next door (which attracts a younger, bottled-beer-drinking crowd). Situated on a pedestrianised street opposite St John's Church, this pub attracts a mixture of faithful regulars and passing trade. It gets quite busy in the evening – especially at weekends – and in the summer tables and chairs are put out in the bustling church square. Excellent food served all day, every day.

 *12–11pm (10.30pm Sun).*

The Yard Bar & Kitchen

Old Brewery Quarter, St Mary Street, Cardiff CF10 1AD
☎ *(029) 2022 7577* Nick Newman (manager)

Three real ales from Cardiff's own Brains brewery are always on offer here – Bitter, SA and Dark.

This large new pub and bar has been recreated out of the old brewery tap pub for the Brains brewery, The Albert, and part of the old brewery itself. The front half of the open plan pub retains The Albert's traditional decor and cosy pub charm; the rear half sports flagstones and incorporates some of the industrial piping left behind when the brewery moved out. Food is served all day, every day from 10am to midnight.

 *10am–1am Mon–Sat; 10am–12.30am Sun.*

CHEPSTOW

Carpenter's Arms

Llanishen, Nr Chepstow, Monmouthshire NP16 6QH
☎ *(01600) 860812* John and Joy Davies

Two pumps are dedicated to real ale at this country freehouse, one a regular and one constantly changing. Timothy Taylor Landlord is a firm favourite; the other pump features Hook Norton Old Hooky, Wadworth 6X or any one of the many beers from small, independent brewers.

The pub, in the small village of Llanishen, dates back to the seventeenth century and features beams, open fires, a lounge and a bar. You won't find a juke box or fruit machines here – just a good, old-fashioned pub welcome. The new landlords are building a patio at the back where they plan to have outdoor tables; work on six B&B rooms is due for completion mid 2005. Food is available lunchtime and evenings (except Sunday evening).

 *12–3pm and 6pm–11pm Tues– Sat (closed Mon); 12–3pm and 7.30pm–10.30pm Sun.*

The Coach & Horses

Welsh Street, Chepstow, Monmouthshire NP6 5LN
☎ *(01291) 622626* Ian Meyrick

A Brains tied pub, with the brewery's ales on three pumps and two guests, changing every week. Regular visitors include Greene King Old Speckled Hen. Additional range of beers available in the summer. This pub takes part in Chepstow's Beer Festival, usually held in June or July.

A family pub with B&B accommodation and food available at lunchtime and evenings in a separate dining area.

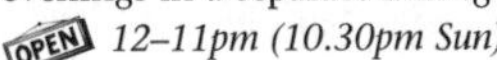 *12–11pm (10.30pm Sun).*

CLYDACH

The Carpenter's Arms

High Street, Clydach, Nr Swansea SA6 5LN
☎ *(01792) 843333* Richie Saunders

Four real ales, mainly local brews, always on offer, often from the Swansea Brewing Company, Bryncelyn Brewery and Tomos Watkin. Young's and Adnams beers also favoured.

A stone-built village pub with two bars and a restaurant. Attracts mainly local clientele (a local cycle club holds regular meetings here) and runs four seasonal beer festivals a year. Food available, bar snacks and à la carte menu, lunchtime and evenings. Just off route 43 of the National Cycle Network.

 *11am–11pm (10.30pm Sun).*

CLYTHA

Clytha Arms

Clytha, Monmouthshire NP7 9BW
☎ *(01873) 840206* Mr and Mrs Canning

Hook Norton Best is among those beers permanently available, plus Brains SA. Three other pumps serve a constantly changing rota of guest ales (up to 200 per year) from breweries such as Freeminer, Felinfoel, RCH, Wye Valley, Jennings, Fuller's, Exmoor and Adnams. The pub also hosts a Welsh beer festival in mid-summer when you'll find up to 24 ales on offer.

A large old dower house with restaurant and traditional bar. Bar and restaurant food available at lunchtime and evenings. Car park, garden, accommodation. Children allowed. Located on the old Abergavenny to Raglan road.

 *6–11pm Mon; 12–3.30pm and 6–11pm Tues–Sat; 12–3.30pm and 6–10.30pm Sun.*

COWBRIDGE

The Bear Hotel

63 High Street, Cowbridge, Vale of Glamorgan CF71 7AF
☎ *(01446) 774814* Kate Walters

Brains SA is always available plus up to four guests (changing regularly) such as Wye Valley Butty Bach, Adnams Broadside and Timothy Taylor Landlord.

Part smart county hotel, part friendly local pub, the Bear Hotel's two bars are always busy with locals and residents. The building dates back to the twelfth century, has open fires and two beer gardens. Children are welcome and bar food is served from 12–9.30pm. Situated right on the main shopping street in Cowbridge where you'll find interesting individual shops and be hard pushed to find a single chain store.

 *12–11pm (10.30pm Sun).*

The Bush Inn

St Hilary, Cowbridge, Vale of Glamorgan CF71 7OP
☎ *(01446) 772745* Mark Hitchcock

Greene King Old Speckled Hen is a regular here, plus scrumpy cider straight from the barrel. A regular guest cask ale is usually available during the summer months.

This is a traditional sixteenth-century inn set in a beautiful village with two friendly locals' bars, a larger side bar with a warming inglenook fireplace and a restaurant in the back. Food is served 12–2.30pm and 6.45–9.30pm Mon–Sat and 12–3pm and 6.30–8.30pm Sun. Children are welcome all day and there is a beer garden at the back of the pub.

 *11am–11pm (10.30pm Sun).*

The Vale of Glamorgan Inn

51–3 High Street, Cowbridge, Vale of Glamorgan CF71 7AE
☎ *(01446) 772252* Alan and Peter John

A freehouse serving three cask ales at any one time. Greene King Old Speckled Hen is among the regulars; guests come from a wide range of independent breweries and change several times a week.

A friendly, locals' pub with one busy bar and a patio beer garden. Children welcome and food served lunchtimes during the week and Saturday (not Sunday).

 *11.30am–11pm Mon–Sat; 12–10.30pm Sun.*

CRAIG PENLLYN

The Barley Mow

Craig Penllyn, Cowbridge, Vale of Glamorgan CF71 1RT
☎ *(01446) 772558* Elia Pellegrotti

A freehouse serving two guest ales from brewers such as Cottage and Wye Valley.

An old Victorian village house with low ceilings and wooden beams, this is a popular pub both with locals and as a Sunday lunch venue. Food lunchtime and evenings Wed–Sun. Small patio beer garden. Well behaved children welcome.

 *11am–11pm (10.30pm Sun).*

CWMBRAN

The Bush

Craig Road, Cwmbran, Torfaen NP44 5AN
☎ *(01633) 483764* Robert Lewis

Beers from the nearby Cwmbran Brewery, such as Crow Valley Bitter and Double Hop, are always available here on at least two pumps.

Country pub in an eighteenth-century building, with one bar and garden. No food. Disco held every other Saturday. Car park. Children welcome. Call or ask for directions.

 *12–3pm and 7–11pm Mon–Fri; all day Sat–Sun.*

EAST ABERTHAW

The Blue Anchor Inn

East Aberthaw, Vale of Glamorgan CF62 3DD
☎ *(01446) 750329* Jeremy Coleman

This Grade II listed freehouse dating k to the thirteenth-century was sadly damaged by fire in early 2004.

Landlord Jeremy Coleman hopes to re-open again in September 2004 and plans to serve the same real ales as before. These included Wadworth 6X, Marston's Pedigree and one, regularly changing guest ale.

GLAN-Y-LLYN

Fagin's Ale & Chop House

Cardiff Road, Glan-y-Llyn, Nr Taff's Well, Cardiff CF15 7RE
☎ *(02920) 811800* Stuart Golding

Between four and six pumps regularly serve cask ales including Shepherd Neame Spitfire and Brains Bitter. In addition you'll find up to eight guest ales available straight from the barrel, such as Greene King Abbot and Old Speckled Hen, plus many more.

A converted terraced house. Bar and restaurant food available at lunchtime and evenings. Function room. Children allowed.

OPEN *11am–11pm Mon–Sat; 12–10.30pm Sun.*

GOVILON

Bridgend Inn

Church Lane, Govilon, Nr Abergavenny, Monmouthshire NP7 9RP
☎ *(01873) 830177*
Judy and Rob Llewellyn-Feasey

Adnams Bitter is regularly on offer plus two guests such as Badger Tanglefoot and Sussex Bitter, although these could come from a wide selection of independent brewers.

A sixteenth-century pub with two bars, beams and outdoor patio area, the Bridgend Inn is situated less than two minutes' walk from the Monmouthshire–Brecon Canal towpath. Popular with visiting boaties, tourists and locals. Children are welcome. Live music every Friday night. Bar meals available lunchtimes and evenings and all day on weekends.

OPEN *12–4pm and 7–11pm Mon–Fri; all day Sat–Sun.*

GOWER

The Greyhound Inn

Old Walls, Gower, Swansea SA3 1HA
☎ *(01792) 391027* Paul Stevens (also of the King's Head Hotel, Llangennith)

A freehouse with a total of six real ale pumps always serving ales including Marston's Pedigree.

Eighteenth-century pub, popular with walkers, locals and holidaymakers. Two bars and a function room. Food available all day including locally caught fresh fish and homemade curries. Beer garden. Children welcome. Live folk music on Sunday nights.

OPEN *11am–11pm Mon–Sat; 12–10.30pm Sun.*

King's Head Hotel

Llangennith, Gower, Swansea SA3 1HU
☎ *(01792) 386212* Chris Stevens

A freehouse serving at least three real ales, often more. Stalwarts include Wadworth 6X, as well as beers from local brewer Tomos Watkin including OSB and Brewery Bitter.

Situated in the centre of a picturesque Gower village, the pub is a Mecca for daytrippers, campers and surfers from nearby Rhossili beach. Food served until 9.30pm daily. Children are welcome until 9pm and the beer garden is a popular suntrap. Buzzing on summer evenings.

OPEN *11am–11pm Mon–Sat; 12–10.30pm Sun.*

GWAELOD-Y-GARTH

Gwaelod-y-Garth Inn

Main Road, Gwaelod-y-Garth, Cardiff CF15 9HH
☎ *(02920) 810408* Barbara Evans

Four cask ale pumps serving regular guest ales such as Greene King Abbot Ale and Jennings Cumberland Ale.

Friendly seventeenth-century freehouse, perched in the shadow of Garth Hill, this is a popular haunt for walkers, who rub shoulders with locals. Food available 12–2.30pm and 6–10pm daily in upstairs restaurant. Beer garden overlooking the valley. Children welcome.

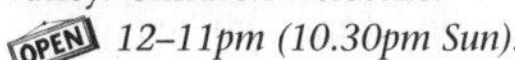

OPEN *12–11pm (10.30pm Sun).*

KENFIG

The Prince of Wales Inn

Kenfig, Bridgend CF33 4PR
☎ *(01656) 740356* Gareth Maund

A freehouse serving up to four real ales from the barrel at any one time, changing constantly, from a huge list that might include Tomos Watkin Cwrw Haf or Wye Valley Dorothy Goodbody's Golden Ale.

An olde-worlde pub with three open fires, a lounge and a function room (which houses the Sunday School). Food is available at lunchtime and evenings. Children allowed.

OPEN *11am–11pm (10.30pm Sun).*

LLANDOGO

The Sloop Inn

Llandogo, Monmouthshire NP5 4TW
☎ *(01594) 530291* Caroline Kendrick

A freehouse with two real ales always available. Recent policy favours Reverend James from Brains and Hook Norton Old Hooky, both popular with the pub's locals.

This pub has recently been refurbished and now has a dining room overlooking the river; there is also a beer garden with swings for children. Set in a beautiful village location in the Wye Valley backing onto the river. Food available every lunchtime and evening. On the A466.

Winter: 12–2.30pm and 5.30–11pm Mon–Fri; 11am–11pm Sat–Sun (10.30pm Sun). Summer: all day, every day.

LLANGYNWYD

The Old House

Llangynwyd, Maesteg, Bridgend CF34 9SB
☎ *(01656) 733310* Richard David

A freehouse always serving Brains and Flower's Original. Usually one or more guest ale, such as Shepherd Neame Spitfire, is on offer during the summer months.

A traditional pub dating back to the twelfth century, run by same family for 36 years. Beautiful panoramic views overlooking wonderful countryside. Large children's play area.

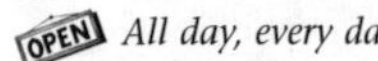
All day, every day.

LLANTWIT MAJOR

The Old Swan Inn

Church Street, Llantwit Major, Vale of Glamorgan CF61 1SB
☎ *(01446) 792230* Geoff Harper (manager)

A freehouse serving a very wide-ranging selection of guest ales which change frequently. Minimum of two guest ales during the week and often four on weekends. Breweries favoured include Shepherd Neame, Everards, Bateman and Tomos Watkin.

The pub, situated opposite the old Town Hall, dates back to the fourteenth century and is one of the oldest buildings in the historic town centre. A busy local with two bars, popular for food – extensive menu served until 9.30pm. Children welcome. Beer garden.

12–11pm (10.30pm Sun).

LLANVIHANGEL CRUCORNEY

Skirrid Mountain Inn

Llanvihangel Crucorney, Abergavenny, Monmouthshire NP7 8DH
☎ *(01873) 890258*
Daryl Hardy and Maria Appleton

There are usually four real ales on offer at this ancient, stone-walled pub. Currently the landlords favour Ushers Best, Marston's Pedigree and Wychwood Hobgoblin, plus one regularly changing guest ale.

Historic, twelfth-century country inn, believed to be the oldest pub in Wales and situated in the beautiful Black Mountains. Food served all day, every day, except Sun and Mon evenings. Car park. Well-behaved children welcome, but no special facilities.

11am–11pm Mon–Sat; 12–10.30pm Sun (closed mid-afternoon on winter weekdays).

LLYSWORNEY

The Carne Arms

Llysworney, Cowbridge, Vale of Glamorgan CF71 7NQ
☎ *(01446) 773553* Matthew Foster

Wychwood Hobgoblin is among the beers always available and up to three guest ales such as Greene King IPA or Old Speckled Hen.

An old village pub popular with locals and passing tourists, there are two bars, inglenook fireplaces and a covered, outdoor seating area. There is a large children's play area and food (bar meals and à la carte menu) is served lunchtime and evenings.

12–2.30pm and 6–11pm Mon–Fri; 12–11pm Sat; 12–10.30pm Sun.

MACHEN

The White Hart Inn

White Hart Lane, Machen, Caerphilly CF83 8QQ
☎ *(01633) 441005* Alan Carter

A village freehouse, home of Carter's Brewery, offering four real ales at any one time; three guests changing frequently and one from the pub's own brewery. The range of beers comes from small and micro-breweries all around the UK.

A very olde-worlde pub built in 1734 featuring oak panelling from an old ship (the captain's cabin came from the Empress of France). Food available at lunchtime and evenings. Play area and patio beer garden. Children allowed. Located just off the main road (A448).

11am–3pm and 6–11pm Mon–Sat; 12–10.30pm Sun; closed 3.30–6pm in winter.

MAMHILAD

The Star Inn

Folly Lane, Mamhilad, Nr Pontypool, Torfaen NP4 0JF
☎ *(01495) 785319* Darren Munt

A freehouse offering two frequently changing guest ales such as Badger's Best and Exmoor Gold.

Seventeenth-century village pub situated opposite a church with reputedly the oldest yew tree in Wales. Two drinking areas around a single bar plus a dining room. Cosy in winter with an open fire and woodburning stove. Beer garden in summer. Popular with walkers and boaty-types from the nearby Monmouthshire and Brecon canal. Food available lunchtimes and evenings. Regular beer festival held in August.

6–11pm Mon; 12–2.30pm and 6–11pm Tues–Fri; 11am–11pm Sat–Sun (10.30pm Sun).

MONKNASH

The Plough & Harrow

12

Monknash, Nr Llantwit Major, Vale of Glamorgan CF71 7QQ
☎ *(01656) 890209* Lynne Moffat

Five regular cask ale pumps often serving Wye Valley Hereford Pale Ale, Shepherd Neame Spitfire and Cottage Golden Arrow, plus guest ales served straight from the barrel. Beers from Bullmastiff are often on offer. Also a selection of bottled real ales, and cask cider (often Weston's Old Rosie).

This lively pub dates back to the twelfth century and is situated next to the ruins of an old priory in the village of Monknash. Two bars, one of which has a huge hearth with roaring fire in the winter. Food served lunchtimes and evenings. Live music is a regular feature on Sunday nights. Large beer garden. Located only a short detour from the Glamorgan Heritage Coast footpath.

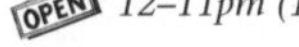
12–11pm (10.30pm Sun).

MONMOUTH

The Old Nag's Head

Granville Street, Monmouth, Monmouthshire
☎ *(01600) 713782* Rhiannon Thomas

Three cask ales are served at this popular pub. One is always from Brains, such as Reverend James or SA; guests include Fuller's London Pride.

The pub, an old toll gate for the town of Monmouth, is near to the River Monnow and popular with local rowers as well as tourists. It has two bars, a beer garden and serves food lunchtimes and evenings.

12–3pm and 6–11pm Mon–Thurs; 12–3pm and 5–11pm Fri; 12–11pm Sat; 12–10.30pm Sun.

MWYNDY

The Barn at Mwyndy

Mwyndy, Nr Llantrisant CF72 8PJ
☎ *(01443) 222333* Mark and Christine Wilby

There are usually five guest beers, which change regularly. These might include ales from Tomos Watkin and local brewer Bullmastiff, as well as beers from further afield like Timothy Taylor Landlord.

Parts of this pub, in a converted barn, date back to the sixteenth century. There is a garden and separate dining area as well as a traditional bar (no juke box, woodburning stove). Holds at least two beer festivals a year. Food available lunchtime and evenings on weekdays, and all day on weekends.

11.30am–2.30pm and 5–11pm Mon–Fri; 11am–11pm Sat; 12–10.30pm Sun.

NEWPORT

St Julian Inn

Caerleon Road, Newport NP18 1QA
☎ *(01633) 243548*
Steve Williams and Mary Nelmes

A Unique Pub Company pub serving three regular beers and up to two guests changed frequently. Regulars include Charles Wells Bombardier; guests could be Adnams Broadside or Wye Valley Butty Bach.

A pretty, family pub in a scenic location with balcony overlooking the River Usk. Food available Mon–Sat lunchtime and evenings. Children allowed.

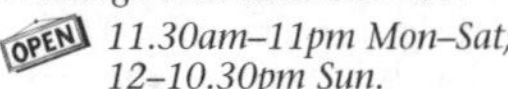
11.30am–11pm Mon–Sat; 12–10.30pm Sun.

The John Wallace Linton

Cambrian Retail Centre, Cambrian Road, Newport NP9 4AD
☎ *(01633) 251752* Paul McDonnell

A JD Wetherspoon's pub with five hand pumps serving a wide range of real ales that change on a weekly basis.

A busy pub with a wide-ranging clientele, old and young. Particularly lively in the evenings. Food available all day. No children. Next to the railway station.

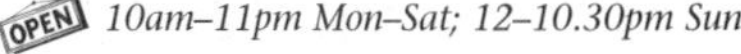
10am–11pm Mon–Sat; 12–10.30pm Sun.

OGMORE

The Pelican In Her Piety

Ogmore, Bridgend CF32 0QP
☎ *(01656) 880049* Steve Fisher
www.pelicanpub.co.uk

Freehouse with six pumps serving Fuller's London Pride and Brains SA, plus one regularly changing guest from independent brewers, such as Wye Valley Hereford Pale Ale.

Unusually named (it's from a local family's coat of arms), eighteenth-century inn situated opposite Ogmore Castle on the river Ewenny. The restaurant serves food 12–2pm and 6–9pm. Child- and dog-friendly. Beer garden with pleasant views across the river.

OPEN *12–11pm (10.30pm Sun).*

PENALLT

The Boat Inn

Lone Lane, Penallt, Monmouth, Monmouthshire NP25 4AJ
☎ *(01600) 712615* Don and Pat Ellis

Wadworth 6X and Greene King IPA are always available straight from the barrel, plus approximately six others also from the barrel. Brewers favoured include nearby Forest of Dean brewer Freeminer and Hereford's Spinning Dog.

A small riverside inn on the England–Wales border built into the hillside, with stone floors and simple decor. Live music on Tuesday and Thursday evenings. Very cosy with no juke box or games machines. Bar food available at lunchtimes and evenings (all day at weekends). Car park on the other side of the river, terraced gardens with ponds. Children allowed. The car park is in Redbrook (Gloucestershire) on the A466, next to a football field. Follow the footpath over an old railway bridge across the Wye.

OPEN *11am–11pm Mon–Sat; 12–10.30pm Sun.*

PONTARDAWE

The Pontardawe Inn

Herbert Street, Pontardawe, Swansea SA8 4ED
☎ *(01792) 830791* Peter Clayton

A freehouse serving four real ales. Regulars are Brains Reverend James, Buckley's Best and Brains Dark, plus a constantly changing guest, often from Wye Valley or Cottage.

An olde-worlde pub with no juke box and no pool table. Four beer festivals are held every year and the pub is very lively during the town's annual folk music festival. Food served at lunchtime and in the evenings in a separate 28-seater restaurant. Children allowed until 9pm. Winner of CAMRA Regional Pub of the Year 2002. Three boules courts.

OPEN *11am–11pm Mon–Sat; 12–10.30pm Sun.*

RAGLAN

The Ship Inn

High Street, Raglan, Monmouthshire NP15 2DY
☎ *(01291) 690635* Jane Roper

A freehouse regularly serving Adnams Broadside or Flower's IPA plus two guest beers, such as Timothy Taylor Landlord, which change frequently.

A sixteenth-century olde-worlde coaching inn with beams and log fires. There is a well in the cobblestoned forecourt. Food available at lunchtime and evenings. Children allowed. Located just off the High Street, opposite the supermarket.

12–11pm Mon; 11.30am–11pm Tues–Sat; 12–10.30pm Sun.

RISCA

The Fox & Hounds

Park Road, Risca, Newport NP11 6PW
☎ *(01633) 612937* Mr and Mrs J Madden

Three pumps serve an ever-changing range of beers, often including something from Everards, Arkells or Stonehenge Ales.

Village pub in an old stone building with beams and a fireplace. Food served 5–7pm Mon–Thurs plus at Fri–Sun lunchtimes. Children allowed. Two double letting rooms. Car park.

OPEN *11am–11pm Mon–Sat; 12–10.30pm Sun.*

RUDRY

Maenllwyd Inn

Rudry, Caerphilly CF83 3EB
☎ *(029) 2088 2372* Alistair Baker

Normally two guest cask ales are on offer at this extremely busy, country freehouse. Examples include Wadworth JCB and Skinner's Spriggan Ale.

A former farmhouse, this village inn has beams, three open fires and one long bar on two levels. People drive from miles around for the food and atmosphere (food is served all day but no bookings taken).

OPEN *12–11pm (10.30pm Sun).*

ST BRIDES MAJOR

The Farmer's Arms

Wick Road, St Brides Major, Vale of Glamorgan CF32 0SE
☎ *(01656) 880224/880329* Nigel Guy

Six cask pumps serving a regular selection including beers such as Greene King Old Speckled Hen.

Nineteenth-century pub with patio garden overlooking the traditional village duck pond. Children welcome all day. Food served 12–2.30pm and 6.30–9.30pm Mon–Sat and 12–3.30pm and 6.30–9.30pm Sun.

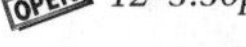
12–3.30pm and 6–11pm (10.30pm Sun).

SEBASTOPOL

The Open Hearth

Wern Road, Sebastopol, Pontypool, Torfaen NP4 5DR
☎ *(01495) 763752* Emma Bennett

You'll find up to nine real ales on offer at any one time here, seven of them guest beers which change frequently. Regular favourites include Greene King Abbot Ale, as well as beers from Hook Norton, Everards and Jennings.

A busy pub on the canal side, with a reputation for good beer and food. Food available 12–2pm and 6.30–10pm every day in a separate non-smoking restaurant. No juke box or pool table. Mixed clientele of all ages. Children welcome, with children's room provided.

11.30am–11pm Mon–Sat; 12–10.30pm Sun.

SHIRENEWTON

The Carpenter's Arms

Shirenewton, Nr Chepstow, Monmouthshire
☎ *(01291) 641231* James Bennett

There are five real ales regularly on offer here including Fuller's London Pride and Wadworth 6X. The landlord says he tries to sell as much good-quality ale as he can, and has generated a strong local following for his well-kept beer.

Traditional country inn crammed with antiques and memorabilia. Profusion of colour from the hanging baskets in summer months. Food served 7–9.30pm Mon–Sat (until 10pm Fri–Sat). Car park. Family room. Outside tables. Located on the B4235 Chepstow/Usk road, just outside the village.

OPEN *11am–3pm and 6–11pm (10.30pm Sun).*

Tredegar Arms

Shirenewton, Nr Chepstow, Monmouthshire NP16 6RQ
☎ *(01291) 641274* Tracey Eastabrook

Three real ale pumps, with beers from Hook Norton and Brains always on offer, plus a guest ale which changes regularly.

A pub since the mid nineteenth-century although the building, which includes two bars and open fires, is considerably older. Situated in the centre of a picturesque Monouthshire village, a popular haunt for locals and occasional passing tourists. Food served lunchtimes and evenings. Children welcome. Outside patio area with seating and tables at the front of the pub.

12–2.30pm and 6–11pm Mon–Fri; 12–11pm Sat; 12–4.30pm and 6–10.30pm Sun.

SIGINGSTONE

The Victoria Inn

Sigingstone, Nr Cowbridge, Vale of Glamorgan CF71 7LP
☎ *(01446) 773943* Eifion Watkins

Tomos Watkins beers are popular at this village local. Whoosh is always available, plus a guest ale, for example, Tomos Watkin Cwrw Haf, although this could be from other independent brewers.

Parts of this friendly pub, in a tucked away Vale village, date back to 1300. Two bars, beer garden, upstairs restaurant. Bar meals are served lunchtimes and evenings.

11.45am–3pm and 6–11pm Mon–Sat; 11.45am–3pm and 7–10.30pm Sun.

SWANSEA

The Park Inn

23 Park Street, Mumbles, Swansea SA3 4DA
☎ *(01792) 366738* Richard Martin

There are five cask ale pumps at this traditional freehouse. Ales from Cottage, Archers and Swansea Brewing Company feature – Three Cliffs is a favourite – and the beers change every week.

Built in a ninteenth-century terraced house in the seaside village of Mumbles. One bar where locals mix with tourists. Children welcome until 9pm, if eating. This pub takes part in the annual Mumbles Beer Festival over the August Bank Holiday weekend.

OPEN *4–11pm Mon–Wed; 12–11pm Thurs–Sat; 12–10.30pm Sun.*

Plough & Harrow

Church Road, Llansamlet, Swansea SA7 9RL
☎ *(01792) 772263* Mike Bolter

Four real ale pumps serving Tomos Watkin beers such as OSB, Whoosh, Merlin and a seasonal Tomos Watkin ale, plus occasional guests.

A village pub with a friendly atmosphere on the outskirts of Swansea, mainly frequented by locals. One large bar, open fire and outside seating. Children welcome. Food served lunchtimes and evenings.

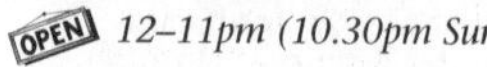 *12–11pm (10.30pm Sun).*

The Potters Wheel

85–6 The Kingsway, Swansea SA1 5JE
☎ *(01792) 465113* Carl Jones

A JD Wetherspoon's pub with up to 10 real ales available including five regulars such as Greene King Abbot and Brains SA, plus at least three guests.

A town-centre pub on Swansea's main clubbing street. No music, games or pool, non-smoking area. Food available all day. Children welcome.

 *10am–11pm Mon–Sat; 12–10.30pm Sun.*

The Queens Hotel

Gloucester Place, Swansea SA1 1TY
☎ *(01792) 521531* Gary Owen

Four real ales regularly available including Theakston Old Peculiar, Theakston Best, Brains Buckley's Best plus one guest ale, often from the local Swansea Brewing Company.

A Victorian pub with original features, in Swansea's Maritime Quarter. It is frequented by locals, tourists and journalists from the nearby *South Wales Evening Post* offices. Photos of old ships decorate the walls. Food is available lunchtimes, when children are also welcome. Pavement tables outside.

 *11am–11pm Mon–Sat; 12–10.30pm Sun.*

The Railway Inn

553 Gower Road, Upper Killay, Swansea SA2 7DS
☎ *(01792) 203946*
Adrian Martin and Rory Gowland

A freehouse with up to six cask ales at any one time. Three beers regularly come from the nearby Swansea Brewing Company, such as Original Wood or Deep Slade Dark. Two to three guests change regularly; favourites include Timothy Taylor Landlord.

Dating back to 1864, this pub was a house until the 1930s. It stands next to the ticket office and station master's house on the old Clyne railway line which ran down the valley into Swansea. The line is now a cycle track and the pub is a popular stop-off point for cyclists, as well as locals and trippers to and from the nearby Gower peninsula. One main bar, separate lounge bar, open fires in the winter and a beer garden (two patios). Children welcome until 7pm.

 *11am–11pm Mon–Sat; 12–10.30pm Sun.*

The Westbourne

1 Bryn-y-Mor Road, Swansea SA1 4JQ
☎ *(01792) 476637* Carley Hines

Six pumps are dedicated to four regular ales and two guests. Greene King Abbot, Marston's Pedigree and Charles Wells Bombardier are among the beers always on offer; guest beers come from a variety of independent brewers.

Previously a striking, three-storey private Victorian house then a hotel, the Westbourne became a pub in 1912. It has two bars and a beer terrace and is situated on the edge of Uplands, traditionally the city's student, literary and arty area. The new landlord plans to hold several beer festivals a year.

 *12–11pm (10.30pm Sun).*

The Woodman Inn

Mumbles Road, Blackpill, Swansea SA3 5AS
☎ *(01792) 402700* Roland Jenkins

Two pumps regularly serving real ale including one beer from Brains and one guest ale changing regularly.

Old pub on the main tourist route to Swansea's beaches, with low beams and old-fashioned charm, attracting regulars and tourists. Children welcome until 8pm.

OPEN *11am–11pm Mon–Sat; 12–10.30pm Sun.*

TINTERN

Cherry Tree Inn

Chapel Hill, Tintern, Monmouthshire NP16 6TH
☎ *(01291) 689292* Stephen Pocock

Beers served straight from the barrel always include a choice of between five and six real ales. Wye Valley Butty Bach makes regular appearances. Guests often come from such brewers such as Cottage, Freeminer and Bullmastiff.

The Cherry Tree has been a pub since the mid-seventeenth century. The original, single room bar has now been joined by an airy new bar and restaurant room. In addition there is a beer garden and outdoor patio; four B&B rooms are newly available too. Children welcome. Make the effort to find this gem of a pub and you'll not be disappointed.

OPEN *12–11pm (10.30pm Sun).*

TONDU

Llynfi Arms

Maesteg Road, Tondu, Bridgend CF32 9DP
☎ *(01656) 720010* Neil Wisenden

One guest beer always available, changing every two weeks. This tends to be from smaller independents such as Cottage or Tomos Watkin.

The pub is close to Tondu railway station, and has two model trains running around the ceiling of the lounge bar. Food served 12–2pm and 7–9.30pm Wed–Sat and 12–2pm Sun. Booking advised Fri–Sun. Children welcome in the lounge bar at lunchtime.

12–4pm and 6–11pm Mon–Thurs; 11am–11pm Fri–Sat; 12–10.30pm Sun.

TRELLECK

The Lion Inn

Trelleck, Nr Monmouth, Monmouthshire NP25 4PA
☎ *(01600) 860322* Tom and Debbie Zsigo

A freehouse with four pumps. Bath Ales SPA is always on offer, plus either Wadworth 6X, Fuller's London Pride or Wye Valley Butty Bach. Plus a weekly guest.

A traditional, stone-fronted, Grade II listed, sixteenth-century typical country pub with open fire, no fruit machines or juke box. Favours traditional pub games such as bar billiards and bar skittles plus many social evenings. Food available every lunchtime and all evenings except Sunday. Well-behaved children and dogs allowed, but no dogs in the lounge.

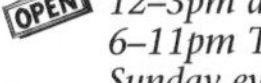

12–3pm and 7–11pm Mon; 12–3pm and 6–11pm Tues–Sat; 12–3pm Sun (closed Sunday evening).

The Trekkers

The Narth, Nr Trelleck, Monmouthshire NP5 4QG
☎ *(01600) 860367* Mr and Mrs Flower

A freehouse with three real ales. Regularly on offer are Ruddles Best Bitter, Felinfoel Double Dragon and Greene King IPA. In addition, one guest available in summer, possibly Trekkers Ale, made by Wye Valley.

A local country pub, in the style of a log cabin, family-orientated with beer garden, swings and skittle alley. Traditional, homemade, British food available in separate dining area lunchtimes and evenings. It is essential to book for Sunday lunch.

All day Thurs–Sun; call for opening times Mon–Wed.

UPPER LLANOVER

The Goose & Cuckoo Inn

Upper Llanover, Abergavenny, Monmouthshire NP7 9ER
☎ *(01873) 880277* Carol and Michael Langley

A freehouse with four pumps dedicated to real ale. Two pumps always serve Brains Reverend James and Breconshire Brewery's County Ale; the other two serve constantly changing guests from brewers such as Cottage and Bullmastiff.

A small, isolated, picturesque country pub with a log fire. The pub is family-orientated and has a collection of animals in the garden for youngsters. No juke box or games machines, traditional games available including quoits, dominoes, cribbage and darts. Beer garden. Food available every lunchtime and evening, but Sunday lunch must be booked. Accommodation is available. Also an impressive 85 malt whiskies at the bar.

11.30am–3pm and 7–11pm Tues–Thurs (closed Mon); all day Fri–Sun.

UPPER TORFORA

The Queen Inn

Upper Cwmbran Road, Upper Torfora, Cwmbran, Torfaen NP44 1SN
☎ *(01633) 484252* Peter Crooks

A guest beer is always available plus others, usually from the nearby Cwmbran Brewery, perhaps Four Seasons, Crow Valley Bitter, The Full Malty, or a seasonal ale. Adnams also favoured.

Country inn on the edge of village in a 150-year-old stone building which is three cottages knocked into one. Food available. Restaurant, bar, lounge and garden. Children allowed. Car park. Off Henleys Way.

12–3pm and 5–11pm (10.30pm Sun).

USK

The Kings Head Hotel

18 Old Market Street, Usk, Monmouthshire NP15 1AL
☎ *(01291) 672963* Stephen Musto

A freehouse with three pumps regularly serving Fuller's London Pride, Timothy Taylor Landlord and Charles Wells Bombardier.

A fifteenth-century pub with accommodation. Open fireplace, function room and restaurant serving food at lunchtime and evenings. Children allowed.

All day, every day.

WICK

The Lamb & Flag

Church Street, Wick, Vale of Glamorgan CF71 7QE
☎ *(01656) 890278* Tim Warrick

Two pumps dedicated to guest real ales such as Cottage Mallard Gold and local brew Bullmastiff Best Bitter.

Traditional sixteenth-century village pub (no juke box, no pool table) with mainly local clientele in the two bars and back lounge, but some tourists do drop in on their way to local beaches like Southerdown and Ogmore. Open fires in winter, outside seating in summer. Food available lunchtimes and evenings Mon–Fri, all day Sat–Sun.

11.30am–3.30pm and 5.30pm–11pm Mon–Thurs; 11.30am–11pm Fri– Sun (10.30pm Sun).

YSTALYFERA

Wern Fawr Inn

47 Wern Road, Ystalyfera, Swansea SA9 2LX
☎ *(01639) 843625* Will Hopton

The home of the Bryncelyn Brewery with a full range of own brews permanently available on three to four pumps. A tiny pub where all the home ales are named on a Buddy Holly theme and include Oh Boy, Peggy's Brew and 2003 CAMRA Welsh beer award winner, Buddy Marvellous.

A village pub dating back to the 1850s with two small bars. Background music is 1960s and 1970s. No food. Beer garden. Children allowed.

7–11pm Mon–Sat; 12–3.30pm and 7–10pm Sun.

THE PUBS

ABERCYCH

The Nag's Head Inn

Abercych, Boncath, Pembrokeshire
☎ *(01239) 841200* Steven Jamieson

A brewpub with Old Emrys brewed on the premises and always available plus three guests at any one time, which could be something like Greene King Old Speckled Hen and Abbot, a Dorothy Goodbody's ale from Wye Valley or anything from a Welsh micro-brewery.

A friendly family-run riverside pub with flagstone floors and wooden beams. Bar and restaurant food available 12–2pm and 6–9pm daily. Separate non-smoking room. Children welcome with a dedicated menu and playground. Large car park. Situated on the B4332 between Cenarth Falls and Boncath.

11.30am–3pm and 6–11.30pm.

FELINFOEL

The Royal Oak

Felinfoel Road, Felinfoel, Carmarthenshire SA14 8LA
☎ *(01554) 751140* Mrs M Cleland

Tied to the nearby Felinfoel Brewery, with two hand pumps serving the Felinfoel ales.

An old-fashioned local opposite the brewery, with food available at lunchtime and evenings. Children allowed.

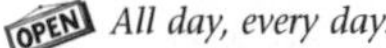
All day, every day.

HAVERFORDWEST

King's Arms Hotel

23 Dew Street, Haverfordwest, Dyfed
☎ *(01437) 763726* Chris Hudd

Six beers always available from a list of approximately 150 brews per year.

An old, beamed and flagstoned pub in the town, just past the library. Street parking, function room. No children.

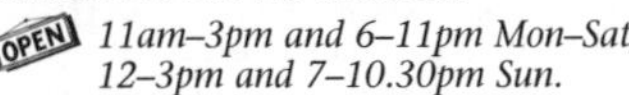
11am–3pm and 6–11pm Mon–Sat; 12–3pm and 7–10.30pm Sun.

HEOL Y PLAS

Ye Olde Red Lion

Heol y Plas, Llannon, Carmarthenshire SA14 6AA
☎ *(01269) 841276* Steven Ireland

A Felinfoel Brewery tied house with two pumps serving Felinfoel ales.

A rural sixteenth-century pub with oak beams and log fires. Non-smoking and smoking dining areas. Food available every evening plus Saturday and Sunday lunchtimes. Children welcome.

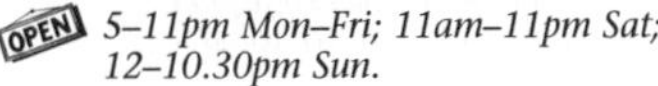
5–11pm Mon–Fri; 11am–11pm Sat; 12–10.30pm Sun.

HOREB

The Waunwyllt Inn

Horeb Road, Five Roads, Horeb, Llanelli, Carmarthenshire SA15 5AQ
☎ *(01269) 860209* Shaun Pawson

A freehouse with four pumps serving a constantly changing selection of real ales. Examples include Shepherd Neame Bishop's Finger, Everards Tiger and others from Cottage and Tomos Watkin.

A popular country inn in a quiet hamlet outside Llanelli. Close to the Celtic Trail cycle route. Large beer garden, non-smoking dining area, five en-suite bedrooms. Food available at lunchtime and evenings. Children allowed. From Llanelli, take the B4309 towards Carmarthen.

11am–11pm Mon–Sat and 12–10.30pm Sun in summer; 12–3pm and 6.30–11pm in winter.

LLANDDAROG

The White Hart Thatched Inn

Llanddarog, Carmarthenshire SA32 8NT
☎ *(01267) 275395* Coles family

Cwrw Blasus ('tasty beer') is just one of the ales brewed and served here.

Beautiful rural village inn dating back to 1371, with open log fire, oak beams and old carved furniture. The antiques create an olde-worlde atmosphere. Delicious homemade meals are served in the dining room, with snacks and sandwiches available throughout the pub. The food is served during all opening times. Car park. Children welcome. On the B4310, just off the A48, not far from the National Botanic Garden of Wales.

11.30am–3pm and 6.30–11pm Mon–Sat; 12–3pm and 7–10.30pm Sun.

LLANDEILO

The Castle Hotel

113 Rhosmaen Street, Llandeilo, Dyfed SA19 6EN
☎ *(01558) 823446 Simon Williams*

A Tomas Watkins tied house with award-winning ales such as Whoosh, Best, Old Style Bitter and Merlin's Stout permanently available. Other seasonal guests rotated on one hand pump.

A town-centre pub with two bars serving five adjoining rooms, 65-seater restaurant, beer garden. Bar and restaurant food served lunchtimes and evenings. Children allowed. Easy, free parking.

OPEN *All day, every day.*

LLANDOVERY

The White Swan

47 High Street, Llandovery, Carmarthenshire SA20 0DE
☎ *(01550) 720816* Ray Miller

A freehouse specialising in beers up to 4.2% ABV. Two always available, changed every two weeks.

A town pub offering darts, pool and a mixed local clientele. No juke box or fruit machines. No food. Children and dogs are welcome. The last pub on the way out of Llandovery, near the supermarket.

OPEN *12–3pm and 7–11pm (10.30pm Sun).*

LLANSAINT

The King's Arms

13 Maes yr Eglyws, Llansaint, Nr Kidwelly, Carmarthenshire SA17 5JE
☎ *(01267) 267487* John and Debbie Morris

A freehouse serving three regularly changing beers.

Separate smoking and non-smoking dining areas – bar and restaurant food served lunchtimes and evenings. Log fire in season, beer garden, car park. Children allowed. Follow signs for Llansaint from Kidwelly – the pub nestles under the church tower. Accommodation available.

OPEN *12–2.30pm and 6.30–11pm (10.30pm Sun); closed Tues lunchtimes.*

MYNYDD Y GARREG

The Prince of Wales

Heol Meinciau, Mynydd y Garreg, Kidwelly, Carmarthenshire SA17 4RP
☎ *(01554) 890522* Gail and Richard Pickett

A freehouse with six beers always available from a list that includes brews from Wye Valley, Bullmastiff and various Welsh micro-breweries. Please phone ahead for details of beers currently on tap. Real cider also available from Easter–Oct.

A 200-year-old cottage pub, in the same ownership since 1989, with a collection of cinema memorabilia and bric-à-brac. Bar and restaurant food available evenings – the restaurant is completely non-smoking. Car park and garden. No children. Take the Mynydd y Garreg turn from the Cydweli bypass, then just over a mile on the right.

OPEN *5–11pm (10.30pm Sun).*

NARBETH

The Kirkland Arms

East Gate, St James Street, Narbeth, Dyfed SA67 7DB
☎ *(01834) 860423* Mr Edger

A Felinfoel Brewery tied pub with guest beers rotated on one pump. These might include York Yorkshire Terrier, Swansea Bishopswood Bitter, Wadworth 6X and many others changed on a weekly basis.

An old, traditional pub with pool table, games machines and beer garden. Fresh rolls and sandwiches served every day. Children allowed.

OPEN *11am–11pm Mon–Sat; 12–10.30pm Sun.*

PEMBROKE

The Castle Inn

17 Main Street, Pembroke, Pembrokeshire SA71 4JS
☎ *(01646) 682883* Nigel Temple

A freehouse usually serving Charles Wells Bombardier and Wadworth 6X plus up to two guests.

A very old pub with long and narrow stone walls and beams. No food. Children allowed.

OPEN *11am–11pm Mon–Sat; 12–10.30pm Sun.*

The First & Last

London Road, Pembroke Dock, Pembrokeshire SA72 6TX
☎ *(01646) 682687* Richard Maynard

A freehouse with Charles Wells Bombardier or Brains SA usually available plus one other.

A local community pub with beer garden. Light lunches only served. Children allowed at lunchtime only.

OPEN *11am–11pm Mon–Sat; 12–10.30pm Sun.*

UPPER CWMTWRCH

The George IV Inn

Upper Cwmtwrch, Swansea Valley SA9 2XH
☎ *(01639) 830938* Roy and June King

Brains SA and Greene King Abbot are regular offerings plus one guest such as Adnams Broadside.

Friendly riverside rural pub and restaurant in a scenic valley in the foothills of West Wales' Black Mountains. Log fire, oak beams, antiques and plenty of olde-worlde atmosphere. Large beer garden and car park. Homemade food prepared in the open-plan kitchen and served during opening hours. Located just off the A4067 Brecon to Swansea road, not far from the famous Dan-yr-Ogof caves.

12–3pm and 6pm–11pm Mon–Sat; 12–3pm and 7pm–10.30pm Sun.

You might think it wouldn't be too difficult to find a bottle of bottle-conditioned beer in the high-street shops but, in fact, it's not that easy. I was certainly hard-pressed to find any in the high-street off-licence chains.

The situation is better – although still patchy – in the supermarkets. Sainsbury's comes out on top, as there is a good chance that you'll find a choice of bottle-conditioned beers at your local store, most of them from national or regional brewers. A couple of them, though, could even be locally brewed, for which Sainsbury's should be applauded. Tesco's offer far less choice, despite sponsoring the Tesco's Challenge competition for small and large brewers. Of the dozen bottled beers on their shelves when I last visited, just two were bottle-conditioned.

'So where are we to buy the gems listed below?' Some micro-breweries run shops on their premises and there are also a handful of specialist off-licences around the country which cater for this growing market.

The Beer Essentials in Horsham, West Sussex is one such off-licence. They keep over 100 different bottled beers in stock, over half of which are bottle-conditioned. The Hogs Back Brewery also supports the bottle-conditioned format by offering a range of their own brewed beers as well as bottle-conditioned beers from around the country.

You can also buy online, which is where askdaisy.net comes in, with its informative tasting notes helping you get the style of beer you enjoy.

Real ale in a bottle, or bottle-conditioned beer, like cask ale, contains live yeast and fermentable sugars. A secondary fermentation takes place in the bottle, which develops the beer naturally and maintains its condition. Despite the almost hysterical passion for sell-by dates nowadays, these beers actually mature in the bottle and are likely to be in prime condition for some time. Beers like Fuller's Vintage Ale, produced in 1997 with a sell-by date of the end of 2000, is drinking beautifully now and probably will do so for a long while yet. Obviously, though, you should make your own decision as to whether your particular bottle is drinkable and will not cause you any upset.

Like cask beer, to allow enjoyment of the full complexity of flavour, bottle-conditioned beers should be between 13–15°C/55–59°F when drunk. The bottle should be allowed to stand for a sufficient period to allow the sediment to drop to the bottom, then poured carefully to prevent the sediment rising and clouding the beer. They should never be drunk straight from the bottle. Some less hoppy, continental beers can be drunk cloudy, but British bottle-conditioned beers generally should not.

The numbers beside the colours give an idea of the depth of colour on a scale of one–20, with one being pale yellow and 20 being the darkest black.

B&T DRAGON SLAYER 4.5% ABV 500 ML
Brewed by B&T Brewery Ltd, The Brewery, Shefford, Bedfordshire SG17 5DZ.
☎ (01462) 815080.
www.banksandtaylor.com
Colour: Golden-yellow (3).
Head: White dense large rocky head.
Aroma: A sweet malty aroma, most unexpected from such a pale beer.
Taste: Initial taste is a delicate yet sweet hop flavour that continues through to the end with a delicate hoppy aftertaste.
Ease of Decanting: Have two glasses ready. Not easy due to the large head, and pouring into one glass from start to finish could be difficult. Best to use the second glass, and watch out for swirls of yeast in the last quarter. Well worth the effort.
Opinion: A pale, delicate, thirst-quenching ale which would be a godsend after a hot curry.

B&T EDWIN TAYLOR'S EXTRA STOUT 4.5% ABV 500 ML
Brewed by B&T Brewery Ltd, The Brewery, Shefford, Bedfordshire SG17 5DZ.
☎ (01462) 815080.
www.banksandtaylor.com
Colour: Black with ruby tints in the light (20).
Head: Pours with a small head with brown, dense bubbles.
Aroma: A very aromatic ale with earthy blackcurrant notes.
Taste: The theme of this B&T stout is definitely malt. The initial taste is smooth and malty, leading to hints of fruit, yet finishing with a subtle yet refreshing hoppy aftertaste.
Ease of Decanting: Quite easy as the head pours small and tight. Keep an eagle eye out for those yeast tendrils in the last quarter of the bottle – a steady hand wins the day.
Opinion: Very nice example of bottle-conditioned stout from a small brewery. Would be a very nice accompaniment to a roast dinner.

BALLARD'S BEST BITTER 4.2% ABV
Brewed by Ballard's Brewery Ltd, The Old Sawmill, Nyewood, Petersfield, Hampshire GU31 5HA. ☎ (01730) 821301.
www.ballardsbrewery.org.uk
Colour: Orange-brown (10).
Head: White, dense bubbles in a large head which keeps growing even after pouring has finished.
Aroma: Delicate toffee apple and caramel aroma.
Taste: Delicate caramel leading to hops on the side of the tongue, with caramel sweetness blending in to produce a slightly burnt, bitter aftertaste.
Ease of Decanting: Difficult. Due to the head growth I couldn't finish pouring it all into a pint glass, so it may need an hour or two in the fridge just to quieten it down a bit before opening. Worth the effort though.
Opinion: Nice beer with sirloin steak and chips.

BALLARD'S NYEWOOD GOLD 5.0% ABV
Brewed by Ballard's Brewery Ltd, The Old Sawmill, Nyewood, Petersfield, Hampshire GU31 5HA. ☎ (01730) 821301.
www.ballardsbrewery.org.uk
Colour: Amber-orange (6).
Head: White dense bubbles in a good head that did not need creating.
Aroma: Sweet and appley.
Taste: Fresh, frothy with apples slightly drying into a subtle cidery finish.
Ease of Decanting: Yeast clung to the base of the bottle. Pour carefully to control the head.
Opinion: An unusually cidery beer, very nice and well worth trying. Would go down well with roast pork and crackling.

BALLARD'S WASSAIL 6.0% ABV 500 ML
Brewed by Ballard's Brewery Ltd, The Old Sawmill, Nyewood, Petersfield, Hampshire GU31 5HA. ☎ (01730) 821301.
www.ballardsbrewery.org.uk
Colour: Burgundy-brown (14).
Head: Brown, small head with dense bubbles.
Aroma: Malty with slight fruit notes.
Taste: Definite taste of molasses and malt, balanced with bitter fruits in the aftertaste.
Ease of Decanting: A nice easy-pouring ale with yeast that clings to the bottom of the bottle and a head that doesn't get too excited on pouring.
Opinion: A lovely beer with game pie.

BARUM BREWERY BARUM BARNSTABLASTA 6.6% ABV
Brewed by Barum Brewery, c/o Reform Inn, Reform Road, Pilton, Barnstable, Devon EX31 1PD. ☎ (01271) 329994.
www.barumbrewery.co.uk
Colour: Oak-burgundy (17).
Head: Small light brown head with small bubbles.
Aroma: Acrid liquorice with blackcurrant.
Taste: Rich blackcurrant and liquorice followed by rich black cherry bitterness that prickles on the tongue, then slides away in a rich black cherry finish.
Ease of Decanting: Yeast was a touch loose at the bottom but the head stayed small, a small amount of care for a huge reward.
Opinion: Packed with flavour, robust enough for liver and bacon with creamy mashed potato.

BARUM BREWERY BARUM BREAKFAST 5.0% ABV
Brewed by Barum Brewery, c/o Reform Inn, Reform Road, Pilton, Barnstable, Devon EX31 1PD. ☎ (01271) 329994.
www.barumbrewery.co.uk
Colour: Ruby-brown (13).
Head: Stayed small, bubbles were white and small.
Aroma: Sweet with slight sulphur tones and a slightly acrid note.
Taste: Smooth initially, sweet like flat Coca Cola maturing to rich fruit cake, then to bitter cherries lightly furring the sides of the tongue in a long aftertaste.
Ease of Decanting: Yeast stayed at the bottom and the head was small, so nice and easy.
Opinion: A very nice beer which would go down well with roast beef and Yorkshire pudding.

BARUM BREWERY BARUM CHALLENGER 5.6% ABV
Brewed by Barum Brewery, c/o Reform Inn, Reform Road, Pilton, Barnstable, Devon EX31 1PD. ☎ (01271) 329994.
www.barumbrewery.co.uk
Colour: Oak-burgundy (17).
Head: White dense bubbles in a large head.
Aroma: Fragrant butterscotch and burnt toffee.
Taste: Frothy burnt toffee taste with butterscotch maturing to bittersweet demerara in a short aftertaste.
Ease of Decanting: Although yeast stayed at the bottom, the large head presented something of a challenge. Persevere, however, as it is well worth the effort.
Opinion: Would go down very nicely with a nice roast pork dinner on a Sunday afternoon.

BARUM BREWERY BARUM ORIGINAL 4.4% ABV
Brewed by Barum Brewery, c/o Reform Inn, Reform Road, Pilton, Barnstable, Devon EX31 1PD. ☎ (01271) 329994.
www.barumbrewery.co.uk
Colour: Dark amber-chestnut (11).
Head: Large head with lots of small dense white bubbles.
Aroma: Slight rubber and glue aroma though very subtle.
Taste: Smooth initial taste maturing to slight soft apple flavour that dries to tart bitter crab apple.
Ease of Decanting: Yeast swirls in the last quarter with a big head make this a challenge, but well worth the effort.
Opinion: Would go down very nicely with fish and chips.

BLUE ANCHOR SPINGO 6.6% ABV 275 ML
Brewed by The Blue Anchor Inn, 50 Coinagehall Street, Helston, Cornwall TR13 8EL. ☎ (01326) 562821.
Colour: Rich burgundy (19).
Head: Brown, dense bubbles in a large head.
Aroma: Sweet forest fruits aroma.
Taste: Initial sensation is prickling on the tongue. The taste is malty caramel with slight liquorice in a short, refreshing aftertaste.
Ease of Decanting: Well-conditioned ale in a small bottle (275 ml), this makes pouring a bit easier. When poured into a pint glass, there is room for the large head with brown dense bubbles.
Opinion: Full-bodied malty ale that would go nice with Irish stew.

BLUE ANCHOR SPINGO MIDDLE 6.6% ABV 500 ML
Brewed by The Blue Anchor Inn, 50 Coinagehall Street, Helston, Cornwall TR13 8EL. ☎ (01326) 562821.
Colour: Orange-brown (10).
Head: Very large white dense head.
Aroma: Burnt sugar and honeycomb, like a spiced fruitcake.
Taste: Smooth with fruit warming on the tongue with a short bitter fruit aftertaste on the middle of the tongue.
Ease of Decanting: Difficult with large head, indicating that this beer is sensitive to temperature. Put in the fridge for an hour to control the head.
Opinion: Malty, easy-drinking ale, nice with a strong Cheddar ploughman's.

BURTON BRIDGE BRAMBLE STOUT 5.0% ABV 500 ML
Brewed by Burton Bridge Brewery, Bridge Street, Burton upon Trent, Staffordshire DE14 1SY. ☎ (01283) 510573.
Colour: Black (20).
Head: Brown, dense, large head.
Aroma: Fruity, blackberry aromas.
Taste: Initial grainy fruit taste which explodes into blackberry sweetness, balanced by fruit bitterness in the aftertaste.
Ease of Decanting: Be careful with this one. Large-headed beer with yeast swirls in the last quarter of the bottle, but well worth the effort.
Opinion: Dark, fruity, interesting ale, good with a nice Stilton ploughman's.

BURTON BRIDGE BURTON PORTER 4.5% ABV 500 ML
Brewed by Burton Bridge Brewery, Bridge Street, Burton upon Trent, Staffordshire DE14 1SY. ☎ (01283) 510573.
Colour: Black with burgundy hints (20).
Head: Brown coloured with small, dense bubbles, stayed small and manageable.
Aroma: Slight vanilla aroma, sweet.
Taste: Fruity initial taste frothing on the tongue leading to vanilla pods and fruit cake, then a short bittersweet fruit aftertaste.
Ease of Decanting: Yeast clings to the base of the bottle and head stays small, so a nice easy pourer.
Opinion: Dark, frothy and easy to drink. Would go down a treat with O'Hagan's sausage and mash.

BUTTS GOLDEN BROWN 5.0% ABV 500 ML
Brewed by Butts Brewery Ltd, Northfield Farm, Wantage Road, Great Shefford, Hungerford, Berkshire RG17 7BY. ☎ (01488) 648133.
Colour: Dark amber-chestnut (11).
Head: White, dense head with small bubbles, pours quite large and clings to side of glass.
Aroma: Slightly sulphury with tar aromas.
Taste: Smooth initial impression leading to fruit with molasses, yet balanced in the aftertaste by bitter fruit and hops.
Ease of Decanting: Not an easy pour, due to the large head, so you will possibly need two glasses and a steady hand. Well worth the effort.
Opinion: Would go down very nicely with a pork pie ploughman's.

COTTAGE NORMAN'S CONQUEST 7.0% ABV 500 ML
Brewed by The Cottage Brewing Co. Ltd., The Old Cheese Dairy, Hornblotton Road, Lovington, Somerset BA7 7PS. ☎ (01963) 240551.
Colour: Dark brown (14).
Head: Dense, white head with fine bubbles.
Aroma: Quite subdued fruit with a slight spirity edge.
Taste: Rich, tasty malt and a surprisingly short, dry finish.
Ease of Decanting: Poured very easily.
Opinion: Would suit a rich beef stew.

CROPTON KING BILLY 3.6% ABV 500 ML
Brewed by Cropton Brewery at The New Inn, Cropton, Pickering, North Yorkshire YO18 8HH. ☎ (01751) 417330
www.croptonbrewery.co.uk
Colour: Light golden (6).
Head: Dense white head.
Aroma: Clean, fresh grassy hops.
Taste: Crisp and dry with a lingering hop finish.
Ease of Decanting: Very easy to pour.
Opinion: Light enough to enjoy at lunchtime with a ham doorstep.

CROPTON MONKMAN'S SLAUGHTER 6.0% ABV 500 ML
Brewed by Cropton Brewery at The New Inn, Cropton, Pickering, North Yorkshire YO18 8HH. ☎ (01751) 417330
www.croptonbrewery.co.uk
Colour: Dark brown (15).
Head: Tight, brown head.
Aroma: Rich, malty and faintly biscuity.
Taste: Complex and rich with a tasty, biscuity sweetness and a long finish.
Ease of Decanting: Quite easy to pour.
Opinion: Great for after dinner with the cheese board.

CROPTON SCORESBY STOUT 4.2% ABV 500 ML
Brewed by Cropton Brewery at The New Inn, Cropton, Pickering, North Yorkshire YO18 8HH. ☎ (01751) 417330
www.croptonbrewery.co.uk
Colour: Black (20).
Head: Dark, inviting head.
Aroma: Roasted but not quite burnt.
Taste: Rich and roasted with a little hop to add balance.
Ease of Decanting: Some care required due to the colour of the beer, but worth the effort.
Opinion: Perfect with steak and mushroom pie and mash.

DURHAM CLOISTER 4.5% ABV 500 ML
Brewed by The Durham Brewery, Unit 5A, Bowburn North Industrial Estate, Bowburn, County Durham DH6 5PF.
☎ (0191) 377 1991.
www.durham-brewery.co.uk
Colour: Golden-orange (4).
Head: Pours up with a large white rocky head, with dense bubbles which subside, clinging to the sides of the glass.
Aroma: Subtle fruity malt aroma.
Taste: A complex ale for its strength, Cloister's initial malty aroma actually gives way to an initial hop taste. The malt sweetness then comes through to balance the hops, then slides away leaving a bitter but not astringent hoppy aftertaste.
Ease of Decanting: Be careful with this one. Not easy to pour due to a large creamy head, but well worth the effort. Yeast disturbs whilst pouring so a steady hand and a sharp eye are required.
Opinion: A complex and quaffable ale that would go down very well with fish and chips.

DURHAM SAINT CUTHBERT 6.5% ABV 500 ML
Brewed by The Durham Brewery, Unit 5A, Bowburn North Industrial Estate, Bowburn, County Durham DH6 5PF.
☎ (0191) 377 1991.
www.durham-brewery.co.uk

Colour: Rich golden amber (8).
Head: White dense bubbles in a medium head.
Aroma: Toffee and caramel.
Taste: Sweet malt initial taste with full-bodied sweetness turning into hops and increasing in bitterness through long aftertaste.
Ease of Decanting: Medium head and yeast that clings to the base of the bottle means that this is a nice easy-pouring ale.
Opinion: A lovely full-bodied ale that would go down very nicely with a pork pie.

FREEMINER SPECULATION 4.8% ABV 500 ML
Brewed by Freeminer Brewery Ltd, Whimsey Road, Steam Mills, Cinderford, Royal Forest of Dean GL14 3JA. ☎ (01594) 827989.
www.freeminer.com
Colour: Reddish brown (12).
Head: Dense white head with small bubbles.
Aroma: Fresh hops and a hint of orange.
Taste: Tasty malt and bitter hops with a long, bitter, slightly citrus finish.
Ease of Decanting: Quite easy to pour.
Opinion: Perfect with spaghetti Bolognese.

FREEMINER TRAFALGAR IPA 6.0% ABV 500 ML
Brewed by Freeminer Brewery Ltd, Whimsey Road, Steam Mills, Cinderford, Royal Forest of Dean GL14 3JA. ☎ (01594) 827989.
www.freeminer.com
Colour: Golden (6).
Head: Very flat head with a few fine bubbles.
Aroma: Spirity malt.
Taste: Toffee and rich fruit. Spirity malt which gives way to bitterness in the finish.
Ease of Decanting: The flat head made this an easy beer to pour.
Opinion: The finishing touch to roast beef with all the trimmings.

FREEMINER WATERLOO 4.5% ABV 500 ML
Brewed by Freeminer Brewery Ltd, Whimsey Road, Steam Mills, Cinderford, Royal Forest of Dean GL14 3JA. ☎ (01594) 827989.
www.freeminer.com
Colour: Reddish brown (12).
Head: White dense bubbles with a small head.
Aroma: Soft fruit
Taste: Refreshing malt and hops with a long, tangy hop finish.
Ease of Decanting: Yeast clings to the base of the bottle and the head is not too big, so a nice easy-pouring ale.
Opinion: Very nice with a cheese ploughman's.

FROG ISLAND CROAK & STAGGER 5.6% ABV 500 ML
Brewed by Frog Island Brewery, The Maltings, Westbridge, St James Road, Northampton NN4 8DU. ☎ (01604) 587772.
www.frogislandbrewery.co.uk
Colour: Oak-burgundy (17).
Head: Small brown head that diminished quickly.
Aroma: Black treacle and molasses.
Taste: Initial acrid bakelite, tarry taste, warming and increasing in bitterness to floral grapefruit zinging the taste buds in a long aftertaste.
Ease of Decanting: Yeast stayed at the bottom and the head stayed small so an easy beer to pour.
Opinion: A robust beer which would complement a nice rabbit stew.

FROG ISLAND FIRE BELLIED TOAD 5.0% ABV 500 ML
Brewed by Frog Island Brewery, The Maltings, Westbridge, St James Road, Northampton NN4 5DU. ☎ (01604) 587772.
www.frogislandbrewery.co.uk
Colour: Rich golden amber (8).
Head: Small white head with large bubbles.
Aroma: Spicy sweetness with a slight parsnip aroma.
Taste: Musty followed by a damp soil mouth-feel and a metallic aftertaste like rusty water.
Ease of Decanting: Yeast rose up on pouring, creating swirls in the last quarter.
Opinion: Frog Island were e-mailed with these tasting notes but have not replied.

FROG ISLAND NATTERJACK 4.8% ABV 500 ML
Brewed by Frog Island Brewery, The Maltings, Westbridge, St James Road, Northampton NN4 5DU. ☎ (01604) 587772.
www.frogislandbrewery.co.uk
Colour: Golden-yellow (3).
Head: Large dense white head.
Aroma: Malt, but with a slight peppery note.
Taste: Warming initially, then metallic-peppery taste with slight notes of plastic, the aftertaste is long and slightly rancid and furry on the sides of the tongue.
Ease of Decanting: Large head, but yeast stayed at the bottom of the bottle, so pour into an oversized glass.
Opinion: Drink at lunch with a pork pie ploughman's to clean the palate.

FULLERS 1845 6.3% ABV 500 ML
Brewed by Fuller, Smith & Turner PLC, Griffin Brewery, Chiswick Lane South, London W4 2QB. ☎ (020) 8996 2000.
www.fullers.co.uk
Colour: Oak-burgundy (17).
Head: Brown dense bubbles in a medium-sized head.
Aroma: Warming winter mulling spices with blackcurrant.
Taste: Frothy initial mouth-feel leading to a warming and pleasant grapefruit bitterness that increases in bitterness through to the aftertaste.
Ease of Decanting: A nice easy-to-pour beer with the yeast staying steadfastly at the bottom of the bottle.
Opinion: A distinctive beer which is one of the best-selling bottle-conditioned beers in the UK. Nice with the traditional London fayre of pie, mash and liquor.

GALE'S FESTIVAL MILD 4.8% ABV 500 ML
Brewed by George Gale & Co. Ltd, The Hampshire Brewery, Horndean, Hampshire PO8 0DA. ☎ (0239) 257 1212.
www.gales.co.uk
Colour: Black with ruby tints (20).
Head: Brown, dense, small head.
Aroma: Malty and fruity, reminiscent of a Belgian Bruin.
Taste: Initial fizz prickling on the tongue leads to bitter fruit taste which tails off in the aftertaste.
Ease of Decanting: Easy to pour due to small head and yeast that clings to the base of the bottle.
Opinion: Unusual mild which seems to use bitter fruit flavours as a substitute for hop bitterness. Nice with an O'Hagan's sausage.

GALE'S HSB 4.8% ABV 500 ML
Brewed by George Gale & Co. Ltd, The Hampshire Brewery, Horndean, Hampshire PO8 0DA. ☎ (0239) 257 1212.
www.gales.co.uk
Colour: Oak-burgundy (17).
Head: Good natural head with small white bubbles .
Aroma: Reminded me of Coca Cola.
Taste: Sweet malt, frothy but with lots of body, maturing to caramel with a hint of burnt currants.
Ease of Decanting: Yeast stayed at the bottom, easy to pour due to the 330 ml bottle.
Opinion: A tasty beer that would accompany liver and onions with mash. Very nice.

GALE'S PRIZE OLD ALE 9.0% ABV 275 ML
Brewed by George Gale & Co. Ltd, The Hampshire Brewery, Horndean, Hampshire PO8 0DA. ☎ (0239) 257 1212.
www.gales.co.uk
Colour: Rich burgundy (19).
Head: Did not pour with a head.
Aroma: Sweet pungent toffee apple.
Taste: Stewed apple and sultana initially, warms the throat and coats the tongue then leaves a sweet fruitcake aftertaste.
Ease of Decanting: After taking the cork out, no problem as the bottle is only 275 ml, no head and yeast that stuck to the base of the bottle.
Opinion: An after-dinner beer to be savoured like a fine port or a brandy, a true classic.

HAMPSHIRE 1066 6.0% ABV 500 ML
Brewed by Hampshire Brewery Ltd, Romsey Industrial Estate, Greatbridge Road, Romsey, Hampshire SO51 0HR. ☎ (01794) 830529.
www.hampshirebrewery.com
Colour: Ruby-brown (13).
Head: Small, dense, clean white head.
Aroma: Like tutti-frutti sweets (remember those?)
Taste: Initially frothy, sweet and light, then cream soda developing into warming bitterness, then into an almondy bitter fruit with an aftertaste of slowly drying malt.
Ease of Decanting: Yeast swirls were evident in the last quarter of the bottle, so pour carefully for a rewarding beer.
Opinion: Surprisingly easy to drink for its strength, would go down nicely with gammon, egg and chips.

HAMPSHIRE GOLD RESERVE 4.8% ABV 500 ML
Brewed by Hampshire Brewery Ltd, Romsey Industrial Estate, Greatbridge Road, Romsey, Hampshire SO51 0HR. ☎ (01794) 830529.
www.hampshirebrewery.com
Colour: Straw (2).
Head: Small head with dense white bubbles.
Aroma: Lemon zest with lime high notes.
Taste: Frothy slight banana, warming spices turn to bitter fruit on the tongue, then hops dry the mouth in a long aftertaste.
Ease of Decanting: Yeast clung to the base of the bottle, the head stayed small, so nice and easy.
Opinion: A very nice beer, would go down nicely with a good chicken tikka.

HAMPSHIRE IRONSIDE 4.2% ABV 500 ML
Brewed by Hampshire Brewery Ltd, Romsey Industrial Estate, Greatbridge Road, Romsey, Hampshire SO51 0HR. ☎ (01794) 830529.
www.hampshirebrewery.com
Colour: Mid-brown(12).
Head: Small head with dense white bubbles.
Aroma: Cream soda with slight hint of vanilla.
Taste: Soft initial impression then caramelised malt drying quite sharply, leaving quite a long acrid aftertaste that furred the tongue.
Ease of Decanting: A nice and easy-to-pour ale.
Opinion: A nice beer to wash down some homemade beef cobbler.

HAMPSHIRE PENDRAGON 4.8% ABV 500 ML
Brewed by Hampshire Brewery Ltd, Romsey Industrial Estate, Greatbridge Road, Romsey, Hampshire SO51 0HR. ☎ (01794) 830529.
www.hampshirebrewery.com
Colour: Oak (16).
Head: White, dense bubbles in a large, but controllable, head.
Aroma: Sweet banana and vanilla aromas.
Taste: Initial impression is of fizz and prickle on the tongue, with subtle malt following through and leading to subtle bananas and a long aftertaste of hops drying and maturing on the tongue.
Ease of Decanting: A careful pour will reward the drinker with a smashing glass of beer. The head can be controlled by slow, careful pouring halfway through, keeping a close eye on those yeasty tendrils.
Opinion: A fruity beer with a long, drying, hoppy aftertaste, lovely with roast pork.

HAMPSHIRE PRIDE OF ROMSEY IPA 4.8% ABV 500 ML
Brewed by Hampshire Brewery Ltd, Romsey Industrial Estate, Greatbridge Road, Romsey, Hampshire SO51 0HR. ☎ (01794) 830529.
www.hampshirebrewery.com
Colour: Copper-brown (9).
Head: White, dense bubbles in a small head which is controllable through the height of the pour.
Aroma: Sweet floral, malty aroma.
Taste: Hops on the middle of the tongue that bitter progressively in a long aftertaste.
Ease of Decanting: Nice and easy to pour, with a controllable head and the yeast clinging to the base of the bottle.
Opinion: Nice bitter ale, a good quencher for a hot vindaloo.

HANBY PREMIUM 4.6% ABV 500 ML
Brewed by Hanby Ales Ltd. New Brewery, Aston Park, Soulton Road, Wem, Shropshire SY4 5SD. ☎ (01939) 232432.
www.hanbyales.co.uk
Colour: Rich golden amber (8).
Head: A large white head with small bubbles.
Aroma: Sweet red rhubarb.
Taste: Bitter black cherry zings through the taste buds increasing in fruitiness through to the end.
Ease of Decanting: Yeast swirls in the last quarter and the large head make this beer a difficult beer to pour, but it's well worth the effort.
Opinion: A beer with bags of taste, it would go down nicely with steak and kidney pie.

HANBY RAINBOW CHASER 4.3% ABV 500 ML
Brewed by Hanby Ales Ltd. New Brewery, Aston Park, Soulton Road, Wem, Shropshire SY4 5SD. ☎ (01939) 232432.
www.hanbyales.co.uk
Colour: Amber (7).
Head: White, small bubbles and controllable.
Aroma: Molasses and fruit cake.
Taste: Bitter honey like a dry mead, dry honey stays throughout finishing in a bitter flourish.
Ease of Decanting: Yeast clings to the bottom and the head stays small, so nice and easy.
Opinion: A nice thirst-quenching beer to be enjoyed on a hot summer's day with a honey-glazed ham baguette.

HANBY SHROPSHIRE STOUT 4.4% ABV 500 ML
Brewed by Hanby Ales Ltd. New Brewery, Aston Park, Soulton Road, Wem, Shropshire SY4 5SD. ☎ (01939) 232432.
www.hanbyales.co.uk
Colour: Black (20).
Head: Brown dense bubbles in a small controllable head.
Aroma: Unusual aromas, biscuity and chocolatey with a slight hint of old sock. Strangely pleasant.
Taste: Bitter blackcurrant initially leading to bitter fruit, drying to a bitter cherry and dark chocolate finish that dries on the tongue, a lingering aftertaste of drying dark chocolate.
Ease of Decanting: Head stayed small and yeast stayed at the base of the bottle making this an easy beer to pour.
Opinion: A complex stout, would be beautiful with organic roast lamb.

HARVEY'S IMPERIAL EXTRA DOUBLE STOUT 9.0% ABV 330 ML
Brewed by Harvey & Sons (Lewes) Ltd, The Bridge Wharf Brewery, 6 Cliffe High Street, Lewes, East Sussex BN7 2AH. ☎ (01273) 480209.
www.harveys.org.uk
Colour: Black (20).
Head: Very brown, dense head like drinking chocolate, which required pouring from height to create.
Aroma: Mulled wine and vintage port.
Taste: Initially smooth velvety mouth-feel, then powerful liquorice and honey warming to a long bitter liquorice aftertaste.
Ease of Decanting: The 330 ml bottle means that there is more room in the pint glass for this beer, yeast stays at the bottom and head has to be created, so a nice easy beer to pour.
Opinion: This beer has the wow factor, savour it like a fine port as an after-dinner drink.

HOGS BACK A OVER T (AROMAS OVER TONGHAM) 9.0% ABV 275 ML
Brewed by Hogs Back Brewery, Manor Farm, The Street, Tongham, Surrey GU10 1DE.
☎ (01252) 783000.
www.hogsback.co.uk
Colour: Oak-burgundy (17).
Head: Small creamy-coloured head with small bubbles.
Aroma: Sweet and alcoholic, like Christmas pudding.
Taste: Smooth thick caramel and molasses matures into liquorice then dries into thick caramel sweetness.
Ease of Decanting: Yeast stayed at the bottom of the bottle, the head was very small and the bottle was small which meant that it fit easily into my pint glass.
Opinion: A barley-wine style of beer, nice after dinner when appreciated like a fine port or brandy.

HOGS BACK BSA (BURMA STAR ALE) 4.5% ABV 500 ML
Brewed by Hogs Back Brewery, Manor Farm, The Street, Tongham, Surrey GU10 1DE.
☎ (01252) 783000.
www.hogsback.co.uk
Colour: Oak-burgundy (17).
Head: Stayed controllable, creamy white dense white bubbles.
Aroma: Subtle Ovaltine aroma, slightly fruity.
Taste: Subtle initial malt, fruit follows through, dries on the tongue, then bitter hops follow in a long aftertaste.
Ease of Decanting: Yeast stayed at the bottom of the bottle and the head can be created to whatever size is required.
Opinion: Nice beer with a cheese ploughman's.

HOGS BACK OTT (OLD TONGHAM TASTY) 6.0% ABV
Brewed by Hogs Back Brewery, Manor Farm, The Street, Tongham, Surrey GU10 1DE.
☎ (01252) 783000.
www.hogsback.co.uk
Colour: Black with burgundy tints (20).
Head: Small head with brown, dense bubbles.
Aroma: Sweet liquorice aroma.
Taste: Frothy, strong liquorice flavour with hops drying on the tongue in a long aftertaste.
Ease of Decanting: Yeast clung to the base of the bottle and the head stayed small and controllable.
Opinion: Would go very nicely with liver and bacon.

HOGS BACK TEA (TRADITIONAL ENGLISH ALE) 4.2% ABV 500 ML
Brewed by Hogs Back Brewery, Manor Farm, The Street, Tongham, Surrey GU10 1DE.
☎ (01252) 783000.
www.hogsback.co.uk
Colour: Orange-brown (10).
Head: Creamy-coloured small head which disappeared into the beer.
Aroma: Citrus zesty pear drops with a touch of blackcurrant.
Taste: Subtle and easy to drink with malt and subtle fruit flavours coming through then drying, then hops hit, then dry in the aftertaste.
Ease of Decanting: Yeast stayed at the bottom of the bottle and head stayed small, so nice and easy.
Opinion: An easy-to-drink bitter that would be a good thirst-quencher for a nice hot Indian curry.

HOGS BACK WOBBLE IN A BOTTLE 7.5% ABV 275 ML
Brewed by Hogs Back Brewery, Manor Farm, The Street, Tongham, Surrey GU10 1DE.
☎ (01252) 783000.
www.hogsback.co.uk
Colour: Ruby-brown (13).
Head: Small head with small dense white bubbles.
Aroma: Citrusy and slightly zesty.
Taste: Sweet caramel to start, then develops into powerful bitter fruits leading to bitter lemon in a

long drying aftertaste.
Ease of Decanting: Yeast clung to the bottom of the bottle and head stayed small, with the unusual 275 ml bottle, no problems to pour.
Opinion: A nice beer to sip and appreciate with roast pork and all the trimmings.

HOP BACK CROP CIRCLE 4.2% ABV 500 ML
Brewed by Hop Back Brewery plc, Unit 22–24 Batten Road Industrial Estate, Downton, Salisbury, Wiltshire SP5 3HU. ☎ (01725) 510986. *www.hopback.co.uk*
Colour: Straw (2).
Head: White dense small bubbles, stayed small and was controllable with care.
Aroma: Aroma of strong bitter lager hops with hints of elderflower.
Taste: Smooth and frothy with light berries changing to light fruit, turning slightly bitter in a short aftertaste.
Ease of Decanting: Yeast behaved impeccably and the head stayed small, though controlled with care, worth the effort.
Opinion: A light and refreshing thirst-quenching bitter which would be a godsend after a hot spicy curry.

HOP BACK SUMMER LIGHTNING 5.0% ABV 500 ML
Brewed by Hop Back Brewery plc, Unit 22–24 Batten Road Industrial Estate, Downton, Salisbury, Wiltshire SP5 3HU. ☎ (01725) 510986. *www.hopback.co.uk*
Colour: Pale straw (2).
Head: Small white head with small bubbles.
Aroma: Hard to describe, it reminded me of freshly mown hay.
Taste: Initial frothy sweetness dries to a fruit salad finish that dries with a slightly bitter aftertaste.
Ease of Decanting: Yeast swirls in the last quarter, so a steady hand is needed.
Opinion: A legendary beer, another good beer to enjoy with a good hot curry.

HOP BACK TAIPHOON LEMON GRASS BEER 4.2% ABV
Brewed by Hop Back Brewery plc, Unit 22–24 Batten Road Industrial Estate, Downton, Salisbury, Wiltshire SP5 3HU. ☎ (01725) 510986. *www.hopback.co.uk*
Colour: Golden-orange (4).
Head: White, dense-bubbled head that stays small and manageable, yet clings to the sides of the glass.
Aroma: Sweet and lemony aroma.
Taste: Initial impression is sweet, light and refreshing with slight warm spice taste after frothing subsides, with a long aftertaste of subtle spice on the tongue.
Ease of Decanting: Yeast clung to the base of the bottle and the head stayed manageable, so a nice easy pour.
Opinion: Nice beer with a Thai curry. Surprisingly refreshing and well worth trying even if the idea of a lemongrass beer does not appeal.

ICENI FEN TIGER 4.2% ABV 500 ML
Brewed by Iceni Brewery, 3 Foulden Road, Ickburgh, Mundford, Norfolk IP26 5BJ. ☎ (01842) 878922.
Colour: Reddish gold (10).
Head: Small tight head.
Aroma: Coriander.
Taste: Fresh grassy hops but the dominant flavour is coriander.
Ease of Decanting: Quite easy to pour.
Opinion: Excellent with a Thai curry.

ICENI FINE SOFT DAY 4.0% ABV 500 ML
Brewed by Iceni Brewery, 3 Foulden Road, Ickburgh, Mundford, Norfolk IP26 5BJ. ☎ (01842) 878922.
Colour: Rich golden amber (8).
Head: White small bubble head that stayed controllable, sunk into beer.
Aroma: Damsons and unripe plums.
Taste: Smooth soft bitter fruits develop their bitterness then dry in a short bitter aftertaste.
Ease of Decanting: Easy to pour, yeast stayed at the bottom of the bottle.
Opinion: An easy-to-drink thirst-quencher, would cool the mouth after a fiery hot curry.

ICENI IT'S A GRAND DAY 4.5% ABV 500 ML
Brewed by Iceni Brewery, 3 Foulden Road, Ickburgh, Mundford, Norfolk IP26 5BJ. ☎ (01842) 878922.
Colour: Copper-brown (9).
Head: White large bubbles formed a small head.
Aroma: Slightly peachy aroma.
Taste: Aromatic initial flavours, slightly perfumy like Parma violet maturing to a flowery taste which is quite sweet but drying.
Ease of Decanting: Yeast stuck to the base of the bottle, the head stayed small so a nice easy beer to decant.
Opinion: A nice thirst-quencher for a hot madras.

ICENI MEN OF NORFOLK 6.2% ABV 500 ML
Brewed by Iceni Brewery, 3 Foulden Road, Ickburgh, Mundford, Norfolk IP26 5BJ. ☎ (01842) 878922.
Colour: Black (20).
Head: A brown head with a mixture of small and large bubbles that was controllable by adjusting the height of the pour.
Aroma: Molasses and rich warm mince pie.
Taste: Blackcurrant and liquorice with bitter cherries coming through and drying on the back of the palate.
Ease of Decanting: A controllable head and yeast that stayed in the bottle made this an easy beer to pour.
Opinion: A nice robust ale that would go down nicely with steak and kidney pudding.

ICENI PORTED PORTER 4.4% ABV 500 ML
Brewed by Iceni Brewery, 3 Foulden Road, Ickburgh, Mundford, Norfolk IP26 5BJ. ☎ (01842) 878922.
Colour: Black (20).
Head: Stayed small, with small brown bubbles.
Aroma: Liquorice with cough mixture, you can smell the port.
Taste: Very smooth initial taste with the port taste coming through, it dries to bitter fruits in the aftertaste.
Ease of Decanting: Yeast stayed at the bottom

and head stayed small so a nice easy beer to pour.
Opinion: Unusual beer in that port has been added to great effect. A nice beer with homemade beef cobbler.

ICENI RED, WHITE AND BLUEBERRY 4.0% ABV 500 ML
Brewed by Iceni Brewery, 3 Foulden Road, Ickburgh, Mundford, Norfolk IP26 5BJ.
☎ (01842) 878922
Colour: Mid-brown (12).
Head: Small head with a mix of large and small white bubbles.
Aroma: Forest berries and fruits.
Taste: Thin initially, bitter and hoppy with delicate underlying fruit, hops zing on the taste buds then draw the juices in a long aftertaste.
Ease of Decanting: Yeast stayed where it should and the head stayed small, so nice and easy to pour.
Opinion: A nice easy-to-drink beer with a cheese ploughman's.

ICENI THETFORD FOREST MILD 3.6% ABV 500 ML
Brewed by Iceni Brewery, 3 Foulden Road, Ickburgh, Mundford, Norfolk IP26 5BJ.
☎ (01842) 878922.
Colour: Black (20).
Head: Brown fizzing head, sunk into beer and disappeared.
Aroma: Liquorice and faint sherry.
Taste: Lively initial bitterness, light and tasty, soft fruit initially, light burnt liquorice follows and ripens into bitter fruit.
Ease of Decanting: Yeast stayed at the bottom and the head stayed small so nothing to fear.
Opinion: A lovely easy-to-drink mild, nice with gammon and eggs.

KELTEK BEHEADED 10.0% ABV 500 ML AND 275 ML
Brewed by Keltek Brewery, Unit 3a, Restormel Industrial Estate, Liddicost Road, Lostwithiel, Cornwall PL22 0HG.
☎ (01208) 871199.
Colour: Dark brown (11).
Head: Dense white head.
Aroma: Rich fruit bread.
Taste: Powerful and full-bodied but relatively dry for the strength, with a long lingering malt finish.
Ease of Decanting: Well conditioned and therefore quite easy to pour.
Opinion: Would suit a rich game stew.

KELTEK KING 5.1% ABV 500 ML
Brewed by Keltek Brewery, Unit 3a, Restormel Industrial Estate, Liddicost Road, Lostwithiel, Cornwall PL22 0HG. ☎ (01208) 871199.
Colour: Pale amber (5).
Head: Small head with white, dense bubbles.
Aroma: Sweet vanilla and toffee.
Taste: Smooth and fruity sweetness maturing to a fruity hop bitterness with a slightly fruit spice (cloves, nutmeg, etc) aftertaste.
Ease of Decanting: Yeast clings to base of bottle and the head stays small, which makes this beer a pleasure to pour.
Opinion: Clean-tasting ale that would go down nicely with fish and chips.

KELTEK KRIPPLE DICK 8.5% ABV 275 ML
Brewed by Keltek Brewery, Unit 3a, Restormel Industrial Estate, Liddicost Road, Lostwithiel, Cornwall PL22 0HG.
☎ (01208) 871199.
Colour: Black with burgundy tints (20).
Head: Small head with dense, brown bubbles.
Aroma: Very alcoholic, like plum pudding steeped in brandy.
Taste: Sweetness suddenly exploding into sweet molasses and brown sugar with a backtaste of warming alcohol.
Ease of Decanting: Yeast clings to the base of bottle and the head stays very controllable, which means pouring from height to achieve head.
Opinion: Strong ale to savour, best drunk after a good meal, as you would a fine port or brandy.

KELTEK REVENGE 7.0% ABV
Brewed by Keltek Brewery, Unit 3a, Restormel Industrial Estate, Liddicost Road, Lostwithiel, Cornwall PL22 0HG.
☎ (01208) 871199.
Colour: Ruby-brown (13).
Head: Have to pour from height to create head, which rapidly disappears into beer.
Aroma: Liquorice with faint cinnamon.
Taste: Molasses creating a velvety mouth-feel leading to masses of bitter fruit which bitters increasingly on the tongue in a long aftertaste.
Ease of Decanting: Yeast clings to the base of the bottle and the head is small and disappearing, so very easy to pour.
Opinion: A lovely beer to enjoy with some nice ripe mature Stilton and biscuits.

MAULDONS BLACK ADDER 5.3% 500 ML
Brewed by Mauldons Brewery, 7 Addison Road, Chiltern Industrial Estate, Sudbury, Suffolk CO10 2YW. ☎ (01787) 311055.
www.mauldons.co.uk
Colour: Black (20).
Head: Small head with brown bubbles that disappeared into the beer.
Aroma: Rich fruity blackcurrant with hints of liquorice.
Taste: Smooth initially, then acrid charcoal and iron, well conditioned, dry acrid creosote flavour dries in a long finish.
Ease of Decanting: Yeast clung to the base of the bottle and the head was small, so easy to pour.
Opinion: A strongly flavoured dark ale, would drink nicely with organic roast lamb with all the trimmings.

MORLAND HENS TOOTH 6.5% ABV 500 ML
Brewed by Greene King PLC, Westgate Brewery, Bury St Edmunds IP33 1QT. ☎ (01284) 763222.
www.greeneking.co.uk
Colour: Ruby-brown (13).
Head: Small dense white head.
Aroma: All-spice with fruity pears, slightly warming to the nose.
Taste: Tart fruit bitterness initially, then pear and melon with slight spice warming, the alcoholic warming comes through with fruit bitterness in the aftertaste.
Ease of Decanting: Small head but yeast swirling in last quarter, so care and attention needed, for which you will be well rewarded.
Opinion: Available in supermarkets, another of the UK's top ten best-selling bottle-conditioned

beers due to the size of the brewer, but when all said and done, a high-quality beer. Try one with some game pie.

OAKLEAF HOLE HEARTED 4.7% ABV 500 ML
Brewed by Oakleaf Brewing Co. Ltd, Westgate Brewery, 7, Clarence Wharf Industrial Estate, Mumby Road, Gosport, Hampshire PO12 1AJ.
☎ (02392) 510148.
www.oakleafbrewing.co.uk
Colour: Light golden (6).
Head: Virtually no head.
Aroma: Flowery hops.
Taste: Fresh grapefruit flavour which is typical of American hop variety, Cascade. Long, dry, hoppy finish.
Ease of Decanting: Very easy to pour.
Opinion: The perfect refresher with a creamy curry.

ORGANIC BREWHOUSE LIZARD POINT 4.0% ABV 500 ML
Brewed by The Organic Brewhouse, Cury Cross Lanes, Helston, Cornwall TR12 7AZ
☎ (01326) 241555.
Colour: Light golden brown (8).
Head: Large dense white head.
Aroma: Clean, fresh, zingy hops.
Taste: Tasty malt and appley fruit with a long malt finish.
Ease of Decanting: Quite easy to pour.
Opinion: Perfect with a roast chicken salad.

ORGANIC BREWHOUSE SERPENTINE 4.5% ABV 500 ML
Brewed by The Organic Brewhouse, Cury Cross Lanes, Helston, Cornwall TR12 7AZ
☎ (01326) 241555.
Colour: Oak-burgundy (17).
Head: Small head with dense white bubbles.
Aroma: Glacé to bitter cherry with hot blackcurrant.
Taste: Marzipan and vanilla matures from sweetness to chocolate malt in the aftertaste, has a nice clean texture.
Ease of Decanting: Yeast stayed at the bottom of the bottle, the head stayed small, so nice and easy.
Opinion: Another of those fine beers that would go down nicely with a nice organic liver and bacon meal.

ORGANIC BREWHOUSE WOLF ROCK 5.0% ABV 500 ML
Brewed by The Organic Brewhouse, Cury Cross Lanes, Helston, Cornwall TR12 7AZ
☎ (01326) 241555.
Colour: Ruby-brown (13).
Head: White small dense bubbled head.
Aroma: Sweet and fruity with pear drops coming through.
Taste: Smooth fruit initially leading through to pear-drop sweetness, then hop bitterness punching through and drying on the palate in a long bitter aftertaste.
Ease of Decanting: Unusually for bottle-conditioned beers, this comes in a clear bottle making it easy to see the yeast: there were swirls in the last quarter though the head was small, so an easy beer to pour.
Opinion: Organic bottle-conditioned beers are rare. Bottle-conditioning definitely improves organic beers as this was the best organic beer I have tasted, would accompany cod and chips very nicely.

PITFIELD BREWERY 1824 MILD ALE 6.5% ABV 500 ML
Brewed by Pitfield Brewery, The Beer Shop, 14 Pitfield Street, Hoxton, London N1 6EY.
☎ (020) 7739 3701.
www.pitfieldbeershop.co.uk
Colour: Very dark brown (18).
Head: Dense, creamy, small white head.
Aroma: Coffee, bitter chocolate and dark sugar.
Taste: Rich, smooth, chocolate malt with a dry, short, coffee finish.
Ease of Decanting: The yeast clung to the bottom of the bottle making this an easy pour despite the colour.
Opinion: Perfect with beef stew and dumplings.

PITFIELD BREWERY 1830 AMBER ALE 6.0% ABV 500 ML
Brewed by Pitfield Brewery, The Beer Shop, 14 Pitfield Street, Hoxton, London N1 6EY.
☎ (020) 7739 3701.
www.pitfieldbeershop.co.uk
Colour: Dark reddish-brown (15) (not really amber!).
Head: Virtually no head at all.
Aroma: Malt whisky and leather.
Taste: Dry malt with a marked taste of brazil nuts and a short dry finish.
Ease of Decanting: Very easy to pour due to the small head.
Opinion: After a big meal, try this with the cheese board.

PITFIELD BREWERY 1896 STOCK ALE 10.0% ABV 500 ML
Brewed by Pitfield Brewery, The Beer Shop, 14 Pitfield Street, Hoxton, London N1 6EY.
☎ (020) 7739 3701.
www.pitfieldbeershop.co.uk
Colour: Golden brown (9).
Head: Large, dense, white head with fine bubbles.
Aroma: Complex, raisin fruit. A bit spirity, like a dessert wine.
Taste: Brown sugar and raisins with a long, lingering dry finish.
Ease of Decanting: A bit tricky to pour but worth the effort.
Opinion: After a really big meal try this powerful beer instead of a port or a brandy. (Note: it's probably worth getting your pyjamas on first!)

PITFIELD BREWERY ORGANIC PITFIELDS ECO WARRIOR 4.5% ABV 500 ML
Brewed by Pitfield Brewery, The Beer Shop, 14 Pitfield Street, Hoxton, London N1 6EY.
☎ (020) 7739 3701.
www.pitfieldbeershop.co.uk
Colour: Rich golden amber (8).
Head: White dense bubbles in a small head.
Aroma: Pear drops, lemonade shandy, slightly lemony with a faint aroma of mushy bananas.
Taste: Sweet velvet taste of Caribbean fruit punch, then extreme fruit bitterness, sweet punch comes through near the end, then finishes with fresh fruity bitterness.
Ease of Decanting: Yeast stays at the bottom and the head is small, so nice and easy.
Opinion: An unusual beer that would go down nicely with coronation chicken.

PITFIELD BREWERY PITFIELD SHOREDITCH STOUT 4.0% ABV 500 ML
Brewed by Pitfield Brewery, The Beer Shop, 14 Pitfield Street, Hoxton, London N1 6EY. ☎ (020) 7739 3701.
www.pitfieldbeershop.co.uk
Colour: Black (20).
Head: Small head with brown small bubbles.
Aroma: Molasses and dark chocolate.
Taste: Bitter chocolate powder maturing to subtle bitter fruits in a short aftertaste.
Ease of Decanting: Yeast stayed at the bottom of the bottle and the head stayed small, so nice and easy to pour.
Opinion: A very clean-tasting stout, nice with a Melton Mowbray pork pie.

RCH ALE MARY 5.0% ABV 500 ML
Brewed by RCH Brewery, West Hewish, Weston-super-Mare, Somerset BS24 6RR.
☎ (01934) 834447.
www.rchbrewery.com
Colour: Rich golden amber (8).
Head: Very large, white, dense head.
Aroma: Fruity and sweet.
Taste: Winter spices initially leading to bitter fruit with slight ginger overtones, then a spiced dry aftertaste.
Ease of Decanting: Difficult due to a large head, though bottoms did not rise into the beer. Worth ensuring that the beer is well cooled before opening to minimise risk of excessive heading.
Opinion: A well-hung pheasant or grouse meal would complement this beer perfectly.

RCH FIREBOX 6.0% ABV 500 ML
Brewed by RCH Brewery, West Hewish, Weston-super-Mare, Somerset BS24 6RR.
☎ (01934) 834447.
www.rchbrewery.com
Colour: Ruby brown (13).
Head: Small tight head.
Aroma: Fresh hops and malt.
Taste: Lots of citrus fruit and bitter hops with a long, bitter, slightly roasted finish.
Ease of Decanting: Quite easy to pour.
Opinion: Perfect with steak and chips.

RCH OLD SLUG PORTER 4.5% ABV 500 ML
Brewed by RCH Brewery, West Hewish, Weston-super-Mare, Somerset BS24 6RR.
☎ (01934) 834447.
www.rchbrewery.com
Colour: Rich burgundy (19).
Head: Medium head, light brown, dense small bubbles stayed throughout, clinging to the sides of the glass.
Aroma: Liquorice with toffee and blackcurrants.
Taste: Bitter fruits quickly lead to very slightly aniseed/liquorice and dark caramel, with sweetness slowly fading, giving a full mouth-feel.
Ease of Decanting: Yeast clings to the base of the bottle and head did not start feeding itself, so a nice easy-pouring ale.
Opinion: Fruity, yet well-balanced with a good finish. Nice beer with game pie or a good goulash.

RCH ON THE TILES 4.0% ABV 500 ML
Brewed by RCH Brewery, West Hewish, Weston-super-Mare, Somerset BS24 6RR.
☎ (01934) 834447.
www.rchbrewery.com
Colour: Straw (2).
Head: Dense white bubbles in a small head.
Aroma: Reminded me of babies' nappies and cardboard.
Taste: Initial froth gives way to faint pears and vanilla, light and short sweet fruit aftertaste.
Ease of Decanting: Yeast stays at the bottom and the head stays small, so a good one for a novice to start with.
Opinion: Light thirst-quenching ale, easy to drink, nice with a hot Thai curry.

RCH PITCHFORK 4.3% ABV 500 ML
Brewed by RCH Brewery, West Hewish, Weston-super-Mare, Somerset BS24 6RR.
☎ (01934) 834447.
www.rchbrewery.com
Colour: Golden (10).
Head: Creamy dense head.
Aroma: Fresh fruit and malt.
Taste: Fresh fruity flavour which develops through to a lingering, bitter hop finish.
Ease of Decanting: Very easy to pour.
Opinion: Great with pasta in a light mushroom sauce.

RINGWOOD FORTYNINER 4.9% ABV 500 ML
Brewed by Ringwood Brewery Ltd, 138 Christchurch Road, Ringwood, Hampshire BH24 3AP. ☎ (01425) 471177.
www.ringwoodbrewery.co.uk
Colour: Orange-brown (10).
Head: Controllable white head with large and small bubbles.
Aroma: Faint aroma of fruity caramel.
Taste: Smooth initial taste, light fruit comes through and dries on the palate.
Ease of Decanting: Yeast stayed sticky and head was controllable, so an easy beer to decant.
Opinion: Surprisingly easy to drink for its strength, a nice beer with fish and chips.

RINGWOOD XXXX PORTER 4.7% ABV 500 ML
Brewed by Ringwood Brewery Ltd, 138 Christchurch Road, Ringwood, Hampshire BH24 3AP. ☎ (01425) 471177.
www.ringwoodbrewery.co.uk
Colour: Black with deep burgundy hints in the light (20).
Head: Dense brown head which needs to be poured from height to create the desired head volume.
Aroma: Faint toffee and banana.
Taste: Creamy, light mouth-feel with sweet caramel and chocolate malt maturing into bitter hops developing long into the aftertaste.
Ease of Decanting: Nice easy-pouring ale with yeast that clings to the base of the bottle and a head that responds to what you like. For example, pour close to the glass for no head or pour from three inches for a large, rocky head – it's up to you.
Opinion: Lovely beer with a nice O'Hagan's sausage and mash.

SALOPIAN ENTIRE BUTT ENGLISH PORTER 4.8% ABV 500 ML
Brewed by Salopian Brewing Co. Ltd, 67 Mytton Oak Road, Shrewsbury, Shropshire SY3 8UQ.
☎ (01743) 248414.
Colour: Black with deep burgundy hints (20).
Head: Medium brown, dense-bubbled head, the size of which is controlled by height of pour.
Aroma: Liquorice and black treacle.
Taste: Frothy initial impression maturing into a dark chocolate and burnt caramel taste, finishing with a bittersweet burnt malt frothing on the sides of the tongue.
Ease of Decanting: Yeast clings to the base of the bottle and the head is easy to control.
Opinion: A lovely beer with a nice pork casserole.

SALOPIAN GINGER SNAP 4.7% ABV 500 ML
Brewed by Salopian Brewing Co. Ltd, 67 Mytton Oak Road, Shrewsbury, Shropshire SY3 8UQ.
☎ (01743) 248414.
Colour: Rich golden amber (8).
Head: White, dense bubbles in a small, controllable head.
Aroma: Lemony ginger and citrus aromas.
Taste: Initial taste is of gingery sweetness, with the spiciness of the ginger burning through in the mid-taste and lingering on the tongue in a long aftertaste.
Ease of Decanting: Yeast clings to the base of the bottle and head stays manageable, so a nice easy beer to pour.
Opinion: A ginger beer for the connoisseur.

SALOPIAN MINSTERLEY 4.5% ABV 500 ML
Brewed by Salopian Brewing Co. Ltd, 67 Mytton Oak Road, Shrewsbury, Shropshire SY3 8UQ.
☎ (01743) 248414.
Colour: Golden-orange (4).
Head: Small, white with large bubbles, subsiding into beer leaving a brown marble effect on top of the liquid.
Aroma: Fruity/toffee, with a slight aroma of tar.
Taste: Starts out with subtle sweet malt flavours which mature into a tart caramel taste that bitters progressively in a long aftertaste.
Ease of Decanting: Easy to pour as head sinks quickly into the beer.
Opinion: Unusual golden ale in which hops might be expected to be the main flavour. Would go very well with duck and orange pie.

SPRINGHEAD CROMWELLS HAT 6.2% ABV 500 ML
Brewed by Springhead Brewery, Unit 3, Sutton Workshops, Old Great North Road, Sutton on Trent, Newark, Nottinghamshire NG23 6QS.
☎ (01636) 821000.
www.springheadfineales.co.uk
Colour: Orange-brown (10).
Head: Very large dense white bubbles.
Aroma: Orange zest and raisins.
Taste: Initial taste of tangy zesty orange peel turning tart and lemony which dries to a warming bitter cherry finish.
Ease of Decanting: A real challenge for the more experienced connoisseur of bottle-conditioned beers. Yeast swirls in the last quarter plus a large head required a steady hand to wait until the head had subsided.
Opinion: Unexpected taste, reminiscent of a Belgian cherry beer. Very good with game pie.

SPRINGHEAD THE LEVELLER 5.0% ABV 500 ML
Brewed by Springhead Brewery, Unit 3, Sutton Workshops, Old Great North Road, Sutton on Trent, Newark, Nottinghamshire NG23 6QS.
☎ (01636) 821000.
www.springheadfineales.co.uk
Colour: Mid-brown (12).
Head: Large head with large, white bubbles.
Aroma: Dryish malt and caramel aromas.
Taste: Initial powerful hops give way to balancing hops in the main taste. A pleasant prickle on the tongue due to excellent conditioning.
Ease of Decanting: Large head and tendrils in the last quarter means that this is a challenging beer to pour, though definitely worth the effort.
Opinion: Excellent accompaniment to a good steak and kidney pie.

SUTHWYK SKEW SUNSHINE ALE 4.6% ABV 500 ML
Brewed by Suthwyk Ales, Offwell Farm, Southwick, Fareham, Hampshire PO17 6DX.
☎ (01392) 325252.
www.suthwykales.com
Colour: Straw (2).
Head: White, dense bubbly large head.
Aroma: Slightly citrus with underlying forest fruit aromas.
Taste: Initial frothy mouth-feel gives way to a sweet malt taste with subtle fruit which matures on the roof of the mouth in a short aftertaste.
Ease of Decanting: Difficult unless kept in the fridge for an hour before pouring. Mine had a very large head and yeast swirls in the last quarter, so be careful. The taste is definitely worth the trouble.
Opinion: Lovely refreshing ale which would go down very well with a nice fresh baguette with ham off the bone and some English mustard.

TEIGNWORTHY BEACHCOMBER 4.5% ABV 500 ML (BOTTLE-CONDITIONED LAGER)
Brewed by Teignworthy Brewery, The Maltings, Teign Road, Newton Abbot, Devon TQ12 4AA.
☎ (01626) 332066.
Colour: Amber (7).
Head: Stayed small, high pour to create the head, white dense bubbles.
Aroma: Fruit salad penny sweets.
Taste: Light bitter fruits maturing to delicate pears with bitter fruit drying the palate in a short aftertaste.
Ease of Decanting: Yeast clung to base of bottle and head controllable by height of pour, so nice and easy to pour.
Opinion: Unusually sweet for a lager but very tasty for it. Would drink nicely with fish and chips.

TEIGNWORTHY EDWIN TUCKERS EAST INDIA PALE ALE 6.5% ABV 500 ML
Brewed by Teignworthy Brewery, The Maltings, Teign Road, Newton Abbot, Devon TQ12 4AA.
☎ (01626) 332066.
Colour: Rich golden amber (8).
Head: Small head with dense white bubbles.
Aroma: Slightly citrusy with sweet caramel.
Taste: Unexpectedly smooth and sweet initial taste, smooth caramel continuing into long warm bitter lingering aftertaste.
Ease of Decanting: Won't take an expert, but not one to pour for the novice, head was controllable, but yeast swirls in the last quarter.

Opinion: Unexpectedly sweet for an IPA, which are traditionally very hoppy, nicely balanced. Would go down well with roast pork.

TEIGNWORTHY EDWIN TUCKERS EMPRESS RUSSIAN PORTER 10.5% ABV 275 ML
Brewed by Teignworthy Brewery, The Maltings, Teign Road, Newton Abbot, Devon TQ12 4AA. ☎ (01626) 332066.
Colour: Thick dense black (20).
Head: Creamy meniscus that broke to a large bubbled head if poured from a height, then disappeared into the beer.
Aroma: Rich, acrid and fruity, like dark rum.
Taste: Dense full soft mouth-feel, initial liquorice with prune developing a hot fermented black treacle tempered by bitter fruit in the aftertaste.
Ease of Decanting: Easy to pour as the bottle is 275 ml, though it was hard to see the yeast due to the darkness of the beer
Opinion: Wow! Full-blooded Russian-style porter, intense and strong, this beer should be drunk like a port, and would go down well after a good meal with some good cheese.

TEIGNWORTHY MALTSTERS ALE 4.5% ABV 500 ML
Brewed by Teignworthy Brewery, The Maltings, Teign Road, Newton Abbot, Devon TQ12 4AA. ☎ (01626) 332066.
Colour: Burgundy-brown (14).
Head: Small head with dense white bubbles.
Aroma: Pineapple with traces of zesty orange and kiwi fruit.
Taste: Bitter fruit developing to bitter cherry drying to a slightly burnt, long grapefruit aftertaste.
Ease of Decanting: Yeast clinging to the base of the bottle and the small head make this a nice easy beer to pour.
Opinion: Would accompany a nice game pie.

TEIGNWORTHY OLD MOGGIE 4.4% ABV 500 ML
Brewed by Teignworthy Brewery, The Maltings, Teign Road, Newton Abbot, Devon TQ12 4AA. ☎ (01626) 332066.
Colour: Dark amber-chestnut (11).
Head: White dense bubbles with a small head.
Aroma: Like tutti-frutti children's sweets leading to a slightly soapy aroma.
Taste: Lots of body, slightly sweet marmalade leading to a long drying bitter aftertaste.
Ease of Decanting: Yeast clung to the base of the bottle and the head stayed small.
Opinion: Would accompany a good cheese board with soft cheeses like a nice mature warm brie.

TEIGNWORTHY REEL ALE 4.0% ABV 500 ML
Brewed by Teignworthy Brewery, The Maltings, Teign Road, Newton Abbot, Devon TQ12 4AA. ☎ (01626) 332066.
Colour: Orange-brown (10).
Head: Small controllable head that needed height to create.
Aroma: Subtle warming spices with vanilla and caramel notes.
Taste: Sweet Malteser, drying to a long bitter fruit taste, then malty and slightly aromatic finish.
Ease of Decanting: Yeast clung to the base of the bottle and head stayed small, so a nice easy one to pour.
Opinion: A well-crafted session beer, would go down nicely with an authentic spaghetti bolognese.

TITANIC CAPTAIN SMITH'S 5.2% ABV 500 ML
Brewed by The Titanic Brewery, Harvey Works, Lingard Street, Burslem, Stoke-on-Trent, Staffordshire ST6 1JL. ☎ (01782) 823447. *www.titanicbrewery.co.uk*
Colour: Ruby-brown (13).
Head: White, large bubble head that disperses into the beer.
Aroma: Flowery and slightly acid hops.
Taste: Strong malt which continues though to a drying hoppy finish.
Ease of Decanting: Small head but tendrils to look out for in the last quarter require that all-important eagle eye.
Opinion: Nice beer to accompany beef cobbler.

TITANIC STOUT 4.5% ABV 500 ML
Brewed by The Titanic Brewery, Harvey Works, Lingard Street, Burslem, Stoke-on-Trent, Staffordshire ST6 1JL. ☎ (01782) 823447. *www.titanicbrewery.co.uk*
Colour: Black with ruby hints in the light (20).
Head: Brown, dense bubbles in a medium-sized head.
Aroma: Dark chocolate and burnt caramel.
Taste: Initial chocolate malt and molasses maturing into bitter chocolate with full smooth mouth-feel, then hop bitterness maturing on the back of the tongue, balancing the chocolate in a long bitter aftertaste.
Opinion: Strongly flavoured stout with long bitter aftertaste, a very nice accompaniment to a strong Cheddar ploughman's.

VALE BREWERY BLACK BEAUTY PORTER 4.3% ABV 500 ML
Brewed by Vale Brewery Co Ltd, Thame Road, Haddenham, Buckinghamshire HP17 8BY. ☎ (01844) 290008. *www.valebrewery.co.uk*
Colour: Black (20).
Head: Small with dense brown bubbles that disappeared into the beer leaving a brown cream meniscus.
Aroma: Rich plum and autumn fruit.
Taste: Surprisingly light initial taste, delicate malt comes through with hops that dry to a blackberry bitter fruit taste, with residual sweetness countering the bitterness.
Ease of Decanting: Small head and yeast clinging to the base of the bottle making this nice and easy to pour.
Opinion: Lovely beer to drink with a beef hotpot.

VALE BREWERY BLACK SWAN DARK MILD 3.3% ABV 500 ML
Brewed by Vale Brewery Co Ltd, Thame Road, Haddenham, Buckinghamshire HP17 8BY. ☎ (01844) 290008. *www.valebrewery.co.uk*
Colour: Dark brown to black (20).
Head: Brown head was created by pouring from height, stayed small.
Aroma: A subtle fruity with acetate tones.
Taste: Thin bitter taste initially, subtle aftertaste of drying chocolate malt.
Ease of Decanting: Yeast stayed at the bottom and the head needed creating, so no problems with this beer.
Opinion: Would go down nicely with steak and kidney pudding.

VALE BREWERY EDGAR'S GOLDEN ALE 4.3% ABV 500 ML
Brewed by Vale Brewery Co Ltd, Thame Road, Haddenham, Buckinghamshire HP17 8BY. ☎ (01844) 290008.
www.valebrewery.co.uk
Colour: Amber (7).
Head: White dense bubbles in a small head.
Aroma: A slightly acrid aroma of fresh cauliflower.
Taste: Initially light, frothy and refreshing, slightly bitter caramelised subtle zesty fruits mature to drying light bitter fruit.
Ease of Decanting: Yeast swirls in the last quarter need to be watched carefully, worth the effort though.
Opinion: A nice beer with a Cheddar ploughman's.

VALE BREWERY GRUMPLING PREMIUM 4.6% ABV 500 ML
Brewed by Vale Brewery Co Ltd, Thame Road, Haddenham, Buckinghamshire HP17 8BY. ☎ (01844) 290008.
www.valebrewery.co.uk
Colour: Orange-brown (10).
Head: Small head with dense white bubbles.
Aroma: Subtle aroma of blackcurrant and pears.
Taste: Subtle initial flavour, smooth, slightly fruity blackberry malt, fruity bitterness zings on the sides of the tongue.
Ease of Decanting: A nice easy beer to pour, with the head staying small and the yeast staying at the bottom of the bottle.
Opinion: Goes down well with a cheese ploughman's and sweet pickle.

VALE BREWERY WYCHERT THE ORIGINAL 3.9% ABV 500 ML
Brewed by Vale Brewery Co Ltd, Thame Road, Haddenham, Buckinghamshire HP17 8BY. ☎ (01844) 290008.
www.valebrewery.co.uk
Colour: Dark amber-chestnut (11).
Head: Small with dense white bubbles.
Aroma: Like pear drops or fresh candyfloss.
Taste: Initially light, frothy and easy to drink, slightly sour malt with burnt toffee malt leading to a long bitter dark chocolate aftertaste that lingers.
Ease of Decanting: Yeast clung to the base of the bottle and the head stayed small, so no problems with this beer.
Opinion: Would go down nicely with O'Hagan's sausage, onions and mash.

VENTNOR OYSTER STOUT 4.5% ABV 500 ML
Brewed by Ventnor Brewery, 119 High Street, Ventnor, Isle of Wight, PO38 1LY. ☎ (01983) 856404.
www.ventnorbrewery.co.uk
Colour: Almost black (19).
Head: Dense, white head.
Aroma: Ozone freshness and slightly fishy.
Taste: Slight hop flavour but dominated by the oysters.
Ease of Decanting: Very easy to pour despite the colour.
Opinion: Not a session beer but absolutely perfect with a steak and mushroom pie.

WICKWAR BOB 4.0% ABV 500 ML
Brewed by Wickwar Brewery Co. The Old Cider Mill, Station Road, Wickwar, Gloucestershire. GL12 8NB. ☎ (01454) 294168.
www.wickwarbrewing.co.uk
Colour: Orange-brown (10).
Head: Small white head.
Aroma: Appetising malt.
Taste: Slightly dry fruit balanced with hops and a long, dry finish.
Ease of Decanting: Easy to pour.
Opinion: A perfect partner for a cheese doorstep.

WICKWAR MR PERRETTS TRADITIONAL STOUT 5.9% ABV 500 ML
Brewed by Wickwar Brewery Co. The Old Cider Mill, Station Road, Wickwar, Gloucestershire. GL12 8NB. ☎ (01454) 294168.
www.wickwarbrewing.co.uk
Colour: Very dark brown (18).
Head: Dark dense head.
Aroma: Coffee and chocolate.
Taste: Bitter chocolate and dark tasty malt.
Ease of Decanting: Pour carefully due to colour.
Opinion: Great with Stilton and biscuits.

WICKWAR STATION PORTER 6.1% ABV 500 ML
Brewed by Wickwar Brewery Co. The Old Cider Mill, Station Road, Wickwar, Gloucestershire. GL12 8NB. ☎ (01454) 294168.
www.wickwarbrewing.co.uk
Colour: Black (20).
Head: Brown, dense bubbles in a small head.
Aroma: Molasses and black treacle.
Taste: Smooth and sweet with subtle black treacle bittering to stringent hops to balance in the aftertaste.
Ease of Decanting: Nice and easy to pour.
Opinion: A sweet beer, would drink nicely with roast pork and crackling.

WOLF BREWERY CAVELL ALE 3.7% ABV 500 ML
Brewed by The Wolf Brewery, 10 Maurice Gaymer Road, Attleborough, Norfolk NR17 2QZ. ☎ (01953) 457775.
www.wolf-brewery.ltd.uk
Colour: Rich golden amber (8).
Head: White, small dense bubbled head.
Aroma: Zest and citrus with warm spices.
Taste: Light and bubbly leading to bitter hops that sour slightly, then dry in the aftertaste.
Ease of Decanting: The yeast clung to the base of the bottle and the head was small, making this an easy ale to pour.
Opinion: Unusually low in alcohol for a bottle-conditioned beer. Would drink nicely with a doorstep off-the-bone ham and pickle sandwich.

WOLF BREWERY GRANNY WOULDN'T LIKE IT 4.8% ABV 500 ML
Brewed by The Wolf Brewery, 10 Maurice Gaymer Road, Attleborough, Norfolk NR17 2QZ. ☎ (01953) 457775.
www.wolf-brewery.ltd.uk
Colour: Rich burgundy (19).
Head: White, dense head that stayed small.
Aroma: Subtle sweet aroma of cinnamon.
Taste: Bitter fruits dry to rich malt leading to a bitter slightly metallic hop aftertaste.
Ease of Decanting: No problem decanting this beer, yeast stayed where you want it (at the bottom of the bottle) and the head stayed small.
Opinion: A nice thirst-quencher after a hot chilli con carne.

WOLF BREWERY STRAW DOGS 4.5% ABV 500 ML

Brewed by The Wolf Brewery, 10 Maurice Gaymer Road, Attleborough, Norfolk NR17 2QZ. ☎ (01953) 457775.
www.wolf-brewery.ltd.uk
Colour: Blonde (5).
Head: Creamy, dense head.
Aroma: Cloves.
Taste: Very refreshing with intense, mouth-filling fruit and a long dry finish.
Ease of Decanting: Very easy to pour.
Opinion: Try this with salami and crusty bread.

WOODFORDE'S GREAT EASTERN 4.3% ABV 500ML

Brewed by Woodforde's Norfolk Ales, Broadland Brewery, Slad Lane, Woodbastwick, Norwich NR13 6SW. ☎ (01603) 720353.
www.woodfordes.co.uk
Colour: Amber (7).
Head: Large bubbles in a large head.
Aroma: Cream soda and vanilla.
Taste: Coats mouth initially in slightly tart, but quite heavy wort sweetness, which matures to a tart bitterness that warms the tongue.
Ease of Decanting: This beer should be poured by the more experienced drinker of bottle-conditioned ales as the head was large and there were yeasty tendrils that stopped the decanting process, leaving a third of the beer still in the bottle.
Opinion: This beer would go down nicely with gammon steak and pineapple.

WOODFORDE'S NELSONS REVENGE 4.5% ABV 500ML

Brewed by Woodforde's Norfolk Ales, Broadland Brewery, Slad Lane, Woodbastwick, Norwich NR13 6SW. ☎ (01603) 720353.
www.woodfordes.co.uk
Colour: Rich golden amber to copper-brown (8 to 9).
Head: Dense white bubbles in a small head.
Aroma: Subtle fruitcake with orange rind notes.
Taste: Slightly tarry and tallowy leading to ripe pears and sour cherries which linger long in the aftertaste on the sides of the tongue.
Ease of Decanting: Nice and easy to pour as the yeast stayed stuck to the base of the bottle.
Opinion: Would go nicely with roast beef and horseradish.

WOODFORDE'S NORFOLK NOG 4.6% ABV 500ML

Brewed by Woodforde's Norfolk Ales, Broadland Brewery, Slad Lane, Woodbastwick, Norwich NR13 6SW. ☎ (01603) 720353.
www.woodfordes.co.uk
Colour: Black with burgundy hints (20).
Head: Small head made of small dense brown bubbles.
Aroma: Caramel and molasses with black treacle.
Taste: Smooth mouth-feel initially, then bitter cherries come through, then dry to a slightly warming aftertaste.
Ease of Decanting: Easy-pouring beer, yeast staying at the bottom of the bottle.
Opinion: Would possibly complement a roast beef ploughman's.

WOODFORDE'S WHERRY 3.8% ABV 500 ML

Brewed by Woodforde's Norfolk Ales, Broadland Brewery, Slad Lane, Woodbastwick, Norwich NR13 6SW. ☎ (01603) 720353.
www.woodfordes.co.uk
Colour: Rich golden amber (8).
Head: Small head made of dense white bubbles.
Aroma: Spice and fruits ranging from grapefruit to lemon.
Taste: Initial cream soda and vanilla, smooth and slightly prickly becoming slightly tart with subtle burnt toffee tempered by vanilla. The aftertaste is bitter and slightly cidery with bitter grapefruit drying and slightly furring the sides of the tongue.
Ease of Decanting: Yeast stayed at the bottom and the head stayed small, so no problems pouring this beer.
Opinion: A complex beer for its strength, a good thirst-quencher as well so would be a welcome alternative to lager after a hot Indian curry.

YOUNG'S SPECIAL LONDON ALE 6.4% ABV 500 ML

Brewed by Young & Co's Brewery plc, The Ram Brewery, High Street, Wandsworth, London SW18 4JD. ☎ (020) 8875 7000.
www.youngs.co.uk
Colour: Ruby-brown (13).
Head: Small white bubbles forming a small head.
Aroma: Caramel and sweet almonds.
Taste: Initial froth reduces to spiced pears leading to summer berries, leading on to drying bitter fruits in a long but pleasant aftertaste.
Ease of Decanting: Yeast swirls in the last quarter mean you have to be careful, but the rewards are great.
Opinion: Available quite widely and one of the top-selling bottle-conditioned beers. This is a quality beer to be enjoyed with a lovely venison pie and mash.

INDEX OF BREWERIES

INDEX OF BREWERIES

INDEX OF BEERS

Pub name: ______________________ Already in the guide? Yes ☐ No ☐
Address: ______________________

Comments: ______________________

Your name: ______________________
Your address: ______________________

Tel: ______________________

Pub name: ______________________ Already in the guide? Yes ☐ No ☐
Address: ______________________

Comments: ______________________

Your name: ______________________
Your address: ______________________

Tel: ______________________

Pub name: ______________________ Already in the guide? Yes ☐ No ☐
Address: ______________________

Comments: ______________________

Your name: ______________________
Your address: ______________________

Tel: ______________________

Pub name: ______ Already in the guide? Yes ☐ No ☐
Address: ______

Comments: ______

Your name: ______
Your address: ______

______ Tel: ______

Pub name: ______ Already in the guide? Yes ☐ No ☐
Address: ______

Comments: ______

Your name: ______
Your address: ______

______ Tel: ______

Pub name: ______ Already in the guide? Yes ☐ No ☐
Address: ______

Comments: ______

Your name: ______
Your address: ______

______ Tel: ______